Pass the CPA Exam
or your money back.* Guaranteed!

Our 4-volume CPA Review textbooks are an integral part of Totaltape's CPA Review System—A system specifically designed to assist you in passing the CPA exam.

100,000 SUCCESSFUL CANDIDATES HAVE ALREADY PASSED WITH THE HELP OF TOTALTAPE'S UNIQUE STUDY SYSTEM

Dear Future CPA:

Passing the CPA exam is an ambitious - but attainable - goal. Effective with the May 1996 examination, the Uniform CPA Exam will be "nondisclosed." This means that the AICPA will no longer release examination questions. Therefore, you are going to need all the help you can get to pass the exam.

With our **25 years of exam preparation experience**, we are uniquely qualified to help you pass the exam. Your purchase of the Totaltape CPA Review System is the first step. We are now celebrating 25 years as America's #1 CPA Review program with this 26th edition, and are proud that Totaltape is the only CPA Review officially licensed as Microsoft® Windows™ compatible.

TOTALTAPE IS THE FIRST AND ONLY CPA REVIEW TO PROVIDE A PERSONAL CHOICE OF FORMATS:

Textbooks The first texts fully updated to the new closed exam content specifications...complete and authoritative—available as a 4-volume set and as individual exam sections.

Audiotapes The most flexible of learning formats, which enable you to gain additional study time, anywhere and anytime.

Videotapes 25 Hot•Spot video lectures highlight difficult to grasp key subjects and demonstrate valuable memory aids.

Software Interactive programs for Windows or MS-DOS are smart, fast and user-friendly. Your complete CPA Review 4-volume textbooks are on-line at the touch of a key.

CD-ROM The ultimate reference source! Our complete Windows software with text on CD-ROM, to view and review time and time again—and the multimedia sights, sounds and motion make learning fun!

The Totaltape CPA Review System also offers a comprehensive range of user features, maintaining leadership as **AMERICA'S BEST SELLING CPA REVIEW SYSTEM SINCE 1971.**

Diagnostic and final exams. Included with all textbooks & software so you can check and monitor your exam preparation progress at all times.

Free personalized help line. If you need clarification of a point, or have a question, our full-time CPA Review experts are only a toll-free call away for one-on-one guidance.

You are now commencing your training to pass the CPA exam. The Totaltape CPA Review System has been developed to help you succeed. We're so confident, we even offer you a simple pledge:

PASS THE CPA EXAM OR YOUR MONEY BACK, GUARANTEED.*

Good luck. I look forward to welcoming you as a fellow CPA.

Sincerely,

Nathan M. Bisk

Nathan M. Bisk, J.D., C.P.A. (FL)
Publisher and Editor-in-Chief

*Purchase of software required. Certain restrictions apply. Call for complete details.

TOTALTAPE'S CPA REVIEW SYSTEM WILL PREPARE YOU FOR THE MOST IMPORTANT EXAM OF YOUR LIFE

Everything You Need to Pass the CPA Exam or Your Money Back. Guaranteed.*

The Company: Committed to Serving You

Since 1971, Bisk Publishing Company's Totaltape CPA Review has been a pioneer in the development of alternative teaching methods for taxation, accounting, auditing and business law education. To accommodate individual study habits, we have developed a variety of learning formats from which to mix-and-match: textbooks, interactive software, videotapes, audiotapes, and a personalized help line. Responding to changing needs and technological advances, **Totaltape became the first to introduce CPA Review software *for Windows*, "textbooks on disk" *for Windows*, and multimedia CD-ROM.**

Here at Totaltape Plaza in our 75,000 square foot facility located in Tampa, Florida, we consult with and employ the nation's leading experts to develop and write our programs. We utilize sophisticated multi-million dollar video and audio studios, word processing, and computer systems to better serve you. And, because all of our operation is under one roof, we offer you low prices and instant service in the form of shipment within 48 hours of receipt of your order. We look forward to serving your educational needs both now and in the future.

The CPA Exam Experts: A Proven Track Record

We have a 75% national passing rate. And more than 100,000 successful subscribers are now CPAs. You can be, too, with the help of Totaltape's CPA Review System. We guarantee it, or your money back.*

The System: What You Get and Why It Works

Personal Choice of Formats—Every individual is different. Different habits. Different preferences. Different schedules. So Totaltape provides you with a variety of learning formats: videotapes, audiotapes, interactive software for Windows or MS-DOS, CD-ROM, and textbooks. Each is as individual as you. But all are designed to effectively meet your study needs; whatever they may be.

Complete and Comprehensive Coverage—Fully updated to the new closed exam content specifications, Totaltape's CPA Review materials zero-in on exactly, and only, what you need to know to pass the CPA exam; the first time you sit. With the current exam changes, you need to prepare harder, smarter, and more efficiently than ever before.

Time Management Techniques—We show you how to create a personalized study schedule to make maximum use of your time, and your intelligence. And, by offering you a variety of learning formats, we also provide you with a diversity of study opportunities. In the car while commuting. At work between appointments. While exercising. At home. Wherever and whenever it's convenient. You maximize your productivity and effectiveness.

Actual Questions, Problems, and Essays—Taken from the most recent CPA exams, our practice questions not only test your understanding of key concepts, they also show you areas tested more frequently on the Uniform CPA Exam. As you work through our multiple choice, objective answer, and essay questions, your exam confidence builds as you apply the knowledge you've learned. Plus, we go a step further and provide you with automatic and immediate feedback to your question responses, telling you whether your answer is right or wrong, and why. And Totaltape is the only software program that will grade your essays.

Diagnostic and Final Exams—Our diagnostic exams serve as "practice" exams, pinpointing your weak areas and showing you where to focus your study efforts for the greatest improvement. Our "retakeable" final exams are your dry run for the actual CPA exam. Do well on our finals, and you can be confident that you'll pass the CPA exam.

Free Personal Help Line Service—Studying on your own? That doesn't mean you have to face the exam alone. Speak one-on-one with the CPAs and Professors who wrote Totaltape's CPA Review program whenever you need help with a topic, or a concept, or have a question. We're the only CPA Review that has the answers you want, when you want them. We're the only CPA Review that provides a free help line. Why? Because our continued success depends on your success. Our materials are so complete and comprehensive, we know your questions will be few and far between. But if and when they do arise, we'll be here to answer them.

**Purchase of software required. Certain restrictions apply. Call for complete details.*

Free Personal Help Line with any CPA Exam Section Simply dial 1-800-874-7599

COMPLETE COVERAGE OF ALL FOUR EXAM SECTIONS

First Materials Updated to the New Closed Exam Content Specifications

FINANCIAL ACCOUNTING & REPORTING

Textbooks or "Textbooks on disk" for Windows or CD-ROM. 986 pages of text; complete, current, and comprehensive. 2,115 recent CPA exam questions, problems, essays, and answers; including analysis of recent exam coverage.
Software for Windows or MS-DOS. 2,115 recent CPA exam questions, problems, essays, and answers; including analysis of recent exam coverage.
Audiotapes. 14 hours of instruction cross-referenced to the textbooks.
Video Hot•Spot Lectures. Including: *Consolidations; FASBs 95 & 109; Leases & Pensions; Bonds & Other Liabilities; Assets; Revenue Recognition/Income Statement Presentation; Inventory.*

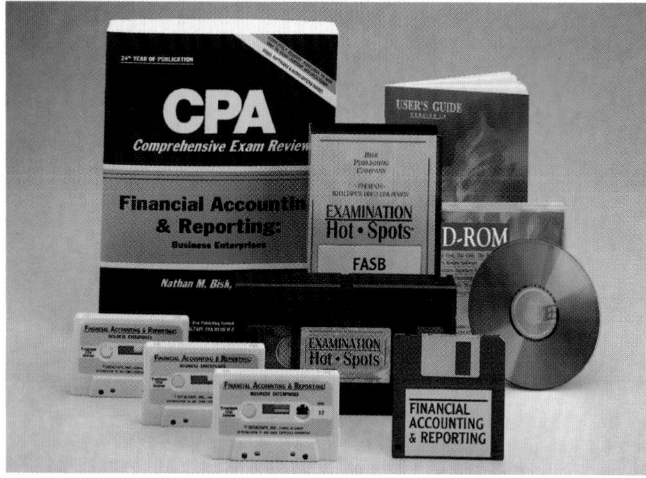

ACCOUNTING & REPORTING

Textbooks or "Textbooks on disk" for Windows or CD-ROM. 598 pages of text; complete, current, and comprehensive. 961 recent CPA exam questions and answers; including analysis of recent exam coverage.
Software for Windows or MS-DOS. 961 recent CPA exam questions and answers; including analysis of recent exam coverage.
Audiotapes. 12 hours of instruction cross-referenced to the textbooks.
Video Hot•Spot Lectures. Including: *Governmental & Nonprofit Accounting; Capital Gains & Losses; Corporate Taxation; Cost Accounting; Managerial Accounting; Estates, Trusts & Partnerships; Individual Taxation: Filing Status, Exemptions & Gross Income; Individual Taxation: Adjustments & Itemized Deductions; Tax Liabilities & Credits.*

AUDITING

Textbooks or "Textbooks on disk" for Windows or CD-ROM. 702 pages of text; complete, current, and comprehensive. 908 recent CPA exam questions, essays, and answers; including analysis of recent exam coverage.
Software for Windows or MS-DOS. 908 recent CPA exam questions, essays, and answers; including analysis of recent exam coverage.
Audiotapes. 12 hours of instruction cross-referenced to the textbooks.
Video Hot•Spot Lectures. Including: *Standard Audit Reports; Audit: Internal Control; Audit Evidence; Other Reports, Reviews & Compilations; EDP Auditing & Stat Sampling.*

BUSINESS LAW & PROFESSIONAL RESPONSIBILITIES

Textbooks or "Textbooks on disk" for Windows or CD-ROM. 696 pages of text; complete, current, and comprehensive. 832 recent CPA exam questions, essays, and answers; including analysis of recent exam coverage.
Software for Windows or MS-DOS. 832 recent CPA exam questions, essays, and answers; including analysis of recent exam coverage.
Audiotapes. 12 hours of instruction cross-referenced to the textbooks.
Video Hot•Spot Lectures. Including: *Contracts & Commercial Paper; Sales & Agency; Bankruptcy; Property & Secured Transactions.*

Call Now for Your Free CPA Review Demos or to Place Your Order 1-800-874-7599

The Only CPA Review Officially Licensed as Microsoft® Windows™ Compatible

YOUR PERSONAL CHOICE OF FORMATS

Totaltape's Flexible Learning Formats Let You Create a Personalized Study System That's Convenient For You

EXAMINATION HOT•SPOT VIDEO SERIES

Used in the Country's Largest Regional Live Reviews

These entertaining and fast paced, 2- to 3-hour video tutorial courses, feature Ivan Fox, Tim Gearty, and Bob Monette; three of the most popular CPA Review instructors in the country. They organize, prioritize, and summarize key concepts vital to your exam success, and demonstrate helpful memory aids, problem-solving tips, and short-cuts learned from more than 50 years combined exam preparation experience.

Watch, Listen, and Learn from the Country's Top-Rated CPA Review Instructors

IVAN FOX, J.D., LL.M., is a Professor of Law at Pace University, where he formerly served as Chairperson of the Law Department. He is a recipient of the Outstanding Teacher Award, and author of the country's best-selling business law text entitled, *Business Law & the Legal Environment.* With more than 20 years of CPA exam preparation experience, Mr. Fox is known as the "Dean" of CPA Law Review.

TIMOTHY F. GEARTY, M.B.A., J.D., C.P.A., is a former Professor of Accounting and currently manages and directs his own tax consulting and CPA practice. He is a frequent lecturer on tax and accounting topics. Mr. Gearty is the lead tax and accounting instructor for the Fox Gearty CPA Review, one of America's largest regional programs. He has over 12 years of experience teaching CPA Review, and is recognized nationally as an expert on the CPA exam.

ROBERT L. MONETTE, J.D., C.P.A., is nationally recognized as an expert on the CPA exam, and currently serves as the owner and instructor of the Gross-Monette CPA Review, the largest CPA Review seminar in Philadelphia. Mr. Monette's background also includes teaching CPA Review in Boston, New York, and New Jersey, where he has helped tens-of-thousands of candidates become CPAs.

Publisher and Editor-in-Chief

NATHAN M. BISK, J.D., C.P.A. (FL) is the Publisher and Editor-in-Chief of the Totaltape CPA Review System. He is both an attorney and a CPA in the State of Florida, and has written and taught CPA Review accounting, auditing, taxation, and business law programs since 1970. Mr. Bisk is also a pioneer in the development of video, audio, software, and CD-ROM Continuing Education programs for accountants and attorneys. He is recognized as the leading expert in the nation on the CPA exam.

Select from 25 New & Current Video Titles:

Capital Gains & Losses. Corporate Taxation. FASBs 95 & 109. Contracts & Commercial Paper. Governmental & Nonprofit Accounting. Standard Audit Reports. Consolidations. Leases & Pensions. Bonds & Other Liabilities. Audit: Internal Control. Audit Evidence. Individual Taxation: Filing Status, Exemptions & Gross Income. Individual Taxation: Adjustments & Itemized Deductions. Cost Accounting. Managerial Accounting. Sales & Agency. Assets. Revenue Recognition/Income Statement Presentation. Other Reports, Reviews & Compilations. Bankruptcy. Estates, Trusts & Partnerships. Tax Liabilities & Credits. Property and Secured Transactions. EDP Auditing & Stat Sampling.
Inventory.

Totaltape's Examination Hot•Spot Videos are the perfect supplement to our other review materials.

Call Now for Your Free Video Demo 1-800-874-7599

INTERACTIVE SOFTWARE FOR WINDOWS & MS-DOS

The Only CPA Review Officially Licensed as Microsoft® Windows™ Compatible

Smart, fast and user-friendly, our latest software *for Windows* includes exclusive features and expanded coverage making it even easier to customize exam preparation to your specific needs. In fact, our software has more features than any other program on the market. Used in the country's largest regional live reviews!

From over 4,000 multiple choice, objective format, and essay questions, you select the actual questions you want to study; questions you've never seen, those you've missed; or the most recent from Uniform CPA Exams. Plus, if you need a fast answer to a specific question, you can pinpoint areas beyond topics and subtopics to microtopics; you can even make on-line notes for future reference.

An Interactive Progress Report keeps you right on track by monitoring your exam preparation from start to finish, with diagnostic analysis pinpointing weak areas that need additional study emphasis. Totaltape CPA Review is the only software that provides instant on-line grades. Just to make certain you are totally prepared, Totaltape's software allows you to take an unlimited number of final exams, covering the complete spectrum of exam questions. Each exam is made up from scratch every time. No two are exactly alike.

"The combination of videos, textbooks and software that I purchased...cannot be beat by any other system on the market."

G.E., Danville, Virgina

"The materials were available when I wanted to study, not when a class was in session, and Totaltape even guarantees that you pass!"

V.S., Chicago, Illinois

"I successfully negotiated all four sections of the Uniform CPA Exam on my first sitting. There is no question that I owe my success in large part to Totaltape."

L.E., West Columbia, South Carolina

"After becoming frustrated with the tremendous amount of time I was wasting in the classroom, I decided to study on my own. Without the aid of your tapes and software, I would not have been able to...achieve success on the exam."

B.S., Pittstown, New Jersey

"I utilized many different review resources. I found that the Totaltape CPA Review videos were the most powerful study aids available anywhere."

P.D., Troy, Michigan

In addition, we are the first publisher to offer our CPA Review "textbooks on disk" *for Windows*. Our entire 4-volume review textbooks are on-line, including the complete question and answer section. With a single click of a button, you can instantly move from question to relevant text coverage, and back again. Or you can use the synchronized text feature which automatically brings up the relevant text every time you answer a question.

At the end of your study session or when you need a break, a handy "bookmark" lets you tag the program and pick up later right where you left off. And remember, every software program is supported by unlimited toll-free technical assistance.

The Only CPA Review Officially Licensed as Microsoft® Windows™ Compatible

Windows is a trademark of Microsoft Corporation.

Call Now for Your Free Software Demo
1-800-874-7599

Look for us on the INTERNET!

Here's how to access Totaltape's home page on the World Wide Web:

http://www.bisk.com

email: bisk@bisk.com

INNOVATIVE MULTIMEDIA CD-ROM

The First and Only CPA Review Materials Available on CD-ROM

State-of-the-art, full-motion video, stereo-sound audio, and animated graphics combined with Totaltape's comprehensive textbook coverage virtually take you from behind your computer and transport you into a classroom setting with America's leading CPA Review Instructors. Totaltape's new CD-ROM CPA Review features our entire software *for Windows* program, including our 4-volume set of textbooks on disk, full search capabilities, and more than 4,000 recent multiple choice, objective format, and essay questions. Plus, you get our exciting new multimedia audiovisual coverage designed exclusively for the upcoming exam. A couple of minutes is all it takes to be up and running with Totaltape's CD-ROM. Hard drive space limited? No problem, you can run the entire program straight off the CD. A dramatic and dynamic way to learn.

FLEXIBLE AUDIOTAPES

Quadruple Your Study Time

More than 50 hours of digitally-recorded audio lectures add insight and analysis to Totaltape's textbook coverage. The flexibility of audiotapes gives you complete control of your study program. Gain as much as two extra days study time per week simply by using our audio lectures in your car while commuting. Move ahead, repeat, review, and re-review as often as necessary until you understand the subject matter. Study on your own time. At your own pace. Whenever and wherever it's convenient for you. Plus, each audio lecture is indexed to help you locate specific topics of interest quickly.

COMPLETE AND AUTHORITATIVE TEXTBOOKS

Available in a 4-Volume Set & Individual Exam Sections
Feature an Extensive Section on the Grading of Writing Skills, Now Worth 5% of Your Grade

Developed and written by the nation's foremost tax, accounting, auditing, and law experts, Totaltape's CPA Review textbooks feature complete and current coverage of every exam section and ALL official CPA exam changes. Available by individual exam section, our textbooks contain more than 3,000 pages of text and over 4,000 recent CPA exam questions, problems, and essays with solutions, including correct and incorrect answer explanations not available from the AICPA. We teach you the most important "how-to's" and exam topics; you get the kind of time-effective training you need to pass the exam. Plus, we show you how to set up a study plan, how to build exam confidence, and how to answer exam questions the way the graders are looking to see them for maximum points.

Call Now for Your Free Audio Demo
1-800-874-7599

Here's how to access Totaltape's home page on the World Wide Web:

http://www.bisk.com

email: bisk@bisk.com

Totaltape CPA Review Order Form

	FINANCIAL ACCOUNTING & REPORTING	QTY	ACCOUNTING & REPORTING	QTY	AUDITING	QTY	BUSINESS LAW & PROFESSIONAL RESPONSIBILITIES	QTY	FULL SET	QTY	TOTAL $
Software *for Windows* with Q&A and Text on Disk	$128.90 CPA2543		$116.90 CPA2513		$116.90 CPA2533		$116.90 CPA2523		$479.60 CPA2503		
Software *for Windows* with Q&A	$89.95 CPA2855		$84.95 CPA2856		$84.95 CPA2857		$84.95 CPA2858		$344.80 CPA2859		
Software for DOS with Q&A*	$89.95 CPA2851		$84.95 CPA2850		$84.95 CPA2853		$84.95 CPA2852		$344.80 CPA2854		
CD-ROM *for Windows* with Q&A, Text on Disk & Multimedia	$138.90 CPA2700		$126.90 CPA2701		$126.90 CPA2702		$126.90 CPA2703		$519.60 CPA2704		
CPA Review Audiotape Lectures	$99.95 CPA2542		$99.95 CPA2512		$99.95 CPA2532		$99.95 CPA2522		$399.80 CPA2502		
CPA Review Examination Hot•Spot Videos	Bonds & Other Liabilities CPA2090		Governmental & Nonprofit Accounting CPA2040		Audit Evidence CPA2110		Contracts & Commercial Paper CPA2050		Examination Hot•Spot Video Series CPA2160		
	Consolidations CPA2020		Capital Gains & Losses CPA2015		Audit: Internal Control CPA2100		Sales & Agency CPA2150		**Money-Saving Discount Available with Purchase of Full Video Set! Call Now for Special Pricing and to Place Your Order.**		
ALL VIDEOS $99.00 each	FASBs 95 & 109 CPA2030		Corporate Taxation CPA2016		Standard Audit Reports CPA2000		Bankruptcy CPA3190				
	Leases & Pensions CPA2080		Individual Taxation: Filing Status, Exemptions & Gross Income CPA2410		Other Reports, Reviews & Compilations CPA3230		Property and Secured Transactions CPA3200				
	Revenue Recognition/ Income Statement Presentation CPA3220		Individual Taxation: Adjustments & Itemized Deductions CPA2310		EDP Auditing & Stat Sampling CPA2548				**CALL FOR NEW TITLES!**		
	Assets CPA3210		Cost Accounting CPA2130								
	Inventory CPA3250		Managerial Accounting CPA2140								
			Estates, Trusts & Partnerships CPA3245								
			Tax Liabilities & Credits CPA2510								
CPA Review Textbooks 4-Volume	$39.95 CPA2551		$32.95 CPA2552		$32.95 CPA2553		$32.95 CPA2554		$138.80 CPA2550		

*5¼ disks available upon request.

HOW TO PASS THE CPA EXAM VIDEO...$60.00 (CPA2560)

TERMS

We ship on account to qualified individuals, firms, bookstores, libraries, institutions, and government agencies with purchase order. Prices subject to change without notice. 10-day refund policy on resaleable textbooks. Rapid delivery via UPS with Air Service to the West Coast.
We ship within 48 hours.

CALL TOLL-FREE
1-800-874-7599

METHOD OF PAYMENT

❑ Check enclosed, ***made payable to Bisk Publishing Company***

Visa❑ MC❑ Amex❑ Discover❑ Exp Date________

Card No____________________

Signature____________________

Name____________________

Address____________________

City__________ State____ Zip______

Day Phone__________ Eve Phone__________

DISCOUNTS
Orders Totaling $1,000 or More...**SAVE 10%**
Orders Totaling $1,400 or More...**SAVE 15%**
Orders Totaling $1,800 or More...**SAVE 25%**

GENERAL SHIPPING CHARGES
Orders up to $499.00 +7% of total
Orders over $500.00 +6% of total

TEXT ONLY SHIPPING CHARGES
Financial Accounting & Reporting, $6.95
All Others, $5.95 each

Additional shipping required for delivery outside the U.S. Call 813-621-6200 for details.

SUBTOTAL	
LESS APPLICABLE DISCOUNT	
IN FL ADD 6½% SALES TAX	
PLUS SHIPPING	
TOTAL DUE	

When ordering please use code #94043

Complete & Mail to: Bisk Publishing Company, TOTALTAPE CPA REVIEW
9417 Princess Palm Avenue, Tampa, FL 33619-8317 Fax Toll-Free 1-800-345-8273 Internet http://www.bisk.com Email bisk@bisk.com

EDITORIAL BOARD

Our Editorial Board Includes the Nation's Leading CPAs, Attorneys and Educators

Publisher and Editor-in-Chief

NATHAN M. BISK, J.D., C.P.A. (FL), has written and taught CPA Review, accounting, auditing, taxation, and business law programs since 1970. He has been a pioneer in the development, writing, and production of audio, video, software, and CD-ROM education programs for accountants and attorneys. He is recognized as the leading expert in the nation on the CPA exam.

Co-Author

PAUL MUNTER, Ph.D, C.P.A. (CO and TX), a 1993 recipient of the FICPA's Outstanding Educator Award, Dr. Munter is the KPMG Peat Marwick Accounting Scholar, Professor of Accounting, and Department Chair at the University of Miami. He has published extensive articles on financial accounting and auditing matters, and was the Texas Society of CPAs first Outstanding Discussion Leader.

Consulting Editors

DONALD C. ALEXANDER, LL.B., LL.D., former IRS Commissioner and a partner in the Washington DC law firm of Akin, Gump, Strauss, Hauer and Feld.

MORTIMER M. CAPLIN, LL.B., J.S.D., LL.D., former IRS Commissioner and a partner in the Washington DC law firm of Caplin and Drysdale.

RICHARD M. FELDHEIM, M.B.A., J.D., LL.M., C.P.A. (NY), has experience as both a CPA with Price Waterhouse & Co. and as a Senior Partner with the Arizona law firm of Wentworth and Lundin.

IVAN FOX, J.D., LL.M., a recipient of the Outstanding Teaching Award, is a Professor of Law at Pace University. With more than 20 years of CPA exam preparation experience, he is recognized as the "Dean" of CPA Law Review.

TIMOTHY F. GEARTY, M.B.A., J.D., C.P.A. (NY), a former Professor of Accounting, is the lead tax and accounting instructor for the Fox Gearty CPA Review, one of America's largest regional programs.

MARILYN F. HUNT, M.A., C.P.A. (FL), is an Accounting Instructor at the University of Central Florida, where she has been CPA Review Program Coordinator for more than 15 years.

ROBERT L. MONETTE, J.D., C.P.A. (PA), currently serves as the owner and instructor of the Gross-Monette CPA Review, the largest live CPA Review seminar in Philadelphia.

THOMAS A. RATCLIFFE, Ph.D., C.P.A. (TX), Professor of Accounting and Department Chair at Troy State University. Recipient of the Alabama Society of CPAs Outstanding Educator Award, and Outstanding Discussion Leader for the past four years.

C. WILLIAM THOMAS, M.B.A., Ph.D., C.P.A. (TX), Professor of Accounting and Department Chair at Baylor University. Nationally-known author with extensive experience teaching Auditing CPA Review.

Call Now for Your Free CPA Review Demos or to Place Your Order 1-800-874-7599

Your Satisfaction is Always Guaranteed!

ENHANCE THE POWER OF YOUR BOOKS with MULTIMEDIA CPA REVIEW MATERIALS

Totaltape CPA Review • Multimedia Discount Coupon

$50 OFF - AUDIO

This coupon is good for $50 off any full set of Totaltape CPA Review on Audio.

To receive your discount, simply detach this coupon and mail it in with the order form located on the opposite page.
Be sure to add the coupon amount to the discount line on the order form.
For faster service, call **1-800-874-7599** or fax your order to us at 1-800-345-8273.
When calling or faxing, be sure to include your Priority Code number.

Priority Code #64522

Totaltape CPA Review • Multimedia Discount Coupon

$50 OFF - SOFTWARE

This coupon is good for $50 off any full set of Totaltape CPA Review on Software.

To receive your discount, simply detach this coupon and mail it in with the order form located on the opposite page.
Be sure to add the coupon amount to the discount line on the order form.
For faster service, call **1-800-874-7599** or fax your order to us at 1-800-345-8273.
When calling or faxing, be sure to include your Priority Code number.

Priority Code #64523

Totaltape CPA Review • Multimedia Discount Coupon

$100 OFF - VIDEO

This coupon is good for $100 off the purchase of 10 or more Totaltape CPA Review Videos.

To receive your discount, simply detach this coupon and mail it in with the order form located on the opposite page.
Be sure to add the coupon amount to the discount line on the order form.
For faster service, call **1-800-874-7599** or fax your order to us at 1-800-345-8273.
When calling or faxing, be sure to include your Priority Code number.

Priority Code #64524

YOUR PERSONAL CHOICE OF FORMATS

Totaltape's flexible learning formats let you create a personalized study system that's convenient for you

Totaltape CPA Review • Multimedia Discount Coupon

$50 OFF - AUDIO

Flexible Audio Tapes

More than 50 hours of digitally-recorded audio lectures
add insight and analysis to Totaltape's textbook coverage.
Each audio lecture is fully indexed to help you locate specific topics of interest.

Bisk Publishing Company • TOTALTAPE CPA REVIEW
9417 Princess Palm Avenue • Tampa, FL 33619 • **1-800-874-7599**

Totaltape CPA Review • Multimedia Discount Coupon

$50 OFF - SOFTWARE

Choose from Innovative Multimedia CD-ROM or Interactive Software for Windows or MS-DOS

Our 4-volume set of textbooks are on disk with the complete question & answer section
and instant on-line grades. You select the actual questions you want to study from over
4,000 multiple choice, objective format, and essay questions
including the most recent from Uniform CPA exams.

Bisk Publishing Company • TOTALTAPE CPA REVIEW
9417 Princess Palm Avenue • Tampa, FL 33619 • **1-800-874-7599**

Totaltape CPA Review • Multimedia Discount Coupon

$100 OFF - VIDEO

Examination Hot • Spot Video Series

These entertaining and fast-paced 2-3 hour video courses,
organize, prioritize, and summarize key concepts vital to your exam success,
and demonstrate helpful memory aids, problem-solving tips, and short-cuts.

Bisk Publishing Company • TOTALTAPE CPA REVIEW
9417 Princess Palm Avenue • Tampa, FL 33619 • **1-800-874-7599**

FREE

MULTIMEDIA DEMOS & UPDATING SUPPLEMENTS

Free CD-ROM CPA Review Demo...
The ultimate reference source. All your exam information on a multimedia CD-ROM disk, to view and review time and time again.

Free Software CPA Review Demo...
Try America's leading CPA Review software yourself and learn how to make your exam preparation easier and more effective than ever before!

Free Video CPA Review Demo...
Get a "sampling" of Totaltape's new Examination Hot•Spot Video Series, featuring America's leading CPA Review instructors—watch, listen and learn as they coach you through the toughest, most challenging, most frequently tested topics on the CPA exam!

Free Audio CPA Review Demo...
See for yourself how flexible and convenient audio cassette instruction truly is with our 60-minute audio sample lecture and accompanying 50-page workbook!

Free Updating Supplement...
Be Sure You're Current for the Upcoming CPA Exam—Reserve Your Copy Today!
You'll receive outlines of new FASB and AICPA pronouncements, and a review of new developments in Business Law and Federal Income Taxation. Plus, we'll alert you to new subject areas or significant changes in exam emphasis. This free supplement applies only to information that is published within six months of our receipt of your updating request. On the card below, check the CPA Review section(s) you have purchased, and we will send your updating supplement(s) when available.

COMPLETE CARD BELOW AND MAIL IT IN TODAY!

Please send the free information that I have checked below...*

- ❑ **Free CD-ROM Demo–(CPA2705)**
- ❑ **Free Software Demo–**(Check One)
  - For Windows ❑ **3½" (CPA1746)**
  - For DOS ❑ **3½" (CPA1735)** ❑ **5¼" (CPA1725)**
- ❑ **Free Video Demo–(CPA2070)**
- ❑ **Free Audio Demo–(CPA1550)**
- ❑ **Free Updating Supplement–**(Check section(s) purchased)
  - ❑ **Financial Accounting & Reporting (CPA2582)**
  - ❑ **Accounting & Reporting (CPA2583)**
  - ❑ **Auditing (CPA2584)**
  - ❑ **Business Law & Professional Responsibilities (CPA2585)**
  - ❑ **Full Set (CPA2581)**

***UPDATING IS AVAILABLE TO ORIGINAL PURCHASERS ONLY**

Name ____________________
Address ____________________
City __________ State _____ Zip _____
Day Phone ( ) ____________________
Eve. Phone ( ) ____________________
Place Purchased ____________________
Date Purchased ____________________

Phone numbers required for UPS delivery.
Orders without phone numbers cannot be processed.

Priority Code #64521

Bisk Publishing Company, TOTALTAPE CPA REVIEW
9417 Princess Palm Avenue, Tampa, FL 33619

MULTIMEDIA DEMOS
&
UPDATING SUPPLEMENTS

• CD-ROM • Software • Video • Audio

Complete card on the reverse side and mail it in today!

NO POSTAGE NECESSARY IF MAILED IN THE UNITED STATES

BUSINESS REPLY MAIL
FIRST-CLASS MAIL PERMIT NO. 7657 TAMPA FL

POSTAGE WILL BE PAID BY ADDRESSEE

BISK PUBLISHING COMPANY
TOTALTAPE CPA REVIEW
9417 PRINCESS PALM AVENUE
PO BOX 31028
TAMPA FL 33633-0421

CPA

Comprehensive Exam Review

Auditing

Nathan M. Bisk, J.D., C.P.A.
Paul Munter, Ph.D., C.P.A.

ACKNOWLEDGEMENTS

EDITORIAL BOARD

Nathan M. Bisk, J.D., C.P.A.
Paul Munter, Ph.D., C.P.A.
Donald C. Alexander, LL.B., LL.D.
Mortimer M. Caplin, LL.B., J.S.D., LL.D.
Richard M. Feldheim, M.B.A., J.D., LL.M., C.P.A.
Ivan Fox, J.D., LL.M.
Timothy F. Gearty, M.B.A., J.D., C.P.A.
Marilyn F. Hunt, M.A., C.P.A.
Robert L. Monette, J.D., C.P.A.
Thomas A. Ratcliffe, Ph.D., C.P.A.
C. William Thomas, M.B.A., Ph.D., C.P.A.

CONTRIBUTING EDITORS

Lowell S. Broom
D.B.A., C.P.A.
University of Alabama at Birmingham

Janet Colbert
Ph.D., C.P.A.
Western Kentucky University

John W. Coughlan
M.A., Ph.D., C.P.A.
C.P.A. School of Washington, Inc.

Paul M. Fischer
Ph.D., C.P.A.
University of Wisconsin—Milwaukee

Ivan Fox
J.D., LL.M.
Pace University

Timothy F. Gearty
M.B.A., J.D., C.P.A.
Fox-Gearty CPA Review

Marilyn F. Hunt
M.A., C.P.A.
University of Central Florida

Janet E. Mercincavage
M.B.A., C.P.A.
King's College

Robert L. Monette
J.D., C.P.A.
Gross-Monette CPA Review

Paul Munter
Ph.D., C.P.A.
University of Miami

Thomas A. Ratcliffe
Ph.D., C.P.A.
Troy State University

James P. Sanford
J.D., C.P.A.
Grand Valley State University

John W. Stevenson
J.D., Ph.D., C.P.A.
Corpus Christi State University

C. William Thomas
M.B.A., Ph.D., C.P.A.
Baylor University

We wish to thank the **American Institute of Certified Public Accountants** and the **Financial Accounting Standards Board** for permission to reprint the following copyright © materials:

1. Uniform CPA Examination Questions and Unofficial Answers Copyright © 1985 through 1996. Reprinted (or adapted) with permission.
2. Accounting Research Bulletins, APB Opinions, APB Statements, and Code of Professional Conduct.
3. FASB Statements, Interpretations, and Statements of Financial Accounting Concepts (SFAC), Copyright © Financial Accounting Standards Board, 401 Merrit 7, P.O. Box 5116, Norwalk, CT 06856, U.S.A. Reprinted with permission. Copies of the complete documents are available from the FASB.
4. Statements on Auditing Standards (SAS), Statements on Standards for Accounting and Review Services (SSARS), Statements on Standards for Management Advisory Services (SSMAS), Statements on Standards for Accountants' Services on Prospective Financial Information, and Statements on Standards for Attestation Engagements.

© 1996, by NATHAN M. BISK, J.D., C.P.A.
Tampa, Florida 33619

TWENTY-SIXTH EDITION

ALL RIGHTS RESERVED. Reproduction in any form expressly prohibited.
Printed in the United States of America.

PREFACE

Our texts provide comprehensive, complete coverage of all the topics tested on all four sections of the CPA Examination, including **Business Law & Professional Responsibilities, Financial Accounting & Reporting, Accounting & Reporting,** and **Auditing**. Used effectively, our materials will enable you to achieve maximum preparedness for the Uniform CPA Examination. Here is a brief summary of the **features** and **benefits** that our texts will provide for you:

1. **New Edition For Closed Exam . . .** Beginning with the May 1996 Exam, the Uniform CPA Examination will be non-disclosed. See page F-5 for a full discussion of this issue. This edition contains up-to-date coverage, including complete coverage of all exam changes. This edition also includes all the latest pronouncements of the AICPA and FASB, the current tax rates, governmental and nonprofit accounting, and other topics that are tested on the CPA exam. Our coverage is based on the new **AICPA Content Specification Outlines for the Uniform CPA Exam,** effective May 1996.

2. **Separate and Complete Volumes . . .** Each text includes multiple choice and other objective questions with solutions, plus essays and problems where appropriate. There is no need to refer to any other volume.

3. **More than 3,000 Pages of Text . . .** As well as a selection of more than 4,000 recent CPA Examination questions, problems, and essays with Unofficial Answers. Solving these questions and problems under test conditions with immediate verification of results instills confidence and reinforces our **SOLUTIONS APPROACH™** to solving exam questions.

4. **Complete Coverage . . .** No extra materials required. We discuss and explain all important AICPA and FASB pronouncements, including all significant ARBs, APBs, SASs, SSARs, SFACs, and FASB materials. We also cite and identify all authoritative sources including the dates of all AICPA Questions and Unofficial Answers covered in our materials.

5. **Detailed Summaries . . .** We set forth the significant testable concepts in each CPA exam topic. These highly readable summaries are written in complete sentences using an outline format to facilitate rapid and complete comprehension. The summaries isolate and emphasize topics historically tested by the CPA examiners.

6. **Emphasis on "How to Answer Questions" and "How to Take the Exam" . . .** We teach you to solve problem, essay, and objective questions using our unique and famous **SOLUTIONS APPROACH.™**

7. **Discussion and Development of . . .** AICPA grading procedures, grader orientation strategies, examination confidence, and examination success.

8. **Unique Objective Question Coverage and Unofficial Answers Updated . . .** We explain ***why*** the multiple choice alternatives are either right or wrong. Plus, we clearly indicate the changes that need to be made in the Unofficial Answers to correctly reflect current business and tax laws and AICPA and FASB pronouncements.

9. **Writing Skills . . .** Financial Accounting and Reporting, Auditing, and Business Law and Professional Responsibilities contain a section to help you brush up on your writing skills, which are now tested on the CPA exam.

10. **Indexes . . .** We have included a comprehensively compiled index for easy topic reference in all four sections.

11. **Trend Analysis of Recent Exams . . .** We include short summaries of all essays and problems given on the most recent exams, to assist you in accurately pinpointing topics tested most frequently.

12. **Diagnostic Exam to Test Your Present Level of Knowledge . . .** And we include a **Final Exam** to test your exam preparedness under actual exam conditions. These testing materials are designed to help you single out for concentrated study the exam topic areas in which you are dangerously deficient.

Our materials are designed for the candidate who has previously studied accounting. Therefore, the rate at which a candidate studies and learns (not merely reads) our material will depend on a candidate's background and aptitude. Candidates who have been out of school for a period of years will need more time to study than recent graduates. The point to remember is that all the material you will need to know to pass the exam is here. All you need to do is apply yourself and learn this material at a rate that is appropriate to your situation. **As a final thought**, keep in mind that test confidence gained through disciplined preparation equals success.

OUR EDITORIAL BOARD INCLUDES THE NATION'S LEADING CPAs, ATTORNEYS AND EDUCATORS!

The Only CPA Review Texts Developed By Full-Time Experts.

Publisher and Editor-in-Chief
NATHAN M. BISK, J.D., C.P.A. (FL), is both an Attorney and a CPA in the State of Florida. He is a graduate of Franklin and Marshall College and the University of Florida College of Law. He is a member of the Florida Institute of CPAs, AICPA, American Accounting Association, National Association of Accountants, Association of Gov't. Accountants, American Association of Attorney-CPAs, Florida Bar, and American Bar Association. His background includes public accounting experience at both Ernst & Young and Arthur Andersen & Co. He is a graduate of the 2-year JET program of Merrill Lynch, Pierce, Fenner & Smith, Inc. Mr. Bisk has written and taught CPA Review, accounting, auditing, taxation, and business law programs since 1970. He has been a pioneer in the development, writing, and production of audio, video, and software Continuing Education programs for accountants and attorneys.

Co-Author
PAUL MUNTER, Ph.D., C.P.A. (CO and TX), is a KPMG Peat Marwick Accounting Scholar, Professor of Accounting and Chairman of the Department of Accounting at the University of Miami. Before joining the faculty at UM, Dr. Munter served as Professor of Accounting at Texas Tech University for 11 years. He has extensively published articles on financial accounting and auditing matters in journals such as the *Journal of Accountancy, CPA Journal, Management Accounting, Accounting Review, Today's CPA,*and *Practical Accountant.* Dr. Munter is a member of the IMA's national teaching faculty and was honored by the Texas Society of CPAs as its first Outstanding Discussion Leader. In addition, he was selected as the Outstanding Educator of the Year by the FICPA. Dr. Munter also teaches CPE courses for accountants in public accounting and industry.

Contributing Editor
IVAN FOX, J.D., LL.M., currently serves as a Professor of Law at Pace University, where he formerly served as Chairperson of the Law Department. He is a recipient of the Outstanding Teaching Award, and author of the country's best-selling business law text entitled, *Business Law & the Legal Environment.* With more than 20 years of CPA exam preparation experience, Mr. Fox is known as the "Dean" of CPA Law Review and is one of the expert instructors on Totaltape's Hot•Spots CPA Review video series.

Contributing Editor
ROBERT L. MONETTE, J.D., C.P.A.(PA), is nationally recognized as an expert on the CPA exam, and currently serves as the owner and instructor of the Gross-Monette CPA Review, the largest live CPA Review seminar in Philadelphia. His background also includes teaching CPA Review in Boston, New York, and New Jersey, where he has helped tens-of-thousands of candidates become CPAs. Mr. Monette is one of the expert instructors on Totaltape's Hot•Spots CPA Review video series.

Contributing Editor
TIMOTHY F. GEARTY, M.B.A., J.D., C.P.A. (NJ), is the lead Accounting and Tax Instructor for the Fox Gearty CPA Review course. He is nationally recognized as an expert on the CPA exam, and is a frequent lecturer on current tax and accounting topics. He has served as a Professor of Accounting at a major university, and worked for a "Big Six" accounting firm. He has over 12 years of experience teaching CPA Review. Mr. Gearty is one of the expert instructors on Totaltape's Hot•Spots CPA Review video series.

Consulting Editor
DONALD C. ALEXANDER, LL.B., LL.D., is a Partner with the law firm of Akin, Gump, Strauss, Hauer and Feld. He has served as Commissioner of the Internal Revenue Service, and currently serves as Director of the United States Chamber of Commerce and Chairman of the Commissioner's Exempt Organizations Advisory Group. Mr. Alexander is an active member of the Tax Advisory Group of the American Law Institute, and is a nationally recognized author of more than 30 articles on federal tax subjects.

YOU WILL LEARN FROM OUR OUTSTANDING EXPERTS . . . WITHOUT LEAVING YOUR HOME OR OFFICE.

Consulting Editor
MORTIMER M. CAPLIN, LL.B., J.S.D., LL.D., is a Senior Partner with the Washington D.C. law firm of Caplin and Drysdale. He has served as Commissioner of the Internal Revenue Service, and serves as a member of the President's Task Force on Taxation. He is a recipient of the Alexander Hamilton Award (the highest award conferred by the Secretary of the Treasury) "for outstanding and unusual leadership during service as a U.S. Commissioner of Internal Revenue." For more than 23 years, Mr. Caplin has been in private practice with his present law firm, and has served as Adjunct Professor for the University of Virginia Law School. He is a nationally acclaimed author of numerous articles on tax and corporate matters.

Consulting Editor
RICHARD M. FELDHEIM, M.B.A., J.D., LL.M., C.P.A. (NY), is a New York CPA as well as an Attorney in New York and Arizona. He holds a Masters in Tax Law from New York University Law School. Mr. Feldheim is a member of the New York State Society of CPAs, AICPA, New York State Bar Association, Association of the Bar of the City of New York, Arizona Bar, and American Bar Association. His background includes practice as both a CPA with Price Waterhouse & Co. and as a Senior Partner with the Arizona law firm of Wentworth & Lundin. He has lectured for the AICPA, the Practising Law Institute, Seton Hall University, and the University of Arizona.

Consulting Editor
MARILYN F. HUNT, M.A., C.P.A. (FL), currently serves as an Accounting instructor at the University of Central Florida, where she has been CPA Review Program Coordinator for more than 15 years. Ms. Hunt is a contributing editor for *The Internal Auditor* magazine and is an author and reviewer for various accounting and CPA Review texts. In addition, she regularly writes questions for the Certified Internal Auditor Examination. Ms. Hunt has conducted CPE programs for the AICPA, the Associated Regional Accounting Firms, the IMA, the Florida Institute of Certified Public Accountants, DisneyWorld, Blue Cross/ Blue Shield, and many local and national CPA firms. Her background includes public accounting experience with Price Waterhouse.

Consulting Editor
THOMAS A. RATCLIFFE, Ph.D., C.P.A. (TX), is Professor of Accounting and Chairman of the Department of Accounting and Finance at Troy State University. Dr. Ratcliffe teaches financial accounting courses and has published more than 100 technical works in accounting and auditing. He received the 1991 Alabama Society of CPAs Outstanding Accounting Educator award and has been named Alabama's Outstanding Discussion Leader and CPE instructor for the past four years. Dr. Ratcliffe serves as a consultant to several CPA firms and was past President of the Southeast Alabama Chapter of the Alabama Society of CPAs. He currently serves as a Council Representative for the Alabama Society of CPAs.

Consulting Editor
C. WILLIAM THOMAS, M.B.A., Ph.D., C.P.A. (TX), currently serves as a Professor and Chairman of the Department of Accounting and Business Law at Baylor University. He is a member of the AICPA, the Texas Society of CPAs, the Central Texas Chapter of CPAs, and the American Accounting Association, where he is past Chairperson for the Southwestern Regional Audit Section. Professor Thomas is a nationally known author and has extensive experience in Auditing CPA Review. In addition, he has received recognition for special audit education and curriculum projects he developed for Coopers & Lybrand. His background includes public accounting experience with KPMG Peat Marwick.

AUDITING

VOLUME III of IV

TABLE OF CONTENTS

NOTES

GETTING STARTED

STEP ONE: READ PART ONE OF THE PRACTICAL ADVICE SECTION AT THE FRONT OF THE BOOK

Part One of the Practical Advice section is designed to familiarize you with the CPA Examination. Included in this section are general comments about the exam, a schedule of future exam dates, the addresses and phone numbers of the state boards of accountancy, and attributes required for exam success.

STEP TWO: TAKE THE DIAGNOSTIC EXAMS

The diagnostic exams are designed to help you determine your strong and weak areas. This in turn will help you design your personalized training plan so that you spend more time in your weak areas and do not waste precious study time in areas where you are already strong. You can take the exams using either the books or CPA Review Software for Windows. CPA Review Software for Windows will automatically score your exams for you and give you a personalized analysis of your strong and weak areas. The books provide you with a worksheet which makes self diagnosis fast and easy.

NOTE: If you took a previous CPA Exam and did not pass one or more sections, we recommend that you analyze these exam sections to help you determine where you need to concentrate your efforts this time around.

STEP THREE: DEVELOP A PERSONALIZED TRAINING PLAN

Now, based on the results from your diagnostic exams, we will show you how to develop your personalized training plan. If you are taking the exam for the first time, and you are the "average" CPA candidate, we recommend that you train for 20 weeks at a minimum of 20 hours per week. This level of intensity should increase during the final four weeks of your training and peak at a minimum of 40 hours the final week before the exam. If you took the exam last time and did not condition (you still have to take all four sections), and you are the "average" CPA candidate, we recommend that you train for 12 weeks at a minimum of 20 hours per week. Again, this level of intensity should increase during the final four weeks of your training and peak at a minimum of 40 hours the final week before the exam. If you have conditioned (you have to take three or less sections), you can adjust these guidelines accordingly.

You are probably wondering what we mean by an "average" candidate. We are referring to the candidate who is just finishing or has just finished his or her academic training, attended a school which has a solid accounting curriculum, and received above average grades in his or her accounting and business law courses. Remember, "average" is a benchmark, many candidates are not "average", so adjust your training plan accordingly.

HOW TO FIND 20 HOURS A WEEK TO STUDY

The typical CPA candidate is a very busy individual. He or she goes to school and/or works full or part time. Some candidates have additional responsibilities such as a spouse, children, a house to take care of--the list can go on and on. Consequently, your first reaction may be, " I don't have 20 hours a week to devote to training for the CPA Exam." Using the chart on the following page, we will show you how to "find" the time that you need to develop your training schedule.

1. Keeping in mind what you would consider to be a typical week; first mark out in black the time that you know you won't be able to study. For example, mark an "X" in each block which represents time that you normally sleep, have a class, work, or have some other type of commitment.

2. Next, in a different color, put a "C" in each block which represents commute time, an "M" in each block which represents when you normally eat your meals, and an "E" in each block which represents when you normally exercise.

3. Now pick one hour each day to relax and give your mind a break. In black, write "BREAK" in one block each day. Do not skip this step. By taking a break, you will study more efficiently and effectively.

4. Count how many blocks are left. Are there 20? If so, in a different color write "STUDY" in 20 blocks. If not, write "STUDY" in the remaining blocks. Now count your "C", "M", and "E" blocks; if needed, these can be used to gain additional study time by using tapes and/or flashcards.

5. If you still do not have 20 blocks, and you scored 70% or more on your diagnostic exams, you may still be able to pass the exam even with your limited study time. If, however, you scored less than 70% on your diagnostic exams, you have 2 options: (1) re-prioritize and make a block which has an "X" in it, available study time; or (2) concentrate on conditioning (passing some but not all of the sections) instead of on passing the entire exam.

TIME AVAILABILITY

	MON	TUES	WED	THURS	FRI	SAT	SUN
1:00 AM							
2:00 AM							
3:00 AM							
4:00 AM							
5:00 AM							
6:00 AM							
7:00 AM							
8:00 AM							
9:00 AM							
10:00 AM							
11:00 AM							
12:00 PM							
1:00 PM							
2:00 PM							
3:00 PM							
4:00 PM							
5:00 PM							
6:00 PM							
7:00 PM							
8:00 PM							
9:00 PM							
10:00 PM							
11:00 PM							
12:00 AM							

HOW TO ALLOCATE YOUR 20 WEEKS

This is where we will develop your overall training plan. We will outline a recommended training plan based on 20 hours per week and 20 weeks of study. The suggested hours of study are based on 20 hours of study time per week. The time allocated to each topic was based on the length of the chapter, the difficulty of the material, and how heavily the topic is tested on the exam (refer to the exam specifications and our frequency analysis found in the Practical Advice section of your book). Keep in mind that this plan is for the "average" CPA candidate. Consequently, you should customize this plan based on the results of your diagnostic exams and level of knowledge in each area tested. For example, if you have not had a course in governmental accounting, you will need to adjust your training plan to allow for more time in this area. Conversely, do not fall into the trap of spending too much time covering an area which is rarely tested on the exam.

RECOMMENDED TRAINING PLAN

		Hours
WEEK 1:	READ PRACTICAL ADVICE SECTION	
	TAKE DIAGNOSTIC EXAMS	
	GET ORGANIZED	
WEEK 2:	CHAPTER 1-- OVERVIEW OF FINANCIAL ACCOUNTING	5
	CHAPTER 2-- CASH, SHORT-TERM INVESTMENTS, AND RECEIVABLES	8
	CHAPTER 3-- INVENTORIES	7
WEEK 3:	WEEKLY REVIEW OF WEEK 2	1
	CHAPTER 4-- PROPERTY, PLANT, AND EQUIPMENT	5
	CHAPTER 5-- INTANGIBLES, R & D, & OTHER ASSETS	4
	CHAPTER 6-- BONDS	4
	CHAPTER 7-- LIABILITIES	6
WEEK 4:	WEEKLY REVIEW OF WEEKS 2 - 3	2
	CHAPTER 34-- STANDARDS AND RELATED TOPICS	2
	CHAPTER 35-- PLANNING THE AUDIT	2
	CHAPTER 8-- LEASES	7
	CHAPTER 9-- PENSIONS	7
WEEK 5:	WEEKLY REVIEW OF WEEKS 2 - 4	2
	CHAPTER 36-- INTERNAL CONTROL	8
	CHAPTER 37-- AUDIT EVIDENCE, PROGRAMS, AND PROCEDURES	7
	CHAPTER 38-- AUDIT SAMPLING PROCEDURES	3
WEEK 6:	WEEKLY REVIEW OF WEEKS 2 - 5	2
	CHAPTER 10-- OWNERS' EQUITY	6
	CHAPTER 11-- REPORTING THE RESULTS OF OPERATIONS	8
	CHAPTER 39-- AUDITING EDP SYSTEMS	4
WEEK 7:	WEEKLY REVIEW OF WEEKS 2 - 6	2
	CHAPTER 12-- REVENUE & EXPENSE RECOGNITION: SPECIAL AREAS	7
	CHAPTER 40-- REPORTS ON AUDITED FINANCIAL STMTS	8
	CHAPTER 41-- OTHER TYPES OF REPORTS	3

		Hours
WEEK 8:	WEEKLY REVIEW OF WEEKS 2 - 7	2
	CHAPTER 13-- ACCOUNTING FOR INCOME TAXES	9
	CHAPTER 14-- STATEMENT OF CASH FLOWS	6
	CHAPTER 15-- FINANCIAL STMT & RATIO ANALYSIS	3
WEEK 9:	WEEKLY REVIEW OF WEEKS 2 - 8	3
	CHAPTER 16-- FINANCIAL REPORTING AND CHANGING PRICES	3
	CHAPTER 17-- FOREIGN OPERATIONS	3
	CHAPTER 18-- EARNINGS PER SHARE	3
	CHAPTER 19-- PARTNERSHIPS & PERSONAL FS	5
	CHAPTER 42-- OTHER PROFESSIONAL SERVICES	3
WEEK 10:	WEEKLY REVIEW OF WEEKS 2 - 9	2
	OVERALL REVIEW OF AUDIT	2
	CHAPTER 20-- BUSINESS COMBINATIONS & CONSOLIDATED FS	10
	CHAPTER 43-- CONTRACTS	6
WEEK 11:	WEEKLY REVIEW OF WEEKS 2 - 10	4
	OVERALL REVIEW OF FINANCIAL ACCOUNTING & REPORTING	6
	CHAPTER 21-- GOVERNMENTAL ACCOUNTING	10
WEEK 12:	WEEKLY REVIEW OF WEEKS 2-11	4
	CHAPTER 44-- SALES	6
	CHAPTER 22-- NON-PROFIT ACCOUNTING	10
WEEK 13:	WEEKLY REVIEW OF WEEKS 2 - 12	4
	CHAPTER 45-- COMMERCIAL PAPER	4
	CHAPTER 46-- DOCUMENTS OF TITLE	2
	CHAPTER 47-- SECURED TRANSACTIONS	4
	CHAPTER 23-- MANUFACTURING COST ELEMENTS & CGMS	3
	CHAPTER 24-- PRODUCT COSTING	3
WEEK 14:	WEEKLY REVIEW OF WEEKS 2 - 13	4
	CHAPTER 25-- STANDARD COSTING	3
	CHAPTER 26-- COST-VOLUME-PROFIT ANALYSIS	3
	CHAPTER 48-- BANKRUPTCY	3
	CHAPTER 49-- SURETYSHIP	3
	CHAPTER 27-- DIRECT (VARIABLE COSTING)	2
	CHAPTER 28-- BUDGETING	2
WEEK 15:	WEEKLY REVIEW OF WEEKS 2 - 14	5
	CHAPTER 29-- QUANTITATIVE METHODS	5
	CHAPTER 30-- FEDERAL TAXATION: INDIVIDUALS	10
WEEK 16:	WEEKLY REVIEW OF WEEKS 2 - 15	5
	CHAPTER 50-- AGENCY	4
	CHAPTER 51-- PARTNERSHIPS	3
	CHAPTER 52-- CORPORATIONS	3
	CHAPTER 53-- ESTATES AND TRUSTS	3
	CHAPTER 54-- REGULATION OF EMPLOYMENT	2
	CHAPTER 31-- FEDERAL TAXATION: PROPERTY	5

		Hours
WEEK 17:	WEEKLY REVIEW OF WEEKS 2 - 16	11
	CHAPTER 32-- FEDERAL TAXATION: CORPORATIONS	10
	CHAPTER 55-- FEDERAL SECURITIES REGULATIONS	3
	CHAPTER 56-- REAL & PERSONAL PROPERTY	4
	CHAPTER 57-- FIRE AND CASUALTY INSURANCE	2
WEEK 18:	WEEKLY REVIEW OF WEEKS 2 - 17	17
	CHAPTER 33-- FEDERAL TAXATION: P'SHIPS., ESTATES, & TRUSTS	4
	CHAPTER 58-- ETHICS & PROFESSIONAL RESPONSIBILITIES	2
	CHAPTER 59-- ACCOUNTANTS' PROFESSIONAL LIABILITIES	3
	OVERALL REVIEW OF ACCOUNTING & REPORTING	5
	OVERALL REVIEW OF BUSINESS LAW & PROFESSIONAL RESPONS.	4
WEEK 19:	REVIEW AREAS YOU STILL FEEL WEAK IN	40+
WEEK 20:	TAKE FINAL EXAMS UNDER EXAM CONDITIONS	8
	DO FINAL REVIEWS	32+

YOUR PERSONALIZED TRAINING PLAN:

WEEK	TASK	DIAGNOSTIC SCORE	ESTIMATED HOURS	DATE COMPLETE	POST-TEST SCORES
1					
2					
3					
4					
5					
6					
7					
8					

WEEK	TASK	DIAGNOSTIC SCORE	ESTIMATED HOURS	DATE COMPLETE	POST-TEST SCORES
9					
10					
11					
12					
13					
14					
15					
16					

WEEK	TASK	DIAGNOSTIC SCORE	ESTIMATED HOURS	DATE COMPLETE	POST-TEST SCORES
17					
18					
19					
20					

NOTES:

STEP FOUR: READ PART TWO OF THE PRACTICAL ADVICE SECTION AT THE FRONT OF YOUR BOOK

Part Two of the Practical Advice section of the book will familiarize you with how the CPA Examination is graded and tell you how you can earn extra points on the exam simply by knowing what the grader is going to look for. In addition, we explain our Solutions Approach, which is an efficient, systematic method of organizing and solving questions found on the CPA Exam. Using this approach will help you maximize your grade on the exam. In Part Two, we also outline the AICPA content specifications for each section of the exam.

STEP FIVE: HOW TO INTEGRATE YOUR REVIEW MATERIALS

In this section we will show you how to integrate the Totaltape CPA review products that you purchased to optimize the effectiveness of your training plan. Find the section that corresponds to the package that you purchased. Then read the material that follows to maximize your training.

BOOKS, AUDIOTAPES, and CPA REVIEW SOFTWARE FOR WINDOWS

This is our most comprehensive review package available. This combination is reserved expressly for the serious CPA candidate. It is intended for those candidates who want to make sure that they pass the exam the first time (or this time, if you have already taken the exam). In addition, by using this package, you are eligible to qualify for Totaltape's money-back guarantee.

How to Use This Package:

1. First take the diagnostic exams using CPA Review Software for Windows. CPA Review Software for Windows automatically scores your exams and tells you what your strong and weak areas are.

In chapters where you are strong (i.e. you scored 65% or better on the diagnostic exam):

2. Begin your study of that chapter by answering the multiple choice questions using CPA Review Software for Windows. Once again, CPA Computer Software for Windows will point out the subtopics where you are strong and where you are weak so that you can focus on your weak subtopics.

3. Read the subsections of the chapter which correspond to your weak areas.

4. At this point, listen to the tape for this chapter to reinforce your weak areas and review your strong areas.

5. Now, using CPA Review Software for Windows, answer the multiple choice questions that you previously answered incorrectly. If you answer 70% or more of the questions correctly, you are ready to move on to the next chapter. If you answer less than 70% of the questions correctly, go back and review the subtopics which are still giving you trouble. Then using CPA Review Software for Windows, answer the questions which you previously answered incorrectly. If you still do not get at least 70% of the questions correct, check the exam specification and frequency charts in the Practical Advice section of your book to find out how heavily this area is tested. If this is an area which is heavily tested, continue reviewing the material and answering questions until you can answer at least 70% of them correctly. Allocate more time than you originally budgeted, if necessary. If this area is not heavily tested, move on, but make a note to come back to this topic later as time allows.

In chapters where you are weak (i.e. you scored less than 65% on the diagnostic exam):

2. Read the chapter in the book.

3. Listen to the taped lecture on this chapter.

4. Re-read the subsections of the chapter which correspond to your weak subtopics.

5. Using CPA Review Software for Windows, answer the multiple choice questions for this chapter. If you answer 70% or more of the questions correctly, you are ready to move on to the next chapter. If you get less than 70% of the questions correct, use your book to review the subtopics where you are weak. Then answer the questions that you previously answered incorrectly. If you still do not get at least 70% correct, check the exam specification and frequency charts in the Practical Advice section of your book to find out how heavily the area is tested. If this is an area which is heavily tested, continue reviewing the material and answering multiple choice questions until you can answer at least 70% correctly. Allocate more time than you originally budgeted, if necessary. If this is not a heavily tested area, move on, but make a note to come back to this area later as time allows.

BOOKS AND CPA REVIEW SOFTWARE FOR WINDOWS

This combination allows you to use the books to review the material and CPA Review Software for Windows to practice exam questions. You can also use the books to practice exam questions when you do not have access to a computer. In addition, by using this package, you are eligible to qualify for Totaltape's money-back guarantee.

How to Use This Package:

1. Take the diagnostic exams using CPA Review Software for Windows. CPA Review Software for Windows automatically scores your exams and tells you what your strong and weak areas are.

In chapters where you are strong (i.e. you scored 65% or better on the diagnostic exam):

2. Begin your study of that chapter by <u>first</u> answering the multiple choice questions using CPA Review Software for Windows. Once again, CPA Review Software for Windows will point out the subtopics where you are strong and where you are weak so that you can focus on your weak subtopics.

3. Read the subsections of the chapter which correspond to your weak areas.

4. Now using CPA Review Software for Windows, answer the multiple choice questions that you previously answered incorrectly. If you answer 70% or more of the questions correctly, you are ready to move on to the next chapter. If you answer less than 70% of the questions correctly, go back and review the subtopics which are still giving you trouble. Then using CPA Review Software for Windows, answer the questions which you previously answered incorrectly. If you still do not get at least 70% of the questions correct, check the exam specification and frequency charts in the Practical Advice section of your book to find out how heavily this area is tested. If this is an area which is heavily tested, continue reviewing the material and answering questions until you can answer at least 70% of them correctly. Allocate more time than you originally budgeted, if necessary. If this area is not heavily tested, move on, but make a note to come back to this topic later as time allows.

In chapters where you are weak (i.e. you scored less than 65% on the diagnostic exam):

2. Read the chapter in the book.

3. Using CPA Review Software for Windows, answer the multiple choice questions for this chapter. If you answer 70% or more of the questions correctly, you are ready to move on to the next chapter. If

you get less than 70% of the questions correct, use your book to review the subtopics where you are weak. Then answer the questions that you previously answered incorrectly. If you still do not get at least 70% correct, check the exam specification and frequency charts in the Practical Advice section of your book to find out how heavily the area is tested. If this is an area which is heavily tested, continue reviewing the material and answering multiple choice questions until you can answer at least 70% correctly. Allocate more time than you originally budgeted, if necessary. If this is not a heavily tested area, move on, but make a note to come back to this area later as time allows.

BOOKS AND AUDIOTAPES

This combination is designed for the candidate who does not have access to a computer to study, who spends time commuting or doing other activities which could take valuable time away from studying, and for those who like to reinforce what they read by listening to a lecture on tape.

How to Use This Package:

1. Take the diagnostic exams found in the Practical Advice section of your book. Using the worksheets provided, score your exams to determine your strong and weak areas.

In chapters where you are strong (i.e. you scored 65% or better on the diagnostic exam):

2. Do the multiple choice questions for that chapter. Using the worksheet provided, analyze your strong and weak areas.

3. Read the subsections of the chapter which correspond to your weak subtopics.

4. At this point, listen to the audiotape on this chapter to reinforce your weak areas and review your strong areas.

5. Answer the multiple choice questions that you previously answered incorrectly. If you answer 70% or more of the questions correctly, you are ready to move on to the next chapter. If you answer less than 70% of the questions correctly, go back and review the subtopics which are still giving you trouble. Then answer the questions that you previously answered incorrectly. If you still do not get at least 70% of the questions correct, check the exam specification and frequency charts in the Practical Advice section of your book to find out how heavily this area is tested. If this is an area which is heavily tested, continue reviewing the material and answering questions until you can answer at least 70% of them correctly. Allocate more time than you originally budgeted, if necessary. If this area is not heavily tested, move on, but make a note to come back to this topic later as time allows.

In chapters where you are weak (i.e. you scored less than 65% on the diagnostic exam):

2. First read the chapter in the book.

3. Now listen to the lecture of this chapter on tape.

4. Re-read the subsections of the chapter which correspond to your weak subtopics.

5. Do the multiple choice questions and score yourself using the worksheet provided. If you answer 70% or more of the questions correctly, you are ready to move on to the next chapter. If you answer less than 70% of the questions correctly, go back and review the subtopics which are still giving you trouble. Then answer the questions which you have previously answered incorrectly. If you still do not get at least 70% of the questions correct, check the exam specification and frequency charts in the Practical Advice section of your book to find out how heavily this area is tested. If this is an area which is heavily tested, continue reviewing the material and answering questions until you can answer

at least 70% of them correctly. Allocate more time than you originally budgeted for if necessary. If this area is not heavily tested, move on, but make a note to come back to this topic later as time allows.

VIDEOTAPES

The videotapes are designed to supplement all of the study packages. Use them to help you study the areas which are most troubling for you. They contain concise, informative lectures, as well as CPA Exam tips, tricks, and techniques which will help you to learn the material and to pass the exam.

STEP SIX: HELPFUL HINTS

♦ HOW TO SPEND YOUR WEEKLY REVIEW TIME

Answer the multiple choice questions and objective format questions that you previously answered incorrectly or merely guessed correctly.

Read through your notes.

Pick one essay question or problem to work.

Read the other essay and problem questions and solutions.

Go through your flashcards.

♦ USE A SEPARATE SHEET OF PAPER TO ANSWER THE MULTIPLE CHOICE QUESTIONS

Do not circle the answer to the multiple choice questions in the book. You should work every multiple choice question at least twice and you do not want to influence your answer by knowing how you previously answered the question.

♦ CIRCLE THE NUMBER OF THE MULTIPLE CHOICE QUESTIONS THAT YOU ANSWER INCORRECTLY OR MERELY GUESS CORRECTLY.

This way you know to answer this question again at a later time.

♦ MAKE NOTES AS YOU STUDY

Make notes and/or highlight when you read the chapters in the book. When possible, make notes when you listen to the tapes. You will find these very useful for your weekly reviews and for your final review.

♦ MAKE FLASHCARDS

Make flashcards for topics which are heavily tested on the exam and/or are giving you trouble. You will find these very useful for your weekly reviews and for your final review. Keep these handy and review them when you are waiting in line or on hold. This will turn nonproductive time into valuable study time.

- HOW TO MOST EFFECTIVELY USE THE AUDIO TAPES

  Use the tapes to turn nonproductive time into valuable study time. For example, play the tapes when you are commuting, exercising, getting ready for school or work, doing laundry, etc. The tapes will help you to memorize and retain key concepts. They will also reinforce what you have read in the books. Get in the habit of listening to the tapes whenever you have a chance. The more times that you listen to each tape, the more familiar you will become with the material and the easier it will be for you to recall it on the exam.

STEP SEVEN: IMPLEMENT YOUR TRAINING PLAN

This is it! You are primed and ready. You have decided which training tools will work best for you and you know how to use them. As you implement your personalized training plan, keep yourself focused. Your goal is to obtain a grade of 75 or better on each section and, thus, pass the CPA Exam. Therefore, you should concentrate on learning new material and reviewing old material only to the extent that it helps you reach this goal. Also, keep in mind that now is not the time to hone your procrastination skills. Utilize the personalized training plan that you developed in step three so that you do not fall behind schedule. Adjust it when necessary if you need more time in one chapter or less time in another. However, make sure to refer to the AICPA content specification and the frequency analysis to make sure that the adjustment is warranted. Above all else, remember that passing the exam is an attainable goal. If, after reading forewords E, F, and G, you do not feel ready to implement your training plan, or if at any point you have problems, call and talk to one of our editors. Our editors have all passed the exam and stand ready to help you do the same. Good luck!

PRACTICAL ADVICE FOR CPA EXAM PREPARATION

Your first step toward an effective CPA Review program is to study the material in this Foreword. It has been carefully developed to provide you with essential information which will help you succeed on the CPA Exam. This material will assist you in organizing an efficient study plan and will demonstrate effective techniques and strategies for taking the CPA Exam.

PART ONE

GENERAL COMMENTS ON THE CPA EXAM

The difficulty and comprehensiveness of the CPA Exam is a well-known fact to all candidates. However, success on the CPA Exam is a reasonable, attainable goal. You should keep this point in mind as you study this Foreword and develop your study plan. A positive attitude toward the examination, combined with determination and discipline, will enhance your opportunity to pass.

Purpose of the CPA Exam

The CPA Exam is designed as a licensing requirement to measure the technical competence of CPA candidates. Although licensing occurs at the State Board level, it is a uniform exam with national acceptance. Generally, passing the CPA Exam in one jurisdiction allows a candidate to obtain a reciprocal certificate or license if they meet all the requirements imposed by the jurisdiction from which reciprocity is being sought.

State Boards also rely upon other means to ensure that candidates possess the necessary technical and character attributes, including interviews, letters of reference, affidavits of employment, ethics examinations, and educational requirements.

Generally speaking, the CPA Exam is essentially an academic examination which tests the breadth of material covered by good accounting curricula; it also appears to emphasize the body of knowledge required for the practice of public accounting. It is to your advantage to take the exam as soon as possible after completing the formal education requirements. We also recommend that you study for the entire examination the first time you take it, since there is a synergistic learning effect to be derived through preparing for all four parts. That is, all sections of the exam share some common subjects (particularly Financial Accounting & Reporting, Accounting & Reporting, and Auditing); so as you study for one section, you are also studying for the others.

State Boards of Accountancy

Certified Public Accountants are licensed to practice by individual State Boards of Accountancy. Application forms and requirements to sit for the CPA Exam should be requested from your individual State Board. IT IS EXTREMELY IMPORTANT THAT YOU COMPLETE THE APPLICATION FORM CORRECTLY AND RETURN IT TO YOUR STATE BOARD BEFORE THE SPECIFIED DEADLINE. Errors and/or delays may result in the rejection of your application. Be extremely careful in filling out the application and be sure to enclose all required materials. In many states, applications must be received by the State Board at least ninety days before the examination date. Requirements as to education, experience, internship, and other matters vary. If you have not already done so, take a moment to call the appropriate State Board for specific and current requirements. Complete the application in a timely manner.

It may be possible to sit for the exam in another state as an out-of-state candidate. Candidates wishing to do so should contact the State Board of Accountancy in their home state. Addresses of State Boards of Accountancy are provided on page F-7 of this section.

Approximately one month before the exam, check to see that your application to sit for the exam has been processed. DON'T ASSUME THAT YOU ARE PROPERLY REGISTERED UNLESS YOU HAVE RECEIVED YOUR CANDIDATE ID NUMBER.

The AICPA publishes a booklet entitled Information for CPA Candidates, usually distributed by State Boards of Accountancy to candidates upon receipt of their applications. To request a complimentary copy, write your State Board or the AICPA, Examination Division, 1211 Avenue of the Americas, New York, NY 10036. The addresses of State Boards are on page F-7.

CPA Exam Schedule

The CPA Exam is given twice a year, on Wednesday and Thursday of the first week of May and November. The projected exam dates for May 1996 through November 1998 are as follows:

1996:	May 8, 9	1997:	May 7, 8	1998:	May 6, 7
	November 6, 7		November 5, 6		November 4, 5

The day and time for each section of the exam is also standardized as follows:

Section	Day	Time	Hours
Business Law & Professional Responsibilities	Wed.	9:00 - 12:00	3 hours
Auditing	Wed.	2:00 - 6:30	4 1/2 hours
Financial Accounting & Reporting--Business Enterprises	Thur.	8:00 - 12:30	4 1/2 hours
Accounting & Reporting--Taxation, Managerial, and Governmental and Not-for-Profit Organizations	Thur.	2:30 - 6:00	3 1/2 hours
			15 1/2 hours

Conditional Status

You will receive four scores. A passing score for each section is 75. Conditional status is granted by the individual State Boards of Accountancy and may vary from state to state. **Conditional status** may be granted to those candidates who receive a passing grade in some, but not all, sections. Some Boards of Accountancy grant conditional status to candidates who pass only one section, while other Boards require that at least two sections be passed before conditional status is awarded. Many Boards require a minimum grade in the sections failed to receive conditional credit for the sections passed.

If you received credit for passing some sections of the CPA Exam before May 1994 and plan to sit for re-examination in May 1994 and thereafter, you will be required to pass new sections of the exam. Candidates that have obtained conditional status by passing some sections of the Examination before May 1994 should check with their Board of Accountancy to determine the new Examination sections they must pass to complete the Examination process. The AICPA's recommendation for transitional conditional status is shown below. Keep in mind that this is only a recommendation. The final determination is up to each State Board of Accountancy.

Examination Sections Before May 1994	Examination Sections May 1994 and After
Accounting Theory	Financial Accounting & Reporting--Business Enterprises
Accounting Practice	Accounting & Reporting--Taxation, Managerial, and Governmental and Not-for-Profit Organizations
Auditing	Auditing
Business Law	Business Law & Professional Responsibilities

The AICPA has recommended that Boards of Accountancy which currently waive the Business Law section for members of the state bar should consider deleting this waiver because the new exam section, Business Law & Professional Responsibilities, also tests candidates' knowledge of the CPA's professional responsibilities to the public and the profession. This subject matter was previously tested in the Auditing section. Once again, candidates should check with their State Board of Accountancy concerning this matter.

Writing Skills Content

Answers to selected essay responses from Business Law & Professional Responsibilities, Auditing, and Financial Accounting & Reporting sections will be used to assess candidates' writing skills. Five percent of the points available on each of these sections will be allocated to writing skills. Effective writing skills include the following six characteristics:

1. Coherent organization.
2. Conciseness.
3. Clarity.
4. Use of standard English.
5. Responsiveness to the requirements of the question.
6. Appropriateness for the reader.

Calculators

Candidates will be provided with calculators at the examination sites for use on the Accounting & Reporting and Financial Accounting & Reporting sections. The purpose of providing calculators is to save the time candidates spend on performing and rechecking manual calculations; it is not intended to allow for more difficult and complex calculations and problems.

Examination Format

The examination will consist of the following sections and formats:

	Format		
Section	4-Option Multiple Choice	Other Objective Answer Formats	Essays or Problems
Financial Accounting & Reporting--Business Enterprises	50-60%	20-30%	20-30%
Accounting & Reporting--Taxation, Managerial, and Governmental and Not-for-Profit Organizations	50-60%	40-50%	---
Auditing	50-60%	20-30%	20-30%
Business Law & Professional Responsibilities	50-60%	20-30%	20-30%

The four sections of the exam cover the following:

1. **Business Law & Professional Responsibilities**--This section covers the legal implications of business transactions generally confronted by CPAs, and the CPA's professional responsibility to the public and the profession (formerly covered in the Auditing section). It comprises 3 hours of the exam, and five percent of the candidate's score on this section is based on writing skills.

2. **Auditing**--This section covers the generally accepted auditing standards, procedures, and related topics. The CPA's professional responsibility is no longer tested in this area. It comprises 4½ hours of the exam, and five percent of the candidate's score on this section is based on writing skills.

3. **Accounting & Reporting**--This section covers federal taxation, managerial accounting, and accounting for governmental and not-for-profit organizations. This section consists of multiple choice and other objective format questions only. It comprises 3½ hours of the exam.

4. **Financial Accounting & Reporting**--This section covers generally accepted accounting principles for business enterprises. It comprises 4½ hours of the exam, and five percent of the candidate's score on this section is based on writing skills.

Reference Materials

All the material you need to know to pass the CPA Exam is in your BISK CPA Comprehensive Review texts! However, should you desire more detailed coverage in any area, you should consult the actual promulgations. Individual copies of recent pronouncements are available from the FASB or AICPA.

To order materials from the FASB or AICPA contact:

FASB Order Department	AICPA Order Department
P.O. Box 5116	P.O. Box 1003
Norwalk, CT 06856-5116	New York, NY 10108-1003
Telephone (203) 847-0700	Telephone (800) 334-6961

The FASB offers a student discount, which varies depending on the publication. The AICPA offers a 30% educational discount, which students may claim by submitting proof of their eligibility (e.g., copy of ID card or teacher's letter). AICPA members get a 20% discount and delivery time will be speedier because members may order by phone.

THE NONDISCLOSED EXAM

Beginning with the May 1996 exam, the Uniform CPA Examination will be nondisclosed. This means that candidates will no longer be allowed to keep (or receive) their examination booklets after the test. Candidates will also be required to sign a statement of confidentiality in which they promise not to reveal questions or answers. The AICPA will continue to distribute *Selected Questions and Unofficial Answers,* but this publication will no longer contain actual questions from previous tests; instead, a sampling of questions which have been chosen as being similar to future test questions will be provided. After the exam, only the Institute will have access to the tests themselves. Totaltape's Editorial Board will continue to update our diagnostic tests for your convenience, with questions based upon the representative items which will be provided, items from previously disclosed tests, and the teaching expertise of our editors.

Background

The AICPA made this change, which was authorized in June 1991 by the Board of Examiners, in order to increase consistency, facilitate possible future computer administration of the test, and improve examination quality by pretesting questions. Because the examination will no longer be completely changed every year, statistical equating methods will be more relevant, and the usefulness of specific questions as indicators of candidates' knowledge can be tested.

Effects on Time Management

Approximately 10% of the multiple choice questions in every section of the May 1996 exam, and every exam thereafter, will be questions which are being pretested. These questions will not be included in candidates' final grades; they are presented only so that the Board of Examiners may evaluate them for effectiveness and possible ambiguity. The Scholastic Achievement Test and the Graduate Record Exam both employ similar but not identical strategies: those tests include an extra section, which is being pretested, and test-takers do not know which section is the one which will not be graded. On the Uniform CPA Examination, however, the extra questions will be mixed in among the graded questions. This will make time management even more crucial. Candidates who are deciding how much time to spend on a difficult multiple choice question must keep in mind that there is a 10% chance that the answer to the question will not affect them either way. Also, candidates should not allow a question that seems particularly difficult or confusing to shake their confidence or affect their attitude towards the rest of the test; it may not even count. However, this experimental 10% will work against candidates who are not sure whether or not they have answered enough questions to earn 75%. Candidates should try for a safety margin, so that they will have accumulated enough correct answers to pass, even though some of their correctly answered questions will not be scored.

Post-Exam Diagnostics

The AICPA Board of Examiners' Advisory Grading Service will provide boards of accountancy with individual diagnostic reports for all candidates along with the candidates' grades. The diagnostic reports will show the candidate's level of proficiency on each examination section. The boards of accountancy may mail the diagnostic reports to candidates along with their grades: candidates should contact the state board in their jurisdiction to find out its policy on this. As before, grades will be mailed approximately 90 days after the examination.

Question Re-evaluation

Candidates who believe that an examination question contains errors which will affect the grading should turn in the Question Comment Form to the proctor before leaving the examination room. Candidates may also fax their complaint to the AICPA Examinations Division, at (201) 938-3443, within 48 hours after taking the examination. Only these two methods of communication will satisfy the requirements of the AICPA. The Advisory Grading Service asks candidates to be as precise as possible about the question and their reason for believing that it should be re-evaluated, and, if possible, to supply references to support their position. Since candidates are no longer able to keep or discuss the examination questions, it is important to remember as much detail as possible about a disputed question.

Discussing the Exam

Remember that candidates will be required to sign a statement of confidentiality in which they promise not to reveal questions or answers. Due to the nondisclosure requirements, Totaltape's editors will no longer be able to address questions about specific examination questions, although we will continue to supply help with similar study problems and questions in our texts.

STATE BOARDS OF ACCOUNTANCY

STATE	ADDRESS	PHONE NUMBER
AL	770 Washington Ave., RSA Plaza, Suite 236, Montgomery 36130	205/242-5700
AK	P.O. Box 110806, Juneau 99811-0806	907/465-2580
AZ	3110 N. 19th Ave., Ste. 140, Phoenix 85015	602/255-3648
AR	101 E. Capitol Avenue, Ste. 430, Little Rock 72201	501/682-1520
CA	2000 Evergreen St., Ste. 250, Sacramento 95815	916/263-3680
CO	1560 Broadway, Ste. 1370, Denver 80202	303/894-7800
CT	30 Trinity St., Hartford 06106	203/566-7835
DE	P.O. Box 1401, Margaret O'Neill Bldg., Dover 19903	302/739-4522
DC	614 H Street, N.W., Room 923, Washington, DC 20001	202/727-7454
FL	2610 N.W. 43rd St., Ste. 1A, Gainesville 32606	904/955-2165
GA	166 Pryor St., S.W., Atlanta 30303	404/656-3941
GU	P.O. Box P, Bank of Guan Building, Ste. 800, Agana, GU 96910	671/472-2910
HI	P.O. Box 3469, Honolulu 96801 or 1010 Richard St., Honolulu 96813	808/586-2694
ID	1109 Main St., Owyhee Plaza #470, Boise 83720	208/334-2490
IL	Univ. of Illinois, 10 Henry Admin. Bldg., 506 S. Wright St., Urbana 61801	217/333-1566
IN	Indiana Gov. Center S. E034, 302 W. Washington St., Indianapolis 46204-2246	317/232-2980
IA	1918 S.E. Hulsizer, Ankeny 50021	515/281-4126
KS	900 S.W. Jackson St., Ste. 556, Topeka 66612-1239	913/296-2162
KY	332 W. Broadway, Ste. 310, Louisville 40202	502/595-3037
LA	1515 World Trade Center, 2 Canal St., New Orleans 70130	504/566-1244
ME	State House Station 35, Augusta 04333	207/582-8700
MD	501 St. Paul Place, Room 902, Baltimore 21202-2272	410/333-6322
MA	100 Cambridge Street, Room 1315, Boston 02202	617/727-1806
MI	Dept. of Commerce, P.O. Box 30018, Lansing 48909	814/238-3066
MN	113 E. 7th St., St. Paul 55101	612/296-7937
MS	961 Highway 80E, Ste. A., Clinton 39056-5246	601/354-7320
MO	3605 Missouri Blvd., P.O. Box 613, Jefferson City 65102	314/751-0012
MT	111 N. Jackson, P.O. Box 200513, Helena 59620-0513	406/444-3739
NE	P.O. Box 94725, Lincoln 68509	402/471-3595
NV	200 S. Virginia, Ste. 670, Reno 89501	702/786-0231
NH	57 Regional Dr., Concord 03301	603/271-3286
NJ	P.O. Box 45000, Newark 07101	201/504-6380
NM	1650 University Blvd., N.E., Ste. 400-A, Albuquerque 87102	505/841-9108
NY	The State Education Dept., Cultural Education Center, Room 3013, Albany 12230	518/474-3836
NC	P.O. Box 12827, Raleigh 27605-2827	919/733-4222
ND	U.N.D., P.O. Box 9037, Grand Forks 58202-9037	701/775-7100
OH	77 S. High St., 18th Floor, Columbus 43266-0301	614/466-4135
OK	4545 N. Lincoln Blvd., Ste. 165, Oklahoma City 73105-3413	405/521-2397
OR	3218 Pringle Rd. S.E., Ste. 110, Salem 97302	503/378-4181
PA	P.O. Box 2649, Harrisburg 17105-2649	717/783-1404
PR	Box 3671, San Juan 00904	809/722-2121
RI	233 Richmond St., Ste. 236, Providence 02903	401/277-3185
SC	P.O. Box 11329, Columbia 29211	803/734-4228
SD	301 E. 14th St., Ste. 200, Sioux Falls 57104	605/367-5770
TN	500 James Robertson Pkwy., 2nd Floor, Nashville 37243-1141	615/741-2550
TX	1033 La Posada, Ste. 340, Austin 78752-3892	512/505-5570
UT	P.O. Box 45805, Salt Lake City 84145	801/530-6628
VT	109 State Street, Montpelier 05609-1106	802/828-2837
VI	P.O. Box Y, Christiansted, St. Croix VI, 00822	809/773-4305
VA	3600 W. Broad Street, 5th Floor, Richmond 23230-4917	804/367-8505
WA	P.O. Box 9131, Olympia 98507-9131	360/664-9192
WV	201 L&S Bldg., 812 Quarrier Street, Charleston 25301	304/558-3557
WI	P.O. Box 8935, Madison 53708-8935	608/266-2112
WY	Barrett Bldg., 2nd Floor, Room 217-218, Cheyenne 82002	307/777-7551

TEN ATTRIBUTES OF EXAMINATION SUCCESS

1. **Positive Mental Attitude**
2. **Development of a Plan**
3. **Adherence to the Plan**
4. **Time Management**
5. **Knowledge**
6. **Examination Grading**
7. **Solutions Approach**
8. **Examination Strategies**
9. **Focus on Ultimate Objective--Passing!**
10. **Examination Confidence**

We believe that successful CPA candidates possess these ten characteristics that contribute to their ability to pass the exam. Because of their importance, we will consider each attribute individually.

1. Positive Mental Attitude

Preparation for the CPA Exam is a long, intense process. A positive mental attitude, above all else, can be the difference between passing and failing.

2. Development of a Plan

The significant commitment involved in preparing for the exam requires a plan. We have prepared a Study Plan in the preceding "Getting Started" section. Take time to read this plan. Whether you use our "Study Plan" or create your own, the importance of this attribute can't be overlooked.

3. Adherence to the Plan

You cannot expect to accomplish a successful and comprehensive review without adherence to your study plan.

4. Time Management

We all lead busy lives, and the ability to budget study time is a key to success. We have outlined steps to budgeting time in the Personalized Training Plan found in the "Getting Started" section.

5. Knowledge

There is a distinct difference between understanding the material and knowledge of the material. A superficial understanding of accounting, auditing, and business law is not enough. You must know the material likely to be tested on the exam. Your BISK text is designed to help you acquire the working knowledge which is essential to exam success.

6. Examination Grading

An understanding of the CPA Exam grading procedure will help you to maximize grading points on the exam. Remember that your objective is to score 75 points on each section. Points are assigned to individual questions by the grader who reads your exam. In essence, your job is to satisfy the grader by writing answers which closely conform to the grading guide. In Part Two, Section 1, we explain AICPA grading procedures and show you how to tailor your answer to the grading guide and thus earn more points on the exam.

7. Solutions Approach

The Solutions Approach is an efficient, systematic method of organizing and solving questions found on the CPA Exam. This Approach will permit you to organize your thinking and your written answers in a logical manner that will maximize your exam score. Candidates who do not use a systematic answering method often neglect to show all their work on difficult problems or essays--work which could earn partial credit if it were presented to the grader in an orderly fashion. The Solutions Approach will help you avoid drawing "blanks" on the exam; with it, you always know where to begin.

Many candidates have never developed an effective problem-solving methodology in their undergraduate studies. The "cookbook" approach, in which students work problems by following examples, is widespread among accounting schools. Unfortunately, it is not an effective problem-solving method for the CPA Exam or for problems you will encounter in your professional career. Our Solutions Approach teaches you to derive solutions independently, without an example to guide you.

We feel that our **Solutions Approach** and grader orientation skills, when properly developed, can be worth at least 10 to 15 points for most candidates. As you can probably imagine, these 10 to 15 points can often make the difference between passing and failing.

The Solutions Approach for objective questions, problems, and essays is outlined in Part Two, Section 2. Examples are worked and explained.

8. Examination Strategies

You should be familiar with the format of the CPA Exam and know exactly what you will do when you enter the examination room. In Part Two, Section 3, we discuss the steps you should take from the time you receive the test booklet, until you hand in your answer sheet. Planning in advance how you will spend your examination time will save you time and confusion on exam day.

9. Focus on Ultimate Objective--Passing!

Your primary goal in preparing for the CPA Exam is to attain a grade of 75 or better on all sections and, thus, pass the examination. Your review should be focused on this goal. Other objectives, such as learning new material or reviewing old material, are important only insofar as they assist you in passing the exam.

10. Examination Confidence

Examination confidence is actually a function of the other nine attributes. If you have acquired a good working knowledge of the material, an understanding of the grading system, a tactic for answering the problems or essays, and a plan for taking the exam, you can go into the examination room confident that you are in control.

PART TWO: SECTION 1

EXAMINATION GRADING AND GRADER ORIENTATION SKILLS

The CPA Exam is prepared and graded by the AICPA Examinations Division. It is administered by the various State Boards of Accountancy.

An understanding of the grading procedure will help you maximize grading points on the CPA Exam. Remember that your objective is to pass the exam. You cannot afford to spend time on activities that will not affect your grade, or to ignore opportunities to increase your points. The following material abstracted from the Information for CPA Candidates booklet summarizes the important substantive aspects of the Uniform CPA Examination itself and the grading procedures used by the AICPA.

Security

The examination is prepared and administered under tight security measures. The candidates' anonymity is preserved throughout the examination and grading process. Unusual similarities in answers among candidates are reported to the appropriate State Boards.

Objective Questions

Objective questions consist of four-option, multiple-choice questions and other objective answer formats, which include: yes-no, true-false, matching, and questions requiring a numerical response. 50 - 60% of Financial Accounting & Reporting will consist of four-option multiple-choice questions. 20 - 30% of this section will consist of non-multiple-choice types of objective questions, designed to broaden the types of knowledge which can be tested.

Objective questions are machine graded. Thus, you will accomplish nothing (and only waste time) by writing explanations beside your answers--only the blackened response is considered by the optical scanner. It is also important to understand that there is no grade reduction for incorrect responses to objective questions--your total objective question grade is determined solely by the number of correct answers. Thus, you should answer every question. If you do not know the answer, make an intelligent guess.

There are two or three formats for questions on each section of the CPA Exam. In the past, difficulty points were assigned to these parts as a means of curving the entire section. Beginning with the May 1994 Exam, this will no longer occur. Instead, difficulty points will be assigned to the exam as a whole, not to each individual question. The point to remember is to avoid getting "bogged down" on one answer. Move along and answer all the questions. Finally, leaving questions unanswered or panic-answering questions due to poor budgeting of test time can mean disaster.

Essay Questions

Essay questions are graded by CPAs and AICPA staff members, using the following procedures as described in the Information for CPA Candidates booklet:

First grading

The first grading is done by graders assigned to individual questions. For example, each problem in the Auditing section will be graded by a different grader. A grader assigned to a single question, which will be graded during the full grading session of six or seven weeks, becomes an expert in the subject matter of the question and in the evaluation of the candidates' answers. Thus, grading is objective and uniform.

The purpose of the first grading is to separate the candidates' papers into three groups: obvious passes, marginal, and obvious failures.

Second grading

Upon completion of the first grading, a second grading is made by reviewers. Obvious passes and failures are subjected to cursory reviews as part of the grading controls. Marginal papers (papers with grades of 70 to 74), however, receive an extensive review. These papers are regraded to grades of 69 or 75.

The graders who make the extensive reviews have had years of experience grading the CPA Examination. They have also participated in the development of the grading bases and have access to item analysis for objective questions, identifying concepts as discriminating (those included by most candidates passing the exam) or as rudimentary (those included by candidates both passing and failing the exam). An important indicator of the competence of the candidate is whether grade points were earned chiefly from discriminating concepts or from rudimentary concepts.

Third grading

After the papers have been through the second grading for all parts of the examination, the resultant grades are listed by candidate number and compared for consistency among subjects. For example, if a candidate passes two subjects and receives a 69 in a third, the 69 paper will receive a third grading in the hope that the candidate, now identified as possessing considerable competence, can have the paper raised to a grade of 75 by finding additional points for which to grant positive credit. This third grading is done by the section head or a reviewer who did not do the second grading of the paper.

Fourth grading

The Director of Examinations applies a fourth grading to papers that have received the third grading but have grades that are inconsistent. The Director knows that the papers have already been subjected to three gradings, and that it would be difficult to find additional points for which the candidates should be given credit. Obviously, very few candidates are passed in this manner, but this fourth grading assures that marginal candidates receive every possible consideration.

Essay Question Example--Grading Guide

Points are assigned to essay questions on the basis of key concepts. A key concept is an idea, thought, or option that can be clearly defined and identified. Through a grading of sample papers, a list of key concepts related to each question is accumulated. These key concepts become the grading bases for the question. That is, your answer will be scored according to the number of key concepts it contains. Note that you need not include all possible key concepts to receive full credit on a question. The total number of grading bases exceeds the point value of the question. For example, a 10-point question may have 15 or more grading bases. Thus, a candidate would not have to provide all the key concepts to get the maximum available points. Conversely, a candidate cannot receive more points even if he or she provides more than 10 key concepts.

To illustrate the grading procedure and the importance of using key concepts in your answers, we will develop a hypothetical grading guide for a question adapted from a past Auditing exam. We will assume that the entire question is worth 10 points.

Example 1

Microcomputer software has been developed to improve the efficiency and effectiveness of the audit. Electronic spreadsheets and other software packages are available to aid in the performance of audit procedures otherwise performed manually.

Required:

Describe the potential benefits to an auditor of using microcomputer software in an audit as compared to performing an audit without the use of a computer. (11/87, Aud., #4)

Now let's look at the unofficial answer. Notice that we have underlined the key concepts in the answer. Later, as we develop a grading guide for the answer, you will see the importance of using key concepts to tailor your answer to parallel the grading guide.

Solution: Advantages of Using a Computer in an Audit

The potential benefits to an auditor of using microcomputer software in an audit as compared to performing an audit without the use of a computer include the following:

1. Time may be saved by eliminating manual footing, cross-footing, and other routine calculations.
2. Calculations, comparisons, and other data manipulations are more accurately performed.
3. Analytical procedures calculations may be more efficiently performed.
4. The scope of analytical procedures may be broadened.
5. Audit sampling may be facilitated.
6. Potential weaknesses in a client's internal control structure may be more readily identified.
7. Preparation and revision of flowcharts depicting the flow of financial transactions in a client's structure may be facilitated.
8. Working papers may be easily stored and accessed.
9. Graphics capabilities may allow the auditor to generate, display, and evaluate various financial and nonfinancial relationships graphically.
10. Engagement-management information such as time budgets and the monitoring of actual time vs. budgeted amounts may be more easily generated and analyzed.
11. Customized working papers may be developed with greater ease.
12. Standardized audit correspondence such as engagement letters, client representation letters, and attorney letters may be stored and easily modified.
13. Supervisory-review time may be reduced.
14. Staff morale and productivity may be improved by reducing the time spent on clerical tasks.
15. Client's personnel may not need to manually prepare as many schedules and otherwise spend as much time assisting the auditor.
16. Computer-generated working papers are generally more legible and consistent.

The grading guide consists of a list of the key concepts relevant to the question, both in key word form and in a detailed phrase. Each concept is assigned a point (more than one point if it is particularly important or fundamental). A point is also given on many questions for neatness and clarity of answer (including the use of proper formats, schedules, etc.). A hypothetical grading guide for our sample question follows.

Example 2--Grading Guide for Essay

STATE____________________________

CANDIDATE NO.______________________

POINTS		KEY WORD CONCEPTS
2	1.	Time saved by eliminating manual calculations.
2	2.	Accuracy.
2	3.	Analytical procedures more efficient.
2	4.	Scope of analytical procedures broadened.
1	5.	Audit sampling facilitated.
1	6.	Potential weaknesses in internal control structure more readily identified.
1	7.	Preparation and revision of flowcharts facilitated.
1	8.	Working papers easily stored and accessed.
1	9.	Graphics capabilities to generate, display, and evaluate financial and nonfinancial relationships graphically.
1	10.	Engagement-management information more easily generated and analyzed.
1	11.	Customized working papers developed with greater ease.
1	12.	Standardized audit correspondence stored and easily modified.
1	13.	Supervisory-review time reduced.
1	14.	Staff morale and productivity improved by reducing time spent on clerical tasks.
1	15.	Client's personnel time assisting auditor decreased.
1	16.	Computer-generated working papers more legible and consistent.
20		

GRADE CONVERSION CHART: POINTS TO GRADE

POINTS	1 2	3 4	5 6	7 8	9 10	11 12	13 14	15 16	17 18	19 20
GRADE	1	2	3	4	5	6	7	8	9	10

Importance of Key Concepts

A grading guide similar to the one in Example 4 is attached to every candidate's paper, with the key concepts or grading bases for each question. On the first grading, answers may be scanned first for key words, then read carefully to ascertain that no key concepts were overlooked. Each key concept in the answer increases the candidate's grade. The candidate's total grade for the question is easily determined by converting raw points, using a conversion chart. For example, a candidate who provides 17 of the 20 key concepts for this question would earn a grade of 9 for the answer. The process is repeated by the second grader and subsequent graders if necessary (i.e., borderline papers).

The point you should notice is that key concepts earn points. The unofficial answer closely conforms to the grading guide, making the grader's task simple. In turn, the unofficial answer also conforms to the format of the question. That is, each answer is numbered and lettered to correspond to the requirements. This should be your standard format.

There are two more points you should observe as you study the unofficial answer for our example. First, the answer is written in standard English, with clear, concise sentences and short paragraphs. A simple listing of key words is unacceptable; the concepts and their interrelationships must be logically presented. Secondly, remember that the unofficial answer represents the most acceptable solution to a question. This is not to say, however, that alternative answers are not considered. During the accumulation of grading bases, many concepts are added to the original "correct answer." Additionally, a paper that is near the passing mark receives a third (and perhaps fourth) grading, at which time individual consideration is given to the merits of each answer.

Parenthetically, we should mention that all the BISK CPA Review essays and problems are solved using the unofficial AICPA answers. Thus, you have ample opportunity to accustom yourself to the favored answer format.

Importance of Writing Skills

At least two essay responses will be graded for writing skills. A response is defined as a part of an essay. Therefore, if an essay question has a **Part a** and a **Part b,** it has two responses. The two responses graded for writing skills may be from the same question or from different questions. Either way, they will be totally independent topics requiring different technical knowledge. Five percent of the candidate's grade for the essay portion of the exam will be allocated to writing skills. For more coverage of this area, refer to the section of your book entitled **Accounting for 5%.**

Grading Implications for CPA Candidates

To summarize this review of the AICPA's grading procedure, we can offer the following conclusions which will help you to satisfy the grader and maximize your score:

1. Attempt an answer on every question.

2. Do not explain answers to multiple choice questions or other objective answer formats.

3. Respond directly to the requirements of the questions.

4. Use of a well-chosen example is an easy way of expressing an understanding of the subject or supporting a conclusion.

5. Use formats favored by the AICPA examiners.

6. Answer all requirements.

7. Develop a **Solutions Approach** to each question type.

8. Essay questions:

   Label your solutions parallel to the requirements.

   Offer reasons for your conclusions.

   Emphasize key words by underlining them.

   Separate grading concepts into individual sentences or paragraphs.

   Do not present your answer in outline format.

9. Allocate your examination time based on AICPA minimum suggested time.

10. Write neatly and legibly to avoid demerits.

PART TWO: SECTION 2

THE SOLUTIONS APPROACH

The **BISK Solutions Approach** is an efficient, systematic method of organizing and solving questions found on the CPA Exam. Remember that all the knowledge in the world is worthless unless you can get it down on paper. Conversely, a little knowledge can go a long way if you use a proper approach. The Solutions Approach was developed by our Editorial Board in 1971; all subsequently developed stereotypes trace their roots from the original "Approach" which we formulated. We feel that our Solutions Approach and grader orientation skills, when properly developed, can be worth at least 10 to 15 points for most candidates. As you can probably imagine, these 10 to 15 points often make the difference between passing and failing.

We will suggest a number of steps for deriving a solution that will help maximize your grade on the exam. Although you should remember the important steps in our suggested approach, don't be afraid to adapt these steps to your own taste and requirements. When you work the questions at the conclusion of each chapter, make sure you use your variation of the Solutions Approach. It is also important for you to attempt to pattern the organization and format of your written solution to the unofficial answer reprinted after the text of the questions. However, DO NOT CONSULT THE UNOFFICIAL ANSWER UNTIL YOU FINISH THE QUESTION. The worst thing you can do is look at old questions and then turn to the answer without working the problem. This will build false confidence and provide no skills in developing a Solutions Approach. Therefore, in order to derive the maximum number of points from an essay solution, you should first apply the Solutions Approach to reading and answering the question, and secondly, write an essay answer using an organization and format identical to that which would be used by the AICPA in writing the unofficial answer to that essay question.

Solutions Approach for Essay Questions

Our **six steps** are as follows:

1. Scan the text of the question for an overview of the subject area and content of the question.
2. Study the question requirements slowly and thoroughly; underline portions of the requirements as needed.
3. Visualize the unofficial answer format based on the requirements of the question.
4. Carefully study the text of the question. Underline important data.
5. Outline the solution in key words and phrases. Be sure to respond to the requirements, telling the grader only what he or she needs to know. You must explain the reasons for your conclusions.
6. Write the solution in the proper format based upon your key word outline. Write legibly in concise, complete sentences. Do not forget to proofread and edit your solution.

Essay Question Example

To illustrate the Solutions Approach for essay questions, we have adapted a question from a past Auditing examination. Key words in the solution are underlined.

Example 1 (15 to 25 minutes)

Cook, CPA, has been engaged to audit the financial statements of General Department Stores, Inc., a continuing audit client, which is a chain of medium-sized retail stores. General's fiscal year will end on June 30, 1993, and General's management has asked Cook to issue the auditor's report by August 1, 1993. Cook will not have sufficient time to perform all of the necessary field work in July 1993, but will have time to perform most of the field work as of an interim date, April 30, 1993.

For the accounts to be tested at the interim date, Cook will also perform substantive tests covering the transactions of the final two months of the year. This will be necessary to extend Cook's conclusions to the balance sheet date.

Required:

a. Describe the factors Cook should consider before applying principal substantive tests to General's balance sheet accounts at April 30, 1993.

b. For accounts tested at April 30, 1993, describe how Cook should design the substantive tests covering the balances as of June 30, 1993, and the transactions of the final two months of the year.

Let's look at the steps you go through to arrive at your solution:

In **Step 1**, you scan the question. Do not read thoroughly, simply get an overview of the subject area and content of the question. You notice the question deals with substantive testing.

In **Step 2**, you study the question requirements thoroughly. **Part a** asks about factors important to the reliance of substantive testing of the balance sheet accounts, while **Part b** refers to the period between the date of testing and year end. Underline key phrases and words.

In **Step 3**, you visualize the format of your solution. The solution will be in paragraph form. **Part a** will discuss the factors considered in the decision to rely on substantive testing. **Part b** will discuss the design of substantive tests to be used and the risks inherent to this area.

In **Step 4**, you carefully study the text of the question, given the requirements you want to satisfy, i.e., read the question carefully. You should mark important information.

In **Step 5**, you outline your answer in keyword form. In your exam preparation, as you work Auditing essays, notice that sometimes you are not asked to make a decision or reach a conclusion, but rather you are asked to identify and discuss all important factors in the situation.

Outline Answer

a. Assess difficulty in controlling incremental audit risk
 consider:
  reliability of accounting records
  management integrity
  business environment
  predictability of year-end balances
  internal control for cutoffs
  availability of information for final two months
  cost of substantive tests necessary to provide level of assurance
 (control risk assessed at < maximum) not required to extend audit conclusions to final two months
  (if control risk = maximum) - during final two months - will effectiveness be impaired?

b. Design of tests
 level of assurance meets audit objectives
  comparison of year-end information to comparable interim
   to identify and investigate unusual amounts
  Other analytical procedures
   to extend conclusions based on interim date to balance sheet date

In **Step 6**, you write your solution in a format similar to the unofficial answer. Notice how clear and concise the AICPA unofficial answers are. There is no doubt as to their decision or the reasoning supporting the decision. Notice also how they answer each requirement separately and in the same order as in the question. Be sure to proofread and edit your solution.

Example 2: Solution

a. Before applying principal substantive tests to balance sheet accounts at April 30, 1993, the interim date, Cook should assess the difficulty in controlling incremental audit risk. Cook should consider whether

- Cook's experience with the reliability of the accounting records and management's integrity has been good;

- Rapidly changing business conditions or circumstances may predispose General's management to misstate the financial statements in the remaining period;
- The year-end balances of accounts selected for interim testing will be predictable;
- General's procedures for analyzing and adjusting its interim balances and for reestablishing proper accounting cutoffs will be appropriate;
- General's accounting system will provide sufficient information about year-end balances and transactions in the final two months of the year to permit investigation of unusual transactions, significant fluctuations, and changes in balance compositions that may occur between the interim and balance sheet dates;
- The cost of the substantive tests necessary to cover the final two months of the year and provide the appropriate audit assurance at year end is substantial.

Assessing control risk at below the maximum would not be required to extend the audit conclusions from the interim date to the year end; however, if Cook assesses control risk at the maximum during the final two months, Cook should consider whether the effectiveness of the substantive tests to cover that period will be impaired.

b. Cook should design the substantive tests so that the assurance from those tests and the tests to be applied as of the interim date, and any assurance provided from the assessed level of control risk, achieve the audit objectives at year end. Such tests should include the comparison of year-end information with comparable interim information to identify and investigate unusual amounts. Other analytical procedures and/or substantive test should be performed to extend Cook's conclusions relative to the assertions tested at the interim date to the balance sheet date.

Solutions Approach for Objective Questions

The **Solutions Approach** is also adaptable to objective questions. We recommend the following framework:

1. Read the "Instructions to Candidates" section on your particular exam to determine if the AICPA's standard is the same. Generally, your objective portion will be determined by the number of correct answers with no penalty for incorrect answers.

2. Read the question carefully, noting exactly what the question is asking. Negative requirements are easily missed. Underline key words and note when the requirement is an exception (e.g., "except for...," or "which of the following does not..."). Perform any intermediate calculations necessary to the determination of the correct answer.

3. Anticipate the answer by covering the possible answers and seeing if you know the correct answer.

4. Read the answers given.

5. Select the best alternative. Very often, one or two possible answers will be clearly incorrect. Of the other alternatives, be sure to select the alternative that **best** answers the question asked.

6. Mark the correct answer on the examination booklet itself. After completing all of the individual questions in an overall question, transfer the answers to the machine readable answer sheet with extreme care. Before you hand in your answer sheet, go back and double check your answers--make sure the answer is correct and make sure the sequence is correct. The AICPA uses answer sheets with varying formats; it is extremely important to follow the correct sequence (across the sheet vs. down or vice versa). READ THE INSTRUCTIONS CAREFULLY.

7. Answer the questions in order. This is a proven, systematic approach to objective test taking. You will generally be limited to a maximum of 2 minutes per question. Under no circumstances should you allow yourself to fall behind schedule. If a question is too difficult, too long, or is a multiple question fact situation, be sure you remain cognizant of the time you are using. If after a minute or so you feel that it is too costly to continue on with a particular question, select the letter answer you tentatively feel is the best answer and go on. Return to these questions at a later time and attempt to finally answer them when you have time for more consideration. If you cannot find a better answer when you return to the question, use your preliminary answer because your first impressions are often correct. However, as you read other question(s), if something about these subsequent questions or answers jogs your memory, return to the previous tentatively answered question(s) and make a note of the idea for later consideration (time permitting).

   Let's consider a multiple choice question adapted from a past Auditing examination:

Example 3

Which of the following are elements of a CPA firm's quality control that should be considered in establishing its quality control policies and procedures?

	Advancement	Inspection	Consultation
a.	Yes	Yes	No
b.	Yes	Yes	Yes
c.	No	No	Yes
d.	Yes	No	Yes

(5/90, Aud., #54)

APPLYING THE SOLUTIONS APPROACH

Let's look at the steps you should go through to arrive at your objective question solution.

In **Step 1** , you must carefully read the "Instructions" which precede your particular objective CPA exam portion.

In **Step 2**, you must read the question and its requirements carefully. Look out for questions which require you to provide those options **not** applicable, **not** true, etc...

In **Step 3**, you must anticipate the correct answer after reading the question but before reading the possible answers.

In **Step 4**, you must read the answer carefully and select the alternative which best answers the question asked. Ideally, the best alternative will immediately present itself because it roughly or exactly corresponds with the answer you anticipated before looking at the other possible choices.

In **Step 5**, you select the best alternative. If there are two close possibilities, make sure you select the **best** one in light of the facts and requirements of the question.

In **Step 6**, you must make sure you accurately mark the correct answer in the proper sequence. If anything seems wrong, stop, go back and double check your answer sheet. As a fail safe mechanism, circle the correct letter on the exam sheet first, before you move it to the answer sheet.

In **Step 7**, you must make sure you answer the questions on the answer sheet in order, with due regard to time constraints.

Example 4-- Unofficial Answer

Solution: The answer is (b). A firm shall consider each of the elements of quality control, to the extent applicable to its practice, in establishing its quality control policies and procedures. These elements include independence, assigning personnel to engagements, consultation, supervision, hiring, professional development, advancement, acceptance and continuance of clients, and inspection (QC 10.07).

Benefits of the Solutions Approach

The **Solutions Approach** may seem cumbersome the first time you attempt it; candidates frequently have a tendency to write as they think. It should be obvious to you that such a haphazard approach will result in a disorganized answer. The Solutions Approach will help you write a solution that parallels the question requirements. It will also help you recall information under the pressure of the exam. The technique assists you in directing your thoughts toward the information required for the answer. Without a Solutions Approach, you are apt to become distracted or confused by details which are irrelevant to the answer. Finally, the Solutions Approach is a faster way to answer exam questions. You will not waste time on false starts or rewrites. The approach may seem time-consuming at first, but as you become comfortable using it, you will see that it actually saves time and results in a better answer.

We urge you to give the **Solutions Approach** a good try by using it throughout your CPA review. As you practice, you may adapt or modify it to your own preferences and requirements. The important thing is to develop a system so that you do not approach exam questions with a storehouse of knowledge that you can not put down on paper.

PART TWO: SECTION 3

EXAMINATION STRATEGIES

The CPA Exam is more than a test of your knowledge and technical competence. It is also a test of your ability to function under psychological pressure. You could easily be thrown off balance by an unexpected turn of events during the days of the exam. Your objective is to avoid surprises and eliminate hassles and distractions which might shake your confidence. You want to be in complete control so that you can concentrate on the exam material, rather than the exam situation. By taking charge of the exam, you will be able to handle pressure in a constructive manner.

The keys to control are adequate preparation and an effective examination strategy.

Overall Preparation

Advance preparation will arm you with the confidence you need to overcome the psychological pressure of the exam. As you complete your comprehensive review, you will cover most of the material that will be tested on the exam; it is unlikely that an essay, problem, or series of objective questions will deal with a topic you have not studied. But if an unfamiliar topic <u>is</u> tested, you will not be dismayed because you have learned to use the Solutions Approach to derive the best possible answer from the knowledge you possess. Similarly, you will not feel pressured to write "perfect" answers, because you understand the grading process. You recognize that there is a limit to the points you can earn for each answer, no matter how much you write.

The components of your advance preparation program have previously been discussed in this Foreword. Briefly summarizing, they include:

1. Comprehensive review materials such as your BISK CPA Review Program.

2. A method for pre-review and ongoing self-evaluation of your level of proficiency.

3. A study plan which enables you to review each subject area methodically and thoroughly.

4. A Solutions Approach for each type of examination question.

5. An understanding of the grading process and grader orientation skills.

CPA Exam Strategies

The second key to controlling the exam is to develop effective strategies for the days during which the exam is given. Your objective is to avoid surprises and frustrations so that you can focus your full concentration on the questions and your answers.

You should be familiar with the format of the CPA Exam and know exactly what you will do when you enter the examination room. Remember to carefully read the instructions on the cover page of the Exam booklet AND for each problem. Disregarding the instructions may mean loss of points.

On the following pages, we discuss the steps you should take from the time you receive the test booklet until the time you hand in your booklet. Planning in advance how you will spend your examination time will save you time and confusion on exam day.

Four topics are very important in a discussion of overall examination strategies. They are:

- Inventory of the examination
- Order of answering questions
- Time budgeting
- Page numbering

Inventory of the Examination

You should spend the first few minutes of the exam surveying the exam booklet and planning your work. Do not plunge head-first into answering the questions without a plan of action. You do not want to risk running out of time, becoming frustrated by a difficult question, or losing the opportunity to answer a question that you could have answered well.

1. Carefully read the "Instructions to Candidates" on the cover page.

2. Note the number of questions/problems and the time allocated to each on the cover page.

3. Once permission is given, go through the booklet and see what topics each question covers. Jot down the topics on the time schedule on the front cover, forming a table of contents.

Your inventory should take no longer than five minutes. The time you spend will help you "settle in" to the examination and develop a feel for your ability to answer the questions.

Order of Answering Questions

Once you have completed your inventory of the exam, the next step is to develop an order for answering the objective questions and problems/essays. We recommend that you begin with the objective questions and then proceed to the essays, beginning with the essay that you feel is the least difficult.

Objective questions comprise a majority of the point value of each section. Because of their objective nature, the correct solution is listed as one of the answer choices. By solving these questions, not only do you gain confidence, but they often involve the same or a related topic to that covered in one of the problems/essays.

A very effective and efficient manner of answering the objective questions is to make two passes through the questions. On the first pass, you should answer those questions that you find the easiest. If you come across a question that you find difficult to solve, mark it and proceed to the next one. This will allow you to avoid wasting precious time and will enable your mind to clear and start anew on your second pass. On the second pass, you should go back and solve those questions you left unanswered on the first pass. Some of these questions you may have skipped over without an attempt, while in others you may have been able to eliminate one or two of the answer choices. Either way, you should come up with an answer on the second pass, even if you have to guess!! After completing all of the individual questions in an overall question, transfer the answers to the machine readable answer sheet with extreme care. Simply make note of those questions that gave you difficulty and then proceed to the problems/essays.

Essay questions should be worked only through the key word outlines on the first pass. Then return to write your essay solution with a fresh look at the question.

Examination Time Budgeting

You must plan how you will use your examination time and adhere faithfully to your schedule. If you budget your time carefully, you should be able to answer all parts of all questions. To demonstrate a realistic time budget, refer again to the time parameters in the examination booklet.

The time limitation on the exam is 4½ hours. You should subtract five minutes for your initial inventory. Assuming you will use the Solutions Approach and there will be two problem/essay type questions, your time budget may be similar to the one below. The actual exam may differ from this scenario so be sure to adjust your time budget to accommodate the number and type of questions asked.

	Minutes
Inventory examination	5
Answer objective questions	180
Key word outline essays (10 min. for each)	40
Write essay solutions (10 min. for each)	40
Review answers	15
	270

Your objective in time budgeting is to avoid running out of time to answer a question. Work quickly but efficiently (i.e., use the Solutions Approach). Remember that when you are answering an essay question, a partial answer is better than no answer at all.

Page Numbering

Follow all instructions on the front of each exam section. Remember to arrange your answers in numerical order and number pages consecutively. The multiple choice answer sheet should be numbered page 1 and the numbering of your other pages should start with page 2. Start every essay question on a new sheet of paper and write on one side. Write "continued" on the bottom of sheets when another answer sheet for the same essay follows.

Psychology of Examination Success

As stated previously, the CPA Exam is in itself a physical and mental strain. You can minimize this strain by avoiding all unnecessary distractions and inconveniences during exam week. For example:

- **Make reservations for lodging well in advance**. It's best to reserve a room for Tuesday night so that you can check in, get a good night's sleep, and locate the exam site early the next morning.

- **Stick to your normal eating, sleeping, and exercise habits**. Eat lightly before the exam, and take small candies with you for quick energy. Watch your caffeine and alcohol intake. If you are accustomed to regular exercise, continue a regular routine during exam week.

- **Visit the examination facilities before the examination** and familiarize yourself with the surroundings.

- **Arrive early for the exam**. Allow plenty of time for unexpected delays. Nothing is more demoralizing than getting caught in a traffic jam ten minutes before the exam is scheduled to begin.

- **Avoid possible distractions**, such as friends and pre-exam conversation, immediately before the exam.

- In general, **you should not attempt to study on the nights before exam sessions**. It's better to relax--go to a movie, read a novel, or watch television. If you feel you must study, spend half an hour or so going over the chapter outlines in the text.

- **Don't discuss exam answers with other candidates**. Someone is sure to disagree with your answer, and if you are easily influenced by his or her reasoning, you can become doubtful of your own ability. Wait and analyze the entire exam yourself after it's all over.

AICPA General Rules Governing Examination

1. Read carefully the identification card assigned to you; sign it; make note of your number for future reference; when it is requested, return the card to the examiner. Only the examination number on your card shall be used on your papers for the purpose of identification. The importance of remembering this number and recording it on your examination paper correctly cannot be overemphasized. If a question calls for an answer involving a signature, do not sign your own name or initials.

2. Seating during the exam is assigned according to your ID number in most states.

3. Answers must be submitted on paper furnished by the Board and must be completed in the total time allotted for each subject stated on the printed examinations. Begin your answer to each question on a separate page.

4. Answers should be written in pencil using No. 2 lead. Neatness and orderly presentation of work are important. Credit cannot be given for answers that are illegible.

5. Use a soft No. 2 lead pencil to blacken the spaces on the answer sheets for the objective-type questions.

6. Supplies furnished by the Board shall remain its property and must be returned whether used or not. You must hand in your printed examination booklet before leaving the examination room or your examination will not be graded.

7. Any reference during the examination to books or other matters or the exchange of information with other persons shall be considered misconduct sufficient to bar you from further participation in the examination.

8. The only aids candidates are permitted to have in the examination room are pens, pencils, and erasers. Calculators will be provided. Handbags and purses must be placed on the floor at candidates' locations during the entire time candidates are taking the exam. Briefcases, files, books, and other material brought to the examination site by candidates must be placed in a designated area before the start of the examination.

9. The fixed time for each session must be observed by all candidates. Each period will start and end promptly. It is the candidate's responsibility to be present and ready at the start of the period and to stop writing when told to do so.

10. Candidates arriving late should not be permitted any extension of time, but may be allowed to take the examination with proctor approval.

11. Smoking is allowed only in designated areas away from the general examination area.

12. No telephone calls are permitted during the examination session.

13. Only two time warnings are given: (1) thirty minutes prior to the end of session, and (2) five minutes prior to the end of session. (Additional warnings are not considered necessary.)

CPA Exam Week Checklist

What to pack for exam week:

1. CPA Exam registration material.

2. Hotel confirmation.

3. Cash and/or a major credit card.

4. Alarm clock--Don't rely on a hotel wake-up call.

5. Comfortable clothing that can be layered to suit varying temperatures.

6. A watch.

7. Appropriate review materials, pencils, erasers, and pencil sharpener.

8. Healthy snack foods.

Evenings before exam sections:

1. Read through your BISK chapter outlines for the next day's section(s).

2. Eat lightly and monitor your intake of alcohol and caffeine. Get a good night's rest.

3. Do not try to cram. A brief review of your notes will help to focus your attention on important points and remind you that you are well prepared, but too much cramming can shatter your self-confidence. If you have reviewed conscientiously, you are already well-prepared for the CPA Exam.

The morning of each exam section:

1. Eat a satisfying breakfast. It will be several hours before your next meal. Eat enough to ward off hunger, but not so much that you feel uncomfortable.

2. Dress appropriately. Wear layers you can take off to suit varying temperatures in the room.

3. Take ample supplies.

4. Arrive at the exam center thirty minutes early. Check in as soon as you are allowed to do so.

What to bring to the exam:

1. ID card--This is your official entrance permit to the exam.

2. Several sharpened No. 2 pencils, erasers, and a small pencil sharpener.

3. A watch.

4. Tissues, small candies, gum, and aspirin.

5. Do not take articles that will not be allowed in the exam room.

During the exam:

1. Always read all instructions and follow the directions of the exam administrator. If you don't understand any written or verbal instructions, or if something doesn't seem right, ASK QUESTIONS. Remember that an error in following directions could invalidate your entire exam.

2. Budget your time. Always keep track of the time and avoid getting too involved with one question.

3. **Satisfy the grader**. Remember that the grader cannot read your mind. You must explain every point. Focus on key words and concepts. Tell the grader what you know, don't worry about any points you don't know.

4. Answer every question, even if you must guess.

5. Use all the allotted time. If you finish a section early, go back and reconsider the more difficult questions.

6. Check the answer sheet frequently to see that the number of each answer corresponds to the number of the question you intended. Many examinees get out of sequence on the answer sheet.

7. Stop working immediately when time is called. You do not want to risk being disqualified just to get one last answer recorded.

8. Get up and stretch if you feel sluggish. Walk around if you are allowed. Breathe deeply; focus your eyes on distant objects to avoid eye strain. Do some exercises to relax muscles in the face, neck, fingers, and back.

9. Take enough time to write neatly and organize your answer. Legible, well-organized answers will impress the grader.

10. Remember that you are well-prepared for the CPA Exam, and that you can expect to pass! A confident attitude will help you overcome examination anxiety.

PART TWO: SECTION 4

AICPA CONTENT SPECIFICATION OUTLINES FOR CPA EXAMS BEGINNING MAY 1996

The AICPA Board of Examiners has developed a revised **Content Specification Outline** of each section of the exam to be tested, effective **May 1996**. These outlines list the areas, groups, and topics to be tested and indicate the approximate percentage of the total test score devoted to each area. The content of the examination is based primarily on the results of two national studies of public accounting practice and the evaluation of CPA practitioners and educators.

Auditing Section

I. Evaluate the Prospective Client and Engagement, Decide Whether to Accept or Continue the Client and the Engagement, Enter Into an Agreement With the Client, and Plan the Engagement (40%)

A. Determine Nature and Scope of Engagement

1. Generally Accepted Auditing Standards
2. Standards for Accounting and Review Services
3. Standards for Attestation Engagements
4. Compliance Auditing Applicable to Governmental Entities and Other Recipients of Governmental Financial Assistance
5. Filings Under Federal Securities Statutes
6. Letters for Underwriters and Certain Other Requesting Parties

B. Assess Engagement Risk and the CPA Firm's Ability to Perform the Engagement

1. Engagement Responsibilities
2. Staffing and Supervision Requirements
3. Quality Control Considerations
4. Management Integrity

C. Communicate With the Predecessor Accountant/Auditor

D. Decide Whether to Accept or Continue the Client and Engagement

E. Enter Into an Agreement With the Client as to the Terms of the Engagement

F. Obtain an Understanding of the Client's Operations, Business, and Industry

G. Perform Analytical Procedures

H. Determine Preliminary Engagement Materiality

I. Assess Inherent Risk and Risk of Misstatements

1. Errors (inadvertent misstatements)
2. Irregularities (intentional misstatements)
3. Illegal Acts by Clients

J. Consider the Internal Control Structure

1. Obtain and Document an Understanding of the Internal Control Structure
2. Assess Control Risk
3. Assess Override and Collusion Risk

K. Consider Other Planning Matters

1. Using the Work of Other Independent Auditors
2. Using the Work of a Specialist
3. Internal Audit Function
4. Related Parties and Related Party Transactions
5. Segment Information
6. Interim Financial Information

L. Identify Financial Statement Assertions and Formulate Audit Objectives

1. Accounting Estimates
2. Routine Financial Statement Balances, Classes of Transactions, and Disclosures
3. Unusual Financial Statement Balances, Classes of Transactions, and Disclosures

M. Determine and Prepare the Work Program Defining the Nature, Timing, and Extent of the Auditor's Procedures

1. Tests of Controls
2. Analytical Procedures
3. Confirmation of Balances and/or Transactions With Third Parties
4. Physical Examination of Inventories and Other Assets
5. Other Tests of Details
6. Substantive Tests Prior to the Balance Sheet Date

II. Obtain and Document Information to Form a Basis for Conclusions (35%)

A. Perform Planned Procedures Including Planned Applications of Audit Sampling

1. Tests of Controls
2. Analytical Procedures
3. Confirmation of Balances and/or Transactions With Third Parties
4. Physical Examination of Inventories and Other Assets
5. Other Tests of Details
6. Substantive Tests Prior to the Balance Sheet Date

B. Evaluate Contingencies and Obtain and Evaluate Lawyer's Letter
C. Review Subsequent Events
D. Obtain Representations From Management
E. Identify Reportable Conditions and Other Control Deficiencies
F. Identify Matters for Communication With Audit Committees
G. Review Unusual Year-End Transactions

III. Review the Engagement to Provide Reasonable Assurance That Objectives are Achieved and Evaluate Information Obtained to Reach and to Document Engagement Conclusions (5%)

A. Perform Analytical Procedures
B. Evaluate the Sufficiency and Competence of Audit Evidence and Document Engagement Conclusions

1. Consider Substantial Doubt About an Entity's Ability to Continue as a Going Concern
2. Evaluate Whether Financial Statements Are Free of Material Misstatements, Either Inadvertent or Intentional, and in Conformity With Generally Accepted Accounting Principles or an Other Comprehensive Basis of Accounting
3. Consider Other Information in Documents Containing Audited Financial Statements

C. Review the Work Performed to Provide Reasonable Assurance That Objectives Are Achieved

IV. Prepare Communications to Satisfy Engagement Objectives (20%)

A. Prepare Reports

1. Reports on Audited Financial Statements
2. Reports on Reviewed and Compiled Financial Statements
3. Reports Required by *Government Auditing Standards*
4. Reports on Compliance With Laws and Regulation
5. Reports on Internal Control
6. Reports on Prospective Financial Information
7. Reports on Other Attestation Engagements
8. Reports on the Processing of Transactions by Service Organizations
9. Reports on Elements of Financial Statements
10. Reports on Supplementary Financial Information
11. Reissuance of Auditors' Reports

B. Prepare Letters and Other Required Communications

1. Errors and Irregularities
2. Illegal Acts
3. Special Reports
4. Communication With Audit Committees
5. Other Reporting Considerations Covered by Statements on Auditing Standards and Statements on Standards for Attestation Engagements

C. Other Matters

1. Subsequent Discovery of Facts Existing at the Date of the Auditor's Report
2. Consideration of Omitted Procedures After the Report Date

AUDITING DIAGNOSTIC EXAMINATION

Time Allowance: 135 to 165 minutes

1. The first general standard requires that an audit of financial statements is to be performed by a person or persons having
   a. Seasoned judgment in varying degrees of supervision and review.
   b. Adequate technical training and proficiency.
   c. Knowledge of the standards of field work and reporting.
   d. Independence with respect to the financial statements and supplementary disclosures. (5/90, Aud., #46)

2. One of a CPA firm's basic objectives is to provide professional services that conform with professional standards. Reasonable assurance of achieving this basic objective is provided through
   a. A system of quality control.
   b. A system of peer review.
   c. Continuing professional education.
   d. Compliance with generally accepted reporting standards. (11/92, Aud., #3)

3. The GAO standards of reporting for governmental financial audits incorporate the AICPA standards of reporting and prescribe supplemental standards to satisfy the unique needs of governmental audits. Which of the following is a supplemental reporting standard for government financial audits?
   a. A written report on the auditor's understanding of the entity's internal control structure and assessment of control risk should be prepared.
   b. Material indications of illegal acts should be reported in a document with distribution restricted to senior officials of the entity audited.
   c. Instances of abuse, fraud, mismanagement, and waste should be reported to the organization with legal oversight authority over the entity audited.
   d. All privileged and confidential information discovered should be reported to the senior officials of the organization that arranged for the audit. (5/91, Aud., #47)

4. Which of the following procedures would an auditor most likely include in the initial planning of a financial statement audit?
   a. Obtaining a written representation letter from the client's management.
   b. Examining documents to detect illegal acts having a material effect on the financial statements.
   c. Considering whether the client's accounting estimates are reasonable in the circumstances.
   d. Determining the extent of involvement of the client's internal auditors. (11/94, Aud., #1)

5. On the basis of audit evidence gathered and evaluated, an auditor decides to increase the assessed level of control risk from that originally planned. To achieve an overall audit risk level that is substantially the same as the planned audit risk level, the auditor would
   a. Increase inherent risk.
   b. Increase materiality levels.
   c. Decrease substantive testing.
   d. Decrease detection risk. (11/93, Aud., #7)

6. Before accepting an audit engagement, a successor auditor should make specific inquiries of the predecessor auditor regarding
   a. Disagreements the predecessor had with the client concerning auditing procedures and accounting principles.
   b. The predecessor's evaluation of matters of continuing accounting significance.
   c. The degree of cooperation the predecessor received concerning the inquiry of the client's lawyer.
   d. The predecessor's assessments of inherent risk and judgments about materiality. (11/91, Aud., #4)

7. After obtaining an understanding of an entity's internal control structure, an auditor may assess control risk at the maximum level for some assertions because the auditor
   a. Believes the internal control policies and procedures are unlikely to be effective.
   b. Determines that the pertinent internal control structure elements are **not** well documented.
   c. Performs tests of controls to restrict detection risk to an acceptable level.
   d. Identifies internal control policies and procedures that are likely to prevent material misstatements. (5/90, Aud., #31)

8. In an audit of financial statements in accordance with generally accepted auditing standards, an auditor is required to

a. Perform tests of controls to evaluate the effectiveness of the entity's accounting system.
b. Determine whether control procedures are suitably designed to prevent or detect material misstatements.
c. Document the auditor's understanding of the entity's internal control structure.
d. Search for significant deficiencies in the operation of the internal control structure. (5/92, Aud., #43)

9. When an auditor increases the planned assessed level of control risk because certain control procedures were determined to be ineffective, the auditor would most likely increase the

a. Extent of tests of details.
b. Level of inherent risk.
c. Extent of tests of controls.
d. Level of detection risk. (5/92, Aud., #37)

10. The ultimate purpose of assessing control risk is to contribute to the auditor's evaluation of the risk that

a. Specified controls requiring segregation of duties may be circumvented by collusion.
b. Entity policies may be overridden by senior management.
c. Tests of controls may fail to identify procedures relevant to assertions.
d. Material misstatements may exist in the financial statements. (11/92, Aud., #8)

11. The objective of tests of details of transactions performed as tests of controls is to

a. Detect material misstatements in the account balances of the financial statements.
b. Evaluate whether an internal control structure policy or procedure operated effectively.
c. Determine the nature, timing, and extent of substantive tests for financial statement assertions.
d. Reduce control risk, inherent risk, and detection risk to an acceptably low level. (11/90, Aud., #41)

12. Which of the following controls most likely would be effective in offsetting the tendency of sales personnel to maximize sales volume at the expense of high bad debt write-offs?

a. Employees responsible for authorizing sales and bad debt write-offs are denied access to cash.
b. Shipping documents and sales invoices are matched by an employee who does **not** have authority to write off bad debts.
c. Employees involved in the credit-granting function are separated from the sales function.
d. Subsidiary accounts receivable records are reconciled to the control account by an employee independent of the authorization of credit. (5/92, Aud., #45)

13. Which of the following controls would be most effective in assuring that recorded purchases are free of material errors?

a. The receiving department compares the quantity ordered on purchase orders with the quantity received on receiving reports.
b. Vendors' invoices are compared with purchase orders by an employee who is independent of the receiving department.
c. Receiving reports require the signature of the individual who authorized the purchase.
d. Purchase orders, receiving reports, and vendors' invoices are independently matched in preparing vouchers. (11/90, Aud., #51)

14. The purpose of segregating the duties of hiring personnel and distributing payroll checks is to separate the

a. Authorization of transactions from the custody of related assets.
b. Operational responsibility from the record keeping responsibility.
c. Human resources function from the controllership function.
d. Administrative controls from the internal accounting controls. (11/91, Aud., #40)

15. A weakness in internal control over recording retirements of equipment may cause an auditor to

a. Trace additions to the "other assets" account to search for equipment that is still on hand but **no** longer being used.
b. Select certain items of equipment from the accounting records and locate them in the plant.
c. Inspect certain items of equipment in the plant and trace those items to the accounting records.
d. Review the subsidiary ledger to ascertain whether depreciation was taken on each item of equipment during the year.(11/89, Aud., #48)

16. Which of the following controls would an entity most likely use in safeguarding against the loss of marketable securities?

a. An independent trust company that has **no** direct contact with the employees who have record keeping responsibilities has possession of the securities.
b. The internal auditor verifies the marketable securities in the entity's safe each year on the balance sheet date.
c. The independent auditor traces all purchases and sales of marketable securities through the subsidiary ledgers to the general ledger.
d. A designated member of the board of directors controls the securities in a bank safe-deposit box. (11/92, Aud., #22)

17. The objectives of the internal control structure for a production cycle are to provide assurance that transactions are properly executed and recorded, and that

a. Independent internal verification of activity reports is established.
b. Transfers to finished goods are documented by a completed production report and a quality control report.
c. Production orders are prenumbered and signed by a supervisor.
d. Custody of work in process and of finished goods is properly maintained.(11/90, Aud., #52)

18. An auditor's communication of internal control structure related matters noted in an audit usually should be addressed to the

a. Audit committee.
b. Director of internal auditing.
c. Chief financial officer.
d. Chief accounting officer. (5/91, Aud., #33)

19. Which of the following statements concerning an auditor's communication of reportable conditions is correct?

a. The auditor should request a meeting with management one level above the source of the reportable conditions to discuss suggestions for remedial action.
b. Any report issued on reportable conditions should indicate that providing assurance on the internal control structure was **not** the purpose of the audit.
c. Reportable conditions discovered and communicated at an interim date should be reexamined with tests of controls before completing the engagement.
d. Suggestions concerning administration efficiencies and business strategies should **not** be communicated in the same report with reportable conditions. (5/92, Aud., #51)

20. Which of the following statements concerning material weaknesses and reportable conditions is correct?

a. An auditor should identify and communicate material weaknesses separately from reportable conditions.
b. All material weaknesses are reportable conditions.
c. An auditor should report immediately material weaknesses and reportable conditions discovered during an audit.
d. All reportable conditions are material weaknesses. (11/90, Aud., #55)

21. In developing a preliminary audit strategy, an auditor should consider

a. Whether the allowance for sampling risk exceeds the achieved upper precision limit.
b. Findings from substantive tests performed at interim dates.
c. Whether the inquiry of the client's attorney identifies any litigation, claims, or assessments **not** disclosed in the financial statements.
d. The planned assessed level of control risk. (11/91, Aud., #8)

22. When one auditor succeeds another, the successor auditor should request the

a. Client to instruct its attorney to send a letter of audit inquiry concerning the status of the prior year's litigation, claims, and assessments.
b. Predecessor auditor to submit a list of internal control weaknesses that have not been corrected.
c. Client to authorize the predecessor auditor to allow a review of the predecessor auditor's working papers.
d. Predecessor auditor to update the prior year's report to the date of the change of auditors. (11/86, Aud., #9)

23. Which of the following audit risk components may be assessed in nonquantitative terms?

	Inherent risk	Control risk	Detection risk
a.	Yes	Yes	No
b.	Yes	No	Yes
c.	No	Yes	Yes
d.	Yes	Yes	Yes

(5/89, Aud., #5)

24. In testing the existence assertion for an asset, an auditor ordinarily works from the
a. Financial statements to the potentially unrecorded items.
b. Potentially unrecorded items to the financial statements.
c. Accounting records to the supporting evidence.
d. Supporting evidence to the accounting records. (11/90, Aud., #17)

25. Which of the following statements is generally correct about the competence of evidential matter?
a. The more effective the internal control structure, the more assurance it provides about the reliability of the accounting data and financial statements.
b. Competence of evidential matter refers to the amount of corroborative evidence obtained.
c. Information obtained indirectly from independent outside sources is more persuasive than the auditor's direct personal knowledge obtained through observation and inspection.
d. Competence of evidential matter refers to the audit evidence obtained from outside the entity. (5/92, Aud., #16)

26. Disclosure of irregularities to parties other than a client's senior management and its audit committee or board of directors ordinarily is not part of an auditor's responsibility. However, to which of the following outside parties may a duty to disclose irregularities exist?

	To the SEC when the client reports an auditor change	To a successor auditor when the successor makes appropriate inquiries	To a government funding agency from which the client receives financial assistance
a.	Yes	Yes	No
b.	Yes	No	Yes
c.	No	Yes	Yes
d.	Yes	Yes	Yes

(5/90, Aud., #55)

27. When an auditor becomes aware of a possible illegal act by a client, the auditor should obtain an understanding of the nature of the act to
a. Evaluate the effect on the financial statements.
b. Determine the reliability of management's representations.
c. Consider whether other similar acts may have occurred.
d. Recommend remedial actions to the audit committee. (11/92, Aud., #4)

28. Which of the following statements ordinarily is included among the written client representations obtained by the auditor?
a. Management acknowledges that there are **no** material weaknesses in the internal control structure.
b. Sufficient evidential matter has been made available to permit the issuance of an unqualified opinion.
c. Compensating balances and other arrangements involving restrictions on cash balances have been disclosed.
d. Management acknowledges responsibility for illegal actions committed by employees. (11/90, Aud., #20)

29. For all audits of financial statements made in accordance with generally accepted auditing standards, the use of analytical procedures is required to some extent

	In the planning stage	As a substantive test	In the review stage
a.	Yes	No	Yes
b.	No	Yes	No
c.	No	Yes	Yes
d.	Yes	No	No

(11/90, Aud., #22)

30. When using the work of a specialist, an auditor may refer to and identify the specialist in the auditor's report if the
a. Auditor expresses a qualified opinion as a result of the specialist's findings.
b. Specialist is **not** independent of the client.
c. Auditor wishes to indicate a division of responsibility.
d. Specialist's work provides the auditor greater assurance of reliability. (5/92, Aud., #22)

31. An auditor should request that an audit client send a letter of inquiry to those attorneys who have been consulted concerning litigation, claims, or

assessments. The primary reason for this request is to provide

a. The opinion of a specialist as to whether loss contingencies are possible, probable, or remote.
b. A description of litigation, claims, and assessments that have a reasonable possibility of unfavorable outcomes.
c. An objective appraisal of management's policies and procedures adopted for identifying and evaluating legal matters.
d. The corroboration of the information furnished by management concerning litigation, claims, and assessments. (5/92, Aud., #23)

32. An auditor's working papers should

a. Not be permitted to serve as a reference source for the client.
b. Not contain critical comments concerning management.
c. Show that the accounting records agree or reconcile with the financial statements.
d. Be considered a primary support for the financial statements being audited. (5/90, Aud., #7)

33. When auditing related party transactions, an auditor places primary emphasis on

a. Confirming the existence of the related parties.
b. Verifying the valuation of the related party transactions.
c. Evaluating the disclosure of the related party transactions.
d. Ascertaining the rights and obligations of the related parties. (5/92, Aud., #31)

34. The negative request form of accounts receivable confirmation is useful particularly when the

	Combined assessed level of inherent and control risk relating to receivables is	Number of small balances is	Consideration by the recipient is
a.	Low	Many	Likely
b.	Low	Few	Unlikely
c.	High	Few	Likely
d.	High	Many	Likely

(5/91, Aud., #9, amended)

35. After accounting for a sequence of inventory tags, an auditor traces a sample of tags to the physical inventory listing to obtain evidence that all items

a. Included in the listing have been counted.
b. Represented by inventory tags are included in the listing.
c. Included in the listing are represented by inventory tags.
d. Represented by inventory tags are bona fide. (11/87, Aud., #34)

36. To establish the existence and ownership of a long-term investment in the common stock of a publicly traded company, an auditor ordinarily performs a security count or

a. Assesses control risk at the minimum level if the auditor has reasonable assurance that the control procedures are being applied as prescribed.
b. Confirms the number of shares owned that are held by an independent custodian.
c. Determines the market price per share at the balance sheet date from published quotations.
d. Confirms the number of shares owned with the issuing company. (5/88, Aud., #22)

37. Which of the following audit procedures is best for identifying unrecorded trade accounts payable?

a. Examining unusual relationships between monthly accounts payable balances and recorded cash payments.
b. Reconciling vendors' statements to the file of receiving reports to identify items received just prior to the balance sheet date.
c. Reviewing cash disbursements recorded subsequent to the balance sheet date to determine whether the related payables apply to the prior period.
d. Investigating payables recorded just prior to and just subsequent to the balance sheet date to determine whether they are supported by receiving reports. (5/91, Aud., #10)

38. Tracing selected items from the payroll register to employee time cards that have been approved by supervisory personnel provides evidence that

a. Internal controls relating to payroll disbursements were operating effectively.
b. Payroll checks were signed by an appropriate officer independent of the payroll preparation process.
c. Only bona fide employees worked and their pay was properly computed.
d. Employees worked the number of hours for which their pay was computed. (5/89, Aud., #33)

39. An advantage of statistical sampling over nonstatistical sampling is that statistical sampling helps an auditor to

a. Eliminate the risk of nonsampling errors.
b. Reduce the level of audit risk and materiality to a relatively low amount.
c. Measure the sufficiency of the evidential matter obtained.
d. Minimize the failure to detect errors and irregularities. (11/90, Aud., #31)

40. To determine the sample size for a test of controls, an auditor should consider the tolerable deviation rate, the allowable risk of assessing control risk too low, and the
a. Expected deviation rate.
b. Upper precision limit.
c. Risk of incorrect acceptance.
d. Risk of incorrect rejection. (11/90, Aud., #58)

41. The risk of incorrect acceptance and the likelihood of assessing control risk too low relate to the
a. Effectiveness of an audit.
b. Efficiency of the audit.
c. Preliminary estimates of materiality levels.
d. Allowable risk of tolerable error. (5/90, Aud., #44)

42. Which of the following activities would most likely be performed in the EDP department?
a. Initiation of changes to master records.
b. Conversion of information to machine-readable form.
c. Correction of transactional errors.
d. Initiation of changes to existing applications. (5/85, Aud., #25)

43. Which of the following most likely represent a significant deficiency in the internal control structure?
a. The systems analyst reviews applications of data processing and maintains systems documentation.
b. The systems programmer designs systems for computerized applications and maintains output controls.
c. The control clerk establishes control over data received by the EDP department and reconciles control totals after processing.
d. The accounts payable clerk prepares data for computer processing and enters the data into the computer. (11/91, Aud., #36)

44. When an auditor tests a computerized accounting system, which of the following is true of the test data approach?
a. Test data must consist of all possible valid and invalid conditions.
b. The program tested is different from the program used throughout the year by the client.
c. Several transactions of each type must be tested.
d. Test data are processed by the client's computer programs under the auditor's control. (11/90, Aud., #28)

45. How does an auditor make the following representations when issuing the standard auditor's report on comparative financial statements?

	Examination of evidence on a test basis	Consistent application of accounting principles
a.	Explicitly	Explicitly
b.	Implicitly	Implicitly
c.	Implicitly	Explicitly
d.	Explicitly	Implicitly

(11/91, Aud., #21)

46. The following explanatory paragraph was included in an auditor's report to indicate a lack of consistency:

> "As discussed in note T to the financial statements, the company changed its method of computing depreciation in 1990."

How should the auditor report on this matter if the auditor concurred with the change?

	Type of opinion	Location of explanatory paragraph
a.	Unqualified	Before opinion paragraph
b.	Unqualified	After opinion paragraph
c.	Qualified	Before opinion paragraph
d.	Qualified	After opinion paragraph

(11/91, Aud., #18)

47. King, CPA, was engaged to audit the financial statements of Newton Company after its fiscal year had ended. King neither observed the inventory count nor confirmed the receivables by direct communication with debtors, but was satisfied concerning both after applying alternative procedures. King's auditor's report most likely contained a(an)
a. Qualified opinion.
b. Disclaimer of opinion.
c. Unqualified opinion.
d. Unqualified opinion with an explanatory paragraph. (11/90, Aud., #2)

48. When an auditor qualifies an opinion because of inadequate disclosure, the auditor should describe the nature of the omission in a separate explanatory paragraph and modify the

	Introductory paragraph	Scope paragraph	Opinion paragraph
a.	Yes	No	No
b.	Yes	Yes	No
c.	No	Yes	Yes
d.	No	No	Yes

(5/91, Aud., #46)

49. Comparative financial statements include the prior year's statements that were audited by a predecessor auditor whose report is not presented. If the predecessor's report was unqualified, the successor should
a. Express an opinion on the current year's statements alone and make **no** reference to the prior year's statements.
b. Indicate in the auditor's report that the predecessor auditor expressed an unqualified opinion.
c. Obtain a letter of representations from the predecessor concerning any matters that might affect the successor's opinion.
d. Request the predecessor auditor to reissue the prior year's report. (11/90, Aud., #10)

50. An auditor issued an audit report that was dual dated for a subsequent event occurring after the completion of field work but before issuance of the auditor's report. The auditor's responsibility for events occurring subsequent to the completion of field work was
a. Extended to subsequent events occurring through the date of issuance of the report.
b. Extended to include all events occurring since the completion of field work.
c. Limited to the specific event referenced.
d. Limited to include only events occurring up to the date of the last subsequent event referenced. (11/91, Aud., #57)

51. After issuing a report, an auditor has **no** obligation to make continuing inquiries or perform other procedures concerning the audited financial statements, unless
a. Information, which existed at the report date and may affect the report, comes to the auditor's attention.
b. Management of the entity requests the auditor to reissue the auditor's report.
c. Information about an event that occurred after the end of field work comes to the auditor's attention.
d. Final determinations or resolutions are made of contingencies that had been disclosed in the financial statements. (11/91, Aud., #20)

52. Six months after issuing an unqualified opinion on audited financial statements, an auditor discovered that the engagement personnel failed to confirm several of the client's material accounts receivable balances. The auditor should first
a. Request the permission of the client to undertake the confirmation of accounts receivable.
b. Perform alternative procedures to provide a satisfactory basis for the unqualified opinion.
c. Assess the importance of the omitted procedures to the auditor's ability to support the previously expressed opinion.
d. Inquire whether there are persons currently relying, or likely to rely, on the unqualified opinion. (11/90, Aud., #35)

53. When an independent CPA assists in preparing the financial statements of a publicly held entity, but has **not** audited or reviewed them, the CPA should issue a disclaimer of opinion. In such situations, the CPA has **no** responsibility to apply any procedures beyond
a. Ascertaining whether the financial statements are in conformity with generally accepted accounting principles.
b. Determining whether management has elected to omit substantially all required disclosures.
c. Documenting that the internal control structure is **not** being relied on.
d. Reading the financial statements for obvious material misstatements. (5/92, Aud., #2)

54. Green, CPA, concludes that there is substantial doubt about JKL Co.'s ability to continue as a going concern. If JKL's financial statements adequately disclose its financial difficulties, Green's auditor's report should

	Include an explanatory paragraph following the opinion paragraph	Specifically use the words "going concern"	Specifically use the words "substantial doubt"
a.	Yes	Yes	Yes
b.	Yes	Yes	No
c.	Yes	No	Yes
d.	No	Yes	Yes

(11/92, Aud., #49)

55. An auditor's special report on financial statements prepared in conformity with the cash basis of accounting should include a separate explanatory paragraph before the opinion paragraph that

a. Justifies the reasons for departing from generally accepted accounting principles.
b. States whether the financial statements are fairly presented in conformity with another comprehensive basis of accounting.
c. Refers to the note to the financial statements that describes the basis of accounting.
d. Explains how the results of operations differ from financial statements prepared in conformity with generally accepted accounting principles. (11/92, Aud., #54)

56. When an accountant issues to an underwriter a comfort letter containing comments on data that have **not** been audited, the underwriter most likely will receive
a. Negative assurance on capsule information.
b. Positive assurance on supplementary disclosures.
c. A limited opinion on "pro forma" financial statements.
d. A disclaimer on prospective financial statements. (5/92, Aud., #8)

57. Which of the following circumstances requires modification of the accountant's report on a review of interim financial information of a publicly held entity?

	An uncertainty	Inadequate disclosure
a.	Yes	Yes
b.	No	No
c.	Yes	No
d.	No	Yes

(5/88, Aud., #48)

58. Which of the following procedures is more likely to be performed in a review engagement of a nonpublic entity than in a compilation engagement?
a. Gaining an understanding of the entity's business transactions.
b. Making a preliminary assessment of control risk.
c. Obtaining a representation letter from the chief executive officer.
d. Assisting the entity in adjusting the accounting records. (5/92, Aud., #35)

59. Which of the following is a prospective financial statement for general use upon which an accountant may appropriately report?
a. Financial projection.
b. Partial presentation.
c. Pro forma financial statement.
d. Financial forecast. (11/87, Aud., #11)

60. An attestation engagement is one in which a CPA is engaged to
a. Issue a written communication expressing a conclusion about the reliability of a written assertion that is the responsibility of another party.
b. Provide tax advice or prepare a tax return based on financial information the CPA has **not** audited or reviewed.
c. Testify as an expert witness in accounting, auditing, or tax matters, given certain stipulated facts.
d. Assemble prospective financial statements based on the assumptions of the entity's management without expressing any assurance.

(11/92, Aud., #60)

ANSWERS TO AUDITING DIAGNOSTIC EXAM

1. b	6. a	11. b	16. a	21. d	26. d	31. d	36. b	41. a	46. b	51. a	56. a
2. a	7. a	12. c	17. d	22. c	27. a	32. c	37. c	42. b	47. c	52. c	57. d
3. a	8. c	13. d	18. a	23. d	28. c	33. c	38. d	43. b	48. d	53. d	58. c
4. d	9. a	14. a	19. b	24. c	29. a	34. a	39. c	44. d	49. b	54. a	59. d
5. d	10. d	15. b	20. b	25. a	30. a	35. b	40. a	45. d	50. c	55. c	60. a

---

PERFORMANCE BY TOPICS

Diagnostic exam question numbers corresponding to each chapter of your Auditing text are listed below. To assess your preparedness for the CPA Exam, record the number and percentage of questions you correctly answered in each topic area.

Chapter 34: Standards and Related Topics

Question #	Correct √
1	
2	
3	

Questions 3

Correct ______
% Correct ______

Chapter 35: Audit Planning

Question #	Correct √
4	
5	
6	

Questions 3

Correct ______
% Correct ______

Chapter 36: Internal Control

Question #	Correct √
7	
8	
9	
10	
11	
12	
13	
14	
15	
16	
17	
18	
19	
20	

Questions 14

Correct ______
% Correct ______

Chapter 37: Audit Evidence, Programs, and Procedures

Question #	Correct √
21	
22	
23	
24	
25	
26	
27	
28	
29	
30	
31	
32	
33	
34	
35	
36	
37	
38	

Questions 18

Correct ______
% Correct ______

Chapter 38: Audit Sampling Procedures

Question #	Correct √
39	
40	
41	

Questions 3

Correct ______
% Correct ______

Chapter 39: Auditing EDP Systems

Question #	Correct √
42	
43	
44	

Questions 3

Correct ______
% Correct ______

Chapter 40: Reports on Audited Financial Statements

Question #	Correct √
45	
46	
47	
48	
49	
50	
51	
52	
53	
54	

Questions 10

Correct ______
% Correct ______

Chapter 41: Other Types of Reports

Question #	Correct √
55	
56	
57	

Questions 3

Correct ______
% Correct ______

Chapter 42: Other Professional Services

Question #	Correct √
58	
59	
60	

Questions 3

Correct ______
% Correct ______

Frequently Tested Areas

Although the new format of the exam and the many changes in content coverage make it difficult to know with certainty what the AICPA will now ask, we can use exam history to highlight those areas which have been emphasized. Based on analysis of past exams, we have identified the following areas as those most heavily tested in the past. We have also identified those tested the least. Keep in mind, however, that there is the potential for **any area to be tested.**

Heavy		Light	
Ch. 36	Internal Control	Ch. 34	Standards and Related Topics
Ch. 37	Audit Evidence, Programs, & Procedures	Ch. 38	Audit Sampling Procedures
Ch. 40	Reports on Audited Financial Statements	Ch. 39	Auditing EDP Systems
Ch. 42	Other Professional Services		

Auditing Coverage by Bisk Chapter

AUDITING
AUTHORITATIVE PRONOUNCEMENTS CROSS-REFERENCES

Section No.	Bisk Chapter Number(s)	Statements on Auditing Standards
AU 110	34	Responsibilities and Functions of the Independent Auditor
AU 150	34	Generally Accepted Auditing Standards
AU 161	34	The Relationship of Generally Accepted Auditing Standards to Quality Control Standards
AU 201	34	Nature of the General Standards
AU 210	34	Training and Proficiency of the Independent Auditor
AU 220	34	Independence
AU 230	34	Due Care in the Performance of Work
AU 310	35	Relationship Between the Auditor's Appointment and Planning
AU 311	35	Planning and Supervision
AU 312	35	Audit Risk and Materiality in Conducting an Audit
AU 313	35	Substantive Tests Prior to the Balance Sheet Date
AU 315	35	Communications Between Predecessor and Successor Auditors
AU 316	35, 41	The Auditor's Responsibility to Detect and Report Errors and Irregularities
AU 317	35, 41	Illegal Acts by Clients
AU 319	34, 41	Consideration of the Internal Control Structure in a Financial Statement Audit
AU 322	37	The Auditor's Consideration of the Internal Audit Function in an Audit of Financial Statements
AU 324	41	Reports on the Processing of Transactions by Service Organizations
AU 325	36, 41	The Communication of Internal Control Structure Related Matters Noted in an Audit
AU 326	37	Evidential Matter
AU 329	37	Analytical Procedures
AU 330	37	The Confirmation Process
AU 331	37	Inventories
AU 332	37	Long-Term Investments
AU 333	37, 40, 41	Client Representations
AU 334	37	Related Parties
AU 336	37	Using the Work of a Specialist
AU 337	37	Inquiry of a Client's Lawyer Concerning Litigation, Claims, and Assessments
AU 339	37, 41	Working Papers
AU 341	40	The Auditor's Consideration of an Entity's Ability to Continue as a Going Concern
AU 342	37	Auditing Accounting Estimates
AU 350	38	Audit Sampling
AU 380	35	Communication With Audit Committees
AU 390	40	Consideration of Omitted Procedures After the Report Date
AU 410	40	Adherence to Generally Accepted Accounting Principles
AU 411	40	The Meaning of *Present Fairly in Conformity With Generally Accepted Accounting Principles* in the Independent Auditor's Report
AU 420	40	Consistency of Application of Generally Accepted Accounting Principles

Section No.	Bisk Chapter Number(s)	Statements on Auditing Standards
AU 431	40	Adequacy of Disclosure in Financial Statements
AU 435	40	Segment Information
AU 504	40	Association With Financial Statements
AU 508	40	Reports on Audited Financial Statements
AU 530	40	Dating of the Independent Auditor's Report
AU 534	41	Reporting on Financial Statements Prepared for Use in Other Countries
AU 543	40	Part of Audit Performed by Other Independent Auditors
AU 544	40	Lack of Conformity With Generally Accepted Accounting Principles
AU 550	40, 42	Other Information in Documents Containing Audited Financial Statements
AU 551	41	Reporting on Information Accompanying the Basic Financial Statements in Auditor-Submitted Documents
AU 552	41	Reporting on Condensed Financial Statements and Selected Financial Data
AU 558	40	Required Supplementary Information
AU 560	40	Subsequent Events
AU 561	40, 41	Subsequent Discovery of Facts Existing at the Date of the Auditor's Report
AU 622	40, 41	Special Reports--Applying Agreed-Upon Procedures to Specified Elements, Accounts, or Items of a Financial Statement
AU 623	41	Special Reports
AU 625	41	Reports on the Application of Accounting Principles
AU 634	41	Letters for Underwriters and Certain Other Requesting Parties
AU 711	41, 42	Filings Under Federal Securities Statutes
AU 722	41	Interim Financial Information
AU 801	41	Compliance Auditing Applicable to Governmental Entities and Other Recipients of Governmental Financial Assistance
AU 901	37	Public Warehouses--Internal Control Structure Policies and Procedures and Auditing Procedures for Goods Held
		Statements on Standards for Attestation Engagements
AT 100	42	Attestation Standards
AT 200	42	Financial Forecasts and Projections
AT 300	42	Reporting on Pro Forma Financial Information
AT 400	41	Reporting on an Entity's Internal Control Structure Over Financial Reporting
AT 500	42	Compliance Attestation
		Statements on Standards for Accounting and Review Services
AR 100	42	Compilation and Review of Financial Statements
AR 200	42	Reporting on Comparative Financial Statements
AR 300	42	Compilation Reports on Financial Statements Included in Certain Prescribed Forms
AR 400	42	Communications Between Predecessor and Successor Accountants
AR 500	41	Reporting on Compiled Financial Statements
AR 600	42	Reporting on Personal Financial Statements Included in Written Personal Financial Plans

Section No.	Bisk Chapter Number(s)	Statements on Quality Control Standards
QC 10	34	System of Quality Control for a CPA Firm
QC 90	34	Quality Control Policies and Procedures for CPA Firms
		Standards for Performing and Reporting on Quality Reviews
QR 100	34	Standards for Performing and Reporting on Quality Reviews
		Other Standards
	34	Government Auditing Standards (Yellow Book)

NOTES

ACCOUNTING FOR 5%

CONTENTS

INTRODUCTION

Writing skills are utilized extensively in interactions with clients, colleagues, and other professionals. In response to the increasing need for good communication skills within the accounting profession, the AICPA began testing candidates on their writing skills with the May 1994 CPA Exam.

To assess candidates' writing skills, answers to selected essay responses from Business Law & Professional Responsibilities, Auditing, and Financial Accounting & Reporting sections will be used. Five percent of the points available on each of these sections will be allocated to writing skills.

If an essay question is divided into parts a, b, and c, for example, each of these parts is considered a separate response. It is possible that only one of these three parts will be graded for writing skills. However, at least two responses from each section will be used for this assessment. These responses may or may not be from the same question, but they will cover different technical areas. Therefore, if a question is graded differently for writing skills, then the number of points allocated to the technical concepts of the essay is reduced so that the total number of points per question does not change.

The AICPA considers the following six characteristics to constitute effective writing and will make its evaluations of candidates' writing skills based on these criteria:

1. **Coherent organization.** Does each paragraph begin with a topic sentence? Are ideas arranged logically, and do they flow smoothly?

2. **Conciseness.** Are complete thoughts presented in the fewest possible words?

3. **Clarity.** Are sentences constructed properly? Are meanings and reasons clear? Are proper technical terminology and key words and phrases used?

4. **Standard English.** Is your work free from nonstandard usage; that is, does it demonstrate proper spelling, punctuation, capitalization, diction, and knowledgeable usage choices?

5. **Responsiveness to the requirements of the question.** Make sure your answers respond directly to the question and are not broad discourses on the general subject.

6. **Appropriateness for the reader.** If not otherwise mentioned in the question, you should assume that the reader is a CPA. Questions asking that you write something for a client or anyone else with less technical knowledge should be answered with that particular audience in mind.

If you are not convinced that the five points in a section will make a significant difference, consider this: of the passing grades in each section, the vast majority are scored at 75, the minimum. For many candidates, therefore, writing skills may determine whether or not they pass a section.

TOTALTIP: When writing your exam answers, write on **every other line only**. This will give you space for editing.

Accounting for 5% has been designed primarily to help CPA candidates polish their writing skills. Beyond this purpose, we hope that it will continue to serve as a useful reference in the future.

Before skipping this Foreword, review at least the following writing samples and the "Writing an Answer to an Exam Question" starting on page G-6. Be sure to take the Diagnostic Quiz beginning on G-8.

WRITING SKILLS SAMPLES

The following problems taken from past exams are answered in various ways to illustrate good, fair, and poor writing skills.

Auditing Problem From Chapter 34--Standards and Related Topics

Feiler, the sole owner of a small hardware business, has been told that the business should have financial statements reported on by an independent CPA. Feiler, having some bookkeeping experience, has personally prepared the company's financial statements and does not understand why such statements should be audited by a CPA. Feiler discussed the matter with Farber, a CPA, and asked Farber to explain why an audit is considered important.--Describe the objectives of an independent audit.

Good: Farber should explain to Feiler that an independent audit is an audit of the financial statements in accordance with certain generally accepted auditing standards. The objective of an ordinary audit is to render an opinion on the fairness, in all material respects, with which the financial statements present financial position, results of operations, and cash flows in conformity with generally accepted accounting principles. The auditor, after an objective evidence-gathering audit, expresses an opinion and "bears witness" to the fair presentation of the financial statements. An independent expert is needed to lend credibility to the financial statements. It would not be meaningful for a company to report on itself without the attestation of an independent party because the company itself might not be objective.

Explanation: This essay begins with an excellent initial sentence that not only introduces the explanation of what an audit consists of but also refers directly to the manner in which the problem was posed (Farber's explanation to Feiler). The technical objectives of conducting an audit are explained, as well as why an objective, independent opinion is important. The passage contains no irrelevant material, and it is clearly and concisely worded with language appropriate for the reader. There are no grammatical or spelling errors.

Fair: Farber tells Feiler that he'd better have an audit done of his financial statements. An audit consists of auditing financial statements in accordance with certain generally accepted auditing standards to render an opinion about the fairness of the statements in presenting the companies financial statements, such as cash flows, financial position, and results of operations. This is acomplished by the auditor who gathers information and does tests. The company need an independent opinion.

Explanation: All things considered, this essay is not bad. It begins with an introductory sentence which could be more comprehensive. The passage covers most of the material it should; however, although it mentions the *need* for an objective opinion, it does not state *why* an objective opinion is needed or beneficial. The language, although accurate, is a little too colloquial. There are also a few grammatical errors.

Poor: An auditor needs to audit financial statements who is independent. A CPA expresses an opinion on the statements which are supposed to be objective and presented fairlly. They must be according to generally accepted accounting principals. Usually audit the balance sheet. Usually the auditor runs some tests on them in order for them to be correct. Farber should tell Feiler that he will get in trouble if he doesn't get his statements properly done.

Explanation: Although some of the necessary material is in this paragraph, it lacks a number of important details. It also is very weak in coherence, the language is marginally standard, and it contains a number of grammatical and spelling errors. Additionally, there are no connecting links between any of the ideas.

PARAGRAPHS

The kind of writing you do for the CPA Exam is called **expository writing** (writing in which something is explained in straightforward terms). Expository writing uses the basic techniques we will be discussing here. Other kinds of writing (i.e., narration, description, argument, and persuasion) will sometimes require different techniques.

Consider a paragraph as a division of an essay that consists of one or more sentences, deals with one point, and begins on a new, indented line. Paragraphs provide a way to write about a subject one point or one thought at a time.

Usually, a paragraph begins with a **topic sentence**. The topic sentence communicates the main idea of the paragraph, and the remainder of the paragraph explains or illuminates that central idea. The paragraph sometimes finishes with a restatement of the topic sentence. This format is easily read by the exam graders.

Often the topic sentence of the first paragraph is the central idea of the entire composition. Each succeeding paragraph then breaks down this idea into subtopics with each of the new topic sentences being the central thought of that subtopic.

Let's take a look at a simple paragraph to see how it's put together.

> The deductibility of home mortgage interest has been under recent review by Congress as a way to raise revenue. There have been two major reasons for this scrutiny. First, with consumer interest soon to be totally nondeductible and with investment interest being limited to net investment income, taxpayers would be motivated to rearrange their finances to maximize their tax deductions. Second, most voters do not own homes costing more than $500,000 and, therefore, putting a cap on mortgage loans does not affect the mass of voters. Given the pressure to raise revenue, two major changes have occurred in this area.

The first sentence of the example is the **topic sentence**. The second sentence introduces the supporting examples which appear in the next two sentences beginning with *first* and *second.* The final sentence of the paragraph acts as a preview to the contents of the next paragraph.

Now, let's examine the makeup of a single paragraph answer to a Business Law Exam essay question.

> Question: Dunhill fraudulently obtained a negotiable promissory note from Beeler by misrepresentation of a material fact. Dunhill subsequently negotiated the note to Gordon, a holder in due course. Pine, a business associate of Dunhill, was aware of the fraud perpetrated by Dunhill. Pine purchased the note for value from Gordon. Upon presentment, Beeler has defaulted on the note.
>
> Required: Answer the following, setting forth reasons for any conclusions stated.
>
> 1. What are the rights of Pine against Beeler?
> 2. What are the rights of Pine against Dunhill?

Examples of possible answers:

> 1. The rights of Pine against Beeler arise from Pine's having acquired the note from Gordon, who was a holder in due course. Pine himself is not a holder in due course because he had knowledge of a

> defense against the note. The rule wherein a transferee, not a holder in due course, acquires the rights of one by taking from a holder in due course is known as the "shelter rule." Through these rights, Pine is entitled to recover the proceeds of the note from Beeler. The defense of fraud in the inducement is a personal defense and not valid against a holder in due course.

The first sentence of the paragraph is the topic sentence in which the basic answer to the question is given. The third and fourth sentence explains the rule governing Pine's rights. (The *shelter rule* would be considered a *key phrase* in this answer.) The final sentence of the paragraph is not really necessary to answer the question but was added as an explanation of what some might mistakenly believe to be the key to the answer.

> 2. As one with the rights of a holder in due course, Pine is entitled to proceed against any person whose signature appears on the note, provided he gives notice of dishonor. When Dunhill negotiated the note to Gordon, Dunhill's signature on the note made him secondarily liable. As a result, if Pine brings suit against Dunhill, Pine will prevail because of Dunhill's secondary liability.

The first sentence of this paragraph restates the fact that Pine has the rights of a holder in due course and what these rights mean. The second sentence explains what happened when Dunhill negotiated the note, and the third sentence states the probable outcome of these results.

Note that in both answers 1. and 2., the sentences hang together in a logical fashion and lead the reader easily from one thought to the next. This is called *coherence*, a primary factor in considerations of conciseness and clarity.

Transitions

To demonstrate how to use **transitions** in a paragraph to carry the reader easily from one thought or example to another, let's consider a slightly longer and more detailed paragraph. The transitions are indicated in italics.

> A concerted effort to reduce book income in response to AMT could have a significant impact on corporations. *For example,* the auditor-client relationship may change. *Currently,* it isn't unusual for corporate management to argue for higher rather than lower book earnings, *while* the auditor would argue for conservative reported numbers. Such a corporate reporting posture may change as a consequence of the BURP adjustment. *Furthermore,* stock market analysts often rely on a price/earnings ratio. Lower earnings for essentially the same level of activity may have a significant effect on security prices.

The first sentence of the paragraph is the topic sentence. The next sentence, beginning with the transition *for example,* introduces the example with a broad statement. The following sentence, beginning with *currently,* gives a specific example to support the basic premise. The sentence beginning *furthermore* leads us into a final example. Without these transitions, the paragraph would be choppy and lack coherence.

What follows is a list of some transitions divided by usage. We suggest you commit some of these to memory so that you will never be at a loss as to how to tie your ideas together.

Transitional Words and Phrases

One idea plus one idea:

again	equally important	in addition	likewise	similarly
also	finally	in the same fashion	moreover	third
and	first	in the same respect	next	thirdly
and then	further	last	second	too
besides	furthermore	lastly	secondly	

To show time or place:

after a time	before	lately	soon
after a while	earlier	later	temporarily
afterwards	eventually	meanwhile	then
as long as	finally	next	thereafter
as soon as	first	of late	thereupon
at last	further	presently	to the left
at length	immediately	second	until
at that time	in due time	shortly	when
at the same time	in the meantime	since	while

To contrast or qualify:

after all	but	in contrast	on the contrary
although true	despite this fact	in spite of	on the other hand
and yet	for all that	nevertheless	otherwise
anyway	however	nonetheless	still
at the same time	in any case	notwithstanding	yet

To introduce an illustration:

for example	in other words	namely	to illustrate
for instance	in summary	specifically	
in fact	incidentally	that is	
in particular	indeed	thus	

To indicate concession:

after all
although this may be true
at the same time
even though
I admit
naturally
of course

To indicate comparison:

in a like manner
likewise
similarly

WRITING AN ANSWER TO AN EXAM QUESTION

Now that we have examined the makeup of an answer to an exam question, let's take an actual question from a past Business Law Exam and see how to go about writing a clear, comprehensive answer, step by step, sentence by sentence. A question similar to the one that follows would very likely be one for which the examiners would choose to grade writing skills.

Question:

> Bar Manufacturing and Cole Enterprises were arch rivals in the high technology industry, and both were feverishly working on a new product which would give the first to develop it a significant competitive advantage. Bar engaged Abel Consultants on April 1, 1983, for one year, commencing immediately, at $7,500 a month to aid the company in the development of the new product. The contract was oral and was consummated by a handshake. Cole approached Abel and offered them a $10,000 bonus for signing, $10,000 a month for nine months, and a $40,000 bonus if Cole was the first to successfully market the new product. In this connection, Cole stated that the oral contract Abel made with Bar was unenforceable and that Abel could walk away from it without liability. In addition, Cole made certain misrepresentations regarding the dollar amount of its commitment to the project, the state of its development, and the expertise of its research staff. Abel accepted the offer.
>
> Four months later, Bar successfully introduced the new product. Cole immediately dismissed Abel and has paid nothing beyond the first four $10,000 payments plus the initial bonus. Three lawsuits ensued: Bar sued Cole, Bar sued Abel, and Abel sued Cole.

Required: Answer the following, setting forth reasons for any conclusions stated.

> Discuss the various theories on which each of the three lawsuits is based, the defenses which will be asserted, the measure of possible recovery, and the probable outcome of the litigation.

Composing an Answer:

<u>Analyze</u> requirements.

<u>Plan</u> on one paragraph for each lawsuit. Each paragraph will contain four elements: theory, defenses, recovery, and outcome.

Paragraph one:

Step 1: Begin with the first lawsuit mentioned, Bar vs. Cole. Write a topic sentence which will sum up the theory of the suit.

> **Topic sentence containing basic theory of the suit:** Bar's lawsuit against Cole will be based upon the intentional tort of wrongful interference with a contractual relationship.

Step 2: Back up this statement with law and facts from the question scenario.

> The primary requirement for this cause of action is a valid contractual relationship with which the defendant knowingly interferes. This requirement is met in the case of Cole.

Step 3: State defenses.

> The contract is not required to be in writing since it is for exactly one year from the time of its making. It is, therefore, valid even though oral.

Step 4: Introduce subject of recovery (damages).

> Cole's knowledge of the contract is obvious.

Step 5: Explain possible problems to recovery.

The principal problem, however, is damages. Since Bar was the first to market the product successfully, it would seem that damages are not present. It is possible there were actual damages incurred by Bar (for example, it hired another consulting firm at an increased price).

Step 6: Discuss possible outcome.

It also might be possible that some courts would permit the recovery of punitive damages since this is an intentional tort.

Thus, the complete paragraph reads as follows:

Bar's lawsuit against Cole will be based upon the intentional tort of wrongful interference with a contractual relationship. The primary requirement for this cause of action is a valid contractual relationship with which the defendant knowingly interferes. The requirement is met in the case of Cole. The contract is not required to be in writing since it is for exactly one year from the time of its making. It is, therefore, valid even though oral. Cole's knowledge of the contract is obvious. The principal problem, however, is damages. Since Bar was the first to market the product successfully, it would seem that damages are not present. It is possible there were actual damages incurred by Bar (for example, it hired another consulting firm at an increased price). It also might be possible that some courts would permit the recovery of punitive damages since this is an intentional tort.

Paragraph two:

Step 1: Discuss second lawsuit mentioned, Bar vs. Abel. Write a topic sentence which will sum up the theory of the suit.

Topic sentence containing basic theory of the suit: Bar's cause of action against Abel would be for breach of contract.

Step 2: State defenses. [*Same as for first paragraph; this could be left out.*]

The contract is not required to be in writing since it is for exactly one year from the time of its making. It is, therefore, valid even though oral.

Step 3: Introduce subject of recovery (damages).

Once again, [*indicating similarity and tying second paragraph to first*] damages would seem to be a serious problem.

Step 4: Explain possible problems to recovery.

Furthermore, punitive damages would rarely be available in a contract action. Finally, Bar cannot recover the same damages twice.

Step 5: Discuss possible outcome.

Hence, if it proceeds against Cole and recovers damages caused by Abel's breach of contract, it will not be able to recover a second time.

Thus, the complete paragraph reads as follows:

Bar's cause of action against Abel would be for breach of contract. [The contract is not required to be in writing since it is for exactly one year from the time of its making. It is, therefore, valid even though oral.] Once again, damages would seem to be a serious problem. Furthermore, punitive damages would rarely be available in a contract action. Finally, Bar cannot recover the same damages twice. Hence, if it proceeds against Cole and recovers damages caused by Abel's breach of contract, it will not be able to recover a second time.

Paragraph three:

Step 1: Discuss third lawsuit mentioned, Abel vs. Cole. Write a topic sentence which will sum up the theory of the suit.

Topic sentence containing basic theory of the suit: Abel's lawsuit against Cole will be based upon fraud and breach of contract.

Step 2: State defenses.

There were fraudulent statements made by Cole with the requisite intent and that were possibly to Abel's detriment. The breach of contract by Cole is obvious.

Step 3: Back up these statements with law and facts from the question scenario.

However, the contract that Cole induced Abel to enter into and which it subsequently breached was an illegal contract, that is, one calling for the commission of a tort.

Step 4: Explain possible problems to recovery and possible outcome.

Therefore, both parties are likely to be treated as wrongdoers, and Abel will be denied recovery.

Thus, the complete paragraph reads as follows:

Abel's lawsuit against Cole will be based upon fraud and breach of contract. There were fraudulent statements made by Cole with the requisite intent and that were possibly to Abel's detriment. The breach of contract by Cole is obvious. However, the contract that Cole induced Abel to enter into and which it subsequently breached was an illegal contract, that is, one calling for the commission of a tort. Therefore, both parties are likely to be treated as wrongdoers, and Abel will be denied recovery.

Paragraph Editing:

After you have written your essay, go back over your work to check for the six characteristics that the AICPA will be looking for; coherent organization, conciseness, clarity, use of standard English, responsiveness to the requirements of the question, and appropriateness to the reader.

DIAGNOSTIC QUIZ

The following quiz is designed to test your knowledge of standard English, and grammar in particular. The correct answers follow the quiz, along with references to the sections which cover that particular area. By identifying the sections that are troublesome for you, you will be able to assess your weaknesses and concentrate on reviewing these areas. Consequently, only a brief review of the areas associated with the items you answered correctly will be necessary. If you simply made a lucky guess, you'd better do a quick review anyway.

Circle the correct choice in the brackets for the following:

1. The company can assert any defenses against third party beneficiaries that [they have/it has] against the promisee.

2. Among those securities [which/that] are exempt from registration under the 1933 Act [are/is] a class of stock given in exchange for another class by the issuer to its existing stockholders without the [issuer's/issuer] paying a commission.

3. This type of promise will not bind the promisor [as/because/since] there is no mutuality of obligation.

4. Under the cost method, treasury stock is presented on the balance sheet as an unallocated reduction of total [stockholders'/stockholders/stockholder's] equity.

5. Jones wished that he [was/were] not bound by the offer he made Smith, while Smith celebrated [his/him] having accepted the offer.

6. [Non-cash/Noncash] investing and financing transactions are not reported in the statement of cash flows because the statement reports only the [affects/effects] of operating, investing, and financing activities that directly [affect/effect] cash flows.

7. Since [its/it's] impossible to predict the future and because prospective financial statements can be [effected/affected] by numerous factors, the accountant must use [judgment/judgement] to estimate when and how conditions are [likely/liable] to change.

8. A common format of bank reconciliation statements [is/are] to reconcile both book and bank balances to a common amount known as the "true balance."

9. Corporations, clubs, churches, and other entities may be beneficiaries so long as they are sufficiently identifiable to permit a determination of [who/whom] is empowered to enforce the terms of the trust.

10. None of the beneficiaries [was/were] specifically referred to in the will.

11. Either Dr. Kline or Dr. Monroe [have/has] been elected to the board of directors.

12. The letter should be signed by Bill and [me/myself].

13. Any trust [which/that] is created for an illegal purpose is invalid.

14. When the nature of relevant information is such that it cannot appear in the accounts, this [principal/principle] dictates that such relevant information be included in the accompanying notes to the financial statements. Financial reporting is the [principal/principle] means of communicating financial information to those outside an entity.

15. The inheritance was divided [between/among] several beneficiaries.

16. Termination of an offer ends the offeree's power to [accept/except] it.

17. The consideration given by the participating creditors is [their/there] mutual promises to [accept/except] less than the full amount of [their/there] claims. Because [their/there] must be such mutual promises [between/among] all the participating creditors, a composition or extension agreement requires the participation of at least two or more creditors.

Follow instructions for each of the following items:

18. The duties assigned to the interns were to accompany the seniors on field work assignments and the organization and filing of the work papers.

    Fix this sentence so that it will read more smoothly. ______________________________

    ____

    ____

19. Circle the correct spelling of the following pairs of words.

    liaison laison — privilege priviledge — supersede supercede

    achieve acheive — occasion occassion — accommodate accomodate

20. Each set of brackets in the following example represents a possible location for punctuation. If you believe a location needs no punctuation, leave it blank; if you think a location needs punctuation, enter a comma, a colon, or a semicolon.

    If the promises supply the consideration [ ] there must be a mutuality of obligation [ ] in other words [ ] both parties must be bound.

ANSWERS TO DIAGNOSTIC QUIZ

Each answer includes a reference to the section that covers what you need to review.

1.	it has	Pronouns—Antecedents, p. G-31.
2.	that; is; issuer's	Subordinating Conjunctions, p. G-35; Verbs —Agreement, p. G-27; Nouns—Gerunds, p. G-30.
3.	because	Subordinating Conjunctions, p. G-35.
4.	stockholders'	Possessive Nouns, p. G-29.
5.	were; his	Verbs, p. G-24, Subjunctive Mood, p. G-25; Nouns—Gerunds, p. G-30.
6.	Noncash; effects; affect	Hyphens, p. G-21; Troublesome Words: Misused or Confused Terminology, p. G-14.
7.	it's; affected; judgment, likely	Troublesome Words: Misused or Confused Terminology, p. G-14; Troublesome Words: Spelling, p. G-21; Diction, List of Words p. G-11.
8.	is	Verbs—Agreement, p. G-27.
9.	who	Pronouns, Who/Whom, p. G-30.
10.	were	Verbs—Agreement with Each/None, p. G-28.
11.	has	Verbs—Agreement, p. G-27.
12.	me	Pronouns, that follow prepositions, p. G-31.
13.	that	Subordinating Conjunctions, p. G-35.
14.	principle; principal	Troublesome Words: Misused or Confused Terminology, p. G-14.
15.	among	Diction, List of Words, p. G-11.
16.	accept	Troublesome Words: Misused or Confused Terminology, p. G-14.

17. their; accept; their; there; among; Troublesome Words: Misused or Confused Terminology, p. G-14, G-16; Diction, List of Words, p. G-11.

18. Two possible answers: Refer to Parallelism, p. G-17.

The duties assigned to the interns were *accompanying* the seniors on field work assignments and *organizing* and filing the work papers.
or
The duties assigned to the interns were to accompany the seniors on field work assignments and *to organize* and *file* the work papers.

19. In every case, the **first choice** is the correct spelling.
Refer to Troublesome Words: Spelling, p. G-21.

20. If the promises supply the consideration [,] there must be a mutuality of obligation [;] in other words [,] both parties must be bound. Refer to Punctuation, p. G-18.

SCORING

Count one point for each item (some numbers contain more than one item) and one point for question number 18 if your sentence came close to the parallelism demonstrated by the answer choices. There are a total of 40 points.

If you scored 37-40, you did very well. A brief review of the items you missed should be sufficient to make you feel fairly confident about your grammar skills.

If you scored 33-36, you did fairly well—better than average—but you should do a thorough review of the items you missed.

If you scored 29-32, your score was average. Since "average" will probably not make it on the CPA Exam, you might want to consider a thorough grammar review, in addition to the items you missed.

If you scored below average (28 or less), you **definitely** should make grammar review a high priority when budgeting your exam study time.

SENTENCE STRUCTURE

A sentence is a statement or question, consisting of a subject and a predicate. A subject, at a minimum is a noun, usually accompanied by one or more modifiers (for example, "The Trial Balance"). A predicate consists, at a minimum, of a verb. Cultivate the habit of a quick verification for a subject, predicate, capitalized first word, and ending punctuation in each sentence of an essay.

A study of sentence structure is essentially a study of grammar but also moves just beyond grammar to diction, syntax, and parallelism. **Diction** is appropriate word choice. **Syntax** is the order of words in a sentence. In **parallelism,** parts of a sentence (or a paragraph) that are parallel in meaning are also parallel in structure. As we discuss how sentences are structured, there will naturally be some overlapping with grammar.

Diction

There is no substitute for a diversified vocabulary. If you have a diversified vocabulary or "a way with words," you are already a step ahead. A good general vocabulary, as well as a good accounting vocabulary, is a prerequisite of the exam. Develop your vocabulary as you review for the exam.

An important aspect of choosing the right words is knowing the audience for whom you are choosing those "perfect words." A perfect word for accountants is not necessarily the perfect word for mechanics or even lawyers or English professors. If a CPA Exam essay question asks you to write a specific document for a reader other than another accountant or CPA, you would need to be very specific but less technical than you would be otherwise.

Anyone who has waded through the statements of the FASB, and other legal and accounting literature knows that the language and sentence structure can be difficult. Nevertheless, accounting, auditing, and related areas do have a certain diction and syntax peculiar unto themselves. Complain as we may about the complexity of the sentence structure, we would be hard-pressed to construct the sentences much differently to convey the same meaning. Promulgations, for instance, are written very carefully so as to avoid possible misinterpretations or misunderstandings. Of course, you are not expected to write like this—for the CPA Exam or in other situations. Find the best word possible to explain clearly and concisely what it is you are trying to say. Often the "right word" is simply just not the "wrong word," so be certain you know the exact meaning of a word before you use it. As an accountant writing for accountants, what is most important is knowing the technical terms and the "key words" and placing them in your sentences properly and effectively. Defining or explaining key words demonstrates to graders that you understand the words you are using and not merely parroting the jargon.

As we work through the rest of this section on structure and organization, we will be giving some examples that will demonstrate how important diction can be.

The following is a list of words that frequently either are mistaken for one another or incorrectly assumed to be more or less synonymous.

Among—preposition, refers to more than two
Between—preposition, refers to two
(Between is used for three or more if the items are considered severally and individually.)

> If only part of the seller's capacity to perform is affected, the seller must allocate deliveries *among* the customers, and he or she must give each one reasonable notice of the quota available to him or her.
>
> *Between* merchants, the additional terms become part of the contract unless one of the following applies ...(This sentence is correct whether there are two merchants or many merchants.)

Amount—noun, an aggregate; total number or quantity
Number—noun, a sum of units; a countable number
Quantity—noun, an indefinite amount or number

> The checks must be charged to the account in the order of lowest *amount* to highest *amount* to minimize the *number* of dishonored checks.
> The contract is not enforceable under this paragraph beyond the *quantity* of goods shown in such writing.

Allude—verb, to state indirectly
Refer—verb, to state clearly and directly

> She *alluded* to the fact that the company's management was unscrupulous.
> She *referred* to his poor management in her report.

Bimonthly—adjective or adverb; every two months
Semimonthly—adjective or adverb; twice a month

> Our company has *bimonthly* meetings.
> We get paid *semimonthly.*

Can—verb (auxiliary), to be able
May—verb (auxiliary), to be permitted

> Treasury shares *may* be sold for whatever the corporation *can* garner.

The distinction between **can** and **may** has virtually disappeared in speech and in informal writing. In formal writing, however, they are not synonymous.

Continual—adjective, that which is repeatedly renewed after each interruption or intermission
Continuous—adjective, that which is uninterrupted in time, space, or sequence

> The *continuous* ramblings of the managing partner caused the other partners to *continually* check the time.

Cost—noun, the amount paid for an item
Price—noun, the amount set for an item
Value—noun, the relative worth, utility, or importance of an item
Worth—noun, value of an item measured by its qualities or by the esteem in which it is held

> The *cost* of that stock is too much.
> The *price* of that stock is $100 a share.
> I place no *value* on that stock.
> That stock's *worth* is overestimated.

Decide—verb, to arrive at a solution
Conclude—verb, to reach a final determination; to exercise judgment

> Barbara *decided* to listen to what the accountant was saying; she then *concluded* that what he was saying was true.

Fewer—adjective, not as many; consisting of or amounting to a smaller number (used of numbers; comparative of few)
Less—adjective, lower rank, degree, or importance; a more limited amount (used of quantity— for the most part)

> My clients require *fewer* consultations than yours do.
> My clients are *less* demanding than yours are.

Good—adjective, of a favorable character or tendency;
noun, something that is good
Well—adverb, good or proper manner; satisfactorily with respect to conduct or action;
adjective, being in satisfactory condition or circumstances

> It was *good* [adjective] of you to help me study for the CPA exam.
> The decision was for the *good* [noun] of the firm.
> He performed that task *well* [adverb].
> His work was *well* [adjective] respected by the other accountants.

Imply—verb, to suggest
Infer—verb, to assume; deduce

> Her report seems to *imply* that my work was not up to par.
> From reading her report, the manager *inferred* that my work was not up to par.

Last—adjective, the end in a series or the next before the present; following all the rest
Latest—adjective, coming or remaining after the usual or proper time; last in time

> The bankrupt corporation issued its *last* prospectus.
> The *latest* quarterly report was issued yesterday.

Liable—adjective, a legal obligation; being exposed or subject to some adverse contingency
Likely—adjective, inclination or probability

If the corporation continues to loose revenue, it is *liable* to fail.
It is *likely* to fail by the first of the year.

Oral—adjective, by the mouth, spoken; not written
Verbal—adjective, relating to or consisting of words
Vocal—adjective, uttered by the voice, spoken; persistence and volume of speech

Hawkins, Inc. made an *oral* agreement to the contract.
One partner gave his *verbal* consent while the other partner was very *vocal* with his objections.

State—verb, to set forth in detail; completely
Assert—verb, to claim positively, sometimes aggressively or controversially
Affirm—verb, to validate, confirm, state positively

The attorney *stated* the facts of the case.
The plaintiff *asserted* that his rights had been violated.
The judge *affirmed* the jury's decision.

Syntax

Errors in syntax occur in a number of ways; the number one way is through hasty composition. The only way to catch errors in word order is to read each of your sentences carefully to make sure that the words you meant to write or type are the words that actually appear on the page and that those words are in the best possible order. The following list should help you avoid errors in both diction and syntax and gives examples where necessary.

Troublesome Words: Misused or Confused Terminology

Accept—verb, to receive or to agree to willingly
Except—verb, to take out or leave out from a number or a whole;
conjunction, on any other condition but that condition

Except for the items we have mentioned, we will *accept* the conditions of the contract.

Advice—noun, information or recommendation
Advise—verb, to recommend, give advice

The accountant *advised* us to take his *advice*.

Affect—verb, to influence or change
(**Note:** affect is occasionally used as a noun in technical writing only.)
Effect—noun, result or cause;
verb, to cause

The *effect* [noun] of Ward, Inc.'s decision to cease operations *affected* many people.
He quickly *effected* [verb] policy changes for office procedures.

All Ready—adjectival phrase, completely prepared
Already—adverb, before now; previously

Although the tax return was *all ready* to be filed, the deadline had *already* passed.

All Right; Alright—adjective or adverb, beyond doubt; very well; satisfactory; agreeable, pleasing
(Although many grammarians insist that **alright** is not a proper form, it is widely accepted.)

Appraise—verb, set a value on
Apprise—verb, inform

Dane Corp. *apprised* him of the equipment's age, so that he could *appraise* it more accurately.

Assure—verb, to give confidence to positively
Ensure—verb, to make sure, certain, or safe
Insure—verb, to obtain or provide insurance on or for; to make certain by taking necessary measures and precautions

The accountant *assured* his client that he would file his return in a timely manner.
He added the figures more than once to *ensure* their accuracy.
She was advised to *insure* her diamond property.

Decedent—noun, a deceased person
Descendant—noun, proceeding from an ancestor or source

The *decedent* left her vast fortune to her *descendants*.

Eminent—adjective, to stand out; important
Imminent—adjective, impending

Although he was an *eminent* businessman, foreclosure on his house was *imminent*.

Its—possessive
It's—contraction, **it is**

The company held *its* board of directors meeting on Saturday. *It's* the second meeting this month.

Percent—used with numbers only
Percentage—used with words or phrases

Each employee received two *percent* of the profits.
They all agreed this was a small *percentage*.

Precedence—noun, the fact of preceding in time, priority of importance
Precedent—noun, established authority;
adjective, prior in time, order, or significance

The board of directors meeting took *precedence* over his going away.
The president set a *precedent* when making that decision.

Principal—noun, a capital sum placed at interest; a leading figure; the corpus of an estate;
adjective, first, most important
Principle—noun, a basic truth or rule

Paying interest on the *principal* [noun] of the loan was explained to the company's *principals* [noun].
The *principal* [adjective] part of ...
She refused to compromise her *principles*.

Than—conjunction, function word to indicate difference in kind, manner, or identity;
preposition, in comparison with (indicates comparison)

Then—adverb, at that time; soon after that (indicates time)

BFE Corp. has more shareholders *than* Hills Corp.
First, we must write the report, and *then* we will meet with the clients.

Their—adjective, of or relating to them or themselves
There—adverb, in or at that place

There were fifty shareholders at the meeting to cast *their* votes.

Placement of Modifiers

Pay close attention to where modifiers are placed, especially adverbs such as **only** and **even**. In speech, inflection aids meaning but, in writing, placing modifiers improperly can be confusing and often changes the meaning of the sentence. The modifier should usually be placed before the word or words it modifies. Consider the following:

She *almost* finished the whole report.
She finished *almost* the whole report.

Only she finished the report.
She *only* finished the report.
She finished *only* the report.

Phrases also must be placed properly, usually, but not always, following the word or phrase they modify. Often, **reading the sentence aloud** will help you decide where the modifier belongs.

(1) Fleming introduced a client to John with a counter-offer.

Analysis: *With a counter-offer* modifies *client*, not *John*, and should be placed after *client*.

(2) The accountant recommended a bankruptcy petition to the client under Chapter 7.

Analysis: *Under Chapter 7* modifies *bankruptcy petition*, not *the client*, and should be placed after *bankruptcy petition*.

Splitting Infinitives

Infinitives are the root verb form (e.g., to be, to consider, to walk). Generally speaking, infinitives should not be split except when to do so makes the meaning clearer.

Awkward: Management's responsibility is to clearly represent its financial position.
Better: Management's responsibility is to represent its financial position clearly.

Exception: Management's responsibility in the future is to better represent its financial position.

Sentence Fragments

To avoid sentence fragments, read over your work carefully. Each sentence needs at least (1) a subject and (2) a predicate.

Unlike the case of a forged endorsement, a drawee bank charged with the recognition of its drawer-customer's signature. (The verb *is*, before the word *charged*, has been left out.)

Parallelism

Parallelism refers to a similarity in structure and meaning of all parts of a sentence or a paragraph. Sentences that violate rules of parallelism will be difficult to read and may obscure meaning. The following are some examples of different **violations** of parallelism.

(1) A security interest can be effected through a financing statement or the creditor's taking possession of it.

Analysis: The two prepositional phrases separated by **or** should be parallel. The sentence may be corrected as follows:

> A security interest can be effected through a financing statement or through possession by the creditor.

(2) The independent auditor should consider whether the scope is appropriate, adequate audit programs and working papers, appropriate conclusions, and reports prepared are consistent with results of the work performed.

Analysis: The clause beginning with **whether** (which acts as the direct object of the verb **should consider**) is faulty. The items mentioned must be similarly constructed to each other. The sentence may be corrected as follows:

> The independent auditor should consider whether the scope is appropriate, audit programs and working papers are adequate, conclusions are appropriate, and reports prepared are consistent with results of the work performed.

(3) The CPA was responsible for performing the inquiry and analytical procedures and that the review report was completed in a timely manner.

Analysis: The prepositional phrase beginning with **for** is faulty. The sentence may be corrected as follows:

> The CPA was responsible for performing the inquiry and analytical procedures and ensuring that the review report was completed in a timely manner.

(4) Procedures that should be applied in examining the stock accounts are as follows:
(1) Review the corporate charter ...
(2) Obtain or preparing an analysis of ...
(3) Determination of authorization for ...

Analysis: All items in a list must be in parallel structure. An example of how the list may be corrected follows:

1. Review the corporate charter ...
2. Obtain or prepare an analysis of ...
3. Determine the authorization for ...

There are many other types of faulty constructions that can creep into sentences—too many to detail here. Furthermore, if any of the above is not clear, syntax may be a problem for you and you might want to consider a more thorough review of this subject.

NUMBERS

The basic rule for writing numbers is to write out the numbers ten and under and use numerals for all the others. More formal writing may dictate writing out all round numbers and numbers under 101. Let style, context of the sentence and of the work, and common sense be your guide.

The partnership was formed 18 years ago.
Jim Bryant joined the firm four years ago.
Baker purchased 200 shares of stock.

When there are two numbers next to each other, alternate the styles.

three 4-year certificates of deposit 5 two-party instruments

Never begin a sentence with numerals, such as:

1989 was the last year that Zinc Co. filed a tax return.

This example can be corrected as follows:

Nineteen hundred and eighty-nine was the last year that Zinc Co. filed a tax return. (For use only in very formal writing)
or
Zinc Co. has not filed a tax return since 1989.

CAPITALIZATION

Under the assumption that most of us know the basic rules for normal capitalization, this section mentions only two special but common areas that seem to cause difficulties.

(1) The first word **after a colon** is capped only when it is the beginning of a complete sentence.

We discussed several possibilities at the meeting: Among them were liquidation, reorganization, and rehabilitation.
We discussed several possibilities at the meeting: liquidation, reorganization, and rehabilitation.

(2) The capitalization of titles and headings is especially tricky. In general, the first word and all other important words, no matter what length they are, should be capped. Beyond this general rule, there are several variations relating to the capitalization of pronouns. The important thing here is to pick a style and use it consistently within a single document, article, etc.

For example, the following pair of headings would both be acceptable depending on the style and consistency of style:

Securities to which SFAS 115 Applies	**or**	Securities to Which SFAS 115 Applies
Issues for Property other than Cash	**or**	Issues For Property Other Than Cash

PUNCTUATION

Period

Probably the two most common errors involving periods occur when incorporating quotation marks and/or parentheses with periods.

(1) When a period is used with closing quotation marks, the period is always placed **inside**, regardless of whether the entire sentence is a quote or only the end of the sentence.

(2) When a period is used with parentheses, the period goes **inside** the closing parenthesis if the entire sentence is enclosed in parentheses. When only the last word or words is enclosed in parentheses, the period goes **outside** the closing parenthesis.

(See Chapter 38, Contracts.)
The answer to that question is in the section on contracts (Chapter 38).

Exclamation Point

An **exclamation point** is used for emphasis and when issuing a command. In many cases, this is determined by the author when he or she wants to convey urgency, irony, or stronger emotion than ordinarily would be inferred.

Colons

A **colon** is used to introduce something in the sentence—a list of related words, phrases, or items directly related to the first part of the sentence; a quotation; a **direct** question; or an example of what was stated in the first part of the sentence. The colon takes the place of **that is** or **such as** and should never be used **with** such phrases.

The accountant discussed two possibilities with the clients: first, a joint voluntary bankruptcy petition under Chapter 7, and second, ...

The following will be discussed: life insurance proceeds; inheritance; and property.

My CPA accounting review book states the following: "All leases that do not meet any of the four criteria for capital leases are operating leases."

Colons are used in formal correspondence after the salutation.

Dear Mr. Bennett:
To Whom it May Concern:

Note: When **that is** or **such as** is followed by a numeric list, it may be followed by a colon.

TOTALTIP: When writing a sentence, if you're not sure whether or not a colon is appropriate, it probably isn't. When in doubt, change the sentence so that you're sure it doesn't need a colon.

Semicolons

A **semicolon** is used in a number of ways:

(1) Use a **semicolon in place of a conjunction** when there are two or more closely related thoughts and each is expressed in a coordinate clause (a clause that could stand as a complete sentence).

A marketable title is one that is free from plausible or reasonable objections; it need not be perfect.

(2) Use a **semicolon** as in the above example **with a conjunction** when the sentence is very long and complex. This promotes **clarity** by making the sentence easier to read.

Should the lease be prematurely terminated, the deposit may be retained only to cover the landlord's actual expenses or damages; ***and*** any excess must be returned to the tenant.

An assignment establishes privity of estate between the lessor and assignee; ***[and]*** therefore, the assignee becomes personally liable for the rent.

(3) When there are commas in a series of items, use a **semicolon** to separate the main items.

Addison, Inc. has distribution centers in Camden, Maine; Portsmouth, New Hampshire; and Rock Island, Rhode Island.

Commas

Informal English, in general, allows much freedom in the placement or the omission of commas, and the overall trend is away from commas. However, standard, formal English provides rules for its usage. Accounting "language" can be so complex that using commas and using them correctly and appropriately is a necessity to avoid obscurity and promote clarity. Accordingly, we encourage you to learn the basics about comma placement.

What follows is not a complete set of rules for commas but should be everything you need to know about commas to make your sentences clear and concise. Because the primary purpose of the comma is to clarify meaning, it is the opinion of the authors that in the case of a complex subject such as accounting, it is better to overpunctuate than to underpunctuate. If you are concerned about overpunctuation, try to reduce an unwieldly sentence to two or more sentences.

(1) Use a **comma** to **separate a compound sentence** (one with two or more independent coordinate clauses joined by a conjunction).

Gil Corp. has current assets of $90,000**,** but the corporation has current liabilities of $180,000.
Jim borrowed $60,000**,** and he used the proceeds to purchase outstanding common shares of stock.

Note: In these examples, a comma would **not** be necessary if the **and** or the **but** were not followed by a noun or pronoun (the subject of the second clause). In other words, if by removing the conjunction, the sentence could be separated into two complete sentences, it needs a comma.

(2) Use a **comma** after an **introductory word or phrase.**

During 1992**,** Rand Co. purchased $960,000 of inventory.
On April 1, 1993**,** Wall's inventory had a fair value of $150,000.

Note: Writers often choose to omit this comma when the introductory phrase is very short. Again, we recommend using the comma. It will never be incorrect in this position.

(3) Use a **comma** after an **introductory adverbial clause.**

Although insurance contracts are not required by the Statute of Frauds to be in writing**,** most states have enacted statutes which now require such.

(4) Use **commas** to separate **items, phrases, or clauses in a series.**

To be negotiable, an instrument must be in writing**,** signed by the maker or drawer**,** contain an unconditional promise or order to pay a sum certain in money on demand or at a specific time**,** and be payable to order or to bearer.

Note: Modern practice often omits the last comma in the series (in the above example, the one before **and**). Again, for the sake of clarity, we recommend using this comma.

(5) In most cases, use a **comma or commas** to separate **a series of adjectives.**

Silt Co. kept their inventory in an old**,** decrepit**,** brick building .
He purchased several outstanding shares of common stock. (*No* commas are needed.)

TOTALTIP: When in doubt as to whether or not to use a comma after a particular adjective, try inserting the word **and** between the adjectives. If it makes sense, use a comma. (In the second example, above, **several and outstanding**, or **outstanding and several** don't make sense.

(6) Use a **comma or commas** to set off any **word or words, phrase, or clause that interrupts the sentence** but does not change its essential meaning.

SLD Industries, as drawer of the instrument, is only secondarily liable.

(7) Use **commas** to set off **geographical names** and **dates**.

Feeney Co. moved its headquarters to Miami, Florida, on August 16, 1992.

Quotation Marks

Quotation marks are used with **direct quotations; direct discourse and direct questions**; and **definitions or explanations of words**. There are other uses of quotation marks that would be used rarely in the accounting profession and, therefore, are not discussed in this review.

Hyphens

Use a **hyphen** to separate words into syllables. It is always best to check a dictionary, because some words do not split where you would imagine.

Modern practice does not normally hyphenate prefixes and their root words, even when both the prefix and the root word begin with vowels. A common exception is when the root word begins with a capital letter or a date or number.

prenuptial	nonexempt	semiannual
pre-1987	nonnegotiable	non-American

Although modern practice is moving away from using hyphens for **compound adjectives** (a noun and an adjective in combination to make a single adjective), clarity dictates that hyphens still be used in many cases.

long-term investments	two-party instrument
a noninterest-bearing note	short-term capital losses

Use a hyphen **only** when the compound adjective or compound adjective-adverb **precedes the noun.**

The well-known company is going bankrupt.
The company is well known for its quality products.

Note: There are certain word combinations that are always hyphenated, always one word, or always two words. Use the dictionary.

The final item we want to mention regarding hyphenation is the **suspended hyphen**. Suspended hyphens are used to avoid repetition in compound adjectives. For example, instead of having to write **himself or herself**, especially when these forms are being used repeatedly as they often must be in our new nongender-biased world, use **him- or herself**.

10-, 15-, and 18-year depreciation	first-, second-, and third-class

SPELLING

Just as many of us believe that arithmetic can always be done by our calculators, we also believe that spelling will be done by our word processors and, therefore, we needn't worry too much about it. There is no doubt that these devices are tremendous boons to writers and others. However, although you soon will be able to use a calculator during the CPA Exam, you will not be able to use a word processor. And like it or not, you will encounter many other situations where a spell-checker will not be available to you, so you'd better be able to **spell!** Also, a spell-checker cannot tell the difference between words that you have misspelled which are nonetheless real words, such as **there** and **their**. (See the list in this section of words often confused.)

Let's hit some highlights here of troublesome spellings with some brief tips that should help you become a better speller.

(1) **IE** or **EI**? If you are still confused by words containing the **ie** or **ei** combinations, you'd better relearn those old rhymes we ridiculed in grade school.

"**i** before **e** except after **c.**" (This works only for words where the ie-ei combination sounds like **ee.**)

ach**ie**ve	bel**ie**ve	ch**ie**f
ceiling	re**cei**ve	re**cei**pt

Of course there are always **exceptions** such as:

either neither seize financier

When **ie** or **ei** have a different sound than **ee**, the above rule does not apply. For example:

fr**ie**nd	s**ie**ve	effic**ie**nt
for**ei**gn	sover**ei**gn	surf**ei**t

(2) **Doubling final consonants**. When an ending (**suffix**) beginning with a vowel is added to a root word that ends in a single consonant, that final consonant is **usually doubled.**

lag—lagging bid—bidding top—topped

The exceptions generally fall under three rules.

First, double only after a short vowel and **not** after a double vowel.

big—bigger	tug—tugging	get—getting
need—needing	keep—keeping	pool—pooled

Second, a **long** vowel (one that "says its own name"), which is almost always followed by a silent **e** that must be dropped to add the suffix, is **not** doubled.

hope—hoping tape—taped rule—ruled

Note: Sometimes, as in the first two examples above, doubling the consonants would create entirely new words.

Third, with root words of two or more syllables ending in a single consonant, double the consonant **only** when the last syllable is the **stressed syllable.**

Double:	beg**in**—beginning, beginner	pre**fer**—preferred, preferring
	re**gret**—regretted, regrettable	ad**mit**—admitted, admittance

Don't Double:	pro**hi**bit—prohibited, prohibitive de**vel**op—developing	**be**nefit—benefited, benefiting **pref**erence—preferable

(3) **Drop** the silent **e** before adding a suffix **beginning with a vowel.**

store—storing   take—taking   value—valuing

Keep the **e** before adding a suffix **beginning with a consonant**, such as:

move—movement   achieve—achievement

Again, there are **exceptions.**

e: mile—mileage   dye—dyeing

No e: argue—argument   due—duly   true—truly
judge—judgment   acknowledge—acknowledgment

(4) Change **y** to **ie** before adding **s** when it is the single final vowel.

country—countries   study—studies   quantity—quantities

Change **y** to **i** before adding other endings **except s.**

busy—business   dry—drier   copy—copier

Exceptions: Keep **y** for the following:

copying   studying   trying

Y is also usually preserved when it follows another vowel.

delays   joys   played

Exceptions:

day—daily   lay—laid   pay—paid   say—said

(5) **Forming Plurals.** The formation of some plurals does not follow the general rule of adding **s** or **es** to the singular. What follows are some of the more troublesome forms.

Some singular nouns that end in **o** form their plurals by adding **s**; some by adding **es.**

ratio**s**   zero**s**   hero**es**   potato**es**

Many nouns taken directly from **foreign languages** retain their original plural. Below are a few of the more common ones.

alumnus—alumni   basis—bases   crisis—crises
criterion—criteria   datum—data   matrix—matrices

Other nouns taken directly from foreign languages have **two acceptable plural forms**: the foreign language plural and the anglicized plural. Here are some of the more common:

medium—media, mediums
formula—formulae, formulas
appendix—appendices, appendixes
memorandum—memoranda, memorandums

Finally, in this foreign language category are some commonly used Latin nouns that form their plurals by adding **es**.

census—censuses
hiatus—hiatuses
consensus—consensuses
prospectus—prospectuses

Troublesome Words: Spelling

Spelling errors occur for different reasons; probably the two most common reasons are confusion with the spelling of similar words or mistaking the British spelling of certain words for the American spelling. The following is a list of commonly misspelled words. You will find those you may have misspelled in taking the Diagnostic Quiz, and you may recognize others you have problems with. Memorize them. And, whenever and wherever possible, have a dictionary handy so that you won't be tempted to guess at spelling.

accommodate	existence	liaison	resistance
achieve	fulfill	occasion	skillful
acknowledgment	irrelevant	paralleled	supersede
bankruptcy	judgment	privilege	surety

GRAMMAR

This section on grammar is intended to be a brief overview only. Consequently, the authors have chosen to focus on items that, in their experience, seem to cause the most problems. If you did not do well on the Diagnostic Quiz at the beginning of "Accounting for 5%," you would be well advised to go over all the material in this section and, if there are areas you still do not feel confident about, you should consider a more thorough grammar study than the review provided here.

VERBS

The verb is the driving force of the sentence: it is the word or words to which all other parts of the sentence relate. When trying to analyze a sentence to identify its grammatical parts or its meaning, or when attempting to amend a sentence, you should always identify the verb or verbs first. A verb expresses action or being.

Action: The accountant *visits* his clients regularly.
Being: Kyle *is* an accountant.

Voice

The **active voice** indicates that the subject of the sentence (the person or thing) does something. The **passive voice** indicates that the subject is acted upon.

Active: *The accountant worked* on the client's financial statements.
Passive: The client's financial statements *were worked on by the accountant.*

For most kinds of writing, the passive voice is considered "weak" and generally should be avoided. For expository writing (properly used for the exam), however, the passive voice is legitimate and is used frequently.

Once the computations *are tested*, mathematical accuracy will be assured.

The most important thing to understand about voice is that it should be consistent; that is, you should avoid shifts from one voice to another, especially within the same sentence as below.

> Taylor Corporation *hired* an independent computer programmer to develop a simplified payroll application for its new computer, and an on-line, data-based microcomputer system *was developed.*

Use the active voice for the entire sentence:

> Taylor Corporation *hired* an independent computer programmer to develop a simplified payroll application for its new computer, and he *developed* an on-line, data-based microcomputer system.

Mood

Common errors in syntax are made when **more than one mood** is used in a single sentence. The first example that follows begins with the **imperative** and shifts to the **indicative**. The second example corrects the sentence by using the imperative in both clauses, and the third example corrects the sentence by using the indicative in both clauses. The fourth example avoids the problem by forming two sentences.

> Pick up (imperative) that work program for me at the printer, and then we will go (indicative) to the client.
> Pick up that work program for me at the printer, and then go to the client with me.
> After you pick up that work program for me at the printer, we will go to the client.
> Pick up that work program for me at the printer. Then we will go to the client.

There are three moods: the indicative, the imperative, and the subjunctive. Most sentences are **indicative**:

> *The percentage-of-completion method is justified.* Declarative indicative.
> *Is the percentage-of-completion method justified?* Interrogative indicative.

Sentences that give a command are called **imperative** sentences:

> Pick up your books!
> Be sure to use the correct method of accounting for income taxes.

The **subjunctive** mood is headed toward extinction. Today's grammar books often disagree on the use of the subjunctive in clauses that express **conditions** or **contingencies**. In other words, in a sentence containing an "if" clause that expresses a **condition, contingency, or a condition clearly contrary to fact**, some books will tell you to use the **subjunctive.** Others will say the **indicative** is the proper form in all cases **except** when expressing a condition clearly contrary to fact. Thus, in standard English today, you will often see the indicative used where previously the subjunctive had been used.

That having been said, let's go over the rules for using the subjunctive that, for the most part, are alive and well.

The subjunctive is usually used to express conditions contrary to fact, contingencies, and wishes, demands, recommendations, requests, and speculations, as in the following examples:

(1) In **if** clauses and some **unless** clauses for **conditions contrary to fact** or **speculations.**

> If the internal control *were* (the indicative is *was*) strong, the auditor would rely on it more.

(2) In clauses beginning with **as if** or **as though** to indicate **conditions or contingencies.**

> The client acted as though he *were* (indicative is *was*) uncomfortable with the statement.

(3) In clauses introduced by **that** for **wishes, demands, indirect requests, and recommendations.**

> Martha wished that no one *were* (indicative is *was*) around to see the client yell at her.

The manager demanded that the workpapers *be* (indicative is *are*) turned in for review before the return is prepared.
The instructor recommends that she *retake* (indicative is *retakes*) the exam.
It is important that the manager *review* (indicative is *reviews*) the workpapers immediately.

(4) In subordinate clauses beginning with **if** followed by the subjunctive verb form, the auxiliary verbs **would, could**, and **should** are usually used to indicate speculations or conditions contrary to fact.

If Harry *were* not over budget, he *would have* checked his work before giving it to the partner.

Warning: Beware of sentences in which the independent clause uses **would have.** The subordinate clause (the **if** clause) **does not also use would have**. The following is an example of a faulty construction which has crept comfortably into the language in recent years:

If I *would have* studied harder, I *would have* passed the exam.

Be sure to use **had** in the **if clause.**

If I *had* studied harder, I *would have* passed the exam.

(5) In certain traditional words and phrases, the subjunctive remains with us, even if modern practice tends not to use it in similar constructions.

Let me *be.*
Far *be* it from me ...
Be that as it *may* ...
If I *were* you ...

> **TOTALTIP**: Use the subjunctive form in clauses beginning with **if**, since it is still viable according to many grammar texts, and still commonly used in formal writing.

Tense

Tense is all about *time.* The **present tense** is used to express action or a state of being that is taking place in the present. The present tense is also used to express an action or a state of being that is habitual and when a definite time in the future is stated.

Dan *is taking* his CPA Exam.
Robin *goes* to the printer once a week.
The new computer *arrives* on Monday.

The **present perfect tense** is used to indicate action that began in the past and has continued to the present.

From the time of its founder, the CPA firm *has celebrated* April 16 with a fabulous dinner party.

The **future tense** is used to indicate action that takes place in the indefinite future.

A plan of reorganization *will determine* the amount and the manner in which the creditors *will be paid*, in what form the business *will continue*, and any other necessary details.

The **future perfect tense** is used to indicate action that has not taken place yet but will take place before a specific future time.

Before Susan arrives at the client's office, the client *will have prepared* the documents she needs.

The **past tense** is used to indicate an action that took place in the past. The **past tense** is also used to indicate a condition or state occurring at a specific time in the past.

The predecessor auditor *resigned* last week.
The company *contacted* its auditor the first of every new year.

The **past perfect tense** is used to indicate an action that is completed before another action that also took place in the past.

The work load *had been* so heavy that she was required to work overtime. (Not *was*)

As you can see by what we have just reviewed, the importance of using the proper tense is to properly indicate **time.** If the proper sequence of tenses is not used, confusion can arise as to what happened when. Consider:

Not getting the raise he was expecting, John was unhappy about the additional work load. [???]
Having not gotten the raise he was expecting, John was unhappy about the additional work load. [Much clearer]

Agreement

We cover **agreement** under the heading of verbs because the verb is the driving force of the sentence and, thus, it is the component with which everything else in the sentence should agree. The first element of agreement to examine is **verb** and **subject**. These two components must agree **in number**. We will see as we move along that **number** is just one of several things to consider when examining the agreement of the components of a sentence.

The subject of the sentence is the noun or pronoun (person, place, or thing) doing the action stated by the verb (in the case of the active voice) or being acted upon by the verb (in the case of the passive voice). Although the subject normally precedes the verb, this is not always the case. Thus, you must be able to identify sentence elements no matter where they happen to fall. This is not a difficult matter, at least most of the time. Consider:

(1) Lewis, Bradford, Johnson & Co. [is or are] the client with the best pay record.

(2) For me, one of the most difficult questions on the exam [was or were] concerned with correcting weaknesses in internal controls.

In both examples, the first choice, the singular verb form, is correct.

In sentence (1), Lewis, Bradford, Johnson & Co. is considered singular in number because we are talking about the company, not Lewis, Bradford, and Johnson per se.

In sentence (2), the verb is also singular because **one** is the subject of the sentence, not **questions**. **Questions** is the object of the preposition **of**. If this seems confusing, rearrange the sentence so that the prepositional phrase appears first, and the agreement of subject and verb will be clearer. Thus:

Of the most difficult questions, one *was concerned* with correcting weaknesses in internal controls.

We will address special problems associated with prepositional phrases in other sections.

Beware of the word **number**. When it is preceded by the word **the**, it is always singular, and when it is preceded by the word **a**, it is always plural.

The number of listings generated by the new EDP system *was* astounding.
A number of listings *were generated* by the new EDP system.

A **compound subject**, even when made up of nouns singular in number, always takes a plural verb.

> The balance sheet, the independent auditor's report, and the quarterly report *are lying* on the desk. (Not *is lying)*

Having used a form of the verb **lie** in the above example, let's mention the difference between **lie** and **lay**.

There are two separate verbs: **to lie**, meaning **to recline**, and **to lay**, meaning **to place or set**.

> He *lies* down to rest.
> He *lays* down the book.

Continuing now with **compound subjects**, let's address the problem of when there are two or more subjects—one (or more) singular and one (or more) plural.

When the sentence contains subjects connected by **or** or **nor**, or **not only ... but also**, the verb should agree with the subject nearer to the verb.

> Either the auditors or the partner *is going* to the client.
> Not only the partner but also the auditors *are going* to the client.

In the case of the first example above, which sounds awkward, simply switch the order of the subjects **(the partner; the auditors)** and use the verb **are going** to make it read better.

When one subject is **positive** and one is **negative**, the verb always agrees with the positive.

> The partner, and not the auditors, *is going* to the client.
> Not the partner but the auditors frequently go to the client.

You should use **singular verbs** with the following: **each, every, everyone, everybody, anyone, anybody, either, neither, someone, somebody, no one, nobody,** and **one**.

> Anybody who wants to go *is* welcome.
> Neither the accountant nor the bookkeeper ever *arrives* on time.
> One never *knows* what to expect.

TOTALTIP: Watch out for the words **each** and **none**. They can trip up even the most careful writer.

Improper placement of **each** in the sentence will confuse the verb agreement.

> The balance sheet, the income statement, and the statement of cash flows each [*has/have*] several errors.

In this example, we know that the verb must be **has** (to agree with **each**), but then again, maybe it should be **have** to agree with the subjects. The problem is that we have a sentence with a compound subject that must take a plural verb, but here it is connected with a singular pronoun (each).

This is a very common error. This particular example may be fixed in one of two ways. First, if the word **each** is not really necessary in the sentence, simply drop it. Second, simply place the word **each** in a better position in the sentence. In the example below, placing the word **each** at the end of the sentence properly connects it to **errors**; also it no longer confuses verb agreement.

> The balance sheet, the income statement, and the statement of cash flows *have* several errors *each.*

The word **none** has special problems all its own. Not too many years ago, it was the accepted rule that every time **none** was the subject of the sentence, it should take a **singular verb**. Most modern grammarians now agree that the plural may be used when followed by a prepositional phrase with a plural object (noun) or with an object whose meaning in the sentence is plural.

None of the statements *were* correct.

When **none** stands alone, some purists believe it should take the singular and others believe that the plural is the proper form when the meaning conveys plurality. Consequently, in the following example, either the singular or plural is generally acceptable.

All the financial statements had been compiled, but none *was* ***or*** *were* correct.

TOTALTIP: When in doubt or when the sentence sounds awkward, use **not one** in place of **none** (with a singular verb, of course).

NOUNS

Nouns are people, places, and things and can occur anywhere in the sentence. Make sure that, when necessary, the nouns are the same in number.

Do the exercises at the end of each chapter by answering the *questions* true or false. (Not singular *question*)
At the end of the engagement, everyone must turn in their *time sheets*. (Not singular *time sheet*)

Possessive Nouns

The basic rule for making a **singular noun** possessive is to add an **apostrophe and an s.** If a singular noun ends in s, **add apostrophe and an s**. To make a **plural noun** possessive, add an **apostrophe alone** when the plural ends in **s** or an **apostrophe and an s** when the plural does not end in an **s**.

Singular:	client*'s*	system*'s*	beneficiary*'s*	*Chris'*
Plural:	client*s'*	system*s'*	beneficiarie*s'*	

A common area of difficulty has to do with **ownership**, that is, when two or more individuals or groups are mentioned as owning something. If the ownership is **not common** to all, apostrophes appear after each individual or group. If the ownership **is common** to all, only the last individual or group in the series takes an apostrophe.

Not common to all: The accountant's and the attorney's offices ...
Common to all: Robert, his brother, and their sons' company ...

TOTALTIP: Most of the confusion associated with possessives seems to be with the plural possessive. Remember to make the noun **plural** first and **possessive** second.

Modern usage tends to make possessive forms into adjectives where appropriate. Thus:

Company's (possessive) management becomes *company* (adjective) management.
A *two weeks'* (possessive) vacation becomes a *two weeks* or *two-week* (both adjectives) vacation.

TOTALTIP: In most instances, either the possessive form or the adjectival form is acceptable. Go with the form that seems most appropriate for that particular sentence.

Gerunds

A gerund is a verb changed to a noun by adding **ing**. A noun preceding a gerund must be possessive so that it may be construed as **modifying the noun.**

Caroline's auditing the financial statements was approved by the partner.

In this example, the subject of the sentence is **auditing**, not Caroline or Caroline's. Since we know that nouns cannot modify nouns, Caroline must become **Caroline's** to create a possessive form which can modify the noun **auditing.**

The same holds true for **gerunds** used as **objects of prepositions**:

The partner objected to *Caroline's auditing* the financial statements.

In this example, **auditing** is the object of the preposition **to.** Caroline's is an appositive (or possessive) form modifying **auditing.**

PRONOUNS

Like Latin where most words have "cases" according to their function in the sentence, English **pronouns** also have cases. Sometimes you may be aware that you are using a case when determining the proper form of the pronoun and sometimes you may not.

He met *his* partner at *their* office.

Let's begin by tackling everybody's favorite: **who** and **whom.** We're going to take some time reviewing this one since it seems to be a major area of confusion.
There is little or no confusion when **who** is clearly the **subject** of the sentence:

Who is going with us?

And little or no confusion when **whom** is clearly (1) the **object** of the sentence or (2) the **object** of the preposition.

(1) Jenny audited *whom*? *Whom* did Jenny audit?

(2) Jenny is working for *whom*? For *whom* is Jenny working?

> **TOTALTIP**: If you are having difficulty with **questions**, try changing them into declarative sentences (statements) and substituting another pronoun. Thus: Jenny audits **them** (objective), obviously not **they** (subjective), or Jenny is working for **her**, obviously not **she**.

Who or **whoever** is the subjective case, and **whom** or **whomever** is the objective case. Common errors occur frequently in two instances: (1) when **who or whoever** is interrupted by a parenthetical phrase and (2) when an entire clause is the subject of a preposition.

(1) *Whoever* she decides is working with her should meet her at six o'clock.

In this example, **she decides** is a parenthetical phrase (one that could be left out of the sentence and the sentence would still be a complete thought). When you disregard **she decides,** you can see that **whoever** is the subject of the sentence, not **she**. The error occurs when **she** is believed to be the subject and **whomever**, the object of **decides.**

(2) Jenny will work with *whoever* shows up first.

This example represents what seems the most problematic of all the areas relating to who or whom. We have been taught to use the objective case after the preposition (in this case **with**). So why isn't **whomever** the correct form in this example? The answer is that it would be the correct form if the sentence ended with the word **whomever**. (**Whomever** would be the object of the preposition **with**.) In this case, it is not the last word but, rather, it is the **subject** of the clause **whoever shows up first**.

TOTALTIP: Again, make the substitution of another pronoun as a test of whether to use the subjective or objective case.

Let's look at a few more examples. See if you are better able to recognize the correct form using the **TOTALTIPS**.

(1) I'm sure I will be comfortable with [*whoever/whomever*] the manager decides to assign.

(2) To [*who/whom*] should she speak regarding that matter?

(3) He always chooses [*whoever/whomever*] in his opinion is the best auditor.

(4) She usually enjoys working with [*whoever/whomever*] the partner assigns.

(5) [*Who/Whom*] should I ask to accompany me?

Let's see how well you did.

(1) **Whomever** is correct. The whole clause after the preposition **with** is the object of the preposition, and **whomever** is the object of the verb **to assign**. Turn the clause around and substitute another pronoun. Thus, **the manager decides to assign *him***.

(2) **Whom** is correct. **Whom** is the object of the preposition **to**. Make the question into a declarative sentence and substitute another pronoun. Thus, **She should speak to *him* regarding that matter**.

(3) **Whoever** is correct. The entire clause **whoever is the best auditor** is the object of the main verb **chooses**. **Whoever** is the subject of that clause. **In his opinion** is a parenthetical phrase and doesn't affect the rest of the sentence.

(4) **Whomever** is correct. The entire clause **whomever the partner assigns** is the object of the preposition **with**, and **whomever** is the object of the verb **assigns**. Again, turn the clause around and substitute another pronoun. Thus, **the partner assigns *him***.

(5) **Whom** is correct. **Whom** is the object of the main verb **ask**. Turn the question into a regular declarative sentence and substitute another pronoun. Thus, **I should ask *her* to accompany me**.

Pronouns that follow prepositions are always in the **objective case**, except when serving as the subject of a clause, as discussed above. The most popular misuse occurs when using a pronoun after the preposition **between**. (**I, he, she, they**, are never used after **between**, no matter where the prepositional phrase falls in the sentence.)

Between you and me, I don't believe our client will be able to continue as a going concern.
That matter is strictly between her and them.

Antecedents

An antecedent is the word or words for which a pronoun stands. Any time a pronoun is used, its antecedent must be clear and agree with the word or words for which it stands.

The accountant placed *his* work in the file.

In this example, **his** is the pronoun with **the accountant** as its antecedent. **His** agrees with **the accountant** in person and number. **His** is used so as not to repeat **the accountant.**

Confusion most often occurs when using indefinite pronouns such as **it, that, this,** and **which.**

The company for *which* he works always mails *its* paychecks on Friday.

In this example, the pronouns **which** and **its** both clearly refer to **the company**. But, what about this sentence?:

The company always mails my paycheck on Friday and *it* is a small one.

Since it is not clear what the antecedent for **it** is, we can't tell for sure whether the company or the paycheck is small.

The following examples demonstrate unclear antecedents and how they may be clarified.

(1) When Claudia visited the client, *she* was ill. (Who was ill?)

When she visited the client, Claudia was ill.
Claudia was ill when she visited the client.
The client was ill when Claudia visited her.

(2) When a forecast contains a range, *it* is not selected in a biased or misleading manner. (The forecast or the range?)

When a forecast contains a range, *the range* is not ...

(3) Wanting to show all his workpapers to the auditors, Tom decided to get *them* all together right away. (To get what or whom together?)

Tom decided to get all his workpapers together right away so he could show them to the auditors.
Tom decided to get the auditors together right away so he could show them all his workpapers.

So far in our discussion of antecedents, we have talked about agreement in person. We have not addressed agreement in **number**. The following examples demonstrate pronouns that **do not agree** in number with their antecedents.

The company issued quarterly financial reports to *their* shareholders. (*Its* is the correct antecedent to agree in number with *company.*)

Each of the methods is introduced on a separate page, so that the student is made aware of *their* importance. (*Its* is the correct antecedent to agree in number with *each.*) **Note: Importance** refers to **each**, the subject of the sentence, not to **methods,** which is the object of the preposition **of**.

When a pronoun refers to singular antecedents that are connected by **or** or **nor**, the pronoun should be **singular**.

Joe or Buddy has misplaced *his* workpapers.
Neither Joe nor Buddy has misplaced *his* workpapers.

When a pronoun refers to a singular and a plural antecedent connected by **or** or **nor**, the pronoun should be **plural.**

Neither Joe nor his associates can locate *their* workpapers.

Pronouns must also agree with their antecedents in **gender**.

The English language has no way of expressing gender-neutral in pronoun agreement and, therefore, it has long been the custom to use **his** as a convenience when referring to both sexes. Originally, it was the feminist movement that focused attention on this "gender bias" in writing and, consequently, there is a growing use of a more cumbersome construction in order not to be offensive to some readers. Thus, when pronouns must agree in gender with noun antecedents, you will be more "politically correct" when you communicate accordingly.

Old: When a new partner's identifiable asset contribution is less than the ownership interest *he* is to receive, the excess capital allowed *him* is considered as goodwill attributable to *him.*

New: When a new partner's identifiable asset contribution is less than the ownership interest *he or she* is to receive, the excess capital allowed *the new partner* is considered as goodwill attributable to *him or her.*

You will note in the above example that **he or she (he/she)** and **him or her (him/her)** have been used only once each and the antecedent **new partner** has been repeated once.

TOTALTIP: The idea is to not overload a single sentence with too many repetitions of each construction. When it seems that **he/she** constructions are overwhelming the sentence, repeat the noun antecedent where possible, even if it sounds a bit labored.

Reflexive pronouns are pronouns that are used for **emphasizing their antecedents** and should **not be used as substitutes** for regular pronouns. The reflexive pronouns are **myself, yourself, himself, herself, itself, ourselves, yourselves, and themselves.**

The financing is being handled by the principals *themselves.* (Demonstrates emphasis)
The partner *himself* will take care of that matter. (Demonstrates emphasis)
My associate and *I* accept the engagement. (Not my associate and *myself...*)
I am fine; how about *you*? (Not how about *yourself?)*

ADJECTIVES AND ADVERBS

Most of us understand that adjectives and adverbs are **modifiers**, but many of us can't tell them apart. And, it is not true that all adverbs end in **ly**. In fact, there are many words that can be used as either depending on their use in the sentence. Consequently, differentiating adjectives from adverbs is really not very important as long as you know how to use them. Understanding, however, that **adjectives modify nouns or pronouns**, and **adverbs modify verbs** and adjectives will help you choose the correct form.

Falcone Co. purchased *two* computers from Wizard Corp., a very *small* manufacturer. (*two* is an adjective describing the noun *computers, very* is an adverb modifying the adjective *small*, and *small* is an adjective describing the noun *manufacturer.*)

Acme advised Mason that it would deliver the appliances on July 2 as *originally* agreed. (*originally* is an adverb describing the verb *agreed.*)

In writing for the CPA Exam, avoid colloquial uses of the adjectives **real** and **sure**. In the following examples, adverbs are called for.

I am *very* (not *real*) sorry that you didn't pass the exam.
He will *surely* (not *sure*) be glad if he passes the exam.

Comparisons using adjectives frequently present problems.

Remember that when comparing two things, the **comparative** (often **er)** form is used, and when comparing more than two, the **superlative** (often **est**) form is used.

> This report is *larger* than the other one.
> This report is the *largest* of them all.

Other types of comparisons indicate **degree**:

> This report is *more* detailed than the others.
> This report is the *most* detailed of them all.

Articles are adjectives and are either **definite—the,** or **indefinite—a** and **an**, and need little discussion for our purposes here. A difficulty does seem to exist, however, in deciding when to use **a** and when to use **an** before certain constructions. We know that **an** precedes most vowels, but when the vowel begins with a **consonant sound**, we should use **a**.

> ***a*** usual adjustment ...
> ***a*** one in a million deal ...

Similarly, when **a** or **an** precedes abbreviations or initials, it is the next **sound** that we should consider, not the next letter. In other words, if the next sound is a vowel sound, **an** should be used.

> *An S.A.* will be used to head up the field work on this engagement.
> *An F.O.B.* contract is a contract indicating that the seller will bear that degree of risk and expense which is appropriate to the F.O.B. terms.

TOTALTIP: Be reasonably sure that your reader will be reading the abbreviations or initials, and not the whole term, title, etc. If that should be the case, stick with **a**.

CONJUNCTIONS

There are three types of conjunctions: coordinating, subordinating, and correlative.

Coordinating conjunctions

Coordinating conjunctions are conjunctions that connect equal elements in a sentence. These conjunctions include **and, but, for, yet, so, or,** and **nor**.

> The partner *and* the manager ...
> The manager wrote the engagement letter *and* the partner signed it.

Examples of common problems involving coordinating conjunctions:

(1) Leaving out the **and**, leading to difficulties with comprehension and clarity.

The accountant studied some of management's representations, marked what she wanted to discuss in the meeting. (The word *and* should be in the place of the comma.)

Mike's summer job entails opening the mail, stamps it with a dater, routing it to the proper person. (Should be: ... opening the mail from other offices, *stamping* it with a dater, *and* routing it to the proper person. **This example also demonstrates a lack of parallelism,** which will be addressed in detail in a later section.)

Omission of **and** is correct when the sentence is a compound sentence (meaning that it contains two independent clauses), in which case a semicolon takes the place of **and**. When the semicolon is used, the ideas of each independent clause should be closely related.

The security is genuine; it has not been materially altered.

(2) Although the rules for **or** and **nor** have become less strict over time, you should understand proper usage for the sake of comprehension and clarity. Most of us are familiar with **either ... or** and **neither ... nor**:

Either the creditor must take possession *or* the debtor must sign a security agreement that describes the collateral.

The company would neither accept delivery of the water coolers, nor pay for them, because Peterson did not have the authority to enter into the contract.

(3) The only mention we want to make concerning the use of the conjunction **so** is simply to discourage using it very often. In many cases, there will be a more appropriate or explicit word or phrase. In other cases, the thought may be better expressed in another way.

She was not able to attend the meeting, *so* quorum was not met.

This example is acceptable; however, the following two examples are better.

She was not able to attend the meeting, *therefore*, quorum was not met.
Since she was unable to attend the meeting, quorum was not met.

Subordinating conjunctions

Subordinating conjunctions are conjunctions that introduce subordinate elements of the sentence. The most common and the ones we want to concentrate on here are **as, since, because, that, which, when, where,** and **while.**

As; Since; Because

Because is the only word of the three that **always** indicates cause. **Since** usually indicates **time** and, when introducing adverbial clauses, may mean either **when** or **because**. **As** should be avoided altogether in these constructions and used only for comparisons. We strongly recommend using the **exact** word to avoid any confusion, especially when **clarity** is essential.

Attachment of the security interest did not occur because Pix failed to file a financing statement. (Specifically indicates *cause.*)
Green has not paid any creditor since January 1, 1992. (Specifically indicates *time.*)

The following example is a typical misuse of the conjunction **as** and demonstrates why **as** should not be used as a substitute for **because:**

As the partners are contributing more capital to the company, the stock prices are going up.

The meaning of this sentence is ambiguous. Are the stock prices going up **while** the partners are contributing capital or are the stock prices going up **because** the partners are contributing more capital?

That; Which

Many people complain about not understanding when to use **that** and when to use **which** than just about anything else. The rule to follow requires that you know the difference between a restrictive and a nonrestrictive clause. A **restrictive clause** is one that must remain in the sentence for the sentence to make sense. A **nonrestrictive** clause is one that may be removed from a sentence and the sentence will still make sense.

That is used with restrictive clauses; *which* is used with nonrestrictive clauses.

(1) An accountant who breaches his or her contract with a client may be subject to liability for damages and losses *which* the client suffers as a direct result of the breach.

(2) As a result, the accountant is responsible for errors resulting from changes *that* occurred between the time he or she prepared the statement and its effective date.

(3) A reply *that* purports to accept an offer but which adds material qualifications or conditions is not an acceptance; rather, it is a rejection and a counter-offer.

In example (1) above, the clause beginning with **which** is nonrestrictive (sentence would make sense without it). In examples (2) and (3), the clauses that follow **that** are restrictive (necessary for the meaning of the sentence).

TOTALTIP: If you can put commas around the clause in question, it is usually nonrestrictive and thus takes **which**. Occasionally, there will be a fine line between what one might consider restrictive or nonrestrictive. In these cases, make your choice based on which sounds better and, if there is another **which** or **that** nearby, let that help your decision. (Unless truly necessary, don't have two or three uses of **which** or two or three uses of **that** in the same sentence.)

When; Where

Most uses of **when** and **where** are obvious. The most common incorrect usage associated with these words occurs when they are used to define something.

(1) Exoneration is *where* the surety takes action against the debtor, which seeks to force the debtor to pay his or her debts.

(2) A fiduciary relationship is *where* the agent acts for the benefit of the principal.

(3) Joint liability is *when* all partners in a partnership are jointly liable for any contract actions against the partnership.

The above three examples are **faulty constructions.** The verb **to be** (**is**, in this case) must be followed by a predicate adjective (an adjective modifying the subject) or a predicate nominative (a noun meaning the same as the subject), **not** an adverbial phrase or clause. These sentences should be rewritten as follows:

(1) Exoneration is *an action* by the surety against the debtor, which seeks to force the debtor to pay his or her debts.

(2) A fiduciary relationship is *the association* of the agent and the principal whereby the agent acts for the benefit of the principal.

(3) Joint liability is *the liability* of all partners in a partnership for any contract actions against the partnership.

While

Formerly, **while** was acceptable only to denote time. Modern practice accepts **while** and **although** as nearly synonymous.

While/Although Acme contends that its agreement with Mason was not binding, it is willing to deliver the goods to Mason.

In the following example, however, **while** is **not** a proper substitution for **although**.

> Under a sale or return contract, the sale is considered as completed *although* it is voidable at the buyer's election.

TOTALTIP: Don't be seduced by what some falsely consider the more "literary" or more "formal" conjunctions such as **as, which,** and **while**. Clarity is important!

Correlative Conjunction

The third type of conjunction is the **correlative conjunction**. We have briefly mentioned and presented examples of **either** ... **or** and **neither** ... **nor** earlier in connection with nouns, verbs, and agreement. Now we want to discuss these correlatives in connection with **parallelism**.

Not only should be followed by **but (also)**.

> In determining whether a mere invitation or an offer exists, the courts generally will look *not only* to the specific language *but also* to the surrounding circumstances, the custom within the industry, and the prior practice between the parties.

Watch out for **placement of correlatives**. Faulty placement leads to faulty construction and obstructs clarity.

> The lawyer *either* is asked to furnish specific information *or* comment as to where the lawyer's views differ from those of management.

Below is the same sentence in much clearer form. Note that the phrases introduced by *either* and *or* are now in parallel construction: *either to furnish ... or to comment.*

> The lawyer is asked *either* to furnish specific information *or to* comment as to where the lawyer's views differ from those of management.

NOTES

CHAPTER 34

STANDARDS AND RELATED TOPICS

CHAPTER 34

STANDARDS AND RELATED TOPICS

I. An Overview of the Audit Function

A. Responsibilities

1. Management is responsible for the contents of financial statements, even if the statements are prepared and/or audited by CPAs. Financial statements are the representation of management of the affects of transactions and events which have affected the organization's financial position and results of operations. Management is also responsible for establishing and maintaining an effective internal control structure and for developing accounting policies.

2. The CPA, as an independent auditor, is responsible for rendering an opinion on the organization's financial statements in accordance with generally accepted auditing standards. The objective of the audit is the expression of an opinion as to the fairness, in all material respects, that the financial position, results of operations, and cash flows are presented fairly in conformity with generally accepted accounting principles. The auditor's responsibility to express an opinion on the financial statements is explicitly stated in the introductory paragraph of the auditor's report.

3. Financial statement users should recognize that the accounting process necessitates the use of estimates and evaluations that affect the fairness of the financial statements. They should also understand the meaning and significance of the auditor's report.

B. Nature of the Audit Function--To independently accumulate and evaluate evidence of an economic entity for the purpose of reporting on the degree of correspondence between information produced and established criteria (e.g., generally accepted accounting principles).

C. Important Determinations by the Auditor

1. Actual Occurrence--Did the transactions summarized in the financial statements actually occur? The auditor makes this determination by vouching items from the financial statements back to the accounts and ultimately to the original transaction documents. This is a downward process in Exhibit 1.

2. No Omissions (Completeness)--Have all transactions that occurred during the period been properly recorded in the accounts and summarized in the financial statements? The auditor makes this determination by tracing items from original transaction documents to the accounts and ultimately to the financial statements. This is an upward process in Exhibit 1.

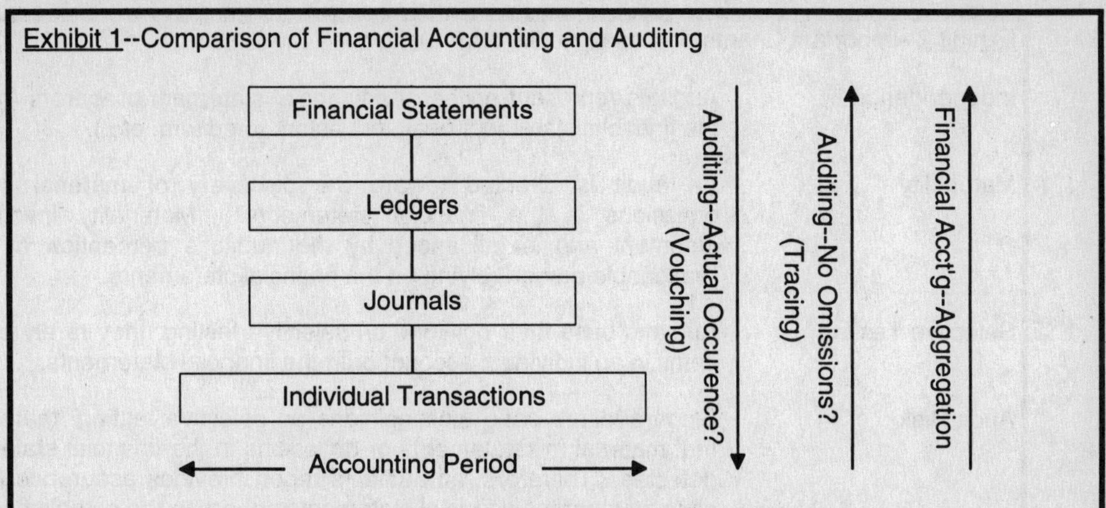
Exhibit 1--Comparison of Financial Accounting and Auditing
Financial Statements
Ledgers
Journals
Individual Transactions
Accounting Period
Auditing--Actual Occurence? (Vouching)
Auditing--No Omissions? (Tracing)
Financial Acct'g--Aggregation
Note that financial accounting is a process of aggregation. Individual transactions are first recorded in journals; subsequently, the data in journals are classified in ledgers; and finally, the data in ledgers are summarized in the financial statements.

D. Steps in the Audit Process

1. Understand the Client--The auditor becomes familiar with the industry in which the client operates and the client's organization and accounting system. Based on this initial understanding, the auditor determines whether to accept the client.

2. Engagement Letter--An engagement letter is issued outlining the nature of the audit, the responsibilities of the client for the financial statements, and the meaning of the auditor's report. Both the auditor and the client sign the engagement letter.

3. Plan the Audit--The auditor must plan the audit to obtain sufficient, competent evidential matter about the financial statement assertions. Planning involves obtaining an understanding of the industry and significant transactions of the client, an assessment of the risk of errors and irregularities occurring, and an understanding of the internal control structure. Additionally, planning will involve a preliminary assessment of audit risk and materiality. The planning should be documented in both a planning memorandum and in a detailed audit program.

4. Substantive Tests--The auditor uses the knowledge provided by the understanding of the internal control structure and the assessed level of control risk in determining the nature, timing, and extent of substantive tests for financial statement assertions. Substantive tests consist of tests of details of transactions and balances, and analytical procedures.

5. Evaluation of Evidence--After all substantive tests have been performed, the auditor analyzes the accumulated evidence to decide whether an audit opinion can be reached.

6. Audit Report--The audit report describes the scope of the audit and states the auditor's conclusion regarding the fairness of the financial statements, including the related disclosures. Consistency in application of accounting principles is implied in the standard auditor's report unless otherwise indicated by the auditor. The audit report should also include any reservations the auditor has regarding the financial statements.

Exhibit 2--Important Characteristics of Audits and Auditors	
Independence	Auditors represent neither the financial statement preparers (management) nor the financial statement users (investors, creditors, etc.).
Materiality	An audit is directed toward the discovery of material misstatements or omissions in the financial statements. Materiality involves professional judgment and is influenced by the auditor's perception of the needs of a reasonable person relying on the financial statements.
Selective Testing	Auditors base their opinions on selective testing; they rarely examine all of the items in an individual account or in the financial statements.
Audit Risk	Since auditors base their opinions on selective testing, there is always a risk that material misstatements or omissions in the financial statements will not be detected. Therefore, an auditor's report provides assurance (not a guarantee) as to whether the financial statements adhere to the established criteria. Even if the auditor examines 100% of an account, the audit still is subject to audit risk.
Overall Opinion	The auditor's opinion relates to the financial statements as a whole rather than individual items within the financial statements.
Presentation	An audit is concerned with financial statement presentation; it is not concerned with the effectiveness of management, or the advisability of investing in the organization.

E. Types of Audits

1. Financial Statement Audit--This is the audit discussed above and throughout the remainder of the text unless otherwise indicated. Its objective is to express an opinion on the fairness, in all material respects, with which the financial statements present the organization's financial position, results of operations, and cash flows in conformity with generally accepted accounting principles (GAAP).

2. Compliance Audit--The purpose of this type of audit is to evaluate an organization's compliance with a defined set of specifications. Common examples include Internal Revenue Service audits to determine whether a taxpayer has complied with applicable provisions of the Internal Revenue Code; audits of governmental units to verify their compliance with applicable state and federal regulations; and verification audits by a CPA to determine a client's compliance with the provisions of a bond or loan indenture.

3. Operational Audit--These audits, usually performed by internal auditors, evaluate the efficiency and effectiveness of some part of an organization in achieving its specific goals vis-a-vis the general goals of an organization. This type of audit involves an evaluation of operating procedures and methods, and usually requires the auditor to issue a report to management recommending ways to improve efficiency and/or effectiveness. A common example would be a review by government auditors (e.g., General Accounting Office auditors) to determine the effectiveness and continued utility of specific government-funded programs. This type of audit is not usually concerned with financial information.

F. Types of Auditors

1. Independent Auditors--These are external auditors (i.e., outside of the organization being audited) who provide an independent, professionally competent evaluation of the financial statements of a client. Additionally, independent CPAs are actively engaged in tax services, consulting services, and other types of financial services for their clients. Consistent with their external audit and advisory responsibilities, CPAs are certified and licensed by the

individual states in which they practice, and many belong to the American Institute of Certified Public Accountants (AICPA).

- The terms "CPA" and "auditor" are frequently used interchangeably. In this text, unless otherwise indicated, the term "auditor" will mean a CPA who is independent of the client.

2. Internal Auditors--Internal auditors work full time for the organization or entity. Some internal auditors perform financial statement audits, while others perform compliance or operational audits. Since internal auditors are not independent in the same sense as a CPA, they cannot issue an audit report for stockholders or other interested outside parties.

   - Organizational Independence--For an internal audit function to be effective, it is important that it be directed to a level of the organization which is above the level being audited. For example, if the internal auditors are based at corporate headquarters and report to the audit committee of the board of directors, the internal audit function would be organizationally independent from a particular plant audited by the internal audit staff.

3. Governmental Auditors--These are auditors who work for the federal, state, or local government. Two of the most commonly mentioned are the following:

   a. General Accounting Office (GAO) Auditors--GAO auditors conduct audits for Congress. While they do a considerable number of compliance audits, they also perform an increasing amount of operational-type audit work.

   b. Internal Revenue Agents--These are auditors who conduct compliance audits for the Internal Revenue Service.

4. Audit Committees--These are special committees formed by the audit client's board of directors to act as a liaison between the board and the independent auditor. Also, they are formed to reinforce the auditor's independence in relation to client management. The following are some of the committee's normal functions:

   a. Select the independent auditor and negotiate appropriate fees.

   b. Review the auditor's overall audit plan.

   c. Review relevant company policies and procedures.

   d. Review the results of the audit and discuss the auditor's management letter.

   e. Consider matters that the auditor believes should be brought to the attention of the shareholders or directors.

II. Generally Accepted Auditing Standards (AU 150.02)

A. General Standards--(*TIC*)

1. ***T***-Technical Training and Proficiency--The audit is to be performed by a person or persons having adequate technical training and proficiency as an auditor.

2. ***I***-Independence--In all matters relating to the assignment, an independence in mental attitude is to be maintained by the auditor or auditors.

3. ***C***-Due Professional Care--Due professional care is to be exercised in the performance of the audit and the preparation of the report.

B. Standards of Field Work--(*PIE*)

1. ***P***-Adequate Planning and Supervision--The work is to be adequately planned and assistants, if any, are to be properly supervised.

2. ***I***-Understanding of the Internal Control Structure--A sufficient understanding of the internal control structure is to be obtained to plan the audit and to determine the nature, timing, and extent of tests to be performed.

3. ***E***-Sufficient Competent Evidential Matter--Sufficient competent evidential matter is to be obtained through inspection, observation, inquiries, and confirmations to afford a reasonable basis for an opinion regarding the financial statements under audit.

C. Standards of Reporting--(*ACDO*)

1. ***A***-Conformity With GAAP--The report shall state whether the financial statements are presented in conformity with generally accepted accounting principles.

2. ***C***-Consistency--The report shall identify those circumstances in which such principles have not been consistently observed in the current period in relation to the preceding period.

3. ***D***-Adequate Informative Disclosure--Informative disclosures in the financial statements are to be regarded as reasonably adequate unless otherwise stated in the report.

4. ***O***-Expression of an Opinion--The report shall contain either an expression of opinion regarding the financial statements, taken as a whole, or an assertion to the effect that an opinion cannot be expressed. When an overall opinion cannot be expressed, the reasons should be stated. In all cases where an auditor's name is associated with financial statements, the report should contain a clear-cut indication of the character of the auditor's work, if any, and the degree of responsibility the auditor is taking.

TotalRecall

GENERALLY ACCEPTED AUDITING STANDARDS

T Training
I Independence
C Care

P Planning
I Internal Control
E Evidence

A Accounting = GAAP
C Consistency
D Disclosure
O Opinion

D. Auditing Procedures vs. Auditing Standards (AU 150.01)

1. Procedures relate to the acts to be performed; for example, the confirmation of a predetermined number of accounts receivable. The auditing procedures used will vary from engagement to engagement.

2. Standards deal with measures of the quality of performance of the auditing procedures and the objectives the procedures are to attain. These include both professional qualities and audit judgment. The auditing standards will not vary from engagement to engagement.

E. Observations on GAAS

1. CPAs are expected to comply with GAAS.

2. The concepts of "materiality" and "audit risk" underlie the application of GAAS, especially the standards of field work and reporting. Materiality and audit risk need to be considered when determining the nature, timing, and extent of audit procedures to be performed, as well as evaluating the results of those procedures.

   a. Materiality is used to determine the effect of misstatements, individually and in the aggregate, on the financial statements taken as a whole. Materiality involves professional judgment of the auditor made in light of the surrounding circumstances, involving both quantitative and qualitative considerations, and the auditor's perception of the needs of a reasonable person relying on the financial statements.

   b. Audit risk is the risk that the auditor may unknowingly fail to modify his or her opinion on financial statements that are materially misstated. Audit risk is reflected in the auditor's report with the statement that the auditor obtained reasonable assurance that the financial statements are free of material misstatements. Audit risk should also be considered at the account and class of transactions level, taking into consideration inherent risk, control risk, and detection risk factors.

3. GAAS are applicable to all services covered by the Statements on Auditing Standards, to the extent that they are relevant. They deal with measures of the quality of performance of the auditor.

4. The general standards are personal in nature. They relate to the qualifications of the auditor and the quality of the work performed (AU 201).

III. The General Standards

A. Training and Proficiency of the Independent Auditor (AU 210)

1. The First General Standard--"The audit is to be performed by a person or persons having adequate technical training and proficiency as an auditor."

2. Proficiency--The auditor holds him- or herself out as being proficient in accounting and auditing. This requires academic training and professional experience. Training is an ongoing process that includes remaining current with new developments taking place in business and in the accounting profession.

B. Independence (AU 220)

1. The Second General Standard--"In all matters relating to the assignment, an independence in mental attitude is to be maintained by the auditor or auditors."

2. Attitude--The attitude implied by independence is that of judicial impartiality or fairness toward clients and others who rely upon the independent auditor's report. The auditor's objective is to ensure that the general public maintain confidence in the independence of the auditor. Independence in attitude also implies the auditor is without bias towards the client.

3. Code of Professional Conduct--Our discussion of the AICPA Code of Professional Conduct includes an in-depth discussion of the area of independence (see Chapter 58, *Business Law and Professional Responsibilities*).

C. Due Care in the Performance of Work (AU 230)

1. The Third General Standard--"Due professional care is to be exercised in the performance of the audit and the preparation of the report."

2. Responsibility of the Independent Auditor--Each person within an independent auditor's organization has the responsibility to exercise due care and to adhere to the standards of field work and reporting. This responsibility necessitates critical review by supervisors of the work done and judgment exercised by those assisting in the audit.

3. Extent of Due Care

a. Fraud--An auditor commits a type of fraud if he or she alleges possessing the degree of skill commonly possessed by other auditors when the auditor actually does not possess such skill.

b. Not Infallible--Due care does not guarantee infallibility in either performance or in matters of pure judgment.

IV. The Relationship of Generally Accepted Auditing Standards to Quality Control Standards (AU 161, SAS 25)

A. Compliance With GAAS--An individual CPA or a firm of CPAs must comply with GAAS in the conduct of its audit practice. The firm should establish quality control policies and procedures which provide reasonable assurance of conforming with GAAS in the conduct of its audit engagements. The nature and extent of the quality control policies and procedures depend on such factors as the firm's size, the degree of operating autonomy that its personnel and its practice offices are allowed, the nature of its practice, its organization, and appropriate cost-benefit considerations.

B. Relationship of GAAS and Quality Control Standards--GAAS relates to the conduct of individual audit engagements. Quality control standards relate to the conduct of a CPA firm's audit practice as a whole. Since a firm's audit practice is composed of individual audit engagements, GAAS and quality control standards are related, and the latter may affect the conduct of individual audit engagements as well as the firm's audit practice as a whole.

V. System of Quality Control for a CPA Firm (SQCS 1)

A. Applicability--Applies to quality control for all auditing and accounting and review services for which professional standards have been established. It does not prescribe provisions for other areas of a firm's practice, such as tax services and management consulting services except to the extent they are part of auditing and accounting and review services. Firms that are members of the AICPA Division for CPA Firms must adhere to quality control standards promulgated by the Institute; and all members of the AICPA may be called upon to justify departures.

B. Definitions

1. Firm--"A proprietorship, partnership, or professional corporation or association engaged in the practice of public accounting, including individual partners or shareholders thereof."

2. Professional Standards--Relate to the professional qualities and performance of individual members of the AICPA. These include AICPA Rules of Conduct, Auditing Standards Board Pronouncements, and pronouncements of the Accounting and Review Services Committee.

3. Personnel--Unless stated otherwise, "personnel" includes all of a firm's professionals who perform auditing and accounting and review services. This includes proprietors, partners, principals, and stockholders or officers of professional corporations, and their professional employees.

C. Reason for Having a System of Quality Control--To give the firm reasonable assurance that it is meeting its responsibility to provide professional services that conform with professional standards.

D. System of Quality Control--Includes the organizational structure of the firm and the policies adopted and procedures established to provide reasonable assurance that the firm is meeting its responsibility to provide professional services that conform with professional standards. Because the organizational structure, policies, and nature of practice will vary from firm to firm, the system should be appropriately comprehensive and suitably designed (i.e., each firm will not have the same system of quality control).

1. Limitations--There are inherent limitations in any system of quality control that can reduce its effectiveness (for example, variance in individual performance and understanding of professional requirements).

2. Foreign Offices--A U.S. firm should have a system of quality control that provides reasonable assurance that work performed by its foreign offices or by its domestic or foreign affiliates or correspondents meets U.S. professional standards.

E. Establishment of Quality Control Policies and Procedures

1. The nature and extent of a firm's quality control procedures will depend on such factors as (a) its size, (b) the degree of autonomy that its personnel and practice offices are allowed, (c) the nature of its practice, (d) its organization, and (e) appropriate cost-benefit considerations.

2. Elements of Quality Control--Each of the following interrelated elements should be considered, to the extent applicable to its practice, in establishing quality control policies and procedures:

   a. Independence--Policies and procedures should be established to provide reasonable assurance that personnel at all organizational levels maintain independence as required by the AICPA's Rules of Conduct.

   b. Assignment of Personnel to Engagements--Policies and procedures for assigning personnel to engagements should be established to provide reasonable assurance that the work will be performed by those who possess the appropriate degree of technical training and proficiency. It is important to consider the nature and extent of supervision that will be required. As a general rule, the need for supervision decreases as more able and experienced personnel are assigned to the engagement.

   c. Consultation--Policies and procedures for consultation should be established to provide the firm with reasonable assurance that when required, personnel will seek assistance and advice from persons having appropriate levels of knowledge, competence, judgment, and authority.

d. Supervision--Policies and procedures for the conduct, supervision, and review of work at all organizational levels should be established to provide reasonable assurance that the work performed will meet the standards of quality established by the firm. The extent of supervision and review that is appropriate in a given circumstance varies with such factors as how complex the subject matter is, how qualified the personnel are, and the degree to which consultation is available and is used. It should be noted that this responsibility is distinct from the responsibility to adequately plan and supervise the work that is done on a particular engagement.

e. Hiring--Policies and procedures for hiring should be established to provide reasonable assurance that those persons hired possess the appropriate characteristics to enable them to perform their work competently.

f. Professional Development--Policies and procedures for professional development should be established to provide reasonable assurance that the personnel will have the knowledge that is required to fulfill those responsibilities assigned and to progress within the firm.

g. Advancement--Policies and procedures for advancing personnel should be established to provide reasonable assurance that those advanced within the firm will be qualified to perform their new responsibilities and that those meeting stated criteria are assigned increased degrees of responsibilities. Qualifications that personnel selected for advancement should possess include character, motivation, intelligence, and judgment.

h. Acceptance and Continuance of Clients--Policies and procedures should be established for making the decision as to whether or not to accept or continue a client (i.e., to minimize the chance of being associated with a client whose management lacks integrity). For example, the auditor should inquire of third parties (i.e., bankers and attorneys) about the prospective clients.

i. Inspection--Policies and procedures for inspections should be established to provide reasonable assurance that the procedures that relate to the above elements are adhered to. The exact type of inspection will depend on the controls that have been established and on the assignment of responsibilities within the firm.

TotalRecall

QUALITY CONTROL

A Assigning Personnel
I Independence
C Consultation
P Professional Development
A Advancement

H Hiring
A Acceptance and Continuance of Clients
S Supervision

I Inspection

F. Assignment of Responsibilities--Responsibilities should be assigned to personnel as needed to effectively implement the quality control policies and procedures.

G. Communication--The quality control policies and procedures should be communicated to personnel in a way that will provide reasonable assurance that they will understand the policies and procedures.

- Documentation--While having written policies and procedures usually enhances the communication, it is not necessarily true that the effectiveness of a firm's system of quality control will be harmed if this is not done. Factors such as the size, structure, and nature of practice of the firm are determining factors in assessing the need to document and, if it is required, the extent of documentation. Usually, it would be expected that a large firm would have more documentation than a small firm and that a multi-office firm's documentation would be more extensive than a single-office firm.

H. Monitoring--A firm must monitor the effectiveness of its system of quality control. This involves evaluating, on a timely basis, its policies and procedures, assignment of responsibilities, and communication of policies and procedures. Such factors as new authoritative pronouncements and/or changes in circumstances (e.g., expansion of practice, opening of new offices, or merging of firms) may necessitate timely modification of policies and procedures, assignment of responsibilities, and the form and extent of communication. Monitoring activities involves, but is not limited to, inspection.

VI. Governmental Auditing Standards

A. Authoritative Bodies

1. General Accounting Office (GAO)--The GAO has published revised *Standards for Audit of Governmental Organizations, Programs, Activities, and Functions.* This publication provides those standards appropriate for audits of government financial assistance programs, and consists of two types of audits, financial and performance.

2. Governmental Accounting Standards Board--The GASB establishes financial accounting and reporting principles for state and local governmental entities.

3. Generally Accepted Government Auditing Standards--In 1988, the Comptroller General of the United States, GAO, issued a revision to the Government Auditing Standards, which is also referred to as the Yellow Book. In 1994, a new revision to the Yellow Book was released which supersedes the 1988 revision. The generally accepted government auditing standards (GAGAS) were developed to guide auditors and provide for reliance on auditors' work in assessing government accountability.

B. Scope

The scope of auditing a government organization should include the following:

1. Financial and Compliance--Which determine (a) whether the financial statements of the entity fairly present the financial position and the results of financial operations in conformity with generally accepted accounting principles and (b) whether the entity has complied with laws and regulations which may have a material effect upon the financial statements. Financial and compliance audits are quite similar to independent financial statement opinion audits, as both are conducted to determine whether financial statements are presented fairly in conformity with GAAP.

2. Economy and Efficiency--Which determines (a) whether the entity is managing and utilizing its resources economically and efficiently, (b) the causes of any inefficient or uneconomical

practices, and (c) whether the entity has complied with laws and regulations concerning matters of economy and efficiency.

3. Program Results--Which determine (a) whether the desired results or benefits established by the legislature or other authorizing body are being achieved, (b) the effectiveness of organizations, programs, activities, or functions, and (c) whether the entity has complied with significant laws and regulations applicable to the program. Program results audits focus on whether the objectives of a program are being met, unlike economy and efficiency audits, which focus on potential cost savings and improvements in the cost-benefit relationship.

C. General Standards

1. Qualifications--The auditors assigned to conduct the audit should collectively possess adequate professional proficiency for the tasks required.

2. Independence--The audit organization and the individual auditors, whether government or public, must be free from impairments to independence, should be organizationally independent, and should maintain an independent attitude and appearance.

3. Due Professional Care--Due professional care should be exercised in conducting the audit and in preparing related reports.

4. Quality Control--Organizations conducting governmental audits should have both an appropriate internal quality control system in place, and participate in external quality control reviews (peer reviews).

D. Examination and Evaluation (Field Work) and Reporting Standards for Financial Audits

1. AICPA Statements on Auditing Standards for field work and reporting are applicable to government financial audits. (Unless GAO specifically excludes them, future statements would also apply.)

2. Additional standards and requirements for government financial and compliance audits include the following:

    a. Standards on Examination and Evaluation

        (1) Planning shall include consideration of the requirements of all levels of government.

        (2) A review is to be made of compliance with applicable laws and regulations.

        (3) A written record of the auditor's work shall be retained in the form of working papers.

        (4) Auditors shall be alert to situations or transactions that could be indicative of fraud, abuse, and illegal expenditures and acts. If such evidence exists, audit steps and procedures should be extended to identify the effect on the entity's financial statements.

    b. Standards on Reporting

        (1) Written audit reports are to be submitted to the appropriate officials of the organization audited and to the appropriate officials of the organizations requiring or arranging for the audits unless legal restrictions or ethical considerations prevent it. Copies of the reports should also be sent to other officials who may be responsible for taking action and to those authorized to

receive reports. Unless restricted by law or regulation, copies should be made available for public inspection.

(2) A statement in the auditor's report that the audit was made in accordance with generally accepted government auditing standards (GAGAS) and GAAS for financial audits will be acceptable language to indicate that the audit was made in accordance with these standards.

(3) Either the auditor's report on the entity's financial statements or a separate report shall contain a statement of positive assurance on those items of compliance tested and negative assurance on those items not tested. It shall also include material instances of noncompliance and instances or indications of fraud, abuse, or illegal acts found during or in connection with the audit.

(4) The auditors shall include a report on their <u>evaluation of internal controls</u> and <u>assessment of control risk</u> made as part of the financial and compliance audit. They shall identify as a minimum (a) the entity's significant internal controls, (b) the controls identified that were not evaluated (the auditor may satisfy this requirement by identifying any significant classes of transactions and related assets not included in the evaluation), and (c) the material weaknesses identified as a result of the evaluation.

(5) Either the auditor's report on the entity's financial statements or a separate report shall contain any other material deficiency findings identified during the audit.

(6) If certain information is prohibited from general disclosure, the report shall state the nature of the information omitted and the requirement that makes the omission necessary.

E. <u>Examination and Evaluation and Reporting Standards for Performance Audits</u>

1. The general standards are the same as for financial and compliance audits.

2. Field Work Standards:

a. Work is to be adequately planned.

b. Assistants are to be properly supervised.

c. A review is to be made of compliance with applicable laws and regulations.

d. During the audit, an evaluation shall be made of the internal control structure (administrative controls) applicable to the organization, program, activity, or function under audit.

e. When audits involve computer-based systems, the auditors shall review the following:

(1) General controls in data processing systems to determine whether (a) the controls have been designed according to management's direction and known legal requirements and (b) the controls are operating effectively to provide reliability of, and security over, the data being processed.

(2) Application controls of installed data processing applications upon which the auditor is relying to assess their reliability in processing data in a timely, accurate, and complete manner.

f. Sufficient, competent, and relevant evidence is to be obtained to afford a reasonable basis for the auditors' judgments and conclusions regarding the organization, program, activity, or function under audit. A written record of the auditors' work shall be retained in the form of working papers.

g. The auditors shall be alert to situations or transactions that could be indicative of fraud, abuse, and illegal acts. If evidence of fraud, abuse, and illegal acts exists, external audit steps and procedures should be taken to identify the effect on the entity's operations and programs.

3. Reporting Standards

a. Written reports indicating the results of each government audit are to be prepared.

b. Written audit reports are to be submitted to the appropriate officials of the organization audited and to the appropriate officials of the organizations requiring or arranging for the audits unless legal restrictions or ethical considerations prevent it. Copies of the reports should also be sent to other officials who may be responsible for taking action on audit findings and recommendations and to others authorized to receive such reports. Unless restricted by law or regulation, copies should be made available for public inspection.

c. Reports are to be issued on or before dates specified by law, regulation, or other special arrangement. Reports are to be issued promptly so as to make the information available for timely use by management and by legislative officials.

d. The report shall include:

(1) A description of the scope and objectives of the audit.

(2) A statement that the audit was made in accordance with generally accepted government auditing standards.

(3) A description of material weaknesses found in the internal control structure (administrative controls).

(4) A statement of positive assurance on those items of compliance tested and negative assurance on those items not tested. This should include significant instances of noncompliance and instances of, or indications of, fraud, abuse, or illegal acts found during, or in connection with, the audit.

(5) Recommendations to improve problem areas noted in the audit.

(6) Views of responsible officials of the organization, program, activity, or function audited concerning the auditors' findings, conclusions, and recommendations. When possible, their views should be obtained in writing.

(7) A description of noteworthy accomplishments, particularly when management improvement in one area may be applicable elsewhere. The report should place primary emphasis on improvement rather than on criticism of the past.

(8) A listing of any issues and questions needing further study and consideration.

(9) If any information has been omitted because it is considered privileged or confidential, a statement should be made describing the nature of the information and the law or other basis under which it is withheld. The report should also indicate if a separate report was issued containing this information.

CHAPTER 34—STANDARDS AND RELATED TOPICS

Problem 34-1 MULTIPLE CHOICE QUESTIONS (30 to 40 minutes)

1. An auditor's responsibility to express an opinion on the financial statements is
a. Implicitly represented in the auditor's standard report.
b. Explicitly represented in the opening paragraph of the auditor's standard report.
c. Explicitly represented in the scope paragraph of the auditor's standard report.
d. Explicitly represented in the opinion paragraph of the auditor's standard report.
(5/92, Aud., #11, 9911)

1A. Which of the following factors most likely would cause an auditor **not** to accept a new audit engagement?
a. An inadequate understanding of the entity's internal control structure.
b. The close proximity to the end of the entity's fiscal year.
c. Concluding that the entity's management probably lacks integrity.
d. An inability to perform preliminary analytical procedures before assessing control risk.
(5/94, Aud., #2, 4667)

2. Which of the following best describes what is meant by the term generally accepted auditing standards?
a. Procedures to be used to gather evidence to support financial statements.
b. Measures of the quality of the auditor's performance.
c. Pronouncements issued by the Auditing Standards Board.
d. Rules acknowledged by the accounting profession because of their universal application. (11/91, Aud., #9, 9911)

2A. Which of the following statements is correct concerning an auditor's responsibilities regarding financial statements?
a. Making suggestions that are adopted about the form and content of an entity's financial statements impairs an auditor's independence.
b. An auditor may draft an entity's financial statements based on information from management's accounting system.
c. The fair presentation of audited financial statements in conformity with GAAP is an implicit part of the auditor's responsibilities.
d. An auditor's responsibilities for audited financial statements are **not** confined to the expression of the auditor's opinion. (11/94, Aud., #19, 5092)

3. The first general standard requires that an audit of financial statements is to be performed by a person or persons having
a. Seasoned judgment in varying degrees of supervision and review.
b. Adequate technical training and proficiency.
c. Knowledge of the standards of field work and reporting.
d. Independence with respect to the financial statements and supplementary disclosures.
(5/90, Aud., #46, 0007)

4. Which of the following elements underlies the application of generally accepted auditing standards, particularly the standards of field work and reporting?
a. Internal control structure.
b. Corroborating evidence.
c. Quality control.
d. Materiality and audit risk.
(11/88, Aud., #2, 0015)

5. An auditor strives to achieve independence in appearance in order to
a. Maintain public confidence in the profession.
b. Become independent in fact.
c. Comply with the generally accepted auditing standards of field work.
d. Maintain an unbiased mental attitude.
(11/87, Aud., #19, 0020)

6. To exercise due professional care an auditor should
a. Attain the proper balance of professional experience and formal education.
b. Design the audit to detect all instances of illegal acts.
c. Critically review the judgment exercised by those assisting in the audit.
d. Examine all available corroborating evidence supporting management's assertions.
(11/92, Aud., #1, 2935)

6A. The third general standard states that due care is to be exercised in the performance of an audit. This standard is ordinarily interpreted to require

a. Thorough review of the existing safeguards over access to assets and records.
b. Limited review of the indications of employee fraud and illegal acts.
c. Objective review of the adequacy of the technical training and proficiency of firm personnel.
d. Critical review of the judgment exercised at every level of supervision.

(5/95, Aud., #23, 5641)

6B. After field work audit procedures are completed, a partner of the CPA firm who has not been involved in the audit performs a second or wrap-up working paper review. This second review usually focuses on

a. The fair presentation of the financial statements in conformity with GAAP.
b. Irregularities involving the client's management and its employees.
c. The materiality of the adjusting entries proposed by the audit staff.
d. The communication of internal control weaknesses to the client's audit committee.

(11/94, Aud., #5, 5078)

7. Quality control for a CPA firm, as referred to in Statements on Quality Control Standards, applies to

a. Auditing services only.
b. Auditing and management advisory services.
c. Auditing and tax services.
d. Auditing and accounting and review services.

(11/85, Aud., #3, 0033)

7A. Which of the following is an element of a CPA firm's quality control system that should be considered in establishing its quality control policies and procedures?

a. Complying with laws and regulations.
b. Using statistical sampling techniques.
c. Assigning personnel to engagements.
d. Considering audit risk and materiality.

(5/94, Aud., #15, 4680)

8. One of a CPA firm's basic objectives is to provide professional services that conform with professional standards. Reasonable assurance of achieving this basic objective is provided through

a. A system of quality control.
b. A system of peer review.
c. Continuing professional education.
d. Compliance with generally accepted reporting standards.

(11/92, Aud., #3, 2937)

8A. The nature and extent of a CPA firm's quality control policies and procedures depend on

	The CPA firm's size	The nature of the CPA firm's practice	Cost-benefit considerations
a.	Yes	Yes	Yes
b.	Yes	Yes	No
c.	Yes	No	Yes
d.	No	Yes	Yes

(5/95, Aud., #5, 5623)

9. A CPA firm evaluates its personnel advancement experience to ascertain whether individuals meeting stated criteria are assigned increased degrees of responsibility. This is evidence of the firm's adherence to which of the following prescribed standards?

a. Quality control.
b. Human resources.
c. Supervision and review.
d. Professional development.

(11/90, Aud., #36, 9911)

10. CPA firms should establish quality control policies and procedures for professional development in order to provide reasonable assurance that

a. Employees promoted possess the appropriate characteristics to perform competently.
b. Personnel will have the knowledge required to fulfill responsibilities assigned.
c. The extent of supervision and review in a given instance will be appropriate.
d. Association with a client whose management lacks integrity will be minimized.

(11/87, Aud., #49, 0022)

11. Which of the following are elements of a CPA firm's quality control that should be considered in establishing its quality control policies and procedures?

	Advancement	Inspection	Consultation
a.	Yes	Yes	No
b.	Yes	Yes	Yes
c.	No	No	Yes
d.	Yes	No	Yes

(5/90, Aud., #54, 0009)

12. A CPA firm should establish procedures for conducting and supervising work at all organizational levels to provide reasonable assurance that the work performed meets the firm's standards of quality. To achieve this goal, the firm most likely would establish procedures for

a. Evaluating prospective and continuing client relationships.
b. Reviewing engagement working papers and reports.
c. Requiring personnel to adhere to the applicable independence rules.
d. Maintaining personnel files containing documentation related to the evaluation of personnel. (11/88, Aud., #11, 9911)

13. A CPA firm's quality control procedures pertaining to the acceptance of a prospective audit client would most likely include

a. Inquiry of management as to whether disagreements between the predecessor auditor and the prospective client were resolved satisfactorily.
b. Consideration of whether sufficient competent evidential matter may be obtained to afford a reasonable basis for an opinion.
c. Inquiry of third parties, such as the prospective client's bankers and attorneys, about information regarding the prospective client and its management.
d. Consideration of whether the internal control structure is sufficiently effective to permit a reduction in the extent of required substantive tests. (5/89, Aud., #4, 0014)

14. The GAO standards of reporting for governmental financial audits incorporate the AICPA standards of reporting and prescribe supplemental standards to satisfy the unique needs of governmental audits. Which of the following is a supplemental reporting standard for government financial audits?

a. A written report on the auditor's understanding of the entity's internal control structure and assessment of control risk should be prepared.
b. Material indications of illegal acts should be reported in a document with distribution restricted to senior officials of the entity audited.
c. Instances of abuse, fraud, mismanagement, and waste should be reported to the organization with legal oversight authority over the entity audited.
d. All privileged and confidential information discovered should be reported to the senior officials of the organization that arranged for the audit. (5/91, Aud., #47, 0002)

15. Which of the following bodies promulgates standards for audits of federal financial assistance recipients?

a. Governmental Accounting Standards Board.
b. Financial Accounting Standards Board.
c. General Accounting Office.
d. Governmental Auditing Standards Board.
(5/89, Aud., #2, 9911)

16. A governmental audit may extend beyond an audit leading to the expression of an opinion on the fairness of financial presentation to include

	Program results	Compliance	Economy & efficiency
a.	Yes	Yes	No
b.	Yes	Yes	Yes
c.	No	Yes	Yes
d.	Yes	No	Yes

(5/88, Aud., #37, 0019)

16A. Which of the following statements is a standard applicable to financial statement audits in accordance with *Government Auditing Standards*?

a. An auditor should assess whether the entity has reportable measures of economy and efficiency that are valid and reliable.
b. An auditor should report on the scope of the auditor's testing of internal controls.
c. An auditor should briefly describe in the auditor's report the method of statistical sampling used in performing tests of controls and substantive tests.
d. An auditor should determine the extent to which the entity's programs achieve the desired level of results. (5/95, Aud., #90, 5708)

17. Which of the following is a documentation requirement that an auditor should follow when auditing in accordance with *Government Auditing Standards?*

a. The auditor should obtain written representations from management acknowledging responsibility for correcting instances of fraud, abuse, and waste.
b. The auditor's working papers should contain sufficient information so that supplementary oral explanations are **not** required.
c. The auditor should document the procedures that assure discovery of all illegal acts and contingent liabilities resulting from noncompliance.
d. The auditor's working papers should contain a caveat that all instances of material errors and irregularities may **not** be identified.
(11/93, Aud., #44, 4281)

18. In reporting on compliance with laws and regulations during a financial statement audit in accordance with *Government Auditing Standards*, an auditor should include in the auditor's report

a. A statement of assurance that all controls over fraud and illegal acts were tested.

b. Material instances of fraud and illegal acts that were discovered.

c. The materiality criteria used by the auditor in considering whether instances of noncompliance were significant.

d. An opinion on whether compliance with laws and regulations affected the entity's goals and objectives. (5/95, Aud., #89, 5707)

19. In performing a financial statement audit in accordance with *Government Auditing Standards,* an auditor is required to report on the entity's compliance with laws and regulations. This report should

a. State that compliance with laws and regulations is the responsibility of the entity's management.

b. Describe the laws and regulations that the entity must comply with.

c. Provide an opinion on overall compliance with laws and regulations.

d. Indicate that the auditor does **not** possess legal skills and **cannot** make legal judgments. (11/93, Aud., #58, 4295)

20. The primary purpose of establishing quality control policies and procedures for deciding whether to accept a new client is to

a. Enable the CPA firm to attest to the reliability of the client.

b. Satisfy the CPA firm's duty to the public concerning the acceptance of new clients.

c. Minimize the likelihood of association with clients whose management lacks integrity.

d. Anticipate before performing any field work whether an unqualified opinion can be expressed. (11/94, Aud., #24, 5097)

Solution 34-1 MULTIPLE CHOICE ANSWERS

Generally Accepted Auditing Standards (AU 150)

1. (b) The basic elements of the introductory paragraph of the auditor's standard report are a statement that financial statements identified in the report were audited and a statement that the financial statements are the responsibility of the Company's management and that the auditor's responsibility is to express an opinion on the financial statements based on the audit (AU 508.08).

1A. (c) AU 319.18 states that concerns about the integrity of the entity's management may be so serious as to cause the auditor to conclude that the risk of management misrepresentations in the financial statements is such that an audit cannot be conducted. The auditor would perform additional procedures to obtain the required understanding of the entity's internal control structure. The auditor may perform alternative procedures to achieve the audit objective he or she has developed. Analytical procedures should be performed in the planning stage of the audit, but they would not replace the tests of controls in gathering evidence to support the assessed level of control risk.

2. (b) AU 150.01 states that auditing standards concern themselves with the auditor's professional qualities but also with the judgment exercised by him or her in the performance of the audit. Auditing standards are issued by the Auditing Standards Board, but that does not describe what is meant by generally accepted auditing standards. Auditing procedures relate to the acts to be performed during an audit. The standards deal with measures of the quality of the performance of the procedures; they are not a strict set of rules.

2A. (b) AU 110.02 states, "The auditor may make suggestions about the form and content of the financial statements or draft them, in whole or in part, based on information from management's accounting system." An auditor may make suggestions about the form and content of the financial statements (AU 110.02). The fair presentation of the financial statements in conformity with GAAP is management's responsibility (AU 110.02). The auditor's responsibility is to express an opinion on the financial statements (AU 110.02).

3. (b) The first general standard states, "The audit is to be performed by a person or persons having adequate technical training and proficiency as an auditor." (AU 150.02.)

4. (d) AU 150.03 states, "Materiality and audit risk underlie the application of all the standards, particularly the standards of field work and reporting."

5. (a) AU 220.03 states, "It is of utmost importance to the profession that the general public maintain confidence in the independence of independent auditors. Public confidence would be impaired by evidence that independence was actually lacking, and it might also be impaired by the existence of circumstances which reasonable people might believe likely to influence independence."

6. (c) The third general standard states, "Exercise of due care requires critical review at every level of supervision of the work done and the judgment exercised by those assisting in the audit." (AU 230.02.) Answers (a), (b), and (d) do not relate to the third general standard regarding due care.

6A. (d) The third general standard states, "Due professional care is to be exercised in the performance of the audit and the preparation of the report," and "The exercise of due care requires critical review at every level of supervision of the work done and the judgment exercised by those assisting in the audit." Safeguards over assets and records and review of indications of fraud and illegal acts are internal control issues specific to one audit. Objective review of the adequacy of the training and proficiency of personnel is a quality control issue.

6B. (a) The secondary review partner usually focuses on the fair presentation of the financial statements in accordance with GAAP. Answers (b), (c), and (d) are usually done by staff directly involved in the audit.

Quality Control

7. (d) QC 10.01 provides that quality control for a CPA firm applies to all auditing and accounting and review services.

7A. (c) QC 10.07 states, "A firm shall consider each of the elements of quality control, which includes: independence; assigning personnel to engagements; supervision... to the extent applicable to its practice, in establishing its quality control policies and procedures." Answer (a) is irrelevant. Answers (b) and (d) would be associated with auditing requirements and procedures.

8. (a) QC 10.02 states, "To provide itself with reasonable assurance of meeting its responsibility to provide professional services that conform with professional standards, a firm shall have a system of quality control." A peer review provides information on whether a CPA firm is following an appropriate quality control system and would not by itself provide reasonable assurance that a CPA firm is providing professional services that conform with professional standards. Continuing professional education is only one of the policies and procedures concerned with the professional development element of quality control. Compliance with generally accepted reporting standards is only one part of the basic objective of providing professional services that conform with professional standards.

8A. (a) AU 161.02 states, "The nature and extent of a firm's quality control policies and procedures depend on factors such as its size,...the nature of its practice,...and appropriate cost-benefit considerations." Answers (b), (c), and (d) are considerations in determining the nature and extent of a CPA firm's quality control policies and procedures.

9. (a) The evaluation of personnel advancement provides evidence of adherence to the broad category of Quality Control Standards (QC 10.07). Answers (c) and (d) are two of the nine elements of those standards. Answer (b) is not a standard by itself or an element of the Quality Control Standards.

10. (b) QC 10.07(f) states, "Policies and procedures for professional development should be established to provide the firm with reasonable assurance that personnel will have the *knowledge required to enable them to fulfill responsibilities assigned.* Continuing professional education and training activities enable a firm to provide personnel with the knowledge required to fulfill responsibilities assigned to them and to progress within the firm." Answer (a) relates to advancement [QC 10.07(g)]. Answer (c) pertains to supervision [QC 10.07(d)]. Answer (d) is concerned with the acceptance and continuance of clients [QC 10.07(h)].

11. (b) A firm shall consider each of the elements of quality control, to the extent applicable to its practice, in establishing its quality control policies and procedures. These elements include independence, assigning personnel to engagements, *consultation*, supervision, hiring, professional development, *advancement*, acceptance and continuance of clients, and *inspection* (QC 10.07).

12. (b) Procedures for conducting and supervising work should include reviewing engagement working papers and reports (QC 90.16). Evaluating client relationships is a part of the acceptance and continuance of clients' quality control standard. Requiring personnel to adhere to independence rules is suggested by the independence quality control standard. Evaluating personnel is a part of the advancement quality control standard.

13. (c) Before accepting a client, a CPA firm should, "inquire of third parties about any information regarding the prospective client and its management and principals that may have a bearing on evaluating the prospective client." (QC 90.24.) The CPA firm should inquire of the *predecessor auditor* as to whether disagreements were resolved satisfactorily (QC 90.24). Answers (b) and (d) are audit steps that would occur *after* accepting the client.

Governmental Auditing Standards

14. (a) Chapter 5, paragraph 17, of the GAO's *Government Auditing Standards* (Yellow Book) states, "The auditors should prepare a written report on their understanding of the entity's internal control structure and the assessment of control risk made as part of a financial statement audit of a financial related audit." The distribution of reports concerning material indications of illegal acts is not limited to the entity's senior officials. In a government financial audit, the auditor is not required to report on instances of abuse, fraud, mismanagement and waste. It is not required that the auditor report all privileged and confidential information to the entity's senior officials.

15. (c) The standards for audits of federally assisted programs may be found in the publication of the U.S. General Accounting Office (GAO) entitled *Standards for Audit of Governmental Organizations, Programs, Activities, and Functions.* The Governmental Accounting Standards Board (GASB) establishes financial accounting principles for state and local government entities. The Financial Accounting Standards Board (FASB) establishes generally accepted accounting principles. The Governmental Auditing Standards Board does not exist.

16. (b) The first standard on government auditing states that the full scope of an audit should include a review and evaluation of the following three elements of a comprehensive audit:

- Financial and Compliance--This element is designed to determine whether the agency audited is (1) exercising appropriate controls over its assets, liabilities, receipts, and expenditures; (2) maintaining the appropriate records of such items; and (3) rendering accurate and useful reports in much the same manner as a traditional financial audit.
- Economy and Efficiency--This element is a review of how efficiently and economically resources are used.
- Program Results--This element is a review to determine whether the desired results of the program are being effectively achieved.

16A. (b) AU 801.37 states, "Governmental Auditing Standards requires that the auditor's report on internal control structure related matters describe the scope of his or her work in obtaining an understanding of the internal control structure and in assessing control risk." For a *performance* audit, an auditor should assess whether the entity has reportable measures of economy and efficiency that are valid and reliable.

17. (b) Included in the field work standards of supplemental working paper requirements for financial audits is the statement that working papers should contain sufficient information so that supplementary oral explanations are not required. Written representations from management are not required. An audit does not ensure that all illegal acts and contingent liabilities resulting from noncompliance will be discovered by the auditor. The auditor's workpapers should include positive statements about the procedures applied and the results of those procedures; thus, there is no requirement that the working papers contain a caveat statement.

18. (b) GAS 5.18 states, "When auditors conclude, based on evidence obtained, that an irregularity or illegal act either has occurred or is likely to have occurred, they should report relevant information. Auditors need not report information about an irregularity or illegal act that is clearly inconsequential. Thus, auditors should present in a report the same irregularities and illegal acts that they report to audit committees under AICPA standards." (The footnote to GAS 5.18 cautions the auditor to take care not to imply that they have made a determination of illegality when they disclose matters that have led them to conclude that an illegal act is likely to have occurred, as the determination of illegality may have to await final decision by a court of law.) Per GAS 5.17, "Auditors should report the scope of their testing of compliance with laws and regulations and of internal controls...[and] whether or not the tests they performed provided sufficient evidence to support an opinion on compliance or internal controls." There is no requirement that *all* controls be tested. Answer (c) is the second best answer; GAS 5.19 requires the auditor to place their findings in proper perspective and identify at least the condition, criteria, and possible asserted effect of noncompliance. Answer (d) is not required in a financial statement audit.

19. (a) Under AU 801.20, which covers reporting under *Government Auditing Standards*, AU 801.24 states that positive assurance consists of a statement by the auditors that the tested items were in compliance with applicable laws and regulations. Negative assurance is a statement that nothing came

to the auditors' attention as a result of specified procedures that caused them to believe the tested items were not in compliance with applicable laws and regulations. The basic elements of a report expressing positive and negative assurance on compliance should include a statement that management is responsible for compliance with laws, regulations, contracts, and grants.

20. (c) QC 90.23 states, "Policies and procedures should be established for deciding whether to accept or continue a client in order to minimize the likelihood of association with a client whose management lacks integrity." A CPA firm does not perform any attestation engagements regarding the reliability of a client, only assertions made by the client. The CPA firm's duty to the public is established in the AICPA's Rules of Conduct. Answer (d) is not required before the acceptance of a new client; the opinions rendered are based upon the results of procedures performed.

PERFORMANCE BY SUBTOPICS

Each category below parallels a subtopic covered in Chapter 34. Record the number and percentage of questions you correctly answered in each subtopic area.

Generally Accepted Auditing Standards (AU 150)

Question #	Correct √
1	
1A	
2	
2A	
3	
4	
5	
6	
6A	
6B	
# Questions	10

Correct ______
% Correct ______

Quality Control

Question #	Correct √
7	
7A	
8	
8A	
9	
10	
11	
12	
13	
# Questions	9

Correct ______
% Correct ______

Governmental Auditing Standards

Question #	Correct √
14	
15	
16	
16A	
17	
18	
19	
20	
# Questions	8

Correct ______
% Correct ______

ESSAY QUESTIONS

Essay 34-2 (15 to 25 minutes)

Cook, CPA, has been engaged to audit the financial statements of General Department Stores, Inc., a continuing audit client, which is a chain of medium-sized retail stores. General's fiscal year will end on June 30, 1993, and General's management has asked Cook to issue the auditor's report by August 1, 1993. Cook will not have sufficient time to perform all of the necessary field work in July 1993, but will have time to perform most of the field work as of an interim date, April 30, 1993.

For the accounts to be tested at the interim date, Cook will also perform substantive tests covering the transactions of the final two months of the year. This will be necessary to extend Cook's conclusions to the balance sheet date.

Required:

a. Describe the factors Cook should consider before applying principal substantive tests to General's balance sheet accounts at April 30, 1993.

b. For accounts tested at April 30, 1993, describe how Cook should design the substantive tests covering the balances as of June 30, 1993, and the transactions of the final two months of the year.

(11/92, Aud., #5)

Essay 34-3 (15 to 25 minutes)

Feiler, the sole owner of a small hardware business, has been told that the business should have financial statements reported on by an independent CPA. Feiler, having some bookkeeping experience, has personally prepared the company's financial statements and does not understand why such statements should be audited by a CPA. Feiler discussed the matter with Farber, a CPA, and asked Farber to explain why an audit is considered important.

Required:

a. Describe the objectives of an independent audit.

b. Identify ten ways in which an independent audit may be beneficial to Feiler. (5/87, Aud., #3)

ESSAY SOLUTIONS

Solution 34-2 Substantive Tests

a. Before applying principal substantive tests to balance sheet accounts at April 30, 1993, the interim date, Cook should assess the difficulty in controlling **incremental audit risk.** Cook should consider whether

- Cook's experience with the **reliability** of the **accounting records** and **management's integrity** has been good;
- Rapidly changing **business conditions** or circumstances may predispose General's management to misstate the financial statements in the remaining period;
- The **year-end balances** of accounts selected for interim testing will be **predictable;**
- General's procedures for **analyzing and adjusting** its interim balances and for reestablishing **proper accounting cutoffs** will be appropriate;
- General's accounting system will provide **sufficient information** about year-end balances and transactions in the final two months of the year to permit investigation of **unusual transactions, significant fluctuations,** and **changes in balance compositions** that may occur between the interim and balance sheet dates;
- The **cost** of the substantive tests necessary to cover the final two months of the year and provide the appropriate audit assurance at year end is **substantial.**

Assessing control risk at **below the maximum** would **not be required** to extend the audit conclusions from the interim date to the year end; however, if Cook assesses control risk **at the maximum** during the final two months, Cook should consider whether the **effectiveness** of the **substantive tests** to cover that period will be **impaired.**

b. Cook should **design the substantive tests** so that the **assurance** from those tests and the tests to be applied as of the **interim date,** and any assurance provided from the assessed level of **control risk,** achieve the **audit objectives at year end.** Such tests should include the **comparison** of **year-end information** with comparable **interim information** to identify and investigate unusual amounts. Other **analytical procedures and/or substantive tests** should be performed to **extend Cook's conclusions** relative to the assertions tested at the **interim date to the balance sheet date.**

Solution 34-3 Objectives and Benefits of an Independent Audit

a. Farber should explain to Feiler that an independent audit is an **audit** of the financial statements in accordance with certain **generally accepted auditing standards**. The objective of an ordinary audit is **to render an opinion on the fairness, in all material respects,** with which the financial statements **present financial position, results of operations, and cash flows in conformity with generally accepted accounting principles**. The auditor, after an objective **evidence-gathering audit,** expresses an opinion and "bears witness" to the fair presentation of financial statements. An independent expert is needed to lend **credibility** to the financial statements. It would not be meaningful for a company to report on itself without the **attestation of an independent party** because the company, itself, might not be **objective.**

b. Farber should inform Feiler of the following ways in which an independent audit can be beneficial:

1. To serve as a basis for the **extension of credit.**
2. To supply credit rating agencies with required information.
3. To serve as a basis for preparation of **tax returns.**

4. To **establish amounts of losses from fire,** theft, burglary, and so forth.
5. To **determine amounts receivable or payable** under
   a. Agreements for **bonuses based on profits.**
   b. **Contracts** for sharing expenses.
   c. Cost-plus contracts.
6. To provide data for proposed changes in financial structure or to supply proper financial data in the event of a proposed **sale or merger**.
7. To serve as a **basis for changes** in accounting or recording practices.
8. To serve as a basis for action in **bankruptcy** and insolvency cases.
9. To determine proper execution of **trust agreements.**
10. To furnish **estates** with information in order to obtain proper settlements and avoid costly litigation.
11. To provide a review of many aspects of the organization's activities and procedures.
12. To establish and/or improve **internal control structure** policies and procedures.
13. To provide important aid in case of **tax audits, court actions**, and so forth.
14. To **discourage employees from planning errors,** irregularities, and so forth, by making them aware of auditor presence.
15. To provide **industry-wide comparisons.**
16. To provide a realistic look at **inventories.**
17. To review adequacy of **insurance coverage**.
18. To provide the **professional knowledge** of an external auditor, which is generally superior to the client's bookkeeping experience.

NOTES

CHAPTER 35

AUDIT PLANNING

CHAPTER 35

AUDIT PLANNING

I. Relationship Between the Auditor's Appointment and Planning (AU 310, as amended by SAS 45)

A. The First Standard of Field Work--"The work is to be adequately planned, and assistants, if any, are to be properly supervised."

- Once the auditor understands the general environment for the audit, a tentative audit plan is developed. Next, the auditor gains an understanding of the client's internal control structure. When the auditor gains an understanding of the internal control structure and decides that the client is auditable, the tentative audit plan is revised and a written audit program is developed to guide the auditor through the audit. The program aids the auditor in the satisfaction of the first standard of field work by showing that the field work was planned. The audit program also provides instructions to assistants, which aids in supervision.

B. Appointment of the Independent Auditor--An early appointment is advantageous. This allows proper planning of the audit so that the work may be performed effectively and efficiently.

C. Appointment Near or After the Year-End Date--Before accepting an engagement near or after the close of the accounting period, the auditor should consider whether it will be possible to obtain evidence sufficient to support an unqualified opinion. If that is not possible, the auditor should discuss the possible scope limitation and the necessity for issuing a qualified opinion or disclaimer of opinion with the potential client.

D. Engagement Letter--Helps ensure that the auditor and the client clearly understand the services the auditor is engaged to perform. It will usually include reference to: (1) the periods covered; (2) assurance that the audit will be performed in accordance with GAAS, but a specific opinion is not guaranteed; (3) any assistance to be rendered by client personnel; (4) management's responsibility for preparing the financial statements; (5) fee basis (6) and other matters the auditor feels need to be included, such as other services. (**NOTE**: Engagement letters are not required by GAAS but are recommended.)

1. Addressee--Usually the audit committee, the board of directors, or the chief executive officer of the client.

2. Client Response--The client is asked to indicate its agreement with the letter by signing a copy and returning it to the auditor.

<u>Exhibit 1</u>--Sample Engagement Letter

(CPA Company Name)

[Date]
Audit Committee
Anonymous Company, Inc.
Route 32
Nowhere, New York 10000

This will confirm our understanding of the arrangements for our audit of the financial statements of Anonymous Company, Inc., for the year ending (date).

We will audit the Company's balance sheet at (date), and the related statements of income, retained earnings, and cash flows for the year then ended, for the purpose of expressing an opinion on them. The financial statements are the responsibility of the Company's management. Our responsibility is to express an opinion on the financial statements based on our audit.

We will conduct our audit in accordance with generally accepted auditing standards. Those standards require that we plan and perform the audit to obtain reasonable assurance about whether the financial statements are free of material misstatement. An audit includes examining, on a test basis, evidence supporting the amounts and disclosures in the financial statements. An audit also includes assessing the accounting principles used and significant estimates made by management, as well as evaluating the overall financial statement presentation. We believe that our audit will provide a reasonable basis for our opinion.

Our procedures will include tests of documentary evidence supporting the transactions recorded in the accounts, tests of the physical existence of inventories, and direct confirmation of receivables and certain other assets and liabilities by correspondence with selected customers, creditors, legal counsel, and banks. At the conclusion of our audit, we will request certain written representations from you about the financial statements and matters related thereto.

Our audit is subject to the inherent risk that material errors and irregularities, including fraud or defalcations, if they exist, will not be detected. However, we will inform you of irregularities that come to our attention, unless they are inconsequential.

If you intend to publish or otherwise reproduce the financial statements and make reference to our firm, you agree to provide us with printers' proofs or masters for our review and approval before printing. You also agree to provide us with a copy of the final reproduced material for our approval before it is distributed.

We will review the Company's federal and state (identify states) income tax returns for the fiscal year ended (date). These returns, we understand, will be prepared by the controller.

Further, we will be available during the year to consult with you on the tax effects of any proposed transactions or contemplated changes in business policies.

Our fee for these services will be at our regular per diem rates, plus travel and other out-of-pocket costs. Invoices will be rendered every two weeks and are payable on presentation.

We are pleased to have this opportunity to serve you.

If this letter correctly expresses your understanding, please sign the enclosed copy where indicated and return it to us.*

Very truly yours,

(CPA Name)

....

Partner

APPROVED:
By:..
Date: ....

---

* Some accountants prefer not to obtain an acknowledgment, in which case their letter would omit the paragraph beginning "If this letter..." and the spaces for the acknowledgment. The first paragraph of their letter might begin as follows: "This letter sets forth our understanding of the terms and objectives of our audit...."

II. Communications Between Predecessor and Successor Auditors (AU 315, SAS 7)

A. Purpose--This Section provides guidance relating to communications between the predecessor and successor auditors when a change in auditors has taken place or is in process.

B. Definitions

1. Predecessor Auditor--The auditor who has resigned or has been terminated.

2. Successor Auditor--The auditor who has accepted the engagement or has been asked to make a proposal for the engagement.

C. Communications--The successor has the responsibility to initiate communication. Either written or oral communication is permissible. The information communicated should be kept confidential, regardless of whether or not the successor accepts the engagement.

1. Communications Before the Successor Accepts the Engagement--The successor auditor should attempt certain communications before accepting the engagement. Since the AICPA Code of Professional Conduct precludes an auditor from disclosing confidential information obtained in an audit engagement unless the client gives permission, the successor should ask the prospective client to authorize the predecessor to respond promptly and fully to the successor's questions. These inquiries should relate to matters the successor feels will help in deciding whether to accept the engagement. These communications would include specific questions regarding facts that bear on: (a) the integrity of management; (b) disagreements between the predecessor and management on accounting principles, auditing procedures, or other significant matters; and (c) the predecessor's understanding about why there was a change in auditors.

   - Response--The predecessor should respond promptly and fully. If the predecessor decides not to respond fully (due to unusual circumstances such as impending litigation), the predecessor should indicate that a limited response is being given. The successor should consider the implications of receiving a limited response in deciding whether or not to accept the engagement.

2. If a prospective client refuses to permit the predecessor to respond or limits the response, the successor auditor should inquire as to the reasons and consider the implications of that refusal in deciding whether to accept that engagement.

3. Other Communications Prior to or Subsequent to Acceptance of the Engagement--These are concerned with assisting the successor with the audit, such as evaluations of consistency in applying accounting principles, inquiries into audit areas which required an inordinate amount

of time, and problems that arose because of the condition of accounting systems or records. The successor may ask the client to authorize the predecessor to allow review of the predecessor's working papers. However, the successor should not make any reference to the predecessor's work as a basis for the successor's own opinion. While it is common for the predecessor to make working papers available, at times the predecessor may feel there are valid reasons for refusing, such as when more than one auditor is considering taking the engagement. See Chapter 40, Part 5, for examples of reports involving predecessor accountants.

D. Financial Statements Reported on by Predecessor--During the course of the audit, it is possible that the successor may become aware of information which leads to a belief that the financial statements reported on by the predecessor may require revision. The successor should ask the client to arrange a meeting with the client, the predecessor, and the successor to resolve the matter. If the client refuses or if the successor is not satisfied, the auditor should consider consulting an attorney.

III. Planning and Supervision (AU 311, SAS 22)

A. Definitions

1. Assistants--Audit firm personnel who perform technical aspects of the engagement but who do not have final responsibility for the audit.

2. Auditor--The professional responsible for the engagement. The auditor is in charge of field work. If there are assistants, the auditor supervises them.

B. Planning--Planning involves the development of an overall strategy for the expected conduct and scope of the audit. The nature, extent, and timing of planning is a function of the size and complexity of the entity, the auditor's experience with the entity, and the auditor's knowledge of the entity's business.

1. Considerations in Planning--The auditor should consider: (a) relevant matters relating to the entity's business and the industry in which it operates; (b) the entity's accounting policies and procedures; (c) planned assessed level of control risk; (d) preliminary estimates of materiality levels; (e) any financial statement items that are likely to require adjustment; (f) any conditions that may necessitate modifying or extending audit tests (e.g., material errors or irregularities or related party transactions); (g) the types of audit reports (e.g., a special report, a report on statements to be filed with the SEC, etc.); and (h) the methods used by the entity to process significant transactions.

2. Procedures in Planning--Procedures that the auditor may consider in planning the audit usually involve a review of client records and discussions with personnel of the client and the audit team. Examples of these procedures include: (a) the review of the auditor's correspondence files, prior year's working papers, permanent files, copies of financial statements, and previous audit reports; (b) discussion with firm personnel who are responsible for providing nonaudit services to the client; (c) inquiry concerning current business developments affecting the entity; (d) reading the interim financial statements for the current year; (e) discussing the type, scope, and timing of the audit with the entity's management, the audit committee, or the board of directors; (f) considering accounting and auditing pronouncements which apply; (g) coordinating the assistance of the entity's personnel in data preparation; (h) determining how, if at all, consultants, specialists, and internal auditors will be used; (i) establishing a time schedule for the engagement; and (j) establishing and coordinating staffing requirements.

3. Written Audit Program--A written audit program is required which sets forth in reasonable detail the necessary audit procedures. Its form and degree of detail will vary from

engagement to engagement, and modification of the audit program may be necessary if circumstances change during the audit.

4. Knowledge of the Client's Business--The auditor must understand the client's business (i.e., the auditor must understand the events, transactions, and practices that may significantly affect the financial statements). This understanding helps to: (a) identify areas that may need special consideration; (b) comprehend the accounting systems; (c) evaluate the reasonableness of estimates; (d) evaluate the reasonableness of representations made by management; and (e) evaluate the appropriateness of the accounting principles used and the adequacy of disclosures. Knowledge of the client's business includes a knowledge of matters relating to its nature, organization, and operating characteristics (e.g., the type of business, types of products and services, locations, and related parties).

5. Knowledge of the Industry--The auditor should consider relevant matters affecting the industry in which the client operates. These would include: (a) economic conditions, (b) government regulations, (c) changes in technology, (d) industry accounting practices, (e) competitive conditions, and (f) available industry trends and ratios.

6. Computer Usage--The extent to which computer processing is used and its complexity may influence the nature, timing, and extent of audit procedures. If specialized skills are needed to evaluate the effect of computer processing on the audit, the auditor should use a specialist. If the use of such a professional is planned, the auditor should have sufficient computer-related knowledge to communicate the objectives, evaluate whether the specified procedures will meet the auditor's objectives, and evaluate the results of the procedures.

C. Supervision--Involves directing assistants in accomplishing the audit objectives and subsequently determining whether those objectives were accomplished. Supervision involves (1) instructing assistants, (2) keeping informed of significant problems they encounter, (3) reviewing their work, and (4) dealing with differences of opinion which arise among firm personnel. The extent of supervision required will vary from situation to situation, depending on the complexity of the subject matter and the qualifications of the persons performing the work.

1. Instruct Assistants--The audit program serves as the basic instructional tool for assistants. The auditor also provides oral instructions to the assistants.

2. Inform Assistants--The auditor should inform assistants of their responsibilities and the objectives of the audit procedures they are to perform in sufficient detail. The assistants should be instructed to bring significant accounting and auditing questions to the auditor's attention.

3. Review Assistants' Work--The auditor should review the work of each assistant to be sure it was adequately performed and that the results obtained are consistent with the conclusions presented in the audit report.

4. Disagreements--Both the auditor and the assistants should be aware of the procedures to be followed when differences of opinion arise on accounting and auditing issues. The procedures should allow assistants to document their disagreements with the conclusions reached if, after appropriate consultation, they believe it necessary to disassociate themselves from the resolution of the matter. The basis for the resolution should also be documented.

IV. Audit Risk and Materiality in Conducting an Audit (AU 312, SAS 47)

A. Nature of Audit Risk--Audit risk is the risk that an auditor may unknowingly fail to modify the opinion on financial statements that are materially misstated. The existence of audit risk is acknowledged in the auditor's standard report in that the auditor obtained "reasonable assurance" that the financial statements are free of material misstatement. Audit risk and materiality should be considered in planning the audit and evaluating the results of audit procedures for determining whether the financial statements taken as a whole are presented fairly.

B. Nature of Materiality

1. The concept of materiality recognizes that some matters affect the fair presentation of financial statements, while others do not.

2. Material misstatements are errors or irregularities which cause the financial statements to not be presented fairly in conformity with GAAP and result from the following:

   a. Misapplications of GAAP.

   b. Omissions of necessary information.

   c. Departures from fact.

TotalRecall

Misapplications of GAAP or Omits of necessary information or Departs from fact	= **MISSTATEMENT**

3. In assessing materiality, misstatements should be considered both individually and in the aggregate. A material misstatement means either an individual misstatement or the aggregate of misstatements which cause a material misstatement of the financial statements.

4. When judging the materiality of misstatements, the auditor must consider their nature and amount in relation to the nature and amount of items in the financial statements. Materiality depends on the circumstances.

5. The auditor's assessment of materiality is a matter of professional judgment. In making this assessment, the auditor should consider the needs of a reasonable person who will rely on the financial statements. A material misstatement is one which would change or influence the judgment of a reasonable person relying on the information contained in the financial statements.

6. Materiality judgments involve both quantitative and qualitative considerations. For example, an illegal payment that is immaterial in amount could be material if there is a reasonable possibility that it could lead to a material contingent liability or a material loss of revenue or if users might find such a payment significant.

C. Planning the Audit--Audit Risk and Materiality Considerations at the Financial Statement Level

1. In planning the audit, the auditor must make a preliminary judgment about the acceptable level of audit risk and materiality.

2. The auditor should plan the audit so that audit risk will be reduced to a low level. The auditor's assessment of audit risk may be in quantitative or nonquantitative terms.

3. Materiality levels include an overall level for each financial statement. However, in planning audit procedures, the auditor should consider materiality in terms of the smallest aggregate level of misstatements that could be considered material to any one of the financial statements.

4. The auditor ordinarily designs audit procedures to detect misstatements that are quantitatively material. It is generally impractical to design audit procedures to detect qualitatively material misstatements. However, the auditor should be alert for qualitatively material misstatements during the course of the audit.

5. A decrease in the acceptable level of audit risk in an account balance or class of transactions or a decrease in the amount of misstatements that the auditor believes could be material would require the auditor to increase the extent and/or effectiveness of the applicable auditing procedures, thereby increasing the likelihood that smaller misstatements would be found.

6. The auditor's assessment of materiality may change as the audit progresses. Thus, materiality levels considered in evaluating audit findings may differ from those used for planning purposes. If significantly lower materiality levels become appropriate in evaluating audit findings, the auditor should reevaluate the sufficiency of the audit procedures performed.

7. In planning the audit, the auditor should consider the nature, cause, and extent of misstatements found in audits of prior periods' financial statements.

D. Planning the Audit--Materiality and Audit Risk Considerations at the Individual Account-Balance or Class-of-Transaction Level

1. There is an inverse relationship between audit risk and materiality considerations. A decrease in either the acceptable level of audit risk or the perceived materiality level of an account balance or class of transactions would require the auditor to do one or more of the following:

   a. Select a more effective auditing procedure (nature).

   b. Perform auditing procedures closer to the balance sheet date (timing).

   c. Increase the extent of a particular auditing procedure (extent).

2. In planning audit procedures for a specific account balance or class of transactions, the auditor should design procedures to detect misstatements which, if aggregated with other misstatements, could be material to the financial statements taken as a whole. The maximum amount of misstatement in any balance or class that could exist without causing a material misstatement of the financial statements may or may not be explicitly stated.

3. The audit risk at the individual account-balance or class-of-transactions level should be low enough that an opinion can be expressed on the financial statements. Thus, audit risk should be considered in determining the scope of auditing procedures for the balance or class.

4. At the account-balance or class-of-transactions level, there are three components of audit risk:

a. Inherent Risk--The susceptibility of an assertion to a material misstatement, assuming that there are no related internal control structure policies or procedures. The risk that misstatement is greater for some assertions than for others. For example, cash is more susceptible to theft than an inventory of coal. External factors also influence inherent risk. For example, technological developments might make a particular product obsolete, thereby causing an overstatement of inventory.

b. Control Risk--The risk that a material misstatement that could occur in an assertion will not be prevented or detected on a timely basis by the entity's internal control structure policies or procedures. That risk is a function of the effectiveness of the design and operation of such policies and procedures. Some control risk will always exist because of the limitations of any internal control structure.

c. Detection Risk--The risk that the auditor will not detect a material misstatement that exists in an assertion. Detection risk is a function of the effectiveness of an auditing procedure and of its application by the auditor. It arises partly from uncertainties that exist when the auditor examines less than 100% of an account balance or class of transactions. Other uncertainties are present even when 100% of the balance or class is examined. For example, the auditor might select an inappropriate procedure, misapply an appropriate procedure, or misinterpret the audit results.

- Detection risk should bear an inverse relationship to inherent and control risk. The less the inherent and control risk the auditor believes exists, the greater the detection risk that can be accepted.

- Inherent risk and control risk differ from detection risk in that they exist independently of the audit, whereas detection risk relates to the auditor's procedures and can be altered by adjusting the nature, timing, and extent of substantive procedures. Thus, the auditor assesses inherent risk and control risk. Detection risk is a function of the nature, timing, and extent of audit procedures.

d. The relationship between audit risk and its three components is expressed in the following model:

$$AR = IR \times CR \times DR$$

where: AR = Audit risk
IR = Inherent risk
CR = Control risk
DR = Detection risk

5. The components of audit risk may be assessed quantitatively or nonquantitatively.

6. The assessment of inherent risk is a matter of professional judgment. Factors which should be considered include those peculiar to the account balance or class of transaction, as well as those pervasive to the financial statements taken as a whole. The effort required to evaluate the inherent risk for a balance or class may exceed the potential reduction in audit procedures that might be derived from such an evaluation. If this is the case, the auditor should assess inherent risk at its maximum level.

7. Professional judgment is also required in the assessment of control risk. The auditor's assessment is based on the sufficiency of evidential matter obtained to support the effectiveness of internal control structure policies or procedures. If the auditor believes such policies or procedures are unlikely to be effective, or if evaluating them would be inefficient, control risk for that assertion is assessed at the maximum level.

8. If the auditor assesses inherent and/or control risk at less than the maximum, there should be an appropriate basis for the assessment. The basis must be documented. The auditor might choose to use materials such as flowcharts, questionnaires, checklists, or narratives to document the basis.

9. The detection risk that an auditor can accept is based on the maximum acceptable level of audit risk and the assessed levels of inherent and control risks. As the assessments of inherent and control risks decrease, the auditor can accept a greater level of detection risk. However, the auditor cannot rely completely on assessments of inherent and control risks to the exclusion of performing substantive tests.

10. The auditor's assessments regarding the levels of inherent and control risks may change as the audit progresses, causing the preliminary judgment concerning materiality to be altered. In such cases, the auditor should reevaluate the planned auditing procedures to be applied.

Exhibit 2--Risk Relationships

Inherent Risk and Control Risk	Acceptable Level of Detection Risk	Substantive Tests
Increase	Decrease	Increase
Decrease	Increase	Decrease

NOTE: A change in substantive tests means to alter the nature, timing, or extent of such tests.

E. Evaluating Audit Findings

1. The auditor should aggregate uncorrected misstatements in a way that enables the auditor to consider whether they materially misstate the financial statements taken as a whole. Misstatements may be aggregated in relation to individual amounts, subtotals, or totals in the financial statements.

2. The aggregation of misstatements in account balances or classes of transactions should include all likely misstatements, and known misstatements (i.e., misstatements specifically identified). Likely misstatements are those which the auditor has projected from the sample results to the population.

3. The risk of material misstatement of the financial statements is generally greater when accounting estimates are involved because of the inherent subjectivity in estimating future events. An estimated amount supported by audit evidence may differ from the estimated amount included in the financial statements. If the difference is reasonable, it would not be considered a likely misstatement. However, if the difference is unreasonable, the auditor should treat the difference as a likely misstatement and aggregate it with other likely misstatements.

   - In some cases, individual accounting estimates may be reasonable, but the cumulative effect of such estimates may cause a misstatement of the financial statements. Thus, the auditor must consider the aggregate effect of accounting estimates.

4. In prior periods, likely misstatements may not have been corrected because they did not materially misstate the financial statements. Those misstatements might affect the current financial statements. If likely misstatements from prior periods, aggregated with likely misstatements arising in the current period, cause a material misstatement of the current period's financial statements, the misstatements from prior periods should be included in the auditor's audit evaluation.

5. If the aggregation of likely misstatements causes the financial statements to be materially misstated, the auditor should request management to correct the material misstatement. If the material misstatement is not corrected, the auditor should issue a qualified or adverse opinion on the financial statements. If the auditor concludes that the aggregation of likely misstatements does not cause the financial statements to be materially misstated, the auditor should recognize that they could still be materially misstated due to further misstatement remaining undetected. This risk is usually reduced by appropriately specifying the acceptable level of detection risk.

V. Substantive Tests Prior to the Balance-Sheet Date (AU 313, SAS 45)

A. Objectives--Audit testing at an interim date allows the auditor to obtain an early consideration of significant matters that may affect the year-end financial statements.

   1. Procedures That Can Be Performed Prior to Year-End--Planning the audit, obtaining an understanding of the internal control structure, assessing control risk, and applying substantive tests to transactions. The potential for increased audit risk becomes greater as the interim period is lengthened.

   2. Dangers--Substantive tests used to cover the period subsequent to the interim test date should be designed so that this potentially increased audit risk can be controlled.

B. Factors to Consider Prior to Applying Principal Substantive Tests at Interim Dates--The auditor should assess the difficulty in controlling the incremental audit risk that may result from the performance of substantive tests at an interim date. This assessment also involves a consideration of the costs of the substantive tests that are necessary to provide the appropriate audit assurance over the period from the interim date to the balance-sheet date.

   1. Assessing Control Risk Below the Maximum--If the auditor assesses control risk at the maximum level for the period from the interim period tests to the balance-sheet date, the auditor should consider whether the effectiveness of the substantive tests covering the period will be impaired. If so, additional audit assurance should be sought or the account should be tested at the balance-sheet date.

   2. Rapidly Changing Business Conditions--The auditor should consider whether the post-interim-date substantive tests would be effective in controlling the incremental audit risk associated with misstated financial statements due to rapidly changing business conditions.

   3. Predictability of the Amount, Relative Significance, and Composition of Account Balance--The auditor should consider the appropriateness of the client's procedures for analyzing and adjusting the accounts at interim dates and for establishing proper cutoffs.

C. Extending Audit Conclusions to the Balance Sheet Date

   1. Substantive Tests Design--The substantive tests designed for the post-interim-date period should be designed so that the audit assurance obtained from the tests, combined with the assurances obtained from the substantive tests performed at the interim date and from the assurance provided from the assessed level of control risk, will achieve the overall audit objectives at the balance-sheet date. Analytical procedures and other substantive tests should provide a reasonable basis for extending the conclusions reached at the interim date to the balance-sheet date.

   2. Misstatements at Interim Dates--The existence of misstatements at the interim date may cause the auditor to modify the nature, timing, or extent of the planned substantive tests to be performed for the post-interim-date period, or the auditor may have to reperform certain procedures at the balance-sheet date.

D. Coordinating the Timing of Auditing Procedures--In deciding how related auditing procedures are to be coordinated, the auditor should consider (1) coordinating the work of related parties, (2) coordinating the testing of interrelated accounts and cutoffs, and (3) asserting control, albeit temporary, over certain negotiable assets, and testing such assets simultaneously with other related items such as cash on hand and in banks.

VI. The Auditor's Responsibility to Detect and Report Errors and Irregularities (AU 316, SAS 53)

A. Responsibility--The auditor should design the audit to provide reasonable assurance of detecting errors and irregularities that are material to the financial statements. Because of the characteristics of irregularities, particularly those involving collusion, a properly designed and executed audit may not detect a material irregularity.

1. Errors refer to unintentional misstatements or omissions of amounts or disclosures in financial statements. Errors may involve the following:

   a. Mistakes in gathering or processing accounting data used to prepare the financial statements.

   b. Incorrect accounting estimates arising from oversight or misinterpretation of facts.

   c. Mistakes in the application of accounting principles relating to amount, classification, manner of presentation, or disclosure.

2. Irregularities refer to intentional misstatements, omissions of amounts, or disclosures in financial statements. Irregularities may include fraudulent financial reporting intended to result in misleading financial statements--called management fraud. Misappropriation of assets called defalcation, is another form of irregularity. Irregularities may also involve the following:

   a. Manipulation, falsification, or alteration of accounting records or supporting documents used to prepare financial statements.

   b. Misrepresentation or intentional omission of events, transactions, or other significant information.

   c. Intentional misapplication of accounting principles relating to amounts, classification, manner of presentation, or disclosure.

B. Audit Planning--The auditor should exercise due care in planning, performing, and evaluating the results of audit procedures. Also, the proper degree of professional skepticism should be maintained.

1. In planning the audit, the auditor must understand the internal control structure of the client, and make an assessment of the risk of material misstatement. An overall judgment regarding the risk that material errors or irregularities may have occurred should be made. Factors to be considered that would tend to increase the risk of misstatements:

   a. Management Characteristics

      (1) Management's operating and financing decisions are dominated by a single person.

      (2) Management's attitude toward financial reporting is unduly aggressive.

      (3) Management (particularly senior accounting personnel) turnover is high.

(4) Management places undue emphasis on meeting earnings projections.

(5) Management's reputation in the business community is poor.

b. Operating and Industry Characteristics

(1) Profitability of entity relative to its industry is inadequate or inconsistent.

(2) Sensitivity of operating results to economic factors (inflation, interest rates, unemployment, etc.) is high.

(3) Rate of change in entity's industry is rapid.

(4) Direction of change in entity's industry is declining with many business failures.

(5) Organization is decentralized without adequate monitoring.

(6) Internal or external matters that raise substantial doubt about the entity's ability to continue as a going concern are present.

c. Engagement Characteristics

(1) Many contentious or difficult accounting issues are present.

(2) Significant difficult-to-audit transactions or balances are present.

(3) Significant and unusual related party transactions not in the ordinary course of business are present.

(4) Nature, cause (if known), or the amount of known and likely misstatements detected in the audit of prior period's financial statements is significant.

(5) A new client with no prior audit history, or sufficient information is not available from the predecessor auditor.

2. Risk factors are strongly influenced by the size, complexity, and ownership characteristics of the entity.

3. The risk of management misrepresentation should be assessed by reviewing information about risk factors and the internal control structure. The following are matters to be considered:

a. Are there known circumstances that may indicate a management predisposition to distort financial statements, such as frequent disputes about aggressive application of accounting principles that increase earnings?

b. Are there indications that management has failed to establish policies and procedures that provide reasonable assurance of reliable accounting estimates, such as personnel who develop estimates appearing to lack necessary knowledge and experience?

c. Are there conditions that indicate lack of control of activities, such as constant crisis conditions in operating or accounting areas?

d. Are there indications of a lack of control over computer processing, such as lack of controls over access to applications that initiate or control the movement of assets (for example, a demand deposit application in a bank)?

e. Are there indications that management has not developed or communicated adequate policies and procedures for security of data or assets, such as not investigating employees in key positions before hiring?

4. The auditor's consideration of risk of material misstatement related to particular assertions at the balance or class of transactions level may be influenced by the following:

   a. Effect of risk factors identified at the financial statement or engagement level on the particular account balance or transaction class.

   b. Complexity and contentiousness of accounting issues and calculations affecting the balance or class.

   c. Frequency or significance of difficult-to-audit transactions affecting balance or class.

   d. Nature, cause, and amount of known and likely misstatements detected in the balance or class in the prior audit.

   e. Susceptibility of related assets to misappropriation.

   f. Competence and experience of personnel assigned to processing data that affect the balance or class.

   g. Size and volume of individual items constituting the balance or class.

5. Management integrity is an important consideration because management can direct subordinates to record transactions or conceal information in a manner which can materially misstate the financial statements.

6. If conditions or circumstances noted in an audit differ adversely from expectations, the auditor must consider the reasons for the difference. The following are examples of such conditions or circumstances:

   a. Analytical procedures disclose significant differences from expectations.

   b. Significant unreconciled differences between a control account and subsidiary records or between a physical count and a related account are not appropriately investigated and corrected on a timely basis.

   c. Confirmation requests disclose significant differences or yield fewer responses than expected.

   d. Supporting records or files that should be readily available are not promptly produced when requested or are not appropriately authorized.

   e. Audit tests detect misstatements that apparently were known to client personnel, but were not voluntarily disclosed to the auditor.

   When such conditions or circumstances exist, the planned scope of audit procedures should be reconsidered.

7. The auditor's overall judgment about the level of risk in an engagement may affect engagement staffing, extent of supervision, overall strategy for expected conduct and scope of audit, and degree of professional skepticism applied.

C. Conclusions

1. If an audit finding is, or may be, an irregularity but is not material in relation to the financial statements, the auditor should

   a. Refer the matter to the appropriate level of management that is at least one level above those involved.

   b. Be satisfied that, in view of the organizational position of the likely perpetrator, the irregularity has no implications for other aspects of the audit or that those implications have been adequately considered.

2. If the audit finding is, or may be, an irregularity which could have a material effect on the financial statements, the auditor should:

   a. Consider the implications for other aspects of the audit.

   b. Discuss the matter and the approach to further investigation with an appropriate level of management that is at least one level above those involved.

   c. Attempt to obtain sufficient competent evidential matter to determine whether, in fact, material irregularities exist and, if so, their effect.

   d. If appropriate, suggest that the client consult with legal counsel on matters concerning questions of law.

D. Audit Report

1. If the auditor concludes that the financial statements have been materially affected by an irregularity, the financial statements should be revised or a qualified or adverse opinion issued with disclosure of all substantive reasons for the opinion.

2. If the auditor is unable to conclude whether possible irregularities may materially affect the financial statements or is precluded from applying necessary procedures, a disclaimer or qualified opinion should be issued and the findings should be communicated to the audit committee or the board of directors.

   - If the client refuses to accept the auditor's report as modified for the circumstances described above, then the auditor should withdraw from the engagement and communicate the reasons to the audit committee or the board of directors.

E. Communications Regarding Errors or Irregularities

1. The auditor should keep the audit committee or board of directors informed regarding findings concerning significant errors and irregularities.

2. The auditor may be required to disclose information regarding irregularities to outside parties. The auditor may wish to consult with legal counsel before discussing findings with outside parties. In the following circumstances, an auditor may need to disclose information:

   a. When the entity reports an auditor change under the appropriate securities law on Form 8-K.

   b. To a successor auditor when the successor makes inquiries in accordance with SAS 7, *Communications Between Predecessor and Successor Auditors.*

   c. In response to a subpoena.

d. To a funding agency or other specified agency in accordance with requirements for the audits of entities that receive financial assistance from a governmental agency.

VII. Illegal Acts by Clients (AU 317, SAS 54)

A. Illegal Acts--Illegal acts are defined as violations of laws or governmental regulations by management or employees acting on behalf of the company. Illegal acts by clients do not include personal misconduct by the entity's personnel unrelated to their business activities.

B. Legal Judgment--The auditor, generally, should leave the determination of the legality of an act to an expert qualified to practice law or to a court of law. The auditor's experience and knowledge of the client and its industry may provide a basis for recognition of acts which may be illegal.

C. Relation to Financial Statements--Generally, the further removed an illegal act is from the events and transactions reflected in the financial statements, the less likely the auditor is to become aware of the act. The auditor normally considers only those laws and regulations having a direct and material effect on the financial statement amounts.

1. An entity may be affected by many laws or regulations relating more to its operating aspects than to the financial statements. An auditor ordinarily does not have sufficient basis for recognizing possible violations of laws and regulations (for example, shipping regulations for tractor-trailers or maritime vessels).

2. The auditor may not become aware of illegal acts which could have an indirect effect on the financial statements unless the client discloses such information, or there is evidence of a governmental agency investigation or enforcement proceeding in the records normally inspected in an audit. Examples would include price fixing, equal employment, and occupational safety and health.

D. Information That May Be Evidence of Illegal Acts--In applying audit procedures, the auditor may encounter information that may raise a question concerning possible illegal acts, such as the following:

1. Unauthorized or improperly recorded transactions.

2. Investigation by a governmental agency.

3. Large payments for unspecified services to consultants.

4. Excessive sales commissions or agents' fees.

5. Unusually large cash payments.

6. Unexplained payments to government officials or employees.

7. Failure to file tax returns.

8. Forced to discontinue operations in a foreign country.

E. Audit Procedures--Normally, an audit conducted in accordance with generally accepted auditing standards does not include procedures specifically designed to detect illegal acts. During the course of an audit, however, other audit procedures may bring illegal acts to the auditor's attention. Such procedures may include the following: reading minutes; inquiring of client's management and legal counsel concerning litigation, claims, and assessments; and performing substantive tests of details of transactions or balances. The auditor should also make inquiries of management concerning the client's compliance with laws and regulations, and the client's policies to prevent illegal acts. The auditor should obtain written representations from management concerning the absence of violations or possible violations of laws or regulations whose effects must be considered for disclosure in the financial statements or as a basis for recording a loss contingency.

1. If a possible illegal act has occurred, the auditor should obtain an understanding of the act, the circumstances under which it occurred, and sufficient information to evaluate its effect on the financial statements. The auditor may wish to consult with the client's legal counsel or other specialists regarding the possible illegal act and its effects, and additional procedures may be applied, if necessary, to obtain further understanding of the acts.

2. Additional audit procedures may include the following:

    a. Examining supporting documents, such as invoices, canceled checks, and agreements, and comparing them with accounting records.

    b. Confirming significant information concerning the matter with the other party to the transaction or with intermediaries, such as banks or lawyers.

    c. Determining whether the transaction has been properly authorized.

    d. Considering whether other similar transactions or events may have occurred, and applying procedures to identify them.

F. Financial Statement Effect--When an illegal act has occurred, the auditor should consider both the quantitative and qualitative materiality of the act on the financial statements as well as the implications for other aspects of the audit, such as the reliability of representations of management. The illegal act may involve contingent liabilities which must be disclosed. The auditor should consider whether material revenue or earnings are derived from transactions involving illegal acts, or if illegal acts create significant unusual risks associated with material revenue or earnings.

The auditor should consider the implications of an illegal act in relation to other aspects of the audit, particularly the reliability of representations of management.

G. Audit Committee--The auditor should ascertain that the audit committee, or those with equivalent authority, are adequately informed about illegal acts that come to the auditor's attention. The communication should describe the act, the circumstances, and the effect on the financial statements. The communication may be written or oral. If oral, the communication should be documented. The auditor need not communicate inconsequential matters.

H. Auditor's Report--If the auditor concludes that an illegal act having a material effect on the financial statements has occurred, and the act has not been properly accounted for or disclosed, the auditor should express a qualified opinion or an adverse opinion, depending on the materiality.

If the auditor is precluded by the client from obtaining sufficient evidential matter to determine whether an illegal act that could be material has, or is likely to have, occurred, (i.e., a scope limitation), the auditor should disclaim an opinion on the financial statements.

If the client refuses to accept the auditor's report as modified, the auditor should withdraw from the engagement and indicate the reasons for doing so in writing to the audit committee or board of directors.

I. Other Considerations--The auditor may decide that withdrawal is necessary when the client does not take remedial action that the auditor considers necessary, even when the illegal act is not material to the financial statements.

Disclosure of illegal acts to outside parties may be necessary in certain circumstances, such as follows:

1. When the entity reports an auditor change under the appropriate securities law on Form 8-K.

2. To a successor auditor when the successor makes inquiries in accordance with SAS 7, *Communications Between Predecessor and Successor Auditors*.

3. In response to a subpoena.

4. To a funding agency or other specified agency in accordance with requirements for the audits of entities that receive financial assistance from a government agency.

The auditor may wish to consult with legal counsel before discussing illegal acts with outside parties.

J. Responsibilities in Other Circumstances--An auditor may accept an engagement that entails, by agreement with the client, a greater responsibility for detecting illegal acts than a typical audit. For example, the auditor may be engaged to test and report on compliance with specific government regulations.

VIII. Communication With Audit Committees (AU 380, SAS 61)

A. Audit Committees--Those responsible for oversight of the financial reporting process. The auditor is responsible for ensuring that the audit committee receives any additional information regarding the scope and results of the audit that may assist the audit committee in overseeing the financial reporting process. The communication is not required to be made before issuance of the report. The communication may be oral or written. Oral communication should be documented by the auditor. Written communication should specify that it is intended solely for the audit committee, board of directors, or management, if appropriate.

B. Matters to be Communicated--The auditor should communicate (1) the level of responsibility assumed under GAAS, and (2) that the audit should provide reasonable, rather than absolute, assurance about the financial statements. The auditor should inform the audit committee of:

- Significant matters related to the internal control structure.
- Selection of or changes in significant accounting policies.
- Management's process in making accounting estimates.
- Adjustments arising from the audit which could have a significant impact on the financial statements.
- Any disagreements, whether or not resolved, with management about matters which, individually or in the aggregate, could have a significant impact on the financial statements.
- Any serious difficulties encountered in dealing with management related to the performance of the audit.
- Responsibility for other information in documents containing financial statements.
- Any consultations management had with other accountants about accounting and auditing matters.
- Any major issues discussed regarding initial or recurring retention of the auditor.

As indicated in Chapter 36, XII., "Communication of Internal Control Structure Related Matters Noted in an Audit," the auditor must also communicate reportable conditions and material weaknesses noted during an audit. It is not necessary to repeat the communication of recurring matters each year, although the auditor should determine if changes in the composition of the audit committee warrant repetition of previously communicated matters.

NOTES

CHAPTER 35—AUDIT PLANNING

Problem 35-1 MULTIPLE CHOICE QUESTIONS (190 to 230 minutes)

1. Which of the following documentation is **not** required for an audit in accordance with generally accepted auditing standards?
a. A client engagement letter that summarizes the timing and details of the auditor's planned field work.
b. The basis for the auditor's conclusions when the assessed level of control risk is below the maximum level.
c. A written audit program setting forth the procedures necessary to accomplish the audit's objectives.
d. An indication that the accounting records agree or reconcile with the financial statements.
(5/92, Aud., #28, 2781)

1A. Which of the following statements would least likely appear in an auditor's engagement letter?
a. Fees for our services are based on our regular per diem rates, plus travel and other out-of-pocket expenses.
b. During the course of our audit we may observe opportunities for economy in, or improved controls over, your operations.
c. Our engagement is subject to the risk that material errors or irregularities, including fraud and defalcations, if they exist, will **not** be detected.
d. After performing our preliminary analytical procedures we will discuss with you the other procedures we consider necessary to complete the engagement. (5/95, Aud., #3, 5621)

2. Which of the following procedures would an auditor **least** likely perform in planning a financial statement audit?
a. Coordinating the assistance of entity personnel in data preparation.
b. Discussing matters that may affect the audit with firm personnel responsible for non-audit services to the entity.
c. Selecting a sample of vendors' invoices for comparison to receiving reports.
d. Reading the current year's interim financial statements. (5/93, Aud., #2, 3898)

2A. Audit programs should be designed so that
a. Most of the required procedures can be performed as interim work.
b. Inherent risk is assessed at a sufficiently low level.
c. The auditor can make constructive suggestions to management.
d. The audit evidence gathered supports the auditor's conclusions. (11/94, Aud., #16, 5089)

2B. Which of the following procedures would an auditor most likely perform in planning a financial statement audit?
a. Inquiring of the client's legal counsel concerning pending litigation.
b. Comparing the financial statements to anticipated results.
c. Examining computer generated exception reports to verify the effectiveness of internal controls.
d. Searching for unauthorized transactions that may aid in detecting unrecorded liabilities.
(5/95, Aud., #4, 5622)

2C. The audit program usually **cannot** be finalized until the
a. Consideration of the entity's internal control structure has been completed.
b. Engagement letter has been signed by the auditor and the client.
c. Reportable conditions have been communicated to the audit committee of the board of directors.
d. Search for unrecorded liabilities has been performed and documented.
(5/95, Aud., #17, 5635)

3. In developing a preliminary audit strategy, an auditor should consider
a. Whether the allowance for sampling risk exceeds the achieved upper precision limit.
b. Findings from substantive tests performed at interim dates.
c. Whether the inquiry of the client's attorney identifies any litigation, claims, or assessments **not** disclosed in the financial statements.
d. The planned assessed level of control risk.
(11/91, Aud., #8, 2276)

3A. An auditor obtains knowledge about a new client's business and its industry to
a. Make constructive suggestions concerning improvements to the client's internal control structure.
b. Develop an attitude of professional skepticism concerning management's financial statement assertions.

c. Evaluate whether the aggregation of known misstatements causes the financial statements taken as a whole to be materially misstated.
d. Understand the events and transactions that may have an effect on the client's financial statements. (5/94, Aud., #4, 4669)

3B. Which of the following factors most likely would influence an auditor's determination of the auditability of an entity's financial statements?
a. The complexity of the accounting system.
b. The existence of related party transactions.
c. The adequacy of the accounting records.
d. The operating effectiveness of control procedures. (11/94, Aud., #2, 5075)

3C. To obtain an understanding of a continuing client's business in planning an audit, an auditor most likely would
a. Perform tests of details of transactions and balances.
b. Review prior-year working papers and the permanent file for the client.
c. Read specialized industry journals.
d. Reevaluate the client's internal control environment. (11/94, Aud., #6, 5079)

3D. In planning an audit of a new client, an auditor most likely would consider the methods used to process accounting information because such methods
a. Influence the design of the internal control structure.
b. Affect the auditor's preliminary judgment about materiality levels.
c. Assist in evaluating the planned audit objectives.
d. Determine the auditor's acceptable level of audit risk. (11/94, Aud., #7, 5080)

4. The element of the audit planning process most likely to be agreed upon with the client before implementation of the audit strategy is the determination of the
a. Timing of inventory observation procedures to be performed.
b. Evidence to be gathered to provide a sufficient basis for the auditor's opinion.
c. Procedures to be undertaken to discover litigation, claims and assessments.
d. Pending legal matters to be included in the inquiry of the client's attorney. (5/90, Aud., #52, 0161)

4A. The element of the audit planning process most likely to be agreed upon with the client before implementation of the audit strategy is the determination of the
a. Evidence to be gathered to provide a sufficient basis for the auditor's opinion.
b. Procedures to be undertaken to discover litigation, claims, and assessments.
c. Pending legal matters to be included in the inquiry of the client's attorney.
d. Timing of inventory observation procedures to be performed. (5/95, Aud., #1, 5619)

4B. Which of the following procedures would an auditor **least** likely perform before the balance sheet date?
a. Confirmation of accounts payable.
b. Observation of merchandise inventory.
c. Assessment of control risk.
d. Identification of related parties. (5/95, Aud., #73, 5691)

5. Which of the following is required documentation in an audit in accordance with generally accepted auditing standards?
a. A written engagement letter formalizing the level of service to be rendered.
b. A flowchart depicting the segregation of duties and authorization of transactions.
c. A written audit program describing the necessary procedures to be performed.
d. A memorandum setting forth the scope of the audit. (11/91, Aud., #53, 2321)

5A. Which of the following procedures would an auditor most likely include in the initial planning of a financial statement audit?
a. Obtaining a written representation letter from the client's management.
b. Examining documents to detect illegal acts having a material effect on the financial statements.
c. Considering whether the client's accounting estimates are reasonable in the circumstances.
d. Determining the extent of involvement of the client's internal auditors. (11/94, Aud., #1, 5074)

6. The audit work performed by each assistant should be reviewed to determine whether it was adequately performed and to evaluate whether the
a. Audit has been performed by persons having adequate technical training and proficiency as auditors.
b. Auditor's system of quality control has been maintained at a high level.

c. Results are consistent with the conclusions to be presented in the auditor's report.
d. Audit procedures performed are approved in the professional standards.
(11/91, Aud., #5, 2273)

6A. An auditor should design the written audit program so that
a. All material transactions will be selected for substantive testing.
b. Substantive tests prior to the balance sheet date will be minimized.
c. The audit procedures selected will achieve specific audit objectives.
d. Each account balance will be tested under either tests of controls or tests of transactions.
(5/95, Aud., #16, 5634)

7. A difference of opinion regarding the results of a sample cannot be resolved between the assistant who performed the auditing procedures and the in-charge auditor. The assistant should
a. Refuse to perform any further work on the engagement.
b. Accept the judgment of the more experienced in-charge auditor.
c. Document the disagreement and ask to be disassociated from the resolution of the matter.
d. Notify the client that a serious audit problem exists. (5/88, Aud., #56, 0209)

7A. The senior auditor responsible for coordinating the field work usually schedules a pre-audit conference with the audit team primarily to
a. Give guidance to the staff regarding both technical and personnel aspects of the audit.
b. Discuss staff suggestions concerning the establishment and maintenance of time budgets.
c. Establish the need for using the work of specialists and internal auditors.
d. Provide an opportunity to document staff disagreements regarding technical issues.
(11/94, Aud., #4, 5077)

7B. Would the following factors ordinarily be considered in planning an audit engagement's personnel requirements?

	Opportunities for on-the-job training	Continuity and periodic rotation of personnel
a.	Yes	Yes
b.	Yes	No
c.	No	Yes
d.	No	No

(5/95, Aud., #6, 5624)

7C. The in-charge auditor most likely would have a supervisory responsibility to explain to the staff assistants
a. That immaterial irregularities are **not** to be reported to the client's audit committee.
b. How the results of various auditing procedures performed by the assistants should be evaluated.
c. What benefits may be attained by the assistant's adherence to established time budgets.
d. Why certain documents are being transferred from the current file to the permanent file.
(5/95, Aud., #7, 5625)

8. Which of the following audit risk components may be assessed in nonquantitative terms?

	Control risk	Detection risk	Inherent risk
a.	Yes	Yes	Yes
b.	No	Yes	Yes
c.	Yes	Yes	No
d.	Yes	No	Yes

(5/93, Aud., #3, 3899)

8A. On the basis of audit evidence gathered and evaluated, an auditor decides to increase the assessed level of control risk from that originally planned. To achieve an overall audit risk level that is substantially the same as the planned audit risk level, the auditor would
a. Increase inherent risk.
b. Increase materiality levels.
c. Decrease substantive testing.
d. Decrease detection risk. (11/93, Aud., #7, 4244)

9. The existence of audit risk is recognized by the statement in the auditor's standard report that the auditor
a. Obtains reasonable assurance about whether the financial statements are free of material misstatement.
b. Assesses the accounting principles used and also evaluates the overall financial statement presentation.
c. Realizes some matters, either individually or in the aggregate, are important, while other matters are **not** important.
d. Is responsible for expressing an opinion on the financial statements, which are the responsibility of management. (11/91, Aud., #6, 2274)

10. As lower acceptable levels of both audit risk and materiality are established, the auditor should plan more work on individual accounts to

a. Find smaller misstatements.
b. Find larger misstatements.
c. Increase the tolerable misstatement in the accounts.
d. Decrease the risk of assessing control risk too low. (11/87, Aud., #27, 9911)

10A. As the acceptable level of detection risk decreases, an auditor may
a. Reduce substantive testing by relying on the assessments of inherent risk and control risk.
b. Postpone the planned timing of substantive tests from interim dates to the year-end.
c. Eliminate the assessed level of inherent risk from consideration as a planning factor.
d. Lower the assessed level of control risk from the maximum level to below the maximum. (5/95, Aud., #12, 5630)

11. The risk that an auditor will conclude, based on substantive tests, that a material error does **not** exist in an account balance when, in fact, such error does exist is referred to as
a. Sampling risk.
b. Detection risk.
c. Nonsampling risk.
d. Inherent risk. (11/91, Aud., #7, 2275)

12. Which of the following audit risk components may be assessed in nonquantitative terms?

	Control risk	Detection risk	Inherent risk
a.	Yes	Yes	No
b.	Yes	No	Yes
c.	Yes	Yes	Yes
d.	No	Yes	Yes

(5/95, Aud., #10, 5628)

12A. Which of the following statements is **not** correct about materiality?
a. The concept of materiality recognizes that some matters are important for fair presentation of financial statements in conformity with GAAP, while other matters are **not** important.
b. An auditor considers materiality for planning purposes in terms of the largest aggregate level of misstatements that could be material to any one of the financial statements.
c. Materiality judgments are made in light of surrounding circumstances and necessarily involve both quantitative and qualitative judgments.
d. An auditor's consideration of materiality is influenced by the auditor's perception of the needs of a reasonable person who will rely on the financial statements. (11/94, Aud., #11, 5084)

12B. Which of the following would an auditor most likely use in determining the auditor's preliminary judgment about materiality?
a. The anticipated sample size of the planned substantive tests.
b. The entity's annualized interim financial statements.
c. The results of the internal control questionnaire.
d. The contents of the management representation letter. (5/95, Aud., #11, 5629)

13. An auditor assesses control risk because it
a. Indicates where inherent risk may be the greatest.
b. Affects the level of detection risk the auditor may accept.
c. Determines whether sampling risk is sufficiently low.
d. Includes the aspects of nonsampling risk that are controllable. (5/91, Aud., #22, 0041)

14. Inherent risk and control risk differ from detection risk in that inherent risk and control risk are
a. Elements of audit risk, while detection risk is **not**.
b. Changed at the auditor's discretion, while detection risk is **not**.
c. Considered at the individual account-balance level, while detection risk is **not**.
d. Functions of the client and its environment, while detection risk is **not**. (5/92, Aud., #57, 2810)

15. A prospective client's refusal to grant a CPA permission to communicate with the predecessor auditor will bear directly on the CPA's ability to
a. Obtain an understanding of the client's internal control structure.
b. Determine the integrity of management.
c. Determine the beginning balances of the current year's financial statements.
d. Establish consistency in application of GAAP between years. (11/85, Aud., #10, 9911)

15A. Hill, CPA, has been retained to audit the financial statements of Monday Co. Monday's predecessor auditor was Post, CPA, who has been notified by Monday that Post's services have been terminated. Under these circumstances, which party should initiate the communications between Hill and Post?

a. Hill, the successor auditor.
b. Post, the predecessor auditor.
c. Monday's controller or CFO.
d. The chairman of Monday's board of directors.

(11/94, Aud., #3, 5076)

16. Before accepting an audit engagement, a successor auditor should make specific inquiries of the predecessor auditor regarding the predecessor's

a. Awareness of the consistency in the application of generally accepted accounting principles between periods.
b. Evaluation of all matters of continuing accounting significance.
c. Opinion of any subsequent events occurring since the predecessor's audit report was issued.
d. Understanding as to the reasons for the change of auditors. (5/88, Aud., #54, 0207)

16A. A successor auditor most likely would make specific inquiries of the predecessor auditor regarding

a. Specialized accounting principles of the client's industry.
b. The competency of the client's internal audit staff.
c. The uncertainty inherent in applying sampling procedures.
d. Disagreements with management as to auditing procedures. (5/95, Aud., #2, 5620)

17. Before accepting an audit engagement, a successor auditor should make specific inquiries of the predecessor auditor regarding

a. Disagreements the predecessor had with the client concerning auditing procedures and accounting principles.
b. The predecessor's evaluation of matters of continuing accounting significance.
c. The degree of cooperation the predecessor received concerning the inquiry of the client's lawyer.
d. The predecessor's assessments of inherent risk and judgments about materiality.

(11/91, Aud., #4, 2272)

17A. Before accepting an engagement to audit a new client, an auditor is required to

a. Make inquiries of the predecessor auditor after obtaining the consent of the prospective client.
b. Obtain the prospective client's signature to the engagement letter.
c. Prepare a memorandum setting forth the staffing requirements and documenting the preliminary audit plan.
d. Discuss the management representation letter with the prospective client's audit committee.

(11/93, Aud., #5, 4242)

18. When one auditor succeeds another, the successor auditor should request the

a. Client to instruct its attorney to send a letter of audit inquiry concerning the status of the prior year's litigation, claims, and assessments.
b. Predecessor auditor to submit a list of internal control weaknesses that have not been corrected.
c. Client to authorize the predecessor auditor to allow a review of the predecessor auditor's working papers.
d. Predecessor auditor to update the prior year's report to the date of the change of auditors.

(11/86, Aud., #9, 0234)

18A. In auditing the financial statements of Star Corp., Land discovered information leading Land to believe that Star's prior year's financial statements, which were audited by Tell, require substantial revisions. Under these circumstances, Land should

a. Notify Star's audit committee and stockholders that the prior year's financial statements **cannot** be relied on.
b. Request Star to reissue the prior year's financial statements with the appropriate revisions.
c. Notify Tell about the information and make inquiries about the integrity of Star's management.
d. Request Star to arrange a meeting among the three parties to resolve the matter.

(5/95, Aud., #18, 5636)

19. Which of the following statements is correct concerning an auditor's required communication with an entity's audit committee?

a. This communication should include disagreements with management about significant audit adjustments, whether or **not** satisfactorily resolved.
b. If matters are communicated orally, it is necessary to repeat the communication of recurring matters each year.
c. If matters are communicated in writing, the report is required to be distributed to both the audit committee and management.
d. This communication is required to occur before the auditor's report on the financial statements is issued. (5/93, Aud., #59, 3955)

19A. Which of the following statements is correct concerning an auditor's required communication with an entity's audit committee?

a. This communication is required to occur before the auditor's report on the financial statements is issued.
b. This communication should include management changes in the application of significant accounting policies.
c. Any significant matter communicated to the audit committee also should be communicated to management.
d. Significant audit adjustments proposed by the auditor and recorded by management need **not** be communicated to the audit committee.

(5/95, Aud., #88, 5706)

19B. An auditor is obligated to communicate a proposed audit adjustment to an entity's audit committee only if the adjustment

a. Has **not** been recorded before the end of the auditor's field work.
b. Has a significant effect on the entity's financial reporting process.
c. Is a recurring matter that was proposed to management the prior year.
d. Results from the correction of a prior period's departure from GAAP. (11/93, Aud., #60, 4297)

19C. Which of the following matters is an auditor required to communicate to an entity's audit committee?

a. The basis for assessing control risk below the maximum.
b. The process used by management in formulating sensitive accounting estimates.
c. The auditor's preliminary judgments about materiality levels.
d. The justification for performing substantive procedures at interim dates.

(11/94, Aud., #84, 5157)

20. Should an auditor communicate the following matters to an audit committee of a public entity?

	Significant audit adjustments recorded by the entity	Management's consultation with other accountants about significant accounting matters
a.	Yes	Yes
b.	Yes	No
c.	No	Yes
d.	No	No

(5/92, Aud., #5, 9911)

20A. An auditor would **least** likely initiate a discussion with a client's audit committee concerning

a. The methods used to account for significant unusual transactions.
b. The maximum dollar amount of misstatements that could exist without causing the financial statements to be materially misstated.
c. Indications of fraud and illegal acts committed by a corporate officer that were discovered by the auditor.
d. Disagreements with management as to accounting principles that were resolved during the current year's audit. (5/95, Aud., #19, 5637)

21. An auditor may compensate for a weakness in the internal control structure by increasing the

a. Level of detection risk.
b. Extent of tests of controls.
c. Preliminary judgment about audit risk.
d. Extent of analytical procedures.

(5/88, Aud., #8, 9911)

22. Under Statements on Auditing Standards, which of the following would be classified as an error?

a. Misappropriation of assets for the benefit of management.
b. Misinterpretation by management of facts that existed when the financial statements were prepared.
c. Preparation of records by employees to cover a fraudulent scheme.
d. Intentional omission of the recording of a transaction to benefit a third party.

(11/86, Aud., #3, 0232)

23. What assurance does the auditor provide that errors, irregularities, and direct effect illegal acts that are material to the financial statements will be detected?

	Errors	Irregularities	Direct effect illegal acts
a.	Limited	Negative	Limited
b.	Limited	Limited	Reasonable
c.	Reasonable	Limited	Limited
d.	Reasonable	Reasonable	Reasonable

(5/92, Aud., #59, 2812)

24. Which of the following statements describes why a properly designed and executed audit may **not** detect a material irregularity?

a. Audit procedures that are effective for detecting an unintentional misstatement may be ineffective for an intentional misstatement that is concealed through collusion.
b. An audit is designed to provide reasonable assurance of detecting material errors, but there is **no** similar responsibility concerning material irregularities.
c. The factors considered in assessing control risk indicated an increased risk of intentional misstatements, but only a low risk of unintentional errors in the financial statements.
d. The auditor did **not** consider factors influencing audit risk for account balances that have effects pervasive to the financial statements taken as a whole. (11/91, Aud., #10, 2278)

25. Because an audit in accordance with generally accepted auditing standards is influenced by the possibility of material misstatements, the auditor should conduct the audit with an attitude of
a. Professional responsiveness.
b. Conservative advocacy.
c. Objective judgment.
d. Professional skepticism.
(11/87, Aud., #24, 0213)

25A. Which of the following statements reflects an auditor's responsibility for detecting errors and irregularities?
a. An auditor is responsible for detecting employee errors and simple fraud, but **not** for discovering irregularities involving employee collusion or management override.
b. An auditor should plan the audit to detect errors and irregularities that are caused by departures from GAAP.
c. An auditor is **not** responsible for detecting errors and irregularities unless the application of GAAS would result in such detection.
d. An auditor should design the audit to provide reasonable assurance of detecting errors and irregularities that are material to the financial statements. (5/95, Aud., #15, 5633)

26. Which of the following circumstances most likely would cause an auditor to consider whether material misstatements exist in an entity's financial statements?
a. Supporting records that should be readily available are frequently **not** produced when requested.
b. Reportable conditions previously communicated have **not** been corrected.
c. Clerical errors are listed on a monthly computer-generated exception report.
d. Differences are discovered during the client's annual physical inventory count.
(11/91, Aud., #12, 2280)

27. Which of the following circumstances is most likely to cause an auditor to consider whether a material misstatement exists?
a. Transactions selected for testing are **not** supported by proper documentation.
b. The turnover of senior accounting personnel is exceptionally low.
c. Management places little emphasis on meeting earnings projections.
d. Operating and financing decisions are dominated by several persons.
(11/90, Aud., #38, 0150)

28. Disclosure of irregularities to parties other than a client's senior management and its audit committee or board of directors ordinarily is not part of an auditor's responsibility. However, to which of the following outside parties may a duty to disclose irregularities exist?

	To the SEC when the client reports an auditor change	To a successor auditor when the successor makes appropriate inquiries	To a government funding agency from which the client receives financial assistance
a.	Yes	Yes	No
b.	Yes	No	Yes
c.	No	Yes	Yes
d.	Yes	Yes	Yes

(5/90, Aud., #55, 0163)

29. Which of the following statements concerning illegal acts by clients is correct?
a. An auditor's responsibility to detect illegal acts that have a direct and material effect on the financial statements is the same as that for errors and irregularities.
b. An audit in accordance with generally accepted auditing standards normally includes audit procedures specifically designed to detect illegal acts that have an indirect but material effect on the financial statements.
c. An auditor considers illegal acts from the perspective of the reliability of management's representations rather than their relation to audit objectives derived from financial statement assertions.
d. An auditor has **no** responsibility to detect illegal acts by clients that have an indirect effect on the financial statements. (5/90, Aud., #58, 0166)

29A. Jones, CPA, is auditing the financial statements of XYZ Retailing, Inc. What assurance does Jones provide that direct effect illegal acts that are material to XYZ's financial statements, and illegal acts that have a material, but indirect effect on the financial statements will be detected?

	Direct effect illegal acts	Indirect effect illegal acts
a.	Reasonable	None
b.	Reasonable	Reasonable
c.	Limited	None
d.	Limited	Reasonable

(5/94, Aud., #6, 4671)

29B. During the annual audit of Ajax Corp., a publicly held company, Jones, CPA, a continuing auditor, determined that illegal political contributions had been made during each of the past seven years, including the year under audit. Jones notified the board of directors about the illegal contributions, but they refused to take any action because the amounts involved were immaterial to the financial statements. Jones should reconsider the intended degree of reliance to be placed on the

a. Letter of audit inquiry to the client's attorney.
b. Prior years' audit programs.
c. Management representation letter.
d. Preliminary judgment about materiality levels.
(11/94, Aud., #12, 5085)

30. The most likely explanation why the audit **cannot** reasonably be expected to bring all illegal acts by the client to the auditor's attention is that

a. Illegal acts are perpetrated by management override of the internal control structure.
b. Illegal acts by clients often relate to operating aspects rather than accounting aspects.
c. The client's internal control structure may be so strong that the auditor performs only minimal substantive testing.
d. Illegal acts may be perpetrated by the only person in the client's organization with access to both assets and the accounting records.
(11/87, Aud., #28, 0216)

31. An auditor of a manufacturer would most likely question whether that client has committed illegal acts if the client has

a. Been forced to discontinue operations in a foreign country.
b. Been an annual donor to a local political candidate.
c. Failed to correct material weaknesses in internal control that were reported after the prior year's audit.
d. Disclosed several subsequent events involving foreign operations in the notes to the financial statements. (11/88, Aud., #12, 0189)

31A. Which of the following characteristics most likely would heighten an auditor's concern about the risk of intentional manipulation of financial statements?

a. Turnover of senior accounting personnel is low.
b. Insiders recently purchased additional shares of the entity's stock.
c. Management places substantial emphasis on meeting earnings projections.
d. The rate of change in the entity's industry is slow. (5/95, Aud., #14, 5632)

32. If specific information comes to an auditor's attention that implies the existence of possible illegal acts that could have a material, but indirect effect on the financial statements, the auditor should next

a. Apply audit procedures specifically directed to ascertaining whether an illegal act has occurred.
b. Seek the advice of an informed expert qualified to practice law as to possible contingent liabilities.
c. Report the matter to an appropriate level of management at least one level above those involved.
d. Discuss the evidence with the client's audit committee, or others with equivalent authority and responsibility. (11/89, Aud., #60, 0172)

33. When an auditor becomes aware of a possible illegal act by a client, the auditor should obtain an understanding of the nature of the act to

a. Evaluate the effect on the financial statements.
b. Determine the reliability of management's representations.
c. Consider whether other similar acts may have occurred.
d. Recommend remedial actions to the audit committee. (11/92, Aud., #4, 2938)

Items 34 and 35 are based on the following information:

During the annual audit of BCD Corp., a publicly held company, Smith, CPA, a continuing auditor, determined that illegal political contributions had been made during each of the past seven years, including the year under audit. Smith notified the board of directors of BCD Corp. of the illegal contributions, but they refused to take any action because the amounts involved were immaterial to the financial statements.

34. Smith should reconsider the intended degree of reliance to be placed on the
a. Management representation letter.
b. Preliminary judgment about materiality levels.
c. Letter of audit inquiry to the client's attorney.
d. Prior years' audit programs.
(11/86, Aud., #14, 9911)

35. Since management took no action, Smith should
a. Report the illegal contributions to the Securities and Exchange Commission.
b. Issue an "except for" qualified opinion or an adverse opinion.
c. Disregard the political contributions since the board of directors were notified and the amounts involved were immaterial.
d. Consider withdrawing from the engagement or dissociating from any future relationship with BCD Corp. (11/86, Aud., #15, 9911)

35A. Which of the following relatively small misstatements most likely could have a material effect on an entity's financial statements?
a. An illegal payment to a foreign official that was **not** recorded.
b. A piece of obsolete office equipment that was **not** retired.
c. A petty cash fund disbursement that was **not** properly authorized.
d. An uncollectible account receivable that was **not** written off. (5/95, Aud., #9, 5627)

36. Morris, CPA, suspects that a pervasive scheme of illegal bribes exists throughout the operations of Worldwide Import-Export, Inc., a new audit client. Morris notified the audit committee and Worldwide's legal counsel, but neither could assist Morris in determining whether the amounts involved were material to the financial statements or whether senior management was involved in the scheme. Under these circumstances, Morris should
a. Express an unqualified opinion with a separate explanatory paragraph.
b. Disclaim an opinion on the financial statements.
c. Express an adverse opinion of the financial statements.
d. Issue a special report regarding the illegal bribes. (5/90, Aud., #57, 0165)

Solution 35-1 MULTIPLE CHOICE ANSWERS

Planning and Supervision (AU 311)

1. (a) AAM 3130.01 states, "In an engagement letter, the firm and the client indicate their mutual understanding and agree to the nature and terms of the engagement. Engagement letters are a matter of sound business practice rather than a professional requirement."

1A. (d) AAM 3130.01 states, "In an engagement letter, the firm and the client indicate their mutual understanding and agree to the nature and terms of the engagement." Answer (a) would be included as part of the terms of the engagement. Answer (b) would be included to indicate the nature of the services the client could expect in the engagement. Answer (c) would be included to establish the mutual understanding of some of the limitations inherent in an audit due to less than 100% testing of all accounts. The auditor would usually not outline to the client the specific procedures to be performed during the audit.

2. (c) Answer (c) is a procedure that would be performed during the actual field work of an audit. Answers (a), (b), and (d) are procedures performed during the planning stage of an audit, AU 311.04.

2A. (d) The primary purpose of the audit is to gather sufficient evidence to support the auditor's conclusions. The design of the audit program has no effect on inherent risk. Procedures *may* be performed prior to the balance sheet date only if the effectiveness of interim work is not likely to be impaired. Suggestions to management are secondary considerations in an audit.

2B. (b) AU 329.06 states that the purpose of applying analytical procedures, for example, comparing recorded amounts to anticipated results, assists the auditor in planning the nature, timing, and extent of auditing procedures that will be used to obtain evidential matter for account balances. Inquiry of the client's legal counsel is an audit procedure that would be performed near the end of the audit engagement. AU 319.17 states that in planning an audit and considering the internal control structure, the auditor is not required to obtain knowledge about operating effectiveness as part of the understanding of the control structure. Answer (d) is a substantive audit procedure that would be performed near the end of the audit engagement to support management's assertion of completeness.

2C. (a) Consideration of the entity's internal control structure is part of the planning of the audit. An engagement letter is recommended, but not required, by GAAS. Reportable conditions are usually communicated to the audit committee during the audit (as they become known) or at the end. The search for unrecorded liabilities is part of the performance of the audit program.

3. (d) In planning the audit, the auditor should consider, among other matters, the planned assessed level of control risk (AU 311.03).

3A. (d) AU 311.06 states that the auditor should obtain a level of knowledge of the entity's business that will enable him or her to plan and perform the audit in accordance with GAAS...and this knowledge should enable him or her to obtain an understanding of the events and transactions that may have a significant effect on the financial statements. Answer (a) would be a possible result of obtaining an understanding of the internal control structure of the client. Answers (b) and (c) would be required of the auditor regardless of the business and industry knowledge obtained about the client.

3B. (c) While the effectiveness of internal controls is of importance to an auditor, if the accounting records are not adequate, the auditor will have nothing to audit.

3C. (b) Since the client is a continuing client, an auditor would most likely review prior-year working papers and the permanent file of the client. Answer (a) involves tests that would be done during the audit. Answer (c) would be helpful for comparison purposes for the industry, but in a more general way. Answer (d) is done after obtaining information about the client's business.

3D. (a) The auditor should obtain sufficient knowledge about the accounting system because the methods influence the design of the internal control structure. Materiality levels, audit objectives, and an auditor's acceptable level of audit risk are independent of the methods used to process accounting information.

4. (a) Procedures that an auditor may consider in planning the audit usually involve review of his or her records relating to the entity and discussion with other firm personnel and personnel of the entity. An example of these procedures would be the establishment of the timing of the audit work (AU 311.04). Answers (b), (c), and (d) would be considered subsequent to the planning process.

4A. (d) Procedures that an auditor may consider in planning the audit usually involve review of his or her records relating to the entity and discussion with other firm personnel and personnel of the entity. An example of these procedures would be the establishment of the timing of the audit work (AU 311.04). The other answers would be considered subsequent to the planning process.

4B. (a) While the confirmation of accounts *receivable* and the other answer options are common audit procedures, confirmation of accounts *payable* is an extended procedure and usually occurs under unusual conditions. AU 330.07 states, "The greater the combined level of risk, the greater the assurance that the auditor needs from substantive tests related to a financial statement assertion....In these situations, the auditor might use confirmation procedures rather than or in conjunction with tests directed toward documents or parties within the entity." In a low risk situation, review of post balance sheet date payments to vendors may adequately substantiate the accounts payable balance.

5. (c) The auditor should prepare a written set of audit programs after considering the nature, extent, and timing of the work to be performed. Such written audit programs should detail the specific audit procedures that are necessary to accomplish the objectives of the audit. Audit programs may change as the audit progresses, to account for unexpected and/or changed conditions (AU 311.05).

5A. (d) Of the procedures listed an auditor is most likely to determine the extent of involvement of the client's internal auditors in the initial planning of a financial statement audit. A written representation letter from the client's management is usually obtained at the end of an audit, not the beginning, thus answer (a) is incorrect. Examining documents and considering the reasonableness of estimates are procedures that are done during the audit.

6. (c) AU 311.13 states, "The work performed by each assistant should be reviewed to determine whether it was adequately performed and to evaluate whether the results are consistent with the conclusions to be presented in the auditor's report."

6A. (c) The auditor should prepare a written set of audit programs. Such written audit programs should detail the specific audit procedures that are necessary to accomplish the objectives of the audit (AU 311.05). All material transactions and all account balances are not required to be tested in all circumstances. Minimizing substantive tests prior to the balance sheet date is not required.

7. (c) AU 9311.37 states, ". . . each assistant has a professional responsibility to bring to the attention of the appropriate individuals in the firm, disagreements or concerns the assistant might have... In addition, each assistant should have a right to document his disagreement if he believes it is necessary to disassociate himself from the resolution of the matter."

7A. (a) In a pre-audit conference, a senior auditor would most likely discuss the technical and personnel aspects of a job. Feedback from the staff would occur later. Establishing the need for specialists and the use of internal auditors is done during the planning stage. Answer (d) is done during field work.

7B. (a) The auditor uses professional judgment in planning an audit engagement's personnel requirements; the auditor has final responsibility and may delegate portions of the audit functions to other firm personnel, referred to in the code as "assistants." Opportunities for on-the-job training as well as continuity and periodic rotation of personnel are all valid factors the auditor may consider in this task.

7C. (b) AU 311 states that the auditor should inform assistants of their responsibilities and the objective of the audit procedures they are to perform in sufficient detail so that they understand what they are doing. Assistants should be informed of matters that affect the procedures the assistants perform, such as the nature of the client's business. The in-charge auditor should instruct assistants to bring to his or her attention significant questions raised during the audit so the in-charge auditor can assess their significance. As the auditor would most likely report to the client's audit committee, the in-charge auditor would not need to outline to assistants what would be included in that report. Answers (c) and (d) are less vital duties than audit procedure objectives.

Audit Risk and Materiality in Conducting an Audit (AU 312)

8. (a) AU 312.21 states that audit risk may be assessed in quantitative terms such as percentages or in nonquantitative terms that range, for example, from a minimum to a maximum. Therefore, all of the elements of audit risk may be assessed in nonquantitative terms.

8A. (d) AU 319.58 states that after considering the level to which the auditor seeks to restrict the risk of a material misstatement in the financial statements and the assessed levels of inherent risk and control risk, the auditor performs substantive tests to restrict detection risk to an acceptable level. As the assessed level of control risk decreases (or increases, for this question), the acceptable level of detection risk increases (or decreases, for this question). To increase control risk while maintaining the same audit risk level, the auditor could also reduce inherent risk. If the auditor were to increase materiality levels, that would reduce the overall audit risk. When the auditor increases control risk and thus decreases detection risk, substantive testing would need to be increased.

9. (a) AU 312.02 states, "The existence of audit risk is recognized by the statement in the auditor's standard report that the auditor obtained 'reasonable assurance' about whether the financial statements are free of material misstatement."

10. (a) A decrease in the level of audit risk that the auditor judges to be appropriate in an account balance or class of transactions or a decrease in the amount of misstatements in the balance or class that he or she believes could be material would require the auditor to increase the extent and effectiveness of the applicable auditing procedures thereby increasing the likelihood that smaller misstatements would be found (AU 312.17). Reduced materiality would allow for smaller, not larger, misstatements. Lower acceptable levels of materiality *decrease* the tolerable misstatement. The risk of assessing control risk too high would *increase* the scope of the substantive tests (AU 350.13).

10A. (b) AU 313.03 states, "Applying principal substantive tests to the details of an asset or liability account as of an interim date rather than as of the balance-sheet date potentially increases the risk that misstatements that may exist at the balance-sheet date will not be detected by the auditor." Postponing the planned timing of substantive tests from interim dates to the year-end decreases detection risk. The auditor should increase substantive testing when the acceptable level of detection risk decreases. Lower levels of acceptable detection risk should not effect the assessments of inherent and control risk. It was likely an assessment of higher levels of inherent or control risk that caused the decrease in acceptable levels of detection risk.

11. (b) AU 312.20(c) states, "Detection risk is the risk that the auditor will not detect a material misstatement that exists in an assertion." Inherent risk is the susceptibility of an assertion to a material

misstatement assuming that there are no related internal control structure policies or procedures [AU 312.20(a)]. Sampling risk arises from the possibility that, when a test of controls or a substantive test is restricted to a sample, the auditor's conclusions may be different from the conclusions he or she would reach if the test were applied in the same way to all items in the account balance or class of transactions (AU 350.10). Nonsampling risk includes all the aspects of audit risk that are not due to sampling (AU 350.11).

12. (c) All three components of audit risk (inherent, control, and detection) may be assessed quantitatively or nonquantitatively (AU 312.21).

12A. (b) AU 312 provides guidance on materiality. The concept of materiality recognizes that some matters affect the fair presentation of financial statements, while others do not. Materiality judgments involve both quantitative and qualitative considerations. In making the assessment of materiality, an auditor should consider the needs of a reasonable person who would rely on the financial statements.

12B. (b) Materiality considerations for planning purposes are generally based on the financial statements to be audited. Alternatively, the auditor may base the assessment of materiality on the entity's annualized interim financial statements (AU 312.14). The anticipated sample size of the planned tests and the internal control questionnaire are, if anything, dependent on materiality, not vice versa. The contents of the management representation letter (with a date the same as the auditor's report) are not always known during the planning stages of the audit.

13. (b) AU 312.25 indicates that the detection risk that the auditor can accept in the design of auditing procedures is based on the level to which he or she seeks to restrict audit risk related to the account balance or class of transactions and on his or her assessment of inherent and control risks. For example, as the auditor's assessment of inherent risk and control risk decreases, the detection risk that he or she can accept increases. The auditor's assessment of control risk will give no indication of the level of inherent risk. Sampling and nonsampling risk are a part of detection risk.

14. (d) Inherent risk is the susceptibility of an assertion to a material misstatement, assuming that there are no related internal control structure policies and procedures. Control risk is the risk that a material misstatement that could occur in an assertion will not be prevented or detected on a timely basis by the entity's internal control structure policies or procedures. Detection risk is the risk that the auditor will not detect a material misstatement that exists in an assertion. Thus, inherent risk and control risk are functions of the client and its environment while detection risk is not. Inherent risk, control risk, and detection risk are all a part of audit risk (AU 312.20). Inherent risk and control risk differ from detection risk in that they exist independently of the audit of financial statements, whereas detection risk relates to the auditor's procedures and can be changed at his or her discretion (AU 312.21). All of the elements of audit risk (inherent risk, control risk, and detection risk) should be considered at the individual account-balance or class-of-transactions level because such consideration directly assists the auditor in determining the scope of auditing procedures for the balance or class of related assertions (AU 312.19).

Communications Between Predecessor and Successor Auditors (AU 315)

15. (b) AU 315.05 states, "If a prospective client refuses to permit the predecessor to respond or limits the response, the successor auditor should inquire as to the reasons and consider the implications of that refusal in deciding whether to accept the engagement." Normally, the successor's inquiries of the predecessor should include, among other things, facts that might bear upon the integrity of management (AU 315.06). The discussion with the predecessor does not bear directly on the successor's ability to consider internal control, determine beginning balances, or establish consistency in the application of GAAP.

15A. (a) Under AU 315.02, successor auditors initiate contact with the predecessor auditor on a new or proposed engagement.

16. (d) AU 315.06 states, "The successor auditor should make specific and reasonable inquiries of the predecessor regarding matters that the successor believes will assist him in determining whether to accept the engagement. His inquiries should include specific questions regarding, among other things, facts that might bear on the integrity of management; on disagreements with management as to accounting principles, auditing procedures, or other similarly significant matters; and on the predecessor's understanding as to the reasons for the change of auditors."

16A. (d) AU 315.06 states, "[The successor auditor's] inquiries should include specific questions regarding, among other things, facts that might bear on the integrity of management: on disagreements with management as to accounting principles, auditing procedures, or other similarly significant matters: and on the predecessor's understanding as to the reasons for the change of auditors." The auditor would use other sources for learning specialized accounting principles of the client's industry and the inherent uncertainty in applying sampling procedures. The competency of the client's internal audit staff should be an evaluation of the current auditor.

17. (a) AU 315.06 states, "(The successor auditor's) inquiries should include specific questions regarding, among other things, facts that might bear on the integrity of management; on disagreements with management as to accounting principles, auditing procedures, or other similarly significant matters; and on the predecessor's understanding as to the reasons for the change of auditors."

17A. (a) AU 315.03 states that prior to acceptance of the engagement, the successor auditor should attempt certain communications such as inquiry of the predecessor auditor. Obtaining an engagement letter is not required; however, it is strongly recommended to establish the agreement between the client and the CPA as to the services to be performed. Answer (c) represents steps to be taken *after* the client has been accepted by the CPA. The management representation letter would be obtained near the completion of the audit.

18. (c) AU 315.09 states, "The successor auditor should request the client to authorize the predecessor to allow a review of the predecessor's working papers."

18A. (d) AU 315.10 states that if during an audit, the successor auditor becomes aware of information that leads the auditor to believe the financial statements reported on by the predecessor auditor may require revision, the successor auditor should request his client to arrange a meeting among the three parties to resolve the matter. If the client refuses or if the successor is not satisfied with the result, the successor auditor should consult with an attorney in determining an appropriate course of action.

Communications With Audit Committee (AU 380)

19. (a) AU 380.11 states that disagreements with management may occasionally arise over application of accounting principles to the entity's specific transactions and events and the basis for management's judgments about accounting estimates. Disagreements may also arise regarding the scope of the audit, disclosures to be included in the entity's financial statements, and the wording of the auditor's report. The auditor should discuss with the audit committee any disagreements with management, whether or not satisfactorily resolved, about matters that individually or in the aggregate could be significant to the entity's financial statements or the auditor's report. The auditor is not required to repeat communications every year unless changes in board members or the passage of time makes it appropriate and timely to report the matters. Written communications are to be distributed to the audit committee or its equivalent. The communications with the audit committee are incidental to the audit, and are not required to occur before the issuance of the auditor's report on the entity's financial statements, so long as the communications occur on a timely basis. There may be occasions when discussion of certain matters with the audit committee prior to the issuance of the report will be desirable.

19A. (b) AU 380.07 states, "The auditor should determine that the audit committee is informed about...changes in significant accounting policies or their application." AU 380.04 states that the communications are not required to occur before the issuance of the auditor's report so long as the communications occur on a timely basis. AU 380.02 states that this reporting does not require communications with management. AU 380.09 states that the auditor should inform the audit committee about adjustments that could have a significant effect on the entity's financial reporting process...whether or not recorded by the entity.

19B. (b) AU 380.09 states that an auditor should inform the audit committee about adjustments arising from the audit that could, in the auditor's judgment, either individually or in the aggregate, have a significant effect on the entity's financial reporting process. Often adjustments are not recorded until after the auditor has completed the field work and the client has approved all adjustments. A recurring matter does not have to be resolved by management; the auditor may report it again in the management letter that is presented with the report. Prior period adjustments are made to the financial statements of the prior period beginning balances due to a mistake in the previous year's report and are not required to be reported to the audit committee.

19C. (b) AU 380.08 notes that the auditor must communicate to the audit committee the process management uses to formulate sensitive accounting estimates.

20. (a) AU 380.09 states, "The auditor should inform the audit committee about adjustments arising

from the audit that could, in his judgment, either individually or in the aggregate, have a significant effect on the entity's financial reporting process." AU 380.12 states, "In some cases, management may decide to consult with other accountants about auditing and accounting matters. When the auditor is aware that such consultation has occurred, he should discuss with the audit committee his views about significant matters that were the subject of such consultation."

20A. (b) While the amount of misstatements that would be material may be discussed with the audit committee, the auditor *must* report the methods used to account for significant unusual transactions (AU 380.07) and disagreements with management, whether or not satisfactorily resolved (AU 380.11). The auditor also has the responsibility to report reportable conditions and material weaknesses. Indications of fraud and illegal acts are listed as examples of material weaknesses in AU 325.21.

The Auditor's Responsibility to Detect and Report Errors and Irregularities (AU 316)

21. (d) The evidential matter required by the third standard of field work is obtained through two general classes of substantive tests: (1) tests of details of transactions and balances and (2) analytical procedures applied to financial information (AU 319.64). Reliance on substantive tests may properly vary with the assessed level of control risk. Therefore, an auditor may compensate for a weakness in the internal control structure by increasing the extent of tests of details of transactions and balances or by increasing the extent of analytical procedures. The detection risk that an auditor can accept is based on the maximum level of audit risk and the perceived levels of inherent and control risks. Because a weakness in the internal control structure increases the auditor's assessment of control risk, the auditor should decrease the level of detection risk. The auditor may compensate for a weakness in the internal control structure by increasing the extent of substantive testing; he or she may not compensate for the weakness by increasing the extent of testing of controls. Audit risk is the risk that the auditor may unknowingly fail to appropriately modify his or her opinion on financial statements that are materially misstated. Increasing the preliminary judgment about audit risk would compound a weakness in the internal control structure.

22. (b) AU 316.02 states, ". . . *errors* refer to *unintentional* misstatements or omissions of amounts or disclosures in financial statements." Answers (a), (c) and (d) are examples of *irregularities* which AU 316.03 defines as ". . . *intentional* misstatements or omissions of amounts or disclosures in financial statements."

23. (d) The auditor should design the audit to provide reasonable assurance of detecting errors and irregularities that are material to the financial statements (AU 316.04). The auditor's responsibility for detecting misstatements resulting from illegal acts having a direct and material effect on the determination of financial statement amounts is the same as that for errors and irregularities (AU 317.05).

24. (a) AU 316.07 states, "Because of the characteristics of irregularities, particularly those involving forgery and collusion, a properly designed and executed audit may not detect a material irregularity. Also, audit procedures that are effective for detecting a misstatement that is unintentional may be ineffective for a misstatement that is intentional and is concealed through collusion between client personnel and third parties or among management or employees of the client."

25. (d) AU 316.08 states, "The auditor should exercise (1) due care in planning, performing, and evaluating the results of audit procedures, and (2) the proper degree of *professional skepticism* to achieve reasonable assurance that material errors or irregularities will be detected."

25A. (d) The auditor should design the audit to provide reasonable assurance of detecting errors and irregularities that are material to the financial statements (AU 316.04). The auditor's responsibility for detecting misstatements resulting from illegal acts that have a direct and material effect on the determination of financial statement amounts is the same as that for errors and irregularities (AU 317.05).

26. (a) AU 316.21 states, "The performance of auditing procedures during the audit may result in the detection of conditions or circumstances that should cause the auditor to consider whether material misstatements exist." One of the examples given of such a circumstance is when supporting records or files that should be readily available are not promptly produced when requested.

27. (a) Performing tests of transactions, with their examination of accounting records and supporting documents, are important procedures that can accomplish both the testing of controls and substantive testing. If the auditor finds transactions that are unsupported by proper documentation, this may cause him or her to question whether the level of audit risk has been sufficiently reduced to allow him or her

the assurance that the financial statements are free of material misstatements. Answers (b), (c), and (d) do not by themselves point to an increased chance of a material misstatement.

28. (d) Disclosure of irregularities to parties other than the client's senior management and its audit committee or board of directors is not ordinarily part of the auditor's responsibility, and would be precluded by the auditor's ethical or legal obligation of confidentiality unless the matter affects his or her opinion on the financial statements. The auditor should recognize, however, that in the following circumstances a duty to disclose outside the client may exist: (1) when the entity reports an auditor change under the appropriate securities law on Form 8-K, (2) to a successor auditor when the successor makes inquiries in accordance with AU 315, (3) in response to a subpoena, and (4) to a funding agency in accordance with requirements for the audits of entities that receive financial assistance from a government agency (AU 316.29).

Illegal Acts by Clients (AU 317)

29. (a) The auditor's responsibility to detect and report misstatements resulting from illegal acts having a direct and material effect on the determination of financial statement amounts is the same as that for errors and irregularities.

29A. (a) AU 316.05 states that the auditor should assess the risk that errors and irregularities may cause the financial statements to contain a material misstatement, and based on that assessment, the auditor should design the audit to provide reasonable assurance of detecting errors and irregularities that are material to the financial statements. AU 317.07 states because of the characteristics of illegal acts having material but indirect effects on the financial statements, an audit made in accordance with generally accepted auditing standards provides no assurance that illegal acts will be detected.

29B. (c) AU 317.16 states, "The auditor should consider the implications of an illegal act in relation to other aspects of the audit, particularly the reliability of representations of management."

30. (b) The laws and regulations pertaining to the entity under audit are often highly specialized and complex. AU 317.06 states that they often relate to the operating aspects of an entity rather than its financial or accounting aspects. Therefore, the audit cannot reasonably be expected to bring to the auditor's attention violations of those types of laws and regulations, unless he or she becomes aware of external evidence, such as a governmental agency investigation or an enforcement proceeding, or obtains information from the client's management or legal counsel drawing his or her attention to such matters.

31. (a) Forced discontinuance of operations in a foreign country may indicate illegal acts. Annual donations to a local politician generally are not illegal. Management may elect not to correct material weaknesses if the cost of correction would exceed the benefit. Disclosure of subsequent events generally would not cause the auditor to question whether illegal acts have occurred.

31A. (c) AU 316.10 lists an undue emphasis on meeting earnings projections by management as a characteristic likely to heighten an auditor's concern about the risk of intentional manipulation of financial statements. A low turnover of senior accountants and a slow rate of industry change would be factors to reassure an auditor concerned about management's intentional manipulation of financial statements. Insiders' recent purchases of the entity's stock is proper and by itself would not indicate questionable motives.

32. (a) AU 317.07 states, "If specific information comes to the auditor's attention that provides evidence concerning the existence of possible illegal acts that could have a material indirect effect on the financial statements, the auditor should apply audit procedures specifically directed to ascertaining whether an illegal act has occurred." Only after determining that an illegal act has occurred would the auditor contemplate the steps in the alternatives.

33. (a) AU 317.10 states, "When the auditor becomes aware of information concerning a possible illegal act, the auditor should obtain an understanding of the nature of the act, the circumstances in which it occurred, and sufficient other information to evaluate the effect on the financial statements." Obtaining an understanding of the act will not necessarily affect the reliability of management's representations (AU 317.12). Consideration of whether other similar acts may have occurred is an additional procedure used, if necessary, by the auditor to obtain further understanding of the nature of the acts. It would not be considered until after the auditor determined the effect of the act on the financial statements (AU 317.11). While the occurrence of illegal acts will be communicated to the audit committee, the auditor will not necessarily recommend remedial actions.

34. (a) AU 317.16 states, "The auditor should consider the implications of an illegal act in relation to

other aspects of the audit, particularly the reliability of representations of management."

35. (d) AU 317.22 states, ". . . the auditor may conclude that withdrawal is necessary when the client does not take the remedial action that the auditor considers necessary in the circumstances even when the illegal act is not material to the financial statements."

35A. (a) AU 317.16 states, "The auditor should consider the implications of an illegal act in relation to other aspects of the audit, particularly the reliability of representations of management." A relatively small misstatement of unretired fixed assets, improperly authorized petty cash fund disbursement, or uncollectible account receivable that was not written off have less impact on the financial statements taken as a whole and, by themselves, do not tend to place doubt on the integrity of management.

36. (b) When the auditor is unable to conclude whether the financial statements are materially misstated due to an illegal act, he or she should disclaim an opinion or issue a qualified opinion on the financial statements.

PERFORMANCE BY SUBTOPICS

Each category below parallels a subtopic covered in Chapter 35. Record the number and percentage of questions you correctly answered in each subtopic area.

Planning and Supervision (AU 311)

Question #	Correct √
1	
1A	
2	
2A	
2B	
2C	
3	
3A	
3B	
3C	
3D	
4	
4A	
4B	
5	
5A	
6	
6A	
7	
7A	
7B	
7C	
# Questions	22
# Correct	______
% Correct	______

Audit Risk and Materiality in Conducting an Audit (AU 312)

Question #	Correct √
8	
8A	
9	
10	
10A	
11	
12	
12A	
12B	
13	
14	
# Questions	11
# Correct	______
% Correct	______

Communications Between Predecessor and Successor Auditors (AU 315)

Question #	Correct √
15	
15A	
16	
16A	
17	
17A	
18	
18A	
# Questions	8
# Correct	______
% Correct	______

Communications With Audit Committee (AU 380)

Question #	Correct √
19	
19A	
19B	
19C	
20	
20A	
# Questions	6
# Correct	______
% Correct	______

The Auditor's Responsibility to Detect and Report Errors and Irregularities (AU 316)

Question #	Correct √
21	
22	
23	
24	
25	
25A	
26	
27	
28	
# Questions	9
# Correct	______
% Correct	______

Illegal Acts by Clients (AU 317)

Question #	Correct √
29	
29A	
29B	
30	
31	
31A	
32	
33	
34	
35	
35A	
36	
# Questions	12
# Correct	______
% Correct	______

OTHER OBJECTIVE FORMAT QUESTION

Problem 35-2 (15 to 25 minutes)

Bond, CPA, is considering audit risk at the financial statement level in planning the audit of Toxic Waste Disposal (TWD) Company's financial statements for the year ended December 31, 1993. TWD is a privately-owned entity that contracts with municipal governments to remove environmental wastes. Audit risk at the financial statement level is influenced by the risk of material misstatements, which may be indicated by a combination of factors related to management, the industry, and the entity.

Required:

Based only on the information below, indicate whether each of the following factors **(Items 1 through 15)** would most likely increase audit risk (I), decrease audit risk (D), or have **no** effect on audit risk (N).

Items to be answered:

Company profile

1. This was the first year TWD operated at a profit since 1989 because the municipalities received increased federal and state funding for environmental purposes.

2. TWD's Board of Directors is controlled by Mead, the majority stockholder, who also acts as the chief executive officer.

3. The internal auditor reports to the controller and the controller reports to Mead.

4. The accounting department has experienced a high rate of turnover of key personnel.

5. TWD's bank has a loan officer who meets regularly with TWD's CEO and controller to monitor TWD's financial performance.

6. TWD's employees are paid biweekly.

7. Bond has audited TWD for five years.

Recent developments:

8. During 1993, TWD changed its method of preparing its financial statements from the cash basis to generally accepted accounting principles.

9. During 1993, TWD sold one half of its controlling interest in United Equipment Leasing (UEL) Co. TWD retained significant interest in UEL.

10. During 1993, litigation filed against TWD in 1988 alleging that TWD discharged pollutants into state waterways was dropped by the state. Loss contingency disclosures that TWD included in prior years' financial statements are being removed for the 1993 financial statements.

11. During December 1993, TWD signed a contract to lease disposal equipment from an entity owned by Mead's parents. This related party transaction is not disclosed in TWD's notes to its 1993 financial statements.

12. During December 1993, TWD completed a barter transaction with a municipality. TWD removed waste from a municipally-owned site and acquired title to another contaminated site at below market price. TWD intends to service this new site in 1994.

13. During December 1993, TWD increased its casualty insurance coverage on several pieces of sophisticated machinery from historical cost to replacement cost.

14. Inquiries about the substantial increase in revenue TWD recorded in the fourth quarter of 1993 disclosed a new policy. TWD guaranteed to several municipalities that it would refund the federal and state funding paid to TWD if any municipality fails federal or state site clean-up inspection in 1994.

15. An initial public offering of TWD's stock is planned for late 1994. (5/94, Aud., #3, 4905-19)

OTHER OBJECTIVE FORMAT SOLUTION

Problem 35-2 Audit Risk

1. (D) The organization's ability to continue as a going concern decreases audit risk.

2. (I) Audit risk is increased when management operating and financial decisions are dominated by one person.

3. (I) Audit risk is increased when the internal auditor reports to the person they are evaluating (i.e., controller).

4. (I) High turnover of accounting personnel increases the potential for errors due to poorly trained personnel and, thus, increases audit risk.

5. (D) The monitoring of financial performance decreases audit risk.

6. (N) The pay period has no effect on audit risk since it has no effect on the possibility for error or irregularities.

7. (D) Audit risk is decreased due to familiarity with the audit history, client industry and client procedures.

8. (I) Changing accounting methods increases audit risk due to the complicated accounting issues involved.

9. (I) The retention of a significant interest, while losing decision-making powers in the operations of the company, results in increased audit risk.

10. (D) The settlement of a contingency reduces audit risk.

11. (I) Related party transactions increase audit risk.

12. (I) Difficult-to-audit transactions, such as the barter transaction, increase audit risk.

13. (N) The increase in casualty insurance coverage has no effect on the possibility of errors and irregularities and, therefore, does not effect audit risk.

14. (I) The guarantee represents a loss contingency which could result in revenue not being realized. Therefore, audit risk is increased.

15. (I) The impending initial public offering could cause an unduly aggressive attitude toward financial reporting and an emphasis on meeting earnings projections in an effort to improve the financial results. Therefore, audit risk is increased.

ESSAY QUESTIONS

Essay 35-3 (15 to 25 minutes)

Dodd, CPA, audited Adams Company's financial statements for the year ended December 31, 1989. On November 1, 1990, Adams notified Dodd that it was changing auditors and that Dodd's services were being terminated. On November 5, 1990, Adams invited Hall, CPA, to make a proposal for an engagement to audit its financial statements for the year ended December 31, 1990.

Required:

a. What procedures concerning Dodd should Hall perform before accepting the engagement?

b. What additional procedures should Hall consider performing during the planning phase of this audit (after acceptance of the engagement) that would **not** be performed during the audit of a continuing client? (11/90, Aud., #2)

Essay 35-4 (15 to 25 minutes)

Reed, CPA, accepted an engagement to audit the financial statements of Smith Company. Reed's discussion with Smith's new management and the predecessor auditor indicated the possibility that Smith's financial statements may be misstated due to the possible occurrence of errors, irregularities, and illegal acts.

Required:

a. Identify and describe Reed's responsibilities to detect Smith's errors and irregularities. Do **not** identify specific audit procedures.

b. Identify and describe Reed's responsibilities to report Smith's errors and irregularities.

c. Describe Reed's responsibilities to detect Smith's material illegal acts. Do **not** identify specific audit procedures.

d. Describe Reed's additional responsibilities to report on errors, irregularities, and illegal acts if this audit were one to which the requirements of Government Auditing Standards apply.
(5/89, Aud., #5)

Essay 35-5 (15 to 25 minutes)

Parker is the in-charge auditor with administrative responsibilities for the upcoming annual audit of FGH Company, a continuing audit client. Parker will supervise two assistants on the engagement and will visit the client before the field work begins.

Parker has started the planning process by preparing a list of procedures to be performed prior to the beginning of field work. The list includes:

1. Review correspondence and permanent files.
2. Review prior year's audit working papers, financial statements, and auditor's reports.
3. Discuss with CPA firm personnel responsible for audit and non-audit services to the client matters that may affect the audit.
4. Discuss with management current business developments affecting the client.

Required:

Complete Parker's list of procedures to be performed prior to the beginning of field work. (5/87, Aud., #5)

Essay 35-6 (15 to 25 minutes)

Audit risk and materiality should be considered when planning and performing an audit of financial statements in accordance with generally accepted auditing standards. Audit risk and materiality should also be considered together in determining the nature, timing, and extent of auditing procedures and in evaluating the results of those procedures.

Required:

a. 1. Define audit risk.
2. Describe its components of inherent risk, control risk, and detection risk.
3. Explain how these components are interrelated.

b. 1. Define materiality.
2. Discuss the factors affecting its determination.
3. Describe the relationship between materiality for planning purposes and materiality for evaluation purposes. (11/86, Aud., #2)

ESSAY SOLUTIONS

Solution 35-3 Communications Between Predecessor and Successor Auditors (AU 315)

a. The procedures Hall should perform before accepting the engagement include the following:

1. Hall should explain to Adams the need to make an **inquiry of Dodd** and should **request permission** to do so.
2. Hall should a**sk Adams to authorize Dodd to respond fully** to Hall's inquiries.
3. If Adams **refuses** to permit Dodd to respond or limits Dodd's response, Hall should **inquire as to the reasons** and **consider** the implications in deciding **whether to accept the engagement.**
4. Hall should make **specific and reasonable inquiries** of Dodd regarding matters Hall believes will assist in determining whether to accept the engagement, including specific questions regarding

- Facts that might bear on the **integrity of management.**
- **Disagreements with management** as to accounting principles, auditing procedures, or other similarly significant matters.
- Dodd's understanding as to the **reasons for the change** of auditors.

5. If Hall receives a **limited response**, Hall should **consider its implications** in deciding whether to accept the engagement.

b. The additional procedures Hall should consider performing during the planning phase of this audit that would not be performed during the audit of a continuing client may include the following:

1. Hall may apply appropriate **auditing procedures** to the account balances at the **beginning of the audit period** and, possibly, to transactions in prior periods.

2. Hall may make **specific inquiries** of Dodd regarding matters Hall believes may affect the conduct of the audit, such as

- **Audit areas** that have **required an inordinate amount of time.**
- **Audit problems** that arose from the **condition** of the **accounting system and records.**

3. Hall may request Adams to authorize Dodd to allow a **review of Dodd's working papers.**

4. Hall should **document compliance** with **firm policy** regarding acceptance of a new client.

5. Hall should start obtaining the **documentation** needed to create a **permanent working paper file.**

Solution 35-4 Errors, Irregularities, and Illegal Acts (AU 316 and AU 317)

a. To satisfy an auditor's responsibilities to **detect Smith's errors and irregularities**, Reed should

- **Assess the risk** that Smith's errors and irregularities may cause its financial statements to contain a **material misstatement.**
- **Design the audit** to provide **reasonable assurance** of **detecting errors** and **irregularities** that are material to the financial statements.
- Exercise **due care in planning, performing, and evaluating** the **results** of audit procedures, and the proper degree of **professional skepticism** to achieve **reasonable assurance** that material errors or irregularities will be detected.

b. To satisfy an auditor's responsibilities to **report Smith's errors and irregularities**, Reed should

- Inform Smith's **audit committee,** or others having equivalent authority and responsibility, about **material irregularities** of which Reed becomes aware.
- Express a **qualified or an adverse opinion** on the financial statements if they are **materially affected by an error or irregularity** and are **not revised.**
- **Disclaim or qualify an opinion** on the financial statements and communicate the findings to the audit committee or the board of directors if the **scope** of the audit has been restricted concerning a possible irregularity.
- Consider **notification** of **outside parties** concerning irregularities in certain circumstances.

c. Reed's responsibilities to **detect** Smith's **illegal acts** that have a material and direct effect on Smith's financial statements are the same as that for errors and irregularities.

Reed's responsibilities to detect Smith's illegal acts that have a material and indirect effect on the financial statements are to be aware of the possibility that such illegal acts may have occurred. If specific **information** comes to Reed's attention that provides evidence concerning the **existence** of such possible illegal acts, Reed should **apply audit procedures specifically directed** to ascertaining whether an illegal act has occurred.

d. In an audit to which GAO standards apply, Reed should additionally

- Determine that instances or apparent indications of **illegal acts** are **reported** to the **funding agency** or other **specified agency.**
- Express **positive assurance** on whether the items tested were in **compliance** with applicable laws and regulations.
- Express **negative assurance** that, except as otherwise noted, **nothing came to Reed's attention** that caused Reed to believe that the untested items were not in compliance with applicable laws and regulations.

Solution 35-5 Audit Procedures Prior to the Beginning of Field Work (AU 311)

Additional procedures to be performed prior to the beginning of field work are:

5. **Read** the current year's **interim financial statements.**
6. Discuss the **scope of the audit** with management of the client.
7. Establish the **timing** of the audit work.
8. Arrange with the client for adequate **working space.**
9. Coordinate the assistance of **client personnel** in data preparation.
10. Establish and coordinate **staffing requirements** including **time budget.**
11. Hold a **planning conference** with assistants assigned to the engagement.

12. Determine the extent of involvement, if any, of **consultants, specialists,** and **internal auditors.**
13. Consider the effects of applicable accounting and auditing **pronouncements**, particularly recent ones.
14. Consider the need for an appropriate **engagement letter.**
15. Prepare documentation setting forth the **preliminary audit plan.**
16. Make preliminary judgment about **materiality levels.**
17. Make **preliminary** judgment about the **assessment of control risk.**
18. Update the prior year's written **audit program.**

Solution 35-6 Audit Risk and Materiality (AU 312)

a. 1. **Audit risk** is the risk that the **auditor** may unknowingly **fail** to appropriately **modify** the auditor's **opinion** of financial statements that are materially misstated.

2. **Inherent risk** is the **susceptibility** of an assertion to a **material misstatement,** assuming that there are no related internal control structure policies or procedures.

Control risk is the risk that a material misstatement that **could occur** in an assertion **will not be prevented or detected** on a timely basis by the entity's internal control structure policies and procedures.

Detection risk is the risk that the **auditor will not detect** a material misstatement that exists in an assertion.

3. **Inherent risk** and **control risk** differ from detection risk in that they **exist independently of the audit** of financial statements, whereas **detection risk** relates to the **auditor's procedures** and can be changed at the auditor's discretion. **Detection risk** should bear an **inverse** relationship to **inherent and control risk.** The less the inherent and control risk the auditor believes exists, the greater the acceptable detection risk. Conversely, the greater the inherent and control risk the auditor believes exists, the less the acceptable detection risk.

b. 1. **Materiality** is the **magnitude** of an **omission or misstatement** of accounting information that, in the light of surrounding circumstances, makes it **probable** that the **judgment** of a reasonable person relying on the information would have been **changed** or **influenced** by the omission or misstatement. This concept recognizes that some matters, either individually or in the aggregate, are important for the fair presentation of financial statements in conformity with generally accepted accounting principles, while other matters are not important.

2. **Materiality** is affected by the **nature** and **amount** of an item in relation to the nature and amount of items in the financial statements under audit, and the auditor's judgment as influenced by the **auditor's perception** of the needs of a reasonable person who will rely on the financial statements.

3. The auditor's judgment about materiality for planning purposes is ordinarily different from materiality for evaluation purposes because the **auditor**, when **planning** an audit, **cannot anticipate** all of the circumstances that may ultimately influence judgment about materiality in evaluating the audit findings at the completion of the audit. If significantly lower materiality levels become appropriate in evaluating the audit findings, the auditor should reevaluate the sufficiency of the audit procedures already performed.

NOTES

CHAPTER 36

INTERNAL CONTROL

CHAPTER 36

INTERNAL CONTROL

PART ONE: THE INTERNAL CONTROL STRUCTURE

I. The Second Standard of Field Work

"A sufficient understanding of the internal control structure is to be obtained to plan the audit and to determine the nature, timing, and extent of tests to be performed."

II. Summary of the Consideration of the Internal Control Structure

A. Obtain an Understanding of (1) the design of relevant internal control structure policies and procedures and (2) whether or not they have been placed in operation. The understanding should include all three elements of the internal control structure: the control environment, the accounting system, and the control procedures.

B. Document the Understanding of the internal control structure obtained to plan the audit.

C. Assess the Control Risk by (1) considering the misstatements that could occur in financial statement assertions, (2) identifying policies and procedures relevant to specific assertions, and (3) performing tests of controls to evaluate the effectiveness of the design and operation of policies and procedures in preventing or detecting material misstatements in assertions. In some cases, the procedures used to obtain an understanding of the control structure and to assess control risk may be performed concurrently.

D. Further Reduction in the Assessed Level of Control Risk--After obtaining the understanding and assessing control risk, the auditor may desire a further reduction in the assessed level of control risk for certain assertions. In such cases, the auditor considers whether sufficient evidential matter exists to support a further reduction and whether the performance of the additional tests would be efficient.

E. Document the Basis for Conclusions About the Assessed Level of Control Risk for financial statement assertions if the auditor chooses to assess control risk at below the maximum level. Otherwise, the auditor need only document the understanding of the internal control structure and the fact that control risk is assessed at the maximum level.

F. Substantive Tests--Use knowledge obtained from an understanding of internal control structure and from assessed level of control risk in designing substantive tests for these assertions.

III. Internal Control Structure

A. Policies and Procedures--An entity's internal control structure consists of the policies and procedures established to provide reasonable assurance that specific entity objectives will be achieved. The fundamental concept behind internal control is the segregation of duties in order to eliminate incompatible functions. Incompatible functions place a person in the position to both perpetrate and conceal errors or irregularities in the normal course of his or her duties. Therefore, a well designed plan of organization separates the duties of authorization, recordkeeping, and custody of the assets. The auditor need consider only those policies and procedures that are relevant to the audit.

INTERNAL CONTROL STRUCTURE

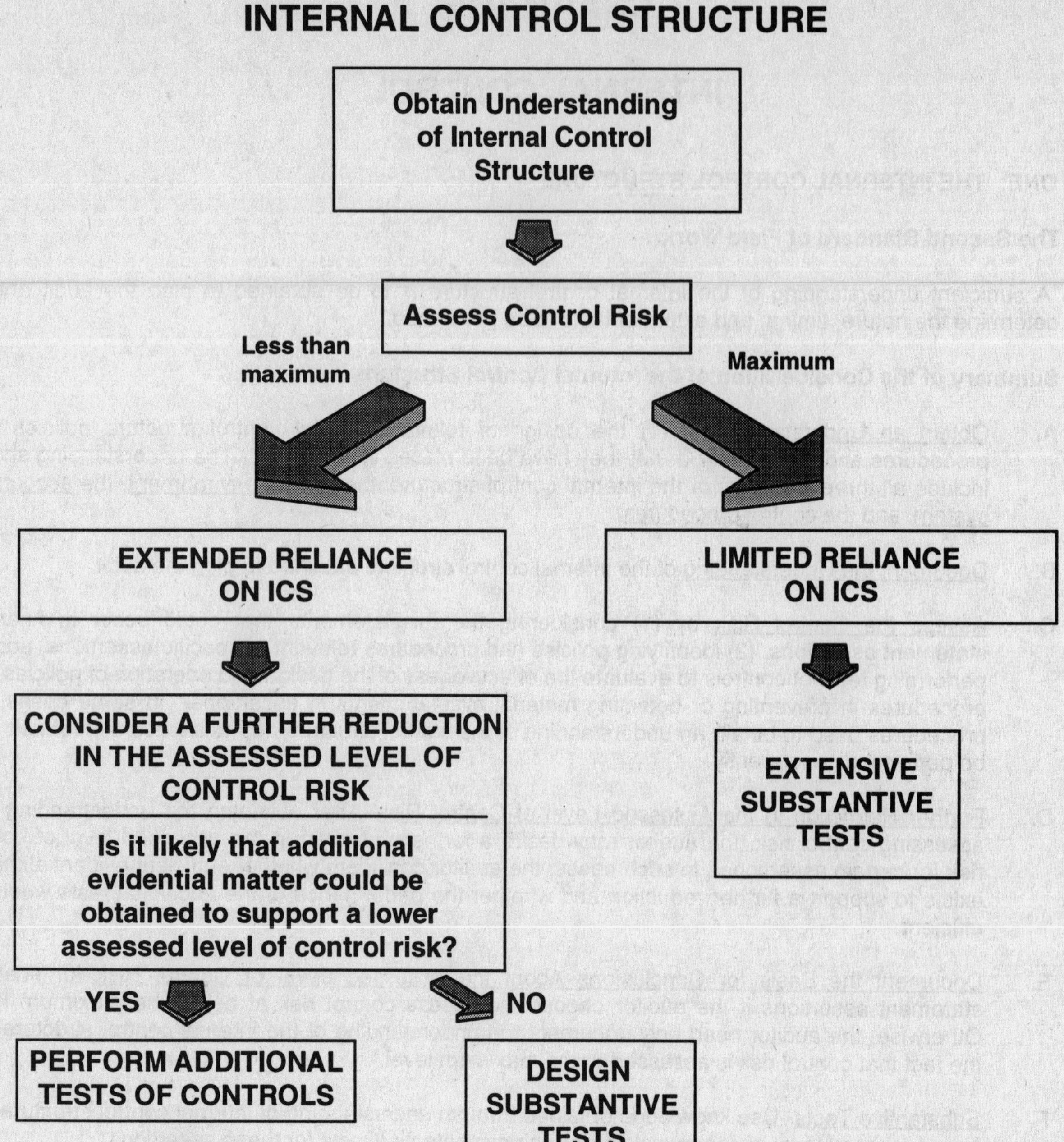

1. Relevant policies and procedures include those that pertain to the entity's ability to record, process, summarize, and report financial data consistent with the assertions embodied in the financial statements. Other policies and procedures may be relevant if they pertain to data the auditor uses to apply auditing procedures.

2. Irrelevant policies and procedures include those concerning the effectiveness, economy, and efficiency of certain management decision-making processes, such as the appropriate price to charge for its products, or whether to spend money for certain research and development or advertising activities. These relate to operational aspects of the client's business.

TotalRecall

BASIC CONCEPTS OF INTERNAL CONTROL STRUCTURE

M Methods of data processing

O Organization and ownership characteristics

D Diversity and complexity of its operations

E Entity's size

R Regulatory and legal requirements

N Nature of its business

B. General Considerations

1. The specific control environment factors, accounting system methods and records, and control procedures that an entity establishes should be considered in the context of the following:

   a. The nature of its business.

   b. Its organization and ownership characteristics.

   c. Its applicable legal and regulatory requirements.

   d. Its methods of processing data.

   e. The size of the entity.

   f. The diversity and complexity of its operations.

2. The responsibility for establishing and maintaining an internal control structure is management's.

3. The concept of reasonable assurance recognizes that the cost of an entity's internal control structure should not exceed the benefits derived. The precise measurement of costs and benefits usually is not possible; hence, management makes both quantitative and qualitative estimates and judgments in evaluating the cost-benefit relationship.

4. Inherent limitations exist with respect to the effectiveness of an entity's internal control structure. Mistakes may occur in the application of certain policies and procedures due to misunderstanding of instructions or personal carelessness. Policies and procedures that require segregation of duties could be circumvented by collusion or by management override.

IV. Elements of the Internal Control Structure

A. Control Environment--Control environment reflects the overall attitude, awareness, and actions of the board of directors, management, owners, and others concerning the importance of control and its emphasis in the entity. It represents the collective effect of various factors on establishing, enhancing, or mitigating the effectiveness of specific policies and procedures. Such factors include the following:

1. Management's philosophy and operating style.

2. The entity's organizational structure.

3. The functioning of the board of directors and its committees, particularly the audit committee.

4. Methods of assigning authority and responsibility.

5. Management's control methods for monitoring and following up on performance, including internal auditing.

6. Personnel policies and practices.

7. Various external influences that affect an entity's operations and practices, such as examinations by bank regulatory agencies.

B. Accounting System--Accounting system consists of the methods and records established to identify, assemble, analyze, classify, record, and report an entity's transactions and to maintain accountability for the related assets and liabilities. An effective accounting system gives appropriate consideration to establishing methods and records that will accomplish the following:

1. Identify and record all valid transactions.

2. Describe, on a timely basis, the transactions in sufficient detail to permit proper classification of transactions for financial reporting.

3. Measure the value of transactions in a manner that permits recording their proper monetary value in the financial statements.

4. Determine the time period in which transactions occurred to permit recording of transactions in the proper accounting period.

5. Present properly the transactions and related disclosures in the financial statements.

C. Control Procedures--Control procedures are those policies and procedures other than those in the control environment and accounting system that management has established to provide reasonable assurance that specific objectives will be achieved. However, they may be integrated into specific components of the control environment and accounting system.

1. Control procedures specify that every transaction should be:

   a. Authorized.

   b. Initiated.

   c. Approved.

   d. Executed.

   e. Recorded.

2. Internal controls will be enhanced if each of these steps is performed by an independent person or department.

3. The following are examples of control procedures:

   a. Preparation of monthly bank reconciliations by an employee not authorized to issue checks or handle cash.

   b. Periodic comparisons between accounting records and physical assets on hand.

   c. Use of pre-numbered sales invoice documents.

V. Consideration of the Internal Control Structure in Planning the Audit

A. Understanding the Internal Control Structure--In making a judgment about the understanding of the internal control structure necessary to plan the audit, the auditor should consider his or her assessment of inherent risk, judgments about materiality, and the complexity and sophistication of the entity's operations and systems. The auditor must also obtain a sufficient understanding of the three elements of the internal control structure to allow for adequate planning of the audit. The understanding should include knowledge about the design of relevant policies and procedures and whether they have been placed in operation. In planning the audit, such knowledge should be used to (1) identify types of misstatements which could occur, (2) consider factors that affect the risk of material misstatement, and (3) design substantive tests. Operating effectiveness is concerned with how the policy or procedure was applied, the consistency with which it was applied, and by whom. The auditor is not required to obtain knowledge about operating effectiveness as part of the understanding of the internal control structure. The auditability of the entity's financial statements may come into question as the auditor obtains the understanding of the internal control structure. Doubts as to the integrity of management or the sufficiency of evidential matter may cause the auditor to conclude that an audit cannot be completed.

1. The auditor should obtain sufficient knowledge of the control environment to understand management's and the board of directors' attitude, awareness, and actions concerning the control environment. The auditor should concentrate on the substance of management's policies and procedures rather than the form, because appropriate policies and procedures may exist but not be followed.

2. The auditor should obtain sufficient knowledge about the accounting system to understand the following:

   a. The classes of transactions in the entity's operations that are significant to the financial statements.

   b. How those transactions are initiated.

   c. The accounting records, supporting documents, machine-readable information, and specific accounts in the financial statements involved in the processing and reporting of transactions.

   d. The accounting processing involved from the initiation of a transaction to its inclusion in the financial statements, including how the computer is used to process data.

   e. The financial reporting process used to prepare the entity's financial statements, including significant accounting estimates and disclosures.

3. The auditor should consider the knowledge about the presence or absence of control procedures in determining whether it is necessary to devote additional attention to obtaining an understanding of control procedures to plan the audit. Ordinarily, audit planning does not require an understanding of the control procedures related to each account balance, transaction class, and disclosure component in the financial statements or to every assertion relevant to those components.

4. A function of internal control is to provide assurance that errors and irregularities may be discovered with reasonable promptness. The auditor's understanding of the internal control structure should either heighten or mitigate the auditor's concern about the risk of material misstatements.

5. Only those controls relevant to financial statement assertions for which the auditor intends to assess control risk at below the maximum level are reviewed, tested, and evaluated.

B. Procedures to Obtain Understanding--The nature and extent of procedures performed generally vary from entity to entity and are influenced by the size and complexity of the entity, and the nature of the particular policy or procedure. The auditor also considers his or her assessments of inherent risk, judgments about materiality, and the complexity and sophistication of the entity's operations and systems. Ordinarily, the procedures used to obtain sufficient knowledge of the design of the relevant policies, procedures, and records pertaining to each of the three internal control structure elements and whether they have been placed in operation would include prior experience with the entity and:

1. Inquiries of appropriate management, supervisory, and staff personnel.

2. Inspection of entity documents and records.

3. Observation of entity activities and operations.

C. Documentation of Understanding--The auditor should document the understanding of the entity's internal control structure elements obtained to plan the audit. The form and extent of this documentation is influenced by the size and complexity of the entity, as well as the nature of the entity's internal control structure. For a large, complex entity, documentation may include flowcharts, questionnaires, or decision tables. For a small, simple entity, documentation in the form of a memorandum may be sufficient.

VI. Consideration of the Internal Control Structure in Assessing Control Risk

A. Risk of Material Misstatement--The risk of material misstatement in financial statement assertions consists of the following:

1. Inherent Risk

2. Control Risk

3. Detection Risk

B. Assessing Control Risk--Assessing control risk is the process of evaluating the effectiveness of an entity's internal control structure policies and procedures in preventing or detecting material misstatements in the financial statements. Control risk should be assessed in terms of financial statement assertions. After obtaining an understanding of the internal control structure, the auditor may assess control risk as follows:

1. At the maximum level for some or all assertions because the auditor believes policies and procedures are unlikely to pertain to an assertion, are unlikely to be effective, or because evaluating their effectiveness would be inefficient. The auditor assesses control risk at the maximum when there is a high probability that a material misstatement that could occur in an assertion will not be prevented or detected on a timely basis by an entity's internal control structure.

2. Below the maximum level, which involves the following:

   a. Identifying specific internal control structure policies and procedures relevant to specific assertions that are likely to prevent or detect material misstatement in those assertions.

   b. Performing tests of controls to evaluate the effectiveness of such policies and procedures.

C. Identifying Internal Control Structure Policies and Procedures--Identifying internal control structure policies and procedures relevant to specific financial statement assertions involves the consideration of whether the policies and procedures have either a pervasive effect on many assertions or a specific effect on an individual assertion. Another consideration is whether the policies and procedures can be either directly or indirectly related to an assertion. The more indirect the relationship, the less effective that policy or procedure may be in reducing control risk for that assertion.

D. Tests of Controls--Procedures directed toward either of the following:

1. The effectiveness of the design of an internal control structure policy or procedure is concerned with whether that policy or procedure is suitably designed to prevent or detect material misstatements in specific financial statement assertions. Tests to obtain such evidential matter ordinarily include the following:

   a. Inquiries of appropriate entity personnel.

   b. Inspection of documents and reports.

   c. Observation of the application of specific internal control structure policies and procedures.

2. The operating effectiveness of an internal control structure policy or procedure is concerned with how the policy or procedure was applied, the consistency with which it was applied during the audit period, and by whom it was applied. These tests ordinarily include procedures such as the following:

   a. Inquiries of appropriate entity personnel.

   b. Inspection of documents and reports.

   c. Observation of the application of specific internal control structure policies and procedures.

   d. Reperformance of the application of the policy or procedure by the auditor.

E. Assessed Level of Control Risk--The assessed level of control risk is the conclusion reached as a result of evaluating control risk. In determining the evidential matter necessary to support a specific assessed level of control risk at below the maximum level, the auditor should consider the characteristics of evidential matter about control risk discussed in Section VIII, following. Generally, the lower the assessed level of control risk, the greater the assurance the evidential matter must provide that the internal control structure policies and procedures relevant to an assertion are designed and operating effectively. The auditor uses the assessed level of control risk (together with the assessed level of inherent risk) to determine the acceptable level of detection risk for financial statement assertions. The auditor then uses the acceptable level of detection risk to determine the nature, timing, and extent of the auditing procedures (i.e., substantive tests) to be used to detect material misstatements in the financial statement assertions.

F. Documentation of the Assessed Level of Control Risk

1. For those financial statement assertions where control risk is assessed at the maximum level, the auditor should document the conclusion that control risk is at the maximum level but need not document the basis for that conclusion.

2. For those assertions where the assessed level of control risk is below the maximum level, the auditor should document the basis for the conclusion that the effectiveness of the design

and operation of internal control structure policies and procedures supports that assessed level.

VII. Relationship of Understanding to Assessing Control Risk

A. Concurrent Performance--Obtaining an understanding of the internal control structure and assessing control risk may be performed concurrently in an audit. For example, the auditor's procedures to obtain an understanding of the control structure may, in some circumstances, also provide evidential matter sufficient to support an assessed level of control risk that is below the maximum level. However, such procedures are not sufficient to support an assessed level of control risk below the maximum level if they do not provide sufficient evidential matter to evaluate the effectiveness of both the design and operating effectiveness of a policy or procedure relevant to an assertion.

B. Further Reduction in the Assessed Level of Control Risk--After obtaining the understanding of the internal control structure and assessing control risk, the auditor may decide to seek a further reduction in the assessed level of control risk for certain assertions. In such cases, the auditor considers whether additional evidential matter sufficient to support a further reduction is likely to be available, and whether it would be efficient to perform tests of controls to obtain that evidential matter. The results of the procedures performed to obtain the understanding of the internal control structure, as well as information obtained from other sources, help the auditor's evaluation. For those assertions for which the auditor performs additional tests of controls, the auditor determines the assessed level of control risk that the results of those tests will support. This assessed level of control risk is used in determining the appropriate detection risk to accept for those assertions and, accordingly, in determining the nature, timing, and extent of substantive tests for such assertions.

VIII. Evidential Matter to Support the Assessed Level of Control Risk

A. Sufficiency of Evidential Matter--When the auditor assesses control risk at below the maximum level, the auditor should obtain sufficient evidential matter to support that assessed level. The sufficiency of the evidential matter is based on the auditor's judgment. The type of evidential matter, its source, its timeliness, and the existence of other evidential matter related to the conclusions to which it leads, all bear on the degree of assurance evidential matter provides. These characteristics influence the nature, timing, and extent of the tests of controls that the auditor applies to obtain evidential matter about control risk. The auditor selects such tests from a variety of techniques such as inquiry, observation, inspection, and reperformance of a policy or procedure that pertains to an assertion. No one specific test of controls is always necessary, applicable, or equally effective in every circumstance.

1. Type of Evidential Matter--The nature of the particular policies and procedures that pertain to an assertion influences the type of evidential matter that is available to evaluate the effectiveness of the design or operation of those policies and procedures.

2. Source of Evidential Matter--Generally, evidential matter about the effectiveness of the design and operation of policies and procedures obtained directly by the auditor, such as through observation, provides more assurance than evidential matter obtained indirectly or by inference, such as through inquiry. Inquiry alone generally will not provide sufficient evidential matter to support a conclusion about the effectiveness of the design or operation of a specific control procedure.

3. Timeliness of Evidential Matter--The timeliness of evidential matter concerns when it was obtained and the portion of the audit period to which it applies. In evaluating the degree of assurance that is provided by evidential matter, the auditor should consider that the evidential matter obtained by some tests of controls, such as observation, pertains only to the point in time at which the auditing procedure was applied. Consequently, such evidential matter may be insufficient to evaluate the effectiveness of the design or operation of internal control structure policies and procedures for periods not subjected to such tests. In such

circumstances, the auditor may decide to supplement these tests with other tests of controls that are capable of providing evidential matter about the entire audit period.

a. Evidential matter about the effective design or operation of internal control structure policies and procedures that was obtained in <u>prior audits</u> may be considered by the auditor in assessing control risk in the current period. The auditor should consider that the longer the time elapsed since the performance of tests of controls to obtain evidential matter about control risk, the less assurance it may provide. When considering evidential matter obtained from prior audits, the auditor should obtain evidential matter in the current period about whether changes have occurred in the internal control structure subsequent to the prior audits, as well as the nature and extent of any such changes.

b. When the auditor obtains evidential matter about the design or operation of internal control structure policies and procedures during an <u>interim period</u>, the auditor should determine what additional evidential matter should be obtained for the remaining period. The auditor should obtain evidential matter about the nature and extent of any significant changes in the internal control structure, including its policies, procedures, and personnel, that occur subsequent to the interim period.

B. <u>Interrelationship of Evidential Matter</u>--The auditor should consider the combined effect of various types of evidential matter relating to the same assertion in evaluating the degree of assurance that evidential matter provides. In some circumstances, a single type of evidential matter may not be sufficient to evaluate the effective design or operation of an internal control structure policy or procedure. For example, because an observation is pertinent only at the point in time at which it is made, the auditor may supplement the observation with inquiries.

1. When evaluating the degree of assurance provided by evidential matter, the auditor should consider the interrelationship of an entity's control environment, accounting system, and control procedures.

2. Generally, when various types of evidential matter support the same conclusion about the design or operation of an internal control structure policy or procedure, the degree of assurance provided increases. Conversely, if various types of evidential matter lead to different conclusions, the assurance provided decreases.

3. An audit of financial statements is a cumulative process; as the auditor assesses control risk, the information obtained may cause the auditor to modify the nature, timing, or extent of the other planned tests of controls for assessing control risk. In addition, information may come to the auditor's attention as a result of performing substantive tests or from other sources during the audit that differs significantly from the information on which the planned tests of controls for assessing control risk were based. In such circumstances, the auditor may need to reevaluate the planned substantive procedures, based on a revised consideration of the assessed level of control risk for all or some of the financial statement assertions.

IX. Correlation of Control Risk With Detection Risk

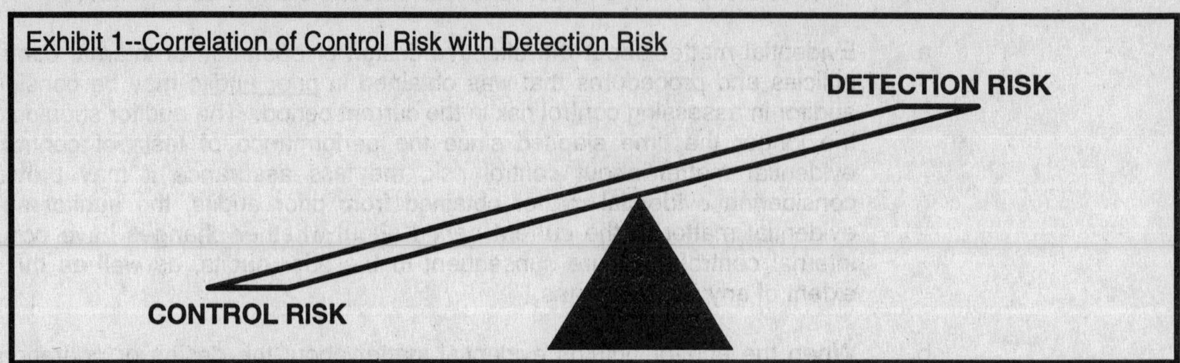

A. Inverse Relationship--After considering the level to which the auditor seeks to restrict the risk of a material misstatement in the financial statements and the assessed levels of inherent risk and control risk, the auditor performs substantive tests to restrict detection risk to an acceptable level. As the assessed level of control risk decreases, the acceptable level of detection risk increases. Accordingly, the auditor may alter the nature, timing, and extent of the substantive tests performed.

B. Requirements for Performing Substantive Tests--The assessed level of control risk cannot be sufficiently low to eliminate the need to perform any substantive tests. Consequently, regardless of the assessed level of control risk, the auditor should perform substantive tests for significant account balances and transaction classes.

C. Types of Substantive Tests--The substantive tests that the auditor performs consist of tests of details of transactions and balances, and analytical procedures. In assessing control risk, the auditor also may use tests of details of transactions as tests of controls. The objective of tests of transactions performed as substantive tests is to detect material misstatements in the financial statements. The objective of tests of details of transactions, performed as tests of controls, is to evaluate whether an internal control structure policy or procedure operated effectively. Although these objectives are different, both may be accomplished concurrently through performance of a test of details on the same transaction.

X. Tools for Obtaining an Understanding and Documenting of the Internal Control Structure

Three tools the auditor may use to obtain an understanding of the internal control structure policies and procedures are the questionnaire, the memorandum (narrative), and the flowchart. (Note that these also provide documentation of the auditor's understanding.)

A. Questionnaire Approach--An internal control questionnaire is simply an enumeration of the matters to be investigated in the auditor's consideration of the internal control structure. It should be designed by persons who are fully conversant with the problems of internal control and who have experience in the kind of structure being reviewed.

1. Sample Questions--While the size and scope of internal control questionnaires will vary, some possible questions for an accounts receivable system are as follows:

a. Are the following functions performed by employees other than accounts receivable bookkeepers?

(1) Handling cash and maintaining cash records.

(2) Opening incoming mail.

(3) Credit and collection.

(4) Review and mailing of statements to customers.

b. Are the accounts receivable ledgers unavailable to the cashier?

c. Are the subsidiary ledgers regularly balanced with the control accounts?

d. Are the subsidiary ledgers occasionally balanced with the control accounts by someone other than the accounts receivable bookkeepers?

e. Are aged trial balances of accounts receivable regularly prepared and submitted for executive approval?

f. Are statements sent at regular intervals to all customers?

2. Advantages of the Questionnaire--One advantage of the internal control questionnaire is that it is easy to complete. Another advantage is that the comprehensive list of questions provides assurance that relevant points will be covered. Also, weaknesses are obvious because they are usually the "no" answers.

3. Problem--A possible problem is that if the questionnaire is too general, it may not be adequate to evaluate a specific structure.

B. Narrative (Memorandum) Approach--The auditor determines what the prescribed system of internal control structure is, and then writes it out in the auditor's own words.

1. Advantages--The narrative is tailor-made for each engagement. Another advantage is that it requires a detailed analysis of the client's internal control structure since the auditor must thoroughly understand the structure in order to describe it.

2. Problems--The narrative approach is very time consuming. Further, it does not have built-in safeguards to prevent the auditor from overlooking some aspect of the internal control structure. In addition, weaknesses in the internal control structure are not always obvious and may not be detected by this approach.

C. Flowchart Approach--An internal control flowchart is a graphic representation of a portion of a company's internal control structure. It shows the segregation of functions, document flows, controls, etc.

1. Advantages--The internal control flowchart is a graphic representation of a structure or a series of sequential processes. It shows the steps required and the flow of documents from person to person in carrying out the functions depicted. Therefore, the tendency to overlook the controls existing between functions or departments is minimized. Another advantage is that the flowchart clearly communicates the structure. The use of a flowchart is especially useful in the evaluation of electronic data processing systems because it avoids much of the terminology that would be present in a narrative. Finally, constructing a flowchart requires the auditor to completely understand the structure.

2. Problem--It takes longer to construct the flowchart than it does to fill out an internal control questionnaire.

3. Flowchart Symbols--Several of the commonly used flowchart symbols are:

DOCUMENT: Paper documents and reports of all kinds, e.g., sales invoices, purchase orders, employee paychecks, and computer-prepared error listings.

COMPUTER OPERATION/PROCESS: Execute defined operations resulting in some change in the information or the determination of flow direction, e.g., checking customer's credit limit.

MANUAL OPERATION: Off-line process that is performed manually, e.g., preparing a three-part sales invoice or manually posting to customer accounts.

MANUAL INPUT: Represents input entered manually at the time of processing, e.g., using a keyboard.

INPUT/OUTPUT: General input/output symbol, e.g., general ledger, can be used regardless of the type of medium or data.

PUNCHED CARD: Input/output function in which the medium is a punched card, e.g., payroll earnings card.

PUNCHED TAPE: Input/output function in which the medium is punched tape.

MAGNETIC TAPE: Input/output function in which the medium is magnetic tape, e.g., master payroll data file.

DISPLAY: Input/output device in which the information is displayed at the time of processing for human use, e.g., display customer number.

ON-LINE STORAGE: Storage that is connected to and under the control of the computer, e.g., disk, drum, magnetic tape, etc.

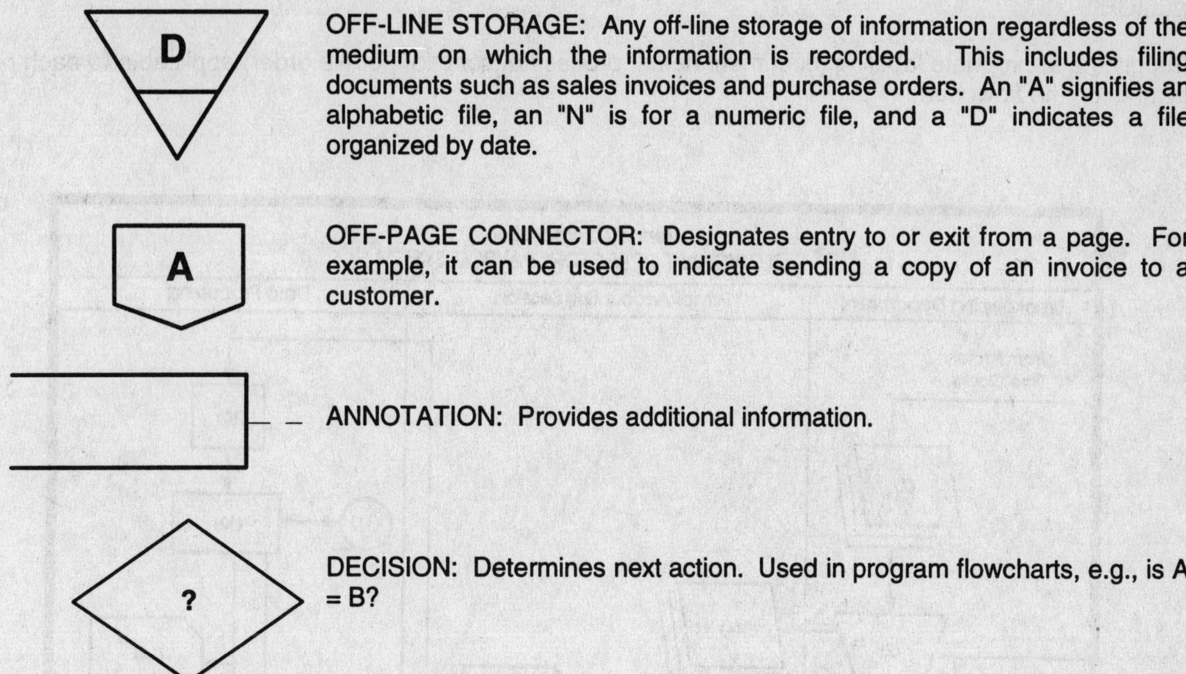

OFF-LINE STORAGE: Any off-line storage of information regardless of the medium on which the information is recorded. This includes filing documents such as sales invoices and purchase orders. An "A" signifies an alphabetic file, an "N" is for a numeric file, and a "D" indicates a file organized by date.

OFF-PAGE CONNECTOR: Designates entry to or exit from a page. For example, it can be used to indicate sending a copy of an invoice to a customer.

ANNOTATION: Provides additional information.

DECISION: Determines next action. Used in program flowcharts, e.g., is A = B?

<u>Example 1</u>--Sample Flowchart

The following flowchart and portion of an essay question taken from a past CPA Auditing Exam illustrate the use of a flowchart for a factory payroll system:

You are reviewing audit workpapers containing a narrative description of the Tenney Corporation's factory payroll system. A portion of that narrative is as follows:

> Factory employees punch time clock cards each day when entering or leaving the shop. At the end of each week, the timekeeping department collects the time cards and prepares duplicate batch-control slips by department showing total hours and number of employees. The time cards and original batch-control slips are sent to the payroll accounting section. The second copies of the batch-control slips are filed by date.
>
> In the payroll accounting section, payroll transaction cards are keypunched from the information on the time cards, and a batch total card for each batch is keypunched from the batch-control slip. The time cards and batch-control slips are then filed by batch for possible reference. The payroll transaction cards and batch total cards are sent to data processing where they are sorted by employee number within batch. Each batch is edited by a computer program which checks the validity of employee number against a master employee tape file and the total hours and number of employees against the batch total card. A detailed printout by batch and employee number is produced which indicates batches that do not balance and invalid employee numbers. This printout is returned to payroll accounting to resolve all differences.
>
> In searching for documentation, you found a flowchart of the payroll system which included all appropriate symbols (American National Standards Institute, Inc.), but was only partially labeled.

Required:

Supply the appropriate labeling (document name, process description, or file order) applicable to each numbered symbol on the flowchart.

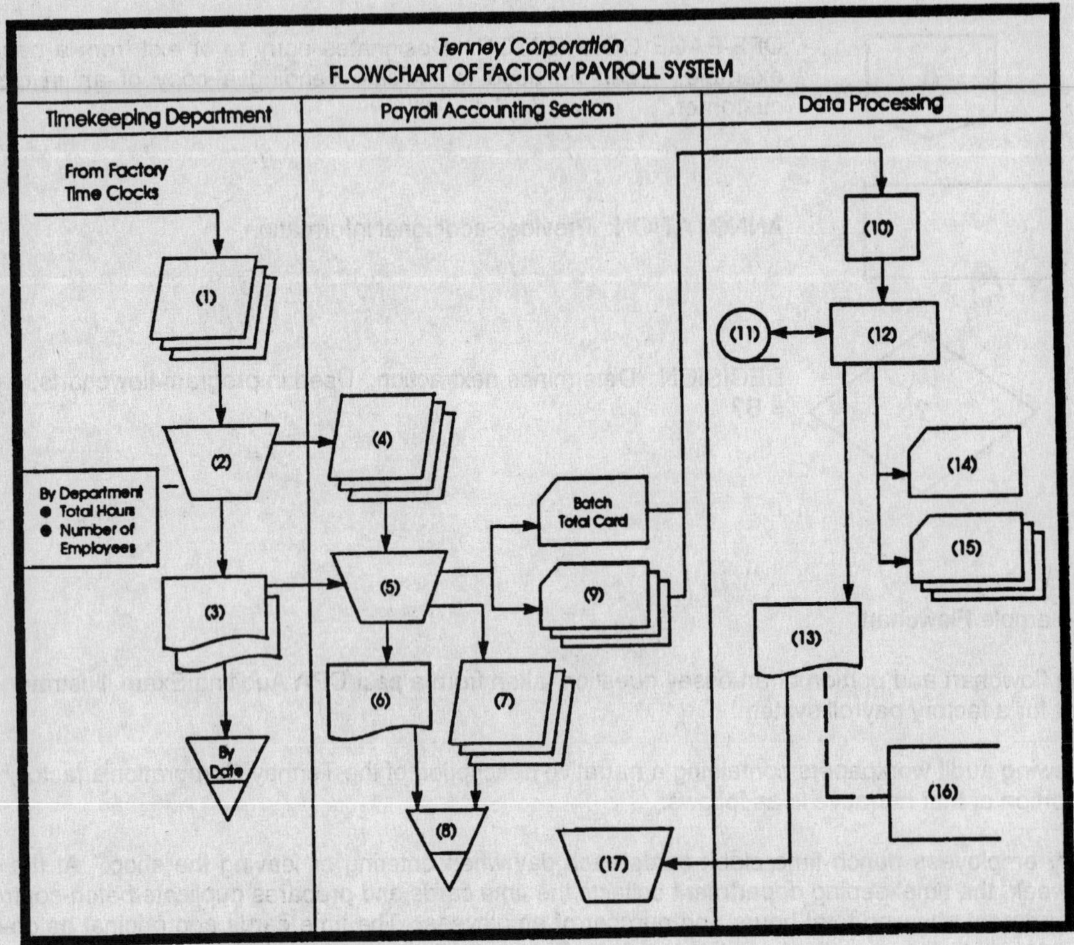

Solution:

(1) Time cards

(2) Prepare batch-control slips

(3) Batch-control slips (the numbers 1 and 2 should be added to indicate first and second copy)

(4) Time cards

(5) Keypunch

(6) Batch-control slip (the number 1 should be added to indicate first copy)

(7) Time cards

(8) By batch

(9) Payroll transaction cards

(10) Sort by employee number within batch

(11) Master employee file

(12) Edit and compare batch total hours and number of employees

(13) Batch listing and exception report

(14) Batch total card

(15) Payroll transaction cards

(16) Exceptions noted:

Unbalanced batch
Invalid employee number

(17) Resolve differences

Summary Flow Chart of Consideration of the Internal Control Structure in a Financial Statement Audit

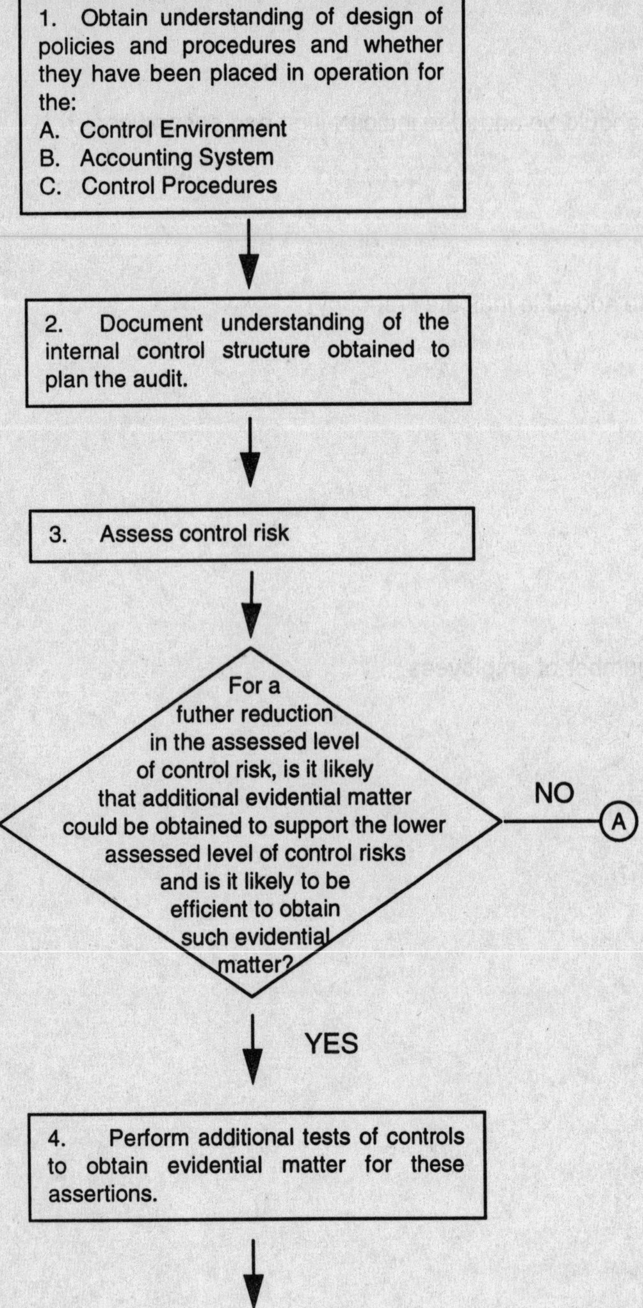
1. Obtain understanding of design of policies and procedures and whether they have been placed in operation for the:
A. Control Environment
B. Accounting System
C. Control Procedures
2. Document understanding of the internal control structure obtained to plan the audit.
3. Assess control risk
For a futher reduction in the assessed level of control risk, is it likely that additional evidential matter could be obtained to support the lower assessed level of control risks and is it likely to be efficient to obtain such evidential matter?
NO
A
YES
4. Perform additional tests of controls to obtain evidential matter for these assertions.

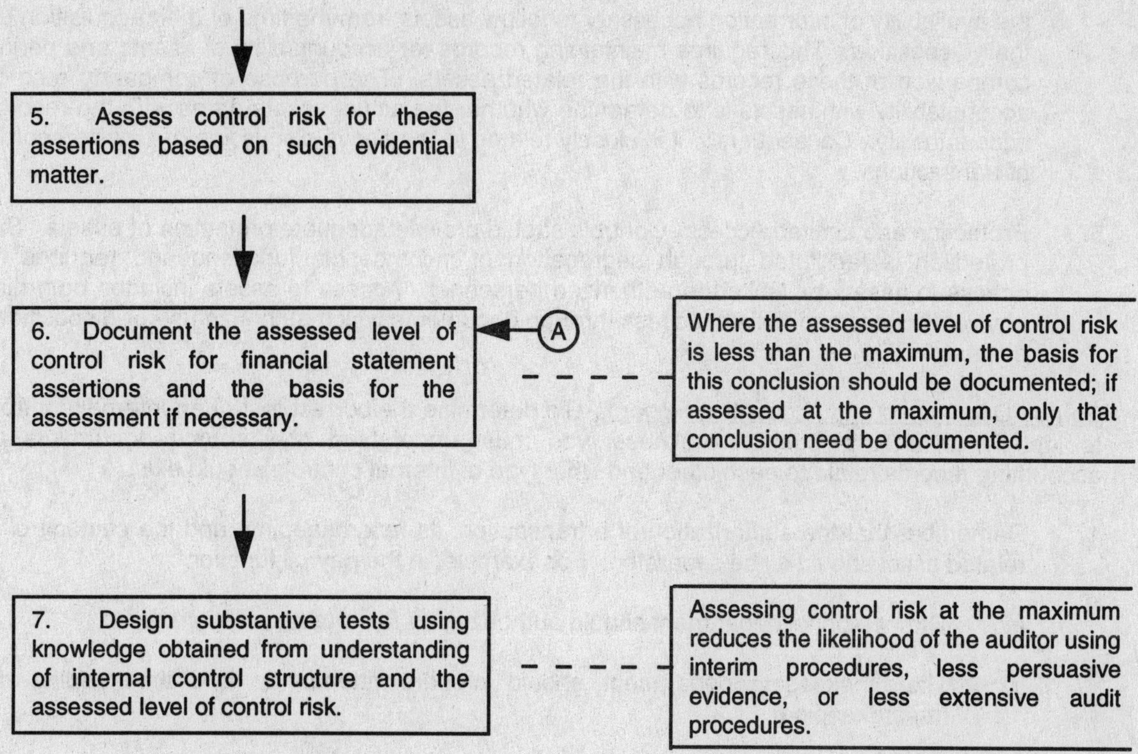

5. Assess control risk for these assertions based on such evidential matter.
6. Document the assessed level of control risk for financial statement assertions and the basis for the assessment if necessary.
A
Where the assessed level of control risk is less than the maximum, the basis for this conclusion should be documented; if assessed at the maximum, only that conclusion need be documented.
7. Design substantive tests using knowledge obtained from understanding of internal control structure and the assessed level of control risk.
Assessing control risk at the maximum reduces the likelihood of the auditor using interim procedures, less persuasive evidence, or less extensive audit procedures.

XI. Internal Control Objectives and Procedures for Specific Transaction Cycles

A. <u>Objectives of Internal Control</u>--A well designed internal control structure should ensure the following: (1) authorization, (2) validity, (3) proper recording, (4) accountability and comparison, and (5) protection and limited access.

1. Authorization--The starting point for establishing accounting control of transactions is appropriate authorization. Obtaining reasonable assurance of appropriate general or specific authorization requires independent evidence that authorizations are issued by persons acting within the scope of their authority and that transactions conform with the terms of the authorizations.

2. Validity--Controls should provide reasonable assurance relative to the validity or existence of assets and liabilities at a given date and whether recorded transactions have occurred during a given period.

3. Proper Recording--The objective of internal control with respect to the proper recording of transactions encompasses several sub-objectives. These include the following:

   a. Completeness--Transactions are not omitted from the accounting records.

   b. Valuation--Transactions are to be recorded at the actual amounts at which they transpired.

   c. Classification--Transactions are to be classified in the appropriate accounts.

   d. Timing--Transactions are to be recorded in the accounting period in which they occurred. Additionally, they are to be recorded as promptly as practicable when recording is necessary to maintain accountability.

4. Accountability and Comparison--The accountability objective of internal control is to assure the availability of information necessary to follow assets from the time of their acquisition until their disposition. This requires maintaining records for accountability of assets and periodic comparison of these records with the related assets. The purpose of comparing recorded accountability with assets is to determine whether the actual assets agree with the recorded accountability. Consequently, it is closely related to the above discussion of proper recording of transactions.

5. Protection and Limited Access--Controls should provide adequate protection of assets. Such protection is facilitated through segregation of incompatible functions and requires that access to assets be limited to authorized personnel. Access to assets includes both direct physical access and indirect access through documents which authorize use or disposition of assets.

B. Source Documents and Accounting Records--To determine the correct test of an internal control or to identify an internal control weakness, you must understand how source documents and accounting records relate to each other and what type of internal controls should exist.

1. Remember that the authorization of a transaction, its recordkeeping, and the custody of the related asset should all be separated. For example, in the payroll function

   a. The personnel department should authorize pay rates (authorization).

   b. The timekeeping department should prepare attendance and timekeeping data (recordkeeping).

   c. The payroll department prepares the payroll (recordkeeping).

   d. The treasurer's department prepares the payroll checks and distributes them to employees (custody).

      - If any person or department was responsible for more than one of these functions, an internal control weakness would exist.

2. Source documents should be pre-numbered and controlled so that they can all be accounted for.

3. Subsidiary ledgers should be reconciled to general ledgers.

4. When attempting to answer a multiple choice question about testing an internal control, first determine what is being asked.

   a. Tracing from a source document to the recorded entry tests the completeness assertion by looking for understatements.

   b. Vouching from a recorded entry to the source document tests the existence assertion by looking for overstatements.

C. Transaction Cycles--Internal control objectives can best be analyzed based on specific business activities or logical groups of transactions. Groupings of similar transactions or functions of an entity are known as transaction cycles. Although classification of a transaction cycle is somewhat arbitrary, the following is representative of the cycles of most businesses:

1. Sales, Receivables, and Cash Receipts Cycle.

2. Purchases, Payables, and Cash Disbursements Cycle.

3. Inventory and Production Cycle.

4. Personnel and Payroll Cycle.

5. Property, Plant, and Equipment Cycle.

Dividing the audit into transaction cycles is known as the cycle approach. The cycle approach combines similar transactions with the ledger balances that result from those transactions. This is more efficient than treating each account balance as a separate segment.

D. Policies and Procedures Within the Transaction Cycles--This section examines the five transaction cycles more closely by relating specific internal control structure policies and procedures within the cycles to the objectives of internal control. Additionally, for each control, an audit test of controls is suggested to evaluate the effectiveness of the policies and procedures.

1. Sales, Receivables, and Cash Receipts Cycle:

Objective	Internal Control	Test of Controls
Authorization	Credit approval occurs before shipment is authorized.	Examine appropriate document for approval.
	Existence of a cash discount policy.	Discuss policy with management. Review sales orders for evidence of compliance.
	Approval of cash discounts and adjustments.	Examine remittance advices for proper approval.
	Sales prices are from authorized price list or executed contract.	Compare sales invoice prices to appropriate price list or contract.
Validity	Prenumbered sales invoices.	Account for numerical sequence of sales invoices.
	Sales are supported by authorized shipping documents and approved customer orders.	Examine supporting bills of lading and customer orders.
	Monthly statements are mailed to customers.	Observe mailing of statements.
	Independent follow-up of customer complaints.	Examine customer correspondence files.
	Separation of the functions of cash handling and recordkeeping.	Observation. Discuss with management and review employee job descriptions.
	Shipment is acknowledged by shipping department.	Examine acknowledgment on sales order copy.

Objective	Internal Control	Test of Controls
Proper Recording	Shipping documents are prenumbered (Completeness).	Accounting for numerical sequence of shipping documents. Trace documents to recording of sales and accounts receivable subsidiary ledger.
	A chart of accounts is used and is adequate (Classification).	Review adequacy and use of proper accounts. Examine sales documents to determine if sales transactions are properly classified.
	Cash receipts are recorded immediately and deposited on a daily basis. (Timing).	Observation. Trace totals to duplicate deposit slips.
	Sales invoices and credit memoranda are prenumbered (Completeness).	Account for numerical sequence of sales invoices and credit memoranda.
	Internal verification of invoice preparation and posting (Valuation, Completeness, Classification).	Observation. Discuss policy with management.
Accountability and Comparison	Independent reconciliation of bank statements.	Observation. Review bank reconciliation.
	Cash register totals are verified by persons not having access to cash or cash records.	Examine documentation of verification.
	Cash receipts are recorded immediately to establish accountability.	Observe the cash receiving process.
	A list of checks is prepared as the mail is opened.	Observation. Compare check listing total to duplicate deposit slip.
Protection and Limited Access	Persons receiving or otherwise handling cash are bonded.	Discuss with management. Review appropriate documentation of bonding.
	Checks are immediately endorsed.	Observation.
	Separation of cash handling and recordkeeping functions.	Observation. Discuss with management and review employee job descriptions.

2. Purchases, Payables, and Cash Disbursements Cycle:

Objective	Internal Control	Test of Controls
Authorization	Appropriate approval is required for all purchases.	Examine supporting documentation for indication of approval (purchase requisition and order).
	Payment approval required before check signing.	Observation. Examine documentation for indication of approval.
	Authorized signatures on checks. Two signatures on large checks.	Select a sample of large disbursements from the cash disbursements journal and examine the correlating canceled checks for two signatures.
Validity	Purchases are supported by purchases requisition, purchase order, receiving report, and vendor invoice.	Examine supporting documentation of vouchers.
	Documentation is canceled to prevent reuse.	Examine documentation for indication of cancellation.
	Receiving reports are prenumbered.	Account for numerical sequence of receiving reports.
	Receiving reports are required before approval of invoice for payment.	Discuss policy with management. Observation. Compare payment approval and receiving report dates.
Proper Recording	Vouchers are prenumbered (Completeness).	Account for numerical sequence of vouchers.
	Internal verification of vendor invoice amounts and calculations. (Valuation).	Examine invoice copy for indication of clerical accuracy verification.
	Transactions are recorded as soon as possible after receiving goods. (Timing).	Compare purchase journal dates to receiving report and invoice dates. (Observation).
	Purchase orders are prenumbered (Completeness).	Account for numerical sequence of purchase orders.
	A chart of accounts is used and is adequate (Classification).	Review adequacy and use of proper accounts. Examine sales documents to determine if sales transactions are properly classified.

Objective	Internal Control	Test of Controls
Accountability and Comparison	Independent reconciliation of bank statement.	Observation. Review bank reconciliation.
	Checks are signed only with appropriate support, by the treasurer, and the treasurer mails the checks.	Observation. Examine canceled check signatures.
	Monthly suppliers' statements are compared to accounts payable.	Examine statements for indication of agreement.
	Receiving department examines quantity and quality of merchandise upon receipt.	Examine copies of receiving reports and purchase orders for indication of goods received.
	Accountability is established for unused and voided checks.	Discuss policy with management.
Protection and Limited Access	Separation of functions between accounts payable and custody of signed checks.	Observation. Review employee job descriptions.
	Checks are prenumbered.	Account for numerical sequence of checks.
	Mechanical check protector is used.	Examine check copies for evidence of check protector use.
	Separation of purchasing department functions from receiving and recordkeeping.	Observation. Review employee job descriptions.
	Physical control of unused checks is properly and securely maintained.	Observation. Discuss policy with management.

3. **Inventory and Production Cycle:**

Objective	Internal Control	Test of Controls
Authorization	Movement of inventory items is authorized by requisitions.	Examine requisitions for indication of approval. Inquire of client personnel.
	Inventory purchases are appropriately authorized.	Select a sample of recorded purchases and vouch to documents authorizing purchase.

Objective	Internal Control	Test of Controls
	Write-offs and write-downs of obsolete inventory are appropriately authorized.	Examine appropriate documentation for indication of authorization.
Validity	Receiving prepares prenumbered receiving reports.	Account for numerical sequence of receiving reports.
	Payment for inventory is approved only after verification of quantity and prices of vendor invoice.	Examine documentation for indication of verification.
Proper Recording	Merchandise receiving reports are matched with vendor invoices (Valuation, Completeness).	Examine vendor invoice copy for indication of agreement with receiving report.
	Purchase orders are prenumbered (Completeness).	Account for numerical sequence of purchase orders.
	Shipping or transfer reports are prenumbered (Completeness).	Account for numerical sequence of reports.
	Movement of inventory items is accounted for on a timely basis by authorized requisitions (Timing, Completeness, Classification).	Compare dates recorded for shipping reports of transferor with receiving report and requisition data of receiving department.
	Clerical accuracy of vendor invoices is checked prior to payment (Valuation).	Examine invoice for indication of accuracy check.
Accountability and Comparison	Receiving department indicates inventory received on prenumbered receiving reports as to description and quantity.	Examine receiving reports.
	Perpetual inventory records maintained for large dollar value items.	Review inventory records. Discuss policy with management.
	Periodic comparison made between inventory records and physical inventory.	Review inventory records for indication of agreement with physical count.
Protection and Limited Access	Inventory is stored under the control of a custodian. Access is limited.	Observation. Discuss procedures with management and custodian.
	Inventory purchasers and handlers are bonded.	Review appropriate documentation of bonding.

Objective	Internal Control	Test of Controls
	Inventory records are maintained separate from the functions of shipping, receiving, and custody.	Observation.
	Physical safeguards against theft and fire exist.	Examine physical safeguards.
	Insurance coverage on inventory is adequate.	Review insurance policies.

4. Personnel and Payroll Cycle:

Objective	Internal Control	Test of Controls
Authorization	Employment is authorized before hiring.	Review hiring policies and verify the hiring authorization of a sample of employees.
	Payment rates (including commissions and bonuses) and hours to be worked are authorized at the appropriate levels.	Examine approval for rates or union contracts and approval for hours to be worked.
	Deduction authorizations are obtained for each payroll deduction.	Review personnel file for authorizations.
	Personnel department authorizes all changes to payroll master file.	Review change authorizations for a sample of changes made during the year.
	Authorized signature(s) is/are required on payroll checks.	Examine payroll checks for evidence of appropriate signature(s).
Validity	Time clock is used to record time worked by employees.	Observation.
	Department head or foreman approves and signs time cards.	Examine time cards for indication of approval.
	A paymaster (with no other payroll responsibilities) distributes payroll checks.	Observation. Discuss policy with management.
	Personnel department keeps personnel files on each employee.	Review personnel files.

Objective	Internal Control	Test of Controls
	Terminations are properly documented.	Review personnel files.
Proper Recording	Accounting procedures require recording payroll transactions as timely as possible (Timing).	Compare time card dates with recording date and paycheck dates for proper timing.
	Job time tickets are reconciled to time clock cards.	Examine job time tickets for indication of reconciliation and/or approval.
	An adequate chart of accounts is maintained including appropriate payroll accounts (Classification).	Review adequacy and use of proper accounts.
	Calculation and amounts of payroll are internally verified. (Completeness, Valuation).	Examine indication of internal verification.
	Account classification of payroll-related transactions is internally verified (Classification).	Review reconciliation of monthly payroll with labor distribution.
Accountability and Comparison	Independent reconciliation of bank statement for imprest payroll account.	Observation. Review reconciliation of bank statement.
	Unclaimed payroll checks are returned to a person responsible for their custody (e.g., internal audit).	Discuss policy with management. Observe distribution of paychecks. Inquire of client personnel.
	Accountability is established for unused and voided payroll account checks.	Discuss policy with management and personnel responsible for check accountability (Observation).
Protection and Limited Access	Separation of personnel, payroll, and timekeeping functions.	Observation. Discuss functions with management.
	Use of a separate imprest payroll account.	Review separate documentation such as bank statements.
	Payroll checks are prenumbered.	Account for numerical sequence of payroll checks.
	Treasurer signs payroll checks.	Observation. Examine canceled payroll checks.

5. Property, Plant, and Equipment Cycle:

Objective	Internal Control	Test of Controls
Authorization	Authorization is required for all purchases over a certain amount.	Discuss policy with management. Review documentation of a sample of large purchases for indication of approval.
Validity	Major purchases require authorization by the board of directors.	Examine documentation of major purchases for approval by board. Review minutes of board meetings.
	Movements or sales of equipment have prior approval.	Examine appropriate documentation for existence of approval.
	Abandonments are reported to accounting department by foremen.	Discuss abandonment policy with management and foremen.
	Purchases are supported by appropriate authorizations, purchase order, receiving report, and vendor invoice.	Examine acquisition files for supporting documentation.
	Policies exist for classification of fixed assets, including a policy for expensing or capitalizing items (Classification).	Examine written policies. Vouch a selected sample of capitalized and expenses disbursements for compliance with policies.
	Policies exist for asset life estimations and depreciation tables used (Valuation, Timing).	Review written policies. Discuss with management. Vouch a sample of items for compliance with policies.
	Depreciation charges are recorded in subsidiary ledgers and amounts are internally verified periodically (Valuation, Completeness).	Examination subsidiary ledgers for appropriate depreciation charges and evidence of internal verification.
	Accounting procedures require timely recording of purchases and associated depreciation (Timing).	Compare receiving report dates, invoice dates, and recording dates for appropriate timing.
Accountability and Comparison	Subsidiary ledgers exist and are used.	Verify the existence of subsidiary ledgers and review entry detail for appropriateness.

Objective	Internal Control	Test of Controls
	The responsibility for small tools is assigned to individual foremen.	Review tool responsibility with management and foremen. Examine the internal verification of the existence of tools.
	Internal verification is performed to examine existence and condition of fixed assets on a periodic basis.	Discuss policy with internal audit. Examine records for indication of verification.
Protection and Limited Access	Equipment has identification numbers to protect against loss.	Examine assets for existence of identification numbers.
	Insurance coverage on property, plant, and equipment is adequate.	Review insurance policies for adequacy of coverage.
	Physical safeguards are available for protection of assets from fire and theft (e.g., fire extinguishers, burglar alarms, etc.).	Examine physical safeguards for adequacy.

XII. Communication of Internal Control Structure Related Matters Noted in an Audit (SAS 60, AU 325)

A. Audit Committee--Communication regarding internal control structure related matters should be directed to the audit committee. If the entity does not have an audit committee, the communication should be directed to individuals with a level of authority and responsibility equivalent to an audit committee such as the board of directors, the board of trustees, or others who may have engaged the auditor. It is then common for these reports to be made available to management.

B. Reportable Conditions--Reportable conditions are those matters that the auditor is required to report to the audit committee. They represent, in the auditor's judgment, significant deficiencies in the design or operation of the internal control structure which could adversely affect the entity's ability to record, process, summarize, and report financial data consistent with the assertions of management in the financial statements. The auditor may identify conditions that are not reportable but decide to communicate such matters for the benefit of management. These constructive suggestions are a desirable by-product of an audit.

C. Identifying Reportable Conditions--The auditor's objective in an audit is to form an opinion on the entity's financial statements. It is not the auditor's duty to search for reportable conditions unless the client has specifically requested that the auditor be alert to such matters. The auditor may notice reportable conditions as a consequence of performing audit procedures. In some cases, management may be aware of certain reportable conditions due to a conscious decision to accept the degree of risk associated with the condition as a result of a cost-benefit analysis. The auditor does not need to report such conditions, provided the audit committee has acknowledged its understanding and consideration of such deficiencies and the associated risks. However, changes in management, changes in the audit committee, or passage of time might make it appropriate and timely to report such matters.

D. Agreed-Upon Criteria--Clients may request the auditor to be alert to matters and to report conditions that go beyond those in a normal audit. The auditor is not precluded from reporting matters that are viewed to be of value to management in the absence of any specific request to do so. Agreed-upon arrangements between the auditor and the client to report conditions noted may include for example, the reporting of matters of less significance than would normally be reported.

E. Reporting Form and Content--Conditions determined by the auditor to be reportable or that are the result of an agreement with the client should be reported to the audit committee, preferably in writing. If the communication is oral, that fact should be documented in the workpapers.

1. Any report issued on reportable conditions should

   a. Indicate that the purpose of the audit was to report on the financial statements and not to provide assurance on the internal control structure.

   b. Include the definition of reportable conditions.

   c. State that the report is solely for the information and use of the audit committee, management, and others within the organization.

   d. Identify reportable conditions noted.

> Exhibit 2--Illustration of Report Encompassing the Above Requirements
>
> In planning and performing our audit of the financial statements of the ABC Corporation for the year ended December 31, 19XX, we considered its internal control structure in order to determine our auditing procedures for the purpose of expressing our opinion on the financial statements and not to provide assurance on the internal control structure. However, we noted certain matters involving the internal control structure and its operation that we consider to be reportable conditions under standards established by the American Institute of Certified Public Accountants. Reportable conditions involve matters coming to our attention relating to significant deficiencies in the design or operation of the internal control structure that, in our judgment, could adversely affect the organization's ability to record, process, summarize, and report financial data consistent with the assertions of management in the financial statements.
>
> [Include paragraph(s) to describe the reportable conditions noted.]
>
> This report is intended solely for the information and use of the audit committee (board of directors, board of trustees, or owners in owner-managed enterprises), management, and others within the organization (or specified regulatory agency or other specified third party).

2. In some instances, the auditor may decide to include statements regarding inherent limitations of the internal control structure in general, and the specific extent and nature of the auditor's consideration of the internal control structure.

3. Because of the potential for misinterpretation of the limited degree of assurance associated with the auditor issuing a written report representing that no reportable conditions were noted during an audit, the auditor should not issue such representations.

4. Timely communication of reportable conditions may be important. The auditor may communicate significant matters during the course of an audit rather than at the conclusion based upon the relative significance of the matters and the urgency of corrective follow-up action.

F. Material Weaknesses--A material weakness is a reportable condition in which the design or operation of the specific internal control structure elements does not reduce to a relatively low level the risk that errors or irregularities in amounts that would be material in relation to the financial statements may occur and not be detected within a timely period by employees in the normal course of performing their assigned functions. The auditor is not required to separately identify material weaknesses from reportable conditions but the auditor may choose to do so or the client may request that it be done.

XIII. Foreign Corrupt Practices Act of 1977

A. Antibribery Provisions--The Act makes it illegal for any U.S. business engaged in interstate commerce to offer a bribe to a foreign official.

- Penalties--Companies are subject to a fine of up to $1,000,000, while individuals are subject to a maximum fine of $10,000 and/or up to 5 years imprisonment.

B. Recordkeeping and Internal Control--The Act requires entities to maintain books, records, and accounts which accurately reflect the transactions and dispositions of the assets of the entity. Entities must also maintain a system of accounting control sufficient to provide reasonable assurance that (1) transactions are executed in accordance with management's authorization, (2) transactions are properly recorded in conformity with GAAP, (3) access to assets is restricted only to those authorized by management, and (4) the recorded accountability for assets is periodically compared to, and reconciled with, the existing assets.

C. Reporting--The Act does not require the auditor to issue a special report on internal control.

PART TWO: INTERNAL CONTROL STRUCTURE QUESTIONNAIRE

On past CPA Exams, candidates have been asked to prepare various segments of an internal control questionnaire in the essay section, or answer multiple choice questions identifying audit procedures that most effectively provide audit evidence of internal control policies and procedures. We will structure this section as the actual questionnaire would appear, starting with the objectives of an internal control structure accompanied by the questions which identify controls to meet the objectives. Questions should generally be worded to require a yes or no answer. It is not necessary that you memorize this information, but you should be familiar with the thought processes involved.

I. Control Environment

Objective--Responsibilities are defined and authority is assigned to specific individuals to permit identification of whether persons are acting within the scope of their authority.

A. Management Philosophy and Operating Style

1. Does management have clear objectives in terms of budget, profit, and other financial and operating goals?

2. Are policies:

   a. Clearly written?

   b. Communicated throughout the entity?

   c. Actively monitored?

3. Does management adequately consider the effects of taking business risks?

B. Organizational Structure

1. Is the organization of the entity clearly defined in terms of lines of authority and responsibility?

2. Does the entity have a current organization chart?

3. Are policies and procedures for authorization of transactions established at adequately high levels?

C. Audit Committee

1. Does the board of directors have an audit committee?

2. Does the audit committee take an active role in overseeing the entity's accounting and financial reporting policies and practices?

3. Does the audit committee:

a. Hold regular meetings?

b. Appoint members with adequate qualifications?

c. Adequately assist the board in meeting its fiduciary responsibilities?

d. Assist the board in maintaining a direct line of communication with the internal and external auditors?

D. Methods of Assigning Authority and Responsibility

1. Does the entity have code of conduct and conflict of interest requirements?

2. Are employees given job descriptions which delineate specific duties, reporting relationships, and constraints?

3. Has the entity developed computer systems documentation which indicates procedures for authorizing transactions and approving systems changes?

E. Management Control Methods

1. Are there regular meetings of the board of directors and are minutes of such meetings prepared on a timely basis?

2. Does the entity have in place planning and reporting systems that:

a. Identify variances from planned performance?

b. Communicate variances to the appropriate management level?

c. Adequately investigate variances?

d. Allow management to take appropriate and timely corrective action?

3. Has the company established a records retention policy and made arrangements for the storage of the information?

F. Internal Audit Function

1. Does the entity have an internal audit function?

2. If the entity has an internal audit function:

   a. Is the internal auditor independent of the activities he or she audits?

   b. Is the internal audit function adequately staffed?

   c. Does the internal auditor document the control structure and perform tests of controls?

   d. Does the internal auditor perform substantive tests of the details of transactions and account balances?

   e. Does the internal auditor document the planning and execution of his or her work?

   f. Does the internal auditor render written reports on his or her findings and conclusions?

   g. Are the internal auditor's reports submitted to the board or to a similar committee?

3. Does management take timely action to correct conditions reported by the internal auditor?

G. Personnel Policies and Procedures

1. Are employees adequately trained?

2. Is performance systematically evaluated?

3. Does the entity dismiss employees on a timely basis for critical violations of control policies?

4. Are employees in positions of trust bonded?

5. Are employees required to take mandatory vacations?

6. Is access to records limited to authorized persons?

II. Accounting System

Objectives--Accounting policies and procedures are determined in accordance with management's authorization.

- Access to the accounting and financial records is limited to minimize opportunity for errors and irregularities and provide reasonable protection from physical hazards.
- Accounting entries are initiated and approved in accordance with management's authorization.
- Accounting entries are appropriately accumulated, classified, and summarized.
- The general ledger and related records permit preparation of financial statements in conformity with GAAP.
- Financial statements with related disclosures are prepared and released in accordance with management's authorization.
- Individuals at appropriate levels consider reliable information in making estimates and judgments required for preparation of the financial statements and related disclosures.

A. General Accounting

1. Does the entity have adequate written statements and explanations of its accounting policies and procedures, such as:

   a. Chart of accounts?

   b. Assignment of responsibilities and delegation of authority?

   c. Explanations of documentation and approval requirements for various types of transactions and journal entries?

2. Is access to the general ledger and related records restricted to those who are assigned general ledger responsibilities?

3. Is appropriate insurance coverage maintained (such as loss of records coverage and fidelity bonding of employees in positions of trust) in accordance with management's authorization?

4. Are all journal entries reviewed and approved?

5. Are all journal entries explained and supported?

6. Are individuals who review and approve journal entries independent of initiation of the entries they are authorized to approve?

B. Preparation of Financial Statements

1. Are the general ledger accounts arranged in orderly groupings which are conducive to efficient statement preparation?

2. Are there adequate instructions and procedures for :

   a. Assignment of specific preparation and review responsibilities?

   b. Accumulation of information on intercompany transactions?

   c. Accumulation of information for footnote disclosure?

3. Are estimates and adjustments to provide valuation allowances reviewed and approved by appropriate levels in the organization independent of the persons originating the estimates and adjustments?

4. Are procedures adequate for the review and comparison of working papers to source data and comparison of elimination and reclassification entries to those made in prior periods?

5. Are financial statements subjected to overall review and comparisons with the prior period and budgeted amounts by appropriate levels of management?

III. Transaction Cycles

Several internal control policies and procedures are common to most, if not all, transaction cycles. Listed in the Appendix at the end of this chapter are general internal control questions that can be asked for most of the transaction cycles indicated. These questions are presented in this format to help you become familiar with the general questions. Specific internal control questions applicable to the individual transaction cycles are included under the transaction cycle titles in the Appendix of this chapter.

A. Revenues and Receivables

Objectives--The types of goods and services provided, the manner in which they will be provided, and the customers to which they will be provided are in accordance with management's authorization.

- The prices and other terms of sales are established in accordance with management's authorization.
- Credit terms and limits are established.
- Goods delivered and services provided are based on orders which have been approved.
- Deliveries of goods and services result in preparation of accurate and timely billings.
- Sales related deductions and adjustments are made in accordance with management's authorization.

1. Are sales orders approved before shipment?

2. Do approved sales orders record the terms of sales in detail?

3. Are unfilled sales commitments periodically reviewed?

4. Is current information on prices, discounts, sales taxes, freight, warranties, and returned goods clearly communicated to the sales and billing personnel (i.e. approved sales catalogs, manuals, and price lists)?

5. Is the credit of prospective customers investigated before it is extended to them?

6. Is there a periodic review of credit limits?

7. Are shipping documents prepared for all shipments?

8. Are goods shipped based on documented sales orders which have been approved?

9. Are shipping documents subjected to:

   a. Timely communication to persons who physically perform the shipping function?

   b. Timely communication to persons who perform the billing function?

10. Are quantities of goods shipped verified, by double counting or comparison with counts by common carriers?

11. Are shipping documents compared with billings to determine that all goods shipped are billed and accounted for?

12. Are sales invoices prepared for all shipments of goods?

13. Are sales invoices:

   a. Matched with approved sales orders?

   b. Matched with shipping documents?

14. Are credit memos:

   a. Pre-numbered and accounted for?

   b. Matched with applicable receiving reports for returns?

c. Approved by a responsible employee independent of the person preparing the credit memo?

15. Are monthly statements reviewed and mailed by a responsible employee who is independent of the accounts receivable and cash functions?

16. Is an aging schedule of past due accounts prepared monthly?

17. Is there documentation of review and analysis of accounts receivable balances for determining valuation allowances and any specific balances to be written-off?

18. Are valuation allowances and write-offs approved?

B. <u>Cash Receipts</u>

Objectives--Access to cash receipts records, accounts receivable records, and billing and shipping records is controlled to prevent the taking of unrecorded cash receipts or abstraction of recorded cash receipts.

- Detailed transaction and account balance records are reconciled with control accounts and bank statements at least monthly for the timely detection and correction of errors.
- All cash receipts are recorded at the correct amounts in the period in which received and are properly classified and summarized.

1. Does the person who opens the mail:

   a. Place restrictive endorsements on all checks received so they are for deposit only?

   b. List all remittances and prepare totals daily?

   c. Forward all remittances to the person who prepares and makes a daily bank deposit?

2. Are currency receipts forwarded daily to the person who prepares the daily bank deposit?

3. Is a summary listing of daily currency receipts forwarded to a person independent of physical handling of remittances and accounts receivable?

4. Are each day's receipts deposited intact daily?

5. Are all employees who handle receipts adequately bonded?

6. Does company policy prohibit the cashing of any accommodation checks (payroll, personal) out of collections?

7. Are bank chargebacks received directly from the bank and investigated by a person independent of the physical handling of collections and posting of accounts receivable subsidiary ledgers?

8. Are entries to the cash receipts journal compared with:

   a. Duplicate deposit slips authenticated by the bank?

   b. Deposits per the bank statement?

   c. Listings prepared when the mail is opened?

9. Is information from remittance documentation adequate for the accurate posting of credits to individual accounts receivable subsidiary records or accounts such as investment income, rents, and sales of property?

10. Are details of collections posted to subsidiary accounts receivable records by a person independent of the general ledger functions, physical handling of collections, and receipt and investigation of bank chargebacks?

C. Purchases and Accounts Payable

Objectives--The types of goods and services to be obtained, the manner in which they are obtained, the vendors from which they are obtained, the quantities to be obtained, and the prices and terms initiated and executed are in accordance with management's authorization.

- Adjustments to vendor accounts and account distributions are made in accordance with management's authorization.
- All goods and services received are accurately accounted for on a timely basis.
- Only authorized goods and services are accepted and paid for.
- Amounts payable for goods and services received are accurately recorded at the correct amounts in the appropriate period and properly classified.
- Access to purchasing, receiving, and accounts payable records is controlled to prevent or detect duplicate or improper payments.

1. Are written purchase orders used for all commitments and do those orders include the vendor description, quantity, quality, price, terms, and delivery requirements for the goods or services ordered?

2. Is there a record of open purchase commitments?

3. Are open purchase orders periodically reviewed and investigated?

4. Are goods received inspected for condition and independently counted, for comparison with the applicable purchase order?

5. Are receiving reports prepared promptly for all goods received?

6. Do receiving reports provide for recording of:

   a. Description, quantity, and acceptability of goods?

   b. Date on which the goods or services are received?

   c. Signature of the individual approving the receipt?

7. Are receiving reports subjected to the following:

   a. Accounting for all receiving reports used?

   b. Copies distributed for timely matching with purchase orders and vendor invoices?

8. Is control established over all invoices received?

9. Are duplicate invoices stamped or destroyed as a precaution against duplicate payment?

10. Are vendors' invoices, prior to payment, compared in detail to purchase orders and receiving reports?

11. Are all available discounts taken?

12. Are there procedures for periodic review and investigation of unprocessed invoices, unmatched purchase orders and receiving reports to provide for follow-up and proper accruals and to result in a proper cutoff for financial reporting purposes?

13. Are vendors' statements reviewed for, and proper follow-up made of, overdue items?

D. Payroll

Objectives--Employees are hired and retained only at rates and benefits determined by management's authorization.

- Payroll withholdings and deductions are based on evidence of appropriate authorization.
- Compensation is made only to company employees at authorized rates and for services rendered.
- Gross pay, withholdings, deductions, and net pay are correctly computed using authorized rates and properly authorized withholding exemptions and deductions.
- Payroll costs and related liabilities are correctly accumulated, classified, and summarized in the accounts in the proper period.
- Comparisons are made of personnel, payroll, and work records at reasonable intervals for timely detection and correction of errors.
- Net pay and related withholdings and deductions are remitted to the appropriate employees when due.
- Functions are assigned so that no single individual is in a position to both perpetrate and conceal errors and irregularities in the normal course of their duties.
- Access to personnel and payroll records is limited.

1. Are all new hires, rates of pay and changes thereto, changes in position, and terminations based on written authorizations by management's criteria?

2. Are appropriate written authorizations obtained from employees for all payroll deductions and withholding exemptions?

3. Are personnel files maintained on individual employees which include appropriate written authorizations for rates of pay, payroll deductions, and withholding exemptions?

4. Are methods for determining premium pay rates for matters such as overtime, night shift work, and employee benefits determined in accordance with management's authorizations?

5. Do employees who perform the payroll processing function receive timely notification of wage and salary rate changes, new hires, changes in position, terminations, and changes in authorized deductions and withholding exemptions?

6. Is there an adequate chart of accounts for determining account distributions for wages and related taxes and controlling liabilities for payroll deductions and taxes withheld?

7. Are clerical operations in the preparation of payrolls verified by re-performance or reconciliation with independent controls over source data?

8. Are piece rate records reconciled with production records, or salesmen's commission records reconciled with recorded sales, or total production hours reconciled with production statistics?

9. Are payroll checks drawn on a separate imprest account, and are deposits equal to the amount of net pay?

10. Is responsibility for custody and follow-up of unclaimed wages assigned to a responsible person independent of personnel, payroll processing, and cash disbursement functions?

11. Are procedures adequate to result in timely and accurate preparation and filing of payroll tax returns and payment of accumulated withholdings and related accrued taxes?

12. Are personnel and payroll records reasonably safeguarded (locked file cabinets, work areas with limited access)?

E. Cash Disbursements

Objectives--Functions are assigned so that no single individual is in a position to both perpetrate and conceal errors or irregularities in the normal course of their duties.

- Disbursements are made only for expenditures incurred in accordance with management's authorization.
- Adjustments to cash accounts are made only in accordance with management's authorizations.
- Disbursements are recorded at correct amounts in the appropriate period and are properly classified in the accounts.
- Access to cash and disbursement records is restricted to minimize opportunities for irregular or erroneous disbursements.
- Comparison of detail records, control accounts, and bank statements are made at reasonable intervals for detection and appropriate disposition of errors or irregularities.

1. Are bank accounts and check signers authorized by the board of directors?

2. Are approved supporting documents presented with the checks to the check signer?

3. Is a mechanical check protector used to inscribe amounts on checks to protect against alteration?

4. Are supporting documents for checks canceled to avoid reuse?

5. Are signed checks independently mailed directly after signing without being returned to persons involved in the invoice processing and check preparation functions?

6. Are all voided checks retained and mutilated?

7. Are there written policies which prohibit making checks payable to cash or bearer, and signing blank checks?

8. Are dual signatures required for large disbursements, and are the signers independent of one another?

9. If a check-signing machine is used, are the keys, signature plate, and operation of the signing machine under control at all times of the official whose signature is on the plate? Are employees who have custody of them independent of voucher and check preparation functions, and are they denied access to blank checks?

10. If cash funds are maintained on the premises, they should be kept on an imprest basis and:

    a. Are they kept in a safe place?

    b. Reasonable in amount?

    c. Controlled by one custodian?

d. Are disbursements supported by vouchers?

e. Are vouchers approved with management's authorization?

f. Are cash funds on a surprise basis counted by someone other than the custodian?

g. Is the custodian independent of cash receipts?

h. Does the custodian have no access to accounting records?

i. Are reimbursements of the cash fund remitted by checks made payable to the order of the custodian?

11. Are old outstanding checks investigated, controlled, and their proper disposition arranged?

F. Inventory and Cost of Sales

Objectives--All production activity and accounting therefor is determined in accordance with management's general or specific authorizations.

- Resources obtained and used in the production process and completed results are accurately recorded on a timely basis.
- Transfer of finished products to customers and other dispositions such as sales of scrap are accurately recorded.
- Inventory, production costs, and costs of sales are accumulated and classified in the accounts to maintain accountability for costs and permit preparation of statements in conformity with GAAP.
- Inventory is protected from unauthorized use or removal.
- Recorded balances of inventory are substantiated and evaluated at reasonable intervals by comparison with quantities on hand.

1. Are production goals and schedules based on accompanying sales forecasts?

2. Are methods and materials to be used based upon product engineering plans and specifications?

3. Does the company have budgeted inventory levels and predetermined reorder points authorized by management?

4. Does the company have policies for identification and disposition of excess or obsolete inventory?

5. Are all adjustments to inventory and cost of sales made in accordance with management's authorizations?

6. Are all dispositions of obsolete or excess inventory approved?

7. Does the chart of accounts provide adequate general ledger control accounts and subsidiary detail for the accumulation and classification of costs of materials, direct labor, and overhead?

8. Is access to the detailed inventory records and control accounts limited to persons responsible for their maintenance, oversight, and internal audit?

9. Are there physical safeguards against theft, fire, and flooding?

10. Is insurance coverage of the inventory maintained and reviewed periodically for adequacy?

11. Do detailed written inventory procedures and instructions exist which have been approved and are they adequately communicated to the persons who perform the physical counts?

12. Are inventory physical counts performed by persons whose duties do not include the physical custody and detailed record keeping of inventory or maintenance of control accounts?

13. Are differences in physical counts and detailed records investigated?

14. Are adjustments of the inventory detail records and control accounts given prior approval by management?

15. Are dispositions of obsolete or excess inventories made in accordance with criteria authorized by management?

G. Property and Equipment

Objectives--Additions and related accumulation of depreciation retirements, and dispositions of property and equipment are made in accordance with management's authorization.

- Transactions involving property and equipment and depreciation are accurately recorded, accumulated, and classified in detail and in control accounts to maintain accountability for the assets.
- Property and equipment is reasonably safeguarded from loss.

1. Are work order forms approved by management for property additions?

2. Are contracts and agreements signed by individuals in accordance with appropriately documented designation by the board of directors?

3. Are detailed records maintained for property and equipment indicating: a description of the assets, their location, cost, acquisition date, date of service, depreciable life and method of depreciation used?

4. Is property and equipment insured and coverage reviewed periodically for additions, disposals, and adequacy?

5. Is there a written capitalization/expense policy for property and equipment purchases?

H. Stockholders' Equity and Capital Accounts

Objectives--Capital transactions are authorized and approved in conformity with the entity's governing document (corporate charter, partnership agreement).

- Transactions and obligations are promptly and accurately recorded.
- Access to records, agreements, and negotiable documents is permitted only in accordance with management's authorization.
- Records, agreements, and documents are subjected to adequate physical safeguards and custodial procedures.
- Dividends are disbursed accurately and in conformity with decisions of the board of directors.

1. Are authorizations and approvals for specific capital transactions appropriately recorded?

2. Are two officials authorized by the board required to sign and countersign stock certificates?

3. Are all stock certificates prepared and approved before issuance within management's authorization?

4. Are appropriate control records maintained for each class of stock on information such as number of shares authorized, issued and outstanding, and the number of shares subject to options, warrants, and conversion privileges?

5. Are timely detailed records maintained on specific stock certificates issued and outstanding for each class of capital stock and the identity of holders of record and the number of shares for each certificate?

6. Are detailed stock certificate records reconciled at reasonable intervals with the control records and the general ledger?

7. Are reconciliations of detailed records with the control records and general ledger performed by persons independent of custody of unissued stock certificates, maintenance of the detailed records, and cash functions?

8. Are unissued stock certificates, reacquired certificates and detailed stockholder records subject to reasonable physical safeguards?

9. Are stock certificates pre-numbered so that all certificates (unissued, issued, and retired) may be accounted for?

10. Are retired stock certificates examined for proper endorsement and effectively canceled by a person whose duties do not include maintenance of the detailed stockholder records?

11. Are treasury stock certificates registered in the name of the company and recorded to be readily distinguished from other outstanding shares?

12. Are dividends declared recorded in the minutes of the board of directors meetings?

13. Do procedures result in an accurate cutoff and accurate listing of stockholders as of the record date?

14. Are total dividends disbursed reconciled to total outstanding shares as of the record date?

NOTES

[APPENDIX: GENERAL INTERNAL CONTROL QUESTIONS
can be found on the following page.]

APPENDIX: GENERAL INTERNAL CONTROL QUESTIONS

General Control Questions	Cash Receipts	Cash Disbursements	Payroll
1. Are forms used which are prenumbered?	Prenumbered Receipts, Cash Register tapes by date	Prenumbered Checks	Prenumbered Payroll Checks
2. Is adequate control maintained of unissued forms to prevent misuse?	Unused Blank Receipts Controlled	Unused Blank Checks Controlled	Unused Blank Payroll Checks Controlled
3. Are policies and procedures in place for the authorization of transactions?	Remittance listing prepared by designated mail opener.	Check signers authorized by board of directors. Authorization for bank accounts to be maintained.	Payroll approved in writing by responsible employee prior to issuance of paychecks.
4. Is approval of transaction obtained prior to processing?	Comparison of remittance listing and validated deposit slip before processing.	Invoice matched to approved receiving report and approved purchase order. Disbursements and bank transfers approved.	Supervisor reviews and approves time cards.
5. Is a proper segregation of duties maintained to reduce potential errors and irregularities?	Employee responsible for preparing remittance lists independent of billing, cash disbursement, and general ledger functions. Employee making deposit independent of cash disbursement, billing, and general ledger functions.	Employee performing bank reconciliation independent of invoice processing, cash disbursements, cash receipts, petty cash, and general ledger functions.	Payroll checks signed by treasurer. Payroll checks distributed by person independent of personnel, payroll preparation, time-keeping, and check preparation.
6. Are all prenumbered forms accounted for?	Detail Cash Receipts Journal	Outstanding check list maintained.	Payroll Journal, Outstanding check list maintained.
7. Is a detailed record of transactions maintained?	Cash Receipts Journal	Check Register, Cash Disbursements Journal	Payroll Journal
8. Are periodic (monthly, annual) reconciliations made between source documents, quantities on hand, subsidiary ledgers, and the general ledger?	Trace cash receipts journal total to bank statement and/or validated deposit slips.	Bank reconciliations, Cash Disbursements Journal reconciled to general ledger.	Time card hours reconciled to job time tickets.
9. Is access to assets and/or accounting records limited?	Mail received by same person daily who is independent of cash, billings, general ledger and shipping functions.	Bank statement received directly by person who will reconcile.	Payroll records and Personnel files kept in locked file cabinets.
10. Are transactions and source documents checked for clerical accuracy?	Remittance list footed and agreed to validated deposit slip.	Checks compared to approved invoice and supporting documents before signing. Discounts, if available, have been taken.	Time card totals checked by supervisor.
11. Is there a proper cut-off of transactions for accurate reporting?	Bank reconciliations are prepared and approved on a timely basis.	Bank reconciliations are prepared and approved on a timely basis.	Bank reconciliations are prepared and approved on a timely basis.

Inventory	Cost of Sales	Fixed Assets	Accounts Receivable	Accounts Payable
Prenumbered: Shipping Documents, Purchase Orders, Receiving Reports	Prenumbered Inventory Requisitions	Prenumbered Purchase Orders	Prenumbered Invoices	Prenumbered Vouchers
Unused Purchase Orders, Receiving Reports, Shipping Documents controlled.	Unused Inventory Requisitions controlled.	Unused Purchased Orders Controlled	Unused Invoices Controlled	Unused Vouchers Controlled
Purchases made in accordance with vendor acceptability. Customer Acceptance/Terms of Sale, credit clearance all pre-established.	Pre-established overhead rates, requisition processing controls	Additions/Retirements have authorization in Board of Directors meeting minutes.	Invoices prepared from approved shipping reports and matching vendor purchase orders.	Authorization by Board of Directors for large purchases (contracts).
Approved purchase order, Approved inventory requisitions, sales orders approved before shipment	Inventory requisitions, overhead rate changes and personnel rate changes are properly approved.	Approval of additions and retirements in writing; Board minutes, manager approval.	Approval noted on invoice.	Invoices and supporting documents approved before payment.
Credit, Sales, Shipping, Billing, Collections, receiving, and general accounting all independent of one another.	Authority to approve inventory requisitions assigned to employees independent of physical custody, and maintenance of inventory records and inventory control accounts.	Responsibility for physical custody assigned to employees independent of maintaining detailed property records and general ledger functions.	Individual responsible for accounts receivable function is independent of cash and general ledger functions.	Vendors' invoices processed by employee independent of purchasing, receiving, shipping, and cash functions.
Purchase Orders, Shipping Documents, Receiving Reports	Work Orders, Inventory Requisitions	Physical asset identification plates numbered consecutively	Numbered sales invoices properly filed.	Numbered vouchers and Purchase Orders maintained in open, pending, or paid files.
Shipment Log, Receiving Log, Purchases Journal	Work-in-Process and Finished Goods journals	Detailed listing of fixed assets maintained	Sales Invoice Register	Purchases Journal and Accounts Payable Subsidiary Ledger maintained
Inventory physically counted annually. Inventory detail records and control accounts reconciled to physical count. Perpetual records reconciled to general ledger and physical counts.	Cost accounting system reconciled to general ledger.	Detailed records of assets compared to actual property and equipment on hand, and reconciled to general ledger.	Accounts receivable subsidiary ledger reconciled to general ledger control account.	Accounts payable subsidiary ledger reconciled with general ledger control account.
Finished goods and merchandise are restricted so that withdrawals are based on approved sales orders.	Releases from storage of raw materials and supplies based upon approved requisitions.	Physical controls such as fences, burglar alarms, fire alarms, security guards, and requisitioning procedures for the use of portable equipment.	Passwords used on computer system limiting data entry to designated individuals.	Passwords used on computer system limiting data entry to designated individuals.
Receiving Reports, Shipping Documents, Purchase Orders	Inventory Requisitions checked	Invoices compared to approved purchase order and totals including taxes and freight are checked for reasonableness.	Sales Invoices	Vendors' Invoices
Inventory received included, goods on consignment included, goods sold but not shipped excluded from inventory totals.	See Inventory	Cash receipts and disbursements checked and compared to bank reconciliation for cut-off.	Shipping documents and related billings compared for proper cut-off.	Receiving reports or service dates and vendor invoices compared prior to recording.

NOTES

CHAPTER 36—INTERNAL CONTROL

Problem 36-1 MULTIPLE CHOICE QUESTIONS (105 to 130 minutes)

1. The ultimate purpose of assessing control risk is to contribute to the auditor's evaluation of the
   a. Factors that raise doubts about the auditability of the financial statements.
   b. Operating effectiveness of internal control policies and procedures.
   c. Risk that material misstatements exist in the financial statements.
   d. Possibility that the nature and extent of substantive tests may be reduced.

(5/93, Aud., #7, 3903)

1A. The primary objective of procedures performed to obtain an understanding of the internal control structure is to provide an auditor with
   a. Knowledge necessary for audit planning.
   b. Evidential matter to use in assessing inherent risk.
   c. A basis for modifying tests of controls.
   d. An evaluation of the consistency of application of management's policies.

(5/95, Aud., #24, 5642)

2. When an auditor assesses control risk below the maximum level, the auditor is required to document the auditor's

	Basis for concluding that control risk is below the maximum level	Understanding of the entity's internal control structure elements
a.	No	No
b.	Yes	Yes
c.	Yes	No
d.	No	Yes

(5/93, Aud., #9, 3905)

2A. Management's attitude toward aggressive financial reporting and its emphasis on meeting projected profit goals most likely would significantly influence an entity's control environment when
   a. The audit committee is active in overseeing the entity's financial reporting policies.
   b. External policies established by parties outside the entity affect its accounting practices.
   c. Management is dominated by one individual who is also a shareholder.
   d. Internal auditors have direct access to the board of directors and entity management.

(5/94, Aud., #19, 4684)

2B. The overall attitude and awareness of an entity's board of directors concerning the importance of the internal control structure usually is reflected in its
   a. Computer-based controls.
   b. System of segregation of duties.
   c. Control environment.
   d. Safeguards over access to assets.

(5/95, Aud., #25, 5643)

2C. When an auditor assesses control risk at the maximum level, the auditor is required to document the auditor's

	Understanding of the entity's accounting system	Basis for concluding that control risk is at the maximum level
a.	No	No
b.	No	Yes
c.	Yes	No
d.	Yes	Yes

(5/95, Aud., #29, 5647)

3. In obtaining an understanding of an entity's internal control structure, an auditor is required to obtain knowledge about the

	Operating effectiveness of policies and procedures	Design of policies and procedures
a.	Yes	Yes
b.	No	Yes
c.	Yes	No
d.	No	No

(5/93, Aud., #12, 3908)

4. Assessing control risk at below the maximum most likely would involve
   a. Changing the timing of substantive tests by omitting interim-date testing and performing the tests at year end.
   b. Identifying specific internal control structure policies and procedures relevant to specific assertions.
   c. Performing more extensive substantive tests with larger sample sizes than originally planned.
   d. Reducing inherent risk for most of the assertions relevant to significant account balances.

(5/93, Aud., #13, 3909)

4A. An auditor should obtain sufficient knowledge of an entity's accounting system to understand the
a. Safeguards used to limit access to computer facilities.
b. Process used to prepare significant accounting estimates.
c. Procedures used to assure proper authorization of transactions.
d. Policies used to detect the concealment of irregularities. (5/94, Aud., #20, 4685)

5. Which of the following is **not** an element of an entity's internal control structure?
a. Control risk.
b. Control procedures.
c. The accounting system.
d. The control environment.
(5/89, Aud., #11, 0086)

5A. When obtaining an understanding of an entity's internal control procedures, an auditor should concentrate on the substance of the procedures rather than their form because
a. The procedures may be operating effectively but may **not** be documented.
b. Management may establish appropriate procedures but **not** enforce compliance with them.
c. The procedures may be so inappropriate that **no** reliance is contemplated by the auditor.
d. Management may implement procedures whose costs exceed their benefits.
(5/94, Aud., #21, 4686)

6. Which of the following most likely would **not** be considered an inherent limitation of the potential effectiveness of an entity's internal control structure?
a. Incompatible duties.
b. Management override.
c. Mistakes in judgment.
d. Collusion among employees.
(5/94, Aud., #22, 4687)

6A. Regardless of the assessed level of control risk, an auditor would perform some
a. Tests of controls to determine the effectiveness of internal control policies.
b. Analytical procedures to verify the design of internal control procedures.
c. Substantive tests to restrict detection risk for significant transaction classes.
d. Dual-purpose tests to evaluate both the risk of monetary misstatement and preliminary control risk. (11/93, Aud., #23, 4260)

7. After obtaining an understanding of an entity's internal control structure and assessing control risk, an auditor may next
a. Perform tests of controls to verify management's assertions that are embodied in the financial statements.
b. Consider whether evidential matter is available to support a further reduction in the assessed level of control risk.
c. Apply analytical procedures as substantive tests to validate the assessed level of control risk.
d. Evaluate whether the internal control structure policies and procedures detected material misstatements in the financial statements.
(11/89, Aud., #40, 0077)

7A. After obtaining an understanding of the internal control structure and assessing control risk, an auditor decided to perform tests of controls. The auditor most likely decided that
a. It would be efficient to perform tests of controls that would result in a reduction in planned substantive tests.
b. Additional evidence to support a further reduction in control risk is **not** available.
c. An increase in the assessed level of control risk is justified for certain financial statement assertions.
d. There were many internal control structure weaknesses that could allow errors to enter the accounting system. (5/95, Aud., #33, 5651)

7B. An auditor may decide to assess control risk at the maximum level for certain assertions because the auditor believes
a. Control policies and procedures are unlikely to pertain to the assertions.
b. The entity's control environment, accounting system, and control procedures are interrelated.
c. Sufficient evidential matter to support the assertions is likely to be available.
d. More emphasis on tests of controls than substantive tests is warranted.
(11/93, Aud., #21, 4258)

8. An auditor uses the knowledge provided by the understanding of the internal control structure and the final assessed level of control risk primarily to determine the nature, timing, and extent of the
a. Attribute tests.
b. Compliance tests.
c. Tests of controls.
d. Substantive tests. (11/90, Aud., #42, 0054)

8A. An auditor uses the assessed level of control risk to

a. Evaluate the effectiveness of the entity's internal control policies and procedures.
b. Identify transactions and account balances where inherent risk is at the maximum.
c. Indicate whether materiality thresholds for planning and evaluation purposes are sufficiently high.
d. Determine the acceptable level of detection risk for financial statement assertions.

(5/94, Aud., #24, 4689)

8B. Which of the following statements concerning control risk is correct?

a. Assessing control risk and obtaining an understanding of an entity's internal control structure may be performed concurrently.
b. When control risk is at the maximum level, an auditor is required to document the basis for that assessment.
c. Control risk may be assessed sufficiently low to eliminate substantive testing for significant transaction classes.
d. When assessing control risk an auditor should **not** consider evidence obtained in prior audits about the operation of control procedures.

(11/93, Aud., #22, 4259)

9. An auditor would most likely be concerned with internal control structure policies and procedures that provide reasonable assurance about the

a. Efficiency of management's decision-making process.
b. Appropriate prices the entity should charge for its products.
c. Methods of assigning production tasks to employees.
d. Entity's ability to process and summarize financial data. (11/91, Aud., #35, 2303)

10. An auditor's primary consideration regarding an entity's internal control structure policies and procedures is whether the policies and procedures

a. Affect the financial statement assertions.
b. Prevent management override.
c. Relate to the control environment.
d. Reflect management's philosophy and operating style. (11/92, Aud., #9, 2943)

10A. In an audit of financial statements, an auditor's primary consideration regarding an internal control policy or procedure is whether the policy or procedure

a. Reflects management's philosophy and operating style.
b. Affects management's financial statement assertions.
c. Provides adequate safeguards over access to assets.
d. Enhances management's decision-making processes. (11/94, Aud., #28, 5101)

11. Which of the following factors are included in an entity's control environment?

	Audit committee	Internal audit function	Organizational structure
a.	Yes	Yes	No
b.	Yes	No	Yes
c.	No	Yes	Yes
d.	Yes	Yes	Yes

(5/91, Aud., #25, 0043)

11A. Which of the following are considered control environment factors?

	Detection risk	Personnel policies and practices
a.	Yes	Yes
b.	Yes	No
c.	No	Yes
d.	No	No

(11/94, Aud., #29, 5102)

12. When considering the internal control structure, an auditor should be aware of the concept of reasonable assurance, which recognizes that

a. Procedures requiring segregation of duties may be circumvented by employee collusion and management override.
b. Establishing and maintaining the internal control structure is an important responsibility of management.
c. The cost of an entity's internal control structure should **not** exceed the benefits expected to be derived.
d. Adequate safeguards over access to assets and records should permit an entity to maintain proper accountability. (11/92, Aud., #7, 2941)

12A. When considering the internal control structure, an auditor should be aware of the concept of reasonable assurance, which recognizes that

a. Internal control policies and procedures may be ineffective due to mistakes in judgment and personal carelessness.
b. Adequate safeguards over access to assets and records should permit an entity to maintain proper accountability.

c. Establishing and maintaining the internal control structure is an important responsibility of management.
d. The cost of an entity's internal control structure should **not** exceed the benefits expected to be derived. (5/95, Aud., #26, 5644)

13. As part of understanding the internal control structure, an auditor is **not** required to
a. Consider factors that affect the risk of material misstatement.
b. Ascertain whether internal control structure policies and procedures have been placed in operation.
c. Identify the types of potential misstatements that can occur.
d. Obtain knowledge about the operating effectiveness of the internal control structure. (5/92, Aud., #40, 2793)

13A. In obtaining an understanding of an entity's internal control structure in a financial statement audit, an auditor is **not** obligated to
a. Determine whether the control procedures have been placed in operation.
b. Perform procedures to understand the design of the internal control structure policies.
c. Document the understanding of the entity's internal control structure elements.
d. Search for significant deficiencies in the operation of the internal control structure. (11/93, Aud., #19, 4256)

14. As a result of sampling procedures applied as tests of controls, an auditor incorrectly assesses control risk lower than appropriate. The most likely explanation for this situation is that
a. The deviation rates of both the auditor's sample and the population exceed the tolerable rate.
b. The deviation rates of both the auditor's sample and the population are less than the tolerable rate.
c. The deviation rate in the auditor's sample is less than the tolerable rate, but the deviation rate in the population exceeds the tolerable rate.
d. The deviation rate in the auditor's sample exceeds the tolerable rate, but the deviation rate in the population is less than the tolerable rate. (11/93, Aud., #20, 4257)

15. The primary objective of procedures performed to obtain an understanding of the internal control structure is to provide an auditor with
a. A basis for modifying tests of controls.
b. An evaluation of the consistency of application of management's policies.
c. Knowledge necessary for audit planning.
d. Evidential matter to use in assessing inherent risk. (5/92, Aud., #41, 2794)

16. In planning an audit of certain accounts, an auditor may conclude that specific procedures used to obtain an understanding of an entity's internal control structure need **not** be included because of the auditor's judgments about materiality and assessments of
a. Control risk.
b. Detection risk.
c. Sampling risk.
d. Inherent risk. (11/90, Aud., #44, 0056)

17. When obtaining an understanding of an entity's control environment, an auditor should concentrate on the substance of management's policies and procedures rather than their form because
a. The auditor may believe that the policies and procedures are inappropriate for that particular entity.
b. The board of directors may **not** be aware of management's attitude toward the control environment.
c. Management may establish appropriate policies and procedures but **not** act on them.
d. The policies and procedures may be so weak that **no** reliance is contemplated by the auditor. (11/89, Aud., #39, 0076)

18. In an audit of financial statements in accordance with generally accepted auditing standards, an auditor is required to
a. Perform tests of controls to evaluate the effectiveness of the entity's accounting system.
b. Determine whether control procedures are suitably designed to prevent or detect material misstatements.
c. Document the auditor's understanding of the entity's internal control structure.
d. Search for significant deficiencies in the operation of the internal control structure. (5/92, Aud., #43, 2796)

19. On the basis of audit evidence gathered and evaluated, an auditor decides to increase the assessed level of control risk from that originally planned. To achieve an overall audit risk level that is substantially the same as the planned audit risk level, the auditor would
a. Decrease substantive testing.
b. Decrease detection risk.
c. Increase inherent risk.
d. Increase materiality levels. (11/94, Aud., #10, 5083)

19A. The ultimate purpose of assessing control risk is to contribute to the auditor's evaluation of the risk that

a. Tests of controls may fail to identify procedures relevant to assertions.
b. Material misstatements may exist in the financial statements.
c. Specified controls requiring segregation of duties may be circumvented by collusion.
d. Entity policies may be overridden by senior management. (11/94, Aud., #30, 5103)

19B. Control risk should be assessed in terms of

a. Specific control procedures.
b. Types of potential irregularities.
c. Financial statement assertions.
d. Control environment factors.

(5/95, Aud., #27, 5645)

19C. Which of the following is a step in an auditor's decision to assess control risk at below the maximum?

a. Apply analytical procedures to both financial data and nonfinancial information to detect conditions that may indicate weak controls.
b. Perform tests of details of transactions and account balances to identify potential errors and irregularities.
c. Identify specific internal control policies and procedures that are likely to detect or prevent material misstatements.
d. Document that the additional audit effort to perform tests of controls exceeds the potential reduction in substantive testing.

(11/94, Aud., #32, 5105)

19D. The likelihood of assessing control risk too high is the risk that the sample selected to test controls

a. Does **not** support the auditor's planned assessed level of control risk when the true operating effectiveness of the control structure justifies such an assessment.
b. Contains misstatements that could be material to the financial statements when aggregated with misstatements in other account balances or transactions classes.
c. Contains proportionately fewer monetary errors or deviations from prescribed internal control structure policies or procedures than exist in the balance or class as a whole.
d. Does **not** support the tolerable error for some or all of management's assertions.

(11/94, Aud., #33, 5106)

19E. Inherent risk and control risk differ from detection risk in that they

a. Arise from the misapplication of auditing procedures.
b. May be assessed in either quantitative or nonquantitative terms.
c. Exist independently of the financial statement audit.
d. Can be changed at the auditor's discretion.

(11/94, Aud., #8, 5081)

20. The acceptable level of detection risk is inversely related to the

a. Assurance provided by substantive tests.
b. Risk of misapplying auditing procedures.
c. Preliminary judgment about materiality levels.
d. Risk of failing to discover material misstatements. (5/91, Aud., #26, 0044)

21. As the acceptable level of detection risk increases, an auditor may change the

a. Assessed level of control risk from below the maximum to the maximum level.
b. Assurance provided by tests of controls by using a larger sample size than planned.
c. Timing of substantive tests from year-end to an interim date.
d. Nature of substantive tests from a less effective to a more effective procedure.

(11/92, Aud., #10, 2944)

22. When an auditor increases the planned assessed level of control risk because certain control procedures were determined to be ineffective, the auditor would most likely increase the

a. Extent of tests of details.
b. Level of inherent risk.
c. Extent of tests of controls.
d. Level of detection risk. (5/92, Aud., #37, 2790)

23. Which of the following types of evidence would an auditor most likely examine to determine whether internal control structure policies and procedures are operating as designed?

a. Confirmations of receivables verifying account balances.
b. Letters of representations corroborating inventory pricing.
c. Attorneys' responses to the auditor's inquiries.
d. Client records documenting the use of EDP programs. (11/92, Aud., #11, 2945)

23A. The objective of tests of details of transactions performed as tests of controls is to

a. Monitor the design and use of entity documents such as prenumbered shipping forms.
b. Determine whether internal control structure policies and procedures have been placed in operation.

c. Detect material misstatements in the account balances of the financial statements.
d. Evaluate whether internal control structure procedures operated effectively.

(11/94, Aud., #42, 5115)

24. To obtain evidential matter about control risk, an auditor ordinarily selects tests from a variety of techniques, including
a. Analysis.
b. Confirmation.
c. Reperformance.
d. Comparison. (11/90, Aud., #45, 0057)

24A. To obtain evidential matter about control risk, an auditor selects tests from a variety of techniques including
a. Inquiry.
b. Analytical procedures.
c. Calculation.
d. Confirmation. (11/94, Aud., #31, 5104)

25. Proper segregation of functional responsibilities in an effective internal control structure calls for separation of the functions of
a. Authorization, execution, and payment.
b. Authorization, recording, and custody.
c. Custody, execution, and reporting.
d. Authorization, payment, and recording.

(11/88, Aud., #32, 0092)

25A. Proper segregation of duties reduces the opportunities to allow persons to be in positions to both
a. Journalize entries and prepare financial statements.
b. Record cash receipts and cash disbursements.
c. Establish internal controls and authorize transactions.
d. Perpetuate and conceal errors and irregularities. (11/94, Aud., #26, 5099)

26. The objective of tests of details of transactions performed as tests of controls is to
a. Detect material misstatements in the account balances of the financial statements.
b. Evaluate whether an internal control structure policy or procedure operated effectively.
c. Determine the nature, timing, and extent of substantive tests for financial statement assertions.
d. Reduce control risk, inherent risk, and detection risk to an acceptably low level.

(11/90, Aud., #41, 9911)

27. In his consideration of an entity's internal control structure, the auditor is basically concerned that the controls provide reasonable assurance that
a. Operational efficiency has been achieved in accordance with management plans.
b. Errors and irregularities have been prevented or detected.
c. Controls have **not** been circumvented by collusion.
d. Management **cannot** override the controls.

(11/88, Aud., #31, 9911)

28. After obtaining an understanding of a client's EDP controls, an auditor may decide not to perform tests of controls related to the control procedures within the EDP portion of the client's internal control system. Which of the following would **not** be a valid reason for choosing to omit tests of controls?
a. The controls duplicate operative controls existing elsewhere in the system.
b. There appear to be major weaknesses that would preclude assessment of control risk on the stated procedure.
c. The time and dollar costs of testing exceed the time and dollar savings in substantive testing if the tests of controls show the controls to be operative.
d. The controls appear adequate.

(5/88, Aud., #4, 9911)

29. Which of the following internal control procedures most likely would assure that all billed sales are correctly posted to the accounts receivable ledger?
a. Daily sales summaries are compared to daily postings to the accounts receivable ledger.
b. Each sales invoice is supported by a prenumbered shipping document.
c. The accounts receivable ledger is reconciled daily to the control account in the general ledger.
d. Each shipment on credit is supported by a prenumbered sales invoice.

(5/94, Aud., #28, 4693)

30. Which of the following procedures most likely would **not** be an internal control procedure designed to reduce the risk of errors in the billing process?
a. Comparing control totals for shipping documents with corresponding totals for sales invoices.
b. Using computer programmed controls on the pricing and mathematical accuracy of sales invoices.

c. Matching shipping documents with approved sales orders before invoice preparation.
d. Reconciling the control totals for sales invoices with the accounts receivable subsidiary ledger. (11/94, Aud., #36, 5109)

31. Immediately upon receipt of cash, a responsible employee should
a. Record the amount in the cash receipts journal.
b. Prepare a remittance listing.
c. Update the subsidiary accounts receivable records.
d. Prepare a deposit slip in triplicate. (11/91, Aud., #41, 2309)

31A. Sound internal control procedures dictate that immediately upon receiving checks from customers by mail, a responsible employee should
a. Add the checks to the daily cash summary.
b. Verify that each check is supported by a prenumbered sales invoice.
c. Prepare a duplicate listing of checks received.
d. Record the checks in the cash receipts journal. (5/95, Aud., #30, 5648)

32. Proper authorization procedures in the revenue cycle usually provide for the approval of bad debt write-offs by an employee in which of the following departments?
a. Treasurer.
b. Sales.
c. Billing.
d. Accounts receivable. (11/90, Aud., #49, 0061)

32A. Proper authorization of write-offs of uncollectible accounts should be approved in which of the following departments?
a. Accounts receivable.
b. Credit.
c. Accounts payable.
d. Treasurer. (11/94, Aud., #35, 5108)

33. Employers bond employees who handle cash receipts because fidelity bonds reduce the possibility of employing dishonest individuals and
a. Protect employees who make unintentional errors from possible monetary damages resulting from their errors.
b. Deter dishonesty by making employees aware that insurance companies may investigate and prosecute dishonest acts.
c. Facilitate an independent monitoring of the receiving and depositing of cash receipts.
d. Force employees in positions of trust to take periodic vacations and rotate their assigned duties. (5/90, Aud., #35, 0073)

34. Which of the following controls most likely would be effective in offsetting the tendency of sales personnel to maximize sales volume at the expense of high bad debt write-offs?
a. Employees responsible for authorizing sales and bad debt write-offs are denied access to cash.
b. Shipping documents and sales invoices are matched by an employee who does **not** have authority to write off bad debts.
c. Employees involved in the credit-granting function are separated from the sales function.
d. Subsidiary accounts receivable records are reconciled to the control account by an employee independent of the authorization of credit. (5/92, Aud., #45, 2798)

35. An entity with a large volume of customer remittances by mail could most likely reduce the risk of employee misappropriation of cash by using
a. Employee fidelity bonds.
b. Independently prepared mailroom prelists.
c. Daily check summaries.
d. A bank lockbox system. (11/92, Aud., #14, 2948)

36. Which of the following internal control procedures most likely would deter lapping of collections from customers?
a. Independent internal verification of dates of entry in the cash receipts journal with dates of daily cash summaries.
b. Authorization of write-offs of uncollectible accounts by a supervisor independent of credit approval.
c. Segregation of duties between receiving cash and posting the accounts receivable ledger.
d. Supervisory comparison of the daily cash summary with the sum of the cash receipts journal entries. (5/93, Aud., #14, 3910)

37. For the most effective internal control, monthly bank statements should be received directly from the banks and reviewed by the
a. Controller.
b. Cash receipts accountant.
c. Cash disbursements accountant.
d. Internal auditor. (11/87, Aud., #53, 0111)

38. To determine whether the internal control structure operated effectively to minimize errors of failure to invoice a shipment, the auditor would select a sample of transactions from the population represented by the

a. Customer order file.
b. Bill of lading file.
c. Open invoice file.
d. Sales invoice file. (11/86, Aud., #22, 9911)

38A. Tracing shipping documents to prenumbered sales invoices provides evidence that
a. No duplicate shipments or billings occurred.
b. Shipments to customers were properly invoiced.
c. All goods ordered by customers were shipped.
d. All prenumbered sales invoices were accounted for. (5/95, Aud., #32, 5650)

39. In assessing control risk for purchases, an auditor vouches a sample of entries in the voucher register to the supporting documents. Which assertion would this test of controls most likely support?
a. Completeness.
b. Existence or occurrence.
c. Valuation or allocation.
d. Rights and obligations. (11/94, Aud., #39, 5112)

40. Which of the following internal control procedures is **not** usually performed in the vouchers payable department?
a. Matching the vendor's invoice with the related receiving report.
b. Approving vouchers for payment by having an authorized employee sign the vouchers.
c. Indicating the asset and expense accounts to be debited.
d. Accounting for unused prenumbered purchase orders and receiving reports. (11/94, Aud., #40, 5113)

41. Mailing disbursement checks and remittance advices should be controlled by the employee who
a. Matches the receiving reports, purchase orders, and vendors' invoices.
b. Signs the checks last.
c. Prepares the daily voucher summary.
d. Agrees the check register to the daily check summary. (5/93, Aud., #18, 3914)

42. In a well-designed internal control structure, the same employee may be permitted to
a. Mail signed checks, and also cancel supporting documents.
b. Prepare receiving reports, and also approve purchase orders.
c. Approve vouchers for payment, and also have access to unused purchase orders.
d. Mail signed checks, and also prepare bank reconciliations. (5/93, Aud., #19, 3915)

42A. In a properly designed internal control structure, the same employee most likely would match vendors' invoices with receiving reports and also
a. Post the detailed accounts payable records.
b. Recompute the calculations on vendors' invoices.
c. Reconcile the accounts payable ledger.
d. Cancel vendors' invoices after payment. (5/94, Aud., #30, 4695)

43. When the shipping department returns non-conforming goods to a vendor, the purchasing department should send to the accounting department the
a. Unpaid voucher.
b. Debit memo.
c. Vendor invoice.
d. Credit memo. (11/92, Aud., #16, 2950)

44. An auditor wishes to perform tests of controls on a client's cash disbursements procedures. If the control procedures leave **no** audit trail of documentary evidence, the auditor most likely will test the procedures by
a. Inquiry and analytical procedures.
b. Confirmation and observation.
c. Observation and inquiry.
d. Analytical procedures and confirmation. (11/90, Aud., #50, 9911)

44A. To provide assurance that each voucher is submitted and paid only once, an auditor most likely would examine a sample of paid vouchers and determine whether each voucher is
a. Supported by a vendor's invoice.
b. Stamped "paid" by the check signer.
c. Prenumbered and accounted for.
d. Approved for authorized purchases. (5/95, Aud., #34, 5652)

45. Which of the following controls would be most effective in assuring that recorded purchases are free of material errors?
a. The receiving department compares the quantity ordered on purchase orders with the quantity received on receiving reports.
b. Vendors' invoices are compared with purchase orders by an employee who is independent of the receiving department.
c. Receiving reports require the signature of the individual who authorized the purchase.
d. Purchase orders, receiving reports, and vendors' invoices are independently matched in preparing vouchers. (11/90, Aud., #51, 9911)

46. An entity's internal control structure requires for every check request that there be an approved voucher, supported by a prenumbered purchase order and a prenumbered receiving report. To determine whether checks are being issued for unauthorized expenditures, an auditor most likely would select items for testing from the population of all
a. Purchase orders.
b. Canceled checks.
c. Receiving reports.
d. Approved vouchers. (11/92, Aud., #17, 2951)

47. For effective internal control, the accounts payable department generally should
a. Obliterate the quantity ordered on the receiving department copy of the purchase order.
b. Establish the agreement of the vendor's invoice with the receiving report and purchase order.
c. Stamp, perforate, or otherwise cancel supporting documentation after payment is mailed.
d. Ascertain that each requisition is approved as to price, quantity, and quality by an authorized employee. (11/92, Aud., #15, 2949)

47A. Which of the following questions would an auditor most likely include on an internal control questionnaire for notes payable?
a. Are assets that collateralize notes payable critically needed for the entity's continued existence?
b. Are two or more authorized signatures required on checks that repay notes payable?
c. Are the proceeds from notes payable used for the purchase of noncurrent assets?
d. Are direct borrowings on notes payable authorized by the board of directors? (11/93, Aud., #32, 4269)

48. In a properly designed accounts payable system, a voucher is prepared after the invoice, purchase order, requisition, and receiving report are verified. The next step in the system is to
a. Cancel the supporting documents.
b. Enter the check amount in the check register.
c. Approve the voucher for payment.
d. Post the voucher amount to the expense ledger. (5/86, Aud., #39, 9911)

49. The authority to accept incoming goods in receiving should be based on a(an)
a. Vendor's invoice.
b. Materials requisition.
c. Bill of lading.
d. Approved purchase order. (5/93, Aud., #17, 3913)

49A. An auditor generally tests the segregation of duties related to inventory by
a. Personal inquiry and observation.
b. Test counts and cutoff procedures.
c. Analytical procedures and invoice recomputation.
d. Document inspection and reconciliation. (5/95, Aud., #31, 5649)

50. Sound internal control procedures dictate that defective merchandise returned by customers should be presented initially to the
a. Accounts receivable supervisor.
b. Receiving clerk.
c. Shipping department supervisor.
d. Sales clerk. (5/93, Aud., #20, 3916)

51. An on-line sales order processing system most likely would have an advantage over a batch sales order processing system by
a. Detecting errors in the date entry process more easily by the use of edit programs.
b. Enabling shipment of customer orders to be initiated as soon as the orders are received.
c. Recording more secure backup copies of the data base on magnetic tape files.
d. Maintaining more accurate records of customer accounts and finished goods inventories. (11/92, Aud., #12, 2946)

52. In obtaining an understanding of a manufacturing entity's internal control structure concerning inventory balances, an auditor most likely would
a. Review the entity's descriptions of inventory policies and procedures.
b. Perform test counts of inventory during the entity's physical count.
c. Analyze inventory turnover statistics to identify slow-moving and obsolete items.
d. Analyze monthly production reports to identify variances and unusual transactions. (11/92, Aud., #19, 2953)

53. Which of the following most likely would be an internal control procedure designed to detect errors and irregularities concerning the custody of inventory?
a. Periodic reconciliation of work in process with job cost sheets.
b. Segregation of functions between general accounting and cost accounting.
c. Independent comparisons of finished goods records with counts of goods on hand.
d. Approval of inventory journal entries by the storekeeper. (5/91, Aud., #29, 9911)

54. Which of the following internal control procedures most likely would prevent direct labor hours from being charged to manufacturing overhead?

a. Periodic independent counts of work in process for comparison to recorded amounts.
b. Comparison of daily journal entries with approved production orders.
c. Use of time tickets to record actual labor worked on production orders.
d. Reconciliation of work-in-process inventory with periodic cost budgets. (5/94, Aud., #32, 4697)

55. Independent internal verification of inventory occurs when employees who

a. Issue raw materials obtain material requisitions for each issue and prepare daily totals of materials issued.
b. Compare records of goods on hand with physical quantities do **not** maintain the records or have custody of the inventory.
c. Obtain receipts for the transfer of completed work to finished goods prepare a completed production report.
d. Are independent of issuing production orders update records from completed job cost sheets and production cost reports on a timely basis. (5/89, Aud., #18, 0089)

56. Which of the following internal control procedures most likely would be used to maintain accurate inventory records?

a. Perpetual inventory records are periodically compared with the current cost of individual inventory items.
b. A just-in-time inventory ordering system keeps inventory levels to a desired minimum.
c. Requisitions, receiving repoıts, and purchase orders are independently matched before payment is approved.
d. Periodic inventory counts are used to adjust the perpetual inventory records. (5/94, Aud., #33, 4698)

57. The objectives of the internal control structure for a production cycle are to provide assurance that transactions are properly executed and recorded, and that

a. Production orders are prenumbered and signed by a supervisor.
b. Custody of work in process and of finished goods is properly maintained.
c. Independent internal verification of activity reports is established.
d. Transfers to finished goods are documented by a completed production report and a quality control report. (11/93, Aud., #28, 4265)

58. An auditor generally tests physical security controls over inventory by

a. Test counts and cutoff procedures.
b. Examination and reconciliation.
c. Inspection and recomputation.
d. Inquiry and observation. (11/87, Aud., #48, 4698)

59. An auditor most likely would assess control risk at the maximum if the payroll department supervisor is responsible for

a. Examining authorization forms for new employees.
b. Comparing payroll registers with original batch transmittal data.
c. Authorizing payroll rate changes for all employees.
d. Hiring all subordinate payroll department employees. (5/94, Aud., #29, 4694)

60. The purpose of segregating the duties of hiring personnel and distributing payroll checks is to separate the

a. Human resources function from the controllership function.
b. Administrative controls from the internal accounting controls.
c. Authorization of transactions from the custody of related assets.
d. Operational responsibility from the record-keeping responsibility. (11/93, Aud., #30, 4267)

61. Which of the following departments most likely would approve changes in pay rates and deductions from employee salaries?

a. Personnel.
b. Treasurer.
c. Controller.
d. Payroll. (11/93, Aud., #31, 4268)

62. If a control total were computed on each of the following data items, which would best be identified as a hash total for a payroll EDP application?

a. Total debits and total credits.
b. Net pay.
c. Department numbers.
d. Hours worked. (11/92, Aud., #20, 2954)

63. Which of the following procedures most likely would be considered a weakness in an entity's internal controls over payroll?

a. A voucher for the amount of the payroll is prepared in the general accounting department based on the payroll department's payroll summary.
b. Payroll checks are prepared by the payroll department and signed by the treasurer.

c. The employee who distributes payroll checks returns unclaimed payroll checks to the payroll department.
d. The personnel department sends employees' termination notices to the payroll department.
(11/92, Aud., #21, 2955)

64. Which of the following symbolic representations indicates that new payroll transactions and the old payroll file have been used to prepare payroll checks, prepare a printed payroll journal, and generate a new payroll file?

a.

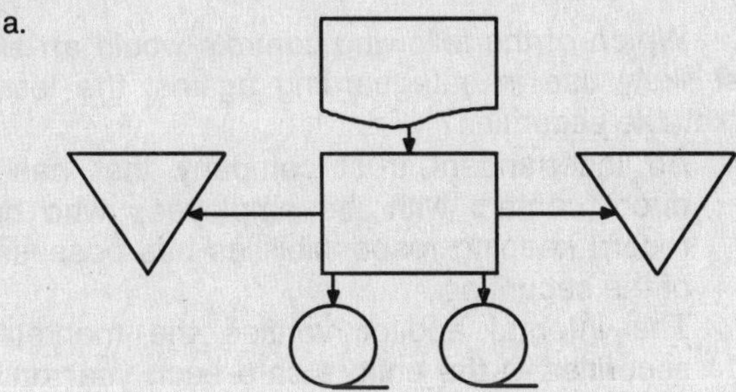

b.

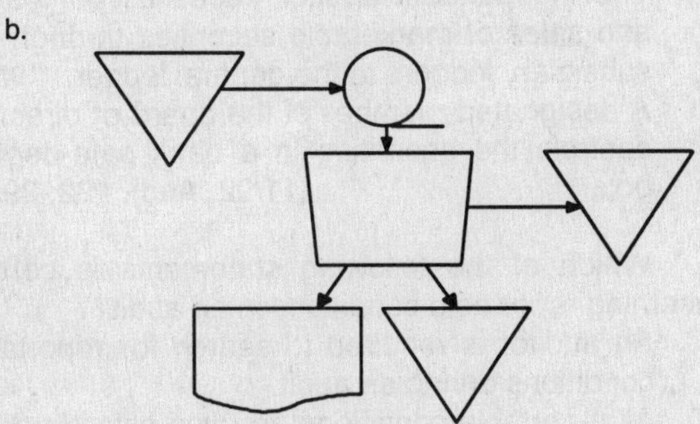

c.

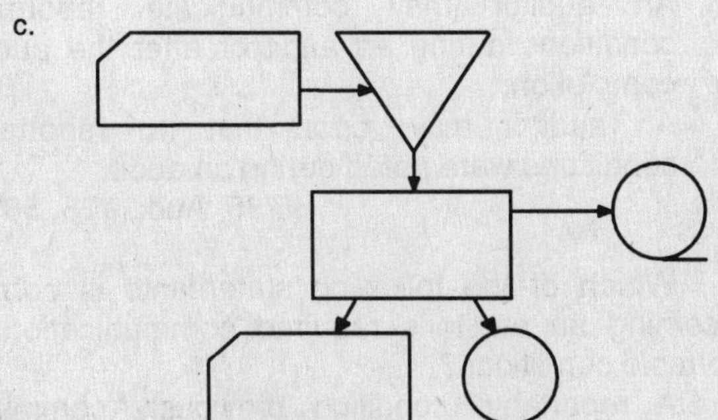

d.

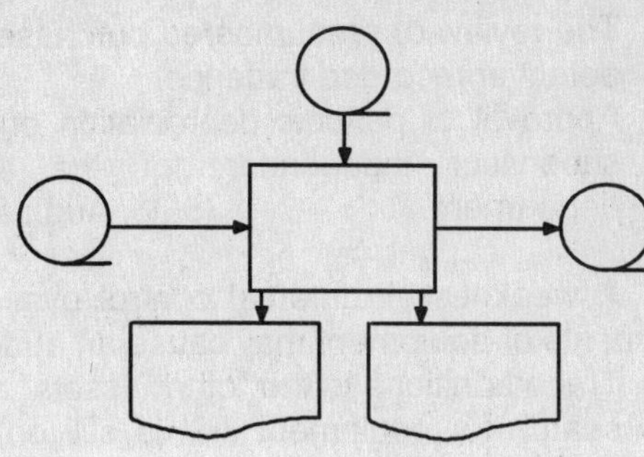

(11/89, Aud., #55, 9911)

65. Which of the following questions would an auditor **least** likely include on an internal control questionnaire concerning the initiation and execution of equipment transactions?
a. Are requests for major repairs approved at a higher level than the department initiating the request?
b. Are prenumbered purchase orders used for equipment and periodically accounted for?
c. Are requests for purchases of equipment reviewed for consideration of soliciting competitive bids?
d. Are procedures in place to monitor and properly restrict access to equipment?
(11/94, Aud., #41, 5114)

66. Equipment acquisitions that are misclassified as maintenance expense most likely would be detected by an internal control procedure that provides for
a. Segregation of duties of employees in the accounts payable department.
b. Independent verification of invoices for disbursements recorded as equipment acquisitions.
c. Investigation of variances within a formal budgeting system.
d. Authorization by the board of directors of significant equipment acquisitions.
(11/93, Aud., #34, 4271)

67. Which of the following internal control procedures most likely would justify a reduced assessed level of control risk concerning plant and equipment acquisitions?
a. Periodic physical inspection of plant and equipment by the internal audit staff.
b. Comparison of current-year plant and equipment account balances with prior-year actual balances.

c. The review of prenumbered purchase orders to detect unrecorded trade-ins.
d. Approval of periodic depreciation entries by a supervisor independent of the accounting department. (5/93, Aud., #21, 3917)

68. A weakness in internal control over recording retirements of equipment may cause an auditor to
a. Trace additions to the "other assets" account to search for equipment that is still on hand but **no** longer being used.
b. Select certain items of equipment from the accounting records and locate them in the plant.
c. Inspect certain items of equipment in the plant and trace those items to the accounting records.
d. Review the subsidiary ledger to ascertain whether depreciation was taken on each item of equipment during the year.
(11/89, Aud., #48, 0081)

69. When there are numerous property and equipment transactions during the year, an auditor who plans to assess control risk at a low level usually performs
a. Analytical procedures for property and equipment balances at the end of the year.
b. Tests of controls and extensive tests of property and equipment balances at the end of the year.
c. Analytical procedures for current-year property and equipment transactions.
d. Tests of controls and limited tests of current-year property and equipment transactions.
(11/92, Aud., #18, 2952)

70. When an entity uses a trust company as custodian of its marketable securities, the possibility of concealing fraud most likely would be reduced if the
a. Trust company has **no** direct contact with the entity employees responsible for maintaining investment accounting records.
b. Securities are registered in the name of the trust company, rather than the entity itself.
c. Interest and dividend checks are mailed directly to an entity employee who is authorized to sell securities.
d. Trust company places the securities in a bank safe-deposit vault under the custodian's exclusive control. (5/94, Aud., #34, 4699)

71. Which of the following procedures most likely would give the greatest assurance that securities held as investments are safeguarded?
a. There is no access to securities between the year-end and the date of the auditor's security count.
b. Proceeds from the sale of investments are received by an employee who does not have access to securities.
c. Investment acquisitions are authorized by a member of the Board of Directors before execution.
d. Access to securities requires the signatures and presence of two designated officials.
(5/93, Aud., #22, 3918)

72. Which of the following controls would an entity most likely use in safeguarding against the loss of marketable securities?
a. An independent trust company that has **no** direct contact with the employees who have record keeping responsibilities has possession of the securities.
b. The internal auditor verifies the marketable securities in the entity's safe each year on the balance sheet date.
c. The independent auditor traces all purchases and sales of marketable securities through the subsidiary ledgers to the general ledger.
d. A designated member of the board of directors controls the securities in a bank safe-deposit box. (11/92, Aud., #22, 2956)

73. Which of the following statements is correct concerning reportable conditions in an audit?
a. An auditor is required to search for reportable conditions during an audit.
b. All reportable conditions are also considered to be material weaknesses.
c. An auditor may communicate reportable conditions during an audit or after the audit's completion.
d. An auditor may report that **no** reportable conditions were noted during an audit.
(5/95, Aud., #38, 5656)

74. Which of the following statements is correct concerning an auditor's required communication of reportable conditions?
a. A reportable condition previously communicated during the prior year's audit that remains uncorrected causes a scope limitation.
b. An auditor should perform tests of controls on reportable conditions before communicating them to the client.

c. An auditor's report on reportable conditions should include a restriction on the distribution of the report.
d. An auditor should communicate reportable conditions after tests of controls, but before commencing substantive tests.
(11/94, Aud., #45, 5118)

75. When communicating internal control structure related matters noted in an audit, an auditor's report issued on reportable conditions should indicate that
a. Errors or irregularities may occur and **not** be detected because there are inherent limitations in any internal control structure.
b. The issuance of an unqualified opinion on the financial statements may be dependent on corrective follow-up action.
c. The deficiencies noted were **not** detected within a timely period by employees in the normal course of performing their assigned functions.
d. The purpose of the audit was to report on the financial statements and **not** to provide assurance on the internal control structure.
(11/93, Aud., #25, 4262)

76. A letter issued on reportable conditions relating to an entity's internal control structure observed during an audit of financial statements should include a
a. Restriction on the distribution of the report.
b. Description of tests performed to search for material weaknesses.
c. Statement of compliance with applicable laws and regulations.
d. Paragraph describing management's evaluation of the effectiveness of the control structure.
(5/93, Aud., #23, 3919)

77. An auditor's communication of internal control structure related matters noted in an audit usually should be addressed to the
a. Audit committee.
b. Director of internal auditing.
c. Chief financial officer.
d. Chief accounting officer. (5/91, Aud., #33, 0050)

77A. An auditor most likely would be responsible for communicating significant deficiencies in the design of the internal control structure
a. To the Securities and Exchange Commission when the client is a publicly held entity.
b. To specific legislative and regulatory bodies when reporting under *Government Auditing Standards*.
c. To court-appointed creditors' committee when the client is operating under Chapter 11 of the Federal Bankruptcy Code.
d. To shareholders with significant influence (more than 20% equity ownership) when the reportable conditions are deemed to be material weaknesses. (5/95, Aud., #76, 5694)

78. The development of constructive suggestions to a client for improvements in its internal control structure is
a. Addressed by the auditor only during a special engagement.
b. As important as establishing a basis for assessing the level of control risk below the maximum.
c. A requirement of the auditor's consideration of the internal control structure.
d. A desirable by-product of an audit engagement.
(5/89, Aud., #6, 0083)

79. Reportable conditions are matters that come to an auditor's attention that should be communicated to an entity's audit committee because they represent
a. Manipulation or falsification of accounting records or documents from which financial statements are prepared.
b. Disclosures of information that significantly contradict the auditor's going concern assumption.
c. Material irregularities or illegal acts perpetuated by high-level management.
d. Significant deficiencies in the design or operation of the internal control structure.
(5/92, Aud., #50, 2803)

79A. Reportable conditions are matters that come to an auditor's attention that should be communicated to an entity's audit committee because they represent
a. Disclosures of information that significantly contradict the auditor's going concern assumption.
b. Material irregularities or illegal acts perpetrated by high-level management.
c. Significant deficiencies in the design or operation of the internal control structure.
d. Manipulation or falsification of accounting records or documents from which financial statements are prepared.
(11/94, Aud., #44, 5117)

80. A previously communicated reportable condition that has not been corrected, ordinarily should be communicated again if

a. The deficiency has a material effect on the auditor's assessment of control risk.
b. The entity accepts that degree of risk because of cost-benefit considerations.
c. The weakness could adversely affect the entity's ability to report financial data.
d. There has been major turnover in upper-level management and the board of directors.

(5/91, Aud., #35, 0052)

81. Which of the following statements concerning an auditor's communication of reportable conditions is correct?

a. The auditor should request a meeting with management one level above the source of the reportable conditions to discuss suggestions for remedial action.
b. Any report issued on reportable conditions should indicate that providing assurance on the internal control structure was **not** the purpose of the audit.
c. Reportable conditions discovered and communicated at an interim date should be reexamined with tests of controls before completing the engagement.
d. Suggestions concerning administration efficiencies and business strategies should **not** be communicated in the same report with reportable conditions. (5/92, Aud., #51, 2804)

82. In general, a material internal control structure weakness may be defined as a condition in which material errors or irregularities may occur and not be detected within a timely period by

a. An independent auditor during the testing of controls phase of the consideration of the internal control structure.
b. Employees in the normal course of performing their assigned functions.
c. Management when reviewing interim financial statements and reconciling account balances.
d. Outside consultants who issue a special-purpose report on internal control.

(5/85, Aud., #5, 9911)

83. Which of the following statements concerning material weaknesses and reportable conditions is correct?

a. An auditor should identify and communicate material weaknesses separately from reportable conditions.
b. All material weaknesses are reportable conditions.
c. An auditor should report immediately material weaknesses and reportable conditions discovered during an audit.
d. All reportable conditions are material weaknesses. (11/90, Aud., #55, 0063)

84. Which of the following representations should **not** be included in a report on internal control structure related matters noted in an audit?

a. Reportable conditions related to the internal control structure design exist, but **none** is deemed to be a material weakness.
b. There are **no** significant deficiencies in the design or operation of the internal control structure.
c. Corrective follow-up action is recommended due to the relative significance of material weaknesses discovered during the audit.
d. The auditor's consideration of the internal control structure would **not** necessarily disclose all reportable conditions that exist.

(11/92, Aud., #23, 2957)

Solution 36-1 MULTIPLE CHOICE ANSWERS

Consideration of the Internal Control Structure in Planning the Audit (AU 319)

1. (c) AU 319.58 states that the ultimate purpose of assessing control risk is to contribute to the auditor's evaluation of the risk that material misstatements exist in the financial statements. Answers (a), (b), and (d), are all by-products of the result of assessing control risk and performing tests of controls.

1A. (a) The second standard of field work is, "A sufficient understanding of the internal control structure is to be obtained to plan the audit..." The other choices are intermediate considerations.

2. (b) AU 319.28 states that the auditor should document the understanding of the entity's internal control structure elements obtained to plan the audit. AU 319.39 states that in addition to the documentation of the understanding of the internal control structure, the auditor should document the basis for his or her conclusions about the assessed

level of control risk. For financial statement assertions where control risk is assessed at the maximum level, the auditor should document his or her conclusion that control risk is at the maximum level but need not document the basis for that conclusion. For assertions where the assessed level of control risk is below the maximum level, the auditor should document the basis for his or her conclusion that the effectiveness of the design and operation of internal control structure policies and procedures supports that assessed level.

2A. (c) The control environment reflects the overall attitude, awareness, and actions of the board of directors, management, owners and others concerning the importance of control and its emphasis in the entity. If management is dominated by one individual who is also a shareholder, aggressive reporting and the achievement of profit goals may be overemphasized to the detriment of proper reporting. Answers (a), (b), and (d) represent examples of good control environment influences on financial statement reporting.

2B. (c) AU 319.09 states, "The control environment reflects the overall attitude, awareness, and actions of the board of directors, management, owners, and others concerning the importance of control and its emphasis in the entity." Computer-based controls, the system of segregation of duties, and safeguards over access to assets are day-to-day details with which board members are unlikely to have as much influence (unless they are also officers).

2C. (c) Regardless of the level of assessed control risk, the auditor must document the understanding of the elements of the internal control structure (AU 319.26). When control risk is assessed at the maximum level, the auditor documents the conclusion that control risk is at the maximum level, but is not required to document the basis for the conclusion (AU 319.39).

3. (b) AU 319.17 does not require the auditor to obtain knowledge about operating effectiveness as part of the understanding of the internal control structure. The section states that the understanding of the entity's internal control structure should include knowledge about the design of relevant policies, procedures, and records, and whether they have been placed in operation by the entity.

4. (b) AU 319.30 states that assessing control risk at below the maximum level involves identifying specific internal control structure policies and procedures relevant to specific assertions that are likely to prevent or detect material misstatements in those assertions. Answers (a) and (c) represent procedures the auditor may perform as the acceptable level of detection risk decreases because the assurance provided from substantive tests should increase. Reducing control risk to below the maximum does not affect the auditor's assessment of inherent risk.

4A. (b) AU 319.10 states, "The accounting system consists of the methods and records established to identify, assemble, analyze, classify, record, and report an entity's transactions and to maintain accountability..." Answers (a), (c), and (d) are all examples of control procedures.

5. (a) An entity's internal control structure consists of three elements: the control environment, the accounting system and the control procedures (AU 319.02). Control risk is one of the three components of audit risk (AU 312.20).

5A. (b) AU 319.20 states, "The auditor should obtain sufficient knowledge of the control environment to understand management's and the board of directors' attitude, awareness, and actions concerning the control environment. The auditor should concentrate on the substance of management's policies, procedures, and related actions rather than their form because management may establish appropriate policies and procedures but not act on them." Depending on the size of the entity, written policies, such as formal credit policies, may not be necessary. Answer (c) would require alternative audit procedures be performed to compensate for the lack of internal control because this would be a result of understanding the substance of a procedure rather than its form, and answer (d) would not affect the auditor's assessment of the performance of control procedures.

6. (a) AU 319.15 states that the potential effectiveness of an entity's internal control structure is subject to inherent limitations such as mistakes in judgment. Policies and procedures that require segregation of duties can be circumvented by collusion among employees and by management override.

6A. (c) AU 319.63 states that ordinarily the assessed level of control risk cannot be sufficiently low to eliminate the need to perform any substantive tests to restrict detection risk for all of the assertions relevant to significant transaction balances. Tests of controls are used in assessing the level of control risk. Analytical procedures are required to be used in the planning stage of the audit. However, they would not be performed to verify the design of internal control procedures. A dual purpose test is a sample that is designed to both assess control risk and to provide substantive testing as to whether a recorded balance or amount is correct, and is not a required procedure.

7. (b) AU 319.04 states, "After obtaining the understanding and assessing control risk, the auditor may desire to seek a further reduction in the assessed level of control risk for certain assertions. In such cases, the auditor considers whether evidential matter sufficient to support a further reduction is likely to be available and whether performing additional tests of controls to obtain such evidential matter would be efficient."

7A. (a) AU 319.43 states that after obtaining an understanding of the internal control structure, the auditor considers if it is efficient to perform tests of controls that would result in a reduction in planned substantive tests. If evidence is not available, tests of controls are not performed. As the assessed level of control risk increases, the auditor is less likely to test controls. If the auditor is aware of many internal control weaknesses, the assessed level of control risk will be high, and controls will not be tested.

7B. (a) AU 319.29 states that the auditor may assess control risk at the maximum level for some or all assertions because he or she believes policies and procedures are unlikely to pertain to an assertion, are unlikely to be effective, or because evaluating their effectiveness would be inefficient. Answer (b) is a true statement, but, it would not be valid reasoning for assessing control risk at the maximum. Answer (d) is incorrect because the opposite would be true when assessing control risk at the maximum. This situation would apply when control risk is assessed at below the maximum.

8. (d) AU 319.05 states, "The auditor uses the knowledge provided by the understanding of the internal control structure and the assessed level of control risk in determining the nature, timing, and extent of substantive tests for financial statement assertions."

8A. (d) AU 319.37 states that the auditor uses the assessed level of control risk to determine the acceptable level of detection risk for financial statement assertions. The effectiveness of control policies and procedures are evaluated by the actual tests of control. Answer (b) is not an objective of assessing control risk. Answer (c) is not a direct result of assessing control risk but a result of performing tests of controls.

8B. (a) AU 319.40 states that although understanding the internal control structure and assessing control risk are discussed separately, they may be performed concurrently in an audit. AU 319.39 states that for financial statement assertions where control risk is assessed at the maximum level, the auditor should document his or her conclusions that control risk is at the maximum level, but need not document the basis for that conclusion. AU 319.63 states that ordinarily the assessed level of control risk cannot be sufficiently low to eliminate the need to perform any substantive tests to restrict detection risk for all of the assertions relevant to significant account balances. Consequently, regardless of the assessed level of control risk, the auditor should perform substantive tests for significant account balances and transaction classes. AU 319.53 states that evidential matter about the effective design or operation of internal control structure policies and procedures that was obtained in prior audits may be considered by the auditor in assessing control risk in the current audit.

9. (d) AU 319.06 states, "Generally, the policies and procedures that are relevant to an audit pertain to the entity's ability to record, process, summarize, and report financial data consistent with the assertions embodied in the financial statements."

10. (a) An auditor's primary consideration is whether an internal control structure policy or procedure affects financial statement assertions (AU 319.08). An entity's policies and procedures cannot be designed in such a way that they would prevent every incidence of management override. The auditor is not solely concerned with the policies and procedures as they relate to the control environment. The auditor is also concerned with the accounting system and control procedures. The auditor is concerned with management's philosophy and operating style as only one factor within the control environment. The auditor is also concerned with the accounting system and control procedures.

10A. (b) AU 319.08 states, "An auditor's primary consideration is whether an internal control structure policy or procedure affects financial statement assertions, rather than its classification into any particular category." Management's philosophy and operating style are elements of the control environment that would influence policies and procedures, but are not the primary consideration. Answer (c) represents physical control over assets, but would not be a control policy applicable to liabilities and is therefore not a primary consideration of general policies and procedures. Control policies should *reflect* management's decision-making processes. Sufficient financial and substantive information would help *enhance* management's decision-making processes.

11. (d) The audit committee, the internal audit function, and the organizational structure are specifically mentioned as factors included in the entity's control environment (AU 319.09).

11A. (c) AU 319.09 states, "The control environment represents the collective effect of various factors on establishing, enhancing, or mitigating the effectiveness of specific policies and procedures. Factors include management's philosophy and operating style, personnel policies and practices, etc." Detection risk is an element of audit risk and is a factor used by the auditor in determining overall audit risk." Detection risk is a factor in determining audit risk, not a factor of the control environment. Personnel policies and practices, not detection risk, is a factor of the control environment.

12. (c) AU 319.14 states, "The concept of reasonable assurance recognizes that the cost of an entity's internal control structure should not exceed the benefits that are expected to be derived." Answers (a), (b), and (d) all represent statements that are not a part of the definition of reasonable assurance.

12A. (d) AU 319.12 states that the concept of reasonable assurance recognizes that the cost of the internal control structure should not exceed the benefits expected to be derived.

13. (d) AU 319.17 states, "Whether an internal control structure policy or procedure has been placed in operation is different from its operating effectiveness. In obtaining knowledge about whether policies, procedures, or records have been placed in operation, the auditor determines that the entity is using them. Operating effectiveness, on the other hand, is concerned with how the policy, procedure, or record was applied, the consistency with which it was applied, and by whom. This section does not require the auditor to obtain knowledge about operating effectiveness as part of the understanding of the internal control structure."

13A. (d) AU 319.02 states that the auditor should obtain a sufficient understanding of each of the three elements in an internal control structure to plan the audit, by performing procedures to understand the design of policies and procedures relevant to audit planning and whether they have been placed in operation. AU 319.26 states that the auditor should document the understanding of the entity's internal control structure elements obtained to plan the audit. The auditor is not obligated to search for significant deficiencies in the operation of the internal control structure in obtaining an understanding of the entity's internal control structure.

14. (c) The audit sample in this case was not representative of the population and indicated a tolerable deviation rate that did not, in fact, exist. This unjustified acceptance of the sample results allowed the auditor to incorrectly assess control risk too low, when in fact the auditor should have done the opposite.

15. (c) AU 319.16 states, "The auditor should obtain a sufficient understanding of each of the three elements of the entity's internal control structure to plan the audit of the entity's financial statements."

16. (d) AU 319.19 states, "In making a judgment about the understanding of the internal control structure necessary to plan the audit, . . . the auditor considers his assessments of inherent risk, his judgments about materiality, and the complexity and sophistication of the entity's operations and systems."

17. (c) AU 319.20 states, "The auditor should obtain sufficient knowledge of the control environment to understand management's and the board of directors' attitude, awareness, and actions concerning the control environment. The auditor should concentrate on the substance of management's policies, procedures, and related actions rather than their form because management may establish appropriate policies and procedures but not act on them."

18. (c) The auditor should document the understanding of the entity's internal control structure elements obtained to plan the audit. The form and extent of this documentation is influenced by the size and complexity of the entity, as well as the nature of the entity's internal control structure.

19. (b) Detection risk has an inverse relationship to control risk. Therefore, if an auditor decides to *increase* the assessed level of control risk from the originally planned level, in order to achieve an equivalent overall level of risk, the detection risk must be *decreased.*

19A. (b) AU 319.61 states, "The ultimate purpose of assessing control risk is to contribute to the auditor's evaluation of the risk that material misstatements exist in the financial statements." Tests of controls are performed on procedures after making a preliminary assessment of control risk and when it is likely and potentially efficient to obtain a lower assessed level of control risk. Thus, tests of controls are not performed to identify procedures, but rather to test procedures relevant to assertions. Answers (c) and (d) are resulting by-products of assessing control risk and performing tests of controls.

19B. (c) AU 319.27-28 discuss assessing control risk in terms of financial statement assertions.

19C. (c) AU 319.30 states, "Assessing control risk at below the maximum level involves identifying specific internal control structure policies and procedures relevant to specific assertions that are likely to prevent or detect material misstatements in those assertions." Analytical procedures are substantive tests required in the planning and review phases of the audit. Tests of details of transactions and account balances represent substantive tests, not tests of controls. Answer (d) represents required documentation when control risk is assessed at the maximum, per AU 319.39.

19D. (a) AU 350.12 states, "The risk of assessing control risk *too high* is the risk that the assessed level of control risk based on the sample is greater than the true operating effectiveness of the control structure policy or procedure." Answer (b) is incorrect because fewer errors or deviations would be discovered; therefore, the auditor would not identify those misstatements. Answer (c) is incorrect because the true operating effectiveness of the control structure would not support such an assessment; the auditor would find fewer errors or deviations. Answer (d) is incorrect because the sample would support the tolerable error for misstatements because the sample would reveal fewer errors or deviations than exist in the balance or class of transactions.

19E. (c) Inherent risk and control risk are present whether or not an audit is done. Detection risk is the risk that a material misstatement is present, and it is not detected during the audit. All three components of audit risk may be assessed in quantitative or qualitative terms. None of these types of risk arise from the misapplication of auditing standards; they are present in any audit. Inherent risk and control risk cannot be changed at the auditor's discretion; the auditor can only change the assessment of the level of the risk.

20. (a) AU 319.37 states, "The auditor uses the acceptable level of detection risk to determine the nature, timing and extent of the auditing procedures to be used to detect material misstatements in the financial statements in the financial statement assertions. Auditing procedures designed to detect such misstatements are referred to in this section as substantive tests. As the acceptable level of detection risk decreases, the assurance provided from substantive tests should increase." The risk of misapplying audit procedures is a part of detection risk. The acceptable level of detection risk is unrelated to the preliminary judgment about materiality levels. The risk of failing to discover material misstatements is detection risk.

21. (c) AU 319.62 states, "As the assessed level of control risk decreases, the acceptable level of detection risk increases. Accordingly, the auditor may alter the nature, timing, and extent of the substantive tests performed." There is an inverse relationship between control risk and detection risk. Thus as the acceptable level of detection risk increases, the assessed level of control risk decreases (AU 319.62). The auditor would change the assurance provided by tests of controls by using a larger sample size than planned when the acceptable level of detection risk decreases (AU 319.38). The auditor would change the nature of substantive tests from a less effective to a more effective procedure when the acceptable level of detection risk decreases (AU 319.38).

22. (a) As the auditor increases the planned assessed level of control risk, he or she would likely increase the extent of tests of details, because the extent of substantive testing would have to be increased due to the weakness of the internal control structure, as evidenced by the ineffective control procedures. Inherent risk would not be affected by a change in the assessment of control risk. It has already been determined that tests of controls were ineffective. The level of detection risk has an inverse relationship with the assessed level of control risk.

23. (d) Tests of controls to obtain evidence about the effectiveness of the design of internal control structure policies and procedures include, among other procedures, inquiries of appropriate client personnel, inspection of documents and reports, and observation of the application of specific internal control structure policies and procedures (AU 319.34). Answers (a), (b), and (c) are substantive tests, not tests of controls.

23A. (d) AU 319.65 states, "The objective of tests of details of transactions performed as tests of controls is to evaluate whether internal control structure procedures operated effectively." Answer (a) would be a substantive test rather than a test of controls. Determining whether internal control policies and procedures have been placed in operation is the objective of obtaining a sufficient understanding of each of the three elements in an entity's control structure. Answer (c) is the objective of tests of details of transactions performed as substantive tests.

24. (c) Reperformance is a type of test of controls in which the auditor duplicates part of, or repeats a section of, the internal controls. This differs from another test of controls called inspection, in which the auditor checks for the existence of some type of documentation in order to draw a conclusion regarding the working of the internal control system. Answers (a), (b), and (d) are examples of substantive tests.

24A. (a) AU 319.47 states, "[Various] characteristics influence the nature, timing, and extent of the tests of controls that the auditor applies to obtain evidential matter about control risk. The auditor selects such tests from a variety of techniques such as inquiry, observation, inspection, and reperformance of a policy or procedure that pertains to an assertion." Answers (b), (c), and (d) each represent a substantive test.

25. (b) Incompatible functions are those that place any person in a position to both perpetrate and conceal errors or irregularities in the normal course of his or her duties. Therefore, a well-designed plan of organization separates the duties of *authorization*, *recordkeeping*, and *custody* of assets.

25A. (d) AU 319.11 states, "[Control procedures] pertain to...the segregation of duties that reduce the opportunities to allow any person to be in a position to both perpetrate and conceal errors or irregularities in the normal course of his [or her] duties." Answers (a), (b), and (c) are incompatible functions that could result in errors or irregularities by the person with these responsibilities.

26. (b) Tests of transactions can accomplish both testing of controls and substantive testing. Tests of controls are accomplished when the auditor examines supporting documentation to determine if the system of internal control is working as prescribed.

27. (b) A function of internal control is to provide assurance that errors and irregularities may be discovered with reasonable promptness. "The auditor's understanding of the internal control structure should either heighten or mitigate the auditor's concern about the risk of material misstatements." (AU 316.10) The consideration of internal control is not concerned with the operational efficiency of the entity. A consideration of internal control will not in itself provide reasonable assurance that a misstatement that is intentional and is concealed through collusion or management intervention has occurred.

28. (d) After obtaining an understanding of the client's EDP controls, the auditor must assess control risk with respect to the EDP portion of the client's internal control structure. If the auditor decides that the controls appear adequate and that he or she will assess control risk at below the maximum level he or she must then perform tests of controls on these controls. The auditor may decide that, although the controls appear adequate, he or she will not perform any tests of controls to determine the assessed level of control risk. The auditor would reach this conclusion if: (1) he or she believes the effort required to assess control risk is greater than the reduction in audit effort that would result from assessing control risk at below the maximum level or (2) he or she believes the controls are redundant because of the existence of other control procedures. The auditor may decide that he or she does not wish to assess control risk for any of the EDP controls because he or she believes the EDP portion of the client's internal control structure is inadequate for his or her purposes (either because of weaknesses or because of the types of controls it includes). The auditor will, therefore, not perform any tests of controls on the EDP controls.

Sales, Receivables, and Cash Receipts Cycle

29. (a) Periodically accounting for the daily sales summaries posting to the accounts receivable ledger helps ensure that all entries affecting the sales and receivables accounts have been recognized and posted. Answer (b) does not ensure that the transaction has been posted to the receivable ledger. Answer (c) would not identify any missed sales summaries not included in the accounts receivable ledger, therefore, allowing those sales to go unposted to the accounts receivable ledger. Answer (d) is concerned with the proper issuance of credit for returned goods and not the posting of sales to the receivable ledger.

30. (d) Answers (a), (b), and (c) are all controls applicable to the billing process. Answer (d) is a control used *after* the billing process.

31. (b) To achieve a proper segregation of duties, immediately upon the receipt of cash, a remittance listing should be prepared by a responsible employee who does not have further access to the cash. Such a listing provides an independent record of the cash received for those who subsequently record the amounts in the cash receipts journal.

31A. (c) By immediately recording the receipt of the checks, the employee is providing evidence of the existence of cash. While each of the procedures in answers (a), (b), and (d) should be performed, preparing a duplicate listing of the checks is of immediate concern.

32. (a) The treasury department acts in a guardianship capacity over assets. Since writing off bad debts involves the safekeeping of those assets, this function should be performed by the treasury department. The sales department does not concern itself with the custody of assets. The billing and accounts receivable departments function in a recording capacity and should not have custody of assets.

32A. (d) The treasury department is independent of the recordkeeping and custodial functions for the accounts receivable. Incompatible functions are those that place any person in a position to both perpetrate and conceal errors or irregularities in the normal course of his or her duties. Therefore, a well-designed plan of organization separates the duties of *authorization*, *recordkeeping*, and *custody* of assets. Answer (a) would not separate the authorization and recordkeeping functions. The authorization for approval of credit and write-off of accounts by the same department could allow for an employee defalcation scheme. Answer (c) is incorrect because this department would not have adequate information to make such a recommendation and could result in the concealment of errors or irregularities.

33. (b) In addition to indemnification in case of loss, fidelity bonds provide a psychological deterrent to employees considering defalcations. The insurance company's investigation before an employee is bonded tends to discourage those with intentions of committing defalcations from accepting jobs requiring bonds. A further deterrent is the employee's knowledge that the insurance company will prosecute in an effort to recover a material loss, whereas the employer might be persuaded to forego prosecution.

34. (c) The most effective control in offsetting the tendency of sales personnel to maximize sales volume at the expense of high bad debt write-offs would be the segregation of duties of those employees involved in the credit-granting function and those employees in the sales function. If this segregation of duties exists, those employees in the credit-granting function should help to screen those potential customers likely to result in high bad-debt write-offs.

35. (d) An entity with a large volume of mail receipts should use a bank lockbox system to reduce the risk of employee misappropriation of cash. Under this type of security system, the bank picks up the mail daily, credits the company for the cash, and sends the remittance advices to the company. Fidelity bonds work as insurance for the employer if an employee misappropriates cash. However, it does not always reduce the risk of misappropriation. Although independently prepared mailroom prelists may be an effective internal control in this situation, this is a less effective control than a lockbox system (the employee still has access to the cash). A summary of checks received daily is not as effective as a lockbox system (the employee still handles the cash).

36. (c) Answer (c) identifies the segregation of custody and reporting as important internal controls. Authorization of write-offs by a supervisor is a good control but would not in itself prevent an employee from misappropriating accounts receivable collections because the supervisor is unfamiliar with the accounts, as indicated in the question, and would, therefore, not be aware of customers who are delinquent in their payments. Answers (a) and (d) are examples of good internal controls but would not by themselves uncover a lapping of collections scheme.

37. (d) Internal verifications of cash balances should generally be made monthly. Recorded cash on hand and petty cash balances should be compared with cash counts, and recorded bank balances should be reconciled to balances shown on bank statements. These verifications should be made by personnel who are not otherwise involved in executing or recording cash transactions to maintain a segregation of functions. The cash receipts accountant, the cash disbursements accountant, and the controller should not reconcile the monthly statements as they are involved in the executing or recording of cash transactions.

38. (b) In this case, the auditor is concerned with minimizing errors of failure to invoice a *shipment*. Therefore, we want to examine the "bill of lading file" since it will indicate the time, description, quantity, etc., of merchandise shipped. The merchandise ordered/sold in the files described in answers (a), (c), and (d) may not have been shipped yet.

38A. (b) Tracing from the source document (shipping document) to the recorded item (invoice) provides evidence of completeness. That is, all shipments should be invoiced. To test for answer (a), the auditor vouches from the sales invoices back to the shipping documents, sales orders, and customer orders. To test for answer (c), the auditor traces forward from the customer order to the sales order to the shipping documents. To test for answer (d), the auditor accounts for a sequence of invoice numbers.

Purchases, Payables, and Cash Disbursements Cycle

39. (b) AU 326.04 states that assertions about existence or occurrence deal with whether assets or liabilities of the entity exist at a given date and whether recorded transactions have occurred during a given period. Thus, management asserts that the purchases reported are the result of transactions occurring through a given date. This would be tested by vouching entries from the voucher register to the supporting documentation. Answer (a) tests the opposite, vouching from the source documents to the financial statement amounts. Assertions about valuation and allocation would be tested by comparing the costs to purchase invoices received from outside vendors. Assertions about rights and obligations are focused more on asset and liability accounts and would be tested primarily by confirmation procedures.

40. (d) Accounting for unused purchase orders and receiving reports by the same department does not provide sufficient segregation of duties for the authorization, custody, and reporting functions of an effective internal control system. The lack of segregation of these items could result in an employee defalcation scheme. Answers (a), (b), and (c) are incorrect because they each represent a procedure that is usually performed in the vouchers payable department.

41. (b) Good internal controls require that the person who last signs the checks keep control of them until they are mailed. Answers (a), (c), and (d) do not provide sufficient segregation of duties for the authorization, custodial, and reporting functions of an effective internal control system.

42. (a) Internal controls are not mitigated by the fact that the individual with the authority to sign checks also cancels the supporting documents. By doing so, the person in authority ensures that the documents are not presented for payment again. Answers (b), (c), and (d) represent situations where there is a lack of segregation of duties for the authorization, custody, and reporting of items that could result in an employee defalcation scheme. The receiving and purchasing departments should not be involved with the custody of assets.

42A. (b) Incompatible functions are those that place any person in a position to both perpetrate and conceal errors or irregularities in the normal course of his or her duties. Therefore, a well-designed plan of organization separates the duties of authorization, record keeping and custody of assets. Answers (a), (c) and (d) would allow the same employee to perform too much of the recordkeeping function to where it becomes possible to conceal irregularities or allow errors to go undetected.

43. (b) When the shipping department returns nonconforming goods to a vendor the purchasing department should send to the accounting department the debit memo. This enables the accounting department to make the appropriate adjustment to the vendor's account. Answers (a) and (c) are incorrect because the accounting department would have no use for the unpaid voucher and the vendor invoice. Answer (d) is incorrect because a credit memo would be provided by the vendor, not by the purchasing department.

44. (c) AU 319.34 indicates that tests of controls to obtain evidential matter relating to whether policies and procedures are suitably designed to prevent or detect material misstatements in financial statement assertions include inquiries, inspection of documents and reports, and observation of the application of the specific policies and procedures. Analytical procedures and confirmation are substantive tests of the accounting records and not tests of controls.

44A. (b) By immediately stamping "paid" on the paid voucher, the check signer prevents the voucher from being paid again. While each of the items in answers (a), (c), and (d) is a recommended practice, none prevent the voucher from being paid again.

45. (d) The most effective controls over recorded purchases occur when supporting forms such as purchase orders, receiving reports, and vendor invoices are compared independently for agreement. For good control, the receiving department should not know the quantity ordered. Answer (b) is a step in the right direction, but does not encompass as many independent comparisons as does answer (d). Answer (c) is an example of incompatible functions. The assets should not be checked in and recorded by the same person who authorized their purchase.

46. (b) When the internal control structure dictates that each check be accompanied by an approved voucher, and supported by a prenumbered purchase order and a prenumbered receiving report, the auditor would select items for testing from the population of all the canceled checks. If the auditor were to consider populations made up of all purchase

orders, receiving reports, or approved vouchers, those canceled checks which were issued without such supporting documentation would not be discovered.

47. (b) The agreement of the documents will verify that the goods were ordered (purchase order), received (receiving report), and the company has been billed (vendor's invoice). The purchasing department, not the accounting department, will obliterate the quantity ordered on the receiving department copy of the purchase order. The individual signing the checks should stamp, perforate, or otherwise cancel supporting documentation. The accounting department should not be responsible for these tasks. The purchasing department, not the accounting department, is involved with the approval of purchase requisitions.

47A. (d) Approved borrowings by the board of directors indicate that transactions must be approved before the recording and custody functions can take place. This is also performed by a party independent of the recording and custody functions.

48. (c) The next step is to approve the voucher for payment. Only after the voucher is approved should the check be written, the supporting documents canceled (to prevent paying the same invoice twice) and the payment posted.

Inventory and Production Cycle

49. (d) A good system of internal controls will include the segregation of duties, such as the comparison of an approved purchase order to items received. Answers (a) and (c) represent documentation included with the order as it is received, without any indication of authorization. Answer (b) represents a form used when goods and materials are taken from the inventory supply to be used or shipped.

49A. (a) To test for appropriate segregation of duties, the auditor makes inquiries and conducts observations. The procedures in answers (b), (c), and (d) are not applicable to testing for segregation of duties.

50. (b) For sound internal controls, all receipts for goods, including returned goods or materials, should be handled by the receiving clerk. Receiving reports should be prepared for all items received. Those employees who have recording responsibilities should not also be given custody of the related assets.

51. (b) In a batch sales order processing system, sales are processed periodically in groups. An on-line sales order processing system would enable processing to take place immediately as an order was placed, thereby allowing shipment of customer orders to be initiated as soon as the order was received. Edit programs may detect errors in either an on-line or a batch processing system. The relative security of backup copies of the data base would not be affected by the type of sales order processing system used. Either system allows the maintenance of accurate records.

52. (a) In obtaining an understanding of a manufacturing entity's internal control structure concerning inventory balances, an auditor would review the entity's descriptions of inventory policies and procedures. The performance of inventory test counts and the analysis of inventory turnover statistics and monthly production reports would be considered subsequent to the auditor obtaining the understanding of the internal control structure.

53. (c) An independent comparison of finished goods records with counts of goods on hand would be an audit procedure designed to detect errors and irregularities concerning custody of the inventory as it would provide an independent reconciliation of the two amounts. Answers (a) and (b) do not consider the inventory itself nor the custody of the inventory. The storekeeper should not have both access to the inventory and authorization responsibilities.

54. (c) Use of time tickets indicates the amount of actual labor employed during the day on a given job. An internal control procedure requiring the use of charging the actual time to the job in progress would help prevent mistakes in the recording of direct and indirect labor. Answers (a) and (d) would indicate variances after improperly charging direct labor to factory overhead, but would not be good preventative measures. Answer (b) would have no effect on identifying misposted direct labor.

55. (b) Incompatible functions are those that place any person in a position to both perpetrate and conceal errors or irregularities in the normal course of his or her duties. Therefore, a well-designed plan of organization separates the duties of *authorization*, *recordkeeping*, and *custody* of assets. Answers (a) and (c) do not separate custody and recordkeeping. Answer (d) would not provide verification of inventory.

56. (d) AU 326.04 states "Assertions about existence or occurrence deal with whether assets or liabilities of the entity exist at a given date and whether recorded transactions have occurred during a

given period." In this question, periodically comparing goods on hand with perpetual inventory records would assist in identifying any potential errors. Answer (a) addresses the valuation of the inventory. Answer (b) would not identify variances in actual inventory on hand compared to the recorded amounts. Answer (c) represents examples of controls necessary for the proper segregation of duties in purchasing inventory.

57. (b) Controlling the access to assets is an important objective of proper inventory control. Answers (a), (c), and (d) are procedures for satisfying inventory control objectives--not actual internal control objectives.

58. (d) Inventory can be stolen, lost, or diverted, potentially resulting in misapplied assets and misstated accounts. As a result, access to inventory should be restricted to personnel authorized by management. Management should establish physical controls over inventory (e.g., fences, locks, inventory control clerks), maintain insurance--both for inventory and for inventory personnel (i.e., fidelity bonds), segregate responsibility for handling inventory from inventory recording, cost accounting, and general accounting, and also restrict access to production, cost accounting, and perpetual inventory records. An auditor generally tests these controls by inquiry and observation. Answers (a), (b), and (c) deal with the testing of inventory *records* (i.e., documents and transactions).

Personnel and Payroll Cycle

59. (c) Incompatible functions are those that place any person in a position to both perpetrate and conceal errors or irregularities in the normal course of his or her duties. Therefore, a well-designed plan of organization separates the duties of authorization, record keeping, and custody of assets. Answers (a) and (d) are similar in that they would place the functions of authorization and custody or personal bias under the control of one person. General accounting should perform the processing of payroll.

60. (c) Incompatible functions are those that place any person in a position to both perpetrate and conceal errors or irregularities in the normal course of his or her duties. Therefore, a well-designed plan of organization separates the duties of authorization, recordkeeping, and custody of assets.

61. (a) The authorization of a transaction, its record keeping, and the custody of the related asset should all be separated. In a payroll function, the treasurer's department would prepare the payroll checks and distribute them to employees (custody), the controller would review the payroll, and the payroll department would prepare the payroll (recordkeeping).

62. (c) Control totals may be used to detect errors in processing when information is batched before entry. One type of control total is a *hash total* which is a total of field amounts for all the records in a batch that are computed for control purposes only. For example, the total of the department numbers would have no intrinsic value. Conversely, the total of hours worked, debits and credits, and net pay are normally computed in the payroll process and have intrinsic meaning in the engagement. Therefore, answers (a), (b), and (d) are incorrect.

63. (c) A weakness in internal control would be evidenced by an employee who distributes payroll checks and who returns unclaimed payroll checks to the payroll department. The treasurer should be given custody of unclaimed paychecks. The accounting department would normally prepare a voucher for the amount of payroll, based on the payroll department's payroll summary. The payroll checks would normally be prepared by the payroll department and signed by the treasurer. The personnel department would normally send employees' termination notices to the payroll department to allow the removal of terminated employees from the payroll.

64. (d) The requirement is to find the symbolic representation which indicates two forms of input (new payroll transactions and the old payroll file) being processed to generate three forms of output (payroll checks, printed payroll journal, and a new payroll file). Answer (a) shows only one input with four forms of output. Answer (b) represents a manual process while the facts given indicate that a printed payroll journal is to be generated. Answer (c) is incorrect, because one of the output functions is shown as a punched card when payroll checks, a printed payroll journal, and a new payroll file should be represented in the output.

Property, Plant, and Equipment Cycle

65. (d) The procedures in place to monitor and properly restrict access to equipment would more likely be *observed* by the auditor than be part of a questionnaire, as this is very important. Answer (a) represents the authorization function of the control structure, which would be included on the internal control questionnaire. Answer (b) represents a procedure to test the accounting and recording function of the control structure, which the auditor would include in the control structure questionnaire.

Requests for competitive bids reduce the possibility of an individual's personal gain at the expense of the business in unusual and material transactions.

66. (c) The investigation of variances within a formal budgeting system would identify any unusual and unanticipated fluctuations in the repairs and maintenance accounts when asset acquisitions are incorrectly recorded there. While the segregation of duties is necessary for good internal controls; however, answer (a) would not ensure that equipment acquisitions were not misclassified. Answer (b) is also a good internal control, but would not ensure that equipment purchases were properly recorded because these invoices only represent those acquisitions which are already properly recorded as fixed assets. Answer (d) would not prevent the recording of the acquisition to the repairs and maintenance accounts, nor would it serve to identify misclassifications.

67. (a) The internal control procedure of the periodic inspection of physical equipment to what is recorded by the internal auditor who does not actively participate in the acquisition or disposal process would allow for a reduction in the scope of the auditor's tests of asset acquisitions. The comparison of account balances and entries is an analytical procedure that would highlight unusual and unanticipated fluctuations; however, it would not indicate acquisitions which were not approved. The review of prenumbered purchase orders would indicate trade-ins or retirements of fixed assets in exchange for new assets; thus, there would be no change in the quantity of fixed assets on hand.

68. (b) The auditor may test the internal control over the recording of retirements by tracing certain items of equipment from the accounting records and locating them in the plant to make sure that they have not been retired. The "other assets" account has nothing to do with the recording of retired assets. Tracing from the plant assets to the books does not consider assets which may appear on the books even though they have been retired. The depreciation of equipment has nothing to do with whether or not the equipment has been retired.

69. (d) AU 319.63 states, " ... regardless of the assessed level of control risk, the auditor should perform *substantive tests* for *significant* account balances and transaction classes." AU 319.30 states, "Assessing control risk at below the maximum level involves ... performing *tests of controls* to evaluate the effectiveness of policies and procedures." An auditor would also perform tests of controls to assess control risk at a low level. The auditor would perform tests of controls to assess control risk at a low level, but would perform only limited substantive tests.

Investing Cycle

70. (a) The fact that only the trust company has access to the securities should prevent unauthorized entity personnel with record keeping responsibility from conspiring or colluding to misappropriate the securities. Trust company employees or management could potentially sell or otherwise mismanage the assets. Answers (c) and (d) put the custody and record keeping functions in the hands of one individual or party which could result in unauthorized transactions of the securities.

71. (d) Custody of investment securities is usually maintained on the company premises or assigned to an outside agent such as a brokerage house. Good internal controls dictate that at least two officers should sign for and be present to access these investments to prevent unauthorized sales. Answer (a) is incorrect because there is no guarantee that unauthorized access to the investments during the time period indicated did not occur. Answers (b) and (c) are good internal controls, but do not address the physical control of the assets as asked for in the question.

72. (a) Of the choices given, the strongest internal control in safeguarding against the loss of marketable securities would be the use of an independent trust company that has no direct contact with the employees who have record keeping responsibilities. The fact that only the trust company has access to the securities should prevent unauthorized entity personnel with record keeping responsibility from conspiring or colluding to misappropriate the securities. In determining appropriate controls in safeguarding an asset against loss, the auditor would start with those controls involving access to the asset in question. Neither verifying the securities in the safe nor tracing all purchases and sales provides evidence as to who has access to, or custody of, the marketable securities. It is not a strong control to allow just one person access to an asset. This enables the individual to take the asset without being discovered.

Communication of Internal Control Structure Related Matters Noted in an Audit (AU 325)

73. (c) AU 325.18 states that reportable conditions may be communicated during the course of the audit or after its completion. AU 325.02 does not require the auditor to search for reportable conditions. AU 325.15 specifies which reportable conditions might

be considered material weaknesses. AU 325.17 prohibits an auditor from reporting that no reportable conditions were noted.

74. (c) AU 325.11 states that any report issued on reportable conditions should include the definition of reportable conditions, indicate that the purpose of the audit was to report on the financial statements and not to provide assurance on the internal control structure, and include a restriction on distribution. The restriction in the report should state that the communication is intended solely for the information and the use of the audit committee, management, and others within the organization. Reportable conditions do not create scope limitations, and management may have made a conscious decision, of which the audit committee is aware, to accept the degree of risk related to the reportable condition due to cost or other considerations. It is the responsibility of management to make the decision concerning costs to be incurred and related benefits of any corrective measures. The auditor's objective in an audit of financial statements is to form an opinion on the entity's financial statements taken as a whole. The auditor is not obligated to search for reportable conditions. Because timely communication may be important, the auditor may choose to communicate significant matters during the course of the audit, rather than after the audit is concluded (AU 325.18). The auditor is not required to perform tests of controls on reportable conditions; however, performing tests of controls in an audit may reveal reportable conditions. AU 325.18 states that, because timely communication may be important, the auditor may choose to communicate significant matters during the course of the audit, rather than after the audit is concluded. The decision on whether an interim communication should be issued would be influenced by the significance of the matters noted and the urgency of corrective follow-up action, not in which stage of the audit the auditor is.

75. (d) AU 325.11 states that any report issued on reportable conditions should indicate that the purpose of the audit was to report on the financial statements and not to provide assurance on the internal control structure. Answers (a), (b), and (c) would not be used in the report on reportable conditions noted.

76. (a) AU 325.10 states that the report on reportable conditions should state that the communication is intended solely for the information and use of the audit committee, management, and others within the organization. Answers (b) and (c) should not be included in the letter. The auditor bases the nature, extent, and timing of his or her substantive tests on the operating effectiveness of the control structure. Management's evaluation of the internal control structure is not reported on by the auditor.

77. (a) AU 325.01 states, "It is contemplated that the communication (of internal control structure matters) would generally be to the audit committee or to individuals with a level of authority and responsibility equivalent to an audit committee in organizations that do not have one, such as the board of directors, the board of trustees, an owner in an owner-managed enterprise, or others who may have engaged the auditor." In some situations, the auditor may report to the director of internal auditing, chief financial officer or chief accounting officer, but whenever possible communication should be made with the audit committee.

77A. (b) AU 801.20 states, "In performing an audit in accordance with Government Auditing Standards, the auditor assumes responsibilities beyond those assumed in an audit conducted in accordance with GAAS to report on compliance with laws and regulations and on the internal control structure." The Yellow Book, *GAO Government Auditing Standards*, 5.21-.23 states that GAGAS require auditors to report irregularities directly to parties outside the auditee if the management of the auditee fails to take remedial steps or does not report the irregularity as soon as practicable to the appropriate entity. Per GAS 5.25, under some circumstances, laws, regulations, or policies may require the auditor to report promptly indications of certain types of irregularities to proper authorities.

78. (d) The auditor is *required* to report to the audit committee all "reportable conditions" (i.e. matters coming to the auditor's attention that, in his or her judgment, should be reported because they represent significant deficiencies in the design or operation of the internal control structure). The auditor may also choose to communicate, for the benefit of management, matters which would not fit the definition of reportable conditions (i.e., constructive suggestions) (AU 325.01-.03). Constructive suggestions would be a desirable by-product of the audit. They need not be limited to special engagements, nor are they required during the consideration of internal control.

79. (d) AU 325.02 states, "Specifically, (reportable conditions) are matters that come to the auditor's attention that, in his judgment, should be communicated to the audit committee because they represent significant deficiencies in the design or operation of the internal control structure, which could adversely

affect the organization's ability to record, process, summarize, and report financial data consistent with the assertions of management in the financial statements."

79A. (c) AU 325.02 states that reportable conditions are matters coming to the auditor's attention that, in his or her judgment, should be communicated to the audit committee because they represent significant deficiencies in the design or operation of the internal control structure, which could adversely affect the organization's ability to record, process, summarize, and report financial data consistent with the assertions of management in the financial statements. Reportable conditions do not necessarily indicate an inability for the entity to continue as a going concern. Answer (b) and (d) represent employee irregularities or illegal acts.

80. (d) AU 325.06 states, "Periodically, the auditor should consider whether, because of changes in management, the audit committee, or simply because of the passage of time, it is appropriate and timely to report (the existence of reportable conditions already known)." Answers (a) and (c) may affect the auditor's judgment about necessary audit procedures, but they would not require the recommunication of a previously communicated reportable condition. There is no point in communicating a reportable condition again if the entity is aware of and accepts the degree of risk associated with the condition.

81. (b) Any report issued on reportable conditions should (1) indicate that the purpose of the audit was to report on the financial statements and not to provide assurance on the internal control structure, (2) include the definition of reportable conditions, and (3) include the appropriate restriction on distribution (AU 325.11).

82. (b) AU 325.15 states, "A material weakness in the internal control structure is a reportable condition in which the design or operation of the specified internal control structure elements do not reduce to a relatively low level the risk that errors or irregularities in amounts that would be material in relation to the financial statements being audited may occur and not be detected within a timely period by employees in the normal course of performing their assigned functions."

83. (b) All material weaknesses are classified as reportable conditions; however, not all reportable conditions are of a serious enough nature to fall into the category of being a material weakness (AU 325.15). The auditor is not required to separately identify and communicate material weaknesses (AU 325.15). The auditor is not required to immediately report these conditions.

84. (b) AU 325.17 states, "Because of the potential for misinterpretation of the limited degree of assurance associated with the auditor issuing a written report representing that no reportable conditions were noted during an audit, the auditor should not issue such representations." *Significant deficiencies* are reportable conditions about which the report does not guarantee do not exist. Answers (a), (c), and (d) are all examples of items that could be included in a report on internal control structure related matters noted in an audit.

PERFORMANCE BY SUBTOPICS

Each category below parallels a subtopic covered in Chapter 36. Record the number and percentage of questions you correctly answered in each subtopic area.

Consideration of the Internal Control Structure in Planning the Audit (AU 319)

Question #	Correct √
1	
1A	
2	
2A	
2B	
2C	
3	
4	
4A	
5	
5A	
6	
6A	
7	
7A	
7B	
8	
8A	
8B	
9	
10	
10A	
11	
11A	
12	
12A	
13	
13A	
14	
15	
16	
17	
18	
19	
19A	
19B	
19C	
19D	
19E	
20	
21	
22	
23	
23A	
24	
24A	
25	
25A	
26	
27	
28	
# Questions	51

Correct ________
% Correct ________

Sales, Receivables, and Cash Receipts Cycle

Question #	Correct √
29	
30	
31	
31A	
32	
32A	
33	
34	
35	
36	
37	
38	
38A	
# Questions	13

Correct ________
% Correct ________

Purchases, Payables, and Cash Disbursements Cycle

Question #	Correct √
39	
40	
41	
42	
42A	
43	
44	
44A	
45	
46	
47	
47A	
48	
# Questions	13

Correct ________
% Correct ________

Inventory and Production Cycle

Question #	Correct √
49	
49A	
50	
51	
52	
53	
54	
55	
56	
57	
58	
# Questions	11

Correct ________
% Correct ________

Personnel and Payroll Cycle

Question #	Correct √
59	
60	
61	
62	
63	
64	
# Questions	6

Correct ________
% Correct ________

Property, Plant, and Equipment Cycle

Question #	Correct √
65	
66	
67	
68	
69	
# Questions	5

Correct ________
% Correct ________

Investing Cycle

Question #	Correct √
70	
71	
72	
# Questions	3

Correct ________
% Correct ________

Communication of Internal Control Structure Related Matters Noted in an Audit (AU 325)

Question #	Correct √
73	
74	
75	
76	
77	
77A	
78	
79	
79A	
80	
81	
82	
83	
84	
# Questions	14

Correct ________
% Correct ________

ESSAY QUESTIONS

Essay 36-2 (15 to 25 minutes)

Field, CPA, is auditing the financial statements of Miller Mailorder, Inc. (MMI) for the year ended January 31, 1995. Field has compiled a list of possible errors and irregularities that may result in the misstatement of MMI's financial statements, and a corresponding list of internal control procedures that, if properly designed and implemented, could assist MMI in preventing or detecting the errors and irregularities.

Required:

For each possible error and irregularity numbered **1 through 15**, select one internal control procedure from the answer list that, if properly designed and implemented, most likely could assist MMI in preventing or detecting the errors and irregularities. Each response in the list of internal control procedures may be selected once, more than once, or not at all.

Possible Errors and Irregularities

1. Invoices for goods sold are posted to incorrect customer accounts.

2. Goods ordered by customers are shipped, but are **not** billed to anyone.

3. Invoices are sent for shipped goods, but are **not** recorded in the sales journal.

4. Invoices are sent for shipped goods and are recorded in the sales journal, but are **not** posted to any customer account.

5. Credit sales are made to individuals with unsatisfactory credit ratings.

6. Goods are removed from inventory for unauthorized orders.

7. Goods shipped to customers do **not** agree with goods ordered by customers.

8. Invoices are sent to allies in a fraudulent scheme and sales are recorded for fictitious transactions.

9. Customers' checks are received for less than the customers' full account balances, but the customers' full account balances are credited.

10. Customers' checks are misappropriated before being forwarded to the cashier for deposit.

11. Customers' checks are credited to incorrect customer accounts.

12. Different customer accounts are each credited for the same cash receipt.

13. Customers' checks are properly credited to customer accounts and are properly deposited, but errors are made in recording receipts in the cash receipts journal.

14. Customers' checks are misappropriated after being forwarded to the cashier for deposit.

15. Invalid transactions granting credit for sales returns are recorded.

Internal Control Procedures

A. Shipping clerks compare goods received from the warehouse with the details on the shipping documents.

B. Approved sales orders are required for goods to be released from the warehouse.

C. Monthly statements are mailed to all customers with outstanding balances.

D. Shipping clerks compare goods received from the warehouse with approved sales orders.

E. Customer orders are compared with the inventory master file to determine whether items ordered are in stock.

F. Daily sales summaries are compared with control totals of invoices.

G. Shipping documents are compared with sales invoices when goods are shipped.

H. Sales invoices are compared with the master price file.

I. Customer orders are compared with an approved customer list.

J. Sales orders are prepared for each customer order.

K. Control amounts posted to the accounts receivable ledger are compared with control totals of invoices.

L. Sales invoices are compared with shipping documents and approved customer orders before invoices are mailed.

M. Prenumbered credit memos are used for granting credit for goods returned.

N. Goods returned for credit are approved by the supervisor of the sales department.

O. Remittance advices are separated from the checks in the mailroom and forwarded to the accounting department.

P. Total amounts posted to the accounts receivable ledger from remittance advices are compared with the validated bank deposit slip.

Q. The cashier examines each check for proper endorsement.

R. Validated deposit slips are compared with the cashier's daily cash summaries.

S. An employee, other than the bookkeeper, periodically prepares a bank reconciliation.

T. Sales returns are approved by the same employee who issues receiving reports evidencing actual return of goods.

(5/95, Aud., #3)

Essay 36-3 (15 to 25 minutes)

Butler, CPA, has been engaged to audit the financial statements of Young Computer Outlets, Inc., a new client. Young is a privately-owned chain of retail stores that sells a variety of computer software and video products. Young uses an in-house payroll department at its corporate headquarters to compute payroll data, and to prepare and distribute payroll checks to its 300 salaried employees. Butler is preparing an internal control questionnaire to assist in obtaining an understanding of Young's internal control structure and in assessing control risk.

Required:

Prepare a "Payroll" segment of Butler's internal control questionnaire that would assist in obtaining an understanding of Young's internal control structure and in assessing control risk. Do **not** prepare questions relating to cash payrolls, EDP applications, payments based on hourly rates, piecework, commissions, employee benefits (pensions, health care, vacations, etc.), or payroll tax accruals other than withholdings.

Use the format in the following example:

Question	*Yes*	*No*
Are paychecks prenumbered and accounted for?		

(5/93, Aud., #3)

Essay 36-4 (15 to 20 minutes)

Smith, CPA, has been engaged to audit the financial statements of Reed, Inc., a publicly held retailing company. Before assessing control risk, Smith is required to obtain an understanding of Reed's control environment.

Required:

a. Identify additional control environment factors (excluding the factor illustrated in the example below) that establish, enhance, or mitigate the effectiveness of specific policies and procedures.

b. For the control environment factors identified in **a,** describe the components that could be of interest to the auditor.

Use the following format:

Management Philosophy and Operating Style

Management philosophy and operating style characteristics may include the following: management's approach to taking and monitoring business risks; management's attitudes and actions toward financial reporting; and management's emphasis on meeting budget, profit, and other financial and operating goals. (11/91, Aud., #3)

Essay 36-5 (15 to 25 minutes)

An auditor is required to obtain a sufficient understanding of each of the elements of an entity's internal control structure. This is necessary to plan the audit of the entity's financial statements and to assess control risk.

Required:

a. For what purposes should an auditor's understanding of the internal control structure elements be used in planning an audit?

b. What is required for an auditor to assess control risk at below the maximum level?

c. What should an auditor consider when seeking a further reduction in the planned assessed level of control risk?

d. What are an auditor's documentation requirements concerning an entity's internal control structure and the assessed level of control risk?

(11/92, Aud., #4)

Essay 36-6 (15 to 20 minutes)

Harris, CPA, has accepted an engagement to audit the financial statements of Grant Manufacturing Co., a new client. Grant has an adequate control environment and a reasonable segregation of duties. Harris is about to assess control risk for the assertions related to Grant's property and equipment.

Required:

Describe the key internal control structure policies and procedures related to Grant's property, equipment and related transactions (additions, transfers, major maintenance and repairs, retirements, and dispositions) that Harris may consider in assessing control risk. (5/92, Aud., #3)

Essay 36-7 (15 to 25 minutes)

During the course of an audit made in accordance with generally accepted auditing standards, an auditor may become aware of matters relating to the client's internal control structure that may be of interest to the client's audit committee or to individuals with an equivalent level of authority and responsibility, such as the board of directors, the board of trustees, or the owner in an owner-managed enterprise.

Required:

a. What are meant by the terms "reportable conditions" and "material weaknesses"?

b. What are an auditor's responsibilities in identifying and reporting these matters?

(5/90, Aud., #3)

Essay 36-8 (15 to 25 minutes)

The flowchart below depicts the activities relating to the purchasing, receiving, and accounts payable departments of Model Company, Inc.

Required:

Based only on the flowchart, describe the internal control procedures (strengths) that most likely would provide reasonable assurance that specific internal control objectives for the financial statement assertions regarding purchases and accounts payable will be achieved. Do **not** describe weaknesses in the internal control structure. (5/91, Aud., #4)

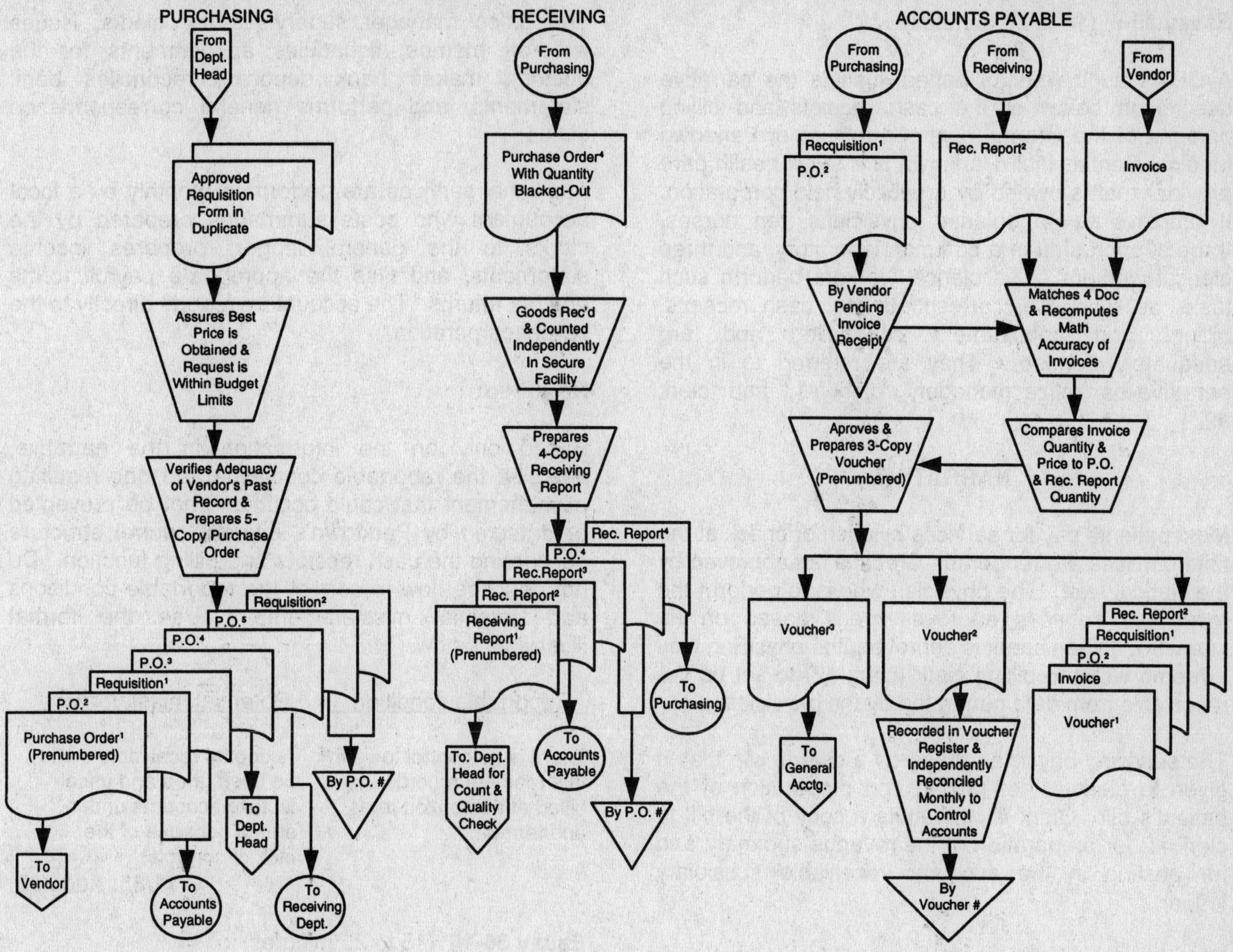
PURCHASING
From Dept. Head
Approved Requisition Form in Duplicate
Assures Best Price is Obtained & Request is Within Budget Limits
Verifies Adequacy of Vendor's Past Record & Prepares 5-Copy Purchase Order
Requisition²
P.O.⁵
P.O.⁴
P.O.³
Requisition¹
P.O.²
Purchase Order¹ (Prenumbered)
To Vendor
To Accounts Payable
To Dept. Head
To Receiving Dept.
By P.O. #
RECEIVING
From Purchasing
Purchase Order⁴ With Quantity Blacked-Out
Goods Rec'd & Counted Independently In Secure Facility
Prepares 4-Copy Receiving Report
Rec. Report⁴
P.O.⁴
Rec.Report³
Rec. Report²
Receiving Report¹ (Prenumbered)
To. Dept. Head for Count & Quality Check
To Accounts Payable
By P.O. #
To Purchasing
ACCOUNTS PAYABLE
From Purchasing
From Receiving
From Vendor
Requisition¹
P.O.²
Rec. Report²
Invoice
By Vendor Pending Invoice Receipt
Matches 4 Doc & Recomputes Math Accuracy of Invoices
Compares Invoice Quantity & Price to P.O. & Rec. Report Quantity
Aproves & Prepares 3-Copy Voucher (Prenumbered)
Voucher³
To General Acctg.
Voucher²
Recorded in Voucher Register & Independently Reconciled Monthly to Control Accounts
By Voucher #
Rec. Report²
Requisition¹
P.O.²
Invoice
Voucher¹

Essay 36-9 (15 to 25 minutes)

A CPA's audit working papers include the narrative description below of the cash receipts and billing portions of the internal control structure of Parktown Medical Center, Inc. Parktown is a small health care provider that is owned by a publicly held corporation. It employs seven salaried physicians, ten nurses, three support staff in a common laboratory, and three clerical workers. The clerical workers perform such tasks as reception, correspondence, cash receipts, billing, and appointment scheduling and are adequately bonded. They are referred to in the narrative as "office manager," "clerk #1," and "clerk #2."

NARRATIVE

Most patients pay for services by cash or check at the time services are rendered. Credit is not approved by the clerical staff. The physician who is to perform the respective services approves credit based on an interview. When credit is approved, the physician files a memo with the billing clerk (clerk #2) to set up the receivable from data generated by the physician.

The servicing physician prepares a charge slip that is given to clerk #1 for pricing and preparation of the patient's bill. Clerk #1 transmits a copy of the bill to clerk #2 for preparation of the revenue summary and for posting in the accounts receivable subsidiary ledger.

The cash receipts functions are performed by clerk #1, who receives cash and checks directly from patients and gives each patient a prenumbered cash receipt. Clerk #1 opens the mail and immediately stamps all checks "for deposit only" and lists cash and checks for deposit. The cash and checks are deposited daily by the office manager. The list of cash and checks together with the related remittance advices are forwarded by clerk #1 to clerk #2. Clerk #1 also serves as receptionist and performs general correspondence duties.

Clerk #2 prepares and sends monthly statements to patients with unpaid balances. Clerk #2 also prepares the cash receipts journal and is responsible for the accounts receivable subsidiary ledger. No other clerical employee is permitted access to the accounts receivable subsidiary ledger. Uncollectible accounts are written off by clerk #2 only after the physician who performed the respective services believes the account to be uncollectible and communicates the write-off approval to the office manager. The office manager then issues a write-off memo that clerk #2 processes.

The office manager supervises the clerks, issues write-off memos, schedules appointments for the doctors, makes bank deposits, reconciles bank statements, and performs general correspondence duties.

Additional services are performed monthly by a local accountant who posts summaries prepared by the clerks to the general ledger, prepares income statements, and files the appropriate payroll forms and tax returns. The accountant reports directly to the parent corporation.

Required:

Based only on the information in the narrative, describe the reportable conditions and one resulting misstatement that could occur and not be prevented or detected by Parktown's internal control structure concerning the cash receipts and billing function. Do not describe how to correct the reportable conditions and potential misstatements. Use the format illustrated below.

Reportable condition	Potential misstatement
There is no control to verify that fees are recorded and billed at authorized rates and terms.	Accounts receivable could be overstated and uncollectible accounts understated because of the lack of controls.

(11/85, Aud., #5)

Essay 36-10 (15 to 25 minutes)

Martin, CPA, has been engaged to express an opinion on Beta Manufacturing Company's internal control structure in effect as of June 1, 1992.

Required:

a. Compare Martin's examination of the internal control structure for the purpose of expressing an opinion on it with the consideration of the internal control structure made as part of an audit of the financial statements made in accordance with generally accepted auditing standards. The comparison should be made as to the (1) scope, (2) purpose, and (3) timing of the engagements, and (4) users of the reports.

b. Identify the major contents of Martin's report expressing an opinion on Beta's internal control structure. Do **not** draft the report.

(5/87, Aud., #4, amended)

Essay 36-11 (15 to 25 minutes)

The flowchart below depicts the activities relating to the sales, shipping, billing, and collecting processes used by Newton Hardware, Inc.

Required:

Identify the weaknesses in the internal control structure relating to the activities of (a) the warehouse clerk, (b) bookkeeper A, and (c) the collection clerk. Do not identify weaknesses relating to the sales clerk or bookkeepers B and C. Do not discuss recommendations concerning the correction of these weaknesses. (5/88, Aud., #4)

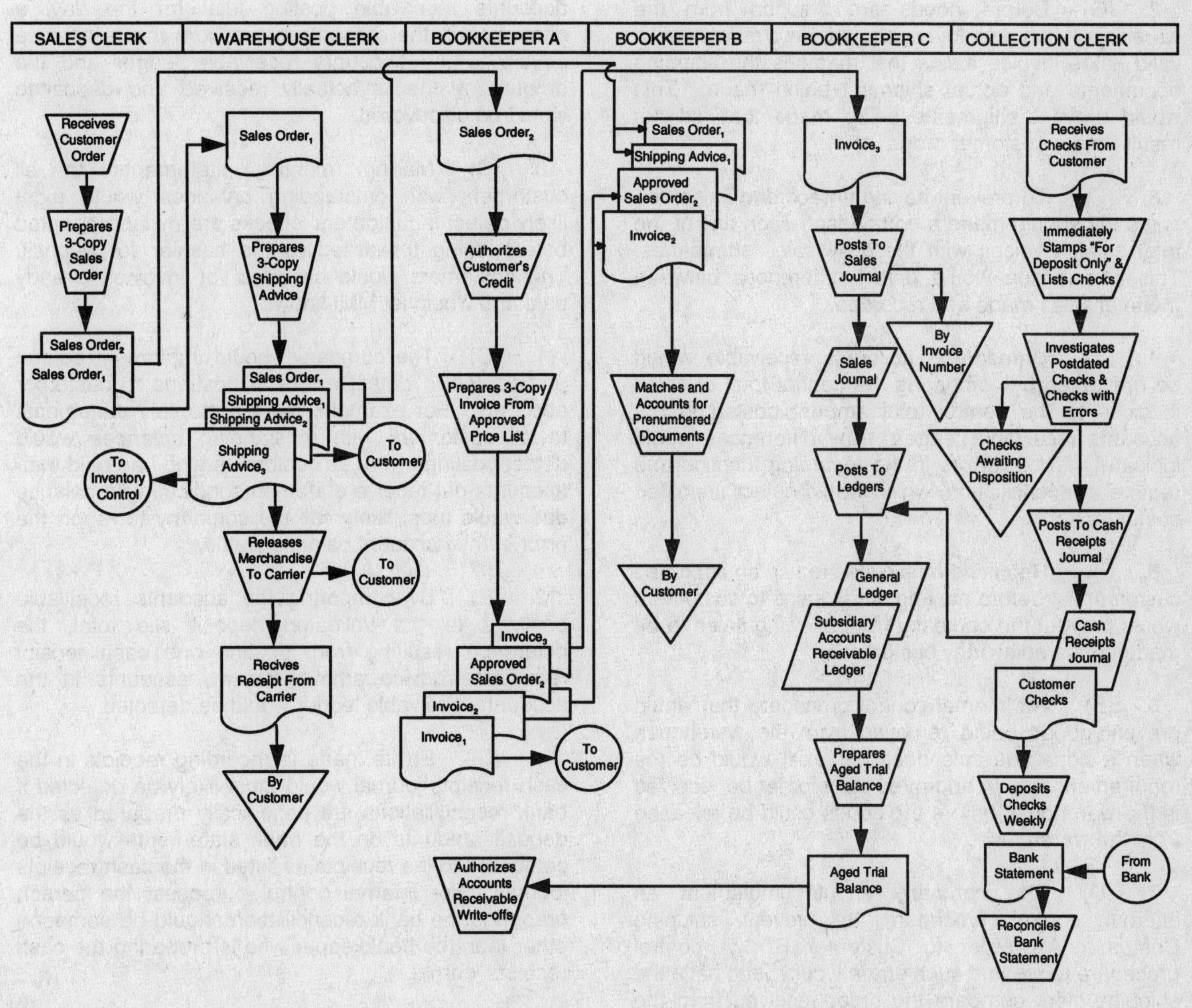

ESSAY SOLUTIONS

Solution 36-2 Procedures

1. (C) The error of posting a customer's payment to the wrong account would be detected when his or her monthly statement was received, indicating a balance due, when payment had already been made.

2. (G) Before goods are shipped from the warehouse, an employee should determine that a valid sales invoice exists that matches the shipping documents and actual shipment being made. This would prevent shipments being made that did not result from a customer order.

3. (F) To prevent having unrecorded sales, the company should make a comparison each day of the total sales invoices with the daily sales summaries. This comparison would detect differences between the total sales made and recorded.

4. (K) Unrecorded accounts receivable would be prevented by comparing the control total of sales invoices to the control total amount posted to the accounts receivable ledger. Any differences would indicate possible errors in the recording function and require a reconciliation, which would detect unposted customer sales.

5. (I) Requiring employees to use an approved customer list before making credit sales to customers would prevent the company from allowing sales to be made to uncreditworthy customers.

6. (B) An internal control procedure that would prevent goods being removed from the warehouse when a bona fide sale does not exist would be the requirement that an approved sales order be received in the warehouse before the goods could be released from the warehouse.

7. (D) The company should implement an internal control procedure to prevent shipping Customer A's order to Customer B. A control procedure to prevent such errors would be to have the shipping clerk compare the order received from the warehouse and prepared for shipping to the approved customer sales order.

8. (L) The company would be able to prevent a fraudulent sales scheme where sales were recorded for fictitious transactions if certain control procedures were in place. For example, requiring an employee not in the sales department to compare customer sales invoices to shipping documents and approved customer orders before invoices were recorded and sent would prevent other than bona fide sales transactions from being recorded.

9. (P) The company would be able to detect errors in postings to customer accounts by placing certain control procedures in place. For example, by comparing the validated bank deposit slip total to the accounts receivable posting total for the day, a difference in the amount posted from the remittance advice to the accounts receivable ledger and the amount of checks actually received and deposited would be discovered.

10. (C) Mailing monthly statements to all customers with outstanding balances would most likely detect if customers' checks are misappropriated before being forwarded to the cashier for deposit. The customers would be billed for invoices already paid and would let MMI know.

11. (C) The company should implement control procedures to detect errors in postings to customer accounts. For example, mailing monthly statements to all customers with outstanding balances would detect posting errors as customers who had paid their accounts but receive statements indicating a balance due would most likely call the company to report the error in their account balance status.

12. (P) By comparing the accounts receivable postings to the validated deposit slip total, the difference resulting from posting one cash receipt remittance advice amount to two accounts in the accounts receivable ledger would be detected.

13. (S) Errors made in recording receipts in the cash receipts journal would most likely be detected if bank reconciliations are periodically prepared as the deposit amounts on the bank statements would be compared to the receipts as listed in the cash receipts journal. For internal control purposes, the person preparing the bank reconciliation should be someone other than the bookkeeper who is preparing the cash receipts journal.

14. (P) The company should implement control procedures to prevent customer checks from being misappropriated before being deposited by the cashier. One procedure to have in place would require comparing the total amount posted to the accounts receivable ledger from the remittance advice to the validated deposit slip. Differences may indicate misappropriation of customer checks because they were not deposited or were deposited to accounts

other than the company's operating account or possibly a bank account unrelated to the company.

15. (N) To prevent invalid transactions granting credit for sales returns from being recorded, internal control procedures should be implemented to require proper authorization of any sales returns. Authorization by the supervisor of the sales department would be appropriate, especially as the sales supervisor's goals are generally higher sales results, and thus, he or she would not likely have a motivation for approving invalid sales returns.

Solution 36-3 Internal Control Questionnaire--Payroll

Young Computer Outlets, Inc.
Payroll
Internal Control Questionnaire

Question	*Yes*	*No*
1. Are **payroll changes** (hires, separations, salary changes, overtime, bonuses, promotions, etc.) properly **authorized and approved**?		
2. Are discretionary payroll **deductions and withholdings authorized** in writing by employees?		
3. Are the employees who perform each of the following payroll functions **independent** of the other five functions? • **personnel and approval of payroll changes** • **preparation** of payroll data • **approval** of payroll • **signing** of paychecks • **distribution** of paychecks • **reconciliation** of payroll account		
4. Are changes in standard data on which payroll is based (hires, separations, salary changes, promotions, deduction and withholding changes, etc.) promptly input to the system to process the payroll?		
5. Is gross pay determined by using **authorized salary rates and time and attendance records**?		
6. Is there a **suitable chart of accounts** and/or established guidelines for determining salary account distribution and for recording payroll withholding liabilities?		
7. Are **clerical operations** in payroll preparation **verified**?		
8. Is **payroll preparation and recording reviewed** by supervisors or internal audit personnel?		
9. Are **payrolls approved** by a responsible official **before** payroll checks are **issued**?		
10. Are payrolls disbursed through an **imprest account**?		
11. Is the payroll **bank account reconciled monthly** to the general ledger?		
12. Are payroll **bank reconciliations** properly **approved** and differences promptly followed up?		
13. Is the custody and follow-up of **unclaimed salary checks** assigned to a responsible official?		
14. Are **differences reported by employees followed up on a timely basis** by persons not involved in payroll preparation?		
15. Are there **procedures** (e.g., tickler files) to assure **proper and timely payment of withholdings** to appropriate bodies and to file required information returns?		
16. Are employee **compensation records reconciled to control accounts**?		
17. Is **access** to personnel and payroll records, checks, forms, signature plates, etc. **limited**?		

Solution 36-4 Control Environment Factors

The control environment factors (excluding the factor illustrated in the example) that establish, enhance, or mitigate the effectiveness of specific policies and procedures, and their components are

Organizational Structure

An entity's organizational structure provides the **overall framework** for planning, directing, and controlling operations. An organizational structure includes consideration of the form and nature of an entity's **organizational units**, including the **data processing organization**, and **related management** functions and **reporting relationships**. In addition, the organizational structure should **assign authority and responsibility** within the entity in an appropriate manner.

Audit Committee/Board of Directors

An effective audit committee takes an **active role** in **overseeing** an entity's accounting and financial **reporting policies and practices**. The committee should **assist the board** of directors in fulfilling its **fiduciary and accountability responsibilities** and should help maintain a direct line of communication between the board and the entity's external and internal auditors.

Methods of Assigning Authority and Responsibility

These methods affect the understanding of reporting relationships and responsibilities established within the entity. Methods of assigning authority and responsibility include consideration of

- **Entity policy regarding** such matters as **acceptable business practices**, conflicts of interest, and **codes of conduct**.
- Assignment of responsibility and delegation of authority to deal with such matters as organizational goals and objectives, operating functions, and regulatory requirements.
- Employee **job descriptions** delineating specific duties, reporting relationships, and constraints.
- **Computer systems documentation** indicating the procedures for authorizing transactions and approving system changes.

Internal Audit Function

The internal audit function is established within an entity to **examine and evaluate the adequacy** and **effectiveness of other internal control structure policies and procedures**. Establishing an effective internal audit function includes consideration of its **authority** and **reporting relationships**, the **qualifications** of its staff, and its **resources**.

Management Control Methods

These methods affect management's direct control over the exercise of authority delegated to others and its ability to effectively supervise overall company activities. Management control methods include consideration of

- **Establishing planning and reporting systems** that set forth management's plans and the results of actual performance. Such systems may include **business planning; budgeting**, forecasting, and profit planning; and responsibility accounting.
- Establishing **methods that identify** the status of **actual performance and exceptions from planned performance**, as well as communicating them to the appropriate levels of management.
- Using such methods at appropriate management levels to **investigate variances from expectations** and to take appropriate and timely **corrective action**.
- Establishing and **monitoring policies for** developing and **modifying accounting systems** and **control procedures**, including the development, modification, and use of any related computer programs and data files.

Personnel Policies and Practices

These polices and practices affect an entity's ability to employ sufficient competent personnel to accomplish its goals and objectives. **Personnel policies** and practices include consideration of an entity's policies and procedures for **hiring, training, evaluating, promoting**, and **compensating** employees, and giving them the resources necessary to **discharge** their assigned responsibilities.

External Influences

These are influences established and exercised by parties outside an entity that affect an entity's operations and practices. They include monitoring and **compliance requirements** imposed by legislative and regulatory bodies, such as examinations by bank regulatory agencies. They also include review and follow-up by parties outside the entity concerning entity actions. External influences are ordinarily outside an entity's authority. Such influences, however, may heighten management's consciousness of and attitude towards the conduct and reporting of an entity's operations and may also prompt management to establish specific internal control structure policies or procedures.

Solution 36-5 Understanding of the Internal Control Structure

a. In **planning** an audit, an auditor's understanding of the internal control structure elements should be used to **identify** the types of **potential misstatements** that could occur, to consider the factors affecting the risk of material misstatement, and to influence the design of substantive tests.

b. An auditor obtains an **understanding of the design** of relevant internal control structure policies and procedures and whether they have been **placed in operation**. Assessing control risk at **below the maximum** level further involves **identifying specific policies and procedures** relevant to specific assertions that are **likely to prevent or detect material misstatements** in those assertions. It also involves performing **tests of controls** to evaluate the operating design and effectiveness of such policies and procedures.

c. When seeking a **further reduction** in the assessed level of **control risk**, an auditor should consider whether **additional evidential matter** sufficient to support a further reduction is **likely to be available**, and whether it would be **efficient to perform tests** of controls to obtain that evidential matter.

d. An auditor should **document the understanding** of an entity's internal control structure elements obtained to plan the audit. The auditor also should **document** the **basis for the auditor's conclusion** about the **assessed level of control risk**. If control risk is assessed at the **maximum level**, the auditor should **document that conclusion**, but it is **not required to document the basis** for that conclusion. However, if the assessed level of control risk is **below the maximum** level, the auditor should **document the basis for the conclusion that the effectiveness** of the design and operation **of internal control structure** policies and procedures **supports that assessed level.**

Solution 36-6 Internal Control Procedures--Property, Plant and Equipment

The key internal control structure policies and procedures related to Grant's property, equipment, and related transactions that Harris may consider in assessing control risk include the following:

- Advance **approval** in accordance with management's criteria is required for property and equipment transactions.
- Approval authority for transactions above an established dollar value is required at a higher level, such as the board of directors.
- Property and equipment transactions are **adequately documented.**
- There are **written policies covering capitalizing expenditures**, classifying **leases**, and determining estimated **useful lives**, salvage values, and methods of depreciation and amortization.
- There are **written policies** covering **retirement procedures** that include serially numbered retirement work orders stating reasons for retirement and bearing appropriate approvals.
- There are adequate policies and procedures to determine whether property and equipment are received and properly recorded, such as a system that matches purchase orders, receiving reports, and vendors' invoices.
- There are adequate procedures to determine whether **dispositions** of property and equipment are **properly accounted for** and proceeds, if any, are received in accordance with management's authorization.
- A property and equipment **subsidiary ledger is maintained** showing additions, retirements, and depreciation, and the ledger is periodically reconciled.
- Property and equipment is **physically inspected** and **reconciled** at reasonable intervals with independently maintained property and equipment records.
- An **annual budget** is prepared and monitored to forecast and **control acquisitions and retirements** of property and equipment.
- Reporting procedures assure prompt **identification and analysis of variances** between **authorized expenditures and actual costs.**
- Property and equipment is protected by adequate **safeguards.**
- Property and equipment is **insured** in accordance with management's authorization.

- Documents evidencing **title and property rights** are periodically **compared with** the detailed property records.
- The **entity employs internal auditors** to test whether the internal control structure policies and procedures are operating effectively.

Solution 36-7 Reportable Conditions/Material Weaknesses (AU 325)

a. **Reportable conditions** are matters that come to an auditor's attention, which, in the auditor's judgment, should be **communicated to the client's audit committee or** its **equivalent** because they represent significant deficiencies in the design or operation of the internal control structure, which could **adversely affect the organization's ability to record, process, summarize, and report** financial data consistent with the assertions of management in the financial statements.

Material weaknesses are reportable conditions in which the **design or operation** of specific internal control structure **elements do not reduce,** to a relatively low level, the **risk that errors or irregularities** in amounts that would be **material** in relation to the financial statements being audited **may occur and not be detected** within a **timely period by employees** in the normal course of performing their assigned functions.

b. An auditor is **required to identify reportable conditions that come to the auditor's attention** in the normal course of an audit, but is **not obligated to search for reportable conditions.** The auditor uses judgment as to which matters are reportable conditions. Provided the audit committee has acknowledged its understanding and consideration of such deficiencies and the associated risks, the auditor may decide certain matters do not need to be reported unless, because of changes in management or the audit committee, or because of the passage of time, it is appropriate to do so.

Conditions noted by the auditor that are considered reportable **should be reported, preferably in writing.** If information is communicated orally, the auditor should **document the communication.** The report should state that the communication is intended solely for the information and use of the audit committee, management, and others within the organization.

The auditor **may identify and communicate separately** those **reportable conditions the auditor considers to be material weaknesses,** but **may not state that no reportable conditions were noted** during the audit. Reportable conditions may be communicated during the course of the audit rather than after the audit is concluded, depending on the relative significance of the matters noted and the urgency of corrective follow-up action.

Solution 36-8 Internal Control Procedures--Purchases and Accounts Payable

The internal control procedures that most likely would provide reasonable assurance that specific control objectives for the financial statement assertions regarding purchases and accounts payable will be achieved are:

1. Proper **authorization of requisitions** by department head is required before purchase orders are prepared.

2. Purchasing department assures that **requisitions are within budget limits** before purchase orders are prepared.

3. The adequacy of each **vendor's** past record as a supplier is **verified.**

4. Secure facilities **limit access** to the goods during the receiving activity.

5. Receiving department makes a blind count of the goods received, independently of any other department.

6. The requisitioning department head independently verifies the quantity and quality of the goods received.

7. **Requisitions, purchase orders,** and **receiving reports** are **matched with vendor invoices** as to quantity and price.

8. Accounts payable department **recomputes** the **mathematical accuracy** of each **invoice.**

9. The **voucher register** is **independently reconciled to** the **control accounts monthly.**

10. All supporting documentation is required for payment and is made available to the treasurer.

11. The purchasing, receiving, and accounts payable **functions are segregated.**

Solution 36-9 Reportable Conditions--Cash Receipts and Billing

The reportable conditions and resulting misstatements, in addition to the example, that could occur and not be prevented or detected by Parktown's internal control structure concerning the cash receipts and billing functions include the following:

Reportable condition	Potential misstatement
The employees who perform services also are permitted to approve credit without an external credit check.	**Uncollectible account expense could be understated** and **accounts receivable could be overstated** because of the lack of an appropriate credit check.
There is no independent verification of the billing process.	Fees earned and accounts receivable may be **understated because not all services performed might be reported** for billing. or Fees earned and accounts receivable may be either overstated or understated because of the use of incorrect price of service data or because of mathematical errors.
The employees who approve credit also approve write-offs of uncollectible accounts.	**Accounts receivable could be understated** and uncollectible accounts expense overstated because **write-offs of accounts receivable could be approved** for accounts **that are,** in fact, **collectible.** or **Accounts receivable could be overstated** and uncollectible accounts expense understated because **write-offs of accounts receivable might not be initiated** for accounts that are uncollectible.
Credit is not granted on the basis of established limits.	**Uncollectible accounts expense could be either understated or overstated** because the **lack of** established **credit limits** may make it **more difficult to identify uncollectible amounts.**
The employee who initially handles cash receipts also prepares billings.	Fees earned and cash receipts or accounts receivable could be understated because of **omitted or inaccurate billing.**
The employee who makes bank deposits also reconciles bank statements.	The **cash balance per books** may be **overstated** because **not all cash is deposited.**
Uncollectible accounts are not determined on the basis of established criteria.	**Uncollectible accounts expense could be either understated or overstated** because of the **lack of** established **write-off criteria.**
Trial balances of the accounts receivable subsidiary ledger are not prepared independently of, or verified and reconciled to, the accounts receivable control account in the general ledger.	Any of fees earned, cash receipts, and uncollectible accounts expense could be either understated or overstated because of undetected differences between the subsidiary ledger and the general ledger. or Fees earned and cash receipts or accounts receivable could be understated because of **failure to record billings, cash receipts, or write-offs accurately.**

Solution 36-10 Reporting on the Internal Control Structure

a. 1. An engagement to express an opinion on an entity's internal control structure and a consideration of the internal control structure made as part of an audit of financial statements in accordance with generally accepted auditing standards generally differ in scope. While the engagement to express an opinion on an entity's internal control structure can be made in conjunction with the consideration made as part of an audit, the **consideration made as part of an audit is more limited in scope.**

2. The engagements also differ in purpose. The auditor's consideration of the internal control structure is an intermediate step in forming an opinion on the financial statements. It establishes a basis for assessment of control risk and for determining the nature, extent and timing of the auditing procedures. The purpose of the accountant's engagement to express an opinion on the internal control structure is to provide assurance about whether the broad objectives of internal control are being achieved.

3. An **engagement to express an opinion** on an entity's **internal control structure can be made as of any date**, while the **auditor's consideration** of the internal control structure **is made in the early stages of an audit.**

4. Ordinarily, the **users of an opinion** on an entity's **internal control structure** are the **client's management** and **third parties**, such as regulatory agencies. The **primary user** of a consideration of the **internal control** structure made **as part of an audit** is the auditor who makes the consideration.

b. The **accountant's report** expressing an **opinion** on an **entity's internal control** structure should contain

1. A **description of the scope** of the engagement.
2. The **date** to which the opinion relates.
3. A statement that the **establishment** and **maintenance** of the structure is the **responsibility of management.**
4. A brief **explanation** of the **broad objectives** and **inherent limitations** of internal controls.
5. The **accountant's opinion** on whether the structure meets the broad objectives of internal control insofar as those objectives pertain to the prevention or detection of material errors or irregularities.
6. The description of any **material weakness.**

Solution 36-11 Internal Control Structure Weaknesses--Sales, Shipping, Billing, and Collecting

The **weaknesses** in Newton Hardware's internal controls include these:

Warehouse Clerk

- Initiates posting to inventory records by preparation of shipping advice.
- **Releases merchandise** to customers **before** proper **approvals** of customers' credit.
- Does **not retain a copy of the shipping advice** for comparison with receipt from carrier.

Bookkeeper A

- Authorizes customers' credit and prepares source documents for posting to customers' accounts.
- **Prepares invoices without notice** that the merchandise was actually shipped and the date it was shipped.
- **Authorizes write-offs** of customer accounts receivable and authorizes **customers' credit.**

Collection Clerk

- **Receives directly** and **records** customers' checks.
- Does not deliver checks excluded from the deposit to an employee independent of the bank deposit for review and disposition.
- Initiates posting of receipts to subsidiary accounts receivable ledger and has **initial access to cash receipts.**
- Does **not deposit** cash receipts **promptly.**
- **Reconciles bank statement** and has initial access to cash receipts.

CHAPTER 37

AUDIT EVIDENCE, PROGRAMS, AND PROCEDURES

CHAPTER 37

AUDIT EVIDENCE, PROGRAMS, AND PROCEDURES

PART ONE: THE THIRD STANDARD OF FIELD WORK

I. Evidential Matter (AU 326, SAS 31)

A. The Third Standard of Field Work

1. The third standard of field work states, "Sufficient competent evidential matter is to be obtained through inspection, observation, inquiries, and confirmations to afford a reasonable basis for an opinion regarding the financial statements under audit."

   - This standard is very broad in nature, and it encompasses Steps 3, 4, 5, and 6 in the audit process, which is outlined in Chapter 34. The consideration of internal control (Steps 3, 4, and 5) is covered by the second standard of field work (see Chapter 36), and such consideration provides evidential matter that has an important effect on the nature, timing, and extent of the auditor's substantive testing (Step 5). Therefore, the auditor's consideration of the client's internal control structure and the results of the auditor's substantive testing together comprise evidential matter that must be both sufficient and competent in order to provide the auditor with a reasonable basis to form an opinion (or to disclaim an opinion) on the financial statements.

2. The sufficiency and competence of evidential matter are subjective issues to be decided by the auditor on the basis of his or her judgment.

3. The evidential matter is obtained through two general classes of substantive tests: (a) tests of details of transactions and balances and (b) analytical procedures applied to financial information. Reliance on substantive tests will vary with the assessed level of control risk. Therefore, an auditor may compensate for a weakness in the internal control structure by increasing the substantive tests.

C Completeness
O Obligations and Rights
V Valuation or Allocation
E Existence or Occurrence
S Statement Presentation & Disclosure

B. Nature of Assertions--Assertions are representations made by management and embodied in the financial statements being audited. There are five broad categories of assertions dealing with the following:

1. Completeness--Deals with whether all accounts and all transactions that should be presented in the financial statements are included and whether all transactions which should be recorded in the accounts actually are.

2. Obligations and Rights--Concerns whether, at a given date, recorded assets indeed represent rights of the entity and liabilities represent obligations.

3. Valuation or Allocation--Deals with whether assets and liabilities are properly valued and whether revenues and expenses are allocated appropriately between periods.

4. Existence or Occurrence--Deals with whether assets or liabilities exist as of a financial statement date and whether recorded transactions did occur during a reporting period.

5. Statement Presentation and Disclosure--Concerns the proper classification, description, and disclosure in the financial statements (including footnotes).

C. Use of Assertions in Developing Audit Objectives and Designing Substantive Tests

1. In obtaining evidential matter in support of financial statement assertions, the auditor should develop specific audit objectives. These objectives should take into consideration the specific circumstances of the entity, including the nature of its economic activity, the accounting practices of the particular industry, and unique aspects of the entity.

2. Once the specific audit objectives have been identified, the auditor must design specific substantive tests to attain those objectives. The design of substantive test procedures is based on considerations such as the following:

   a. The risk of material misstatement of the financial statements, including the assessed levels of control risk, and the expected effectiveness and efficiency of such tests.

   b. The nature and materiality of the items being tested.

   c. The kinds and competence of available evidential matter.

   d. The nature of the audit objective to be achieved.

Exhibit 1--Obtaining Evidential Matter

Management's Assertions → *Specific Audit Objectives* → *Audit Procedures*

D. Nature of Evidential Matter--Evidential matter supporting financial statement assertions consists of the underlying accounting data and all corroborating information available to the auditor.

1. Underlying Accounting Data--Includes books of original entry, subsidiary ledgers, supporting schedules, etc. By itself, accounting data does not constitute sufficient evidential matter; yet, it provides a necessary step in translating the raw economic events into financial statements. As such, the propriety and accuracy of accounting data must be ascertained as a prerequisite to forming an opinion on the financial statements.

   The auditor tests the underlying accounting data by analysis and review, by retracing the procedural steps in the accounting process, by recalculation and redevelopment of allocations and schedules, and by reconciling related types of information.

2. Corroborating Evidential Matter--Includes documents such as checks, invoices, contracts, and minutes of meetings; confirmations and other written representations; and information obtained by the auditor from observation, inquiry, inspection, physical examination, or any other appropriate sources.

E. Competence of Evidential Matter--Competent evidence is both valid and relevant. The validity of evidential matter is highly dependent upon the circumstances under which it is obtained. Subject to exceptions for certain specific circumstances, however, the following generalizations can be made (AU 326.19):

1. "When evidential matter can be obtained from independent sources outside an entity, it provides greater assurance of reliability for the purposes of an independent audit than that secured solely within the entity."

2. "The more effective the internal control structure, the more assurance it provides about the reliability of the accounting data and financial statements."

3. "The independent auditor's direct personal knowledge, obtained through physical examination, observation, computation, and inspection, is more persuasive than information obtained indirectly."

F. Sufficiency of Evidential Matter

1. The independent auditor's objective is to obtain sufficient evidential matter to provide a reasonable basis for forming an opinion on the financial statements.

   a. The amounts and kinds of evidence needed are a matter of professional judgment. In exercising this judgment, the auditor considers both the materiality of the item in question and the inherent risk of the item.

   b. In most cases, it will be necessary to rely on evidence that is persuasive rather than convincing. An auditor is seldom convinced beyond all doubt with respect to all of the financial statements being audited. Remember, audit risk is reduced to a low level; it cannot be reduced to zero.

2. An auditor works within time/cost constraints. Professional judgment is required to determine whether the evidence obtained is sufficient to form an opinion. Audit risk and cost/benefit relationships may be considered in deciding whether to obtain a particular kind of evidence.

   - The degree of difficulty and expense involved in testing a particular item, however, is not, by itself, a valid basis for omitting the test.

G. Evaluation of Evidential Matter--The basis for evaluation is whether specific audit objectives have been achieved. The search for evidential matter should be thorough and its analysis should be unbiased. If the audit evidence does not provide a basis for an opinion relative to any assertion of material significance, the auditor must obtain sufficient competent evidential matter. Failure to do so will result in a qualified opinion or a disclaimer of opinion due to scope limitation.

II. The Auditor's Consideration of the Internal Audit Function in an Audit of Financial Statements (AU 322, SAS 65)

A. Background--This Statement provides the auditor with guidance on considering the work of internal auditors and on using internal auditors to provide direct assistance to the auditor in an audit performed in accordance with GAAS.

B. Roles of the Auditor and the Internal Auditors--To fulfill the responsibility to obtain sufficient competent evidential matter to provide a reasonable basis for the opinion of the entity's financial statements, the auditor maintains independence from the entity. To fulfill the responsibility for providing analyses, evaluations, recommendations, and other information to the entity's management and board of directors or to others with equivalent authority, internal auditors maintain objectivity with respect to the activity being audited.

C. Obtaining an Understanding of the Internal Audit Function

1. When obtaining an understanding of the internal control structure, the auditor should obtain an understanding of the internal audit function sufficient to identify those internal audit activities that are relevant to planning the audit.

2. An external auditor will usually perform financial audits to enable him or her to attest to the fairness of an entity's financial statements. Internal auditors may also perform these financial audits as well as procedural and operational audits which are usually beyond the scope of the

external audit. Therefore, a comprehensive internal audit program will be more detailed and cover more areas than an independent auditor's audit program.

3. The auditor ordinarily should make inquiries of appropriate management and internal audit personnel about the internal auditors' (a) organizational status within the entity; (b) application of professional standards; (c) audit plan, including the nature, timing, and extent of audit work; and (d) access to records and whether there are limitations on the scope of their activities.

4. Internal audit activities relevant to an audit of the entity's financial statements are those that provide evidence about the design and effectiveness of internal control structure policies and procedures that pertain to the entity's ability to record, process, summarize, and report financial data consistent with the assertions embodied in the financial statements or that provide direct evidence about potential misstatements of such data. The results of the following procedures should be helpful to the auditor in assessing the relevancy of internal audit activities (a) considering knowledge from prior-year audits, (b) reviewing how the internal auditors allocate their audit resources to financial or operating areas in response to their risk assessment process, and (c) reading internal audit reports to obtain detailed information about the scope of internal audit activities.

5. If the auditor concludes that some of the internal auditors' activities are relevant to the audit and that it would be efficient to consider how the internal auditors' work might affect the nature, timing, and extent of audit procedures, the auditor should assess the competence and objectivity of the internal audit in light of the intended effect of the internal auditors' work on the audit.

   a. Competence of Internal Auditors

      (1) Education level and professional experience.

      (2) Professional certification and continuing education.

      (3) Evaluation of internal auditors' performance.

      (4) Supervision and review of internal auditors' activities.

      (5) Quality of working paper documentation, reports, and recommendations.

   b. Objectivity of Internal Auditors

      (1) The organizational status of the internal auditor.

      (2) What organizational level does the internal auditor report to (the higher, the more objective).

      (3) Amount of access to the board of directors or audit committee.

      (4) Whether the board of directors, the audit committee, or the owner-manager oversees employment of the internal auditors.

      (5) Policies to maintain internal auditor's objectivity about areas audited.

D. Coordination of the Audit Work With Internal Auditors

1. Hold periodic meetings.

2. Schedule audit work.

3. Provide access to internal auditors' working papers.

4. Review audit reports.

5. Discuss possible audit issues.

E. Evaluating the Effectiveness of the Internal Auditors' Work involves determining whether

1. The scope of work is appropriate.

2. Audit programs are adequate.

3. Working papers adequately document work performed, including evidence of supervision and review.

4. Conclusions are appropriate.

5. Reports are consistent with the results of the work performed.

F. Testing the Internal Auditors' Work--The external auditor should test the internal auditors' work by examining some of the controls, transactions, or balances that the internal auditors examined, or similar evidence not actually examined by the internal auditors.

G. Using Internal Auditors to Provide Direct Assistance, the external auditor should assess the internal auditors' competence and objectivity, and supervise, review, evaluate, and test the work performed. The auditor should inform the internal auditors of their responsibilities, the objectives of the procedures, and matters that may affect the nature, timing, and extent of audit procedures. The internal auditor should also be informed of the need to bring all significant accounting and auditing issues identified to the external auditor's attention.

III. Client Representations (AU 333, SAS 19)

A. Written Representations--In order to comply with GAAS, the auditor must obtain certain written representations from management. These are considered to be part of the evidential matter but are not a substitute for the application of auditing procedures. The written representations (1) confirm the oral representations that were given to the auditor during the engagement, (2) serve as documentation of the continuing appropriateness of the representations, and (3) reduce the chance of misunderstanding between the auditor and the client.

1. Corroborating Procedures--The auditor frequently performs auditing procedures in order to corroborate the substance of the written representations. For example, even though procedures will be performed to test the adequacy of the disclosure of related party transactions, the auditor will also obtain a written representation from client management that it has no knowledge of any related party transactions which have not been disclosed. In some cases, however, there cannot be any corroboration. For example, since other audit procedures would probably not reveal subjective intent, the auditor should obtain written representations of management's intent to discontinue a line of business (and corroborate the representation by reading the minutes).

2. Auditor's Reliance--It is <u>reasonable</u> for the auditor to rely on the written representations of management <u>unless</u> audit procedures provide evidential matter that indicates otherwise. However, the auditor must maintain an appropriate level of professional skepticism.

B. <u>Specific Representations</u>--The specific written representations that are to be obtained by the auditor will depend on the <u>circumstances</u> of the engagement and on the <u>nature</u> and <u>basis</u> of presentation of the financial statements.

a. Materiality--Except for items which do not directly relate to amounts included in the financial statements, management's representations may be limited to matters that are considered <u>material</u> (either collectively or individually), <u>as long as</u> management and the auditor have reached agreement on the limits of materiality.

b. Other Written Representations--The auditor may decide that other matters in addition to those usually indicated may require written representation. For example, written representations should be obtained concerning unaudited interim financial information accompanying the audited financial statements.

C. <u>Consolidated Financial Statements</u>--When consolidated financial statements are involved, the parent company management's written representations should specify that they pertain to the consolidated financial statements and, if applicable, to the separate financial statements of the parent.

D. <u>Address, Date, and Signature</u>

1. Address--Should be addressed to the auditor.

2. Date--The same date as the auditor's report (the last day of field work).

3. Signature--Signed by members of management whom the auditor feels are responsible for and knowledgeable of the matters being represented--<u>normally</u> the chief executive officer and the chief financial officer.

E. <u>Representations From Others</u>--Written representations are occasionally obtained from client employees other than management. <u>For example</u>, representations as to the completeness of the minutes of the stockholders' meeting may be obtained from the keeper of the minutes.

F. <u>Scope Limitations</u>--A scope limitation sufficient to preclude an unqualified opinion is present if management <u>refuses</u> to furnish the auditor with a written representation the auditor feels is essential. This refusal may impair the auditor's ability to rely on management's other representations.

- Restriction on Auditing Procedures--The auditor should <u>qualify</u> the opinion or <u>disclaim</u> an opinion because of a scope limitation if precluded by the client from performing a procedure considered necessary, even though management has given representations concerning the matter. For example, the auditor would need to confirm accounts receivable even though management has given its written representation that accounts receivable are fairly stated.

Exhibit 2--Sample Representation Letter

(Date of Auditor's Report)

(To Independent Auditor)

In connection with your audit of the (identification of financial statements) of (name of client) as of (date) and for the (period of the audit) for the purpose of expressing an opinion as to whether the (consolidated) financial statements present fairly, in all material respects, the financial position, results of operations, and cash flows of (name of client) in conformity with generally accepted accounting principles (other comprehensive basis of accounting), we confirm, to the best of our knowledge and belief, the following representations made to you during your audit.

(**NOTE:** Items 1., 2., and 3., below, are required on all audits per SAS 19.)

1. We are responsible for the fair presentation in the (consolidated) financial statements of financial position, results of operations, and cash flows in conformity with generally accepted accounting principles (other comprehensive basis of accounting).

2. We have made available to you all:

   a. Financial records and related data.

   b. Minutes of the meetings of stockholders, directors, and committees of directors, or summaries of actions of recent meetings for which minutes have not yet been prepared.

3. There have been no:

   a. Irregularities involving management or employees who have significant roles in the internal control structure.

   b. Irregularities involving other employees that could have a material effect on the financial statements.

   c. Communications from regulatory agencies concerning noncompliance with, or deficiencies in, financial reporting practices that could have a material effect on the financial statements.

4. We have no plans or intentions that may materially affect the carrying value or classification of assets and liabilities.

5. The following have been properly recorded or disclosed in the financial statements:

   a. Related party transactions and related amounts receivable or payable, including sales, purchases, loans, transfers, leasing arrangements, and guarantees.

   b. Capital stock repurchase options or agreements or capital stock reserved for options, warrants, conversions, or other requirements.

   c. Arrangements with financial institutions involving compensating balances or other arrangements involving restrictions on cash balances and line-of-credit or similar arrangements.

   d. Agreements to repurchase assets previously sold.

(continued on next page)

6. There are no:

   a. Violations or possible violations of laws or regulations whose effects should be considered for disclosure in the financial statements or as a basis for recording a loss contingency.

   b. Other material liabilities or contingencies that are required to be accrued or disclosed by Statement of Financial Accounting Standards No. 5.

7. There are no unasserted claims or assessments that our lawyer has advised us are probable of assertion and must be disclosed in accordance with Statement of Financial Accounting Standards No. 5.

8. There are no material transactions that have not been properly recorded in the accounting records underlying the financial statements.

9. Provision, when material, has been made to reduce excess or obsolete inventories to their estimated net realizable value.

10. The company has satisfactory title to all owned assets, and there are no liens or encumbrances on such assets nor has any asset been pledged.

11. Provision has been made for any material loss to be sustained in the fulfillment of, or from inability to fulfill, any sales commitments.

12. Provision has been made for any material loss to be sustained as a result of purchase commitments for inventory quantities in excess of normal requirements or at prices in excess of the prevailing market prices.

13. We have complied with all aspects of contractual agreements that would have a material effect on the financial statements in the event of noncompliance.

14. No events have occurred subsequent to the balance sheet date that would require adjustment to, or disclosure in, the financial statements.

(Name of Chief Executive Officer and Title)

(Name of Chief Financial Officer and Title)

IV. Analytical Procedures (AU 329, SAS 56)

A. Analytical Procedures--Analytical procedures are important audit tools. Procedures consist of evaluations of financial information made by a study of plausible relationships among both financial and nonfinancial data. The procedures range from simple comparisons to complex models.

To utilize analytical procedures, the auditor must understand financial relationships and have a knowledge of the client and its industry.

1. Analytical procedures are used for the following purposes:

   a. To assist the auditor in planning the nature, timing, and extent of other auditing procedures. (This is required by GAAS.)

b. As a substantive test to obtain evidential matter about particular assertions related to account balances or classes of transactions. (Not a required GAAS procedure but commonly used.)

c. As an overall review of the financial information in the final review stage of the audit. (This is also required by GAAS.)

2. Analytical procedures involve comparisons of recorded amounts, or ratios developed from recorded amounts, to expectations developed by the auditor. The auditor develops expectations by identifying relationships that are reasonably expected to exist from understanding the client and the industry in which the client operates. The following are examples of sources of information for developing expectations:

a. Financial information for comparable prior periods giving consideration to known changes.

b. Anticipated results, for example, budgets, or forecasts including extrapolations from interim or annual data.

c. Relationships among elements of financial information within the period.

d. Information regarding the industry in which the client operates, for example, gross margin information.

e. Relationships of financial information with relevant nonfinancial information.

B. Planning the Audit--The purpose of applying analytical procedures in planning the audit is to assist in planning the nature, timing, and extent of substantive tests. Analytical procedures should focus on enhancing the auditor's understanding of the client's business and the transactions and events that have occurred since the last audit date, and identifying areas that may represent specific risks relevant to the audit.

C. Analytical Procedures Used as Substantive Tests--The auditor's reliance on substantive tests to achieve an audit objective related to a particular assertion (representation by management) may be derived from tests of details, from analytical procedures, or from a combination of both. The expected effectiveness and efficiency of an analytical procedure in identifying potential misstatements depends on, among other things, the nature of the assertion, the plausibility and predictability of the relationship, the availability and reliability of the data used to develop the expectation, and the precision of the expectation. For example, the auditor may use inventory turnover figures to evaluate the salability of inventory.

D. Plausibility and Predictability of the Relationship--A basic premise underlying the application of analytical procedures is that plausible relationships among data may reasonably be expected to exist and continue in the absence of known conditions to the contrary.

Relationships are more predictable in a stable environment, while relationships in a dynamic environment lose predictability. Relationships involving income statement accounts are usually more predictable than those involving only balance sheet accounts because income statement accounts represent transactions over a period of time, while balance sheet accounts represent amounts as of a point in time.

E. Reliability of Data--The reliability of the data used by the auditor to develop expectations should be appropriate for the desired level of assurance from the analytical procedures. The auditor should assess the reliability of the data by considering the source of the data and the conditions under which it was gathered. The following factors influence the auditor's consideration of the reliability of data for purposes of achieving audit objectives:

1. Whether the data was obtained from independent sources outside the entity or from sources within the entity.

2. Whether sources within the entity were independent of those who are responsible for the amount being audited.

3. Whether the data was developed under a reliable system with adequate controls.

4. Whether the data was subjected to audit testing in the current or prior year.

5. Whether the expectations were developed using data from a variety of sources.

F. Precision of the Expectation--The expectation should be precise enough to provide the desired level of assurance that differences that may be potential material misstatements, individually or when aggregated with other misstatements, would be identified for the auditor to investigate. The auditor's identification and consideration of factors that significantly affect the amount being audited and the level of detail of data used to develop expectations affect the precision of the expectations. Greater detail of data increases reliability of expectations. For example, using monthly amounts will generally be more effective than annual amounts.

G. Investigation and Evaluation of Significant Differences--In planning the analytical procedures as a substantive test, the auditor should consider the amount of difference from the expectation that can be accepted without further investigation.

The auditor should evaluate significant unexpected differences. If an explanation for the difference cannot be obtained, the auditor should obtain sufficient evidence about the assertion by performing other audit procedures to determine whether the difference is likely to be a misstatement.

H. Analytical Procedures Used in Overall Review--Analytical procedures are used in the overall review stage to assist the auditor in assessing conclusions reached and in evaluating the overall financial statement presentation. The overall review would generally include reading the financial statements and notes and considering the adequacy of evidence gathered in response to unusual or unexpected balances identified in planning the audit or in the course of the audit, and unusual or unexpected balances or relationships that were not previously identified. The results of an overall review may indicate that additional evidence may be needed. Also, use of analytical procedures in the overall review helps the auditor in the going concern assessment.

V. Using the Work of a Specialist (AU 336, SAS 73)

A. Definition--A specialist is a person (or firm) possessing special skill or knowledge in a particular field other than accounting or auditing. Specialists include, but are not limited to, actuaries, appraisers, engineers, environmental consultants, and geologists. Additionally, SAS 73 applies to attorneys engaged as specialists in situations other than to provide services to a client concerning litigation, claims, or assessments to which SAS 12, *Inquiry of a Client's Lawyer Concerning Litigation, Claims, and Assessments*, applies. For example, attorneys may be engaged by a client or by the auditor as specialists in a variety of other circumstances, including interpreting the provisions of a contractual agreement. Examples of those not included for the purposes of this Section would be members of the auditor's staff, client, credit or plant managers, and internal auditors.

B. Applicability of SAS 73--The guidance provided in SAS 73 applies to audits of financial statements prepared in accordance with GAAP and to engagements performed under SAS 62, *Special Reports*, including a comprehensive basis of accounting other than GAAP.

C. Decision to Use the Work of a Specialist--The auditor's education and experience enable him or her to be knowledgeable about business matters in general, but the auditor is not expected to have the expertise of a person trained for or qualified to engage in the practice of another profession or occupation. During the audit, however, an auditor may encounter complex or subjective matters potentially material to the financial statements. Such matters may require special skill or knowledge and in the auditor's judgment require using the work of a specialist to obtain competent evidential matter. Examples of the types of matters that the auditor may decide require him or her to consider using the work of a specialist include, but are not limited to, the following:

1. Valuation (i.e., special-purpose inventories, high-technology materials or equipment, pharmaceutical products, complex financial instruments, real estate, restricted securities, works of art, and environmental contingencies).

2. Determination of physical characteristics relating to quantity on hand or condition (i.e., quantity or condition of minerals, mineral reserves, or materials stored in stockpiles).

3. Determination of amounts derived by using specialized techniques or methods (i.e., actuarial determinations for employee benefits obligations and disclosures, and determination of insurance loss reserves).

4. Interpretation of technical requirements, regulations, or agreements (i.e., the potential significance of contracts or other legal documents, or legal title to property).

D. Engaging and Using a Specialist--Specialist Engaged by Management--Management may engage or employ a specialist and the auditor may use that specialist's work as evidential matter in performing substantive tests to evaluate material financial statement assertions. Alternatively, management may engage a specialist employed by the auditor's firm to provide advisory services and the auditor may use that specialist's work as evidential matter in performing substantive tests to evaluate material financial statement assertions.

E. Engaging and Using a Specialist--Specialist Engaged by Auditor--The auditor may engage a specialist and use that specialist's work as evidential matter in performing substantive tests to evaluate material financial statement assertions.

F. Selecting a Specialist--The auditor should evaluate the professional qualifications of the specialist to determine that the specialist possesses the necessary skill or knowledge in the particular field. The auditor should consider the following:

1. The professional certification, license, or other recognition of the competence of the specialist in his or her field.

2. The reputation and standing of the specialist in the views of peers and others familiar with the specialist's capability or performance.

3. The specialist's experience in the type of work under consideration.

4. The auditor should obtain an understanding of the nature of the work performed or to be performed by the specialist. This understanding should cover the following:

   (a) The objectives and scope of the specialist's work.

   (b) The specialist's relationship to the client.

   (c) The methods or assumptions used.

   (d) A comparison of the methods or assumptions used with those used in the preceding period.

(e) The appropriateness of using the specialist's work for the intended purpose.

(f) The form and content of the specialist's findings.

G. Evaluating the Objectivity of a Specialist--The auditor should evaluate the relationship of the specialist to the client, including circumstances that might impair the objectivity of the specialist. Such circumstances include situations in which the client has the ability (through employment, ownership, contractual right, family relationship, or otherwise) to directly or indirectly control or significantly influence the specialist.

1. When a specialist does not have a relationship with the client, the specialist's work will usually provide the auditor with greater assurance.

2. If the specialist has a relationship to the client, the auditor should assess the risk that the specialist's objectivity might be impaired. If the auditor believes the relationship might impair the specialist's objectivity, the auditor should perform additional procedures with respect to some or all of the specialist's assumptions, methods, or findings to determine that the findings are not unreasonable or should engage another specialist for that purpose.

H. Evaluating the Work of the Specialist--The appropriateness and reasonableness of methods and assumptions used and their application are the responsibility of the specialist. The auditor should obtain an understanding of the methods and assumptions used by the specialist to determine whether the findings are suitable for corroborating the assertions in the financial statements. The auditor should consider whether the specialist's findings support the related assertions in the financial statements and, depending on the auditor's assessment of control risk, make appropriate tests of data provided to the specialist. Ordinarily, the auditor would use the work of the specialist unless the auditor's procedures lead him or her to believe that the findings are unreasonable in the circumstances. If the auditor believes the findings are unreasonable, he or she should apply additional procedures, which may include obtaining the opinion of another specialist.

I. Auditor's Conclusions and Additional Procedures--If the auditor determines that the specialist's findings support the related assertions in the financial statements, he or she may reasonably conclude that sufficient competent evidential matter has been obtained. If there is a material difference between the specialist's findings and the assertions in the financial statements, the auditor should apply additional procedures. If after applying the additional procedures, the auditor is unable to resolve the matter, the auditor should obtain the opinion of another specialist, unless it appears to the auditor that the matter cannot be resolved. A matter that has not been resolved will ordinarily cause the auditor to qualify the opinion or disclaim an opinion. The auditor may conclude that the assertions in the financial statements are not in conformity with GAAP. In that event, the auditor should express a qualified or adverse opinion.

J. Effect on the Auditor's Report--Normally, the auditor should not refer to the work or findings of the specialist. Such a reference might be misunderstood to be a qualification of the auditor's opinion or a division of responsibility, neither of which is intended. Further, there may be an inference that the auditor making such reference performed a more thorough audit than an auditor not making such reference. Reference to and identification of the specialist may be made in the auditor's report only if the auditor believes such reference will facilitate an understanding of the reason for an explanatory paragraph or the departure from the unqualified opinion. Reporting alternatives are:

1. Unqualified opinion--No reference to the specialist.

2. Qualified or disclaimer of opinion--Scope limitation, the auditor is unable to obtain sufficient, competent evidential matter (as discussed in I., above)--No reference to the specialist.

3. Qualified or adverse opinion--Auditor concludes there is a departure from GAAP (as discussed in I., above)--Refer to specialist in explanatory paragraph only if doing so will help clarify the reason for the qualification or adverse opinion.

VI. Inquiry of a Client's Lawyer Concerning Litigation, Claims, and Assessments (AU 337, SAS 12)

A. Accounting Considerations--Management has the responsibility to adopt policies and procedures that will identify, evaluate, and account for litigation, claims, and assessments as a basis for the preparation of financial statements in conformity with GAAP.

B. Auditing Considerations--The auditor should obtain evidential matter relating to (1) the existence of conditions or circumstances which indicate a possible loss from litigation, claims, and assessments, (2) the period in which the underlying cause for legal action occurred, (3) the probability of an unfavorable outcome, and (4) the amount or range of the potential loss.

1. Audit Procedures--Management is the primary source of information about these matters. Therefore, the auditor should:

a. Inquire of and discuss with management the client's policies and procedures for identifying, evaluating, and accounting for litigation, claims, and assessments.

b. Obtain from management a description and evaluation of litigation, claims, and assessments that existed at the balance sheet date and during the time until management furnishes the information. Further, the auditor should obtain assurance, usually in writing, that the client disclosed all such matters that are required to be disclosed by SFAS 5, *Accounting for Contingencies.*

c. Examine appropriate documents in the possession of the client that relate to these contingencies, including correspondence and invoices from lawyers.

d. Obtain assurance from management, ordinarily in writing, that it has disclosed all unasserted claims the lawyer feels are probable of assertion and that must be disclosed in accordance with SFAS 5.

(1) Inform Lawyer--With the client's permission, the auditor should inform the lawyer that the client has given the auditor this assurance.

(2) Regular Audit Procedures--The auditor will find that some of the regular audit procedures (e.g., reading the minutes of the board of directors meetings, sending bank confirmations, reading contracts and loan agreements, and inspecting documents for guarantees by the client) may also disclose possible litigation, claims, and assessments.

2. Letter of Audit Inquiry to a Client's Lawyer--The auditor should request client management to send a letter of inquiry to those lawyers consulted by management concerning litigation, claims, and assessments (however, the letter should be physically mailed by the auditor). This serves to corroborate the information furnished by management. Additionally, this corroboration may be provided by information from inside legal counsel. However, such information is not a substitute for information which outside counsel refuses to furnish.

a. Contents--Some of the matters that should be covered in a letter of audit inquiry include the following:

(1) Identification of the company, subsidiaries, and audit date.

(2) A management-prepared list and evaluation of pending or threatened litigation, claims, and assessments with which the lawyer has been substantially involved

(if management prefers, they may request the lawyer to prepare the list). The lawyer is asked either to furnish the following information or to comment as to where the lawyer's views differ from management's of:

(a) A description of the matter, progress to date, and the action the company plans to take.

(b) An evaluation of the likelihood of an unfavorable outcome and, if possible, an estimate of the amount or range of potential loss.

(c) An identification of any missing items or a statement that the list is complete.

(3) A management-prepared list describing and evaluating unasserted claims and assessments which management considers are probable of assertion and which have at least a reasonable probability of unfavorable outcome. For example, due to the negligence of client personnel, a customer may have suffered a serious injury. It is possible the client may expect a lawsuit and may have consulted the lawyer in that regard. The lawyer would be requested to comment on those areas where the lawyer's views differ from those of management.

(4) A statement by the client management that it understands it will be notified by the lawyer when an unasserted claim or assessment of the type requiring financial disclosure per SFAS 5 comes to the attention of the lawyer. The communication should also include a request that the lawyer confirm this understanding.

(5) A request that the lawyer specifically indicate the nature of, and the reason for, any limitations on the response.

b. Materiality--No inquiry needs to be made concerning matters not considered material as long as the auditor specifies a materiality amount in the letter.

c. Conference--If the client's lawyers provide the auditor with the information in a conference, the auditor should document the information received.

d. Change of Lawyers--If there has been a change of lawyers or a lawyer has resigned, the auditor should consider the need to inquire of the reasons for the change since lawyers may be required to resign when clients fail to follow their advice on matters of disclosure.

Exhibit 3--Sample Inquiry Letter to Legal Counsel

In connection with an audit of our financial statements at (balance sheet date) and for the (period) then ended, management of the Company has prepared, and furnished to our auditors (name and address of auditors), a description and evaluation of certain contingencies, including those set forth below involving matters with respect to which you have been engaged and to which you have devoted substantive attention on behalf of the Company in the form of legal consultation or representation. These contingencies are regarded by management of the Company as material for this purpose (management may indicate a materiality limit if an understanding has been reached with the auditor). Your response should include matters that existed at (balance sheet date) and during the period from that date to the date of your response.

(continued on next page)

Pending or Threatened Litigation (excluding unasserted claims)

[Ordinarily the information would include the following: (1) the nature of the litigation, (2) the progress of the case to date, (3) how management is responding or intends to respond to the litigation (for example, to contest the case vigorously or to seek an out-of-court settlement), and (4) an evaluation of the likelihood of an unfavorable outcome and an estimate, if one can be made, of the amount or range of potential loss.] Please furnish to our auditors such explanation, if any, that you consider necessary to supplement the foregoing information, including an explanation of those matters as to which your views may differ from those stated and an identification of the omission of any pending or threatened litigation, claims, and assessments or a statement that the list of such matters is complete.

Unasserted Claims and Assessments (considered by management to be probable of assertion, and that, if asserted, would have at least a reasonable possibility of an unfavorable outcome)

[Ordinarily management's information would include the following: (1) the nature of the matter, (2) how management intends to respond if the claim is asserted, and (3) an evaluation of the likelihood of an unfavorable outcome and an estimate, if one can be made, of the amount or range of potential loss.] Please furnish to our auditors such explanation, if any, that you consider necessary to supplement the foregoing information, including an explanation of those matters as to which your views may differ from those stated.

We understand that whenever, in the course of performing legal services for us with respect to a matter recognized to involve an unasserted possible claim or assessment that may call for financial statement disclosure, if you have formed a professional conclusion that we should disclose or consider disclosure concerning such possible claim or assessment, as a matter of professional responsibility to us, you will so advise us and will consult with us concerning the question of such disclosure and the applicable requirements of Statement of Financial Accounting Standards No. 5. Please specifically confirm to our auditors that our understanding is correct.

Please specifically identify the nature of and reasons for any limitation on your response.

[The auditor may request the client to inquire about additional matters, for example, unpaid or unbilled charges or specified information on certain contractually assumed obligations of the company, such as guarantees of indebtedness of others.]

3. Lawyer's Response Limited--The lawyer may limit the response to those matters which the lawyer had been <u>substantially involved</u> with and which are considered to be <u>material</u> (provided the lawyer and the auditor have agreed on what will be considered material). The refusal of a lawyer to furnish the information requested in an inquiry letter is a <u>limitation</u> on the <u>scope</u> of the audit which is sufficient to preclude an unqualified opinion if not satisfactorily resolved.

4. Other Limitations on a Lawyer's Response--Due to the inherent uncertainties present, the lawyer may feel unable to respond to the likelihood of an unfavorable outcome and/or to the amount or range of potential loss on one or more items. The auditor is then faced with an uncertainty which will be resolved in the future but which cannot be reasonably estimated at the present time. If the effect on the financial statements could be material, the auditor may be required to add an explanatory paragraph to the report because of the uncertainty.

5. The refusal of a client to allow necessary communications with a lawyer is a scope limitation that usually results in a disclaimer of opinion.

C. Dates (Auditing Interpretation: AU 9337)--The client's letter should specify the date by which the lawyer's response should be sent to the auditor and should also request the lawyer to specify the effective date of the response. The latest date of the period covered by the lawyer's response (the "effective date") should be as close as possible to the date of the auditor's completion of field work. If the lawyer's response does not specify an effective date, the auditor can assume it is the date of the response.

VII. Working Papers (AU 339, SAS 41)

A. Function and Nature of Working Papers

1. Working papers are records kept by the auditor of the (a) procedures applied, (b) tests performed, (c) information obtained, and (d) pertinent conclusions reached in the engagement.

2. Examples include audit programs, analyses, memoranda, letters of confirmation and representation, abstracts of company documents, and schedules or commentaries prepared or obtained by the auditor. Working papers also may be in the form of data stored on tapes, films, or other media.

3. There are two types of working paper files:

   a. Current files contain evidence of the entity's current account balances (e.g., bank reconciliation or recomputation of depreciation expense).

   b. Permanent files contain items of continuing interest (e.g., articles of incorporation, a pension plan contract, a flowchart of internal controls).

B. Requirement

1. The auditor is required to prepare and maintain working papers that are designed to meet the circumstances of a particular engagement.

2. The information contained in working papers constitutes the principal record of the work that the auditor has done and the conclusions that have been reached concerning significant matters.

C. Purposes of Working Papers

1. To provide the principal support for the auditor's report, including the auditor's representation regarding observance of the standards of field work, which is implicit in the reference in the report to GAAS.

2. To aid the auditor in the conduct and supervision of the audit.

D. Content of Working Papers

1. The quantity, type, and content of working papers for a particular engagement are a matter of judgment. The auditor's judgment may be affected by the following factors:

   a. The nature of the engagement.

   b. The nature of the auditor's report.

   c. The nature of the financial statements, schedules, or other information on which the auditor is reporting.

d. The nature and condition of the client's records.

e. The assessed level of control risk.

f. The needs in the particular circumstances for supervision and review of the work.

2. The quantity, type, and content of working papers should be sufficient to show that the accounting records agree or reconcile with the financial statements or other information reported on and that the applicable standards of field work have been observed.

3. Working papers ordinarily include documentation showing that:

   a. The work has been adequately planned and supervised, thereby indicating observance of the first standard of field work.

   b. A sufficient consideration of the internal control structure has been performed to plan the audit and to determine the nature, timing, and extent of tests to be performed.

   c. The audit evidence obtained, the auditing procedures applied, and the testing performed have provided sufficient competent evidential matter to afford a reasonable basis for an opinion, thereby indicating observance of the third standard of field work.

4. Detailed audit working papers are subdivided and grouped by financial statement accounts, which are filed in order of appearance in the financial statements. Working papers for each asset, liability, and equity account begin with a lead schedule summarizing the account's balance per the general ledger, and then show adjusting and reclassification entries, and the final balance per audit. The lead schedule also includes the auditor's conclusions about whether the account is fairly stated.

E. Ownership and Custody of Working Papers

1. Working papers are the property of the auditor. Some states have statutes that designate the auditor as the owner of the working papers. The auditor's rights of ownership, however, are subject to ethical limitations relating to the confidential relationship with clients.

2. Certain auditor's working papers may sometimes serve as a useful reference source for the client, but the working papers should not be regarded as a part of, or a substitute for, the client's accounting records.

3. The auditor should adopt reasonable procedures for safe custody of the working papers and should retain them for a period sufficient to meet the needs of the practice and to satisfy any legal requirements of records retention.

VIII. Related Parties (AU 334, SAS 45)

A. Definition--Related parties include (1) the reporting entity; (2) its affiliates; (3) principal owners (owner of record or known beneficial owner of more than 10% of the voting interests), management, and members of their immediate families; (4) equity-method investees; (5) trusts for the benefit of employees, such as pension or profit-sharing trusts that are managed by, or under the trusteeship of, management; and (6) any other party that can exercise significant influence over the reporting entity, or over which the reporting entity can exercise significant influence. Examples of related party transactions include parent-subsidiary transactions and transactions among subsidiaries of a common parent. Transactions between related parties are considered related party transactions even if they are not given accounting recognition (e.g., a parent providing free services a subsidiary).

B. Accounting Considerations--Related party transactions should be adequately and properly disclosed in conformity with GAAP. Recognition should be given to their economic substance rather than merely their legal form. Transactions that may indicate the existence of related party transactions include the following:

1. Borrowing or lending money without charging interest or at an interest rate significantly different from current market rates.

2. Selling real estate at a price considerably different from its appraised value.

3. Exchanging property for similar property in a nonmonetary transaction.

4. Making loans without scheduled repayment terms.

C. Audit Procedures--The auditor should be aware of the possible existence of such transactions and of any common ownership or management control relationships and may decide there is a need for additional procedures to determine their existence in certain cases. The auditor should be aware that business structure and operating style are occasionally deliberately designed to obscure related party transactions. The auditor should gain an understanding of management and the business in order to evaluate the possible existence of related party transactions. Related party transactions should not be assumed to be outside of the normal course of business unless there is applicable evidence.

1. Motivating Conditions--The following are examples of conditions which may motivate manipulation of related party transactions:

   a. Lack of sufficient working capital or credit to continue in business.

   b. An urgent desire for a continued favorable earnings record to support the price of the company's stock.

   c. An overly optimistic earnings forecast.

   d. Dependence on a single (or a relatively few) products, customers, or transactions for the ongoing success of the business.

   e. A declining industry that is experiencing a large number of business failures.

   f. Excess capacity.

   g. Significant litigation, especially between stockholders and management.

   h. Significant dangers of obsolescence because of being in a high technology industry.

2. Determining the Existence of Related Parties--The auditor will want to audit material transactions between related parties and the client. To determine the existence of less obvious relationships, the auditor may decide to apply one or more specific procedures such as the following:

   a. Evaluation of the company's procedures for identifying and properly accounting for related party transactions.

   b. Request of appropriate management personnel the names of all related parties and inquire whether any transaction occurred with these parties during the period (should be documented in the management representation letter).

c. Review SEC filings, etc., for the names of related parties and for other businesses in which officers and directors occupy directorship or management positions.

d. Determine the names of all pensions and trusts established for the benefit of employees and the names of their officers and trustees. They will be considered related parties if managed by or under the trusteeship of the client's management.

e. Review stockholder listings of closely held companies in order to identify principal stockholders.

f. Review the workpapers from prior years for the names of known related parties.

g. Inquire of the predecessor, principal, or other auditors of related parties as to their knowledge of existing relationships.

h. Review the period's material investment transactions to determine if any related party transactions were created.

3. Identifying Material Related Party Transactions--The following procedures may help the auditor identify material transactions with known related parties or which may indicate previously undetermined relationships:

a. Provide the names of related parties to the audit staff so they can watch for transactions with those parties.

b. Review the minutes of the board of directors' meetings (and other executive or operating committees) to see if any material transactions were authorized or discussed.

c. Review proxy and other material filed with the SEC.

d. Review "conflict-of-interests" statements obtained by the company from its management.

e. Review the extent and nature of transactions with major customers, suppliers, etc.

f. Consider whether nonmonetary transactions, such as free accounting or management expertise, are being provided but not recorded.

g. Review the accounting records for large, unusual, or nonrecurring transactions or balances. Special attention should be paid to transactions that are recognized at or near the end of the reporting period.

h. Review confirmations of compensating balance arrangements.

i. Review invoices from law firms that have performed regular or special services.

j. Review loans receivable and payable confirmations to see if any are guaranteed by parties that may be considered related parties.

4. Examining Identified Related Party Transactions--Once related party transactions have been identified, the auditor should apply whatever procedures considered necessary to obtain reasonable satisfaction as to their purpose, nature, and effect on the financial statements. In extending inquiry beyond the range of management, the auditor should:

a. Obtain an understanding of the business purpose of the transaction.

b. Examine pertinent documents such as invoices, contracts, and receiving and shipping documents.

c. Determine whether appropriate officials, such as the board of directors, have approved the transaction.

d. Test the amounts to be disclosed (or considered to be disclosed) in the financial statements for reasonableness.

e. Consider having intercompany balances audited on the same date. The auditors would then exchange relevant information.

f. Inspect or confirm the transferability and value of collateral.

g. Perform additional procedures needed to fully understand the particular transaction. The auditor would:

(1) Confirm the amounts and terms of the transactions (including guarantees) with the other parties.

(2) Inspect evidence that is in the possession of the other party (or parties) to the transaction.

(3) Confirm or discuss significant information with such intermediaries as banks, guarantors, or attorneys.

(4) If there is reason to believe that transactions lacking substance were conducted with any unfamiliar customers, businesses, etc., the auditor should refer to financial publications, trade journals, credit agencies, etc., to verify the lack of substance.

(5) Obtain information on the financial capability of the other party (parties) with respect to material uncollected balances, guarantees, and other obligations.

D. Disclosure--The auditor must evaluate the competence and sufficiency of evidence concerning related parties. This evaluation involves all the information available so that, using professional judgment, the auditor can determine the adequacy of the related party disclosures.

- Unless a transaction with a related party is of a routine nature, it is generally not possible to determine whether a particular transaction would have taken place had the parties not been related. As a result, it is quite difficult to determine if the terms were equivalent to those that prevail in arm's-length transactions. However, if the financial statements contain a representation that a material transaction was carried out at arm's-length bargaining and the representation is unsubstantiated by management, the auditor should, depending upon the materiality of the unsubstantiated representations, express a qualified or adverse opinion because of a departure from GAAP.

PART TWO: AUDIT PROGRAMS AND PROCEDURES

I. Review of Audit Evidence

A. Calculations by the Auditor--For example, the auditor may recompute a tax liability or depreciation. In addition to verifying the amount in the financial records, this procedure also contributes to the auditor's understanding of the summarization of the data in the financial statements.

B. Analytical Procedures (Interrelationships Within the Data)--The interrelationships among the various data are investigated to provide evidence of reasonable presentation in the financial statements. For example, the auditor may examine the ratio of interest expense to long-term debt, the ratio of accounts receivable to sales, and the gross profit ratios for a period of several years. Alternatively, the auditor may match several associated accounts and audit the data simultaneously (e.g., purchases and accounts payable, accounts receivable and sales).

C. Documents (Authoritative)--Authoritative documents such as vendor's invoices, time cards, receiving reports, and purchase orders provide support for recording transactions in journals and are used to authorize transactions.

1. Internally Prepared vs. Externally Prepared--In general, authoritative documents prepared by third parties are a better form of evidence than those prepared by the client.

2. Internal Control--Authoritative documents prepared under a good internal control structure are generally considered better evidence than those prepared under a weak internal control structure.

D. Subsequent Events--The occurrence of events subsequent to the financial statement date is especially important evidence regarding cut-off work on year-end balances. An important use of subsequent evidence is the search for unrecorded liabilities. In analyzing the cash disbursements made after the year-end, the auditor is looking for items which were a liability at year-end but which were not recorded and disclosed in the financial statements.

E. Client's Statements--The auditor frequently must rely on statements made by the client. The client's explanations must be evaluated as to the treatment of various items and as to the reasoning that supports certain judgmental decisions.

F. Records (Subsidiary)--Subsidiary records add to the evidential matter supporting the financial statement generation process. Subsidiary ledgers for accounts receivable, inventory, and fixed assets are examples of the types of evidence the auditor evaluates.

G. Internal Control--Can be thought of as a form of audit evidence since the auditor considers the internal control structure in reaching conclusions concerning the fairness of the financial statements. The strength of internal control affects the nature, timing, and extent of the auditing procedures that will be performed. Therefore, under a strong internal control structure, the auditor may require less audit evidence than under a weak internal control structure.

H. Physical Evidence--Examples include counting cash, counting inventory, and observing fixed assets such as buildings and machines.

I. Third Party Statements--Statements by third parties are strong types of evidence since they are prepared by independent parties. Examples include accounts receivable confirmations, confirmations from insurance brokers concerning the status of various insurance policies, confirmations of the number of shares outstanding from registrars, and confirmations of account balances by banks.

REVIEW OF AUDIT EVIDENCE

C Calculations by the auditor
A Analytical procedures
D Documents (authoritative)

S Subsequent events
C Client statements
R Records (subsidiary)
I Internal control
P Physical evidence
T Third party statements

II. General Approach to the Audit of Specific Accounts

A. In General--At this stage in the audit process, the auditor performs substantive testing. Such testing involves procedures which are designed to determine the accuracy of the dollar amounts reported in the financial statements. Substantive testing entails analytical procedures (see IV. of Part One) and tests of details--either tests of transactions or tests of balances.

1. Tests of Transactions--These tests are performed to determine whether the entity's transactions are correctly recorded and summarized in the accounting records. Many of these tests can be performed simultaneously with the tests of controls of the internal control structure (i.e., dual-purpose tests).

2. Tests of Balances--These tests are primarily concerned with monetary misstatements in the account balances. Tests of balances can be distinguished from tests of transactions because the tests of balances relate to individual accounts, whereas the tests of transactions relate to the different transaction cycles.

B. Audit Program--A list of audit procedures that should be comprehensive enough to enable the gathering of evidence indicating the satisfaction of the audit objectives of the particular account(s). The program should also be concise and understandable so that anyone examining the working papers can evaluate the work performed.

C. Audit of Specific Accounts--A general approach to the audit of specific accounts includes the following steps and considerations:

1. Audit Objectives--Consider the objectives of the audit of the specific account. In other words, what does the auditor want to determine through the audit procedures? There there are seven audit objectives that must be addressed in the audit of each and every account. These objectives are as follows:

   a. The transactions must be properly classified.

   b. The data must be accurate in amount.

   c. The transactions must be recorded at proper values.

   d. The item must actually exist.

   e. The transactions must be recorded on a timely basis.

   f. The assets and liabilities must be owned by the client.

   g. The financial statements must properly disclose the outcome of transactions.

   h. All transactions have been recorded--completeness.

TotalRecall

AUDIT OBJECTIVES

C The transactions must be properly **classified.**

A The data must be **accurate** in amount.

V The transactions must be recorded at proper **values.**

E The item of interest must actually **exist.**

T The transactions must be recorded on a **timely** basis.

O The assets and liabilities must be **owned** by the client.

D The financial statements must properly **disclose** the outcome of transactions.

C All transactions have been recorded--**completeness.**

2. Internal Control--Visualize and understand the control environment accounting system, control environment and control procedures that are designed into the structure. A good technique is to visualize the physical flow of the goods and the resulting accounting entries and records.

3. Audit Evidence--Determine which of the forms of audit evidence are applicable in the particular situation. Audit evidence must be both valid and relevant.

4. Audit Procedures--Determine the types of audit procedures that will be required to obtain the audit evidence.

   a. Interim Tests vs. Year-End Tests--Some tests, including tests of controls, can be done during the year, rather than at year-end. Therefore, the audit program may be broken into two parts, one dealing with interim procedures and the other with year-end procedures. Note that interim work consists primarily of procedural work.

   b. Cost/Benefit Analysis--The audit procedures must be justifiable in terms of their cost/benefit relationship. This will include consideration of (1) the materiality of the account being audited, (2) the materiality of possible misstatements, and (3) the audit risk associated with the account. For example, certain items such as cash have a much greater risk associated with them than accounts such as land. In general, the more material an account and its possible misstatements, the higher the audit risk and the more extensive the audit procedures should be.

Exhibit 4--Management Assertions and Audit Objectives

Definition	Management Assertion	Audit Objective
All Transactions Recorded	Completeness	Completeness
Assets and Liabilities "Owned" and "Owed"	Obligations and Rights	Ownership/Authorization
Accuracy of Amounts in Financial Statements	Valuation or Allocation	1. Estimates are reasonable and realistic 2. Good cutoff obtained 3. Mechanical accuracy reliable
Recorded Transactions Exist	Existence	Validity
Reporting Standards--GAAP, Consistency, Disclosure	Statement Presentation and Disclosure	1. Adequate disclosure 2. G/L classification reasonable

III. Standardized Audit Procedures

A. In General--Many past CPA Exams have contained essay questions in which the candidate was required to develop an audit program for a particular account or transaction cycle. Composing such an audit program is greatly simplified if the candidate has knowledge of the key terms used in describing audit procedures. The following is a listing of such key words:

TotalRecall

STANDARDIZED AUDIT PROCEDURES

T	**TRACING**	**Follow transaction from supporting documentation to accounting records.**
R	**RECONCILE**	**Account for difference between two amounts.**
A	**ANALYZE**	**Search for unexpected trends or the lack of expected deviations.**
F	**FOOT**	**Recompute column totals within financial statements and individual accounts.**
I	**INSPECT**	**Physically confirm the existence of assets such as stock certificates**
C	**CONFIRM**	**Confirmation of certain account balances with third parties.**
C	**CONSIDER**	**internal control structure.**
I	**INQUIRE**	**Make inquiries of client management and employees.**
V	**VOUCHING**	**Examine documentation which supports entries in the accounting records.**
I	**INVESTIGATE**	**Look for cause of detected irregularities discovered in testing.**
C	**COUNT**	**Physical count of inventories on hand and fixed assets owned.**
S	**SUBSEQUENT EVENTS**	**Events occurring after the year-end which may have an effect on the financial statements.**

B. Standardized Audit Procedures--The following are frequently used audit procedures. Because they are in general form, each procedure in an audit program should specify the account balance or transaction to which it applies (e.g., vouch sales journal entries to the bills of lading).

1. Consider internal control, assess control risk.

2. Evaluate whether transactions are properly recorded in conformity with GAAP.

3. Reconcile detail records and data with the general ledger.

4. Confirm and observe for proper segregation of duties and actual practice.

5. Test posting from the journals to the ledgers.

6. Compare the beginning balance in an account with the ending balance from the previous period.

7. Scan the accounts for unusual items.

8. Investigate unusual items.

9. Test for proper authorizations.

10. Vouch (i.e., examine) source documents.

11. Inquire about significant accounts and events.

12. Test for adequate disclosures.

13. Foot and cross-foot.

14. Test for interrelationships between certain accounts and between certain amounts (i.e., perform analytical procedures).

15. Recalculate significant figures.

16. Review cut-off dates.

17. Examine subsequent events.

18. Make inquiries of client personnel.

19. Obtain written representations from management.

20. Read the minutes of the Board of Directors' meetings and committee meetings of the Board.

21. Make inquiries of client's attorney.

C. Guidelines for Tracing or Vouching--Exam questions frequently require you to determine the purpose of tracing or vouching given documents through the accounting process.

1. Tracing From Source Documents to Ledgers--Provides evidence of completeness (i.e., all transactions are recorded and the ledger accounts are not understated). This is indicated by the upward arrow in Exhibit 5, below.

2. Vouching From Ledgers to Source Documents--Provides evidence of existence (i.e., all transactions summarized in the ledgers actually occurred, the ledgers contain no unsupported entries, and ledger balances are not overstated). This is indicated by the downward arrow in Exhibit 5, below.

Exhibit 5--Guidelines for Tracing or Vouching

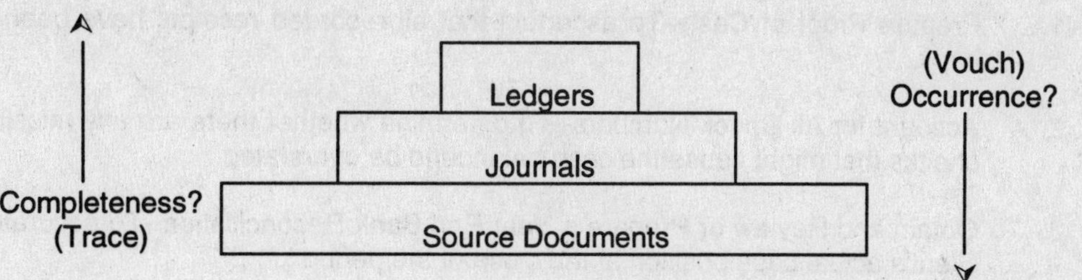

IV. Audit of Cash

A. Audit Objectives--The objectives of the audit of the cash account are to ensure (1) there are adequate internal control structure policies and procedures over cash, (2) all cash that should be in the custody of the client is (existence), (3) all of the cash in custody of the client is properly recorded (completeness), and (4) the cash in the custody of the client is properly disclosed in the financial statements.

B. Subfunctions--Subfunctions for cash include (1) accounts receivable, (2) accounts payable, (3) cash sales, and (4) general ledger accounting.

C. Kiting--This is the practice whereby an employee who is embezzling funds makes a transfer of funds from a bank account in one bank to a bank account in another bank near the end of the period. The transfer is effected through the use of a check and, therefore, does not show up as a withdrawal from the first bank until the check clears. It is listed as a deposit in transit on the receiving bank's books but not as an outstanding check on the disbursing bank's books. As a result, the overall cash balance is temporarily overstated at the balance sheet date and the embezzlement is not detected.

> Example 1--Kiting
>
> Allen Richards is the bookkeeper for Diversified, Inc. Diversified has two bank accounts--one in the First Federal Bank of Starke and another in the Fourth National Bank of Gainesville. On a hot tip from Allen's investment broker, Allen writes himself a $5,000 check on the First Federal account, makes no entry, and purchases stock in STCG, Inc. Shortly thereafter, STCG, Inc. is subjected to SEC investigation and all trading in its stock is frozen. As the end of the year nears, Allen's predicament remains unchanged. To cover the defalcation, Allen writes a $5,000 check on the Fourth National account on December 31 and deposits it in the First Federal account on the same day. Furthermore, he makes no entry in the cash disbursements journal and fails to list the check as outstanding on the year-end bank reconciliation. Since the check will not show up as a decrease in the Fourth National account until it clears, that account will still reflect the same account balance without the check deduction, and the First Bank will reflect the $5,000 deposited as of December 31. The money "appears" to be in both accounts, when in reality, only due to the delay in transaction posting, it is not.

D. Sample Audit Procedures for Cash--The following audit procedures are generally performed during the audit of the cash account to obtain supporting evidence of the objectives defined for the following assertions:

Obtain an Understanding of Relevant Internal Control Structure Policies and Procedures and Assess Control Risk--In order to ascertain the nature, timing, and extent of substantive tests to be applied.

Completeness

1. Prepare Proof of Cash--To ascertain that all recorded receipts have been deposited in the bank.

2. Account for All Check Numbers--To determine whether there are any missing or outstanding checks that might cause the cash balance to be overstated.

3. Obtain and Review or Prepare a Year-End Bank Reconciliation--To accurately determine the client's actual cash position at the close of the period.

4. Obtain a Bank Cutoff Statement Directly From the Bank--To ascertain whether the items on the year-end reconciliation have cleared the bank and, therefore, were valid. Bank cutoff statements are generally requested for one to two weeks after year end. After finishing this procedure, the cutoff bank statement is given to the client. This procedure is useful for detecting kiting between account balances.

Obligations and Rights

5. Investigate Any Checks Made to Cash or Bearer--To determine the propriety of the disbursement.

Valuation or Allocation

6. Trace a Sample of Entries in the Cash Receipts Journal to the A/R Subsidiary Ledger, Duplicate Deposit Ticket, and General Ledger--In order to determine whether the cash is accurately stated.

Existence or Occurrence

7. Count All Cash on Hand Simultaneously--To ensure that no cash is counted more than once (coordinate with count of marketable securities on hand).

8. Investigate NSF Checks and Other Debit Memos--Because these may be an indication of the covering up of a cash shortage.

9. Prepare a Schedule of Bank Transfers--Around year-end to help detect kiting.

10. Confirm the Existence of Year-End Bank Balances--Of the following:

    a. Amounts on deposit.

    b. Direct liabilities.

    c. Contingent liabilities on notes discounted.

    d. Other direct or contingent liabilities.

    e. Other security agreements.

Statement Presentation and Disclosure

11. Determine If Any Cash Is Restricted--So that the restricted balance is properly classified on the balance sheet, and requirements of compensating balance agreements are properly disclosed.

V. Audit of Accounts Receivable and Sales

A. Audit Objectives--To ascertain the following: (1) adequate control structure policies and procedures exist; (2) all sales and receivables that should be recorded are properly recorded (completeness); (3) only sales and receivables that should be recorded are recorded (existence); and (4) accounts receivable are presented at approximate realizable valuation.

B. Subfunctions--After the audit objectives for an audit area are specified, they should be broken into subfunctions. For accounts receivable and sales, possible subfunctions include: (1) credit granting, (2) billing, (3) shipping, (4) cash receipts, (5) detailed ledger bookkeeping, and (6) general ledger accounting.

C. Broad Outline of an Audit Program for Accounts Receivable and Sales

1. Interim Work--Possibilities include (a) obtaining understanding of the internal control structure (may include walking through a transaction, inquiry, and observation), and (b) performing tests of control as to operating effectiveness.

2. Year-End Work--Sales--(a) Analytical procedures (including ratio and trend analysis), (b) review sales cutoff and consignment sales, and (c) review sales returns and allowances and sales discounts.

3. Year-End Work--Accounts Receivable--(a) Review aged trial balance, (b) confirm accounts receivable by positive and/or negative confirmations, and (c) review bad debts allowance and expense.

D. Confirmation of Accounts Receivable (AU 330, SAS 67)--Confirmation of accounts receivable is a generally accepted auditing procedure (although not a standard). Therefore, if the procedure is not performed, the auditor must document the reason.

1. Extent and Method of Confirmation--The extent and method of confirmation will be determined by the auditor after considering (a) the effectiveness of internal control; (b) the possibility of disputes, inaccuracies, and irregularities in the accounts; (c) the expected degree of cooperation by the debtor; (d) the probability that the debtor will be able to confirm the amounts involved; and (e) the materiality of the amounts involved.

2. Auditor's Responsibility--Confirmation requests should always be mailed by the auditor. In addition, the auditor's firm should receive all requests. These procedures diminish the possibility that the confirmation requests could be altered by the client, either during the mailing process or upon receipt.

3. Positive Form of Confirmation Request--Requests a response concerning whether or not the customer is in agreement with the client's records. The positive request may also be blank, requesting the recipient to indicate balances and furnish other information. The positive form is preferable when individual account balances are relatively large or when there is reason to believe that a substantial number of the accounts may be disputed or that errors and/or irregularities exist.

   - Nonresponse--Generally requires the use of follow-up requests such as additional mailings or telephone calls. In cases where there is still no response to requests dealing with significant accounts, alternative procedures should be used to obtain adequate evidence. These additional procedures may involve the examination of documents such as subsequent cash receipts, sales invoices, and shipping documents.

4. Negative Form of Confirmation Request--Requests a response only in cases where the customer disagrees with the stated balance. The negative form is useful when the assessed

level of control risk is low, when a large number of small balances are involved, and when the auditor has no reason to believe the persons receiving the requests are unlikely to give them consideration.

- Nonresponse--An inherent weakness in the negative form is that a nonresponse does not necessarily mean that the balance is accurate. Rather, a nonresponse may have nothing to do with the correctness or incorrectness of the balance. The response form may simply have not been returned by the debtor or may have been lost enroute from the debtor to the auditor.

5. A combination of the two forms may be appropriate in some situations, with the positive form used for large balances and the negative form for small balances.

6. Subject of Confirmation--Confirmations may deal with the account balance or with individual items. The latter are useful when the customer may not be in a position to confirm the total account balance owed to the client. This occurs frequently when sales or contracts are made with governmental agencies.

E. Lapping--This is one of the most common types of fraud, and it involves the delay in the recording of a cash receipt in order to cover up an existing shortage in the actual cash on hand. Lapping is made possible through either bad internal control (i.e., having the same employee handle both the cash and the accounts receivable records) or collusion. In order to detect a lapping scheme, the auditor must compare the name, amounts, and dates shown on the customers' remittance advices with entries in the cash receipts journal and the related deposit slips.

F. Sample Audit Procedures for A/R and Sales--The following procedures (and the purpose behind each procedure) are generally performed during the audit of accounts receivable and sales to obtain supporting evidence of the objectives defined for the following assertions:

Obtain an Understanding of Relevant Internal Control Structure Policies and Procedures and Assess Control Risk--In order to ascertain the nature, timing, and extent of substantive tests to be applied.

Completeness

1. Compare a Sample of Shipping Documents to the Related Sales Invoices--For the purpose of discovering orders which have been shipped but not billed. (Cutoff tests should be performed both at the confirmation date and balance sheet date, if different.)

> Example 2--Lapping
>
> Georgia Thomas is the bookkeeper for Farley Fabrics (a retail cloth distributor), and her duties consist of receiving the checks from the customers and recording the payments in the A/R subsidiary ledger. On January 8th, Georgia hears the president talk about a one-time purchase of a unique fabric by Colin's Casuals. She also hears that Colin's is going to make a $640 purchase. The next day, Colin's Casuals submits its order for that $640 of fabric. With all of this in mind, Georgia embezzles $640 of that day's payments received from Mama's Moo Moos and Jabba's Jammies (both of whom are regular customers of Farley). Georgia makes no entries in the accounts. Five days later, Colin's Casuals pays its bill, and Georgia credits the payments to Mama's and Jabba's accounts. Colin does no more business with Farley and, at the end of the year, Georgia writes-off Colin's receivable as uncollectible.

2. Reconcile a Sample of Cash Register Tapes and Sales Tickets With the Sales Journals--So that evidence is gathered that shows that all sales have been recorded--and recorded accurately.

3. Perform Analytical Procedures--For example, a gross profit test, to determine that all sales have been recorded and classified correctly. Investigate any unexpected fluctuations.

Obligations and Rights

4. Review Sales Discount Procedures and Documentation--To determine that discounts were granted only for payments received within the discount period.

5. Vouch Debits in Individual A/R Accounts to Sales Invoices--In order to determine whether the sale actually occurred.

6. Review Sales and Receipts Occurring Near Year-End--In order to ascertain that such transactions were recorded in the proper time period and were valid transactions.

Valuation or Allocation

7. Test Foot the Sales Journal and Reconcile With Postings to the General Ledger--To find out if the sales figures were brought forward accurately.

8. Vouch Debit Entries in the Allowance for Doubtful Accounts to the Individual Accounts and Original Write-Off Authorizations--So that it can be determined that such write-offs were properly reflected in the accounts and were authorized.

9. Prepare or Obtain an Aged A/R Schedule--(a) To help identify accounts that should be written off, (b) to determine the reasonableness of the bad-debt expense and allowance for doubtful accounts, and (c) to aid the confirmation of A/R.

10. Investigate Any Unusual Items, Transactions, or Amounts--To determine the substance behind, and treatment of, such items, transactions, and amounts.

11. Recalculate and Review Bad-Debt Expense and Allowance--For reasonableness of expense and adequacy of the allowance.

12. Examine cash receipts after the balance sheet date to provide evidence of collectibility at the balance sheet date.

Existence or Occurrence

13. Examine All Aspects of a Sample of Sales Transactions--In order to determine whether the internal control procedures are being applied properly (i.e., perform tests of controls directed toward operating effectiveness). This procedure includes the following:

    a. Comparing the sales invoice with the customer's purchase order.

    b. Checking for proper credit approval.

    c. Comparing prices on sales invoice with those on price list. Ascertaining the propriety of discounts granted to purchasers.

    d. Recomputing extensions and footings.

    e. Checking the recording in the sales journal and the posting of the sale in the A/R subsidiary ledger.

14. Confirm A/R on a Test Basis--To verify the existence and accuracy of the account balances and that the receivables are the rights of the company.

Statement Presentation and Disclosure

15. Review Loan Agreements--For pledging of accounts and agreements, for any factoring of accounts, and for disclosure purposes.

VI. Audit of Inventory

A. Audit Objectives--To ascertain (1) the inventory exists and the client owns it (existence and rights), (2) it is priced correctly, (3) the quantities shown are reasonable (rights), (4) the computations used to arrive at the inventory dollar amounts are accurate (valuation), and (5) there is adequate disclosure in the financial statements.

B. Subfunctions--Subfunctions for inventory include (1) purchasing, (2) receiving, (3) storing, (4) processing, (5) shipping, (6) detailed bookkeeping, and (7) general ledger accounting.

C. Evidence for Inventories (AU 331)--The observation of the taking of the inventory is a generally accepted auditing procedure (although not a standard). Therefore, if an observation is not performed, the auditor must document the reason.

1. Periodic Inventory--When the client determines its inventory quantities entirely by means of a physical count at or near the balance sheet date, the auditor ordinarily must be present at the count. The auditor should use suitable observations, tests, and inquiries to become satisfied that the method of accounting for inventory is effective and that the client's claims as to the quantities and physical condition are reliable.

2. Perpetual Inventory System--When a good perpetual inventory system is maintained in which the client periodically compares the inventory records with the physical counts, the auditor should observe the counting and comparing. However, this can be done either during the period (assuming an adequate system of internal control over inventory and the assessed level of control risk is low) or at or after the end of the period.

3. Advanced Methods--Some companies have developed highly effective inventory methods (using statistical sampling) which make annual counts of each item of inventory unnecessary. In these cases, the auditor must be present at such partial countings as considered necessary. The auditor must also be satisfied that the inventory method will produce results which are comparable to those which would be obtained by an annual count of physical inventory.

   - Statistical Sampling--If the inventory plan is based on statistical sampling, the auditor must be satisfied that the plan has statistical validity and is properly applied, and that the resulting precision and reliability are statistically reasonable.

4. Sufficient Audit Evidence--Tests of the accounting records are not sufficient evidence as to current inventories. Rather, the auditor will always have to make or observe some physical counts of the inventory, apply appropriate tests to the intervening transactions, and review any client counts and procedures relating to the physical inventory.

5. Auditor Has Not Audited Prior Inventories--When auditing financial statements covering the current period and one or more periods for which the auditor has not observed or made some physical counts of prior inventories, the auditor must be satisfied as to the prior period's inventory with appropriate tests. These tests might include tests of prior transactions, review of prior record counts, and gross profit tests. An example of this type of situation would be the first audit of a new client who has opening inventory.

6. Inventories Held in Public Warehouses--In some cases, inventories will be held in public warehouses or by other outside custodians. In these situations, direct written confirmation from the custodian is acceptable when the inventory is not material. When the amounts are

substantial, relative to current or total assets, the auditor should undertake one or more of the following procedures: (a) test the owner's control procedures for investigating the warehouse and evaluating its performance; (b) obtain an independent accountant's report on the warehouse's control procedures relevant to custody of goods and, if applicable, pledging of receipts, or apply alternative procedures at the warehouse to gain reasonable assurance that information received from the warehouse is reliable; (c) observe physical counts wherever reasonable and practicable; and finally (d) obtain confirmations from lenders in cases where warehouse receipts have been pledged as collateral.

7. Outside Inventory-Taking Firm (AU 9508)--Some companies (e.g., retail stores, hospitals, and automobile dealers) use outside firms of nonaccountants who specialize in the taking of physical inventories to count, list, price, and subsequently compute the total dollar amount of the inventory. While the use of an outside firm will ordinarily reduce the work, it is not, by itself, a satisfactory substitute for the auditor's observation or taking of physical counts. In this situation, the auditor's primary concern will be to evaluate the effectiveness of the outside firm's procedures. Therefore, the auditor would (a) examine its inventory program, (b) observe its procedures and controls, (c) make or observe some physical counts of the inventory, (d) recompute calculations of the submitted inventory on a test basis, and (e) apply appropriate tests to the intervening transactions.

D. Sample Audit Procedures for Inventory--The following audit procedures are typically performed during the audit of the inventory account to obtain supporting evidence of the objectives defined for the following assertions:

Obtain an Understanding of Relevant Internal Control Structure Policies and Procedures and Assess Control Risk--In order to ascertain the nature, timing, and extent of substantive tests to be applied.

Completeness

1. Account for the Numerical Sequence of Inventory Purchase Requisitions--To ascertain that none are missing, thereby helping to assure that no unauthorized purchases were made.

2. Trace a Sample of Receiving Reports for Inventory to the Perpetual Inventory Records--To determine that all shipments were properly reflected in the accounts. (This cutoff test must be performed at the inventory observation date and at the balance sheet date, if different.)

3. Perform Analytical Procedures on Cost of Goods Sold--To determine if significant fluctuations exist which would necessitate audit investigation; perform procedures to test turnover and compare gross margin of current year with that of prior year to test for overstatement or understatement.

4. Account for Inventory Tags and Count Sheets--To verify the inventory has completely been accounted for.

5. Trace Test Counts of Inventory Items From the Floor to the Client's Inventory Listing--To ensure all items of inventory have been counted and included in the total inventory balance.

Obligations and Rights

6. Vouch a Sample of Inventory Requisitions to Customer or Department Order--So that evidence is obtained that all requisitions are valid.

7. Review Purchase and Sales Cutoffs--To ascertain that ending inventory is properly valued and that the inventory transactions are recorded in the proper time period.

8. Review Inventory on Consignment (as both consignee and consignor)--To determine the inventory actually owned by the client.

9. Confirm Inventory Held at Public Warehouses and With Third Parties--To identify other inventory actually owned by the client.

Valuation or Allocation

10. Test Pricing Method Used by the Client--So that the proper inventory value is attained.

11. Apply Lower-of-Cost-or-Market Rule--So that the proper inventory value and any losses are recognized and disclosed.

12. Perform analytical procedures such as: gross profit percentage calculations; inventory turnover ratios; and number of days sales in inventory ratio analysis.

In addition, inventory audit procedures for a manufacturing client could include the following:

13. Test Cost Accumulation Process--So that the ending inventory and cost-of-goods-sold are properly valued.

14. Review the Overhead Allocations and Rates--For accuracy when compared with actual experience.

Existence or Occurrence

15. For the Physical Inventory:

    a. Review the Client's Plan for Taking the Physical Inventory--In order to determine whether the necessary information will be obtained.

    b. Observe the Physical Count--To become satisfied that the counting methods are effective and the client's representations are reliable.

    c. Trace Client's Physical Counts to Perpetual Records and Inventory Sheets--In order to test the accuracy of the perpetual records.

    d. Vouch the Validity of the Perpetual Records and Inventory Sheets Against the Physical Count--In order to determine that items in the perpetual records exist and quantities are correct.

    e. Test Inventory Sheet and Perpetual Record Computation for Clerical Accuracy--Thereby helping to ascertain that the inventory is properly valued and quantities are correct.

    f. Make Random Test Counts--To assure that the counts made by the client are accurate. Test counts of inventory items should also be traced to client's inventory sheets and to client's final inventory compilation report.

16. Vouch a Sample of Additions to Perpetual Inventory to Supporting Receiving Reports--To assure that the recorded inventory was actually received.

Statement Presentation and Disclosure

17. Review Purchase and Sales Commitments--To determine whether there is a need to accrue a loss and disclose its relevant facts.

18. Determine Whether Any Inventory Has Been Pledged--To assure that such facts are properly disclosed in the financial statements.

VII. Audit of Fixed Assets

A. Audit Objectives--The objectives of the audit of fixed assets are: (1) ascertain the adequacy of internal control structure policies and procedures over fixed assets, (2) verify the existence and ownership of the fixed assets, and (3) ascertain the adequacy of valuation and disclosure of the fixed assets in the financial statements.

B. Subfunctions--Subfunctions for fixed assets include (1) depreciation, (2) financing, (3) detailed ledger bookkeeping, and (4) general ledger accounting.

C. Sample Audit Procedures for Fixed Assets--The following procedures are normally performed during the audit of fixed assets to obtain supporting evidence of the objectives defined for the following assertions:

Obtain an Understanding of Relevant Internal Control Structure Policies and Procedures and Assess Control Risk--In order to ascertain the nature, timing, and extent of substantive tests to be applied.

Completeness

1. Vouch--From fixed assets to the plant and equipment subsidiary ledger--To determine that the assets are recorded.

2. Obtain or Prepare an Analysis of the Repair and Maintenance Expense Account--To consider if any items should be classified as capital expenditures.

3. Review Rental Revenue and Property Tax Expense--By obtaining a map of rented and leased property. This procedure will help determine the accuracy of the rental revenue and tax expense accounts by exposing all the client's real property, thereby enabling a thorough evaluation.

Obligations and Rights

4. Verify the Client's Ownership of the Assets--By examining titles to the fixed assets.

5. Review Lease Agreements--For determining whether assets should be capitalized.

Valuation or Allocation

6. Reconcile the Plant and Equipment Subsidiary Ledger With the General Ledger--To determine that the accounting for the plant and equipment transactions was consistent.

7. Recalculate--The accounting for retirements of fixed assets.

8. Review Depreciation Methods--For consistency with prior periods.

9. Review Useful Lives--For appropriateness and consistency with prior periods.

10. Recalculate--Depreciation computations.

Existence or Occurrence

11. Trace--From the plant and equipment subsidiary ledger to the fixed assets--To determine that the assets actually exist.

12. Vouch Acquisitions--To purchase orders or contracts approved by appropriate personnel.

Statement Presentation and Disclosure

13. Review Loan Agreements--To verify any loans collateralized by property or equipment for proper disclosure.

VIII. Audit of Long-Term Investments

A. Audit Objectives--The objectives of the audit of long-term investments are: (1) ascertain the adequacy of internal control structure policies and procedures over long-term investments; (2) ascertain whether the investments are accounted for in conformity with GAAP; (3) ascertain the adequacy of financial statement disclosure of such investments; (4) determine whether a loss in value of such investments should be considered as temporary or permanent; and (5) obtain evidence as to the existence of securities by inspection and/or confirmation.

B. Subfunctions--Subfunctions for long-term investments include (1) financing, (2) cash, (3) detailed ledger bookkeeping, and (4) general ledger accounting.

C. Evidence for Long-Term Investments (AU 332.04-.05)--The auditor is concerned with gathering sufficient competent evidence pertaining to the existence, ownership, and cost of long-term investments, as well as their carrying amounts, or valuation, on the balance sheet.

1. Evidence of the existence, ownership, and cost of long-term investments can be obtained from the accounting records and documents of the investor. In the case of securities, such evidence can be corroborated through inspection or, when appropriate, confirmation from an independent custodian. In the case of loans, bonds, and similar debt obligations, evidence should be corroborated through written confirmation from the debtor or trustee.

2. Evidence of the carrying amount of long-term investments and income and losses attributable to such investments can be obtained from the following sources:

   a. Audited Financial Statements--Generally provide sufficient evidential matter, when the statements have been audited by an independent auditor, regarding equity in underlying net assets and results of operation of investee, as well as corroboration of investments in bonds and other debt instruments.

   b. Unaudited Financial Statements--Provide insufficient information. However, the investor's auditor may utilize the investee's auditor for the purpose of applying auditing procedures to the unaudited statements, thereby obtaining sufficient evidence.

   c. Market Quotations--If the market is reasonably broad and active, such quotations ordinarily constitute sufficient competent evidence as to the current market value of unrestricted securities.

   d. Published Dividend Records--These provide the strongest evidence supporting dividends earned on marketable equity securities.

D. The Equity Method of Accounting (AU 332.06-.15)--APB Opinion 18 requires the use of the equity method by an investor whose investment in voting stock gives it the ability to exercise significant influence over operating and financial policies of the investee. If the investor owns 50% or more of the investee's voting stock, the ability to exercise significant influence is presumed to exist. The auditor must be satisfied as to the correctness of the accounting method adopted by the investor (i.e., cost or equity method).

E. Sample Audit Program for Long-Term Investments--The following audit procedures are generally performed during the audit of long-term investments to obtain supporting evidence of the objectives defined for the following assertions:

Obtain an Understanding of Relevant Internal Control Structure Policies and Procedures and Assess Control Risk--In order to ascertain the nature, timing, and extent of substantive tests to be applied.

Completeness

1. Obtain or Prepare an Account Analysis for the Long-Term Investment and Related Revenue or Loss Accounts--This procedure allows the auditor to

   a. Establish the accuracy of the individual debits and credits occurring during the year, and

   b. Prove the validity of the year-end balance in the accounts.

2. Perform Analytical Procedures--By comparing dividends, interest and other investment income with those of prior years to ascertain the reasonableness of the completeness of recorded investment income. Calculate the percentage of accrued investment income to total investments and estimate total accrued income based on current investments.

Obligations and Rights

3. Verify Purchases and Sales of Securities During the Year and For a Short Period Subsequent to the Balance Sheet Date--This procedure allows the auditor to determine whether all of the securities are accounted for in the accounting records.

Valuation or Allocation

4. Investigate Method of Accounting for Equity Securities--To determine whether such securities should be accounted for under the cost or equity method.

5. Determine FMV of Securities on Balance Sheet Date--This procedure provides evidence as to the proper carrying amount of debt securities and equity securities accounted for under the cost method, and may also be necessary for disclosure purposes.

6. Verify the Interest Earned on Bonds--By recomputing the interest earned on the basis of the face amount, interest rate, and period held.

7. Examine Financial Statements of Investee Companies--To determine gains and losses from investments in equity securities, as well as the carrying amounts of securities accounted for under the equity method.

8. Test calculations of premium and discount amortization for accuracy.

Existence or Occurrence

9. Inspect securities on hand and compare serial numbers with those shown in previous year's working papers. This procedure will help identify any undisclosed sales or purchases of investments. (Coordinate with cash count to prevent substitution.)

10. Obtain Confirmation of Securities From Third-Party Custodian--In order to provide evidence as to the existence of such investments.

Statement Presentation and Disclosure

11. Examine Financial Presentation of Long-Term Investments--To determine whether GAAP is followed.

12. Inquire of management and review loan documents as to possible pledging of securities for appropriate disclosure purposes.

IX. Audit of Accounts Payable, Purchases, and Other Liabilities

A. Audit Objectives--The objectives of the audit of payables and purchases are to ensure the following: (1) there are adequate internal control structure policies and procedures over payables and purchases; (2) all transactions that should be recorded are recorded (completeness); (3) those transactions that are recorded are recorded properly (valuation); and (4) the financial statement presentation is adequate (disclosure and obligation).

B. Subfunctions--Subfunctions for payables and purchases include (1) purchasing, (2) receiving, (3) payment, (4) detailed ledger bookkeeping, and (5) general ledger accounting.

C. Sample Audit Procedures for A/P, Purchases, and Other Liabilities--The following audit procedures are commonly performed during the audit of the A/P, purchasing, and other liabilities accounts to obtain supporting evidence of the objectives defined for the following assertions:

Obtain an Understanding of Relevant Internal Control Structure Policies and Procedures and Assess Control Risk--In order to ascertain the nature, timing, and extent of substantive tests to be applied.

Completeness

1. Perform Search for Unrecorded Liabilities--To ascertain that all payables have been recorded in the proper period. This search is performed, at the balance sheet date, in the following areas:

   a. Unmatched invoices and unbilled receiving reports.

   b. Significant payments subsequent to the end of the period may indicate liabilities that existed at the end of the period.

   c. Invoices received after the end of the period may have been for goods received at or before the end of the period.

   d. Customer deposits recorded as credits to A/R.

   e. Unbilled professional fees at the end of the period under audit.

   f. Perform inventory receiving cutoff test.

2. Perform Analytical Procedures--To assess the reasonableness of balances. Compare the average number of days purchases in accounts payable at the end of the current year to prior years. Compare purchases divided by payables to payables divided by total current liabilities for the current and prior years. Compare payables and purchases to budgeted or forecasted amounts.

Obligations and Rights

3. Vouch--The paid check and invoice from the vendor to the receiving report to determine if any payments were made for goods that were not received.

4. Review the Cutoff of Purchases, Returns, and Disbursements--To determine that transactions are recorded in the proper periods.

Valuation or Allocation

5. Obtain a listing of A/P and reconcile with general ledger A/P balance.

6. Recalculate the Extensions and Footings on Customer Invoices--To determine whether such invoices were accurately priced and computed.

7. Trace Vendor Invoices to Voucher Register and Checks to Check Register--To determine that all payables and related disbursements have been properly recorded.

8. Foot Voucher Register and Trace to General Ledger--To substantiate the entries in the general ledger.

9. Reclassify debit balances as receivables and review for collectibility.

10. Recalculate Other (Accrued) Liabilities--To test computations for reasonableness and consistent treatment when compared to prior years. Examples include property and income taxes, commissions, profit-sharing and pension plans, and warranties.

Existence or Occurrence

11. Vouch Purchase Requisitions of a Sample of Purchase Orders--To determine if any unrequested purchases were made.

12. Confirm--Accounts payable balances with vendors, although not a generally accepted auditing procedure, confirm in cases of suspected fraud, sloppy or missing records, or suspected understatements.

13. Inspect copies of notes and other agreements.

Statement Presentation and Disclosure

14. Review Purchase Commitments--To determine whether there are any losses to be accrued and/or disclosed.

X. Audit of Payroll

A. Audit Objectives--The objectives of the audit of payroll are: (1) ascertain the adequacy of internal control over payroll, (2) verify that all employees included in the payroll actually exist and work for the client (existence), (3) verify the accuracy of the payroll computations (valuation), and (4) ascertain the adequacy of disclosure in the financial statements.

B. Subfunctions--Subfunctions for payroll include (1) personnel, (2) production, (3) detailed ledger bookkeeping, and (4) general ledger accounting.

C. Sample Audit Procedures for Payroll--The following audit procedures are usually performed during the audit of the payroll accounts to obtain supporting evidence of the objectives defined for the following assertions:

Obtain an Understanding of Relevant Internal Control Structure Policies and Procedures and Assess Control Risk--In order to ascertain the nature, timing, and extent of substantive tests to be applied.

Completeness

1. Review Time Reports and Piecework or Commission Records--To determine that such reports and records agree with production records.

Obligations and Rights

2. Verify Payroll Deductions--To ascertain that they are computed accurately and that they agree with withholding authorizations.

3. Review Accounting for Unclaimed Wages--To ascertain that they are being properly classified.

4. Examine Payroll Cutoff--To determine that wages were reported in the proper time period.

5. Analyze Officers' Compensation--To determine that salaries agree with contracts, minutes of directors' meeting, or other authorization.

Valuation or Allocation

6. Recompute Payroll Register--To determine its accuracy.

7. Trace Items From the Payroll Register to Employee Time Cards--To verify employees worked the number of hours for which pay was computed.

8. Observe the Use of the Time Clocks by the Employees--To be assured that each employee punches only one time card.

9. Compare Payroll Expenses With Prior Periods and Investigate Differences--So as to determine the accuracy and validity of the expense.

10. Perform Analytical Procedures--To determine reasonableness of balances. Calculate ratios to determine whether accounts relate to each other in the manner expected. If relationships vary significantly from expected results, additional substantive tests of account balances may be necessary.

11. Review the results of audits of related pension and profit-sharing plans.

Existence or Occurrence

12. Review Payroll Checks and Bank Reconciliations--To determine that all checks were cashed.

13. Review the Payroll Register--To determine if all payroll transactions were recorded.

14. Examine Personnel Records--To determine that a name, salary rate, and job position all exist for each employee on the payroll.

15. On a Surprise Basis, Observe the Distribution of the Paychecks--To determine that every name on the company payroll is that of a bona fide employee presently working.

Statement Presentation and Disclosure

16. Review Related Tax Expense and Liability, Unemployment Insurance, and Other Payroll Deduction Accounts--To determine accuracy and proper classification in the financial statements.

XI. Audit of Long-Term Liabilities

A. Audit Objectives--The objectives of the audit of long-term liabilities are: (1) ascertain the adequacy of internal control structure policies and procedures over long-term liabilities; (2) verify that all long-term liabilities are recorded properly (existence and obligation); (3) verify that interest expense is correctly computed and that other contractual obligations are satisfied (valuation); and (4) ascertain the adequacy of disclosure of long-term liabilities in the financial statements.

B. Subfunctions--Subfunctions for long-term liabilities include (1) financing, (2) fixed assets, (3) cash, (4) detailed ledger bookkeeping, and (5) general ledger accounting.

C. Sample Audit Procedures for Long-Term Liabilities--The following audit procedures are normally performed during the audit of long-term liabilities to obtain supporting evidence of the objectives defined for the following assertions:

Obtain an Understanding of Relevant Internal Control Structure Policies and Procedures and Assess Control Risk--In order to ascertain the nature, timing, and extent of substantive tests to be applied.

Completeness

1. Obtain or Prepare an Account Analysis for the Long-Term Debt, Discount, Premium, and Related Interest Accounts--This procedure allows the auditor to:

    a. Verify the payment or other disposition of the debt listed as outstanding at the beginning of the period.

    b. Establish the accuracy of the individual debits and credits occurring during the year.

    c. Prove the validity of the year-end balance in the accounts.

2. Perform Analytical Procedures--By comparing current amortization amounts to prior actual and current budgeted amounts. Compare current interest costs to prior actual and current budgeted amounts. Compare current and noncurrent debt obligations to prior actual and current budgeted amounts.

3. Review bank confirmation for indication of loans and other commitments, including any unrecorded debt.

Obligations and Rights

4. Review Cutoff--To determine that transactions recorded at the end of the year are recorded in the proper period.

Valuation or Allocation

5. Verify Interest Computations and Amortization of Premiums and/or Discounts--To determine whether such amounts were properly and accurately disclosed. This procedure also aids in the discovery of undisclosed liabilities.

Existence or Occurrence

6. Confirm with the creditor the transactions of the period and compliance with the contractual provisions. This procedure provides evidence that the transactions actually occurred and that the transactions were properly carried out, e.g., deposits into a sinking fund.

Statement Presentation and Disclosure

7. Review the Contractual Provisions and Supporting Documents of Long-Term Debt--To determine that details of the debt instruments correspond to those in the account analysis and that such details are accurately disclosed in the financial statements. Supporting documents include note and loan agreements, bond indentures, and lease agreements.

XII. Audit of Stockholders' Equity

A. <u>Audit Objectives</u>--The objectives of the audit of stockholders' equity are: (1) ascertain the adequacy of internal control over stock transactions, stock certificates, and receipts payments; (2) verify that the transactions are properly authorized and comply with applicable regulations; (3) verify that the transactions are recorded in conformity with GAAP; and (4) ascertain the adequacy of <u>disclosure</u> of stockholders' equity in the financial statements.

B. <u>Subfunctions</u>--Subfunctions for stockholders' equity include (1) financing, (2) cash, (3) detailed ledger bookkeeping, and (4) general ledger accounting.

C. <u>Sample Audit Procedures for Stockholders' Equity</u>--The following audit procedures are normally performed during the audit of stockholders' equity to obtain supporting evidence of the objectives defined for the following assertions:

Obtain an Understanding of Relevant Internal Control Structure Policies and Procedures and Assess Control Risk--In order to ascertain the nature, timing, and extent of substantive tests to be applied.

Completeness

1. Obtain or Prepare an Account Analysis for All Accounts--To outline the historical picture of corporate capital and any changes to corporate capital.

2. Account for All Certificate Numbers--To determine that no unauthorized securities were issued during the period.

3. Perform Analytical Procedures--By computing the return on stockholders' equity, the book value per share, and the dividend payout ratio and comparing them to those of prior years. Compare current year dividend amounts and balances for common and preferred stock and additional paid-in capital to those of prior years.

Obligations and Rights

4. Vouch All Retirements of Securities--To ascertain that no certificates were fraudulently reissued.

5. Review Compliance With Stock Option Plans and Other Restrictions on Capital Stocks--This procedure allows the auditor to do the following:

   a. Determine the adequacy of disclosure with respect to these arrangements.

   b. Verify the number of shares issued during the year through conversion or exercise of convertible stocks and bonds, stock options, and stock warrants.

   c. Ascertain whether the shares held in reserve exceed the shares authorized but unissued.

   d. Determine that the call provisions of preferred stock are accurately carried out.

6. Review Minutes of Board of Directors' Meetings--To verify that stock and dividend transactions have been properly authorized.

Valuation or Allocation

7. Account for All Proceeds From Security Issues--To determine whether the transactions were accounted for in accordance with underwriting contracts, state stock issuance permits, and SEC registration statements.

8. Analyze Treasury Stock Transactions--To determine that such transactions were properly authorized and recorded in conformity with GAAP.

9. Reconcile Subsidiary Ledger With General Ledger Control Account--To establish the amount of outstanding stock and to rule out the possibility of an over-issuance of shares.

10. Reconcile Dividend Distributions and Verify Dividend Calculations--To ascertain the accurate dividend amount and to discover any declared, but yet unpaid, dividends.

Existence or Occurrence

11. Confirm Shares Outstanding With Registrar--To ascertain whether the corporate records are accurate and that stock is issued in accordance with the authorization of the board of directors and the articles of incorporation.

Statement Presentation and Disclosure

12. Analyze the Retained Earnings Account--To determine whether it is accurately disclosed in the financial statements, and determine the amount of any restrictions on retained earnings that result from loans, other agreements, or state law.

13. Analyze Prior-Period Adjustments--To ascertain whether they are valid and are treated properly in the financial statements and determine the amount of any restrictions on retained earnings that result from loans, other agreements, or state law.

XIII. Audit of Accounting Estimates (AU 342, SAS 57)

A. Audit Objectives--The objectives of auditing accounting estimates is to provide reasonable assurance that (1) all accounting estimates which could be material to the financial statements have been developed, (2) the estimates are reasonable, and (3) the estimates are in conformity with applicable accounting principles and are properly disclosed.

1. Accounting estimates are used when the measurement of some amounts or the valuations of some accounts is uncertain pending the outcome of future events.

2. Estimates are also used when relevant data concerning events that have already occurred cannot be accumulated on a timely, cost-effective basis.

B. Developing Accounting Estimates--Management is responsible for establishing the process for preparing accounting estimates. Generally this consists of the following:

1. Identifying situations which require accounting estimates.

2. Identifying relevant factors.

3. Accumulating relevant, sufficient, and reliable data on which to base the estimate.

4. Developing assumptions based on management's judgment of the most likely circumstances and events.

5. Determining estimated amounts based on the assumptions.

6. Determining the estimate is presented in conformity with applicable accounting principles and that disclosure is adequate.

C. Internal Control Structure--The internal control structure may reduce the risk of material misstatements of accounting estimates. Some relevant features of the structure include the following:

1. Management communication of the need for proper accounting estimates.

2. Accumulation of relevant, sufficient, and reliable data on which to base an accounting estimate.

3. Preparation of estimates by qualified personnel.

4. Adequate review and approval of accounting estimates by appropriate levels of authority.

5. Comparison of prior accounting estimates with subsequent results to assess the reliability of the process used to develop estimates.

6. Consideration by management of whether the resulting accounting estimate is consistent with the operational plans of the entity.

D. Procedures

1. To determine whether management has identified all accounting estimates which could be material to the financial statements, the auditor should evaluate information regarding the following: changes made or planned in the entity's business; changes in the method of accumulating information; litigation, claims, and assessments; minutes of meetings; and regulatory or examination reports.

2. The auditor must evaluate the reasonableness of accounting estimates, and consider them with an attitude of professional skepticism. The auditor should understand how management develops estimates. The auditor should develop an independent expectation of the estimate based on knowledge of the entity and its industry. The historical experience of the entity in making past estimates should be considered.

3. Management's process of developing accounting estimates should be reviewed and tested. The auditor should consider performing the following procedures:

   a. Identify controls over the preparation of accounting estimates and supporting data which may be useful in the evaluation.

   b. Identify the sources of data and factors that management used and consider whether such data and factors are relevant, reliable, and sufficient for the purpose.

   c. Evaluate whether the assumptions are consistent with each other, the supporting data, historical data, and industry data.

   d. Consider whether changes in business or industry may cause other factors to become significant.

   e. Consider whether there are additional factors which should be evaluated.

   f. Evaluate historical data used to develop assumptions to assess whether data is comparable and consistent with data of the period being audited.

CHAPTER 37—AUDIT EVIDENCE, PROGRAMS, AND PROCEDURES

Problem 37-1 MULTIPLE CHOICE QUESTIONS (190 to 230 minutes)

1. Which of the following procedures would provide the most reliable audit evidence?
a. Inquiries of the client's internal audit staff held in private.
b. Inspection of prenumbered client purchase orders filed in the vouchers payable department.
c. Analytical procedures performed by the auditor on the entity's trial balance.
d. Inspection of bank statements obtained directly from the client's financial institution.
(5/93, Aud., #26, 3922)

1A. Which of the following types of audit evidence is the most persuasive?
a. Prenumbered client purchase order forms.
b. Client work sheets supporting cost allocations.
c. Bank statements obtained from the client.
d. Client representation letter.
(5/95, Aud., #39, 5657)

2. An auditor most likely would review an entity's periodic accounting for the numerical sequence of shipping documents and invoices to support management's financial statement assertion of
a. Existence or occurrence.
b. Rights and obligations.
c. Valuation or allocation.
d. Completeness. (5/93, Aud., #27, 3923)

3. In evaluating the adequacy of the allowance for doubtful accounts, an auditor most likely reviews the entity's aging of receivables to support management's financial statement assertion of
a. Existence or occurrence.
b. Valuation or allocation.
c. Completeness.
d. Rights and obligations. (5/93, Aud., #29, 3925)

4. Which of the following statements concerning audit evidence is correct?
a. To be competent, audit evidence should be either persuasive or relevant, but need **not** be both.
b. The measure of the validity of audit evidence lies in the auditor's judgment.
c. The difficulty and expense of obtaining audit evidence concerning an account balance is a valid basis for omitting the test.
d. A client's accounting data can be sufficient audit evidence to support the financial statements. (11/93, Aud., #36, 4273)

5. Which of the following statements concerning evidential matter is correct?
a. Competent evidence supporting management's assertions should be convincing rather than merely persuasive.
b. An effective internal control structure contributes little to the reliability of the evidence created within the entity.
c. The cost of obtaining evidence is **not** an important consideration to an auditor in deciding what evidence should be obtained.
d. A client's accounting data **cannot** be considered sufficient audit evidence to support the financial statements. (5/91, Aud., #1, 0121)

5A. In designing written audit programs, an auditor should establish specific audit objectives that relate primarily to the
a. Timing of audit procedures.
b. Cost-benefit of gathering evidence.
c. Selected audit techniques.
d. Financial statement assertions.
(5/94, Aud., #8, 4673)

6. Each of the following might, by itself, form a valid basis for an auditor to decide to omit a test **except** for the
a. Difficulty and expense involved in testing a particular item.
b. Assessed level of control risk for the relevant financial statement assertions.
c. Irrelevance of the test.
d. Relationship between the cost of obtaining evidence and its usefulness.
(5/89, Aud., #1, 0173)

7. In testing the existence assertion for an asset, an auditor ordinarily works from the
a. Financial statements to the potentially unrecorded items.
b. Potentially unrecorded items to the financial statements.
c. Accounting records to the supporting evidence.
d. Supporting evidence to the accounting records.
(11/90, Aud., #17, 0136)

8. An auditor selects a sample from the file of shipping documents to determine whether invoices were prepared. This test is performed to satisfy the audit objective of

a. Accuracy.
b. Completeness.
c. Control.
d. Existence. (11/87, Aud., #56, 9911)

9. Audit evidence concerning segregation of duties ordinarily is best obtained by
a. Performing tests of transactions that corroborate management's financial statement assertions.
b. Observing the employees as they apply control procedures.
c. Obtaining a flowchart of activities performed by available personnel.
d. Developing audit objectives that reduce control risk. (5/93, Aud., #10, 3906)

10. Which of the following statements is generally correct about the competence of evidential matter?
a. The more effective the internal control structure, the more assurance it provides about the reliability of the accounting data and financial statements.
b. Competence of evidential matter refers to the amount of corroborative evidence obtained.
c. Information obtained indirectly from independent outside sources is more persuasive than the auditor's direct personal knowledge obtained through observation and inspection.
d. Competence of evidential matter refers to the audit evidence obtained from outside the entity. (5/92, Aud., #16, 2769)

10A. Which of the following presumptions is correct about the reliability of evidential matter?
a. Information obtained indirectly from outside sources is the most reliable evidential matter.
b. To be reliable, evidential matter should be convincing rather than persuasive.
c. Reliability of evidential matter refers to the amount of corroborative evidence obtained.
d. An effective internal control structure provides more assurance about the reliability of evidential matter. (11/94, Aud., #47, 5120)

11. An auditor most likely would analyze inventory turnover rates to obtain evidence concerning management's assertions about
a. Existence or occurrence.
b. Rights and obligations.
c. Presentation and disclosure.
d. Valuation or allocation. (11/92, Aud., #29, 2963)

12. To satisfy the valuation assertion when auditing an investment accounted for by the equity method, an auditor most likely would
a. Inspect the stock certificates evidencing the investment.
b. Examine the audited financial statements of the investee company.
c. Review the broker's advice or canceled check for the investment's acquisition.
d. Obtain market quotations from financial newspapers or periodicals. (11/91, Aud., #44, 2312)

13. An auditor most likely would inspect loan agreements under which an entity's inventories are pledged to support management's financial statement assertion of
a. Existence or occurrence.
b. Completeness.
c. Presentation and disclosure.
d. Valuation or allocation. (11/92, Aud., #28, 2962)

14. The objective tests of details of transactions performed as substantive tests is to
a. Detect material misstatements in the financial statements.
b. Evaluate whether management's policies and procedures operated effectively.
c. Identify specific financial statement assertions that satisfy the audit objectives.
d. Verify that significant deficiencies in the accounting system are discovered. (11/91, Aud., #47, 9911)

14A. An auditor most likely would extend substantive tests of payroll when
a. Payroll is extensively audited by the state government.
b. Payroll expense is substantially higher than in the prior year.
c. Overpayments are discovered in performing tests of details.
d. Employees complain to management about too much overtime. (5/94, Aud., #49, 4714)

14B. Which of the following circumstances most likely would cause an auditor to consider whether material misstatements exist in an entity's financial statements?
a. Management places little emphasis on meeting earnings projections.
b. The board of directors makes all major financing decisions.
c. Reportable conditions previously communicated to management are **not** corrected.
d. Transactions selected for testing are **not** supported by proper documentation. (11/94, Aud., #13, 5086)

15. When assessing an internal auditor's competence, a CPA ordinarily obtains information about all of the following **except**
a. Quality of working paper documentation.
b. Educational level and professional experience.
c. Audit programs and procedures.
d. Access to information about related parties.
(5/93, Aud., #6, 3902)

15A. When assessing the internal auditors' competence, the independent CPA should obtain information about the
a. Organizational level to which the internal auditors report.
b. Educational background and professional certification of the internal auditors.
c. Policies prohibiting the internal auditors from auditing areas where relatives are employed.
d. Internal auditors' access to records and information that is considered sensitive.
(11/94, Aud., #25, 5098)

16. When assessing an internal auditor's objectivity, an independent auditor should
a. Evaluate the adequacy of the internal auditor's audit programs.
b. Inquire about the internal auditor's educational background and professional certification.
c. Consider the organizational level to which the internal auditor reports.
d. Review the internal auditor's working papers.
(11/92, Aud., #6, 2940)

16A. In assessing the competence and objectivity of an entity's internal auditor, an independent auditor **least** likely would consider information obtained from
a. Discussions with management personnel.
b. External quality reviews of the internal auditor's activities.
c. Previous experience with the internal auditor.
d. The results of analytical procedures.
(11/94, Aud., #68, 5141)

17. Miller Retailing, Inc., maintains a staff of three full-time internal auditors who report directly to the controller. In planning to use the internal auditors to provide assistance in performing the audit, the independent auditor most likely will
a. Place limited reliance on the work performed by the internal auditors.
b. Decrease the extent of the tests of controls needed to support the assessed level of detection risk.
c. Increase the extent of the procedures needed to reduce control risk to an acceptable level.
d. Avoid using the work performed by the internal auditors. (5/90, Aud., #28, 0157)

17A. An internal auditor's work would most likely affect the nature, timing, and extent of an independent CPA's auditing procedures when the internal auditor's work relates to assertions about the
a. Existence of contingencies.
b. Valuation of intangible assets.
c. Existence of fixed asset additions.
d. Valuation of related party transactions.
(5/95, Aud., #59, 5677)

18. During an audit an internal auditor may provide direct assistance to an independent CPA in

	Obtaining an understanding of the internal control structure	Performing tests of controls	Performing substantive tests
a.	No	No	No
b.	Yes	No	No
c.	Yes	Yes	No
d.	Yes	Yes	Yes

(5/95, Aud., #60, 5678)

19. Which of the following statements best describes how a detailed audit program of a CPA who is engaged to audit the financial statements of a large publicly held company compares with the audit client's comprehensive internal audit program?
a. The comprehensive internal audit program is substantially identical to the audit program used by the CPA because both cover substantially identical areas.
b. The comprehensive internal audit program is less detailed and covers fewer areas than would normally be covered by the CPA.
c. The comprehensive internal audit program is more detailed and covers areas that would normally **not** be covered by the CPA.
d. The comprehensive internal audit program is more detailed although it covers fewer areas than would normally be covered by the CPA.
(5/89, Aud., #7, 0175)

20. Which of the following documentations is required for an audit in accordance with generally accepted auditing standards?
a. An internal control questionnaire.
b. A client engagement letter.
c. A planning memorandum or checklist.
d. A client representation letter.
(11/89, Aud., #30, 0170)

21. When considering the use of management's written representations as audit evidence about the completeness assertion, an auditor should understand that such representations

a. Complement, but do not replace, substantive tests designed to support the assertion.
b. Constitute sufficient evidence to support the assertion when considered in combination with the assessment of control risk.
c. Are not part of the evidential matter considered to support the assertion.
d. Replace the assessment of control risk as evidence to support the assertion.
(11/87, Aud., #32, 0218)

22. A purpose of a management representation letter is to reduce
a. Audit risk to an aggregate level of misstatement that could be considered material.
b. An auditor's responsibility to detect material misstatements only to the extent that the letter is relied on.
c. The possibility of a misunderstanding concerning management's responsibility for the financial statements.
d. The scope of an auditor's procedures concerning related party transactions and subsequent events. (5/93, Aud., #32, 3928)

23. The primary source of information to be reported about litigation, claims, and assessments is the
a. Client's lawyer.
b. Court records.
c. Client's management.
d. Independent auditor. (11/93, Aud., #39, 4276)

24. Which of the following statements ordinarily is included among the written client representations obtained by the auditor?
a. Compensating balances and other arrangements involving restrictions on cash balances have been disclosed.
b. Management acknowledges responsibility for illegal actions committed by employees.
c. Sufficient evidential matter has been made available to permit the issuance of an unqualified opinion.
d. Management acknowledges that there are **no** material weaknesses in the internal control.
(5/94, Aud., #54, 4719)

25. A written client representation letter most likely would be an auditor's best source of corroborative information of a client's plans to
a. Terminate an employee pension plan.
b. Make a public offering of its common stock.
c. Settle an outstanding lawsuit for an amount less than the accrued loss contingency.
d. Discontinue a line of business.
(5/89, Aud., #34, 0183)

26. To which of the following matters would materiality limits **not** apply in obtaining written management representations?
a. The availability of minutes of stockholders' and directors' meetings.
b. Losses from purchase commitments at prices in excess of market value.
c. The disclosure of compensating balance arrangements involving related parties.
d. Reductions of obsolete inventory to net realizable value. (5/95, Aud., #66, 5684)

27. "There are no violations or possible violations of laws or regulations whose effects should be considered for disclosure in the financial statements or as a basis for recording a loss contingency." The foregoing passage most likely is from a (an)
a. Client engagement letter.
b. Report on compliance with laws and regulations.
c. Management representation letter.
d. Attestation report on an internal control structure. (11/94, Aud., #64, 5137)

28. In planning a new engagement, which of the following is **not** a factor that affects the auditor's judgment as to the quantity, type, and content of working papers?
a. The type of report to be issued by the auditor.
b. The content of the client's representation letter.
c. The auditor's estimated occurrence rate of attributes.
d. The auditor's preliminary evaluations of risk based on decisions with the client.
(5/90, Aud., #50, 0160)

29. The date of the management representation letter should coincide with the date of the
a. Balance sheet.
b. Latest interim financial information.
c. Auditor's report.
d. Latest related party transaction.
(5/95, Aud., #67, 5685)

30. An entity's income statements were misstated due to the recording of journal entries that involved debits and credits to an unusual combination of expense and revenue accounts. The auditor most likely could have detected this irregularity by
a. Tracing a sample of journal entries to the general ledger.
b. Evaluating the effectiveness of the internal control structure policies and procedures.

c. Investigating the reconciliations between controlling accounts and subsidiary records.
d. Performing analytical procedures designed to disclose differences from expectations. (11/94, Aud., #14, 5087)

31. For all audits of financial statements made in accordance with generally accepted auditing standards, the use of analytical procedures is required to some extent

	In the planning stage	As a substantive test	In the review stage
a.	Yes	No	Yes
b.	No	Yes	No
c.	No	Yes	Yes
d.	Yes	No	No

(11/90, Aud., #22, 0141)

31A. The objective of performing analytical procedures in planning an audit is to identify the existence of
a. Unusual transactions and events.
b. Illegal acts that went undetected because of internal control weaknesses.
c. Related party transactions.
d. Recorded transactions that were **not** properly authorized. (5/94, Aud., #5, 4670)

32. Analytical procedures used in planning an audit should focus on
a. Identifying possible scope limitations and gathering evidence in assessing control risk environmental factors.
b. Enhancing the understanding of the entity's business and the transactions and events that have occurred since the last audit.
c. Aggregating data at a low level and substantiating management's assertions that are embodied in the financial statements.
d. Discovering material weaknesses in the internal control structure and reporting them to the entity's management for corrective action. (5/92, Aud., #58, 2811)

33. An auditor's analytical procedures most likely would be facilitated if the entity
a. Corrects material weaknesses in internal control before the beginning of the audit.
b. Develops its data from sources solely within the entity.
c. Segregates obsolete inventory before the physical inventory count.
d. Uses a standard cost system that produces variance reports. (11/91, Aud., #48, 2316)

33A. An accountant should perform analytical procedures during an engagement to

	Compile a nonpublic entity's financial statements	Review a nonpublic entity's financial statements
a.	No	No
b.	Yes	Yes
c.	Yes	No
d.	No	Yes

(5/94, Aud., #59, 4724)

34. Analytical procedures used in the overall review stage of an audit generally include
a. Considering unusual or unexpected account balances that were **not** previously identified.
b. Performing tests of transactions to corroborate management's financial statement assertions.
c. Gathering evidence concerning account balances that have **not** changed from the prior year.
d. Retesting control procedures that appeared to be ineffective during the assessment of control risk. (11/92, Aud., #32, 2966)

34A. Analytical procedures used in the overall review stage of an audit generally include
a. Gathering evidence concerning account balances that have **not** changed from the prior year.
b. Retesting control procedures that appeared to be ineffective during the assessment of control risk.
c. Considering unusual or unexpected account balances that were **not** previously identified.
d. Performing tests of transactions to corroborate management's financial statement assertions. (5/95, Aud., #47, 5665)

34B. Analytical procedures used in planning an audit should focus on
a. Reducing the scope of tests of controls and substantive tests.
b. Providing assurance that potential material misstatements will be identified.
c. Enhancing the auditor's understanding of the client's business.
d. Assessing the adequacy of the available evidential matter. (5/95, Aud., #8, 5626)

35. Which of the following comparisons would be most useful to an auditor in evaluating the results of an entity's operations?
a. Prior year accounts payable to current year accounts payable.
b. Prior year payroll expense to budgeted current year payroll expense.

c. Current year revenue to budgeted current year revenue.
d. Current year warranty expense to current year contingent liabilities. (5/91, Aud., #5, 0125)

35A. Which of the following would **not** be considered an analytical procedure?
a. Estimating payroll expense by multiplying the number of employees by the average hourly wage rate and the total hours worked.
b. Projecting an error rate by comparing the results of a statistical sample with the actual population characteristics.
c. Computing accounts receivable turnover by dividing credit sales by the average net receivables.
d. Developing the expected current-year sales based on the sales trend of the prior five years. (5/95, Aud., #48, 5666)

36. Which of the following tends to be most predictable for purposes of analytical procedures applied as substantive tests?
a. Relationships involving balance sheet accounts.
b. Transactions subject to management discretion.
c. Relationships involving income statement accounts.
d. Data subject to audit testing in the prior year. (5/92, Aud., #20, 2773)

37. An auditor compares 1985 revenues and expenses with those of the prior year and investigates all changes exceeding 10%. By this procedure the auditor would be most likely to learn that
a. Fourth quarter payroll taxes were not paid.
b. The client changed its capitalization policy for small tools in 1985.
c. An increase in property tax rates has not been recognized in the client's accrual.
d. The 1985 provision for uncollectible accounts is inadequate because of worsening economic conditions. (5/86, Aud., #33, 9911)

38. An auditor's decision either to apply analytical procedures as substantive tests or to perform tests of transactions and account balances usually is determined by the
a. Availability of data aggregated at a high level.
b. Relative effectiveness and efficiency of the tests.
c. Timing of tests performed after the balance sheet date.
d. Auditor's familiarity with industry trends. (11/92, Aud., #31, 2965)

39. Which of the following statements concerning analytical procedures is correct?
a. Analytical procedures may be omitted entirely for some financial statement audits.
b. Analytical procedures used in planning the audit should **not** use nonfinancial information.
c. Analytical procedures usually are effective and efficient for tests of controls.
d. Analytical procedures alone may provide the appropriate level of assurance for some assertions. (11/91, Aud., #42, 2310)

40. Which of the following factors would **least** influence an auditor's consideration of the reliability of data for purposes of analytical procedures?
a. Whether the data were processed in an EDP system or in a manual accounting system.
b. Whether sources within the entity were independent of those who are responsible for the amount being audited.
c. Whether the data were subjected to audit testing in the current or prior year.
d. Whether the data were obtained from independent sources outside the entity or from sources within the entity. (5/90, Aud., #2, 0151)

41. An auditor who uses the work of a specialist may refer to the specialist in the auditor's report if the
a. Specialist's findings provide the auditor greater assurance of reliability about management's representations.
b. Auditor adds an explanatory paragraph to an unqualified opinion describing an uncertainty resulting from the specialist's findings.
c. Auditor's use of the specialist's findings is different from that of prior years.
d. Specialist is a related party whose findings fully corroborate management's financial statement assertions. (5/93, Aud., #33, 3929)

42. Which of the following statements concerning the auditor's use of the work of a specialist is correct?
a. If the auditor believes that the determinations made by the specialist are unreasonable, only a qualified opinion may be issued.
b. If the specialist is related to the client, the auditor is still permitted to use the specialist's findings as corroborative evidence.
c. The specialist need **not** have an understanding of the auditor's corroborative use of the specialist's findings.
d. The specialist may be identified in the auditor's report when the auditor issues an unqualified opinion. (5/91, Aud., #7, 0126)

42A. Which of the following statements is correct concerning an auditor's use of the work of a specialist?

a. The work of a specialist who is related to the client may be acceptable under certain circumstances.
b. If an auditor believes that the determinations made by a specialist are unreasonable, only a qualified opinion may be issued.
c. If there is a material difference between a specialist's findings and the assertions in the financial statements, only an adverse opinion may be issued.
d. An auditor may **not** use a specialist in the determination of physical characteristics relating to inventories. (5/95, Aud., #61, 5679)

42B. Which of the following statements is correct about the auditor's use of the work of a specialist?

a. The specialist should **not** have an understanding of the auditor's corroborative use of the specialist's findings.
b. The auditor is required to perform substantive procedures to verify the specialist's assumptions and findings.
c. The client should **not** have an understanding of the nature of the work to be performed by the specialist.
d. The auditor should obtain an understanding of the methods and assumptions used by the specialist. (11/94, Aud., #65, 5138)

43. In using the work of a specialist, an understanding should exist among the auditor, the client, and the specialist as to the nature of the specialist's work. The documentation of this understanding should cover

a. A statement that the specialist assumes **no** responsibility to update the specialist's report for future events or circumstances.
b. The conditions under which a division of responsibility may be necessary.
c. The specialist's understanding of the auditor's corroborative use of the specialist's findings.
d. The auditor's disclaimer as to whether the specialist's findings corroborate the representations in the financial statements. (11/92, Aud., #33, 2967)

43A. In using the work of a specialist, an auditor may refer to the specialist in the auditor's report if, as a result of the specialist's findings, the auditor

a. Becomes aware of conditions causing substantial doubt about the entity's ability to continue as a going concern.
b. Desires to disclose the specialist's findings, which imply that a more thorough audit was performed.
c. Is able to corroborate another specialist's earlier findings that were consistent with management's representations.
d. Discovers significant deficiencies in the design of the entity's internal control structure that management does **not** correct. (5/95, Aud., #62, 5680)

44. An auditor should obtain evidential matter relevant to all the following factors concerning third-party litigation against a client **except** the

a. Period in which the underlying cause for legal action occurred.
b. Probability of an unfavorable outcome.
c. Jurisdiction in which the matter will be resolved.
d. Existence of a situation indicating an uncertainty as to the possible loss. (11/88, Aud., #53, 0191)

44A. A client's lawyer is unable to form a conclusion about the likelihood of an unfavorable outcome of pending litigation because of inherent uncertainties. If the litigation's effect on the client's financial statements could be material, the auditor most likely would

a. Issue a qualified opinion in the auditor's report because of the lawyer's scope limitation.
b. Withdraw from the engagement because of the lack of information furnished by the lawyer.
c. Disclaim an opinion on the financial statements because of the materiality of the litigation's effect.
d. Add an explanatory paragraph to the auditor's report because of the uncertainty. (5/95, Aud., #64, 5682)

45. Which of the following is **not** an audit procedure that the independent auditor would perform concerning litigation, claims, and assessments?

a. Obtain assurance from management that it has disclosed all unasserted claims that the lawyer has advised are probable of assertion and must be disclosed.
b. Confirm directly with the client's lawyer that all claims have been recorded in the financial statements.

c. Inquire of and discuss with management the policies and procedures adopted for identifying, evaluating, and accounting for litigation, claims, and assessments.
d. Obtain from management a description and evaluation of litigation, claims, and assessments existing at the balance sheet date. (11/91, Aud., #60, 2328)

46. An auditor should request that an audit client send a letter of inquiry to those attorneys who have been consulted concerning litigation, claims, or assessments. The primary reason for this request is to provide
a. The opinion of a specialist as to whether loss contingencies are possible, probable, or remote.
b. A description of litigation, claims, and assessments that have a reasonable possibility of unfavorable outcomes.
c. An objective appraisal of management's policies and procedures adopted for identifying and evaluating legal matters.
d. The corroboration of the information furnished by management concerning litigation, claims, and assessments. (5/92, Aud., #23, 2776)

46A. The primary reason an auditor requests letters of inquiry be sent to a client's attorneys is to provide the auditor with
a. The probable outcome of asserted claims and pending or threatened litigation.
b. Corroboration of the information furnished by management about litigation, claims, and assessments.
c. The attorneys' opinions of the client's historical experiences in recent similar litigation.
d. A description and evaluation of litigation, claims, and assessments that existed at the balance sheet date. (11/94, Aud., #66, 5139)

47. The scope of an audit is **not** restricted when an attorney's response to an auditor as a result of a client's letter of audit inquiry limits the response to
a. Matters to which the attorney has given substantive attention in the form of legal representation.
b. An evaluation of the likelihood of an unfavorable outcome of the matters disclosed by the entity.
c. The attorney's opinion of the entity's historical experience in recent similar litigation.
d. The probable outcome of asserted claims and pending or threatened litigation. (11/90, Aud., #19, 0138)

47A. The refusal of a client's attorney to provide information requested in an inquiry letter generally is considered
a. Grounds for an adverse opinion.
b. A limitation on the scope of the audit.
c. Reason to withdraw from the engagement.
d. Equivalent to a reportable condition. (5/95, Aud., #63, 5681)

48. The refusal of a client's attorney to provide a representation on the legality of a particular act committed by the client is generally
a. Sufficient reason to issue a "subject to" qualified opinion.
b. Considered to be a scope limitation.
c. Insufficient reason to modify the auditor's report due to the attorney's obligation of confidentiality.
d. Proper grounds to withdraw from the engagement. (5/88, Aud., #59, 9911)

49. Which of the following documentation is required for an audit in accordance with generally accepted auditing standards?
a. A flowchart or an internal control questionnaire that evaluates the effectiveness of the entity's internal control policies and procedures.
b. A client engagement letter that summarizes the timing and details of the auditor's planned field work.
c. An indication in the working papers that the accounting records agree or reconcile with the financial statements.
d. The basis for the auditor's conclusions when the assessed level of control risk is at the maximum level for all financial statement assertions. (5/93, Aud., #38, 3934)

49A. Which of the following documentation is **not** required for an audit in accordance with generally accepted auditing standards?
a. A written audit program setting forth the procedures necessary to accomplish the audit's objectives.
b. An indication that the accounting records agree or reconcile with the financial statements.
c. A client engagement letter that summarizes the timing and details of the auditor's planned field work.
d. The basis for the auditor's conclusions when the assessed level of control risk is below the maximum level. (11/94, Aud., #15, 5088)

50. Although the quantity and content of audit working papers vary with each particular engagement, an auditor's permanent files most likely include

a. Schedules that support the current year's adjusting entries.
b. Prior years' accounts receivable confirmations that were classified as exceptions.
c. Documentation indicating that the audit work was adequately planned and supervised.
d. Analyses of capital stock and other owners' equity accounts. (5/93, Aud., #39, 4276)

50A. The permanent file of an auditor's working papers generally would **not** include
a. Bond indenture agreements.
b. Lease agreements.
c. Working trial balance.
d. Flowchart of the internal control structure.
(11/94, Aud., #17, 5090)

51. Which of the following factors most likely would affect an auditor's judgment about the quantity, type, and content of the auditor's working papers?
a. The assessed level of control risk.
b. The likelihood of a review by a concurring (second) partner.
c. The number of personnel assigned to the audit.
d. The content of the management representation letter. (11/92, Aud., #35, 2969)

51A. Which of the following factors would **least** likely affect the quantity and content of an auditor's working papers?
a. The condition of the client's records.
b. The assessed level of control risk.
c. The nature of the auditor's report.
d. The content of the representation letter.
(11/94, Aud., #73, 5146)

52. Which of the following statements ordinarily is correct concerning the content of working papers?
a. Whenever possible, the auditor's staff should prepare schedules and analyses rather than the entity's employees.
b. It is preferable to have negative figures indicated in red figures instead of parentheses to emphasize amounts being subtracted.
c. It is appropriate to use calculator tapes with names or explanations on the tapes rather than writing separate lists onto working paper.
d. The analysis of asset accounts and their related expense or income accounts should **not** appear on the same working paper.
(5/92, Aud., #24, 2777)

53. The audit working paper that reflects the major components of an amount reported in the financial statements is the
a. Interbank transfer schedule.
b. Carryforward schedule.
c. Supporting schedule.
d. Lead schedule. (11/91, Aud., #52, 2320)

54. An auditor ordinarily uses a working trial balance resembling the financial statements without footnotes, but containing columns for
a. Reclassifications and adjustments.
b. Reconciliations and tickmarks.
c. Accruals and deferrals.
d. Expense and revenue summaries.
(5/91, Aud., #12, 0131)

54A. An auditor ordinarily uses a working trial balance resembling the financial statements without footnotes, but containing columns for
a. Cash flow increases and decreases.
b. Audit objectives and assertions.
c. Reclassifications and adjustments.
d. Reconciliations and tickmarks.
(11/94, Aud., #72, 5145)

54B. When an auditor tests a computerized accounting system, which of the following is true of the test data approach?
a. Several transactions of each type must be tested.
b. Test data are processed by the client's computer programs under the auditor's control.
c. Test data must consist of all possible valid and invalid conditions.
d. The program tested is different from the program used throughout the year by the client.
(5/95, Aud., #72, 5690)

55. Working papers ordinarily would not include
a. Initials of the in-charge auditor indicating review of the staff assistants' work.
b. Cutoff bank statements received directly from the banks.
c. A memo describing the internal control structure.
d. Copies of client inventory count sheets.
(5/88, Aud., #29, 0203)

55A. An auditor's working papers serve mainly to
a. Provide the principal support for the auditor's report.
b. Satisfy the auditor's responsibilities concerning the Code of Professional Conduct.
c. Monitor the effectiveness of the CPA firm's quality control procedures.
d. Document the level of independence maintained by the auditor.
(5/95, Aud., #71, 5689)

56. An auditor most likely would modify an unqualified opinion if the entity's financial statements include a footnote on related party transactions
a. Disclosing loans to related parties at interest rates significantly below prevailing market rates.
b. Describing an exchange of real estate for similar property in a nonmonetary related party transaction.
c. Stating that a particular related party transaction occurred on terms equivalent to those that would have prevailed in an arm's-length transaction.
d. Presenting the dollar-volume of related party transactions and the effects of any change in the method of establishing terms from prior periods. (5/93, Aud., #44, 3940)

57. When auditing related party transactions, an auditor places primary emphasis on
a. Confirming the existence of the related parties.
b. Verifying the valuation of the related party transactions.
c. Evaluating the disclosure of the related party transactions.
d. Ascertaining the rights and obligations of the related parties. (5/92, Aud., #31, 2784)

57A. When auditing related party transactions, an auditor places primary emphasis on
a. Ascertaining the rights and obligations of the related parties.
b. Confirming the existence of the related parties.
c. Verifying the valuation of the related party transactions.
d. Evaluating the disclosure of the related party transactions. (5/95, Aud., #68, 5686)

57B. Which of the following auditing procedures most likely would assist an auditor in identifying related party transactions?
a. Retesting ineffective internal control procedures previously reported to the audit committee.
b. Sending second requests for unanswered positive confirmations of accounts receivable.
c. Reviewing accounting records for nonrecurring transactions recognized near the balance sheet date.
d. Inspecting communications with law firms for evidence of unreported contingent liabilities. (5/94, Aud., #57, 4722)

58. After discovering that a related party transaction exists, the auditor should be aware that the
a. Substance of the transaction could be significantly different from its form.
b. Adequacy of disclosure of the transaction is secondary to its legal form.
c. Transaction is assumed to be outside the ordinary course of business.
d. Financial statements should recognize the legal form of the transaction rather than its substance. (5/87, Aud., #33, 0230)

59. An auditor searching for related party transactions should obtain an understanding of each subsidiary's relationship to the total entity because
a. This may permit the audit of intercompany account balances to be performed as of concurrent dates.
b. Intercompany transactions may have been consummated on terms equivalent to arm's-length transactions.
c. This may reveal whether particular transactions would have taken place if the parties had **not** been related.
d. The business structure may be deliberately designed to obscure related party transactions. (5/89, Aud., #42, 0185)

60. Which of the following most likely would indicate the existence of related parties?
a. Writing down obsolete inventory just before year end.
b. Failing to correct previously identified internal control structure deficiencies.
c. Depending on a single product for the success of the entity.
d. Borrowing money at an interest rate significantly below the market rate. (11/92, Aud., #40, 2974)

61. After identifying related party transactions, an auditor most likely would
a. Substantiate that the transactions were consummated on terms equivalent to those prevailing in arms-length transactions.
b. Discuss the implications of the transactions with third parties, such as the entity's attorneys and bankers.
c. Determine whether the transactions were approved by the board of directors or other appropriate officials.
d. Ascertain whether the transactions would have occurred if the parties had **not** been related. (11/91, Aud., #56, 2324)

61A. After determining that a related party transaction has, in fact, occurred, an auditor should

a. Add a separate paragraph to the auditor's standard report to explain the transaction.
b. Perform analytical procedures to verify whether similar transactions occurred, but were **not** recorded.
c. Obtain an understanding of the business purpose of the transaction.
d. Substantiate that the transaction was consummated on terms equivalent to an arm's-length transaction. (11/94, Aud., #69, 5142)

62. The primary purpose of sending a standard confirmation request to financial institutions with which the client has done business during the year is to
a. Detect kiting activities that may otherwise **not** be discovered.
b. Corroborate information regarding deposit and loan balances.
c. Provide the data necessary to prepare a proof of cash.
d. Request information about contingent liabilities and secured transactions.
(5/93, Aud., #34, 3930)

63. An auditor ordinarily sends a standard confirmation request to all banks with which the client has done business during the year under audit, regardless of the year-end balance. A purpose of this procedure is to
a. Provide the data necessary to prepare a proof of cash.
b. Request a cutoff bank statement and related checks be sent to the auditor.
c. Detect kiting activities that may otherwise **not** be discovered.
d. Seek information about contingent liabilities and security agreements.
(11/90, Aud., #25, 0144)

64. The primary evidence regarding year-end bank balances is documented in the
a. Standard bank confirmations.
b. Bank reconciliations.
c. Interbank transfer schedule.
d. Bank deposit lead schedule.
(11/90, Aud., #27, 0146)

65. Which of the following cash transfers results in a misstatement of cash at December 31, 1987?

	Bank Transfer Schedule			
	Disbursement		Receipt	
Transfer	Recorded in books	Paid by bank	Recorded in books	Received by bank
a.	12/31/87	01/04/88	12/31/87	12/31/87
b.	01/04/88	01/05/88	12/31/87	01/04/88
c.	12/31/87	01/05/88	12/31/87	01/04/88
d.	01/04/88	01/11/88	01/04/88	01/04/88

(5/88, Aud., #26, 0200)

Items 66 and 67 are based on the following:

The information below was taken from the bank transfer schedule prepared during the audit of Fox Co.'s financial statements for the year ended December 31, 1991. Assume all checks are dated and issued on December 30, 1991.

	Bank Accounts		Disbursement Date		Receipt Date	
Check No.	From	To	Per books	Per bank	Per books	Per bank
101	National	Federal	Dec. 30	Jan. 4	Dec. 30	Jan. 3
202	County	State	Jan. 3	Jan. 2	Dec. 30	Dec. 31
303	Federal	American	Dec. 31	Jan. 3	Jan. 2	Jan. 2
404	State	Republic	Jan. 2	Jan. 2	Jan. 2	Dec. 31

66. Which of the following checks might indicate kiting?
a. #101 and #303.
b. #202 and #404.
c. #101 and #404.
d. #202 and #303. (5/92, Aud., #26, 2779)

67. Which of the following checks illustrate deposits/transfers in transit at December 31, 1991?
a. #101 and #202.
b. #101 and #303.
c. #202 and #404.
d. #303 and #404. (5/92, Aud., #27, 2780)

68. Which of the following procedures would an auditor most likely perform for year-end accounts receivable confirmations when the auditor did **not** receive replies to second requests?
a. Review the cash receipts journal for the month prior to the year end.
b. Intensify the study of the internal control structure concerning the revenue cycle.
c. Increase the assessed level of detection risk for the existence assertion.
d. Inspect the shipping records documenting the merchandise sold to the debtors.
(5/93, Aud., #35, 3931)

68A. Which of the following audit procedures would an auditor most likely perform to test controls relating to management's assertion concerning the completeness of sales transactions?

a. Verify that extensions and footings on the entity's sales invoices and monthly customer statements have been recomputed.
b. Inspect the entity's reports of prenumbered shipping documents that have **not** been recorded in the sales journal.
c. Compare the invoiced prices on prenumbered sales invoices to the entity's authorized price list.
d. Inquire about the entity's credit granting policies and the consistent application of credit checks.

(5/94, Aud., #27, 4692)

69. The negative request form of accounts receivable confirmation is useful particularly when the

	Combined assessed level of inherent and control risk relating to receivables is	Number of small balances is	Consideration by the recipient is
a.	Low	Many	Likely
b.	Low	Few	Unlikely
c.	High	Few	Likely
d.	High	Many	Likely

(5/91, Aud., #9, amended, 0128)

69A. In auditing accounts receivable the negative form of confirmation request most likely would be used when

a. Recipients are likely to return positive confirmation requests without verifying the accuracy of the information.
b. The combined assessed level of inherent and control risk relative to accounts receivable is low.
c. A small number of accounts receivable are involved but a relatively large number of errors are expected.
d. The auditor performs a dual purpose test that assesses control risk and obtains substantive evidence.

(11/94, Aud., #52, 5135)

70. Negative confirmation of accounts receivable is less effective than positive confirmation of accounts receivable because

a. A majority of recipients usually lack the willingness to respond objectively.
b. Some recipients may report incorrect balances that require extensive follow-up.
c. The auditor **cannot** infer that all nonrespondents have verified their account information.
d. Negative confirmations do **not** produce evidential matter that is statistically quantifiable.

(11/89, Aud., #27, 0168)

70A. In which of the following circumstances would the use of the negative form of accounts receivable confirmation most likely be justified?

a. A substantial number of accounts may be in dispute and the accounts receivable balance arises from sales to a few major customers.
b. A substantial number of accounts may be in dispute and the accounts receivable balance arises from sales to many customers with small balances.
c. A small number of accounts may be in dispute and the accounts receivable balance arises from sales to a few major customers.
d. A small number of accounts may be in dispute and the accounts receivable balance arises from sales to many customers with small balances.

(11/93, Aud., #40, 4277)

70B. Which of the following statements is correct concerning the use of negative confirmation requests?

a. Unreturned negative confirmation requests rarely provide significant explicit evidence.
b. Negative confirmation requests are effective when detection risk is low.
c. Unreturned negative confirmation requests indicate that alternative procedures are necessary.
d. Negative confirmation requests are effective when understatements of account balances are suspected.

(5/95, Aud., #45, 5663)

71. Cooper, CPA, is auditing the financial statements of a small rural municipality. The receivable balances represent residents' delinquent real estate taxes. The internal control structure at the municipality is weak. To determine the existence of the accounts receivable balances at the balance sheet date, Cooper would most likely

a. Send positive confirmation requests.
b. Send negative confirmation requests.
c. Examine evidence of subsequent cash receipts.
d. Inspect the internal records such as copies of the tax invoices that were mailed to the residents.

(5/89, Aud., #29, 0178)

71A. An auditor's purpose in reviewing credit ratings of customers with delinquent accounts receivable most likely is to obtain evidence concerning management's assertions about

a. Valuation or allocation.
b. Presentation and disclosure.
c. Existence or occurrence.
d. Rights and obligations.

(11/94, Aud., #50, 5123)

72. When an auditor does **not** receive replies to positive requests for year-end accounts receivable confirmations, the auditor most likely would

a. Inspect the allowance account to verify whether the accounts were subsequently written off.
b. Increase the assessed level of detection risk for the valuation and completeness assertions.
c. Ask the client to contact the customers to request that the confirmations be returned.
d. Increase the assessed level of inherent risk for the revenue cycle. (5/95, Aud., #46, 5664)

73. Which of the following most likely would be detected by an auditor's review of a client's sales cut-off?

a. Shipments lacking sales invoices and shipping documents.
b. Excessive write-offs of accounts receivable.
c. Unrecorded sales at year end.
d. Lapping of year-end accounts receivable. (5/92, Aud., #25, 2778)

73A. Tracing bills of lading to sales invoices provides evidence that

a. Shipments to customers were recorded as sales.
b. Recorded sales were shipped.
c. Invoiced sales were shipped.
d. Shipments to customers were invoiced. (5/92, Aud., #44, 9911)

74. Which of the following most likely would give the most assurance concerning the valuation assertion of accounts receivable?

a. Tracing amounts in the subsidiary ledger to details on shipping documents.
b. Comparing receivable turnover ratios to industry statistics for reasonableness.
c. Inquiring about receivables pledged under loan agreements.
d. Assessing the allowance for uncollectible accounts for reasonableness. (5/92, Aud., #19, 2772)

75. Which of the following auditing procedures most likely would provide assurance about a manufacturing entity's inventory valuation?

a. Testing the entity's computation of standard overhead rates.
b. Obtaining confirmation of inventories pledged under loan agreements.
c. Reviewing shipping and receiving cutoff procedures for inventories.
d. Tracing test counts to the entity's inventory listing. (11/94, Aud., #48, 5131)

75A. While observing a client's annual physical inventory, an auditor recorded test counts for several items and noticed that certain test counts were higher than the recorded quantities in the client's perpetual records. This situation could be the result of the client's failure to record

a. Purchase discounts.
b. Purchase returns.
c. Sales.
d. Sales returns. (5/95, Aud., #52, 5670)

76. When auditing inventories, an auditor would **least** likely verify that

a. The financial statement presentation of inventories is appropriate.
b. Damaged goods and obsolete items have been properly accounted for.
c. All inventory owned by the client is on hand at the time of the count.
d. The client has used proper inventory pricing. (5/93, Aud., #28, 9911)

77. A client maintains perpetual inventory records in both quantities and dollars. If the assessed level of control risk is high, an auditor would probably

a. Insist that the client perform physical counts of inventory items several times during the year.
b. Apply gross profit tests to ascertain the reasonableness of the physical counts.
c. Increase the extent of tests of controls of the inventory cycle.
d. Request the client to schedule the physical inventory count at the end of the year. (5/91, Aud., #11, 0130)

77A. A client maintains perpetual inventory records in both quantities and dollars. If the assessed level of control risk is high, an auditor would probably

a. Increase the extent of tests of controls of the inventory cycle.
b. Request the client to schedule the physical inventory count at the end of the year.
c. Insist that the client perform physical counts of inventory items several times during the year.
d. Apply gross profit tests to ascertain the reasonableness of the physical counts. (11/94, Aud., #58, 5141)

78. An auditor most likely would make inquiries of production and sales personnel concerning possible obsolete or slow-moving inventory to support management's financial statement assertion of

a. Valuation or allocation.
b. Rights and obligations.
c. Existence or occurrence.
d. Presentation and disclosure. (5/95, Aud., #43, 5661)

79. Which of the following audit procedures probably would provide the most reliable evidence concerning the entity's assertion of rights and obligations related to inventories?

a. Trace test counts noted during the entity's physical count to the entity's summarization of quantities.
b. Inspect agreements to determine whether any inventory is pledged as collateral or subject to any liens.
c. Select the last few shipping advices used before the physical count and determine whether the shipments were recorded as sales.
d. Inspect the open purchase order file for significant commitments that should be considered for disclosure.

(5/92, Aud., #17, 2770)

79A. An auditor most likely would inspect loan agreements under which an entity's inventories are pledged to support management's financial statement assertion of

a. Presentation and disclosure.
b. Valuation or allocation.
c. Existence or occurrence.
d. Completeness. (5/95, Aud., #40, 5658)

80. An auditor selected items for test counts while observing a client's physical inventory. The auditor then traced the test counts to the client's inventory listing. This procedure most likely obtained evidence concerning management's assertion of

a. Rights and obligations.
b. Completeness.
c. Existence or occurrence.
d. Valuation. (5/94, Aud., #41, 4706)

80A. To gain assurance that all inventory items in a client's inventory listing schedule are valid, an auditor most likely would trace

a. Inventory tags noted during the auditor's observation to items listed in the inventory listing schedule.
b. Inventory tags noted during the auditor's observation to items listed in receiving reports and vendors' invoices.
c. Items listed in the inventory listing schedule to inventory tags and the auditor's recorded count sheets.
d. Items listed in receiving reports and vendors' invoices to the inventory listing schedule.

(5/95, Aud., #53, 5671)

81. Which of the following combinations of procedures would an auditor most likely perform to obtain evidence about fixed asset additions?

a. Inspecting documents and physically examining assets.
b. Recomputing calculations and obtaining written management representations.
c. Observing operating activities and comparing balances to prior period balances.
d. Confirming ownership and corroborating transactions through inquiries of client personnel. (11/92, Aud., #27, 2961)

81A. In testing plant and equipment balances, an auditor examines new additions listed on an analysis of plant and equipment. This procedure most likely obtains evidence concerning management's assertion of

a. Completeness.
b. Existence or occurrence.
c. Presentation and disclosure.
d. Valuation or allocation. (5/94, Aud., #42, 4707)

82. An auditor analyzes repairs and maintenance accounts primarily to obtain evidence in support of the audit assertion that all

a. Noncapitalizable expenditures for repairs and maintenance have been recorded in the proper period.
b. Expenditures for property and equipment have been recorded in the proper period.
c. Noncapitalizable expenditures for repairs and maintenance have been properly charged to expense.
d. Expenditures for property and equipment have **not** been charged to expense.

(11/94, Aud., #62, 5135)

83. In performing a search for unrecorded retirements of fixed assets, an auditor most likely would

a. Inspect the property ledger and the insurance and tax records, and then tour the client's facilities.
b. Tour the client's facilities, and then inspect the property ledger and the insurance and tax records.
c. Analyze the repair and maintenance account, and then tour the client's facilities.
d. Tour the client's facilities, and then analyze the repair and maintenance account.

(5/95, Aud., #55, 5673)

84. Determining that proper amounts of depreciation are expensed provides assurance about management's assertions of valuation or allocation and

a. Presentation and disclosure.
b. Completeness.

c. Rights and obligations.
d. Existence or occurrence.
(11/94, Aud., #51, 5134)

85. In confirming with an outside agent, such as a financial institution, that the agent is holding investment securities in the client's name, an auditor most likely gathers evidence in support of management's financial statement assertions of existence or occurrence and
a. Valuation or allocation.
b. Rights and obligations.
c. Completeness.
d. Presentation and disclosure.
(5/95, Aud., #44, 5662)

86. An auditor would most likely verify the interest earned on bond investments by
a. Vouching the receipt and deposit of interest checks.
b. Confirming the bond interest rate with the issuer of the bonds.
c. Recomputing the interest earned on the basis of face amount, interest rate, and period held.
d. Testing the internal controls over cash receipts.
(5/89, Aud., #30, 0179)

86A. Which of the following pairs of accounts would an auditor most likely analyze on the same working paper?
a. Notes receivable and interest income.
b. Accrued interest receivable and accrued interest payable.
c. Notes payable and notes receivable.
d. Interest income and interest expense.
(5/95, Aud., #70, 5688)

86B. In testing long-term investments, an auditor ordinarily would use analytical procedures to ascertain the reasonableness of the
a. Completeness of recorded investment income.
b. Classification between current and noncurrent portfolios.
c. Valuation of marketable equity securities.
d. Existence of unrealized gains or losses in the portfolio. (5/93, Aud., #31, 3927)

87. To establish the existence and ownership of a long-term investment in the common stock of a publicly traded company, an auditor ordinarily performs a security count or
a. Assesses control risk at the minimum level if the auditor has reasonable assurance that the control procedures are being applied as prescribed.
b. Confirms the number of shares owned that are held by an independent custodian.
c. Determines the market price per share at the balance sheet date from published quotations.
d. Confirms the number of shares owned with the issuing company. (5/88, Aud., #22, 0198)

87A. In establishing the existence and ownership of a long-term investment in the form of publicly-traded stock, an auditor should inspect the securities or
a. Correspond with the investee company to verify the number of shares owned.
b. Inspect the audited financial statements of the investee company.
c. Confirm the number of shares owned that are held by an independent custodian.
d. Determine that the investment is carried at the lower of cost or market.
(11/94, Aud., #49, 5132)

88. Which of the following is the most effective audit procedure for verification of dividends earned on investments in marketable equity securities?
a. Tracing deposit of dividend checks to the cash receipts book.
b. Reconciling amounts received with published dividend records.
c. Comparing the amounts received with preceding year dividends received.
d. Recomputing selected extensions and footings of dividend schedules and comparing totals to the general ledger. (5/87, Aud., #31, 0228)

89. Which of the following is a substantive test that an auditor most likely would perform to verify the existence and valuation of recorded accounts payable?
a. Investigating the open purchase order file to ascertain that prenumbered purchase orders are used and accounted for.
b. Receiving the client's mail, unopened, for a reasonable period of time after the year end to search for unrecorded vendor's invoices.
c. Vouching selected entries in the accounts payable subsidiary ledger to purchase orders and receiving reports.
d. Confirming accounts payable balances with known suppliers who have zero balances.
(5/93, Aud., #36, 3932)

89A. To determine whether accounts payable are complete, an auditor performs a test to verify that all merchandise received is recorded. The population of documents for this test consists of all
a. Payment vouchers.
b. Receiving reports.
c. Purchase requisitions.
d. Vendor's invoices. (11/93, Aud., #26, 4263)

89B. In auditing accounts payable, an auditor's procedures most likely would focus primarily on management's assertion of
a. Existence or occurrence.
b. Presentation and disclosure.
c. Completeness.
d. Valuation or allocation. (11/93, Aud., #37, 4274)

89C. Cutoff tests designed to detect purchases made before the end of the year that have been recorded in the subsequent year most likely would provide assurance about management's assertion of
a. Valuation or allocation.
b. Existence or occurrence.
c. Completeness.
d. Presentation and disclosure. (5/95, Aud., #42, 5660)

90. Which of the following questions would most likely be included in an internal control questionnaire concerning the completeness assertion for purchases?
a. Is an authorized purchase order required before the receiving department can accept a shipment or the vouchers payable department can record a voucher?
b. Are purchase requisitions prenumbered and independently matched with vendor invoices?
c. Is the unpaid voucher file periodically reconciled with inventory records by an employee who does **not** have access to purchase requisitions?
d. Are purchase orders, receiving reports, and vouchers prenumbered and periodically accounted for? (5/92, Aud., #46, 2799)

90A. Which of the following internal control procedures is **not** usually performed in the treasurer's department?
a. Verifying the accuracy of checks and vouchers.
b. Controlling the mailing of checks to vendors.
c. Approving vendors' invoices for payment.
d. Canceling payment vouchers when paid. (11/93, Aud., #27, 4264)

91. To determine whether accounts payable are complete, an auditor performs a test to verify that all merchandise received is recorded. The population of documents for this test consists of all
a. Vendor's invoices.
b. Purchase orders.
c. Receiving reports.
d. Canceled checks. (5/90, Aud., #36, 9911)

92. An auditor performs a test to determine whether all merchandise for which the client was billed was received. The population for this test consists of all
a. Merchandise received.
b. Vendors' invoices.
c. Canceled checks.
d. Receiving reports. (5/88, Aud., #6, 0195)

93. Which of the following procedures is **least** likely to be performed before the balance sheet date?
a. Testing of internal control over cash.
b. Confirmation of receivables.
c. Search for unrecorded liabilities.
d. Observation of inventory. (11/90, Aud., #24, 0143)

93A. Which of the following procedures would an auditor most likely perform in obtaining evidence about subsequent events?
a. Determine that changes in employee pay rates after year end were properly authorized.
b. Recompute depreciation charges for plant assets sold after year end.
c. Inquire about payroll checks that were recorded before year end but cashed after year end.
d. Investigate changes in long-term debt occurring after year end. (5/95, Aud., #65, 5683)

94. In an audit of contingent liabilities, which of the following procedures would be **least** effective?
a. Reviewing a bank confirmation letter.
b. Examining customer confirmation replies.
c. Examining invoices for professional services.
d. Reading the minutes of the board of directors. (5/89, Aud., #35, 0184)

95. An auditor most likely would perform substantive tests of details on payroll transactions and balances when
a. Cutoff tests indicate a substantial amount of accrued payroll expense.
b. The assessed level of control risk relative to payroll transactions is low.
c. Analytical procedures indicate unusual fluctuations in recurring payroll entries.
d. Accrued payroll expense consists primarily of unpaid commissions. (5/93, Aud., #37, 3933)

95A. When control risk is assessed as low for assertions related to payroll, substantive tests of payroll balances most likely would be limited to applying analytical procedures and
a. Observing the distribution of paychecks.
b. Footing and crossfooting the payroll register.
c. Inspecting payroll tax returns.
d. Recalculating payroll accruals. (5/95, Aud., #54, 5672)

96. The sampling unit in a test of controls pertaining to the existence of payroll transactions ordinarily is a(an)
a. Clock card or time ticket.
b. Employee Form W-2.
c. Employee personnel record.
d. Payroll register entry. (5/90, Aud., #39, 0159)

97. An auditor vouched data for a sample of employees in a payroll register to approved clock card data to provide assurance that
a. Payments to employees are computed at authorized rates.
b. Employees work the number of hours for which they are paid.
c. Segregation of duties exists between the preparation and distribution of the payroll.
d. Internal controls relating to unclaimed payroll checks are operating effectively.
(5/95, Aud., #37, 5655)

98. An auditor's program to examine long-term debt should include steps that require
a. Examining bond trust indentures.
b. Inspecting the accounts payable subsidiary ledger.
c. Investigating credits to the bond interest income account.
d. Verifying the existence of the bondholders.
(11/89, Aud., #28, 0169)

99. An auditor's program to examine long-term debt most likely would include steps that require
a. Comparing the carrying amount of the debt to its year-end market value.
b. Correlating interest expense recorded for the period with outstanding debt.
c. Verifying the existence of the holders of the debt by direct confirmation.
d. Inspecting the accounts payable subsidiary ledger for unrecorded long-term debt.
(5/91, Aud., #8, 0127)

100. In auditing long-term bonds payable, an auditor most likely would
a. Perform analytical procedures on the bond premium and discount accounts.
b. Examine documentation of assets purchased with bond proceeds for liens.
c. Compare interest expense with the bond payable amount for reasonableness.
d. Confirm the existence of individual bondholders at year-end. (11/94, Aud., #60, 5133)

101. During an audit of an entity's stockholders' equity accounts, the auditor determines whether there are restrictions on retained earnings resulting from loans, agreements, or state law. This audit procedure most likely is intended to verify management's assertion of
a. Existence or occurrence.
b. Completeness.
c. Valuation or allocation.
d. Presentation and disclosure.
(5/92, Aud., #18, 2771)

102. An auditor should trace corporate stock issuances and treasury stock transactions to the
a. Numbered stock certificates.
b. Articles of incorporation.
c. Transfer agent's records.
d. Minutes of the board of directors.
(5/88, Aud., #27, 0201)

103. In performing tests concerning the granting of stock options, an auditor should
a. Confirm the transaction with the Secretary of State in the state of incorporation.
b. Verify the existence of option holders in the entity's payroll records or stock ledgers.
c. Determine that sufficient treasury stock is available to cover any new stock issued.
d. Trace the authorization for the transaction to a vote of the board of directors.
(11/94, Aud., #61, 5134)

104. The primary responsibility of a bank acting as registrar of capital stock is to
a. Ascertain that dividends declared do **not** exceed the statutory amount allowable in the state of incorporation.
b. Account for stock certificates by comparing the total shares outstanding to the total in the shareholders subsidiary ledger.
c. Act as an independent third party between the board of directors and outside investors concerning mergers, acquisitions, and the sale of treasury stock.
d. Verify that stock is issued in accordance with the authorization of the board of directors and the articles of incorporation.
(5/91, Aud., #32, 0133)

105. In auditing intangible assets, an auditor most likely would review or recompute amortization and determine whether the amortization period is reasonable in support of management's financial statement assertion of
a. Valuation or allocation.
b. Existence or occurrence.
c. Completeness.
d. Rights and obligations. (5/95, Aud., #41, 5659)

106. Which of the following procedures would an auditor ordinarily perform first in evaluating management's accounting estimates for reasonableness?
a. Develop independent expectations of management's estimates.
b. Consider the appropriateness of the key factors or assumptions used in preparing the estimates.
c. Test the calculations used by management in developing the estimates.
d. Obtain an understanding of how management developed its estimates. (5/95, Aud., #69, 5687)

107. Which of the following procedures would an auditor most likely perform in auditing the statement of cash flows?
a. Compare the amounts included in the statement of cash flows to similar amounts in the prior year's statement of cash flows.
b. Reconcile the cutoff bank statements to verify the accuracy of the year-end bank balances.
c. Vouch all bank transfers for the last week of the year and first week of the subsequent year.
d. Reconcile the amounts included in the statement of cash flows to the other financial statements' balances and amounts. (5/95, Aud., #56, 5674)

108. In determining whether transactions have been recorded, the direction of the audit testing should be from the
a. General ledger balances.
b. Adjusted trial balance.
c. Original source documents.
d. General journal entries. (5/95, Aud., #57, 5675)

Solution 37-1 MULTIPLE CHOICE ANSWERS

Evidential Matter (AU 326)

1. (d) AU 326.18 states that the validity of evidential matter in auditing is more reliable when the evidential matter can be obtained from independent sources outside the entity. This is because it provides greater assurance of reliability for the purposes of an independent audit than evidential matter secured solely within the entity. Answers (a), (b), and (c) are all examples of auditing procedures performed on information obtained from within the entity.

1A. (c) Despite the bank statements being handled by the client, they originate outside the entity and are therefore the most persuasive of the choices. Both purchase orders and work sheets originate within the client. The client representation letter only documents oral representations the client has made.

2. (d) AU 326.05 states that assertions about completeness deal with whether all transactions and accounts that should be presented in the financial statements are so included. Periodically accounting for the numerical sequence of documents and invoices helps ensure that all entries affecting those accounts have been recognized and posted. Answer (a) deals with whether assets or liabilities of the entity exist at a given date and whether recorded transactions have occurred during a given period. Answer (b) deals with whether assets are the rights of the entity and liabilities are the obligations of the entity at a given date. Answer (c) deals with whether asset, liability, revenue, and expense components have been included in the financial statements at appropriate amounts.

3. (b) AU 326.07 states that valuation and allocation deals with whether asset, liability, revenue, and expense components have been included in the financial statements at appropriate amounts. An example would be management's assertion that trade accounts receivable included in the balance sheet are stated at net realizable value. Answer (a) deals with whether assets or liabilities of the entity exist at a given date and whether recorded transactions have occurred during a given period. Answer (c) deals with whether all transactions and accounts that should be presented in the financial statements are so included. Answer (d) deals with whether assets are the rights of the entity and liabilities are the obligations of the entity at a given date.

4. (b) AU 326.02 states that the measure of the validity of evidential matter for audit purposes lies in the judgment of the auditor. AU 326.19 states that for evidence to be competent, it must be both valid and relevant. AU 326.22 states that the matter of difficulty and expense involved in testing a particular item is not in itself a valid basis for omitting the test. AU 326.15 states that by itself, accounting data cannot be considered sufficient support for financial statements.

5. (d) AU 326.15 states, "By itself, accounting data cannot be considered sufficient support for financial statements . . ." The auditor should also acquire corroborative evidence to support the financial statement assertions. In a great majority of cases, the auditor finds it necessary to rely on evidence that is persuasive rather than convincing. Even an experienced auditor is seldom convinced beyond all doubt with respect to all aspects of the statements being audited (AU 326.20). The more effective the internal control structure, the more assurance it provides about the reliability of the accounting data and financial statements [AU 326.19(c)]. An auditor typically works within economic limits; his or her opinion, to be economically useful, must be formed within a reasonable length of time and at a reasonable cost.

5A. (d) AU 326.09 states that the auditor develops specific audit objectives for obtaining evidential matter in support of financial statement assertions. Answers (a), (b), and (c) are all considerations of the substantive and analytical procedures necessary to satisfy the audit objectives.

6. (a) "The matter of difficulty and expense involved in testing a particular item is not in itself a valid basis for omitting the test." (AU 326.22) In selecting particular substantive tests to achieve the audit objectives he or she has developed, an auditor considers, among other things, the risk of material misstatement of the financial statements, including the assessed levels of control risk, and the expected effectiveness and efficiency of such tests (AU 326.11). "There should be a rational relationship between the cost of obtaining evidence and the usefulness of the information obtained" (AU 326.22).

7. (c) In testing the existence assertion for an asset, the auditor would start with the accounting records themselves to determine that the assets recorded on the client's books do exist. Further evidence of the asset existence would then be found in the supporting evidence.

8. (b) This test is performed to satisfy the audit objective of completeness. The primary purpose of this objective is to establish whether all transactions that should have been recorded by the client are included in the accounts.

9. (b) AU 326.19 states that the competence of evidential matter depends upon the circumstances under which it is obtained and the independent auditor's direct personal knowledge, obtained through physical examination, observation, computation, and inspection, is more persuasive than information obtained indirectly. Performing tests of transactions tests segregation of duties from the past which may not be operating currently. A flowchart reflects the ideal operating conditions of the company, established at a point in time, which may not be representative of the actual processing procedures being performed. Audit objectives cannot in themselves reduce control risk.

10. (a) AU 326.19(b) states, "The more effective the internal control structure, the more assurance it provides about the reliability of the accounting data and financial statements."

10A. (d) AU 326.19(b) states, "The more effective the internal control structure, the more assurance it provides about the reliability of the accounting data and financial statements." AU 326.19(a) states, "When evidential matter can be obtained from independent sources outside an entity, it provides greater assurance of reliability for the purposes of an independent audit. Information obtained directly, not indirectly, from outside sources would provide the most reliable evidence." Per AU 326.20, the auditor finds it necessary to rely on evidence that is persuasive rather than convincing. An auditor typically works within economic limits; his or her opinion, to be economically useful, must be performed within a reasonable length of time and at a reasonable cost. Thus, the amount and kinds of evidential matter required to support an informed opinion are matters for the auditor to determine exercising his or her professional judgment. In most cases, the auditor finds it necessary to rely on information that is persuasive rather than convincing.

11. (d) Assertions about valuation or allocation deal with whether asset, liability, revenue, and expense components have been included in the financial statements at appropriate amounts. Analysis of inventory turnover rates would provide evidence as to the valuation of inventory in the financial statements. Answers (a), (b), and (c) are all incorrect because existence or occurrence, rights and obligations, and presentation and disclosure are less directly related to inventory rates than is valuation or allocation.

12. (b) The valuation assertion for an investment accounted for by the equity method can generally be satisfied by referring to the audited financial statements of the investee company.

13. (c) Assertions about presentation and disclosure deal with whether particular components of the financial statements are properly classified, described and disclosed. An auditor would inspect loan

agreements under which an entity's inventories are pledged in order to ensure that the inventory amount presented in the financial statements is actually owned by the client. Answers (a), (b), and (d) are all incorrect because existence or occurrence, completeness, and valuation or allocation are less directly related to the pledging of an entity's inventories than is presentation and disclosure.

14. (a) Substantive tests are designed to detect material misstatements, existing in the financial statements, by providing direct evidence regarding management's assertions.

14A. (c) Most of the auditor's work in forming his or her opinion on financial statements consists of obtaining and evaluating evidential matter concerning the assertions in such financial statements. The auditor's objective is to obtain sufficient competent evidential matter to provide him or her with a reasonable basis for forming an opinion. The amount and kinds of evidential matter required to support an informed opinion are matters for the auditor to determine based upon his or her professional judgment. Answer (a) would not indicate the need for additional substantive testing because the auditor uses his or her own judgment based upon the evidence obtained from his or her own tests. Answer (b) could be the result of nonaccounting factors, such as opening up of a new branch, or hiring additional employees for new contracts received. Answer (d) could be a reason supporting an increase in payroll from one year to the next, but would not indicate the need for additional testing.

14B. (d) The auditor would most likely consider whether material misstatements exist when transactions selected for testing are not supported by proper documentation. Reduced emphasis on meeting earnings projections would be a factor *decreasing* the likelihood of overstatements of earnings and assets (the most frequent misstatement). Having the board of directors making all major financing decisions would decrease the incentive for management to use questionable reporting by reducing the amount of management's responsibility. Reportable conditions previously communicated to management may not have been corrected because of an unfavorable cost-benefit relationship.

The Auditor's Consideration of the Internal Audit Function in an Audit of Financial Statements (AU 322)

15. (d) Answer (d) does not address the internal auditor's competence, but rather the internal auditor's scope of authority for performing procedures on the transactions of the entity. AU 322.90 lists answers (a), (b), and (c) as factors the auditor should consider in assessing the internal auditor's competence.

15A. (b) AU 322.09 states, "When assessing the internal auditor's competence, the auditor should obtain information about such factors as...professional certification and the educational level and professional experience of the internal auditor." Answers (a), (c), and (d) are incorrect because this information is used in assessing the internal auditor's objectivity.

16. (c) When assessing an internal auditor's objectivity, an independent auditor should obtain information about such factors as whether the internal auditor has direct access and reports regularly to the board of directors, the audit committee, or the owner-manager (AU 322.10). Answers (a), (b), and (d) are all incorrect because they refer to factors to consider in assessing the *competence* of the internal auditor, not the internal auditor's objectivity (AU 322.09).

16A. (d) Answers (a), (b), and (c) are all specifically mentioned in AU 322.11 as items the auditor considers in assessing the internal auditor's competence and objectivity.

17. (a) If the independent auditor decides that the work performed by internal auditors may have a bearing on his or her own procedures, he or she should assess the competence and objectivity of internal auditors and evaluate their work. When assessing the internal auditor's objectivity, the auditor should determine the organizational status of the internal auditor responsible for the internal audit function, including (1) whether the internal auditor reports to an officer of sufficient status to ensure broad audit coverage and adequate consideration of, and action on, the findings and recommendations of the internal auditors; (2) whether the internal auditor has direct access and reports regularly to the board of directors, the audit committee, or the owner-manager; and (3) whether the board of directors, the audit committee, or the owner-manager oversees employment decisions related to the internal auditor (AU 322.10). In this case, the independent auditor would only place limited reliance on the work of the internal auditors because the internal auditors report to the corporate controller and may be reluctant to report weaknesses in the controller's activities.

17A. (c) The existence of fixed asset additions is an example of audit assertions where the work of an internal auditor would be relevant. Per <u>SAS 65</u>, AU 322.07, "Relevant activities are those that provide evidence about the design and effectiveness of internal control structure policies and procedures that pertain to the entity's ability to record, process, summarize, and report financial data consistent with the assertions embodied in the financial statements or that provide direct evidence about potential misstatements of such data." The existence of contingencies, the valuation of intangible assets, and the valuation of related party transactions are all examples of assertions that have higher degrees of subjectivity involved and do not necessarily pertain to the entity's ability to record, process, summarize, and report. For such assertions, per AU 322.21, "the consideration of internal auditors' work cannot alone reduce audit risk to an acceptable level to eliminate the necessity to perform tests of those assertions directly by the auditor."

18. (d) According to SAS 65, AU 322.27, "In performing an audit, the auditor may request direct assistance from the internal auditors...[including] assist[ance]...in obtaining an understanding of the internal control structure or in performing tests of controls or substantive tests..."

19. (c) A CPA (or external auditor) will usually perform *financial* compliance audits to enable him to attest to the fairness of an entity's financial statements. Internal auditors may also perform these financial compliance audits, as well as *procedural* compliance audits and *operational* audits which are usually beyond the realm of concern of the CPA. Therefore, a comprehensive internal audit program will be more detailed and cover more areas than the independent CPA's audit program.

Client Representations (AU 333)

20. (d) The independent auditor is required to obtain written representations from management as a part of an audit performed in accordance with generally accepted auditing standards (AU 333.01). Generally accepted auditing standards do not require an internal control questionnaire, a client engagement letter, or a planning memorandum or checklist.

21. (a) AU 333.02 states, "During an audit, management makes many representations to the auditor, both oral and written, in response to specific inquiries or through the financial statements. Such representations from management are part of the evidential matter the independent auditor obtains, but they are *not a substitute* for the application of those auditing procedures necessary to afford a reasonable basis for his opinion on the financial statements. Written representations from management ordinarily confirm oral representations given to the auditor, indicate and document the continuing appropriateness of such representations, and reduce the possibility of misunderstanding concerning the matters that are the subject of the representations."

22. (c) AU 333.02 states that written representations from management ordinarily reduce the possibility of misunderstanding concerning the matters that are the subject of the representations, i.e., the financial statements. The auditor does not reduce audit risk or the scope of audit procedures performed based on the representations made in the management representation letter. A representation letter does not reduce the auditor's responsibility to detect material misstatements in the audit.

23. (c) AU 337.05 states that since the events or conditions that should be considered in the accounting for, and reporting of, litigation, claims, and assessments are matters within the direct knowledge, and often control, of management of an entity, that management is then the primary source of information about such matters. Although a letter of audit inquiry to the client's lawyer is the auditor's primary means of obtaining *corroboration* of the information furnished by management concerning litigation, claims, and assessments, it is not the primary means of obtaining that information, as indicated above.

24. (a) AU 333.04 deals with client representations and lists compensating balances and other restrictions on cash balances as one of the representations obtained by the auditor, if appropriate to the client's business.

25. (d) AU 333.03 states, "In some cases involving written representations, the corroborating information that can be obtained by the application of auditing procedures other than inquiry is limited. When a client plans to discontinue a line of business, for example, the auditor may not be able to obtain information through other auditing procedures to corroborate the plan or intent. Accordingly, the auditor should obtain a written representation to provide confirmation of management's intent." Plans to terminate an employee pension plan, make a stock offering, or settle a lawsuit for an amount less than the accrued loss contingency would usually be seen in the minutes of the board meetings.

26. (a) According to AU 333.05, management's representations may be limited to matters that are considered material. Materiality limitations would not apply to those representations that are not directly related to amounts included in the financial statements, such as the availability of minutes of stockholders' and directors' meetings. Answers (b), (c), and (d) relate directly to amounts included in the

financial statements and thus the materiality limits would apply.

27. (c) AU 333A.05 provides an example of a sample management representation letter and the types of assertions that should be made. Among these assertions is *that no violations or possible violations of laws or regulations whose effects should be considered for disclosure in the financial statements or as a basis for recording a loss contingency.*

28. (b) AU 333.09 states, "Because the auditor is concerned with events occurring through the date of his report that may require adjustment to or disclosure in the financial statements, the representations should be dated as of the date of the auditor's report." Hence, the auditor would not be able to consider the client's representation letter in the planning of a new engagement.

29. (c) According to AU 333.10 (SAS 19), the management representation letter should be dated as of the date of the auditor's report.

Analytical Procedures (AU 329)

30. (d) Performing analytical procedures designed to disclose differences from expectations would be the most likely way to detect unusual entries. Evaluating the effectiveness of the internal control would not ordinarily detect journal entries with unusual combinations of accounts. Investigating the reconciliations between controlling accounts and subsidiary records would mostly expose the auditor to only typical, recurring journal entries. Tracing a sample of journal entries to the general ledger would most likely not be among the early work of an audit, and thus, the unusual entries would most likely already be detected.

31. (a) AU 329.04 indicates that analytical procedures are to be used to some extent in the planning of the audit and in the final review stages. The use of analytical procedures as a substantive test is not mandated, but can be "more effective or efficient than tests of details for achieving substantive audit objectives."

31A. (a) AU 329.06 states "the objective of the procedures is to identify such things as the existence of unusual transactions and events..." Answers (b), (c), and (d) would not necessarily be discovered in the performance of analytical procedures, but would more likely be discovered in the performance of substantive tests.

32. (b) The analytical procedures used in planning the audit should focus on (1) enhancing the auditor's understanding of the client's business and the transactions and events that have occurred since the last audit date, and (2) identifying areas that may represent specific risks relevant to the audit (AU 329.06).

33. (d) The objective of analytical procedures is to identify the existence of unusual transactions and events, amounts, ratios, and trends, that may identify matters having financial statement and audit planning ramifications. The use of a standard cost system that produces variance reports allows the auditor an opportunity to compare the output from the standard cost system with the financial information presented by management (AU 329.06).

33A. (d) AR 100.12 states that for a compilation of financial statements the accountant is not required to make inquiries or perform other procedures to verify, corroborate, or review information supplied by the entity. AR 100.04 states that a review of financial statements involves performing inquiry and analytical procedures that provide the accountant with a reasonable basis for expressing limited assurance that there are no material modifications that should be made to the statements in order for them to be in conformity with GAAP. Therefore, answers (a), (b), and (c) are incorrect.

34. (a) AU 329.22 states, "The overall review would generally include reading the financial statements and notes and considering the adequacy of evidence gathered in response to unusual or unexpected balances identified in planning the audit or in the course of the audit ..." Analytical procedures do not include performing tests of transactions. Analytical procedures in the overall review stage of the audit are more concerned with unexplained changes to account balances. The auditor would not likely gather evidence about account balances that had not changed from the prior year. The retesting of control procedures relates more directly to tests of controls than it does to analytical procedures.

34A. (c) AU 329.22 states, "The objective of analytical procedures used in the overall review stage of the audit is to assist the auditor in assessing the conclusions reached and in the evaluation of the overall financial statement presentation.... The overall review would generally include reading the financial statements and notes and considering...unusual or unexpected balances or relationships that were not previously identified." The other options are activities to be done before the overall review stage.

34B. (c) AU 329.06 states, "The purpose of applying analytical procedures in planning the audit is to assist in planning the nature, timing, and extent of auditing procedures that will be used to obtain evidential matter for specific account balances or classes of transactions. To accomplish this, the analytical procedures used in planning the audit should focus on enhancing the auditor's understanding of the client's business and the transactions and events that have occurred since the last audit date..." Consideration of reductions in the scope of test of controls and substantive tests occurs after the auditor understands the client's business. The audit as a whole provides reasonable assurance that potential material misstatements will be identified. Assessing the adequacy of available evidential matter can occur only after examination of evidential matter, not in the planning stage.

35. (c) A comparison of current year revenue to budgeted current year revenue would provide an evaluation of the entity's expected results for the year. Comparisons between prior year amounts and current year amounts are not as likely to provide useful information about current year results. Also, the study of accounts payable, payroll expense, warranty expense and contingent liabilities would not, by themselves, provide sufficient evidence to evaluate an entity's results of operations.

35A. (b) Analytical procedures consist of evaluations of financial information made by a study of plausible relationships among both financial and nonfinancial data. Projecting an error rate is not an evaluation of financial information.

36. (c) AU 329.14 states, "Relationships involving income statement accounts tend to be more predictable than relationships involving only balance sheet accounts since income statement accounts represent transactions over a period of time, whereas balance sheet accounts represent amounts as of a point in time. Relationships involving transactions subject to management discretion are sometimes less predictable."

37. (b) A comparison of revenues and expenses with those of the prior year is likely to reveal a change in the capitalization policy for small tools. For instance, if tools costing less than $25 were formerly expensed and the policy is changed to $100, this is likely to show a substantial increase in the amount of tools expensed during the period. Answer (a) concerns a liability account, Payroll Taxes Payable, not a revenue or expense account. Failure to recognize the property tax increase would make the account balances comparable and so the auditor would *not* investigate.

38. (b) AU 329.09 states, "The auditor's reliance on substantive tests to achieve an audit objective related to a particular assertion may be derived from tests of details, from analytical procedures, or from a combination of both. The decision about which procedure or procedures to use to achieve a particular audit objective is based on the auditor's judgment on the expected effectiveness and efficiency of the available procedures." An auditor's decision whether to apply analytical procedures or to perform tests of transactions and account balances is not solely determined by the availability of data aggregated at a high level, the timing of tests performed after the balance sheet date, or the auditor's familiarity with industry trends.

39. (d) AU 329.10 states, "For some assertions, analytical procedures are effective in providing the appropriate level of assurance. For other assertions, however, analytical procedures may not be as effective or efficient as tests of details in providing the desired level of assurance."

40. (a) AU 329.16 states, "The following factors influence the auditor's consideration of the reliability of data for purposes of achieving audit objectives: Whether the data was obtained from independent sources outside the entity or from sources within the entity; Whether sources within the entity were independent of those who are responsible for the amount being audited; Whether the data was developed under a reliable system with adequate controls; Whether the data was subjected to audit testing in the current or prior year; Whether the expectations were developed using data from a variety of sources." Whether the data were processed in an EDP system or in a manual accounting system would generally not influence the auditor's consideration of the reliability of data for purposes of analytical procedures.

Using the Work of a Specialist (AU 336)

41. (b) AU 336.12 states that if the auditor, as a result of the report or findings of the specialist, decides to add an explanatory paragraph describing an uncertainty, reference to and identification of the specialist may be made in the auditor's report if the auditor believes such reference will facilitate an understanding of the reason for the explanatory paragraph or the departure from the unqualified opinion. Otherwise, when expressing an unqualified opinion, the auditor should not refer to the work or findings of the specialist as this might be

misunderstood to be a qualification of the auditor's opinion or a division of responsibility, neither of which is intended. Answer (a) may be a reason for deciding to use the work of a specialist but would not be a reason for referring to the specialist in the report. The auditor would use for his or her current year report the report on the results of the specialist's findings in the period being reported on, not on the results of prior-period findings. The auditor ordinarily should attempt to obtain a specialist who is unrelated to the client. However, if the specialist is related, the auditor should consider performing additional procedures with respect to some or all of the related specialist's assumptions, methods, or findings to determine that the findings are not unreasonable.

42. (b) AU 336.06 states, "Ordinarily, the auditor should attempt to obtain a specialist who is unrelated to the client. However, when the circumstances so warrant, work of a specialist having a relationship to the client may be acceptable." AU 336.08 expands on this and states, "If the specialist is related to the client, the auditor should consider performing additional procedures with respect to some or all of the related specialist's assumptions, methods, or findings to determine that the findings are not unreasonable or engage an outside specialist for that purpose." The auditor may also disclaim an opinion when sufficient competent evidential matter cannot be obtained (AU 336.09). The specialist should have an understanding of the auditor's use of the specialist's findings (AU 336.07). The specialist should not be referred to when the auditor expresses an unqualified opinion (AU 336.11).

42A. (a) While, according to AU 336.06 (SAS 11), the "work of a specialist unrelated to the client will usually provide the auditor with greater assurance of reliability because of the absence of a relationship that might impair objectivity," "when circumstances so warrant, work of a specialist having a relationship to the client may be acceptable." If an auditor believes that the determinations made by a specialist are unreasonable, or if there is a material difference between a specialist's findings and the assertions in the financial statements, per AU 336.09, the auditor "should apply additional procedures." If the matters cannot be resolved, the auditor may conclude that he or she should qualify the opinion or disclaim an opinion. Per AU 336.03, an example of a matter that the auditor may decide *requires* the use of the work of a specialist is in the determination of physical characteristics relating to inventories.

42B. (d) AU 336.08, regarding the use of a specialist's findings, indicates that *an auditor should obtain an understanding of the methods and assumptions used by the specialist.*

43. (c) AU 336.07 states, "An understanding should exist among the auditor, the client, and the specialist as to the nature of the work to be performed by the specialist. Preferably, the understanding should be documented and should cover the following: (a) The objectives and scope of the specialist's work; (b) The specialist's representations as to his relationship, if any, to the client; (c) The methods or assumptions to be used; (d) A comparison of the methods or assumptions to be used with those used in the preceding period; (e) *The specialist's understanding of the auditor's corroborative use of the specialist's findings in relation to the representations in the financial statements*; (f) The form and content of the specialist's report ..."

43A. (a) Per SAS 73, par. 16, "The auditor may, as a result of the report or findings of the specialist, decide to add explanatory language to his or her standard report or depart from an unqualified opinion. Reference to and identification of the specialist may be made in the auditor's report if the auditor believes such reference will facilitate an understanding of the reason for the explanatory paragraph or the departure from the unqualified opinion." If, as a result of the use of the specialist, the auditor concludes that conditions exist that cause substantial doubt about the entity's ability to continue as a going concern and the auditor believes a reference to the specialists will facilitate an understanding of the reason for the reference to this conclusion, the auditor may refer to the specialist in the auditor's report. Disclosure of the specialist's findings, implying that a more thorough audit was performed is not appropriate, per SAS 73, par. 15. If a specialist's findings are consistent with management's representations and corroborate another specialist's earlier findings, there would be no need to disclose the findings of the specialist for the reasons above. Internal control is generally not a matter that would require the use of a specialist, as described in SAS 73, par. 7.

Inquiry of a Client's Lawyer Concerning Litigation, Claims, and Assessments (AU 337)

44. (c) AU 337.04 states, "With respect to litigation, claims, and assessments, the independent auditor should obtain evidential matter relevant to the following factors: (1)The existence of a condition, situation or set of circumstances indicating an uncertainty as to the possible loss to an entity arising from litigation, claims, and assessments. (2) The period in which the underlying cause for legal action occurred. (3) The degree of probability of an

unfavorable outcome. (4) The amount or range of potential loss."

44A. (d) According to AU 337.14 (SAS 12), when a client's lawyer is unable to form a conclusion about the likelihood of an unfavorable outcome of pending litigation because of inherent uncertainties and the effect on the financial statements could be material, the auditor will ordinarily conclude that an explanatory paragraph should be added to the report.

45. (b) AU 337.06 states, "An auditor does not possess legal skills and, therefore, cannot make legal judgments concerning information coming to his attention. Accordingly, the auditor should request the *client's management* to send a letter of inquiry to those lawyers with whom management consulted concerning litigation, claims, and assessments." The auditor would not confirm directly with the client's lawyer.

46. (d) AU 337.08 states, "A letter of audit inquiry to the client's lawyer is the auditor's primary means of obtaining corroboration of the information furnished by management concerning litigation, claims, and assessments."

46A. (b) AU 337.08 states that the letter of inquiry to the client's attorney is the primary means the auditor has to obtain corroboration of information furnished by management concerning litigation, claims, and assessments. The terms mentioned in answers (a) and (c) might be covered by the attorney, but are not the primary reasons the auditor makes the request. The items in answer (d) are normally furnished by management (or management may request that the attorney prepare the description and evaluation); they are not the primary reason the auditor sends a letter of inquiry.

47. (a) AU 337.12 states, "A lawyer may appropriately limit his response to matters to which he has given substantive attention in the form of legal consultation or representation." Incorrect answers (b) and (d) are addressed in AU 337.13 where it indicates these are sufficient to cause a scope limitation. Answer (c) is also incorrect, as it may lead the auditor to conclude that the financial statements are affected by an uncertainty which is not susceptible to a reasonable estimate (AU 337.14).

47A. (b) According to AU 337.12 (SAS 12), "A lawyer's refusal to furnish the information requested in an inquiry letter...would be a limitation on the scope of the audit sufficient to preclude an unqualified opinion." The auditor would need to use alternate procedures to obtain evidence to satisfy the auditor on litigation or potential litigation issues before issuing an unqualified opinion. Such a refusal *and the results of other procedures* may result in the auditor determining to issue an adverse opinion, or to withdraw from the engagement, or to include disclosures in the financial statements or report to management and/or the audit committee.

48. (b) AU 337.13 states, "A lawyer's refusal to furnish the information requested in an inquiry letter either in writing or orally would be a limitation on the scope of the audit sufficient to preclude an unqualified opinion." A lawyer's response to such an inquiry, along with other auditing procedures, provides the auditor with sufficient evidential matter to satisfy her- or himself concerning the accounting for and reporting of pending and threatened litigation, claims, and assessments.

Working Papers (AU 339)

49. (c) AU 339.05 states that the quantity, type, and content of working papers vary with the circumstances, but they should be sufficient to show that the accounting records agree or reconcile with the financial statements. Documentation of the internal control structure design of relevant policies, procedures, and records pertaining to each of the three internal control structure elements is required. The auditor is not required to document the operating effectiveness of the control policies and procedures. Obtaining an engagement letter is a recommended auditing procedure but is not required. Where control risk is assessed at the maximum level, the auditor should document his or her conclusion that control risk is at the maximum level, but need not document the basis for that conclusion.

49A. (c) Client engagement letters are a matter of sound business practice, rather than a professional requirement. AU 311.05 states that a written audit program establishing auditing procedures to accomplish the audit's objectives is necessary. AU 326.14 states that the basic accounting data and all corroborating information support the financial statements. Without an indication that the accounting records agree or reconcile with the financial statements, the auditor cannot express an opinion upon them. AU 319.39 states the basis for the auditor's conclusions is required to be documented when the assessed level of control risk is below the maximum level.

50. (d) AU 339 states that working papers serve mainly to provide the principal support for the auditor's report, including his representation regarding observance of the standards of field work, and aid the

auditor in the conduct and supervision of the audit. Answers (a), (b), and (c) would be found in the current working paper files. Permanent files contain items of continuing interest, for example, articles of incorporation, pension plan contracts, flowcharts of internal controls, and records of stockholders' equity and capital accounts.

50A. (c) AU 339 states that working papers serve mainly to provide principal support for the auditor's report. Permanent files contain items of continuing interest. A working trial balance would not have continuing interest.

51. (a) AU 319.39 states, "The nature and extent of the auditor's documentation are influenced by the assessed level of control risk used, the nature of the entity's internal control structure, and the nature of the entity's documentation of its internal control structure." Answers (b), (c), and (d) represent factors that would not likely affect the auditor's judgment about the quantity, type, and content of the working papers.

51A. (d) The matters noted in answers (a), (b), and (c) would all have a significant impact on the quantity and content of the auditor's working papers. While the content of the representation letter may affect the quantity and content of the auditor's working papers, the effect is minimal.

52. (c) Among the examples of timesaving considerations in workpaper content listed in the AICPA Audit and Accounting Manual is that the auditor should consider using adding machine tape instead of separate lists, and may enter names or explanations on the tapes where appropriate (AAM 6300.03).

53. (d) Detailed audit working papers are subdivided and grouped by financial statement accounts, which in turn are filed in order of appearance in the financial statements. Working papers for each asset, liability, and equity account begin with a lead schedule summarizing the account's balance per the general ledger, and then showing adjusting and reclassification entries, and the final balance per audit. The lead schedule also includes the auditor's conclusion about whether the account is fairly stated.

54. (a) The working trial balance is a list of accounts in the client's general ledger that, at a minimum, contains columns for reclassifications and adjustments. Reconciliations and tickmarks are usually found within the supporting working papers. Accruals and deferrals would normally be found in supporting schedules within the working papers. Expense and revenue summaries are not part of the working trial balance, but may be a supporting workpaper included in the audit workpapers as a whole.

54A. (c) Worksheets contain reclassification and adjustments columns. The items in answers (a), (b), and (d) are included in the audit workpapers, but are not included in the working trial balance.

54B. (b) In the test data approach to testing a computerized accounting system, test data are processed by the client's computer programs under the auditor's control. The auditor will determine how many transactions and what types of transactions to test which may or may not include several transactions of each type. The auditor need not include test data for all possible valid and invalid conditions. The object of the test is to test the client's program that is used throughout the year and the auditor must take steps to make sure that the program being tested is the one that is actually used in routine processing; thus, a different program would not be tested.

55. (b) A cutoff bank statement is a statement covering a specified number of business days (usually 7 to 10) following the end of the client's fiscal year. The client will request that the bank prepare such a statement and deliver it to the auditors. Most auditors do not actually prepare a second bank reconciliation, but merely examine the cutoff statement closely to see that the year-end reconciling items, such as deposits in transit and outstanding checks, have cleared the bank in the interval since the balance sheet date. When the auditor has completed his or her auditing procedures, the cutoff bank statement is given to the client. Answers (a), (c), and (d) are normally included in the working papers.

55A. (a) According to AU 339.02 (SAS 41), working papers serve mainly to provide the principal support for the auditor's report and to aid the auditor in the conduct and supervision of the audit.

Related Parties (AU 334)

56. (c) AU 334.12 states that except for routine transactions, it will generally not be possible to determine whether a particular transaction would have taken place if the parties had not been related, or assuming it would have taken place what the terms and manner of settlement would have been. Accordingly, it is difficult to substantiate representations that a transaction was consummated on terms equivalent to those that prevail in arm's-

length transactions. If such a representation is included in the financial statements and the auditor believes that the representation is unsubstantiated by management, he or she should express a qualified or adverse opinion because of a departure from GAAP, depending on materiality. The disclosure of loans below market value is additional support for items included in the financial statements. Describing the exchange of real estate or presenting the dollar volume of related party transactions and any changes in the method of establishing terms from prior periods are all typical disclosure items that should be included in the financial statements for them to be in conformity with GAAP.

57. (c) AU 334.02 states, "The auditor should view related party transactions within the framework of existing pronouncements, placing primary emphasis on the adequacy of disclosure."

57A. (d) According to AU 334.02 (SAS 45), an auditor places primary emphasis on the adequacy of disclosure when auditing related party transactions. Answers (a), (b), and (c) are among the possible audit procedures used to evaluate the adequacy of related party disclosure.

57B. (c) AU 334.08 lists procedures that are intended to provide guidance for identifying material transaction with parties known to be related and for identifying material transactions that may be indicative of the existence of previously undetermined relationships, including reviewing accounting records for large, unusual, or nonrecurring transactions or balances, paying particular attention to transactions recognized at or near the end of the reporting period. Answers (b) and (d) are audit procedures that would be helpful in obtaining audit evidence in support of financial statement amounts. Answer (a) is an audit procedure that identifies whether previously reported internal control weaknesses have been corrected.

58. (a) Concerning transactions involving related parties, AU 334.02 states, ". . . the auditor should be aware that the substance of a particular transaction could be significantly different from its form and that financial statements should recognize the substance of particular transactions rather than merely their legal form."

59. (d) When searching for related party transactions, the auditor should obtain an understanding of each subsidiary's relationship to the total entity because ". . . business structure and operating style are occasionally deliberately designed to obscure related party transactions." (AU 334.05) Answers (a), (b), and (c) are not reasons for an auditor to obtain an understanding of each subsidiary's relationship to the total entity (AU 334.05).

60. (d) AU 334.03 states, "Transactions that because of their nature may be indicative of the existence of related parties include: (a) *Borrowing or lending on an interest-free basis or at a rate of interest significantly above or below market rates prevailing at the time of the transaction*; (b) selling real estate at a price that differs significantly from its appraised value; (c) exchanging property for similar property in a nonmonetary transaction; (d) making loans with no scheduled terms for when or how the funds will be repaid."

61. (c) After related party transactions are identified, the auditor should apply procedures that provide further information regarding the transaction. One such procedure is to determine whether the transaction has been approved by the board of directors or other appropriate officials (AU 334.09).

61A. (c) AU 334.09 notes that after identifying related party transactions, the auditor should obtain an understanding of the business purpose of the transactions. The other answers are all procedures that may be performed later.

Audit of Cash

62. (b) AU 326.19 states that for audit evidence to be competent, it must be both valid and relevant. When evidential matter can be obtained from independent sources outside an entity, it provides greater assurance of reliability for the purposes of an independent audit than that secured solely within the entity. Answers (a), (c), and (d) represent audit procedures that may be performed and evidence that can be obtained as a by-product of receiving the standard confirmation; however, they do not represent the primary purpose for obtaining the confirmation.

63. (d) A standard bank confirmation not only yields information regarding ending account balances, but also requests information on contingent liabilities and security agreements with the bank (AU 337.09). A bank confirmation does not provide the information necessary to prepare a proof of cash. A cutoff bank statement is usually requested separately. A bank confirmation does not allow the discovery of kiting activities.

64. (a) or (b) Depending on the level of service, either the bank confirmations or the bank reconciliations provide primary evidence of the year-end bank balance. In an audit engagement, the best evidence would probably be the bank confirmation

from an independent third party. If financial statements are being compiled, however, no confirmation is required and the bank reconciliation would provide the primary evidence. A bank deposit lead schedule is not primary evidence by itself.

65. (b) This bank transfer results in an overstatement of cash at December 31, 1987. The receipt of the transfer was recorded in the books on 12/31/87, thus increasing that bank account's cash balance on that date. However, the disbursement of the transfer was not recorded in the books until 1/4/88; thus, that bank account's cash balance was not decreased until after the financial statement date. The bank transfers indicated in answers (a), (c), and (d) do not result in a misstatement of cash. The books recorded the disbursement and receipt of each of these bank transfers in the same fiscal year.

66. (b) The term kiting refers to the practice of transferring cash between or among various bank accounts, with recording of the cash receipt (deposit) being made on a timely basis, while the recording of the disbursement (withdrawal) is delayed. Thus, for a period of time, the amount of the check could appear in two different accounts simultaneously. In this question, note that the *receipt* of check #202 was recorded (per the books) at 12/30, while the disbursement was not recorded (per the books) until 1/3. Also, note that check #404 (written from State Bank) was received by the bank on 12/31 but was not recorded on the Fox Co.'s books until 1/2.

67. (b) Deposits/transfers in transit refer to checks which have been recorded on the entity's books but have not yet cleared the bank. In this question, note that checks #101 and #303 were disbursed (per books) at the end of December, but were not received by the bank until early January.

Audit of Accounts Receivable and Sales

68. (d) AU 330.32 states that the nature of alternative procedures varies according to the account and assertion in question. In the examination of accounts receivable, alternative procedures may include examination of subsequent cash receipts, shipping documents, or other client documentation to provide evidence for the existence assertion. Answers (b) and (c) are procedures and considerations that would be made in the planning stages of the audit.

68A. (b) AU 326.05 states that assertions about completeness deal with whether all transactions and accounts that should be presented in the financial statements are so included. Periodically accounting for the numerical sequence of documents and invoices helps ensure that all entries affecting those accounts have been recognized and posted. Answer (a) is a clerical test for accuracy. Answer (c) relates to management's assertion of accuracy and valuation. Answer (d) is a test of controls for authorization of credit prior to the sale being approved.

69. (a) AU 331.20 states the negative form requests the recipient to respond only if he or she disagrees with the information stated on the request. Negative confirmation requests may be used to reduce audit risk to an acceptable level when (a) the combined assessed level of inherent and control risk is low, (b) a large number of small balances is involved, and (c) the auditor has no reason to believe that the recipients of the requests are unlikely to give them consideration.

69A. (b) Negative confirmations are more likely to be used in auditing accounts receivable *when the combined assessed level of inherent and control risk is low,* according to AU 330.20.

70. (c) A positive confirmation request asks the debtor to respond whether or not he is in agreement with the information given. The negative form of confirmation request asks the debtor to respond only if he disagrees with the information given (AU 330.20). An inherent weakness in the negative form is that a nonresponse does not necessarily mean that the balance is accurate. Rather a nonresponse may have nothing to do with the correctness or incorrectness of the balance. The response form may simply have not been returned by the debtor or may have been lost enroute from the debtor to the auditor.

70A. (d) AU 330.20 states that negative confirmation requests may be used to reduce audit risk to an acceptable level when (1) the combined assessed level of inherent risk and control risk is low, (2) a large number of small balances is involved, and (3) the auditor has no reason to believe that the recipients of the requests are unlikely to give them consideration.

70B. (a) AU 330.22 states that unreturned negative confirmations do not provide explicit evidence. AU 330.20 notes that negative confirmations may be effective when three criteria are met; one of the criteria is that the combined assessed level of inherent and control risk is low. AU 330.31 notes that for unreturned positive confirmations, alternative procedures are used. The auditor would be more likely to use positive confirmations, which provide more persuasive evidence, if understatements are suspected.

71. (a) The positive (confirmation) form is preferable when individual account balances are relatively large or when there is reason to believe that there may be a substantial number of accounts in dispute or with inaccuracies or irregularities. In this case, inaccuracies and irregularities are likely since the internal control structure is weak. Negative confirmations are used when the assessed level of control risk is low. With weak internal controls, the auditor needs to obtain third party verification.

71A. (a) AU 326.07 states that assertions about valuation deal with whether assets (among other components) are included in financial statements at appropriate amounts. An auditor's primary purpose in reviewing credit ratings of customers with delinquent accounts receivable is to obtain evidence relating to valuation. If the valuation account is too low, net accounts receivable would be too high, and the assets would, therefore, be overstated.

72. (c) Nonresponse to positive requests for accounts receivable confirmations generally requires the use of follow-up requests, such as additional mailings or telephone calls. It is appropriate that the auditor ask the client to contact the customers. In cases where there is still no response to requests dealing with significant accounts, alternative procedures should be used to obtain adequate evidence, as discussed in AU 330.31 and .32 (SAS 67). These additional procedures may involve the examination of documents such as subsequent cash receipts, sales invoices, and shipping documents. While nonresponse increases risks associated with the audit, it is the auditor's responsibility to apply alternative procedures to keep the risks within acceptable levels.

73. (c) In general, cut-off tests are used to detect unrecorded transactions at the end of the period. In this question, the auditor would most likely detect unrecorded sales for the year by reviewing a sales cut-off to determine that sales were recorded in the period in which title to the goods passed to the customer. Such a review would not reveal shipments lacking invoices, excessive write-offs of accounts receivable, or lapping of year-end accounts receivable.

73A. (d) Tracing bills of lading to sales invoices provides evidence that shipments to customers were invoiced. Tracing bills of lading to sales invoices will not provide evidence as to the recorded amount of sales or whether the sales were actually shipped.

74. (d) AU 326.07 states, "Assertions about valuation or allocation deal with whether asset, liability, revenue, and expense components have been included in the financial statements at appropriate amounts. For example, . . . management asserts that trade accounts receivable included in the balance sheet are stated at net realizable value." One step in assuring that receivables are valued properly would thus be to assess the allowance for uncollectible accounts for reasonableness.

Audit of Inventory

75. (a) The procedure in answer (a) helps provide assurance about valuation of inventory. The procedures in answers (b), (c), and (d) provide assurance regarding existence.

75A. (d) Physical counts of inventory items higher than the recorded quantities in perpetual inventory records could be the result of the failure to record sales returns in the books when sales return items were returned to inventory. Failure to record purchase discounts would have nothing to do with the recorded *quantities* in the records. Failure to record purchase returns and sales would result in the physical counts being *lower* than the quantities in the perpetual records.

76. (c) When auditing inventory, the auditor needs to obtain evidence supporting management's assertions of presentation and disclosure, answer (a), and valuation, answers (b) and (d). It would not be unusual for the client to have inventory out on consignment or held in a warehouse beyond the client's premises. Also, some of the inventory items could be in transit at the inventory date. The auditor needs to obtain confirmation or perform other auditing procedures to support management's assertions as to the existence and valuation of these assets, but they would not necessarily need to be on hand.

77. (d) When the assessed level of control risk is high and the auditor has not satisfied himself as to inventories in the client's possession, tests of the accounting records or other procedures will not be sufficient for him to become satisfied as to quantities. In this case, it will always be necessary for the auditor to make, or observe, physical counts of the inventory on which the balance sheet inventory is based (AU 331.12).

77A. (b) Normally when perpetual inventory records are well-kept and physical count comparisons are made on a regular basis an auditor may perform inventory observation during or after the end of the period being audited. However, an auditor would probably request that the physical inventory count be done at the end of the year, since the auditor does not have much confidence in the ability of the internal controls present to detect errors when control risk is high.

78. (a) The cost of obsolete or slow-moving inventory may have to be written down or written off; this affects the valuation assertion. The assertions of rights and obligations, existence or occurrence, and presentation and disclosure are not affected by obsolete or slow-moving items.

79. (b) Inspecting agreements to determine whether any inventory is pledged as collateral or subject to any liens would provide the accountant with evidence concerning the assertions about rights and obligations which deal with whether assets are the rights of the entity and liabilities are the obligations of the entity at a given date.

79A. (a) The account scrutinized in this question is inventory (not loans payable). The valuation, existence, and completeness of the inventory are not in question. The inventory is collateral for the loan; disclosure is the issue.

80. (b) AU 326.05 states that completeness deals with whether all transactions and accounts that should be presented in the financial statements are so included. For example, management asserts that all purchases of goods and services are recorded and included in the financial statements. By tracing from the inventory floor to the records, the auditor is checking for completeness. Answer (a) would deal with the rights to the inventory which would be evidenced by vendor invoices. Answer (c) would be tested by vouching or going from the inventory list to the floor to identify the assets are in existence. Answer (d) deals with extending the counts at the proper amount in the financial statements which would be tested by multiplying the inventory count of an item by its cost based on a vendor's invoice.

80A. (c) To gain assurance that all items in a client's inventory listing schedule are valid, an auditor most likely would trace items listed in the listing schedule to inventory tags and the auditor's recorded count sheets. To trace the inventory tags to the listing schedule and to trace items listed in receiving reports and vendors' invoices to the listing schedule would provide assurance that all the inventory items are on the schedule, but would not give assurance that all of the items on the schedule are valid; some items on the schedule may not exist. Tracing tags to receiving reports and vendors' invoices does not involve the inventory listing schedule and thus does not provide any assurances related to the listing schedule.

Audit of Fixed Assets

81. (a) To obtain evidence about fixed asset additions, the auditor would most likely inspect related documents and physically examine the assets. The other procedures might be considered by the auditor, but they would not provide direct evidence that the fixed asset additions actually exist.

81A. (b) AU 326.04 states that assertions about existence deal with whether assets exist at a given date. Answer (a) deals with whether all items in the plant and equipment inventory are included in the financial statements and would be tested by examining all plant and equipment items at the balance sheet date. Answer (c) deals with reporting the amounts in the financial statements. Answer (d) deals with whether the assets and related accounts such as depreciation have been included in the financial statements at appropriate amounts.

82. (d) The repairs and maintenance expense accounts are analyzed by an auditor in obtaining evidence regarding the completeness of fixed assets, since there is the possibility that items were expensed that should have been capitalized. Therefore, answer (d) is correct.

83. (a) In the search for unrecorded retirements of fixed assets, an auditor most likely would inspect the property ledger and the insurance and tax records before touring the client's facilities. If an asset on the ledger has been retired and the auditor is looking for it on the tour, the retirement will most likely be discovered. If the tour is taken before inspecting the ledger and other records, generally only the assets still in use will be reviewed and retired assets would not as likely be discovered, especially if they physically were not still in the facilities. Analyzing the repair and maintenance account would be useful in considering if any items should be classified as capital expenditures but would not likely be useful in searching for unrecorded retirements of assets.

84. (a) Since recording depreciation is necessary for the financial statements to conform with GAAP, after valuation and allocation, the secondary purpose of determining that the proper amount of depreciation was expensed is presentation and disclosure.

Audit of Long-Term Investments

85. (b) In accordance with AU 332.04, an auditor confirms with an outside agent that the agent is holding investment securities in the client's name on deposit, pledged, or in safekeeping to support

assertions pertaining to the existence, ownership and cost (not valuation). Ownership assertions include rights and obligations. The auditor would check valuation with a listing of market values, as not all agents undertake to value the securities that they hold. Completeness would not be confirmed, as an entity might have more than one agent or have some securities in transit. Presentation and disclosure would depend, in part, on the nature of the securities, not that they are being held.

86. (c) The auditor would most likely verify the interest earned on bonds by recomputing the interest earned on the basis of the face amount, interest rate, and period held. After determining the interest earned by recomputing, the auditor would vouch the receipt and deposit of interest checks. Confirming the bond interest rate with the issuer would not be necessary. Testing the internal controls over cash receipts would not verify the interest earned on bonds.

86A. (a) The auditor would most likely analyze on the same working paper pairs of accounts that are directly related to each other, such as notes receivable and interest income. Answers (b), (c), and (d) do not have accounts in common and would not likely be analyzed on the same working paper.

86B. (a) Analytical tests as a source of information for developing expectations include analysis of the relationships among elements of financial information within the period. Answers (b), (c), and (d) represent management's assertions of disclosure, valuation and existence which would be verified by substantive tests applied to the respective accounts.

87. (b) AU 332.04 states, "Evidential matter pertaining to the existence, ownership, and cost of long-term investments includes accounting records and documents of the investor relating to their acquisition. In the case of investments in the form of securities (such as stocks, bonds, and notes), this evidential matter should be corroborated by inspection of the securities, or, in appropriate circumstances, by written confirmation from an independent custodian of securities on deposit, pledged, or in safekeeping." The auditor should examine sufficient evidential matter supporting the existence and ownership of a long-term investment (AU 332.02). Determining the market price of the shares at the balance sheet date establishes the carrying amount of the securities, not their existence or ownership. Answer (d) is also incorrect. Confirming the number of shares owned with the issuing company is not a generally accepted auditing procedure.

87A. (c) AU 332.04 states, "Evidential matter pertaining to the existence, ownership, and cost of long-term investments includes accounting records and documents of the investor relating to their acquisitions." In the case of investments in the form of securities (such as stocks, bonds, and notes), this evidential matter should be corroborated by inspection of the securities, or by written confirmation from an independent custodian of securities on deposit, pledged, or in safekeeping. Shares owned and signed over to new owners or purchased from other investors would not always be made known to the issuing company on a timely basis. Inspecting the financial statements of the investee company would not indicate the number of shares owned and who the owners are. Per SFAS 115, investment securities are to be reported at market value, not the lower of cost or market.

88. (b) Audit evidence obtained from independent sources outside the entity is generally more persuasive than evidence obtained by examining the entity's records. Thus, the *strongest* evidence supporting dividends earned on marketable equity securities is provided by published dividend records such as might appear in financial publications.

Audit of Accounts Payable, Purchases, and Other Liabilities

89. (c) In order to verify the existence and valuation of the accounts payable account, the auditor should go to the source documents. These would include purchase orders and receiving reports. Answer (a) pertains to the completeness assertion and whether or not management has included all obligations in the account. Answer (b) is not a standard auditing procedure but deals with determining whether management has included all obligations for the rights and obligations assertions in the account. Answer (d) also pertains to determining whether or not there are any unrecorded obligations of the company not recorded in the account.

89A. (b) To verify that all merchandise received is recorded, the auditor would trace from the receiving reports to the related records. Payment vouchers, purchase requisitions, and vendor's invoices would not provide evidence that the related merchandise was actually received.

89B. (c) AU 326.05 states that assertions about completeness deal with whether all transactions and accounts that should be presented in the financial statements are so included. Because liabilities have the inherent risk of being understated, substantive tests and tests of controls are directed towards determining that all liabilities of the company as of the balance sheet date are properly included.

89C. (c) AU 326.05 states, "Assertions about completeness deal with whether all transactions and accounts that should be presented in the financial statements are so included. For example, management asserts that all purchases of goods and services are recorded and are included in the financial statements." AU 326.10 states, "There is not necessarily a one-to-one relationship between audit objectives and procedures. Some auditing procedures may relate to more than one objective." The primary focus of cutoff tests is completeness.

90. (d) AU 326.05 states, "Assertions about completeness deal with whether all transactions and accounts that should be presented in the financial statements are so included." One step in assuring this would be the periodic reconciliation of prenumbered purchase orders, receiving reports, and vouchers.

90A. (c) Incompatible functions are those that place any person in a position to both perpetrate and conceal errors or irregularities in the normal course of his or her duties. Therefore, a well-designed plan of organization separates the duties of authorization, record keeping, and custody of assets. The treasurer would generally perform the other procedures indicated in answers (a), (b), and (d).

91. (c) To verify that all merchandise received is recorded, the auditor would trace from the receiving reports to the related records. Vendor's invoices, purchase orders, and canceled checks would not provide evidence that the related merchandise was actually received.

92. (b) The objective of the auditor's test is to determine whether all merchandise for which the client was billed was received. The population for this test consists of all vendor's invoices (bills for merchandise). The auditor would select a sample of vendor's invoices and then trace them to supporting receiving reports to assure that the merchandise for which the client was billed was received.

93. (c) To discover unrecorded liabilities as of the balance sheet date, the auditor usually examines cash disbursements made in the subsequent period. This procedure would not be performed at an earlier time. The other answers are procedures that are frequently performed before the balance sheet date.

93A. (d) Per AU 560.12, the "auditor should perform other auditing procedures with respect to the period after the balance-sheet date for the purpose of ascertaining the occurrence of subsequent events that may require adjustment or disclosure..." including [AU 560.12 (b)(ii)] investigating changes in long-term debt after year end. Other auditing procedures are applied to transactions occurring after the balance-sheet date (AU 560.11) for the purpose of assurance that proper cutoffs have been made, and for the purpose of obtaining information to aid in the evaluation of the assets and liabilities as of the balance-sheet date. Answer (a) is a test of internal control.

94. (b) The least effective procedure for detecting contingent liabilities would be examining customer confirmation replies which would normally provide information on accounts receivable. Bank confirmations and the minutes of board meetings could provide information about contingent liabilities. Invoices for professional services would show lawyer's expenses which may provide information as to possible contingent liabilities.

Audit of Payroll

95. (c) Analytical procedures performed in the planning stages of an audit assist the auditor in determining the nature, extent, and timing of other substantive tests that may be necessary in performing the audit of various account balances. Answers (a) and (d) are examples of possible outcomes from performing substantive procedures. A reduction in the assessed level of control risk generally indicates that the auditor may reduce the extent of substantive tests performed in the audit.

95A. (d) Substantive tests of payroll balances when control risk is assessed as low most likely would be limited to applying analytical procedures and recalculating payroll accruals to assure the accuracy of the payroll liabilities. Observing the distribution of paychecks, recomputing the payroll register and inspecting payroll tax returns would be of greater importance if control risk related to payroll was assessed as high. In such case, these procedures would be required to assure the accuracy, and other assertions, related to payroll accounts.

96. (d) AU 326.04 states, "Assertions about existence or occurrence deal with whether assets or liabilities of the entity exist at a given date and whether *recorded transactions* have occurred during a given period." In this case, the auditor would consider the recorded transactions in the payroll register. Answers (a), (b), and (c) would not provide evidence

as to what payroll transactions were actually recorded. The clock card or time ticket would provide evidence for the completeness assertion, not the existence assertion.

97. (b) To test for the appropriate number of hours worked, the auditor examines clock card data. To test for answer (a), the auditor checks personnel records. To test for answers (c) and (d), the auditor uses inquiries and observation.

Audit of Long-Term Liabilities

98. (a) An auditor's program to examine long-term debt should include steps that require examining supporting documentation for all debt (and debt equivalents) and related interest expense (for example, note and loan agreements, bond indentures, lease agreements, correspondence from legal counsel, etc.).

99. (b) An auditor's program to examine long-term debt should include a step where the auditor reconciles interest expense with debt outstanding during the year (period). This step would provide information as to the completeness and valuation of the account balance. The auditor is not concerned with the year-end market value of the debt. The auditor would not verify the existence of the holders of the debt by direct confirmation. Outstanding balances, terms, and conditions are confirmed with the credit grantor or independent trustee. The search for unrecorded liabilities would generally be made by scanning cash disbursements made in the period following the balance sheet date. Also, the accounts payable subsidiary ledger would not likely provide evidence as to long-term liabilities.

100. (c) One of the audit objectives of long-term liabilities is to verify that interest expense is correctly computed and that other contractual obligations are satisfied. Therefore, the auditor would most likely compare interest expense with the bond payable to see if it is reasonable, and thereby test valuation. This procedure could also aid in the discovery of undisclosed liabilities.

Audit of Stockholders' Equity

101. (d) AU 326.08 states, "Assertions about presentation and disclosure deal with whether particular components of the financial statements are properly classified, described, and disclosed." AAM 5400.150 specifically lists as one of the substantive test procedures relating to the presentation and disclosure of retained earnings the following, "Determine the amount of restrictions, if any, on retained earnings at end of period which result from loans, other agreements, or state law."

102. (d) One of the auditor's objectives in his examination of owners' equity is to determine that all transactions during the year affecting owners' equity accounts were properly authorized and recorded. In the case of a corporation, changes in capital stock accounts should receive formal advance approval by the *board of directors*. The substantive tests for verifying an entry in a Capital Stock account, therefore, should include tracing the entry to an authorization in the minutes of the directors' meetings. Answers (a), (b), and (c) are incorrect because the auditor should not trace an entry to the Capital Stock account to these documents for an authorization of the transaction.

103. (d) One of the primary objectives in testing related to Stockholder's Equity and Capital accounts is to verify that capital transactions are appropriately authorized and approved. The granting of stock options would require board of director approval because it could affect the number of shares outstanding.

104. (d) The primary responsibility of a registrar of capital stock is to verify that securities are properly issued, recorded, and transferred.

Audit of Accounting Estimates

105. (a) Amortization allocates the cost of the intangible to the periods in which the benefit is received and yields an appropriate valuation of the intangible in those periods. Amortization is not relevant to the existence or occurrence, completeness, or rights and obligations assertions.

106. (d) Regarding management's accounting estimates, AU 342.10 (SAS 57) states, "In evaluating reasonableness, the auditor should obtain an understanding of how management developed the estimate." Based on that understanding, the auditor should use at least one of several approaches which include review and test the process used by management to develop the estimate, and develop an independent expectation of the estimate. In reviewing and testing management's process, an auditor would consider the appropriateness of the key factors or assumptions used in preparing the estimates (AU 342.11).

General

107. (d) A reconciliation between the amounts included in the cash flow statement and other financial

statements would be a procedure the auditor would perform because the cash flow statement amounts are a result of the transactions reflected in and the changes in balances on the other financial statements. Relationships between current year and prior year amounts due do not necessarily exist as can be expected on the balance sheet and income statement. This procedure would provide more audit evidence in the overall review stage of the audit for the balance sheet and income statement. Answer (b) is an audit procedure an auditor would perform in auditing the cash balance on the balance sheet. Answer (c) is a procedure the auditor would perform in auditing the cash balance for the balance sheet presentation.

108. (c) To determine whether transactions have been recorded (completeness), audit procedures include tracing from supporting documentation to accounting records. Testing from the general ledger balances, the adjusted trial balance, and general journal entries (vouching) would all provide evidence of existence (occurrence).

PERFORMANCE BY SUBTOPICS

Each category below parallels a subtopic covered in Chapter 37. Record the number and percentage of questions you correctly answered in each subtopic area.

Evidential Matter (AU 326)

Question #	Correct √
1	
1A	
2	
3	
4	
5	
5A	
6	
7	
8	
9	
10	
10A	
11	
12	
13	
14	
14A	
14B	
# Questions	19

\# Correct ______
% Correct ______

The Auditor's Consideration of the Internal Audit Function in an Audit of Financial Statements (AU 322)

Question #	Correct √
15	
15A	
16	
16A	
17	
17A	
18	
19	
# Questions	8

\# Correct ______
% Correct ______

Client Representations (AU 333)

Question #	Correct √
20	
21	
22	
23	
24	
25	
26	
27	
28	
29	
# Questions	10

\# Correct ______
% Correct ______

Analytical Procedures (AU 329)

Question #	Correct √
30	
31	
31A	
32	
33	
33A	
34	
34A	
34B	
35	
35A	
36	
37	
38	
39	
40	
# Questions	16

\# Correct ______
% Correct ______

Using the Work of a Specialist (AU 336)

Question #	Correct √
41	
42	
42A	
42B	
43	
43A	
# Questions	6

\# Correct ______
% Correct ______

Inquiry of a Client's Lawyer Concerning Litigation, Claims, and Assessments (AU 337)

Question #	Correct √
44	
44A	
45	
46	
46A	
47	
47A	
48	
# Questions	8

\# Correct ______
% Correct ______

Working Papers (AU 339)

Question #	Correct √
49	
49A	
50	
50A	
51	
51A	
52	
53	
54	
54A	
54B	
55	
55A	
# Questions	13

\# Correct ______
% Correct ______

Related Parties (AU 334)

Question #	Correct √
56	
57	
57A	
57B	
58	
59	
60	
61	
61A	
# Questions	9

\# Correct ______
% Correct ______

Audit of Cash

Question #	Correct √
62	
63	
64	
65	
66	
67	

Questions 6

Correct ________
% Correct ________

Audit of Accounts Receivable and Sales

Question #	Correct √
68	
68A	
69	
69A	
70	
70A	
70B	
71	
71A	
72	
73	
73A	
74	

Questions 13

Correct ________
% Correct ________

Audit of Inventory

Question #	Correct √
75	
75A	
76	
77	
77A	
78	
79	
79A	
80	
80A	

Questions 10

Correct ________
% Correct ________

Audit of Fixed Assets

Question #	Correct √
81	
81A	
82	
83	
84	

Questions 5

Correct ________
% Correct ________

Audit of Long-Term Investments

Question #	Correct √
85	
86	
86A	
86B	
87	
87A	
88	

Questions 7

Correct ________
% Correct ________

Audit of Accounts Payable, Purchases, and Other Liabilities

Question #	Correct √
89	
89A	
89B	
89C	
90	
90A	
91	
92	
93	
93A	
94	

Questions 11

Correct ________
% Correct ________

Audit of Payroll

Question #	Correct √
95	
95A	
96	
97	

Questions 4

Correct ________
% Correct ________

Audit of Long-Term Liabilities

Question #	Correct √
98	
99	
100	

Questions 3

Correct ________
% Correct ________

Audit of Stockholders' Equity

Question #	Correct √
101	
102	
103	
104	

Questions 4

Correct ________
% Correct ________

Audit of Accounting Estimates

Question #	Correct √
105	
106	

Questions 2

Correct ________
% Correct ________

General

Question #	Correct √
107	
108	

Questions 2

Correct ________
% Correct ________

OTHER OBJECTIVE FORMAT QUESTION

Problem 37-2 (15 to 25 minutes)

To support financial statement assertions, an auditor develops specific audit objectives. The auditor then designs substantive tests to satisfy or accomplish each objective.

Required:

Items 1 through 10 represent audit objectives for the investments, accounts receivable, and property and equipment accounts. To the right of each set of audit objectives is a listing of possible audit procedures for that account. For each audit objective, select the audit procedure that would primarily respond to the objective. Select only one procedure for each audit objective. A procedure may be selected only once or not at all.

Items to be answered:

Audit Objectives for Investments

1. Investments are properly described and classified in the financial statements.

2. Recorded investments represent investments actually owned at the balance sheet date.

3. Investments are properly valued at the lower of cost or market at the balance sheet date.

Audit Procedures for Investments

A. Trace opening balances in the subsidiary ledger to prior year's audit working papers.

B. Determine that employees who are authorized to sell investments do not have access to cash.

C. Examine supporting documents for a sample of investment transactions to verify that prenumbered documents are used.

D. Determine that any impairments in the price of investments have been properly recorded.

E. Verify that transfers from the current to the noncurrent investment portfolio have been properly recorded.

F. Obtain positive confirmations as of the balance sheet date of investments held by independent custodians.

G. Trace investment transactions to minutes of the Board of Directors' meetings to determine that transactions were properly authorized.

Audit Objectives for Accounts Receivable

4. Accounts receivable represent all amounts owed to the entity at the balance sheet date.

5. The entity has legal right to all accounts receivable at the balance sheet date.

6. Accounts receivable are stated at net realizable value.

7. Accounts receivable are properly described and presented in the financial statements.

Audit Procedures for Accounts Receivable

A. Analyze the relationship of accounts receivable and sales and compare it with relationships for preceding periods.

B. Perform sales cut-off tests to obtain assurance that sales transactions and corresponding entries for inventories and cost of goods sold are recorded in the same and proper period.

C. Review the aged trial balance for significant past due accounts.

D. Obtain an understanding of the business purpose of transactions that resulted in accounts receivable balances.

E. Review loan agreements for indications of whether accounts receivable have been factored or pledged.

F. Review the accounts receivable trial balance for amounts due from officers and employees.

G. Analyze unusual relationships between monthly accounts receivable balances and monthly accounts payable balances.

Audit Objectives for Property & Equipment

8. The entity has legal right to property and equipment acquired during the year.

9. Recorded property and equipment represent assets that actually exist at the balance sheet date.

10. Net property and equipment are properly valued at the balance sheet date.

Audit Procedures for Property & Equipment

A. Trace opening balances in the summary schedules to the prior year's audit working papers.

B. Review the provision for depreciation expense and determine that depreciable lives and methods used in the current year are consistent with those used in the prior year.

C. Determine that the responsibility for maintaining the property and equipment records is segregated from the responsibility for custody of property and equipment.

D. Examine deeds and title insurance certificates.

E. Perform cut-off tests to verify that property and equipment additions are recorded in the proper period.

F. Determine that property and equipment is adequately insured.

G. Physically examine all major property and equipment additions. (11/92, Aud., #2)

OTHER OBJECTIVE FORMAT SOLUTION

Solution 37-2 Audit Procedures--Investments, Accounts Receivable, and Property and Equipment

1. (E) Of the choices given, the best audit procedure to ensure that investments are properly described and classified in the financial statements is to verify that transfers from the current to the noncurrent investment portfolio have been properly recorded.

2. (F) Of the choices given, the best audit procedure to ensure that recorded investments represent investments actually owned at the balance sheet date is to obtain positive confirmations as of the balance sheet date of investments held by independent custodians.

3. (D) Of the choices given, the best audit procedure to ensure that investments are properly valued at the lower of cost or market at the balance sheet date is to determine that any impairments in the price of investments have been properly recorded.

4. (B) Of the choices given, the best audit procedure to ensure that accounts receivable represent all amounts owed to the entity at the balance sheet date is to perform sales cut-off tests to obtain assurance that sales transactions and corresponding entries for inventories and costs of goods sold are recorded in the same and proper period.

5. (E) Of the choices given, the best audit procedure to ensure that the entity has legal right to all accounts receivable at the balance sheet date is to review loan agreements for indications of whether accounts receivable have been factored or pledged.

6. (C) Of the choices given, the best audit procedure to ensure that accounts receivable are

stated at net realizable value is to review the aged trial balance for significant past due accounts.

7. (F) Of the choices given, the best audit procedure to ensure that accounts receivable are properly described and presented in the financial statements is to review the accounts receivable trial balance for amounts due from officers and employees.

8. (D) Of the choices given, the best audit procedure to ensure that the entity has legal right to property and equipment acquired during the year is to examine deeds and title insurance certificates.

9. (G) Of the choices given, the best audit procedure to ensure that recorded property and equipment represent assets that actually exist at the balance sheet date is to physically examine all major property and equipment additions.

10. (B) Of the choices given, the best audit procedure to ensure that net property and equipment are properly valued at the balance sheet date is to review the provision for depreciation expense and determine that depreciable lives and methods used in the current year are consistent with those used in the prior year.

ESSAY QUESTIONS

Essay 37-3 (15 to 25 minutes)

Hart, an assistant accountant with the firm of Better & Best, CPAs, is auditing the financial statements of Tech Consolidated Industries, Inc. The firm's audit program calls for the preparation of a written management representation letter.

Required:

a. 1. In an audit of financial statements, in what circumstances is the auditor required to obtain a management representation letter?

2. What are the purposes of obtaining the letter?

b. 1. To whom should the representation letter be addressed and as of what date should it be dated?

2. Who should sign the letter and what would be the effect of their refusal to sign the letter?

c. In what respects may an auditor's other responsibilities be relieved by obtaining a management representation letter? (11/93, Aud., #4)

Essay 37-4 (15 to 25 minutes)

Cole & Cole, CPAs, are auditing the financial statements of Consolidated Industries Co. for the year ended December 31, 1992. On April 2, 1993, an inquiry letter to J. J. Young, Consolidated's outside attorney, was drafted to corroborate the information furnished to Cole by management concerning pending and threatened litigation, claims, and assessments, and unasserted claims and assessments. On May 6, 1993, C. R. Brown, Consolidated's Chief Financial Officer, gave Cole a draft of the inquiry letter below for Cole's review before mailing it to Young.

Required:

Describe the omissions, ambiguities, and inappropriate statements and terminology in Brown's letter below.

May 6, 1993

J. J. Young, Attorney at Law
123 Main Street
Anytown, USA

Dear J. J. Young:

In connection with an audit of our financial statements at December 31, 1992, and for the year then ended, management of the Company has prepared, and furnished to our auditors, Cole & Cole, CPAs, 456 Broadway, Anytown, USA, a description and evaluation of certain contingencies, including those set forth below involving matters with respect to which you have been engaged and to which you have devoted substantive attention on behalf of the Company in the form of legal consultation or representation. Your response should include matters that existed at December 31, 1992. Because of the confidentiality of all these matters, your response may be limited.

In November 1992, an action was brought against the Company by an outside salesman alleging breach of contract for sales commissions and pleading a second cause of action for an accounting with respect to claims for fees and commissions. The causes of action claim damages of $300,000, but the

Company believes it has meritorious defenses to the claims. The possible exposure of the Company to a successful judgment on behalf of the plaintiff is slight. In July 1988, an action was brought against the Company by Industrial Manufacturing Co. (Industrial) alleging patent infringement and seeking damages of $20,000,000. The action in U. S. District Court resulted in a decision on October 16, 1992, holding that the Company infringed seven Industrial patents and awarded damages of $14,000,000. The Company vigorously denies these allegations and has filed an appeal with the U. S. Court of Appeals for the Federal Circuit. The appeal process is expected to take approximately two years, but there is some chance that Industrial may ultimately prevail.

Please furnish to our auditors such explanation, if any, that you consider necessary to supplement the foregoing information, including an explanation of those matters as to which your views may differ from those stated and an identification of the omission of any pending or threatened litigation, claims, and assessments or a statement that the list of such matters is complete. Your response may be quoted or referred to in the financial statements without further correspondence with you.

You also consulted on various other matters considered pending or threatened litigation. However, you may not comment on these matters because publicizing them may alert potential plaintiffs to the strengths of their cases. In addition, various other matters probable of assertion that have some chance of an unfavorable outcome, as of December 31, 1992, are unasserted claims and assessments.

C. R. Brown
Chief Financial Officer (5/93, Aud., #5)

Essay 37-5 (15 to 25 minutes)

Larkin, CPA, has been engaged to audit the financial statements of Vernon Distributors, Inc., a continuing audit client, for the year ended September 30, 1991. After obtaining an understanding of Vernon's internal control structure, Larkin assessed control risk at the maximum level for all financial statement assertions concerning investments. Larkin determined that Vernon is unable to exercise significant influence over any investee and none are related parties.

Larkin obtained from Vernon detailed analyses of its investments in domestic securities showing:

- The classification between current and noncurrent portfolios;
- A description of each security, including the interest rate and maturity date of bonds and par value and dividend rate on stocks;
- A notation of the location of each security, either in the Treasurer's safe or held by an independent custodian;
- The number of shares of stock or face amount of bonds held at the beginning and end of the year;
- The beginning and ending balances at cost and at market, and the unamortized premium or discount on bonds;
- Additions to and sales from the portfolios for the year, including date, number of shares, face amount of bonds, cost, proceeds, and realized gain or loss;
- Valuation allowances at the beginning and end of the year and changes therein;
- Accrued investment income for each investment at the beginning and end of the year, and income earned and collected during the year.

Larkin then prepared the following partial audit program of substantive auditing procedures:

1. Foot and crossfoot the analyses.
2. Trace the ending totals to the general ledger and financial statements.
3. Trace the beginning balances to the prior year's working papers.
4. Obtain positive confirmation as of the balance sheet date of the investments held by any independent custodian.
5. Determine that income from investments has been properly recorded as accrued or collected by reference to published sources, by computation, and by tracing to recorded amounts.
6. For investments in nonpublic entities, compare carrying value to information in the most recently available audited financial statements.
7. Determine that all transfers between the current and noncurrent portfolios have been properly authorized and recorded.
8. Determine that any other-than-temporary decline in the price of an investment has been properly recorded.

Required:

a. Identify the primary financial statement assertion relative to investments that would be addressed by each of the procedures #4 through #8 and describe the primary audit objective of performing those procedures. Use the format illustrated below.

Primary Assertion	Objective

b. Describe three additional substantive auditing procedures Larkin should consider in auditing Vernon's investments. (11/91, Aud., #4)

Essay 37-6 (15 to 25 minutes)

Taylor, CPA, has been engaged to audit the financial statements of Palmer Co., a continuing audit client. Taylor is about to perform substantive audit procedures on Palmer's goodwill (excess of cost over the fair value of net assets purchased) that was acquired in prior years' business combinations. An industry slowdown has occurred recently and purchased operations have not met profit expectation.

During the planning process, Taylor determined that there is a high risk that material misstatements in the assertions related to goodwill could occur. Taylor obtained an understanding of the internal control structure and assessed control risk at the maximum level for the assertions related to goodwill.

Required:

a. Describe the substantive audit procedures Taylor should consider performing in auditing Palmer's goodwill. Do **not** discuss Palmer's internal control structure.

b. Describe the two significant assertions that Taylor would be most concerned with relative to Palmer's goodwill. Do **not** describe more than two. (5/91, Aud., #3)

Essay 37-7 (15 to 25 minutes)

Kane, CPA, is auditing Star Wholesaling Company's financial statements and is about to perform substantive audit procedures on Star's trade accounts payable balances. After obtaining an understanding of Star's internal control structure for accounts payable, Kane assessed control risk at near the maximum. Kane requested and received from Star a schedule of the trade accounts payable prepared using the trade accounts payable subsidiary ledger (voucher register).

Required:

Describe the substantive audit procedures Kane should apply to Star's trade accounts payable balances. Do **not** include procedures that would be applied only in the audit of related party payables, amounts withheld from employees, and accrued expenses such as pension cost and interest. (11/90, Aud., #4)

Essay 37-8 (15 to 25 minutes)

Bell, CPA, was engaged to audit the financial statements of Kent Company, a continuing audit client. Bell is about to audit Kent's Payroll transactions. Kent uses an in-house payroll department to compute payroll data, and prepare and distribute payroll checks.

During the planning process, Bell determined that the inherent risk of overstatement of payroll expense is high. In addition, Bell obtained an understanding of the internal control structure and assessed control risk at the maximum level for payroll-related assertions.

Required:

Describe the audit procedures Bell should consider performing in the audit of Kent's payroll transactions to address the risk of overstatement. Do **not** discuss Kent's internal control structure. (11/89, Aud., #2)

Essay 37-9 (15 to 25 minutes)

Edwards, CPA, is engaged to audit the financial statements of Matthews Wholesaling for the year ended December 31, 1988. Edwards obtained and documented an understanding of the internal control structure relating to the accounts receivable and assessed control risk relating to accounts receivable at the maximum level. Edwards requested and obtained from Matthews an aged accounts receivable schedule listing the total amount owed by each customer as of December 31, 1988, and sent positive confirmation requests to a sample of the customers.

Required:

What additional substantive audit procedures should Edwards consider applying in auditing the accounts receivable? (5/89, Aud., #4)

Essay 37-10 (15 to 25 minutes)

Temple, CPA, is auditing the financial statements of Ford Lumber Yards, Inc. a privately held corporation with 300 employees and five stockholders, three of whom are active in management. Ford has been in business for many years, but has never had its financial statements audited. Temple suspects that the substance of some of Ford's business transactions differ from their form because of the pervasiveness of related party relationships and transactions in the local building supplies industry.

Required:

Describe the audit procedures Temple should apply to identify related party relationships and transactions. (11/88, Aud., #2)

Essay 37-11 (15 to 25 minutes)

MLG Company's auditor received directly from the banks, confirmations and cutoff statements with related checks and deposit tickets for MLG's three general-purpose bank accounts. The auditor determined that internal control over cash was satisfactory and control risk could be assessed at below the maximum level. The proper cutoff of external cash receipts and disbursements was established. No bank accounts were opened or closed during the year.

Required:

Prepare the audit program of substantive procedures to verify MLG's bank balances. Ignore any other cash accounts. (11/87, Aud., #3)

Essay 37-12 (15 to 25 minutes)

Jones, CPA, the continuing auditor of Sussex, Inc., is beginning the audit of the common stock and treasury stock accounts. Jones has decided to assess control risk at the maximum level.

Sussex has no par, has no stated value common stock, and acts as its own registrar and transfer agent. During the past year Sussex both issued and reacquired shares of its own common stock, some of which the company still owned at year-end. Additional common stock transactions occurred among the shareholders during the year.

Common stock transactions can be traced to individual shareholders' accounts in a subsidiary ledger and to a stock certificate book. The company has not paid any cash or stock dividends. There are no other classes of stock, stock rights, warrants, or option plans.

Required:

What substantive audit procedures should Jones apply in examining the common stock and treasury stock accounts? (5/86, Aud., #2)

Essay 37-13 (15 to 25 minutes)

Pierce, an independent auditor, was engaged to audit the financial statements of Mayfair Construction Incorporated for the year ended December 31, 1983. Mayfair's financial statements reflect a substantial amount of mobile construction equipment used in the firm's operations. The equipment is accounted for in a subsidiary ledger. Pierce considered the internal control structure and assessed control risk at below the maximum level.

Required:

Identify the substantive audit procedures which Pierce should utilize in examining mobile construction equipment and related depreciation in Mayfair's financial statements. (11/84, Aud., #2)

Essay 37-14 (15 to 25 minutes)

Green, CPA, is considering audit risk at the financial statement level in planning the audit of National Federal Bank (NFB) Company's financial statements for the year ended December 31, 1990. Audit risk at the financial statement level is influenced by the risk of material misstatements, which may be indicated by a combination of factors related to management, the industry, and the entity. In assessing such factors, Green has gathered the following information concerning NFB's environment.

<u>Company profile</u>:

NFB is a federally insured bank that has been consistently more profitable than the industry average by marketing mortgages on properties in a prosperous rural area, which has experienced considerable growth in recent years. NFB packages its mortgages and sells them to large mortgage investment trusts. Despite recent volatility of interest rates, NFB has been able to continue selling its mortgages as a source of new lendable funds.

NFB's board of directors is controlled by Smith, the majority stockholder, who also acts as the chief executive officer. Management at the bank's branch offices has authority for directing and controlling

NFB's operations and is compensated based on branch profitability. The internal auditor reports directly to Harris, a minority shareholder, who also acts as chairman of the board's audit committee. The accounting department has experienced little turnover in personnel during the five years Green has audited NFB. NFB's formula consistently underestimates the allowance for loan losses, but its controller has always been receptive to Green's suggestions to increase the allowance during each engagement.

Recent developments:

During 1990, NFB opened a branch office in a suburban town thirty miles from its principal place of business. Although this branch is not yet profitable due to competition from several well-established regional banks, management believes that the branch will be profitable by 1992.

Also, during 1990, NFB increased the efficiency of its accounting operations by installing a new, sophisticated computer system.

Required:

Based only on the information above, describe the factors that most likely would have an effect on the risk of material misstatements. Indicate whether each factor increases or decreases the risk. Use the format illustrated below.

Environmental factor	Effect on risk of material misstatements
Branch management has authority for directing and controlling operations	Increase

(5/91, Aud., #5)

Essay 37-15 (15 to 25 minutes)

Kent, CPA, is engaged in the audit of Davidson Corp.'s financial statements for the year ended December 31, 1989. Kent is about to commence auditing Davidson's employee pension expense, but Kent's preliminary inquiries concerning Davidson's defined benefit pension plan lead Kent to believe that some of the actuarial computations and assumptions are so complex that they are beyond the competence ordinarily required of an auditor. Kent is considering engaging Park, an actuary, to assist with this portion of the audit.

Required:

a. What are the factors Kent should consider in the process of selecting Park?

b. What are the matters that should be understood among Kent, Park, and Davidson's management as to the nature of the work to be performed by Park?

c. May Kent refer to Park in the auditor's report if Kent decides to issue an unqualified opinion? Why?

d. May Kent refer to Park in the auditor's report if Kent decides to issue other than an unqualified opinion as a result of Park's findings? Why?

(5/90, Aud., #5)

Essay 37-16 (15 to 25 minutes)

Analytical procedures consist of evaluations of financial information made by a study of plausible relationships among both financial and nonfinancial data. They range from simple comparisons to the use of complex models involving many relationships and elements of data. They involve comparisons of recorded amounts, or ratios developed from recorded amounts, to expectations developed by the auditors.

Required:

a. Describe the broad purposes of analytical procedures.

b. Identify the sources of information from which an auditor develops expectations.

c. Describe the factors that influence an auditor's consideration of the reliability of data for purposes of achieving audit objectives. (11/89, Aud., #3)

Essay 37-17 (15 to 25 minutes)

The purpose of all auditing procedures is to gather sufficient competent evidence for an auditor to form an opinion regarding the financial statements taken as a whole.

Required:

a. In addition to the example below, identify and describe five means or techniques of gathering audit evidence used to evaluate a client's inventory balance.

Technique	Description
Observation	An auditor watches the performance of some function, such as a client's annual inventory count.

b. Identify the five general assertions regarding a client's inventory balance and describe one **different** substantive auditing procedure for each assertion. Use the format illustrated below.

Assertion	Substantive Auditing Procedure

(11/88, Aud., #5)

Essay 37-18 (15 to 25 minutes)

Young, CPA, is considering the procedures to be applied concerning a client's loss contingencies relating to litigation, claims, and assessments.

Required:

What substantive audit procedures should Young apply when testing for loss contingencies relating to litigation, claims, and assessments? (5/88, Aud., #3)

Essay 37-19 (15 to 25 minutes)

The CPA firm of Wright & Co. is in the process of auditing William Corporation's 1984 financial statements. The following open matters must be resolved before the audit can be completed:

(1) No audit work has been performed on nonresponses to customer accounts receivable confirmation requests. Both positive and negative confirmations were used. A second request was sent to debtors who did not respond to the initial positive request.

(2) The client representation letter has not been completed and signed by William's management. Wright has started to outline the content of the representation letter and believes the following matters should be included in the letter:

Management should acknowledge whether or not

- All material transactions have been properly reflected in the financial statements.
- It is aware of irregularities that could have a material effect on the financial statements or that involve management employees.
- Events have occurred subsequent to the balance sheet date that would require adjustment to, or disclosure in, the financial statements.
- There are any communications from regulatory agencies concerning noncompliance with, or deficiencies in, financial reporting practices.
- The company has complied with all aspects of contractual agreements that would have a material effect on the financial statements in the event of noncompliance.
- There are any plans or intentions that may materially affect the carrying value or classification of assets or liabilities.
- There are any losses from sales commitments.
- There are any losses from purchase commitments for inventory quantities in excess of requirements or at prices in excess of market.
- There are any agreements to repurchase assets previously sold.
- There are any violations or possible violations of laws or regulations whose effects should be considered for disclosure in the financial statements or as a basis for recording a loss contingency.
- There are any capital stock repurchase options or agreements or capital stock reserved for options, warrants, conversions, or other requirements.

Required:

a. What alternative audit procedures should Wright consider performing on the nonresponses to customer accounts receivable confirmation requests?

b. Identify the other matters that Wright would expect to be included in William's management representation letter. (11/85, Aud., #4)

Essay 37-20 (25 to 35 minutes)

King, CPA, is auditing the financial statements of Cycle Co., an entity that has receivables from customers, which have arisen from the sale of goods in the normal course of business. King is aware that the confirmation of accounts receivable is generally accepted auditing procedure.

Required:

a. Under what circumstances could King justify omitting the confirmation of Cycle's accounts receivable?

b. In designing confirmation requests, what factors are likely to affect King's assessment of the reliability of confirmations that King sends?

c. What alternative procedures would King consider performing when replies to positive confirmation requests are **not** received? (5/94, Aud., #5)

ESSAY SOLUTIONS

Solution 37-3 Client Representations (AU 333)

a. 1. An auditor is required to obtain a written management representation letter as part of every audit performed in accordance with generally accepted auditing standards.

2. The purposes of obtaining a written management representation letter are to:

- Confirm the oral representations given to the auditor.
- Indicate and document the continuing appropriateness of management's representations.
- Reduce the possibility of misunderstanding concerning the matters that are the subject of the representations.
- Complement the other auditing procedures by corroborating the information discovered in performing those procedures.
- Obtain evidence concerning management's future plans and intentions, e.g., when refinancing debt or discontinuing a line of business.

b. 1. The representation letter should be addressed to the auditor and dated as of the date of the auditor's report.

2. The letter should be signed by members of management whom the auditor believes are responsible for and knowledgeable, directly or through others in the organization, about the matters covered by the representation. Their refusal to sign the letter would constitute a limitation on the scope of the audit sufficient to preclude an unqualified opinion and affect the auditor's ability to rely on other management representations.

c. Obtaining a management representation letter does not relieve an auditor of any other responsibility for planning or performing an audit. Accordingly, an auditor should still perform all the usual tests to corroborate representations made by management.

Solution 37-4 Legal Inquiry Letter for Litigation, Claims, and Assessments

The omissions, ambiguities, and inappropriate statements and terminology in Brown's letter are as follows:

1. The **action** that Consolidated **intends to take** concerning each suit (for example, to contest the matter vigorously, to seek an out-of-court settlement, or to an appeal an adverse decision) is omitted.

2. A **description of the progress** of each case to date is omitted.

3. An **evaluation** of the **likelihood of an unfavorable outcome** of each case is omitted.

4. An **estimate**, if one can be made, of the **amount or range of potential loss** of each case is omitted.

5. The various **other pending or threatened litigation** on which Young was consulted is not identified and included.

6. The **unasserted claims and assessments** probable of assertion that have a reasonable possibility of an unfavorable outcome are not identified.

7. Consolidated's understanding of Young's responsibility to advise Consolidated concerning the **disclosure of unasserted possible claims or assessments** is omitted.

8. **Materiality** (or the limits of materiality) is not addressed.

9. The reference to a **limitation** on Young's response **due to confidentiality is inappropriate.**

10. Young is not requested to identify the nature of and **reasons for any limited response.**

11. **Young is not requested to include matters that existed after December 31, 1992**, up to the date of Young's response.

12. The **date** by which Young's **response is needed** is not indicated.

13. The reference to Young's response possibly being quoted or referred to in the financial statements is inappropriate.

14. **Vague terminology** such as "slight" and "some chance" is included where "remote" and "possible" are more appropriate.

15. There is **no inquiry about** any unpaid or **unbilled charges**, services, or disbursements.

Solution 37-5 Audit Procedures--Investments

a.

Primary Assertion	Objective
4. Existence or occurrence	To determine that the custodian holds the securities as identified in the confirmation.
5. Completeness	To determine that all income and related collections from the investments are properly recorded.
6. Valuation or allocation	To determine that the market or other value of the investments is fairly stated.
7. Presentation and disclosure	To determine that the financial statement presentation and disclosure of investments is in conformity with generally accepted accounting principles consistently applied.
8. Valuation or allocation	To determine that the market or other value of the investments is fairly stated and the loss is properly recognized and recorded.

b. Larkin should consider applying the following additional substantive auditing procedures in auditing Vernon's investments:

- **Inspect** securities on hand in the presence of the custodian.
- **Examine supporting evidence** (broker's advices, etc.) for transactions between the balance sheet date and the inspection date.
- Obtain **confirmation** from the issuers or trustees for investments in nonpublic entities.
- **Examine** contractual **terms** of debt securities and preferred stock.
- Determine that sales and purchases were properly **approved** by the Board of Directors or its designee.
- **Examine** broker's advices in support of transactions or **confirm transactions** with broker.
- Determine that **gains and losses** on dispositions have been **properly computed**.
- **Trace** payments for purchases to canceled checks, and proceeds from sales to entries in the cash receipts journal.
- Determine that the **amortization** of premium and discount on bonds has been **properly computed.**
- **Determine** that **market value** for both current and long-term portfolios has been properly computed by tracing quoted market prices to competent published or other sources.
- **Compute the unrealized** gains and losses on both current and long-term portfolios for marketable equity securities.
- Determine that the unrealized **gains and losses** on the current portfolio have been **properly classified** in the income statement, and the unrealized gains and losses on the noncurrent portfolio have been properly classified in the equity section of the balance sheet.
- **Ascertain whether** any investments are **pledged** as collateral or encumbered by liens, and, if so, are properly **disclosed.**

Solution 37-6 Audit Procedures--Goodwill

a. Taylor should consider performing the following procedures in the audit of Palmer's goodwill:

- **Trace the totals** in the account analysis for each significant acquisition to the general ledger;
- Trace the **opening balance** to the audit working papers for the **preceding year**;
- **Examine supporting documents** for evidence of continued **ownership** of the acquisitions that resulted in excess of costs over fair value of net assets;
- Review the **reasonableness and consistency** of application of the method of amortization used;
- Determine that the **amortization period** is **reasonable**;
- **Recompute amortization**;
- Determine that the **carrying amount does not exceed** amounts properly allocable to **future** periods;
- **Assess** whether there has been a **permanent impairment** of value;
- **Trace amounts amortized** during the period to the related general ledger expense accounts;
- **Examine evidence supporting additions and reductions** during the year (e.g., contingency payments properly capitalizable, reductions due to recovery of preacquisition taxes, etc.);
- Ascertain whether goodwill and amortization are **properly described and classified** in the financial statements and **disclosed in the notes** to the financial statements.

b. The **two** significant assertions that Taylor would be most concerned with relative to Palmer's goodwill are **valuation or allocation**, and **presentation and disclosure**. Taylor would be most concerned with the risk of the loss of recoverability of the goodwill's market value due to not meeting profit expectations, and the risk of inadequate disclosure or presentation in the financial statements.

Solution 37-7 Audit Procedures--Trade Accounts Payable

The substantive audit procedures Kane should apply to Star's trade accounts payable balances include the following:

- **Foot** the schedule of the trade accounts payable.
- **Agree** the total of the **schedule** to the **general ledger** trial balance.
- **Compare** a sample of individual account balances from the **schedule** with the accounts payable subsidiary **ledger**.
- **Compare** a sample of **individual account** balances from the **accounts payable subsidiary** ledger with the **schedule.**
- Investigate and **discuss** with management any **old** or **disputed** payables.
- Investigate debit balances and, if significant, **consider** requesting positive confirmations and propose **reclassification** of the amounts.
- **Review the minutes** of board of directors' meetings and any **written agreements** and inquire of key employees as to whether any assets are pledged to collateralize payables.
- Perform **cut-off** tests.
- Perform **analytical procedures.**

Confirm or verify recorded accounts payable balances by:

- **Reviewing** the voucher register or subsidiary accounts payable **ledger** and consider confirming payables of a sample of vendors.
- Requesting a sample of vendors to provide statements of account balances as of the date selected.
- **Investigating and reconciling differences** discovered during the confirmation procedures.
- **Testing** a sample of unconfirmed **balances** by examining the **related vouchers,** invoices, purchase orders, and receiving reports.

Perform a **search for unrecorded liabilities** by:

- Examining a file of receiving **reports unmatched** with vendors' invoices, searching for items received before the balance sheet date but not yet billed or on the schedule.
- **Inspecting files** of **unprocessed invoices,** purchase orders, and vendors' statements.
- **Reviewing support for the cash disbursements journal**, the voucher register, or canceled checks for disbursements after the balance sheet date to identify transactions that should have been recorded at the balance sheet date, but were not.
- **Inquiring** of key employees about additional sources of unprocessed invoices or other trade payables.

Solution 37-8 Audit Procedures--Payroll

Bell should consider performing the following procedures in the audit of Kent's payroll transactions:

Select a **sample of payments to employees** from the **payroll register** and compare each selected transaction to the related documents and records examining

- Evidence in support of **authorization of rate** of pay.
- Evidence in support of **time** on which compensation was based, such as approved **time cards or attendance records.**
- Evidence in support of proper **authorization** of payroll **withholdings.**
- Evidence in support of payments, such as **canceled payroll checks.**
- Evidence in support of **account distribution.**
- The **clerical accuracy** of the transaction.
- The entry to the employee's records used to summarize employee compensation for payroll reporting purposes.

Obtain the **payroll register** for a selected period and

- Test the **arithmetical accuracy** of the payroll register.
- Determine whether **payroll** was **approved** in accordance with management's prescribed procedures.
- **Trace totals** per the **register** to postings in the **general ledger.**
- **Observe** the **distribution** of payroll checks.
- **Review** the **accounting for unclaimed wages.**
- **Observe** a sample of **employees** in the performance of their **duties.**
- Perform **analytical procedures.**

Solution 37-9 Audit Procedures--Accounts Receivable

Edwards should consider applying the following additional substantive audit procedures:

- Test the **accuracy** of the aged accounts receivable schedule.
- Send **second requests** for all **unanswered positive confirmation requests.**
- Perform **alternative auditing procedures** for unanswered second confirmation requests.
- **Reconcile and investigate exceptions** reported on the confirmations.
- **Project the results** of the sample confirmation procedures to the **population** and evaluate the confirmation results.
- Determine whether any accounts receivable are owed by employees or related parties.
- Test the **cutoff of sales**, cash receipts, and sales returns and allowances.
- Evaluate the **reasonableness of the allowance** for doubtful accounts.
- Perform **analytical procedures** for accounts receivable (e.g., accounts receivable to credit sales, allowance for doubtful accounts to accounts receivable, sales to returns and allowances, doubtful accounts expense to net credit sales).
- Identify differences, if any, between the book and tax basis for the allowance for doubtful accounts and related expense.
- **Review activity after the balance sheet date** for unusual transactions.
- Determine that the **presentation and disclosure** of accounts receivable is in conformity with generally accepted accounting principles consistently applied.

Solution 37-10 Audit Procedures--Related Party Transactions (AU 334)

The audit procedures Temple should apply to identify Ford's related party relationships and transactions include the following:

- Evaluate the company's procedures for **identifying and properly reporting** related party relationships and transactions.
- **Request** from management the **names of all related parties** and inquire whether there were any transactions with these parties during the period.
- **Review tax returns** and filings with other regulatory agencies for the names of related parties.
- Determine the **names of all pension plans** and other trusts and the names of their officers and trustees.
- Review **stock certificate book** to identify the stockholders.
- Review material investment transactions to determine whether the investments created related party relationships.
- Review the **minutes of board of directors' meetings**.
- Review **conflict-of-interest statements** obtained by the company from its management.
- Review the extent and nature of business transacted with major customers, suppliers, borrowers, and lenders.
- Consider whether transactions are occurring, but are not being given proper accounting recognition, e.g., personal use of company vehicles, interest-free loans, etc.
- Review accounting records for **large, unusual, or nonrecurring transactions** or balances, paying particular attention to transactions recognized at or near the end of the reporting period.
- **Review confirmations of compensating balance arrangements** for indications that balances are or were maintained for or by related parties.
- Review **invoices from law firms** that have performed services for the company for indications of the existence of related party relationships or transactions.
- Review **confirmations of loans receivable and payable** for indications of **guarantees**, and determine their nature and the relationships, if any, of the guarantors to the reporting entity.

Solution 37-11 Audit Procedures--Bank Balances

The auditor should:

- Review answers to questions on confirmation requests to determine proper recognition in accounting records and the necessity for financial statement disclosure.
- Make **inquiries as to compensating balances** and restrictions.
- **Obtain copies** of the **bank reconciliations** as of the balance sheet date, and
- **Trace** the adjusted book balances to the general ledger balances.
- **Compare** the bank balances to the opening balances on the cutoff bank statements.
- Compare the bank balances to the balances on the confirmations.
- Trace amounts of **deposits in transit** to the cutoff bank statements and ascertain whether the **time lags** are reasonable.
- Verify the **clerical accuracy** of the reconciliations.

- Obtain explanation for **unusual reconciling items**, including checks drawn to "bearer," "cash," and related parties.
- Trace checks dated prior to the **end of the period** that were returned with the cutoff statements to the **list of outstanding checks.**
- **Investigate outstanding checks** that did not clear with the cutoff bank statements.
- Examine a sample of checks for payee, amount, date, authorized signatures, and endorsements to determine any irregularities from company policy or accounting records.
- **Prepare a bank transfer schedule** from a review of the cash receipts and disbursements journals, bank statements, and related paid checks for the last few days before and the first few days after the year-end, and
- Review the schedule to determine that the deposit and disbursement of each transfer is recorded in the proper period.
- Trace **incomplete transfers** to the schedule of **outstanding checks and deposits in transit.**

Solution 37-12 Audit Procedures--Common Stock and Treasury Stock

The substantive audit procedures that Jones should apply in examining the common stock and treasury stock accounts are as follows:

- **Review the corporate charter** to verify details of the common stock such as authorized shares, par value, etc.
- **Obtain** or prepare an **analysis of changes** in common stock and treasury stock accounts.
- **Compare** opening **balances with prior year's** working papers.
- **Foot the total shares outstanding** in the stockholders' ledger and stock certificate book.
- Determine **authorization for common stock issuances** and **treasury stock transactions** by inspecting the minutes of the board of directors' meetings.
- Verify capital stock issuances by examining supporting documentation and tracing entries into the records.
- Verify treasury stock transactions by examining supporting documentation and tracing entries into the records.
- **Examine** all **certificates canceled** during the year.
- **Inspect all treasury stock certificates owned** by the client.
- **Reconcile** the details of the individual certificates in the stock certificate book with the individual shareholders' accounts in the stockholders' ledger.
- **Compare** the totals in the stockholders' ledger and the stock certificate book to the balance sheet presentation.
- **Recompute the weighted average number** of shares outstanding.
- **Compare** the **financial statement presentation** and disclosure with generally accepted accounting principles.
- Determine the existence of, and proper accounting for, common stock and treasury stock transactions occurring since year-end.
- **Obtain written representations** concerning common and treasury stock in the client representation letter.

Solution 37-13 Audit Procedures--Mobile Equipment and Related Depreciation

Substantive audit procedures that Pierce should use in examining Mayfair's mobile construction equipment and related depreciation would include the following:

- Determine that the equipment account is **properly footed.**
- Determine that the **subsidiary accounts agree** with controlling accounts.
- Obtain, or **prepare, an analysis of changes** in the account during the year.
- Determine that **beginning-of-year balances agree with the prior year's ending balances.**
- **Inspect documents** in support of **additions** during the year.
- **Inspect documents** in support of **retirements** during the year.
- **Analyze repairs and maintenance** for possible reclassifications.
- Determine the propriety of accounting for **equipment not in current use.**
- Test the accuracy of equipment and accounting records by:
    - Selecting items from the accounting records and **verifying their physical existence.**
    - Selecting items of equipment and locating them in the accounting records.
- Evaluate the **reasonableness of estimated lives** and methods of depreciation used.
- **Test the calculation of depreciation** expense and accumulated depreciation expense and accumulated depreciation balance.
- **Perform analytical procedures** such as comparing depreciation expense to balance sheet

accounts for proper relationship and comparing the current year's depreciation expense with prior year's depreciation expense.

- Evaluate the **financial statement presentation and disclosures** for conformity with generally accepted accounting principles.
- **Review insurance coverage.**

Solution 37-14 Factors Affecting Risk of Material Misstatement

The factors most likely to have an effect on the risk of material misstatements and their resulting effect include the following:

Environmental factor	Effect on risk of material misstatements
Governmental regulation over the banking industry is extensive.	Decrease
NFB operates profitably in a growing prosperous area.	Decrease
Overall **demand for the industry's product** is high.	Decrease
Interest rates have been **volatile** recently.	Increase
The **availability of funds** for additional mortgages is **promising**.	Decrease
The **principal shareholder** is also the **chief executive officer** and controls the board of directors.	Increase
Branch **management is compensated based on branch profitability**.	Increase
The **internal auditor reports directly to the chairman of the board's audit committee**, a minority shareholder.	Decrease
The **accounting department** has experienced **little turnover** in personnel recently.	Decrease
NFB is a **continuing audit client**.	Decrease
Management **fails to establish proper procedures** to provide reasonable assurance of reliable **accounting estimates**.	Increase
Management has been receptive to Green's **suggestions** relating to accounting adjustments.	Decrease
NFB recently **opened a new branch** office that is **not yet profitable**.	Increase
NFB recently installed a **new sophisticated computer system**.	Increase

Solution 37-15 Use of a Specialist

a. The factors Kent should consider in the process of selecting Park include

- **Park's professional certification**, license, or other recognition of Park's competence.
- **Park's reputation** and standing in the view of **Park's peers** and others familiar with Park's capability or performance.
- **Park's relationship**, if any, to Davidson Corporation.

b. The understanding among Kent, Park, and Davidson's management as to the nature of the work to be performed by Park should cover

- The **objectives and scope** of Park's work.
- Park's representations as to Park's relationship, if any, to Davidson.
- The **methods** or **assumptions** to be **used**.
- A comparison of the methods or assumptions to be used with those used in the preceding period.
- Park's **understanding** of Kent's **corroborative use of Park's findings.**
- The form and content of Park's report that would enable Kent to evaluate Park's findings.

c. Kent **may not refer to Park in the auditor's report** if Kent decides to issue an unqualified opinion. Such a reference might be **misunderstood** to be a **qualification**, a **division of responsibility**, or an **inference that a more thorough audit was performed.**

d. Kent **may refer** to Park in the auditor's report **if** Kent decides to **issue other than an unqualified opinion** as a result of Park's findings. Reference is permitted if it will facilitate an understanding of the reason for the modification.

Solution 37-16 Analytical Procedures (AU 329)

a. Analytical procedures are used for these broad purposes:

- To assist the auditor in **planning the nature, timing, and extent** of other auditing procedures.
- As a **substantive test** to obtain **evidential matter** about particular **assertions** related to account balances or classes of transactions.
- As an **overall review** of the financial information in the final review stage of the audit.

b. An auditor's expectations are developed from the following sources of information:

- Financial information for **comparable prior periods** giving consideration to known changes.

- **Anticipated results**--for example, budgets, forecasts, and extrapolations.
- **Relationships** among elements of financial information **within the period.**
- **Information regarding the industry** in which the client operates.
- **Relationships** of financial information **with** relevant **nonfinancial information.**

c. The factors that influence an auditor's consideration of the reliability of data for purposes of achieving audit objectives are whether the

- Data were **obtained from independent sources** outside the entity or from sources within the entity.
- **Sources within the entity were independent** of those who are responsible for the amount being audited.
- Data were **developed under a reliable system** with adequate controls.
- Data were **subjected to audit testing** in the current or prior year.
- Expectations were developed using data from a variety of sources.

Solution 37-17 Gathering Audit Evidence/Audit Procedures--Inventory

a. The means or techniques of gathering audit evidence, in addition to the example, are as follows:

Technique	Description
Inquiry	An auditor questions client personnel about events and conditions, such as obsolete inventory.
Confirmation	An auditor obtains acknowledgments in writing from third parties of transactions or balances, such as inventory in public warehouses or on consignment.
Calculation or Recomputation	An auditor recomputes certain amounts, such as the multiplication of quantity times price to determine inventory amounts.
Analysis	An auditor combines amounts in meaningful ways to allow the application of audit judgment, such as the determination of whether a proper inventory cutoff was performed.
Inspection	An auditor examines documents relating to transactions and balances, such as shipping and receiving records to establish ownership of inventory.
Comparison	An auditor relates two or more amounts, such as inventory cost in perpetual inventory records to costs as shown on vendor invoices as part of the evaluation of whether inventory is priced at the lower of cost or market.

b. Substantive auditing procedures that would satisfy the five general assertions regarding a client's inventory balance include the following:
(one different procedure required for each assertion)

Assertion	Substantive Auditing Procedure
1. Existence or Occurrence	• **Observe physical inventory** counts. • **Obtain confirmation** of inventories at locations outside the entity. • Test inventory transactions between a preliminary physical inventory date and the balance sheet date. • **Review perpetual inventory records**, production records, and purchasing records for indications of current activity. • **Compare inventories** with a current sales catalog and subsequent sales and delivery reports. • Use the work of specialists to corroborate the nature of specialized products.
2. Completeness	• **Observe physical inventory counts.** • Apply **analytical procedures** to the relationship of inventory balances to recent purchasing, production, and sales activities. • Test shipping and receiving cutoff procedures. • **Obtain confirmation** of inventories at locations outside the entity. • **Trace test counts** recorded during the physical inventory observation to the inventory listing. • **Account for all inventory tags** and count sheets used in recording the physical inventory counts. • Test the clerical accuracy of inventory listings. • **Reconcile physical counts to perpetual records** and general ledger balances and investigate significant fluctuations.
3. Rights and Obligations	• **Observe physical inventory counts.** • Obtain confirmation of inventory at locations outside the entity. • **Examine paid vendors' invoices**, consignment agreements, and contracts. • **Test shipping and receiving cutoff procedures.**
4. Valuation or Allocation	• **Examine paid vendors' invoices.** • Review direct labor rates. • **Test the computation** of standard overhead rates. • Examine analyses of purchasing and manufacturing standard cost variances. • Examine an analysis of **inventory turnover.** • Review **industry experience and trends.** • Apply **analytical procedures** to the relationship of inventory balances to anticipated sales volume. • **Tour the plant.** • Inquire of production and sales personnel concerning possible excess or obsolete inventory items. • **Obtain current market value** quotations. • Review current market value quotations. • **Examine sales after year-end** and open purchase order commitments.
5. Presentation and Disclosure	• **Review drafts** of the financial statements. • Compare the **disclosures** made in the financial statements to the requirements of generally accepted accounting principles. • Obtain confirmation of inventories pledged under loan agreements.

Solution 37-18 Audit Procedures--Loss Contingencies

The substantive audit procedures that Young should apply when testing for loss contingencies relating to litigation, claims, and assessments include the following:

- **Read minutes** of meetings of stockholders, directors, and committees.
- **Read contracts, loan agreements, leases,** and other documents.
- Read **correspondence with taxing** and other governmental **agencies.**
- Read **correspondence with insurance** and bonding **companies.**
- Read confirmation replies for information concerning guarantees.

- **Discuss with management** the entity's **policies and procedures** for identifying, evaluating, and accounting for litigation, claims, and assessments.
- **Obtain from management** or inside general counsel a **description and evaluation of litigation, claims, and assessments.**
- Obtain **written assurance from management** that the financial statements include all accruals and disclosures required by Statement of Financial Accounting Standards No. 5.
- **Examine documents** in the client's possession concerning litigation, claims, or assessments, including correspondence from lawyers.
- Obtain an analysis of **professional fee expenses and review supporting invoices** for indications of contingencies.
- Request the client's management to prepare for transmittal a **letter of inquiry to** those **lawyers** consulted by the client concerning litigation, claims, and assessments.
- Compare the lawyer's response to the items in the letter of inquiry to the description and evaluation of litigation, claims, and assessments obtained from management.
- Determine that the financial statements include **proper accruals and disclosures** of the contingencies.

Solution 37-19 Accounts Receivable Confirmations (AU 330)/Client Representations (AU 333)

a. Since recipients of negative accounts receivable confirmations are requested to respond only if they disagree with the information in the confirmation, no additional audit procedures are necessary on nonresponses to negative accounts receivable confirmations.

For **nonresponses to positive** confirmations, Wright should consider performing the following alternative audit procedures:

- The use of **other means**, e.g., **telephone inquiry**, or directly communicating with the debtor.
- Examination of evidence of **subsequent cash receipts.**
- Examination of evidence of customer orders, duplicate **sales invoices**, and **shipping documents.**
- **Examination** of William's files involving **correspondence with the customers.**

b. The other matters that Wright would expect to be included in William's management representation letter are whether or not

- **Management acknowledges responsibility for the fair presentation** in the financial statements of financial positions, results of operations, and cash flows in conformity with generally accepted accounting principles (or other comprehensive basis of accounting).
- **All financial records** and data were made **available.**
- The accountant has been **furnished with copies of all minutes** of meetings of stockholders, board of directors, and committees of the board of directors (or other similar bodies).
- The company has **satisfactory title to all owned assets**, and whether there are **liens** or **encumbrances** on such assets or any pledging of assets.
- **Provision**, when material, has been **made** to **reduce excess or obsolete inventories** to their estimated net realizable value.
- There are **related party transactions** or related party **receivables or payables** that have not been properly disclosed in the financial statements.
- There are **compensating balances** or other arrangements involving restrictions on cash balances.
- **Unasserted claims or assessments** that management's counsel has advised are probable of assertion have been disclosed in accordance with Statement of Financial Accounting Standards No. 5.
- There are **other** material liabilities or **gain or loss contingencies** that are required to be accrued or disclosed.

Solution 37-20 Audit Procedures--Accounts Receivable

a. Although there is a presumption that King will request the confirmation of Cycle's accounts receivable, King could justify omitting this procedure if Cycle's accounts receivable are **immaterial to its financial statements**. King could also justify omitting this procedure if the **expected response rates** to properly designed confirmation requests **will be inadequate**, or if **responses will be unreliable.** In these circumstances, King may determine that the use of confirmations would be **ineffective.**

Additionally, King could justify omitting the confirmation of Cycle's accounts receivable if King's **combined assessed level of inherent** and **control**

risk is low and the **assessed level, in conjunction** with the **evidence** expected to be **provided by analytical procedures** or other **substantive tests of details**, is **sufficient to reduce audit risk** to an **acceptably low level** for the applicable financial assertions.

b. Among the factors likely to affect the **reliability of confirmations** that King sends is King's decision in choosing the confirmation form. Some positive forms **request agreement or disagreement with information stated** on the form; other positive forms, known as **blank forms**, request the respondent to **fill in the balance or furnish other information**; **negative forms request** a response **only if there is disagreement** with the information stated on the request.

King's prior experience with Cycle or similar clients is also likely to affect reliability because King probably would have **prior knowledge** of the **expected confirmation response rates**, inaccurate **information on prior years' confirmations**, and **misstatements identified during prior audits.**

The **nature of the information** being confirmed may affect the **competence of the evidence** obtained as well as the response rate. For example, Cycle's **customers' accounting systems** may permit confirmation of individual transactions, but not account balances, or vice versa.

Additionally, King's sending of each confirmation request to the **proper respondent** will likely provide meaningful and competent evidence. Each request should be sent to a person who King believes is **knowledgeable about the information** to be confirmed.

c. The nature of the alternative procedures King would apply when replies to positive confirmation request are not received varies according to the account and assertion in question. Possible alternative procedures include **examining subsequent cash receipts**, and **matching** such **receipts with the actual items being paid.** King would also consider **inspecting Cycle's shipping documents or invoices**, or Cycle's **customers' purchase orders** on file. **Inspecting correspondence** between Cycle and its customers could provide additional evidence. King may also establish the existence of Cycle's customers by **reference to credit sources** such as Dun & Bradstreet.

CHAPTER 38

AUDIT SAMPLING PROCEDURES

CHAPTER 38

AUDIT SAMPLING PROCEDURES

I. Introduction

A. Definition--Audit sampling is defined by SAS 39 as the application of an audit procedure to less than 100% of the items within an account balance or class of transactions (the audit population) with the intent of drawing conclusions about the population based on the results of the sample.

1. The underlying principle of sampling is that the results of a sample yield information about the population from which the sample was taken. Sampling, therefore, can be looked upon as an effective and efficient method of gathering audit evidence.

2. Absent sampling, an auditor would examine every item comprising an account balance or every transaction occurring within a class of transactions. The cost would (a) be prohibitive due to the amount of time required to perform the examination and (b) far outweigh the benefit obtained. Sampling provides the auditor with a means of obtaining information, but at a much lower cost.

B. Attributes Sampling--In the auditor's consideration of internal control, tests are performed on the client's internal control policies and procedures in order to determine the degree to which the client's employees have complied (i.e., tests of controls). These tests involve the determination of the rate of occurrence of some characteristic (i.e., attribute), in a population. The attribute of interest is frequently a deviation from the particular control procedure. Thus, the auditor takes a sample from the population, computes the deviation rate in the sample, and draws conclusions about the true population deviation rate.

C. Variables Sampling--In performing the tests of details of transactions and account balances (i.e., substantive tests), the auditor is concerned with the dollar amounts reported in the financial statements. Thus, the auditor draws a sample from the population of interest, determines the proper dollar value of the items sampled, and makes inferences, based upon projection of the sample results to the population, about the fairness of the amounts reported in the financial statements.

D. Dual-Purpose Sampling

1. In some circumstances, the auditor may design a test that will be used for dual purposes--tests of controls directed toward operation and substantive testing as to whether a recorded balance or amount of transactions is correct. A dual-purpose sample is a sample that is designed to both assess control risk and to provide a substantive objective. Because the auditor will have begun substantive procedures before determining whether the tests of controls support the initial assessment of control risk, an auditor planning to use a dual-purpose sample would have made a preliminary assessment that there is an acceptably low risk that the rate of deviations in the population exceeds the maximum acceptable rate without altering the assessment of control risk.

2. Objectives--A dual-purpose sample has two objectives:

   a. To assess control risk.

   b. To test whether the recorded monetary amounts of a transaction are correct.

3. Low Risk Factor--Generally, the auditor who plans to use this type of sample believes that there is an acceptably low risk that the rate of deviations from prescribed internal control policies and procedures in the population is greater than the tolerable rate.

4. Size--The size of the sample should be the larger of the samples that would have been designed for the two separate purposes.

II. Audit Sampling (AU 350, SAS 39)

A. Purpose and Scope--SAS 39 provides guidelines on the use of sampling in an audit. The Third Standard of Field Work requires sufficient competent evidential matter to be obtained through inspection, observation, inquiries, and confirmations to afford a reasonable basis for an opinion on the financial statements. The use of audit sampling relates to this standard.

1. Audit sampling is the application of an audit procedure to less than 100% of the items within an account balance or class of transactions for the purpose of evaluating some characteristic of the balance or class.

2. There are two general approaches to audit sampling: statistical and nonstatistical. Both require the auditor to use professional judgment.

3. The sufficiency of evidential matter is determined by the size and design of an audit sample (among other factors).

a. Size--Depends on both the objectives and efficiency of the sample.

b. Design--Relates to the efficiency of the sample; for example, one sample is more efficient than another if it achieves the same objectives with a smaller sample size.

4. The competence of evidential matter is determined by audit judgment--not the design and evaluation of an audit sample.

B. Uncertainty and Audit Sampling--In the Third Standard of Field Work, the concept of a "reasonable basis for an opinion" suggests some degree of uncertainty or audit risk. There are some situations in which the surrounding factors do not justify the acceptance of any amount of sampling risk, and, therefore, all related data is examined. The theory of sampling is well established in auditing practice because it is unusual to find instances where 100% of the items need to be examined for each account balance and class of transactions.

1. Audit Risk--The uncertainty inherent in applying audit procedures is referred to as audit risk (see Chapter 35). Using professional judgment, the auditor evaluates numerous factors to assess inherent risk and control risk, and performs substantive tests to reduce detection risk to an appropriate level.

2. Aspects of Audit Risk--Audit risk includes both uncertainties due to sampling as well as uncertainties due to factors other than sampling.

a. Sampling risk results from the possibility that if a test is restricted to a sample, the conclusions reached may be different than the conclusions that may result if the entire population is examined. The smaller the sample size is, the greater the sampling risk becomes, thus sampling risk varies inversely with sample size.

b. Nonsampling risk includes all aspects of audit risk not due to sampling. Nonsampling risk can be reduced by adequate planning and supervision of audit work, and adherence to quality control standards. For example:

(1) Incorrect audit procedures for a given objective.

(2) Nonrecognition of misstatements, making the procedure ineffective.

C. Assessing Sampling Risk--The judgment of the auditor should be used to assess sampling risk.

1. Substantive Tests of Details--The auditor is concerned with two aspects of sampling risk while performing substantive tests:

   a. The Risk of Incorrect Acceptance (Beta Risk)--The risk that the sample supports the conclusion that the recorded account balance is not materially misstated when it is, in fact, materially misstated.

   b. The Risk of Incorrect Rejection (Alpha Risk)--The risk that the sample supports the conclusion that the recorded account balance is materially misstated when, in fact, it is not materially misstated.

2. Tests of Internal Control--The auditor is concerned with two aspects of sampling risk while performing tests of controls:

   a. The Risk of Assessing Control Risk Too Low--The risk that the assessed level of control risk based on the sample is less than the true operating effectiveness of the control structure policy or procedure.

   b. The Risk of Assessing Control Risk Too High--The risk that the assessed level of control risk based on the sample is greater than the true operating effectiveness of the control structure policy or procedure.

3. The risk of incorrect rejection and the risk of assessing control risk too high on internal control relate to the efficiency of the audit. Thus, if the auditor assesses control risk too high, additional substantive tests will be performed beyond what is necessary. The risk of incorrect acceptance and the risk of assessing control risk too low on internal control relate to the effectiveness of the audit in the detection of existing material misstatements. This could potentially result in materially misstated financial statements from not expanding substantive audit tests to a necessary level.

Exhibit 1

For Tests of Control Procedures

Auditor's Assessment of Control Risk Is:	Client's Control Risk Is: Less Than Maximum	Client's Control Risk Is: Maximum
Less than Maximum Level	Correct Decision (1)	Incorrect Decision (2)
Maximum Level	Incorrect Decision (3)	Correct Decision (4)

(continued on next page)

For Substantive Tests

Indication of Sample Results	Client's Book Value Is: Not Fairly Stated	Fairly Stated
Accept Book Value	Correct Decision (5)	Incorrect Decision (6)
Reject Book Value	Incorrect Decision (7)	Correct Decision (8)

(2) Assessing Control Risk Too Low (effectiveness)
(3) Assessing Control Risk Too High (efficiency)
(6) Incorrect Acceptance (effectiveness)
(7) Incorrect Rejection (efficiency)

D. Sample Selection--Items for sampling should be chosen in such a way that the sample can be representative of the population. The auditor should ensure that all items have an opportunity to be selected. The following are commonly used selection procedures:

1. Haphazard Sampling.

2. Random sampling.

3. Systematic sampling.

4. Stratified sampling.

5. Block sampling. Note, however, that block sampling does not meet the requirements for a representative sample.

6. Probability-proportional-to-size (PPS) sampling.

E. Sampling in Tests of Internal Controls

1. Planning a Sample--The auditor should take the following into consideration:

   a. The relationship of the sample to the objective of the test of controls. For many tests of controls, such as those concerning segregation of duties, sampling does not apply.

   b. The maximum rate of deviations from prescribed control structure policies and procedures that would support the auditor's planned assessed level of control risk.

      - This is the tolerable rate which is assessed by considering the relationship of procedural deviations to (1) the planned assessed level of control risk and (2) the degree of assurance desired by the evidential matter in the sample.

c. The auditor's allowable risk of assessing control risk too low.

- When the degree of assurance desired by the sample is high, the auditor should allow for a low level of sampling risk (that is, the risk of assessing control risk too low).

d. Characteristics of the population, that is, the items comprising the account balance or class of transactions of interest.

- To determine sample size for a test of controls, the auditor should consider (1) the tolerable rate of deviation from the control structure policies or procedures being tested, (2) the likely rate of deviations, and (3) the allowable risk of assessing control risk too low.

2. Professional Judgment--The auditor must apply professional judgment in determining these factors in order to determine the sample size.

3. Performance and Evaluation--In performing audit procedures on items included in a sample and in evaluating sample results, the auditor should repeat the same steps that are outlined for substantive testing. However, in tests of controls, if the accountant is unable to perform all tests, it is considered a <u>deviation</u>.

- If the auditor concludes that the sample results do not support the planned assessed level of control risk for an assertion, the auditor should reevaluate the nature, timing, and extent of substantive procedures based on a revised consideration of the assessed level of control risk.

F. <u>Sampling in Substantive Tests of Details</u>

1. Planning a Sample--The auditor should consider the following:

a. Relationship of the sample to the relevant audit objectives.

b. Preliminary judgments of materiality levels.

c. Auditor's allowable risk of incorrect acceptance.

d. Characteristics of the population, that is, the items comprising the account balance or class of transactions of interest.

e. Planning a Sample for a Substantive Test--The auditor should consider how much monetary misstatement in the related account balance may exist without causing the financial statements to be materially misstated. This is called the <u>tolerable misstatement</u> or tolerable error for the sample.

2. Designing a Sample--The auditor should consider the audit objectives to be achieved and decide on the procedure to be applied which will achieve those objectives.

a. The auditor should conclude that the population being sampled is appropriate for the audit objective.

b. The <u>extent</u> of substantive tests required to obtain sufficient evidential matter under the Third Standard should vary with the auditor's assessed level of control risk.

3. Professional Judgment--The auditor may be able to reduce the needed sample size by separating the population into relatively homogenous groups on the basis of some characteristic related to the specific audit objective. (<u>For example</u>, dividing accounts

receivable into several groups based on the size of the individual account balances.) The required sample size will also be influenced by (a) the auditor's assessment of the tolerable misstatement, (b) the allowable risk of incorrect acceptance, and (c) the characteristics of the population.

4. Performance and Evaluation

a. Procedures that are appropriate to the particular audit objective should be applied to each sample item. If certain selected sample items cannot be examined, the auditor's treatment of these unexpected items will depend upon their effect on the auditor's evaluation of the sample. If the auditor's evaluation of the sample results would not be altered by considering those unexamined items to be misstated, it is not necessary to examine the items. However, if considering those unexamined items to be misstated would lead to a conclusion that the balance or class contains material misstatements, the auditor should consider alternative procedures, and should consider whether the inability to examine the items has implications in relation to the auditor's assessed level of control risk or degree of reliance on management representations. Note that this applies to substantive testing, not to tests of controls.

b. The auditor should compare total projected misstatement with the tolerable misstatement.

(1) The auditor's judgment is a necessary factor in this evaluation for both statistical and nonstatistical sampling.

(2) In addition to the evaluation of the frequency and amounts of monetary misstatements, consideration should be given to the qualitative aspects of the misstatements. Specifically, the nature and cause of the misstatement and the possible relationship of the misstatement to other phases of the audit.

(3) When the auditor evaluates whether the financial statements taken as a whole may be materially misstated, projected misstatement results for all audit sampling applications, and all known misstatements from nonsampling applications should be considered in the aggregate along with other relevant audit evidence.

G. Audit Risk

1. The appendix to SAS 39, *Audit Sampling*, provides a model that expresses the general relationship of audit risk to the extent of necessary substantive tests of details. Because the acceptable level of audit risk is a matter of professional judgment, the model is not intended to be a mathematical formula including all factors that may influence the determination of individual risk components. However, the model may be useful for planning appropriate risk levels for audit procedures to achieve the desired audit risk. The model is:

$$AR = IR \times CR \times AP \times TD.$$

AR = The allowable audit risk that monetary misstatements equal to tolerable misstatements might remain undetected for the account balance or class of transactions and related assertions after the auditor has completed all audit procedures deemed necessary.

IR = Inherent risk is the susceptibility of an assertion to a material misstatement assuming there are no related internal control structure policies or procedures.

CR = Control risk is the risk that material misstatements that could occur in an assertion will not be prevented or detected on a timely basis by the entity's internal control structure policies and procedures. If the auditor believes that control structure policies and procedures would prevent or detect misstatements equal to tolerable misstatements about half the time, the auditor would assess this risk as 50 percent.

AP = The auditor's assessment of the risk that analytical procedures and other relevant substantive tests would fail to detect misstatements that could occur in an assertion equal to tolerable misstatement, given that such misstatements occur and are not detected by the internal control structure.

TD = The allowable risk of incorrect acceptance for the substantive test of details, given that misstatements equal to tolerable misstatement occur in an assertion and are not detected by the internal control structure or analytical procedures and other relevant substantive tests.

The auditor can mathematically compute TD if the auditor first assigns an acceptable audit risk (AR) and subjectively quantifies the judgment risks (IR and AP). To compute TD, the model must be restated.

$$TD = AR \div (IR \times CR \times AP)$$

Example 1--An illustration of the use of the audit risk model.

Assume the auditor is planning a sampling application to test a client's accounts receivable voucher register. If AR = .05 and IR = 1.0 and the auditor has subjectively assessed CR and AP equal to 50% and 30%, respectively, then the auditor can use the model to compute an appropriate level of risk of incorrect acceptance (sampling risk).

$$TD = AR/(IR \times CR \times AP)$$
$$TD = .05/(1.0 \times .5 \times .3)$$
$$TD = .33 \text{ (or 33\%)}$$

III. Classical Sample Selection Methods

A. Judgmental (Haphazard) Sampling--The auditor uses professional judgment to decide how many and which items should be included in the sample. (i.e., the items included in the sample are selected without any conscious bias and without any special reason for including or omitting items from the sample).

1. It does **not** consist of sampling units selected in a careless manner; rather, the sample is selected in a manner the auditor expects to be representative of the population. For example, the auditor decides to select 100 accounts from a population of 1,000 accounts based on the auditor's judgment as to how many and which specific accounts should be included in the sample.

2. While haphazard sampling is useful for nonstatistical sampling, it is not used for statistical sampling because it does not allow the auditor to measure the probability of selecting the combination of sampling units.

B. Random Number Sampling--The auditor may select a random sample by matching random numbers generated by a computer or selected from a random number table with, for example, document numbers. With this method, every item in the population has the same probability of being selected as every other item in the population, and every sample has the same probability of being selected as every other sample of the same size.

1. With/Without Replacement--With random number and other sample selection methods, the auditor may sample with or without replacement (i.e., with or without replacing an item in the population after its value or attribute has been selected). Sampling with replacement may result in the appearance of a particular item in the sample more than once. In actual practice, the auditor generally chooses the without replacement approach.

2. This approach is useful for both statistical and nonstatistical sampling.

C. Systematic Sampling--For this method, the auditor determines a uniform interval by dividing the number of physical units in the population by the sample size. A random number is selected as a starting point for the first interval, and one item is selected throughout the population at each of the uniform intervals from the starting point (every n^{th} item). For example, if the auditor wishes to select 100 items from a population of 20,000 items, the uniform interval is every 200th item. First the auditor selects a random starting point (a random number from 1 to 200) and then selects every 200th item from the random start, including the random start item.

1. Because a random start is used, the systematic method provides a sample that allows every sampling unit in the population an equal chance of being selected. If the population is arranged randomly, systematic selection is essentially the same as random number selection. However, unlike random number sampling, this method may not always give every possible combination of sampling units the same probability of being selected. For example, a population of employees on a payroll for a construction company might be organized by teams; each team consisting of a crew leader and nine other workers. A selection of every tenth employee will either list every crew leader or no crew leaders, depending on the random start. No combination would include both crew leaders and other employees. In these circumstances, the auditor may consider using a different sample selection method such as random selection or making a systematic selection with multiple starts. For example, in the case related to payroll cited above, the auditor could use an interval of 50 rather than 10. This would require that the auditor select 5 different random starting points and move through the population 5 different times.

2. This method is useful for both statistical and nonstatistical sampling.

D. Stratified Sampling--The population is divided into groups, called strata, according to some common characteristic, and then random sampling is applied to each stratum. For example, the auditor may divide the client's accounts receivable into three strata--those with balances of $2,000 and above, those with balances between $500 and $2,000, and those with balances of $500 and below. The auditor might positively confirm the whole population of accounts with balances of $2,000 and above, positively confirm a random sample of the accounts with balances between $500 and $2,000, and negatively confirm a random sample of those accounts with balances of $500 and below. The primary objective of stratified sampling is to decrease the effect of variance in the total population, thereby reducing sample size.

1. The mean-per-unit method is a classical variables sampling technique that uses the sample average to project the total population dollar value by multiplying the sample average by the number of items in the population. A smaller sample size can be obtained by stratifying a highly variable population into segments. These segments will then have a minimum of variability within segments and variability between segments will be eliminated. As a result, the total sample size of all combined segments will be less. This is accomplished without a loss of reliability or precision. Therefore, stratified MPU sampling may be more efficient than unstratified MPU because it usually produces an estimate having the desired level of precision, with a smaller sample size.

2. This approach can be used for both statistical and nonstatistical sampling. It is particularly useful in reducing the overall sample size when the auditor is using the MPU (mean-per-unit) approach on populations that include sampling units (such as individual customer receivable balances) that have a wide range of dollar values.

E. Block Sampling--A block sample consists of selecting contiguous transactions. For example, a block sample from a population of all vouchers processed for the year 19XX might be all vouchers processed on February 3, May 17, and July 19, 19XX. This sample includes only three sampling units out of 250 business days because the sampling unit, in this case, is a period of time rather than an individual transaction. A sample with so few blocks is generally not adequate to reach a reasonable audit conclusion. Although a block sample might be designed with enough blocks to minimize this limitation, using such samples might be inefficient. If an auditor decides to use a block sample, special care should be exercised to control sampling risk in designing that sample. Block sampling should not be used with statistical sampling approaches. Block sampling is often used to evaluate changes in control procedures by examining all transactions at that time.

IV. Statistical and Nonstatistical Sampling

A. Basic Concept--Statistical sampling is based on the assumption that, within a given confidence level and allowance for sampling risk, a randomly selected sample of items from a population will reflect the same characteristics that occur in the population. Therefore, auditors may draw valid conclusions based on data derived from a relatively small sample of the total population. The distinguishing feature of statistical sampling methods as opposed to nonstatistical methods is that the user is able to provide a mathematical measurement of the degree of uncertainty that results from examining only part of a population. That is, statistical sampling allows an auditor to measure sampling risk.

B. Similarities--Both statistical and nonstatistical sampling involve examining less than the whole body of data to express a conclusion about the total body of data. Both methods involve audit judgment in planning and performing a sampling procedure and evaluating the results of the sample. Both provide sufficient, competent, evidential matter. Also, the audit procedures involved in examining the selected items in a sample generally do not depend on the sampling approach used.

C. Benefits of Statistical Sampling--The auditor must choose between statistical and nonstatistical sampling. This choice is primarily a cost/benefit consideration. Because either nonstatistical or statistical sampling can provide sufficient evidential matter, the auditor chooses between them after considering their relative cost and effectiveness in the circumstances. Statistical sampling helps the auditor to (1) design an efficient sample, (2) measure the sufficiency of the evidential matter obtained, and (3) evaluate the sample results. If audit sampling, either nonstatistical or statistical, is used, some sampling risk is always present. One benefit of statistical sampling is that it uses the laws of probability to measure sampling risk. Another benefit of statistical sampling is that it provides a model for determining sample size while explicitly recognizing relevant factors such as risk of assessing control risk too low, tolerable misstatement, and the expected population deviation rate. With nonstatistical sampling, on the other hand, the auditor implicitly recognizes the relevant factors while determining the sample size based on his or her own judgment and experience.

D. Costs of Statistical Sampling--Statistical sampling might involve additional costs for (1) training auditors, (2) designing individual samples to meet the statistical requirements, and (3) selecting the items to be examined. For example, if the individual balances comprising an account balance to be tested are not maintained in an organized pattern, it might not be cost effective for an auditor to select items in a way that would satisfy the requirements of a properly designed statistical sample.

E. Distinguishing Feature--A properly designed nonstatistical sampling application can provide results that are as effective as those from a properly designed statistical sampling application. The one difference is that statistical sampling allows the sampling risk associated with the sampling procedure to be quantified.

F. Selecting a Sampling Approach--Statistical or nonstatistical approaches can provide sufficient evidential matter.

1. Because either can provide sufficient evidential matter, the auditor chooses between statistical or nonstatistical sampling after considering their relative cost and effectiveness in the specific situation.

2. Statistical sampling helps to: (a) Design efficient samples, (b) Measure the sufficiency of evidential matter, (c) Evaluate sample results.

V. Attributes Sampling

A. Operating Effectiveness of Internal Control Policies and Procedures

1. In performing tests of controls, the auditor is frequently interested in determining the rate of deviation from prescribed internal control policies and procedures. The sampling plan generally used in this situation is attribute sampling.

Test of Controls → Attribute Sampling → Deviation Rate

2. The attribute of interest is normally a control procedure. For example, the auditor may be concerned with estimating the percentage of purchase orders that do not have proper authorization.

3. A weakness in internal control does not necessarily mean that there will be a misstatement in the financial statements. If a material misstatement occurs and it is not detected by internal controls or substantive tests, only then will the financial statements be misstated.

4. The auditor should determine the maximum rate of deviations from the prescribed internal control policy and procedure that he or she would be willing to accept without altering the planned assessed level of control risk. This is referred to as the tolerable rate.

B. Methods

1. Attribute Estimation Method--A sample is selected and its attribute error rate is determined. This rate serves as an estimate of the error rate in the population and allows the auditor to make statistical statements about the population attribute error rate.

2. Acceptance Sampling Method--A special case of estimation of attributes. An acceptance sampling table, which utilizes the population size, sample size, and number of errors found in the sample, is used to make a statistical statement that the error rate in the population is not greater than a specified error rate. For example, based on sample results, an auditor may obtain 95% confidence that the actual error rate in the population does not exceed 8%.

3. Sequential Sampling--The sample is selected in several steps, with each step conditional on the results of previous steps.

4. Discovery Sampling Method--A special case of acceptance sampling. The objective is to attain a specified level of confidence that, if the error rate in the population is at least a certain percentage, the sample will include at least one instance of failure to comply with the control procedure being audited. For example, discovery sampling can be used to determine how large a sample needs to be for the auditor to have 95% confidence that, if the error rate in the population is 1% or higher, the auditor's sample will include at least one example of an error. What if a sample of the determined size is selected and no error found? The auditor then has 95% confidence that the error rate in the population is less than 1%.

   - Discovery sampling is frequently used when the auditor expects an extremely low error rate, usually zero. It is often used in testing for critical problems such as forgery. If a forgery is found, the auditor would discontinue sampling and investigate further.

C. <u>Steps</u>--The following general steps are appropriate for attributes sampling in tests of controls with prescribed internal control procedures.

1. Determine the Objective--In a compliance test of control procedures, the objective is to compare the actual deviation rate to the tolerable rate. It should be remembered that the purpose of the test is to provide reasonable assurance that internal controls are operating in an effective manner.

2. Determine the Tolerable Rate--This is the maximum rate of deviations from the prescribed internal control procedure (i.e., maximum misstatement rate) that the auditor is willing to accept without altering the assessment of control risk on the particular internal control procedure and is a judgmental decision. Therefore, the tolerable rate is a function of both the expected level of control risk and the degree of assurance desired. Thus, an increase in the tolerable rate would allow a reduction in sample size. If, after performing the sampling application, the auditor finds that the rate of deviations from the prescribed control procedure is close to or exceeds the tolerable rate, the auditor normally would decide that there is an unacceptably high risk that the deviation rate for the population exceeds the tolerable rate. In such cases, the auditor should consider modifying the assessed level of control risk.

3. Determine the Confidence (Reliability) Level--This is a judgmental decision that quantifies the level of sampling risk the auditor is willing to accept. The auditor's willingness to accept sampling risk is determined to a large extent by the nature of the other test that the auditor intends to perform that would complement the test of controls.

4. Determine the Expected Population Deviation Rate--This is the expected rate of occurrence of deviations from the prescribed internal control procedure (i.e., the expected error rate). <u>The expected population deviation rate should not exceed the tolerable rate</u>. If prior to testing, the auditor believes that the actual deviation rate is higher than the tolerable rate, the auditor generally omits testing of that control procedure and either seeks to obtain assurance by testing other relevant internal control structure policies and procedures, or assesses control risk at the maximum level for the related financial statement assertion. The auditor estimates the expected population deviation rate, considering such factors as results of the prior years' tests and the overall control environment. Prior years' results should be considered in light of changes in the entity's internal control structure and changes in personnel.

5. Consider the Effect of Population Size--When a sample is small in relation to the population, the population size has little or no effect on the determination of an appropriate sample size. If the sample size is greater than 10% of the population size, which is rarely the case, a <u>finite population correction factor</u> may be used. However, the finite population correction factor tends to <u>decrease</u> the sample size. Therefore, most auditors ignore the factor because any error in sample size that results will be on the conservative side. **NOTE**: The finite population correction factor is not given in this text because it has not been asked on past exams.

6. Determine the Method of Selecting the Sample--The sample should be representative of the population, and all items should have chance of being selected. The various methods for selecting samples are discussed in III., above.

7. Compute the Sample Size--Sample sizes can be computed by the use of formulas, computer software, and, most often, sample size tables. Consideration should be given to the following when determining sample size:

   a. Assessing Control Risk Too Low--As discussed earlier, there is an <u>inverse</u> relationship between the risk of assessing control risk too low and sample size.

b. Tolerable Deviation Rate--The maximum rate of deviation from a prescribed control policy or procedure that the auditor is willing to accept without modifying the planned level of control risk.

<u>Example 2</u>--Assume the auditor would like to assess control risk at below the maximum level. Assume also that in this case, in order to do this, the auditor must have 95% confidence that the actual population deviation rate (i.e., the percentage of vouchers that are paid without being approved) is not greater than 6%. Therefore, the tolerable rate is 6%; i.e., the auditor will be able to assess control risk at below the maximum level as long as the auditor can conclude with 95% confidence that not more than 6% of the unpaid vouchers lack approval. Based on the error rate observed in last year's sample, the auditor expects a population deviation rate of only 1.50% this year. Using Table 1, 103 vouchers should be examined to yield the desired confidence about the population error rate.

<u>Table 1</u>

5% Risk of Assessing Control Risk Too Low
(with number of expected errors in parentheses)

Expected Population Deviation	Tolerable Rate										
Rate	2%	3%	4%	5%	6%	7%	8%	9%	10%	15%	20%
0.00%	149(0)	99(0)	74(0)	59(0)	49(0)	42(0)	36(0)	32(0)	29(0)	19(0)	14(0)
.25	236(1)	157(1)	117(1)	93(1)	78(1)	66(1)	58(1)	51(1)	46(1)	30(1)	22(1)
.50	*	157(1)	117(1)	93(1)	78(1)	66(1)	58(1)	51(1)	46(1)	30(1)	22(1)
.75	*	208(2)	117(1)	93(1)	78(1)	66(1)	58(1)	51(1)	46(1)	30(1)	22(1)
1.00	*	*	156(2)	93(1)	78(1)	66(1)	58(1)	51(1)	46(1)	30(1)	22(1)
1.25	*	*	156(2)	124(2)	78(1)	66(1)	58(1)	51(1)	46(1)	30(1)	22(1)
1.50	*	*	192(3)	124(2)	103(2)	66(1)	58(1)	51(1)	46(1)	30(1)	22(1)
1.75	*	*	227(4)	153(3)	103(2)	88(2)	77(2)	51(1)	46(1)	30(1)	22(1)
2.00	*	*	*	181(4)	127(3)	88(2)	77(2)	68(2)	46(1)	30(1)	22(1)
2.25	*	*	*	208(5)	127(3)	88(2)	77(2)	68(2)	61(2)	30(1)	22(1)
2.50	*	*	*	*	150(4)	109(3)	77(2)	68(2)	61(2)	30(1)	22(1)
2.75	*	*	*	*	173(5)	109(3)	95(3)	68(2)	61(2)	30(1)	22(1)
3.00	*	*	*	*	195(6)	129(4)	95(3)	84(3)	61(2)	30(1)	22(1)
3.25	*	*	*	*	*	148(5)	112(4)	84(3)	61(2)	30(1)	22(1)
3.50	*	*	*	*	*	167(6)	112(4)	84(3)	76(3)	40(2)	22(1)
3.75	*	*	*	*	*	185(7)	129(5)	100(4)	76(3)	40(2)	22(1)
4.00	*	*	*	*	*	*	146(6)	100(4)	89(4)	40(2)	22(1)
5.00	*	*	*	*	*	*	*	158(8)	116(6)	40(2)	30(2)
6.00	*	*	*	*	*	*	*	*	179(11)	50(3)	30(2)
7.00	*	*	*	*	*	*	*	*	*	68(5)	37(3)

* Sample size is too large to be cost-effective for most audit applications.

NOTE: This table assumes a large population.

Exhibit 2--The effect on sample size when other factors are changed.

Increase in	Effect on Sample Size
Risk of assessing control risk too low	Decrease
Population	Slight increase for increased populations, generally little or no effect
Tolerable rate	Decrease
Expected deviation rate	Increase

Note: This is frequently tested on the CPA Exam.

8. Select and Audit the Sample Items--Audit procedures should be applied to the items in the sample to determine deviations from the prescribed control procedures previously identified. Deviations should be grouped according to whether they are occurring with some regularity or are isolated events. In cases where selected items cannot be examined, they should be counted as deviations from control procedures. This occurs, for example, when documentation used to test for the procedures has been misplaced, lost, or destroyed. Voided items would generally be replaced by another randomly selected item, if it was properly voided.

9. Evaluate the Sample Results--The results of the sample must be analyzed in order to make an inference about the population error rate. This can be done by formula, but is most often accomplished by tables or even computer programs. Tables will be used to further illustrate the evaluation process.

   a. The first step in the evaluation of the results is tabulating the number of deviations found and comparing this to the number of deviations expected to occur using the sample size determined from the above table. The expected number of deviations is the parenthetical number found next to each sample size. In cases where the deviations found are less than the number that would be expected (the parenthetical number) it can be assumed that the risk of assessing control risk too low and the allowance for sampling risk is not more than the tolerable rate.

   b. When the actual deviations are more than those that would be expected according to the parenthetical number in the table above, the auditor can calculate the maximum deviation rate in the population using a table similar to the one below. The table below is for evaluating sample results for a 5% risk of assessing control risk too low or a 95% confidence level.

   c. No one table can accommodate an evaluation of every possible size and number of deviations, and the auditor will often need to use other references to find appropriate tables. Computer programs can also be used. In cases where a particular sample size does not appear in a table, it is always a good idea to be conservative by using the next smaller sample size shown on the table that is available.

Table 2

Statistical Sample Results Evaluation
Upper Limit at 5% of Assessing Control Risk Too Low

Actual Number of Deviations Found

Sample Size	0	1	2	3	4	5	6	7	8	9	10
25	11.3	17.6	*	*	*	*	*	*	*	*	*
30	9.5	14.9	19.6	*	*	*	*	*	*	*	*
35	8.3	12.9	17.0	*	*	*	*	*	*	*	*
40	7.3	11.4	15.0	18.3	*	*	*	*	*	*	*
45	6.5	10.2	13.4	16.4	19.2	*	*	*	*	*	*
50	5.9	9.2	12.1	14.8	17.4	19.9	*	*	*	*	*
55	5.4	8.4	11.1	13.5	15.9	18.2	*	*	*	*	*
60	4.9	7.7	10.2	12.5	14.7	16.8	18.8	*	*	*	*
65	4.6	7.1	9.4	11.5	13.6	15.5	17.4	19.3	*	*	*
70	4.2	6.6	8.8	10.8	12.6	14.5	16.3	18.0	19.7	*	*
75	4.0	6.2	8.2	10.1	11.8	13.6	15.2	16.9	18.5	20.0	*
80	3.7	5.8	7.7	9.5	11.1	12.7	14.3	15.9	17.4	18.9	*
90	3.3	5.2	6.9	8.4	9.9	11.4	12.8	14.2	15.5	16.8	18.2
100	3.0	4.7	6.2	7.6	9.0	10.3	11.5	12.8	14.0	15.2	16.4
125	2.4	3.8	5.0	6.1	7.2	8.3	9.3	10.3	11.3	12.3	13.2
150	2.0	3.2	4.2	5.1	6.0	6.9	7.8	8.6	9.5	10.3	11.1
200	1.5	2.4	3.2	3.9	4.6	5.2	5.9	6.5	7.2	7.8	8.4

* Over 20 percent

NOTE: This table presents upper limits as percentages. This table assumes a large population.

Example 3--To illustrate, assume that only one error is discovered from the 103 sample items selected in Example 2. Use of Table 2, above, reveals that there is no corresponding sample size for 103 items, so the next lowest (100 sample size) is used. The intersection of the sample size and the number of deviations found reveals the maximum population deviation rate in this case is 4.7%. Since this maximum population deviation rate is less than the tolerable rate of 6%, it can be concluded that within a 95% reliability level, the control is functioning as required.

10. Reach an Overall Conclusion--The auditor uses professional judgment to reach an overall conclusion about the effect of the evaluation of the test of controls on the nature, timing, and extent of planned substantive tests. If the sample results, along with other relevant evidential matter, support the assessed level of control risk, the auditor generally does not need to modify planned substantive tests. If the sample results do not support the assessed level of control risk, the auditor would ordinarily either perform tests of controls on other relevant internal controls for which control risk can be assessed at below the maximum level, or assess control risk at a higher, or the maximum, level and modify the nature, timing, and/or extent of substantive testing. In addition to the evaluation of the frequency and amounts of monetary misstatements, consideration should be given to the qualitative aspects of the misstatements. These would include the nature and cause of the misstatements. For example, were there differences in principle or applications or differences due to misunderstanding of instructions or carelessness? Also, consideration should be given to the possible relationship of the misstatements to other phases of the audit.

11. Document the Sampling Procedure--Documentation might include such items as follows:

    a. A description of the prescribed control procedure being tested.

    b. The objectives of the test, including the relationship to planned substantive testing.

c. The definition of the population and sampling unit.

d. The definition of the deviation condition (i.e., what is considered a deviation from prescribed internal control policies and procedures).

e. The rationale for the confidence level, the tolerable rate, and the expected population deviation rate used in the application.

f. The method of sample size determination.

g. The method of sample selection.

h. A description of the sampling procedure performed and a listing of compliance deviations identified in the sample.

i. The evaluation of the sample and a summary of the overall conclusion.

VI. Classical Variables Sampling

A. Substantive Tests of Details--Substantive tests are performed by the auditor to either detect misstatements or obtain evidence about the validity and propriety of the accounting treatment of transactions and balances. In substantive testing, the auditor is primarily interested in dollar amounts. An example of a substantive test is the use of a sample from the accounts receivable subsidiary ledger to estimate the balance in the control account. The traditional method of performing substantive tests of details is by variables sampling.

Substantive Tests → Variables Sampling → Dollar Amount

B. Methods

1. Simple Extension (Mean-Per-Unit Approach)--A method of estimating variables in which the auditor finds the average audited value for the items in the sample and then estimates the population value by multiplying the average sample value by the size of the population. For example, if the mean of a sample of 50 accounts is calculated to be $100 and there are 1,000 accounts in the population, the total value of the 1,000 accounts would be estimated at $100,000 [i.e., ($100 per account) x (1,000 accounts)] plus or minus an allowance for sampling error that is statistically determined. Note that the auditor needs to know the audited values of the items in the sample but does not need to know their book values.

2. Difference Estimation--The auditor first finds the average difference between the audited value and the book value of the items in the sample. This average difference is then multiplied by the size of the population in order to estimate the difference between the book value of the population and its actual value. For example, if the average difference between the book value and audited value for each account in a sample of 100 accounts is $10 and if there are 10,000 accounts in the population, the auditor will estimate that there is a $100,000 difference between the book value of the population and the actual value (i.e., $10 x 10,000 accounts) plus or minus an allowance for sampling risk that is statistically determined. The interval, so determined, is then compared against the precision required (i.e., against the amount of acceptable difference) in order to decide if the account appears to be reasonably stated.

3. Ratio Method--The auditor uses sample results to estimate the ratio of audited value to book value. This ratio is then applied to the population to estimate the actual value. Ratio estimation should be used when each population item has a book value, an audited value may be ascertained for each sample item, and differences occur frequently. For example, if the auditor finds that the average ratio of audited value to book value for the sample is 1.05 and if the book value for the population is $100,000, the actual value for the population can

be estimated to be $105,000 (i.e., 1.05 x $100,000) plus or minus an allowance for sampling risk.

C. Steps--The following general steps are appropriate in substantive tests of details.

1. Determine the Objectives--It is important for the auditor to specify the purpose of the test because this will determine the population of the test. For example, the purpose may be to prove the existence of an account balance or to show that the account is complete.

2. Define the Population--The auditor must match the objectives of the test to the appropriate population. The population is made up of the account balances or class of transactions of interest to the auditor. Defining the population involves consideration of the individual sampling units of the entire population, whether or not the entire population is available to be picked, and the identification of those items that are individually significant. Those items that are individually significant may be accounts that are large enough to exceed the level of tolerable deviation by themselves. These would not be included in the population available for sampling, but should be tested separately.

3. Determine the Confidence Level--The confidence level for the auditor's substantive tests will generally vary inversely with the assessed level of control risk (i.e., the stronger internal control is judged to be, the lower the assessed level of control risk, thereby affecting the extent of substantive tests). The confidence level for a particular substantive test is a matter of judgment, but the auditor should consider the overall confidence level in making the determination. This confidence level is related to the auditor's assessment of sampling risk.

4. Determine the Expected Standard Deviation of the Population, or the Expected Amount of Misstatement Directly in Dollar Value--This is also a matter of judgment, frequently based on the prior year's audit or on the results of a small pilot sample. As expected misstatement increases, a larger sample size is required.

5. Determine the Tolerable Misstatement--The tolerable misstatement is the maximum monetary misstatement that may exist without causing the financial statements to be materially misstated. This is a judgmental value which should closely relate to the auditor's preliminary estimates of materiality levels. As tolerable misstatement increases, sample size decreases.

6. Select a Method of Audit Sampling--These can be either statistical or nonstatistical. If statistical sampling is used, either PPS or classical variables techniques would be used.

7. Compute the sample size by using a sample size table, formula, or computer software. The sample size formula for substantive testing is as follows:

$$n = \frac{c^2 \times s^2 \times N^2}{A^2} = \frac{c^2 \times s^2}{a^2}$$

Where:

n = Size of the sample.

c = Confidence (reliability) coefficient. This is the number of standard deviations that corresponds to the selected confidence level.

s = Standard deviation of the population (usually the standard deviation of a small pilot sample or the standard deviation found in previous years).

N = Size of the population.

A = Population allowance for sampling error (tolerable misstatement less expected amount of misstatement).

a = Allowance for sampling error per population item.

Example 4--An auditor wishes to apply statistical sampling as part of substantive testing of the accounts receivable control account. The account has a book value of $500,000 and is composed of 5,000 individual accounts. Assume that the auditor determines that 90% confidence is necessary in the results of substantive testing for this account, and that the auditor sets total allowance for sampling error (precision) at $40,000. Next, the auditor takes a small pilot sample in order to estimate the standard deviation of the population. Assume the pilot sample has a standard deviation of $40. This information can be summarized as follows:

n = ?

N = 5,000

c = 1.64 (i.e., the number of standard deviations corresponding to 90% for a normal distribution--Standard deviations table not included.)

A = $40,000

$$a = \frac{\$40{,}000}{5{,}000} = \$8$$

s = $40

Substituting this information into the sample size formula and solving the equation gives the following results:

$$n = \frac{(1.64)^2\ (\$40)^2}{(\$8)^2} = 67.24 \approx 68 \text{ accounts}$$

Therefore, the auditor should take a random sample of 68 accounts from the population of 5,000 accounts receivable in order to have 90% confidence that the inference based on the sample results will be within $40,000 of the true (actual) value of accounts receivable. That is, if a population of 5,000 accounts actually has a standard deviation of $40, 90% of the possible samples of 68 accounts will yield estimates that are within $40,000 of the actual value of accounts receivable. It is important to remember how the variable sampling factors affect the sample size.

Exhibit 3--Summary of sampling factor relationships.

Decrease in	Effect on Sample Size
Confidence (reliability) coefficient	Decrease
Tolerable misstatement	Increase
Expected standard deviation of the population	Decrease
Risk-Incorrect Acceptance	Increase
Risk-Incorrect Rejection	Increase

8. Select and audit the sample items.

9. Evaluate the Sample Results--The auditor computes the actual sampling error (precision) and confidence level attained by the sample.

   a. Estimate the population value (multiply the sample mean by the population size).

b. Compute the actual sampling error (i.e., precision) by solving the sample size formula for A.

$$A = \frac{c \times s \times N}{\sqrt{n}}$$

c. Compute the actual confidence level by solving the sample size formula for c.

$$c = \frac{A \times \sqrt{n}}{s \times N}$$

> Example 5--Assume the auditor selects a sample of 68 accounts as described in Example 2. The auditor would audit these accounts to determine the actual value of each account, then compute the average audited balance. Assume that the average audited balance is $95 per account. The estimated population value is $475,000 ($95 x 5,000 accounts). If the standard deviation of the sample is assumed to be $40, we can compute the actual sampling error (precision) as follows:
>
> $$A = \frac{c \times s \times N}{\sqrt{n}} = \frac{(1.64)\ (\$40)\ (5{,}000)}{\sqrt{68}} = \$39{,}775 \approx \$40{,}000$$
>
> And the confidence level coefficient as follows:
>
> $$c = \frac{A \times \sqrt{n}}{s \times N} = \frac{\$40{,}000 \times \sqrt{68}}{(\$40)\ (5{,}000)} = 1.649 \approx 1.65$$
>
> Thus, the auditor can rely on the results of the test, with 90% confidence that it yields an estimated value for accounts receivable that differs from the true value by no more than $40,000.

10. Reach an Overall Conclusion--The auditor should project the results of the sample to the population from which the sample was taken before evaluating the results of the sample. The client may adjust the book value of the account to correct the misstatements actually found in the sample and any misstatements discovered in any 100%-examined items. The total projected misstatement after the book value has been adjusted should be compared with the tolerable misstatement. If the auditor considers the projected misstatement unacceptable, the auditor should take appropriate action (for example, performing other substantive tests on the account). Note that the auditor also considers the qualitative aspects of misstatements (i.e., misstatements in amount vs. misapplication of accounting principle, or errors vs. irregularities) in reaching an overall conclusion.

11. Document the Sampling Procedure--Documentation might include the following:

    a. The objectives of the test and a description of other audit procedures related to those objectives.

    b. The definition of the population and the sampling unit, including how the auditor considered completeness of the population.

    c. The definition of a misstatement.

    d. The rationale for the risk of incorrect acceptance, the risk of incorrect rejection, the tolerable misstatement, and the expected population deviation amount used in the application.

e. The audit sampling technique used.

f. The method of sample selection.

g. A description of the performance of the sampling procedure and a listing of misstatements identified in the sample.

h. The evaluation of the sample and a summary of the overall conclusion.

VII. Probability-Proportional-to-Size Sampling (PPS)

PPS is a form of variables sampling that uses attribute sampling theory and is used for substantive testing. The sampling unit is not an individual account or transaction, but an individual dollar in an account balance (a logical unit).

A. Distinguishing Features--PPS sampling has two unique properties:

1. The audit population is automatically stratified by monetary value.

2. Larger dollar amounts have a higher probability of being selected. Therefore, overstatements are more likely to be detected than understatements. Hence, PPS sampling is most appropriate when an auditor desires testing for material overstatements. PPS sampling is ineffective in searching for unrecorded items. The probability of an item being selected is directly proportional to its dollar value.

> Example 6
>
> X Co.'s account receivable balance is \$2,000,000 — The population is 2,000,000
> Customer Y has a balance of \$120,000 — The sampling unit is 1
>
> Customer Y has a 6% chance of being selected
>
> 120,000 / 2,000,000 = 6%

B. Advantages of the PPS Sampling Method--Sample sizes in low-error environments tend to be relatively small because their approach does not use standard deviations (which tend to be large in most credit environments) in determining sample size. This method also reduces audit work because several dollars selected will appear in the same sample item (for example, a customer's account balance) and, therefore, the same audit procedures often determine the audited value of more than one sample item. Also, this approach does not require a high number of errors to be observed in the sample for the results to be statistically valid, as is the case with Difference Estimation and Ratio Estimation.

C. Disadvantages of the PPS Sampling Method--An understatement is less likely to be discovered than an overstatement, since those accounts receivable with higher dollar values have a greater chance of being selected. Therefore, PPS sampling is generally considered inappropriate for liability accounts. Also, special consideration must be given to zero and negative balance accounts which are usually excluded from the PPS sample. A third disadvantage occurs when the population has a high expected misstatement rate; the auditor may obtain sample sizes larger than those required by classical variables sampling.

D. Determining Sample Size--Requires that the auditor determine a reliability factor for overstatement errors, a tolerable rate, and an expected error rate.

1. Reliability Factor for Overstatement Errors--Can be determined from tables after specifying the expected number of overstatement errors and the risk of incorrect acceptance. The

auditor controls the risk of incorrect acceptance by specifying the risk level for the sampling plan.

a. PPS sampling is most appropriate when no errors are expected. Therefore, zero is the appropriate estimate for the number of overstatement errors.

b. The risk of incorrect acceptance is a matter of professional judgment. With PPS sampling, it represents an auditor's risk that book value is not materially overstated when material monetary overstatements exist.

Table 3

Reliability Factors for Errors of Overstatement

Number of Overstatement Errors	Risk of Incorrect Acceptance								
	1%	5%	10%	15%	20%	25%	30%	37%	50%
0	4.61	3.00	2.31	1.90	1.61	1.39	1.21	1.00	.70
1	6.64	4.75	3.89	3.38	3.00	2.70	2.44	2.14	1.68
2	8.41	6.30	5.33	4.72	4.28	3.93	3.62	3.25	2.68
3	10.05	7.76	6.69	6.02	5.52	5.11	4.77	4.34	3.68
4	11.61	9.16	8.00	7.27	6.73	6.28	5.90	5.43	4.68
5	13.11	10.52	9.28	8.50	7.91	7.43	7.01	6.49	5.68
6	14.57	11.85	10.54	9.71	9.08	8.56	8.12	7.56	6.67
7	16.00	13.15	11.78	10.90	10.24	9.69	9.21	8.63	7.67
8	17.41	14.44	13.00	12.08	11.38	10.81	10.31	9.68	8.67
9	18.79	15.71	14.21	13.25	12.52	11.92	11.39	10.74	9.67
10	20.15	16.97	15.41	14.42	13.66	13.02	12.47	11.79	10.67
11	21.49	18.21	16.60	15.57	14.78	14.13	13.55	12.84	11.67
12	22.83	19.45	17.79	16.72	15.90	15.22	14.63	13.89	12.67
13	24.14	20.67	18.96	17.86	17.02	16.32	15.70	14.93	13.67
14	25.45	21.89	20.13	19.00	18.13	17.40	16.77	15.97	14.67
15	26.75	23.10	21.30	20.13	19.24	18.49	17.84	17.02	15.67
16	28.03	24.31	22.46	21.26	20.34	19.58	18.90	18.06	16.67
17	29.31	25.50	23.61	22.39	21.44	20.66	19.97	19.10	17.67
18	30.59	26.70	24.76	23.51	22.54	21.74	21.03	20.14	18.67
19	31.85	27.88	25.91	24.63	23.64	22.81	22.09	21.18	19.67
20	33.11	29.07	27.05	25.74	24.73	23.89	23.15	22.22	20.67

Example 7A--Using Table 3, if the auditor's risk of incorrect acceptance for Co. X is 5% and the number of overstatement errors is 0, then the reliability factor for errors of overstatement is 3.00.

2. The tolerable rate (or tolerable error) is the maximum monetary error that may exist in an account balance without causing the financial statements to be materially misstated. Thus, tolerable error in PPS sampling is closely related to the auditor's planned level of materiality. The sampling interval and the sample size can be determined using the following formulas:

$$\textit{Sampling Interval} = \frac{\textit{Tolerable Misstatement}}{\textit{Reliability Factor for the Error of Overstatement}}$$

$$\textit{Sampling Size} = \frac{\textit{Population}}{\textit{Sampling Interval}}$$

> Example 7B--Continuing example 7:
>
> The tolerable misstatement is $60,000;
>
> therefore, the sampling interval is $20,000.
>
> (60,000 / 3.00 = 20,000)
>
> The sample size is 100.
>
> (2,000,000 / 20,000 = 100)

3. Expected Error Rate--If some errors are expected, the sample interval can be computed by determining the expected error rate.

   a. $$\textit{Expected Error Rate} = \frac{\textit{Expected Misstatement}}{\textit{Population}}$$

> Example 7C--In our example let's assume that we determine that the expected misstatement for Co. X is $10,000 based on our prior experience with the client.
>
> Our expected error rate is .005 (10,000 / 2,000,000 = .005).
>
> Remember that our tolerable rate is 3.
>
> Using Table 1, our sample size is 157.
>
> The sampling interval is then computed by dividing the population by the sample size.
>
> (2,000,000 / 157 = 12,739)

   b. In cases where the expected error rate is not shown on the table, the auditor would use the sample size for the next higher percentage. If the tolerable rate percentage is not found, it would be appropriate to select the sample size for the next smaller percentage shown. This follows the accounting convention of conservatism.

E. Select and Audit the Sample Item--Systematic sampling selection is most often used. Audit procedures are then employed to determine the value of each sample item.

F. Evaluate the Sample Results--Misstatements from the sample should be projected to the population to calculate an allowance for sampling risk. This allowance for sampling risk is a calculation with an incremental allowance for projected errors (misstatements). If the sample contains less than 100 percent errors, the formula for determining the upper limits is as follows:

$$\begin{matrix}\textit{Upper limit} \\ \textit{for errors} \\ \textit{(Misstatements)}\end{matrix} = \begin{matrix}\textit{Projected} \\ \textit{errors} \\ \textit{(Misstatements)}\end{matrix} + \begin{matrix}\textit{Basic} \\ \textit{precision}\end{matrix} + \begin{matrix}\textit{Incremental allowance} \\ \textit{for projected} \\ \textit{errors (Misstatements)}\end{matrix}$$

1. The upper limit on misstatement is calculated by adding the projected misstatement, the basic precision and the incremental allowance.

   a. Projected misstatements are calculated for each sample item depending on whether the recorded book value is less than or greater than the sampling interval. If less than, the difference between the recorded value and the audited value is divided by the recorded value to arrive at a percentage error known as "tainting." The projected misstatement is the "tainting" percentage multiplied by the sampling interval.

b. Basic precision is calculated by multiplying the reliability factor by the sampling interval.

c. An incremental allowance for projected misstatement is calculated using only those errors in logical units less than the sampling interval. These are ranked from highest to lowest (in terms of tainting %), considering the incremental changes in reliability factors for the actual number of errors found.

2. Finishing the evaluation procedure involves comparing the upper limit on errors to the previously estimated tolerable error. If the upper limit on misstatements is less than the tolerable misstatement, such as above, it can be concluded that the total population is not misstated by an amount greater than the originally estimated tolerable misstatement, at the specified risk of incorrect acceptance.

3. If the upper limit on misstatements is greater than the tolerable misstatement, then the sample result does not support the conclusion that the population is not misstated by more than the tolerable misstatement. This may occur if the population was not represented by the sample, the sample was too small due to an excessively low expectation of misstatement, or if the population itself was misstated.

4. In cases where the recorded book value is greater than the sampling interval, the projected misstatement is equal to the actual error.

5. If no errors are found, both the projected errors and the incremental allowance for projected errors would be zero. Therefore, the auditor could conclude that the recorded amount of accounts is not overstated by more than the tolerable error estimated earlier because the only factor with a value other than zero would be the basic precision.

Exhibit 4--Assume that audit procedures reveal four errors. The projected misstatement total is calculated first, followed by the other two components of the upper limits, precision and the incremental allowance for projected misstatement.

a. Projected Misstatement:

(1) Book value	(2) Audited value	(3) Tainting % (1) – (2) ÷ (1)	(4) Sampling interval	(5) Projected error (3) x (4)
$ 500	$ 450	.10	$12,739	$1,274
11,000	10,340	.06	12,739	764
5,700	5,625	.013	12,739	166
25,350	23,350	--	--	2,000
				$4,204

(continued on next page)

b. Basic precision: 3 x $12,739 = $38,217

c. Incremental allowance:

(1)	(2)	(3)	(4)
Projected error	Reliability factor (from table)	Incremental change in reliability factor (from table) (increment–1)	Incremental allowance (3) x (1)
$1,274	4.75	.75 [1]	$ 956
764	6.30	.55 [2]	420
166	7.76	.46 [3]	76
			$1,452

NOTE: To isolate the incremental allowance using Table 3, the quantity 1 must be subtracted from each of the incremental changes.

[1] 4.75 – 3.00 – 1.00 = .75 [2] 6.30 – 4.75 – 1.00 = .55 [3] 7.76 – 6.30 – 1.00 = .46

Projected misstatement	$ 4,204
Precision	38,217
Incremental allowance	1,452
Upper limit	$43,873

In this example, it can be concluded that the audited sample supports the conclusion that the population is not misstated by more than the tolerable misstatement.

APPENDIX: KEY TERMS

1. Allowance for sampling error (precision; sampling error)--A measure of the closeness of a sample estimate to the corresponding population characteristic for a specified sampling risk.

2. Alpha risk--See risk of incorrect rejection and risk of assessing control risk too high.

3. Attribute--Any characteristic that is either present or absent. In tests of controls directed toward operating effectiveness, the presence or absence of evidence of the application of a specified internal control policy or procedure is sometimes referred to as an attribute.

4. Attributes sampling--A statistical procedure based on estimating whether the rate of occurrence of a particular attribute in a population exceeds a tolerable rate.

5. Audit sampling--The application of an audit procedure to less than 100 percent of the items within an account balance or class of transactions for the purpose of evaluating some characteristic of the balance or class.

6. Block sample (cluster sample)--A sample consisting of contiguous transactions.

7. Beta risk--See risk of incorrect acceptance and risk of assessing control risk too low.

8. Classical variables sampling--A sampling approach that measures sampling risk using the variation of the underlying characteristic of interest. This approach includes methods such as mean-per-unit, ratio estimation, and difference estimation.

9. Confidence level (reliability level)--The complement of the applicable sampling risk (see risk of incorrect acceptance, risk of assessing control risk too low, risk of incorrect rejection, and risk of assessing control risk too high). In practice, the confidence level is often set equal to the complement of the risk of incorrect rejection (i.e., to the complement of the alpha risk).

10. Difference estimation--A classical variables sampling technique that uses the total difference between audited values and individual book values to estimate the total dollar error in a population and an allowance for sampling error.

11. Dollar-unit sampling--See probability-proportional-to-size sampling.

12. Expected population deviation rate--An anticipation of the deviation rate in the entire population. It is used in determining an appropriate sample size for an attributes sample.

13. Haphazard sample--A sample consisting of sampling units selected by the auditor without any special reason for including or omitting particular items.

14. Mean-per-unit method--A classical variables sampling technique that uses the sample average to project the total population dollar value by multiplying the sample average by the number of items in the population.

15. Nonsampling risk--All aspects of audit risk not due to sampling.

16. Nonstatistical sampling--A sampling technique for which the auditor considers sampling risk in evaluating an audit sample without using statistical theory to measure that risk.

17. Population (field; universe)--The items comprising the account balance or class of transactions, or a portion of that balance or class of interest. The population excludes individually significant items of which the auditor has decided to examine 100 percent or other items that will be tested separately.

18. Precision--See allowance for sampling errors.

19. Probability-proportional-to-size (PPS) sampling (Dollar-unit sampling; CMA sampling)--A variables sampling procedure that uses attributes theory to express a projection of the error in a population in dollar amounts.

20. Random sample--A sample drawn so that every combination of the same number of items in the population has an equal probability of selection.

21. Ratio estimation--A classical variables sampling technique that uses the ratio of audited values to book values in the sample to estimate the total dollar value of the population and an allowance for sampling error.

22. Reliability level--See confidence level.

23. Risk of incorrect acceptance (beta risk; type II misstatement)--The risk that the sample supports the conclusion that the recorded account balance is not materially misstated when it is, in fact, materially misstated.

24. Risk of incorrect rejection (alpha risk; type I misstatement)--The risk that the sample supports the conclusion that the recorded account balance is materially misstated when, in fact, it is not.

25. Risk of assessing control risk too low--The risk that the assessed level of control risk based on the sample is less than the true operating effectiveness of the control structure policies or procedures.

26. Risk of assessing control risk too high--The risk that the assessed level of control risk based on the sample is greater than the true operating effectiveness of the control structure policies or procedures.

27. Sample--Items selected from a population to reach a conclusion about the population.

28. Sampling risk--The risk that the auditor's conclusion based on a sample may be different from the conclusion the auditor would reach if the test were applied in the same way to the entire population. For tests of controls, sampling risk is the risk of assessing control risk too high or too low. For substantive testing, sampling risk is the risk of incorrect acceptance or rejection.

29. Sequential sampling--A sampling plan for which the sample is selected in several steps, with each step conditional on the results of the previous steps.

30. Standard deviation--A measure of the dispersion among the respective values of a particular characteristic as measured for all items in the population for which a sample estimate is developed.

31. Statistical sampling--Audit sampling that uses the laws of probability for selecting and evaluating a sample from a population for the purpose of reaching a conclusion about the population.

32. Stratification--Division of the population into relatively homogeneous groups.

33. Systematic sampling--A method of drawing a sample in which every n^{th} item is drawn from one or more random starts.

34. Tolerable misstatement--An estimate of the maximum monetary misstatement that may exist in an account balance or class of transactions without causing the financial statements to be materially misstated.

35. Tolerable rate--The maximum population rate of deviations from a prescribed control procedure that the auditor will tolerate without modifying the nature, timing, or extent of substantive testing.

36. Variables sampling--Statistical sampling that reaches a conclusion on the monetary amounts of a population.

CHAPTER 38—AUDIT SAMPLING PROCEDURES

Problem 38-1 MULTIPLE CHOICE QUESTIONS (50 to 60 minutes)

1. Which of the following courses of action would an auditor most likely follow in planning a sample of cash disbursements if the auditor is aware of several unusually large cash disbursements?
a. Increase the sample size to reduce the effect of the unusually large disbursements.
b. Continue to draw new samples until all the unusually large disbursements appear in the sample.
c. Set the tolerable rate of deviation at a lower level than originally planned.
d. Stratify the cash disbursements population so that the unusually large disbursements are selected. (11/92, Aud., #39, 2973)

1A. Which of the following courses of action would an auditor most likely follow in planning a sample of cash disbursements if the auditor is aware of several unusually large cash disbursements?
a. Set the tolerable rate of deviation at a lower level than originally planned.
b. Stratify the cash disbursements population so that the unusually large disbursements are selected.
c. Increase the sample size to reduce the effect of the unusually large disbursements.
d. Continue to draw new samples until all the unusually large disbursements appear in the sample. (11/94, Aud., #55, 5128)

2. An auditor is performing substantive tests of pricing and extensions of perpetual inventory balances consisting of a large number of items. Past experience indicates numerous pricing and extension misstatements. Which of the following statistical sampling approaches is most appropriate?
a. Unstratified mean-per-unit.
b. Probability-proportional-to-size.
c. Stop or go.
d. Ratio estimation. (5/89, Aud., #41, 9911)

2A. In confirming a client's accounts receivable in prior years, an auditor found that there were many differences between the recorded account balances and the confirmation replies. These differences, which were not misstatements, required substantial time to resolve. In defining the sampling unit for the current year's audit, the auditor most likely would choose
a. Individual overdue balances.
b. Individual invoices.
c. Small account balances.
d. Large account balances. (5/95, Aud., #49, 5667)

3. Which of the following statistical sampling plans does not use a fixed sample size for testing of controls purposes?
a. Dollar-unit sampling.
b. Sequential sampling.
c. PPS sampling.
d. Variable sampling. (5/88, Aud., #18, 0263)

4. When performing a test of controls with respect to control over cash receipts, an auditor may use a systematic sampling technique with a start at any randomly selected item. The biggest disadvantage of this type of sampling is that the items in the population
a. Must be systematically replaced in the population after sampling.
b. May systematically occur more than once in the sample.
c. Must be recorded in a systematic pattern before the sample can be drawn.
d. May occur in a systematic pattern, thus destroying the sample randomness. (11/86, Aud., #20, 0267)

5. An auditor may decide to increase the risk of incorrect rejection when
a. Increased reliability from the sample is desired.
b. Many differences (audit value minus recorded value) are expected.
c. Initial sample results do **not** support the planned level of control risk.
d. The cost and effort of selecting additional sample items is low. (11/92, Aud., #38, 2972)

5A. While performing a test of details during an audit, an auditor determined that the sample results supported the conclusion that the recorded account balance was materially misstated. It was, in fact, not materially misstated. This situation illustrates the risk of
a. Assessing control risk too high.
b. Assessing control risk too low.
c. Incorrect rejection.
d. Incorrect acceptance. (5/94, Aud., #43, 4708)

6. To determine the sample size for a test of controls, an auditor should consider the tolerable deviation rate, the allowable risk of assessing control risk too low, and the
a. Expected deviation rate.
b. Upper precision limit.
c. Risk of incorrect acceptance.
d. Risk of incorrect rejection. (11/90, Aud., #58, 0249)

6A. The sample size of a test of controls varies inversely with

	Expected population deviation rate	Tolerable rate
a.	Yes	Yes
b.	No	No
c.	Yes	No
d.	No	Yes

(5/94, Aud., #44, 4709)

6B. In determining the sample size for a test of controls, an auditor should consider the likely rate of deviations, the allowable risk of assessing control risk too low, and the

a. Tolerable deviation rate.
b. Risk of incorrect acceptance.
c. Nature and cause of deviations.
d. Population size. (5/95, Aud., #35, 5653)

7. The risk of incorrect acceptance and the likelihood of assessing control risk too low relate to the

a. Effectiveness of an audit.
b. Efficiency of the audit.
c. Preliminary estimates of materiality levels.
d. Allowable risk of tolerable error.

(5/90, Aud., #44, 0254)

7A. As a result of tests of controls, an auditor assessed control risk too low and decreased substantive testing. This assessment occurred because the true deviation rate in the population was

a. Less than the risk of assessing control risk too low, based on the auditor's sample.
b. Less than the deviation rate in the auditor's sample.
c. More than the risk of assessing control risk too low, based on the auditor's sample.
d. More than the deviation rate in the auditor's sample. (5/95, Aud., #28, 5646)

8. In the audit of the financial statements of Delta Company, the auditor determines that in performing a test of controls, the compliance rate in the sample does not support the assessed level of control risk when, in fact, the compliance rate in the population does justify the assessed level of control risk. This situation illustrates the risk of

a. Assessing control risk too low.
b. Assessing control risk too high.
c. Incorrect rejection.
d. Incorrect acceptance. (11/86, Aud., #21, 9911)

9. The diagram following depicts the auditor's estimated maximum deviation rate compared with the tolerable rate, and also depicts the true population deviation rate compared with the tolerable rate.

	True state of population	
Auditor's estimate based on sample results	**Deviation rate is less than tolerable rate**	**Deviation rate exceeds tolerable rate**
Maximum deviation rate is less than tolerable rate	I.	III.
Maximum deviation rate exceeds tolerable rate	II.	IV.

As a result of tests of controls, the auditor assesses control risk higher than necessary and thereby increases substantive testing. This is illustrated by situation

a. I.
b. II.
c. III.
d. IV. (5/92, Aud., #39, 2792)

10. Given random selection, the same sample size, and the same precision requirement for the testing of two unequal populations, the risk of assessing control risk too low on the smaller population is

a. The same as assessing control risk too low for the larger population.
b. Higher than assessing control risk too low for the larger population.
c. Lower than assessing control risk too low for the larger population.
d. Indeterminate relative to assessing control risk too low for the larger population.

(11/84, Aud., #57, 9911)

10A. When using confirmations to provide evidence about the completeness assertion for accounts payable, the appropriate population most likely would be

a. Vendors with whom the entity has previously done business.
b. Amounts recorded in the accounts payable subsidiary ledger.
c. Payees of checks drawn in the month after the year end.
d. Invoices filed in the entity's open invoice file.

(11/94, Aud., #53, 5126)

11. In which of the following cases would the auditor be most likely to conclude that all of the items in an account under consideration should be examined rather than tested on a sample basis?

	The measure of tolerable misstatement is	Misstatement frequency is expected to be
a.	Large	Low
b.	Small	High
c.	Large	High
d.	Small	Low

(5/83, Aud., #1, 9911)

11A. Which of the following sample planning factors would influence the sample size for a substantive test of details for a specific account?

	Expected amount of misstatements	*Measure of tolerable misstatement*
a.	No	No
b.	Yes	Yes
c.	No	Yes
d.	Yes	No

(11/94, Aud., #56, 5129)

12. An advantage of statistical sampling over nonstatistical sampling is that statistical sampling helps an auditor to

a. Minimize the failure to detect errors and irregularities.
b. Eliminate the risk of nonsampling errors.
c. Reduce the level of audit risk and materiality to a relatively low amount.
d. Measure the sufficiency of the evidential matter obtained. (5/93, Aud., #42, 3938)

12A. An advantage of using statistical over non-statistical sampling methods in tests of controls is that the statistical methods

a. Can more easily convert the sample into a dual-purpose test useful for substantive testing.
b. Eliminate the need to use judgment in determining appropriate sample sizes.
c. Afford greater assurance than a nonstatistical sample of equal size.
d. Provide an objective basis for quantitatively evaluating sample risk. (5/95, Aud., #36, 5654)

13. Stratified mean per unit (MPU) sampling is a statistical technique that may be more efficient than unstratified MPU because it usually

a. May be applied to populations where many monetary errors are expected to occur.
b. Produces an estimate having a desired level of precision with a smaller sample size.
c. Increases the variability among items in a stratum by grouping sampling units with similar characteristics.
d. Yields a weighted sum of the strata standard deviations that is greater than the standard deviation of the population.

(11/90, Aud., #30, 0247)

13A. In statistical sampling methods used in substantive testing, an auditor most likely would stratify a population into meaningful groups if

a. Probability proportional to size (PPS) sampling is used.
b. The population has highly variable recorded amounts.
c. The auditor's estimated tolerable misstatement is extremely small.
d. The standard deviation of recorded amounts is relatively small. (5/95, Aud., #50, 5668)

14. A principal advantage of statistical methods of attribute sampling over nonstatistical methods is that they provide a scientific basis for planning the

a. Risk of assessing control risk too low.
b. Tolerable rate.
c. Expected population deviation rate.
d. Sample size. (11/89, Aud., #54, 0260)

15. Which of the following statements is correct concerning the auditor's use of statistical sampling?

a. An auditor needs to estimate the dollar amount of the standard deviation of the population to use classical variables sampling.
b. An assumption of PPS sampling is that the underlying accounting population is normally distributed.
c. A classical variables sample needs to be designed with special considerations to include negative balances in the sample.
d. The selection of zero balances usually does **not** require special sample design considerations when using PPS sampling.

(5/88, Aud., #34, 0265)

16. Which of the following statistical sampling methods is most useful to auditors when performing tests of controls?

a. Ratio estimation.
b. Variable sampling.
c. Difference estimation.
d. Discovery sampling. (5/86, Aud., #30, 0268)

17. Using statistical sampling to assist in verifying the year-end accounts payable balance, an auditor has accumulated the following data:

	Number of accounts	Book balance	Balance determined by the auditor
Population	4,100	$ 5,000,000	?
Sample	200	$ 250,000	$300,000

Using the ratio estimation technique, the auditor's estimate of year-end accounts payable balance would be

a. $6,150,000.
b. $6,000,000.
c. $5,125,000.
d. $5,050,000. (11/84, Aud., #14, 9911)

18. In planning a statistical sample for a test of controls, an auditor increased the expected population deviation rate from the prior year's rate because of the results of the prior year's tests of controls and the overall control environment. The auditor most likely would then increase the planned

a. Tolerable rate.
b. Allowance for sampling risk.
c. Risk of assessing control risk too low.
d. Sample size. (11/92, Aud., #25, 2959)

19. Which of the following statements is correct concerning statistical sampling in tests of controls?

a. Deviations from control procedures at a given rate usually result in misstatements at a higher rate.
b. As the population size doubles, the sample size should also double.
c. The qualitative aspects of deviations are **not** considered by the auditor.
d. There is an inverse relationship between the sample size and the tolerable rate. (5/92, Aud., #53, 2806)

20. What is an auditor's evaluation of a statistical sample for attributes when a test of 50 documents results in 3 deviations if tolerable rate is 7%, the expected population deviation rate is 5%, and the allowance for sampling risk is 2%?

a. Modify the planned assessed level of control risk because the tolerable rate plus the allowance for sampling risk exceeds the expected population deviation rate.
b. Accept the sample results as support for the planned assessed level of control risk because the sample deviation rate plus the allowance for sampling risk exceeds the tolerable rate.
c. Accept the sample results as support for the planned assessed level of control risk because the tolerable rate less the allowance for sampling risk equals the expected population deviation rate.
d. Modify the planned assessed level of control risk because the sample deviation rate plus the allowance for sampling risk exceeds the tolerable rate. (5/92, Aud., #54, 2807)

Items 21 and 22 are based on the following:

An auditor desired to test credit approval on 10,000 sales invoices processed during the year. The auditor designed a statistical sample that would provide 1% risk of assessing control risk too low (99% confidence) that not more than 7% of the sales invoices lacked approval. The auditor estimated from previous experience that about 2½% of the sales invoices lacked approval. A sample of 200 invoices was examined and 7 of them were lacking approval. The auditor then determined the achieved upper precision limit to be 8%.

21. In the evaluation of this sample, the auditor decided to increase the level of the preliminary assessment of control risk because the

a. Tolerable rate (7%) was less than the achieved upper precision limit (8%).
b. Expected deviation rate (7%) was more than the percentage of errors in the sample (3½%).
c. Achieved upper precision limit (8%) was more than the percentage of errors in the sample (3½%).
d. Expected deviation rate (2½%) was less than the tolerable rate (7%). (11/90, Aud., #59, 0250)

22. The allowance for sampling risk was

a. 5½%.
b. 4½%.
c. 3½%.
d. 1%. (11/90, Aud., #60, 0251)

23. As a result of tests of controls, an auditor assessed control risk too low and decreased substantive testing. This assessment occurred because the true deviation rate in the population was

a. More than the risk of assessing control risk too low based on the auditor's sample.
b. More than the deviation rate in the auditor's sample.
c. Less than the risk of assessing control risk too low based on the auditor's sample.
d. Less than the deviation rate in the auditor's sample. (5/93, Aud., #11, 3907)

24. In performing tests of controls over authorization of cash disbursements, which of the following statistical sampling methods would be most appropriate?
a. Variables.
b. Stratified.
c. Ratio.
d. Attributes. (5/93, Aud., #25, 3921)

24A. For which of the following audit tests would an auditor most likely use attribute sampling?
a. Making an independent estimate of the amount of a LIFO inventory.
b. Examining invoices in support of the valuation of fixed asset additions.
c. Selecting accounts receivable for confirmation of account balances.
d. Inspecting employee time cards for proper approval by supervisors.
(5/94, Aud., #17, 4682)

25. The expected population deviation rate of client billing misstatements is 3%. The auditor has established a tolerable rate of 5%. In the review of client invoices the auditor should use
a. Stratified sampling.
b. Variable sampling.
c. Discovery sampling.
d. Attribute sampling. (11/87, Aud., #58, 0266)

26. An auditor is testing internal control procedures that are evidenced on an entity's vouchers by matching random numbers with voucher numbers. If a random number matches the number of a voided voucher, that voucher ordinarily should be replaced by another voucher in the random sample if the voucher
a. Constitutes a deviation.
b. Has been properly voided.
c. Cannot be located.
d. Represents an immaterial dollar amount.
(5/90, Aud., #43, 0253)

27. Which of the following factors is generally **not** considered in determining the sample size for a test of controls?
a. Population size.
b. Tolerable rate.
c. Risk of assessing control risk too low.
d. Expected population deviation rate.
(5/89, Aud., #24, 0262)

28. Which of the following factors does an auditor generally need to consider in planning a particular audit sample for a test of controls?
a. Number of items in the population.
b. Total dollar amount of the items to be sampled.
c. Acceptable level of risk of assessing control risk too low.
d. Tolerable misstatement. (5/88, Aud., #19, 9911)

29. Samples to test internal control structure procedures are intended to provide a basis for an auditor to conclude whether
a. The control procedures are operating effectively.
b. The financial statements are materially misstated.
c. The risk of incorrect acceptance is too high.
d. Materiality for planning purposes is at a sufficiently low level. (5/91, Aud., #40, 0246)

30. In performing testing of controls, the auditor will normally find that
a. The level of risk is directly proportionate to the rate of misstatement.
b. The rate of deviations in the sample exceeds the rate of misstatement in the accounting records.
c. The rate of misstatement in the sample exceeds the rate of deviations.
d. All unexamined items result in misstatements in the accounting records. (5/85, Aud., #35, 9911)

30A. Which of the following statements is correct concerning statistical sampling in tests of controls?
a. As the population size increases, the sample size should increase proportionately.
b. Deviations from specific internal control procedures at a given rate ordinarily result in misstatements at a lower rate.
c. There is an inverse relationship between the expected population deviation rate and the sample size.
d. In determining tolerable rate, an auditor considers detection risk and the sample size.
(11/94, Aud., #27, 5100)

31. Which of the following most likely would be an advantage in using classical variables sampling rather than probability-proportional-to-size (PPS) sampling?
a. An estimate of the standard deviation of the population's recorded amounts is **not** required.
b. The auditor rarely needs the assistance of a computer program to design an efficient sample.
c. Inclusion of zero and negative balances generally does **not** require special design considerations.
d. Any amount that is individually significant is automatically identified and selected.
(5/93, Aud., #43, 3939)

32. When using classical variables sampling for estimation, an auditor normally evaluates the sampling results by calculating the possible error in either direction. This statistical concept is known as

a. Precision.
b. Reliability.
c. Projected error.
d. Standard deviation. (5/91, Aud., #18, 0244)

32A. The use of the ratio estimation sampling technique is most effective when

a. The calculated audit amounts are approximately proportional to the client's book amounts.
b. A relatively small number of differences exist in the population.
c. Estimating populations whose records consist of quantities, but **not** book values.
d. Large overstatement differences and large understatement differences exist in the population. (5/95, Aud., #51, 5669)

33. Which of the following sampling methods would be used to estimate a numerical measurement of a population, such as a dollar value?

a. Discovery sampling.
b. Numerical sampling.
c. Sampling for attributes.
d. Sampling for variables. (5/92, Aud., #29, 2782)

33A. Which of the following sampling methods would be used to estimate a numerical measurement of a population, such as a dollar value?

a. Attributes sampling.
b. Stop-or-go sampling.
c. Variables sampling.
d. Random-number sampling. (11/94, Aud., #54, 5127)

34. When planning a sample for a substantive test of details, an auditor should consider tolerable misstatement for the sample. This consideration should

a. Be related to the auditor's business risk.
b. Not be adjusted for qualitative factors.
c. Be related to preliminary judgments about materiality levels.
d. Not be changed during the audit process. (5/90, Aud., #51, 0255)

35. A number of factors influence the sample size for a substantive test of details of an account balance. All other factors being equal, which of the following would lead to a larger sample size?

a. Assessing control risk at the minimum level.
b. Greater reliance on analytical procedures.
c. Smaller expected frequency of misstatements.
d. Smaller measure of tolerable misstatements. (5/88, Aud., #33, 0264)

36. Which of the following statements is correct concerning probability-proportional-to-size (PPS) sampling, also known as dollar-unit sampling?

a. The sampling distribution should approximate the normal distribution.
b. Overstated units have a lower probability of sample selection than units that are understated.
c. The auditor controls the risk of incorrect acceptance by specifying that risk level for the sampling plan.
d. The sampling interval is calculated by dividing the number of physical units in the population by the sample size. (5/91, Aud., #17, 0243)

37. In a probability-proportional-to-size sample with a sampling interval of $5,000, an auditor discovered that a selected account receivable with a recorded amount of $10,000 had an audit amount of $8,000. If this were the only error discovered by the auditor, the projected error of this sample would be

a. $1,000.
b. $2,000.
c. $4,000.
d. $5,000. (5/92, Aud., #30, 2783)

38. Hill has decided to use probability-proportional-to-size (PPS) sampling, sometimes called dollar-unit sampling, in the audit of a client's accounts receivable balances. Hill plans to use the following PPS sampling table:

TABLE
Reliability Factors for Errors of Overstatement

Number of overstatement misstatements	Risk of incorrect acceptance 1%	5%	10%	15%	20%
0	4.61	3.00	2.31	1.90	1.61
1	6.64	4.75	3.89	3.38	3.00
2	8.41	6.30	5.33	4.72	4.28
3	10.05	7.76	6.69	6.02	5.52
4	11.61	9.16	8.00	7.27	6.73

Additional Information

Tolerable misstatement (net of effect of expected misstatement)	$ 24,000
Risk of incorrect acceptance	20%
Number of misstatements allowed	1
Recorded amount of accounts receivable	$240,000
Number of accounts	360

What sample size should Hill use?

a. 120
b. 108
c. 60
d. 30 (11/87, Aud., #38, 9911)

Solution 38-1 MULTIPLE CHOICE ANSWERS

Audit Sampling (AU 350)

1. (d) In the circumstances described, the auditor would likely wish to examine 100% of the large disbursements, while examining a sample of all others. Stratification of the unusually large disbursements into a single group and all others into another group would obviously facilitate the approach the auditor would likely wish to use. Simply increasing the sample size would not serve to guarantee the large disbursements would be selected. Also the phrase "reduce the effect of the unusually large disbursements" is meaningless. Answer (b) is incorrect because it would not be as efficient as (d) and could destroy the randomness of the process. The tolerable *rate* is relevant only in an attribute sampling plan (internal control) in which the dollar value of the population item would not be of importance. Decreasing the tolerable rate would simply increase sample size.

1A. (b) In planning a sample of cash disbursements if the auditor is aware of several unusually large cash disbursements, the auditor will most likely stratify the sample to include the unusually large disbursements. By stratifying the sample, the auditor will decrease the effect of the variances in the total population, and therefore be able to reduce the number of items in the sample.

2. (d) Ratio estimation should be used when (1) each population item has a book value, (2) an audited value may be ascertained for each sample item, and (3) *differences occur frequently*. Answers (a), (b), and (c) are less effective methods when frequent misstatements are expected.

2A. (b) It is easiest to reconcile differences and for customers to research the auditor's questions on an individual invoice level. The designation of a sampling unit depends on the type of applied auditing procedures. The auditor considers which sampling unit leads to the most efficient and effective application, given the circumstances. In the case of a high number of expected differences in amounts for accounts receivable confirmations, if the auditor selects the customer balance as a sampling unit, the auditor may need to test each individual transaction supporting that balance in the event of a contradictory report from the customer.

3. (b) Sequential sampling does not use a fixed sample size. Under sequential sampling, the sample is selected in several steps, with each step conditional on the results of the previous steps. Variables sampling methods reach a conclusion as to the monetary amounts of a population and are used for substantive testing purposes; they are not useful in estimating the frequency of deviations or exceptions from a prescribed internal control policy or procedure for testing of controls purposes. Probability-proportional-to-size (PPS) sampling (also known as dollar-unit sampling) is a variables sampling method, and, therefore, for the reasons discussed above, is not suitable for use in testing of controls.

4. (d) When using the systematic sampling technique, the auditor determines a uniform interval by dividing the number of physical units in the population by the sample size. A random number is selected as a starting point for the first interval, and one item is selected throughout the population at each of the uniform intervals from the starting point. The randomness of the sample can be destroyed if the items in the population occur in a systematic pattern. *For example*, a population of employees on a payroll for a construction company might be organized by teams; each team consists of a crew leader and nine other workers. A selection of every tenth employee will list either every crew leader or no crew leaders, depending on the random start. No combination would include both crew leaders and other employees.

5. (d) The risk of incorrect rejection is the risk that the auditor will conclude that an account balance is materially misstated when, in fact, it is not. When this error occurs, the auditor will generally extend his/her audit procedures and would eventually discover that the original conclusion of a material misstatement was incorrect. The cost of this mistake is the cost of the additional procedures that were necesssary to discover that the original conclusion was erroneous. If, however, the cost and effort of those additional procedures is low, the auditor may well decide to use a high risk of incorrect rejection

because doing so will reduce original sample size. If the desired results are achieved with the original small sample, overall audit cost will be lowered. If an incorrect rejection occurs, however, the incremental cost incurred would not be excessive. An increase in the desired reliability would likely result in a decrease (not increase) in the risk of incorrect rejection. The number of differences expected should have no bearing on the risk of incorrect rejection specified. The "risk of incorrect rejection" is not a concept associated with tests of controls. "Risk of underreliance" would be the corresponding risk that is associated with control testing.

5A. (c) AU 350.12 states the risk of incorrect rejection is the risk that the sample supports the conclusion that the recorded account balance is materially misstated when it is not materially misstated. The risk of assessing control risk too high is the risk that the assessed level of control risk based on the sample is greater than the true operating effectiveness of the control structure policy or procedure. The risk of assessing control risk too low is just the opposite. The risk of incorrect acceptance is the risk that the sample supports the conclusion that the recorded account balance is not materially misstated when it is materially misstated.

6. (a) AU 350.38 states, ". . . to determine the number of items to be selected for a particular sample for a test of controls, the auditor should consider the tolerable rate of deviation from the control structure policies or procedures being tested, *the likely rate of deviation*, and the allowable risk of assessing control risk too low." It further states, "An auditor applies professional judgment to relate these factors in determining the appropriate sample size." The upper precision range is arrived at after the sample size is determined. Answers (c) and (d) are both aspects of sampling risk having to do with substantive tests of details (AU 350.12).

6A. (d) In statistical sampling for tests of controls, there is an inverse relationship between the sample size and the tolerable rate, but an increase in the expected population deviation rate would require a corresponding increase in sample size.

6B. (a) The tolerable deviation rate is one of three factors used to determine the appropriate sample size for a test of controls (AU 350.38). The risk of incorrect acceptance and the nature and cause of deviations are considered in determining the sample size for variables (substantive) testing. The population size is only used in determining the sample size for very small populations for variables tests.

7. (a) AU 350.14 states, "The risk of incorrect acceptance and the risk of assessing control risk too low relate to the effectiveness of an audit in detecting an existing material misstatement." If the auditor incorrectly accepts an account as being materially accurate or incorrectly concludes that control risk is below the maximum, additional procedures that may detect this incorrect conclusion are either eliminated or reduced and the audit would prove ineffective in detecting misstatements. Audit efficiency is related to the risk of incorrect rejection or the risk of assessing control risk as too high. Answers (c) and (d) are factors in determining sample size and are determined independently of other risk factors.

7A. (d) If the sample deviation rate is lower than the true deviation rate in the population, the auditor mistakenly assesses control risk too low. The result is that detection risk is allowed to rise too high and substantive testing is decreased.

8. (b) The following definitions are provided in AU 350.12: The risk of *incorrect acceptance* is the risk that the sample supports the conclusion that the recorded account balance is not materially misstated when it is materially misstated. The risk of *incorrect rejection* is the risk that the sample supports the conclusion that the recorded account balance is materially misstated when it is not materially misstated. The risk of *assessing control risk too low* is the risk that the assessed level of control risk based on the sample is less than the true operating effectiveness of the control structure policy or procedure. The risk of *assessing control risk too high* is the risk that the assessed level of control risk based on the sample is greater than the true operating effectiveness of the control structure policy or procedure.

9. (b) The risk of assessing control risk too high is the risk that the assessed level of control risk based on the sample is greater than the true operating effectiveness of the control structure policy or procedure. This would be evidenced by a situation in which the auditor, based on tests of controls, estimates that the maximum deviation rate exceeds the tolerable rate when in fact the true state of the population is that the deviation rate is less than the tolerable rate.

10. (c) The risk of assessing control risk too low is the risk that the assessed level of control risk based on the sample is less than the true operating effectiveness of the control structure policy or procedure (AU 350.12). All things being equal, a sample taken from a smaller population will be more representative of the population than a sample of the same size taken from a larger population. Thus, the

risk that the sample taken from the smaller population will yield a result different from the result obtained had the entire population been examined is *lower* than such a risk inherent in sampling from a larger population.

10A. (a) In performing a search for unrecorded liabilities, one of the procedures performed is to send requests of confirmation of zero liabilities to previous vendors. These liabilities would be tend to be unrecorded, if they did indeed exist. Sending out confirmations to payees of checks drawn in the month after year-end provides evidence of the timing, not regarding the completeness, of accounts payable.

11. (b) The *tolerable misstatement* is the maximum degree of misstatement that the auditor is willing to accept in a sample. If the tolerable misstatement is small and the expected frequency of misstatements is high, then the auditor may decide to examine every item in an attempt to detect most or all of the misstatements. If the measure of tolerable misstatement was large, or if misstatement frequency was expected to be low, then the auditor could afford to test on a sample basis and run the risk that some misstatements would not be detected.

11A. (b) AU §350.48 lists both the expected size and amount of misstatements, and the measure of tolerable misstatement as influencing the sample size of a substantive test of details for a specific account.

Statistical and Nonstatistical Sampling

12. (d) AU 350.04 indicates that both statistical and nonstatistical sampling plans can provide sufficient, competent, evidential matter if properly applied. However, only the statistical sampling plan allows the auditor to measure the sampling risk. This sampling risk indicates the risk that the sample chosen is not representative of the population as a whole. Either statistical or nonstatistical sampling can be used to reduce the risk of failing to detect errors and irregularities. Both types of sampling are subject to nonsampling errors (procedural mistakes or human error). Both methods of sampling may be used to reduce audit risk but neither would affect materiality.

12A. (d) Statistical sampling methods provide an objective basis for quantitatively evaluating sampling risk. Statistical methods do not necessarily more easily convert a test of controls into a dual-purpose test. Judgment is used in determining the appropriate sample size for both statistical and nonstatistical samples. Neither statistical or nonstatistical methods would be expected to yield sample sizes for a test of controls and a substantive test of equal size.

13. (b) A smaller sample size can be obtained by stratifying a highly variable population into segments. These segments will then have a minimum of variability within segments and variability between segments will be eliminated. As a result, the total sample size of all combined segments will be less. This is accomplished without a loss of reliability or precision. The number of expected errors is not a consideration when deciding to use stratified sampling. Answer (c) is incorrect since using stratified sampling causes a decrease in variability. The calculation identified in answer (d) is meaningless.

13A. (b) Stratified sampling can be particularly useful in reducing the overall sample size on populations that have a wide range of dollar values (or highly variable recorded amounts). The primary objective is to decrease the effect of variance in the total population, thereby reducing sample size. Probability-proportional-to-size sampling insures items with large amounts all make it into the sample, but does not do so by stratifying the population. The estimated tolerable misstatement and standard deviation are irrelevant to a decision to stratify or not.

14. (d) The principal advantage of statistical over nonstatistical sampling can be expressed in several ways. One such expression is that statistical sampling provides a scientific (mathematical) basis for determining sample size while nonstatistical sampling does not. Answers (a), (b), and (c) are factors used in determining sample sizes for tests of controls but are determined on the basis of auditor judgment rather than scientifically.

15. (a) The factors affecting sample size when using classical variables sampling are (1) desired precision, (2) desired sample reliability, (3) variability among item values in the population (the estimate of the population's standard deviation) and (4) population size. PPS is a non-parametric method that does not assume a normal distribution. PPS plans require special design to deal with negative balances and zero balances because sample selection is based on the *cumulative sum* of dollars of the population. Negative figures distort the cumulative sum and zero balances would not be considered without special adjustments in a PPS plan. Classical variables techniques are unaffected by either zero balances or negative balances.

16. (d) In testing of controls, the auditor is in fact sampling attributes, for instance, whether an internal control procedure was correctly performed or not. Of the answers listed, only (d) deals with *attribute* sampling; the other three choices listed concern variables sampling.

17. (b) Under the ratio estimation technique, the auditor uses sample results to estimate the ratio of audited value to book value. The ratio is then applied to the population book value to estimate the audited value of the population. The sample "audited value/book value" ratio equals 1.2:1 ($300,000 ÷ $250,000). When this ratio is applied to the population book balance of $5,000,000, an estimated $6,000,000 audited value results.

18. (d) Whenever the auditor increases the expected population deviation rate it is evidence that the confidence in the controls of the client has also decreased. As a result, the auditor will want to consider more items from the designated population. Consequently, the size of the sample would be increased. An increase in the expected population deviation rate would have no effect on the tolerable rate. The allowance for sampling risk is mathematically calculated and is not affected by the expected population rate and is not a "planned" factor. The auditor's planned risk of assessing control risk too low is more of a function of the other types of tests planned on a given account than the expected deviation rate. If anything, however, the planned level of risk for assessing control risk too low would be *decreased* as a result of an increase in the expected deviation rate.

19. (d) In statistical sampling in tests of controls there is an inverse relationship between the sample size and the tolerable rate. Deviations from pertinent control procedures at a given rate ordinarily would be expected to result in misstatements at a *lower* rate (AU 350.35). The sample size is not in direct proportion to the population size. In addition to the evaluation of the frequency of deviations from pertinent procedures, consideration should be given to the qualitative aspects of the deviations (AU 350.42).

20. (d) The auditor should modify his or her planned assessed level of control risk when the sample deviation rate plus the allowance for sampling risk exceeds the tolerable rate. In this question, the deviation rate of 6% (3 deviations among 50 documents) plus the allowance for sampling risk of 2% is greater than the given tolerable rate of 7%.

21. (a) The auditor would increase the preliminary assessment of control risk because the achieved upper precision limit of 8% (sample error rate plus an allowance for sampling risk) exceeded the tolerable error rate of 7% (determined by professional judgment). Therefore, the results of the test did not allow the auditor to conclude with 99% confidence that the error rate in the population did not exceed 7%. All other answers describe comparisons that are meaningless.

22. (b) The allowance for sampling risk is the difference between the observed sample rate and the achieved upper precision limit. The observed sample rate was 3.5% (7/200). Therefore, the allowance for sampling risk would be 4.5% (8% – 3.5%). The planning allowance for sampling risk was also 4.5% (7% – 2.5%).

Attributes Sampling

23. (b) The auditor would assess control risk too low if his sample results, at a specified confidence level, projected an error rate in the population (say 7%) that was less than the tolerable rate (say 8%) when in fact the true error rate in the population (say 9%) exceeded the tolerable rate. Because the projected error rate is calculated by *adding* an allowance for sampling risk (say 3%) to the observed sample error rate (say 4%), the true population rate (9%) would certainly be more than the observed deviation rate (4%) in the auditor's sample in the circumstances described. Answers (a) and (c) describe meaningless comparisons. If the true population rate was less than even the deviation rate in the auditor's sample any original assessment of a low control risk would have been accurate.

24. (d) When performing tests of controls, the auditor is looking for the deviation rate from established control procedures set by the client. Thus, the auditor performs attributes sampling procedures. Answers (a) and (c) represent substantive sampling procedures. Answer (b) describes a selection method that is not relevant to attribute sampling.

24A. (d) Attribute sampling is generally used in determining the rate of deviation from prescribed internal control policies and procedures. Testing for supervisory approval of time cards would be a test of internal controls over authorization for pay. Answers (b) and (c) represent substantive tests. Answer (a) is not an example of sampling.

25. (d) Attribute sampling provides evidence of the rate of occurrence of a specified characteristic in a population at auditor-specified levels of precision and reliability. Variable sampling is used by the auditor to estimate the total dollar amount of a population at auditor-specified levels of precision and reliability. Discovery sampling is a form of attribute sampling that is designed to locate at least one exception if the rate of occurrence in the population is at or above a specified rate. This method is used to search for critical occurrences that may indicate the existence of

an irregularity, and is appropriate when the expected occurrence rate is quite low (usually near zero) and the auditor wants a sample that will provide a specified chance to observe one occurrence. Answer (a) is incorrect, as the population is not divided into groups according to a common characteristic.

26. (b) In an auditor's test of transactions, if a random number matches the number of a voided voucher, that voucher ordinarily should be replaced by another voucher in the random sample if the voucher has been properly voided. The voucher would be counted as an error and would not be replaced if it constituted a deviation or could not be located. The materiality of the dollar amount is irrelevant because the focus in a test of controls is whether or not procedures are properly performed, not the dollar value of the transaction being tested.

27. (a) AU 350.31 states, "When planning a particular audit sample for a test of controls, the auditor should consider (1) the relationship of the sample to the objective of the test of controls, (2) the maximum rate of deviations from prescribed internal control structure policies or procedures that would support his planned assessed level of control risk, (3) the auditor's allowable risk of assessing control risk too low, and (4) characteristics of the population."

28. (c) In planning a particular audit sample for a test of controls, the auditor should consider: (1) the relationship of the sample to the objective of the test of controls; (2) the maximum rate of deviations from prescribed internal control structure policies or procedures that would support his or her planned assessed level of control risk (the tolerable *rate*); (3) the auditor's allowable risk of assessing control risk too low; and (4) characteristics of the population, that is, the items comprising the account balance or class of transactions of interest (AU 350.31). The population size has little or no effect on determining sample size except for very small populations. Answers (b) and (d) are incorrect: these factors, although considered in determining sample size for substantive tests, are not considered in determining sample size for tests of controls. (**NOTE**: Tolerable rate is not the same as tolerable misstatement.)

29. (a) "Rather than using the sample to estimate an unknown, the auditor's objective is generally to corroborate the accuracy of certain client data, such as data about account balances or classes of transactions, or to evaluate the internal accounting controls over the processing of data" (AICPA Audit Sampling Guide, p. 12). Thus, the auditor is concerned with whether the control procedures are operating effectively. Answers (b) and (c) relate to substantive tests rather than to tests of controls. Materiality is based on the auditor's judgment, not on sampling procedures.

30. (b) Failure of an internal control procedure would not always result in an error in recording the transaction. For example, the failure to properly void an invoice when it is paid (deviation) would not always result in the invoice being paid more than once (misstatement). Deviations at a given rate ordinarily would be expected to result in misstatements at a lower rate (AU 350.35). Answer (c) implies the opposite proposition. There is no direct proportionality between the level of risk and the rate of misstatement in the population. The sampled items will probably yield a misstatement rate that is representative of the misstatement rate in the unsampled items.

30A. (b) AU 350.35 states, "Deviations from pertinent control procedures at a given rate ordinarily would be expected to result in misstatements at a lower rate." The sufficiency of audit sample sizes is determined by factors such as the assessments of control risk, inherent risk, and risk for other substantive tests related to a given assertion, and other factors as listed in all AU 350.08. Population size is not a determining factor. The relationship between the expected population deviation rate and sample size is direct, not inverse. In determining tolerable rate, an auditor should consider control risk and the degree of assurance desired by the evidential matter, per AU 350.34.

Variables Sampling

31. (c) A disadvantage of PPS sampling to classical variables sampling is that special consideration must be given to zero and negative balance accounts because they are usually excluded from the PPS sample. Answers (a), (b), and (d) are advantages of PPS sampling.

32. (a) In classical variables sampling for estimation, precision represents the range within which the sample result is expected to be accurate. Hence, it provides a calculation of the maximum acceptable error in either direction. Reliability varies inversely with the assessed level of control risk and is a measure of the probability the sample result will fall within the precision range as mentioned above. Projected error is the anticipated deviation rate, based on the sample, in the entire population. The standard deviation is a measure of the dispersion among the relative values of a particular characteristic.

32A. (a) The use of the ratio estimation sampling technique is most effective when the calculated audit amounts are approximately proportional to the client's book amounts. The auditor uses sample results to estimate the ratio of audited value to book value, which is then applied to the population to estimate the actual value. Ratio estimation should be used when each population item *has a book value*, an audited value may be ascertained for each sample item, and *differences occur frequently.* Large overstatement or understatement differences would reduce the effectiveness of this technique.

33. (d) Variables sampling is used if the auditor desires to reach a conclusion about a population in terms of a dollar amount. Variables sampling is generally used to answer either of these questions: (1) How much? (generally described as dollar-value estimation) or (2) Is the account materially misstated? (generally described as hypothesis testing). Discovery sampling is a technique for determining sample size and is usually used in testing internal control compliance rates (not dollar values). Sampling for attributes describes the methodology used for estimating the rate of compliance (or noncompliance) with internal control procedures (not dollar values). Answer (b) is a meaningless detractor.

33A. (c) Substantive tests of details are performed by the auditor to either detect misstatements or obtain evidence about the validity and propriety of the accounting treatment of transactions and balances. In substantive testing, the auditor is primarily interested in dollar amounts, and the traditional method of performing substantive tests is by variables sampling.

34. (c) AU 350.18 states, "Tolerable misstatement is a planning concept and is related to the auditor's preliminary judgments about materiality levels in such a way that tolerable misstatement, combined for the entire audit plan, does not exceed those estimates." Materiality judgments (tolerable misstatements) are not affected by the auditor's business risk. Judgments about materiality (tolerable misstatements) are subjective and do involve consideration of qualitative as well as quantitative factors (AU 312.27) and ordinarily will change during the process of conducting an audit as the auditor develops new evidence (AU 312.15).

35. (d) Tolerable misstatement is an estimate of the maximum monetary misstatement that may exist in an account balance or class of transactions without causing the financial statements to be materially misstated. The sample size for a substantive test of details of an account balance is inversely related to the measure of tolerable misstatement. The smaller the measure of tolerable misstatement, the larger the sample size. Low control risk would allow the auditor to accept more detection risk which would allow the use of smaller sample sizes. The auditor's acceptable level of detection risk is achieved by performing any combination of tests of details and analytical procedures. Therefore, if greater reliance was placed on analytical procedures, less assurance would need to be derived from tests of details and *smaller* sample sizes would be appropriate. The sample size for a substantive test of details of an account balance is directly related to the expected frequency of misstatements. The smaller the expected frequency of misstatements, the smaller the sample size.

Probability-Proportional-to-Size Sampling (PPS)

36. (c) In PPS sampling, the auditor achieves control over the risk of incorrect acceptance by specifying the level of risk he or she is willing to assume. PPS sampling does not require direct consideration of the standard deviation of dollar amounts to determine the appropriate sample. The book value of the unit determines how probable it is that it will be included in the sample, not whether it is over or understated. The sampling interval is calculated by dividing the book value of the population by the sample size.

37. (b) In PPS sampling, when the recorded amount ($10,000) is greater than the sampling interval ($5,000), the projected error equals the actual error ($2,000).

38. (d) This is one of several approaches that can be used to determine sample size when errors are expected, but it is the only approach possible with the information given.

$$\textit{Sampling Interval} = \frac{\textit{Tolerable Misstatement}}{\textit{Reliability Factor for Misstatement of Overstatement}}$$

$$= \frac{\$24,000}{3.00} = \mathbf{\$8,000}$$

$$\textit{Sample Size} = \frac{\textit{Recorded Amount}}{\textit{Sample Interval}}$$

$$= \frac{\$240,000}{\$8,000} = \mathbf{30}$$

PERFORMANCE BY SUBTOPICS

Each category below parallels a subtopic covered in Chapter 38. Record the number and percentage of questions you correctly answered in each subtopic area.

Audit Sampling (AU 350)

Question #	Correct √
1	
1A	
2	
2A	
3	
4	
5	
5A	
6	
6A	
6B	
7	
7A	
8	
9	
10	
10A	
11	
11A	
# Questions	19

\# Correct ______
% Correct ______

Statistical and Nonstatistical Sampling

Question #	Correct √
12	
12A	
13	
13A	
14	
15	
16	
17	
18	
19	
20	
21	
22	
# Questions	13

\# Correct ______
% Correct ______

Attributes Sampling

Question #	Correct √
23	
24	
24A	
25	
26	
27	
28	
29	
30	
30A	
# Questions	10

\# Correct ______
% Correct ______

Variables Sampling

Question #	Correct √
31	
32	
32A	
33	
33A	
34	
35	
# Questions	7

\# Correct ______
% Correct ______

Probability-Proportional-to-Size Sampling (PPS)

Question #	Correct √
36	
37	
38	
# Questions	3

\# Correct ______
% Correct ______

ESSAY QUESTIONS

Essay 38-2 (15 to 25 minutes)

Mead, CPA, was engaged to audit Jiffy Co.'s financial statements for the year ended August 31, 1993. Mead is applying sampling procedures.

During the prior years' audits, Mead used classical variables sampling in performing tests of controls on Jiffy's accounts receivable. For the current year Mead decided to use probability-proportional-to-size (PPS) sampling (also known as dollar-unit sampling) in confirming accounts receivable because PPS sampling uses each account in the population as a separate sampling unit. Mead expected to discover many overstatements, but presumed that the PPS sample still would be smaller than the corresponding size for classical variables sampling.

Mead reasoned that the PPS sample would automatically result in a stratified sample because each account would have an equal chance of being selected for confirmation. Additionally, the selection of negative (credit) balances would be facilitated without special considerations.

Mead computed the sample size using the risk of incorrect acceptance, the total recorded book amount of the receivables, and the number of misstated accounts allowed. Mead divided the total recorded book amount of the receivables by the sample size to determine the sampling interval. Mead then calculated the standard deviation of the dollar amounts of the accounts selected for evaluation of the receivables.

Mead's calculated sample size was 60 and the sampling interval was determined to be $10,000. However, only 58 different accounts were selected because two accounts were so large that the sampling interval caused each of them to be selected twice. Mead proceeded to send confirmation requests to 55 of the 58 customers. Three selected accounts each had insignificant recorded balances under $20. Mead ignored these three small accounts and substituted the three largest accounts that had not been selected in the sample. Each of these accounts had balances in excess of $7,000, so Mead sent confirmation requests to those customers.

The confirmation process revealed two differences. One account with an audited amount of $3,000 had been recorded at $4,000. Mead projected this to be a $1,000 misstatement. Another account with an audited amount of $2,000 had been recorded at $1,900. Mead did not count the $100 difference because the purpose of the test was to detect overstatements.

In evaluating the sample results, Mead determined that the accounts receivable balance was not overstated because the projected misstatement was less than the allowance for sampling risk.

Required:

Describe each incorrect assumption, statement, and inappropriate application of sampling in Mead's procedures. (11/93, Aud., #5)

Essay 38-3 (15 to 25 minutes)

Baker, CPA, was engaged to audit Mill Company's financial statements for the year ended September 30, 1991. After obtaining an understanding of Mill's internal control structure, Baker decided to obtain evidential matter about the effectiveness of both the design and operation of the policies and procedures that may support a low assessed level of control risk concerning Mill's shipping and billing functions. During the prior years' audits Baker used nonstatistical sampling but for the current year Baker used a statistical sample in the tests of controls to eliminate the need for judgment.

Baker wanted to assess control risk at a low level, so a tolerable rate of deviation or acceptable upper precision limit (UPL) of 20% was established. To estimate the population deviation rate and the achieved UPL, Baker decided to apply a discovery sampling technique of attribute sampling that would use a population expected error rate of 3% for the 8,000 shipping documents, and decided to defer consideration of allowable risk of assessing control risk too low (risk of overreliance) until evaluating the sample results. Baker used the tolerable rate, the population size, and the expected population error rate to determine that a sample size of 80 would be sufficient. When it was subsequently determined that the actual population was about 10,000 shipping documents, Baker increased the sample size to 100.

Baker's objective was to ascertain whether Mill's shipments had been properly billed. Baker took a sample of 100 invoices by selecting the first 25 invoices from the first month of each quarter. Baker then compared the invoices to the corresponding prenumbered shipping documents.

When Baker tested the sample, eight errors were discovered. Additionally, one shipment that should have been billed at $10,443 was actually billed at $10,434. Baker considered this $9 to be immaterial and did not count it as an error.

In evaluating the sample results Baker made the initial determination that a reliability level of 95% (risk of assessing control risk too low 5%) was desired and, using the appropriate statistical sampling table, determined that for eight observed deviations from a sample size of 100, the achieved UPL was 14%. Baker then calculated the allowance for sampling risk to be 5%, the difference between the actual sample deviation rate (8%) and the expected error rate (3%). Baker reasoned that the actual sample deviation rate (8%) plus the allowance for sampling risk (5%) was less than the achieved UPL (14%); therefore, the sample supported a low level of control risk.

Required:

Describe each incorrect assumption, statement, and inappropriate application of attribute sampling in Baker's procedures. (11/91, Aud., #5)

Essay 38-4 (15 to 25 minutes)

Sampling for attributes is often used to allow an auditor to reach a conclusion concerning a rate of occurrence in a population. A common use in auditing is to test the rate of deviation from a prescribed internal control policy or procedure to determine whether planned assessed level of control risk is appropriate.

Required:

a. When an auditor samples for attributes, identify the factors that should influence the auditor's judgment concerning the determination of

1. Acceptable level of risk of assessing control risk too low,
2. Tolerable deviation rate, and
3. Expected population deviation rate.

b. State the effect on sample size of an increase in each of the following factors, assuming all other factors are held constant:

1. Acceptable level of risk of assessing control risk too low,
2. Tolerable deviation rate, and
3. Expected population deviation rate.

c. Evaluate the sample results of a test for attributes if authorizations are found to be missing on 7 check requests out of a sample of 100 tested. The population consists of 2500 check requests, the tolerable deviation rate is 8%, and the acceptable level of risk of assessing control risk too low is low.

d. How may the use of statistical sampling assist the auditor in evaluating the sample results described in **c.**, above? (11/88, Aud., #3)

Essay 38-5 (15 to 25 minutes)

Edwards has decided to use probability-proportional-to-size (PPS) sampling, sometimes called dollar-unit sampling, in the audit of a client's accounts receivable balance. Few, if any, misstatements of account balance overstatement are expected.

Edwards plans to use the following PPS sampling table:

TABLE
Reliability Factors for Errors of Overstatement

Number of overstatement misstatements	Risk of incorrect acceptance 1%	5%	10%	15%	20%
0	4.61	3.00	2.31	1.90	1.61
1	6.64	4.75	3.89	3.38	3.00
2	8.41	6.30	5.33	4.72	4.28
3	10.05	7.76	6.69	6.02	5.52
4	11.61	9.16	8.00	7.27	6.73

Required:

a. Identify the advantages of using PPS sampling over classical variables sampling.

NOTE: Requirements **b.** and **c.** are **not** related.

b. Calculate the sampling interval and the sample size Edwards should use given the following information:

Tolerable misstatement	$ 15,000
Risk of incorrect acceptance	5%
Number of misstatements allowed	0
Recorded amount of accounts receivable	$300,000

c. Calculate the total projected misstatement if the following three misstatements were discovered in a PPS sample:

	Recorded amount	Audit amount	Sampling interval
1st misstatement	$ 400	$ 320	$ 1,000
2nd misstatement	500	0	1,000
3rd misstatement	3,000	2,500	1,000

(5/87, Aud., #3)

Essay 38-6 (15 to 25 minutes)

Smith, CPA, has decided to assess control risk at below the maximum level for an audit client's internal controls affecting receivables. Smith plans to use sampling to obtain substantive evidence concerning the reasonableness of the client's accounts receivable balances. Smith has identified the first few steps in an outline of the sampling plan as follows:

1. Determine the audit objectives of the test.
2. Define the population.
3. Define the sampling unit.
4. Consider the completeness of the population.
5. Identify individually significant items.

Required:

Identify the remaining steps which Smith should include in the outline of the sampling plan. Illustrations and examples need not be provided. (5/86, Aud., #5)

Essay 38-7 (15 to 25 minutes)

One of the generally accepted auditing standards states that sufficient competent evidential matter is to be obtained through inspection, observation, inquiries, and confirmation to afford a reasonable basis for an opinion regarding the financial statements under audit. Some degree of uncertainty is implicit in the concept of "a reasonable basis for an opinion," because the concept of sampling is well established in auditing practice.

Required:

a. Explain the auditor's justification for accepting the uncertainties that are inherent in the sampling process.

b. Discuss the uncertainties which collectively embody the concept of audit risk.

c. Discuss the nature of the sampling risk and nonsampling risk. Include the effect of sampling risk on substantive tests of details and on tests of controls. (5/85, Aud., #5)

ESSAY SOLUTIONS

Solution 38-2 PPS and Classical Variables Sampling Errors

The incorrect assumptions, statements, and inappropriate applications of sampling are as follows:

1. Classical variables sampling is **not designed for tests of controls.**
2. PPS sampling uses **each dollar** in the population, not each account, as a **separate sampling unit.**
3. PPS sampling is **not efficient** if **many misstatements** are **expected** because the sample size can become larger than the corresponding sample size for classical variables sampling as the expected amount of misstatement increases.
4. Each account does not have an equal chance of being selected; the probability of selection of the accounts is **proportional** to the **accounts' dollar amounts.**
5. PPS sampling requires **special consideration for negative (credit) balances.**
6. **Tolerable misstatement** was **not considered** in calculating the sample size.
7. **Expected** (anticipated) **misstatement** was **not considered** in calculating the sample size.
8. The **standard deviation** of the dollar amounts is **not required** for PPS sampling.
9. The three selected accounts with **insignificant balances should not have been ignored or replaced** with other accounts.
10. The account with the $1,000 difference (recorded amount of $4,000 and audited amount of $3,000) was **incorrectly projected** as a **$1,000 misstatement**; projected misstatement for this difference was actually **$2,500 ($1,000 ÷ $4,000 × $10,000 interval).**
11. The **difference** in the understated account (recorded amount of $1,900 and audited amount of $2,000) **should not have been omitted** from the calculation of projected misstatement.
12. The **reasoning** (the comparison of projected misstatement with the allowance for sampling risk) concerning the decision that the receivable balance was not overstated was **erroneous.**

Solution 38-3 Attribute Sampling Procedures

1. Statistical sampling **does not eliminate** the **need for professional judgment.**
2. The **tolerable rate of deviation** or acceptable upper precision limit (UPL) is **too high (20%)** if Baker plans to assess control risk at a **low level (substantial reliance).**
3. **Discovery sampling** is **not an appropriate sampling technique** in this attribute sampling application.
4. The sampling technique employed is **not discovery sampling.**
5. The **increase** in the **population size** has **little or no effect** on determining sample size.
6. Baker failed to consider the **allowable risk** of assessing control risk too low (**risk of overreliance**) in **determining the sample size.**
7. The population from which the sample was chosen (invoices) was an **incorrect population.**
8. The sample selected was **not randomly selected.**
9. Baker failed to consider the difference of an immaterial amount to be an **error.**
10. The **allowance for sampling risk** was **incorrectly calculated.**
11. Baker's reasoning concerning the decision that the sample **supported a low assessed level of control risk** was **erroneous.**

Solution 38-4 Sampling for Attributes/Sample Size

a. 1. In determining an **acceptable level of risk of assessing control risk too low**, an auditor should consider the **importance** of the control to be tested in determining the **extent** to which substantive tests will be **restricted** and the **planned assessed level of control risk.**

2. In determining the **tolerable deviation rate**, an auditor should consider the planned assessed level of control risk for the controls to be tested and how **materially** the financial statements would be affected if the control does not function properly. For example, **how likely** is the control to **prevent** or **detect material misstatements.**

3. In determining the **expected population deviation rate**, an auditor should consider the results of **prior years' tests**, the **overall control environment**, or **utilize a preliminary sample.**

b. 1. There is a **decrease** in sample size if the **acceptable level of risk of assessing control risk too low** is **increased.**

2. There is a **decrease** in sample size if the **tolerable deviation rate is increased.**

3. There is an **increase** in sample size if the **population deviation rate is increased.**

c. For a **low risk of assessing control risk too low** it is generally appropriate to reconsider the planned assessed level of control risk as the **calculated estimate of the population deviation rate** identified in the sample (7%) **approaches the tolerable deviation rate** (8%). This is because there may be an **unacceptably high sampling risk** that these sample results could have occurred with an **actual population deviation rate higher than the tolerable deviation rate.**

d. If statistical sampling is used, an allowance for sampling risk can be calculated. If the **calculated estimate of the population deviation rate** plus the allowance for sampling risk is **greater than the tolerable deviation rate**, the sample results should be interpreted as **not supporting** the assessed level of control risk for the control.

Solution 38-5 Probability-Proportional-to-Size Sampling

a. The advantages of PPS sampling over classical variables sampling are as follows:

- PPS sampling is generally **easier to use** than classical variables sampling.
- **Size** of a PPS sample is **not based on the estimated variation** of audited amounts.
- PPS sampling automatically results in a **stratified sample.**
- **Individually significant** items are automatically **identified.**
- If no misstatements are expected, PPS sampling will usually result in a **smaller sample** size than classical variables sampling.
- A PPS sample can be **easily designed** and sample **selection can begin before the complete population is available.**

b.

$$\textit{Sampling Interval} = \frac{\textit{Total Misstatement}}{\textit{Reliability Factor for Misstatement of Overstatement}}$$

$$= \frac{\$15,000}{3.00} = \mathbf{\$5,000}$$

$$\textit{Sample Size} = \frac{\textit{Recorded Amount}}{\textit{Sampling Interval}}$$

$$= \frac{\$300,000}{\$5,000} = \mathbf{60}$$

c.

	Recorded amount	Audit amount	Tainting	Sampling interval	Projected misstatement
1st misstatement	$ 400	$ 320	20%	$1,000	$ 200
2nd misstatement	500	0	100%	1,000	1,000
3rd misstatement	3,000	2,500	*	1,000	500
Total projected misstatement					$1,700

* The recorded amount is greater than the sampling interval; therefore, the **projected misstatement equals the actual misstatement.**

Solution 38-6 Steps in a Sampling Plan

The remaining steps are as follows:

6. Treat the individually significant items as a **separate population.**
7. **Choose** an audit **sampling technique.**
8. **Determine** the **sample size,** giving consideration for--
   a. **Variations** within the population.
   b. **Acceptable level of risk.**
   c. **Tolerable misstatement.**
   d. **Expected** amount of **misstatement.**
   e. **Population size.**
9. Determine the **method** of selecting a representative sample.
10. **Select** the sample items.
11. **Apply** appropriate **audit procedures** to the sample items.
12. **Evaluate** the sample **results.**
    a. **Project** the **misstatement** to the population and consider sampling risk.
    b. Consider the **qualitative aspects** of misstatements and reach an **overall conclusion.**
13. **Document** the sampling procedure.

Solution 38-7 Audit Risk/Sampling Risk and Nonsampling Risk

a. The auditor's justification for accepting the uncertainties that are inherent in the sampling process are based upon the premise that the

- **Cost** of examining all of the financial data would usually **outweigh** the **benefit** of the **added reliability** of a complete (100%) examination.
- **Time required** to examine **all** of the financial data would usually preclude issuance of a **timely** auditor's report.

b. The uncertainties inherent in applying auditing procedures are collectively referred to as audit risk.

Audit risk, with respect to a particular account balance or class of transactions, is the risk that there is a **monetary misstatement greater than tolerable misstatement** in the balance or class that the auditor fails to detect. Audit risk is a combination of three types of risks as follows:

- **Inherent risk** is the risk that misstatements **will occur** in the accounting system.
- **Control risk** is the risk that material misstatements **will not be detected** by the client's **internal control structure.**
- **Detection risk** is the risk that any material misstatements that occur **will not be detected by the auditor.**

Ultimate audit risk includes both uncertainties due to sampling and uncertainties due to factors other than sampling. These aspects of audit risk are referred to as **sampling risk** and **nonsampling risk**, respectively.

c. Sampling risk arises from the possibility that, when a test of control or a substantive test is restricted to a sample, the auditor's conclusions may be different from the conclusions that might be reached if the test were applied in the same way to all items in the account balance or class of transactions. That is, a **particular sample may contain proportionately more or less monetary misstatements** or **deviations** than exist in the balance or class as a whole.

Nonsampling risk includes all the aspects of audit risk that are not due to sampling. An auditor may apply a procedure to all transactions or balances and still fail to detect a material misstatement or a material internal control weakness. Nonsampling risk includes the possibility of selecting **audit procedures** that are **not appropriate** to achieve the specific objective, or **failing to recognize misstatements** in documents examined, which would **render the procedure ineffective** even if all items were examined.

The auditor should apply professional judgment in assessing sampling risk. In performing substantive tests of details the auditor is concerned with two aspects of sampling risk:

- **The risk of incorrect acceptance** is the risk that the sample **supports the conclusion** that the recorded account balance is not materially misstated **when it is materially misstated.**
- **The risk of incorrect rejection** is the risk that the sample **supports the conclusion** that the recorded account balance is materially misstated **when it is not materially misstated.**

The auditor is also concerned with two aspects of sampling risk in performing tests of controls:

- The **risk of assessing control risk too low** is the risk that the assessed level of control risk based on the sample is **less than the true operating effectiveness** of the control structure policy or procedure.
- The **risk of assessing control risk too high** is the risk that the assessed level of control risk based on the sample is **greater than the true operating effectiveness** of the control structure policy or procedure.

The **risk of incorrect acceptance** and the **risk of assessing control risk too low** relate to the **effectiveness** of an audit in detecting an existing material misstatement. The **risk of incorrect rejection** and the **risk of assessing control risk too high** relate to the **efficiency** of the audit.

CHAPTER 39

AUDITING EDP SYSTEMS

CHAPTER 39

AUDITING EDP SYSTEMS

I. Elements of an EDP-Based System

A. Electronic Data Processing (EDP)--An EDP-based system includes (1) hardware, (2) software, (3) documentation, (4) personnel, (5) data, and (6) controls.

B. Significant Differences Between EDP Activities and Non-EDP Activities

1. Less Documentation--Many control procedures in EDP systems do not leave documentary evidence of performance.

2. Information in Machine-Readable Form--Files and records are usually in machine-readable form and cannot be read without using the computer.

3. Decrease in Human Involvement in Transaction Handling--Computers may obscure errors that a human would notice while handling the transaction.

4. More Reliable--EDP systems are more reliable than manual systems because all of the data is subjected to the same controls. Manual systems are subject to human error on a random basis. Computer processing virtually eliminates computational errors associated with manual processing.

5. Specialized EDP Knowledge--In order to perform an audit per GAAS, an auditor may need specialized EDP knowledge.

6. Difficulty of Change--It is harder to change an EDP system once it is implemented than it is to change a manual system. Therefore, the auditor will want to become familiar with a new EDP system at an early stage of the development process so that the auditor can anticipate possible future audit problems.

C. Computer Hardware--Physical EDP equipment.

Exhibit 1--Computer Hardware Configuration

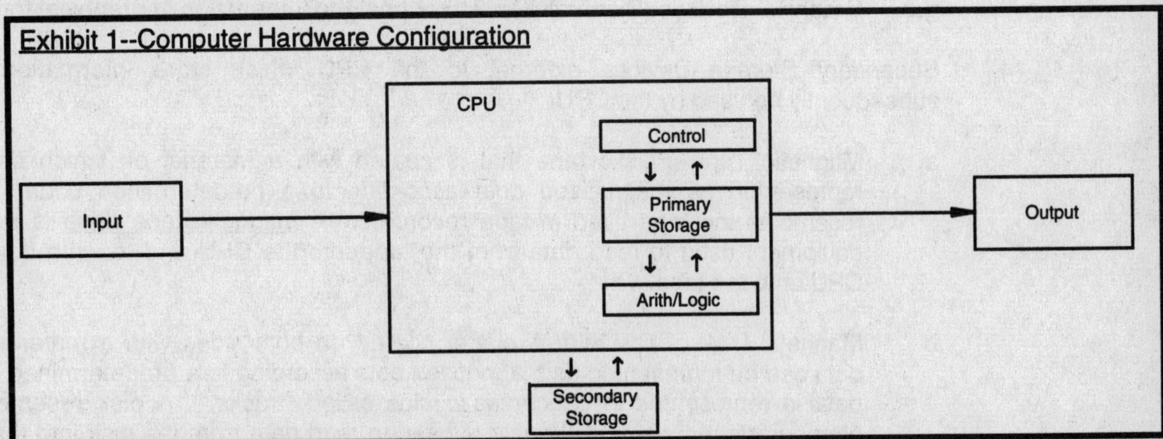

1. Central Processing Unit (CPU, Mainframe)--Primary hardware component. The actual processing of data occurs in the CPU. It contains primary storage, a control unit, and an arithmetic/logic unit.

a. Primary Storage (Main Memory)--Portion of the CPU that holds the program, data, and results (intermediate and final) during processing; therefore, this includes only temporary storage. The primary storage contains the data and program steps that are being processed by the CPU and is divided into RAM (random access memory) and ROM (read only memory).

b. Control Unit--Portion of the CPU which controls and directs the operations of the computer. It interprets the instructions from the program (in order) and directs the computer system to carry them out.

c. Arithmetic/Logic Unit--Portion of the CPU which has special circuitry for performing arithmetic calculations and logical operations.

2. Peripheral Equipment--Data processing equipment that is not physically a part of the CPU but which may be placed under the control of the CPU, i.e., which may be accessed directly by the CPU. Examples include magnetic tape, disk drives, and printers.

3. Input/Output Devices--Devices for transferring data in and out of the CPU into primary storage. Examples include the following:

a. Keyboard--Typewriter-type device that is connected to the CPU and can enter information directly into the primary storage.

b. Magnetic Tape Reader--Senses information recorded as magnetized spots on magnetic tape (e.g., the magnetic strips used on credit cards and ATM cards).

c. Magnetic Ink Character Recognition (MICR)--Senses information recorded in special magnetized ink. MICR is commonly used by the banking industry for check processing.

d. Optical Character Recognition (OCR)--Senses printed information through the use of light-sensitive devices.

e. High-Speed Printers--Print output on computer paper including invoices and checks.

f. Cathode Ray Tube (CRT)--Television screen that displays the information.

g. Graphical Devices (Plotters)--Display or print the information in graphical form.

4. Secondary Storage--Devices external to the CPU which store information that can subsequently be used by the CPU.

a. Magnetic Tape--Plastic tape that is coated with a material on which data can be represented as magnetized dots according to a predetermined code. It closely resembles the tape used in tape recorders. A magnetic tape drive is the piece of equipment used to read data from the tape into the CPU and to write data from the CPU onto the tape.

b. Magnetic Disk or Diskette--A platter coated on both sides with a material on which data can be represented as magnetized dots according to a predetermined code. The data is represented in concentric circles called "tracks." A disk resembles an LP phonograph record. A disk drive is used to read data from the disk into the CPU and to write data from the CPU onto the disk.

c. Off-Line Storage--Not in direct communication with the CPU. Therefore, human intervention is needed before the data can be processed by the computer. For example, a magnetic tape which is stored in the tape vault must be manually mounted on the magnetic tape drive before it can be accessed by the CPU.

d. On-Line Storage--In direct communication with the CPU. Therefore, human intervention is not needed before the data can be processed by the computer. For example, a magnetic disk mounted in a magnetic disk drive can be accessed by the CPU without any need for human intervention.

e. Sequentially Accessible--Requires the reading of all data between the starting point and the information desired. Magnetic tape and paper tape are sequentially accessible. For example, if customer records are arranged in alphabetical order on a reel of magnetic tape, and none of the tape has been read yet, most of the tape would have to be read to get to the information on Joe Zablonski.

f. Randomly Accessible (Direct Access)--Data records can be accessed directly. Magnetic disks are an example. For example, if the customer records are stored in a file on a magnetic disk, the disk drive could go directly to Joe Zablonski's record without having to read any of the other customer records.

g. Laser Disks--Also referred to as CD-ROM. Data records can be accessed directly. Substantially more information can be stored on laser disks than on magnetic disks.

5. Additional terms

a. Downtime--Time when the computer is not functioning. This may be caused by equipment problems or maintenance.

b. Maintenance of the hardware involves servicing the equipment. Scheduled maintenance is routine servicing. Unscheduled maintenance arises when there are unanticipated problems with the system.

c. Decision tables emphasize the relationships among conditions and actions, and present decision choices. Decision tables often supplement systems flowcharts.

D. Computer Software--Programs, routines, documentation, manuals, etc., that make it possible for the computer system to process the data and operate efficiently.

1. Program--Set of instructions that the computer follows to accomplish a specified task (e.g., accounts receivable update program, inventory management program, and payroll program).

2. Programming Languages

a. Machine Language--Language the computer understands. It is very detailed, in binary form (i.e., only 0s and 1s), and changes for different types of computers.

b. Symbolic Language (Machine-Oriented Assembler Language)--Similar to machine language except that symbols are used to make the coding of the instructions easier for the programmer. The computer does not understand a program written in symbolic language. Therefore, it must be translated into machine language before it can be executed. An assembler program is a program (software) that translates the program written in symbolic language (called the "source program") into a program written in machine language (called the "object program"). This can be illustrated as follows:

SOURCE PROGRAM (Symbolic language) → *ASSEMBLER* → *OBJECT PROGRAM (Machine language)*

c. High-Level Languages--The higher the level, the closer the programming language comes to reading like English. FORTRAN, COBOL, PL/1, and BASIC are common examples of procedure-oriented languages. Again, the computer does not understand a program written in a high-level language. Therefore, the program must be translated into machine language before it can be executed--this is called compiling the program.

(1) Compiler Program--A program (software) that translates the program written in a high-level language (called the "source program") into a program written in machine language (called the "object program"). This is illustrated by the following diagram:

SOURCE PROGRAM (FORTRAN, COBOL, etc.) → *COMPILER* → *OBJECT PROGRAM (Machine language)*

(2) Interpreter Program--A program that translates a high-level language, e.g., BASIC, into an object program line by line.

3. Programming Terms and Names

a. Systems Programs (Supervisory Programs)--Perform the functions of coordinating and controlling the overall operation of the computer system. Three common types of systems programs are as follows:

(1) Operating Systems--Manages the coordinating and scheduling of various application programs and computer functions. Examples include the following:

(a) Multiprocessing--Allows the execution of two or more programs at the same time and requires the utilization of more than one CPU.

(b) Multiprogramming--A program is processed until some type of input or output is needed. The operating system then hands the process over to a piece of peripheral equipment, and the CPU begins executing other program instructions. Processing speed is enhanced considerably, making it appear as if more than one program is being processed at the same time, while utilizing only one CPU.

(c) Virtual Storage--The operating system divides a program into segments (called pages) and brings only those sections of the program into memory as needed to execute the instructions. This saves memory and processing cost because the majority of the program remains in less expensive secondary storage.

(2) Utility Program (Utility Routine)--Standard program for performing routine functions, e.g., sorting and merging.

(3) Library Program (Library Routine)--Programs and subroutines which are frequently used by other programs. They are kept within the system and "called up" (i.e., used) whenever necessary. One example is generating random numbers.

b. Application Programs--Designed to perform the processing of a specific application. For example, an accounts receivable update program is an application program that processes accounts receivable data to update the accounts receivable master file.

c. Edit--Refers to the addition, deletion, and/or rearrangement of data. Input editing refers to the editing of the data before it is processed and output editing refers to the editing of data after it is outputted.

d. Patch--Addition of a new part to a program. It may be added to correct or update a program. For example, if a new government regulation affecting withholding tax becomes effective, a patch may be added to the payroll program to provide for this. A patch may also be added for a fraudulent purpose. For example, an employee might insert a patch into a payroll program to print an extra check.

e. Pass (Run)--Complete cycle of input, processing, and output in the execution of a computer program.

f. Program Maintenance--Refers to making changes in the program in order to keep it current and functioning properly. For example, maintenance of the payroll program may involve modifying it because of changes in the social security law or to provide for a greater number of employees.

Exhibit 2--Data Hierarchy

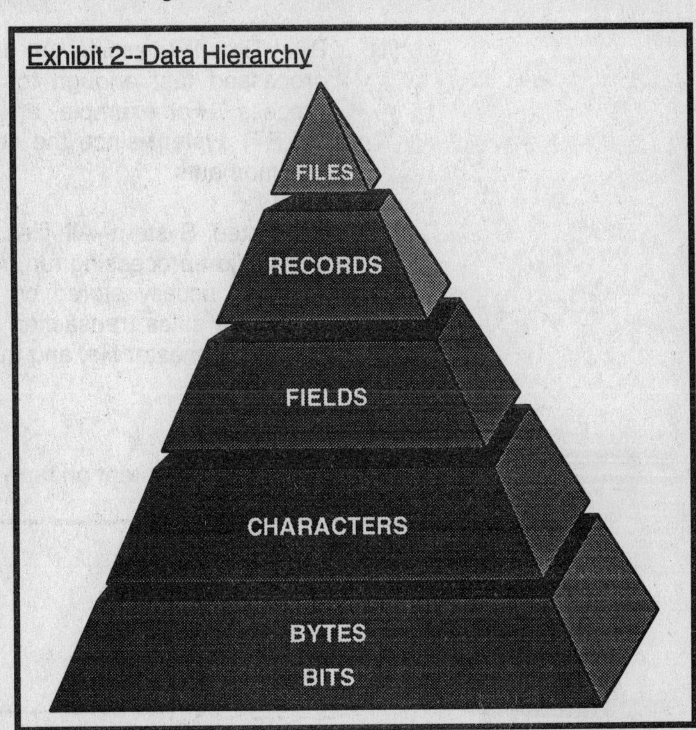

E. Data Organization and Processing

1. Storage of data can be represented by the following hierarchy:

a. Bit--A binary digit (0 or 1, represented by a positive or negative charge, on or off, etc.), representing the smallest unit of data possible.

b. Byte--A group of bits which represents a single character, whether alphabetic, numeric, or alphanumeric.

c. Characters--Alphabetic, numeric, and special characters (e.g., periods, commas, and hyphens).

d. Field--Group of related characters. For example, a customer name.

e. Record--Group of related fields. For example, a customer record would include fields for customer number, name, address, etc.

f. File--Group of related records.

(1) Master File--Contains relatively permanent data. For example, the accounts receivable master file would contain a record for each customer and each record would include fields for customer number, name, address, credit limit, amount owed, etc.

(2) Transaction (Detail) File--Contains current, temporary data. The transaction file is used to update the master file. For example, the day's charge sales would be accumulated on a transaction file that would be used to update the accounts receivable master file during an update run.

2. Transaction Processing Modes--Transactions may be processed either in batches or on-line.

a. Batch Processing--Transactions to be processed are accumulated in groups (batches) before processing and are then processed as a batch. Batch processing frequently involves sequential access to the data files. For example, a company may accumulate a day's charge sales before processing them against the master file during the night. Before they are processed, the transactions would be sorted into the order of the records on the master file. One disadvantage of batch processing is that, because of the time delays, errors may not be detected immediately.

b. On-Line Processing--Transactions are processed and the file is updated as the transactions occur. On-line processing usually involves files that can be directly accessed. For example, a cash register terminal may automatically update the inventory file when a sale is made.

(1) Real-Time Processing--An on-line system is operating in real-time if the data is processed fast enough to get the response back in time to influence the process. For example, an airline reservation system is an on-line, real-time (OLRT) system since the customer receives reservations after waiting only a few moments.

(2) Integrated System--All files affected by a transaction are up-dated in one transaction-processing run, rather than having a separate run for each file. The files are usually stored on magnetic disks. For example, in an integrated system, a sales transaction may update the sales summary file, the accounts receivable master file, and the inventory file during one processing run.

3. File Updating

a. Updating a master file kept on tape is illustrated in Exhibit 3.

Exhibit 3

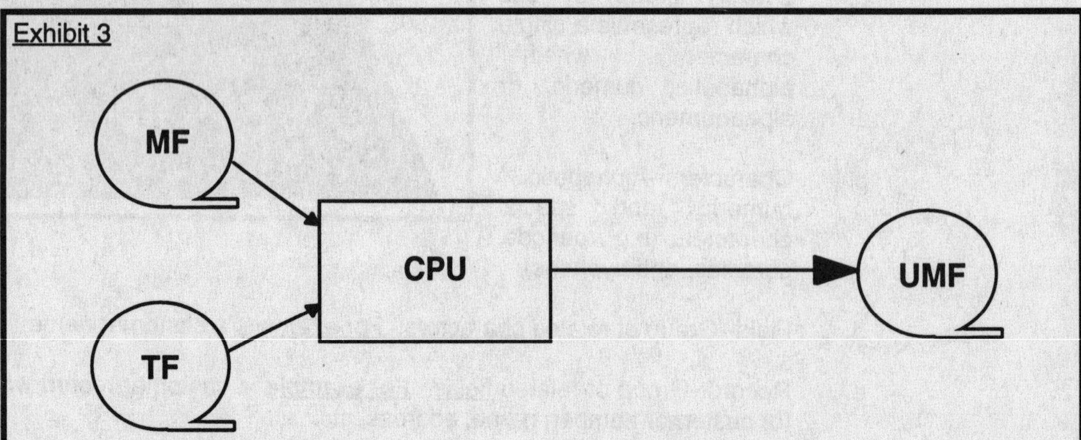

Three reels of tape are required: the master file (MF), the transaction file (TF), and the reel that becomes the updated master file (UMF). There are three basic steps in the updating process. First, records are read into the CPU from the master file (MF) and the transaction file (TF). Second, the records from the master file are updated in the CPU. Third, the updated records are written onto the output reel to form the updated master file (UMF). It is important to note that after updating is complete, all three tapes will still be intact. The updating process is most efficient when the transaction file has been sorted into the same order as the master file.

b. There are four basic steps in the process of updating a record in a master file that is kept on a magnetic disk. First, a transaction enters the CPU. Second, the record to be updated is read from its location on the disk into the CPU. Third, the record is up-dated in the CPU. Fourth, the updated record is written onto the disk in the same location as the original record. The result is that the original record is replaced by the updated record. This results in the original record being erased. This can be contrasted with the updating of a tape file (Exhibit 3, above) in which the original record still exists on the original tape after the updating process.

4. Processing Outside of the Client--While many companies have their own equipment (either leased or purchased) to do their processing within the company (i.e., in-house), others utilize outside processors. Several common arrangements are as follows:

   a. Block Time--Client rents a certain block of computer time from an outside party. For example, a company may rent time from a bank that does not utilize its computer system 24 hours per day.

   b. Time Sharing--A number of users share a computer system. Each may have a terminal which it can use to access a CPU located outside of the client. Each user can access the system whenever it wishes.

   c. Service Bureau--An outside organization that provides a wide range of data processing services for a fee.

5. Management Information Systems (MIS)--The information system within an organization which provides management with the information needed for planning and control. This involves an integration of the functions of gathering and analyzing data, and reporting (i.e., communicating) the results to management in a meaningful form.

6. Data Base System

   a. Data Base--A structured set of interrelated files combined to eliminate redundancy of data items within the files and to establish logical connections between data items. For example, within personnel and payroll files, some of the data in the two records will be the same (i.e., redundant); in a data base system, these files would be combined to eliminate the redundant data.

   b. Data Base Management System (DBMS)--A set of programs (software) which manages the data base (i.e., creates, accesses, and maintains the data base).

F. <u>Guidelines for Development and Implementation of Computer-Based Systems</u>

1. The CPA sometimes becomes involved in the development and implementation of a computer-based application system. The CPA may do the work or may work with client personnel (systems analysts, programmers, etc.). The development and implementation process involves the following phases:

   a. Systems Analysis or (Feasibility Study)--The system's overall objectives and requirements are clearly determined. The existing system is then studied to see if it is adequately meeting them. Broad alternative approaches are also considered.

   b. Systems Design

      (1) General Systems Design--The alternative approaches are evaluated in more detail and a specific proposal is developed for implementing the alternative that is felt to be best.

      (2) Detailed System Design--The recommended system is designed in detail. This includes designing files, determining resource requirements, and developing plans for the following phases.

c. Program Specifications and Implementation Planning--Detailed specifications are developed for the computer programs that will be required, and plans are made for testing the program and implementing the system.

(1) Hardware Installation

(2) Coding and Debugging Programs--Programmers write and test the required programs.

(3) Training Users

(4) Systems Testing--The system is tested thoroughly. The results of the tests are compared with the specifications and requirements of the system; i.e., does it do what it is supposed to do?

(5) Conversion and Volume Testing--Conversion is done from the old system to the new system. This involves such things as converting and verifying files and data. Frequently, conversion involves parallel processing (i.e., parallel operations) in which the old system and the new system are run at the same time with the actual data for the period and the results compared. This checks the new system and avoids disaster if the new system fails the first time it is used.

d. Implementation--The system is turned over to the user.

2. Once the system is operating routinely, it is reviewed to be sure it is attaining the original objectives set for it, and to correct any problems.

II. The Effects of Computer Processing on the Audit of Financial Statements (SAS 48)

A. Objectives Do Not Change--An auditor's objectives do not change when auditing an EDP system. The ultimate objective is still to express an opinion on the fairness of presentation of the financial statements. The auditor must still (1) become familiar with the client, (2) plan the engagement, (3) consider internal control, (4) perform tests of controls, (5) perform substantive tests, (6) evaluate the evidence, and (7) express an opinion.

B. Procedures May Change--While the audit objectives do not change, the audit procedures used to accomplish them may change.

C. Planning the Engagement--The auditor should consider matters such as the following:

1. The extent to which the computer is used in each significant accounting application.

2. The complexity of the entity's computer operations, including the use of an outside service center.

3. The organizational structure of the computer processing activities.

4. The availability of data.

5. The use of computer-assisted audit techniques (CAAT) to increase the efficiency of performing audit procedures.

If specific skills are needed, and a specialist is used, the auditor should have sufficient computer-related knowledge to (a) communicate the objectives of the other professional's work, (b) evaluate whether the specified procedures will meet the auditor's objectives, and (c) evaluate the results of the procedures applied as they relate to the nature, timing, and extent of other planned audit procedures. The auditor's responsibilities with respect to using such a professional are equivalent to those for other assistants.

D. Analytical Procedures--An additional factor in the planning and performing of analytical procedures is the increased availability of data that is used by management. Such computer prepared data and analyses, although not necessarily a part of the basic accounting records, may be valuable sources of information (e.g., budget and variance information).

E. The Auditor's Consideration of Internal Control

1. Basic Concepts--The characteristics that distinguish computer processing from manual processing include the following:

a. Transaction Trails--Some computer systems are designed so that a complete transaction trail that is useful for audit purposes might exist for only a short period of time or only in computer-readable form. This trail is used to monitor the system, answer queries, and deter irregularities.

b. Uniform Processing of Transactions--Computer processing uniformly subjects like transactions to the same processing instructions. Consequently, computer processing virtually eliminates the occurrence of clerical error normally associated with manual processing. Conversely, errors will result in all like transactions being processed incorrectly.

c. Segregation of Functions--Many internal control procedures once performed by separate individuals in manual systems may be concentrated in systems that use computer processing. Therefore, an individual who has access to the computer may be in a position to perform incompatible functions. As a result, other control procedures may be necessary in computer systems to achieve the control objectives ordinarily accomplished by segregation of functions in manual systems.

d. Potential for Errors and Irregularities--Decreased human involvement in handling transactions processed by computers can reduce the potential for observing errors and irregularities. Errors or irregularities occurring during the design or changing of application programs can remain undetected for long periods of time.

e. Potential for Increased Management Supervision--Computer systems offer management a wide variety of analytical tools that may be used to review and supervise the operations of the company. The availability of these additional controls may serve to enhance the entire internal control structure on which the auditor may wish to assess control risk at below the maximum level. For example, comparisons by management of budget to actual results and the response by management to unusual fluctuations indicate management's monitoring of the ongoing operations as a prevention of unfavorable crisis situations.

f. Initiation or Subsequent Execution of Transactions by Computer--The authorization of "automatic" transactions or procedures may not be documented in the same way as those initiated in a manual accounting system, and management's authorization of those transactions may be implicit in its acceptance of the design of the computer system.

g. Dependence of Other Controls on Controls Over Computer Processing--Computer processing may produce reports and other output that are used in performing manual control procedures. The effectiveness of these manual control procedures can be dependent on the effectiveness of controls over the completeness and accuracy of computer processing.

2. Accounting Control Procedures--Where computer processing is used in significant accounting applications, internal accounting control procedures are sometimes defined by classifying control procedures into two types: general and application control procedures.

   a. General Controls--Those controls that relate to all or many computerized accounting applications and often include control over the development, modification, and maintenance of computer programs and control over the use of and changes to data maintained on computer files. When an auditor anticipates assessing control risk at a low level, the auditor would initially focus on these general controls.

   b. Application Controls--Those controls that relate to specific computerized accounting applications, i.e., input, processing, and output controls for an accounts payable application.

3. Review of the Structure--Because of the increased concentration of functions within the computer processing operation, the auditor's concern over the interdependence of control procedures is generally greater than it is in a manual system. In fact, application controls are often dependent upon general controls. Accordingly, it may be more efficient to review the design of general controls before reviewing the specific application controls.

4. Tests of Control--Some internal control procedures consist of the approval or independent review of documents that evidence transactions. If an accounting application is processed by computer, those procedures performed by an application program frequently do not provide visible evidence indicating the control procedures performed. Furthermore, the application program may not perform <u>any</u> procedures subsequent to the original processing of the transactions.

   a. Tests of controls on the procedures performed by a computer may be made provided that the computer produces <u>visible evidence</u> to (1) verify that the procedures were in operation and (2) evaluate the propriety of their performance.

   b. With respect to incompatible functions, a computer processing system should include (1) adequate segregation of incompatible functions within the data processing department, (2) segregation between data processing and user department personnel who perform review procedures, and (3) adequate control over access to data and computer programs.

5. Assessing Control Risk--After obtaining an understanding of the client's EDP controls, the auditor must assess control risk for the EDP portion of the client's internal control structure. The procedures that the auditor would use are the same as for a manual system and would include inquiries, observations, and inspections.

F. <u>Evidential Matter</u>--The auditor can use either manual audit procedures, computer-assisted audit techniques, or a combination of both to obtain sufficient, competent evidential matter. However, in some accounting systems that use a computer for processing significant accounting applications, it may be difficult or impossible for the auditor to obtain certain data for inspection, inquiry, or confirmation without computer assistance.

III. General Controls (GC)

A. <u>Organization and Operation Controls</u>

1. **GC 1:** Segregation of functions between the EDP department and users.

2. **GC 2:** Provision for general authorization over the execution of transactions (prohibiting the EDP department from initiating or authorizing transactions).

3. **GC 3:** Part of proper internal control is the segregation of functions within the EDP department. Among the various functions that should be segregated are the following:

TotalRecall

SEGREGATION OF FUNCTIONS WITHIN THE EDP DEPARTMENT

C	CONTROL GROUP	Responsible for internal control within EDP department.
O	OPERATORS	Convert data into machine readable form.
P	PROGRAMMER	Develops and writes the computer programs. Responsible for debugging of programs. Writes the run manual.
A	ANALYST	Designs the overall system and prepares the system flowchart.
L	LIBRARIAN	Keeps track of program and file use. Maintains storage of all data and backups. Controls access to programs.

a. Systems Analysis--Systems analysts investigate a business system and decide how the computer can be applied. This includes designing the system, deciding what the programs will do, and determining how the outputs should appear.

b. Programming

(1) Applications programmers write, test, and debug the application programs from the specifications provided by the systems analyst.

(2) Systems programmers implement, modify, and debug the software necessary to make the hardware operate.

c. Input Preparation--Process of converting the input data into machine-readable form. Input methods include key-to-tape (i.e., keying the information directly onto the magnetic tape), key-to-disk, and OCR.

d. Computer Operations--Computer operators physically run the equipment. This includes loading (i.e., entering) the program and data into the computer at the correct time, mounting tapes and disks on the appropriate tape and disk drives, and dealing with problems that occur during processing.

e. Librarians--Provide control over the various programs, data tapes, disks, and documentation (manuals, etc.) when they are not in use; also, librarians are responsible for restricting access to EDP materials to authorized personnel only. Library-control software may be used in some systems to keep control over programs, data, etc., that is kept on-line.

f. Data Integrity--Data must be safeguarded for maximum control. To this end, users are given passwords or IDs to ensure that only authorized persons can access selected data. These passwords and IDs are frequently changed to further ensure the integrity of the system and its data. Passwords can be used to limit access to the entire system and to limit what the individual can access and/or change once in the system.

g. Data Base Administrator--The data base administrator is responsible for maintaining the data base and restricting its access to authorized personnel.

- Audit Effect of a Small EDP Environment--In a small EDP environment, many of the computer personnel functions are combined for a small number of employees. In these situations, two key functions that should be segregated are the applications programmer and the operator. When these functions are not segregated, irregularities and errors in EDP can be perpetrated and concealed because the programmer knows exactly what the EDP system is capable of performing.

B. Systems Development and Documentation Controls

1. **GC 4:** The procedures for system design, including the acquisition of software packages, should require active participation by representatives of the users and, as appropriate, the accounting department and internal auditors.

2. **GC 5:** Each system should have written specifications which are reviewed and approved by an appropriate level of management and used in the applicable user departments.

3. **GC 6:** Systems testing should be a joint effort of users and EDP personnel and should include both the manual and computerized phases of the system.

4. **GC 7:** Final approval should be obtained prior to placing a new system into operation.

5. **GC 8:** All master file and transaction file conversions should be controlled to prevent unauthorized changes and to provide accurate and complete results.

6. **GC 9:** After a new system has been placed in operation, all program changes should be approved before implementation to determine whether they have been authorized, tested, and documented.

7. **GC 10:** Management should require various levels of documentation and establish formal procedures to define the system at appropriate levels of detail.

   - Audit Effect of a Weakness in Systems Development and Documentation Controls--Auditor will usually have to spend more time in order to understand the system and evaluate the controls.

C. Hardware and Systems Software Controls

1. Hardware Controls--Controls that are built into the computer.

   a. Parity Bit (Redundant Character Check)--In odd parity, an odd number of magnetized dots (on tape, disk, etc.) should always represent each character. When recording data, the computer automatically checks this. Then, when reading the data, the computer checks to see if there is still an odd number. In even parity, an even number of magnetized dots is used to represent each character. For example, the use of a parity bit would probably discover a distortion caused by dust on a tape or a distortion caused by sending data over telephone lines.

   b. Echo Check--CPU sends a signal to activate an input or output device in a certain manner. The device then sends a signal back to verify activation. The CPU then compares the signals.

   c. Hardware Check--Computer checks to make sure the equipment is functioning properly. For example, periodically the computer may search for circuits that are going bad.

d. Boundary Protection--Keeps several files or programs separate when they share a common storage. For example, in time-sharing, several users may share primary storage. Boundary protection would prevent their data and/or programs from becoming mixed and from accessing each other's data.

2. **GC 11:** The control features inherent in the computer hardware, operating system, and other supporting software should be utilized to the maximum possible extent to provide control over operations and to detect and report hardware malfunctions.

3. **GC 12:** Systems software should be subjected to the same control procedures as those applied to the installation of, and changes to, application programs.

- Audit Effect of a Weakness in Hardware and Systems Software Controls--May seriously affect the auditor's assessed level of control risk.

D. Access Controls

1. Physical Access Controls--Only authorized personnel should have access to the facilities housing EDP equipment, files and documentation.

2. Electronic Access Controls--Access control software and other sophisticated devices are available to limit system access.

3. **GC 13:** Access to program documentation should be limited to those persons who require it in the performance of their duties.

4. **GC 14:** Access to data files and programs should be limited to those individuals authorized to process or maintain particular systems.

5. **GC 15:** Access to computer hardware should be limited to authorized individuals.

- Audit Effect of a Weakness in Access Controls--Weakness increases the opportunity for unauthorized modifications of files and programs and misuse of the system; i.e., weaknesses decrease the integrity of the system.

E. Data and Procedural Controls

1. File Labels

a. External Labels--Human-readable labels attached to the outside of a secondary storage device, indicating the name of the file, expiration date, etc.

b. Internal Labels--Labels in machine-readable form.

(1) Header Label--Appears at the beginning of the file and contains such information as the file name, identification number, and the tape reel number.

(2) Trailer Label--Appears at the end of the file and contains such information as a count of the number of the records in the file and an end-of-file code.

2. File Protection Ring--A plastic ring that must be attached to a reel of magnetic tape before the tape drive will write on the tape. Since writing on magnetic tape automatically erases the data already there, the file protection ring guards against the inadvertent erasure of the information on the tape.

3. File Protection Plans

a. Duplicate Files--The most important data files are duplicated and the duplicates are stored away from the computer center.

b. Grandfather-Father-Son (or Vice Versa) Retention Concept--The master file is updated at the end of each day by the day's transaction file, illustrated in Exhibit 4.

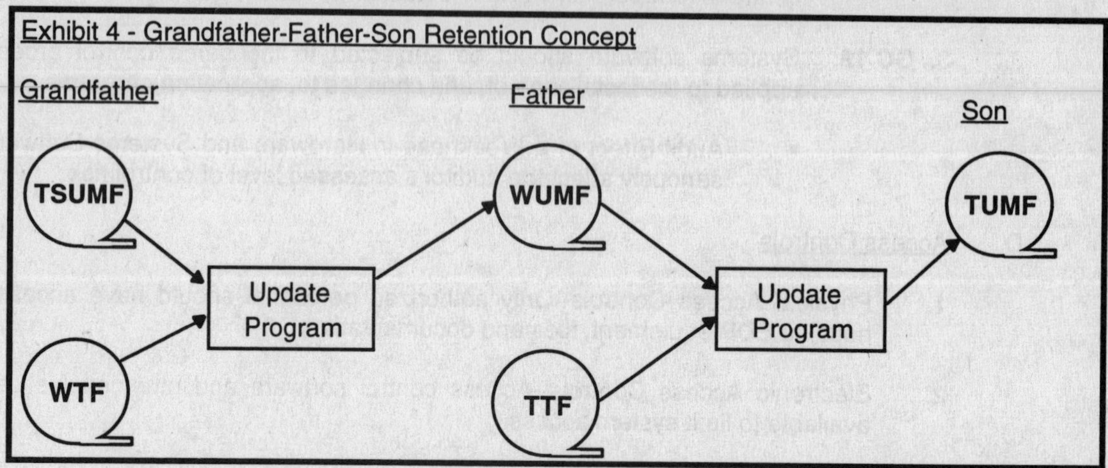

After updating on Thursday, the Thursday updated master file (TUMF) is the son, the Wednesday updated master file (WUMF) is the father, and the Tuesday updated master file (TSUMF) is the grandfather. These three files plus Wednesday's and Thursday's transaction files (WTF and TTF, respectively) are retained. If there is a problem during Friday's update run, the TUMF can be regenerated by running the copy of the WUMF with Thursday's transaction file. If necessary the WUMF could be reconstructed by processing TSUMF with Wednesday's transaction file. Once updating is completed on Friday, Friday's updated master file (FUMF) becomes the son, TUMF becomes the father and WUMF becomes the grandfather. Therefore, at that time, TSUMF and Wednesday's transaction file can be erased.

c. Disk Reconstruction Plan--The problem is that in updating a record in a disk file, the record is read from the disk into the CPU, altered, and then written back to its previous location on the disk, thereby erasing the preupdated record. Therefore, a "disk dump" is used in which a copy of the contents of the disk is made on magnetic tape periodically, say each morning. Then, as the day's transactions are processed against the disk file, copies of the transactions are recorded on another tape. If it becomes necessary to reconstruct the disk file at any time during the day, the old file can be read from the tape to the disk and reupdated with the transactions from the transaction tape.

4. Physical Safeguards

a. Maintenance of Proper Physical Environment--Avoid extremes in temperature, humidity, dust, etc.

b. Environment Free From Possibility of Natural Disasters--Includes proper fire-proofing and locating the computer in a safe place (for example, not in the basement if there is a danger of flooding).

c. Backup Facilities--Arrangements should be made to use other equipment in the case of serious problems. Backup arrangements are frequently made with service bureaus or with computer installations of subsidiaries.

d. Control Access to the Computer Room--Only authorized personnel should have access. For example, computer operators would be authorized to be in the computer room, but programmers would not be. Further, there should always be at least two people in the computer room at all times. A weakness in the internal control structure exists when a client uses microcomputers, because the operators may be able to remove hardware and software components and modify them at home.

5. **GC 16:** A control function should be responsible for receiving all data to be processed, for ensuring that all data are recorded, for following up on errors detected during processing to see that the transactions are corrected and resubmitted by the proper party, and for verifying the proper distribution of output.

6. **GC 17:** A written manual of systems and procedures should be prepared for all computer operations and should provide for management's general or specific authorizations to process transactions.

7. **GC 18:** Internal auditors or some other independent group within an organization should review and evaluate proposed systems at critical stages of development.

8. **GC 19:** On a continuing basis, internal auditors or some other independent group within an organization should review and test computer processing activities.

- Audit Effect of Weaknesses in Data and Procedural Controls--Serious weaknesses can affect the auditor's assessment of control risk when establishing the scope of the substantive testing.

IV. Application Controls (AC)

A. Input Controls--Input controls are designed to provide reasonable assurance that data received by EDP have been properly authorized, converted into machine sensible form, identified and that data have not been lost, suppressed, added, duplicated, or otherwise improperly changed. Basic categories of input to be controlled are (1) transaction entry, (2) file maintenance transactions (e.g., changing sales prices on a product master file), (3) inquiry transactions (e.g., how many units of a particular inventory item are on hand), and (4) error correction transactions.

1. **AC 1:** Only properly authorized and approved input, prepared in accordance with management's general or specific authorization, should be accepted for processing by EDP.

2. **AC 2:** The system should verify all significant codes used to record data.

3. **AC 3:** Conversion of data into machine-sensible form should be controlled.

4. Common Errors in Conversion--Keying errors and the losing or dropping of records.

5. Input Control Techniques

a. Control Totals--A total is computed and then recomputed at a later time. The totals are compared and should be the same. Control totals can be used as input, processing, and output controls.

(1) Financial Total--Has financial meaning in addition to being a control. For example, the dollar amount of accounts receivable to be updated can be compared with a computer-generated total of the dollar amount of updates read from the tape.

(2) Hash Total--Has meaning only as a control. For example, a total of the account numbers of those accounts which should have been updated can be compared with a computer-generated total of those account numbers actually entered.

(3) Record Count (Document Count)--A count of the number of transactions processed. For example, the computer can be programmed to print the total number of A/R records actually inputted.

b. Computer Editing--Computers can be programmed to perform a wide range of edit tests (i.e., edit checks) on records as they are being entered into the system. If a particular record does not meet the test, it would not be processed. Edit tests include the following:

(1) Limit (Reasonableness) Test--A particular field of an input transaction record is checked to be sure it is not greater (or smaller) than a prespecified amount, or that it is within a prespecified range of acceptable values. For example, "hours worked" on a payroll record may be checked to be sure it does not exceed 50 hours.

(2) Valid Field and/or Character Test--The particular field is examined to be sure it is of the proper size and composition. For example, if a customer account number should be seven numeric digits appearing in the first 7 spaces of the record, the first 7 spaces can be examined to be sure there are 7 numerals there.

(3) Valid Number or Code Test--Verifies that a particular number or code is one of those that is recognized by the system. For example, if a company has 5 retail outlets and records sales by using a location code of 1-5, the computer can check to be sure the code digit on the transaction record is a 1, 2, 3, 4, or 5.

(4) Sequence Check--If the input records should be in some particular sequence, the computer can be programmed to verify the sequence. For example, after sorting, the day's transaction file that is being entered should be in ascending order by customer account number.

(5) Missing Data Test--Verifies that all of the data fields actually contain data. For example, a point-of-sale terminal may be programmed not to accept a transaction unless the clerk has entered 10 pieces of required data.

(6) Valid Transaction Test--Since there are only a certain number of transaction types that would be expected for most files, the computer can be programmed to verify that a particular transaction is an appropriate type for a particular file. For example, in the case of inventory, the only valid transaction may be to debit the inventory account when inventory is added and credit the account when inventory is taken away.

(7) Valid Combination of Fields--Checks to be sure a certain combination of fields is reasonable. For example, a large retail outlet may program its computer to check the reasonableness of the product code field and the quantity-sold field. This would disclose a clerical error that resulted in a sale being entered for 10 television sets when only 1 was sold; i.e., it is not reasonable that one customer would purchase 10 television sets.

(8) Check Digit (Self-Checking Digit)--Digit (determined according to a prespecified mathematical routine) that is added to the end of a piece of numeric data to permit the numeric data to be checked for accuracy during input, processing, or output. For example, a customer account number may be 1234. A check digit could be formed by adding the first and third digits and using the sum. Since

the sum of the two digits is 4 (i.e., 1 + 3), the check digit is 4. It is added to the end of the number that is assigned to the customer. The new customer account number becomes 12344. The computer can be programmed to verify the check digit at appropriate times. For instance, if the number is accidentally entered as 13244, the check digit would not match and the transaction would not be accepted. In practice, the mathematical routine is more complex than the one illustrated here.

(9) Valid Sign Test--A particular field can be checked to be sure it has the proper sign. For example, the quantity received in an inventory record should not be negative.

6. **AC 4:** Movement of data between one processing step and another, or between departments, should be controlled.

7. **AC 5:** The correction of all errors detected by the application system and the resubmission of corrected transactions should be reviewed and controlled.

- Error Log (Error Listing)--A computer-prepared list of those transactions that were not processed because of some error condition (e.g., an invalid customer account number). When an error is encountered, the usual procedure is for the computer to not process the erroneous transaction but to skip it and continue processing the valid transactions rather than to halt processing altogether. A control function should be responsible for following up on errors detected during processing to see that the transactions are corrected and resubmitted by the proper party. This control function should ideally be delegated to a special EDP control group which is independent from system analysis, programming, and operation.

B. Processing Controls (**NOTE**: Many of the input controls are also valid processing controls.)

1. **AC 6:** Control totals should be produced and reconciled with input control totals.

2. **AC 7:** Controls should prevent processing the wrong file, detect errors in file manipulation, and highlight operator-caused errors.

3. **AC 8:** Limit and reasonableness checks should be incorporated within programs.

4. **AC 9:** Run-to-run controls should be verified at appropriate points in the processing cycle.

C. Output Controls--Primarily balancing, visual scanning or verification, and distribution.

1. **AC 10:** Output control totals should be reconciled with input and processing controls.

2. **AC 11:** Output should be scanned and tested by comparison to original source documents.

3. **AC 12:** Systems output should be distributed only to authorized users.

D. Audit Effect of a Weakness in Application Controls--Must be considered in relation to the particular application and to the total audit. Controls in the categories of input, processing, and output must be considered in relation to each other; i.e., a strong control in processing may compensate for a weakness in input.

V. Documentation of an EDP-Based System

A. Purpose--Documentation is an important aspect of control as well as of communication. It generally provides (1) an understanding of the system's objectives, concepts, and output, (2) a source of information for systems analysts and programmers when involved in program maintenance and revision, (3) information that is needed for a supervisory review, (4) a basis for training new personnel, (5) a means of communicating common information, (6) a source of information about accounting controls, and (7) a source of information that will aid in providing continuity in the event experienced personnel leave.

DOCUMENTATION OF AN EDP SYSTEM

O **Operations Documentation**--Information provided to the computer operator. Used to obtain an understanding of the functions performed by the operator and to determine how data is processed.

P **Problem Definition Documentation**--Permits the auditor to gain a general understanding of the system without having to become involved in the details of the programs.

S **Systems Documentation**--Provides sufficient information to trace accounting data from its original entry to system output.

O **Operator Documentation**--Documentation should be prepared that will indicate the jobs run and any operator interaction.

U **User Documentation**--Description of the input required for processing and an output listing. Auditor may use it to gain an understanding of the functions performed by the user and the general flow of information.

P **Program Documentation**--Primarily used by systems analysts and programmers to provide a control over program corrections and revisions. May be useful to auditor in determining the current status of a program.

B. Problem Definition Documentation--Permits the auditor to gain a general understanding of the system without having to become involved in the details of the programs. Contents include the following:

1. Description of the reasons for implementing the system.
2. Description of the operations performed by the system.
3. Project proposals.
4. Evidence of approval of the system and subsequent changes (for example, a particular individual may have to sign a form to indicate these).
5. A listing of the assignment of project responsibilities.

C. Systems Documentation--Provides sufficient information to trace accounting data from its original entry to system output. Contents include the following:

1. A description of the system.
2. Systems flowcharts.
3. Input descriptions.
4. Output descriptions.
5. File descriptions.
6. Descriptions of controls.
7. Copies of authorizations and their effective dates for systems changes that have been implemented.

- Systems Flowchart--Flowchart showing the flow of data through the system and the interrelationships between the processing steps and computer runs.

D. Program Documentation--Primarily used by systems analysts and programmers to provide a control over program corrections and revisions. However, it may be useful to the auditor to determine the current status of a program. Contents include the following:

1. Brief narrative description of the program.
2. Program flowchart, decision table, or detailed logic narrative.
   a. Program Flowchart--Shows the steps followed by the program in processing the data.
   b. Decision Table--Describes a portion of the logic used in the program. Although it is not always used, it can replace or supplement the program flowchart.
   c. Detailed Logic Narrative--Narrative description of the logic followed by a program.
3. Source statements (i.e., a listing of the program instructions) or parameter listings.
4. List of control features.
5. Detailed description of file formats and record layouts.
6. Table of code values used to indicate processing requirements.
7. Record of program changes, authorizations, and effective dates.
8. Input and output formats.
9. Operating instructions.
10. Descriptions of any special features.

E. Operations Documentation--Information provided to the computer operator. It can be used by the auditor to obtain an understanding of the functions performed by the operator and to determine how data is processed. Contents include the following:

1. A brief description of the program.
2. Description of the inputs and outputs that are required (e.g., the forms used).
3. Sequence of cards, tapes, disks, and other files.
4. Set-up instructions and operating system requirements.
5. Operating notes listing program messages, halts, and action necessary to signal the end of jobs.
6. Control procedures to be performed by operations.
7. Recovery and restart procedures (to be used for hardware or software malfunctions).
8. Estimated normal and maximum run time.
9. Instructions to the operator in the event of an emergency.

F. User Documentation--Description of the input required for processing and an output listing. Auditor may use it to gain an understanding of the functions performed by the user and the general flow of information. Contents include the following:

1. A description of the system.

2. Description of the input and output.

3. List of control procedures and an indication of the position of the person performing the procedures.

4. Error correction procedures.

5. Cutoff procedures for submitting the data to the EDP department.

6. A description of how the user department should check reports for accuracy.

G. Operator Documentation--Documentation should be prepared that will indicate the jobs run and any operator interaction.

1. Daily Computer Log--May be manually prepared by the computer operator. It indicates the jobs run, the time required, who ran them, etc.

2. Console Log--A listing of all interactions between the console and the CPU. Prepared by the computer as messages are entered from the console, it can be a valuable control for detecting unauthorized intervention of the computer operator during the running of a program. It also shows how the operator responded to processing problems.

H. Audit Impact--If reliable documentation is not available, the auditor must find other sources of information.

VI. Consideration of Accounting Controls in EDP-Based Applications

A. The Auditor's Consideration of Control Policies and Procedures in EDP-Based Applications--Is represented by the following flowchart. This flowchart is a simplified illustration and does not portray all possible decision paths.

Exhibit 5

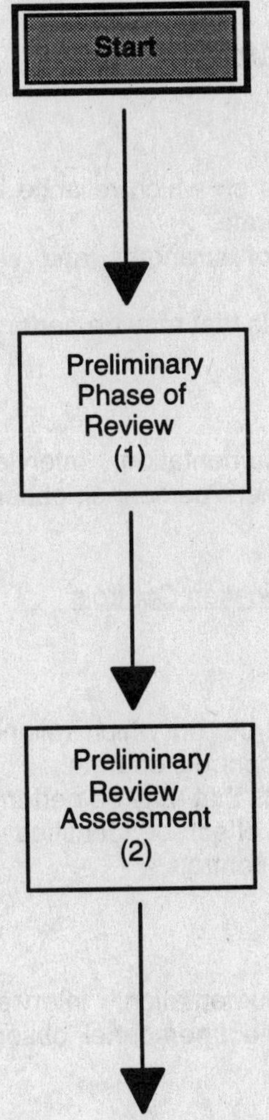

1. Preliminary Phase of the Review

Purpose:

- Understand accounting system including both EDP and non-EDP segments:
  - Flow of transactions and significance of output.
  - Extent to which EDP is used in significant accounting applications.
  - Basic structure of accounting control, including both EDP and user controls.

Methods:

Inquiry and discussion, observation, review of documentation, tracing of transactions, control questionnaires and checklists.

2. Preliminary Phase of the Review--Assessment

Purpose:

- Assess significance of EDP and non-EDP accounting controls.
- Determine extent of additional review within EDP.
- Assess control risk and develop preliminary substantive tests.

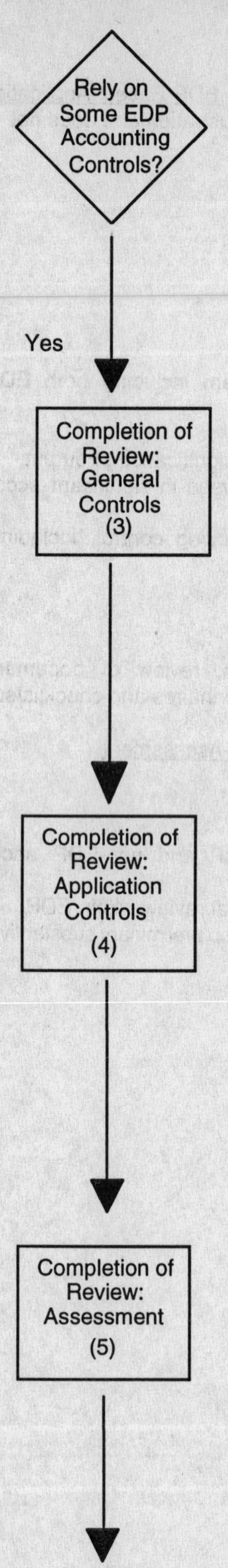

Method:

Judgment.

3. Completion of Review—General Controls

Purpose:

- Identify general controls on which reliance is planned and determine how they operate.
- Determine the effect of strengths and weaknesses on application controls.
- Consider tests of controls that may be performed.

Methods:

Detailed examination of documentation; interviewing internal auditors, EDP and user department personnel; observing operation of general controls.

4. Completion of Review--Application Controls

Purpose:

- Identify application controls on which reliance is planned, and determine how the controls operate.
- Consider tests of controls that may be performed.
- Consider the potential effect of identified strengths and weaknesses on tests of controls.

Methods:

Detailed examination of documentation; interviewing internal auditors, EDP, and user department personnel; observing operation of application controls.

5. Completion of Review--Assessment

Purpose:

For each significant accounting application:

- Consider the types of errors or irregularities that could occur.
- Determine the accounting control procedures that prevent or detect such errors and irregularities.
- Assess effectiveness of EDP and non-EDP accounting controls.

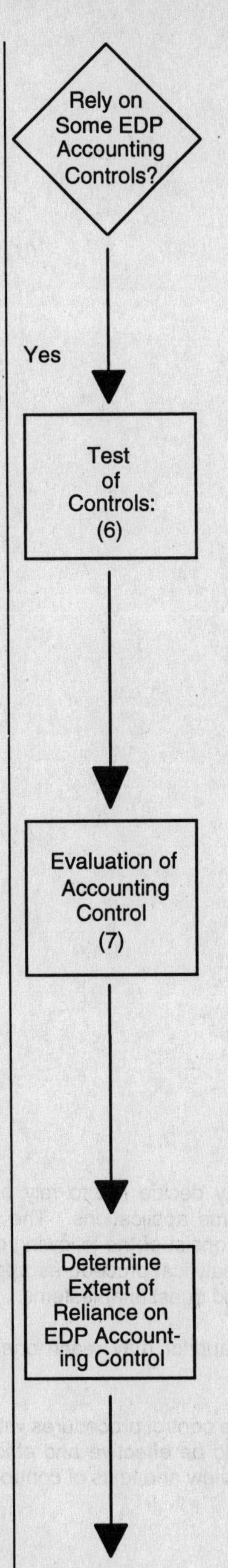

Method:

Judgment.

6. Test of Controls

Purpose:

- Determine whether the necessary control procedures are prescribed and followed satisfactorily.
- Provide reasonable assurance that controls are functioning properly.
- Consider and, to the extent appropriate, document when, how, and by whom controls are provided.

7. Evaluation of Accounting Control

Purpose:

For each significant account application:

- Consider the types of errors or irregularities that could occur.
- Determine the accounting control procedures that prevent or detect such errors and irregularities.
- Determine whether the necessary control procedures are prescribed and followed satisfactorily.
- Evaluate weaknesses and assess their effect on the nature, timing, and extent of substantive procedures.

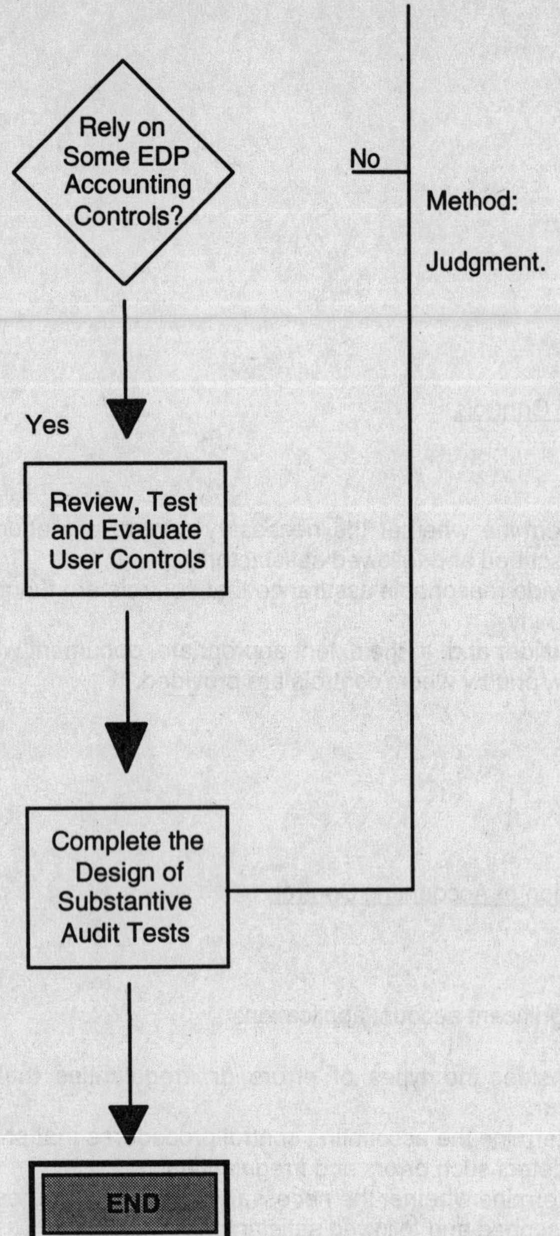

NOTE: At any point after the preliminary phase of the review, the auditor may decide not to rely on EDP accounting controls (i.e., assess control risk at the maximum level) for all or some applications. The auditor would then complete the design of the substantive audit tests. Substantive tests consist of the following classes of audit procedures: (1) tests of details of transactions and balances, and (2) analytical procedures applied to significant ratios and trends and resulting in investigation of unusual fluctuations and questionable items.

B. Amplification of Phase (2): Preliminary Review Assessment--The auditor may reach one of the following conclusions:

1. Control Risk Assessed at Below the Maximum Level--There are control procedures within the EDP portions of the application that the auditor believes would be effective and efficient to test the controls. The auditor would continue with additional review and tests of controls.

2. Control Risk Assessed at the Maximum Level--There are sufficient weaknesses or the auditor does not believe it is efficient to test control procedures. The auditor would assess the impact these weaknesses could have on the financial statements and would accomplish the audit objectives by other means. Bear in mind, this situation may lead to a conclusion that the entity is not auditable if sufficient evidence does not exist outside the EDP environment.

3. Decision Not to Extend Procedures--Even though the controls appear adequate, the auditor may decide not to extend the preliminary review and not to perform tests of controls. This may happen when

   a. Effort Required--The auditor concludes that the audit effort required to complete the review and to test controls is greater than the reduction in audit effort that would result from relying on the controls.

   b. Redundant Controls--The auditor concludes that the control procedures are redundant because of the existence of other accounting control procedures.

C. Work Papers--Work papers for a consideration of EDP controls may include (1) narratives, flowcharts, or other representations of the flow of data in the system, (2) descriptions and evidence of the various controls, (3) questionnaires or checklists which were used in the audit, (4) descriptions of significant computer files, (5) documentation and analysis of the results of the tests of controls that were performed, (6) examples of forms and computer printouts, (7) write-ups of interviews conducted with employees, (8) assessments, evaluations, and conclusions reached concerning the adequacy of accounting control, and (9) comments on elements of accounting control affecting the nature, extent, and timing of other audit procedures.

VII. General Auditing Approaches

A. Auditing Around (Without) the Computer--The computer is treated as a "black box" that is ignored for all practical purposes. The auditor concentrates on input and output; i.e., if the inputs are correct and the outputs are correct, what went on within the computer must also be correct. The auditor does not test or directly examine the computer program, nor use the computer to perform the tests. Rather, the auditor relies on computer-prepared documents and printouts, which provide a visible audit trail which can be used in performing the audit procedures.

1. Type of System--Auditing around the computer is appropriate for simple systems that provide extensive printouts of processing, i.e., systems that provide a good audit trail.

2. Testing of Controls--Extensive use is made of the error listing (error log) to verify the existence and functioning of the control procedures. For example, if the error listing shows that a payroll transaction was not processed because the "hours-worked" field exceeded the limit allowed, the auditor has evidence that the limit test exists and is functioning. The auditor will also trace transactions from the source documents (for example, a sales slip) through processing to their final place in the accounts and reports. Note, however, that while computer-generated output is being used, the computer is not being used as an audit tool.

3. Substantive Testing--The computer-prepared output is used as a basis for substantive testing. For example, the auditor may select a sample of accounts receivable to be confirmed from a computer-prepared listing of all the individual accounts receivable.

B. Auditing Through (With) the Computer--The computer is used to perform tests of controls and substantive testing. The auditor places emphasis on the input data and the processing of the data. While output is not ignored, the auditor reasons that if the input is correct and the processing is correct, then the output must be correct.

1. Type of System--As a system becomes more complex, more processing is done within the computer and more data files are kept only in machine-readable form. This causes the audit

trail to disappear. When this happens, auditing through the computer is really the only alternative open to the auditor.

2. Auditing Through the Computer--Techniques

TotalRecall

AUDITING THROUGH THE COMPUTER

W Writing own program
E Embedded audit modules
T Tagging

C Client-prepared program
U Utility programs (utility routines)
P Program comparison

T Test data (test deck)
R Review of program logic
I Integrated test facility (ITF, minicompany approach)
P Parallel simulation
P Program tracing

a. Test Data (Test Deck)--Auditor prepares a series of fictitious transactions (test data), some of which are valid and some of which contain errors that should be detected by the controls the auditor wants to test. The auditor uses the client's programs to process the test data and then examines the output to check processing, including the computer-prepared error listing. For example, if the payroll program is not supposed to process payroll data for employees whose employee time card indicates they have worked more than 60 hours per week, the auditor's test data would contain at least one time card with more than 60 hours worked on it. If the control is working, the particular transaction should not be processed but should appear on the computer-prepared error listing. Problems--There are at least three potential problems with using test data: (1) Care must be exercised to prevent the fictitious data from becoming part of the client's real data files. (2) Time and care are required to prepare the test data so that it will test for the things that could really go wrong and that are of interest to the auditor. (3) The auditor must take steps to make sure that the program being tested (i.e., the program testing the fictitious data) is the one that is actually used in routine processing.

b. Parallel Simulation--Once the auditor has checked a program, the auditor must determine that the client continues to use it. Parallel simulation involves processing actual client data through an auditor's software program, possibly using the client's computer. After processing the data, the auditor compares the output with output obtained from the client. Two techniques that can be used to help the auditor verify that the program being used for routine processing is the one that has been checked are as follows:

(1) Controlled Processing--The auditor observes (i.e., controls) an actual processing run and compares the results against those expected.

(2) Controlled Reprocessing--The auditor tests a program and keeps a copy of the program. At some future point in time, the auditor has the client use the auditor's control copy of the program to process some actual transactions. The results are compared with those from the client's routine processing run. For example, the auditor may have a control copy of the payroll program. The auditor would select the time cards and payroll data for several employees and have them processed using the control copy. The auditor would then compare the results of gross pay, net pay, withholding, etc., from the program with those that were attained by the payroll program the client had just used. Problem--A major problem is for the auditor to keep the control copy of the program current.

c. Integrated Test Facility (ITF, Minicompany Approach)--Auditor creates a fictitious entity within the client's actual data files. The fictitious data is then processed for the entity as part of the client's regular data processing. For example, if the auditor wants to test the accounts receivable update program, the auditor could create a fictitious customer's account receivable in the client's actual accounts receivable master file. During the period under audit, the auditor would occasionally introduce transactions for the fictitious customer. For instance, the "customer" would make credit purchases, would overpay the account, would not pay the account, would make purchase returns, etc. These transactions would be processed as part of the client's normal processing. Since the auditor knows what effect the various transactions should have on the accounts receivable, the auditor can check the status of the account at any time to verify that transactions are being processed correctly, i.e., that the application programs are working as they should.

(1) Advantage Over Test Data--Two of the main advantages of ITF over the use of test data are that the auditor introduces fictitious data throughout the period (approaches continuous auditing) and it is processed along with the client's other "live" (i.e., actual) data.

(2) Problems--Several potential problems relating to the use of ITF are as follows:

(a) Since the data is part of the client's data files, it may accidentally be included in the financial statements and reports that are prepared. To avoid this, the auditor may wish to introduce reversing entries to reverse the effects of the fictitious transactions (for example, to remove the "sales" made to the fictitious customer from the sales account) or the auditor may have the statement preparation program modified to skip the fictitious account when preparing the financial statements. Or, the auditor may decide to use small dollar amounts so that even if they are not removed, they will not have a material effect.

(b) Time, effort, and skill are required to make the fictitious entity operational and make sure the transactions processed against it will test the conditions and controls the auditor is interested in.

(c) There is also the problem of secrecy, since the auditor's confidence in the technique will decrease if the client's data preparation and computer operations personnel know that the entity is fictitious and that the transactions for it are being introduced by the auditor in order to audit compliance.

d. Tagging--Selected transactions are "tagged" (i.e., are specially marked) at the auditor's direction. Then, as they are processed, additional documentation is displayed (or printed) so that the auditor can see how the transactions are handled as they are processed, i.e., it allows the auditor to examine the transactions at the intermediate steps in processing which are normally done within the computer but not displayed.

e. Review of Program Logic--Auditor reviews the application program's documentation including the flowcharts and possibly the program listing, to obtain a sufficient understanding of the logic of the program in order to evaluate it. This may be time consuming. Unless the auditor specifically believes there is a logic error in the program, other audit techniques will probably be more efficient.

f. Program Comparison--The auditor-controlled copy of the program is compared with the program the client is currently using (usually done on a surprise basis). While the auditor may do this manually, there is software available to do it. A major drawback is the problem of the auditor's maintaining a current copy of the program; i.e., routine maintenance (updating) by programmers may mean that the auditor's copy does not agree with the copy being used, and it is the auditor's copy that is wrong.

g. Tracing (Program Tracing, Tracing Software)--Prints a listing of the program instructions (steps) that were executed in processing a transaction. The auditor must be familiar with the programming language in which the client's application program is written. Even then, it may be time consuming to follow through the program listing.

h. Utility Programs (Utility Routines)--Standard programs furnished by the computer manufacturer for performing common data processing functions such as (1) changing the media a file is stored on (e.g., tape-to-disk, disk-to-tape, tape-to-paper), (2) modifying the data by changing or deleting records within a file, (3) creating or destroying a file, (4) changing the name or password of a file, (5) printing the contents of a file so it may be inspected visually, (6) sorting a file, and (7) merging two or more files. Utility programs may be more technical than GAS (discussed below). Therefore, the auditor may have to be more technically proficient with EDP to use them efficiently. The auditor must also be sure the utility program has not been altered. Consideration should be given as to whether the use of a utility routine will decrease the audit time or if GAS may be more appropriate.

i. Embedded Audit Modules--Sections of program code included in the client's application program to collect audit data for the auditor. For example, at the auditor's direction, a file may be created of all sales transactions that are for more than $100. This monitors the client's system as transactions are actually processed. It can be hard to install once the application program is operational. Thus, it may be most efficiently included during system design.

j. Writing Own Program--Auditor writes a program for the specific substantive test to be performed. The major drawback is the time and effort required to get the program operational.

k. Client-Prepared Program--The client (often the internal audit staff) may have written programs to do the same things the auditor would like to do. Therefore, the auditor may be able to use the programs. However, first the auditor must test them to make sure that they do what they are supposed to do and that their integrity can be relied on.

VIII. Generalized Audit Software

(Primary Source: AICPA Audit Guide; *Computer Assisted Audit Techniques*)

A. Generalized Audit Software (GAS)--A set of programs or routines (i.e., a software package) specifically designed to perform certain data processing functions that are useful to the auditor. The auditor learns how to use the GAS and then can use it on the data files of a variety of clients. The auditor need only briefly describe the organization of each client's files to the GAS, also known as General Purpose Audit Software, General Purpose Computer Audit Software. This is the most prevalently used computer-assisted audit technique.

B. Reasons for Using GAS

1. Enables the Auditor to Use a Large Variety of Data in Making Audit Decisions--Much of a client's data is retained only in machine-readable form. GAS makes it possible for the auditor to access the data, analyze it, and present the results in a meaningful and convenient form.

2. Enables the Auditor to Deal Effectively With Large Quantities of Data--GAS lets the auditor examine more data in more detail. For example, given an insurance company that has a policy file maintained on disk, the auditor can use GAS to perform mathematical tests on

each of the policy records in the file. If auditing the file manually, the auditor would be forced to examine only a sample of the policies.

3. Lessens the Auditor's Dependence on Client EDP Personnel--The auditor can do much of the computerized testing; i.e., the auditor does not need to rely on client EDP personnel for the programs needed.

4. Produces economies in the audit while, at the same time, increasing audit quality.

5. Access to Data--Enables the auditor to gain access and test information stored in the client's files without having to acquire a complete understanding of the client's EDP system.

C. Audit Tasks Performed by GAS--While the exact procedures performed will vary with particular software packages, audit software is used to accomplish six basic types of audit tasks:

1. Examining Records for Quality, Completeness, Consistency, and Correctness--GAS can be instructed to scan the records in a file and print those that are exceptions to auditor-specified criteria.

   - Examples: (1) Reviewing accounts receivable balances for amounts that are over the credit limit, (2) reviewing inventory quantities for negative or unreasonably large balances, (3) reviewing payroll files for terminated employees, and (4) reviewing bank demand deposit files for unusually large deposits or withdrawals.

2. Testing Calculations and Making Computations--GAS can test the accuracy of mathematical computations and can perform quantitative analyses to evaluate the reasonableness of client representations.

   - Examples: (1) Recalculating the extensions of inventory items, depreciation amounts, the accuracy of sales discounts, and interest, and (2) determining the accuracy of the net pay computations for employees.

3. Comparing Data on Separate Files--GAS can be used to determine if identical information on separate files agrees.

   - Examples: (1) Comparing changes in accounts receivable balances between two dates with details of sales and cash receipts on transaction files, (2) comparing payroll details with personnel records, and (3) comparing current and prior-period inventory files to assist in reviewing for obsolete or slow-moving items.

4. Selecting, Printing, and Analyzing Audit Samples--GAS can select statistical samples (random, stratified, etc.), print the items for the auditor's working papers or on special confirmation forms, and then, when the results are known (for example, when the confirmations are returned), analyze the data statistically.

   - Examples: (1) Select and print accounts receivable confirmations, (2) select inventory items for observation, and (3) select fixed asset additions for vouching.

5. Summarizing or Resequencing Data and Performing Analyses--GAS can reformat and aggregate data in a variety of ways.

   - Examples: (1) Refooting account files, (2) testing accounts receivable aging, (3) preparing general ledger trial balances, (4) summarizing inventory turnover statistics for obsolescence analysis, and (5) resequencing inventory items by location to facilitate physical observations.

6. Comparing Data Obtained Through Other Audit Procedures With Company Records--Manually-gathered audit evidence can be converted to machine-readable form and then GAS can compare it to other machine-readable data.

   - Examples: (1) Comparison of inventory test counts with perpetual records and (2) comparison of creditor statements with accounts payable files.

D. Examples

1. Inventories--Potential applications of GAS in the audit of inventory:

   a. Determine the inventory items that should be reduced for quick sale, according to company policy.

   b. Merge last year's inventory file with this year's and list those items which have unit costs of more than $100 which have increased by more than 10%.

   c. Test for quantities on hand in excess of units sold during a period and list possible obsolete inventory items.

   d. Select a sample of inventory items for a physical count and reconcile to the perpetual records.

   e. Scan the sequence of inventory tag numbers and print a list of any missing numbers.

   f. Select a random sample of inventory items for price testing and test the price.

   g. Perform a net-realizable value test on year-end inventory quantities, using unit selling price data, and list any items where inventory cost exceeds net realizable value.

2. Accounts Receivable--Potential applications of GAS in the audit of accounts receivable:

   a. Select and list accounts according to auditor-defined past-due conditions (e.g., over $5,000 and more than 90 days past-due).

   b. List a random sample of past-due accounts to use in determining if follow-up procedures conform to company policy.

   c. Select a sample of customer accounts for confirmation and have the computer print the confirmation requests.

   d. Determine if the accounts receivable master file balance agrees with the general ledger and independently prove a company-prepared aging of accounts.

   e. Match subsequent cash collections with accounts receivable records and independently age receivables not yet paid several weeks after the trial balance date.

   f. Compare amounts due from individual customers with their approved credit limits and print a list of customers with balances in excess of their authorized amounts.

   g. Print, for review and follow-up, a list of accounts for which collection efforts have been temporarily suspended.

E. Feasibility of Using GAS--When deciding whether to use GAS in particular situations, the auditor should consider the following:

1. Nature of the Audit Area and Audit Approach--In some cases, the use of GAS may be the only feasible approach to attain the audit objective, for example, in complex systems with invisible audit trails.

2. Significance of Audit Effort and Timing--GAS may permit the auditor to complete an audit procedure quicker than any other alternative.

3. Availability of Data--Some data is only in machine-readable form. Other data is not in machine-readable form and would, therefore, have to be converted before GAS could be applied to it.

4. Degree of Client Cooperation--Does the client support the use of GAS or oppose its use?

5. Availability of Qualified Staff Personnel--Does the auditor or staff possess the necessary technical expertise to use GAS on the system being audited? For example, an auditor may be experienced in using GAS on relatively simple systems, but not on complex systems.

6. Economic Considerations--While GAS can accomplish many things for the auditor, it has costs associated with its use such as staff hours, technical review hours, mechanical assistance hours, confirmations and other forms, keypunch and verification expense, and computer time.

F. Steps in Planning the Application--The following steps should be followed in planning the use of GAS:

1. Set the objectives of the GAS application.

2. Determine the reports and other output requirements.

3. Review the content, accessibility, etc., of client data files.

4. Identify client personnel who may provide administrative or technical assistance.

5. Determine need for equipment and supplies.

6. Determine the degree of audit control needed so that the auditor will have confidence that the GAS is processed correctly.

7. Prepare application budgets and timetables.

G. Steps in Using GAS--The auditor will go through a series of steps in applying GAS:

1. Determine Routines--Determine the specific GAS routines to be used and the particular order in which to use them for the particular application. The auditor does not have to use all of the routines available. Any routine can be used as many times as the auditor wishes.

2. Complete Coding Sheets--The auditor completes coding sheets which describe the routines to use and the order in which to use them. They are also used to describe the client's system and data files to GAS. These are then keypunched onto cards.

3. Processing--The GAS, the auditor's instruction cards, and the client's data files are entered into the computer and processed. The auditor should maintain physical control over the GAS (i.e., it should be kept in the auditor's possession) and should be present in the computer room when it is run. The auditor should also be present to receive the output directly from the computer.

4. Use Output--The auditor uses the output of the GAS processing in the audit.

H. Statistical Sampling--This section is adapted from the AICPA audit guide entitled *Audit Sampling.* See also Chapter 38.

1. Advantages

a. Computer programs have been developed to assist the auditor in planning and evaluating sampling procedures. These programs overcome the limitations of tables and perform calculations, such as a standard deviation computation, that are difficult and time-consuming to perform manually.

b. Computer programs are flexible. For example, they can calculate sample sizes for different sampling techniques. They can help the auditor select a random sample. They can evaluate samples covering single or multiple locations and can offer many more options for the auditor's planning considerations. These programs generally have built-in controls over human errors. For example, programs can be designed to include controls to identify unreasonable input.

c. The printed output is generally written in nontechnical language that can be easily understood by an auditor. The printout can be included in the auditor's working papers as documentation of the sampling procedure.

2. Time-Sharing Programs

a. General Considerations

(1) Individual time-sharing applications for a statistical sampling procedure are relatively inexpensive. An auditor who decides to use computer time-sharing in performing statistical sampling may need to pay a small, minimum monthly fee to receive a confidential user code and password to access a vendor's library of statistical sampling programs.

(2) Time-sharing programs are available from a variety of sources, including vendors who make their programs available to all auditors. In selecting a time-sharing program, the auditor should obtain reasonable assurance that the program is suitable. The considerations listed in IX. B. through E., below, may assist the auditor in making that determination.

b. Appropriateness of Program

(1) Programs offered by time-sharing vendors generally are developed by the vendors, by third parties for the vendor, or by CPA firms. In most circumstances, more than one statistical theory may be acceptable for use in developing programs. The auditor should inquire which theory was used in order to determine whether that theory is appropriate for the auditor's specific purpose.

(2) The extent of a vendor's testing of its programs varies significantly. It is important for the auditor to determine the extent of such tests before using the programs. For example, the auditor should inquire whether the programs were tested with data that an auditor may encounter both in usual and in rare, but possible, circumstances.

(3) The auditor should also consider making inquiries about the business reputation of the vendor and the qualifications of the program developer. Vendors have significant differences in philosophies about their responsibility to the user of their programs. The extent to which the vendor is willing to assume

responsibility for the programs may indicate the degree to which the vendor believes the programs are suitable for an auditor's purpose.

c. Program Controls--Statistical sampling software should contain basic control features that, for example, reject negative numbers where inapplicable or alert the auditor to inappropriately high risk levels or tolerable rates. The auditor should also inquire whether documentation of the controls is available for review. The software also should contain prompts to lead an auditor who is new to statistical sampling through the various input requirements and alternatives.

d. Vendor Services--A clear and comprehensive user manual should accompany each program. The auditor also should consider if the availability of programs will meet the needs based on work hours and the location of the auditor's offices. For example, some vendors make their programs available twenty-four hours a day. The auditor should consider the amount of technical support available from the vendor when programs are used.

e. Convenience--Many time-sharing vendors provide simple operating instructions designed to meet the needs of the auditor. The program instructions should indicate the program's capabilities. The amount of required input should be minimal and free of complex, special codes. The printout reports should be concise and readily understandable to the auditor.

3. Batch Programs

a. Uses of Batch Programs--Batch programs are especially useful where the company's records are in computer-readable form and the auditor wishes to perform other procedures along with the statistical procedures. For example, the auditor may wish to print confirmation requests at the same time the auditor selects a sample of items to be confirmed using a random selection technique. Many batch processing computer-assisted auditing packages contain routines for statistical sampling to allow this flexibility. Batch processing normally leaves a relatively easy to follow audit trail.

b. General Considerations in Using Batch Programs

(1) Batch programs can be purchased, leased, or internally developed and are usually stored on magnetic tape. Instruction manuals, which describe the program, its use, and the output to be produced generally accompany purchased or leased programs.

(2) Auditors often find it practical to use batch programs on the client's computer system. In circumstances in which the auditor does not believe this is practical, the auditor may decide to use his or her own computer or a service bureau computer system to process the batch programs.

(3) The use of batch programs generally requires the preparation of a description of the input data file and parameter cards. The file description is needed to instruct the program where data is located. The parameter cards are used to relay instructions to the program and instruct the program as to how to process data or as to what statistical routine to execute.

(4) In order to execute the program, the user needs only to combine the file description and parameters with the program and to process the appropriate data file.

(5) Many of the criteria used in the selection of a time-sharing program, described above, apply to selection of a batch program.

IX. Auditing Special Systems

A. On-Line, Real Time (OLRT) Systems--Transactions are processed and files updated as transactions occur. The data is processed fast enough to get the response back in time to influence the process. Common examples include airline reservations systems in which the customer receives the reservations after waiting only a few moments and point-of-sale (POS) terminals in retail stores where a customer's credit limit is checked while the customer waits.

1. OLRT systems have several common characteristics:

   a. On-line terminals are usually used.

   b. Data Files--Usually disk files.

   c. A supervisory program (software) is used to manage the OLRT system.

2. General Controls--Hardware controls that control the transmittal of the transactions from the terminal to the CPU and back are important (for example, a parity bit). Documentation of the transaction is often produced as a by-product of processing. For example, in point-of-sale terminals, a multicopy sales receipt is usually prepared when the transaction is processed. Further, many terminals automatically prepare an input log (input listing) which includes the code number of the employees who entered the data as well as information about the transactions.

3. Programmed Application Controls--Because of the nature of OLRT systems, these are very important. They include the following:

   a. Passwords--In some systems, only certain passwords can input certain kinds of transactions or access certain data files. For example, a salesman could input sales orders under a password but the salesman could not change the payroll records.

   b. Input Edit Tests--Limit and reasonableness tests, valid customer number tests, missing data tests, etc. Transactions that are found to contain an error will not be accepted for processing and the clerk will be notified immediately. Normal error correction is through correction and resubmission.

   c. Control Totals--Control totals can be prepared by the terminal and later checked against totals prepared by the CPU, e.g., the number of transactions processed or the dollar value of sales processed for a day. Either of these totals could also be checked against the copies of the sales slips.

4. Because of the technical complexity of OLRT systems, the auditor will need more technical expertise to consider internal control. Care must also be exercised not to disrupt the system. Techniques such as test data, ITF, and tagging may be used. GAS may be used to perform substantive tests on the data files.

B. Mini- and Microcomputer Systems--The basic control and audit considerations in a small computer environment are the same as those in a larger and more complex EDP system. However, the emphasis on specific procedures the auditor uses needs to be adapted to fit the minicomputer environment.

1. Planning--Since the number of data records that can be stored on magnetic media in a minicomputer system is limited, audit trails are often retained for a limited period of time. Therefore, the auditor must plan the audit steps to take place when sufficient supporting information is available.

2. General Controls

   a. Segregation of Functions--Often, segregation of functions within the EDP department and between the EDP department and user departments does not exist to a significant extent in a small business system. Users may even perform EDP functions. The most desirable segregation controls in this environment would include (1) segregation between data entry and processing or (2) segregation between EDP and user transaction authorization. The auditor should assist management in identifying and implementing alternative or compensating controls where separation of functions does not exist. When the auditor finds weaknesses in segregation, the audit program should include more substantive tests.

   b. System Design and Documentation--Since the choice of software in these smaller systems is influenced by the hardware, users should be involved in the selection of both hardware and software. Although access to program documentation should be limited, it is difficult to enforce in many small computer environments where the data processing group is small. Regardless, there may be times when the auditor may not be able to rely upon the documentation in such an environment.

   c. File Conversion and System Testing--Frequently, an organization's initial EDP applications include the use of a small business computer system. File conversion and system testing are particularly important in these initial applications and, therefore, should influence the auditor in the audit. Before relying on the contents of converted files, the auditor should evaluate the controls used to ensure against lost or distorted data during conversion. If the auditor determines that sufficient user system testing has not been performed by the client, the auditor should perform procedures that will allow for sufficient testing of the system.

   d. Hardware Control--Limiting access to computer hardware is difficult in the small computer environment. Often, these systems lack controls which would prevent access to the actual hardware. Such a situation may cause the auditor to reduce reliance on stored data records. However, good application controls can usually compensate for problems caused by the absence or ineffectiveness of hardware controls.

   e. Software Control--All program changes should be authorized, tested, and documented. However, in some small data processing environments, the auditor will not be able to rely on program change controls. Thus, the auditor may find it appropriate to obtain a copy of the original software directly from the manufacturer. It is also important to control the disk with stored data when not in use. Files should be copied or backed up to ensure against loss of data. The use of hard disk drives calls for access protection with the use of passwords, IDs, and the like.

3. Application Controls--Most application controls have the same relevance in the minicomputer environment as they do in larger EDP systems. The following are problems characteristic of small computer environments:

   a. Many of the protection controls available in larger systems to prohibit file manipulation or processing errors are not available in minicomputer systems.

   b. Limit (reasonableness) checks are not generally adapted to specific situations since most small system software is purchased through outside vendors.

   c. The auditor should look for the existence of external labels on software. Review of the client's storage and use procedures would also be appropriate.

d. Most data is not converted into machine-readable form before input into the mini- or microcomputer system. This should cause the auditor to be more concerned with data input controls and less concerned with data conversion controls.

e. In the smaller organizations or situations which generally characterize these environments, there is usually less movement of data between departments. Also, data processing personnel are familiar with system output users. Therefore, the auditor may be less concerned with controls over movement of data between departments and the distribution of output to authorized users than if the auditor was in a larger EDP environment.

C. Client Uses an EDP Service Center (Service Bureau)--The service center provides EDP services to its clients for a fee. Processing of client data occurs at the service center and the client's computerized master files are usually maintained at the center.

TotalRecall

EDP SERVICE CENTER CONTROLS

T Transmission
E Error correction
A Audit trail
M Master file changes
O Output
S Security

1. Certain controls are particularly important because of the nature of the client-EDP service center relationship.

a. Transmission--Document counts, hash totals, financial totals, etc., may be used to control the transmission of data to and from the client's office.

b. Master File Changes--Printout of all master file changes should be sent to the client. Control counts of master file records and control totals of items within master file records may be used.

c. Error Correction--Client should receive an error printout (i.e., error listing) which identifies all of the errors that occurred in the system. Correction, review, and approval procedures should be established and used.

d. Output--Output must be restricted to the client. An output distribution list (which indicates who should receive the output) and control tests on samples of output may be used.

e. Audit Trail--An audit trail must be maintained. This may be done through proper filing and sequencing of original transaction documents, and also through periodic printouts of journal and ledger balances.

f. Security--Service center must have adequate controls to protect the client's data (while being stored and during processing). Further, there must be adequate reconstruction procedures so that the client's data files can be reconstructed (i.e., recreated) if all or part of them are destroyed.

2. Audit Procedures

a. Review the client's controls.

b. Evaluate Some Processed Transactions--To evaluate control and processing.

c. Evaluate the Controls and Security of the Service Center--A service center sometimes hires a CPA to issue a report on its internal control structure and security. An auditor whose client uses the service center may rely on this report, or if the auditor feels it is inadequate, the auditor may visit the service center to observe the operations.

D. Time-Sharing Systems--A time-sharing center rents time on its central computer to a number of users. Each user has one or more input and output devices at its place of business. The user usually accesses the central computer over telephone lines and operates in an on-line, real-time mode. To each user, it seems as if they are the only one using the system. User files and programs are maintained at the time-sharing center.

1. Controls are needed (a) to prevent alteration and destruction of the client's programs and data files, (b) to prevent the unauthorized use of the client's programs and data files, (c) to reconstruct the data files and other data in the event of a catastrophe or computer breakdown, and (d) to guard against inaccurate transmission of data between the client's terminal and the CPU, and vice versa.

2. Common controls include programmed application controls (as discussed earlier), control totals for data transmission, control totals for processing, boundary protection features (to prevent programs from entering storage, both primary and secondary, that they are not authorized to enter), and the use of passwords or codes which must be furnished by the user each time the user wants to access programs and files.

3. Audit considerations are primarily the same as previously discussed for on-line, real-time systems. Additionally, the auditor may decide to visit the time-sharing center to review its controls if the auditor (a) feels that a large amount of the client's important financial data is processed there and (b) is not able to determine from other sources (such as the review of another auditor) the quality of the center's control and compliance procedures.

E. Distributed Systems are a network of remote computer sites where small computers are connected to the main computer system.

1. Advantages include a reduced work load on the main computer, since edit and processing functions can be performed at the small computer station, and increased efficiency from faster turnaround of information.

2. Audit considerations are that access at each location should be well controlled and audited separately to verify the integrity of the data processed. Also, because users may have both authorization and recording duties, compensating controls should exist for this lack of segregation of duties.

NOTES

CHAPTER 39—AUDITING EDP SYSTEMS

Problem 39-1 MULTIPLE CHOICE QUESTIONS (60 to 75 minutes)

1. Which of the following characteristics distinguishes computer processing from manual processing?
a. Computer processing virtually eliminates the occurrence of computational error normally associated with manual processing.
b. Errors or irregularities in computer processing will be detected soon after their occurrences.
c. The potential for systematic error is ordinarily greater in manual processing than in computerized processing.
d. Most computer systems are designed so that transaction trails useful for audit purposes do not exist. (11/88, Aud., #36, 0289)

2. Which of the following activities would most likely be performed in the EDP department?
a. Initiation of changes to master records.
b. Conversion of information to machine-readable form.
c. Correction of transactional errors.
d. Initiation of changes to existing applications. (5/85, Aud., #25, 0304)

3. Mill Co. uses a batch processing method to process its sales transactions. Data on Mill's sales transaction tape are electronically sorted by customer number and are subjected to programmed edit checks in preparing its invoices, sales journals, and updated customer account balances. One of the direct outputs of the creation of this tape most likely would be a
a. Report showing exceptions and control totals.
b. Printout of the updated inventory records.
c. Report showing overdue accounts receivable.
d. Printout of the sales price master file. (5/93, Aud., #16, 3912)

4. Errors in data processed in a batch computer system may **not** be detected immediately because
a. Transaction trails in a batch system are available only for a limited period of time.
b. There are time delays in processing transactions in a batch system.
c. Errors in some transactions cause rejection of other transactions in the batch.
d. Random errors are more likely in a batch system than in an on-line system. (5/89, Aud., #12, 0284)

5. An auditor would **least** likely use computer software to
a. Construct parallel simulations.
b. Access client data files.
c. Prepare spreadsheets.
d. Assess EDP control risk. (5/93, Aud., #40, 3936)

6. Which of the following statements most likely represents a disadvantage for an entity that keeps microcomputer-prepared data files rather than manually prepared files?
a. Attention is focused on the accuracy of the programming process rather than errors in individual transactions.
b. It is usually easier for unauthorized persons to access and alter the files.
c. Random error associated with processing similar transactions in different ways is usually greater.
d. It is usually more difficult to compare recorded accountability with physical count of assets. (5/94, Aud., #16, 4681)

7. Which of the following most likely represents a significant deficiency in the internal control structure?
a. The systems analyst reviews applications of data processing and maintains systems documentation.
b. The systems programmer designs systems for computerized applications and maintains output controls.
c. The control clerk establishes control over data received by the EDP department and reconciles control totals after processing.
d. The accounts payable clerk prepares data for computer processing and enters the data into the computer. (11/91, Aud., #36, 2304)

8. Which of the following computer documentations would an auditor most likely utilize in obtaining an understanding of the internal control structure?
a. Systems flowcharts.
b. Record counts.
c. Program listings.
d. Record layouts. (5/90, Aud., #27, 0278)

9. An auditor who is testing EDP controls in a payroll system would most likely use test data that contain conditions such as

a. Deductions **not** authorized by employees.
b. Overtime **not** approved by supervisors.
c. Time tickets with invalid job numbers.
d. Payroll checks with unauthorized signatures.

(5/89, Aud., #16, 0286)

10. Which of the following would most likely be a weakness in the internal control structure of a client that utilizes microcomputers rather than a larger computer system?

a. Employee collusion possibilities are increased because microcomputers from one vendor can process the programs of a system from a different vendor.
b. The microcomputer operators may be able to remove hardware and software components and modify them at home.
c. Programming errors result in all similar transactions being processed incorrectly when those transactions are processed under the same conditions.
d. Certain transactions may be automatically initiated by the microcomputers and management's authorization of these transactions may be implicit in its acceptance of the system design. (11/88, Aud., #38, 9911)

11. Which of the following constitutes a weakness in the internal control of an EDP system?

a. One generation of backup files is stored in an off-premises location.
b. Machine operators distribute error messages to the control group.
c. Machine operators do **not** have access to the complete systems manual.
d. Machine operators are supervised by the programmer. (5/84, Aud., #13, 0311)

12. Which of the following is **not** a major reason for maintaining an audit trail for a computer system?

a. Deterrent to irregularities.
b. Monitoring purposes.
c. Analytical procedures.
d. Query answering. (11/91, Aud., #24, 2292)

13. An auditor anticipates assessing control risk at a low level in a computerized environment. Under these circumstances, on which of the following procedures would the auditor initially focus?

a. Programmed control procedures.
b. Application control procedures.
c. Output control procedures.
d. General control procedures.

(5/92, Aud., #36, 2789)

14. When an accounting application is processed by computer, an auditor **cannot** verify the reliable operation of programmed control procedures by

a. Manually comparing detail transaction files used by an edit program to the program's generated error listings to determine that errors were properly identified by the edit program.
b. Constructing a processing system for accounting applications and processing actual data from throughout the period through both the client's program and the auditor's program.
c. Manually reperforming, as of a point in time, the processing of input data and comparing the simulated results to the actual results.
d. Periodically submitting auditor-prepared test data to the same computer process and evaluating the results. (11/89, Aud., #31, 0279)

15. Computer systems are typically supported by a variety of utility software packages that are important to an auditor because they

a. May enable unauthorized changes to data files if **not** properly controlled.
b. Are very versatile programs that can be used on hardware of many manufacturers.
c. May be significant components of a client's application programs.
d. Are written specifically to enable auditors to extract and sort data. (11/89, Aud., #38, 0281)

16. Misstatements in a batch computer system caused by incorrect programs or data may **not** be detected immediately because

a. Errors in some transactions may cause rejection of other transactions in the batch.
b. The identification of errors in input data typically is **not** part of the program.
c. There are time delays in processing transactions in a batch system.
d. The processing of transactions in a batch system is **not** uniform. (11/94, Aud., #37, 5110)

17. Matthews Corp. has changed from a system of recording time worked on clock cards to a computerized payroll system in which employees record time in and out with magnetic cards. The EDP system automatically updates all payroll records. Because of this change

a. A generalized computer audit program must be used.
b. Part of the audit trail is altered.
c. The potential for payroll-related fraud is diminished.
d. Transactions must be processed in batches.

(5/86, Aud., #1, 0296)

18. Which of the following controls most likely would assure that an entity can reconstruct its financial records?
a. Hardware controls are built into the computer by the computer manufacturer.
b. Backup diskettes or tapes of files are stored away from originals.
c. Personnel who are independent of data input perform parallel simulations.
d. System flowcharts provide accurate descriptions of input and output operations.
(5/93, Aud., #8, 3904)

19. To obtain evidence that on-line access controls are properly functioning, an auditor most likely would
a. Create checkpoints at periodic intervals after live data processing to test for unauthorized use of the system.
b. Examine the transaction log to discover whether any transactions were lost or entered twice due to a system malfunction.
c. Enter invalid identification numbers or passwords to ascertain whether the system rejects them.
d. Vouch a random sample of processed transactions to assure proper authorization.
(5/93, Aud., #41, 3937)

20. Which of the following is a general control that would most likely assist an entity whose systems analyst left the entity in the middle of a major project?
a. Grandfather-father-son record retention.
b. Input and output validation routines.
c. Systems documentation.
d. Check digit verification.(11/91, Aud., #32, 2300)

21. An auditor would most likely be concerned with which of the following controls in a distributed data processing system?
a. Hardware controls.
b. Systems documentation controls.
c. Access controls.
d. Disaster recovery controls.
(5/91, Aud., #16, 0273)

22. To obtain evidence that user identification and password controls are functioning as designed, an auditor would most likely
a. Attempt to sign on to the system using invalid user identifications and passwords.
b. Write a computer program that simulates the logic of the client's access control software.
c. Extract a random sample of processed transactions and ensure that the transactions were appropriately authorized.
d. Examine statements signed by employees stating that they have **not** divulged their user identifications and passwords to any other person. (11/89, Aud., #32, 9911)

23. The possibility of erasing a large amount of information stored on magnetic tape most likely would be reduced by the use of
a. File protection rings.
b. Check digits.
c. Completeness tests.
d. Conversion verification.
(11/89, Aud., #42, 0282)

24. Which of the following controls is a processing control designed to ensure the reliability and accuracy of data processing?

	Limit test	Validity check test
a.	Yes	Yes
b.	No	No
c.	No	Yes
d.	Yes	No

(11/94, Aud., #38, 5111)

25. If a control total were to be computed on each of the following data items, which would best be identified as a hash total for a payroll EDP application?
a. Hours worked.
b. Total debits and total credits.
c. Net pay.
d. Department numbers. (11/88, Aud., #45, 9911)

26. The completeness of EDP-generated sales figures can be tested by comparing the number of items listed on the daily sales report with the number of items billed on the actual invoices. This process uses
a. Check digits.
b. Control totals.
c. Validity tests.
d. Process tracing data. (5/87, Aud., #13, 0292)

27. Which of the following is an example of a check digit?
a. An agreement of the total number of employees to the total number of checks printed by the computer.
b. An algebraically determined number produced by the other digits of the employee number.
c. A logic test that ensures all employee numbers are nine digits.
d. A limit check that an employee's hours do not exceed 50 hours per work week.
(5/85, Aud., #24, 0303)

28. An EDP input control is designed to ensure that
a. Machine processing is accurate.
b. Only authorized personnel have access to the computer area.
c. Data received for processing are properly authorized and converted to machine readable form.
d. Electronic data processing has been performed as intended for the particular application. (11/84, Aud, #9, 0306)

29. An auditor most likely would introduce test data into a computerized payroll system to test internal controls related to the
a. Existence of unclaimed payroll checks held by supervisors.
b. Early cashing of payroll checks by employees.
c. Discovery of invalid employee I.D. numbers.
d. Proper approval of overtime by supervisors.
(5/94, Aud., #31, 4696)

30. One of the major problems in an EDP system is that incompatible functions may be performed by the same individual. One compensating control for this is the use of
a. A self-checking digit system.
b. Echo checks.
c. A computer log.
d. Computer-generated hash totals.
(5/86, Aud., #14, 0297)

31. Decision tables differ from program flowcharts in that decision tables emphasize
a. Ease of manageability for complex programs.
b. Logical relationships among conditions and actions.
c. Cost benefit factors justifying the program.
d. The sequence in which operations are performed. (5/92, Aud., #55, 2808)

32. Which of the following statements is **not** true of the test data approach to testing an accounting system?
a. Test data are processed by the client's computer programs under the auditor's control.
b. The test data need consist of only those valid and invalid conditions that interest the auditor.
c. Only one transaction of each type need be tested.
d. The test data must consist of all possible valid and invalid conditions. (11/93, Aud., #18, 4255)

33. When an auditor tests a computerized accounting system, which of the following is true of the test data approach?
a. Test data must consist of all possible valid and invalid conditions.
b. The program tested is different from the program used throughout the year by the client.
c. Several transactions of each type must be tested.
d. Test data are processed by the client's computer programs under the auditor's control.
(11/90, Aud., #28, 0274)

33A. When an auditor tests a computerized accounting system, which of the following is true of the test data approach?
a. Several transactions of each type must be tested.
b. Test data are processed by the client's computer programs under the auditor's control.
c. Test data must consist of all possible valid and invalid conditions.
d. The program tested is different from the program used throughout the year by the client. (5/95, Aud., #72, 5690)

34. Processing data through the use of simulated files provides an auditor with information about the operating effectiveness of control policies and procedures. One of the techniques involved in this approach makes use of
a. Controlled reprocessing.
b. An integrated test facility.
c. Input validation.
d. Program code checking.
(11/92, Aud., #36, 2970)

Item 35 is based on the following flowchart:

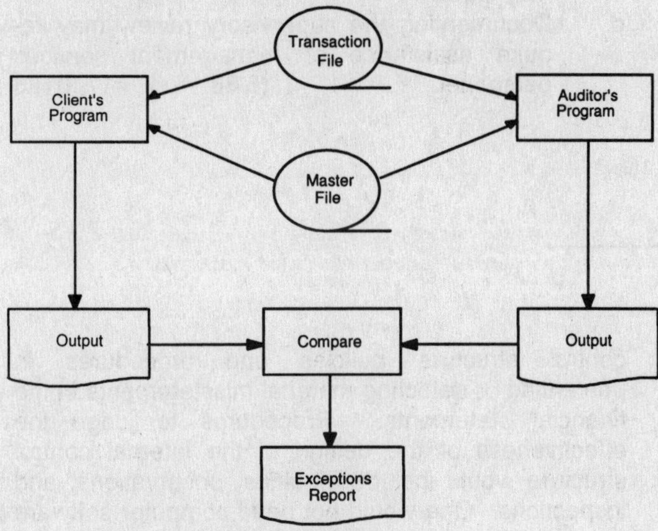

35. The preceding flowchart depicts
a. Program code checking.
b. Parallel simulation.
c. Integrated test facility.
d. Controlled reprocessing.
(11/88, Aud., #59, 9911)

36. Which of the following methods of testing application controls utilizes a generalized audit software package prepared by the auditors?
a. Parallel simulation.
b. Integrated testing facility approach.
c. Test data approach.
d. Exception report tests. (11/84, Aud., #11, 0308)

36A. Which of the following computer-assisted auditing techniques allows fictitious and real transactions to be processed together without client operating personnel being aware of the testing process?
a. Integrated test facility.
b. Input controls matrix.
c. Parallel simulation.
d. Data entry monitor. (11/94, Aud., #70, 5143)

37. An auditor most likely would test for the presence of unauthorized EDP program changes by running a
a. Program with test data.
b. Check digit verification program.
c. Source code comparison program.
d. Program that computes control totals.
(11/92, Aud., #37, 2971)

38. A primary advantage of using generalized audit software packages to audit the financial statements of a client that uses an EDP system is that the auditor may
a. Substantiate the accuracy of data through self-checking digits and hash totals.
b. Reduce the level of required tests of controls to a relatively small amount.
c. Access information stored on computer files while having a limited understanding of the client's hardware and software features.
d. Consider increasing the use of substantive tests of transactions in place of analytical procedures. (11/93, Aud., #43, 4280)

39. An auditor using audit software probably would be **least** interested in which of the following fields in a computerized perpetual inventory file?
a. Economic order quantity.
b. Warehouse location.
c. Date of last purchase.
d. Quantity sold. (5/91, Aud., #15, 0272)

40. The least likely use by the auditor of generalized audit software is to
a. Perform analytical procedures on the client's data.
b. Access the information stored on the client's EDP files.
c. Identify weaknesses in the client's EDP controls.
d. Test the accuracy of the client's computations.
(11/86, Aud., #35, 0295)

41. In a computerized payroll system environment, an auditor would be **least** likely to use test data to test controls related to
a. Missing employee numbers.
b. Proper approval of overtime by supervisors.
c. Time tickets with invalid job numbers.
d. Agreement of hours per clock cards with hours on time tickets. (5/91, Aud., #31, 0049)

42. The two requirements crucial to achieving audit efficiency and effectiveness with a microcomputer are selecting
a. The appropriate audit tasks for microcomputer applications and the appropriate software to perform the selected audit tasks.
b. The appropriate software to perform the selected audit tasks and client data that can be accessed by the auditor's microcomputer.
c. Client data that can be accessed by the auditor's microcomputer and audit procedures that are generally applicable to several clients in a specific industry.
d. Audit procedures that are generally applicable to several clients in a specific industry and the appropriate audit tasks for microcomputer applications. (11/88, Aud., #57, 9911)

43. Using microcomputers in auditing may affect the methods used to review the work of staff assistants because
a. Supervisory personnel may not have an understanding of the capabilities and limitations of microcomputers.
b. Working paper documentation may **not** contain readily observable details of calculations.
c. The audit field work standards for supervision may differ.
d. Documenting the supervisory review may require assistance of management services personnel. (5/88, Aud., #17, 0196)

Solution 39-1 MULTIPLE CHOICE ANSWERS

The Effects of Computer Processing on the Audit of Financial Statements (SAS 48)

1. (a) An advantage of computer processing is that it does virtually eliminate computational errors. Errors or irregularities are not detected more quickly when computer processing is used. The potential for systematic errors is greater in computer processing than in manual processing. Transaction trails useful for audit purposes are created but the data may be available for only a short period of time.

2. (b) The EDP department normally converts data (which is initially prepared elsewhere) into machine-readable form. The following duties are considered incompatible in the case of EDP personnel: (1) transaction origination or correction; (2) transaction authorization; (3) initial data preparation; (4) custody or control over non-EDP assets; (5) authorization or change of controls; and (6) origination of master file changes.

3. (a) The computer process has built-in edit checks to generate exceptions and control totals. Answers (b) and (c) are generated from programs that utilize the information from the sales batch processing system, but are not directly produced from the sales system. Answer (d) represents information that is input into the computer system as a basis for the edit checks.

4. (b) There are time delays when data is processed in batches, so errors may not be detected immediately. Transaction trails are available for an indefinite period of time. The time delays in processing cause a delay in error detection. Random errors are no more likely in a batch system than in an on-line system.

5. (d) After obtaining an understanding of the client's EDP controls, the auditor must assess control risk for the EDP portion of the client's internal control structure. Assessing control risk is the process of evaluating the effectiveness of an entity's internal control structure policies and procedures in preventing or detecting material misstatements in the financial statements. Procedures to judge the effectiveness of the design of the internal control structure would include inquiries, observations, and inspections. One would not need computer software to accomplish this task. Gaining access to client data files, preparing spreadsheets, and constructing parallel simulations would all make use of computer software.

6. (b) Many internal control procedures once performed by separate individuals in manual systems may be concentrated in systems that use computer processing. Therefore, an individual who has access to the computer may be in a position to perform incompatible functions. Answers (a) and (c) are false statements. Detailed ledger accounts may be maintained as easily with microcomputer data files as with manually prepared files.

7. (b) A weakness in internal control exists where an individual is in a position to both perpetrate and conceal an error or irregularity. Hence, a systems programmer should not be given any control over the review or distribution of the output of the EDP system.

8. (a) An auditor is likely to use systems flowcharts in obtaining an understanding of the internal control structure. Systems flowcharts show the flow of data through the system and the interrelationships between the processing steps and computer runs. A record count is an input control technique. Program listings are the source statements or language of the client's programs. Record layouts are the input and output formats.

9. (c) An auditor testing EDP controls in a payroll system would most likely use test data containing time tickets with invalid job numbers. The computer should be programmed to compare job numbers on the time tickets with a list of valid, authorized job numbers. Answers (a) and (b) relate

to preparation of data before it enters the EDP system. Answer (d) relates to controls after data processing has taken place.

10. (b) Both large computer systems and microcomputers are vulnerable to employee collusion and programming errors. Microcomputer hardware and software could be removed from the place of business unlike large computer systems.

11. (d) The programmer knows exactly what the EDP system is capable of performing. By having the programmer supervise the operators, he or she is in a position to both perpetrate and conceal errors or irregularities, without the operators having any cognizance of any problems. Therefore, the programming function should be totally segregated from the EDP operating function. Answers (a), (b), and (c) are all examples of good internal controls over an EDP system.

12. (c) Analytical procedures involve the analysis of the plausible relationship among both financial and nonfinancial data. A lack of an accounting audit trail for a computer system would not preclude the auditor from performing analytical procedures. The purpose of an audit trail would be to monitor the system, answer queries, and deter irregularities.

13. (d) When an auditor anticipates assessing control risk at a low level in a computerized environment, generally, the auditor would initially focus on general control procedures, which are those controls that relate to all or many computerized accounting activities and often include control over the development, modification, and maintenance of computer programs and control over the use of and changes to data maintained on computer files.

14. (c) The auditor would not be able to verify the reliable operation of programmed control procedures by the reperformance of the processing of the *client's* input data through the *client's* computer program as it would produce the same output as that created by the client. The auditor would be able to verify the reliable operation of control procedures when he or she is submitting auditor-prepared test data to the client's computer process, submitting actual data to the auditor's computer program, or utilizing an edit program as these would allow the auditor to make comparisons between the client's expected output, using the client's data and computer program, and the auditor's expected results using auditor-prepared data, the auditor's computer program, and the auditor's edit program.

15. (a) Utility programs are used to perform tasks such as copying, sorting, merging, and printing. This type of software is usually easily accessible and can lead to unauthorized changes if not properly controlled. Answers (b) and (c) do not have any special importance to the auditor. Utility software is not written specifically for auditors.

16. (c) There are time delays when data is processed in batches, so errors may not be detected immediately. The time delays in processing cause a delay in error detection. The identification of errors in input data would be identified through various means such as the use of batch totals and would generally be made part of the program. The processing of transactions in a batch system is uniform; for example, all sales invoices would be part of a group of transactions entered together in a batch system.

17. (b) When time clock cards are used, they constitute a form of physical evidence that can be examined in determining the proper amount of wage expense. By changing to an EDP system, part of the audit trail is altered--although not necessarily destroyed. The EDP system can be audited in numerous ways that don't require the use of a generalized audit program. The potential for payroll fraud may or may not change depending on the internal controls incorporated into the new payroll system. The system automatically updates the payroll records whenever anyone punches in or out. Batch processing is eliminated in this system.

General Controls (GC)

18. (b) Backup files stored off-site are an effective means of preserving data in the event of a catastrophe or other loss of information requiring the reconstruction of the material. Answer (a) refers to controls manufactured into the computer; answer (c) refers to internal controls practiced within the company; and answer (d) refers to internal controls directed at the flow of processing information through the company.

19. (c) Password controls, used in restricting access to computers, are designed to preclude access capabilities of those employees whose regular functions are incompatible with computer use. To obtain evidence that user identification and password controls are functioning as designed, an auditor would most likely examine a sample of invalid passwords or numbers to determine whether the computer is recognizing the invalid passwords and rejecting access. Answer (a) checks the level of authorization an employee has once within the

system rather than access to the on-line system. Answer (b) is a procedure for determining the completeness of transaction processing. Answer (d) does not address whether the on-line access is being limited or circumvented.

20. (c) When an entity's systems analyst leaves the entity in the middle of a major project, the greatest assistance in continuing the project could be obtained from systems documentation that adequately describes the systems operations and procedures up to that point in time. Given good documentation, a new systems analyst could immediately begin to understand the systems operations.

21. (c) A distributed data processing system is one in which many different users have access to the main computer through various computer locations. Thus, access controls, which restrict access to the main computer, are necessary to maintain a strong internal control structure, since those with access to the computer are in a position to perform incompatible functions. Hardware controls, systems documentation controls, and disaster recovery controls would not be as important in assessing control risk and would not likely present unusual problems in a distributed system.

22. (a) To obtain evidence that user identification and password controls are functioning as designed, an auditor would most likely attempt to sign-on to the system using invalid user identifications and passwords. Writing a similar program would be an inefficient procedure. Ensuring that past transactions were properly authorized has no bearing on future transactions. It is possible that controls are weak but they have not yet been circumvented. Information obtained from the client is not as persuasive as evidence obtained directly by the auditor.

23. (a) A file protection ring is a plastic ring that must be attached to a reel of magnetic tape before the tape drive will write on the tape. Since writing on magnetic tape automatically erases the data already there, the file protection ring guards against the inadvertent erasure of the information on the tape. A check digit is an example of a computer editing process designed to detect inaccurate input data. Answer (c) is incorrect because the term "completeness test" does not exist. Conversion verification involves the reinputting of data in order to test its accuracy.

Application Controls (AC)

24. (a) Computers can be programmed to perform a wide range of edit tasks on records as they are being inputted into the system. If a particular record does not meet the test, it would not be processed. Edit tests include limit tests, validity check tests, check digit tests, etc.

25. (d) *Control totals* may be used to detect errors in input or processing when information is batched before entry. One type of control total is a *hash total* which is a total of field amounts for all the records in a batch that are computed for control purposes only. For example, the total of the department numbers would have no intrinsic value. Conversely, the total of hours worked, debits and credits, and net pay are normally computed in the payroll process and have intrinsic meaning in the engagement.

26. (b) The use of control totals is an example of a processing control which is designed to provide reasonable assurances that EDP has been performed as intended for the particular application, i.e., that all transactions are processed as authorized, that no authorized transactions were omitted, and that no unauthorized transactions were added. A *check digit* is a number that is added at the end of a numerical entry to check its accuracy. A *validity test*, is designed to ensure that only data meeting specific criteria are allowed. Answer (d) apparently refers to "tagging" of data, a technique used by auditors to follow a transaction through the processing cycle.

27. (b) A check digit is a digit that is added to a code or identification number and determined through some procedure using the other digits in the code or number. It is one of the six major categories of data validation procedures. The other categories are echo checks, stored data comparison, logic tests, control totals, and output review. A document count is a type of control total. A limit check is a type of logic test.

28. (c) Input controls are designed to provide reasonable assurance that data received by EDP have been properly authorized, converted into machine sensible form and identified and that data have not been lost, suppressed, added, duplicated, or otherwise improperly changed. Answer (a) describes an output control. Answer (d) describes a processing control. Answer (b) describes an access control.

29. (c) An auditor testing computer controls in a payroll system would most likely use test data

containing invalid employee I.D. numbers. The computer should be programmed to compare employee I.D. numbers with a list of valid, authorized employee numbers. Answer (d) relates to preparation of data before it enters the computer system. Answers (a) and (b) relate to controls after data processing has taken place.

Documentation of an EDP-Based System

30. (c) A computer log provides evidence as to which employees used the computer system and the operations performed by them. As a result, the computer log will protect against unauthorized use of the EDP system, and it will provide an audit trail with respect to incompatible operations performed by the same individual. Incompatible functions are the concern of general controls, i.e., controls that relate to all EDP activities. A self-checking digit system and computer-generated hash totals are input controls, i.e., they relate to application controls. An echo check is a hardware control aimed at determining whether the computer is operating properly. It has no effect on the control over incompatible functions.

31. (b) A systems flowchart shows the flow of data through the system and the interrelationships between the processing steps and computer runs. A decision table describes a portion of the logic used in the program.

Auditing Through the Computer--Techniques

32. (d) Test data is processed by the client's computer programs under the auditor's control. It need consist of only those valid and invalid conditions that interest the auditor, and only one transaction of each type need be tested. Answer (d) is correct because the test data does not have to consist of all possible valid and invalid conditions, because the cost of performing such testing would outweigh the benefits, and the auditor should focus on those conditions that could lead to material misstatements in the financial statements.

33. (d) Under the test data method, the auditor prepares input data with known errors. Because the auditor knows what the output *should* be, the test data method is aimed at testing the procedures contained within the program. If the actual output varies from what is expected, the auditor knows that the program is not functioning properly. It is important for the auditor to be sure that the program used to test the data was the same as that used by the client during the period under audit. Answers (a) and (c) are not requirements of the test data approach. The program *should* be the same as that used throughout the year.

33A. (b) In the test data approach to testing a computerized accounting system, test data are processed by the client's computer programs under the auditor's control. The auditor will determine how many transactions and what types of transactions to test which may or may not include several transactions of each type. The auditor need not include test data for all possible valid and invalid conditions. The object of the test is to test the client's program that is used throughout the year and the auditor must take steps to make sure that the program being tested is the one that is actually used in routine processing; thus, a different program would not be tested.

34. (b) Processing data through the use of simulated files makes use of an integrated test facility. Using this method, the auditor creates a fictitious entity within the client's actual data files. He or she then processes fictitious data for the entity as part of the client's regular data processing. Controlled reprocessing involves the processing of the client's actual data through the auditor's controlled copy of the client's program. Input validation is concerned only that the inputted data is accurate. Program code checking involves analysis of the client's actual program.

35. (b) In parallel simulation, the auditor compares the results of the client's processing with results obtained by using the client's input and files and the auditor's own program. In program code checking, the auditor reviews the client's program documentation, including a narrative description and the source code. An integrated test facility includes processing of dummy records with the client's records using the client's program. In controlled reprocessing, the auditor maintains control over the reprocessing of previously processed results using a version of the program the auditor has tested and compares the computer output of the original processing and reprocessing.

36. (a) Parallel simulation involves creating a model of the EDP system to be tested. The auditor reviews the application system to gain an understanding of its functioning and then utilizes a generalized audit software package to create a model or simulation of the application processing. Answers (b), (c), and (d) all utilize the client's software.

36A. (a) An integrated test facility (ITF) processes fictitious data with real data in order to test computer controls; client personnel are unaware of the testing. An input control matrix documents controls and their presence. Parallel simulation processes client input data on an auditor-controlled program to test controls; test data is not utilized. The term "data entry monitor" is not commonly used.

37. (c) A source code comparison program could be used to compare the original code written for a specific program to the current code in use for that program. Thus, it would make note of any differences in the program from the time it was originally written. Test data would generally be used to test the output of the program but would provide no evidence as to whether the program code had been changed. A check digit program involves the use of a digit that is added to the end of a piece of numeric data to permit the data to be checked for accuracy during input, processing, or output. Control totals are totals computed at different times in the computer process and are used as input, processing, and output controls. They would not provide evidence as to whether any changes were made to the original program code.

Generalized Audit Software

38. (c) In the AICPA Audit Guide entitled "Computer Assisted Audit Techniques," one of the reasons for using generalized audit software is that it enables the auditor to gain access and test information stored in the client's files without having to acquire a complete understanding of the client's EDP system. Answer (a) is an example of using control totals to test data input. Answer (b) is the result of assessing control risk and applying preliminary tests of controls. Answer (d) describes additional auditing procedures to be applied to classes of transactions that may have a material impact on the financial statements which would not be an advantage to the auditor.

39. (a) Audit software for a perpetual inventory file would include fields such as warehouse location, date of last purchase, and quantity sold since these fields would have a bearing on the audit of the inventory balance as recorded in the computerized perpetual inventory file. On the other hand, the economic order quantity would be less likely to provide information as to the actual quantity of inventory to be reported in the financial statements, since it is simply a useful guideline which can be used in ordering inventory. The client's *actual* orders of inventory would be much more useful.

40. (c) Generalized audit software (GAS) is generally used to perform tasks involving the manipulation of high volumes of data but requiring little judgment. Thus, GAS is used to select items from a client file meeting specific criteria, to test computations for mathematical accuracy, to compare amounts and ratios, etc. To identify weaknesses in internal controls, the auditor primarily relies on observation, inquiry of client personnel, reading of procedures manuals, tracing of transactions, etc.

41. (b) Proper approval of overtime would most likely be made by inspection of the related documents and reports to assess whether the authorization policy was applied. The computerized system would be unable to make such a judgment. The computerized payroll system could be utilized to test controls related to missing employee numbers, time tickets with invalid job numbers, and agreement of hours per clock cards with hours on time tickets.

Small Business Computers--Control and Audit Considerations

42. (a) Microcomputers may be used to prepare trial balances, to perform analytical procedures, for automated working papers, word processing, and graphics, among other uses. With the appropriate software, applied to the appropriate audit tasks, microcomputers can improve audit efficiency and effectiveness.

43. (b) Working paper documentation may not contain readily observable details of calculations because these calculations would be performed by the computer. If supervisory personnel do not have an understanding of the capabilities and limitations of microcomputers, the auditor should seek the assistance of a professional possessing such skills, who may be either on the auditor's staff or an outside professional. The auditor's responsibilities with respect to using such a professional are equivalent to those for other assistants. The audit field work standards for supervision do not differ when microcomputers are used in an audit.

PERFORMANCE BY SUBTOPICS

Each category below parallels a subtopic covered in Chapter 39. Record the number and percentage of questions you correctly answered in each subtopic area.

The Effects of Computer Processing on the Audit of Financial Statements (SAS 48)

Question #	Correct √
1	
2	
3	
4	
5	
6	
7	
8	
9	
10	
11	
12	
13	
14	
15	
16	
17	
# Questions	17
# Correct	_______
% Correct	_______

General Controls (GC)

Question #	Correct √
18	
19	
20	
21	
22	
23	
# Questions	6
# Correct	_______
% Correct	_______

Application Controls (AC)

Question #	Correct √
24	
25	
26	
27	
28	
29	
# Questions	6
# Correct	_______
% Correct	_______

Documentation of an EDP-Based System

Question #	Correct √
30	
31	
# Questions	2
# Correct	_______
% Correct	_______

Auditing Through the Computer--Techniques

Question #	Correct √
32	
33	
33A	
34	
35	
36	
36A	
37	
# Questions	8
# Correct	_______
% Correct	_______

Generalized Audit Software

Question #	Correct √
38	
39	
40	
41	
# Questions	4
# Correct	_______
% Correct	_______

Small Business Computers--Control and Audit Considerations

Question #	Correct √
42	
43	
# Questions	2
# Correct	_______
% Correct	_______

OTHER OBJECTIVE FORMAT QUESTION

Problem 39-2 (15 to 25 minutes)

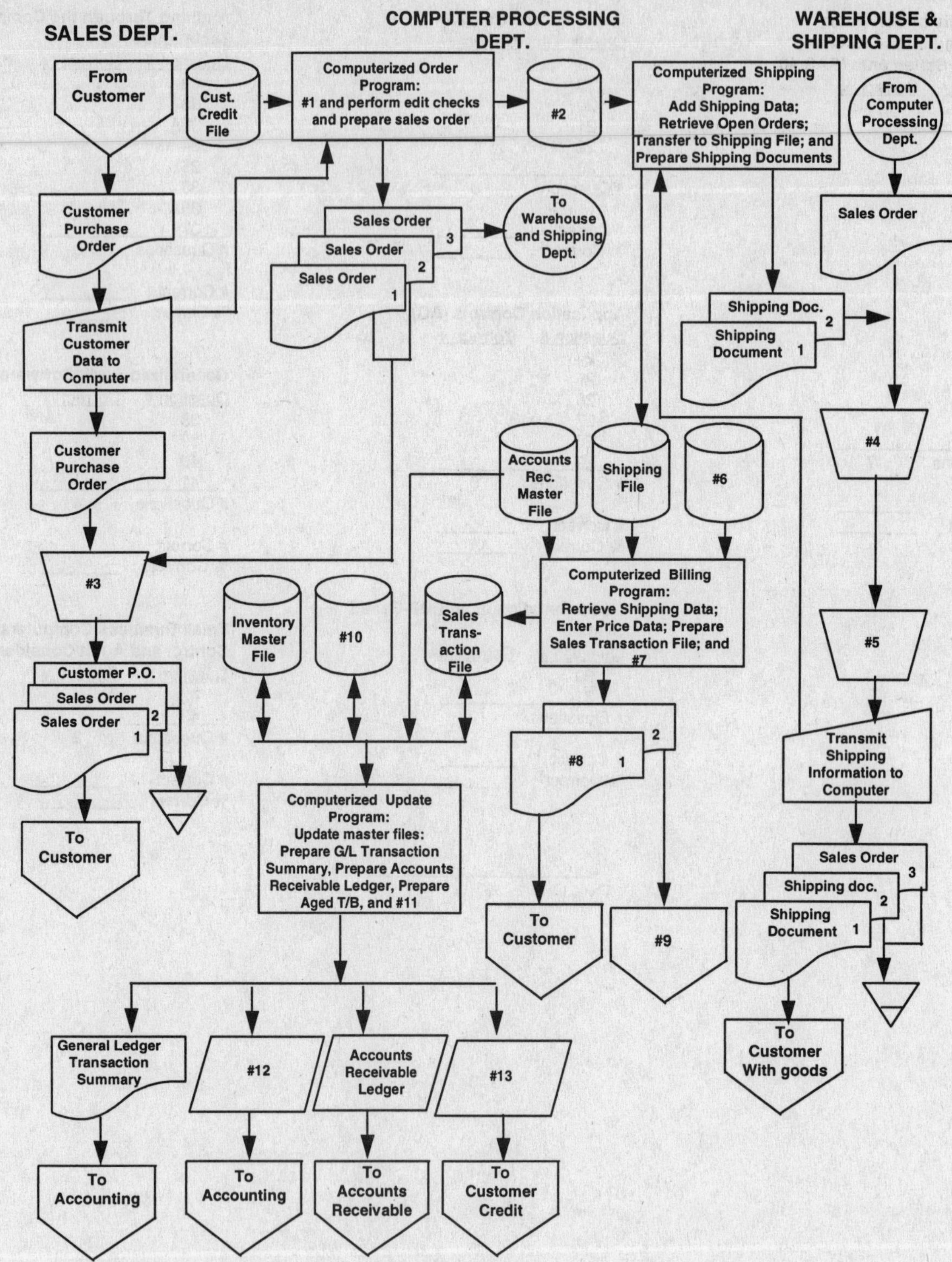

Required:

The accompanying flowchart depicts part of a client's revenue cycle. Some of the flowchart symbols are labeled to indicate control procedures and records. **For each symbol numbered 1 through 13**, select one response from the answer lists below. Each response in the lists may be selected once or **not** at all.

Answer Lists

Operations and control procedures

A. Enter shipping data
B. Verify agreement of sales order and shipping document
C. Write off accounts receivable
D. To warehouse and shipping department
E. Authorize account receivable write-off.
F. Prepare aged trial balance
G. To sales department
H. Release goods for shipment
I. To accounts receivable department
J. Enter price data
K. Determine that customer exists
L. Match customer purchase order with sales order
M. Perform customer credit check
N. Prepare sales journal
O. Prepare sales invoice

Documents, journals, ledgers, and files

P. Shipping document
Q. General ledger master file
R. General journal
S. Master price file
T. Sales journal
U. Sales invoice
V. Cash receipts journal
W. Uncollectible accounts file
X. Shipping file
Y. Aged trial balance
Z. Open order file

(11/93, Aud., #2)

OTHER OBJECTIVE FORMAT SOLUTION

Solution 39-2 Flowcharts

1. (M) Before preparing a sales order, the computer processing department should perform a credit check to determine that the sale will be made to a creditworthy customer. This information may be obtained from the customer credit file or from outside sources.

2. (Z) Once the sales order has been prepared, it will be recorded and placed in the open order file.

3. (L) This manual operation represents the process of matching customer purchase orders with sales orders for agreement.

4. (B) This manual operation represents matching the shipping document with the sales order for agreement.

5. (H) Once the shipping document and sales order have been matched, the goods will be released for shipment.

6. (S) In order to prepare the customer bill, the computerized billing program will retrieve the shipping data from the shipping file and enter the price data from the master price file.

7. (O) Once the shipping data and price data have been retrieved and the sale to the customer generated, the sales invoice will be prepared.

8. (U) This document represents the duplicate copy sales invoice generated by the computerized billing program.

9. (I) One copy of the sales invoice will be sent to the customer, and one will be sent to the accounts receivable department as support for the entry to the accounts receivable ledger--to be held until remittance is made by the customer.

10. (Q) The computer processing department will (daily, weekly, or monthly) update the master files, such as the accounts receivable ledger, the inventory master file, the sales transaction file, and the general ledger master file.

11. (N) The computer processing department will prepare, based upon the update program, an accounts receivable ledger, an aged trial balance, a general ledger transaction summary, and a sales journal.

12. (T) This output function represents the sales journal which was generated by the computerized update program for either the day, week, or month, depending upon the frequency of report generation established by management.

13. (Y) This output report represents the aged trial balance generated by the computerized update program, which combined information from the general ledger master file, the sales transaction file, and the inventory master file.

ESSAY QUESTIONS

Essay 39-3 (15 to 25 minutes)

Microcomputer software has been developed to improve the efficiency and effectiveness of the audit. Electronic spreadsheets and other software packages are available to aid in the performance of audit procedures otherwise performed manually.

Required:

Describe the potential benefits to an auditor of using microcomputer software in an audit as compared to performing an audit without the use of a computer.

(11/87, Aud., #4)

Essay 39-4 (15 to 25 minutes)

Ajax Inc., an audit client, recently installed a new EDP system to process more efficiently the shipping, billing, and accounts receivable records. During interim work, an assistant completed the consideration of the internal control structure. The assistant determined the following information concerning the new EDP system and the processing and control of shipping notices and customer invoices.

Each major computerized function, e.g., shipping, billing, accounts receivable, etc., is permanently assigned to a specific computer operator who is responsible for making program changes, running the program, and reconciling the computer log. Responsibility for the custody and control over the magnetic tapes and system documentation is randomly rotated among the computer operators on a monthly basis to prevent any one person from having access to the tapes and documentation at all times. Each computer programmer and computer operator has access to the computer room via a magnetic card and a digital code that is different for each card. The systems analyst and the supervisor of the computer operators do not have access to the computer room.

The EDP system documentation consists of the following items: program listing, error listing, logs, and record layout. To increase efficiency, batch totals and processing controls are omitted from the system.

Ajax ships its products directly from two warehouses which forward shipping notices to general accounting. There, the billing clerk enters the price of the item and accounts for the numerical sequence of the shipping notices. The billing clerk also prepares daily adding machine tapes of the units shipped and the sales amounts. Shipping notices and adding machine tapes are forwarded to the computer department for processing. The computer output consists of:

- A three-copy invoice that is forwarded to the billing clerk, and
- A daily sales register showing the aggregate totals of units shipped and sales amounts that the computer operator compares to the adding machine tapes.

The billing clerk mails two copies of each invoice to the customer and retains the third copy in an open invoice file that serves as a detail accounts receivable record.

Required:

Describe one specific recommendation for correcting each weakness in the internal control in the new EDP system and for correcting each weakness or inefficiency in the procedures for processing and controlling shipping notices and customer invoices.

(11/86, Aud., #4)

Essay 39-5 (15 to 25 minutes)

Johnson, CPA, was engaged to audit the financial statements of Horizon Incorporated which has its own computer installation. During the preliminary review, Johnson found that Horizon lacked proper segregation of the programming and operating functions. As a result, Johnson intensified the consideration of the internal control surrounding the computer and concluded that the existing compensating general controls provided reasonable assurance that the objectives of the internal control structure were being met.

Required:

a. In a properly functioning EDP environment, how is the separation of the programming and operating functions achieved?

b. What are the compensating general controls that Johnson most likely found? **Do not discuss hardware and application controls.**

(11/81, Aud., #4)

Essay 39-6 (15 to 25 minutes)

Brown, CPA, is auditing the financial statements of Big Z Wholesaling, Inc., a continuing audit client, for the year ended January 31, 1992. On January 5, 1992, Brown observed the tagging and counting of Big Z's physical inventory and made appropriate test counts. These test counts have been recorded on a computer file. As in prior years, Big Z gave Brown two computer files. One file represents the perpetual inventory (FIFO) records for the year ended January 31, 1992. The other file represents the January 5 physical inventory count.

Assume:

- Brown issued an unqualified opinion on the prior year's financial statements.
- All inventory is purchased for resale and located in a single warehouse.
- Brown has appropriate computerized audit software.
- The perpetual inventory file contains the following information in item number sequence:
    - Beginning balances at February 1, 1991; item number, item description, total quantity, and prices.
    - For each item purchased during the year: date received, receiving report number, vendor, item number, item description, quantity, and total dollar amount.
    - For each item sold during the year: date shipped, invoice number, item number, item description, quantity shipped, and dollar amount of the cost removed from inventory.
    - For each item adjusted for physical inventory count differences: date, item number, item descriptions, quantity, and dollar amount.
- The physical inventory file contains the following information in item number sequence: tag number, item number, item description, and count quantity.

Required:

Describe the substantive auditing procedures Brown may consider performing with computerized audit software using Big Z's two computer files and Brown's computer file of test counts. The substantive auditing procedures described may indicate the reports to be printed out for Brown's follow-up by subsequent application of manual procedures. Do **not** describe subsequent manual auditing procedures.

Group the procedures by those using (1) the perpetual inventory file and (2) the physical inventory and test count files.

(5/92, Aud., #4)

Essay 39-7 (15 to 25 minutes)

Talbert Corporation hired an independent computer programmer to develop a simplified payroll application for its newly purchased computer. The programmer developed an on-line, data-based microcomputer system that minimized the level of knowledge required by the operator. It was based upon typing answers to input cues that appeared on the terminal's viewing screen, examples of which follow:

A. Access routine:
   1. Operator access number to payroll file?
   2. Are there new employees?

B. New employees routine:
   1. Employee name?
   2. Employee number?
   3. Social security number?
   4. Rate per hour?
   5. Single or married?
   6. Number of dependents?
   7. Account distribution?

C. Current payroll routine:
   1. Employee number?
   2. Regular hours worked?
   3. Overtime hours worked?
   4. Total employees this payroll period?

The independent auditor is attempting to verify that certain input validation (edit) checks exist to ensure that errors resulting from omissions, invalid entries, or other inaccuracies will be detected during the typing of answers to the input cues.

Required:

Identify the various types of input validation (edit) checks the independent auditor would expect to find in the EDP system. Describe the assurances provided by each identified validation check. Do not discuss the review and evaluation of these controls.

(5/84, Aud., #4)

ESSAY SOLUTIONS

Solution 39-3 Advantages of Using a Computer in an Audit

The potential benefits to an auditor of using microcomputer software in an audit as compared to performing an audit without the use of a computer include the following:

1. **Time** may be **saved** by eliminating manual footing, cross-footing, and other routine calculations.
2. **Calculations,** comparisons, and other data manipulations are **more accurately performed.**
3. **Analytical procedures** calculations may be **more efficiently performed.**
4. The **scope** of analytical procedures may be **broadened.**
5. Audit **sampling** may be **facilitated.**
6. Potential **weaknesses** in a client's internal control structure may be more readily **identified**.
7. Preparation and **revision of flowcharts** depicting the flow of financial transactions in a client's structure may be **facilitated.**
8. **Working papers** may be easily **stored** and accessed.
9. **Graphics capabilities** may allow the auditor to generate, display, and evaluate various financial and nonfinancial relationships graphically.
10. Engagement-management information such as **time budgets** and the monitoring of **actual time vs. budgeted amounts** may be more easily generated and analyzed.
11. **Customized working papers** may be developed with greater ease.
12. **Standardized audit correspondence,** such as engagement letters, client representation letters, and attorney letters **may be stored and easily modified.**
13. **Supervisory-review time** may be **reduced.**
14. Staff morale and productivity may be improved by reducing the time spent on clerical tasks.
15. **Client's personnel may not need to manually prepare** as many **schedules** and otherwise spend as much time assisting the auditor.
16. Computer-generated **working papers** are generally **more legible and consistent.**

Solution 39-4 Recommendations for Correcting Internal Control Weaknesses in an EDP System

Recommendations for correcting weaknesses in the internal controls in the new EDP system and weaknesses and inefficiencies in the procedures for processing and controlling shipping notices and customer invoices:

- The functions of **programming, machine operations**, and **control** should be **assigned to different employees.**
- **Computer log** should be **reconciled** by the **computer operations supervisor** or other independent employee.
- **Access** to tapes and documentation should be **controlled** by an independent employee or through the use of a restricted authorization code.
- **Programmers' access** to computers should be **limited** to testing and debugging.
- The supervisor of the computer operators should have access to the computer room.
- The EDP system's documentation should also include flowcharts, computer programs, and operator instructions.
- **Batch totals** (control totals, hash totals, record counts) **should be utilized** to assure that data have been properly authorized and not lost or otherwise improperly changed.
- **Processing controls** should be put in place to assure that misstatements in the input records will be detected when processing occurs. Among the possible processing controls are

completeness tests, validation tests, sequence tests, and limit or reasonableness tests.

- The **price list** should be **placed on a master file** in the computer and matched with product numbers on the shipping notices to obtain appropriate prices.
- The **computer** should be **programmed to review the numerical sequence of shipping notices** and list missing numbers.
- The billing clerk or other designated control clerk should retain the adding machine tapes or a copy of them to compare the total with the daily sales register.
- Copies of **invoices** should be **forwarded** by the computer department to the mailroom clerk **for mailing** to the customers.
- An individual who is independent of billing and cash collections should maintain the accounts receivable records, or if the records are updated by the computer department, there should be an independent review by general accounting.
- The accounts receivable records maintained manually in an open file should be more efficiently maintained on magnetic tape.

Solution 39-5 Separation of Programming and Operating Functions

a. The primary internal control objectives in separating the programming and operating functions are achieved by **preventing programmer access** to the **computer** (except during designated testing periods) or to input or output documents and by **preventing operator access to operating programs** and operating program documentation, or by **preventing operators from writing or changing programs.**

b. Johnson is likely to find the following **mitigating** controls that are particularly important and that should exist when the programming and operating functions are not separated:

- Joint **operation by two or more operators.**
- **Rotation** of operator **duties.**
- Use of a **computer activity log book.**
- Comparison of computer times to an average or norm.
- Investigation of all **excess computer time** (errors).
- Adequate **supervision** of all EDP operations.
- Periodic comparison of program code value to a control value.
- Periodic **comparison of all programs with control copies.**
- **Required vacations** for all employees.

Solution 39-6 Auditing Procedures--Inventory

The **substantive auditing procedures** Brown may consider performing include the following:

Using the **perpetual** inventory file,

- **Recalculate the beginning and ending balances** (prices x quantities), foot, and print out a report to be used to reconcile the totals with the general ledger (or agree beginning balance with the prior year's working papers).
- **Calculate the quantity balances** as of the physical inventory date **for comparison to** the **physical inventory file**. (Alternatively, update the physical inventory file for purchases and sales from January 6 to January 31, 1992, for comparison to the perpetual inventory at January 31, 1992.)
- Select and print out a **sample of items received and shipped** for the periods (a) before and after January 5 and 31, 1992, **for cut-off testing**, (b) between January 5 and January 31, 1992, **for vouching or analytical procedures,** and (c) prior to January 5, 1992, **for tests of details** or analytical procedures.
- Compare quantities sold during the year to quantities on hand at year end. Print out a **report of items for which turnover is less than expected**. (Alternatively, calculate the number of days' sales in inventory for selected items.)
- **Select items** noted as possibly **unsalable** or **obsolete** during the physical inventory observation and print out information about purchases and sales for further consideration.
- **Recalculate** the prices used to value the year-end FIFO inventory by matching prices and quantities to the most recent purchases.
- Select a **sample** of **items for comparison** to **current sales prices.**
- **Identify** and print out **unusual transactions.** (These are transactions other than purchases or sales for the year, or physical inventory adjustments as of January 5, 1992.)
- **Recalculate the ending inventory** (or selected items) by taking the beginning balances plus purchases, less sales, (quantities and/or amounts) and print out the differences.
- **Recalculate the cost of sales** for selected items sold during the year.

Using the **physical inventory** and test count files,

- **Account for all inventory tag numbers** used and print out a report of missing or duplicate numbers for follow-up.
- **Search for tag numbers** noted during the physical inventory observation as being **voided or not used.**
- **Compare the physical inventory file to the file of test counts** and print out a report of differences for auditor follow-up.
- Combine the quantities for each item appearing on more than one inventory tag number for comparison to the perpetual file.
- **Compare** the **quantities** on the file to the calculated quantity balances on the perpetual inventory file as of January 5, 1992. (Alternatively, compare the physical inventory file updated to year end to the perpetual inventory file.)
- **Calculate the quantities and dollar amounts of the book-to-physical adjustments** for each item and the total adjustment. Print out a report to reconcile the total adjustment to the adjustment recorded in the general ledger before the year end.
- Using the calculated book-to-physical adjustments for each item, compare the quantities and dollar amounts of each adjustment to the perpetual inventory file as of January 5, 1992, and print out a report of differences for follow-up.

Solution 39-7 Input Validation (Edit) Checks

The following **edit checks** might be used to **detect errors** during the typing of answers to the input cues:

- **Password**--Ensures that the operator is authorized to access computer programs and files.
- **Numeric check**--Ensures that numbers are entered into and accepted by the system where only numbers are required to be entered, e.g., numbers 0-9 in social security number.
- **Alphabetic check**--Ensures that letters are entered into and accepted by the system where only letters are required to be entered, e.g., letters A-Z in employee name.
- **Special-character check**--Ensures that only specific special characters are entered into and accepted by the system where only these special characters are required to be entered, e.g., dashes between numbers in social security number.
- **Sign check**--Ensures that positive or negative signs are entered into and accepted by the system where only such signs are required to be entered or that the absence of a positive or negative sign appears where such an absence is required, e.g., hours worked.
- **Arithmetic check**--Ensures the validity of the result of a mathematical computation, e.g., total employees for period equal number of employee numbers in system.
- **Validity check**--Ensures that only authorized data codes will be entered into and accepted by the system where only such authorized data codes are required, e.g., authorized employee account numbers.
- **Limit (reasonableness) check**--Ensures that only data within predetermined limits will be entered into and accepted by the system, e.g., rate per hour cannot be lower than the minimum set by law or higher than the maximum set by management.
- **Self-checking digit**--Ensures that only data within predetermined limits will be entered into and accepted by the system.
- **Size check**--Ensures that only data using fixed or defined field lengths will be entered into and accepted by the system, e.g., number of dependents requires exactly two digits.
- **Missing-data check**--Ensures that no blanks will be entered into and accepted by the system when data should be present, e.g., an "S" or "M" is entered in response to single or married.
- **Overflow check**--Ensures that no digits are dropped if a number becomes too large for a variable during processing, e.g., hourly rates "on size errors" are detected.
- **Control-total check**--Ensures that no unauthorized changes are made to specified data or data fields and all data have been entered.
- **Logic check**--Ensures that spurious data are rejected, e.g., no negative regular hours.

CHAPTER 40

REPORTS ON AUDITED FINANCIAL STATEMENTS

CHAPTER 40

REPORTS ON AUDITED FINANCIAL STATEMENTS

PART ONE: REPORTING STANDARDS

I. The First Standard of Reporting--Adherence to GAAP (AU 410)

"The report shall state whether the financial statements are presented in conformity with generally accepted accounting principles."

A. Opinion, Not Fact--This standard requires an opinion by the auditor, not a statement of absolute fact.

B. Meaning of GAAP--GAAP is described in *Meaning of "Present Fairly in Conformity With Generally Accepted Accounting Principles" in the Independent Auditor's Report* (AU 411, SAS 69)

1. GAAP--A technical accounting term encompassing the conventions, rules, and procedures that are needed to define accepted accounting practice at a particular time.

2. GAAP includes broad guidelines and detailed practices and procedures.

C. Audit Judgment--Audit judgment determines which accounting principles should be used in any situation.

1. General Acceptance--Independent auditors agree on the existence of a body of accounting principles, and they are experts in those accounting principles and the determination of their general acceptance. Nevertheless, the determination that a particular accounting principle is generally accepted may be difficult because no single reference source exists for all principles.

2. The sources of established accounting principles for entities other than governmental entities that are generally accepted in the United States are as follows:

   a. Category (a)--Pronouncements of an authoritative body designated by the AICPA Council to establish accounting principles, pursuant to Rule 203 of the AICPA Code of Professional Conduct. This includes unsuperseded FASB Statements and Interpretations, APB Opinions, and AICPA Accounting Research Bulletins. Rule 203 provides that an unqualified opinion should not be expressed if the financial statements contain a material departure from such pronouncements unless, due to unusual circumstances, adherence to the pronouncements would make the statements misleading. Therefore, Rule 203 implies that application of officially established accounting principles results in the fair presentation of financial position, results of operations, and cash flows in conformity with GAAP.

   b. Category (b)--Pronouncements of bodies composed of expert accountants that follow a due process procedure, including broad distribution of proposed accounting principles for public comment, for the intended purpose of establishing accounting principles or describing existing practices that are generally accepted. This category is composed of FASB Technical Bulletins, and, if cleared by the FASB, AICPA Industry Audit and Accounting Guides and AICPA Statements of Position.

   c. Category (c)--Pronouncements of bodies, organized by a body referred to in category (a) and composed of expert accountants, that deliberate accounting issues in public forums for the purpose of interpreting or establishing accounting principles or describing existing accounting practices that are generally accepted, or pronouncements referred to in category (b) that have been cleared by a body referred to in category (a) but have not been exposed to public comment. This category is composed of AICPA Practice Bulletins that have been cleared by the FASB and consensus positions of the FASB Emerging Issues Task Force (EITF).

d. Category (d)--Practices or pronouncements widely recognized as being generally accepted because they exemplify prevalent practice in a particular industry, or the knowledgeable application to specific circumstances of pronouncements that are generally accepted. These include AICPA accounting interpretations and implementation guides published by the FASB staff, and practices that are widely recognized and prevalent either generally or in the industry.

3. In cases where the accounting treatment of a transaction or event is not specified by a pronouncement under Rule 203, the auditor should consider whether the accounting treatment is specified by another source of established accounting principles. In cases where a conflict arises between accounting principles from category (b), (c), or (d), the auditor should follow the treatment specified by the source in the <u>higher</u> category. For example, category (b) should be followed before categories (c) or (d).

4. At times, due to the evolution of new businesses transactions, there will not be an established accounting principle for reporting a specific transaction or event. When this occurs, an accounting principle that appears appropriate when applied in a manner similar to the application of an established principle to an analogous transaction or event should be selected.

5. Other accounting literature may also be considered in the absence of pronouncements or other established accounting principles. The appropriateness of other accounting literature depends on its relevance to particular circumstances, the specificity of the guidance, and the general recognition of the issuer or author as an authority.

6. A separate, but parallel hierarchy exists for state and local governmental units composed of four categories or levels of authority similar to those for nongovernmental entities.

   a. Category (a)--Consists of GASB Statements and Interpretations, as well as AICPA and FASB pronouncements made applicable to state and local governmental entities by GASB Statements or Interpretations.

   b. Category (b)--Consists of GASB Technical Bulletins and when <u>cleared</u> by the GASB, AICPA Statements of Position and Industry Auditing and Accounting Guides, to the extent the AICPA makes these latter documents applicable to state and local governmental units.

   c. Category (c)--Consists of AICPA Practice Bulletins to the extent these bulletins are made applicable to state and local governmental entities and cleared by the GASB. Also included are consensus positions of a group of accountants organized by the GASB that attempt to reach consensus positions on accounting issues applicable to state and local governmental entities.

   d. Category (d)--Consists of questions and answers published by the GASB staff, as well as practices that are widely recognized and prevalent in state and local government.

Exhibit 1--GAAP Hierarchy

Nongovernmental Entities	State and Local Governments
CATEGORY A (LEVEL ONE)	
FASB Statements of Financial Accounting Standards	GASB Statements
FASB Interpretations	GASB Interpretations
APB Opinions	AICPA and FASB Pronouncements if made applicable to state and local governments by GASB Statement or Interpretations
AICPA Accounting Research Bulletins	
CATEGORY B (LEVEL TWO)	
FASB Technical Bulletins	GASB Technical Bulletins
AICPA Industry Audit and Accounting Guides and Statements of Position	AICPA Industry Audit and Accounting Guides and Statements of Position if made applicable to state and local governments by AICPA
CATEGORY C (LEVEL THREE)	
EITF Consensuses	GASB EITF Consensuses (not yet organized by GASB)
AICPA Practice Bulletins	AICPA Practice Bulletins if made applicable to state and local governments by AICPA
CATEGORY D (LEVEL FOUR)	
AICPA Accounting Interpretations	"Qs and As" published by GASB staff
"Qs and As" published by FASB staff	Prevalent practice
Prevalent practice	

II. The Second Standard of Reporting--Consistency of Application of GAAP (AU 420)

"The report shall identify those circumstances in which such principles have not been consistently observed in the current period in relation to the preceding period."

A. Objective--The objective of the second standard is to provide assurance that (1) comparability has not been materially affected by changes in accounting principles, and (2) if comparability has been materially affected, that the auditor appropriately discloses the changes and their effects.

B. Accounting Changes Affecting Consistency

1. Change in Accounting Principle--Per APB Opinion No. 20, a change in accounting principle arises (a) from the use of a generally accepted accounting principle that is different from the one previously used (e.g., changing from the straight-line method of computing depreciation to the units-of-production method) or (b) from the use of a different method of applying a generally accepted accounting principle (e.g., changing the method of allocating manufacturing overhead to inventory from direct labor hours to machine hours). The auditor must recognize the change in the report if it has a material effect on the financial statements (i.e., the auditor will add an explanatory paragraph to an unqualified opinion). This is not a qualification of the audit opinion. If management has not provided reasonable justification for a change in accounting principle, the auditor's opinion should express an exception to the change having been made without reasonable justification. This would result in a qualified opinion. In addition, the auditor should continue to express the exception with respect to the financial statements for as long as they are presented and reported on.

2. Change in the Reporting Entity--Recognition is required in the auditor's report, as an explanatory paragraph with an unqualified opinion, because of lack of consistency. The following situations represent changes in the reporting entity:

   a. The presentation of consolidated or combined statements in place of the statements of individual companies.

   b. A change in specific subsidiaries which comprise the group of companies for which the consolidated statements are presented. (However, a change does not result from the creation, cessation, purchase, or disposition of a subsidiary.)

   c. A change in the companies that are included in combined financial statements.

   d. A change among the cost, equity, and consolidation methods of accounting for subsidiaries or other investments in common stock.

   e. A pooling is a change in the reporting entity.

3. Correction of an Error in Principle--This involves changing from an accounting principle that is not generally accepted to one that is (including correcting a mistake in the application of a principle). This type of change is accounted for as a correction of an error. Also, it will necessitate a changed audit opinion.

4. Change in Principle That Is Inseparable From a Change in Estimate--When the effect of a change in accounting principle cannot be separated from a change in estimate, the accounting for the change is handled as a change in estimate, but still requires recognition in the audit report for consistency.

5. Changes in Presentation of Cash Flows--An enterprise should disclose its policy for determining which items are treated as cash equivalents. Any change to that policy is a change in accounting principle that is reported by restating financial statements for earlier years presented for comparative purposes.

C. Changes Not Affecting Consistency--The following changes do not affect the consistency of application of accounting principles and, therefore, do not require recognition in the auditor's report as to a lack of consistency. However, if material, they may require disclosure in the financial statements.

1. Changes in Accounting Estimates--Even though accounting estimates will be changed as circumstances change, estimates such as expected salvage values and service lives of fixed assets are a normal part of doing business.

2. Error Correction That Does Not Involve an Accounting Principle--The correction of an error in previously issued financial statements that resulted from mathematical mistakes, oversight, or misunderstanding of facts is considered an error correction that does not involve an accounting principle.

3. Changes in Classification and Reclassification--The classification of items in previously issued financial statements should be adapted to increase comparability with current financial statements.

4. Substantially Different Transactions or Events--A consistency problem does not arise when the use of a different accounting principle is required because the transactions and events being processed are clearly different from those in the previous period.

5. Changes Expected to Have a Material Future Effect--When an accounting change does not affect the current year's financial statements but is expected to have a substantial effect in later years, it should be disclosed in the notes to the financial statements of the year of change.

6. While the changes above do not require the addition of an explanatory paragraph in the auditor's report because of lack of consistency, the opinion must be qualified if adequate disclosure in the financial statements is not made.

D. Periods to Which the Consistency Standard Applies--When reporting only on the current period's financial statements, the auditor should obtain sufficient, competent, evidential matter about the consistency of accounting principles with the previous period even though the prior-period financial statements are not presented. When the auditor has not audited the financial statements of the preceding year, the auditor should adopt procedures that are practicable and reasonable in the circumstances to be assured that the accounting principles are consistent between the current and the preceding year.

When reporting on the financial statements of two or more years that are presented for comparative purposes, the auditor should report on a lack of consistency between the years. The auditor should also report on a lack of consistency between the years and the year prior to the earliest year presented. The auditor is not required to report on a lack of consistency if the change is at the beginning of the earliest year presented and the change was accounted for by retroactive restatement.

III. The Third Standard of Reporting--Adequacy of Disclosure in Financial Statements (AU 431)

"Informative disclosures in the financial statements are to be regarded as reasonably adequate unless otherwise stated in the report."

A. Disclosure of Material Matters

1. Financial statements presented in conformity with GAAP must contain adequate disclosure of material matters. Adequate disclosure includes the form, arrangement, and content of the statements and notes, including the terminology used, amount of detail, classification of items, and the bases of amounts set forth. In determining whether a particular matter should be disclosed, the auditor should consider the circumstances and facts of which the auditor is aware at the time.

2. Failure by management to include information required by GAAP in the financial statements will result in the auditor expressing a qualified or adverse opinion on the statements. If practicable, the auditor should provide the information in the report, unless its omission from the report is sanctioned by a specific SAS. "Practicable" means that the information can reasonably be obtained from the client's accounts and records, and that providing it in the report does not require the auditor to assume the position of preparer of financial information.

For instance, an auditor is not expected to provide a basic financial statement or segment information omitted by management.

B. Confidential Information

In conducting an audit of financial statements and in other areas of work with the client, the auditor uses confidential information provided by the client. Thus, the auditor should not disclose--without management's consent--information not required to be disclosed in financial statements to comply with GAAP.

IV. The Fourth Standard of Reporting--Association With Financial Statements (AU 504)

"The report shall either contain an expression of opinion regarding the financial statements, taken as a whole, or an assertion to the effect that an opinion cannot be expressed. When an overall opinion cannot be expressed, the reasons therefor should be stated. In all cases where an auditor's name is associated with financial statements, the report should contain a clear-cut indication of the character of the auditor's work and the degree of responsibility, if any, the auditor is taking."

A. Objective--The objective of the fourth standard is to prevent any misinterpretation of the degree of responsibility which the auditor is assuming when his or her name is associated with financial statements.

B. Financial Statements Taken as a Whole--Reference to the financial statements taken as a whole applies equally to a complete set of financial statements and to an individual financial statement, such as a balance sheet, and also applies to the current period as well as any prior periods that are presented on a comparative basis.

PART TWO: REPORTS ON AUDITED FINANCIAL STATEMENTS

I. Types of Opinions

A. Unqualified Opinion (Standard Report)--Issued when the auditor feels the financial statements fairly present, in all material respects, the financial position, results of operations, and cash flows in conformity with GAAP (including adequate disclosure). The audit must have been conducted in accordance with GAAS. Exhibit 2 summarizes the necessary conditions for an unqualified opinion.

Exhibit 2--Necessary Conditions for an Unqualified Opinion

1. No departures from GAAP.
2. Disclosures in financial statements (footnotes) are adequate and complete.
3. No unusual uncertainties (contingencies) surrounding the financial statements.
4. No scope limitations.
5. GAAP must be consistently followed between periods.
6. Independent.

B. Explanatory Language Added to the Auditor's Report--Certain circumstances, while not affecting the auditor's unqualified opinion on the financial statements, may require that the auditor add an explanatory paragraph (or other explanatory language) to the report. Explanatory language would be added when part of the audit is performed by other independent auditors; or when change in consistency, material uncertainty, going concern, or emphasis of a matter issues exist.

C. Qualified Opinion--States that the financial statements present fairly, in all material respects, the results of operations, financial position, and cash flows in conformity with GAAP "except for" the effects of the matter to which the qualification relates, and qualification due to a scope limitation.

D. Adverse Opinion--Expressed when, in the auditor's judgment, the financial statements taken as a whole do not fairly present the financial position, results of operations, or cash flows in conformity with GAAP.

E. Disclaimer of Opinion--States that the auditor does not express an opinion on the financial statements, typically due to scope limitations.

II. Standard Report (AU 508, SAS 58)

NOTE: It is recommended that candidates be thoroughly familiar with the standard report since audit report questions appear frequently on the CPA Exam.

The auditor's standard report states that the financial statements present fairly, in all material respects, an entity's financial position, results of operations, and cash flows in conformity with GAAP. The auditor may express this opinion only when an audit conducted according to GAAS has been completed and the necessary conditions are met. The auditor's standard report identifies the financial statements audited in an opening, introductory paragraph, describes the nature of an audit in a scope paragraph, and expresses the auditor's opinion in a separate opinion paragraph. The basic elements of the report include the following:

A. Title--A title that includes the word, "independent."

B. Introductory Paragraph

1. A statement that the financial statements identified in the report were audited.

2. A statement that the financial statements are the responsibility of the Company's management and that the auditor's responsibility is to express an opinion on the financial statements based on the audit.

C. Scope Paragraph

1. A statement that the audit was conducted in accordance with GAAS.

2. A statement that GAAS requires that the auditor plan and perform the audit to obtain reasonable assurance about whether the financial statements are free of material misstatement.

3. A statement that an audit includes:

   a. Examining, on a test basis, evidence supporting the amounts and disclosures in the financial statements.

   b. Assessing the accounting principles used and significant estimates made by management.

   c. Evaluating the overall financial statement presentation.

4. A statement that the auditor believes that the audit provides a reasonable basis for the auditor's opinion.

D. Opinion Paragraph

1. An opinion as to whether the financial statements present fairly, in all material respects, the financial position of the Company as of the balance sheet date and the results of its operations and its cash flows for the period then ended in conformity with GAAP.

2. The manual or printed signature of the auditor's firm.

3. The date of the audit report.

<u>Exhibit 3</u>--The Form of the Auditor's Standard Report for a Single Year

<u>Independent Auditor's Report</u>

(Introductory paragraph)

We have audited the accompanying balance sheet of X Company as of December 31, 19XX, and the related statements of income, retained earnings, and cash flows for the year then ended. These financial statements are the responsibility of the Company's management. Our responsibility is to express an opinion on these financial statements based on our audit.

(Scope paragraph)

We conducted our audit in accordance with generally accepted auditing standards. Those standards require that we plan and perform the audit to obtain reasonable assurance about whether the financial statements are free of material misstatement. An audit includes examining, on a test basis, evidence supporting the amounts and disclosures in the financial statements. An audit also includes assessing the accounting principles used and significant estimates made by management, as well as evaluating the overall financial statement presentation. We believe that our audit provides a reasonable basis for our opinion.

(Opinion paragraph)

In our opinion, the financial statements referred to above present fairly, in all material respects, the financial position of X Company as of (at) December 31, 19XX, and the results of its operations and its cash flows for the year then ended in conformity with generally accepted accounting principles.

(Signature)

(Date)

E. <u>Address</u>--Addressed to the <u>company</u>, to its <u>board of directors</u>, or to its <u>stockholders</u>. If the auditor is retained to audit the financial statements of a company that is not the auditor's client, the report would be addressed to the client and not to the directors or stockholders of the company being audited.

F. <u>Date</u>--Generally, the date upon which the auditor's field work is completed.

G. <u>Explanatory Language Added to the Auditor's Standard Report</u>--There are certain circumstances which, while not affecting the auditor's unqualified opinion, may require that the auditor add explanatory language to the standard report. These circumstances include the following:

1. *Part of Audit Performed by Other Independent Auditors* (AU 543)

   a. Principal Auditor--Sometimes the auditor will be in a position where other independent auditors have audited the financial statements of subsidiaries, divisions, branches, components, or investments that are included in the financial statements the auditor is auditing. The auditor must first decide whether the auditor has participated sufficiently to be the principal auditor (i.e., to report on the financial statements).

b. Whether to Make Reference to the Other Auditor--As principal auditor, the auditor must then decide whether to take responsibility for the work of the other auditor as it relates to the expression of an opinion. If the auditor decides to take responsibility, the principal auditor does not make any reference to the other auditor's examination in the report. If the auditor does not assume this responsibility, the auditor should make reference to the other auditor's examination and clearly indicate the division of responsibility in the audit report.

(1) Decision Not to Make Reference--The principal auditor must be satisfied of the other auditor's independence, professional reputation, and the quality and scope of the audit performed. This position is usually appropriate when: (a) the other auditor is an associated or correspondent firm; (b) the other auditor was retained by the principal auditor; (c) the principal auditor takes steps necessary to be satisfied of the other auditor's work; or (d) the other auditor audited an immaterial portion of the financial statements.

(2) Decision to Make Reference--The principal auditor's report should clearly indicate, in the introductory, scope, and opinion paragraphs, the division of responsibility between the portion of the financial statements covered by the principal auditor's own audit and that covered by the audit of the other auditor. The portion examined by the other auditor should be indicated (e.g., dollar amounts or percentages of total assets, total revenues, etc.). The other auditor may only be named if: (a) the other auditor has given permission, and (b) the other auditor's report is included.

Exhibit 4--Report Indicating a Division of Responsibility

Independent Auditor's Report

(Introductory paragraph)

We have audited the consolidated balance sheets of ABC Company as of December 31, 19X2 and 19X1, and the related consolidated statements of income, retained earnings, and cash flows for the years then ended. These financial statements are the responsibility of the company's management. Our responsibility is to express an opinion on these financial statements based on our audits. We did not audit the financial statements of B Company, a wholly owned subsidiary, which statements reflect total assets of $______ and $______ as of December 31, 19X2 and 19X1, respectively, and total revenues of $______ and $______ for the years then ended. Those statements were audited by other auditors whose report has been furnished to us, and our opinion, insofar as it relates to the amounts included for B Company, is based solely on the report of other auditors.

(Scope paragraph)

We conducted our audits in accordance with generally accepted auditing standards. Those standards require that we plan and perform the audit to obtain reasonable assurance about whether the financial statements are free of material misstatements. An audit includes examining on a test basis, evidence supporting the amounts and disclosures in the financial statements. An audit also includes assessing the accounting principles used and significant estimates made by management, as well as evaluating the overall financial statements presentation. We believe that our audits and other auditors' reports provide a reasonable basis for our opinion.

(continued on next page)

> (Opinion paragraph)
>
> In our opinion, based on our audits and other auditors' reports, the consolidated financial statements referred to above present fairly, in all material respects, the financial position of ABC Company as of December 31, 19X2 and 19X1, and the results of its operations and its cash flows for the years then ended in conformity with generally accepted accounting principles.

c. Other Procedures--Regardless of whether or not reference is made, the principal auditor should inquire as to the professional reputation and independence of the other auditors and should attempt to achieve a proper coordination of their activities.

2. Justifiable Departure From a Promulgated Accounting Principle (Rule 203)--In the rare circumstance where the auditor can demonstrate that due to unusual circumstances the financial statements would be misleading if promulgated GAAP were applied, the auditor must describe the departure, its approximate effects, if practicable, and the reasons why compliance would result in a misleading statement.

   In this situation, it is appropriate for the auditor to express an unqualified opinion on the financial statements with an explanatory paragraph.

3. Lack of Consistency--The auditor's standard report implies that the accounting principles have been consistently applied between periods. In these cases, the auditor should not refer to consistency in the report. If there has been a change affecting consistency, the auditor should refer to the change in an explanatory paragraph of the report. The explanatory paragraph, following the opinion paragraph, should identify the nature of the change and refer the reader to the note in the financial statements that discusses the change in detail. An unqualified opinion would be expressed. The auditor's concurrence with a change is implicit unless the auditor takes exception to the change.

> Exhibit 5--Change in Accounting Principle (following opinion paragraph)
>
> As discussed in Note X to the financial statements, the Company changed its method of computing depreciation in 19X2.

4. Uncertainties--A matter involving an uncertainty is one that is expected to be resolved at a future date when sufficient competent evidential matter concerning its outcome should become available. In some instances, the outcome of future events may affect the financial statements. Since management may not always be able to estimate the effect of such events, the auditor must consider the likelihood of a material loss resulting from the resolution of the uncertainty.

   a. Remote Likelihood of a Material Loss--In this case, the auditor would not add an explanatory paragraph to the report because of the matter.

   b. Probable Chance of Material Loss--If management is unable to provide a reasonable estimate of the amount or range of a material probable loss, the auditor should add an explanatory paragraph to the report. This is not, however, a substitute for accrual if a reasonable estimate is available. If management makes a reasonable accrual for the potential loss, the auditor would decide whether an explanatory paragraph would be appropriate depending upon the materiality of the loss and the likelihood of its occurrence.

   c. Reasonable Possibility of Material Loss--When the chance of material loss is more than remote but less than probable, in deciding whether to add an explanatory paragraph, the auditor would consider the magnitude by which the amount of the potential loss exceeds the auditor's judgment about materiality and the likelihood of its occurrence.

If the auditor concludes that an explanatory paragraph is warranted, it should be included (following the opinion paragraph) in the report. The explanatory paragraph should include a description of the matter giving rise to the uncertainty and should indicate that its outcome cannot be determined. The separate paragraph may be shortened by making reference to financial statement notes. No reference should be made to the uncertainty in the introductory, scope, or opinion paragraphs. If, however, the uncertainty is not properly accounted for or disclosed, the auditor should issue a qualified or adverse opinion.

> Exhibit 6--Uncertainty: Explanatory Paragraph (following the opinion paragraph)
>
> As discussed in Note X to the financial statements, the Company is a defendant in a lawsuit alleging infringement of certain patent rights and claiming royalties and punitive damages. The Company has filed a counteraction, and preliminary hearings and discovery proceedings on both actions are in progress. The ultimate outcome of the litigation cannot presently be determined. Accordingly, no provision for any liability that may result upon adjudication has been made in the accompanying financial statements.

5. Going Concern Questions--The audit report should include an explanatory paragraph following the opinion paragraph if the auditor concludes that substantial doubt about the entity's ability to continue as a going concern does exist. If the auditor concludes that the entity's disclosures regarding its ability to continue as a going concern for a reasonable time are inadequate, misleading, or a departure from GAAP, a qualified or an adverse opinion should be issued.

> Exhibit 7--Going Concern Uncertainty: Explanatory paragraph (following the opinion paragraph)
>
> The accompanying financial statements have been prepared assuming that the Company will continue as a going concern. As discussed in Note X to the financial statements, the Company has suffered recurring losses from operations and has a net capital deficiency, raising substantial doubt about its ability to continue as a going concern. Management's plans in regard to these matters are also described in Note X. The financial statements do not include any adjustments that might result from the outcome of this uncertainty.

6. Emphasis of a Matter--The auditor may wish to emphasize a matter regarding the financial statements even though the auditor intends to express an unqualified opinion. For example, the auditor may wish to emphasize that the entity is a component of a larger business enterprise or that it has had significant transactions with related parties. The auditor may wish to mention an important subsequent event. This should be presented in a separate paragraph in the auditor's report with an unqualified opinion.

III. Departure From Unqualified Opinion

A. Qualified Opinions--Qualified opinions are expressed when the auditor finds that there is a lack of sufficient competent evidential matter, or when other restrictions on the scope of the audit have led the auditor to conclude that the auditor cannot express an unqualified opinion and the auditor has decided not to disclaim an opinion, or when there is a departure from GAAP, the effect of which is material, and the auditor has concluded not to express an adverse opinion.

When the auditor expresses a qualified opinion, the auditor should disclose all of the substantive reasons in one or more separate explanatory paragraph(s) preceding the opinion paragraph of the report. A qualified opinion should include the word *except* or *exception* in a phrase such as *except for* or *with the exception of.* Phrases such as *subject to* and *with the foregoing explanation* are not clear or forceful enough and should not be used.

1. Scope Limitations--Restrictions on the scope of an audit, whether imposed by the client or by circumstances, may require the auditor to express a qualified opinion. The decision depends upon the auditor's assessment of the importance of the omitted procedure(s) in relation to the financial statements. When a significant scope limitation is imposed by the client, the auditor would normally disclaim an opinion on the financial statements. If a qualified opinion is expressed, the reasons should be explained in the audit report in an explanatory paragraph (preceding the opinion paragraph) and referred to in both the scope and opinion paragraphs. The wording in the opinion paragraph should indicate that the qualification pertains to the possible effects on the financial statements and not to the scope limitation itself. Examples of scope limitations include the following situations:

   a. The auditor is unable to observe physical inventories or apply alternative procedures to verify their balances.

   b. The client refuses to permit its attorney to furnish information requested in a letter of audit inquiry.

Exhibit 8--Scope Limitations

Independent Auditor's Report

(Same first paragraph as the standard report)

Except as discussed in the following paragraph, we conducted our audits in accordance with generally accepted auditing standards. Those standards require that we plan and perform the audit to obtain reasonable assurance about whether the financial statements are free of material misstatement. An audit includes examining, on a test basis, evidence supporting the amounts and disclosures in the financial statements. An audit also includes assessing the accounting principles used and significant estimates made by management, as well as evaluating the overall financial statement presentation. We believe that our audits provide a reasonable basis for our opinion.

We were unable to obtain audited financial statements supporting the Company's investment in a foreign affiliate stated at $____ and $____ at December 31, 19X2 and 19X1, respectively, or its equity in earnings of that affiliate of $____ and $____, which is included in net income for the years then ended as described in Note X to the financial statements; nor were we able to satisfy ourselves as to the carrying value of the investment in the foreign affiliate or the equity in its earnings by other auditing procedures.

In our opinion, except for the effects of such adjustments, if any, as might have been determined to be necessary had we been able to examine evidence regarding the foreign affiliate investment and earnings, the financial statements referred to in the first paragraph above present fairly, in all material respects, the financial position of X Company as of December 31, 19X2 and 19X1, and the results of its operations and its cash flows for the years then ended in conformity with generally accepted accounting principles.

Limited Reporting Engagements--The auditor is not precluded from reporting on only one of the basic financial statements and not the others. A scope limitation would not exist if the auditor is able to apply all the procedures to the one financial statement the auditor considers necessary. Such engagements involve limited reporting objectives.

2. Departure From Generally Accepted Accounting Principles--When financial statements are materially affected by a departure from GAAP, the auditor should express a qualified or an adverse opinion. Materiality, significance of an item to the entity, pervasiveness of the

misstatement, and the effect of the misstatement on the financial statements as a whole, must be considered in deciding whether to express a qualified or an adverse opinion. When the auditor expresses a qualified opinion, the auditor should disclose, in a separate explanatory paragraph(s) preceding the opinion paragraph, the substantive reasons that have led the auditor to conclude that there is a departure from GAAP. The opinion paragraph should include appropriate qualifying language and should refer to the explanatory paragraph(s). The explanatory paragraph(s) should also disclose the principal effects of the matter on the financial position, results of operations and cash flows, if practicable. If the effects cannot be determined, the report should so state.

Exhibit 9--Departure From GAAP

Independent Auditor's Report

(Same first and second paragraphs as the standard report)

The company has excluded, from property and debt in the accompanying balance sheets, certain lease obligations that, in our opinion, should be capitalized in order to conform with generally accepted accounting principles. If these lease obligations were capitalized, property would be increased by $_____ and $_____, long-term debt by $_____ and $_____ , and retained earnings by $_____ and $_____ as of December 31, 19X2 and X1, respectively. Additionally, net income would be increased (decreased) by $_____ and $_____, and earnings per share would be increased (decreased) by $_____ and $_____, respectively, for the years then ended.

In our opinion, except for the effects of not capitalizing certain lease obligations as discussed in the preceding paragraph, the financial statements referred to above present fairly, in all material respects, the financial position of X Company as of December 31, 19X2 and 19X1, and the results of its operations and its cash flows for the years then ended in conformity with generally accepted accounting principles.

3. Inadequate Disclosure--If information which is essential for a fair presentation of financial statements in conformity with GAAP is not disclosed in the financial statements or accompanying notes, the auditor should express a qualified or an adverse opinion, and should provide the information in the report if practicable, unless its omission from the auditor's report is recognized as appropriate by a specific SAS.

Exhibit 10--Report Qualified for Inadequate Disclosure

Independent Auditor's Report

(Same first and second paragraphs as the standard report)

The Company's financial statements do not disclose (describe the nature of the omitted disclosures). In our opinion, disclosure of this information is required by generally accepted accounting principles.

In our opinion, except for the omission of the information discussed in the preceding paragraph, . . .

The auditor is not required to prepare a basic financial statement and include it in the report if the company's management declines to present the statement. In the case of, for example, the omission of a cash flow statement, a qualified opinion would be appropriate, with an explanatory paragraph added preceding the opinion paragraph.

Exhibit 11--Report Qualified Because Management Declined to Present a Basic Financial Statement

Independent Auditor's Report

We have audited the accompanying balance sheets of X Company as of December 31, 19X2 and 19X1, and the related statements of income and retained earnings for the years then ended. These financial statements are the responsibility of the Company's management. Our responsibility is to express an opinion on these financial statements based on our audit.

(Same second paragraph as the standard report)

The Company declined to present a statement of cash flows for the years ended December 31, 19X2 and 19X1. Presentation of such statement summarizing the Company's operating, investing, and financing activities is required by generally accepted accounting principles.

In our opinion, except that the omission of a statement of cash flows results in an incomplete presentation as explained in the preceding paragraph, the financial statements referred to above present fairly, in all material respects, the financial position of X Company as of December 31, 19X2 and 19X1, and the results of its operations for the years then ended in conformity with generally accepted accounting principles.

4. Accounting Changes--The auditor should evaluate a change in accounting principle to be satisfied that (a) the newly adopted accounting principle is a generally accepted accounting principle, (b) the method of accounting for the effect of the change is in conformity with GAAP, and (c) management's justification for the change is reasonable. If a change in accounting principle does not meet these conditions, the auditor should express a qualified opinion, or if the effect of the change is sufficiently material, an adverse opinion should be expressed.

Exhibit 12--Report Qualified for Accounting Change Not Reasonably Justified by Management

Independent Auditor's Report

(Same first and second paragraphs as the standard report)

As disclosed in Note X to the financial statements, the Company adopted, in 19X2, the first-in, first-out method of accounting for its inventories, whereas it previously used the last-in, first-out method. Although use of the first-in, first-out method is in conformity with generally accepted accounting principles, in our opinion, the Company has not provided reasonable justification for making this change as required by generally accepted accounting principles.

In our opinion, except for the change in accounting principle discussed in the preceding paragraph, the financial statements referred to above present fairly, in all material respects, the financial position of X Company as of December 31, 19X2 and 19X1, and the results of its operations and its cash flows for the years then ended in conformity with generally accepted accounting principles.

B. Adverse Opinions--State that financial statements do not present fairly the financial position, the results of operations, or cash flows in conformity with GAAP. When the auditor expresses an adverse opinion, the auditor should disclose in a separate explanatory paragraph(s) preceding the opinion paragraph of the report (1) all the substantive reasons for the adverse opinion, and (2) the principal effects of the subject matter of the adverse opinion on financial position, results of operations, and cash flows, if practicable. If the effects are not reasonably determinable, the report should so state. When an adverse opinion is expressed, the opinion paragraph should include a direct reference to a separate paragraph that discloses the basis for the adverse opinion.

Exhibit 13--Adverse Opinion

Independent Auditor's Report

(Same first and second paragraphs on the standard report)

As discussed in Note X to the financial statements, the Company carries its property, plant and equipment accounts at appraisal values, and provides depreciation on the basis of such values. Further, the Company does not provide for income taxes with respect to differences between financial income and taxable income arising because of the use, for income tax purposes, of the installment method of reporting gross profit from certain types of sales. Generally accepted accounting principles require that property, plant, and equipment be stated at an amount not in excess of cost, reduced by depreciation based on such amount, and that deferred income taxes be provided.

Because of the departures from generally accepted accounting principles identified above, as of December 31, 19X2 and 19X1, inventories have been increased $_____ and $_____ by inclusion in manufacturing overhead of depreciation in excess of that based on cost; property, plant, and equipment, less accumulated depreciation, is carried at $_____ and $_____ in excess of an amount based on the cost to the Company; and deferred income taxes of $_____ and $_____ have not been recorded, resulting in an increase of $_____ and $_____ in retained earnings and in appraisal surplus of $_____ and $_____, respectively. For the years ended December 31, 19X2 and 19X1, cost of goods sold has been increased $_____ and $_____, respectively, because of the effects of the depreciation accounting referred to above and deferred income taxes of $_____ and $_____ have not been provided, resulting in an increase in net income of $_____ and $_____, respectively.

In our opinion, because of the effects of the matters discussed in the preceding paragraphs, the financial statements referred to above do not present fairly, in conformity with generally accepted accounting principles, the financial position of X Company as of December 31, 19X2 and 19X1, or the results of its operations or its cash flows for the years then ended.

C. Disclaimer of Opinion--States that the auditor does not express an opinion on the financial statements. It is appropriate when the auditor has not performed an audit sufficient in scope to enable the auditor to form an opinion on the financial statements. If a scope limitation is the reason for the disclaimer, the auditor should indicate in a separate paragraph the reasons for the scope limitation. The auditor should state that the scope of the audit was not sufficient to warrant the expression of an opinion, but the auditor should not identify the procedures that were performed nor include the paragraph describing the characteristics of an audit (that is, the scope paragraph). A disclaimer of opinion should not be expressed when the auditor believes, on the basis of the audit, that there are material departures from GAAP.

Exhibit 14--Disclaimer of Opinion Due to Scope Limitation

Independent Auditor's Report

We were engaged to audit the accompanying balance sheets of X Company as of December 31, 19X2 and 19X1, and the related statements of income, retained earnings, and cash flows for the years then ended. These financial statements are the responsibility of the Company's management.

(Second (scope) paragraph of standard report should be omitted)

The Company did not make a count of its physical inventory in 19X2 or 19X1, stated in the accompanying financial statements at $_____ as of December 31, 19X2, and at $_____ as of December 31, 19X1. Further, evidence supporting the cost of property and equipment acquired prior to December 31, 19X1, is no longer available. The Company's records do not permit the application of other auditing procedures to inventories or property and equipment.

Since the Company did not take physical inventories and we were not able to apply other auditing procedures to satisfy ourselves as to inventory quantities and the cost of property and equipment, the scope of our work was not sufficient to enable us to express, and we do not express, an opinion on these financial statements.

D. Piecemeal Opinions--Piecemeal opinions are expressions of opinion as to certain identified items in the financial statements. Piecemeal opinions should not be expressed when the auditor has disclaimed an opinion or has expressed an adverse opinion on the financial statements taken as a whole because piecemeal opinions tend to overshadow or contradict a disclaimer of opinion or an adverse opinion. Therefore, piecemeal opinions are inappropriate and should not be issued in any situation.

IV. Reports on Comparative Financial Statements

A. Auditor's Standard Report--An auditor's standard report includes statements of the current period and those of one or more prior periods that are presented on a comparative basis. Therefore, a continuing auditor, an auditor who has audited the current period's financial statements and those of one or more immediately preceding periods, will update the report (re-express an opinion) on the individual financial statements of those prior periods. The updated opinion may differ from that previously given if circumstances warrant a change. During the audit of the current period financial statements, the auditor should be alert for circumstances or events that affect the prior-period financial statements.

Exhibit 15--Auditor's Standard Report-Comparative Financial Statements

Independent Auditor's Report

We have audited the accompanying balance sheets of X Company as of December 31, 19X4 and 19X3, and the related statements of income, retained earnings, and cash flows for the years then ended. These financial statements are the responsibility of the Company's management. Our responsibility is to express an opinion on these financial statements based on our audits.

We conducted our audits in accordance with generally accepted auditing standards. Those standards require that we plan and perform the audit to obtain reasonable assurance about whether the financial statements are free of material misstatement. An audit includes examining, on a test basis, evidence supporting the amounts and disclosures in the financial statements.

(continued on next page)

> An audit also includes assessing the accounting principles used and significant estimates made by management, as well as evaluating the overall financial statement presentation. We believe that our audits provide a reasonable basis for our opinion.
>
> In our opinion, the financial statements referred to above present fairly, in all material respects, the financial position of X Company as of December 31, 19X4 and 19X3, and the results of its operations and its cash flows for the years then ended in conformity with generally accepted accounting principles.

B. Report With Differing Opinions--The auditor's report on the comparative statements applies to the individual financial statements that are presented. Therefore, the same type of opinion is not required (qualified, unqualified, etc.) on all of the statements. When it is not, the auditor should (1) disclose all of the substantive reasons for the modified opinion (or for disclaiming an opinion) in a separate explanatory paragraph of the report, and (2) in the opinion paragraph, include an appropriate modification (or disclaimer of opinion) along with a reference to the explanation.

> Exhibit 16--Standard Report on Prior-Year Financial Statements and a Qualified Opinion on Current-Year Statements
>
> Independent Auditor's Report
>
> (Same first and second paragraphs as the standard report)
>
> The Company has excluded, from property and debt in the accompanying 19X2 balance sheet, certain lease obligations that were entered into in 19X2 which, in our opinion, should be capitalized in order to conform with generally accepted accounting principles. If these lease obligations were capitalized, property would be increased by $_____, long-term debt by $_____, and retained earnings by $_____ as of December 31, 19X2, and net income and earnings per share would be increased (decreased) by $_____ and $_____, respectively, for the year then ended.
>
> In our opinion, except for the effects on the 19X2 financial statements of not capitalizing certain lease obligations as described in the preceding paragraph, the financial statements referred to above present fairly, in all material respects, the financial position of ABC Company as of December 31, 19X2 and 19X1, and the results of its operations and its cash flows for the years then ended in conformity with generally accepted accounting principles.

C. Subsequent Restatement of Prior-Period Financial Statements to Conform With GAAP--If the auditor, during the current audit, becomes aware of circumstances or events that affect the financial statements of a prior period, the auditor should consider such matters when updating the report. If an auditor has previously qualified the opinion on the financial statements of a prior period because of a departure from GAAP, and the prior period financial statements are restated in the current period to conform with GAAP, the updated report of the prior period should indicate that the statements have been restated and should express an unqualified opinion with respect to the restated financial statements. If the auditor decides to express a different opinion than that previously expressed, the auditor should disclose all the substantive reasons for the different opinion in a separate explanatory paragraph(s) preceding the opinion paragraph of the report. The explanatory paragraph should disclose (1) the date of the auditor's previous report, (2) the type of opinion previously expressed, (3) the circumstances or events that caused the auditor to express a different opinion, and (4) that the auditor's updated opinion on the financial statements of the prior period is different from the auditor's previous opinion on those statements.

Exhibit 17--Changed Opinion

Independent Auditor's Report

(Same first and second paragraphs as the standard report)

In our report dated March 1, 19X2, we expressed an opinion that the 19X1 financial statements did not fairly present financial position, results of operations, and cash flows in conformity with generally accepted accounting principles because of two departures from such principles: (1) the Company carried its property, plant and equipment at appraisal values, and provided for depreciation on the basis of such values, and (2) the Company did not provide for deferred income taxes with respect to differences between income for financial reporting purposes and taxable income. As described in Note X, the Company has changed its method of accounting for these items and restated its 19X1 financial statements to conform with generally accepted accounting principles. Accordingly, our present opinion on the 19X1 financial statements, as presented herein, is different from that expressed in our previous report.

In our opinion, the financial statements referred to above present fairly, in all material respects, the financial position of X Company as of December 31, 19X2 and 19X1, and the results of its operations and its cash flows for the years then ended in conformity with generally accepted accounting principles.

D. Report of the Predecessor Auditor

1. Predecessor Auditor's Report Reissued--In this case, the predecessor auditor should consider whether the opinion previously issued on the financial statements of the prior period is still appropriate. This should include (a) reading the financial statements of the current period; (b) comparing the statements reported on with those that are being presented for comparative purposes; and (c) obtaining a letter of representation from the successor auditor as to whether the successor's audit found anything that might have a material effect on (or require disclosure in) the prior period's statements. If the predecessor becomes aware of circumstances that may affect the predecessor's own previous opinion, the predecessor should inquire about the event and may want to perform tests such as reviewing the working papers of the successor auditor in regard to the matter. The predecessor must then decide whether to revise the opinion.

   - Predecessor Auditor's Report--When the predecessor reissues the report, the predecessor should use the same date as that of the predecessor's own previous report to avoid any implication that the predecessor examined any records, transactions, or events after that date. The predecessor should not refer to the work or report of the successor auditor. If the predecessor revises the report or if the financial statements are restated, the report should be dual-dated.

2. Predecessor Auditor's Report Not Presented--If the financial statements of a prior period are presented for comparative purposes but the report of the predecessor auditor is not presented, the successor auditor should modify the introductory paragraph of the report to indicate (a) that another auditor audited the prior-period financial statements; (b) the date of the predecessor's report; (c) the type of report issued by the predecessor auditor; and (d) if the report was other than standard, and the substantive reasons therefor.

Exhibit 18--Successor Auditor's Report When the Predecessor's Report Is Not Presented

We have audited the balance sheet of ABC Company as of December 31, 19X2, and the related statements of income, retained earnings, and cash flows for the year then ended. These financial statements are the responsibility of the Company's management. Our responsibility is to express an opinion on these financial statements based on our audit. The financial statements of ABC Company as of December 31, 19X1, were audited by other auditors whose report dated March 31, 19X2, expressed an unqualified opinion on those statements.

(Same second paragraph as the standard report)

In our opinion, the 19X2 financial statements referred to above present fairly, in all material respects, the financial position of ABC Company as of December 31, 19X2, and the results of its operations and its cash flows for the year then ended in conformity with generally accepted accounting principles.

a. If the predecessor auditor's opinion was other than a standard report, the successor auditor should describe the nature of and the reasons for the explanatory paragraph added to the predecessor's report of the opinion qualification. Following is an illustration of the wording that may be used:

   . . . were audited by other auditors whose report, dated March 1, 19X2, on those statements included an explanatory paragraph that described the litigation discussed in Note X to the financial statements.

b. If the financial statements of the prior period have been restated, the introductory paragraph should indicate that a predecessor auditor reported on the financial statements of the prior period before restatement. In addition, if the successor auditor is engaged to audit and applies sufficient procedures to satisfy the appropriateness of the restatement adjustments, the successor may also include the following paragraph in the report:

   We also audited the adjustments described in Note X that were applied to restate the 19X1 financial statements. In our opinion, such adjustments are appropriate and have been properly applied.

E. Summary of Various Audit Opinions

1. Unqualified

   a. All Necessary Conditions for an Unqualified Opinion Are Met--Standard report issued (See Exhibit 2).

   b. Part of Audit Performed by Other Auditor

      (1) Principal Auditor Takes Responsibility for Other Auditor's Work--Standard report issued.

      (2) Principal Auditor Does Not Take Responsibility for Other Auditor's Work--Make reference to other auditor and clearly indicate division of responsibility (do not name unless other gives permission and other's report is included). Introductory, scope, and opinion paragraphs should all be changed to reflect this. No explanatory paragraph.

c. Justifiable Departure From GAAP (rare)--Add explanatory paragraph. Describe departure, approximate effects, and reasons why compliance would result in misleading statement.

d. Uncertainties

(1) Remote--Standard report issued.

(2) Probable--Explanatory paragraph if not estimable; if estimable, management should accrue, or this would be a departure from GAAP (resulting in a qualified or adverse opinion).

e. Doubt About Ability to Continue as a Going Concern--Explanatory paragraph.

f. Lack of Consistency

(1) If Material Effect--Explanatory paragraph added.

(2) If Immaterial--Standard report issued.

g. Emphasis of a Matter--Explanatory paragraph added.

NOTE: When an explanatory paragraph is necessary, it should be placed after the opinion paragraph.

2. Qualified

Explanatory paragraph added preceding the opinion paragraph, words such as *except for* or *with the exception of* used.

a. Scope Limitation--If significant, disclaim; otherwise, explanatory paragraph preceding opinion paragraph added and referred to in scope and opinion paragraphs. This does not refer the reader to footnotes for details.

b. Material Departure From GAAP--Qualified or adverse depending on materiality, significance of item to entity, pervasiveness of misstatement, and effect of misstatement on statements taken as a whole. If qualified, explanatory paragraph added preceding opinion paragraph and referred to in opinion.

c. Inadequate Disclosure--Qualified or Adverse--Explanatory paragraph added and referred to in opinion.

d. Inappropriate Accounting Changes--Qualified or Adverse--Explanatory paragraph preceding opinion paragraph added and referred to in opinion.

3. Adverse

Explanatory paragraph preceding opinion paragraph. Explanatory paragraph added and referred to in adverse opinion.

4. Disclaimer

Explanatory paragraph preceding opinion paragraph. If a scope limitation, scope paragraph omitted, explanatory paragraph added and referred to in disclaimer of opinion.

5. Comparative

Qualified Prior Year, Standard in Current Year--Explanatory paragraph preceding opinion, referred to in opinion paragraph: "except for. . . "

Qualified Prior Year, Change Made in Current Year to Conform to GAAP--Explanatory paragraph preceding opinion, standard opinion paragraph.

6. Predecessor Auditor

If predecessor report is not presented with comparative statements, modify introductory paragraph, no change to scope paragraph, only express opinion on audited (current year, by successor) statements.

Exhibit 19--Conditions Requiring Modification of Report

Reasons for Modification*	Opinion Expressed	Explanatory Paragraph	Opinion Paragraph
GAAP Departure	Qualified or Adverse	Before opinion paragraph to explain the departure and amount(s)	Modified to provide qualifying language and refer to explanatory paragraph(s)
Inadequate Disclosure	Qualified or Adverse	Before opinion paragraph to explain missing disclosure	Modified to provide qualifying language and refer to explanatory paragraph(s)
Scope Limitation	Qualified or Disclaimer	Before opinion paragraph to explain scope limitation and potential monetary effects	Modified to provide qualifying language or to provide disclaimer**
Uncertainty	Unqualified (disclaimer is allowed)	After opinion paragraph to describe uncertainty and refer reader to the financial statement footnote	Not modified
Going Concern Uncertainty	Unqualified (disclaimer is allowed)	After opinion paragraph to describe going concern using wording "substantial doubt" about entity's ability to continue as a going concern and refer reader to the financial statement footnote	Not modified
Consistency Violation (if properly accounted for and disclosed, if not, treat as GAAP departure)	Unqualified	After opinion paragraph describing accounting change and referring reader to financial statement footnote	Not modified
Emphasis of a Matter	Unqualified	After opinion paragraph describing matter and referring reader to financial statement footnote	Not modified

(continued on next page)

Exhibit 19--Conditions Requiring Modification of Report (continued)

Reasons for Modification*	Opinion Expressed	Explanatory Paragraph	Opinion Paragraph
Reliance on Another Auditor	Unqualified	Division of responsibility indicated in introductory paragraph including significance of portion of entity done by other auditor	Modified to refer to other auditor
Changed Opinion on Prior Period Information	Unqualified	After opinion paragraph to describe reason for different opinion	Not modified

* Assuming item is material

** Qualified opinion requires modification of second paragraph (using "except for" language). Disclaimer requires modification of introductory paragraph and the second paragraph (scope) is NOT included.

V. Dating of the Auditor's Report (AU 530)

A. Date of the Auditor's Report--Generally, the date of the report is the date the auditor completes the field work. The auditor does not have responsibility to make any inquiries or to conduct any audit procedures after this date (with the exception of filings under the Securities Act of 1933).

B. Subsequent Events--If the auditor becomes aware of an event requiring adjustment (Type I subsequent event) of the financial statements that occurred after the date of the report but before it is issued, the statements should be adjusted or the opinion should be qualified. If the adjustment is made without any disclosure in the financial statements, the report is still dated as of the last day of field work. If the adjustment is made and is disclosed in the financial statements or if the audit report is qualified because of a lack of adjustment, the auditor may dual-date the report by dating the report as of the last day of field work except for the subsequent event which is dated later. The auditor may become aware of a new event requiring disclosure (Type II subsequent event) (such as a lawsuit filed after the balance sheet date but before the financial statements are issued.) If disclosure is not made, the audit opinion would be qualified. If disclosure is made, the auditor may dual-date the report. If dual-dating is used, the responsibility for any events that occurred after the auditor completed the field work is limited to the particular subsequent event that is dual-dated. If the auditor chooses, the later date may be used for the entire report. However, the auditor's responsibility for events occurring after the completion of field work will then extend to the later date.

C. Reissuance of Auditor's Report--When an auditor reissues a report, the original report date should be used. This implies that there has been no audit past this date. When events that occurred subsequent to the date of the report require modification of the statements or the opinion, a dual-date is appropriate. If events that occurred subsequent to the date of the report only require disclosure in the financial statements, the events may be disclosed in a note to the statements and the date of the original report may be used.

VI. Subsequent Events (AU 560)

A. Subsequent Events--These are events or transactions having a material effect on the financial statements that occur after the balance sheet date, but before the financial statements and the auditor's report are issued. Subsequent events are of two types:

1. Type I: Require Adjustment--Subsequent events that provide additional evidence about conditions that existed at the date of the balance sheet and affect the estimates used in preparing the financial statements require adjustment of the financial statements. Examples include a loss on an uncollectible trade account because a customer went bankrupt shortly

sheet date was not adequate to meet obligations), and the settlement of litigation for an amount different from the amount recorded in the accounts (as long as the reason for the litigation occurred prior to the balance sheet date).

2. Type II: Do Not Require Adjustment--Subsequent events that provide evidence about conditions that did not exist at the balance sheet date but arose after that date, do not require adjustment of the financial statements. The conditions should be disclosed if their disclosure is required to keep the financial statements from being misleading. In some cases, pro forma statements may be prepared. Occasionally, the auditor may decide to include an explanatory paragraph in the report to draw the attention of the reader to the event.

   - Examples--Events requiring disclosure (but not adjustment) include (1) sale of a bond or capital stock issue; (2) purchase of a business; (3) settlement of litigation arising from events that occurred subsequent to the balance sheet date; (4) loss of plant or inventories as a result of a fire or flood; and (5) losses on receivables resulting from conditions that arose after the balance sheet date (such as a customer's major casualty loss).

B. Reissuance of Financial Statements--Events that occur between the time of the original issuance of the statements and the time of reissuance of the statements (for example, in reports filed with a regulatory agency) should not result in an adjustment of the financial statements unless the adjustment would meet the criteria for the correction of an error or the criteria for prior-period adjustments.

C. Auditing Procedures in the Subsequent Period--The subsequent period extends from the balance sheet date to the date of the auditor's report. Certain audit procedures should be performed after the balance sheet date to assure a proper cutoff and to evaluate the balances of certain asset and liability accounts. Additional auditing procedures should be applied to the period after the balance sheet date to identify subsequent events that may require adjustment or disclosure. These generally include (1) reading the latest interim financial statements and comparing them with the financial statements being reported on; (2) discussing with management the existence of substantial contingent liabilities, any significant change in stockholders' equity items, the current status of financial statement items that were accounted for on a tentative basis, and the existence of any unusual adjustments made after the balance sheet date; (3) reading the minutes of the board of directors' and stockholders' meetings; (4) inquiring of the client's legal counsel about litigation, claims, and assessments; (5) obtaining a letter of representation from management, dated as of the date of the auditor's report, as to whether any subsequent events occurred that would require adjustment to or disclosure in the statements; and (6) making any additional inquiries and performing any procedures that are considered necessary by the auditor.

VII. Subsequent Discovery of Facts Existing at the Date of the Auditor's Report (AU 561)

A. Responsibility--The auditor may, after the date of the report, become aware of facts that existed at that date and which might have affected the report had the auditor been aware of them. However, the auditor does not have any obligation to perform auditing procedures or make inquiries after the report date unless the auditor becomes aware of this type of information. When the auditor becomes aware of information which relates to financial statements previously reported on by the auditor, but which was not known at the date of the report, and which is of such a nature and from such a source that the auditor would have investigated it had the auditor been aware of it during the audit, the auditor should, as soon as practicable, determine whether the information is reliable and whether the facts existed at the date of the report. In this case, the auditor should discuss the matter with the appropriate level of the client's management, and request cooperation in the investigation into the matter. The auditor should consult an attorney when encountering these circumstances because of legal implications that may be involved, including the confidentiality of auditor-client communications.

B. Preventing Future Reliance on the Report--When the subsequently discovered information is found both to be reliable and to have existed at the report date, the auditor should take action if the nature and effect of the matter are such that the report would have been affected by the information had it been known, and such that the auditor believes there are persons currently relying on, or likely to rely on, the financial statements. To prevent future reliance on the report, the auditor should advise the client to make appropriate disclosure of the newly discovered information, and the effect of the facts to the persons relying on, or likely to rely on, the statements.

1. Client Cooperates--If the client cooperates, the method used will depend on the circumstances.

   a. Revise and Reissue--The statements should be revised and reissued if the effect of the subsequently discovered information can be determined promptly. The reasons for the revision will usually be described in a note to the statements and referred to in the auditor's report.

   b. Statements of a Subsequent Period--If the issuance of financial statements and the auditor's report for a subsequent period is imminent, appropriate revision can be made in such statements.

   c. Notification by Client--If the effect on the statements cannot be promptly determined but it appears the statements will be revised after investigation, the client should notify persons who are relying (or are likely to rely) on the statements and report that they should not do so, and that revised statements and the report will be issued when the investigation is complete.

2. Client Does Not Cooperate--If the client does not cooperate, the auditor should notify the board of directors that unless the client cooperates, the auditor will (a) notify the client that the auditor's report cannot be associated with the financial statements, (b) notify regulatory agencies that the auditor's report should not be relied upon, and (c) notify each person the auditor knows is relying on the statements and report that they should no longer do so.

   - Guidelines for Disclosure to Persons Other Than Client--When the auditor must make a disclosure and the auditor has been able to make a satisfactory investigation and determine that the information is reliable, the disclosure should include a description of the nature of the subsequently acquired information and describe the effect of the information on the financial statements and the report. The disclosure should be as factual and precise as possible, but it should not contain any comment on the conduct or motive of any person. When the auditor has been prevented from making a satisfactory investigation, the auditor need not provide detailed information but can indicate that additional information, which the client has not helped substantiate, has come to the auditor's attention, and if true, the auditor believes the report should no longer be relied upon. No such disclosure should be made unless the auditor believes that the financial statements are likely to be misleading.

VIII. Consideration of Omitted Procedures After the Report Date (AU 390)

A. Responsibility--The auditor may conclude, after the date of the report, that one or more auditing procedures that was considered necessary at that date were omitted from the audit, even though there is no indication that the financial statements are not fairly presented in conformity with GAAP or another comprehensive basis of accounting. Although the auditor does not have any responsibility to perform a retrospective review of the work performed, the omission of a necessary auditing procedure may be disclosed when the reports and working papers relating to the engagement are subjected to post-issuance review (e.g., a firm's internal inspection program or peer review).

B. Assessment--Upon concluding that a necessary auditing procedure has been omitted, the auditor should assess the importance of the omitted procedure to the auditor's present ability to support a previously expressed opinion regarding the financial statements in question. This assessment can be aided by (1) reviewing the working papers, (2) discussing the audit circumstances with engagement personnel and others, and (3) reevaluating the overall scope of the audit. The results of other procedures that were applied may tend to compensate for or make less important the omitted procedure.

C. Course of Action--If the auditor concludes that the omission of the necessary procedure impairs the present ability to support the previously expressed opinion, and the auditor believes that there are persons currently relying, or likely to rely, on the report, the auditor should proceed as follows:

1. If the Omitted Procedure(s) Can Be Applied--The auditor should promptly apply the omitted procedure(s) or alternative procedures that would provide a satisfactory basis for the auditor's opinion. If, as a result, the auditor becomes aware of facts existing at the date of the report that would have affected that report had the auditor been aware of them, then the auditor should take steps to prevent future reliance on the report.

2. If the Auditor Is Unable to Apply the Previously Omitted Procedures--The auditor should consult an attorney to determine an appropriate course of action concerning responsibilities to the client, regulatory authorities, if any, having jurisdiction over the client, and persons relying, or likely to rely, on the report.

IX. Association With Financial Statements (AU 504, SAS 26)

A. Background--The Fourth Standard of Reporting seeks to avoid any misunderstanding as to the responsibility the accountant is assuming when his or her name is associated with financial statements when it states,

". . . In all cases where an auditor's name is associated with financial statements, the report should contain a clear-cut indication of the character of the auditor's work, and the degree of responsibility the auditor is taking."

B. Objective of SAS 26--The objective is to provide reporting guidance to a CPA who is associated with the audited or unaudited financial statements of a public entity or with the audited financial statements of a nonpublic entity.

- SSARS--Statements on Standards for Accounting and Review Services apply to the unaudited financial statements of a nonpublic entity.

C. Association--The CPA is associated with an entity's financial statements when the CPA (1) has agreed to the use of his or her name in a report, document, or written communication that contains the financial statements; and/or (2) submits financial statements that the CPA has prepared (or assisted in preparing) to the client or to others (even if the CPA does not append his or her name to the financial statements).

- Tax Returns, etc.--Association does not occur when the CPA prepares data, such as tax returns, solely for submission to taxing authorities since these do not constitute financial statements.

D. Disclaimer of Opinion on Unaudited Financial Statements--When associated with a public entity's financial statements that the CPA has not audited or reviewed, the CPA should issue the following disclaimer:

The accompanying balance sheet of X Company as of December 31, 19X1, and the related statements of income, retained earnings, and cash flows for the year then ended were not audited by us and, accordingly, we do not express an opinion on them.

(Signature and date)

Note that this disclaimer is different from a disclaimer of opinion due to a scope limitation as discussed earlier.

1. Disclaimer may accompany, or may be placed directly on, the unaudited financial statements.

2. Each page of the statements should be marked as *unaudited.*

3. Responsibility--CPA's only responsibility is to read the financial statements for obvious material misstatements.

4. Procedures--The CPA should not describe any procedures that may have been applied, since to do so might give the impression that the CPA audited or reviewed the financial statements.

5. Inclusion of Name--When a CPA learns that a client who is a public entity plans to include the CPA's name in a client-prepared written communication that will contain financial statements that the CPA has not audited or reviewed, the CPA should ask (a) that his or her name not be used or (b) that the client clearly mark the financial statements as *unaudited* and that a notation be made that the auditor does not express an opinion on them. If the client refuses, the CPA may need to consult legal counsel as to appropriate actions.

E. Disclaimer of Opinion on Unaudited Financial Statements Prepared on a Comprehensive Basis of Accounting Other Than GAAP

1. Modification of Disclaimer--The unaudited disclaimer applies except that the identification of the financial statements should be modified to conform to SAS 62, *Special Reports*, as follows:

> Exhibit 20--Financial Statements Prepared on the Cash Basis
>
> The accompanying statement of assets and liabilities resulting from cash transactions of XYZ Corporation as of December 31, 19X1, and the related statement of revenues collected and expenses paid during the year then ended were not audited by us and, accordingly, we do not express an opinion on them.
>
> (Signature and date)

2. Note to Financial Statements--Should describe the difference between the basis of presentation and GAAP. The monetary effect of such differences does not need to be stated.

F. Disclaimer of Opinion When the CPA Is Not Independent

1. The Second General Standard requires independence in mental attitude.

2. Disclaim an Opinion--Since the CPA cannot be in accordance with GAAS if the CPA is not independent, the CPA should disclaim an opinion and clearly state that he or she is not independent (the CPA should not give the reasons for this lack of independence).

   a. Nonpublic Entity--The CPA should follow SSARS when the financial statements are those of a nonpublic entity.

b. Public Entity--Paragraphs 1. through 4. of D., above, should be followed except that the disclaimer should be modified so that it clearly indicates the CPA is not independent. The reasons for lack of independence should not be described. For example:

We are not independent with respect to XYZ Company, and the accompanying balance sheet as of December 31, 19X1, and the related statements of income, retained earnings, and cash flows for the year then ended were not audited by us and, accordingly, we do not express an opinion on them.

(Signature and date)

G. Circumstances Requiring a Modified Disclaimer--If the CPA feels the unaudited financial statements do not conform to GAAP (which includes adequate disclosure), the CPA should ask the client to revise the statements. If the client refuses, the CPA should describe the departure in a disclaimer by (1) specifically referring to the nature of the departure and (2) if practicable, stating the effects of the departure on the financial statements or including the information that is needed in order to provide adequate disclosure.

1. If the effects of the departure cannot be reasonably determined, the CPA should state this in the disclaimer. In the case of inadequate disclosure, it may not be practicable for the CPA to include the omitted disclosures in the disclaimer.

2. If the client refuses to revise the statements or accept the disclaimer describing the departure, the CPA should refuse to be associated with the statements. The CPA may find it necessary to withdraw from the engagement.

H. Audited and Unaudited Financial Statements Presented in Comparative Form

1. Documents Filed With the SEC--Unaudited financial statements presented in comparative form with audited financial statements should be clearly marked "unaudited." The auditor's report should not refer to the unaudited statements.

2. In Documents Other Than Those Filed With the SEC--The unaudited financial statements should be clearly marked to indicate they have not been audited and either (a) the report on the prior period should be reissued or (b) the current period's report should contain a separate paragraph which describes the responsibility assumed for the financial statements of the prior period. In either case, the CPA should consider any information that has come to his or her attention during the CPA's current engagement that would help in evaluating the current form and presentation of the prior-period information.

a. Current Period Financial Statements Unaudited, Prior Period Financial Statements Audited--If a separate paragraph is to be used, it should state (1) the prior-period's statements were previously audited; (2) the date of the previous report; (3) the type of opinion that was previously expressed; (4) if it was not unqualified, the substantive reasons for this; and (5) that no auditing procedures have been performed after the date of the previous report.

Exhibit 21--Separate Paragraph

The financial statements for the year ended December 31, 19X1, were audited by us (other accountants) and we (they) expressed an unqualified opinion on them in our (their) report dated March 1, 19X2, but we (they) have not performed any auditing procedures since that date.

b. Financial Statements of the Prior Period Were Not Audited--If a separate paragraph is to be used, it should (1) state the service that was performed in the prior period; (2) state the date of the report on that service; (3) describe any material modifications noted in that report; and (4) state that the scope of the service was less than that of an audit and, therefore, does not provide a basis for the expression of an opinion on the financial statements taken as a whole. When the financial statements are those of a public entity, the separate paragraph should include a disclaimer of opinion or a description of a review. When the prior period statements are for a nonpublic entity and were compiled or reviewed, the separate paragraph should contain an appropriate description of the compilation or review. The unaudited financial statements should be clearly marked to indicate their status.

> Exhibit 22--Separate Paragraph When a Review Was Performed on Financial Statements of the Prior Period and Current Year's Statements Audited
>
> The 19X1 financial statements were reviewed by us (other accountants) and our (their) report thereon, dated March 1, 19X2, stated we (they) were not aware of any material modifications that should be made to those statements for them to be in conformity with generally accepted accounting principles. However, a review is substantially less in scope than an audit and does not provide a basis for the expression of an opinion on the financial statements taken as a whole.

> Exhibit 23--Separate Paragraph When a Compilation Was Performed on Financial Statements of the Prior Period
>
> The 19X1 financial statements were compiled by us (other accountants) and our (their) report thereon, dated March 1, 19X2, stated we (they) did not audit or review those financial statements and, accordingly, express no opinion or other form of assurance on them.

I. Negative Assurance--The CPA should not include statements in the disclaimer that would give negative assurance except as specifically permitted by the AICPA. One permissible area is letters for underwriters.

X. Consideration of an Entity's Ability to Continue as a Going Concern (AU 341, SAS 59)

A. Responsibility--Continuation of an entity as a going concern is assumed in financial reporting in the absence of significant information to the contrary. The auditor is responsible for evaluating information gathered during the audit to determine whether there is substantial doubt about the entity's ability to continue as a going concern for a reasonable period of time. (A reasonable period of time is defined as a period not to exceed one year from the date of the financial statements.)

1. The auditor's evaluation is based on knowledge of events and relevant conditions preceding or existing at the time of the field work.

2. Key information to be considered includes the entity's inability to meet its obligations in a timely manner without substantial disposal of assets outside the normal course of business, restructuring of debt, externally forced revisions of operations, or similar actions. Some examples of nonfinancial factors include the possible loss of key personnel, suppliers, and/or major customers.

B. Audit Procedures--Audit procedures do not need to be designed specifically to identify conditions and events that, when considered in the aggregate, may indicate substantial doubt about the entity's ability to continue as a going concern. The results of auditing procedures designed and performed to achieve other audit objectives should be sufficient for that purpose. The following are examples of procedures which may identify such conditions and events:

1. Analytical procedures.
2. Review of subsequent events.
3. Review of compliance with the terms of debt and loan agreements.
4. Reading of minutes of meetings of stockholders, board of directors, and major committees of the board.
5. Inquiry of an entity's legal counsel about litigation, claims, and assessments.
6. Confirmation with related and third parties of the details of arrangements to provide or maintain financial support.
7. Procedures such as those listed above may identify conditions and events that, when considered in the aggregate, indicate that substantial doubt may exist. Such conditions and events include the following:
    a. Negative Trends--For example, working capital deficiencies, recurring operating losses, negative cash flows from operating activities, or adverse key financial ratios.
    b. Other Indications of Possible Financial Difficulties--For example, default on loan or similar agreements, arrearages in dividends, denial of usual trade credit from suppliers, restructuring of debt, noncompliance with statutory capital requirements, need to seek new sources or methods of financing, or to dispose of substantial assets.
    c. Internal Matters--For example, work stoppages or other labor difficulties, substantial dependence on the success of a particular project, uneconomic long-term commitments, or need to significantly revise operations.
    d. External Matters That Have Occurred--For example, legal proceedings, legislation, or similar matters that might jeopardize an entity's ability to operate; loss of a key franchise, license, or patent; loss of a principal customer or supplier; or uninsured or underinsured catastrophe such as a drought, earthquake, or flood.

C. Conclusions--If, after completing the audit, the auditor finds that conditions and events exist that, when considered in the aggregate, indicate that there could be substantial doubt about the entity's ability to continue as a going concern for a reasonable period of time, the following steps should be taken:

1. The auditor should obtain any additional information available about the conditions and events or about mitigating factors including management's plans.
2. The auditor must consider management's plans in order to evaluate the likelihood of successful implementation.
3. The auditor should consider the adequacy of the disclosure of the doubt about the entity's ability to continue and include an explanatory paragraph following the opinion paragraph in the audit report.
4. If the auditor concludes that substantial doubt does not exist, the auditor should consider the disclosure of the information that triggered concern about the entity's ability to continue as a going concern for a reasonable period of time and outline mitigating circumstances including management's plans.

D. Management's Plans--Management's plans for dealing with the adverse effects of the conditions and events must be considered when there is substantial doubt regarding the entity's ability to continue.

The auditor should obtain information about the plans and decide whether it is likely the adverse effects will be mitigated for a reasonable period of time and that such plans can be effectively implemented. The auditor's consideration relating to management's plans may include the following:

1. Plans to Dispose of Assets

    a. Restrictions on disposal of assets, such as covenants limiting such transactions in loan or similar agreements or encumbrances against assets.

    b. Apparent marketability of assets that management plans to sell.

    c. Possible direct or indirect effects of disposal of assets.

2. Plans to Borrow Money or Restructure Debt

    a. Availability of debt financing, including existing or committed credit arrangements, such as lines of credit or arrangements for factoring receivables or sale-leaseback of assets.

    b. Existing or committed arrangements to restructure or subordinate debt or to guarantee loans to the entity.

    c. Existing restrictions on additional borrowing or the sufficiency of available collateral.

3. Plans to Reduce or Delay Expenditures

    a. Apparent feasibility of plans to reduce overhead or administrative expenditures, to postpone maintenance or research and development projects, or to lease rather than purchase assets.

    b. Possible direct or indirect effects of reduced or delayed expenditures.

4. Plans to Increase Ownership Equity

    a. Apparent feasibility of plans to increase ownership equity, including existing or committed arrangements to raise additional capital.

    b. Existing or committed arrangements to reduce current dividend requirements or to accelerate cash distributions from affiliates or other investors.

E. Prospective Financial Information--When prospective financial information is significant to management's plans, the auditor should request management to provide that information and should consider the adequacy of support for significant assumptions underlying that information. The auditor should give particular attention to assumptions that are (1) material to the prospective financial statements, (2) especially sensitive or susceptible to change, or (3) inconsistent with historical trends. The auditor's consideration should include reading the information and the underlying assumptions, comparing the prospective information in prior periods with actual results, and comparing prospective information for the current period with actual results to date.

F. Disclosure--If the auditor concludes that substantial doubt about the entity's ability to continue as a going concern exists, the auditor must consider disclosure of the conditions or events in the financial statements. Information that might be disclosed include the following:

1. Pertinent conditions and events giving rise to the assessment of substantial doubt about the entity's ability to continue as a going concern for a reasonable period of time.

2. The possible effects of such conditions and events.

3. Management's evaluation of the significance of those conditions and events and any mitigating factors.

4. Possible discontinuance of operations.

5. Management's plans (including relevant prospective financial information).

6. Information about the recoverability or classification of recorded asset amounts or the amounts or classification of liabilities.

G. Audit Report--The audit report should include an explanatory paragraph following the opinion paragraph if the auditor concludes that substantial doubt about the entity's ability to continue as a going concern does exist. If the auditor concludes that the entity's disclosures regarding its ability to continue as a going concern for a reasonable time are inadequate, misleading, or a departure from GAAP, a qualified or an adverse opinion should be issued.

H. Comparison With Prior Financial Statements--Substantial doubt about an entity's ability to continue as a going concern that arose in the current period should not affect the auditor's report on the financial statements of prior periods used for comparison with current financial statements. If substantial doubt existed in the prior period, but has been alleviated in the current period, the explanatory paragraph following the opinion paragraph in the auditor's report should not be repeated.

I. Future Occurrences--The auditor is not expected to predict future conditions or events. If an entity ceases to exist within a year of receiving an audit report which does not refer to substantial doubt about the entity's ability to continue as a going concern, it does not necessarily indicate an inadequate performance by the auditor. The absence of a reference to substantial doubt should not be interpreted as an assurance of the entity's ability to continue as a going concern.

PART THREE: REPORTING ON CERTAIN ADDITIONAL INFORMATION

I. Other Information in Documents Containing Audited Financial Statements (AU 550)

A. Applicability--Applies to: (1) annual reports for owners of the company, annual reports of charitable organizations that are distributed to the public, and annual reports filed with regulatory authorities under the Securities Exchange Act of 1934; or (2) other documents the auditor devotes attention to at the client's request. This section does not apply to reports filed under the Securities Act of 1933 or to other information on which the auditor is engaged to express an opinion.

B. Responsibilities--Auditor's responsibility does not extend beyond the financial information that has been identified in the report. The auditor has no obligation to perform any procedures to corroborate other information that is contained in documents (e.g., annual report) that contain the financial statements the auditor is reporting on. However, the auditor should read the information and consider whether there appear to be any material inconsistencies between the other data (or its presentation) and the financial statements.

1. Material Inconsistency--When the auditor concludes that a material inconsistency exists, the auditor must decide whether the financial statements, the report, or both require revision. If the auditor decides that they do not, but that the other information does require revision, the client should be requested to revise the other information. If the client refuses, the auditor should consider revising the report to describe the material inconsistency, withholding the use of the report in the document, and, possibly, withdrawing from the engagement.

2. Material Misstatement--While reading the other information, the auditor may become aware of information the auditor believes is a material misstatement of fact although it is not a material inconsistency. The matter should be discussed with the client. If the auditor continues to feel there is a material misstatement, the auditor should propose that the client consult with some other party such as its legal counsel. If the auditor still is not satisfied, consideration should be given to notifying the client of these views in writing and consulting with legal counsel.

II. Supplementary Information Required by the FASB or the GASB (AU 558, SAS 52)

A. Applicability--Some FASB (Financial Accounting Standards Board) and GASB (Governmental Accounting Standards Board) requirements call for supplementary information outside of the basic financial statements. SAS 52 applies to an audit conducted according to GAAS of financial statements that are included in a document that should contain such information. It does not apply if the auditor has been engaged to audit the supplementary information.

1. Voluntary Inclusion--Although not required to do so, a company may decide to include supplementary information the FASB or the GASB requires of others in a document of its own that contains audited financial statements. In this situation, this Statement applies unless (a) the client clearly indicates that the auditor has not applied the procedures that are contained in this Statement, or (b) the auditor includes a disclaimer on the information in the report on the audited financial statements.

2. *Other Information in Documents Containing Audited Financial Statements* (AU 550, SAS 8), applies when the information is included voluntarily, but the auditor does not apply the procedures described in this Statement.

B. Involvement With Information Outside of the Financial Statements--While GAAS does not require the auditor to audit information that is outside the basic financial statements, the auditor's responsibility with respect to this information depends on the information and the documents in which they appear. For example, SAS 8 applies to other information that is included in annual reports but not required by the FASB.

C. Involvement With Supplementary Information Required by the FASB or the GASB--This information is unique from other types of information presented outside of the basic financial statements because (1) the FASB or the GASB consider the information to be an essential part of the financial reporting of certain entities, and (2) guidelines for measuring and presenting the information have been established. Therefore, the auditor should apply certain limited procedures to the supplementary information. Any deficiencies in, or the omission of, such information should be reported.

1. Procedures--The auditor should first consider whether the FASB or the GASB requires supplementary information in the circumstances. If so, the auditor should ordinarily:

   a. Inquire of Management about the methods used in preparing the information. This includes (1) whether FASB or GASB prescribed guidelines were followed in measuring and presenting the information; (2) whether there has been a change (from the prior period) in the methods used in measuring and presenting the information (and if so, the reasons why); and (3) any significant assumptions or interpretations that underlie the measurement or presentation.

   b. Compare the information for consistency with (1) the responses management gives to the inquiries above; (2) the audited financial statements; and (3) other knowledge that was obtained during the audit engagement.

   c. Consider whether representations in the supplementary information required by the FASB or the GASB should be included in specific written representations from management gathered per SAS 19 (AU 333), *Client Representations.*

   d. Apply additional procedures if prescribed by other Statements for specific types of supplementary information required by the FASB or GASB.

   e. Make additional inquiries if the auditor feels the information gathered through the foregoing procedures may not meet the guidelines.

2. Circumstances That Require Reporting--The auditor usually will <u>not</u> refer to the supplementary information or to the auditor's limited procedures in the audit report, since the auditor has not audited the information and it is not a required part of the basic financial statements. However, an explanatory paragraph should be added to the report if (a) supplementary information required by the FASB or GASB is omitted (the auditor does not need to present the information); (b) the auditor feels that the measurement or presentation is materially different from that prescribed by the FASB or GASB; (c) the auditor cannot complete the procedures prescribed in 1., above; or (d) the auditor is unable to remove substantial doubts about whether the supplementary information conforms to prescribed guidelines. The occurrence of any of these four circumstances will not affect the auditor's opinion on the basic financial statements since the supplementary information does not affect the standards that apply to the basic statements. Furthermore, the auditor need not present the supplementary information if it is omitted by the entity. Additional paragraphs that might be included in the auditor's report are presented below.

<u>Exhibit 24</u>--Omission of Supplementary Information Required by the FASB or GASB

The (Company or Government Unit) has not presented (describe the supplementary information required by the FASB or GASB in the circumstances) that the (Financial or Governmental) Accounting Standards Board has determined is necessary to supplement, although not required to be part of, the basic financial statements.

<u>Exhibit 25</u>--Material Departures From Guidelines

The (specifically identify the supplementary information) on page XX is not a required part of the basic financial statements, and we did not audit and do not express an opinion on such information. However, we have applied certain limited procedures, which consisted principally of inquiries of management regarding the methods of measurement and presentation of the supplementary information. As a result of such limited procedures, we believe that the (specifically identify the supplementary information) is not in conformity with guidelines established by the (Financial or Governmental) Accounting Standards Board because (describe the material departure[s] from the FASB or GASB guidelines).

<u>Exhibit 26</u>--Prescribed Procedures Not Completed

The (specifically identify the supplementary information) on page XX is not a required part of the basic financial statements, and we did not audit and do not express an opinion on such information. Further, we were unable to apply to the information certain procedures prescribed by professional standards because (state the reasons).

a. Facts Known to the Auditor--Even if the auditor cannot complete the prescribed procedures, the auditor may feel that the supplementary information has not been properly measured and/or presented. In this case, the auditor should suggest appropriate revision and, if not revised, the auditor should describe the nature of any material departure(s) in the audit report.

b. Client Disclosure--The auditor should <u>expand</u> the report to include a <u>disclaimer</u> on the supplementary information if the client includes statements with the supplementary information that the auditor performed some procedures on the information, but fails to state that an opinion is not expressed by the auditor on the information.

c. Presentation of Supplementary Information--Generally, supplementary information required by the FASB or GASB should be presented distinct from the audited financial statements and should be separately identified from other information outside of the financial statements (and which is not required by the FASB or GASB).

- If management chooses to include the supplementary information in the basic financial statements, the information should be clearly marked as unaudited. If it is not so marked, the audit report should be expanded to include a disclaimer on the supplementary information.

III. Segment Information (AU 435, SAS 21)

A. *Financial Reporting for Segments of a Business Enterprise* (SFAS 14)--Requires that certain information about an entity's operation in different industries, its foreign operations and export sales, and its major customers be included in annual financial statements.

B. Objective of Auditing Procedures Applied to Segment Information--Provides the auditor with a reasonable basis for concluding whether the information is presented in conformity with SFAS 14 in relation to the financial statements taken as a whole. The auditor performing an audit of financial statements in accordance with generally accepted auditing standards considers segment information, as other informative disclosures, in relation to the financial statements taken as a whole, and is not required to apply auditing procedures that would be necessary to express a separate opinion on the segment information.

C. Auditing Procedures When Financial Statements Include Segment Information

1. The materiality of the segment information should be evaluated primarily by relating the dollar magnitude of the information to the financial statements taken as a whole, along with certain qualitative judgments. The auditor applies the concept of materiality in determining the nature, timing, and extent of the auditing procedures.

2. In planning the audit, the auditor should modify or redirect selected audit tests to be applied to the financial statements taken as a whole when necessary. Factors such as the following should be considered by the auditor in determining whether the procedures should be modified or redirected:

   a. Internal control structure and the degree of integration, centralization, and uniformity of the accounting records.

   b. The nature, number, and relative size of industry segments and geographic areas.

   c. The nature and number of subsidiaries or divisions in each industry segment and geographic area.

   d. The accounting principles used for the industry segments and geographic areas.

   The tests of the underlying accounting records should include consideration of whether the entity's revenue, operating expenses, and identifiable assets are appropriately classified among industry segments and geographic areas.

3. The auditor should also apply the following procedures to segment information presented in financial statements:

   a. Inquire of management concerning its methods of determining segment information, and evaluate the reasonableness of those methods.

   b. Inquire as to the bases of accounting for sales and transfers among industry segments and among geographic areas, and test, to the extent considered necessary, those sales or transfers for conformity with the bases of accounting disclosed.

   c. Test the disaggregation of the entity's financial statements into segment information. The tests should include the following:

(1) An evaluation of the entity's application of the various percentage tests specified in SFAS 14. (These percentage tests relate mainly to the reportability of the segments.)

(2) Application of analytical procedures to the segment information to identify and provide a basis for inquiry about relationships and individual items that appear to be unusual.

d. Inquire as to the methods of allocating operating expenses incurred and identifiable assets used jointly by two or more segments, evaluate whether those methods are reasonable, and test the allocations to the extent considered necessary.

e. Determine whether the segment information has been presented consistently from period to period and, if not, whether the nature and effect of the inconsistency are disclosed and, if applicable, whether the information has been retroactively restated in conformity with SFAS 14.

D. The Auditor's Standard Report on Financial Statements--Prepared in conformity with generally accepted accounting principles implicitly applies to segment information included in those statements in the same manner that it applies to other informative disclosures in the financial statements that are not clearly marked as "unaudited." The auditor's standard report would not refer to segment information unless the audit revealed a misstatement or omission, or a change in accounting principle, relating to the segment information that is material in relation to the financial statements taken as a whole, or the auditor was unable to apply the auditing procedures that are considered necessary in the circumstances.

E. Misstatement in the Segment Information--If the audit reveals a misstatement in the segment information that is material in relation to the financial statements taken as a whole and that misstatement is not corrected, the auditor should modify his or her opinion (qualified or adverse) on the financial statements because of a departure from generally accepted accounting principles. The following is an example of an auditor's report qualified because of a misstatement of segment information.

Exhibit 27

(Same first and second paragraphs as the standard report)

(Explanatory paragraph)

With respect to the segment information in Note X, $_____ of the operating expenses of Industry A were incurred jointly by Industries A and B. In our opinion, generally accepted accounting principles require that those operating expenses be allocated between Industries A and B. The effect of the failure to allocate those operating expenses has been to understate the operating profit of Industry A and to overstate the operating profit of Industry B by an amount that has not been determined.

(Opinion paragraph)

In our opinion, except for the effects of not allocating certain common operating expenses between Industries A and B, as discussed in the preceding paragraph, the financial statements referred to above present fairly . . .

F. Omission of Segment Information--If the entity declines to include in the financial statements part or all of the segment information that the auditor believes is required to be disclosed, the auditor should modify the opinion on the financial statements because of inadequate disclosure and should describe the type of information omitted. The auditor is not required to provide the omitted information in the report. The following is an example of an auditor's report qualified because of an omission of segment information.

> Exhibit 28
>
> (Same first and second paragraphs as the standard report)
>
> (Explanatory paragraph)
>
> The Company declined to present segment information for the year ended December 31, 19XX. In our opinion, presentation of segment information concerning the Company's operations in different industries, its foreign operations and export sales, and its major customers, is required by generally accepted accounting principles. The omission of segment information results in an incomplete presentation of the Company's financial statements.
>
> (Opinion paragraph)
>
> In our opinion, except for the omission of segment information, as discussed in the preceding paragraph, the financial statements referred to above present fairly . . .

G. Consistency--SFAS 14 requires that the nature and effect of the following changes be disclosed in the period of change:

1. A change in the basis of accounting for sales or transfers among industry segments or among geographic areas, or in the methods of allocating operating expenses or identifiable assets among industry segments or geographic areas.

2. A change in the method of determining or presenting a measure of profitability for some or all of the segments.

3. A change in accounting principle.

4. A change requiring retroactive restatement due to the following:

   a. The financial statements of the entity as a whole have been retroactively restated.

   b. The method of grouping products and services into industry segments or of grouping foreign operations into geographic areas is changed, and the change affects the segment information disclosed.

If the nature and effect of a change are not disclosed or, if applicable, the segment information is not retroactively restated, the auditor should modify the opinion because of the departure from generally accepted accounting principles. The following is an example of an auditor's report qualified because of an entity's failure to disclose the nature and effect of a change in the basis of accounting for sales between industry segments.

Exhibit 29

(Same first and second paragraph as the standard report)

(Explanatory paragraph)

In 19XX, the Company changed the basis of accounting for sales between its industry segments from the market price method to the negotiated price method, but declined to disclose the nature and effect of this change on its segment information. In our opinion, disclosure of the nature and effect of this change, which has not been determined, is required by generally accepted accounting principles.

(Opinion paragraph)

In our opinion, except for the omission of the information discussed in the preceding paragraph, the financial statements referred to above present fairly . . .

H. Scope Limitation Regarding Segment Information--An entity may represent to the auditor that it does not have industry segments, foreign operations, export sales, or major customers required to be disclosed by SFAS 14. If the auditor is unable to reach a conclusion, based on knowledge of the entity's business, whether the entity has such industry segments, foreign operations, export sales, or major customers, and the entity declines to develop the information the auditor considers necessary to reach a conclusion, the auditor should indicate in the scope paragraph of the report the limitation on the audit and should qualify the opinion on the financial statements taken as a whole. The following is an example of an auditor's report qualified because of the auditor's inability to conclude whether the entity is required to present segment information.

Exhibit 30

(Same first paragraph as the standard report)

(Scope paragraph)

. . . Except as discussed in the following paragraph, we conducted our audit in accordance with . . .

(Explanatory paragraph)

The Company has not developed the information we consider necessary to reach a conclusion as to whether the presentation of segment information concerning the Company's operations in different industries, its foreign operations and export sales, and its major customers, is necessary to conform to generally accepted accounting principles.

(Opinion paragraph)

In our opinion, except for the possible omission of segment information, the financial statements referred to above present fairly . . .

I. Auditor Is Unable to Apply Auditing Procedures to Reported Segment Information--The auditor should also qualify the opinion on the financial statements taken as a whole if the auditor is unable to apply to reported segment information the auditing procedures that the auditor considers necessary in the circumstances. The following is an example of an auditor's report qualified because the entity has specified that the auditor should not apply to reported segment information the auditing procedures that the auditor considered necessary in the circumstances.

<u>Exhibit 31</u>

(Scope paragraph)

. . . Except as discussed in the following paragraph, we conducted our audit in accordance with . . .

(Explanatory paragraph)

In accordance with the Company's request, our audit of the financial statements did not include the segment information presented in Note X concerning the Company's operations in different industries, its foreign operations and export sales, and its major customers.

(Opinion paragraph)

In our opinion, except for the effects of such adjustments or disclosures, if any, as might have been determined to be necessary had we applied to the segment information the procedures we considered necessary in the circumstances, the financial statements referred to above present fairly . . .

J. <u>Reporting Separately on Segment Information</u>--An audit of segment information for the purpose of reporting on it separately is more extensive than if the same information were considered in conjunction with an audit of the financial statements taken as a whole. This is true because, in a separate report on segment information, the measurement of materiality is related to the segment information itself rather than the financial statements taken as a whole. Whether segment information is presented voluntarily or because it is required, the auditor's report on the segment information should state whether it is presented in conformity with generally accepted accounting principles.

NOTES

CHAPTER 40—REPORTS ON AUDITED FINANCIAL STATEMENTS

Problem 40-1 MULTIPLE CHOICE QUESTIONS (125 to 150 minutes)

1. The first standard of reporting requires that "the report shall state whether the financial statements are presented in conformity with generally accepted accounting principles." This should be construed to require
a. A statement of fact by the auditor.
b. An opinion by the auditor.
c. An implied measure of fairness.
d. An objective measure of compliance.
(11/83, Aud., #16, 9911)

2. Several sources of GAAP consulted by an auditor are in conflict as to the application of an accounting principle. Which of the following should the auditor consider the most authoritative?
a. FASB Technical Bulletins.
b. AICPA Accounting Interpretations.
c. FASB Statements of Financial Accounting Concepts.
d. AICPA Technical Practice Aids.
(11/93, Aud., #52, 4289)

3. Which of the following requires recognition in the auditor's opinion as to consistency?
a. The correction of an error in the prior year's financial statements resulting from a mathematical mistake in capitalizing interest.
b. The change from the cost method to the equity method of accounting for investments in common stock.
c. A change in the estimate of provisions for warranty costs.
d. A change in depreciation method which has **no** effect on current year's financial statements but is certain to affect future years.
(5/86, Aud., #50, 0382)

4. In which of the following situations would the auditor **not** issue a report that contains an explanatory paragraph identifying a lack of consistency?
a. A change in the method of accounting for specific subsidiaries that comprise the group of companies for which consolidated statements are presented.
b. A change from an accounting principle that is **not** generally accepted to one that is generally accepted.
c. A change in the percentage used to calculate the provision for warranty expense.
d. Correction of a mistake in the application of a generally accepted accounting principle.
(5/85, Aud., #6, 9911)

5. If a client makes a change in accounting principle that is inseparable from the effect of a change in estimate, this material event should be accounted for as a change in
a. Estimate and the auditor would report a consistency exception.
b. Principle and the auditor would report a consistency exception.
c. Estimate and the auditor would **not** modify the report.
d. Principle and the auditor would **not** modify the report.
(5/83, Aud., #29, 9911)

6. Miller Co. uses the first-in, first-out method of costing for its international subsidiary's inventory and the last-in, first-out method of costing for its domestic inventory. Under these circumstances, Miller should issue an auditor's report with an
a. "Except for" qualified opinion.
b. Unqualified opinion.
c. Explanatory paragraph as to consistency.
d. Opinion modified as to consistency.
(11/91, Aud., #28, 2296)

7. If the financial statements, including accompanying notes, fail to disclose information that is required by generally accepted accounting principles, the auditor should express either a(an)
a. "Except for" qualified opinion or an adverse opinion.
b. Adverse opinion or a "subject to" qualified opinion.
c. "Subject to" qualified opinion or an unqualified opinion with a separate explanatory paragraph.
d. Unqualified opinion with a separate explanatory paragraph or an "except for" qualified opinion.
(5/87, Aud., #42, 0370)

7A. In which of the following circumstances would an auditor be most likely to express an adverse opinion?
a. The chief executive officer refuses the auditor access to minutes of board of directors' meetings.
b. Tests of controls show that the entity's internal control structure is so poor that it **cannot** be relied upon.

c. The financial statements are **not** in conformity with the FASB Statements regarding the capitalization of leases.
d. Information comes to the auditor's attention that raises substantial doubt about the entity's ability to continue as a going concern.

(5/94, Aud., #87, 4752)

8. Which of the following representations does an auditor make explicitly and which implicitly when issuing an unqualified opinion?

	Conformity with GAAP	Adequacy of disclosure
a.	Explicitly	Explicitly
b.	Implicitly	Implicitly
c.	Implicitly	Explicitly
d.	Explicitly	Implicitly

(5/88, Aud., #43, 0363)

9. Green, CPA, was engaged to audit the financial statements of Essex Co. after its fiscal year had ended. The timing of Green's appointment as auditor and the start of field work made confirmation of accounts receivable by direct communication with the debtors ineffective. However, Green applied other procedures and was satisfied as to the reasonableness of the account balances. Green's auditor's report most likely contained a(an)

a. Unqualified opinion.
b. Unqualified opinion with an explanatory paragraph.
c. Qualified opinion due to a scope limitation.
d. Qualified opinion due to a departure from generally accepted auditing standards.

(5/93, Aud., #50, 3946)

10. The fourth standard of reporting requires the auditor's report to contain either an expression of opinion regarding the financial statements taken as a whole or an assertion to the effect that an opinion cannot be expressed. The objective of the fourth standard is to prevent

a. Misinterpretations regarding the degree of responsibility the auditor is assuming.
b. An auditor from reporting on one basic financial statement and **not** the others.
c. An auditor from expressing different opinions on each of the basic financial statements.
d. Restrictions on the scope of the examination, whether imposed by the client, or by the inability to obtain evidence.

(11/90, Aud., #7, 0325)

10A. For an entity that does **not** receive governmental financial assistance, an auditor's standard report on financial statements generally would **not** refer to

a. Significant estimates made by management.
b. An assessment of the entity's accounting principles.
c. Management's responsibility for the financial statements.
d. The entity's internal control structure.

(5/94, Aud., #71, 4736)

10B. When single-year financial statements are presented, an auditor ordinarily would express an unqualified opinion in an unmodified report if the

a. Auditor is unable to obtain audited financial statements supporting the entity's investment in a foreign affiliate.
b. Entity declines to present a statement of cash flows with its balance sheet and related statements of income and retained earnings.
c. Auditor wishes to emphasize an accounting matter affecting the comparability of the financial statements with those of the prior year.
d. Prior year's financial statements were audited by another CPA whose report, which expressed an unqualified opinion, is **not** presented.

(5/94, Aud., #74, 4739)

11. How are management's responsibility and the auditor's responsibility represented in the standard auditor's report?

	Management's responsibility	Auditor's responsibility
a.	Explicitly	Explicitly
b.	Implicitly	Implicitly
c.	Implicitly	Explicitly
d.	Explicitly	Implicitly

(11/89, Aud., #3, 0343)

12. How does an auditor make the following representations when issuing the standard auditor's report on comparative financial statements?

	Examination of evidence on a test basis	Consistent application of accounting principles
a.	Explicitly	Explicitly
b.	Implicitly	Implicitly
c.	Implicitly	Explicitly
d.	Explicitly	Implicitly

(11/91, Aud., #21, 2289)

13. When management does **not** provide reasonable justification that a change in accounting principle is preferable and it presents comparative financial statements, the auditor should express a qualified opinion

a. Only in the year of the accounting principle change.
b. Each year that the financial statements initially reflecting the change are presented.
c. Each year until management changes back to the accounting principle formerly used.
d. Only if the change is to an accounting principle that is **not** generally accepted.
(11/89, Aud., #14, 0350)

13A. Which paragraphs of an auditor's standard report on financial statements should refer to generally accepted auditing standards (GAAS) and generally accepted accounting principles (GAAP) in which paragraphs?

	GAAS	GAAP
a.	Opening	Scope
b.	Scope	Scope
c.	Scope	Opinion
d.	Opening	Opinion

(5/94, Aud., #77, 4742)

13B. The existence of audit risk is recognized by the statement in the auditor's standard report that the
a. Auditor is responsible for expressing an opinion on the financial statements, which are the responsibility of management.
b. Financial statements are presented fairly, in all material respects, in conformity with GAAP.
c. Audit includes examining, on a test basis, evidence supporting the amounts and disclosures in the financial statements.
d. Auditor obtains reasonable assurance about whether the financial statements are free of material misstatement. (11/94, Aud., #9, 5082)

14. In which of the following circumstances would an auditor most likely add an explanatory paragraph to the standard report while **not** affecting the auditor's unqualified opinion?
a. The auditor is asked to report on the balance sheet, but **not** on the other basic financial statements.
b. There is substantial doubt about the entity's ability to continue as a going concern.
c. Management's estimates of the effects of future events are unreasonable.
d. Certain transactions **cannot** be tested because of management's records retention policy.
(5/93, Aud., #47, 3943)

15. When an entity changes its method of accounting for income taxes, which has a material effect on comparability, the auditor should refer to the change in an explanatory paragraph added to the auditor's report. This paragraph should identify the nature of the change and
a. Explain why the change is justified under generally accepted accounting principles.
b. Describe the cumulative effect of the change on the audited financial statements.
c. State the auditor's explicit concurrence with or opposition to the change.
d. Refer to the financial statement note that discusses the change in detail.
(5/93, Aud., #49, 3945)

16. In the auditor's report, the principal auditor decides not to make reference to another CPA who audited a client's subsidiary. The principal auditor could justify this decision if, among other requirements, the principal auditor
a. Issues an unqualified opinion on the consolidated financial statements.
b. Learns that the other CPA issued an unqualified opinion on the subsidiary's financial statements.
c. Is unable to review the audit programs and working papers of the other CPA.
d. Is satisfied as to the independence and professional reputation of the other CPA.
(5/93, Aud., #55, 3951)

16A. A principal auditor decides not to refer to the audit of another CPA who audited a subsidiary of the principal auditor's client. After making inquiries about the other CPA's professional reputation and independence, the principal auditor most likely would
a. Add an explanatory paragraph to the auditor's report indicating that the subsidiary's financial statements are **not** material to the consolidated financial statements.
b. Document in the engagement letter that the principal auditor assumes **no** responsibility for the other CPA's work and opinion.
c. Obtain written permission from the other CPA to omit the reference in the principal auditor's report.
d. Contact the other CPA and review the audit programs and working papers pertaining to the subsidiary. (5/95, Aud., #77, 5695)

17. In which of the following situations would an auditor ordinarily issue an unqualified audit opinion without an explanatory paragraph?
a. The auditor wishes to emphasize that the entity had significant related party transactions.
b. The auditor decides to make reference to the report of another auditor as a basis, in part, for the auditor's opinion.

c. The entity issues financial statements that present financial position and results of operations, but omits the statement of cash flows.
d. The auditor has substantial doubt about the entity's ability to continue as a going concern, but the circumstances are fully disclosed in the financial statements. (11/90, Aud., #6, 0324)

17A. An auditor includes a separate paragraph in an otherwise unmodified report to emphasize that the entity being reported on had significant transactions with related parties. The inclusion of this separate paragraph
a. Is considered an "except for" qualification of the opinion.
b. Violates generally accepted auditing standards if this information is already disclosed in footnotes to the financial statements.
c. Necessitates a revision of the opinion paragraph to include the phrase "with the foregoing explanation."
d. Is appropriate and would **not** negate the unqualified opinion. (5/94, Aud., #69, 4734)

18. When a principal auditor decides to make reference to another auditor's audit, the principal auditor's report should always indicate clearly, in the introductory, scope, and opinion paragraphs, the
a. Magnitude of the portion of the financial statements audited by the other auditor.
b. Disclaimer of responsibility concerning the portion of the financial statements audited by the other auditor.
c. Name of the other auditor.
d. Division of responsibility.(11/89, Aud., #1, 0341)

18A. Reference in a principal auditor's report to the fact that part of the audit was performed by another auditor most likely would be an indication of the
a. Divided responsibility between the auditors who conducted the audits of the components of the overall financial statements.
b. Lack of materiality of the portion of the financial statements audited by the other auditor.
c. Principal auditor's recognition of the other auditor's competence, reputation, and professional certification.
d. Different opinions the auditors are expressing on the components of the financial statements that each audited. (5/94, Aud., #65, 4730)

19. In which of the following situations would a principal auditor **least** likely make reference to another auditor who audited a subsidiary of the entity?
a. The other auditor was retained by the principal auditor and the work was performed under the principal auditor's guidance and control.
b. The principal auditor finds it impracticable to review the other auditor's work or otherwise be satisfied as to the other auditor's work.
c. The financial statements audited by the other auditor are material to the consolidated financial statements covered by the principal auditor's opinion.
d. The principal auditor is unable to be satisfied as to the independence and professional reputation of the other auditor.
(11/91, Aud., #30, 2298)

20. If an auditor is satisfied that there is only a remote likelihood of a loss resulting from the resolution of a matter involving an uncertainty, the auditor should express a(an)
a. Unqualified opinion.
b. Unqualified opinion with a separate explanatory paragraph.
c. Qualified opinion or disclaimer of opinion, depending upon the materiality of the loss.
d. Qualified opinion or disclaimer of opinion, depending on whether the uncertainty is adequately disclosed. (5/91, Aud., #44, 0315)

21. An explanatory paragraph following the opinion paragraph of an auditor's report describes an uncertainty as follows:

As discussed in Note X to the financial statements, the Company is a defendant in a lawsuit alleging infringement of certain patent rights and claiming damages. Discovery proceedings are in progress. The ultimate outcome of the litigation cannot presently be determined. Accordingly, no provision for any liability that may result upon adjudication has been made in the accompanying financial statements.

What type of opinion should the auditor express under these circumstances?
a. Unqualified.
b. "Subject to" qualified.
c. "Except for" qualified.
d. Disclaimer. (5/90, Aud., #12, 0333)

22. When there has been a change in accounting principle that materially affects the comparability of the comparative financial statements presented and the auditor concurs with the change, the auditor should

	Concur explicitly with the change	Issue an "except for" qualified opinion	Refer to the change in an explanatory paragraph
a.	No	No	Yes
b.	Yes	No	Yes
c.	Yes	Yes	No
d.	No	Yes	No

(11/90, Aud., #8, 0326)

22A. When there has been a change in accounting principles, but the effect of the change on the comparability of the financial statements is **not** material, the auditor should

a. Refer to the change in an explanatory paragraph.
b. Explicitly concur that the change is preferred.
c. Not refer to consistency in the auditor's report.
d. Refer to the change in the opinion paragraph.

(5/94, Aud., #73, 4738)

23. The following explanatory paragraph was included in an auditor's report to indicate a lack of consistency:

"As discussed in note T to the financial statements, the company changed its method of computing depreciation in 1990."

How should the auditor report on this matter if the auditor concurred with the change?

	Type of opinion	Location of explanatory paragraph
a.	Unqualified	Before opinion paragraph
b.	Unqualified	After opinion paragraph
c.	Qualified	Before opinion paragraph
d.	Qualified	After opinion paragraph

(11/91, Aud., #18, 2286)

24. The auditor who wishes to point out that the entity has significant transactions with related parties should disclose this fact in

a. An explanatory paragraph to the auditor's report.
b. An explanatory footnote to the financial statements.
c. The body of the financial statements.
d. The "Summary of significant accounting policies" section of the financial statements.

(11/87, Aud., #58, 9911)

25. An auditor includes a separate paragraph in an otherwise unqualified report to emphasize that the financial statements are not comparable to those of prior years due to a court-ordered divestiture that is already fully explained in the notes to the financial statements. The inclusion of this paragraph

a. Should be followed by an "except for" consistency modification in the opinion paragraph.
b. Requires a revision of the opinion paragraph to include the phrase "with the foregoing explanation."
c. Is **not** appropriate and may confuse the readers or lead them to believe the report was qualified.
d. Is appropriate and would **not** negate the unqualified opinion. (11/88, Aud., #17, 9911)

26. Eagle Company's financial statements contain a departure from generally accepted accounting principles because, due to unusual circumstances, the statements would otherwise be misleading. The auditor should express an opinion that is

a. Unqualified but **not** mention the departure in the auditor's report.
b. Unqualified and describe the departure in a separate paragraph.
c. Qualified and describe the departure in a separate paragraph.
d. Qualified or adverse, depending on materiality, and describe the departure in a separate paragraph. (11/90, Aud., #12, 0329)

26A. When financial statements contain a departure from GAAP because, due to unusual circumstances, the statements would otherwise be misleading, the auditor should explain the unusual circumstances in a separate paragraph and express an opinion that is

a. Unqualified.
b. Qualified.
c. Adverse.
d. Qualified or adverse, depending on materiality.

(5/94, Aud., #75, 4740)

27. Management believes and the auditor is satisfied that the chance of a material loss resulting from the resolution of a lawsuit is more than remote but less than probable. Which of the following matters should the auditor consider in deciding whether to add an explanatory paragraph?

	Likelihood that the loss is closer to probable than remote	Magnitude by which the loss exceeds the auditor's materiality
a.	Yes	Yes
b.	Yes	No
c.	No	Yes
d.	No	No

(11/93, Aud., #47, 4284)

27A. Management believes and the auditor is satisfied that a material loss probably will occur when pending litigation is resolved. Management is unable to make a reasonable estimate of the amount or range of the potential loss, but fully discloses the situation in the notes to the financial statements. If management does **not** make an accrual in the financial statements, the auditor should express a(an)

a. Qualified opinion due to a scope limitation.
b. Qualified opinion due to a departure from GAAP.
c. Unqualified opinion with an explanatory paragraph.
d. Unqualified opinion in a standard auditor's report. (5/94, Aud., #86, 4751)

28. If a publicly held company issues financial statements that purport to present its financial position and results of operations but omits the statement of cash flows, the auditor ordinarily will express a(an)

a. Disclaimer of opinion.
b. Qualified opinion.
c. Review report.
d. Unqualified opinion with a separate explanatory paragraph. (5/93, Aud., #46, 3942)

29. A limitation on the scope of an audit sufficient to preclude an unqualified opinion will usually result when management

a. Is unable to obtain audited financial statements supporting the entity's investment in a foreign subsidiary.
b. Refuses to disclose in the notes to the financial statements related party transactions authorized by the Board of Directors.
c. Does **not** sign an engagement letter specifying the responsibilities of both the entity and the auditor.
d. Fails to correct a reportable condition communicated to the audit committee after the prior year's audit. (5/93, Aud., #56, 3952)

29A. Due to a scope limitation, an auditor disclaimed an opinion on the financial statements taken as a whole, but the auditor's report included a statement that the current asset portion of the entity's balance sheet was fairly stated. The inclusion of this statement is

a. Not appropriate because it may tend to overshadow the auditor's disclaimer of opinion.
b. Not appropriate because the auditor is prohibited from reporting on only one basic financial statement.
c. Appropriate provided the auditor's scope paragraph adequately describes the scope limitation.
d. Appropriate provided the statement is in a separate paragraph preceding the disclaimer of opinion paragraph. (5/94, Aud., #72, 7437)

30. Delta Life Insurance Co. prepares its financial statements on an accounting basis insurance companies use pursuant to the rules of a state insurance commission. If Wall, CPA, Delta's auditor, discovers that the statements are **not** suitably titled, Wall should

a. Disclose any reservations in an explanatory paragraph and qualify the opinion.
b. Apply to the state insurance commission for an advisory opinion.
c. Issue a special statutory basis report that clearly disclaims any opinion.
d. Explain in the notes to the financial statements the terminology used. (5/93, Aud., #57, 3953)

31. In which of the following situations would an auditor ordinarily choose between expressing an "except for" qualified opinion or an adverse opinion?

a. The auditor did **not** observe the entity's physical inventory and is unable to become satisfied as to its balance by other auditing procedures.
b. The financial statements fail to disclose information that is required by generally accepted accounting principles.
c. The auditor is asked to report only on the entity's balance sheet and **not** on the other basic financial statements.
d. Events disclosed in the financial statements cause the auditor to have substantial doubt about the entity's ability to continue as a going concern. (5/93, Aud., #58, 3954)

32. Tech Company has disclosed an uncertainty due to pending litigation. The auditor's decision to issue a qualified opinion rather than an unqualified opinion with an explanatory paragraph most likely would be determined by the

a. Lack of sufficient evidence.
b. Inability to estimate the amount of loss.
c. Entity's lack of experience with such litigation.
d. Lack of insurance coverage for possible losses from such litigation. (11/90, Aud., #5, 0323)

33. Which of the following phrases should be included in the opinion paragraph when an auditor expresses a qualified opinion?

	When read in connection with Note X	With the foregoing explanation
a.	Yes	No
b.	No	Yes
c.	Yes	Yes
d.	No	No

(11/92, Aud., #46, 2980)

34. An auditor was unable to obtain audited financial statements or other evidence supporting an entity's investment in a foreign subsidiary. Between which of the following opinions should the entity's auditor choose?
a. Adverse and unqualified with an explanatory paragraph added.
b. Disclaimer and unqualified with an explanatory paragraph added.
c. Qualified and adverse.
d. Qualified and disclaimer.
(5/91, Aud., #42, 9911)

34A. When qualifying an opinion because of an insufficiency of audit evidence, an auditor should refer to the situation in the

	Opening (introductory) paragraph	Scope paragraph
a.	No	No
b.	Yes	No
c.	Yes	Yes
d.	No	Yes

(5/94, Aud., #88, 7453)

34B. When disclaiming an opinion due to a client-imposed scope limitation, an auditor should indicate in a separate paragraph why the audit did not comply with generally accepted auditing standards. The auditor should also omit the

	Scope paragraph	Opinion paragraph
a.	No	Yes
b.	Yes	Yes
c.	No	No
d.	Yes	No

(11/93, Aud., #46, 4283)

35. An auditor may reasonably issue an "except for" qualified opinion for a(an)

	Scope limitation	Unjustified accounting change
a.	Yes	No
b.	No	Yes
c.	Yes	Yes
d.	No	No

(11/91, Aud., #16, 2284)

36. Restrictions imposed by a client prohibit the observation of physical inventories, which account for 35% of all assets. Alternative audit procedures cannot be applied, although the auditor was able to examine satisfactory evidence for all other items in the financial statements. The auditor should issue a(an)
a. "Except for" qualified opinion.
b. Disclaimer of opinion.
c. Unqualified opinion with a separate explanatory paragraph.
d. Unqualified opinion with an explanation in the scope paragraph. (11/89, Aud., #4, 9911)

36A. Park, CPA, was engaged to audit the financial statements of Tech Co., a new client, for the year ended December 31, 1993. Park obtained sufficient audit evidence for all of Tech's financial statement items except Tech's opening inventory. Due to inadequate financial records, Park could not verify Tech's January 1, 1993, inventory balances. Park's opinion on Tech's 1993 financial statements most likely will be

	Balance sheet	Income statement
a.	Disclaimer	Disclaimer
b.	Unqualified	Disclaimer
c.	Disclaimer	Adverse
d.	Unqualified	Adverse

(5/94, Aud., #76, 7441)

37. A limitation on the scope of an audit sufficient to preclude an unqualified opinion will usually result when management
a. Presents financial statements that are prepared in accordance with the cash receipts and disbursements basis of accounting.
b. States that the financial statements are **not** intended to be presented in conformity with generally accepted accounting principles.
c. Does **not** make the minutes of the Board of Directors' meetings available to the auditor.
d. Asks the auditor to report on the balance sheet and **not** on the other basic financial statements. (11/89, Aud., #7, 0345)

38. An auditor decides to issue a qualified opinion on an entity's financial statements because a major inadequacy in its computerized accounting records prevents the auditor from applying necessary procedures. The opinion paragraph of the auditor's report should state that the qualification pertains to
a. A client-imposed scope limitation.
b. A departure from generally accepted auditing standards.
c. The possible effects on the financial statements.
d. Inadequate disclosure of necessary information. (11/93, Aud., #49, 4286)

39. When a qualified opinion results from a limitation on the scope of the audit, the situation should be described in an explanatory paragraph
a. Preceding the opinion paragraph and referred to only in the scope paragraph of the auditor's report.
b. Following the opinion paragraph and referred to in both the scope and opinion paragraphs of the auditor's report.
c. Following the opinion paragraph and referred to only in the scope paragraph of the auditor's report.
d. Preceding the opinion paragraph and referred to in both the scope and opinion paragraphs of the auditor's report. (5/90, Aud., #22, 0340)

40. When an auditor qualifies an opinion because of a scope limitation, which paragraph(s) of the auditor's report should indicate that the qualification pertains to the possible effects on the financial statements and **not** to the scope limitation itself?
a. The scope paragraph and the separate explanatory paragraph.
b. The separate explanatory paragraph and the opinion paragraph.
c. The scope paragraph only.
d. The opinion paragraph only.
(5/87, Aud., #50, 0373)

41. When an auditor qualifies an opinion because of the inability to confirm accounts receivable by direct communication with debtors, the wording of the opinion paragraph of the auditor's report should indicate that the qualification pertains to the
a. Limitation on the auditor's scope.
b. Possible effects on the financial statements.
c. Lack of sufficient competent evidential matter.
d. Departure from generally accepted auditing standards. (5/91, Aud., #45, 0316)

42. An auditor has been asked to report on the balance sheet of Kane Company but not on the other basic financial statements. The auditor will have access to all information underlying the basic financial statements. Under these circumstances, the auditor
a. May accept the engagement because such engagements merely involve limited reporting objectives.
b. May accept the engagement but should disclaim an opinion because of an inability to apply the procedures considered necessary.
c. Should refuse the engagement because there is a client-imposed scope limitation.
d. Should refuse the engagement because of a departure from generally accepted auditing standards. (11/87, Aud., #1, 0365)

43. When the client fails to include information that is necessary for the fair presentation of financial statements in the body of the statements or in the related footnotes, it is the responsibility of the auditor to present the information, if practicable, in the auditor's report and issue a(n)
a. Qualified opinion or a disclaimer of opinion.
b. Qualified opinion or an adverse opinion.
c. Adverse opinion or a disclaimer of opinion.
d. Qualified opinion or an unqualified opinion.
(5/83, Aud., #28, 9911)

43A. An auditor concludes that a client's illegal act, which has a material effect on the financial statements, has not been properly accounted for or disclosed. Depending on the materiality of the effect on the financial statements, the auditor should express either a(an)
a. Adverse opinion or a disclaimer of opinion.
b. Qualified opinion or an adverse opinion.
c. Disclaimer of opinion or an unqualified opinion with a separate explanatory paragraph.
d. Unqualified opinion with a separate explanatory paragraph or a qualified opinion.
(5/95, Aud., #13, 5631)

44. Under which of the following circumstances would a disclaimer of opinion **not** be appropriate?
a. The financial statements fail to contain adequate disclosure of related party transactions.
b. The client refuses to permit its attorney to furnish information requested in a letter of audit inquiry.
c. The auditor is engaged after fiscal year-end and is unable to observe physical inventories or apply alternative procedures to verify their balances.
d. The auditor is unable to determine the amounts associated with illegal acts committed by the client's management. (11/92, Aud., #48, 2982)

45. When an auditor qualifies an opinion because of inadequate disclosure, the auditor should describe the nature of the omission in a separate explanatory paragraph and modify the

	Introductory paragraph	Scope paragraph	Opinion paragraph
a.	Yes	No	No
b.	Yes	Yes	No
c.	No	Yes	Yes
d.	No	No	Yes

(5/91, Aud., #46, 0317)

46. Tread Corp. accounts for the effect of a material accounting change prospectively when the inclusion of the cumulative effect of the change is required in the current year. The auditor would choose between expressing a(an)

a. Qualified opinion or a disclaimer of opinion.
b. Disclaimer of opinion or an unqualified opinion with an explanatory paragraph.
c. Unqualified opinion with an explanatory paragraph and an adverse opinion.
d. Adverse opinion and a qualified opinion.

(11/90, Aud., #14, 0330)

47. In which of the following circumstances would an auditor be most likely to express an adverse opinion?

a. Information comes to the auditor's attention that raises substantial doubt about the entity's ability to continue as a going concern.
b. The chief executive officer refuses the auditor access to minutes of board of directors' meetings.
c. Tests of controls show that the entity's internal control structure is so poor that it **cannot** be relied upon.
d. The financial statements are **not** in conformity with the FASB Statements regarding the capitalization of leases. (11/90, Aud., #3, 9911)

48. An auditor most likely would issue a disclaimer of opinion because of

a. Inadequate disclosure of material information.
b. The omission of the statement of cash flows.
c. A material departure from generally accepted accounting principles.
d. Management's refusal to furnish written representations. (5/91, Aud., #53, 0319)

49. When comparative financial statements are presented, the fourth standard of reporting, which refers to financial statements "taken as a whole," should be considered to apply to the financial statements of the

a. Periods presented plus one preceding period.
b. Current period only.
c. Current period and those of the other periods presented.
d. Current and immediately preceding period only.

(5/84, Aud., #90, 9911)

49A. An auditor expressed a qualified opinion on the prior year's financial statements because of a lack of adequate disclosure. These financial statements are properly restated in the current year and presented in comparative form with the current year's financial statements. The auditor's updated report on the prior year's financial statements should

a. Be accompanied by the auditor's original report on the prior year's financial statements.
b. Continue to express a qualified opinion on the prior year's financial statements.
c. Make **no** reference to the type of opinion expressed on the prior year's financial statements.
d. Express an unqualified opinion on the restated financial statements of the prior year.

(5/94, Aud., #90, 4755)

50. When reporting on comparative financial statements, which of the following circumstances ordinarily should cause the auditor to change the previously issued opinion on the prior year's financial statements?

a. The prior year's financial statements are restated following a pooling of interests in the current year.
b. A departure from generally accepted accounting principles caused an adverse opinion on the prior year's financial statements and those statements have been properly restated.
c. A change in accounting principle caused the auditor to make a consistency modification in the current year's auditor's report.
d. A scope limitation caused a qualified opinion on the prior year's financial statements but the current year's opinion was properly unqualified.

(11/90, Aud., #11, 0328)

50A. Comparative financial statements include the financial statements of the prior year that were audited by a predecessor auditor whose report is not presented. If the predecessor's report was qualified, the successor should

a. Indicate the substantive reasons for the qualification in the predecessor auditor's opinion.
b. Request the client to reissue the predecessor's report on the prior year's statements.
c. Issue an updated comparative audit report indicating the division of responsibility.
d. Express an opinion only on the current year's statements and make **no** reference to the prior year's statements. (11/93, Aud., #48, 4285)

51. The predecessor auditor, who is satisfied after properly communicating with the successor auditor, has reissued a report because the audit client desires comparative financial statements. The predecessor auditor's report should make

a. Reference to the report of the successor auditor only in the scope paragraph.
b. Reference to the work of the successor auditor in the scope and opinion paragraphs.

c. Reference to both the work and the report of the successor auditor only in the opinion paragraph.
d. No reference to the report or the work of the successor auditor. (5/90, Aud., #13, 0334)

52. A former client requests a predecessor auditor to reissue an audit report on a prior period's financial statements. The financial statements are not restated and the report is not revised. What date(s) should the predecessor auditor use in the reissued report?
a. The date of the prior-period report.
b. The date of the client's request.
c. The date of reissue.
d. The dual-dates. (11/89, Aud., #23, 0352)

53. Comparative financial statements include the prior year's statements that were audited by a predecessor auditor whose report is not presented. If the predecessor's report was unqualified, the successor should
a. Express an opinion on the current year's statements alone and make **no** reference to the prior year's statements.
b. Indicate in the auditor's report that the predecessor auditor expressed an unqualified opinion.
c. Obtain a letter of representations from the predecessor concerning any matters that might affect the successor's opinion.
d. Request the predecessor auditor to reissue the prior year's report. (11/90, Aud., #10, 0327)

54. When a predecessor auditor reissues the report on the prior period's financial statements at the request of the former client, the predecessor auditor should
a. Indicate in the introductory paragraph of the reissued report that the financial statements of the subsequent period were audited by another CPA.
b. Obtain an updated management representation letter and compare it to that obtained during the prior period audit.
c. Compare the prior period's financial statements that the predecessor reported on with the financial statements to be presented for comparative purposes.
d. Add an explanatory paragraph to the reissued report stating that the predecessor has **not** performed additional auditing procedures concerning the prior period's financial statements. (5/92, Aud., #3, 2756)

54A. Before reissuing the prior year's auditor's report on the financial statements of a former client, the predecessor auditor should obtain a letter of representations from the
a. Former client's management.
b. Former client's attorney.
c. Former client's board of directors.
d. Successor auditor. (11/94, Aud., #77, 5150)

55. An auditor issued an audit report that was dual dated for a subsequent event occurring after the completion of field work but before issuance of the auditor's report. The auditor's responsibility for events occurring subsequent to the completion of field work was
a. Extended to subsequent events occurring through the date of issuance of the report.
b. Extended to include all events occurring since the completion of field work.
c. Limited to the specific event referenced.
d. Limited to include only events occurring up to the date of the last subsequent event referenced. (11/91, Aud., #57, 2325)

55A. In May 1994, an auditor reissues the auditor's report on the 1992 financial statements at a continuing client's request. The 1992 financial statements are not restated and the auditor does not revise the wording of the report. The auditor should
a. Dual date the reissued report.
b. Use the release date of the reissued report.
c. Use the original report date on the reissued report.
d. Use the current-period auditor's report date on the reissued report. (5/94, Aud., #66, 4731)

56. Wilson, CPA, completed the field work of the audit of Abco's December 31, 1991, financial statements on March 6, 1992. A subsequent event requiring adjustment to the 1991 financial statements occurred on April 10, 1992, and came to Wilson's attention on April 24, 1992. If the adjustment is made without disclosure of the event, Wilson's report ordinarily should be dated
a. March 6, 1992.
b. April 10, 1992.
c. April 24, 1992.
d. Using dual dating. (5/92, Aud., #12, 2765)

57. If an auditor dates the auditor's report on financial statements for the year ended December 31, 1984, as of February 10, 1985, except for Note J, as to which the date is March 3, 1985, the auditor is taking responsibility for
a. All subsequent events occurring through March 3, 1985.
b. All subsequent events occurring through February 10, 1985 only.

c. All subsequent events occurring through February 10, 1985, and the specific subsequent event referred to in Note J through March 3, 1985.
d. Only the specific subsequent event referred to in Note J through March 3, 1985.

(11/85, Aud., #54, 9911)

58. The auditor's report should be dated as of the date on which the
a. Report is delivered to the client.
b. Field work is completed.
c. Fiscal period under audit ends.
d. Review of the working papers is completed.

(11/84, Aud., #6, 0386)

59. Which of the following procedures should an auditor generally perform regarding subsequent events?
a. Compare the latest available interim financial statements with the financial statements being audited.
b. Send second requests to the client's customers who failed to respond to initial accounts receivable confirmation requests.
c. Communicate material weaknesses in the internal control structure to the client's audit committee.
d. Review the cut-off bank statements for several months after the year end.

(5/93, Aud., #45, 3941)

59A. Zero Corp. suffered a loss that would have a material effect on its financial statements on an uncollectible trade account receivable due to a customer's bankruptcy. This occurred suddenly due to a natural disaster ten days after Zero's balance sheet date, but one month before the issuance of the financial statements and the auditor's report. Under these circumstances,

	The financial statements should be adjusted	The event requires financial statement disclosure, but **no** adjustment	The auditor's report should be modified for a lack of consistency
a.	Yes	No	No
b.	Yes	No	Yes
c.	No	Yes	Yes
d.	No	Yes	No

(5/94, Aud., #53, 4718)

60. A client acquired 25% of its outstanding capital stock after year-end and prior to completion of the auditor's field work. The auditor should
a. Advise management to adjust the balance sheet to reflect the acquisition.
b. Issue pro forma financial statements giving effect to the acquisition as if it had occurred at year-end.
c. Advise management to disclose the acquisition in the notes to the financial statements.
d. Disclose the acquisition in the opinion paragraph of the auditor's report.

(5/87, Aud., #48, 0372)

60A. An auditor issued an audit report that was dual dated for a subsequent event occurring after the completion of field work but before issuance of the auditor's report. The auditor's responsibility for events occurring subsequent to the completion of field work was
a. Limited to include only events occurring up to the date of the last subsequent event referenced.
b. Limited to the specific event referenced.
c. Extended to subsequent events occurring through the date of issuance of the report.
d. Extended to include all events occurring since the completion of field work.

(11/94, Aud., #67, 5140)

61. An auditor is concerned with completing various phases of the audit after the balance-sheet date. This "subsequent period" extends to the date of the
a. Auditor's report.
b. Final review of the audit working papers.
c. Public issuance of the financial statements.
d. Delivery of the auditor's report to the client.

(5/86, Aud., #43, 0381)

61A. Which of the following events occurring after the issuance of an auditor's report most likely would cause the auditor to make further inquiries about the previously issued financial statements?
a. A technological development that could affect the entity's future ability to continue as a going concern.
b. The discovery of information regarding a contingency that existed before the financial statements were issued.
c. The entity's sale of a subsidiary that accounts for 30% of the entity's consolidated sales.
d. The final resolution of a lawsuit explained in a separate paragraph of the auditor's report.

(11/93, Aud., #59, 4296)

62. After issuing a report, an auditor has **no** obligation to make continuing inquiries or perform other procedures concerning the audited financial statements, unless

a. Information, which existed at the report date and may affect the report, comes to the auditor's attention.
b. Management of the entity requests the auditor to reissue the auditor's report.
c. Information about an event that occurred after the end of field work comes to the auditor's attention.
d. Final determinations or resolutions are made of contingencies that had been disclosed in the financial statements. (11/91, Aud., #20, 2288)

63. After an audit report containing an unqualified opinion on a nonpublic client's financial statements was issued, the client decided to sell the shares of a subsidiary that accounts for 30% of its revenue and 25% of its net income. The auditor should
a. Determine whether the information is reliable and, if determined to be reliable, request that revised financial statements be issued.
b. Notify the entity that the auditor's report may no longer be associated with the financial statements.
c. Describe the effects of this subsequently discovered information in a communication with persons known to be relying on the financial statements.
d. Take **no** action because the auditor has **no** obligation to make any further inquiries. (11/88, Aud., #28, 9911)

64. Subsequent to the issuance of the auditor's report, the auditor became aware of facts existing at the report date that would have affected the report had the auditor then been aware of such facts. After determining that the information is reliable, the auditor should next
a. Notify the board of directors that the auditor's report must **no** longer be associated with the financial statements.
b. Determine whether there are persons relying or likely to rely on the financial statements who would attach importance to the information.
c. Request that management disclose the effects of the newly discovered information by adding a footnote to subsequently issued financial statements.
d. Issue revised pro forma financial statements taking into consideration the newly discovered information. (5/87, Aud., #56, 0375)

64A. Subsequently to the issuance of an auditor's report, the auditor became aware of facts existing at the report date that would have affected the report had the auditor then been aware of such facts. After determining that the information is reliable, the auditor should next
a. Determine whether there are persons relying or likely to rely on the financial statements who would attach importance to the information.
b. Request that management disclose the newly discovered information by issuing revised financial statements.
c. Issue revised pro forma financial statements taking into consideration the newly discovered information.
d. Give public notice that the auditor is **no** longer associated with financial statements. (11/94, Aud., #89, 5162)

65. Soon after Boyd's audit report was issued, Boyd learned of certain related party transactions that occurred during the year under audit. These transactions were not disclosed in the notes to the financial statements. Boyd should
a. Plan to audit the transactions during the next engagement.
b. Recall all copies of the audited financial statements.
c. Determine whether the lack of disclosure would affect the auditor's report.
d. Ask the client to disclose the transactions in subsequent interim statements. (11/89, Aud., #22, 9911)

66. An auditor concludes that the omission of a substantive procedure considered necessary at the time of the audit may impair the auditor's present ability to support the previously expressed opinion. The auditor need **not** apply the omitted procedure if
a. The risk of adverse publicity or litigation is low.
b. The results of other procedures that were applied tend to compensate for the procedure omitted.
c. The auditor's opinion was qualified because of a departure from generally accepted accounting principles.
d. The results of the subsequent period's tests of controls make the omitted procedure less important. (5/89, Aud., #44, 0354)

66A. On March 15, 1994, Kent, CPA, issued an unqualified opinion on a client's audited financial statements for the year ended December 31, 1993. On May 4, 1994, Kent's internal inspection program disclosed that engagement personnel failed to observe the client's physical inventory. Omission of this procedure impairs Kent's present ability to support the unqualified opinion. If the stockholders are currently relying on the opinion, Kent should first

a. Advise management to disclose to the stockholders that Kent's unqualified opinion should **not** be relied on.
b. Undertake to apply alternative procedures that would provide a satisfactory basis for the unqualified opinion.
c. Reissue the auditor's report and add an explanatory paragraph describing the departure from generally accepted auditing standards.
d. Compensate for the omitted procedure by performing tests of controls to reduce audit risk to a sufficiently low level.

(5/94, Aud., #70, 4735)

67. An auditor concludes that an audit procedure considered necessary at the time of the audit had been omitted. The auditor should assess the importance of the omitted procedure to the ability to support the previously expressed opinion. Which of the following would be **least** helpful in making that assessment?

a. A discussion with the client about whether there are persons relying on the auditor's report.
b. A reevaluation of the overall scope of the audit.
c. A discussion of the circumstances with engagement personnel.
d. A review of the other audit procedures that were applied that might compensate for the one omitted. (5/87, Aud., #47, 0371)

67A. An auditor is considering whether the omission of a substantive procedure considered necessary at the time of an audit may impair the auditor's present ability to support the previously expressed opinion. The auditor need **not** apply the omitted procedure if the

a. Financial statements and auditor's report were **not** distributed beyond management and the board of directors.
b. Auditor's previously expressed opinion was qualified because of a departure from GAAP.
c. Results of other procedures that were applied tend to compensate for the procedure omitted.
d. Omission is due to unreasonable delays by client personnel in providing data on a timely basis. (5/95, Aud., #85, 5703)

68. An auditor concludes that a substantive auditing procedure considered necessary during the prior period's audit was omitted. Which of the following factors would most likely cause the auditor promptly to apply the omitted procedure?

a. There are **no** alternative procedures available to provide the same evidence as the omitted procedure.
b. The omission of the procedure impairs the auditor's present ability to support the previously expressed opinion.
c. The source documents needed to perform the omitted procedure are still available.
d. The auditor's opinion on the prior period's financial statements was unqualified.

(5/92, Aud., #33, 2786)

69. Six months after issuing an unqualified opinion on audited financial statements, an auditor discovered that the engagement personnel failed to confirm several of the client's material accounts receivable balances. The auditor should first

a. Request the permission of the client to undertake the confirmation of accounts receivable.
b. Perform alternative procedures to provide a satisfactory basis for the unqualified opinion.
c. Assess the importance of the omitted procedures to the auditor's ability to support the previously expressed opinion.
d. Inquire whether there are persons currently relying, or likely to rely, on the unqualified opinion. (11/90, Aud., #35, 0332)

70. When an independent CPA is associated with the financial statements of a publicly held entity but has **not** audited or reviewed such statements, the appropriate form of report to be issued must include a (an)

a. Regulation S-X exemption.
b. Report on pro forma financial statements.
c. Unaudited association report.
d. Disclaimer of opinion. (11/94, Aud., #76, 5149)

71. When unaudited financial statements of a nonpublic entity are presented in comparative form with audited financial statements in the subsequent year, the unaudited financial statements should be clearly marked to indicate their status and

I. The report on the unaudited financial statements should be reissued.
II. The report on the audited financial statements should include a separate paragraph describing the responsibility assumed for the unaudited financial statements.

a. I only.
b. II only.
c. Both I and II.
d. Either I or II. (5/94, Aud., #89, 4754)

72. When an independent CPA assists in preparing the financial statements of a publicly held entity, but has **not** audited or reviewed them, the CPA should issue a disclaimer of opinion. In such situations, the CPA has **no** responsibility to apply any procedures beyond

a. Ascertaining whether the financial statements are in conformity with generally accepted accounting principles.
b. Determining whether management has elected to omit substantially all required disclosures.
c. Documenting that the internal control structure is **not** being relied on.
d. Reading the financial statements for obvious material misstatements. (5/92, Aud., #2, 2755)

73. An auditor may **not** issue a qualified opinion when

a. A scope limitation prevents the auditor from completing an important audit procedure.
b. The auditor's report refers to the work of a specialist.
c. An accounting principle at variance with generally accepted accounting principles is used.
d. The auditor lacks independence with respect to the audited entity. (5/89, Aud., #52, 0359)

74. If an accountant concludes that unaudited financial statements on which the accountant is disclaiming an opinion also lack adequate disclosure, the accountant should suggest appropriate revision. If the client does **not** accept the accountant's suggestion, the accountant should

a. Issue an adverse opinion and describe the appropriate revision in the report.
b. Make reference to the appropriate revision and issue a modified report expressing limited assurance.
c. Describe the appropriate revision to the financial statements in the accountant's disclaimer of opinion.
d. Accept the client's inaction because the statements are unaudited and the accountant has disclaimed an opinion.
(11/86, Aud., #52, 9911)

75. Davis, CPA, believes there is substantial doubt about the ability of Hill Co. to continue as a going concern for a reasonable period of time. In evaluating Hill's plans for dealing with the adverse effects of future conditions and events, Davis most likely would consider, as a mitigating factor, Hill's plans to

a. Accelerate research and development projects related to future products.
b. Accumulate treasury stock at prices favorable to Hill's historic price range.
c. Purchase equipment and production facilities currently being leased.
d. Negotiate reductions in required dividends being paid on preferred stock.
(5/93, Aud., #53, 3949)

76. Green, CPA, concludes that there is substantial doubt about JKL Co.'s ability to continue as a going concern. If JKL's financial statements adequately disclose its financial difficulties, Green's auditor's report should

	Include an explanatory paragraph following the opinion paragraph	Specifically use the words "going concern"	Specifically use the words "substantial doubt"
a.	Yes	Yes	Yes
b.	Yes	Yes	No
c.	Yes	No	Yes
d.	No	Yes	Yes

(11/92, Aud., #49, 2983)

77. The adverse effects of events causing an auditor to believe there is substantial doubt about an entity's ability to continue as a going concern would most likely be mitigated by evidence relating to the

a. Ability to expand operations into new product lines in the future.
b. Feasibility of plans to purchase leased equipment at less than market value.
c. Marketability of assets that management plans to sell.
d. Committed arrangements to convert preferred stock to long-term debt. (5/91, Aud., #43, 0314)

78. An auditor concludes that there is substantial doubt about an entity's ability to continue as a going concern for a reasonable period of time. If the entity's disclosures concerning this matter are adequate, the audit report may include a(an)

	Disclaimer of opinion	"Except for" qualified opinion
a.	Yes	Yes
b.	No	No
c.	No	Yes
d.	Yes	No

(11/89, Aud., #9, 0346)

79. Which of the following audit procedures would most likely assist an auditor in identifying conditions and events that may indicate there could be substantial doubt about an entity's ability to continue as a going concern?

a. Review compliance with the terms of debt agreements.
b. Confirmation of accounts receivable from principal customers.
c. Reconciliation of interest expense with debt outstanding.
d. Confirmation of bank balances.
(11/89, Aud., #29, 0353)

79A. Which of the following auditing procedures most likely would assist an auditor in identifying conditions and events that may indicate substantial doubt about an entity's ability to continue as a going concern?
a. Inspecting title documents to verify whether any assets are pledged as collateral.
b. Confirming with third parties the details of arrangements to maintain financial support.
c. Reconciling the cash balance per books with the cut-off bank statement and the bank confirmation.
d. Comparing the entity's depreciation and asset capitalization policies to other entities in the industry. (5/94, Aud., #55, 4720)

80. If the auditor concludes that the entity's disclosures with respect to the entity's ability to continue as a going concern for a reasonable period of time are inadequate, the independent auditor should issue a(n)
a. Adverse opinion or a disclaimer of opinion.
b. Unqualified opinion with a consistency modification.
c. Qualified opinion or an adverse opinion.
d. Qualified opinion or a disclaimer of opinion.
(Editorial Board, 9911)

81. If substantial doubt about the entity's ability to continue as a going concern for a reasonable period of time existed at the date of prior period financial statements that are presented on a comparative basis, and that doubt has been removed in the current period, the explanatory paragraph included in the auditor's report on the financial statements of the prior period should
a. Be repeated in the current year's report.
b. Not be repeated in the current year's report.
c. Be repeated in the current year's report with an additional paragraph stating that the substantial doubt has been removed.
d. Be removed from the prior year's report.
(Editorial Board, 9911)

82. Which of the following statements is correct with respect to the auditor's consideration of an entity's ability to continue as a going concern?
a. The auditor has a responsibility to evaluate whether there is substantial doubt about the entity's ability to continue as a going concern for a reasonable period of time, not to exceed the date of the financial statements being audited.
b. If there is absence of reference to substantial doubt in the auditor's report, this should be viewed as assurance as to an entity's ability to continue as a going concern.
c. It is not necessary for the auditor to design audit procedures solely to identify conditions and events that, when considered in the aggregate, indicate there could be substantial doubt about the entity's ability to continue as a going concern for a reasonable period of time.
d. The auditor's workpapers must include evidential matter which provides assurance that the entity will continue as a going concern.
(Editorial Board, 9911)

83. Which of the following conditions or events most likely would cause an auditor to have substantial doubt about an entity's ability to continue as a going concern?
a. Cash flows from operating activities are negative.
b. Research and development projects are postponed.
c. Significant related party transactions are pervasive.
d. Stock dividends replace annual cash dividends.
(11/94, Aud., #71, 5154)

84. When an auditor concludes there is substantial doubt about a continuing audit client's ability to continue as a going concern for a reasonable period of time, the auditor's responsibility is to
a. Issue a qualified or adverse opinion, depending upon materiality, due to the possible effects on the financial statements.
b. Consider the adequacy of disclosure about the client's possible inability to continue as a going concern.
c. Report to the client's audit committee that management's accounting estimates may need to be adjusted.
d. Reissue the prior year's auditor's report and add an explanatory paragraph that specifically refers to "substantial doubt" and "going concern." (5/94, Aud., #62, 4727)

85. When audited financial statements are presented in a client's document containing other information, the auditor should

a. Perform inquiry and analytical procedures to ascertain whether the other information is reasonable.
b. Add an explanatory paragraph to the auditor's report without changing the opinion on the financial statements.
c. Perform the appropriate substantive auditing procedures to corroborate the other information.
d. Read the other information to determine that it is consistent with the audited financial statements. (11/92, Aud., #57, 2991)

86. Investment and property schedules are presented for purposes of additional analysis in an auditor-submitted document. The schedules are not required parts of the basic financial statements, but accompany the basic financial statements. When reporting on such additional information, the measurement of materiality is the
a. Same as that used in forming an opinion on the basic financial statements taken as a whole.
b. Lesser of the individual schedule of investments or schedule of property taken by itself.
c. Greater of the individual schedule of investments or schedule of property taken by itself.
d. Combined total of both the individual schedules of investments and property taken as a whole. (5/94, Aud., #63, 4728)

87. An auditor concludes that there is a material inconsistency in the other information in an annual report to shareholders containing audited financial statements. If the auditor concludes that the financial statements do **not** require revision, but the client refuses to revise or eliminate the material inconsistency, the auditor may
a. Revise the auditor's report to include a separate explanatory paragraph describing the material inconsistency.
b. Issue an "except for" qualified opinion after discussing the matter with the client's board of directors.
c. Consider the matter closed, since the other information is **not** in the audited financial statements.
d. Disclaim an opinion on the financial statements after explaining the material inconsistency in a separate explanatory paragraph. (11/94, Aud., #86, 5159)

88. What is an auditor's responsibility for supplementary information, such as segment information, which is outside the basic financial statements, but required by the FASB?
a. The auditor has **no** responsibility for required supplementary information as long as it is outside the basic financial statements.
b. The auditor's only responsibility for required supplementary information is to determine that such information has **not** been omitted.
c. The auditor should apply certain limited procedures to the required supplementary information, and report deficiencies in, or omissions of, such information.
d. The auditor should apply tests of details of transactions and balances to the required supplementary information and report any material misstatements in such information. (5/94, Aud., #82, 4747)

89. If management declines to present supplementary information required by the Governmental Accounting Standards Board (GASB), the auditor should issue a(an)
a. Adverse opinion.
b. Qualified opinion with an explanatory paragraph.
c. Unqualified opinion.
d. Unqualified opinion with an additional explanatory paragraph. (5/90, Aud., #25, 0399)

90. When a publicly held company refuses to include in its audited financial statements any of the segment information that the auditor believes is required, the auditor should issue a(an)
a. Unqualified opinion with a separate explanatory paragraph emphasizing the matter.
b. "Except for" qualified opinion because of inadequate disclosure.
c. Adverse opinion because of the lack of conformity with generally accepted accounting principles.
d. Disclaimer of opinion because of the significant scope limitation. (5/89, Aud., #55, 0360)

91. The objective of auditing procedures applied to segment information is to provide the auditor with a reasonable basis for concluding whether
a. The information is useful for comparing a segment of one enterprise with a similar segment of another enterprise.
b. Sufficient evidential matter has been obtained to allow the auditor to be associated with the segment information.
c. A separate opinion on the segment information is necessary due to inconsistent application of accounting principles.
d. The information is presented in conformity with the FASB Statement on segment information in relation to the financial statements taken as a whole. (11/87, Aud., #4, 0366)

Solution 40-1 MULTIPLE CHOICE ANSWERS

The Meaning of "Present Fairly in Conformity With GAAP" in the Independent Auditor's Report (AU 411)

1. (b) AU 410.02 states, "The first reporting standard is construed not to require a statement of fact by the auditor, but an opinion as to whether the financial statements are presented in conformity with such principles [GAAP]." The auditor must also judge whether the financial statements are presented fairly within the framework of GAAP (AU 411.03), not some implied measure of fairness. The audit report contains the auditor's *subjective* opinion concerning the financial statement presentation.

2. (a) SAS 69, (AU 411) establishes the new GAAP hierarchy which indicates that FASB Technical Bulletins are in the second category. Answer (b) is included in the fourth category. AU 411.11 states that in the absence of a pronouncement covered by Rule 203 or another source of established accounting principles, the auditor may consider other accounting literature, depending on its relevance in the circumstances. Other accounting literature includes FASB Statements of Financial Accounting Concepts and AICPA Technical Practice Aids.

Consistency of Application of GAAP (AU 420)

3. (b) The objective of the consistency standard is to (1) give assurance that the comparability of financial statements between periods has not been affected by changes in accounting principles, and (2) if comparability has been materially affected by such changes, provide appropriate reporting of the change (AU 420.02). Answer (b) concerns a change in accounting principle, and so it should be given recognition in the auditor's report. Answer (a) concerns the correction of an error, not a change in principle. Likewise, answer (c) involves a change in estimate, not in principle. Answer (d) is also incorrect because the change does not materially affect the comparability of the financial statements. Such changes should be disclosed in the notes to the financial statements, not in the auditor's report (AU 420.17).

4. (c) "Accounting estimates (such as service lives and salvage values of depreciable assets and *provisions for warranty costs*, uncollectible receivables, and inventory obsolescence) are necessary in the preparation of financial statements. Accounting estimates change as new events occur and as additional experience and information are acquired. This type of accounting change is required by altered conditions that affect comparability but do not involve the consistency standard." Answers (a), (b), and (d) are examples of a change in reporting entity, a change in accounting principle, and a correction of an error in principle, respectively (AU 420.07-.11). These changes require the addition of an explanatory paragraph to the auditor's report to identify a lack of consistency (AU 420.06).

5. (a) AU 420.12 states, "The effect of a change in accounting principle may be inseparable from the effect of a change in estimate. Although the accounting for such a change is the *same as that accorded a change only in estimate*, a change in principle is involved. Accordingly, this type of change requires recognition in the auditor's report through the addition of an explanatory paragraph."

6. (b) In some cases, a company's business operations may be such as to make it desirable to apply one of the acceptable methods of determining cost to one portion of the inventory, or components thereof, while applying a different method to another portion of the inventory. Under these circumstances, the consistency of the financial statements is not affected. Consequently, an unqualified opinion is appropriate (ARB 43).

Types of Opinions

7. (a) If the financial statements, including the accompanying notes, omit information that is required by GAAP, the auditor should express a qualified or an adverse opinion. (AU 431.03) The "subject to" opinion should no longer be used. An unqualified opinion could not be expressed when there is inadequate disclosure.

7A. (c) This is a departure from GAAP; if the departure has a material, pervasive effect, an adverse opinion is appropriate (AU 508.67). Answer (a) is a scope limitation problem and could result in a disclaimer (AU 508.70). The situation in (b) will result in expanding substantive tests or determining that the entity is not auditable. AU 341.12 notes that the situation in (d) will result in the addition of an explanatory paragraph.

8. (d) As stated in AU 508.10, an unqualified opinion states that the financial statements present fairly, in all material respects, financial position, results of operations and cash flows in conformity with generally accepted accounting principles (which include adequate disclosure).

9. (a) When an auditor is able to satisfy him- or herself as to accounts receivable by applying alternative procedures, AU 508.42 indicates, "there has been no significant scope limitation, and the auditor is free to issue an unqualified opinion without reference to the omitted procedures or the alternative procedures used." An explanatory paragraph is used to emphasize a matter, report on a departure from a promulgated accounting principle, uncertainty, or to report a lack of consistency. The auditor did not encounter a scope limitation as the auditor was able to satisfy him- or herself as to the accounts receivable balance. A qualified opinion may be issued for a material departure from GAAP but not GAAS.

Standard Report

10. (a) AU 508.05 states, "The objective of the fourth standard is to prevent misinterpretation of the degree of responsibility the auditor is assuming when his name is associated with financial statements." It further states, ". . . the reference to the financial statements taken as a whole, applies equally to a complete set of financial statements, as well as an individual statement, and that different opinions may be expressed on each of the financial statements as circumstances warrant."

10A. (d) AU 508.08 identifies the basic elements of the audit report; item *f.(2)* includes assessing the accounting principles used and significant estimates made by management, item *c.* indicates a statement that the financial statements are the responsibility of the Company's management, and item *h.* includes an opinion as to whether the financial statements present fairly, in all material respects,...in conformity with generally accepted accounting principles. Answers (a), (b), and (c) are included in the report.

10B. (d) Since single-year financial statements are presented, an auditor need not modify his or her report to indicate that the prior year statements were audited by other auditors. The inability to obtain audited financial statements supporting an entity's investment in a foreign affiliate represents a scope limitation resulting in a qualified opinion or a disclaimer of opinion. The entity's omission of the statement of cash flows would result in a qualified opinion. While emphasis of a matter does not preclude the issuance of an unqualified opinion, the report must be modified to include a separate paragraph discussing the matter.

11. (a) The basic elements of the auditor's standard report include *explicit* statements to the effect that the financial statements are the responsibility of the company's management and that the auditor's responsibility is to express an opinion on the financial statements based on his or her audit (AU 508.08).

12. (d) Among the basic elements of the standard auditor's report on comparative financial statements is a statement that an audit includes examining on a test basis, evidence supporting the amounts and disclosures in the financial statements (AU 508.08). The auditor's standard report implies that the auditor is satisfied that the comparability of financial statements between periods has not been materially affected by changes in accounting principles and that such principles have been consistently applied between or among periods (AU 508.34).

13. (b) If management has not provided reasonable justification for a change in accounting principle, the auditor's opinion should express an exception to the change having been made without reasonable justification. In addition, the auditor should continue to express his or her exception with respect to the financial statements for the year of change as long as they are reported on and presented (AU 508.66).

13A. (c) AU 508.08 presents the standard form of the auditor's report. GAAS is referred to in the scope paragraph; GAAP is referred to in the opinion paragraph.

13B. (d) The statement that the auditor obtains *reasonable* assurance about whether the financial statements are free of material misstatement recognizes the existence of audit risk. Answers (a), (b), and (c) do not recognize the existence of audit risk.

Explanatory Language Added to the Auditor's Standard Report

14. (b) AU 341.12 provides guidance on the auditor's considerations in deciding whether an explanatory paragraph needs to be added to his or her report because of a matter involving the uncertainty as to an entity's ability to continue as a going concern. Answers (a), (c), and (d) are examples of when a qualified, adverse, or disclaimer opinion should be issued.

15. (d) AU 508.34 states that if there has been a change in accounting principles or in the method of their application that has a material effect on the comparability of the company's financial statements, the auditor should refer to the change in an explanatory paragraph, identify the nature of the change, and refer the reader to the note in the

financial statements that discussed the change in detail. The justification of the change should not be given, the justification is implied by the statement in the auditor's report that the financial statements are presented fairly. The auditor would not describe the effect of the change in the audit report nor his or her concurrence because this is also implied in the auditor's opinion.

16. (d) AU 543.04 states that if the principal auditor is able to satisfy him- or herself as to the independence and professional reputation of the other auditor, he or she may be able to express an opinion on the financial statements taken as a whole without making reference in the report to the audit of the other auditor. Issuing an unqualified opinion would be the result of deciding not to make reference to the other CPA, not the reason for not making reference. If the report of the other auditor is other than a standard report, the principal auditor should decide whether the reason for the departure from the standard report is of such nature and significance in relation to the financial statements on which the principal auditor is reporting that it would require recognition in his or her own report. Whether or not the other CPA issued an unqualified opinion does not determine whether the auditor should make reference to the other auditor. Answer (c) is an example of justification for making reference to the other auditor in the audit report and indicating the divided responsibility between the auditors who conducted the audits of the various components of the overall financial statements.

16A. (d) According to AU 543.05, the principal auditor would be able to decide not to refer to the audit by another CPA of a subsidiary of the principal auditor's client when, among other things, the principal auditor takes steps necessary to satisfy himself/herself as to the audit performed by the other auditor and the reasonableness of the inclusion in the client's financial statements. The steps the principal auditor might take would most likely include contacting the other CPA and reviewing the audit programs and working papers pertaining to the subsidiary. Adding an explanatory paragraph to the report when the subsidiary's statements are not material to the consolidated statements would not be appropriate. By not referring to the audit of the subsidiary, the CPA is not dividing his responsibility for the financial statements as a whole. The CPA would not need written permission from the other CPA to omit the reference.

17. (b) If reference is made to the report of another auditor as a basis, in part, for the opinion, this divided responsibility is indicated in the introductory, scope, and opinion paragraphs of the report (AU 508.12).

17A. (d) AU 508.37 states, "In some circumstances, the auditor may wish to emphasize a matter regarding the financial statements, but intends to express an unqualified opinion. Examples include situations where the auditor may wish to emphasize that the entity is a component of a larger business enterprise, or that it has had significant transactions with related parties..." Answer (a) would not require "except for" wording in the auditor's report. The information may be included in both places. Typically, more detail regarding the matter is provided in the footnotes. AU 508.37 states specifically that phrases such as "with the foregoing explanation" should not be used in the opinion paragraph in a situation of this type.

18. (d) AU 543.07 states, "When the principal auditor decides that he [or she] will make reference to the audit of the other auditor, his [or her] report should indicate clearly, in the introductory, scope and opinion paragraphs, the division of responsibility as between that portion of the financial statements covered by his [or her] own audit and that covered by the audit of the other auditor."

18A. (a) AU 543.07 states that when the principal auditor decides to make reference to the audit of another auditor who performed part of the audit, his or her report should indicate clearly the division of responsibility as between that portion of the statements covered by his or her own audit and that covered by the audit of the other auditor. If the portion examined by the other auditor is immaterial, there would be no need for a division of responsibilities in the principal auditor's report [AU 543.05(d)]. The principal auditor should make inquiries concerning the professional reputation and independence of the other auditor whether or not the principal auditor decides to make reference to the other auditor (AU 543.10). The principal auditor would not automatically be required to make reference to the other auditor. If the reason for the departure from a standard report is not material in relation to such financial statements and the other auditor's report is not presented, the principal auditor need not make reference in his or her report to such departure (AU 543.15).

19. (a) The principal auditor would not make reference to another auditor who audited a subsidiary of the entity when the other auditor was retained by the principal auditor and the work was performed under the principal auditor's guidance and control. To do so may cause a reader to misinterpret the degree

of responsibility being assumed by the respective auditors (AU 543.05).

20. (a) AU 508.24 states, "If management believes and the auditor is satisfied that there is only a remote likelihood of a material loss resulting from resolution of a matter involving an uncertainty, the auditor would not add an explanatory paragraph to his report because of the matter." Thus, an unqualified opinion would be appropriate in this situation, and an explanatory paragraph or qualification of the opinion would be unnecessary.

21. (a) AU 508.11 states, "Certain circumstances, while not affecting the auditor's unqualified opinion, may require that the auditor add an explanatory paragraph (or other explanatory language) to his [or her] standard report. These circumstances include: . . . The financial statements are affected by uncertainties concerning future events, the outcome of which is not susceptible of reasonable estimation at the date of the auditor's report."

22. (a) When there has been a change in an accounting principle which has a material effect on the company's financial statements, an explanatory paragraph is added which identifies the change and makes reference to the note in the financial statements that discusses the change. The auditor's concurrence with the change is implied by the issuance of an unqualified opinion. Further, this explanatory paragraph is required in succeeding reports on financial statements as long as the year of the change is reported on (AU 508.34-.36).

22A. (c) AU 508.34 states that the auditor should not refer to consistency in his or her report when there has been no change in accounting principles or there has been a change in an accounting principle whose effect on the comparability of the financial statements is *not* material. A change in accounting principles that has a *material* effect on the comparability of the company's financial statements is referred to in an explanatory paragraph of the audit report. The auditor's concurrence with a change is implicit unless he or she takes exception to the change in expressing his or her opinion as to fair presentation of the financial statements in conformity with generally accepted accounting principles. The change in accounting principle is only referred to in the opinion paragraph if the auditor does not concur with the change.

23. (b) If there has been a change in accounting principles or in the method of their application that has a material effect on the comparability of the company's financial statements, the auditor should refer to the change in an explanatory paragraph of his or her report. Such explanatory paragraph (following the opinion paragraph) should identify the nature of the change and refer the reader to the note in the financial statements that discusses the change in detail (AU 508.34).

24. (a) If the auditor wishes to emphasize a matter regarding the financial statements while, at the same time, expressing an unqualified opinion, then the explanatory information may be presented in a separate paragraph of the auditor's report. For example, the auditor may wish to emphasize that the entity had *significant* related party transactions (AU 508.37). The auditor reports on the financial statements as they are prepared by management. The auditor does not *add* to such statements.

25. (d) "In some circumstances, the auditor may wish to emphasize a matter regarding the financial statements, but nevertheless intends to express an unqualified opinion . . . he [or she] may wish to emphasize an unusually important subsequent event or an accounting matter affecting the comparability of the financial statements with those of the preceding period. Such explanatory information should be presented in a separate paragraph of the auditor's report." (AU 508.37) Phrases such as "with the foregoing explanation" and "except for" should *not* be used in the opinion paragraph when the auditor is simply emphasizing a matter (AU 508.37).

26. (b) Rule 203 of the Code of Professional Conduct requires members to follow GAAP whenever possible. However, if by following GAAP the financial statements would be misleading, the member can comply with the rule by, "describing the departure, its approximate effects, if practicable, and the reasons why compliance with the principle would result in a misleading statement." This should be done in a separate paragraph, or paragraphs, of the auditor's report, and an unqualified opinion issued (AU 411.06). The departure from GAAP should be mentioned. Answers (c) and (d) are situations in which an unqualified opinion is appropriate.

26A. (a) AU 508.14 and .15 state that if the statements or data contain a departure from the reporting requirements of Rule 203 and the member can demonstrate that due to unusual circumstances the financial statements would otherwise have been misleading, the member can comply with the rule by describing the departure, its approximate effects, and the reasons why compliance with the principle would result in a misleading statement. The auditor's report should include, in a separate paragraph, the information required by the rule and it would still be appropriate for him or her to express an unqualified opinion with respect to the conformity of the financial statements with GAAP.

27. (a) AU 508.26 states that if management believes and the auditor is satisfied that the chance of a material loss resulting from resolution of a matter involving an uncertainty is more than remote but less than probable, the auditor should consider the following in deciding whether to add an explanatory paragraph to the report: (1) the magnitude by which the amount of reasonably possible loss exceeds the auditor's judgment about materiality and (2) the likelihood of occurrence of a material loss, i.e., whether that likelihood is closer to remote or to probable.

27A. (c) This situation is covered in AU 508.25. Answer (a) is incorrect because there was no limitation on the scope of the work. Answer (b) is incorrect because there was not a departure from GAAP. An unqualified report, is not appropriate because an uncertainty requiring an explanatory paragraph exists.

Departures From Unqualified Opinions (AU 508)

28. (b) AU 508.57 states that the omission of a basic financial statement, such as the statement of cash flows, is a departure from GAAP and requires the auditor to express a qualified or an adverse opinion, depending on materiality, the significance of the item to the entity, the pervasiveness of the misstatement, and the effect of the misstatement on the financial statements as a whole. Disclaimer opinions are issued for scope limitations and separate explanatory paragraphs added to an unqualified opinion are, for the emphasis of a matter, uncertainties, and changes in accounting principles. A review report opinion would be changed for the omission of a required basic financial statement.

29. (a) AU 508.39 states that the auditor can determine that he or she is able to express an unqualified opinion only if the audit has been conducted in accordance with GAAS and if he or she has therefore been able to apply all the procedures he or she considers necessary in the circumstances. Restrictions on the scope of his or her work, the inability to obtain sufficient competent evidential matter, or an inadequacy in the accounting records may require him or her to qualify or disclaim an opinion. Answer (b) is incorrect because an unqualified opinion may be issued in such circumstances, but an explanatory paragraph and language would be added to the report stating that disclosures required by GAAP have not been presented. An engagement letter is not a required procedure to be performed in order for the financial statements to be in conformity with GAAP, but it is a recommended procedure. Reportable conditions are the responsibility of management and management's decisions concerning costs to be incurred and related benefits. Provided the audit committee has acknowledged its understanding and consideration of such deficiencies and the associated risks, the auditor may decide the matter does not need to be repeated.

29A. (a) AU 508.73 states that piecemeal opinions (expressions of opinion as to certain identified items in financial statements) should not be expressed when the auditor has disclaimed an opinion because piecemeal opinions tend to overshadow a disclaimer of opinion. The auditor may issue an audit report on only one basic financial statement. When disclaiming an opinion due to a scope limitation, the scope paragraph is omitted from the audit report. The inclusion of the statement is inappropriate in any paragraph of the audit report.

30. (a) AU 623.06 states that the auditor should consider whether the financial statements that he or she is reporting on are suitably titled. If the auditor believes that the financial statements are not suitably titled, the auditor should disclose his or her reservations in an explanatory paragraph of the report and qualify the opinion. The auditor should not rely on someone else for his or her opinion. The opinion should be qualified; a disclaimer opinion is issued when there has been a scope limitation. Terms such as balance sheet, statement of financial position, statement of income, statement of operations, and statement of cash flows or similar titles are generally understood to be applicable only to financial statements that are intended to present financial position, results of operations, or cash flows in conformity with GAAP. Therefore, explanatory language in the notes to the financial statements is insufficient.

31. (b) AU 508.50 states that when financial statements are materially affected by a departure from GAAP and the auditor has audited the statements in accordance with generally accepted auditing standards, he or she should express a qualified opinion. In deciding whether the effects of a departure from GAAP are sufficiently material to require either a qualified or adverse opinion, one factor to be considered is the dollar magnitude of such effects. Answer (a) represents a scope limitation which would result in a disclaimer of opinion. Answer (c) is an example of an "except for" qualified opinion, but not an adverse opinion. Answer (d) is an

example of a situation where an explanatory paragraph would be added to an unqualified opinion.

32. (a) The auditor's decision to qualify his or her opinion rather than issue an unqualified opinion with an explanatory paragraph indicates that sufficient evidential matter was not obtained which would resolve the uncertainty, its presentation, or disclosure in the financial statements, or which would indicate that the financial statements are not in conformity with GAAP (AU 508.38). Answers (b), (c), and (d) are measurements of the uncertainty, which would be disclosed in footnotes and in a final paragraph of the report.

33. (d) Neither phrase should be used when the auditor is expressing a qualified opinion. AU 508.39 states, "Phrases such as *subject to* and *with the foregoing explanation* are not clear or forceful enough and should not be used. Since accompanying notes are part of the financial statements, wording such as *fairly presented, in all material respects, when read in conjunction with Note 1* is likely to be misunderstood and should not be used."

34. (d) AU 508.40 states, "Restrictions on the scope of [an auditor's] audit, whether imposed by the client or by circumstances, such as an inability to obtain sufficient competent evidential matter, or an inadequacy in the accounting records, may require him [or her] to qualify his [or her] opinion or to disclaim an opinion." An adverse opinion is appropriate only when, in the auditor's judgment, the financial statements are materially misstated, such as when there is a departure from GAAP. An unqualified opinion is not appropriate when there is a scope limitation.

34A. (d) AU 508.43 notes that in a qualified opinion resulting from a scope limitation, the scope and opinion paragraphs are modified and an explanatory paragraph is added.

34B. (d) AU 508.71 states that when disclaiming an opinion because of a scope limitation, the auditor should not identify the procedures that were performed nor include the paragraph describing the characteristics of an audit (i.e., the scope paragraph), because to do so may tend to overshadow the disclaimer. The disclaimer of opinion paragraph would be included as the opinion paragraph.

35. (c) AU 508.40 states, "Restrictions on the scope of the (auditor's) audit, whether imposed by the client or by circumstances, such as the timing of his [or her] work, the inability to obtain sufficient competent evidential matter, or an inadequacy in the accounting records, may require him [or her] to qualify his [or her] opinion or to disclaim an opinion." If management has not provided reasonable justification for a change in accounting principle, the auditor should express a qualified opinion or, if the effect of the change is sufficiently material, the auditor should express an adverse opinion on the financial statements (AU 508.60).

36. (b) AU 508.42 states, "When restrictions that significantly limit the scope of the audit are *imposed by the client*, ordinarily the auditor should disclaim an opinion on the financial statements."

36A. (b) AU 508.05 and .76 allow the auditor to express differing opinions on the balance sheet and income statement. The opinion on the balance sheet is unqualified because the ending inventory is fairly stated. The opinion on the income statement is a disclaimer because of an inability to obtain sufficient audit evidence (a scope limitation) regarding cost of goods sold (because beginning inventory has a significant impact on cost of goods sold).

37. (c) AU 508.42 states, "When restrictions that significantly limit the scope of the audit are *imposed by the client*, ordinarily the auditor should disclaim an opinion on the financial statements." The auditor is not precluded from reporting on financial statements prepared in accordance with the cash receipts and disbursements basis of accounting. Answer (a) is simply an example of an other comprehensive basis of accounting and would require a special report (AU 623.01). Answer (b) contemplates a departure from GAAP, not a scope limitation. The auditor is not precluded from reporting on one basic financial statement and not on the others. These engagements do not involve scope limitations if the auditor's access to information underlying the basic financial statements is not limited and if he or she is able to apply all necessary procedures (AU 508.47).

38. (c) AU 508.44 states that when an auditor qualifies his or her opinion because of a scope limitation, the opinion paragraph should indicate that the qualification pertains to the possible effects on the financial statements and not to the scope limitation itself. There are no reporting requirements for departures from GAAS; however, there are separate reporting requirements for departures from GAAP.

39. (d) AU 508.43 states, "When a qualified opinion results from a limitation on the scope of the audit or an insufficiency of evidential matter, the situation should be described in an explanatory paragraph preceding the opinion paragraph and

referred to in both the scope and opinion paragraphs of the auditor's report."

40. (d) Only the opinion paragraph should indicate that the qualification pertains to the possible effects on the financial statements and *not* to the scope limitation itself. The qualifying language generally used reads as follows: "In our opinion, except for the effects of such adjustments, if any, as might have been determined to be necessary . . ." (AU 508.44).

41. (b) AU 508.46 states, "When an auditor qualifies his opinion because of a scope limitation, the wording in the opinion paragraph should indicate that the qualification pertains to the possible effects on the financial statements and not to the scope limitation itself." The lack of sufficient competent evidential matter and the departure from GAAS should be stated in the separate paragraph preceding the opinion paragraph.

42. (a) AU 508.47 states, "The auditor may be asked to report on one basic financial statement and not on the others. For example, he [or she] may be asked to report on the balance sheet and not on the (other statements). These engagements do not involve scope limitations if the auditor's access to information underlying the basic financial statements is not limited and if he [or she] applies all the procedures he [or she] considers necessary in the circumstances; rather, such engagements involve *limited reporting objectives*."

43. (b) Information essential for a fair presentation in conformity with generally accepted accounting principles should be set forth in the financial statements. If the financial statements, including the accompanying notes, fail to disclose information that is required by generally accepted accounting principles, the auditor should express a *qualified* or an *adverse* opinion because of a departure from those principles and should provide the information in the report, if practicable (AU 508.55).

43A. (b) Whenever an auditor concludes that the financial statements do not represent the activities and position of an entity in conformity with GAAP, the auditor must either issue an adverse or qualified opinion, depending on the materiality of the discrepancy. Disclaimers of opinions are reserved for scope limitations, lack of independence, and nonperformance of an audit. An unqualified opinion, with or without explanation, should never be given on financial statements containing a material departure from GAAP. Unqualified opinions with explanations are reserved for situations when part of the audit is performed by other independent auditors, when the statements would be misleading if a particular GAAP were followed, when uncertainties exist, when there is a lack of consistency, and when the auditor wants to emphasize a matter.

44. (a) If the financial statements, including accompanying notes, fail to disclose information that is required by GAAP (such as the disclosure of related party transactions), the auditor should express a qualified or adverse opinion (AU 508.55). A disclaimer of opinion should not be expressed when the auditor believes, on the basis of the audit, that there are material departures from GAAP (AU 508.70). Answers (b), (c), and (d) all represent scope limitations that may lead to a disclaimer of opinion.

45. (d) AU 508.56 illustrates the proper treatment of an opinion qualified due to inadequate disclosure and the resulting modification of the opinion paragraph. The scope and introductory paragraphs are not affected.

46. (d) "If an entity accounts for the effect of a change prospectively when GAAP requires restatement or the inclusion of the cumulative effect of the change in the year of change, a subsequent year's financial statements could improperly include a charge or credit that is material to those statements. This situation requires that the auditor express a qualified or an adverse opinion." (AU 508.65)

47. (d) Adverse opinions are expressed when, in the auditor's judgment, the financial statements taken as a whole are not presented fairly in conformity with generally accepted accounting principles (AU 508.67). Here, financial statements are not in conformity with FASB statements in regard to the capitalization of leases, and are, therefore, not in conformity with generally accepted accounting principles. Answer (a) concerns an uncertainty, which generally requires a qualified opinion, not an adverse opinion. Answer (b) concerns a scope limitation, thus it is likely to result in a qualified opinion or a disclaimer of opinion. If the internal control structure cannot be relied upon (i.e., control risk must be assessed at the maximum level for all assertions), the auditor will simply expand the scope of his or her other audit procedures accordingly.

48. (d) AU 508.70 states, "A disclaimer of opinion states that the auditor does not express an opinion on the financial statements. It is appropriate when the auditor has not performed an audit sufficient in scope to enable him to form an opinion on the financial statements." In addition, AU 508.42 states, "When restrictions that significantly limit the scope of

the audit are imposed by the client, ordinarily the auditor should disclaim an opinion on the financial statements." Answers (a), (b), and (c) are all departures from GAAP and should be accounted for with a qualified or an adverse opinion.

Reports on Comparative Financial Statements

49. (c) AU 508.74 states, "Reference in the fourth reporting standard to the financial statements taken as a whole applies not only to the financial statements of the current period, but also to those of one or more prior periods that are presented on a comparative basis with those of the current period." The expression relates only to the statements of the periods presented. Answers (b) and (d) limit the application of the expression to the current period or current and immediately preceding periods, respectively.

49A. (d) The auditor expresses the appropriate opinion (unqualified) for the restated prior year statements and adds an explanatory paragraph (AU 508.78). The auditor is not required to attach the original report. A qualified opinion is no longer appropriate. Because the auditor notes the type of opinion previously issued in the current year's report, (c) is incorrect.

50. (b) AU 508.77 indicates that an auditor who becomes aware of events or circumstances which affect the financial statements of a prior period has a responsibility to consider these effects when updating his or her report. In this case, those statements which last year carried an adverse opinion have been restated, and are now in conformity with GAAP. Therefore, the updated report on the financial statements of the prior period should indicate that they have been restated, and an unqualified opinion issued.

50A. (a) AU 508.83 states that if the financial statements of a prior period have been audited by a predecessor auditor whose report is not presented, the successor auditor should indicate in the introductory paragraph of his or her report that the financial statements of the prior period were audited by another auditor and, if the report was other than a standard report, the substantive reasons therefor. The auditor would ask the client to request the predecessor auditor to reissue his or her report. The successor auditor would only report on the current period statements, not on the prior period; thus, no comparative audit report would be issued.

51. (d) A predecessor auditor who reissues a report because the audit client desires comparative statements should not refer in the reissued report to the report or work of the successor auditor (AU 508.80).

52. (a) AU 508.82 states, "A predecessor auditor's knowledge of the current affairs of his or her former client is obviously limited in the absence of a continuing relationship. Consequently, when reissuing a report on prior-period financial statements, a predecessor auditor should use the date of the previous report to avoid any implication that he [or she] has examined any records, transactions, or events after that date. If the predecessor auditor revises his [or her] report or if the financial statements are restated, he [or she] should dual-date the report."

53. (b) AU 508.83 states, "The successor auditor should indicate in the introductory paragraph of his [or her] report (1) that the financial statements of the prior period were audited by another auditor, (2) the date of his [or her] report, (3) the type of report issued by the predecessor auditor, and (4) if the report was other than a standard report, the substantive reasons therefor." Reference to the prior year's statements should be made. Representations made by the predecessor are not sufficient for the expression of an opinion on both years. The client, and not the predecessor auditor, would request the reissuance of the prior year's report (AU 508.79).

54. (c) AU 508.80 states, "Before reissuing (or consenting to the reuse of) a report previously issued on the financial statements of a prior period, a predecessor auditor should consider whether his previous report on those statements is still appropriate. Either the current form or manner of presentations of the financial statements of the prior period or one or more subsequent events might make a predecessor auditor's previous report inappropriate. Consequently, a predecessor auditor should (1) read the financial statements of the current period, (2) compare the prior-period financial statements that he [or she] reported on with the financial statements to be presented for comparative purposes, and (3) obtain a letter of representations from the successor auditor." Answer (b) could be perceived as performing additional audit procedures and would be insufficient for the performance of an audit in accordance with GAAS. The predecessor auditor should not refer in his or her reissued report to the report or the work of the successor auditor (AU 508.80). Answer (d) is incorrect because no explanatory paragraph of this nature would be added to the report.

54A. (d) A letter of representation from the successor auditor is required by AU 508.80. The other parties mentioned would not issue such a letter.

Dating of the Auditor's Report (AU 530)

55. (c) When "dual dating" an audit report, the auditor's responsibility for events occurring subsequent to the completion of field work is limited to the specific event referenced in the note, or otherwise disclosed (AU 530.05).

55A. (c) AU 530.06 states that an independent auditor may be requested by his or her client to furnish additional copies of a previously issued report. Use of the original report date in a reissued report removes any implication that records, transactions, or events after that date have been examined or reviewed. Dual dating is used when the auditor makes reference to a subsequent event disclosed in the financial statements which occurs after completion of the fieldwork, but before issuance of the report (AU 530.03). The release date is never used in dating the report on financial statements. The current period report date would only be used for comparative financial statement dating.

56. (a) AU 530.03 states, "In case a subsequent event of the type requiring adjustment of the financial statements occurs after the date of the independent auditor's report but before its issuance, and the event comes to the attention of the auditor, the financial statements should be adjusted or the auditor should qualify his opinion. When the adjustment is made without disclosure of the event, the report should ordinarily be dated (as of the date of the completion of the field work)." Answers (b), (c), and (d) are incorrect because other methods, including dual dating, would be considered when disclosure of the event is made, either in a note or in the auditor's report.

57. (c) When an auditor dual-dates the audit report, his or her responsibility for events occurring subsequent to the completion of field work is limited to the specific event referred to in the identified note (AU 530.05). The auditor is otherwise responsible for all subsequent events occurring up to the date of completion of the field work, which is the date of the auditor's report (AU 530.01). Answers (a), (b), and (d) either limit or expand the responsibility that the auditor takes when the report is dual-dated.

58. (b) Generally, the date of completion of field work should be used as the date of the auditor's report (AU 530.01). The auditor cannot be certain of the date on which the report is delivered to the client. Most of the audit work, for which the auditor is responsible, occurs after the end of the fiscal period under audit. The auditor may have to perform more audit work after the working papers are reviewed. The auditor must take responsibility for such additional audit work.

Subsequent Events

59. (a) AU 560.12 states that the auditor should perform other auditing procedures with respect to the period after the balance-sheet date for the purpose of ascertaining the occurrence of subsequent events that may require adjustment or disclosure essential to a fair presentation of the financial statements. The auditor should generally read the latest available interim financial statements and compare them with the financial statements. Answers (b), (c), and (d) are all examples of procedures which should be performed during the planning and field work stages of the audit for verification of matters and balances pertaining to the year-end presentation.

59A. (d) AU 560.05 states that the second type of subsequent event which includes losses on receivables resulting from conditions arising subsequent to the balance sheet date, provide evidence with respect to conditions that did not exist at the date of the balance sheet being reported on but arose subsequent to that date. These events should not result in adjustment of the financial statements. Some, however, may be of such a nature that disclosure of them is required to keep the financial statements from being misleading. Consistency is implied in the auditor's report, and a subsequent event does not give rise to a report modification for consistency.

60. (c) Section 560 of the AICPA Auditing Standards identifies two types of events occurring subsequent to the balance sheet date but before the statements are issued ("subsequent events"): *Type 1* events provide additional evidence with respect to conditions that *existed at the balance sheet date; Type 2* events concern conditions that *did not exist at the balance sheet date* but arose subsequent to that date. Type 2 events should not result in adjustment to the financial statements, but may be of such nature that disclosure of them is required to keep the financial statements from being misleading (AU 560.05). Management--not the auditor--is responsible for presenting the financial statements, including appropriate disclosures.

60A. (b) AU 530.05 notes than when using dual dating, the auditor's responsibility for events occurring subsequent to the completion of field work is limited to the specific event disclosed. Under no circumstances does the auditor's responsibility extend to the date of the last subsequent event. Responsibility for subsequent events does not extent through the date of report issuance and does not extend past the completion of field work.

61. (a) There is a period after the balance sheet date with which the auditor must be concerned in completing various phases of his or her audit. This period is known as the "subsequent period" and is considered to extend to the date of the auditor's report. Its duration will depend upon the practical requirements of each audit and may vary from a relatively short period to one of several months (AU 560.10).

61A. (b) An auditor generally has no obligation to make any further or continuing inquiries or to perform any other auditing procedures unless new information that might affect the audit report comes to the auditor's attention. No responsibility exists for events occurring after the end of field work in situations in which the report has been issued (AU 561.04); however, answer (b) is based on factors which existed at the date of the auditor's report.

Subsequent Discovery of Facts Existing at the Date of the Auditor's Report (AU 561)

62. (a) AU 561.03 states, "After he has issued his report, the auditor has no obligation to make any further or continuing inquiry or perform any other auditing procedures with respect to the audited financial statements covered by that report, unless new information which may affect his report comes to his attention."

63. (d) "After he has issued his report, the auditor has no obligation to make any further or continuing inquiry or perform any other auditing procedures with respect to the audited financial statements covered by that report, unless new information which may affect his report comes to his attention." (AU 561.03) The decision to sell the shares was made *after* the audit report was issued. Therefore, the auditor has no obligation to make further inquiries. Answers (a), (b) and (c) would be considered only when the subsequently discovered information was found to have existed at the date of the auditor's report.

64. (b) If the auditor becomes aware of information which would have affected financial statements previously reported on by him or her and the information is found to be reliable and to have existed at the date of the auditor's report, he or she should take action to prevent future reliance on the financial statements (AU 561.05). Therefore, the auditor must *first* attempt to determine whether there are persons relying or likely to rely on the financial statements who would attach importance to such information, so that they may be notified.

64A. (a) According to AU 561.05, after determining that information regarding subsequent discovery of facts is reliable, the auditor next determines if people are relying on the information who would believe the information is important.

65. (c) When the auditor becomes aware of information which relates to financial statements previously reported on by him or her, but which was not known to him or her at the date of the report, and which is of such a nature and from such a source that he or she would have investigated it had it come to his or her attention during the course of the audit, the auditor should, as soon as practicable, undertake to determine whether the information is reliable and whether the facts existed at the date of the report. When the subsequently discovered information is found both to be reliable and to have existed at the date of the auditor's report, the auditor should take action to determine if the nature and effect of the matter are such that (1) the report would have been affected if the information had been known at the date of the report and had not been reflected in the financial statements and (2) the auditor believes there are persons currently relying or likely to rely on the financial statements who would attach importance to the information (AU 561.04-.05).

Consideration of Omitted Procedures After the Report Date (AU 390)

66. (b) The auditor does not need to apply the omitted procedure if, "the results of other procedures that were applied . . . compensate for the one omitted or make its omission less important." (AU 390.04) Answers (a), (c), and (d) would not exempt the auditor from applying the omitted procedure.

66A. (b) AU 390.05 states that if the auditor concludes that the omission of a procedure considered necessary at the time of the audit in the circumstances then existing impairs his or her present ability to support the previously expressed opinion regarding the financial statements, and the auditor believes there are persons currently relying on the report, he or she should promptly undertake to apply the omitted procedure or alternative procedures that would provide a satisfactory basis for the opinion. Answer (a) is a procedure to be followed when the auditor determines, after attempting to perform procedures, that the audit report with an unqualified opinion is inappropriate. Answer (c) would not be an alternative in any situation. Answer (d) would not be feasible and would not eliminate the need to perform some auditing procedures beyond tests of controls.

67. (a) When an auditor concludes that an audit procedure considered necessary has been omitted, the first concern should be to determine whether the previously issued opinion can still be supported. A review of the working papers, discussion of the circumstances with engagement personnel and others, and a reevaluation of the overall scope of the audit may be helpful in making this assessment. If the opinion can still be supported, no further action is necessary. Otherwise, if the auditor believes there are persons relying on the report, then the auditor must promptly undertake the omitted procedures or alternative procedures (AU 390.04). A determination of whether or not there are persons relying on the report [answer (a)] would provide no evidence to the auditor in assessing the importance of the omitted procedure.

67A. (c) AU 390.04 states that the results of other procedures that were applied during the audit may tend to compensate for the one omitted or make its omission less important. Other compensating procedures may compensate for the one omitted, regardless of whether the financial statements had been released or not. Qualification of the report does not reduce the auditor's responsibility to perform required procedures or those the auditor considers necessary. Client delays do not justify omitting audit procedures considered necessary to perform the audit.

68. (b) AU 390.05 states, "If the auditor concludes that the omission of a procedure considered necessary at the time of the audit in the circumstances then existing impairs his present ability to support his previously expressed opinion regarding the financial statements taken as a whole, and he believes there are persons currently relying, or likely to rely, on his report, he should promptly undertake to apply the omitted procedure or alternative procedures that would provide a satisfactory basis for his opinion."

69. (c) AU 390.04 states, "When the auditor concludes that an auditing procedure considered necessary at the time of the audit in the circumstances then existing was omitted from his audit of financial statements, he should assess the importance of the omitted procedure to his present ability to support his previously expressed opinion regarding those financial statements taken as a whole." Answers (a), (b), and (d) are steps that can be performed after the required assessment.

Association With Financial Statements (AU 504)

70. (d) A disclaimer of opinion is the appropriate report in this situation, per AU 504.05. The other reports noted are not appropriate.

71. (d) AU 504.15 allows either alternative I or II.

72. (d) When an accountant is associated with the financial statements of a public entity, but has not audited or reviewed such statements, the form of report to be issued is a disclaimer of opinion. The disclaimer of opinion is the means by which the accountant complies with the fourth standard of reporting when associated with unaudited financial statements in those circumstances. When an accountant disclaims an opinion, he or she has no responsibility to apply any procedures beyond reading the financial statements for obvious material misstatements (AU 504.05).

73. (d) "When an accountant is not independent, any procedures he might perform would not be in accordance with generally accepted auditing standards, and he would be precluded from expressing an opinion on such statements." (AU 504.09) An auditor may issue a qualified opinion due to a scope limitation (AU 508.38). The auditor may refer to the work of a specialist when issuing a qualified opinion if the auditor believes such reference will facilitate an understanding of the reason for the qualification of his or her opinion (AU 336.12). A qualified opinion may be issued due to a departure from generally accepted accounting principles (AU 508.38).

74. (c) "If the accountant concludes on the basis of facts known to him that the unaudited financial statements on which he is disclaiming an opinion are not in conformity with generally accepted accounting principles, which include adequate disclosure, he should suggest appropriate revision; failing that, he should describe the departure in his disclaimer of opinion." (AU 504.11) When an auditor disclaims an opinion, he or she cannot, by definition, issue an adverse opinion or a modified opinion.

The Auditor's Consideration of an Entity's Ability to Continue as a Going Concern (AU 341)

75. (d) AU 341.07 states that once the auditor believes there is substantial doubt about the ability of the entity to continue as a going concern for a reasonable period of time, the auditor should consider management's plans for dealing with the adverse effects of the conditions and events including management's plans to increase ownership equity by committing to negotiate to reduce current dividend

requirements. Management should be looking for ways to reduce or delay expenditures. The purchase of treasury stock requires the outlay of cash and will not improve the ownership equity position. The purchasing of equipment requires a further outlay of cash or the encumbrance of more debt.

76. (a) AU 341.12 states, "If, after considering identified conditions and events and management's plans, the auditor concludes that *substantial doubt* about the entity's ability to continue as a *going concern* for a reasonable period of time remains, the audit report should include an *explanatory paragraph* (following the opinion paragraph) to reflect that conclusion." Therefore, the auditor's report should include all three items.

77. (c) AU 341.07 states, "If the auditor believes there is substantial doubt about the ability of the entity to continue as a going concern for a reasonable period of time, he should consider management's plans for dealing with the adverse effects of the conditions and events. The auditor should obtain information about the plans and consider whether it is likely the adverse effects will be mitigated for a reasonable period of time and that such plans can be effectively implemented. The auditor's considerations relating to management plans may include the following: apparent marketability of assets that management plans to sell." Answers (a), (b), and (d) would not increase the company's revenues or decrease expenses, thereby improving the financial health of the entity.

78. (d) If, after considering identified conditions and events and management's plans, the auditor concludes that substantial doubt about the entity's ability to continue as a going concern for a reasonable period of time remains, the audit report should include an explanatory paragraph (following the opinion paragraph) to reflect that conclusion. The inclusion of the explanatory paragraph should serve adequately to inform the users of the statements. However, the auditor is not precluded from declining to express an opinion in cases involving uncertainties (AU 341.12).

79. (a) AU 341.05 lists the following examples of auditing procedures which may identify conditions and events that, when considered in the aggregate, indicate there could be substantial doubt about the entity's ability to continue as a going concern for a reasonable period of time: (1) analytical procedures, (2) review of subsequent events, (3) *review of compliance with the terms of debt and loan agreements*, (4) reading of minutes of meetings of stockholders, board of directors, and important committees of the board, (5) inquiry of an entity's legal counsel about litigation, claims, and assessments, and (6) confirmation with related and third parties of the details of arrangements to provide or maintain financial support.

79A. (b) AU 341.05 lists the following examples of auditing procedures which may identify conditions and events that, when considered in the aggregate, indicate there could be substantial doubt about the entity's ability to continue as a going concern for a reasonable period of time: (1) analytical procedures...(6) confirmation with related and third parties of the details of arrangements to provide or maintain financial support. Pledging assets as collateral does not indicate an inability to continue as a going concern. The auditor may, however, discover by confirming related loans outstanding that the payments have become overdue. Answers (c) and (d) would not uncover any evidence about an entity's ability to continue as a going concern.

80. (c) AU 340.14 states, "If the auditor concludes that the entity's disclosures with respect to the entity's ability to continue as a going concern for a reasonable period of time are inadequate, a departure from generally accepted accounting principles exists. This may result in either a qualified (except for) or an adverse opinion."

81. (b) AU 340.16 states, "If substantial doubt about the entity's ability to continue as a going concern for a reasonable period of time existed at the date of prior period financial statements that are presented on a comparative basis, and that doubt has been removed in the current period, the explanatory paragraph included in the auditor's report (following the opinion paragraph) on the financial statements of the prior period should not be repeated."

82. (c) "A reasonable period of time" is considered to extend up to one year beyond the date of the financial statements (AU 340.02). The absence of reference to substantial doubt in an auditor's report should <u>not</u> be viewed as providing assurance as to an entity's ability to continue as a going concern (AU 340.04). Continuation of an entity as a going concern is assumed in financial reporting in the absence of significant information to the contrary (AU 340.01).

83. (a) Negative cash flows from operating activities is specifically mentioned as an example of a condition that, when considered with other events, may indicate there is substantial doubt about an entity's ability to continue as a going concern.

84. (b) AU 341.10 states that when the auditor concludes there is substantial doubt about the entity's

ability to continue as a going concern for a reasonable period of time, the auditor should consider the possible effects on the financial statements and the adequacy of the related disclosure. AU 341.14 states the auditor would issue a qualified or adverse opinion if the auditor concludes that the entity's disclosure with respect to the ability to continue as a going concern is inadequate. The auditor may report such adjustments to the audit committee, however, further action is required to deal specifically with the going concern issue, regardless of the changes to any unrelated or related accounting estimates. AU 341.15 states that substantial doubt about the entity's ability to continue as a going concern for a reasonable period of time that arose in the current period does not imply that a basis for such doubt existed in the prior period and should not affect the auditor's report on the financial statements of the prior period presented on a comparative basis.

Other Information in Documents Containing Audited Financial Statements (AU 550)

85. (d) AU 550.04 states, "The auditor's responsibility with respect to information in a document does not extend beyond the financial information identified in his report, and the auditor has no obligation to perform any procedures to corroborate other information contained in a document. However, he should read the other information and consider whether such information, or the manner of its presentation, is materially inconsistent with information, or the manner of its presentation, appearing in the financial statements." The auditor has no obligation to perform inquiry, analytical procedures, or other substantive auditing procedures to corroborate other information in a document. An explanatory paragraph would only be considered if the auditor concludes that there is a material inconsistency in the other information, and the other information is not revised to eliminate the material inconsistency.

86. (a) AU 551.07 states that when reporting on additional information included in auditor-submitted documents, the measurement of materiality is the same as that used in forming an opinion on the basic financial statements taken as a whole. Answers (b) and (c) are irrelevant and neither would be used as a basis for determining materiality. The total of both statements would most likely be too high a materiality level to set, creating the possibility that no individual items would be tested.

87. (a) The situation is specifically dealt with in AU 550.04 and the appropriate manner to handle the matter is answer (a). Answers (b), (c), and (d) are not appropriate ways to address the situation.

Supplementary Information Required by the Financial Accounting Standards Board (SAS 52)

88. (c) AU 551.15 presents the auditor's responsibilities for supplementary information. AU 551.15 gives auditors certain responsibilities for supplementary information. The responsibilities extend beyond determining that the supplementary information has not been omitted. Answer (d) is incorrect because the procedures noted are those used to audit the financial statements, not the supplementary information.

89. (d) Since the required supplementary information does not change the standards of financial accounting and reporting used for the preparation of the entity's basic financial statements, the auditor's opinion on the fairness of presentation of such financial statements in conformity with generally accepted accounting principles is not affected. Hence, if management declines to present supplementary information required by the GASB, the auditor should issue an unqualified opinion with an additional explanatory paragraph (AU 558.08).

Segment Information (AU 435)

90. (b) "If the entity declines to include in the financial statements part or all of the segment information that the auditor believes, based on his knowledge of the entity's business, is required to be disclosed, the auditor should modify (i.e., express a qualified or adverse opinion) his opinion on the financial statements because of *inadequate disclosure* and should describe the type of information omitted." (AU 435.10) The auditor should modify his or her opinion on the financial statements (AU 435.10). The opinion is modified due to inadequate disclosure, *not* a departure from generally accepted accounting principles (AU 435.10) or inadequate disclosure, *not* a scope limitation (AU 435.10).

91. (d) AU 435.03 states, "The objective of auditing procedures applied to segment information is to provide the auditor with a reasonable basis for concluding whether the information is presented in conformity with FASB Statement No. 14 in relation to the financial statements taken as a whole."

PERFORMANCE BY SUBTOPICS

Each category below parallels a subtopic covered in Chapter 40. Record the number and percentage of questions you correctly answered in each subtopic area.

The Meaning of "Present Fairly in Conformity With GAAP" in the Independent Auditor's Report (AU 411)

Question #	Correct √
1	
2	
# Questions	2
# Correct	______
% Correct	______

Consistency of Application of GAAP (AU 420)

Question #	Correct √
3	
4	
5	
6	
# Questions	4
# Correct	______
% Correct	______

Types of Opinions

Question #	Correct √
7	
7A	
8	
9	
# Questions	4
# Correct	______
% Correct	______

Standard Report

Question #	Correct √
10	
10A	
10B	
11	
12	
13	
13A	
13B	
# Questions	8
# Correct	______
% Correct	______

Explanatory Language Added to the Auditor's Standard Report

Question #	Correct √
14	
15	
16	
16A	
17	
17A	
18	
18A	
19	
20	
21	
22	
22A	
23	
24	
25	
26	
26A	
27	
27A	
# Questions	20
# Correct	______
% Correct	______

Departures From Unqualified Opinions (AU 508)

Question #	Correct √
28	
29	
29A	
30	
31	
32	
33	
34	
34A	
34B	
35	
36	
36A	
37	
38	
39	
40	
41	
42	
43	
43A	
44	
45	
46	
47	
48	
# Questions	26
# Correct	______
% Correct	______

Reports on Comparative Financial Statements

Question #	Correct √
49	
49A	
50	
50A	
51	
52	
53	
54	
54A	
# Questions	9
# Correct	______
% Correct	______

Dating of the Auditor's Report (AU 530)

Question #	Correct √
55	
55A	
56	
57	
58	
# Questions	5
# Correct	______
% Correct	______

Subsequent Events

Question #	Correct √
59	
59A	
60	
60A	
61	
61A	
# Questions	6
# Correct	______
% Correct	______

Subsequent Discovery of Facts Existing at the Date of the Auditor's Report (AU 561)

Question #	Correct √
62	
63	
64	
64A	
65	
# Questions	5
# Correct	______
% Correct	______

Consideration of Omitted Procedures After the Report Date (AU 390)

Question #	Correct √
66	
66A	
67	
67A	
68	
69	
# Questions	6
# Correct	______
% Correct	______

Association With Financial Statements (AU 504)

Question #	Correct √
70	
71	
72	
73	
74	
# Questions	5
# Correct	______
% Correct	______

The Auditor's Consideration of an Entity's Ability to Continue as a Going Concern (AU 341)

Question #	Correct √
75	
76	
77	
78	
79	
79A	
80	
81	
82	
83	
84	
# Questions	11
# Correct	______
% Correct	______

Other Information in Documents Containing Audited Financial Statements (AU 550)

Question #	Correct √
85	
86	
87	
# Questions	3
# Correct	
% Correct	

Supplementary Information Required by the Financial Accounting Standards Board (SAS 52)

Question #	Correct √
88	
89	
# Questions	2
# Correct	
% Correct	

Segment Information (AU 435)

Question #	Correct √
90	
91	
# Questions	2
# Correct	
% Correct	

OTHER OBJECTIVE FORMAT QUESTIONS

Problem 40-2 (15 to 25 minutes)

Required:

Items 1 through 7 present various independent factual situations an auditor might encounter in conducting an audit. List A represents the types of opinions the auditor ordinarily would issue and List B represents the report modifications (if any) that would be necessary. For each situation, select one response from List A and one from List B. Select as the **best** answer for each item, the action the auditor normally would take. The types of opinions in List A and the report modifications in List B may be selected once, more than once, or not at all.

Assume:

- The auditor is independent.
- The auditor previously expressed an unqualified opinion on the prior year's financial statements.
- Only single-year (not comparative) statements are presented for the current year.
- The conditions for an unqualified opinion exist unless contradicted in the factual situations.
- The conditions stated in the factual situations are material.
- No report modifications are to be made except in response to the factual situation.

Items to be answered:

1. In auditing the long-term investments account, an auditor is unable to obtain audited financial statements for an investee located in a foreign country. The auditor concludes that sufficient competent evidential matter regarding this investment cannot be obtained.

2. Due to recurring operating losses and working capital deficiencies, an auditor has substantial doubt about an entity's ability to continue as a going concern for a reasonable period of time. However, the financial statement disclosures concerning these matters are adequate.

3. A principal auditor decides to take responsibility for the work of another CPA who audited a wholly owned subsidiary of the entity and issued an unqualified opinion. The total assets and revenues of the subsidiary represent 17% and 18%, respectively, of the total assets and revenues of the entity being audited.

4. An entity issues financial statements that present financial position and results of operations but omits the related statement of cash flows. Management discloses in the notes to the financial statements that it does not believe the statement of cash flows to be a useful financial statement.

5. An entity changes its depreciation method for production equipment from the straight-line to a units-of-production method based on hours of utilization. The auditor concurs with the change although it has a material effect on the comparability of the entity's financial statements.

6. An entity is a defendant in a lawsuit alleging infringement of certain patent rights. However, the ultimate outcome of the litigation cannot be reasonably estimated by management. The auditor believes there is a reasonable possibility of a significant material loss, but the lawsuit is adequately disclosed in the notes to the financial statements.

7. An entity discloses in the notes to the financial statements certain lease obligations. The auditor believes that the failure to capitalize these leases is a departure from generally accepted accounting principles.

List A
Types of Opinions

A. An "except for" qualified opinion.

B. An unqualified opinion.

C. An adverse opinion.

D. A disclaimer of opinion.

E. Either an "except for" qualified opinion or an adverse opinion.

F. Either a disclaimer of opinion or an "except for" qualified opinion.

G. Either an adverse opinion or a disclaimer of opinion.

List B
Report Modifications

H. Describe the circumstances in an explanatory paragraph **preceding** the opinion paragraph **without modifying** the three standard paragraphs.

I. Describe the circumstances in an explanatory paragraph **following** the opinion paragraph **without modifying** the three standard paragraphs.

J. Describe the circumstances in an explanatory paragraph **preceding** the opinion paragraph and **modify** the **opinion** paragraph.

K. Describe the circumstances in an explanatory paragraph **following** the opinion paragraph and **modify** the **opinion** paragraph.

L. Describe the circumstances in an explanatory paragraph **preceding** the opinion paragraph and **modify** the **scope** and **opinion** paragraphs.

M. Describe the circumstances in an explanatory paragraph **following** the opinion paragraph and **modify** the **scope** and **opinion** paragraphs.

N. Describe the circumstances within the **scope** paragraph without adding an explanatory paragraph.

O. Describe the circumstances within the **opinion** paragraph without adding an explanatory paragraph.

P. Describe the circumstances within the **scope** and **opinion** paragraphs without adding an explanatory paragraph.

Q. Issue the **standard** auditor's report **without modification.** (5/92, Aud., #61-67)

Problem 40-3 (15 to 25 minutes)

Perry & Price, CPAs, audited the consolidated financial statements of Bond Company for the year ended December 31, 1993, and expressed an adverse opinion because Bond carried its plant and equipment at appraisal values, and provided for depreciation on the basis of such values.

Perry & Price also audited Bond's financial statements for the year ended December 31, 1994. These consolidated financial statements are being presented on a comparative basis with those of the prior year and an unqualified opinion is being expressed.

Smith, the engagement supervisor, instructed Adler, an assistant on the engagement, to draft the auditor's report on May 3, 1995, the date of completion of the field work. In drafting the report below, Adler considered the following:

- Bond recently changed its method of accounting for plant and equipment and restated its 1993 consolidated financial statements to conform with GAAP. Consequently, the CPA firm's present opinion on those statements is different (unqualified) from the opinion expressed on May 12, 1994.
- Larkin & Lake, CPAs, audited the financial statements of BX, Inc., a consolidated subsidiary of Bond, for the year ended December 31, 1994. The subsidiary's financial statements reflected total assets and revenues of 2% and 3%, respectively, of the consolidated totals. Larkin & Lake expressed an unqualified opinion and furnished Perry & Price with a copy of the auditor's report. Perry & Price has decided to assume responsibility for the work of Larkin & Lake insofar as it relates to the expression of an opinion on the consolidated financial statements taken as a whole.

- Bond is a defendant in a lawsuit alleging patent infringement. This is adequately disclosed in the notes to Bond's financial statements, but no provision for liability has been recorded because the ultimate outcome of the litigation cannot presently be determined.

Auditor's Report

We have audited the accompanying consolidated balance sheets of Bond Company and subsidiaries as of December 31, 1994 and 1993, and the related consolidated statements of income, retained earnings, and cash flows for the years then ended. These financial statements are the responsibility of the Company's management. Our responsibility is to express an opinion on these financial statements based on our audits.

We conducted our audits in accordance with generally accepted auditing standards. Those standards require that we plan and perform the audit to obtain reasonable assurance about whether the financial statements are free of material misstatement. An audit includes examining, on a test basis, evidence supporting the amounts and disclosures in the financial statements. An audit also includes assessing the accounting principles used, as well as evaluating the overall financial statement presentation. We believe that our audits provide a reasonable basis for our opinion.

In our previous report, we expressed an opinion that the 1993 financial statements did not fairly present financial position, results of operations, and cash flows in conformity with generally accepted accounting principles because the Company carried its plant and equipment at appraisal values and provided for depreciation on the basis of such values. As described in Note 12, the Company has changed its method of accounting for these items and restated its 1993 financial statements to conform with generally accepted accounting principles. Accordingly, our present opinion on the 1993 financial statements, as presented herein, is different from that expressed in our previous report.

In our opinion, the consolidated financial statements referred to above present fairly, in all material respects, the financial position of Bond Company and subsidiaries as of December 31, 1994 and 1993, and the results of its operations and its cash flows for the years then ended in conformity with generally accepted accounting principles except for the change in accounting principles with which we concur and the uncertainty, which is discussed in the following explanatory paragraph.

The Company is a defendant in a lawsuit alleging infringement of certain patent rights. The Company has filed a counteraction, and preliminary hearings and discovery proceedings are in progress. The ultimate outcome of the litigation cannot presently be determined. Accordingly, no provision for any liability that may result upon adjudication has been made in the accompanying financial statements.

Perry & Price, CPAs
May 3, 1995

Required:

Smith reviewed Adler's draft and indicated in the *Supervisor's Review Notes* below that there were deficiencies in Adler's draft. **Items 1 through 15** represent the deficiencies noted by Smith. For each deficiency, indicate whether Smith is correct or incorrect in the criticism of Adler's draft.

Supervisor's Review Notes

1. The report is improperly titled.
2. All the basic financial statements are **not** properly identified in the introductory paragraph.
3. There is **no** reference to the American Institute of Certified Public Accountants in the introductory paragraph.
4. Larkin & Lake are **not** identified in the introductory and opinion paragraphs.
5. The subsidiary, BX Inc., is **not** identified and the magnitude of BX's financial statements is **not** disclosed in the introductory paragraph.
6. The report does **not** state in the scope paragraph that generally accepted auditing standards require analytical procedures to be performed in planning an audit.
7. The report does **not** state in the scope paragraph that an audit includes assessing the internal control structure.
8. The report does **not** state in the scope paragraph that an audit includes assessing significant estimates made by management.
9. The date of the previous report (May 12, 1994) is **not** disclosed in the first explanatory paragraph.

10. It is inappropriate to disclose in the first explanatory paragraph the circumstances that caused Perry & Price to express a different opinion on the 1993 financial statements.

11. The concurrence with the accounting change is inappropriate in the opinion paragraph.

12. Reference to the (litigation) uncertainty should **not** be made in the opinion paragraph.

13. Bond's disclosure of the (litigation) uncertainty in the notes to the financial statements is **not** referred to in the second explanatory paragraph.

14. The letter of inquiry to Bond's lawyer concerning litigation, claims, and assessments is **not** referred to in the second explanatory paragraph.

15. The report is **not** dual dated, but it should be because of the change of opinion on the 1993 financial statements. (5/95, Aud., #2)

OTHER OBJECTIVE FORMAT SOLUTIONS

Solution 40-2 Types of Opinions/Report Modifications

1. (F) List A, (L) List B. AU 508.40 states, "Restrictions on the scope of (an auditor's) audit, whether imposed by the client or by the circumstances, such as an inability to obtain sufficient competent evidential matter, or an inadequacy in the accounting records, may require the auditor to qualify his opinion or to disclaim an opinion." Further, it is noted in AU 508.42 that a "common scope restriction involves accounting for long-term investments when the auditor has not been able to obtain audited financial statements of an investee."

   AU 508.43 states, "When a qualified opinion results from a limitation on the scope of the audit or an insufficiency of evidential matter, the situation should be described in an explanatory paragraph preceding the opinion paragraph and referred to in both the scope and opinion paragraphs of the auditor's report."

2. (B) List A, (I) List B. A substantial doubt about an entity's ability to continue as a going concern is listed in AU 508.11 as one of the circumstances which does not affect the auditor's unqualified opinion, but may require the addition of an explanatory paragraph.

   AU 341.12 states, "If, after considering identified conditions and events and management's plans, the auditor concludes that substantial doubt about the entity's ability to continue as a going concern for a reasonable period of time remains, the audit report should include an explanatory paragraph (following the opinion paragraph) to reflect that conclusion." Inadequate disclosure with respect to an entity's ability to continue as a going concern is a departure from GAAP, resulting in either an "except for" qualified opinion or an adverse opinion (AU 341.14). In this case, however, because it was concluded that financial statement disclosures were adequate, an unqualified opinion with an explanatory paragraph is appropriate.

3. (B) List A, (Q) List B. If the principal auditor is able to satisfy him- or herself as to the independence and professional reputation of the other auditor and takes steps considered appropriate to satisfy him- or herself as to the audit performed by the other auditor, he or she may express an unqualified opinion on the financial statements taken as a whole (AU 543.04).

   AU 543.03 states, "If the auditor decides that it is appropriate for him to serve as the principal auditor, he must then decide whether to make reference in his report to the audit performed by another auditor. If the principal auditor decides to assume responsibility for the work of the other auditor insofar as that work relates to the principal auditor's expression of an opinion taken as a whole, no reference should be made to the other auditor's work or report."

4. (A) List A, (J) List B. AU 508.58 states, "The auditor is not required to prepare a basic financial statement and include it in his report if the company's management declines to present the statement." Accordingly, the auditor should issue an "except for" qualified

opinion. The circumstances surrounding the qualification are to be reported in a separate paragraph preceding the opinion paragraph. The opinion paragraph itself should then be modified using the appropriate "except for" wording, making reference to the separate explanatory paragraph.

5. (B) List A, (I) List B. Since the auditor concurs with the change in accounting principle, he or she does not take exception to the change in expressing his or her opinion as to fair presentation of the financial statements in conformity with generally accepted accounting principles. Therefore, the auditor may express an unqualified opinion.

   Changes in accounting principle having a material effect on the financial statements require recognition in the independent auditor's report through the addition of an explanatory paragraph (following the opinion paragraph). Such explanatory paragraph should identify the nature of the change and refer the reader to the note in the financial statements that discusses the change in detail (AU 508.34).

6. (B) List A, (I) List B. AU 508.17 states, "If the auditor has not obtained sufficient evidential matter to support management's assertions about the nature of a matter involving an uncertainty and its presentation or disclosure in the financial statements, he should consider the need to express a qualified opinion or to disclaim an opinion because of a scope limitation." In this question, however, the lawsuit and possible outcome have been adequately described in the notes to the financial statements. Thus, an unqualified opinion is appropriate. AU 508.26 indicates that if management believes, and the auditor is satisfied that the possibility of a material loss resulting from the resolution of an uncertainty is reasonably possible then consideration must be given to adding an explanatory paragraph. One consideration is the likelihood of a material loss occurring and another concerns the amount that a reasonably possible loss may exceed materiality limits. As either of these two considerations increase, the likelihood of the auditor adding an explanatory paragraph also increases. AU 508.31 states, "If, after applying the (appropriate) criteria, the auditor has concluded that he should include an explanatory paragraph in his report, he should describe the matter giving rise to the uncertainty in the explanatory paragraph (following the opinion paragraph) and indicate that its outcome cannot presently be determined. No reference to the uncertainty should be made in the introductory, scope, or opinion paragraphs of his report."

7. (E) List A, (J) List B. AU 508.49 and 508.50 state, "When financial statements are materially affected by a departure from generally accepted accounting principles and the auditor has audited the statements in accordance with generally accepted auditing standards he should express a qualified or an adverse opinion." Factors to consider when deciding whether to issue either of these two opinions include: (1) the dollar magnitude of the effect, (2) the qualitative and quantitative aspects of the departure, (3) the pervasiveness of the misstatement, and (4) the effects on the other financial statements. AU 508.51 and 508.68 indicate that the auditor should disclose, in a separate explanatory paragraph preceding the opinion paragraph, all the substantive reasons for a departure from generally accepted accounting principles and that the opinion paragraph should include appropriate qualifying language.

Solution 40-3 Report Deficiencies

1. (C) A proper title contains the words *independent auditors' report.*

2. (I) The introductory paragraph contains all the necessary references to the audited financial statements.

3. (I) Reference to the American Institute of Certified Public Accountants does not belong anywhere in the report.

4. (I) Perry & Price have decided to assume responsibility for the work of Larkin & Lake as it relates to the expression of an opinion on the consolidated financial statements taken as a whole. In this circumstance it is inappropriate for Perry & Price to refer to Larkin & Lake anywhere in the report.

5. (I) The subsidiary and its magnitude need not be referred to anywhere in the auditor's report.

6. (I) The auditor's report need not state anywhere the requirements of GAAS.

7. (I) The auditor's report need not state anywhere the evaluation of the internal control structure is part of an audit.

8. (C) The auditor's report should state in the scope paragraph that an audit includes assessing significant estimates made by management.

9. (C) When a client subsequently restates prior period financial statements to conform with GAAP, and the auditor decides to express a different opinion than that previously expressed, the auditor should disclose all the substantive reasons for the different opinion in a separate explanatory paragraph preceding the opinion paragraph of the report, that should include: (1) the date of the auditor's previous report; (2) the type of opinion previously expressed; (3) the circumstances or events that caused the auditor to express a different opinion; and (4) that the auditor's updated opinion on the financial statements is different from the auditor's previous opinion on those financial statements.

10. (I) See the explanation to 5/95, Aud., #99.

11. (C) The opinion paragraph should contain only the opinion. Concurrence is assumed if the restated opinion is favorable, and therefore no such explicit statement is necessary in other paragraphs.

12. (C) No reference to any uncertainties should be made in the introductory, scope, or opinion paragraphs. Reference to the uncertainty should be made in a separate explanatory paragraph following the opinion paragraph.

13. (C) The particular note describing the uncertainty should be referred to in the auditor's report. The auditor may describe the uncertainty, but must still refer to the note (AU 508.32).

14. (I) Letters of inquiry to a client's lawyer concerning litigation, claims, and assessments is covered by <u>SAS 12</u>, AU 337. No reference should be made in the auditor's report to such a letter. <u>SAS 73</u> allows mention of a specialist, such as a lawyer, in an auditor's report only when the report is qualified and only when the reference to the specialist will increase the reader's understanding of the qualification, such as in the interpretation of a contractual agreement. <u>SAS 73</u> does not cover letters of inquiry to a client's lawyer.

15. (I) Reports are dual dated in response to a change in opinion when there has been a subsequent event. Changing the financial statements to conform to GAAP is not considered a subsequent event in this context.

ESSAY QUESTIONS

Essay 40-4 (15 to 25 minutes)

The auditor's report below was drafted by Miller, a staff accountant of Pell & Pell, CPAs, at the completion of the audit of the consolidated financial statements of Bond Co. for the year ended July 31, 1993. The report was submitted to the engagement partner who reviewed the audit working papers and properly concluded that an unqualified opinion should be issued. In drafting the report, Miller considered the following:

- Bond's consolidated financial statements for the year ended July 31, 1992, are to be presented for comparative purposes. Pell previously audited these statements and appropriately rendered an unmodified report.
- Bond has suffered recurring losses from operations and has adequately disclosed these losses and management's plans concerning the losses in a note to the consolidated financial statements. Although Bond has prepared the financial statements assuming it will continue as a going concern, Miller has substantial doubt about Bond's ability to continue as a going concern.
- Smith & Smith, CPAs, audited the financial statements of BC Services, Inc., a consolidated subsidiary of Bond, for the year ended July 31, 1993. The subsidiary's financial statements reflected total assets and revenues of 15% and 18%, respectively, of the consolidated totals. Smith expressed an unqualified opinion and furnished Miller with a copy of the auditor's report. Smith also granted permission to present the report together with the principal auditor's report. Miller decided not to present Smith's report with that of Pell, but instead to make reference to Smith.

<u>Independent Auditor's Report</u>

We have audited the consolidated balance sheets of Bond Co. and subsidiaries as of July 31, 1993, and 1992, and the related consolidated statements of income and retained earnings for the years then ended. Our responsibility is to express an opinion on these financial statements based on our audits. We did not audit the financial statements of BC Services, Inc., a wholly-owned subsidiary. Those statements were audited by Smith & Smith, CPAs, whose report has been furnished to us, and our opinion, insofar as it relates to the amounts included for BC Services, Inc., is based solely on the report of Smith & Smith.

We conducted our audits in accordance with generally accepted auditing standards. Those standards require that we plan and perform the audit to obtain reasonable assurance about whether the financial statements are free of material misstatement. An audit includes assessing control risk, the accounting principles used, and significant estimates made by management, as well as evaluating the overall financial statement presentation. We believe that our audits provide a reasonable basis for our opinion.

In our opinion, based on our audits and the report of Smith & Smith, CPAs, the consolidated financial statements referred to above present fairly, in all material respects except for the matter discussed below, the financial position of Bond Co. as of July 31, 1993, and 1992, and the results of its operations for the years then ended.

The accompanying consolidated financial statements have been prepared with the disclosure in Note 13 that the company has suffered recurring losses from operations. Management's plans in regard to those matters are also discussed in Note 13. The financial statements do not include any adjustments that might result from the outcome of this uncertainty.

Pell & Pell, CPAs
November 4, 1993

Required:

Identify the deficiencies in the auditor's report as drafted by Miller. Group the deficiencies by paragraph and in the order in which the deficiencies appear. Do **not** redraft the report. (11/93, Aud., #3)

Essay 40-5 (15 to 25 minutes)

Post, CPA, accepted an engagement to audit the financial statements of General Co., a new client. General is a publicly held retailing entity that recently replaced its operating management. In the course of applying auditing procedures, Post discovered that General's financial statements may be materially misstated due to the existence of irregularities.

Required:

a. Describe Post's responsibilities on the circumstances described above.

b. Describe Post's responsibilities for reporting on General's financial statements and other communications if Post is precluded from applying necessary procedures in searching for irregularities.

c. Describe Post's responsibilities for reporting on General's financial statements and other communications if Post concludes that General's financial statements are materially affected by irregularities.

d. Describe the circumstances in which Post may have a duty to disclose irregularities to third parties outside General's management and its audit committee. (5/93, Aud., #4)

Essay 40-6 (15 to 25 minutes)

The auditors' report below was drafted by Moore, a staff accountant of Tyler & Tyler, CPAs, at the completion of the audit of the financial statements of Park Publishing Co., Inc., for the year ended September 30, 1992. The report was submitted to the engagement partner who reviewed the audit working papers and properly concluded that an unqualified opinion should be issued. In drafting the report, Moore considered the following:

- During fiscal year 1992, Park changed its depreciation method. The engagement partner concurred with this change in accounting principle and its justification and Moore included an explanatory paragraph in the auditor's report.
- The 1992 financial statements are affected by an uncertainty concerning a lawsuit, the outcome of which cannot presently be estimated. Moore has included an explanatory paragraph in the auditors' report.
- The financial statements for the year ended September 30, 1991, are to be presented for comparative purposes. Tyler & Tyler previously audited these statements and expressed an unqualified opinion.

Independent Auditors' Report

To the Board of Directors of Park Publishing Co., Inc.:

We have audited the accompanying balance sheets of Park Publishing Co., Inc. as of September 30, 1992, and 1991, and the related statements of income and cash flows for the years then ended. These financial statements are the responsibility of the company's management.

We conducted our audits in accordance with generally accepted auditing standards. Those standards require that we plan and perform the audit to obtain reasonable assurance about whether the financial statements are fairly presented. An audit includes examining, on a test basis, evidence supporting the amounts and disclosures in the financial statements. An audit also includes assessing significant estimates made by management, as well as evaluating the overall financial statement presentation. We believe that our audits provide a basis for determining whether any material modifications should be made to the accompanying financial statements.

As discussed in Note X to the financial statements, the company changed its method of computing depreciation in fiscal 1992.

In our opinion, except for the accounting change, with which we concur, the financial statements referred to above present fairly, in all material respects, the financial position of Park Publishing Co., Inc. as of September 30, 1992, and the results of its operations and its cash flows for the year then ended in conformity with generally accepted accounting principles.

As discussed in Note Y to the financial statements, the company is a defendant in a lawsuit alleging infringement of certain copyrights. The company has filed a counteraction, and preliminary hearings on both actions are in progress. Accordingly, any provision for liability is subject to adjudication of this matter.

Tyler & Tyler, CPAs
November 5, 1992

Required:

Identify the deficiencies in the auditors' report as drafted by Moore. Group the deficiencies by paragraph and in the order in which the deficiencies appear. Do **not** redraft the report. (11/92, Aud., #3)

Essay 40-7 (15 to 25 minutes)

Green, CPA, is auditing the financial statements of Taylor Corporation for the year ended December 31, 1989. Green plans to complete the field work and sign the auditor's report about May 10, 1990. Green is concerned about events and transactions occurring after December 31, 1989 that may affect the 1989 financial statements.

Required:

a. What are the general types of subsequent events that require Green's consideration and evaluation?

b. What are the auditing procedures Green should consider performing to gather evidence concerning subsequent events? (5/90, Aud., #4)

Essay 40-8 (15 to 25 minutes)

The auditor's report below was drafted by a staff accountant of Jones & Jones, CPAs, at the completion of the audit engagement on the financial statements of Adams Mining, Inc., for the year ended December 31, 1988. It was submitted to the engagement partner who reviewed matters thoroughly and properly concluded that a qualified opinion should be issued because Adams is a defendant in a lawsuit alleging infringement of certain mining rights. The outcome of this material uncertainty cannot be reasonably estimated and is fully disclosed in the consolidated financial statements.
The financial statements for the year ended December 31, 1988 are to be presented for comparative purposes. Jones & Jones previously audited these statements and expressed a qualified opinion because of the aforementioned lawsuit.

On January 31, 1989, Adams acquired a new subsidiary, Harris Coal, Inc. Disclosure of this subsequent event was properly made in Note T to the consolidated financial statements.

To the Board of Directors of Adams Mining, Inc.:

We have audited the consolidated balance sheets of Adams Mining, Inc. and subsidiaries as of December 31, 1988 and 1987, and the related consolidated statements of income, retained earnings, and cash flows for the years then ended. These financial statements are the responsibility of the Company's management. Our responsibility is to express an opinion on these financial statements based on our audit. We did not audit the financial statements of Ford Realty, Inc. a consolidated subsidiary. These statements were audited by King & Co., CPAs, whose report has been furnished to us, and is not presented separately herein. Our opinion, insofar as it relates to the amounts included for Ford Realty is based solely upon the report of King.

We conducted our audits in accordance with generally accepted auditing standards. Those standards require that we plan and perform the audit to obtain reasonable assurance about whether the financial statements are free of material misstatements. An audit also includes assessing the accounting principles used and significant estimates made by the auditor, as well as evaluating the overall financial statement presentation. We believe that our audits and the report of other auditors provide a reasonable basis for our opinion.

Due to the complex nature and magnitude of the Company's mineral holdings, we retained the geological engineering firm of Silver & Gold to attest to the value of the Company's mining inventory and mineral reserves. As a result, the specialist's findings fully support the related representations in the consolidated financial statements.

In our opinion, except for the effects on the consolidated financial statements of a lawsuit in which the Company is a defendant alleging infringement of certain mining rights, the consolidated financial statements referred to above present fairly, in all material respects, the financial position as of December 31, 1988, and the related consolidated statements of income and retained earnings for the year then ended, in conformity with generally accepted accounting principles.

Jones & Jones, CPAs
April 10, 1988, except for Note T as
to which the date is January 31, 1989.

Required:

Identify the deficiencies contained in the auditor's report as drafted by the staff accountant. Group the deficiencies by paragraph. Do **not** redraft the report.
(5/88, Aud., #5)

Essay 40-9 (15 to 25 minutes)

On September 30, 1988, White & Co., CPAs, was engaged to audit the consolidated financial statements of National Motors, Inc. for the year ended December 31, 1988. The consolidated financial statements of National had not been audited the prior year. National's inadequate inventory records precluded White from forming an opinion as to the proper or consistent application of generally accepted accounting principles to inventory balances on January 1, 1988. Therefore, White decided not to express an opinion on the results of operations for the year ended December 31, 1988. National elected not to present comparative financial statements.
Rapid Parts Company, a consolidated subsidiary of National, was audited for the year ended December 31, 1988, by Green & Co., CPAs. Green completed its field work on February 28, 1989, and submitted an unqualified opinion on Rapid's financial statements on March 7, 1989. Rapid's statements reflect total assets and revenues constituting 22% and 25%, respectively, of the consolidated totals of National. White decided not to assume responsibility for the work of Green. Green's report on Rapid does not accompany National's consolidated statements.

White completed its field work on March 28, 1989, and submitted its auditor's report to National on April 4, 1989.

Required:

Prepare White and Company's auditor's report on the consolidated financial statements of National Motors, Inc.
(11/86, Aud., #5)

Essay 40-10 (15 to 25 minutes)

Brown & Brown, CPAs, was engaged by the board of directors of Cook Industries, Inc. to audit Cook's calendar year 1988 financial statements. The following report was drafted by an audit assistant at the completion of the engagement. It was submitted to Brown, the partner with client responsibility for review, on March 7, 1989, the date of the completion of field work. Brown has reviewed matters thoroughly and properly concluded that an adverse opinion was appropriate.

Brown also became aware of a March 14, 1989, subsequent event which the client has properly disclosed in the notes to the financial statements. Brown wants responsibility for subsequent events to be limited to the specific event referred to in the applicable note to the client's financial statements.

The financial statements of Cook Industries, Inc., for the calendar year 1987 were examined by predecessor auditors who also expressed an adverse opinion and have not reissued their report. The financial statements for 1987 and 1988 are presented in comparative form.

Independent Auditor's Report

To the President of Cook Industries, Inc.:

We have audited the financial statements of Cook Industries, Inc., as of December 31, 1988. These financial statements are the responsibility of the Company's management. Our responsibility is to express an opinion on these financial statements based on our audit.

We conducted our audit in accordance with generally accepted auditing standards. Those standards require that we plan and perform the audit to obtain reasonable assurance about whether the financial statements are free of material misstatement. An audit includes examining, on a test basis, evidence supporting the amounts and disclosures in the financial statements. As discussed in Note K to the financial statements, the Company has properly disclosed a subsequent event dated March 14, 1989. We believe that our audit provides a reasonable basis for our opinion.

As discussed in Note G to the financial statements, the Company carries its property and equipment at appraisal values, and provides depreciation on the basis of such values. Further, the company does not provide for income taxes with respect to differences between financial income and taxable income arising because of the use, for income tax purposes, of the installment method of reporting gross profit from certain types of sales.

In our opinion, the financial statements referred to above do not present fairly the financial position of Cook Industries, Inc., as of December 31, 1988, or the results of its operations and cash flows for the year then ended.

Brown & Brown, CPAs
March 7, 1989

Required:

Identify the deficiencies in the draft of the proposed report. Do **not** redraft the report or discuss corrections. (5/86, Aud., #3)

Essay 40-11 (15 to 25 minutes)

The CPA firm of May & Marty has audited the consolidated financial statements of BGI Corporation. May & Marty performed the audit of the parent company and all subsidiaries except for BGI-Western Corporation, which was audited by the CPA firm of Dey & Dee. BGI-Western constituted approximately 10% of the consolidated assets and 6% of the consolidated revenue.

Dey & Dee issued an unqualified opinion on the financial statements of BGI-Western. May & Marty will be issuing an unqualified opinion on the consolidated financial statements of BGI.

Required:

a. What procedures should May & Marty consider performing with respect to Dey & Dee's audit of BGI-Western's financial statements that will be appropriate whether or not reference is to be made to the other auditors?

b. Describe the various circumstances under which May & Marty could take responsibility for the work of Dey & Dee and make no reference to Dey & Dee's audit of BGI-Western in May & Marty's auditor's report on the consolidated financial statements of BGI. (11/85, Aud., #2)

Essay 40-12 (15 to 25 minutes)

Devon Incorporated engaged Smith to audit its financial statements for the year ended December 31, 1988. The financial statements of Devon Incorporated for the year ended December 31, 1987, were audited by Jones whose March 31, 1988, auditor's report expressed an unqualified opinion. This report of Jones is not presented with the 1988-1987 comparative financial statements.

Smith's working papers contain the following information that does not appear in footnotes to the 1988 financial statements as prepared by Devon Incorporated:

- One director appointed in 1988 was formerly a partner in Jones' accounting firm. Jones' firm provided financial consulting services to Devon during 1984 and 1983, for which Devon paid approximately $1,600 and $9,000, respectively.
- The company refused to capitalize certain lease obligations for equipment acquired in 1988. Capitalization of the leases in conformity with generally accepted accounting principles would have increased assets and liabilities by $312,000 and $387,000, respectively, and decreased retained earnings as of December 31, 1988, by $75,000, and would have decreased net income and earnings per share by $75,000 and $.75, respectively, for the year then ended. Smith has concluded that the leases should have been capitalized.

- During the year, Devon changed its method of valuing inventory from the first-in, first-out method to the last-in, first-out method. This change was made because management believes LIFO more clearly reflects net income by providing a closer matching of current costs and current revenues. The change had the effect of reducing inventory at December 31, 1988 by $65,000 and net income and earnings per share by $38,000 and $.38, respectively, for the year then ended. The effect of the change on prior years was immaterial; accordingly, there was no cumulative effect of the change. Smith firmly supports the company's position.

After completion of the field work on February 28, 1989, Smith concludes that the expression of an adverse opinion is not warranted.

Required:

Prepare the body of Smith's report dated February 28, 1989, and addressed to the Board of Directors to accompany the 1988-1987 comparative financial statements. (11/84, Aud., #5)

Essay 40-13 (25 to 35 minutes)

On November 19, 1994, Wall, CPA, was engaged to audit the financial statements of Trendy Auto Imports, Inc. for the year ended December 31, 1994. Wall is considering Trendy's ability to continue as a going concern.

Required:

a. Describe Wall's basic responsibility in considering Trendy's ability to continue as a going concern.

b. Describe the audit procedures Wall most likely would perform to identify conditions and events that may indicate that Trendy has a going concern problem.

c. Describe the management plans that Wall should consider that could mitigate the adverse effects of Trendy's financial difficulties if Wall identified conditions and events that indicated a potential going concern problem. (5/95, Aud., #5)

ESSAY SOLUTIONS

Solution 40-4 Report Deficiencies--Going Concern Uncertainty/Other Auditors

Deficiencies in Miller's draft are as follows:

Within the opening (introductory) paragraph

- The **statement of cash flows** is not identified in this paragraph or in the opinion paragraph.
- The financial statements are not stated to be the **responsibility of management.**
- The magnitude of the portion of the consolidated financial statements audited by the **other auditors** is not disclosed.
- Smith **may not be named** in this paragraph or in the opinion paragraph unless Smith's report is presented together with Pell's report.

Within the second (scope) paragraph

- The statement "An audit includes **examining, on a test basis, evidence supporting the amounts and disclosures in the financial statements**" is omitted.
- It is inappropriate to state that an audit includes "**assessing control risk.**"
- **Reference to the audit of the other auditors** as part of the basis for the opinion is omitted.

Within the third (opinion) paragraph

- Use of the phrase "**except for the matter discussed below**" is inappropriate.
- Reference to "**conformity with generally accepted accounting principles**" is omitted.

Within the fourth (explanatory) paragraph

- The terms "**substantial doubt**" and **going concern**" are omitted.

Solution 40-5 Reporting Irregularities

a. If Post discovers that General's financial statements may be materially misstated due to the **existence of irregularities,** Post should consider the **implications** for other aspects of the audit and discuss the matter and approach to further investigation with an **appropriate level of management that is at least one level above those involved** with the irregularities. Post should also attempt to obtain sufficient competent evidential matter to determine whether, in fact, material irregularities exist and, if so, their effect. Post may suggest that General consult with its legal counsel on matters concerning questions of law.

b. If Post is **precluded from applying necessary procedures,** Post should **disclaim or qualify** an opinion on the financial statements and **communicate** these findings to General's **audit committee** or its **board of directors**.

c. If Post concludes that General's financial statements **are materially affected** by irregularities, Post should insist that the **financial statements be revised** and, if they are not, express a **qualified or** an **adverse** opinion on the financial statements, disclosing all the substantive reasons for such an opinion. Additionally, Post should adequately inform General's audit committee or its board of directors about the irregularities.

d. Post may have a duty to disclose irregularities to **third parties** outside General's management and its audit committee in the following circumstances:

- When General reports an **auditor change** under the appropriate securities law.
- When a **successor auditor appropriately makes inquiries** of a predecessor auditor.
- When responding to a **subpoena.**
- When **communicating with a funding or other specified agency,** as required for entities that receive financial assistance from a government agency.

Solution 40-6 Report Deficiencies--Uncertainty and Accounting Change

Deficiencies in the auditors' report are as follows:

First (Introductory) Paragraph

1. The statement of retained earnings is not identified.
2. The auditor's responsibility to express an opinion is omitted.

Second (Scope) Paragraph

3. The auditor obtains reasonable assurance about whether the financial statements are **"free of material misstatement,"** not **"fairly presented."**
4. The auditors' assessment of the accounting principles used is omitted.
5. An audit provides a **"reasonable basis for an opinion,"** not a "basis for determining whether any material modifications should be made."

Third (First Explanatory) Paragraph

6. An explanatory paragraph added to the report to describe a change in accounting principle (**lack of consistency**) should **follow** the **opinion paragraph, not precede** it.

Fourth (Opinion) Paragraph

7. The phrase "except for" should not be used.
8. The auditor's concurrence with the change in accounting principles is implicit and should not be mentioned.
9. Reference to the prior year's (1991) financial statements is omitted.

Fifth (Second Explanatory) Paragraph

10. The fact that the outcome of the lawsuit cannot presently be estimated is omitted.
11. It is inappropriate to state that "provision for any liability is subject to adjudication" because the report is ambiguous as to whether a liability has been recorded.

Solution 40-7 Subsequent Events (AU 560)

a. The first type of subsequent event includes those events that provide **additional evidence concerning conditions that existed at the balance sheet date** and affect the estimates inherent in the process of preparing financial statements. This type of subsequent event **requires that the financial statements** be adjusted for any changes in estimates resulting from the use of such additional evidence.

The second type of subsequent event consists of those events that provide evidence concerning **conditions that did not exist** at the balance sheet date but **arose subsequent** to that date. These events should **not result in adjustment** to the financial statements but may be such that **disclosure** is required to keep the financial statements from being misleading.

b. The auditing procedures Green should consider performing to gather evidence concerning subsequent events include the following:

- **Compare** the latest available **interim statements** with the financial statements being audited.

- Ascertain whether the interim statements were prepared on the same basis as the audited financial statements.
- Inquire whether any contingent liabilities or commitments existed at the balance sheet date or the date of inquiry.
- **Inquire** whether there was any significant **change** in the capital stock, long-term debt, or working capital to the date of inquiry.
- **Inquire** about the current status of **items** in the audited financial statements that were accounted for on the basis of **tentative, preliminary, or inconclusive data**.
- Inquire about any unusual adjustments made since the balance sheet date.
- **Read or inquire about** the **minutes** of meetings of stockholders or the board of directors.
- Inquire of the client's **legal counsel** concerning litigation, claims, and assessments.
- Obtain a **management representation letter**, dated as of the date of Green's report, as to whether any subsequent events would require adjustment or disclosure.
- Make such additional inquiries or perform such additional procedures Green considers necessary and appropriate.

Solution 40-8 Report Deficiencies--Other Auditors, Use of Specialist

The auditor's report contains the following deficiencies:

Introductory Paragraph

1. The magnitude of the portions of the **financial statements audited** by the other auditor is **not disclosed.**
2. The **other auditor should not be named** unless the other auditor's report is presented together with that of the principal auditor.

Scope Paragraph

3. The statement that, **"An audit includes examining, on a test basis, evidence supporting the amounts and disclosures in the financial statements,"** is omitted.
4. An audit includes assessing the **accounting principles used** and **significant estimates made by "management," not** by **"the auditor."**

Explanatory Paragraph

5. Reference to the specialist should not be made if the auditor does not modify the opinion as a result of the findings of the specialist.
6. All the substantive **reasons** for the **qualified opinion** are not disclosed in a separate **explanatory paragraph.**

Opinion Paragraph

7. **Reference to the other auditor** is not made in the opinion paragraph.
8. The company whose financial statements were audited is not identified in the opinion paragraph.
9. The draft does not refer to both years (1987 and 1988) in the opinion paragraph.
10. The draft does not refer to results of operations or cash flows.

Date

11. Dual-dating should not be used when a subsequent event occurs before field work is completed.

Solution 40-9 Audit Report--Other Auditors, Scope Limitation

To the Board of Directors of National Motors, Inc.:

We have audited the consolidated balance sheet of National Motors, Inc. and subsidiaries as of December 31, 1988, and the related consolidated statements of income, retained earnings, and cash flows for the year then ended. These financial statements are the responsibility of the Company's management. Our responsibility is to express an opinion on these financial statements based on our audit. **We did not audit** the financial statements of Rapid Parts Company, a consolidated subsidiary, which statements reflect total assets and revenues constituting 22 percent and 25 percent, respectively, of the related consolidated totals. **Those statements were audited by other auditors** whose report has been furnished to us, and **our opinion**, insofar as it relates to the amounts included for Rapid Parts Company, **is based solely upon the report of the other auditors.**

Except as explained in the following paragraph, we conducted our audit in accordance with generally accepted auditing standards. Those standards require that we plan and perform the audit to obtain reasonable assurance about whether the financial statements are free of material misstatement. An audit includes examining, on a test basis, evidence supporting the amounts and disclosures in the financial statements. An audit also includes assessing the accounting principles used and significant estimates made by management, as well as evaluating the overall financial statement presentation. **We believe that our audits and the report of other auditors provide a reasonable basis for our opinion.**

We did not observe the taking of the physical inventory as of December 31, 1987, since that date was prior to our appointment as auditors for National Motors, Inc. and we were unable to satisfy ourselves regarding inventory quantities by means of other auditing procedures. Inventory amounts as of December 31, 1987, enter into the determination of net income and cash flows for the year ended December 31, 1988.

Because of the matter discussed in the **preceding paragraph**, the **scope** of our work was **not sufficient** to enable us to express, and **we do not express**, an opinion on the results of operations and cash flows for the year ended December 31, 1988.

In our opinion, based on our audit and the report of the other auditors, **the balance sheet referred to above presents fairly**, in all material respects, the financial position of National Motors, Inc. and subsidiaries as of December 31, 1988, in conformity with generally accepted accounting principles.

White & Co.
March 28, 1989

Solution 40-10 Report Deficiencies--Subsequent Event, Departure From GAAP, Predecessor Auditors

Deficiencies in the audit assistant's draft include the following:

1. The report is improperly addressed to the president.
2. The introductory paragraph does not identify the financial statements examined, i.e., balance sheet, and statements of income, retained earnings, and cash flows.
3. The scope paragraph does not make reference to "assessing the accounting principles used and significant estimates made by management, as well as evaluating the overall financial statement presentation."
4. Reference to "Note K" pertaining to a subsequent event is inappropriate in the scope paragraph. If the auditor wishes to emphasize this matter, such explanatory information should be presented in a separate paragraph of the auditor's report.
5. There is **no reference to the predecessor auditors** in the introductory paragraph as required when the statements are in comparative form.
6. There is no reference that an adverse opinion was expressed by the predecessor auditors, nor is there a description of the nature of and reasons for the predecessors' adverse opinion.
7. The separate **explanatory paragraph** does not make reference to the requirements of generally accepted accounting principles, i.e., property and equipment should be stated at an amount not in excess of cost, and deferred income taxes should be provided. Therefore, all of the **substantive reasons for the adverse opinion have not been disclosed.**
8. The separate explanatory paragraph does not disclose either the monetary effects of the violations of generally accepted accounting principles or that the effects are not reasonably determinable.
9. The opinion paragraph does not include a direct reference to the separate explanatory paragraph that discloses the basis for the adverse opinion.
10. The **opinion** paragraph **does not make reference to "conformity with generally accepted accounting principles."**
11. The auditor's report is **not properly dual-dated.**

Solution 40-11 Other Auditors (AU 543)

a. In order for May & Marty to satisfy itself about the independence and professional reputation of Dey & Dee and assure itself that there has been coordination of activities between the two auditors in order to achieve a proper review of matters affecting consolidation, May & Marty, whether or not it makes reference to Dey & Dee's audit, should consider performing the following procedures:

Make **inquiries about the professional reputation** and standing of Dey & Dee to one or more of the following:

- AICPA, applicable state society of CPAs, and/or local chapter.
- Other appropriate sources such as other practitioners, bankers, and other credit grantors.

Obtain a representation from Dey & Dee that it is independent under the requirements of the AICPA and, if appropriate, the requirements of the SEC. Ascertain through **communication with Dey & Dee that**

- Dey & Dee is aware that the **BGI-Western financial statements are to be included** in the BGI consolidated financial statements on which May & Marty will report, and that **Dey & Dee's report will be relied upon** by May & Marty.
- Dey & Dee is familiar with GAAP and GAAS and will conduct its audit in accordance therewith.
- Dey & Dee has knowledge of the relevant financial reporting requirements for statements and schedules to be filed with regulatory agencies such as the SEC, if appropriate.
- A review will be made of matters affecting elimination of intercompany transactions and accounts and, if appropriate in the circumstances, the uniformity of accounting practices among components included in the financial statements.

b. May & Marty could adopt the position of **not making reference to Dey & Dee's audit** of BGI-Western if **May & Marty is able to satisfy itself about the independence and professional reputation** of Dey & Dee and takes steps it considers appropriate to satisfy itself as to Dey & Dee's audit of BGI-Western. Ordinarily, May & Marty would be able to adopt the position of **not making reference** to Dey & Dee's audit when **any one of the following conditions exists**:

- **Dey & Dee is an associate or correspondent firm** and its work is acceptable to May & Marty based on May & Marty's knowledge of the professional standards and competence of Dey & Dee; or
- **Dey & Dee is retained by May & Marty** and the work is performed under May & Marty's guidance and control; or
- **May & Marty takes steps it considers necessary to satisfy itself as to Dey & Dee's audit**. Such steps may include a visit to Dey and Dee to discuss Dey and Dee's audit procedures or a review of Dey and Dee's audit programs and/or working papers. In addition, May and Marty is satisfied about the reasonableness of the statements of BGI-Western for purposes of inclusion in BGI's consolidated financial statements; or
- **BGI-Western's financial statements are not a material part** of BGI's consolidated financial statements.

Solution 40-12 Audit Report--Accounting Change, Departure From GAAP

To the Board of Directors of Devon Incorporated:

We have audited the balance sheet of Devon Incorporated as of December 31, 1988, and the related statements of income, retained earnings, and cash flows for the year then ended. These financial statements are the responsibility of the Company's management. Our responsibility is to express an opinion on these financial statements based on our audit. The financial statements of Devon Incorporated for the year ended December 31, 1987, **were audited by other auditors** whose report dated March 31, 1988, expressed an unqualified opinion on those statements.

We conducted our audit in accordance with generally accepted auditing standards. Those standards require that we plan and perform the audit to obtain reasonable assurance about whether the balance sheet is free of material misstatement. An audit includes examining, on a test basis, evidence supporting the amounts and disclosures in the balance sheet. An audit also includes assessing the accounting principles used and significant estimates made by management, as well as evaluating the overall balance sheet presentation. We believe that our audit provides a reasonable basis for our opinion.

During the year, **Devon changed its method of valuing inventory** from the first-in, first-out method to the last-in, first-out method. This **change was made because** management believes LIFO more clearly reflects net income by providing a closer matching of current costs and current revenues. The **change had the effect** of reducing inventory at December 31, 1988, by $65,000, and net income and earnings per share by $38,000 and $.38, respectively, for the year then ended. The **effect of the change on prior years was immaterial;** accordingly, there was **no cumulative effect** of the change.

The **company has excluded from property and debt** in the accompanying balance sheet **certain lease obligations, which**, in our opinion, **should be capitalized** in order to conform with generally accepted accounting principles. **If these lease obligations were capitalized**, assets would be increased by $312,000 and liabilities by $387,000, and retained earnings would be decreased by $75,000 as of December 31, 1988; net income and earnings per share would be decreased by $75,000 and $.75, respectively, for the year then ended.

In our opinion, **except for the effects of not capitalizing lease obligations**, and **except for not disclosing the change in inventory methods** as discussed in the preceding paragraphs, the financial statements referred to above present fairly, in all material respects, the financial position of Devon, Inc. as of December 31, 1988, and the results of its operations and its cash flows for the year then ended, in conformity with generally accepted accounting principles.

Smith, CPA
February 29, 1989

Solution 40-13 Going Concern

a. Wall has a responsibility to evaluate whether there is substantial doubt about Trendy's ability to continue as a going concern for a **reasonable period of time, not to exceed one year** beyond the date of Trendy's audited financial statements. This evaluation is based on Wall's knowledge of **conditions and events that exist at**, or have **occurred before,** the **completion of field work.**

b. While it is **not necessary** that Wall design **specific audit procedures solely to identify conditions and events** that may indicate Trendy's has a **going concern problem,** Wall most likely would perform **analytical procedures** to identify ratios and **patterns** indicative of present and future financial difficulties.

Wall most likely would review any debt and **loan agreements** to ascertain whether Trendy is complying with their terms. Additionally, if there are any **agreements with stockholders or creditors** to provide or maintain financial support, **confirmation of the details** of these arrangements would be appropriate.

Wall's **review of subsequent events** near the completion of field work also would produce evidence about Trendy's financial difficulties. Wall would especially focus on **reading the minutes of the directors' meetings, inquiring** of Trendy's legal **counsel** concerning litigation, and reading the **latest interim financial statements.**

c. Wall should **consider** any **management plans** to increase sales, reduce costs, or dispose of assets that could mitigate the adverse effects of Trendy's financial difficulties. The **marketability** of the assets, any **restrictions** on their disposal and the possible **operational effects** of their disposal should be considered in evaluating whether such plans can be effectively implemented.

If management plans to borrow money or restructure its debts, Wall should consider several factors including the **availability of financing**, the **possibility of restructuring** or subordinating debt, the effects of **existing borrowing restrictions,** and the **sufficiency of collateral.**

Wall should evaluate any management plans to **reduce or delay expenditures**, such as overhead or administrative expenditures. The **postponement** of maintenance and R&D, and the leasing of assets ordinarily purchased also may be feasible.

Wall also should consider any plans to increase ownership equity and **raise capital.** Arrangements to **reduce current dividend requirements** or **accelerate cash distributions from subsidiaries** or **cash infusions from investors** also may be possible.

NOTES

CHANGE ALERT

SAS 74, ***Compliance Auditing Considerations in Audits of Governmental Entities and Recipients of Governmental Financial Assistance,*** was issued by the Auditing Standards Board in February 1995 and is effective for fiscal periods ending after December 31, 1994. SAS 74 supersedes SAS 68. SAS 74 was issued to provide general guidance to the auditor, as opposed to the specific guidance in SAS 68. Coverage of SAS 74 is included in Chapter 41.

SAS 75, ***Engagements to Apply Agreed-Upon Procedures to Specified Elements, Accounts, or Items of a Financial Statement,*** was issued by the Auditing Standards Board in September 1995 (in tandem with SSAE No. 4) and is effective for reports dated after April 30, 1996. SAS 75 supersedes SAS 35. SAS 75 should be used when applying agreed-upon procedures to specific parts of a financial statement. SAS 75 does **not** permit negative assurance. Coverage of SAS 75 is included in Chapter 41.

SSAE No. 4, ***Agreed-Upon Procedures Engagements,*** was issued by the Auditing Standards Board in September 1995 (in tandem with SAS 75) and is effective for reports dated after April 30, 1996. SSAE No. 4 provides direction when applying agreed-upon procedures to nonfinancial information. SSAE No. 4 does **not** permit negative assurance. Coverage of SSAE No. 4 is included in Chapter 41.

SAS 76, ***Amendments to SAS No. 72, Letters for Underwriters and Certain Other Requesting Parties,*** was issued by the Auditing Standards Board in September 1995 and is effective for letters released after April 30, 1996. SAS 76 precludes the accountant from providing a comfort letter if an appropriate representation letter is not provided. Coverage of SAS 76 is included in Chapter 41.

CHAPTER 41

OTHER TYPES OF REPORTS

CHAPTER 41

OTHER TYPES OF REPORTS

I. Reporting on Information Accompanying the Basic Financial Statements in Auditor-Submitted Documents (AU 551, SAS 29 and 52)

TotalRecall

GUIDELINES FOR AUDITOR'S REPORT

A **Audit** made to form opinion on financial statements taken as whole

S **State** (or disclaim) opinion as to whether accompanying information is fairly stated in all material respects in relation to basic financial statements taken as a whole

A **Accompanying** information not a required part of financial statements

I **Identify** accompanying information

R **Report** on accompanying information may be added to standard audit report or may appear in separate auditor-submitted document

A. Overview--These statements provide guidance on reporting when the auditor submits to a client, or others, a document containing information in addition to the basic financial statements and the audit report.

1. These statements apply to information that is presented outside the basic financial statements and is not required by GAAP. Such information includes additional details or explanations of items in or related to the basic financial statements, consolidating information, historical summaries of items extracted from the basic financial statements, statistical data, and other material, some of which may be from sources outside the accounting system or outside the entity.

2. These statements do not apply in instances where the client merely includes the auditor's standard report in a document containing the basic financial statements and other information which the auditor has not been engaged to report upon. In such instances, according to SAS 8, *Other Information in Documents Containing Audited Financial Statements*, the auditor is required to read the information to ensure that it is consistent with the audited financial statements. Only if there is an inconsistency will the auditor report on the other information (exception reporting only).

B. Objectives--The objectives of the auditor's report on information accompanying the basic financial statements are the same as the report on the basic financial statements (i.e., to describe the character of the work and the degree of responsibility, if any, the auditor is taking).

1. In achieving these objectives, the following guidelines are applicable:

   a. The report should state that the audit has been made for the purpose of forming an opinion on the basic financial statements taken as a whole.

   b. The report should identify the accompanying information. (Identification may be by descriptive title or page number of the document.)

   c. The report should state that the accompanying information is presented for purposes of additional analysis and is not a required part of the basic financial statements.

   d. The report should include either an opinion on whether the accompanying information is fairly stated in all material respects in relation to the basic financial statements taken as a whole or a disclaimer of opinion, depending on whether the information has been subjected to the auditing procedures applied in the audit of the basic financial statements. The auditor may express an opinion on a portion of the accompanying information and disclaim an opinion on the remainder.

e. The report on the accompanying information may be added to the auditor's standard report on the basic financial statements or may appear separately in the auditor-submitted document.

2. Materiality Considerations--The purpose of an audit in accordance with GAAS is to provide an opinion on the fairness of the basic financial statements taken as a whole. If the auditor decides to express an opinion on the additional information accompanying financial statements, the same materiality level used for the financial statements should be used. Accordingly, the auditor would not need to apply additional procedures on the additional information taken by itself.

3. Misstatements--If the auditor believes that the additional information is materially misstated, in relation to the financial statements, the auditor should discuss it with management and propose that the information be revised. If the client will not agree to a revision, the auditor should do the following:

a. Modify the report on the accompanying information and describe the misstatement.

b. Refuse to include the information in the document.

C. Effects of Report--If the auditor modifies the report on the basic financial statements, the auditor should consider the effects on any related accompanying information (see Exhibit 3). When the auditor expresses an adverse opinion or disclaims an opinion on the basic financial statements, the auditor should disclaim an opinion on all accompanying information.

Exhibit 1--Auditing Procedures Performed on Accompanying Information

Our audit was conducted for the purpose of forming an opinion on the basic financial statements taken as a whole. The (identify accompanying information) is presented for purposes of additional analysis and is not a required part of the basic financial statements. Such information has been subjected to the auditing procedures applied in the audit of the basic financial statements and, in our opinion, is fairly stated in all material respects in relation to the basic financial statements taken as a whole.

Exhibit 2--Disclaimer on Accompanying Information

Our audit was conducted for the purpose of forming an opinion on the basic financial statements taken as a whole. The (identify accompanying information) is presented for purposes of additional analysis and is not a required part of the basic financial statements. Such information has not been subjected to the auditing procedures applied in the audit of the basic financial statements, and, accordingly, we express no opinion on it.

Exhibit 3--Reporting on Accompanying Information to Which a Qualification in the Auditor's Report on the Basic Financial Statements Applies

Our audit was made for the purpose of forming an opinion on the basic financial statements taken as a whole. The schedules of investments (page 7), property (page 8) and other assets (page 9) as of December 31, 19XX, are presented for purposes of additional analysis and are not a required part of the basic financial statements. The information in such schedules has been

(continued on next page)

> subjected to the auditing procedures applied in the audit of the basic financial statements, and, in our opinion, except for the effects on the schedule of investments of not accounting for the investments in certain companies by the equity method as explained in the third paragraph of this report, such information is fairly stated in all material respects in relation to the basic financial statements taken as a whole.

D. Supplementary Information Required by FASB or GASB Pronouncements

1. When supplementary information required by the FASB or GASB is presented outside the basic financial statements in an auditor-submitted document, the auditor should disclaim an opinion on the information unless he or she has been engaged to audit and express an opinion on it.

> Exhibit 4--Disclaimer on Required Supplementary Information Presented Outside the Basic Statements
>
> The (identify the supplementary information) on page XX is not a required part of the basic financial statements but is supplementary information required by the (Financial or Governmental) Accounting Standards Board. We have applied certain limited procedures, which consisted principally of inquiries of management regarding the methods of measurement and presentation of the supplementary information. However, we did not audit the information, and express no opinion on it.

2. Also, the auditor's report should be expanded if required supplementary information is omitted, the auditor has concluded that the measurement or presentation of the supplementary information departs materially from guidelines prescribed by the FASB or GASB, the auditor is unable to remove substantial doubts about whether the supplementary information conforms to prescribed guidelines, or the auditor is unable to complete the procedures prescribed by SAS 52.

E. Consolidating Information

1. An auditor may be engaged to provide an opinion on consolidated financial statements on which consolidating information is also provided (e.g., the individual amounts making up the consolidated totals). The auditor must be satisfied that the consolidating information is suitably identified. If the consolidating information has not been separately audited, the auditor's report should read as follows:

> Exhibit 5--Consolidating Information
>
> Our audit was conducted for the purpose of forming an opinion on the consolidated financial statements taken as a whole. The consolidating information is presented for purposes of additional analysis of the consolidated financial statements rather than to present the financial position, results of operations, and cash flows of the individual companies. The consolidating information has been subjected to the auditing procedures applied in the audit of the consolidated financial statements, and, in our opinion, is fairly stated in all material respects in relation to the consolidated financial statements taken as a whole.

2. An auditor may be engaged to form an opinion on both the consolidated statements and the separate statements of the components of a consolidated group. In this case, the auditor's responsibility with respect to the separate financial statements is the same as the responsibility for the consolidated statements.

II. Special Reports (AU 623, SAS 62)

A. Special Reports (Special Purpose Reports)--Auditor's reports that apply only to (1) financial statements prepared in conformity with a comprehensive basis of accounting other than GAAP (OCBOA); (2) specified elements, accounts, or items of a financial statement; (3) compliance with aspects of contractual agreements or regulatory requirements related to audited financial statements; (4) incomplete presentation; or (5) financial information presented in prescribed forms or schedules that require a prescribed form of auditor's report.

B. Reports on Financial Statements Prepared in Conformity With OCBOA--GAAS apply whenever an auditor conducts an audit of and reports on any financial statement.

1. Comprehensive Basis Other Than GAAP (OCBOA)--A comprehensive basis other than GAAP is (a) a basis that is used to comply with the requirements or financial provisions of a government regulatory agency, but only for filing with that agency (e.g., State insurance commission rules for insurance companies); (b) a basis used (or expected to be used) for filing the client's income tax return for the period covered by the financial statements; (c) the cash receipts and disbursements basis (including modifications to cash basis that have substantial support); and (d) a definite set of criteria having substantial support that is applied to all material financial statement items, (e.g., price-level basis of accounting).

2. Auditor's Report--Should include the following:

a. A title that includes the word "independent."

b. Paragraph One--States the following:

(1) The financial statements were audited.

(2) The financial statements are the responsibility of the company's management and that the auditor is responsible for expressing an opinion.

c. Paragraph Two--States the following:

(1) The audit was conducted in accordance with GAAS.

(2) GAAS require that the auditor plan and perform the audit to obtain reasonable assurance about whether the financial statements are free of material misstatement.

(3) An audit includes examining evidence on a test basis, assessing the accounting principles used and significant estimates made by management, and evaluating the financial statement presentation.

d. Paragraph Three--States the following:

(1) The basis of presentation, and refers to the note that describes the basis.

(2) That the basis of presentation is a comprehensive basis of accounting other than GAAP.

e. Paragraph Four expresses the auditor's opinion on the financial statements in accordance with the OCBOA basis.

f. Restrictive Paragraph--States that the distribution of the report is restricted to those within the entity and for filing with the regulatory agency. This paragraph is used when the financial statements are prepared in conformity with the requirements of a government regulatory agency.

g. Signature of the auditor's firm.

h. Date of the auditor's report.

i. Titles of the Financial Statements--"Balance sheet," "statement of financial position," "statement of income," "statement of operations," "statement of cash flows," etc., apply only to statements prepared in conformity with GAAP. Suitable titles should be given to financial statements prepared in conformity with a comprehensive basis of accounting other than GAAP. For example, an appropriate title for a cash-basis financial statement might be "statement of assets and liabilities arising from cash transactions," and an appropriate title for a financial statement prepared on a statutory basis might be "statement of income--statutory basis." The auditor should disclose reservations in an explanatory paragraph of the report and qualify the opinion in cases where the auditor believes the financial statements are not appropriately titled.

Exhibit 6--Financial Statements Prepared on the Cash Basis

Independent Auditor's Report

We have audited the accompanying statements of assets and liabilities arising from cash transactions of XYZ company as of December 31, 19X2 and 19X1, and the related statements of revenue collected and expenses paid for the years then ended. These financial statements are the responsibility of the Company's management. Our responsibility is to express an opinion on these financial statements based on our audits.

We conducted our audits in accordance with generally accepted auditing standards. Those standards require that we plan and perform the audit to obtain reasonable assurance about whether the financial statements are free of material misstatement. An audit includes examining, on a test basis, evidence supporting the amounts and disclosures in the financial statements. An audit also includes assessing the accounting principles used and significant estimates made by management, as well as evaluating the overall financial statement presentation. We believe that our audits provide a reasonable basis for our opinion.

As described in Note X, these financial statements were prepared on the basis of cash receipts and disbursements, which is a comprehensive basis of accounting other than generally accepted accounting principles.

In our opinion, the financial statements referred to above present fairly, in all material respects, the assets and liabilities arising from cash transactions of XYZ Company as of December 31, 19X2 and 19X1, and the revenue collected and expenses paid during the years then ended, on the basis of accounting described in Note X.

C. Reports on Specified Elements, Accounts, or Items of a Financial Statement

1. Reports Expressing an Opinion on One or More Specified Elements, Accounts, or Items of a Financial Statement--Examples include rentals, royalties, a profit participation, or a provision for income taxes.

   a. GAAS--The ten generally accepted auditing standards are applicable with the exception of the first standard of reporting which is applicable only when the specified elements, accounts, or items are intended to be presented in conformity with GAAP.

   b. Extent of Audit--An engagement to express an opinion on one or more specified elements, accounts, or items may be undertaken as a separate engagement or in conjunction with an audit of the financial statements. Since an opinion is being expressed on each of the specified elements, accounts, or items encompassed by the auditor's report, materiality must be related to each of the specified elements, accounts, or items. Therefore, the audit will usually be more extensive in regard to the element, account, or item than it would be if the only objective were to express an opinion on the financial statements taken as a whole. The auditor must consider any interrelationships among the specified elements, accounts, or items being reported on and other items in the financial statements.

c. Not a Piecemeal Opinion--When the auditor has expressed an adverse opinion or disclaimed an opinion on the financial statements taken as a whole, the auditor should not report on specified elements, accounts, or items which are included in those statements if the effect is to express a piecemeal opinion. However, the auditor should be able to report on one or more specified elements, accounts, or items provided that a major portion of the financial statements is not involved. In this case, the report should not accompany the financial statements.

Exhibit 7--Report Relating to Royalties

Independent Auditor's Report

We have audited the accompanying schedule of royalties applicable to engine production of the Q Division of XYZ Corporation for the year ended December 31, 19X2, under the terms of a license agreement dated May 14, 19XX, between ABC Company and XYZ Corporation. This schedule is the responsibility of XYZ Corporation's management. Our responsibility is to express an opinion on this schedule based on our audit.

We conducted our audit in accordance with generally accepted auditing standards. Those standards require that we plan and perform the audit to obtain reasonable assurance about whether the schedule of royalties is free of material misstatement. An audit includes examining, on a test basis, evidence supporting the amounts and disclosures in the schedule. An audit also includes assessing the accounting principles used and significant estimates made by management, as well as evaluating the overall schedule presentation. We believe that our audit provides a reasonable basis for our opinion.

We have been informed that, under XYZ Corporation's interpretation of the agreement referred to in the first paragraph, royalties were based on the number of engines produced after giving effect to a reduction for production retirements that were scrapped, but without a reduction for field returns that were scrapped, even though the field returns were replaced with new engines without charge to customers.

In our opinion, the schedule of royalties referred to above presents fairly, in all material respects, the number of engines produced by the Q Division of XYZ Corporation during the year ended December 31, 19X2, and the amount of royalties applicable thereto, under the license agreement referred to above.

This report is intended solely for the information and use of the boards of directors and management of XYZ Corporation and ABC Company and should not be used for any other purpose.

2. Agreed-Upon Procedure Engagements

a. SAS 75 and SSAE No. 4 were issued jointly to address situations when accountants are asked to perform agreed-upon procedure engagements.

(1) An agreed-upon procedure engagement is one in which a practitioner is engaged by a client to issue a report of findings based on specific procedures

performed related to a financial statement element, account, or item (a financial statement component) or other written assertion provided by the client.

(2) SAS 75, *Engagements to Apply Agreed-Upon Procedures to Specified Elements, Accounts, or Items of a Financial Statement*, supersedes SAS 35, *Special Reports--Applying Agreed-Upon Procedures to Specified Elements, Accounts, or Items of a Financial Statement.* An example of an assertion where SAS 75 would be applicable would be that the gross income component of a statement of operations is represented to be presented according to the rules of a regulatory agency.

(3) SSAE No. 4, *Agreed-Upon Procedures Engagements*, extends the applicability of attestation standards to circumstances where the practitioner is engaged to apply agreed-upon procedures to a written assertion provided by the client where that written assertion does not relate to a financial statement component. An example of an assertion where SSAE No. 4 would be applicable would be a statement that the documentation of employee evaluations included in personnel files as of a certain date is dated within the time frame set forth in the entity's personnel policy.

(4) Neither pronouncement is applicable to engagements under the scope of the following: (a) SAS 62, *Special Reports*, (b) SAS 70, *Reports on the Processing of Transactions by Service Organizations*, (c) SAS 72, *Letters for Underwriters and Certain Other Requesting Parties*, as amended by SAS 76, (d) SAS 74, *Compliance Auditing Considerations in Audits of Governmental Entities and Recipients of Governmental Financial Assistance.*

b. Before accepting an engagement to issue a report:

(1) Under both pronouncements, the following conditions must be met:

(a) The practitioner is independent.

(b) The practitioner and the specified users of the report agree upon procedures for their purposes.

(c) The specified users take responsibility for the sufficiency of the agreed-upon procedures for their purposes.

(d) The procedures to be applied to the specific subject matter are expected to result in reasonably consistent findings using the criteria.

(e) The specific subject matter to which the procedures are to be applied is subject to reasonably consistent estimation or measurement.

(f) Evidential matter related to the specific subject matter to which the procedures are applied is expected to exist to provide a reasonable basis for expressing the findings in the practitioner's report.

(g) Where applicable, the practitioner and the specified users agree on any materiality limits for reporting purposes.

(h) Use of the report is restricted to specified users.

(2) Under SAS 75, the basis of accounting of the financial statement component(s) must also be clearly evident to the specified users and the practitioner.

(3) Under SSAE No. 4, the following conditions must also be met:

(a) The responsible party will provide the assertion in writing to the practitioner prior to the issuance of his or her report.

(b) Criteria to be used in the determination of findings are agreed upon between the practitioner and the specified users.

(c) For agreed-upon procedures engagements on prospective financial information, the prospective financial statements include a summary of significant assumptions.

(d) For agreed-upon procedures engagements performed pursuant to SSAE No. 3, management evaluates the entity's compliance with specified requirements or the effectiveness of the entity's internal control structure over compliance.

(e) The client is required to provide a written assertion that is capable of reasonably consistent estimation or measurement. As such, the components may be presented in a schedule or statement or in the practitioner's report, appropriately identifying what is being presented and the point in time or the time period covered. (In contrast, under a SAS 75 engagement, financial statement components implicitly or explicitly contain the assertion(s) to be tested by the practitioner.) If no written assertion is provided by the client, a SSAE No. 4 engagement may not be performed.

c. The practitioner and the specified users must agree upon the procedures performed or to be performed and the specified users must take responsibility for the sufficiency of the agreed-upon procedures for their purposes.

(1) Ordinarily the practitioner should communicate directly with and obtain affirmative acknowledgment from each of the specified users. For example, this may be accomplished by meeting with the specified users or by distributing a draft of the anticipated report or a copy of an engagement letter to the specified users and obtaining their agreement.

(2) If the practitioner is not able to communicate directly with all of the specified users, the practitioner may satisfy these requirements by applying any one or more of the following or similar procedures: (a) compare the procedures to be applied to written requirements of the specified users. (b) discuss the procedures to be applied with appropriate representatives of the specified users involved. (c) review relevant contracts with or correspondence from the specified users.

(3) The practitioner should not report on an engagement when specified users do not agree upon the procedures performed or to be performed and do not take responsibility for the sufficiency of the procedures for their purposes.

(4) The practitioner should establish a clear understanding regarding the terms of engagement, preferably in an engagement letter. Engagement letters should be addressed to the client, and in some circumstances also to all specified users. Matters that might be included in such an engagement letter are the following: (a) Nature of the engagement, (b) Identification of or reference to the financial statement components and the party responsible for them, (c) Identification of specified users, (d) Specified users' acknowledgment of their responsibility for the sufficiency of the procedures, (e) Responsibilities of the practitioner, (f)

Reference to applicable AICPA standards, (g) Agreement on procedures by enumerating (or referring to) the procedures, (h) Disclaimers expected to be included in the practitioner's report, (i) Use restrictions, (j) Assistance to be provided to the accountant, (k) Involvement of a specialist, (l) Agreed-upon materiality limits, (m) For SAS 75 engagements, the basis of accounting of the financial statement components.

(5) Specified users are responsible for the sufficiency (nature, timing, and extent) of the agreed-upon procedures, because they best understand their own needs. The specified users assume the risk that such procedures might be insufficient for their purposes. Additionally, the specified users assume the risk that they might misunderstand or otherwise inappropriately use findings properly reported by the practitioner.

d. The responsibility of the practitioner is to carry out the procedures and report the findings in accordance with the applicable general, fieldwork, and reporting standards.

(1) The practitioner assumes the risk that misapplication of the procedures may result in inappropriate findings being reported. Further, the practitioner assumes the risk that appropriate findings may not be reported or may be reported inaccurately. The practitioner's risks can be reduced through adequate planning and supervision and due professional care in performing the procedures, determining the findings, and preparing the report.

(2) The practitioner should have adequate knowledge in the specific subject matter of the specified financial statement components, including the basis of accounting. He or she may obtain such knowledge through formal or continuing education, practical experience, or consultation with others.

(3) The practitioner has no responsibility to determine the differences between the agreed-upon procedures to be performed and the procedures that the practitioner would have determined to be necessary had he or she been engaged to perform another form of engagement. The procedures that the practitioner agrees to perform pursuant to an engagement to apply agreed-upon procedures may be more or less extensive than the procedures that the practitioner would determine to be necessary had he or she been engaged to perform another form of engagement.

(4) The procedures that the practitioner and the specified users agree upon may be as limited or as extensive as the specified users desire. However, mere reading of an assertion or specified information does not constitute a procedure sufficient to permit a practitioner to report on the results of applying agreed-upon procedures. In some circumstances, the procedures agreed upon evolve or are modified over the course of the engagement. In general, there is flexibility in determining the procedures as long as the specified users acknowledge responsibility for the sufficiency of such procedures for their purposes. Matters that would be agreed upon include the nature, timing, and extent of the procedures.

(5) The practitioner should **not** agree to perform procedures that are overly subjective and thus possibly open to varying interpretations. Terms of uncertain meaning (e.g., general review, limited review, reconcile, check, or test) should not be used in describing the procedures unless such terms are defined within the agreed-upon procedures. The practitioner should obtain evidential matter from applying the agreed-upon procedures to provide a reasonable basis for the finding or findings expressed in his or her report, but need not perform

additional procedures outside the scope of the engagement to gather additional evidential matter.

(6) Examples of appropriate procedures include: (a) Execution of a sampling application after agreeing on relevant parameters. (b) Inspection of specified documents evidencing certain types of transactions or detailed attributes thereof. (c) Confirmation of specific information with third parties. (d) Comparison of documents, schedules, or analyses with certain specified attributes. (e) Performance of specific procedures on work performed by others. (f) Performance of mathematical computations.

(7) Examples of inappropriate procedures include: (a) Mere reading of the work performed by others solely to describe their findings. (b) Evaluating the competency or objectivity of another party. (c) Obtaining an understanding about a particular subject. (d) Interpreting documents outside the scope of the practitioner's professional expertise.

(8) In certain circumstances, it may be appropriate or necessary for the practitioner to involve a specialist in the performance of one or more of the agreed-upon procedures. The practitioner and the specified users explicitly should agree to the involvement of the specialist and the practitioner's report should describe the nature of any assistance provided by the specialist.

e. The responsible party's refusal to furnish written representations determined by the practitioner to be appropriate for the engagement constitutes a limitation on the performance of the engagement. In these circumstances, the practitioner should do one of the following: (1) disclose in the report the inability to obtain representations from the responsible party, (2) withdraw from the engagement, or , (3) change the engagement to another form of engagement.

f. The practitioner should prepare and maintain work papers in connection with an engagement to apply agreed-upon procedures under SAS 75 and SSAE No. 4. Such work papers should be appropriate to the circumstances and the practitioner's needs on the engagement to which they apply.

(1) Although the quantity, type, and content of work papers vary with the circumstances, ordinarily they should indicate that: (a) the work was adequately planned and supervised, and (b) evidential matter was obtained to provide a reasonable basis for the finding or findings expressed in the practitioner's report.

(2) Work papers are the property of the practitioner, and some states have statutes or regulations that designate the practitioner as the owner of the work papers. The practitioner's rights of ownership, however, are subject to ethical limitations relating to confidentiality. The practitioner should adopt reasonable procedures for safe custody of his or her work papers and should retain them for a period of time sufficient to meet the needs of his or her practice and satisfy any pertinent legal requirements of records retention. Certain of the practitioner's work papers sometimes may serve as a useful reference source for his or her client, but the work papers should not be regarded as part of, or a substitute for, the client's records.

g. The practitioner's report on applying agreed-upon procedures should be in the form of procedures and findings.

(1) The practitioner's report should contain the following elements:

(a) For both SAS 75 and SSAE No. 4 engagements: (1) A title that includes the word "independent." (2) Identification of specified users. (3) A statement that the procedures performed were those agreed to by the specified users identified in the report. (4) Reference to standards established by the AICPA. (5) A statement that the sufficiency of the procedures solely is the responsibility of the specified users and a disclaimer of responsibility for the sufficiency of those procedures. (6) A list of the procedures performed (or reference thereto) and related findings. (7) Where applicable, a description of any agreed-upon materiality limits. (8) A statement of restrictions on the use of the report because it is intended to be used solely by the specified users. (9) Where applicable, reservations or restrictions concerning procedures or findings. (10) Where applicable, a description of the nature of the assistance provided by a specialist.

(b) For SAS 75 engagements: (1) Reference to the financial statement components of an identified entity and the character of the engagement. (2) The basis of accounting of the financial statement component, unless clearly evident. (3) A statement that the practitioner was not engaged to, and did not, perform an audit of the financial statement components; a disclaimer of opinion on the financial statement components and a statement that if the practitioner had performed additional procedures, other matters might have come to his or her attention that would have been reported. (4) A disclaimer of opinion on the effectiveness of the internal control structure over financial reporting or any part thereof when the practitioner has performed procedures applicable to internal controls.

(c) For SSAE No. 4 engagements: (1) Reference to the assertion and the character of the engagement. (2) A statement that the practitioner was not engaged to, and did not, perform an examination of the assertion, a disclaimer of opinion on the assertion, and a statement that if the practitioner had performed additional procedures, other matters might have come to his or her attention that would have been reported. (3) For an agreed-upon procedures engagement on prospective financial information, all items included in SSAE No. 1.

(2) The date of completion of the agreed-upon procedures should be used as the date of the practitioner's report. A practitioner may find a representation letter to be a useful and practical means of obtaining representations from the parties responsible for the specified financial statement components. The need for such a letter may depend on the nature of the engagement and the specified users. Examples of matters that might appear in the representation letter include a statement that the responsible party has disclosed to the practitioner:

(a) For a SAS 75 engagement, (1) all known matters contradicting the basis of accounting for the financial statement components, and (2) any communication from regulatory agencies affecting the financial statement components.

(b) For a SSAE No. 4 engagement, (1) All known matters contradicting the assertion, and (2) any communication from regulatory agencies affecting the assertion.

(3) In SSAE No. 4 engagements, the responsible party's refusal to furnish written representations determined by the practitioner to be appropriate for the engagement constitutes a limitation on the performance of the engagement. In such circumstances, the practitioner should do one of the following: (a)

disclose in his or her report the inability to obtain representations from the responsible party, (b) withdraw from the engagement, and (c) change the engagement to another form of engagement.

(4) The practitioner should **not** provide negative assurance about whether the financial statement components or assertions are fairly stated in relation to established or stated criteria.

(a) In SAS 75 engagements, for example, the practitioner should not include a statement in the report that "nothing came to my attention that caused me to believe that the specified element, account, or item of a financial statement is not fairly stated in accordance with generally accepted accounting principles."

(b) In SSAE No. 4 engagements, for example, the practitioner should not include a statement in his or her report that "nothing came to my attention that caused me to believe that the assertion is not fairly stated in accordance with (established or stated) criteria."

(5) The practitioner should report all findings from application of the agreed-upon procedures. The concept of materiality does not apply to findings to be reported in an agreed-upon procedures engagement unless the definition of materiality is agreed to by the specified users. Any agreed-upon materiality limits should be described in the practitioner's report.

Exhibit 8--Report in Connection With an Agreed-Upon Procedures Engagement

Independent Practitoners' Report

Board of Directors
X Company

We have applied certain agreed-upon procedures, as discussed below, to accounting records of Y Company, Inc., as of December 31, 19XX, solely to assist you in connection with the proposed acquisition of Y Company, Inc., in accordance with the standards established by the AICPA. These procedures were agreed-upon by the users of this report. The sufficiency of the procedures solely is the responsibility of the specified users. We disclaim any responsibility for the sufficiency of these procedures. It is understood that this report is solely for your information and is not to be referred to or distributed for any purpose to anyone who is not a member of management of X Company. Our procedures and findings are as follows:

(1) We reconciled cash on deposit with the following banks to the balances in the respective general ledger accounts and obtained confirmation of the related balances from the banks.

Bank	Balance Per General Ledger
ABC National Bank	$ 5,000
DEF State Bank	13,776
XYZ Trust Company--regular account	86,912
XYZ Trust Company--payroll account	5,000

(continued on next page)

(2) We obtained an aged trial balance of the accounts receivable subsidiary records, traced the age and amounts of approximately 10 percent of the accounts to the accounts receivable ledger, and added the trial balance and compared the total with the balance in the general ledger control account. We mailed requests for positive confirmation of balances to 150 customers. The differences disclosed in confirmation replies were minor in amount and nature, and we reconciled them to our satisfaction. The results are summarized as follows:

Accounts Receivable
Aging and Confirmation Results

	Account Balance	Requested	Received
Current:	$156,000	$ 76,000	$ 65,000
Past due:			
Less than one month	60,000	30,000	19,000
One to three months	36,000	18,000	10,000
Over three months	48,000	48,000	8,000
	$300,000	$172,000	$102,000

We were not engaged to, and did not, perform an audit of the financial statement components. Therefore we disclaim any opinion on the financial statement components. If we had performed additional procedures, other matters might have come to our attention that would have been reported. This report relates only to the accounts and items specified above and does not extend to any financial statements of Y Company, Inc., taken as a whole.

April 13, 199X (date of the completion of the agreed-upon procedures)
Olive & Oil, CPAs (signature)

D. Reports on Compliance With Aspects of Contractual Agreements or Regulatory Requirements Related to Audited Financial Statements--Contractual agreements sometimes require entities to furnish compliance reports which are prepared by independent auditors (e.g., a loan agreement may contain provisions relating to payments to be made into a sinking fund and the maintenance of a specified current ratio).

1. Negative Assurance--The auditor normally gives negative assurance regarding compliance with the agreements. This may be done by using a separate report or it may be added to one or more paragraphs of the report accompanying the financial statements. Negative assurance should be given only when the auditor has audited the financial statements to which the agreements or requirements relate and the report will be restricted to the named parties.

2. Report--The auditor's report should include the following:

   a. A title that includes the word "independent."

   b. Paragraph One--The financial statements were audited in accordance with GAAS and includes the date of the auditor's report on those financial statements. Any departure from the standard report should also be disclosed.

   c. Paragraph Two--A reference to the specific covenants or paragraphs of the agreement, provides negative assurance relative to the compliance with the applicable covenants insofar as they relate to accounting matters, and specifies that the negative assurance is being given in connection with the audit of the financial statements.

   d. Paragraph Three--A description and source of significant interpretations, if any, made by the company's management relating to the provisions of a relevant agreement.

e. Paragraph Four--Restricts the distribution of the report to those within the entity and the parties to the contract or agreement or for filing with the regulatory agency.

f. Signature of the auditor's firm.

g. The date.

> Exhibit 9--Report on Compliance With Contractual Provisions Given in a Separate Report
>
> We have examined the balance sheet of XYZ Company as of December 31, 19X2, and the related statements of income, retained earnings, and cash flows for the year then ended, and have issued our report thereon dated February 16, 19X3. Our examination was made in accordance with generally accepted auditing standards and, accordingly, included such tests of the accounting records and such other auditing procedures as we considered necessary in the circumstances.
>
> In connection with our examination, nothing came to our attention that caused us to believe that the Company failed to comply with the terms, covenants, provisions or conditions of Sections XX to XX, inclusive, of the Indenture dated July 21, 19X0, with ABC Bank. However, it should be noted that our examination was not directed primarily toward obtaining knowledge of such noncompliance.

E. Incomplete Presentation Otherwise in Conformity With GAAP or OCBOA--This information might include a situation where a buy-sell agreement requires that assets and liabilities be presented in accordance with GAAP, but it only includes those items that will be sold and transferred under the agreement rather than all the entity's assets and liabilities. This does constitute a financial statement in the limited circumstances addressed by SAS 62.

1. The auditor's materiality judgment would be in relation to the presentation taken as a whole. Additionally, since these presentations often include items which are the same as (or similar to) information provided in a complete set of financial statements, similar disclosures should be made. (This is also true if the presentation is based on OCBOA information.)

2. The financial presentation should be appropriately titled so that no confusion exists (terms such as balance sheet, income statement, statement of cash flows should not be used).

3. The audit report should include:

a. A responsibility paragraph that:

(1) identifies the financial information being reported on.

(2) states the responsibilities of management and of the auditor.

b. A scope paragraph.

c. An explanatory paragraph that:

(1) explains what the financial presentation is intended to present and refers the reader to a note which describes the basis of the financial presentation.

(2) states that the financial presentation is not intended to be a complete set of financial information in accordance with GAAP.

d. An opinion paragraph.

e. A paragraph restricting the distribution of the report. This restrictive paragraph cannot be used when the information is filed with a regulatory agency such that the information will be distributed to the public (such as a prospectus filed with the Securities and Exchange Commission).

F. Financial Statements Prepared on a Basis Prescribed by Agreement Which is Not in Conformity With GAAP--In other engagements, the auditor may be asked to report on a financial statement or set of financial statements which are not prepared in accordance with GAAP or OCBOA. For example, a loan application may call for financial statements, however, the inventory is to be valued at sales price; or in an acquisition agreement, the financial statements may request that fixed assets and inventories be measured at their liquidation values.

1. An auditor can be associated with the information using the reporting requirements specified.

2. The auditor would need to consider the adequacy of the disclosures associated with the financial statements and in expressing an opinion, materiality is considered at the financial statement level.

3. The auditor's report will include the following:

   a. A responsibility paragraph.

   b. A scope paragraph.

   c. An explanatory paragraph that:

      (1) explains what the financial statement(s) is intended to present and refers to the note which describes that basis for the presentation.

      (2) states that the financial statement(s) is not intended to be a presentation in conformity with GAAP.

   d. A paragraph that includes a description and the source of significant interpretations made by management.

   e. An opinion paragraph.

   f. A paragraph that restricts the distribution of the report.

G. Financial Information Presented in Prescribed Forms or Schedules--Regulatory bodies, government agencies, and others sometimes use printed forms or schedules which prescribe the form of the auditor's report. A problem arises if the prescribed report does not conform to the applicable professional reporting standards of the public accounting profession (e.g., calling for assertions that are not consistent with the auditor's function).

1. Procedures--Insertion of additional wording can make some report forms acceptable; other report forms require complete revision.

2. Assertions--If a printed report calls for an assertion the auditor believes is not justified, the auditor should either reword the form or attach a separate report.

III. Letters for Underwriters

A. Filings Under Federal Securities Statutes (AU 711, SAS 37)--The financial representations contained in documents filed with the SEC are the responsibility and representations of management. However, the Securities Act of 1933 imposes responsibility on an auditor for false or misleading financial statements (or for omissions which make them misleading) in an effective registration statement prepared or certified by the CPA.

1. Auditor's Defense--The auditor must prove that (a) there were reasonable grounds to believe (and the auditor did believe) that the statements in the registration statement were true and that there was no omission of a material fact at the date of the registration statement or (b) that the part of the registration statement that is in question did not fairly represent the auditor's statement as an expert or was not fairly copied or extracted from the report or valuation.

   - Reasonableness Standard--The standard of reasonableness is that standard which would be used by a prudent person in the management of his or her own property.

2. Date--The auditor's responsibility extends to the effective date of the registration statement.

3. Use of Name--The auditor should be sure his or her name is not used in a way that may indicate that the auditor's responsibility is greater than it really is.

4. Subsequent Events Procedures in 1933 Act Filings--The auditor should extend subsequent event procedures from the date of the report to the effective date of the registration statement. The auditor can rely, for the most part, on inquiries of responsible officials and employees. The auditor should perform the auditing procedures used to assess the existence of subsequent events (e.g., inquiry of management, reading of minutes, etc.) and, in addition, should (a) read the entire prospectus and other pertinent portions of the registration statement, and (b) obtain written confirmation from officers and other executives regarding subsequent events that have a material effect on the audited financial statements included in the registration statement or which require disclosure in order to keep the statements from being misleading.

5. Response to Subsequent Events and Subsequently Discovered Facts--If the auditor discovers (a) subsequent events requiring adjustment or disclosure or (b) facts existing at the time of the report which might have affected the report had the auditor known about them, the auditor should do the following:

   a. Ask management to revise the statements and/or add the required disclosures.

   b. If management refuses, modify the report accordingly and consider obtaining advice from legal counsel.

6. Reports Based on a Review of Interim Financial Information--The SEC requires that when a report based on a review of interim financial information is presented or incorporated in a registration statement by reference, a clarification should be made that the review report is not a "report" or "part" of the registration statement within the meaning of Sections 7 and 11 of the Securities Act of 1933.

7. Two or More Auditors--A registration statement filed with the SEC may contain the reports of two or more auditors for different periods. An auditor who has not audited the financial statements for the most recent period has a responsibility for events that have a material effect on the financial statements the auditor reported on that occurred during the period running from the date of the report until the effective date of the registration statement. The auditor generally should (a) read the pertinent portions of the prospectus and registration statement and (b) obtain a letter of representation from the successor auditor about subsequent events about which the successor has become aware.

B. Letters for Underwriters and Certain Other Requesting Parties (AU 634, SAS 72)--This Statement provides guidance to accountants for reporting on the results of and performing engagements to issue letters for underwriters and certain other requesting parties, commonly referred to as comfort letters, in connection with financial statements and financial statement schedules contained in registration statements filed with the SEC under the Securities Act of 1933.

1. The service of accountants providing letters for underwriters developed following enactment of the Act. Section 11 of the Act provides that underwriters, among others, could be liable if any part of a registration statement contains material omissions or misstatements. The Act also provides for an affirmative defense for underwriters if it can be demonstrated that, after a reasonable investigation, the underwriter has reasonable grounds to believe that there were no material omissions or misstatements. Consequently, underwriters request accountants to assist them in developing a record of reasonable investigation. An accountant's issuance of a comfort letter is one procedure that may be used to establish that an underwriter has conducted a reasonable investigation.

2. Applicability

   a. Using a statutory due diligence defense under Section 11 of the Act, a comfort letter may be addressed to parties other than a named underwriter, only when a law firm or attorney for the requesting party issues a written opinion to the accountants that states that such party has a due diligence defense under Section 11 of the Act. An attorney's letter indicating that a party "may" be deemed to be an underwriter, or has liability substantially equivalent to that of an underwriter under the securities laws, would not meet this requirement. If the requesting party in a securities offering registered pursuant to the Act, other than a named underwriter cannot provide such a letter, he or she must provide a representation letter for the accountant to provide them with a comfort letter. The letter should be addressed to the accountants, signed by the requesting party, and contain the following:

      > This review process, applied to the information relating to the issuer, is substantially consistent with the due diligence review process that we would perform if this placement of securities were being registered pursuant to the Securities Act of 1933. We are knowledgeable with respect to the due diligence review process that would be performed if this placement of securities were being registered pursuant to the Act.

   b. *Amendments to Statement on Auditing Standards No. 72, Letters for Underwriters and Certain Other Requesting Parties* (SAS 76) provides auditors with reporting guidance and an example letter when certain parties request a comfort letter but do not provide a representation letter as described in SAS 72. The key consideration is whether the accountant should provide comfort to a party with a "due diligence" defense even if the other party does not provide appropriate representations. The substance of the amendments to SAS 72 is to preclude the accountant from providing a comfort letter if an appropriate representation letter is not provided. SAS 76 was issued by the ASB in September 1995 and is effective for letters released after April 30, 1996.

3. General

   a. In requesting comfort letters, underwriters are generally seeking assistance on matters of importance to them. They wish to perform a "reasonable investigation" of financial and accounting data not "expertized" as a defense against possible claims under Section 11 of the Act. Accountants will normally be willing to assist the underwriter, but the assistance accountants can provide by way of comfort letters is subject to limitations. One limitation is that independent accountants can properly comment in their professional capacity only on matters to which their professional expertise is substantially relevant. Another limitation is that procedures short of an audit, such as those contemplated in a comfort letter, provide the accountants with a basis for expressing, at the most, negative assurance.

   b. Comfort letters are not required under the Act, and copies are not filed with the SEC. It is nonetheless a common condition of an underwriting agreement in connection with the offering for sale of securities registered with the SEC under the Act that the accountants are to furnish a comfort letter. Because the underwriter will expect the accountants to furnish a comfort letter of a scope to be specified in the underwriting agreement, a draft of that agreement should be furnished to the accountants so that they can indicate whether they will be able to furnish a letter in acceptable form. It is a desirable practice for the accountants, promptly after they have received the draft of the agreement, to prepare a draft of the form of the letter they expect to furnish. The draft should deal with all matters to be covered in the final letter.

c. Accountants, when issuing a letter under the guidance provided in this Section, may not issue any additional letters or reports to the underwriter or the other requesting parties, in connection with the offering or placement of securities, in which the accountants comment on items for which commenting is otherwise precluded by this statement, such as square footage of facilities.

4. Format and contents of comfort letters

a. The following list illustrates the subjects that may be covered in a comfort letter:

(1) The independence of the accountants.

(2) Whether the audited financial statements and financial statement schedules included in the registration statement comply as to form in all material respects with the applicable accounting requirements of the Act and the related published rules and regulations.

(3) Unaudited financial statements, condensed interim financial information, capsule financial information, pro forma financial information, financial forecasts, and changes in selected financial statement items during a period subsequent to the date and period of the latest registration statement.

(4) Tables, statistics, and other financial information included in the registration statement.

(5) Negative assurance as to whether certain nonfinancial statement information, included in the registration statement, complies as to form in all material respects with Regulation S-K.

b. The letter ordinarily is dated on or shortly before the date on which the registration statement becomes effective.

c. The letter should not be addressed or given to any parties other than the client and the named underwriter, broker-dealer, financial intermediary, or buyer or seller. The appropriate addressee is the intermediary who has negotiated the agreement with the client, and with whom the accountants will deal in discussions regarding the scope and sufficiency of the letter.

d. When the report on the audited financial statements and financial statement schedules included in the registration statement departs from the standard report, the accountants should refer to that fact in the comfort letter and discuss the subject matter of the paragraph.

e. The underwriter occasionally requests the accountants to repeat in the comfort letter their report on the audited financial statements included in the registration statement. Because of the special significance of the date of the accountants' report, the accountants should not repeat their opinion. The underwriter sometimes requests negative assurance regarding the accountants' report. Because accountants have a statutory responsibility with respect to their opinion as of the effective date of a registration statement, and because the additional significance, if any, of negative assurance is unclear and such assurance may therefore give rise to misunderstanding, accountants should not give negative assurance.

f. The accountants may refer in the introductory paragraphs of the comfort letter to the fact that they have issued reports on: (1) Condensed financial statements that are derived from audited financial statements; (2) Selected financial data; (3) Interim financial information; (4) Pro forma financial information; and (5) A financial forecast.

g. The accountants should not comment in a comfort letter on: (1) Unaudited condensed interim financial information; (2) Capsule financial information; (3) A financial forecast when historical financial statements provide a basis for one or more significant assumptions for the forecast; or (4) Changes in capital stock, increases in long-term debt, and decreases in selected financial statement items. These may be commented upon if the accounts have obtained knowledge of a client's internal control structure policies and procedures as they relate to the preparation of both annual and interim financial information.

h. Accountants should not comment in a comfort letter on pro forma financial information unless they have an appropriate level of knowledge of the accounting and financial reporting practices of the entity. This would ordinarily have been obtained by the accountant's audit or review of historical financial statements of the entity for the most recent annual or interim period for which the pro forma financial information is presented.

5. Disclosure of subsequently discovered matters--Accountants who discover matters that may require mention in the final comfort letter but that are not mentioned in the draft letter that has been furnished to the underwriter, such as changes, increases, or decreases in specified items not disclosed in the registration statement will naturally want to discuss them with their client so that consideration can be given to whether disclosure should be made in the registration statement. If disclosure is not to be made, the accountants should inform the client that the matters will be mentioned in the comfort letter and should suggest that the underwriter be informed promptly.

IV. Reporting on an Entity's Internal Control Structure Over Financial Reporting (SSAE No. 2)

A. Purpose--This Statement provides guidance to the CPA ("practitioner") who is engaged to examine and report on (attest to) management's written assertion about the effectiveness of an entity's internal control structure over financial reporting as of a point in time.

B. Written Assertion--Management may present its written assertion about the effectiveness of the entity's internal control structure in either of two forms:

1. A separate report that will accompany the practitioner's report.

2. A representation letter to the practitioner (in this case, however, the practitioner should restrict the use of his or her report to management and others within the entity and, if applicable, to specified regulatory agencies).

C. Objective and Examination Steps--The practitioner's objective in an engagement to examine and report on management's assertion about the effectiveness of the entity's internal control structure is to express an opinion about whether management's assertion regarding the effectiveness of the entity's internal control structure is fairly stated, in all material respects, based upon certain specified control criteria. Performing an examination of management's assertion about the effectiveness of an entity's internal control structure involves the following steps:

1. Planning the engagement,

2. Obtaining an understanding of the internal control structure,

3. Evaluating the design effectiveness of internal control structure policies and procedures,

4. Testing and evaluating the operating effectiveness of internal control structure policies and procedures, and

5. Forming an opinion on management's assertion about the effectiveness of the entity's internal control structure.

D. Reportable Conditions and Material Weaknesses--A practitioner engaged to examine and report on management's assertion about the effectiveness of the entity's internal control structure should communicate reportable conditions to the audit committee or its equivalent, such as the board of directors, an owner or the party who engaged the practitioner, and identify the reportable conditions that are also considered to be material weaknesses. Such communication should preferably be made in writing. The auditor should not issue any representation that no reportable conditions were noted during the examination because of the potential for misinterpretation.

E. Reporting Standards--The form of the practitioner's report depends on the manner in which management presents its written assertion. If management's assertion is presented in a separate report that accompanies the practitioner's report, the practitioner's report is considered appropriate for general distribution. If management presents its assertion only in a representation letter to the practitioner, the practitioner should restrict the distribution of his or her report to management, to others within the entity, and if applicable, to specified regulatory agencies.

Exhibit 10--Practitioner's Report on Management's Assertion Presented in a Separate Report

Independent Accountant's Report

(Introductory paragraph)

We have examined management's assertion (identify management's assertion, for example, "that W Company maintained an effective internal control structure over financial reporting as of December 31, 19XX") included in the accompanying (title of management report).

(Scope paragraph)

Our examination was made in accordance with standards established by the American Institute of Certified Public Accountants and, accordingly, included obtaining an understanding of the internal control structure over financial reporting, testing, and evaluating the design and operating effectiveness of the internal control structure, and such other procedures as we considered necessary in the circumstances. We believe that our examination provides a reasonable basis for our opinion.

(Inherent limitations paragraph)

Because of inherent limitations in any internal control structure, errors or irregularities may occur and not be detected. Also, projections of any evaluation of the internal control structure over financial reporting to future periods are subject to the risk that the internal control structure may become inadequate because of changes in conditions, or that the degree of compliance with the policies or procedures may deteriorate.

(continued on next page)

(Opinion paragraph)

In our opinion, management's assertion (identify management's assertion, for example, "that W Company maintained an effective internal control structure over financial reporting as of December 31, 19XX") is fairly stated, in all material respects, based upon (identify stated or established criteria).

As in audits of financial statements, the practitioner may issue qualified, adverse, and disclaimers of opinion by making the appropriate revisions to the above report depending on the details of the situation. Examples of situations requiring modification to the standard report would include cases where the following conditions exist:

1. There is a material weakness in the entity's internal control structure.

2. There is a restriction on the scope of the engagement.

3. The practitioner decides to refer to the report of another practitioner as the basis, in part, for the practitioner's own report.

4. A significant subsequent event has occurred since the date of management's assertion.

5. Management presents an assertion about the effectiveness of only a segment of the entity's internal control structure.

6. Management presents an assertion only about the suitability of design of the entity's internal control structure.

7. Disagreements with management exist.

8. Management's assertion is based upon criteria established by a regulatory agency without following due process.

F. Consideration of Internal Control Structure--An auditor's consideration of the internal control structure in a financial statement audit is more limited than that of a practitioner engaged to examine management's assertion about the effectiveness of the entity's internal control structure. However, knowledge the practitioner obtains about the entity's internal control structure as part of the examination of management's assertion may serve as the basis for his or her understanding of the internal control structure in an audit of the entity's financial statements. Also, the practitioner may consider the results of tests of controls performed in connection with an examination of management's assertion, as well as any material weaknesses identified, when assessing control risk in the audit of the entity's financial statement.

V. Special-Purpose Reports on the Processing of Transactions by Service Organizations (SAS 70)

A. Purpose--This Statement provides guidance on the factors an independent auditor should consider when auditing the financial statements of an entity that uses a service organization to process certain transactions. This Statement also provides guidance for independent auditors who issue reports on the processing of transactions by a service organization for use by other auditors.

B. Definitions

1. User Organization--The entity that has engaged a service organization and whose financial statements are being audited.

2. User Auditor--The auditor who reports on the financial statements of the user organization.

3. Service Organization--The entity (or a segment of that entity) that provides services to the user organization. Services could include the processing of payroll information by a service

organization for other companies or the processing of checks and daily paperwork for banks by a service organization.

4. Service Auditor--The auditor who reports on the processing of transactions by a service organization.

C. Responsibilities of Service Auditors for Special-Purpose Reports

1. The service auditor is responsible for the representations in his or her report and for exercising due care in the application of procedures that support those representations. The service auditor's work should be performed in accordance with the general standards and relevant field work and reporting standards. The service auditor should be independent from the service organization. However, the service auditor is not required to be independent with regard to each client organization.

2. The type of engagement to be performed and the type of report to be prepared should be established by the service organization. The service auditor may issue either of the following types of reports:

   a. Reports on Policies and Procedures Placed in Operation--A service auditor's report on a service organization's description of the policies and procedures that may be relevant to a user organization's internal control structure. The auditor reports on whether the policies and procedures were suitably designed to achieve specified control objectives and on whether the controls have been placed in operation as of a specific date.

   b. Reports on Policies and Procedures Placed in Operation and Tests of Operating Effectiveness--A service auditor's report on a service organization's description of the policies and procedures that may be relevant to a user organization's internal control structure. Like the report above, the auditor reports on whether such policies and procedures were suitably designed to achieve specified control objectives and on whether they had been placed in operation as of a specific date. However, the auditor also reports on whether the policies and procedures that were tested were operating with sufficient effectiveness to provide reasonable, but not absolute, assurance that the related control objectives were achieved during the period specified.

D. Format and Content of Special-Purpose Reports--A report expressing an opinion on a description of policies and procedures placed in operation at a service organization should contain the following:

1. A specific reference to the applications, services, products or other aspects of the service organization covered.

2. A description of the scope and nature of the service auditor's procedures.

3. Identification of the party specifying the control objectives.

4. An indication that the purpose of the service auditor's engagement was to obtain reasonable assurance about whether the service organization's description presents fairly, in all material respects, the aspects of the service organization's policies and procedures that may be relevant to a user organization's internal control structure; that the policies and procedures were suitably designed to achieve specified control objectives; and that such policies and procedures had been placed in operation as of a specific date.

5. A disclaimer of opinion on the operating effectiveness of the policies and procedures.

6. The service auditor's opinion on whether the description presents fairly, in all material respects, the relevant aspects of the service organization's policies and procedures that had

been placed in operation as of a specific date and whether, in the service auditor's opinion, the policies and procedures were suitably designed to provide reasonable assurance that the specified control objectives would be achieved if those policies and procedures were complied with satisfactorily.

7. A statement of the inherent limitations of the potential effectiveness of the policies and procedures at the service organization and of the risk of projecting to future periods any evaluation of the description.

8. Identification of the parties for whom the report is intended.

Exhibit 11--Report on the Policies and Procedures Placed in Operation at a Service Organization

To XYZ Service Organization:

We have examined the accompanying description of the _______ application of XYZ Service Organization. Our examination included procedures to obtain reasonable assurance about whether (1) the accompanying description presents fairly, in all material respects, the aspects of XYZ Service Organization's policies and procedures that may be relevant to a user organization's internal control structure, (2) the control structure policies and procedures included in the description were suitably designed to achieve the control objectives specified in the description, if those policies and procedures were complied with satisfactorily, and (3) such policies and procedures had been placed in operation as of ________. The control objectives were specified by _______. Our examination was performed in accordance with standards established by the American Institute of Certified Public Accountants and included those procedures we considered necessary in the circumstances to obtain a reasonable basis for rendering our opinion.

We did not perform procedures to determine the operating effectiveness of policies and procedures for any period. Accordingly, we express no opinion on the operating effectiveness of any aspects of XYZ Service Organization's policies and procedures, individually or in the aggregate.

In our opinion, the accompanying description of the aforementioned application presents fairly, in all material respects, the relevant aspects of XYZ Service Organization's policies and procedures that had been placed in operation as of ______. Also, in our opinion, the policies and procedures, as described, are suitably designed to provide reasonable assurance that the specified control objectives would be achieved if the described policies and procedures were complied with satisfactorily.

The description of polices and procedures at XYZ Service Organization is as of ___________ and any projection of such information to the future is subject to the risk that, because of change, the description may no longer portray the system in existence. The potential effectiveness of specific policies and procedures at the Service Organization is subject to inherent limitations and, accordingly, errors or irregularities may occur and not be detected. Furthermore, the projection of any conclusions, based on our findings, to future periods is subject to the risk that changes may alter the validity of such conclusions.

This report is intended solely for use by the management of XYZ Service Organization, its customers, and the independent auditors of its customers.

E. Considerations of the User Auditor in Using a Service Auditor's Report

1. In considering whether the service auditor's report is satisfactory for his or her purposes, the user auditor should make inquiries concerning the service auditor's professional reputation.

2. If the user auditor believes that the service auditor's report may not be sufficient to meet his or her objectives, the user auditor may supplement his or her understanding of the service auditor's procedures and conclusions by discussing with the service auditor the scope and results of the service auditor's work. If the user auditor believes it is necessary, he or she may contact the service organization, through the user organization, to request that the service auditor perform agreed-upon procedures at the service organization, or the user auditor may perform such procedures.

3. The user auditor should not make reference to the report of the service auditor as a basis, in part, for his or her own opinion on the user organization's financial statements.

VI. Interim Financial Information (SAS 71)

A. General--SAS 71 provides guidance as to the nature, timing, and extent of procedures to be applied for a review of interim financial information (i.e., financial information or statements for less than a full year or for a twelve-month period ending on a date other than the entity's fiscal year end) and on the resulting report. It also establishes certain communication requirements.

B. Applicability--SAS 71 applies to the following:

1. Reviews of interim financial information presented alone (including interim financial statements and summarized interim financial data) that purports to comply with APB Opinion No. 28.

2. Reviews of interim financial information that accompanies, or is included in a note to audited financial statements.

3. Regulation S-K of the SEC--SAS 71 also provides guidance on reporting when certain quarterly data required by Regulation S-K are not presented or are presented but have not been reviewed.

C. Understanding With the Client--An understanding as to the nature of the procedures to be performed should be established, usually in the form of an engagement letter which includes the following:

1. A general description of the procedures.

2. A statement that the procedures are substantially less in scope than an audit performed in accordance with GAAS.

3. An explanation that the financial information is the responsibility of the company's management.

4. A description of the form of the report, if any.

D. Objective of a Review of Interim Financial Information--To provide the CPA with a basis for reporting whether material modifications are needed to make the information conform with GAAP. This differs substantially from the objective of an audit.

E. Knowledge of Internal Control Structure Policies and Procedures--SAS 71 requires that, for an accountant to perform a review of interim financial information, there must exist a sufficient knowledge of the client's internal control structure policies and procedures as they relate to the prepa of both annual and interim financial information to

1. Identify types of potential material misstatements in the interim financial information and consider the likelihood of their occurrence.

2. Select the inquiries and analytical procedures that will provide the accountant with a basis for reporting whether material modifications should be made for such information to conform with GAAP.

F. Procedures for a Review of Interim Financial Information--Because interim financial information is made available more quickly than annual information, many costs and expenses are estimated to a greater extent than for annual financial statements. Also, the interim information is related to the annual financial information (e.g., accruals at the end of an interim period are affected by the estimate of the results of operations for the remainder of the annual period).

1. Nature of Procedures--Primarily inquiries and analytical procedures.

a. Inquiry About the Internal Control Structure--Inquiry concerning (1) how the system works, and (2) any significant changes in the internal control structure.

b. Analytical Procedures--Applied to interim financial information to provide a basis for inquiring about unusual items. These procedures consist of (1) comparing the financial information with the immediately preceding interim period and with the corresponding previous period(s), (2) comparing actual results with anticipated results, and (3) studying the relationships of those elements that can be expected to conform to predictable patterns. The CPA should consider the types of matters that required accounting adjustments in the preceding year or quarters.

c. Reading Minutes--Reading the minutes of meetings of the stockholders, board of directors, and committees of the board of directors.

d. Reading the Interim Financial Information--To determine whether it conforms to GAAP.

e. Obtaining Reports From Other Accountants--If any have reviewed the interim financial information of significant components of the reporting entity, its subsidiaries, or other investees.

f. Inquiring of Officers and Other Executives--To determine (1) whether the interim financial information conforms to GAAP consistently applied, (2) any changes in the company's business activities or accounting practices, (3) questions that have arisen during the review procedures, and (4) subsequent events (subsequent to the date of the interim financial information).

g. Obtaining Written Representations--From management, concerning management's responsibility for the financial information, completeness of the minutes, subsequent events, etc.

2. Timing of Procedures--Performing some of the work before the end of the interim period (a) usually permits the work to be carried out more efficiently, and (b) permits early consideration of accounting matters that affect the interim financial information.

3. Extent of Procedures--The extent to which the CPA applies the procedures listed above depends on the following:

a. The accountant's knowledge of changes in accounting practices or in the nature or volume of business activity.

b. Inquiry concerning litigation, claims, and assessments.

c. Questions raised in performing other procedures.

d. Modification of review procedures.

G. Reporting on Interim Financial Information Presented Alone

1. Form of Report--The report should consist of (a) a statement that the review conformed to the standards for a review of interim financial information, (b) an identification of the information reviewed, (c) a description of the procedures for a review, (d) a statement that the scope of a review is substantially less than that of an audit and that an opinion on the financial statements, taken as a whole, is not expressed, and (e) a statement as to whether the CPA is aware of any material modifications needed to make the financial information conform with GAAP.

   a. Addressee--Addressed to the company, its board of directors, or its stockholders.

   b. Date--Date of completion of the review.

   c. "Unaudited"--Each page of the interim financial information should be clearly marked "unaudited."

> Exhibit 12--Report on Interim Financial Information
>
> We have reviewed the accompanying (describe the information or statement reviewed) of ABC Company and consolidated subsidiaries as of September 30, 19X1, and for the three-month and nine-month periods then ended. These financial statements (information) are (is) the responsibility of the company's management.
>
> We conducted our review in accordance with standards established by the American Institute of Certified Public Accountants. A review of interim financial information consists principally of applying analytical procedures to financial data, and making inquiries of persons responsible for financial and accounting matters. It is substantially less in scope than an audit conducted in accordance with generally accepted auditing standards, the objective of which is the expression of an opinion regarding the financial statements taken as a whole. Accordingly, we do not express such an opinion.
>
> Based on our review, we are not aware of any material modifications that should be made to the accompanying financial (information or statements) for them (it) to be in conformity with generally accepted accounting principles.

   d. Other Accountants--May use and make reference to the report of another accountant. The reference indicates a division of responsibility for performing the review.

2. Circumstances Requiring Modification of the CPA's Report--Neither an uncertainty nor a lack of consistency in applying accounting principles would result in a modified report as long as the matters are adequately disclosed in the interim financial information or statements. However, a modification is required if a change in accounting principle is not in conformity with GAAP.

   a. Departure From GAAP--Report should be modified when the interim financial information is materially affected by a departure from GAAP. The nature of the departure and, if practicable, its effects should be disclosed.

<u>Exhibit 13</u>--Departure From GAAP

(Explanatory third paragraph)

Based on information furnished to us by management, we believe that the Company has excluded from property and debt in the accompanying balance sheet certain lease obligations that should be capitalized to conform with generally accepted accounting principles. This information indicates that if these lease obligations were capitalized at September 30, 19X1, property would be increased by $_____, long term debt by $______, and net income and earnings per share would be increased (decreased) by $_____ , $_____, $_____, and $_____, respectively, for the three-month and nine-month periods then ended.

(Concluding paragraph)

Based on our review, with the exception of the matter(s) described in the preceding paragraph(s), we are not aware of any material modifications that should be made to the accompanying financial (information or statements) for them (it) to be in conformity with generally accepted accounting principles.

b. Inadequate Disclosure--Report should be modified and, if practicable, the needed information should be included.

<u>Exhibit 14</u>--Inadequate Disclosure

(Explanatory third paragraph)

Management has informed us that the Company is presently contesting deficiencies in federal income taxes proposed by the Internal Revenue Service for the years 19X1 through 19X3 in the aggregate amount of approximately $____, and that the extent of the company's liability, if any, and the effect on the accompanying (information or statements) are (is) not determinable at this time. The (information or statements) fail to disclose these matters, which we believe are required to be disclosed in conformity with generally accepted accounting principles.

(Concluding paragraph)

Based on our review, with the exception of the matter(s) described in the preceding paragraph(s), we are not aware of any material modifications that should be made to the accompanying financial (information or statements) for them (it) to be in conformity with generally accepted accounting principles.

H. <u>Client's Representation Concerning a Review of Interim Financial Information</u>--The CPA may be asked to review interim financial information so that the client can make that representation in documents issued to stockholders or to third parties or in Form 10-Q (a quarterly report filed with the SEC). When the client represents that the CPA made such a review, the CPA should request that the CPA's report be included.

I. <u>Reporting on Interim Financial Information Presented in a Note to Audited Financial Statements</u>--SEC Regulation S-K requires some companies to include a note containing selected quarterly financial information in their audited financial statements. In addition, other companies may choose to do so.

1. If the CPA has audited the annual financial statements for which the quarterly information required by Regulation S-K is presented, the CPA should review the quarterly information as indicated in F., above. If unable to perform such review, see J. 2., below.

2. If the quarterly data is voluntarily presented, the auditor should review it (as in F., above) or the auditor should expand the report to state the data has not been reviewed.

J. Circumstances Requiring Modification of the Auditor's Report

1. The interim financial information is not required by GAAP and has not been audited; therefore, the auditor ordinarily will not modify the report on the audited financial statements to refer to the quarterly data.

2. The auditor's report on the annual statements should be modified, however, if the quarterly data either (a) has been omitted or (b) has not been reviewed.

3. The auditor's report should also be expanded when the following occurs:

a. The interim financial information is not marked "unaudited."

b. The interim information is voluntarily presented but has not been reviewed and is not appropriately marked as such.

c. The interim information does not conform to GAAP.

d. The information, although reviewed, fails to indicate that a review is substantially less in scope than an audit performed per GAAS.

K. Communication With Audit Committees--If the accountant becomes aware of matters that cause him or her to believe that interim financial information is probably materially misstated as a result of a departure from GAAP, the accountant should discuss the matter with the appropriate level of management as soon as practicable. If, in the accountant's judgment, management does not respond appropriately within a reasonable time period, the accountant should notify the audit committee, or its equivalent, of the matter. The communication can be written or oral. If oral, the communication should be documented in the working papers. If, in the accountant's judgment, the audit committee does not respond appropriately within a reasonable time period, the accountant should consider whether to resign from the engagement and whether to remain as the entity's auditor.

L. Subsequent Events--Subsequent discovery of facts that existed at the date of the auditor's report should be handled in accordance with AU 561 (see Chapter 40).

VII. Reporting on Condensed Financial Statements and Selected Financial Data (AU 552, SAS 42)

A. Purpose--This Statement provides guidance on reporting in a client-prepared document on condensed financial statements that are derived from audited financial statements of a public entity which are required to be filed with a regulatory agency. This Statement also provides such guidance for selected financial data that are derived from any audited financial statement and are presented in a document that either includes audited financial statements or incorporates such statements by reference to information filed with a regulatory agency.

B. Condensed Financial Statements

1. Condensed financial statements are presented in considerably less detail than statements presented in conformity with GAAP. Therefore, they should be read in conjunction with the entity's most recent complete financial statements.

2. Because condensed financial statements do not constitute a fair presentation of financial position, results of operations, and cash flows in conformity with GAAP, the auditor engaged to report on such statements should not report in the same manner as the auditor reported on the complete financial statements from which the condensed statements are derived.

3. The report on condensed financial statements that are derived from financial statements that the auditor has audited should indicate the following:

   a. That the auditor has audited and expressed an opinion on the complete financial statements.

   b. The date of the auditor's report on the complete financial statements, thereby removing any implication that records, transactions, or events after that date have been audited.

   c. The type of opinion expressed.

   d. Whether, in the auditor's opinion, the information set forth in the condensed financial statements is fairly stated in all material respects in relation to the complete financial statements from which it has been derived.

4. If a client makes a statement in a client-prepared document that both names the auditor and states that condensed financial statements have been derived from audited financial statements, the auditor is not required to report on the condensed financial statements provided that they are included in a document that either contains the audited financial statements or incorporates such statements by reference to the information filed with a regulatory agency. If such a statement is included in a client-prepared document of a public entity, and that document neither contains the audited financial statements nor incorporates such statements by reference to the information filed with a regulatory agency, the auditor should request the client to do either of the following:

   a. Delete the auditor's name from the document.

   b. Include the auditor's report on the condensed financial statements as described in 3., above.

   If the client does not comply with the auditor's request, the auditor should consider other appropriate actions, such as consulting legal counsel.

5. Condensed financial statements derived from audited financial statements of a public entity may be presented on a comparative basis with interim financial information as of a subsequent date that is accompanied by the auditor's review report. In such a case, the auditor should report on the condensed financial statements of each period in a manner appropriate for the type of service rendered in each period.

C. Selected Financial Data

1. Selected financial data are not a required part of the basic financial statements, and the entity's management is responsible for determining the specific selected financial data to be presented. However, under regulations of the SEC, certain reports must include, for each of the last five fiscal years, selected financial data in accordance with regulation S-K (although there is no SEC requirement for the auditor to report on such selected financial data).

2. If the auditor is engaged to report on the selected financial data, the report should be limited to data that are derived from audited financial statements. If the selected data includes both data derived from audited statements and other information (such as the number of employees or square footage of facilities), the report should specifically identify the data on which the auditor is reporting and should indicate the same items as mentioned in B.3., above. Of course, the auditor is not precluded from expressing an opinion on one or more of the specified elements, accounts, or items of a financial statement in accordance with the provisions of SAS 62, *Special Reports*, as discussed in II., above.

3. If the selected financial data are derived from financial statements that were audited by another independent auditor, the report on the selected financial data should state so, and the auditor should not express an opinion on that data.

4. The following is an example of an auditor's report that includes an additional paragraph because the auditor is also engaged to report on selected financial data for the 5-year period ended December 31, 19X5, in a client-prepared document that includes audited financial statements:

<u>Exhibit 15</u>

We have audited the accompanying consolidated balance sheets of ABC Company and subsidiaries as of December 31, 19X5 and 19X4, and the related consolidated statements of income, retained earnings, and cash flows for each of the three years in the period ended December 31, 19X5. These financial statements are the responsibility of the company's management. Our responsibility is to express an opinion on these financial statements based on our audits.

We conducted our audits in accordance with generally accepted auditing standards. Those standards require that we plan and perform the audit to obtain reasonable assurance about whether the financial statements are free of material misstatement. An audit includes examining, on a test basis, evidence supporting the amounts and disclosures in the financial statements. An audit also includes assessing the accounting principles used and significant estimates made by management, as well as evaluating the overall financial statement presentation. We believe that our audits provided a reasonable basis for our opinion.

In our opinion, the consolidated financial statements referred to above present fairly, in all material respects, the financial position of the ABC Company and subsidiaries as of December 31, 19X5 and 19X4, and the results of its operations and their cash flows for each of the three years in the period ended December 31, 19X5, in conformity with generally accepted accounting principles.

We have also previously audited, in accordance with generally accepted auditing standards, the consolidated balance sheets as of December 31, 19X3, 19X2, and 19X1, and the related consolidated statements of income, retained earnings, and cash flows for the years ended December 31, 19X2 and 19X1 (none of which are presented herein); and we expressed unqualified opinions on those consolidated financial statements.

In our opinion, the information set forth in the selected financial data for each of the five years in the period ended December 31, 19X5, appearing on page XX is fairly stated in all material respects in relation to the consolidated financial statements from which it has been derived.

5. In situations where the client names the independent auditor in a client-prepared document and states that the selected financial data are derived from financial statements audited by the named auditor, the auditor is <u>not</u> required to report on the selected financial data <u>provided that</u> the document either contains audited financial statements or incorporates such statements by reference to information filed with a regulatory agency. If the client-document is lacking these characteristics, the auditor should do either of the following:

   a. Request that neither the auditor's name nor reference to the auditor be associated with the information.

   b. Disclaim an opinion on the selected information and request that the disclaimer be included in the document.

If the client does not comply, the client should be advised that there is no consent to either the use of the auditor's name or the reference to the auditor, and the auditor should consider a consultation with legal counsel.

VIII. Reports on the Application of Accounting Principles (AU 625, SAS 50)

A. General -This Statement outlines the required procedures for accountants in public practice who report or give either written or oral advice on the following:

1. The application of accounting principles to specific completed or uncompleted transactions.

2. The type of opinion which may be rendered on an entity's financial statements.

3. The application of accounting principles to factual or circumstantial hypothetical transactions.

This Statement provides guidelines to those accountants who provide consultation either to management of an entity or to intermediaries such as lenders, major suppliers, underwriters, or regulatory agencies.

B. Applicability Exceptions--This Statement does not apply to the following:

1. An accountant who has been engaged to do the following:

   a. Report on financial statements.

   b. Assist in litigation involving accounting matters.

   c. Provide expert testimony in accounting-related litigation.

   d. Give advice to another accountant in public practice.

2. Communications such as position papers.

   a. Position papers include newsletters, articles, speeches or lectures, and text of speeches or lectures.

   b. Position papers do not include communications intended to provide guidance on the application of accounting principles to a specific transaction.

C. Evaluating and Reporting Procedures

1. The accountant should be capable of making reasonable professional judgments.

   a. Due care in performing the engagement must be exercised.

   b. The accountant should have adequate technical training and proficiency to make the required judgments.

   c. Work should be adequately planned.

   d. Assistants should be properly supervised.

   e. Sufficient information should be gathered to provide a reasonable basis for a professional judgment.

2. When preparing the report and the included opinion, the accountant should consider the following:

a. Who is the requester of the report.

b. The circumstances under which the request is made.

c. The purpose of the request.

d. The intended use of the report.

3. Prior to making a judgment, the accountant should do the following:

a. Obtain an understanding of the form and substance of the transactions involved.

b. Review applicable generally accepted accounting principles.

c. Consult with other professionals or experts if necessary.

d. Perform research on the products to ascertain and consider the existence of creditable precedents or analogies.

4. Evaluation Procedures for Determining the Type of Opinion Which May Be Rendered

a. The reporting accountant who has been engaged by the principal or intermediary to give advice has the responsibility to consult with the continuing accountant who prepares or audits the financial statements to determine the following:

(1) The form and substance of transactions.

(2) How the management applied accounting principles to similar transactions.

(3) If management disputes the method of accounting recommended by the continuing accountant.

(4) If the continuing accountant has reached a different conclusion on the application of accounting principles or type of opinion.

b. The responsibilities of the continuing accountant to respond to the reporting accountant are the same as the responsibilities of a predecessor auditor to a successor auditor.

(1) Explain to the principal the need to consult, and request permission to do so.

(2) Request permission for the continuing accountant to respond to inquiries fully and in detail.

D. Reporting Standards of the Written Report

1. The report should be addressed to the principals or to the intermediary.

2. The first part of the report should describe the engagement.

a. Include a brief description of the nature of the engagement and state that the engagement was performed in accordance with acceptable AICPA standards.

b. Describe the transactions, relevant facts, circumstances, assumptions, and sources of information.

(1) Identify principals to specific transactions.

(2) Describe hypothetical transactions.

(3) Describe nonspecific principals such as Company A, Company B.

c. Describe the appropriate accounting principles or the type of opinion, and the reasons for the reporting accountant's conclusion.

3. The last part of the report should include specific statements.

a. State that responsibility for proper accounting rests with the preparers of the financial statements who should consult with their continuing accountants.

b. State that any difference in the facts, circumstances, or assumptions presented may change the report.

4. Use the report shown in Exhibit 16, below, to assist in preparing a proper report on application of accounting principles or the type of opinion.

Exhibit 16--Report on Application of Accounting Principles or Type of Opinion

(Introduction)

We have been engaged to report on the appropriate application of generally accepted accounting principles to the specific (hypothetical) transaction described below. This report is being issued to the ABC Company (XYZ Intermediaries) for assistance in evaluating accounting principles for the described specific (hypothetical) transaction. Our engagement has been conducted in accordance with standards established by the American Institute of Certified Public Accountants.

(Description of transaction)

The facts, circumstances, and assumptions relevant to the specific (hypothetical) transaction as provided to us by the management of the ABC Company (XYZ Intermediaries) are as follows:

(Appropriate accounting principles)

[Text discussing principles]

(Concluding comments)

The ultimate responsibility for the decision on the appropriate application of generally accepted accounting principles for an actual transaction rests with the preparers of financial statements, who should consult with their continuing accountants. Our judgment on the appropriate application of generally accepted accounting principles for the described specific (hypothetical) transaction is based solely on the facts provided to us as described above. Should these facts and circumstances differ, our conclusion may change.

IX. Reporting on Financial Statements Prepared for Use in Other Countries (AU 534, SAS 51)

A. Applicability--This Statement provides guidelines for an independent auditor engaged to report on financial statements of a U.S. entity for use outside the United States, given the following conditions.

1. Financial statements are prepared in conformity with generally accepted accounting principles of another country.

2. The entity is organized or domiciled in the U.S.

3. The auditor practices in the United States.

B. Purpose and Use of Financial Statements--Such financial statements may be prepared when, for example

1. The statements will be included in the financial statements of a non-U.S. parent.

2. The entity has substantial non-U.S. investors.

3. Capital is to be raised in another country.

C. General and Fieldwork Standards--The auditor should comply with the general and field work standards of U.S. generally accepted auditing standards. The U.S. procedures may need to be modified, however, to apply when there are differences in accounting principles generally accepted in another country and U.S. GAAP. Examples of this include:

1. Accounting principles generally accepted in another country may require that certain assets be revalued to adjust for the effects of inflation—in which case, the auditor should perform procedures to test the revaluation adjustments.

2. Another country's accounting principles may not require or permit recognition of deferred taxes—consequently, procedures for testing deferred tax balances would not be applicable.

D. Auditor's Understanding and Knowledge--The auditor should understand the accounting principles and auditing standards generally accepted in the other country and the legal responsibilities involved.

1. The auditor may obtain such knowledge by reading the applicable statutes, professional literature, and codification of accounting principles and auditing standards generally accepted in that country.

2. If the accounting principles of another country are not established with sufficient authority or by general acceptance, the auditor may report on the financial statements if:

   a. The auditor judges the client's principles and practices to be appropriate, and

   b. The client's principles and practices are disclosed in a clear and comprehensive manner.

3. The auditor should consider consulting with persons having expertise in the accounting principles and auditing standards of the other country.

4. The International Accounting Standards established by the International Accounting Standards Committee may be used.

E. Reporting Standards--The auditor may prepare either a U.S.-style or foreign-style report, or both.

1. A U.S.-style report which is modified to the accounting principles is preferred.

   a. The report should include, in addition to standard required items:

(1) A note to the financial statements which describes the basis of preparation including the nationality of the accounting principles.

(2) A note that says the audit was made in accordance with GAAS of the U.S. (and the auditing standards of the other country, if appropriate).

b. The following is an example of an opinion expressed on financial statements prepared in conformity with accounting principles generally accepted in another country in a U.S.-style report:

> Exhibit 17
>
> We have audited the balance sheet of the International Company as of December 31, 19XX, and the related statements of income, retained earnings, and cash flows for the year then ended, which, as described in Note X, have been prepared on the basis of accounting principles generally accepted in (name of country). These financial statements are the responsibility of the Company's management. Our responsibility is to express an opinion on these financial statements based on our audit.
>
> We conducted our audit in accordance with auditing standards generally accepted in the United States (and in [name of country]). U.S. standards require that we plan and perform the audit to obtain reasonable assurance about whether the financial statements are free of material misstatement. An audit includes examining, on a test basis, evidence supporting the amounts and disclosures in the financial statements. An audit also includes assessing the accounting principles used and significant estimates made by management, as well as evaluating the overall financial statement presentation. We believe that our audit provides a reasonable basis for our opinion.
>
> In our opinion, the financial statements referred to above present fairly, in all material respects, the financial position of the International Company at December 31, 19XX, and the results of its operations and cash flows for the year then ended, in conformity with accounting principles generally accepted in (name of country).

c. Although the report is intended for use only outside the U.S., this is not intended to preclude limited use of the financial statements to parties (such as banks) within the U.S. that deal directly with the entity.

2. The standard report of another country may be used, provided that the following is evident:

a. The standard report is used by auditors in the other country, given similar circumstances.

b. The auditor understands the meaning and implications of the report with respect to different customs and different word interpretations.

c. The auditor is in the position to make the attestations contained in the report.

d. When using a standard report of a foreign country which is similar to the one used in the U.S., the country name should be added to the report to avoid erroneous interpretation due to a different custom or culture.

3. Use of both a U.S.-style and a foreign-style report.

a. The auditor should include a note such as the one below which describes the differences between U.S. GAAP and the foreign GAAP.

We also have reported separately on the financial statements of International Company for the same period presented in conformity with accounting principles generally accepted in (name of country). (The significant differences between the accounting principles accepted in [name of country] and those generally accepted in the United States are summarized in Note X.)

X. Compliance Auditing Considerations in Audits of Governmental Entities and Recipients of Governmental Financial Assistance (SAS 74)

A. Applicability--SAS 74 is applicable when an auditor is engaged to audit a governmental entity and engaged to test and report on compliance with laws and regulations under *Government Auditing Standards* (the Yellow Book) or in certain other circumstances involving governmental financial assistance, such as single or organization-wide audits or program-specific audits under certain federal or state audit regulations. Specifically, SAS 74 provides general guidance to auditors in:

1. Applying the provisions of SAS 54, *Illegal Acts by Clients*, relative to detecting misstatements resulting from illegal acts related to laws and regulations that have a direct and material effect on the determination of financial statement amounts in audits of the financial statements of governmental entities and other recipients of governmental financial assistance.

2. Performing a financial audit in accordance with *Government Auditing Standards*, issued by the Comptroller General of the United States.

3. Performing a single or organization-wide audit or a program-specific audit in accordance with federal audit requirements.

4. Communicating with management if the auditor becomes aware that the entity is subject to an audit requirement that may not be encompassed in the terms of the engagement.

B. Guidance--The auditor should design the audit to provide reasonable assurance that the financial statements are free of material misstatements resulting from violations of laws and regulations that have a direct and material effect on the determination of financial statement amounts.

1. The auditor should obtain an understanding of the possible effects on financial statements of laws and regulations that are generally recognized by auditors to have a direct and material effect on the determination of amounts in an entity's financial statements.

2. The auditor should assess whether management has identified laws and regulations that have a direct and material effect on the determination of amounts in the entity's financial statements and obtain an understanding of the possible effects on the financial statements of such laws and regulations.

3. The auditor may consider performing the following procedures in assessing such laws and regulations and in obtaining an understanding of their possible effects on the financial statements:

   a. Consider knowledge about such laws and regulations obtained from prior years' audits.

   b. Discuss such laws and regulations with the entity's chief financial officer, legal counsel, or grant administrators.

   c. Obtain written representation from management regarding the completeness of management's identification.

d. Review the relevant portions of any directly related agreements, such as those related to grants and loans.

e. Review the minutes of meetings of the legislative body of the governing board of the governmental entity being audited for the enactment of laws and regulations that have a direct and material effect on the determination of amounts in the governmental entity's financial statements.

f. Inquire of the office of the federal, state, or local auditor or other appropriate audit oversight organization about the laws and regulations applicable to entities within their jurisdiction, including statutes and uniform reporting requirements.

g. Review information about compliance requirements and state and local policies and procedures.

4. *Government Auditing Standards* require the auditor to design the audit to provide reasonable assurance of detecting material misstatements resulting from noncompliance with provisions of contracts or grant agreements that have a direct and material effect on the financial statements. For financial audits, *Government Auditing Standards* prescribes fieldwork and reporting standards beyond those required by GAAS. The general standards of *Government Auditing Standards* relate to qualifications of the staff, independence, due professional care, and quality control.

5. These audits generally have the following elements in common:

a. The audit is to be conducted in accordance with GAAS and *Government Auditing Standards*.

b. The auditor's consideration of the internal control structure is to include obtaining and documenting an understanding of the internal control structure established to ensure compliance with the laws and regulations applicable to the federal financial assistance. In some instances, federal audit regulations mandate a "test of controls" to evaluate the effectiveness of the design and operation of the policies and procedures in preventing or detecting material noncompliance.

c. The auditor is to issue a report on the consideration of the internal control structure.

d. The auditor is to determine and report on whether the federal financial assistance has been administered in accordance with applicable laws and regulations (compliance requirements).

6. A recipient of federal financial assistance may be subject to a single or organization-wide audit or to a program-specific audit. A number of federal audit regulations permit the recipient to "elect" to have a program-specific audit, whereas other federal audit regulations require a program-specific audit in certain circumstances. In planning the audit, the auditor should determine and consider the specific federal audit requirements applicable to the engagement, including the issuance of additional reports.

7. In evaluating whether an entity has complied with laws and regulations that, if not complied with, could have a material effect on each major federal financial assistance program, the auditor should consider the effect of identified instances of noncompliance on each such program. In doing so, the auditor should consider:

a. The frequency of noncompliance identified in the audit.

b. The adequacy of the primary recipient's system of monitoring subrecipients and the possible effect on the program of any noncompliance identified by the primary recipient or the auditors of the subrecipients.

c. Whether any instances of noncompliance identified in the audit resulted in "questioned costs," and if they did, whether questioned costs are material to the program.

CHAPTER 41—OTHER TYPES OF REPORTS

Problem 41-1 MULTIPLE CHOICE QUESTIONS (40 to 50 minutes)

1. Which of the following best describes the auditor's reporting responsibility concerning information accompanying the basic financial statements in an auditor-submitted document?

a. The auditor has **no** reporting responsibility concerning information accompanying the basic financial statements.
b. The auditor should report on the information accompanying the basic financial statements only if the auditor participated in its preparation.
c. The auditor should report on the information accompanying the basic financial statements only if the auditor did **not** participate in its preparation.
d. The auditor should report on all the information included in the document.

(5/93, Aud., #48, 3944)

2. Information accompanying the basic financial statements in an auditor-submitted document should **not** include

a. An analysis of inventory by location.
b. A statement that the allowance for doubtful accounts is adequate.
c. A statement that the depreciable life of a new asset is 20 years.
d. An analysis of revenue by product line.

(5/88, Aud., #50, 9911)

3. If information accompanying the basic financial statements in an auditor-submitted document has been subjected to auditing procedures, the auditor may include in the auditor's report on the financial statements an opinion that the accompanying information is fairly stated in

a. Conformity with standards established by the AICPA.
b. Accordance with generally accepted auditing standards.
c. Conformity with generally accepted accounting principles.
d. All material respects in relation to the basic financial statements taken as a whole.

(11/91, Aud., #31, 2299)

3A. If information accompanying the basic financial statements in an auditor-submitted document has been subjected to auditing procedures, the auditor may include in the auditor's report on the financial statements an opinion that the accompanying information is fairly stated in

a. Accordance with generally accepted auditing standards.
b. Conformity with generally accepted accounting principles.
c. All material respects in relation to the basic financial statements taken as a whole.
d. Accordance with attestation standards expressing a conclusion about management's assertions.

(5/95, Aud., #87, 5705)

4. Helpful Co., a nonprofit entity, prepared its financial statements on an accounting basis prescribed by a regulatory agency solely for filing with that agency. Green audited the financial statements in accordance with generally accepted auditing standards and concluded that the financial statements were fairly presented on the prescribed basis. Green should issue a

a. Qualified opinion.
b. Standard three paragraph report with reference to footnote disclosure.
c. Disclaimer of opinion.
d. Special report.

(11/91, Aud., #17, 2285)

5. An auditor's special report on financial statements prepared in conformity with the cash basis of accounting should include a separate explanatory paragraph before the opinion paragraph that

a. Justifies the reasons for departing from generally accepted accounting principles.
b. States whether the financial statements are fairly presented in conformity with another comprehensive basis of accounting.
c. Refers to the note to the financial statements that describes the basis of accounting.
d. Explains how the results of operations differ from financial statements prepared in conformity with generally accepted accounting principles.

(11/92, Aud., #54, 2988)

5A. An auditor's report on financial statements prepared on the cash receipts and disbursements basis of accounting should include all of the following **except**

a. A reference to the note to the financial statements that describes the cash receipts and disbursements basis of accounting.
b. A statement that the cash receipts and disbursements basis of accounting is **not** a comprehensive basis of accounting.
c. An opinion as to whether the financial statements are presented fairly in conformity with the cash receipts and disbursements basis of accounting.
d. A statement that the audit was conducted in accordance with generally accepted auditing standards. (5/95, Aud., #82, 5700)

6. If the auditor believes that financial statements prepared on the entity's income tax basis are **not** suitably titled, the auditor should
a. Issue a disclaimer of opinion.
b. Explain in the notes to the financial statements the terminology used.
c. Issue a compilation report.
d. Disclose his or her reservations in an explanatory paragraph of the report and qualify the opinion. (11/87, Aud., #8, 9911)

6A. When an auditor reports on financial statements prepared on an entity's income tax basis, the auditor's report should
a. Disclaim an opinion on whether the statements were examined in accordance with generally accepted auditing standards.
b. Not express an opinion on whether the statements are presented in conformity with the comprehensive basis of accounting used.
c. Include an explanation of how the results of operations differ from the cash receipts and disbursements basis of accounting.
d. State that the basis of presentation is a comprehensive basis of accounting other than GAAP. (5/94, Aud., #83, 4748)

7. An accountant who is **not** independent of a client is precluded from issuing a
a. Report on consulting services.
b. Compilation report on historical financial statements.
c. Compilation report on prospective financial statements.
d. Special report on compliance with contractual agreements. (11/90, Aud., #37, 0393)

8. An accountant may accept an engagement to apply agreed-upon procedures that are not sufficient to express an opinion on one or more specified accounts or items of a financial statement provided that
a. The accountant's report does **not** enumerate the procedures performed.
b. The financial statements are prepared in conformity with a comprehensive basis of accounting other than generally accepted accounting principles.
c. Distribution of the accountant's report is restricted.
d. The accountant is also the entity's continuing auditor. (11/88, Aud., #24, 2933)

9. Which of the following matters is covered in a typical comfort letter?
a. Negative assurance concerning whether the entity's internal control procedures operated as designed during the period being audited.
b. An opinion regarding whether the entity complied with laws and regulations under *Government Auditing Standards* and the Single Audit Act of 1984.
c. Positive assurance concerning whether unaudited condensed financial information complied with generally accepted accounting principles.
d. An opinion as to whether the audited financial statements comply in form with the accounting requirements of the SEC. (5/93, Aud., #51, 3947)

9A. Which of the following statements is correct concerning letters for underwriters, commonly referred to as comfort letters?
a. Letters for underwriters are required by the Securities Act of 1933 for the initial public sale of registered securities.
b. Letters for underwriters typically give negative assurance on unaudited interim financial information.
c. Letters for underwriters usually are included in the registration statement accompanying a prospectus.
d. Letters for underwriters ordinarily update auditors' opinions on the prior year's financial statements. (5/95, Aud., #86, 5704)

10. When an independent accountant's report based on a review of interim financial information is presented in a registration statement, a prospectus should include a statement about the accountant's involvement. This statement should clarify that the
a. Accountant is **not** an "expert" within the meaning of the Securities Act of 1933.
b. Accountant's review report is **not** a "part" of the registration statement within the meaning of the Securities Act of 1933.

c. Accountant performed only limited auditing procedures on the interim financial statements.
d. Accountant's review was performed in accordance with standards established by the American Institute of CPAs.

(5/90, Aud., #24, 0398)

11. The Securities and Exchange Commission has authority to
a. Prescribe specific auditing procedures to detect fraud concerning inventories and accounts receivable of companies engaged in interstate commerce.
b. Deny lack of privity as a defense in third-party actions for gross negligence against the auditors of public companies.
c. Determine accounting principles for the purpose of financial reporting by companies offering securities to the public.
d. Require a change of auditors of governmental entities after a given period of years as a means of ensuring auditor independence.

(11/88, Aud., #14, 9911)

12. Comfort letters ordinarily are signed by the client's
a. Independent auditor.
b. Underwriter of securities.
c. Audit committee.
d. Senior management. (11/92, Aud., #58, 2992)

13. When an accountant issues to an underwriter a comfort letter containing comments on data that have **not** been audited, the underwriter most likely will receive
a. Negative assurance on capsule information.
b. Positive assurance on supplementary disclosures.
c. A limited opinion on "pro forma" financial statements.
d. A disclaimer on prospective financial statements. (5/92, Aud., #8, 2761)

14. An independent accountant, without auditing an entity's financial statements, may accept an engagement to express an opinion on the entity's internal controls in effect

	As of a specified date	During a specified period of time
a.	Yes	Yes
b.	Yes	No
c.	No	Yes
d.	No	No

(5/89, Aud., #22, 0408)

15. An accountant has been engaged to report on an entity's internal controls without performing an audit of the financial statements. What restrictions, if any, should the accountant place on the use of this report?
a. This report should be restricted for use by management.
b. This report should be restricted for use by the audit committee.
c. This report should be restricted for use by a specified regulatory agency.
d. The accountant does **not** need to place any restrictions on the use of this report.

(11/89, Aud., #51, 0407)

15A. Which of the following conditions is necessary for a practitioner to accept an attest engagement to examine and report on an entity's internal control structure over financial reporting?
a. The practitioner anticipates relying on the entity's internal control structure in a financial statement audit.
b. Management presents its written assertion about the effectiveness of the internal control structure.
c. The practitioner is a continuing auditor who previously has audited the entity's financial statements.
d. Management agrees **not** to present the practitioner's report in a general-use document to stockholders. (11/94, Aud., #18, 5091)

16. How do the scope, procedures, and purpose of an engagement to express an opinion on an entity's system of internal accounting control compare to those for obtaining an understanding of the internal control structure and assessing control risk as part of an audit?

	Scope	Procedures	Purpose
a.	Similar	Different	Similar
b.	Different	Similar	Similar
c.	Different	Different	Different
d.	Different	Similar	Different

(5/90, Aud., #40, 0400)

17. An accountant's report expressing an opinion on an entity's internal controls should state that

a. Only those controls on which the accountant intends to rely were reviewed, tested, and evaluated.
b. The establishment and maintenance of the internal controls is the responsibility of management.
c. The study and evaluation of the internal controls was conducted in accordance with generally accepted auditing standards.
d. Distribution of the report is restricted for use only by management and the board of directors. (5/92, Aud., #52, 9911)

18. An accountant's report expressing an unqualified opinion on an entity's system of internal accounting control should contain a
a. Description of the difference between the expression of an opinion on the system and the assessment of control risk made as part of an audit.
b. Statement that the establishment and maintenance of the system is the responsibility of management.
c. Statement that the distribution of the accountant's report is limited to the entity's management and its board of directors.
d. Description of the material weaknesses that may permit errors or irregularities to occur and **not** be detected. (5/91, Aud., #36, 0387)

18A. Snow, CPA, was engaged by Master Co. to examine and report on management's written assertion about the effectiveness of Master's internal control structure over financial reporting. Snow's report should state that
a. Because of inherent limitations of any internal control structure, errors or irregularities may occur and **not** be detected.
b. Management's assertion is based on criteria established by the American Institute of Certified Public Accountants.
c. The results of Snow's tests will form the basis for Snow's opinion on the fairness of Master's financial statements in conformity with GAAP.
d. The purpose of the engagement is to enable Snow to plan an audit and determine the nature, timing, and extent of tests to be performed. (11/94, Aud., #46, 5119)

19. An accountant's report expressing an unqualified opinion on an entity's system of internal accounting control should state that the
a. Engagement is different in purpose and scope from obtaining an understanding of the internal control structure and assessing control risk as part of an audit.
b. Accountant's opinion does **not** necessarily increase the reliability of the entity's financial statements unless they are audited.
c. System taken as a whole is sufficient to meet the broad objectives pertaining to preventing or detecting material errors or irregularities.
d. Accountant did **not** apply procedures in the engagement that duplicate those procedures previously applied in assessing control risk as part of an audit. (11/90, Aud., #56, 0394)

19A. In reporting on an entity's internal control structure over financial reporting, a practitioner should include a paragraph that describes the
a. Documentary evidence regarding the control environment factors.
b. Changes in the internal control structure since the prior report.
c. Potential benefits from the practitioner's suggested improvements.
d. Inherent limitations of any internal control structure. (5/95, Aud., #84, 5702)

20. Cain Company's management engaged Bell, CPA, to express an opinion on Cain's system of internal accounting control. Bell's report described several material weaknesses and potential errors and irregularities that could occur. Subsequently, management included Bell's report in its annual report to the Board of Directors with a statement that the cost of correcting the weaknesses would exceed the benefits. Bell should
a. Not express an opinion as to management's cost-benefit statement.
b. Advise the Board that Bell either agrees or disagrees with management's statement.
c. Advise management that Bell's report was restricted for use only by management.
d. Advise both management and the Board that Bell was withdrawing the opinion. (11/90, Aud., #57, 0395)

21. The objective of a review of interim financial information of a public entity is to provide an accountant with a basis for reporting whether
a. A reasonable basis exists for expressing an updated opinion regarding the financial statements that were previously audited.
b. Material modifications should be made to conform with generally accepted accounting principles.

c. The financial statements are presented fairly in accordance with standards of interim reporting.
d. The financial statements are presented fairly in accordance with generally accepted accounting principles. (5/93, Aud., #54, 3950)

21A. The objective of a review of interim financial information of a public entity is to provide an accountant with a basis for reporting whether
a. Material modifications should be made to conform with generally accepted accounting principles.
b. A reasonable basis exists for expressing an updated opinion regarding the financial statements that were previously audited.
c. Condensed financial statements or pro forma financial information should be included in a registration statement.
d. The financial statements are presented fairly in accordance with generally accepted accounting principles. (5/95, Aud., #83, 5701)

22. Which of the following procedures ordinarily should be applied when an independent accountant conducts a review of interim financial information of a publicly held entity?
a. Verify changes in key account balances.
b. Read the minutes of the board of directors' meeting.
c. Inspect the open purchase order file.
d. Perform cut-off tests for cash receipts and disbursements. (11/92, Aud., #51, 2985)

22A. An independent accountant's report is based on a review of interim financial information. If this report is presented in a registration statement, a prospectus should include a statement clarifying that the
a. Accountant's review report is **not** a part of the registration statement within the meaning of the Securities Act of 1933.
b. Accountant assumes **no** responsibility to update the report for events and circumstances occurring after the date of the report.
c. Accountant's review was performed in accordance with standards established by the Securities and Exchange Commission.
d. Accountant obtained corroborating evidence to determine whether material modifications are needed for such information to conform with GAAP. (5/94, Aud., #64, 4729)

23. Which of the following circumstances requires modification of the accountant's report on a review of interim financial information of a publicly held entity?

	An uncertainty	Inadequate disclosure
a.	Yes	Yes
b.	No	No
c.	Yes	No
d.	No	Yes

(5/88, Aud., #48, 0410)

24. Reporting on the internal control structure under *Government Auditing Standards* differs from reporting under generally accepted auditing standards in that *Government Auditing Standards* requires a
a. Written report describing the entity's internal control structure procedures specifically designed to prevent fraud, abuse, and illegal acts.
b. Written report describing each reportable condition observed including identification of those considered material weaknesses.
c. Statement of negative assurance that the internal control structure procedures **not** tested have an immaterial effect on the entity's financial statements.
d. Statement of positive assurance that internal control structure procedures designed to detect material errors and irregularities were tested. (5/93, Aud., #24, 3920)

24A. Because of the pervasive effects of laws and regulations on the financial statements of governmental units, an auditor should obtain written management representations acknowledging that management has
a. Identified and disclosed all laws and regulations that have a direct and material effect on its financial statements.
b. Implemented internal control policies and procedures designed to detect all illegal acts.
c. Expressed both positive and negative assurance to the auditor that the entity complied with all laws and regulations.
d. Employed internal auditors who can report their findings, opinions, and conclusions objectively without fear of political repercussion. (5/94, Aud., #84, 4749)

24B. An auditor notes reportable conditions in a financial statement audit conducted in accordance with *Government Auditing Standards*. In reporting on the internal control structure, the auditor should state that

a. Expressing an opinion on the entity's financial statements provides **no** assurance on the internal control structure.
b. The auditor obtained an understanding of the design of relevant policies and procedures, and determined whether they have been placed in operation.
c. The specified government funding or legislative body is responsible for reviewing the internal control structure as a condition of continued funding.
d. The auditor has **not** determined whether any of the reportable conditions described in the report are so severe as to be material weaknesses.

(5/94, Aud., #85, 4750)

25. An auditor most likely would be responsible for assuring that management communicates significant deficiencies in the design of the internal control structure.

a. To a court-appointed creditors' committee when the client is operating under Chapter 11 of the Federal Bankruptcy Code.
b. To shareholders with significant influence (more than 20% equity ownership) when the reportable conditions are deemed to be material weaknesses.
c. To the Securities and Exchange Commission when the client is a publicly held entity.
d. To specific legislative and regulatory bodies when reporting under *Government Auditing Standards.* (5/93, Aud., #52, 3948)

26. Tell, CPA, is auditing the financial statements of Youth Services Co. (YSC), a not-for-profit organization, in accordance with *Government Auditing Standards.* Tell's report on YSC's compliance with laws and regulations is required to contain statements of

	Positive assurance	Negative assurance
a.	Yes	Yes
b.	Yes	No
c.	No	Yes
d.	No	No

(5/93, Aud., #60, 3956)

27. When engaged to audit a not-for-profit organization in accordance with *Government Auditing Standards*, an auditor is required to prepare a written report on compliance with laws and regulations that includes

a. All material and immaterial instances of noncompliance with laws and regulations.
b. All instances or indications of illegal acts that could result in criminal prosecution.
c. A description of all material weaknesses noted during the engagement.
d. An explanation of the inherent limitations of the internal control structure.

(5/92, Aud., #10, 2763)

27A. An auditor was engaged to conduct a performance audit of a governmental entity in accordance with *Government Auditing Standards.* These standards do **not** require, as part of this auditor's report

a. A statement of the audit objectives and a description of the audit scope.
b. Indications or instances of illegal acts that could result in criminal prosecution discovered during the audit.
c. The pertinent views of the entity's responsible officials concerning the auditor's findings.
d. A concurrent opinion on the financial statements taken as a whole.

(11/94, Aud., #90, 5163)

28. When engaged to audit a governmental entity in accordance with *Government Auditing Standards*, an auditor prepares a written report on the internal control structure

a. In all audits, regardless of circumstances.
b. Only when the auditor has noted reportable conditions.
c. Only when requested by the governmental entity being audited.
d. Only when requested by the federal government funding agency.

(5/92, Aud., #1, 9911)

29. When reporting on an entity's internal control structure under *Government Auditing Standards*, an auditor should issue a written report that includes a

a. Statement of negative assurance that nothing came to the auditor's attention that caused the auditor to believe reportable conditions were present.
b. Statement of positive assurance that the results of tests indicate that the internal control structure either can, or cannot, be relied on to reduce control risk to an acceptable level.
c. Description of the weaknesses considered to be reportable conditions and the strengths that the auditor can rely on in reducing the extent of substantive testing.
d. Description of the scope of the auditor's work in obtaining an understanding of the internal control structure and in assessing control risk.

(11/92, Aud., #24, 9911)

30. In an audit in accordance with *Government Auditing Standards*, an auditor is required to report

on the auditor's tests of the entity's compliance with applicable laws and regulations. This requirement is satisfied by designing the audit to provide

a. Positive assurance that the internal control policies and procedures tested by the auditor are operating as prescribed.
b. Reasonable assurance of detecting misstatements that are material to the financial statements.
c. Negative assurance that reportable conditions communicated during the audit do **not** prevent the auditor from expressing an opinion.
d. Limited assurance that the internal control structure designed by management will prevent or detect errors, irregularities, and illegal acts.

(5/92, Aud., #32, 2785)

30A. Wolf is auditing an entity's compliance with requirements governing a major federal financial assistance program in accordance with *Government Auditing Standards.* Wolf detected noncompliance with requirements that have a material effect on the program. Wolf's report on compliance should express

a. No assurance on the compliance tests.
b. Reasonable assurance on the compliance tests.
c. A qualified or adverse opinion.
d. An adverse or disclaimer of opinion.

(11/94, Aud., #85, 5158)

31. The concept of materiality for financial statements audited under the Single Audit Act of 1984 differs from materiality in an audit in accordance with generally accepted auditing standards. Under the Act, materiality is

a. Determined by the federal agency requiring the audit.
b. Ignored, because all account balances, regardless of size, are fully tested.
c. Determined separately for each major federal financial assistance program.
d. Calculated without consideration of the auditor's risk assessment.

(11/92, Aud., #42, 2976)

32. Kent is auditing an entity's compliance with requirements governing a major federal financial assistance program in accordance with the Single Audit Act. Kent detected noncompliance with requirements that have a material effect on that program. Kent's report on compliance should express a(an)

a. Unqualified opinion with a separate explanatory paragraph.
b. Qualified opinion or an adverse opinion.
c. Adverse opinion or a disclaimer of opinion.
d. Limited assurance on the items tested.

(5/91, Aud., #60, 0391)

33. An auditor may report on condensed financial statements that are derived from complete audited financial statements if the

a. Auditor indicates whether the information in the condensed financial statements is fairly stated in all material respects.
b. Condensed financial statements are presented in comparative form with the prior year's condensed financial statements.
c. Auditor describes the additional review procedures performed on the condensed financial statements.
d. Condensed financial statements are distributed only to management and the board of directors.

(11/91, Aud., #29, 2297)

33A. In the standard report on condensed financial statements that are derived from a public entity's audited financial statements, a CPA should indicate that the

a. Condensed financial statements are prepared in conformity with another comprehensive basis of accounting.
b. CPA has audited and expressed an opinion on the complete financial statements.
c. Condensed financial statements are **not** fairly presented in all material respects.
d. CPA expresses limited assurance that the financial statements conform with GAAP.

(11/94, Aud., #87, 5160)

34. A CPA is permitted to accept a separate engagement (**not** in conjunction with an audit of financial statements) to audit an entity's

	Schedule of accounts receivable	Schedule of royalties
a.	Yes	Yes
b.	Yes	No
c.	No	Yes
d.	No	No

(11/93, Aud., #56, 4293)

35. The financial statements of KCP America, a U.S. entity, are prepared for inclusion in the consolidated financial statements of its non-U.S. parent. These financial statements are prepared in conformity with the accounting principles generally accepted in the parent's country and are for use only in that country. How may KCP America's auditor report on these financial statements?

I. A U.S.-style report (unmodified).
II. A U.S.-style report modified to report on the accounting principles of the parent's country.
III. The report form of the parent's country.

	I	II	III
a.	Yes	No	No
b.	No	Yes	No
c.	Yes	No	Yes
d.	No	Yes	Yes

(5/91, Aud., #49, 0389)

36. Hill, CPA, is auditing the financial statements of Helping Hand, a not-for-profit organization that receives financial assistance from governmental agencies. To detect misstatements in Helping Hand's financial statements resulting from violations of laws and regulations, Hill should focus on violations that

a. Could result in criminal prosecution against the organization.
b. Involve reportable conditions to be communicated to the organization's trustees and the funding agencies.
c. Have a direct and material effect on the amounts in the organization's financial statements.
d. Demonstrate the existence of material weaknesses in the organization's internal control structure. (11/92, Aud., #56, 2990)

37. In connection with a proposal to obtain a new client, an accountant in public practice is asked to prepare a written report on the application of accounting principles to a specific transaction. The accountant's report should include a statement that

a. Any difference in the facts, circumstances, or assumptions presented may change the report.
b. The engagement was performed in accordance with Statements on Standards for Consulting Services.
c. The guidance provided is for management use only and may **not** be communicated to the prior or continuing auditors.
d. Nothing came to the accountant's attention that caused the accountant to believe that the accounting principles violated GAAP.

(5/94, Aud., #67, 4732)

38. Before reporting on the financial statements of a U.S. entity that have been prepared in conformity with another country's accounting principles, an auditor practicing in the U.S. should

a. Understand the accounting principles generally accepted in the other country.
b. Be certified by the appropriate auditing or accountancy board of the other country.
c. Notify management that the auditor is required to disclaim an opinion on the financial statements.
d. Receive a waiver from the auditor's state board of accountancy to perform the engagement.

(11/94, Aud., #88, 5161)

39. Lake, CPA, is auditing the financial statements of Gill Co. Gill uses the EDP Service Center, Inc. to process its payroll transactions. EDP's financial statements are audited by Cope, CPA, who recently issued a report on EDP's internal control structure. Lake is considering Cope's report on EDP's internal control structure in assessing control risk on the Gill engagement. What is Lake's responsibility concerning making reference to Cope as a basis, in part, for Lake's own opinion?

a. Lake may refer to Cope only if Lake is satisfied as to Cope's professional reputation and independence.
b. Lake may refer to Cope only if Lake relies on Cope's report in restricting the extent of substantive tests.
c. Lake may refer to Cope only if Lake's report indicates the division of responsibility.
d. Lake may **not** refer to Cope under the circumstances above. (5/94, Aud., #36, 4701)

Solution 41-1 MULTIPLE CHOICE ANSWERS

Reporting on Information Accompanying the Basic Financial Statements in Auditor-Submitted Documents (AU 551)

1. (d) AU 551.04 states that when an auditor submits a document containing audited financial statements to his or her client or to others, the auditor has a responsibility to report on all the information included in the document. AU 551.04 also states that the auditor's responsibility with respect to information in a document does not extend beyond the financial information identified in his or her report, and the auditor has no obligation to perform any procedures to corroborate other information contained in a document.

2. (b) Information accompanying the basic financial statements in an auditor-submitted document is presented outside the basic financial statements and is not considered necessary for presentation of financial position, results of operations, or cash flows in conformity with GAAP. Such information includes additional details or explanations of items in or related to the basic financial statements [see answers (a), (c), and (d) for examples] (AU 551.03). The adequacy of the allowance for doubtful accounts is implied in the financial statements and would not be necessary as additional information.

3. (d) An auditor's report on information accompanying the basic financial statements in an auditor-submitted document should include either an opinion on whether the accompanying information is fairly stated in all material respects in relation to the basic financial statements taken as a whole, or a disclaimer of opinion, depending on whether the information has been subjected to the auditing procedures applied in the audit of the basic financial statements. In this case, since the information had been subjected to auditing procedures a disclaimer of opinion was not appropriate (AU 551.06).

3A. (c) AU 551.06 presents guidelines that apply to an auditor's report on information accompanying the basic financial statements and states, "The report should include either an opinion on whether the accompanying information is fairly stated in all material respects in relation to the basic financial statements taken as a whole, or a disclaimer of opinion..." The auditor's opinion is on whether the statements are fairly stated in conformity with generally accepted accounting principles, not GAAS; however, the audit has been performed for the purpose of forming an opinion on the basic financial statements and does not extend to the accompanying information. The auditor's opinion on fair presentation in conformity with GAAP relates to the basic financial statements and does not extend to the accompanying information. The auditor does not express a conclusion on management's assertions in his or her opinion, and the attestation standards relate to a separate reporting engagement.

Special Reports (AU 623)

4. (d) Special reports include those that are related to financial statements prepared on an accounting basis prescribed by a regulatory agency solely for filing with that agency.

5. (c) According to AU 623.05 and 623.08, an auditor's report on financial statements prepared in conformity with a comprehensive basis of accounting other than GAAP should include a separate paragraph which appears just before the opinion paragraph that (1) states the basis of presentation and refers to the note to the financial statements that describes the basis and (2) states that the basis of presentation is OCBOA. Answers (a) and (d) do not apply to this type of report. A statement about whether the financial statements are fairly presented in conformity with another comprehensive basis of accounting is *part of the opinion paragraph*, not a separate explanatory paragraph.

5A. (b) The auditor's report would not include a statement that the cash receipts and disbursements schedule is not a comprehensive basis of accounting, because the cash basis is a comprehensive basis of accounting (OCBOA); it is only a comprehensive basis of accounting other than GAAP. AU 623.05(d) states that the auditor's report should include a paragraph that refers to the note to the financial statements that describes the cash basis of accounting. AU 623.05(e) states that the report should include a paragraph that expresses the auditor's opinion on whether the financial statements are presented fairly. AU 623.05(c) states that the report should include a paragraph that states that the audit was conducted in accordance with GAAS.

6. (d) When financial statements are intended to be presented in conformity with a "comprehensive basis of accounting other than generally accepted accounting principles," the auditor should consider whether the financial statements he or she is reporting on are suitably titled. If the auditor believes that the financial statements are not suitably titled, he or she should disclose his or her reservations in an

explanatory paragraph of the report and qualify the opinion (AU 623.07).

6A. (d) AU 623.05 presents this requirement. The auditor utilized GAAS in the examination; thus, there is no need for a disclaimer. Answer (b) is incorrect because an opinion is presented. The auditor is not required to include the explanation described in answer (c).

7. (d) AU 623.19 states, "Entities may be required by contractual agreements, such as certain bond indentures and loan agreements, or by regulatory agencies to furnish compliance reports by independent auditors." A lack of independence would not preclude an accountant from issuing compilation reports (AR 100.22) or a report on consulting services.

8. (c) AU 622.01 states, "An accountant may accept an engagement in which the scope is limited to applying to one or more specified elements, accounts, or items of a financial statement agreed-upon procedures that are not sufficient to enable him to express an opinion on the specified elements, accounts, or items, provided (1) the parties involved have a clear understanding of the procedures to be performed and (2) distribution of the report is to be restricted to named parties involved."

Letters for Underwriters

9. (d) AU 634.05 states that is it advisable to accompany any discussion of procedures with a clear statement that the accountant cannot furnish any assurance regarding the sufficiency of the procedures for the underwriter's purposes, and it is advisable for the comfort letter to contain a statement to this effect. In the comfort letter, the accountant may comment on compliance as to form with requirements under published SEC rules and regulations. An opinion regarding *Government Auditing Standards* does not apply when discussing comfort letters.

9A. (b) Per AU 634.63, Example A, a typical comfort letter includes a statement regarding the accountant's independence, an opinion regarding whether the audited financial information included or incorporated by reference complies to the Securities Act of 1933, *negative assurance on unaudited condensed interim financial information* included or incorporated by reference, and negative assurance on whether there has been any later changes in specified accounts in the financial statement items included in the registration statement. Per AU 634.13, "Comfort letters are not required under the Act [Securities Act of 1933, par. .01], and copies are not filed with the SEC." Comfort letters ordinarily express an opinion regarding the audited financial statements' compliance with the Act, which is not an "update" of the audit opinion.

10. (b) AU 711.09 states, "The Securities and Exchange Commission requires that, when an independent accountant's report based on a review of interim financial information is presented or incorporated by reference in a registration statement, a prospectus that includes a statement about the independent accountant's involvement should clarify that his or her review report is not a "report" or "part" of the registration statement within the meaning of Sections 7 and 11 of the Securities Act of 1933."

11. (c) The SEC has the authority to prescribe the accounting and reporting requirements for companies under its jurisdiction. However, the SEC has looked to the private sector for leadership in establishing and improving accounting principles and standards through the FASB. The SEC does not have the authority to prescribe specific auditing procedures, deny lack of privity as a defense in third-party actions, or require a change of auditors of governmental entities.

12. (a) In connection with audited financial statements and schedules included in a registration statement to be filed with the SEC, a client may request the services of an independent auditor. One of these services is the issuance of comfort letters for underwriters (AU 634.01). The underwriter of securities receives the comfort letter. The client and senior management do not sign the comfort letter.

13. (a) When an accountant issues to an underwriter a comfort letter containing comments on data that have not been audited, the underwriter most likely will receive negative assurance on capsule information in regard to conformity with generally accepted accounting principles [AU 634.22(a)]. However, negative assurance should not be given, with respect to capsule information, unless the accountants have obtained knowledge of the client's accounting and financial reporting practices and its internal control structure relating to the preparation of financial statements [AU 634.19(f)]. This problem gave no indication that such knowledge was not obtained.

Reporting on Internal Control Structure

14. (a) An accountant may be engaged to express an opinion on an entity's internal controls in effect as of a specified date or during a specified period of time (AU 642.02).

15. (d) When an accountant has been engaged to report on an entity's internal controls without performing an audit of the financial statements, he or she does not need to place any restrictions on the use of the report (AU 642.03).

15A. (b) AT 400.10 states, "A practitioner may examine and report on management's assertion about the effectiveness of an entity's internal control structure if...(d.) management presents its written assertion about the effectiveness of the entity's internal control structure." Answer (a) is not a requirement for accepting the engagement. Answer (c) is not a requirement; this engagement can be performed for new clients and may be a revenue-generating source of new business. Answer (d) is not required for acceptance of the engagement, but would be part of the reporting requirements if management's assertion is presented only in a representation letter to the practitioner.

16. (d) An engagement to express an opinion on an entity's system of internal accounting control and a consideration of the internal control structure made as part of an audit differ in purpose and generally differ in scope (AU 642.09). However, the procedures are similar in nature (AU 642.11).

17. (b) AU 642.38 states, "The accountant's report expressing an opinion on an entity's system of internal accounting control should contain ... A statement that the establishment and maintenance of the system is the responsibility of management."

18. (b) AU 642.38 states, "The accountant's report expressing an opinion on an entity's system of internal accounting control should contain a statement that the establishment and maintenance of the system is the responsibility of management." The report would not contain a comparison with an assessment of control risk made as part of an audit and would not contain a description of potential misstatements. Unlike a report based on communication of internal control structure related matters noted in an audit, a limitation of the use of the report is not necessary.

18A. (a) AT 400.50 states that the practitioner's report should include a paragraph stating that, because of inherent limitations of any internal control structure, errors or irregularities may occur and not be detected. This statement would be made regardless of whether management makes its assertion in a separate report or in a representation letter to the practitioner. Answer (b) is incorrect because management's assertion should be based on control criteria. Management evaluates the effectiveness of the entity's internal control structure using reasonable criteria for effective internal control structures established by a recognized body. This criteria is referred to as the control criteria and could be issued by the AICPA, regulated agencies, etc. The report should include the practitioner's opinion on whether management's assertion about the effectiveness of the entity's internal control structure over financial reporting is fairly stated, in all material respects, based on the control criteria. No reference should be made as to an opinion on the financial statements in conformity with GAAP. Per AT 400.50, the report should include a statement that the examination was made in accordance with standards established by the AICPA and that the practitioner believes the examination provides a reasonable basis for his or her opinion on management's assertion; thus, the examination was not performed for planning an audit.

19. (c) AU 642.38 states, "The accountant's report expressing an opinion on an entity's system of internal accounting control should contain the accountant's opinion on whether the system taken as a whole was sufficient to meet the broad objectives of internal accounting control insofar as those objectives pertain to the prevention or detection of errors or irregularities in amounts that would be material in relation to the financial statements."

19A. (d) AT 400.50 states that the practitioner's report should include a paragraph describing the inherent limitations of any internal control structure. AT 400.50 states that the practitioner's report should include a statement that the engagement included testing and evaluating the design and effectiveness of the control structure. Evidence obtained would not be reported. Answer (b) is incorrect because the practitioner is reporting on the current year controls only. The practitioner would not include suggested improvements in his or her report.

20. (a) AU 642.41 states, "If a document that contains an accountant's opinion identifying a material weakness also includes a statement by management asserting that the cost of correcting the weakness would exceed the benefits of reducing the risk of errors or irregularities, the accountant should not express any opinion as to management's statement."

Interim Financial Information

21. (b) AU 722.09 states that the objective of a review of interim financial information is to provide the accountant with a basis for reporting whether material modifications should be made for such information to conform with GAAP. The auditor or accountant would add to a review report an additional paragraph indicating the previous period financial statements

had been audited but that no auditing procedures have been applied since the date of the audit report. To state that the opinion has been updated and a reasonable basis exists for such an updated opinion should not be done. The report should not state that the statements are presented fairly in accordance with standards of interim reporting or generally accepted accounting principles, because "presents fairly" is terminology used in the audit opinion.

21A. (a) AU 722.09 states that the objective of a review of interim financial information is to provide the accountant with a basis for reporting whether material modifications should be made for such information to conform with GAAP. Only the statements under current review should be reported on. The objective of the review is to provide the accountant with a basis for reporting whether material modifications should be made, not whether condensed statements or pro forma information should be included. In a review, the accountant supplies only limited assurance and would not provide an opinion stating the financial statements are presented fairly.

22. (b) Among the procedures set forth in AU 722.08 for a review of interim financial information is to "read the minutes of meetings of stockholders, board of directors, and committees of the board of directors to identify actions that may affect the interim financial information." Answers (a), (c), and (d) are not among the procedures normally applied in a review of interim financial information.

22A. (a) AU 711.09 states that when an independent accountant's report based on a review of interim financial information is presented in a registration statement, a prospectus that includes a statement about the accountant's involvement should clarify that his or her review report is not a "report" or "part" of the registration statement within the meaning of the Securities Act of 1933. The accountant does have a responsibility to follow the guidance in AU 560 and 561 regarding subsequent events and the disclosure or adjustment requirements included therein. There are no standards established by the SEC which the auditor must comply with. The accountant does not obtain corroborating evidence in a review engagement.

23. (d) AU 722.22 states, "The circumstances that require modification of the accountant's report on a review of interim financial information arise from departures from generally accepted accounting principles, which include *adequate disclosure*. Normally, neither an *uncertainty* nor a lack of consistency in the application of accounting principles affecting interim financial information would cause the accountant to add an explanatory paragraph to his report provided that the interim financial information or statements appropriately disclose such matters."

Reporting Under *Government Auditing Standards*

24. (b) AU 801.33 states that *Government Auditing Standards* requires a written report on the internal control structure in all audits; whereas GAAS require communication only when the auditor has noted reportable conditions. The auditor is not required to report on the description of the entity's internal control structure procedures. The auditor should not issue the representations in answer (c) because of the potential for misinterpretation of the limited degree of assurance associated with the auditor's issuing a written report representing that no reportable conditions were noted. No positive assurance should be given for the same reason as answer (c).

24A. (a) AU 333.04 and 317.05 present and discuss the items which should be included in management's representations. The items in (b), (c) and (d) are not listed in AU 333.04 as items which should be in the representation.

24B. (b) AU 801.40, item *g*, presents this requirement. Other requirements for the auditor's report on the internal control structure in these circumstances are in AU 801.40. None of the items listed in (a), (c), and (d) are on the list.

25. (d) AU 801.33 states that the auditor is required to prepare a written report on the internal control structure in all audits when reporting under *Government Auditing Standards*. The auditor is not required to report on the types of situations in answers (a) and (c). The auditor is required to report reportable conditions noted in an audit to the audit committee or to individuals with a level of authority and responsibility equivalent to an audit committee, not to shareholders.

26. (a) Reports on Compliance with laws and regulations should contain positive assurance consisting of a statement by the auditor that the tested items were in compliance with applicable laws and regulations, and negative assurance stating that nothing came to the auditor's attention as a result of specified procedures that caused him or her to believe the untested items were not in compliance with applicable laws and regulation, as indicated in the *Government Auditing Standards* (the Yellow Book) and at AU 801.24.

27. (b) *Government Auditing Standards* include the following requirement to report on compliance with laws and regulations: The auditors should prepare a written report on their tests of compliance with applicable laws and regulations. This report, which may be included in either the report on the financial audit or a separate report, should contain a statement of positive assurance on those items which were tested for compliance and negative assurance on those items not tested. It should include all material instances of noncompliance, and all instances or indications of illegal acts which could result in a criminal prosecution (AU 801.18).

27A. (d) *Governmental Auditing Standards* do not require an opinion on the financial statements taken as a whole, when the engagement is a *performance* audit. GAS does require a statement of the audit scope, indications of illegal acts discovered during the audit, and the views of the responsible officials concerning the auditor's findings in the auditor's report.

28. (a) AU 801.30 states, "*Government Auditing Standards* requires a written report on the internal control structure in all audits." This differs from reporting under generally accepted auditing standards which states that the auditor should communicate--orally or in written form--those matters coming to the auditor's attention that in his or her judgment, should be communicated to the audit committee because they represent significant deficiencies in the design or operation of the internal control structure, which could adversely effect the organization's ability to record, process, summarize and report financial statement data consistent with the assertions of management in the financial statements (AU 325.02).

29. (d) When the auditor has conducted an audit in accordance with *Government Auditing Standards*, the auditor's report on the internal control structure should contain a description of the scope of the auditor's work, stating that the auditor obtained an understanding of the design of relevant policies and procedures, determined whether those policies and procedures have been placed in operation, and assessed control risk [AU 801.40(g)]. Answers (a), (b), and (c) represent information that is not included in such a report.

30. (b) In an audit in accordance with *Governmental Auditing Standards* an auditor is required to report on the auditor's test of the entity's compliance with applicable laws and regulations. Among the basic elements of such a report is a statement that the standards require that the auditor plan and perform the audit to obtain reasonable assurance about whether the financial statements are free of material misstatement [AU 801.21(c)].

30A. (c) When an auditor detects noncompliance with requirements that have a material effect on a program, the auditor should express a qualified or adverse opinion. A disclaimer is appropriate only when an audit has not been done. Reasonable assurance on tests is implicit not express.

Responsibilities Under the Single Audit Act

31. (c) AU 801.48 states, "An amount that is material to one major federal financial assistance program may not be material to a major federal financial assistance program of a different size or nature. Also, what is material to a particular major federal financial assistance program might change from one period to another." Answer (a) is incorrect because materiality is not determined by the federal agency requiring the audit. All account balances are not tested. The auditor's risk assessment would be a factor in determining materiality.

32. (b) AU 801.85 states, "When the audit of an entity's compliance with requirements governing a major federal financial assistance program detects noncompliance with those requirements that the auditor believes have a material effect on the program, the auditor should express a qualified or adverse opinion."

33. (a) The auditor's report on condensed financial statements that are derived from financial statements that he or she has audited should indicate (1) that the auditor has audited and expressed an opinion on the complete financial statements, (2) the date of the auditor's report on the complete financial statements, (3) the type of opinion expressed, and (4) whether, in the auditor's opinion, the information set forth in the condensed financial statements is fairly stated in all material respects in relation to the complete financial statements from which it has been derived (AU 552.05).

Miscellaneous

33A. (b) The example report in AU 552.06 covers this situation. Answer (b) is correct; answers (a), (c), and (d) are not.

34. (a) AU 623.13 states that an engagement to express an opinion on one or more specified elements, accounts, or items of a financial statement may be undertaken either as a separate engagement or in conjunction with an audit of financial statements.

35. (d) AU 534.07 states, "If financial statements prepared in conformity with accounting principles generally accepted in another country are prepared for use *only* outside the United States, the auditor may report using either (1) a U.S.-style report modified to report on the accounting principles of another country or (2) if appropriate, the report form of the other country." An unmodified U.S.-style report would be inappropriate in this situation.

36. (c) AU 801.17 concerning not-for-profit organizations and business enterprises that receive federal financial assistance states, "An auditor [has a] responsibility to detect material misstatements of financial statements resulting from violations of laws and regulations that have a direct and material effect on the determination of financial statement amounts ..." Answers (a), (b), and (d) do not represent the focus that is stated in AU 801.11.

37. (a) AU 625.08 states the accountant's written report should include a statement that any differences in the facts, circumstances, or assumptions presented may change the report. Consulting services differ fundamentally from the CPA's function of attesting to assertions of other parties. In consulting services the practitioner develops findings, conclusions, and recommendations. The nature and scope of work is different and the work is generally performed only for the use and benefit of the client. AU 625.08 states that the report should contain a statement that the responsibility for the proper accounting treatment rests with the preparers of the financial statements, who should consult with their continuing accountants. The accountant should not make the type of statement in answer (d) in any report; it is implied unless there is a departure from GAAP when reference to the departure would be made.

38. (a) Per AU 534.05, the auditor must understand the accounting principles of the other country. The auditor does not have to be certified in the other country, disclaim an opinion, or receive a waiver from the State Board of Accountancy.

39. (d) AU 324.24 states, "In reporting on his or her audit of the financial statements, the user auditor should not make reference to the report of the service auditor as a basis, in part, for his or her own opinion."

PERFORMANCE BY SUBTOPICS

Each category below parallels a subtopic covered in Chapter 41. Record the number and percentage of questions you correctly answered in each subtopic area.

Reporting on Information Accompanying the Basic Financial Statements in Auditor-Submitted Documents (AU 551)

Question #	Correct √
1	
2	
3	
3A	
# Questions	4

Correct ______
% Correct ______

Special Reports (AU 623)

Question #	Correct √
4	
5	
5A	
6	
6A	
7	
8	
# Questions	7

Correct ______
% Correct ______

Letters for Underwriters

Question #	Correct √
9	
9A	
10	
11	
12	
13	
# Questions	6

Correct ______
% Correct ______

Reporting on Internal Control Structure

Question #	Correct √
14	
15	
15A	
16	
17	
18	
18A	
19	
19A	
20	
# Questions	10

Correct ______
% Correct ______

Interim Financial Information

Question #	Correct √
21	
21A	
22	
22A	
23	
# Questions	5

Correct ______
% Correct ______

Reporting Under *Government Auditing Standards*

Question #	Correct √
24	
24A	
24B	
25	
26	
27	
27A	
28	
29	
30	
30A	
# Questions	11

Correct ______
% Correct ______

Responsibilities Under the Single Audit Act

Question #	Correct √
31	
32	
33	
# Questions	3

Correct ______
% Correct ______

Miscellaneous

Question #	Correct √
33A	
34	
35	
36	
37	
38	
39	
# Questions	7

Correct ______
% Correct ______

ESSAY QUESTIONS

Essay 41-2 (15 to 25 minutes)

Toxic Waste Disposal Co., Inc. (TWD) is a not-for-profit organization that receives grants and fees from various state and municipal governments as well as grants from several federal government agencies.

TWD engaged Hall & Hall, CPAs, to audit its financial statements for the year ended July 31, 1991, in accordance with *Government Auditing Standards*. Accordingly, the auditors' reports are to be submitted by TWD to the granting government agencies, which make the reports available for public inspection.

The auditors' separate report on compliance with laws and regulations that was drafted by a staff accountant of Hall & Hall at the completion of the engagement contained the statements below. It was submitted to the engagement partner who reviewed matters thoroughly and properly concluded that no material instances of noncompliance were identified.

1. A statement that the audit was conducted in accordance with generally accepted auditing standards and with *Government Auditing Standards* issued by the Comptroller General of the United States.
2. A statement that the auditors' procedures included tests of compliance.
3. A statement that the standards require the auditors to plan and to perform the audit to detect all instances of noncompliance with applicable laws and regulations.
4. A statement that management is responsible for compliance with laws, regulations, contracts, and grants.
5. A statement that the auditors' objective was to provide an opinion on compliance with the provisions of laws and regulations equivalent to

that to be expressed on the financial statements.

6. A statement of positive assurance that the results of the tests indicate that, with respect to the items tested, the entity complied, in all material respects, with the provisions of laws, regulations, contracts, and grants.
7. A statement of negative assurance that, with respect to items tested, nothing came to the auditors' attention that caused the auditors to believe that the entity had not complied, in all material respects, with the provisions of laws, regulations, contracts, and grants.
8. A statement that the report is intended only for the information of the specific legislative or regulatory bodies, and that this restriction is intended to limit the distribution of the report.

Required:

For each of the above statements, indicate whether each is an appropriate or inappropriate element within the report on compliance with laws and regulations. If a statement is **not** appropriate, explain why.

(11/91, Aud., #2)

Essay 41-3 (15 to 25 minutes)

The auditor's report below was drafted by a staff accountant of Baker and Baker, CPAs, at the completion of the audit of the comparative financial statements of Ocean Shore Partnership for the years ended December 31, 1990 and 1989. Ocean Shores prepares its financial statements on the income tax basis of accounting. The report was submitted to the engagement partner who reviewed matters thoroughly and properly concluded that an unqualified opinion should be expressed.

Auditor's Report

We have audited the accompanying statements of assets, liabilities, and capital--income tax basis of Ocean Shore Partnership as of December 31, 1990 and 1989, and the related statements of revenue and expenses--income tax basis and changes in partners' capital accounts--income tax basis for the years then ended.

We conducted our audits in accordance with standards established by the American Institute of Certified Public Accountants. Those standards require that we plan and perform the audit to obtain reasonable assurance about whether the financial statements are free of material misstatement. An audit includes examining, on a test basis, evidence supporting the amounts and disclosures in the financial statements. An audit also includes assessing the accounting principles used as well as evaluating the overall financial statement presentation.

As described in Note A, these financial statements were prepared on the basis of accounting the Partnership uses for income tax purposes. Accordingly, these financial statements are not designed for those who do not have access to the Partnership's tax returns.

In our opinion, the financial statements referred to above present fairly, in all material respects, the assets, liabilities, and capital of Ocean Shore Partnership as of December 31, 1990 and 1989, and its revenue and expenses and changes in partners' capital accounts for the years then ended, in conformity with generally accepted accounting principles applied on a consistent basis.

Baker and Baker, CPAs
April 3, 1991

Required:

Identify the deficiencies contained in the auditors' report as drafted by the staff accountant. Group the deficiencies by paragraph, where applicable. Do **not** redraft the report.

(5/91, Aud., #2)

Essay 41-4 (Estimated time--25 to 35 minutes)

Hart, CPA, has been approached by Unidyne Co. to accept an attest engagement to examine and report on management's written assertion about the effectiveness of Unidyne's internal control structure over financial reporting as of June 30, 1995, the end of its fiscal year.

Required:

a. Describe the required conditions that must be met for Hart to accept an attest engagement to examine and report on management's assertion about the effectiveness of Unidyne's internal control structure.

b. Describe the broad engagement activities that would be involved in Hart's performing an examination of management's assertion about the effectiveness of Unidyne's internal control structure.

c. Describe the other types of attest services that Hart may provide and those specifically **not** permitted in connection with Unidyne's internal control structure.

(5/95, Aud., #4)

Essay 41-5 (15 to 25 minutes)

Martin, CPA, has been engaged to express an opinion on Beta Manufacturing Company's internal controls in effect as of June 1, 1987.

Required:

a. Compare Martin's engagement to express an opinion on the internal controls with the consideration of the internal control structure made as part of an audit of the financial statements in accordance with generally accepted auditing standards. The comparison should be made as to the (1) scope, (2) purpose, (3) timing of the engagements, and (4) users of the reports.

b. Identify the major contents of Martin's report expressing an opinion on Beta's internal controls. Do **not** draft the report. (5/87, Aud., #4)

Essay 41-6 (15 to 25 minutes)

Young and Young, CPAs, completed an audit of the financial statements of XYZ Company, Inc. for the year ended June 30, 1983, and issued a standard unqualified auditor's report dated August 15, 1983. At the time of the engagement the Board of Directors of XYZ requested a special report attesting to the adequacy of the provision for federal and state income taxes and the related accruals and deferred income taxes as presented in the June 30, 1983, financial statements.

Young and Young submitted the appropriate special report on August 22, 1983.

Required:

Prepare the special report that Young and Young should have submitted to XYZ Company, Inc. (5/84, Aud., #2)

ESSAY SOLUTIONS

Solution 41-2 Government Audit Reports

1. Statement 1 is **appropriate.**
2. Statement 2 is **appropriate.**
3. Statement 3 is **not appropriate** because the auditors are **required** to **plan** and **perform** the audit to **provide reasonable assurance** of **detecting instances of noncompliance** having a **direct** and **material effect** on the financial statements, **not all instances** of noncompliance.
4. Statement 4 is **appropriate.**
5. Statement 5 is **not appropriate** because **rendering an opinion** is a **higher level of reporting** than the **positive** and **negative assurance** required by *Government Auditing Standards*.
6. Statement 6 is **appropriate.**
7. Statement 7 is **not appropriate** because **negative assurance** applies to **items not tested.**
8. Statement 8 is **not appropriate** because *Government Auditing Standards* require that, unless restricted by law or regulation, copies of the reports should be made **available for public inspection.**

Solution 41-3 Income Tax Basis Audit Report

The auditors' report contains the following deficiencies:

1. **"Independent"** is **omitted** from the title of the auditors' report.

<u>**Introductory paragraph**</u>

2. **Management's responsibility** for the financial statements is omitted.
3. The auditors' **responsibility** to **express** an **opinion** on the financial statements is **omitted.**

<u>**Scope paragraph**</u>

4. **"Generally accepted auditing standards"** should be referred to, not standards established by the AICPA.
5. Reference to assessing **"significant estimates made by management"** is **omitted.**
6. The concluding statement that the auditors **"believe that our audits provide a reasonable basis for our opinion"** is **omitted.**

Explanatory paragraph

7. Reference to the income tax basis of accounting as **"a comprehensive basis of accounting other than generally accepted accounting principles"** is **omitted.**
8. The statement that the financial statements are **"not designed for those who do not have access to the Partnership tax returns"** is **inappropriate.**

Opinion paragraph

9. **"The income tax basis of accounting described in Note A"** should be referred to, not "generally accepted accounting principles."
10. There should be **no reference** to **consistency unless** the accounting principles **have not been applied consistently.**

Solution 41-4 Internal Control

a. Hart may accept the attest engagement to examine and report on management's assertion about the effectiveness of Unidyne's internal control structure over financial reporting only if Unidyne's **management accepts responsibility** for the structure's effectiveness. Management then would evaluate the structure's effectiveness using **reasonable benchmarks** or criteria established by a **recognized body** such as the AICPA, COSO, or a **regulatory agency.**

b. Performing an examination of management's assertion about the effectiveness of Unidyne's internal control structure initially would involve **planning** the engagement, which includes developing an **overall strategy** for the scope and performance of the engagement. Hart then would **obtain an understanding** of Unidyne's internal control structure by making **inquiries** of management and employees, by **inspecting** documents, and by **observing** Unidyne's activities and operations.

Next, Hart would **test** and **evaluate** the **design effectiveness** of the internal control structure policies and procedures within each element (**control environment, accounting system,** and **control procedures**) of the structure, and then test and evaluate the **operating effectiveness** of the policies and procedures. Hart would perform tests of **relevant controls** to obtain evidence that supports the report's opinion by focusing on **how** the policies and procedure are applied, the **consistency** with which they are applied, and **by whom** they are applied.

Finally, Hart would **consider all the evidence** obtained, including the results of tests of controls and any control deficiencies identified, in forming an opinion on management's assertion about the effectiveness of Unidyne's internal control structure.

c. In addition to the proposed engagement to **examine and report** on management's written assertion about the effectiveness of Unidyne's internal control structure over financial reporting, Hart may also be engaged to perform **agreed-upon procedures** relating to management's assertion about the effectiveness of Unidyne's internal control structure. Hart's report on agreed-upon procedures would be in the form of procedures and findings.

Hart should not accept an engagement to **review and report** on management's assertion about the effectiveness of Unidyne's internal control structure or provide **negative assurance** about whether management's assertion is fairly stated in an agreed-upon procedures engagement.

Solution 41-5 Reporting on Internal Controls (AU 642)

a. 1. An engagement to express an opinion on an entity's internal controls and the consideration of the internal control structure made as part of an audit of financial statements in accordance with generally accepted auditing standards **generally differ in scope.** While the engagement to express an opinion on the entity's internal controls can be made **in conjunction with** the consideration made as part of an audit, the consideration made as part of an audit is more **limited in scope** since only those controls **applicable to the financial statement assertions** for which control risk is **assessed at below the maximum level will be tested. Internal controls** for **assertions** for which control risk is **assessed at the maximum level** will **generally not be tested.**

2. The engagements also **differ in purpose.** The auditor's consideration of the internal control structure is an **intermediate step** in forming an opinion on the financial statements. It established a **basis for assessing control risk** and for **determining** the **nature, extent,** and **timing** of the **auditing procedures.** The purpose of the accountant's engagement to express an opinion on the internal controls is to **provide assurance** about whether the **broad objectives of internal controls are being achieved.**

3. An engagement to express an opinion on an entity's internal controls can be made as of **any date,** while the auditor's consideration of the internal control structure is made in the **early stages** of an

audit with review to determine the effectiveness **throughout** the period.

4. Ordinarily, the users of an opinion on an entity's internal controls are the **client's management** or **third parties**, such as **regulatory agencies.** The **primary user** of a consideration of the internal control structure **made as part of an audit** is the **auditor** who makes the consideration.

b. The accountant's report expressing an opinion on an entity's internal controls should contain:

1. A **description** of the **scope** of the engagement.
2. The **date** to which the opinion relates.
3. A statement that the **establishment and maintenance of the controls is the responsibility of management.**
4. A brief **explanation** of the **broad objectives** and **inherent limitations** of internal control.
5. The accountant's **opinion on whether the broad objectives of internal control are being met insofar as those objectives pertain to the prevention or detection of material errors or irregularities.**
6. The **description** of any **material weakness.**

Solution 41-6 Special Reports (AU 623)

Board of Directors
XYZ Company, Inc.

We have audited, in accordance with generally accepted auditing standards, the financial statements of XYZ Company, Inc., **for the year ended June 30, 1983**, and have issued our report thereon dated August 15, 1983. We have also audited the **current and deferred provision** for the Company's federal and state income taxes for the year ended June 30, 1983, included in those financial statements, and the related asset and liability tax accounts as of June 30, 1983. This income tax information is **the responsibility of the Company's management.** Our **responsibility** is to **express an opinion on it based on our audit.**

We conducted our audit of the income tax information **in accordance with generally accepted auditing standards.** Those standards require that we **plan** and **perform** the audit to obtain **reasonable assurance** about whether the federal and state income tax accounts are **free of material misstatement**. An **audit includes examining, on a test basis, evidence supporting the amounts and disclosures** related to the federal and state income tax accounts. An audit also includes **assessing the accounting principles** used and **significant estimates** made by management, as well as **evaluating the overall presentation** of the federal and state income tax accounts. We believe that our audit provides a **reasonable basis for our opinion.**

In our opinion, the Company **has paid** or, in all material respects, **made adequate provision** in the financial statements referred to above for the payment of all federal and state income taxes and for related accruals and deferred income taxes that could be **reasonably estimated at the time of our audit** of the financial statements of XYZ Company, Inc., **for the year ended June 30, 1983.**

August 15, 1983

Young and Young
Certified Public Accountants

NOTES

CHAPTER 42

OTHER PROFESSIONAL SERVICES

CHAPTER 42

OTHER PROFESSIONAL SERVICES

PART ONE: ACCOUNTING AND REVIEW SERVICES

Statements on Standards for Accounting and Review Services (SSARS) are issued by the Accounting and Review Services Committee.

I. Compilation and Review of Financial Statements (SSARS 1)

A. Applicability--Applies when the CPA is associated with the unaudited financial statements of a nonpublic entity.

B. Definitions

1. Nonpublic Entity--An entity other than one (a) whose securities are traded in a public market (i.e., on a stock exchange or in the over-the-counter market, including those quoted only locally or regionally); (b) that has filed with a regulatory agency in preparation for the sale, in a public market, of any class of its securities; or (c) that is a subsidiary, corporate joint venture, or other entity controlled by an entity described in (a) or (b).

2. Financial Statements--Balance sheet, statement of income, statement of cash flows, etc. Financial forecasts, projections, and financial presentations included in tax returns are not considered financial statements for SSARS 1. The method by which the statement was prepared (e.g., manual, computer, etc.) is irrelevant in defining a financial statement.

3. Compilation of Financial Statements--Presenting information that is the representation of management in the form of financial statements without undertaking to express any assurance on the statements. The CPA may perform other accounting services (e.g., preparing a working trial balance) to enable the CPA to compile the financial statements.

4. Review of Financial Statements--Performing inquiry and analytical procedures to provide a reasonable basis for the CPA to express limited assurance that there are no material modifications that need to be made to the financial statements in order for them to be in conformity with GAAP or, if applicable, with some other comprehensive basis of accounting. The CPA may need to perform a compilation and/or other accounting services to review the financial statements.

   a. Review vs. Compilation--The objective of a review is to express limited assurance. A compilation does not contemplate any assurance.

   b. Review vs. Audit--An audit provides the basis for expression of an opinion on the financial statements taken as a whole. A review aims for limited assurance. A review does not contemplate obtaining an understanding of the internal control structure or assessing control risk.

C. General Requirements--The CPA must issue either a compilation report or a review report whenever a compilation or review of the nonpublic entity's financial statements in compliance with SSARS 1 has been completed. The CPA cannot issue any unaudited financial statements to the client or others unless the CPA has at least complied with the provisions that apply to a compilation.

1. More Than One Service--Whenever the CPA performs more than one level of service (e.g., a compilation and a review or a review and an audit), the CPA should issue the report for the highest level of service rendered.

2. Use of Name--The CPA's name should not appear in documents or written communications containing the unaudited statements unless the CPA has compiled or reviewed them and the report is included, or there is a clear indication in the documents that the CPA has not compiled or reviewed the statements and the CPA assumes no responsibility for them. If an accountant becomes aware that his or her name has been used improperly, the client should be advised that the use of the accountant's name is inappropriate, and the accountant should consider consulting an attorney.

3. Typing and Reproducing--The CPA must, at a minimum, comply with the provisions applicable to a compilation when submitting unaudited financial statements of a nonpublic entity to his or her client or others. Submission of financial statements is defined as presenting to a client or others financial statements that the accountant has:

   a. Generated, either manually or through the use of computer software, or

   b. Modified by materially changing account classification, amounts, or disclosures directly on client-prepared financial statements.

   The following services do not constitute a submission of financial statements:

   a. Reading client-prepared financial statements.

   b. Typing or reproducing client-prepared financial statements, without modification, as an accommodation to a client.

   c. Proposing correcting journal entries or disclosures to the financial statements, either orally or in written form, that materially change client-prepared financial statements, as long as the accountant does not directly modify the client-prepared financial statements.

   d. Preparing standard monthly journal entries (e.g., standard entries for depreciation and expiration of prepaid expenses).

   e. Providing a client with a financial statement format that does not include dollar amounts, to be used by the client to prepare financial statements.

   f. Advising a client about the selection or use of computer software that the client will use to generate financial statements.

   g. Providing the client with the use of or access to computer hardware or software that the client will use to generate financial statements.

4. Accounting Services--SSARS 1 does not apply to such accounting services as (a) preparing a working trial balance, (b) assisting in adjusting the books, (c) consulting on accounting and tax matters, (d) preparing tax returns, (e) providing manual or automated bookkeeping or data processing services (unless the output is in the form of financial statements), or (f) processing financial data for the clients of other accounting firms.

D. Engagement Letter--The CPA must reach an understanding, preferably in writing, with the client as to the services to be performed. An engagement letter is recommended. It should include (1) a description of the nature and limitations of the compilation or review, (2) a description of the report that the CPA expects to render, and (3) a statement that the engagement cannot be relied upon to disclose errors, irregularities or illegal acts, and that the CPA will inform the appropriate level of management of any material errors of which the CPA becomes aware, and any irregularities or illegal acts that come to his or her attention, unless they are inconsequential.

E. Compilation of Financial Statements--The following guidelines apply to a compilation engagement:

1. Knowledge of the Accounting Principles and Practices of the Industry--To compile financial statements that are appropriate in form for a particular industry, the CPA must understand the accounting principles and practices of the client's industry. The CPA need not possess this knowledge when accepting the engagement as long as the CPA can acquire it through AICPA industry guides, industry publications, talking with other practitioners, etc.

2. Knowledge About the Client--The CPA must possess a general understanding of the nature of the client's business transactions, the form of its accounting records, the stated qualifications of its accounting personnel, the accounting basis used for the financial statements, and the form and content of the financial statements. This knowledge is usually acquired through experience with the client or inquiry of the client's personnel. It provides a basis for the CPA to assess the need to perform any accounting services of the type described in C.4., above, when compiling the financial statements.

3. Not Required to Verify, Corroborate, or Review Information Supplied--The CPA is not required to make additional inquiries or to perform any other procedures designed to verify, corroborate, or review the information that the client supplies for a compilation. However, if the information furnished appears to be incorrect, incomplete, or otherwise unsatisfactory, the CPA should request additional or revised information. If the client refuses to provide it, the CPA should withdraw from the compilation engagement.

4. Reading the Compiled Financial Statements--Before issuing the compilation report, the CPA should read the compiled financial statements to be sure they appear to be appropriate in form and free from obvious material errors (such as math mistakes and mistakes in applying accounting principles, including inadequate disclosure).

5. Reporting on Compiled Financial Statements

   a. Statements compiled by the CPA should be accompanied by a report stating that (1) a compilation has been performed in accordance with Statements on Standards for Accounting and Review Services issued by the AICPA, (2) a compilation is limited to presenting, in the form of financial statements, information that is the representation of management, and (3) the statements have not been audited or reviewed and, therefore, no opinion or other form of assurance is expressed on them.

   b. The report should not mention any other procedures the CPA may have performed.

   c. The report should be dated as of the date of completion of the compilation.

   d. Each page of the financial statement should contain a reference such as "See Accountant's Compilation Report."

   e. The CPA is not precluded from issuing a compilation report on one financial statement (e.g., balance sheet) and not on the others.

> <u>Exhibit 1</u>--Standard Report for a Compilation
>
> I (We) have compiled the accompanying balance sheet of XYZ Company as of December 31, 19XX, and the related statements of income, retained earnings, and cash flows for the year then ended, in accordance with Statements on Standards for Accounting and Review Services issued by the American Institute of Certified Public Accountants.
>
> A compilation is limited to presenting, in the form of financial statements, information that is the representation of management (owners). I (We) have not audited or reviewed the accompanying financial statements and, accordingly, do not express an opinion or any other form of assurance on them.

6. Reporting on Financial Statements That Omit Substantially All Disclosures--The CPA may be asked to compile financial statements that omit substantially all the disclosures required by GAAP (or another comprehensive basis of accounting). The CPA can do so as long as the CPA feels the omissions are not designed to mislead the users of the statements and the CPA clearly indicates in the report that the disclosures are omitted.

> <u>Exhibit 2</u>--Additional Paragraph When the Financial Statements Omit Substantially All Disclosures
>
> Management has elected to omit substantially all the disclosures required by generally accepted accounting principles. If the omitted disclosures were included in the financial statements, they might influence the user's conclusions about the company's financial position, results of operations, and cash flows. Accordingly, these financial statements are not designed for those who are not informed about such matters.

   a. Include Selected Disclosures--If the client omits most disclosures but does disclose a few matters in the form of notes to the financial statements, the disclosures should be labeled "Selected Information--Substantially All Disclosures Required by Generally Accepted Accounting Principles Are Not Included."

   b. Comprehensive Basis Other Than GAAP--When the financial statements are prepared on a comprehensive basis of accounting other than GAAP and the basis is <u>not</u> disclosed in the statements (including the notes), the basis <u>must be</u> disclosed in the CPA's report.

7. Reporting When the Accountant Is Not Independent--The CPA may compile financial statements with which the CPA is not independent. While the reason for this lack of independence should not be disclosed, the <u>last</u> paragraph of the report should specifically disclose the lack of independence:

   I am (we are) not independent with respect to XYZ Company.

F. <u>Review of Financial Statements</u>--The CPA uses inquiry and analytical procedures to provide a basis for expressing <u>limited assurance</u> that the financial statements do not contain material deviations from GAAP (or, where applicable, from another comprehensive basis of accounting). The CPA must be independent when engaged to perform a review of financial statements. The following guidelines apply to a review engagement:

1. Knowledge of the Accounting Principles and Practices of the Industry--Required so that the CPA can determine and apply proper inquiry and analytical procedures. However, this does not prevent an accountant from accepting a review engagement for an entity in an industry in which the accountant has no previous experience. The accountant has a responsibility to obtain the required level of knowledge.

2. Knowledge of the Client's Business--The CPA needs a general understanding of the client's business including organization; operating characteristics; nature of assets, liabilities, revenues, and expenses; production, distribution, and compensation methods; types of products and services; operating locations; and material transactions with related parties. This is normally obtained through experience with the client (or its industry) and inquiry of client personnel.

3. Inquiry and analytical procedures usually consist of the following:

   a. Inquiries as to Accounting Principles and Practices--Inquiries should be made concerning the client's accounting principles and practices, including methods used in applying them. Inquiries should be made concerning the client's procedures for recording, classifying, and summarizing transactions, and for accumulating information to be disclosed in the financial statements.

   b. Analytical Procedures--Designed to identify relationships and individual items that appear to be unusual. They consist of (1) comparison of the current financial statements with those of comparable prior periods, (2) comparison of the financial statements with anticipated results such as budgets and forecasts, and (3) examination of those elements of the financial statements that can reasonably be expected to conform to a predictable pattern over time (e.g., changes in sales and accounts receivable, and changes in depreciation and property, plant, and equipment).

   c. Inquiries About Important Meetings--Inquiries should be made as to actions taken at meetings of such groups as stockholders, board of directors, and committees of the board of directors that may have an effect on the financial statements.

   d. Reading the Financial Statements--The CPA should read the financial statements to see if they appear to be in conformity with GAAP.

   e. Obtain Reports From Other Accountants--The financial statements of the client should include an accounting for all significant components (unconsolidated subsidiaries, investees, etc.). If other accountants have audited or reviewed the financial statements, the CPA should obtain their reports. The CPA may decide to refer to the other accountants' work in the report and, if so, should indicate the magnitude of the portion of the financial statements the other accountants audited or reviewed.

   f. Additional Inquiries--Inquiries should be made of individuals who have responsibility for financial accounting matters concerning (1) whether the financial statements have been prepared in conformity with GAAP consistently applied, (2) changes in the client's business activities or accounting principles and practices, (3) matters about which questions have arisen from applying the foregoing procedures, and (4) events subsequent to the date of the financial statements that would have a material effect on the financial statements.

   g. Representation Letter--The CPA must obtain a representation letter from the client to complete a review.

4. One Statement Only--An accountant may be asked to issue a review report on one financial statement such as a balance sheet and not on other related financial statements (i.e., statements of income, retained earnings, and cash flows). The accountant may do so if the scope of his or her inquiry and analytical procedures has not been restricted.

5. Review Is Not an Audit--In performing a review, it is not intended that the CPA will (a) obtain an understanding of the internal control structure or assess control risk, (b) test accounting records and responses to inquiries through obtaining corroborating evidential matter, or (c) perform certain other procedures normally performed during an audit. Because of this, the

accountant may not become aware of all the significant matters an audit would disclose. Yet, if the accountant becomes aware that information is incorrect, incomplete, or otherwise unsatisfactory, the accountant should perform whatever additional procedures are necessary to permit the accountant to achieve limited assurance that the financial statements do not contain material deviations from GAAP (or, where applicable, from another comprehensive basis of accounting).

6. Working Papers--Form and content are not specified by SSARS 1. However, the workpapers should describe the matters covered by the inquiry and analytical procedures, and any unusual matters considered during the review (including how they were disposed of).

7. Reporting on Reviewed Financial Statements

   a. Report Content--The financial statements that have been reviewed should be accompanied by a report which states that (1) the review was performed in accordance with Statements on Standards for Accounting and Review Services issued by the AICPA; (2) all of the information included in the financial statements is the representation of management; (3) a review consists primarily of inquiries of company personnel and analytical procedures applied to the financial data; (4) the scope of a review is substantially less than an audit, the objective of which is to express an opinion on the financial statements taken as a whole and, therefore, no such opinion is expressed; and (5) except for those modifications indicated in the report, the CPA is not aware of any material modifications needed in order for the financial statements to conform to GAAP (or, if applicable, to another comprehensive basis of accounting).

   b. Any other procedures the CPA may have performed (including those performed in connection with a compilation of the financial statements) should not be described in the report.

   c. The report should be dated as of the completion of the inquiry and analytical procedures.

   d. Each page of the financial statements should contain a reference, such as "See Accountant's Review Report."

   e. In those cases where the CPA cannot perform the inquiry and analytical procedures the CPA considers necessary or the client does not provide the accountant with a representation letter, a review report cannot be issued.

8. Reporting When the CPA Is Not Independent--The CPA cannot issue a review report if the CPA is not independent (however, the CPA may be able to issue a compilation report).

Exhibit 3--Standard Report for a Review

I (We) have reviewed the accompanying balance sheet of XYZ Company as of December 31, 19XX, and the related statements of income, retained earnings, and cash flows for the year then ended, in accordance with Statements on Standards for Accounting and Review Services issued by the American Institute of Certified Public Accountants. All information included in these financial statements is the representation of the management (owners) of XYZ Company.

(continued on next page)

> A review consists principally of inquiries of company personnel and analytical procedures applied to financial data. It is substantially less in scope than an audit in accordance with generally accepted auditing standards, the objective of which is the expression of an opinion regarding the financial statements taken as a whole. Accordingly, I (we) do not express such an opinion.
>
> Based on my (our) review, I am (we are) not aware of any material modifications that should be made to the accompanying financial statements in order for them to be in conformity with generally accepted accounting principles.

G. Departures From GAAP--Applies to both compilations and reviews. The CPA may become aware of a departure from GAAP that is material to the financial statements. Appropriate action includes the following:

1. Requesting Client to Revise--The CPA should always first ask the client to revise the financial statements so that they conform with GAAP.

2. Modification of Standard Report--If the statements are not revised and if the departure is not the omission of substantially all disclosures from financial statements that have been compiled (see E.6., above), the CPA should consider whether the departure can be adequately disclosed by modifying the standard report. If it can, a separate paragraph should be used to disclose the departure and its effects (if they have been determined by management or are known through the CPA's procedures).

   a. If management has not determined the effects of the departure, the CPA is not required to determine them if the CPA does not already know the effects, as long as the CPA states in the report that no such determination was made.

   b. The CPA would not usually modify the report because of an uncertainty including an uncertainty about an entity's ability to continue as a going concern, or an inconsistency in the application of accounting principles if the financial statements provide adequate disclosure. However, the accountant is not precluded from emphasizing such a matter in a separate paragraph of the report.

> Exhibit 4--Compilation and Review Reports That Disclose Departures From GAAP
>
> **Compilation Report**
>
> I (We) have compiled the accompanying balance sheet of XYZ Company as of December 31, 19XX, and the related statements of income, retained earnings, and cash flows for the year then ended, in accordance with Statements on Standards for Accounting and Review Services issued by the American Institute of Certified Public Accountants.
>
> A compilation is limited to presenting, in the form of financial statements, information that is the representation of management (owners). I (We) have not audited or reviewed the accompanying financial statements and, accordingly, do not express an opinion or any other form of assurance on them. However, I (we) did become aware of a departure (certain departures) from generally accepted accounting principles that is (are) described in the following paragraph(s).
>
> (continued on next page)

(Separate paragraph)

As disclosed in note X to the financial statements, generally accepted accounting principles require that land be stated at cost. Management has informed me (us) that the company has stated its land at appraised value and that, if generally accepted accounting principles had been followed, the land account and stockholders' equity would have been decreased by $500,000.

or

A statement of cash flows for the year ended December 31, 19XX, has not been presented. Generally accepted accounting principles require that such a statement be presented when financial statements purport to present financial position and results of operations. (**NOTE**: The first paragraph should be modified accordingly when a statement of cash flows is not presented.)

Review Report

I (We) have reviewed the accompanying balance sheet of XYZ Company as of December 31, 19XX, and the related statements of income, retained earnings, and cash flows for the year then ended, in accordance with Statements on Standards for Accounting and Review Services issued by the American Institute of Certified Public Accountants. All information included in these financial statements is the representation of the management (owners) of XYZ Company.

A review consists principally of inquiries of company personnel and analytical procedures applied to financial data. It is substantially less in scope than an audit in accordance with generally accepted auditing standards, the objective of which is the expression of an opinion regarding the financial statements taken as a whole. Accordingly, I (we) do not express such an opinion.

Based on my (our) review, with the exception of the matter(s) described in the following paragraph(s), I am (we are) not aware of any material modifications that should be made to the accompanying financial statements in order for them to be in conformity with generally accepted accounting principles.

(Separate paragraph)

As disclosed in note X to the financial statements, generally accepted accounting principles require that inventory cost consists of material, labor, and overhead. Management has informed me (us) that the inventory of finished goods and work in process is stated in the accompanying financial statements at material and labor cost only, and that the effects of this departure from generally accepted accounting principles on financial position, results of operations, and cash flows have not been determined.

or

As disclosed in note X to the financial statements, the company has adopted (description of newly adopted method), whereas it previously used (description of previous method). Although the (description of newly adopted method) is in conformity with generally accepted accounting principles, the company does not appear to have reasonable justification for making a change as required by Opinion No. 20 of the Accounting Principles Board.

3. A CPA can <u>not</u> issue a review report on financial statements that omit substantially all disclosures required by GAAP.

4. Withdrawal--In cases where the CPA believes the deficiencies cannot be adequately disclosed by modifying the report, the CPA should withdraw from the compilation or review engagement and not provide any further services regarding those financial statements. The CPA may want to consult with legal counsel.

H. Subsequent Discovery of Facts Existing at Date of Report--After the date of the compilation or review report, the CPA may become aware that facts may have existed at that date which, had the CPA been aware of them, might have caused the CPA to believe that the information the client supplied was incorrect, incomplete, or otherwise unsatisfactory. The CPA should consult Section 561 of SAS 1 (see Chapter 40) to help determine the course of action (allowing for differences between the CPA's engagement and an audit). The CPA also should consider consulting with an attorney.

I. Supplementary Information--In cases where the basic financial statements are accompanied by information that is presented for purposes of supplementary analysis, the CPA should clearly indicate the responsibility, if any, that the CPA is taking with respect to the information.

1. Review--In the review report (or in a separate report), the CPA may indicate that the supplementary information was subjected to the same review procedures as the financial statements and the CPA is not aware of any material modifications that should be made to it, or the CPA may indicate that the data is presented only for supplementary purposes and has not been subjected to the review procedures applied to the financial statements, but was compiled from information that is the representation of management (and no opinion or any other form of assurance is given).

2. Compilation--The compilation report should include the supplementary data when the accountant has compiled the supplementary information to be presented with the basic financial statements.

J. Change in Engagement From Audit to Review or Compilation, or Review to Compilation--Before the audit (review) engagement has been completed, the client may ask the CPA to change the engagement to a review or a compilation.

1. Considerations--In reaching a decision, the CPA should consider (a) the client's reason for making the request (especially if either the client or circumstances have imposed a restriction on the scope of the audit or review), (b) the amount of audit (review) effort needed to complete the audit (review), and (c) the estimated additional cost to complete the audit (review).

2. Reasonable Basis for Changing--A change in the circumstances that caused the client to require an audit (or review), or a misunderstanding concerning the nature of an audit, review, or compilation would usually be considered acceptable reasons for changing. For example, the client's bank may have decided to accept reviewed financial statements in place of audited financial statements.

3. Restriction on Scope of Engagement--The CPA should consider whether the information affected by the scope restriction may be incorrect, incomplete, or otherwise unsatisfactory. When the accountant has been engaged to audit an entity's financial statements, the accountant would ordinarily be precluded from issuing a review or a compilation report when the client has prohibited correspondence with the client's legal counsel. If in an audit or a review engagement a client does not provide the accountant with a signed representation letter, the accountant would be precluded from issuing a review report on the financial statements and would ordinarily be precluded from issuing a compilation report on the financial statements.

4. Audit Procedures Are Substantially Complete or the Cost to Complete the Audit (Review) Is Relatively Insignificant--In these circumstances, the CPA should consider carefully the propriety of changing the engagement.

5. Report--When the CPA decides that a change in engagement is appropriate and the requirements for a compilation or a review have been met, the CPA should issue an appropriate compilation or review report. It should not include any reference to the original engagement, any auditing or review procedures that may have been performed, or any scope limitations that resulted in the changed engagement.

II. Reporting on Comparative Financial Statements (SSARS 2)

A. Applicability--Applies when reporting on comparative financial statements of a nonpublic entity when the financial statements of one or more periods presented have been compiled or reviewed per SSARS 1.

B. Definitions

1. Comparative Financial Statements--Financial statements of two or more periods which are presented in a columnar format.

2. Continuing Accountant--Engaged to audit, review, or compile the current period's financial statements and has audited, reviewed, or compiled those of one or more consecutive periods immediately prior to the current period.

3. Updated Report--Issued by the continuing accountant. It takes into account information the continuing accountant becomes aware of during the current engagement. In it, the continuing accountant will either re-express the previous conclusion on the prior-period statements or, in some cases, express a different conclusion on the prior-period statements as of the date of the continuing accountant's current report.

4. Reissued Report--Issued after the date of the original report, but bearing the same date as the original report. If it must be revised because of the effects of specific events, it should be dual-dated, using the original date and a separate date that applies to the effects of such events.

C. General Requirements--The CPA should issue an appropriate report which covers each of the periods presented in the comparative financial statements.

1. Separate Pages--It is permissible for the client to include client-prepared financial statements of some periods that have not been audited, reviewed, or compiled by the CPA on separate pages of a document containing financial statements on which the CPA has issued an audit, review, or compilation report, provided that they are accompanied by an indication from the client that the CPA has not audited, reviewed, or compiled those statements and, therefore, the CPA does not assume any responsibility for them.

   - Columnar Form--If the CPA becomes aware that, within the comparative financial statements, the client has included in a columnar format some information that the CPA has not audited, reviewed, or compiled and some that the CPA has, and the report on the latter or the CPA's name is included in the documents containing the comparative statements, the CPA should advise the client that this is inappropriate. The CPA should consider appropriate action, including, if necessary, consultation with legal counsel.

2. Modified Report--When financial statements are presented for comparative purposes in columnar form, the CPA may issue an unmodified report on some statements and a modified report on others.

3. Omission of Disclosures--Statements that omit substantially all GAAP disclosures are not comparable to financial statements that include such disclosures. Therefore, the CPA should not issue a report on comparative statements when statements for some, but not all, of the periods presented omit substantially all the disclosures required by GAAP.

4. Reference--A reference such as "See Accountant's Report" should be included on each page of the comparative financial statements.

D. Continuing Accountant's Standard Report--Form depends on the level of service (compilation or review) provided with respect to the financial statements presented.

1. Same or Higher Level of Service in the Current Period--The continuing CPA should update the report on the financial statements of a prior period that are presented with those of the current period when the CPA (a) compiled the prior-period statements and the current-period statements, (b) compiled the prior-period statements and reviewed the current statements, or (c) reviewed the prior-period statements and the current-period statements.

> Exhibit 5--Compilation Each Period
>
> I (We) have compiled the accompanying balance sheets of XYZ Company as of December 31, 19X2 and 19X1 and the related statements of income, retained earnings, and cash flows for the years then ended, in accordance with Statements on Standards for Accounting and Review Services issued by the American Institute of Certified Public Accountants.
>
> A compilation is limited to presenting, in the form of financial statements, information that is the representation of management (owners). I (We) have not audited or reviewed the accompanying financial statements and, accordingly, do not express an opinion or any other form of assurance on them.
>
> February 1, 19X3

> Exhibit 6--Review Each Period
>
> I (We) have reviewed the accompanying balance sheets of XYZ Company as of December 31, 19X2 and 19X1, and the related statements of income, retained earnings, and cash flows for the years then ended, in accordance with Statements on Standards for Accounting and Review Services issued by the American Institute of Certified Public Accountants. All information included in these financial statements is the representation of the management (owners) of XYZ Company.
>
> A review consists principally of inquiries of company personnel and analytical procedures applied to financial data. It is substantially less in scope than an audit in accordance with generally accepted auditing standards, the objective of which is the expression of an opinion regarding the financial statements taken as a whole. Accordingly, I (we) do not express such an opinion.
>
> Based on my (our) reviews, I am (we are) not aware of any material modifications that should be made to the accompanying financial statements in order for them to be in conformity with generally accepted accounting principles.
>
> March 1, 19X3

Exhibit 7--Review in the Current Period and Compilation in the Prior Period

I (We) have reviewed the accompanying balance sheet of XYZ Company as of December 31, 19X2, and the related statements of income, retained earnings, and cash flows for the year then ended, in accordance with Statements on Standards for Accounting and Review Services issued by the American Institute of Certified Public Accountants. All information included in these financial statements is the representation of the management (owners) of XYZ Company.

A review consists principally of inquiries of company personnel and analytical procedures applied to financial data. It is substantially less in scope than an audit in accordance with generally accepted auditing standards, the objective of which is the expression of an opinion regarding the financial statements taken as a whole. Accordingly, I (we) do not express such an opinion.

Based on my (our) review, I am (we are) not aware of any material modifications that should be made to the 19X2 financial statements in order for them to be in conformity with generally accepted accounting principles.

The accompanying 19X1 financial statements of XYZ Company were compiled by me (us). A compilation is limited to presenting, in the form of financial statements, information that is the representation of management (owners). I (We) have not audited or reviewed the 19X1 financial statements and, accordingly, do not express an opinion or any other form of assurance on them.

March 1, 19X3

2. Lower Level of Service in the Current Period--A continuing CPA who has compiled the current-period financial statements and previously reviewed those of the prior period(s) presented for comparative purposes should either issue a compilation report or a combined report.

   a. Issue a Compilation Report--The auditor should include in the compilation report on the current-period financial statements a paragraph that describes the responsibility the auditor is assuming for the prior-period statements. The description should include (1) the date of the original report, and (2) a statement that the auditor has not performed any procedures pertaining to the review engagement after that date.

Exhibit 8--Descriptive Paragraph That May Be Added to a Compilation Report on the Current-Period Financial Statements Describing the Responsibilities Assumed When Prior-Period Financial Statements Were Reviewed

The accompanying 19X1 financial statements of XYZ Company were previously reviewed by me (us) and my (our) report dated March 1, 19X2, stated that I was (we were) not aware of any material modifications that should be made to those statements in order for them to be in conformity with generally accepted accounting principles. I (We) have not performed any procedures in connection with that review engagement after the date of my (our) report on the 19X1 financial statements.

   b. Combined Report--Alternatively, the auditor may combine the compilation report on the current-period financial statements with the reissued review report on the prior--period financial statements. The combined report should contain a statement that the auditor has not performed any procedures pertaining to the review after the date of the review report. Alternatively, the CPA may separately present the compilation report on the current statements and the review report on the prior period.

E. Continuing Accountant's Changed Reference to a Departure From GAAP--Circumstances or events may come to the CPA's attention during the current engagement which affect the prior-period financial statements that are presented (including the adequacy of their disclosure). If the CPA's report on the comparative statements includes a changed reference to a departure from GAAP, a separate explanatory paragraph should be included in the report indicating the date of the CPA's previous report, the circumstances or events that caused the CPA to refer to the change, and, when applicable, that the prior-period financial statements have been changed.

- Changed Reference--Includes a reference that is different from the one made in the previous report, the removal of a prior reference, or the inclusion of a new reference.

Exhibit 9--Explanatory Paragraph Reflecting a Changed Reference to a Departure from GAAP

In my (our) previous (compilation) (review) report dated March 1, 19X2, on the 19X1 financial statements, I (we) referred to a departure from generally accepted accounting principles because the company carried its land at appraised values. However, as disclosed in note X, the company has restated its 19X1 financial statements to reflect its land at cost in conformity with generally accepted accounting principles.

F. Predecessor's Compilation or Review Report--At the client's request, a predecessor CPA may reissue the compilation or review report on the prior-period financial statements. However, the CPA does not have to do so.

1. Predecessor's Compilation or Review Report Not Presented--When a predecessor CPA has compiled or reviewed the financial statements of a prior period (that are presented for comparative purposes) but does not reissue the compilation or review report, the successor CPA should either (a) include an additional paragraph(s) in the report on the current-period financial statements which makes reference to the predecessor's report on the prior-period financial statements; or (b) perform a compilation, review, or audit of the prior-period financial statements and issue an appropriate report.

    - Making Reference to Predecessor's Report--The additional paragraph(s) should include (1) a statement that another accountant compiled or reviewed the prior-period financial statements (the predecessor should not be named); (2) the date of the predecessor's report; (3) a description of the standard form of disclaimer or limited assurance that appeared in the report; and (4) a description of any modifications which were made to the standard report and of any paragraphs that were included to emphasize a matter(s) in the financial statements.

Exhibit 10--Additional (Last) Paragraph When the Predecessor Reviewed the Prior-Period Financial Statements

The 19X1 financial statements of XYZ Company were reviewed by other accountants whose report, dated March 1, 19X2, stated that they were not aware of any material modifications that should be made to those statements in order for them to be in conformity with generally accepted accounting principles.

Exhibit 11--Additional Paragraph When the Predecessor Compiled the Prior-Period Financial Statements

The 19X1 financial statements of XYZ Company were compiled by other accountants whose report, dated February 1, 19X2, stated that they did not express an opinion or any other form of assurance on those statements.

2. Predecessor's Compilation or Review Report Reissued--A predecessor should consider whether the report on the prior-period financial statements is still appropriate before the predecessor reissues it. In this regard, the predecessor should consider (a) the current form and manner of presentation of the prior-period financial statements, (b) subsequent events that the predecessor was not aware of at the time of the original report, and (c) if there are any changes in the financial statements that would require the predecessor to either add or delete modifications to the standard report.

   a. Procedures--Before reissuance of the compilation or review report of a prior period, the predecessor should (1) read the current-period financial statements and the report of the successor CPA; (2) compare the prior-period financial statements with those that were previously issued and with those of the current period; and (3) obtain a letter from the successor indicating whether any matters came to his or her attention which, in the successor's opinion, might have a material effect on the prior-period statements, including disclosures. The predecessor should not refer to the successor's letter or report in the reissued report.

   b. If the predecessor becomes aware of information that may affect the financial statements of the prior period and/or the report on them, the predecessor should make inquiries or perform analytical procedures similar to the ones the predecessor would have performed at the date of the report on the prior-period statements had the predecessor been aware of the information, and perform any other necessary procedures. Examples include discussion with the successor and/or review of the successor's working papers on the matter. The predecessor should follow the guidance in E., above, and c. and d., below, if the predecessor decides that the report should be revised.

   c. The date of the previous report should be used when reissuing a report. This avoids any connotation that the predecessor performed any procedures (other than those in a. and b., above) after that date. Dual-dating is appropriate if the predecessor revised the report or if the financial statements are restated (e.g., "March 15, 19X1 except for note X, as to which the date is March 31, 19X2").

      - Written Statement From Former Client--The predecessor should obtain a written statement from the former client that states the information currently acquired and its effect on the prior-period financial statements and, if applicable, includes an expression of the former client's understanding of the information's effect on the predecessor's reissued report.

   d. The predecessor should not reissue the report if the predecessor is unable to complete the procedures described in a., b., and c., above. The predecessor may want to consult legal counsel in deciding the appropriate course of action.

3. Changed Prior-Period Financial Statements--Either the predecessor or the successor should report on prior-period financial statements that have been changed.

   a. Predecessor--When reporting, the predecessor should adhere to F.2., above.

   b. Successor--When reporting, the successor should comply with SSARS 1 (or perform an audit). The successor should not refer to the predecessor's previously issued report in the successor's report.

   c. Restatement Not Involving a Change in Accounting Principle--It is possible that the restatement may be for reasons other than a change in accounting principles or their application, e.g., a revision to correct an error. In this case, as long as the financial statements adequately disclose the matter, the CPA may decide to include an explanatory paragraph in the report, concerning the restatement. However, the CPA should not modify the report beyond this.

G. Reporting When One Period Is Audited

1. Current-Period Financial Statements Are Audited--SASs apply when reporting on comparative financial statements in which the current-period statements have been audited and those for one or more prior periods have been compiled or reviewed. AU 504.15 states that when unaudited financial statements are presented in comparative form with audited financial statements, the financial statements that have not been audited should be clearly marked to indicate their status and either (a) the report on the prior period should be reissued or (b) the report on the current period should include as a separate paragraph an appropriate description of the responsibility assumed for the unaudited financial statements.

2. Prior-Period Financial Statements Are Audited--When a nonpublic entity's current-period financial statements have been compiled or reviewed and the prior-period statements (presented for comparative purposes) have been audited, an appropriate compilation or review report should be issued on the current-period statements. In addition, either the prior-period report should be reissued or a separate paragraph should be added to the current-period's report.

   - Separate Paragraph--If a separate paragraph is used, it should describe the responsibility the CPA is assuming for the financial statements of the prior period. Specifically, it should indicate (1) that the prior-period's financial statements were audited previously; (2) the date of the previous report; (3) the type of opinion that was previously expressed; (4) if the previous opinion was not unqualified, the substantive reasons for this; and (5) that no auditing procedures have been performed since the date of the previous report.

Exhibit 12--Separate Paragraph

The financial statements for the year ended December 31, 19X1, were audited by us (other accountants) and we (they) expressed an unqualified opinion on them in our (their) report dated March 1, 19X2, but we (they) have not performed any auditing procedures since that date.

H. Reporting on Financial Statements That Previously Did Not Omit Substantially All Disclosures--Even though a CPA may have compiled, reviewed, or audited financial statements that did not omit substantially all the disclosures required by GAAP, the CPA may later be asked to compile financial statements for the same period that do omit substantially all the disclosures required by GAAP so that the statements can be presented in comparative financial statements. In this case, the CPA may report on these statements as long as an additional paragraph is included in the report which indicates the nature of the previous service and the date of the previous report.

Exhibit 13--Prior-Period Statements Omitting Substantially All Disclosures Compiled From Previously Reviewed Statements

I (We) have compiled the accompanying balance sheet of XYZ Company as of December 31, 19XX, and the related statements of income, retained earnings, and cash flows for the year then ended, in accordance with Statements on Standards for Accounting and Review Services issued by the American Institute of Certified Public Accountants.

(continued on next page)

> A compilation is limited to presenting, in the form of financial statements, information that is the representation of management (owners). I (We) have not audited or reviewed the accompanying financial statements and, accordingly, do not express an opinion or any other form of assurance on them.
>
> Management has elected to omit substantially all the disclosures required by generally accepted accounting principles. If the omitted disclosures were included in the financial statements, they might influence the user's conclusions about the company's financial position, results of operations, and cash flows. Accordingly, these financial statements are not designed for those who are not informed about such matters.
>
> The accompanying 19X1 financial statements were compiled by me (us) from financial statements that did not omit substantially all the disclosures required by generally accepted accounting principles and that I (we) previously reviewed as indicated in my (our) report dated March 1, 19X2.
>
> February 1, 19X3

I. Change of Status--Public/Nonpublic Entity--A question arises as to whether SAS or SSARS applies when the status of an entity changes, for example, if it is a public entity in the current period, but was a nonpublic entity in the prior period.

1. The current status of the entity governs when the CPA is reporting on comparative financial statements for either interim or annual periods.

2. If a previously issued report is not appropriate for the current status of the entity, it should not be reissued or referred to in the report on the current-period statements.

    - Examples--It is not appropriate to reissue or refer to the compilation or review report on the prior-period financial statements if the entity is a public entity in the current period but was a nonpublic entity in the prior period (SAS should be followed). If the entity is nonpublic in the current period, but was public in the prior period (and its statements were audited), G.2., above, should be followed. If an entity is currently nonpublic and an unaudited disclaimer was issued for the prior period, the disclaimer should not be reissued or referred to in the report on the current statements.

III. Compilation Reports on Financial Statements Included in Certain Prescribed Forms (SSARS 3)

A. Applicability--The requirements of SSARS 1 and SSARS 2 are applicable when the unaudited financial statements of a nonpublic entity are included in a prescribed form. This statement amends SSARS 1 and SSARS 2 to provide for an alternative form of standard compilation report when the prescribed form or related instructions call for departure from generally accepted accounting principles (GAAP) by specifying a measurement principle not in conformity with GAAP or by failing to request the disclosures required by GAAP. This statement also provides additional guidance applicable to reports on financial statements included in a prescribed form.

B. Definition--A prescribed form is any standard preprinted form designed or adopted by the body to which it is to be submitted, for example, forms used by industry trade associations, credit agencies, banks, and governmental and regulatory bodies other than those concerned with the sale or trading of securities. A form designed or adopted by the entity whose financial statements are to be compiled is not considered to be a prescribed form.

C. Procedures--There is a presumption that the information required by a prescribed form is sufficient to meet the needs of the body that designed or adopted the form and that there is no need for that body to be advised of departures from GAAP required by the prescribed form or related instructions. Therefore, without a requirement or a request for a review report on the financial statements included in a prescribed form, the following form of standard compilation report may be used when the unaudited financial statements of a nonpublic entity are included in a prescribed form that calls for a departure from GAAP:

> Exhibit 14
>
> I (We) have compiled the [identification of financial statements, including period covered and name of entity] included in the accompanying prescribed form in accordance with Statements on Standards for Accounting and Review Services issued by the American Institute of Certified Public Accountants.
>
> My (Our) compilation was limited to presenting in the form prescribed by (name of body) information that is the representation of management (owners). I (We) have not audited or reviewed the financial statements referred to above and, accordingly, do not express an opinion or any other form of assurance on them.
>
> These financial statements (including related disclosures) are presented in accordance with the requirements of [name of body], which differ from generally accepted accounting principles. Accordingly, these financial statements are not designed for those who are not informed about such differences.

D. Departures From GAAP--If the accountant becomes aware of a departure from GAAP other than departures that may be called for by the prescribed form or related instructions, the accountant should follow the guidance in SSARS 1 regarding such departures. The sentence introducing the separate paragraph of the report disclosing the departure might read as follows: "However, I did become aware of a departure from generally accepted accounting principles that is not called for by the prescribed form or related instructions, as described in the following paragraph."

E. Departures From Other Requirements--If the accountant becomes aware of a departure from the requirements of the prescribed form or related instructions, the accountant should consider that departure as the equivalent of a departure from GAAP in determining its effect on the report.

F. Preprinted Forms Not Conforming With SSARS--The accountant should not sign a preprinted report form that does not conform with the guidance in this statement or SSARS 1, as amended, whichever is applicable. In such circumstances, the accountant should append an appropriate report to the prescribed form.

IV. Communications Between Predecessor and Successor Accountants (SSARS 4)

A. Overview--This Statement provides guidance to a successor accountant who decides to communicate with a predecessor accountant regarding acceptance of an engagement to compile or review the financial statements of a nonpublic entity. It requires the predecessor accountant to respond promptly and fully in the event of such communications in ordinary circumstances. This Statement also provides guidance on additional inquiries a successor accountant may wish to make of a predecessor, and the predecessor's responses to facilitate the conduct of the successor's compilation or review engagement. It also requires a successor accountant who becomes aware of information that leads him or her to believe the financial statements reported on by the predecessor accountant may require revision to request that the client communicate this information to the predecessor accountant.

B. Definitions

1. Successor Accountant--An accountant who has been invited to make a proposal for an engagement to compile or review financial statements or who has accepted such an engagement.

2. Predecessor Accountant--An accountant who has resigned or who has been notified that his or her services have been terminated and who, at a minimum, was engaged to compile the financial statements of the entity for the prior year or for a period ended within twelve months of the date of the financial statements to be compiled or reviewed by the successor.

C. Inquiries Regarding Acceptance of an Engagement

1. A successor accountant is not required to communicate with a predecessor accountant in connection with acceptance of a compilation or review engagement, but a successor may decide to do so, for example, when circumstances such as the following exist:

   a. The information obtained about the prospective client and its management and principals is limited or appears to require special attention.

   b. The change in accountants takes place substantially after the end of the accounting period for which financial statements are to be compiled or reviewed.

   c. There have been frequent changes in accountants.

2. Except as permitted by the AICPA Rules of Conduct, an accountant is precluded from disclosing any confidential information obtained during a professional engagement without the consent of the client. Accordingly, when the successor accountant decides to communicate with the predecessor, the successor should request the client:

   a. Permit the successor to make inquiries of the predecessor accountant, and

   b. Authorize the predecessor accountant to respond fully to those inquiries.

      - If the client refuses to comply fully with this request, the successor accountant should consider the reasons for, and implications of, that refusal in connection with acceptance of the engagement.

3. When the successor accountant decides to communicate with the predecessor, inquiries may be oral or written and ordinarily would include inquiries concerning the following:

   a. Information that might bear on the integrity of management (owners).

   b. Disagreements with management (owners) about accounting principles or the necessity for the performance of certain procedures.

   c. The cooperation of management (owners) in providing additional or revised information, if necessary.

   d. The predecessor's understanding of the reason for the change of accountants.

4. The predecessor accountant should respond promptly and fully, on the basis of known facts, when the predecessor receives inquiries of the type described in C.3., above, as distinguished from other inquiries discussed in D.1. and 2. However, if the predecessor decides, due to unusual circumstances such as impending litigation, not to respond fully, the predecessor should indicate that his or her response is limited. The successor accountant should consider the reasons for, and implications of, such a response in connection with acceptance of the engagement.

D. Other Inquiries

1. The successor accountant may wish to make other inquiries of the predecessor to facilitate the conduct of the compilation or review engagement. Examples of such inquiries, which

may be made either before or after acceptance of the engagement, might include questions about prior periods regarding the following:

a. Inadequacies noted in the entity's underlying financial data.

b. The necessity to perform other accounting services.

c. Areas that have required an inordinate amount of time in prior periods.

2. A successor accountant also may wish to obtain access to the predecessor's working papers. In these circumstances, the successor should request the client to authorize the predecessor to allow such access. It is customary in such circumstances for the predecessor to be available to the successor for consultation and to make available certain working papers. The predecessor and successor should agree on those working papers that are to be made available and those that may be copied. Ordinarily, the predecessor should provide the successor access to working papers relating to matters of continuing accounting significance and those related to contingencies. Valid business reasons (including, but not limited to, unpaid fees), however, may lead the predecessor to decide not to allow access to the working papers.

3. The successor accountant should not refer to the report or work of a predecessor accountant in his or her own report, except as specifically permitted by SSARS 2 or SAS 26 regarding the financial statements of a prior period.

E. Financial Statements Reported on by Predecessor Accountant--If during the engagement the successor accountant becomes aware of information that leads to a belief that financial statements reported on by the predecessor accountant may require revision, the successor should request the client to communicate this information to the predecessor accountant. SSARS 1 provides guidance to the predecessor accountant in determining an appropriate course of action. If the client refuses to communicate with the predecessor or if the successor accountant is not satisfied with the predecessor's course of action, the successor would be well advised to consult with an attorney.

V. Reporting on Personal Financial Statements Included in Written Personal Financial Plans (SSARS 6)

A. Requirements--An accountant may submit a written personal financial plan containing unaudited personal financial statements to a client without complying with the requirements of SSARS 1, as amended, when both of the following conditions exist:

1. The accountant establishes an understanding with the client that the financial statements will be used solely to assist the client and the client's advisers to develop the client's personal financial goals and objectives, and will not be used to obtain credit or for any purposes other than developing these goals and objectives.

2. Nothing comes to the accountant's attention during the engagement that would cause the accountant to believe that the financial statements will be used to obtain credit or for any purposes other than developing the client's financial goals and objectives.

B. Written Report--An accountant using the exemption provided by this statement should issue a written report. The following is an illustration of such a report:

The accompanying Statement of Financial Condition of X, as of December 31, 19XX, was prepared solely to help you develop your personal financial plan. Accordingly, it may be incomplete or contain other departures from generally accepted accounting principles and should not be used to obtain credit or for any purposes other than developing your financial plan. We have not audited, reviewed, or compiled the statement.

PART TWO: FINANCIAL FORECASTS AND PROJECTIONS

I. Overview

A. Applicability--In their *Statement on Standards for Accountants' Services on Prospective Financial Information*, the AICPA sets forth standards and provides guidance concerning performance and reporting for engagements to examine, compile, or apply agreed-upon procedures to prospective financial statements. The standards and guidance in this Statement apply to an accountant who either (1) submits to the client or others, prospective financial statements that the accountant has assembled or assisted in assembling, or (2) reports on prospective financial statements, if such statements are, or reasonably might be, expected to be used by a third party. In deciding whether the prospective financial statements are, or reasonably might be, expected to be used by a third party, the accountant may rely on either the written or oral representation of the responsible party, unless contradictory information comes to his or her attention.

B. Definitions

1. Prospective Financial Statements--Either financial forecasts or financial projections that include the summaries of significant assumptions and accounting policies (does not include pro forma financial statements or partial presentations).

2. Financial Forecast--Prospective financial statements that present, to the best of the responsible party's knowledge and belief, an entity's expected financial position, results of operations, and cash flows. A financial forecast may be expressed in specific monetary amounts as a single-point estimate of forecasted results or as a range, where the responsible party selects key assumptions to form a range within which it reasonably expects, to the best of its knowledge and belief, the item or items subject to the assumptions to actually fall.

3. Financial Projection--Prospective financial statements that present, to the best of the responsible party's knowledge and belief, given one or more hypothetical assumptions, an entity's expected financial position, results of operations, and cash flows. A financial projection is sometimes prepared to present one or more hypothetical courses of action for evaluation. It answers the question, "What would happen if . . . ?" A financial projection is based on the responsible party's assumptions reflecting conditions it expects would exist and the course of action it expects would be taken, given one or more hypothetical assumptions. It may also contain a range.

4. Entity--Any unit, existing or to be formed, for which financial statements could be prepared in conformity with generally accepted accounting principles or another comprehensive basis of accounting.

5. Hypothetical Assumption--An assumption used in a financial projection to present a condition or course of action that is not necessarily expected to occur, but is consistent with the purpose of the projection.

6. Responsible Party--The person or persons who are responsible for the assumptions underlying the prospective financial statements. The responsible party usually is management, but it can be persons outside the entity who do not currently have the authority to direct operations.

7. Assembly--The manual or computer processing of mathematical or other clerical functions related to the presentation of the prospective financial statements.

8. Key Factors--The significant matters on which an entity's future results are expected to depend. Key factors are the bases for assumptions.

9. Materiality--Materiality is a concept that is judged in the light of the expected range of reasonableness of the information; therefore, users should not expect prospective information to be as precise as historical information.

II. Uses of Prospective Financial Statements

A. General Use--Refers to the use of the statements by persons with whom the responsible party is not negotiating directly. As a result, since they are unable to ask questions of the responsible party, the presentation most useful to them is one that portrays, to the best of the responsible party's knowledge and belief, the expected results. Thus, only a financial forecast is appropriate for general use.

B. Limited Use--Refers to the use of prospective financial statements by the responsible party alone or by the responsible party and third parties with whom the responsible party is negotiating directly. Third-party recipients of prospective financial statements intended for limited use can ask questions of the responsible party and negotiate terms directly with it. Any type of prospective financial statements that would be useful in the circumstances would normally be appropriate for limited use. Thus, the presentation may be a financial forecast or a financial projection.

III. Compilation of Prospective Financial Statements

A. General Provisions

1. A compilation of prospective financial statements is a professional service that involves (a) assembling, to the extent necessary, the prospective financial statements based on the responsible party's assumptions, (b) performing the required compilation procedures, including reading the statements and considering whether they are appropriate and whether they are presented in conformity with AICPA presentation guidelines, and (c) issuing a compilation report.

   A compilation is not intended to provide assurance on the prospective financial statements or the assumptions underlying such statements. Because of the limited nature of the accountant's procedures, a compilation does not provide assurance that the accountant will become aware of significant matters that might be disclosed by more extensive procedures.

2. Summary of Significant Assumptions--Since this is essential to the reader's understanding of prospective financial statements, the accountant should not compile prospective financial statements that exclude disclosure of the summary of significant assumptions. Also, the accountant should not compile a financial projection that excludes (a) an identification of the hypothetical assumptions or (b) a description of the limitations on the usefulness of the presentation.

3. Standards applicable to a compilation of prospective financial statements:

   a. The compilation should be performed by a person or persons having adequate technical training and proficiency to compile prospective financial statements.

   b. Due professional care should be exercised in the performance of the compilation and the preparation of the report.

   c. The work should be adequately planned, and assistants, if any, should be properly supervised.

   d. Applicable compilation procedures should be performed as a basis for reporting on the compiled prospective financial statements.

e. The report based on the accountant's compilation of prospective financial statements should conform to the applicable guidance in this Statement.

B. Working Papers--Although it is not possible to specify the form or content of the working papers that an accountant should prepare in connection with a compilation of prospective financial statements because of the different circumstances of individual engagements, the accountant's working papers ordinarily should indicate that (1) the work was adequately planned and supervised, and (2) the required compilation procedures were performed as a basis for the compilation report.

C. Reports on Compiled Prospective Financial Statements

1. The accountant's standard report on a compilation of prospective financial statements should include the following:

a. An identification of the prospective financial statements presented by the responsible party.

b. A statement that the accountant has compiled the prospective financial statements in accordance with standards established by the American Institute of Certified Public Accountants.

c. A statement that a compilation is limited in scope and does not enable the accountant to express an opinion or any other form of assurance on the prospective financial statements or the assumptions.

d. A caveat that the prospective results may not be achieved.

e. A statement that the accountant assumes no responsibility to update the report for events and circumstances occurring after the date of the report.

Exhibit 15--Compilation Report on a Forecast That Does Not Contain a Range

We have compiled the accompanying forecasted balance sheet, statements of income, retained earnings, and cash flows of XYZ Company as of December 31, 19XX, and for the year then ending, in accordance with standards established by the American Institute of Certified Public Accountants.

A compilation is limited to presenting in the form of a forecast information that is the representation of management and does not include evaluation of the support for the assumptions underlying the forecast. We have not audited the forecast and, accordingly, do not express an opinion or any other form of assurance on the accompanying statements or assumptions. Furthermore, there will usually be differences between the forecasted and actual results, because events and circumstances frequently do not occur as expected, and those differences may be material. We have no responsibility to update this report for events and circumstances occurring after the date of this report.

2. When the Presentation Is a Projection--The accountant's report should include a separate paragraph that describes the limitations on the usefulness of the presentation.

Exhibit 16--Compilation Report on a Projection That Does Not Contain a Range

We have compiled the accompanying projected balance sheet, statements of income, retained earnings, and cash flows of XYZ Company as of December 31, 19XX, and for the year then ending, in accordance with standards established by the American Institute of Certified Public Accountants.

(continued on next page)

> The accompanying projection and this report were prepared for [state special purpose, for example, "the DEF National Bank for the purpose of negotiating a loan to expand XYZ Company's plant,"] and should not be used for any other purpose.
>
> A compilation is limited to presenting in the form of a projection information that is the representation of management and does not include evaluation of the support for the assumptions underlying the projection. We have not audited the projection and, accordingly, do not express an opinion or any other form of assurance on the accompanying statements or assumptions. Furthermore, even if [describe hypothetical assumption, for example, "the loan is granted and the plant is expanded,"] there will usually be differences between the projected and actual results, because events and circumstances frequently do not occur as expected, and those differences may be material. We have no responsibility to update this report for events and circumstances occurring after the date of this report.

3. When the Prospective Financial Statements Contain a Range--The accountant's standard report should also include a separate paragraph that states that the responsible party has elected to portray the expected results of one or more assumptions as a range.

> Exhibit 17--Separate Paragraph for a Compiled Forecast Containing a Range
>
> As described in the summary of significant assumptions, management of XYZ company has elected to portray forecasted [describe financial statement element or elements for which the expected results of one or more assumptions fall within a range, and identify the assumptions expected to fall within a range, for example, "revenue at the amounts $X,XXX and $Y,YYY, which is predicated upon occupancy rates of XX percent and YY percent of available apartments,"] rather than as a single point estimate. Accordingly, the accompanying forecast presents forecasted financial position, results of operations, and cash flows [describe one or more assumptions expected to fall within a range, for example, "at such occupancy rates"]. However, there is no assurance that the actual results will fall within the range [describe one or more assumptions expected to fall within a range, for example, "occupancy rates"] presented.

4. Date--The date of completion of the accountant's compilation procedures should be used as the date of the report.

5. Lack of Independence--An accountant may compile prospective financial statements for an entity with respect to which an accountant is not independent. In such circumstances, the accountant should specifically disclose this lack of independence; however, the reason for the lack of independence should not be described. When the accountant is not independent, the accountant may give the standard compilation report, but should include the following sentence after the last paragraph:

   We are not independent with respect to XYZ Company.

6. Emphasis of a Matter--In some circumstances, an accountant may wish to expand the report to emphasize a matter regarding the prospective financial statements. Such information may be presented in a separate paragraph of the accountant's report. However, the accountant should exercise care that emphasizing such a matter does not give the impression that the accountant is expressing assurance or expanding the degree of responsibility the accountant is taking regarding such information.

D. Modifications of the Standard Compilation Report

- An entity may request an accountant to compile prospective financial statements that contain presentation deficiencies or omit disclosures other than those relating to significant assumptions. The accountant may compile such prospective financial statements provided the deficiency or omission is clearly indicated in the report and is not, to the accountant's knowledge, undertaken with the intention of misleading those who might reasonably be expected to use such statements.

- If the compiled prospective financial statements are presented on a comprehensive basis of accounting other than generally accepted accounting principles and do not include disclosure of the basis of accounting used, the basis should be disclosed in the accountant's report.

> Exhibit 18--Separate Paragraph for a Forecast in Which the Summary of Significant Accounting Policies Has Been Omitted
>
> Management has elected to omit the summary of significant accounting policies required by the guidelines for presentation of a forecast established by the American Institute of Certified Public Accountants. If the omitted disclosures were included in the forecast, they might influence the user's conclusions about the Company's financial position, results of operations, and cash flows for the forecast period. Accordingly, this forecast is not designed for those who are not informed about such matters.

IV. Examination of Prospective Financial Statements

A. General Provisions

1. An examination of prospective financial statements is a professional service that involves (a) evaluating the preparation of the prospective financial statements, (b) evaluating the support underlying the assumptions, (c) evaluating the presentation of the prospective financial statements for conformity with AICPA presentation guidelines, and (d) issuing an examination report.

   As a result of the examination, the accountant has a basis for reporting on whether, in the accountant's opinion, (a) the assumptions provide a reasonable basis for the responsible party's forecast, or whether the assumptions provide a reasonable basis for the responsible party's projection, given the hypothetical assumptions, and (b) whether the prospective financial statements are presented in accordance with AICPA guidelines.

2. The accountant should be independent; have adequate technical training and proficiency to examine prospective financial statements; adequately plan the engagement and supervise the work of assistants, if any; and obtain sufficient evidence to provide a reasonable basis for the examination report.

B. Working Papers--The accountant's working papers in connection with the examination of prospective financial statements should be appropriate to the circumstances and the accountant's needs on the engagement to which they apply. Although the quantity, type, and content of working papers vary with the circumstances, they ordinarily should indicate that (1) the work was adequately planned and supervised, (2) the process by which the entity develops its prospective financial statements was considered in determining the scope of the examination, and (3) sufficient evidence was obtained to provide a reasonable basis for the accountant's report.

C. Reports on Examined Prospective Financial Statements

1. The accountant's standard report on an examination of prospective financial statements should include the following:

   a. An identification of the prospective financial statements presented.

   b. A statement that the examination of the prospective financial statements was made in accordance with AICPA standards, and a brief description of the nature of such an examination.

c. The accountant's opinion that the prospective financial statements are presented in accordance with AICPA presentation guidelines and that the underlying assumptions provide a reasonable basis for the forecast or a reasonable basis for the projection given the hypothetical assumptions.

d. A caveat that the prospective results may not be achieved.

e. A statement that the accountant assumes no responsibility to update the report for events and circumstances occurring after the date of the report.

2. When an accountant examines a projection, the accountant's opinion regarding the assumptions should be conditioned on the hypothetical assumptions; that is, the accountant should express an opinion on whether the assumptions provide a reasonable basis for the projection given the hypothetical assumptions. Also, the report should include a separate paragraph that describes the limitations on the usefulness of the presentation.

Exhibit 19--Standard Report on an Examination of a Projection That Does Not Contain a Range

We have examined the accompanying projected balance sheet, statements of income, retained earnings, and cash flows of XYZ Company as of December 31, 19XX, and for the year then ending. Our examination was made in accordance with standards for an examination of a projection established by the American Institute of Certified Public Accountants and, accordingly, included such procedures as we considered necessary to evaluate both the assumptions used by management and the preparation and presentation of the projection.

The accompanying projection and this report were prepared for [state special purpose, for example, "the DEF National for the purpose of negotiating a loan to expand XYZ Company's plant,"] and should not be used for any other purpose.

In our opinion, the accompanying projection is presented in conformity with guidelines for presentation of a projection established by the American Institute of Certified Public Accountants, and the underlying assumptions provide a reasonable basis for management's projection [describe the hypothetical assumption, for example, "assuming the granting of the requested loan to expand XYZ Company's plant as described in the summary of significant assumptions."]. However, even if [describe hypothetical assumption, for example, "the loan is granted and the plant is expanded,"] there will usually be differences between the projected and actual results, because events and circumstances frequently do not occur as expected, and those differences may be material. We have no responsibility to update this report for events and circumstances occurring after the date of this report.

Exhibit 20--Standard Report on an Examination of a Forecast That Does Not Contain a Range

We have examined the accompanying forecasted balance sheet, statements of income, retained earnings, and cash flows of XYZ Company as of December 31, 19XX, and for the year then ending. Our examination was made in accordance with standards for an examination of a forecast established by the American Institute of Certified Public Accountants and, accordingly, included such procedures as we considered necessary to evaluate both the assumptions used by management and the preparation and presentation of the forecast.

In our opinion, the accompanying forecast is presented in conformity with guidelines for presentation of a forecast established by the American Institute of Certified Public Accountants, and the underlying assumptions provide a reasonable basis for management's forecast. However, there will usually be differences between the forecasted and actual results, because events and circumstances frequently do not occur as expected, and those differences may be material. We have no responsibility to update this report for events and circumstances occurring after the date of this report.

3. When the prospective financial statements contain a range, the accountant's standard report should also include a separate paragraph that states that the responsible party has elected to portray the expected results of one or more assumptions as a range.

> Exhibit 21--Separate Paragraph for a Forecast That Contains a Range
>
> As described in the summary of significant assumptions, management of XYZ Company has elected to portray forecasted (describe financial statement element or elements for which the expected results of one or more assumptions fall within a range, and identify assumptions expected to fall within a range, for example, "revenue at the amounts of $X,XXX and $Y,YYY, which is predicated upon occupancy rates of XX percent and YY percent of available apartments"), rather than as a single point estimate. Accordingly, the accompanying forecast presents forecasted financial position, results of operations and cash flows (describe one or more assumptions expected to fall within a range, for example, "at such occupancy rates."). However, there is no assurance that the actual results will fall within the range of (describe one or more assumptions expected to fall within a range; for example, "occupancy rates") presented.

4. Date--The date of completion of the accountant's examination procedures should be used as the date of the report.

D. Modifications to the Accountant's Opinion

1. Qualified Opinion--In a qualified opinion, the accountant should state, in a separate paragraph, all the substantive reasons for modifying the opinion and describe the departure from AICPA presentation guidelines. The accountant's opinion should include the words "except" or "exception" as the qualifying language and should refer to the separate explanatory paragraph.

> Exhibit 22--Separate Paragraph and Qualifying Language for a Forecast
>
> The forecast does not disclose reasons for the significant variation in the relationship between income tax expense and pretax accounting income as required by generally accepted accounting principles.
>
> In our opinion, except for the omission of the disclosure of the reasons for the significant variation in the relationship between income tax expense and pretax accounting income as discussed in the preceding paragraph, the accompanying forecast is presented in conformity with . . .

2. Adverse Opinion--In an adverse opinion, the accountant should state, in a separate paragraph, all the substantive reasons for the adverse opinion. The accountant's opinion should state that the presentation is not in conformity with presentation guidelines and should refer to the explanatory paragraph. When applicable, the accountant's opinion paragraph should also state that, in the accountant's opinion, the assumptions do not provide a reasonable basis for the prospective financial statements.

> Exhibit 23--Adverse Opinion for a Forecast
>
> We have examined the accompanying forecasted balance sheet, statements of income, retained earnings, and cash flows of XYZ Company as of December 31, 19XX, and for the year then ending. Our examination was made in accordance with standards for an examination of a financial forecast established by the American Institute of Certified Public Accountants and, accordingly, included such procedures as we considered necessary to evaluate both the assumptions used by management and the preparation and presentation of the forecast.
>
> (continued on next page)

> As discussed under the caption "Sales" in the summary of significant forecast assumptions, the forecasted sales include, among other things, revenue from the Company's federal defense contracts continuing at the current level. The Company's present federal defense contracts will expire in March 19XX. No new contracts have been signed and no negotiations are under way for new federal defense contracts. Furthermore, the federal government has entered into contracts with another company to supply the items being manufactured under the Company's present contracts.
>
> In our opinion, the accompanying forecast is not presented in conformity with guidelines for presentation of a financial forecast established by the American Institute of Certified Public Accountants because management's assumptions, as discussed in the preceding paragraph, do not provide a reasonable basis for management's forecast. We have no responsibility to update this report for events or circumstances occurring after the date of this report.

- If the presentation, including the summary of significant assumptions, fails to disclose assumptions that, at the time, appear to be significant, the accountant should describe the assumptions in the report and issue an adverse opinion. The accountant should not examine a presentation that omits all disclosures of assumptions. Also, the accountant should not examine a financial projection that omits (1) an identification of the hypothetical assumptions or (2) a description of the limitations on the usefulness of the presentation.

3. Disclaimer of Opinion--In a disclaimer of opinion, the accountant's report should indicate, in a separate paragraph, the respects in which the examination did not comply with standards for an examination. The accountant should state that the scope of the examination was not sufficient to enable an opinion to be expressed concerning the presentation or the underlying assumptions, and the accountant's disclaimer of opinion should include a direct reference to the explanatory paragraph.

> <u>Exhibit 24</u>--Disclaimer of Opinion
>
> We have examined the accompanying forecasted balance sheet, statements of income, retained earnings, and cash flows of XYZ company as of December 31, 19XX, and for the year then ending. Except as explained in the following paragraph, our examination was made in accordance with standards for an examination of a financial forecast established by the American Institute of Certified Public Accountants and, accordingly, included such procedures as we considered necessary to evaluate both the assumptions used by management and the preparation and presentation of the forecast.
>
> As discussed under the caption "Income From Investee" in the summary of significant forecast assumptions, the forecast includes income from an equity investee constituting 23 percent of forecasted net income, which is management's estimate of the Company's share of the investee's income to be accrued for 19XX. The investee has not prepared a forecast for the year ending December 31, 19XX, and we were therefore unable to obtain suitable support for this assumption.
>
> Because, as described in the preceding paragraph, we are unable to evaluate management's assumption regarding income from an equity investee and other assumptions that depend thereon, we express no opinion concerning the presentation of or the assumptions underlying the accompanying forecast. We have no responsibility to update this report for events and circumstances occurring after the date of this report.

- When there is a <u>scope limitation</u> and the accountant <u>also</u> believes there are <u>material departures</u> from the presentation guidelines, those departures should be described in the accountant's report.

E. Other Modifications to the Standard Examination Report

1. Emphasis of a Matter--In some circumstances, the accountant may wish to emphasize a matter regarding the prospective financial statements but nevertheless intends to issue an unqualified opinion. The accountant may present other information and comments the accountant wishes to include, such as explanatory comments or other informative material, in a separate paragraph of the report.

2. Evaluation Based in Part on a Report of Another Accountant--When the principal accountant decides to refer to the report of another accountant as a basis, in part, for the principal accountant's own opinion, the principal accountant should disclose that fact in stating the scope of the examination and should refer to the report of the other accountant in expressing the opinion. Such a reference indicates the division of responsibility for the performance of the examination.

3. Reporting When the Examination Is Part of a Larger Engagement--When the accountant's examination of prospective financial statements is part of a larger engagement, for example, a financial feasibility study or business acquisition study, it is appropriate to expand the report on the examination of the prospective financial statements to describe the entire engagement.

V. Applying Agreed-Upon Procedures to Prospective Financial Statements

A. General Provisions

1. An accountant may accept an engagement to apply agreed-upon procedures to prospective financial statements provided that (a) the specified users involved have participated in establishing the nature and scope of the engagement and take responsibility for the adequacy of the procedures to be performed, (b) distribution of the report is to be to the specified users involved, and (c) the prospective financial statements include a summary of significant assumptions.

2. The accountant's procedures generally may be as limited or extensive as the specified users desire, as long as the specified users take responsibility for their adequacy. However, mere reading of prospective financial statements does not constitute a procedure sufficient to permit an accountant to report on the results of applying agreed-upon procedures to such statements.

3. To satisfy the requirement that the specified users involved participate in establishing the nature and scope of the engagements, the accountant ordinarily should meet with the specified users involved to discuss the procedures to be followed. This discussion may include describing, to the specified users, procedures that are frequently followed in similar types of engagements. Sometimes the accountant may not be able to discuss the procedures directly with all the specified users who will receive the report. In these circumstances, the accountant may satisfy the above requirement by applying one of the following or similar procedures:

   a. Discuss the applicable procedures with appropriate representatives of the users involved, such as legal counsel or a trustee.

   b. Review relevant correspondence from the specified users.

   c. Compare the procedures to be applied to written requirements.

   d. Distribute a draft of the report or a copy of the client's engagement letter to the users involved.

B. Working Papers--The accountant's working papers ordinarily should indicate that (1) the work was adequately planned and supervised, and (2) the agreed-upon procedures were performed as a basis for the report.

C. Reports on the Results of Applying Agreed-Upon Procedures

1. The accountant's report on the results of applying agreed-upon procedures should include the following:

a. Indicate the prospective financial statements covered by the accountant's report.

b. Indicate that the report is limited in use, intended solely for the specified users, and should not be used by others.

c. Enumerate the procedures performed and refer to conformity with the arrangements made with the specified users.

d. If the agreed-upon procedures are less than those performed in an examination, state that the work performed was less in scope than an examination of prospective financial statements in accordance with AICPA standards and disclaim an opinion on whether the presentation of the prospective financial statements is in conformity with AICPA presentation guidelines and on whether the underlying assumptions provide a reasonable basis for the forecast, or a reasonable basis for the projection given the hypothetical assumptions.

e. State the accountant's findings.

f. Include a caveat that the prospective results may not be achieved.

g. State that the accountant assumes no responsibility to update the report for events and circumstances occurring after the date of the report.

2. Also, the accountant may wish to state in the report that he or she makes no representation about the sufficiency of the procedures for the specified users' purposes.

3. When the accountant reports on the results of applying agreed-upon procedures, the accountant should not express any form of negative assurance on the prospective financial statements taken as a whole.

PART THREE: ATTESTATION STANDARDS

I. Codification of Statements on Standards for Attestation Engagements (SSAE No. 1)

A. Applicability--This Statement provides that an accountant who is engaged to issue or does issue a written communication that expresses a conclusion about the reliability of a written assertion that is the responsibility of another party should either examine, review, or apply agreed-upon procedures to the assertion in accordance with this Statement. This statement was originally issued in three separate unnumbered releases and later codified and combined as SSAE No. 1.

B. Definition--An attest engagement is one in which a practitioner is engaged to issue or does issue a written communication that expresses a conclusion about the reliability of a written assertion that is the responsibility of another party.

1. The following are not attest engagements:

   a. Management consulting services.

   b. Client advocacy engagements (e.g., representing a client before the IRS).

   c. Tax return preparation and tax advice services.

   d. Compilations of financial statements.

   e. Engagements to assist a client in the preparation of information other than financial statements.

   f. Engagements to testify as an expert witness.

   g. Where a practitioner is engaged to provide expert opinion on certain points of principle (e.g., tax law, GAAP) applied to a specific factual situation, but where the practitioner does not undertake to provide any assurance on the facts provided by the other party.

2. An attest engagement may be part of a larger engagement, for example, a feasibility study or business acquisition study that includes an examination of prospective financial information. In such circumstances, these standards apply only to the attest portion of the engagement.

II. The Attestation Standards (AT 100, SSAE No. 1)

The attestation standards and related interpretive commentary are intended to provide guidance that will enhance both consistency and quality in the performance of attestation engagements. The attestation standards are a natural extension of the ten generally accepted auditing standards; however, they are much broader in scope and apply to a growing array of attest engagements, such as reports on internal control structure, descriptions of computer software, and on compliance with statutory, regulatory, and contractual requirements. The attestation standards do not supersede any existing standards. The Accounting and Review Services Committee, Auditing Standards Board, and Management Advisory Services Executive Committee are the senior technical committees of the Institute designated to issue enforceable standards under the AICPA's Code of Professional Conduct concerning attestation services in their respective areas of responsibility.

A. General Standards

1. The engagement shall be performed by a practitioner or practitioners having adequate technical training and proficiency in the attest function.

   - The level and type of training and proficiency required to provide attest services is different from the training and proficiency required to prepare an assertion. Attest services are analytical, critical, investigative, and concerned with the basis and support for the assertions. Proficiency as an attester begins with formal education and extends into subsequent experience.

2. The engagements shall be performed by a practitioner or practitioners having adequate knowledge in the subject matter of the assertion.

   - The practitioner may obtain adequate knowledge through formal or continuing education or through self-study; however, the practitioner does not have to personally acquire all the knowledge necessary in the subject matter to be qualified to judge an assertion's reliability. The practitioner may use specialists, provided that the practitioner has enough knowledge of the subject matter (1) to communicate to the specialist the objectives of the work, and (2) to evaluate the specialist's work to determine if the objectives were achieved.

3. The practitioner shall perform an engagement only if there is reason to believe that the following two conditions exist:

   a. The assertion is capable of evaluation against reasonable criteria that either has been established by a recognized body or is stated in the presentation of the assertion in a sufficiently clear and comprehensive manner for a knowledgeable reader to be able to understand.

      - There must be reasonable criteria against which an assertion can be evaluated. Reasonable criteria is both relevant and reliable. Criteria promulgated by a body designated by Council under the AICPA Code of Professional Conduct is considered reasonable criteria. Criteria issued by regulatory agencies and other bodies of experts that follow due-process procedures is also considered reasonable. On the other hand, criteria issued by industry associations and other groups should be critically examined for reasonableness. Such criteria should be clearly described in the presentation.

   b. The assertion is capable of reasonably consistent estimation or measurement using such criteria.

      - Competent persons using the same or similar measurement and disclosure criteria ordinarily should be able to obtain materially similar estimates or measurements. However, competent persons will not always reach the same conclusions because (a) such estimates and measurements often require the exercise of considerable professional judgment, and (b) a slightly different evaluation of the facts could yield a significant difference in the presentation of a particular assertion. An assertion estimated or measured using criteria promulgated by a body designated by Council under the AICPA Code of Professional Conduct is considered, by definition, to be capable of reasonably consistent estimation or measurement.

4. In all matters relating to the engagement, an independence in mental attitude shall be maintained by the practitioner or practitioners.

   - Practitioners should be independent in <u>appearance</u> as well as in <u>fact</u>. Independence implies a judicial impartiality.

5. Due professional care shall be exercised in the performance of the engagement.

   - Exercise of due care requires critical review at every level of supervision of the work done and the judgment exercised by those assisting in the engagement, including the preparation of the report. The practitioner is understood as possessing the degree of skill commonly possessed by others in the same employment.

B. <u>Standards of Field Work</u>

1. The work shall be adequately planned and assistants, if any, shall be properly supervised.

   a. Factors to be considered by the practitioner in planning an attest engagement include (1) the presentation criteria to be used, (2) the anticipated level of attestation risk related to the assertions on which the practitioner will report, (3) preliminary judgments about materiality levels for attest purposes, (4) the items within a presentation of assertions that are likely to require revision or adjustment, (5) conditions that may require extension or modification of attest procedures, and (6) the nature of the report expected to be issued.

b. The work performed by each assistant should be reviewed to determine if it was adequately performed and to evaluate whether the results are consistent with the conclusions to be presented in the practitioner's report.

2. Sufficient evidence shall be obtained to provide a reasonable basis for the conclusion that is expressed in the report.

a. The level of evidence deemed "sufficient" will depend on the nature of the attest services being provided. An "examination" will require more evidence than a "review." Furthermore, different types of evidence will generally be required to satisfy the "sufficiency" requirement. An examination engagement will generally include search and verification procedures, whereas the procedures used in a review engagement generally will be limited to inquiries and analytical procedures.

b. As a general rule, the Statement establishes the following hierarchy of evidential matter:

(1) Evidence obtained from independent sources outside an entity provides greater assurance of an assertion's reliability than evidence secured solely from within the entity.

(2) Information obtained from the independent attester's direct personal knowledge (such as through physical examination, observation, computation, operating tests, or inspection) is more persuasive than information obtained indirectly.

(3) Assertions developed under effective internal controls are more reliable than those developed in the absence of internal controls.

C. Standards of Reporting

1. The report shall identify the assertion being reported on and state the character of the engagement.

a. The statement of the character of an attest engagement that is designed to result in a general-distribution report (i.e., an examination or a review) includes two elements: (1) a description of the nature and scope of the work performed, and (2) a reference to the professional standards governing the engagement.

b. The statement of the character of an attest engagement in which the practitioner applies agreed-upon procedures should refer to conformity with the arrangements made with the specified user(s). Such engagements are designed to accommodate the specific needs of the parties in interest and should be described by identifying the procedures agreed upon by such parties.

2. The report shall state the practitioner's conclusion about whether the assertion is presented in conformity with the established or stated criteria against which it was measured.

a. The practitioner should consider the idea of materiality in applying this standard. Materiality is determined by the relative size of a misstated or omitted fact, rather than by its absolute amount. Materiality would consider whether a reasonable person relying on the presentation of assertions would be influenced by the inclusion or correction of an individual assertion.

b. General-distribution attest reports should be limited to two levels of assurance: one based on a reduction of attestation risk to an appropriately low level (an "examination") and the other based on a reduction of attestation risk to a moderate level (a "review"). See III., below.

(1) Examinations--Practitioner's conclusion should be expressed in the form of a positive opinion.

(2) Reviews--Conclusion should be expressed in the form of negative assurance.

3. The report shall state all of the practitioner's significant reservations about the engagement and the presentation of the assertion.

   a. "Reservations about the engagement" refers to any unresolved problem the practitioner had in complying with the standards and guidance applicable to attestation services. An unqualified conclusion should not be expressed if the practitioner has been unable to apply all the procedures considered necessary or, if applicable, those procedures agreed-upon with the user(s).

   b. Restrictions on the scope of the engagement, whether imposed by the client or by other circumstances, may require the practitioner to qualify the report, to disclaim any assurance, or to withdraw from the engagement. The decision as to the appropriate course of action depends on an assessment of the effect of the omitted procedure(s) on the practitioner's ability to express assurance on the presentation of assertions.

      - When restrictions that significantly limit the scope of the engagement are imposed by the client, the practitioner generally should disclaim any assurance on the presentation of assertions or withdraw from the engagement.

4. The report on an engagement to evaluate an assertion that has been prepared in conformity with agreed-upon criteria or on an engagement to apply agreed-upon procedures should contain a statement limiting its use to the parties who have agreed upon such criteria or procedures.

5. Levels of Assurance--This Statement provides for three types of attestation engagements: examinations, reviews, and applications of agreed-upon procedures. Reports on examination or review engagements may be distributed to the general public. Reports on agreed-upon procedures should be restricted to the parties who have agreed to the specified procedures.

6. Examinations

   a. Examinations represent the highest level of assurance. A report on an examination engagement should clearly state whether in the practitioner's opinion, the presentation of assertions is presented in conformity with established or stated criteria.

   b. A report presenting a positive opinion on a presentation of assertions taken as a whole may nevertheless be qualified or modified for some aspect of the presentation or the engagement. In addition, such reports may emphasize a matter relating to the attest engagement or the presentation of assertions.

Exhibit 25--Report on Examination of a Presentation of Assertions

We have examined the accompanying (identify the presentation of assertions--for example, Statement of Investment Performance Statistics of XYZ Fund for the year ended December 31, 19X1). Our examination was made in accordance with standards established by the American Institute of Certified Public Accountants and, accordingly, included such procedures as we considered necessary in the circumstances.

(continued on next page)

(Additional paragraph[s] may be added to emphasize certain matters relating to the attest engagement or the presentation of assertions.)

In our opinion, the (identify the presentation of assertions--for example, Statement of Investment Performance Statistics) referred to above presents (identify the assertion--for example, the investment performance of XYZ Fund for the year ended December 31, 19X1) in conformity with (identify established or stated criteria--for example, the measurement and disclosure criteria set forth in Note 1).

6. Reviews

a. A review report should provide limited assurance. That is, the practitioner's conclusion should state whether any information came to the practitioner's attention on the basis of the work performed that indicates that the assertions are not presented in all material respects in conformity with established or stated criteria. If the assertions are not modified to correct for any such information, the incorrect information should be described in the practitioner's report.

b. A limited assurance report should do the following: (1) indicate that the work performed was less in scope than an examination, (2) disclaim a positive opinion on the assertions, and (3) contain a statement of limitations on the use of the report when it has been prepared in conformity with specified criteria that have been agreed upon by the asserter and user(s) because it is intended solely for specified parties.

Exhibit 26--Review Report Expressing Limited Assurance

We have reviewed the accompanying (identify the presentation of assertions--for example, Statement of Investment Performance Statistics of XYZ Fund for the year ended December 31, 19X1). Our review was conducted in accordance with Statements on Standards for Accounting and Review Services issued by the American Institute of Certified Public Accountants.

A review is substantially less in scope than an examination, the objective of which is the expression of an opinion on the (identify the presentation of assertions--for example, Statement of Investment Performance Statistics). Accordingly, we do not express such an opinion.

(Additional paragraph[s] may be added to emphasize certain matters relating to the attest engagement or the presentation of assertions.)

Based on our review, nothing came to our attention that caused us to believe that the accompanying (identify the presentation of assertions--for example, Statement of Investment Performance Statistics) is not presented in conformity with (identify the established or stated criteria--for example, the measurement and disclosure criteria set forth in Note 1).

7. Agreed-Upon Procedures

a. Reports on engagements consisting of applying agreed-upon procedures to a presentation of assertions should be in the form of a summary of findings, negative assurance, or both. Furthermore, the practitioner's report should contain the following:

(1) A statement of limitations on the use of the report because it is intended solely for the use of specified parties (see the fourth reporting standard).

(2) A summary or list of the specific procedures performed (or reference thereto) to notify the reader what the reported findings or negative assurances are based on.

b. A practitioner's report on the application of agreed-upon procedures ordinarily should also indicate that the work performed was less in scope than an examination and disclaim a positive opinion on the assertions.

c. The level of assurance provided in a report on the application of agreed-upon procedures depends on the nature and scope of the practitioner's procedures as agreed upon with the specified parties to whom the report is restricted. Furthermore, such parties must understand that they take responsibility for the adequacy of the attest procedures (and, therefore, the amount of assurance provided) for their purpose.

<u>Exhibit 27</u>--Report on Agreed-Upon Procedures

To ABC, Inc., and XYZ Fund

We have applied the procedures enumerated below to the accompanying (identify the presentation of assertions--for example, Statement of Investment Performance Statistics of XYZ Fund for the year ended December 31, 19X1). These procedures, which were agreed to by ABC, Inc., and XYZ Fund, were performed solely to assist you in evaluating (identify the assertion--for example, the investment performance of XYZ Fund). This report is intended solely for your information and should not be used by those who did not participate in determining the procedures.

(Include paragraph to enumerate procedures and findings.)

These agreed-upon procedures are substantially less in scope than an examination, the objective of which is the expression of an opinion on the (identify the presentation of assertions--for example, Statement of Investment Performance Statistics). Accordingly, we do not express such an opinion.

Based on the application of the procedures referred to above, nothing came to our attention that caused us to believe that the accompanying (identify the presentation of assertions--for example, Statement of Investment Performance Statistics) is not presented in conformity with (identify the established, stated, or agreed-upon criteria--for example, the measurement and disclosure criteria set forth in Note 1). Had we performed additional procedures, or had we made an examination of the (identify the presentation of assertions--for example, Statement of Investment Performance Statistics), other matters might have come to our attention that would have been reported to you.

III. Pro Forma Financial Information (AT 300, <u>SSAE No. 1</u>)

This Statement gives guidance to accountants engaged to examine or review and report on pro forma financial information.

Pro forma financial information is used to show what the significant effects on historical financial information <u>might have</u> been if a consummated or proposed transaction or event had occurred at an earlier date. Pro forma financial information is generally used to show the effects of transactions such as a business combination, change in capitalization, the disposition of a significant portion of a business, a change in the form of business organization, or the proposed sale of securities and the application of proceeds.

Pro forma adjustments should be based on management's assumptions and should consider all significant effects directly attributable to the transaction or event. Pro forma information should be labeled as such to distinguish it from historical financial information. The transaction or event reflected in the pro forma information should be described, as well as the source of the historical information upon which it is based, the significant assumptions used, and any significant uncertainties about those assumptions. The presentation should indicate that the pro forma information should be read in conjunction with the historical data. The presentation should also state that the pro forma financial information does not necessarily indicate the results that would have been attained had the transaction actually taken place earlier.

When pro forma financial information is presented outside the basic financial statements but within the same document, and the accountant is not engaged to report on the pro forma financial information, the accountant's responsibilities are described in SAS 8, *Other Information in Documents Containing Audited Financial Statements* (AU 550), and in SAS 37, *Filings Under Federal Securities Statutes* (AU 711).

A. Requirements--An accountant may agree to report on an examination or a review of pro forma financial information if the following conditions are met:

   1. The document containing pro forma information includes, or incorporates by reference, complete historical financial statements of the entity for the most recent year, or for the preceding year if financial statements for the most recent year are not yet available. Also, interim pro forma financial information must include, or incorporate by reference, historical interim financial information, which may be condensed, for that period. In the case of a business combination, the document should include (or incorporate by reference) the appropriate historical financial information for the significant constituent parts of the combined entity.

   2. The historical financial statements of the entity (or, in the case of a business combination, of each significant constituent part of the combined entity) on which the pro forma financial information is based must have been audited or reviewed. The accountant's attestation risk relating to the pro forma financial information is affected by the scope of the engagement providing the accountant with assurance about the underlying historical financial information to which the pro forma adjustments are applied. Therefore, the level of assurance given by the accountant on the pro forma financial information should be limited to the level of assurance provided on the historical financial statements, or, in the case of a business combination, the lowest level of assurance provided on the underlying historical financial statements of any significant constituent part of the combined entity. For example, if the underlying historical financial statements of each significant constituent part of the combined entity have been audited at year-end and reviewed at an interim date, the accountant may perform an examination or a review of the pro forma financial information at year-end, but is limited to performing a review of the pro forma financial information at the interim date. Finally, when there is a business combination, the accountant should have an appropriate level of knowledge of the accounting and financial reporting practices of each significant constituent part of the combined entity.

B. Examination Objective--The objective of the accountant's examination procedures applied to pro forma financial information is to provide reasonable assurance as to whether the following exists:

   1. Management's assumptions provide a reasonable basis for presenting the significant effects directly attributable to the underlying transaction or event.

   2. The related pro forma adjustments give appropriate effect to those assumptions.

   3. The pro forma column reflects the proper application of those adjustments to the historical financial statements.

C. Review Objective--The objective of the accountant's review procedures is to provide negative assurance as to whether any information came to the auditor's attention to cause a belief of the following:

   1. Management's assumptions do not provide a reasonable basis for presenting the significant effects directly attributable to the transaction or event.

2. The related pro forma adjustments do not give appropriate effect to those assumptions.

3. The related pro forma column does not reflect the proper application of those adjustments to the historical financial statements.

D. Procedures--The procedures the accountant should apply to the assumptions and pro forma adjustments for either an examination or a review engagement, other than those applied to the historical financial statements, are as follows:

1. Obtain an understanding of the underlying transaction or event, for example, by reading relevant contracts and minutes of meetings of the board of directors, and by making inquiries of appropriate officials of the entity or, in some cases, of the entity acquired or to be acquired.

2. Obtain a level of knowledge of each significant constituent part of the combined entity in a business combination that will enable the accountant to perform the required procedures. Procedures to obtain this knowledge may include communicating with other accountants who have audited or reviewed the historical financial information on which the pro forma financial information is based. Matters that may be considered include accounting principles and financial reporting practices followed, transactions between the entities, and material contingencies.

3. Discuss with management their assumptions regarding the effects of the transaction or event.

4. Evaluate whether pro forma adjustments are included for all significant effects directly attributable to the transaction or event.

5. Obtain sufficient evidence in support of such adjustments. The evidence required to support the level of assurance given is a matter of professional judgment. The accountant typically would obtain more evidence in an examination engagement than in a review engagement. Examples of evidence that the accountant might consider obtaining are purchase, merger, or exchange agreements; appraisal reports; debt agreements; employment agreements; actions of the board of directors; and existing or proposed legislation or regulatory actions.

6. Evaluate whether management's assumptions that underlie the pro forma adjustments are presented in a sufficiently clear and comprehensive manner. Also, evaluate whether the pro forma adjustments are consistent with each other and with the data used to develop them.

7. Determine that computations of pro forma adjustments are mathematically correct, and that the pro forma column reflects the proper application of those adjustments to the historical financial statements.

8. Obtain written representations from management concerning the following:

    a. Responsibility for the assumptions used in determining the pro forma adjustments.

    b. Belief that the assumptions provide a reasonable basis for presenting all the significant effects directly attributable to the transaction or event.

    c. Belief that the related pro forma adjustments give appropriate effect to those assumptions.

    d. Belief that the pro forma column reflects the proper application of those adjustments to the historical financial statements.

    e. Belief that the significant effects directly attributable to the transaction or event are appropriately disclosed in the pro forma financial information.

9. Read the pro forma financial information and evaluate whether:

   a. The underlying transaction or event, the pro forma adjustments, the significant assumptions, and the significant uncertainties, if any, about those assumptions have been appropriately described.

   b. The source of the historical financial information on which the pro forma financial information is based has been appropriately identified.

E. Report--The accountant's report on pro forma financial information should be dated as of the completion of the appropriate procedures. The report on pro forma financial information may be added to the accountant's report on historical financial information, or it may appear separately. If the reports are combined and the date of completion of the procedures for the examination or review of the pro forma financial information is after the date of completion of the field work for the audit or review of the historical financial information, the combined report should be dual-dated.

The report on pro forma financial information should include the following:

1. An identification of the pro forma financial information.

2. A reference to the financial statements from which the historical financial information is derived and a statement as to whether such financial statements were audited or reviewed.

3. A statement that the examination or review was made in accordance with standards established or, "Statements on Standards for Accounting and Review Services issued", respectively, by the American Institute of Certified Public Accountants. If a review is performed, the report should include the following statement: "A review is substantially less in scope than an examination, the objective of which is the expression of an opinion on the pro forma financial information. Accordingly, we do not express such an opinion."

4. A separate paragraph explaining the objective of pro forma financial information and its limitations.

5. If an examination of pro forma financial information has been performed, the report should include the accountant's opinion as to whether management's assumptions provide a reasonable basis for presenting the significant effects directly attributable to the transaction or event, whether the related pro forma adjustments give appropriate effect to those assumptions, and whether the pro forma column reflects the proper application of those adjustments to the historical financial statements.

6. If a review of pro forma financial information has been performed, the report should include the accountant's conclusion as to whether any information came to the accountant's attention to cause a belief that management's assumptions do not provide a reasonable basis for presenting the significant effects directly attributable to the transaction or event, or that the related pro forma adjustments do not give appropriate effect to those assumptions, or that the pro forma column does not reflect the proper application of those adjustments to the historical financial statements.

Since a pooling-of-interests business combination is accounted for by combining historical amounts retroactively, pro forma adjustments for a proposed transaction generally affect only the equity section of the pro forma condensed balance sheet. Also, due to the requirements of APB Opinion No. 16, *Business Combinations*, a pooling-of-interests would not ordinarily involve a choice of assumptions by management. Accordingly, a report on a proposed pooling transaction need not address management's assumptions unless the pro forma financial information includes adjustments to conform the accounting principles of the combining entities.

Restrictions on the scope of the engagement, significant uncertainties about the assumptions that could materially affect the transaction or event, reservations about the propriety of the assumptions and the conformity of the presentation with those assumptions (including inadequate disclosure of significant matters), or other reservations may require the accountant to qualify the opinion, render an adverse opinion, disclaim an opinion or withdraw from the engagement. The accountant should disclose all substantive reasons for any report modifications. Uncertainty as to whether the transaction or event will be consummated would not ordinarily require a report modification.

Exhibit 28--Example of a Report on Examination of Pro Forma Financial Information

We have examined the pro forma adjustments reflecting the transaction (or event) described in Note 1 and the application of those adjustments to the historical amounts in the assembly of the accompanying pro forma condensed balance sheet of X Company as of December 31, 19X1, and the pro forma condensed statement of income for the year then ended. The historical condensed financial statements are derived from the historical financial statements of X Company, which were audited by us, and of Y Company, which were audited by other accountants, appearing elsewhere herein (or incorporated by reference). Such pro forma adjustments are based upon management's assumptions described in Note 2. Our examination was made in accordance with standards established by the American Institute of Certified Public Accountants and, accordingly, included such procedures as we considered necessary under the circumstances.

The objective of this pro forma financial information is to show what the significant effects on the historical financial information might have been had the transaction (or event) occurred at an earlier date. However, the pro forma condensed financial statements do not necessarily indicate the results of operations or related effects on financial position that would have been attained had the above-mentioned transaction (or event) occurred earlier.

(Additional paragraph[s] may be added to emphasize certain matters relating to the attest engagement.)

In our opinion, management's assumptions provide a reasonable basis for presenting the significant efforts directly attributable to the above-mentioned transaction (or event) described in Note 1, the related pro forma adjustments give appropriate effect to those assumptions, and the pro forma column reflects the proper application of those adjustments to the historical financial statement amounts in the pro forma condensed balance sheet as of December 31, 19X1, and the pro forma condensed statement of income for the year then ended.

Exhibit 29--Example of Report on Review of Pro Forma Financial Information

We have reviewed the pro forma adjustments reflecting the transaction (or event) described in Note 1 and the application of those adjustments to the historical amounts in the assembly of the accompanying pro forma condensed balance sheet of X Company as of March 31, 19X2, and the pro forma condensed statement of income for the three months then ended. These historical condensed financial statements are derived from the historical unaudited financial statements of X Company, which were reviewed by us, and of Y Company, which were reviewed by other accountants, appearing elsewhere herein (or incorporated by reference). Such pro forma adjustments are based on management's assumptions as described in Note 2. Our review was conducted in accordance with Statements on Standards for Accounting and Review Services issued by the American Institute of Certified Public Accountants.

A review is substantially less in scope than an examination, the objective of which is the expression of an opinion on management's assumptions, the pro forma adjustments and the application of those adjustments to historical financial information. Accordingly, we do not express such an opinion.

(continued on next page)

> The objective of this pro forma financial information is to show what the significant effects on the historical information might have been had the transaction (or event) occurred at an earlier date. However, the pro forma condensed financial statements do not necessarily indicate the results of operations or related effects on financial position that would have been attained had the above-mentioned transaction (or event) occurred earlier.
>
> (Additional paragraph[s] may be added to emphasize certain matters relating to the attest engagement.)
>
> Based on our review, nothing came to our attention that caused us to believe that management's assumptions do not provide a reasonable basis for presenting the significant effects directly attributable to the above-mentioned transaction (or event) described in Note 1, that the related pro forma adjustments do not give appropriate effect to those assumptions, or that the pro forma column does not reflect the proper application of those adjustments to the historical financial statement amounts in the pro forma condensed balance sheet as of March 31, 19X2, and the pro forma condensed statement of income for the three months then ended.

IV. Reporting on Internal Control Structure Over Financial Reporting (AT400, SSAE No. 2)

This Statement supersedes Statement on Auditing Standards No. 30, *Reporting on Internal Accounting Control*, and provides guidance to accountants engaged to examine and report on management's written assertion about the effectiveness of an entity's internal control structure over financial reporting as of a point in time. Detailed coverage of this Statement is included in Chapter 41.

V. Compliance Attestation (AT 500, SSAE No. 3)

A. Applicability

1. SSAE No. 3 provides guidance for engagements related to management's written assertion about either (a) an entity's compliance with requirements of specified laws, regulations, rules, contracts, or grants, or (b) the effectiveness of an entity's internal control structure over compliance with specified requirements. Management's assertions may relate to compliance requirements that are either financial or nonfinancial.

2. SSAE No. 3 does not supersede existing literature, therefore it does not affect engagements covered by existing literature such as SASs or Governmental Auditing Standards.

3. SSAE No. 3 is not applicable unless management presents a written assertion.

B. Appropriate Engagements--Practitioners may be engaged to perform agreed-upon procedures to assist users in evaluating management's written assertion about compliance with specified requirements and/or the effectiveness of an entity's internal control structure over compliance. Practitioners also may be engaged to examine management's written assertion about the entity's compliance with specified requirements. Practitioners should not accept engagements to perform reviews of management's assertion about an entity's compliance with specified requirements or about the effectiveness of an entity's internal control structure over compliance.

1. Practitioners may perform an engagement related to management's written assertion about an entity's compliance with specified requirements or about the effectiveness of the internal control structure over compliance when the following conditions are met:

   a. Management accepts responsibility for the entity's compliance with specified requirements and the effectiveness of the entity's internal control structure over compliance.

   b. Management evaluates the entity's compliance with specified requirements or the effectiveness of the entity's internal control structure over compliance.

2. Practitioners may perform agreed-upon procedures if, in addition to the foregoing conditions, the following conditions are met:

   a. Management makes an assertion about the entity's compliance with specified requirements or the effectiveness of the entity's internal control structure over compliance. The assertion should be in a representation letter to the practitioner and also may be in a separate report that will accompany the practitioner's report.

   b. The agreed-upon procedures (1) are applied to the assertion (or its subject matter) that is capable of evaluation against reasonable criteria and (2) are expected to result in findings that are capable of reasonably consistent estimation or measurement.

3. Practitioners may perform an examination if, in addition to the general conditions, the following conditions are met:

   a. Management makes an assertion about the entity's compliance with specified requirements. If the practitioner's report is intended for general use, the assertion should be in a representation letter to the practitioner and in a separate report that will accompany the practitioner's report. If use of the practitioner's report will be restricted to those within the entity and a specified regulatory agency, the assertion might be only in a representation letter.

   b. Management's assertion is capable of evaluation against reasonable criteria that either have been established by a recognized body or are stated in the assertion in a sufficiently clear and comprehensive manner for a knowledgeable reader to understand them, and the assertion is capable of reasonably consistent estimation or measurement using such criteria.

   c. Sufficient evidential matter exists or could be developed to support management's evaluation.

C. <u>Management Responsibilities</u>--Management is responsible for ensuring that the entity complies with the requirements applicable to its activities. That responsibility includes: (1) identifying applicable compliance requirements, (2) establishing and maintaining internal control structure policies and procedures to provide reasonable assurance that the entity complies with those requirements, (3) evaluating and monitoring the entity's compliance, and (4) specifying reports that satisfy legal, regulatory, or contractual requirements.

D. <u>Agreed-Upon Procedures Engagement</u>--The objective of the practitioner's agreed-upon procedures is to present specific findings to assist users in evaluating management's assertion about an entity's compliance with specified requirements or about the effectiveness of an entity's internal control structure over compliance based on procedures agreed-upon by the users of the report.

1. In these engagements, the practitioner's procedures generally may be as limited or as extensive as the specified users desire as long as the specified users: (a) participate in establishing the procedures to be performed and (b) take responsibility for the adequacy of such procedures for their purposes.

2. Practitioners' reports on agreed-upon procedures should be in the form of procedures and findings. Practitioners should <u>not</u> provide negative assurance about whether management's assertion is fairly stated. The practitioner's report, which ordinarily should be addressed to the entity, should contain:

a. A title that includes the word independent.

b. A statement that the procedures, which were agreed to by the specified users of the report, were performed to assist the users in evaluating management's assertion about the entity's compliance to specified requirements or about the effectiveness of its internal control structure over compliance.

c. A reference to management's assertion about the entity's compliance with specified requirements, or about the effectiveness of an entity's internal control structure over compliance, including the period or point in time addressed in management's assertion.

d. A statement that the sufficiency of the procedures is solely the responsibility of the parties specifying the procedures and a disclaimer of responsibility for the sufficiency of those procedures.

e. A list of the procedures performed and related findings.

f. A statement that the work performed was less in scope than an examination of management's assertion about compliance with specified requirements or about the effectiveness of an entity's internal control structure over compliance, a disclaimer of opinion, and a statement that if additional procedures had been performed, other matters might have come to the practitioner's attention that would have been reported.

g. A statement of limitations on the use of the report because it is intended solely for the use of the specified parties.

E. Examination Engagement--The objective of the practitioner's examination procedures applied to management's assertion about an entity's compliance with specified requirements is to express an opinion about whether management's assertion is fairly stated in all material respects based on established or agreed-upon criteria. To express such an opinion, practitioners accumulate sufficient evidence in support of management's assertion about the entity's compliance with specified requirements, thereby limiting attestation risk to an appropriately low level.

1. For purposes of a compliance examination, the components of risk are defined as follows:

a. Inherent Risk--The risk that material noncompliance with specified requirements could occur, assuming there are no related internal control structure policies or procedures.

b. Control Risk--The risk that material noncompliance that could occur will not be prevented or detected on a timely basis by the entity's internal control structure policies and procedures.

c. Detection Risk--The risk that the practitioner's procedures will lead him or her to conclude that material noncompliance does not exist when, in fact, such noncompliance does exist.

2. In an examination of management's assertion about an entity's compliance with specified requirements, the practitioner's consideration of materiality is different from that in an audit of financial statements in accordance with GAAS. In an examination of management's assertion about an entity's compliance with specified requirements, the practitioner's consideration of materiality is affected by (a) the nature of management's assertion and the compliance requirements, which may or may not be quantifiable in monetary terms, (b) the nature and frequency of noncompliance identified with appropriate consideration of sampling risks, and (c) qualitative considerations, including the needs and expectations of the report's users.

3. In performing an examination engagement, practitioners should exercise due care in planning, performing, and evaluating the results of their examination procedures and the proper degree of professional skepticism to achieve reasonable assurance that material noncompliance will be detected. In these examination engagements, the practitioner should:

   a. Obtain an understanding of the specified compliance requirements.

   b. Plan the engagement.

   c. Consider relevant portions of the entity's internal control structure over compliance.

   d. Obtain sufficient evidence including testing compliance with specified requirements.

   e. Consider subsequent events.

   f. Form an opinion about whether management's assertion about the entity's compliance with specified requirements is fairly stated in all material respects based on the established or agreed-upon criteria.

4. When management presents its assertion in a separate report that will accompany the practitioner's report, the practitioner's report, which is addressed to the entity, should include:

   a. A title that includes the word independent.

   b. A reference to management's assertion about the entity's compliance with specified requirements, including the period covered by management's assertion.

   c. A statement that compliance with the requirements addressed in management's assertion is the responsibility of the entity's management and that the practitioner's responsibility is to express an opinion on management's assertion about compliance with those requirements based on the examination.

   d. A statement that the examination was made in accordance with standards established by the AICPA and included examining, on a test basis, evidence about the entity's compliance with those requirements and performing such other procedures as the practitioner considered necessary in the circumstances. Additionally, the report should include a statement that the practitioner believes the examination provides a reasonable basis for his or her opinion and a statement that the examination does not provide a legal determination on the entity's compliance.

   e. The practitioner's opinion on whether management's assertion is fairly stated, in all material respects, based on established or agreed-upon criteria.

VI. Agreed-Upon Procedures Engagements (SSAE No. 4)

This statement was issued in September 1995 to provide direction when applying agreed-upon procedures to nonfinancial information. Coverage of SSAE No. 4 is included in Chapter 41.

NOTES

CHAPTER 42—OTHER PROFESSIONAL SERVICES

Problem 42-1 MULTIPLE CHOICE QUESTIONS (50 to 60 minutes)

1. Blue Co., a privately held entity, asked its tax accountant, Cook, a CPA in public practice, to reproduce Blue's internally prepared interim financial statements on Cook's microcomputer when Cook prepared Blue's quarterly tax return. Cook should **not** submit these financial statements to Blue unless, as a minimum, Cook complies with the provisions of
a. Statements on Responsibilities in Tax Practice.
b. Statements on Standards for Accounting and Review Services.
c. Statements on Responsibilities in Unaudited Financial Services.
d. Statements on Standards for Attestation Engagements. (5/91, Aud., #58, 0417)

1A. North Co., a privately held entity, asked its tax accountant, King, a CPA in public practice, to generate North's interim financial statements on King's microcomputer when King prepared North's quarterly tax return. King should **not** submit these financial statements to North unless, as a minimum, King complies with the provisions of
a. Statements on Standards for Accounting and Review Services.
b. Statements on Standards for Unaudited Financial Services.
c. Statements on Standards for Consulting Services.
d. Statements on Standards for Attestation Engagements. (5/94, Aud., #9, 4674)

2. Which of the following accounting services may an accountant perform **without** being required to issue a compilation or review report under the Statements on Standards for Accounting and Review Services?

I. Preparing a working trial balance.
II. Preparing standard monthly journal entries.

a. I only.
b. II only.
c. Both I and II.
d. Neither I nor II. (11/92, Aud., #5, 2939)

3. The authoritative body designated to promulgate standards concerning an accountant's association with unaudited financial statements of an entity that is **not** required to file financial statements with an agency regulating the issuance of the entity's securities is the
a. Financial Accounting Standards Board.
b. General Accounting Office.
c. Accounting and Review Services Committee.
d. Auditing Standards Board.
(11/90, Aud., #40, 0006)

4. Which of the following statements is correct concerning both an engagement to compile and an engagement to review a nonpublic entity's financial statements?
a. The accountant does **not** contemplate obtaining an understanding of the internal control structure.
b. The accountant must be independent in fact and appearance.
c. The accountant expresses **no** assurance on the financial statements.
d. The accountant should obtain a written management representation letter.
(11/91, Aud., #59, 2327)

4A. A CPA is required to comply with the provisions of *Statements on Standards for Accounting and Review Services* when

	Processing financial data for clients of other CPA firms	Consulting on accounting matters
a.	Yes	Yes
b.	Yes	No
c.	No	Yes
d.	No	No

(11/93, Aud., #12, 4249)

4B. Statements on Standards for Accounting and Review Services (SSARS) require an accountant to report when the accountant has
a. Typed client-prepared financial statements, without modification, as an accommodation to the client.
b. Provided a client with a financial statement format that does **not** include dollar amounts, to be used by the client in preparing financial statements.
c. Proposed correcting journal entries to be recorded by the client that change client-prepared financial statements.
d. Generated, through the use of computer software, financial statements prepared in accordance with a comprehensive basis of accounting other than GAAP.
(11/94, Aud., #22, 5095)

5. Which of the following procedures is **not** usually performed by the accountant during a review engagement of a nonpublic entity?

a. Inquiring about actions taken at meetings of the board of directors that may affect the financial statements.
b. Issuing a report stating that the review was performed in accordance with standards established by the AICPA.
c. Reading the financial statements to consider whether they conform with generally accepted accounting principles.
d. Communicating any material weaknesses discovered during the consideration of the internal control structure.

(11/92, Aud., #45, 2979)

6. When an accountant performs more than one level of service (for example, a compilation and a review, or a compilation and an audit) concerning the financial statements of a nonpublic entity, the accountant generally should issue the report that is appropriate for

a. The lowest level of service rendered.
b. The highest level of service rendered.
c. A compilation engagement.
d. A review engagement. (11/89, Aud., #5, 0427)

6A. When providing limited assurance that the financial statements of a nonpublic entity require **no** material modifications to be in accordance with generally accepted accounting principles, the accountant should

a. Assess the risk that a material misstatement could occur in a financial statement assertion.
b. Confirm with the entity's lawyer that material loss contingencies are disclosed.
c. Understand the accounting principles of the industry in which the entity operates.
d. Develop audit programs to determine whether the entity's financial statements are fairly presented. (5/95, Aud., #58, 5676)

7. Must a CPA in public practice be independent in fact and appearance when providing the following services?

	Compilation of personal financial statements	Preparation of a tax return	Compilation of a financial forecast
a.	No	No	No
b.	No	No	Yes
c.	Yes	No	No
d.	No	Yes	No

(5/92, Aud., #56, 2809)

8. When compiling the financial statements of a nonpublic entity, an accountant should

a. Review agreements with financial institutions for restrictions on cash balances.
b. Understand the accounting principles and practices of the entity's industry.
c. Inquire of key personnel concerning related parties and subsequent events.
d. Perform ratio analyses of the financial data of comparable prior periods.

(11/92, Aud., #44, 2978)

8A. Which of the following procedures is ordinarily performed by an accountant in a compilation engagement of a nonpublic entity?

a. Reading the financial statements to consider whether they are free of obvious mistakes in the application of accounting principles.
b. Obtaining written representations from management indicating that the compiled financial statements will **not** be used to obtain credit.
c. Making inquiries of management concerning actions taken at meetings of the stockholders and the board of directors.
d. Applying analytical procedures designed to corroborate management's assertions that are embodied in the financial statement components. (5/95, Aud., #75, 5693)

9. Which of the following statements should **not** be included in an accountant's standard report based on the compilation of an entity's financial statements?

a. A statement that the compilation was performed in accordance with Statements on Standards for Accounting and Review Services issued by the American Institute of CPAs.
b. A statement that the accountant has **not** audited or reviewed the financial statements.
c. A statement that the accountant does **not** express an opinion but expresses only limited assurance on the financial statements.
d. A statement that a compilation is limited to presenting, in the form of financial statements, information that is the representation of management. (5/92, Aud., #5, amended, 2758)

9A. Compiled financial statements should be accompanied by an accountant's report stating that

a. A compilation includes assessing the accounting principles used and significant management estimates, as well as evaluating the overall financial statement presentation.
b. The accountant compiled the financial statements in accordance with Statements on Standards for Accounting and Review Services.

c. A compilation is substantially less in scope than an audit in accordance with GAAS, the objective of which is the expression of an opinion.
d. The accountant is **not** aware of any material modifications that should be made to the financial statements to conform with GAAP.
(5/95, Aud., #78, 5696)

10. How does an accountant make the following representations when issuing the standard report for the compilation of a nonpublic entity's financial statements?

	The financial statements have **not** been audited	The accountant has compiled the financial statements
a.	Implicitly	Implicitly
b.	Explicitly	Explicitly
c.	Implicitly	Explicitly
d.	Explicitly	Implicitly

(11/91, Aud., #26, 2294)

10A. Which of the following representations does an accountant make implicitly when issuing the standard report for the compilation of a nonpublic entity's financial statements?
a. The accountant is independent with respect to the entity.
b. The financial statements have **not** been audited.
c. A compilation consists principally of inquiries and analytical procedures.
d. The accountant does **not** express any assurance on the financial statements.
(11/93, Aud., #54, 4291)

11. If compiled financial statements presented in conformity with the cash receipts and disbursements basis of accounting do **not** disclose the basis of accounting used, the accountant should
a. Recompile the financial statements using generally accepted accounting principles.
b. Disclose the basis in the notes to the financial statements.
c. Clearly label each page "Unaudited."
d. Disclose the basis of accounting in the accountant's report. (5/90, Aud., #59, 0402)

11A. Compiled financial statements should be accompanied by a report stating that
a. A compilation is substantially less in scope than a review or an audit in accordance with generally accepted auditing standards.
b. The accountant does **not** express an opinion but expresses only limited assurance on the compiled financial statements.
c. A compilation is limited to presenting in the form of financial statements information that is the representation of management.
d. The accountant has compiled the financial statements in accordance with standards established by the Auditing Standards Board.
(5/94, Aud., #78, 4743)

11B. Miller, CPA, is engaged to compile the financial statements of Web Co., a nonpublic entity, in conformity with the income tax basis of accounting. If Web's financial statements do **not** disclose the basis of accounting used, Miller should
a. Disclose the basis of accounting in the accountant's compilation report.
b. Clearly label each page "Distribution Restricted—Material Modifications Required."
c. Issue a special report describing the effect of the incomplete presentation.
d. Withdraw from the engagement and provide **no** further services to Web.
(11/94, Aud., #81, 5154)

12. Jones Retailing, a nonpublic entity, has asked Winters, CPA, to compile financial statements that omit substantially all disclosures required by generally accepted accounting principles. Winters may compile such financial statements provided the
a. Reason for omitting the disclosures is explained in the engagement letter and acknowledged in the management representation letter.
b. Financial statements are prepared on a comprehensive basis of accounting other than generally accepted accounting principles.
c. Distribution of the financial statements is restricted to internal use only.
d. Omission is **not** undertaken to mislead the users of the financial statements and is properly disclosed in the accountant's report.
(11/92, Aud., #52, 2986)

12A. An accountant's standard report on a compilation of a projection should **not** include a
a. Statement that a compilation of a projection is limited in scope.
b. Disclaimer of responsibility to update the report for events occurring after the report's date.
c. Statement that the accountant expresses only limited assurance that the results may be achieved.
d. Separate paragraph that describes the limitations on the presentation's usefulness.
(11/93, Aud., #57, 4294)

12B. An accountant may compile a nonpublic entity's financial statements that omit all of the disclosures required by GAAP only if the omission is

I. Clearly indicated in the accountant's report.
II. Not undertaken with the intention of misleading the financial statement users.

a. I only.
b. II only.
c. Both I and II.
d. Either I or II. (5/94, Aud., #79, 4744)

13. During a review of the financial statements of a nonpublic entity, an accountant becomes aware of a lack of adequate disclosure that is material to the financial statements. If management refuses to correct the financial statement presentations, the accountant should

a. Issue an adverse opinion.
b. Issue an "except for" qualified opinion.
c. Disclose this departure from generally accepted accounting principles in a separate paragraph of the report.
d. Express only limited assurance of the financial statement presentations. (5/90, Aud., #19, 0422)

14. Clark, CPA, compiled and properly reported on the financial statements of Green Co., a nonpublic entity, for the year ended March 31, 1991. These financial statements omitted substantially all disclosures required by generally accepted accounting principles (GAAP). Green asked Clark to compile the statements for the year ended March 31, 1992, and to include all GAAP disclosures for the 1992 statements only, but otherwise present both years' financial statements in comparative form. What is Clark's responsibility concerning the proposed engagement?

a. Clark may **not** report on the comparative financial statements because the 1991 statements are **not** comparable to the 1992 statements that include the GAAP disclosures.
b. Clark may report on the comparative financial statements provided the 1991 statements do **not** contain any obvious material misstatements.
c. Clark may report on the comparative financial statements provided an explanatory paragraph is added to Clark's report on the comparative financial statements.
d. Clark may report on the comparative financial statements provided Clark updates the report on the 1991 statements that do **not** include the GAAP disclosures. (5/92, Aud., #4, 2757)

15. An accountant has been asked to compile the financial statements of a nonpublic company on a prescribed form that omits substantially all the disclosures required by generally accepted accounting principles. If the prescribed form is a standard preprinted form adopted by the company's industry trade association, and is to be transmitted only to such association, the accountant

a. Need **not** advise the industry trade association of the omission of all disclosures.
b. Should disclose the details of the omissions in separate paragraphs of the compilation report.
c. Is precluded from issuing a compilation report when all disclosures are omitted.
d. Should express limited assurance that the financial statements are free of material misstatement. (5/89, Aud., #47, 0435)

15A. When an accountant is engaged to compile a nonpublic entity's financial statements that omit substantially all disclosures required by GAAP, the accountant should indicate in the compilation report that the financial statements are

a. Not designed for those who are uninformed about the omitted disclosures.
b. Prepared in conformity with a comprehensive basis of accounting other than GAAP.
c. Not compiled in accordance with Statements on Standards for Accounting and Review Services.
d. Special-purpose financial statements that are **not** comparable to those of prior periods. (11/94, Aud., #82, 5155)

16. When providing limited assurance that the financial statements of a nonpublic entity require **no** material modifications to be in accordance with generally accepted accounting principles, the accountant should

a. Understand the accounting principles of the industry in which the entity operates.
b. Develop audit programs to determine whether the entity's financial statements are fairly presented.
c. Assess the risk that a material misstatement could occur in a financial statement assertion.
d. Confirm with the entity's lawyer that material loss contingencies are disclosed. (11/91, Aud., #58, 2326)

17. Performing inquiry and analytical procedures is the primary basis for an accountant to issue a
a. Report on compliance with requirements governing major federal assistance programs in accordance with the Single Audit Act.
b. Review report on prospective financial statements that present an entity's expected financial position, given one or more hypothetical assumptions.
c. Management advisory report prepared at the request of a client's audit committee.
d. Review report on comparative financial statements for a nonpublic entity in its second year of operations. (5/91, Aud., #59, 0418)

18. Which of the following procedures is usually performed by the accountant in a review engagement of a nonpublic entity?
a. Sending a letter of inquiry to the entity's lawyer.
b. Comparing the financial statements with statements for comparable prior periods.
c. Confirming a significant percentage of receivables by direct communication with debtors.
d. Communicating reportable conditions discovered during the study of the internal control structure. (5/92, Aud., #34, 2787)

19. Which of the following inquiry or analytical procedures ordinarily is performed in an engagement to review a nonpublic entity's financial statements?
a. Analytical procedures designed to test the accounting records by obtaining corroborating evidential matter.
b. Inquiries concerning the entity's procedures for recording and summarizing transactions.
c. Analytical procedures designed to test management's assertions regarding continued existence.
d. Inquiries of the entity's attorney concerning contingent liabilities. (11/92, Aud., #43, 2977)

19A. What type of analytical procedure would an auditor most likely use in developing relationships among balance sheet accounts when reviewing the financial statements of a nonpublic entity?
a. Trend analysis.
b. Regression analysis.
c. Ratio analysis.
d. Risk analysis. (5/95, Aud., #74, 5692)

20. Which of the following procedures is more likely to be performed in a review engagement of a nonpublic entity than in a compilation engagement?
a. Gaining an understanding of the entity's business transactions.
b. Making a preliminary assessment of control risk.
c. Obtaining a representation letter from the chief executive officer.
d. Assisting the entity in adjusting the accounting records. (5/92, Aud., #35, 2788)

21. Each page of a nonpublic entity's financial statements reviewed by an accountant should include the following reference:
a. See Accountant's Review Report.
b. Reviewed, No Accountant's Assurance Expressed.
c. See Accompanying Accountant's Footnotes.
d. Reviewed, No Material Modifications Required. (11/88, Aud., #22, 9911)

21A. Each page of a nonpublic entity's financial statements reviewed by an accountant should include the following reference:
a. See Accompanying Accountant's Footnotes.
b. Reviewed, **No** Material Modifications Required.
c. See Accountant's Review Report.
d. Reviewed, **No** Accountant's Assurance Expressed. (5/95, Aud., #81, 5699)

22. An accountant who reviews the financial statements of a nonpublic entity should issue a report stating that a review
a. Is substantially less in scope than an audit.
b. Provides negative assurance that the internal control structure is functioning as designed.
c. Provides only limited assurance that the financial statements are fairly presented.
d. Is substantially more in scope than a compilation. (11/89, Aud., #6, 0428)

23. The standard report issued by an accountant after reviewing the financial statements of a nonpublic entity states that
a. A review includes assessing the accounting principles used and significant estimates made by management.
b. A review includes examining, on a test basis, evidence supporting the amounts and disclosures in the financial statements.
c. The accountant is **not** aware of any material modifications that should be made to the financial statements.
d. The accountant does **not** express an opinion or any other form of assurance on the financial statements. (11/92, Aud., #53, 2987)

23A. When unaudited financial statements are presented in comparative form with audited financial statements in a document filed with the Securities and Exchange Commission, such statements should be

	Marked as "unaudited"	Withheld until audited	Referred to in the auditor's report
a.	Yes	No	No
b.	Yes	No	Yes
c.	No	Yes	Yes
d.	No	Yes	No

(11/93, Aud., #50, 4287)

23B. Which of the following procedures would an accountant **least** likely perform during an engagement to review the financial statements of a nonpublic entity?

a. Observing the safeguards over access to and use of assets and records.
b. Comparing the financial statements with anticipated results in budgets and forecasts.
c. Inquiring of management about actions taken at the board of directors' meetings.
d. Studying the relationships of financial statement elements expected to conform to predictable patterns. (11/94, Aud., #74, 5147)

23C. Which of the following procedures should an accountant perform during an engagement to review the financial statements of a nonpublic entity?

a. Communicating reportable conditions discovered during the assessment of control risk.
b. Obtaining a client representation letter from members of management.
c. Sending bank confirmation letters to the entity's financial institutions.
d. Examining cash disbursements in the subsequent period for unrecorded liabilities.

(11/94, Aud., #75, 5148)

23D. Gole, CPA, is engaged to review the 1994 financial statements of North Co., a nonpublic entity. Previously, Gole audited North's 1993 financial statements and expressed an unqualified opinion. Gole decides to include a separate paragraph in the 1994 review report because North plans to present comparative financial statements for 1994 and 1993. This separate paragraph should indicate that

a. The 1994 review report is intended solely for the information of management and the board of directors.
b. The 1993 auditor's report may **no** longer be relied on.
c. No auditing procedures were performed after the date of the 1993 auditor's report.
d. There are justifiable reasons for changing the level of service from an audit to a review.

(11/94, Aud., #79, 5152)

24. Moore, CPA, has been asked to issue a review report on the balance sheet of Dover Co., a nonpublic entity. Moore will not be reporting on Dover's statements of income, retained earnings, and cash flows. Moore may issue the review report provided the

a. Balance sheet is presented in a prescribed form of an industry trade association.
b. Scope of the inquiry and analytical procedures has **not** been restricted.
c. Balance sheet is **not** to be used to obtain credit or distributed to creditors.
d. Specialized accounting principles and practices of Dover's industry are disclosed.

(5/95, Aud., #79, 5697)

24A. May an accountant accept an engagement to compile or review the financial statements of a not-for-profit entity if the accountant is unfamiliar with the specialized industry accounting principles, but plans to obtain the required level of knowledge before compiling or reviewing the financial statements?

	Compilation	Review
a.	No	No
b.	Yes	No
c.	No	Yes
d.	Yes	Yes

(5/94, Aud., #46, 4711)

24B. An accountant has been engaged to review a nonpublic entity's financial statements that contain several departures from GAAP. If the financial statements are **not** revised and modification of the standard review report is **not** adequate to indicate the deficiencies, the accountant should

a. Withdraw from the engagement and provide **no** further services concerning these financial statements.
b. Inform management that the engagement can proceed only if distribution of the accountant's report is restricted to internal use.
c. Determine the effects of the departures from GAAP and issue a special report on the financial statements.
d. Issue a modified review report provided the entity agrees that the financial statements will **not** be used to obtain credit.

(11/94, Aud., #20, 5093)

24C. Baker, CPA, was engaged to review the financial statements of Hall Co., a nonpublic entity. During the engagement Baker uncovered a complex scheme involving client illegal acts and irregularities that materially affect Hall's financial statements. If Baker believes that modification of the standard review report is **not** adequate to indicate the deficiencies in the financial statements, Baker should

a. Disclaim an opinion.
b. Issue an adverse opinion.
c. Withdraw from the engagement.
d. Issue a qualified opinion.
(5/95, Aud., #80, 5698)

25. If requested to perform a review engagement for a nonpublic entity in which an accountant has an immaterial direct financial interest, the accountant is
a. Independent because the financial interest is immaterial and, therefore, may issue a review report.
b. Not independent and, therefore, may **not** be associated with the financial statements.
c. Not independent and, therefore, may **not** issue a review report.
d. Not independent and, therefore, may issue a review report, but may **not** issue an auditor's opinion. (11/89, Aud., #57, 0012)

25A. If requested to perform a review engagement for a nonpublic entity in which an accountant has an immaterial direct financial interest, the accountant is
a. Not independent and, therefore, may **not** be associated with the financial statements.
b. Not independent and, therefore, may **not** issue a review report.
c. Not independent and, therefore, may issue a review report, but may **not** issue an auditor's opinion.
d. Independent because the financial interest is immaterial and, therefore, may issue a review report. (5/95, Aud., #20, 5638)

26. An accountant who had begun an audit of the financial statements of a nonpublic entity was asked to change the engagement to a review because of a restriction on the scope of the audit. If there is reasonable justification for the change, the accountant's review report should include reference to the

	Original engagement that was agreed to	Scope limitation that caused the changed engagement
a.	Yes	Yes
b.	Yes	No
c.	No	Yes
d.	No	No

(5/92, Aud., #6, 2759)

26A. An accountant who had begun an audit of the financial statements of a nonpublic entity was asked to change the engagement to a review because of a restriction on the scope of the audit. If there is reasonable justification for the change, the accountant's review report should include reference to the

	Scope limitation that caused the changed engagement	Original engagement that was agreed to
a.	Yes	No
b.	No	Yes
c.	No	No
d.	Yes	Yes

(11/94, Aud., #78, 5151)

27. Statements on Standards for Accounting and Review Services establish standards and procedures for which of the following engagements?
a. Assisting in adjusting the books of account for a partnership.
b. Reviewing interim financial data required to be filed with the SEC.
c. Processing financial data for clients of other accounting firms.
d. Compiling an individual's personal financial statement to be used to obtain a mortgage.
(11/91, Aud., #13, 2281)

28. One of the conditions required for an accountant to submit a written personal financial plan containing unaudited financial statements to a client without complying with the requirements of SSARS 1 (*Compilation and Review of Financial Statements*) is that the
a. Client agrees that the financial statements will **not** be used to obtain credit.
b. Accountant compiled or reviewed the client's financial statements for the immediate prior year.
c. Engagement letter acknowledges that the financial statements will contain departures from generally accepted accounting principles.
d. Accountant expresses limited assurance that the financial statements are free of any material misstatements. (5/89, Aud., #45, 0434)

28A. Kell engaged March, CPA, to submit to Kell a written personal financial plan containing unaudited personal financial statements. March anticipates omitting certain disclosures required by GAAP because the engagement's sole purpose is to assist Kell in developing a personal financial plan. For March to be exempt from complying with the requirements of SSARS 1, *Compilation and Review of Financial Statements*, Kell is required to agree that the
a. Financial statements will **not** be presented in comparative form with those of the prior period.
b. Omitted disclosures required by GAAP are **not** material.
c. Financial statements will **not** be disclosed to a non-CPA financial planner.
d. Financial statements will **not** be used to obtain credit. (5/95, Aud., #21, 5639)

29. Which of the following is a prospective financial statement for general use upon which an accountant may appropriately report?
a. Financial projection.
b. Partial presentation.
c. Pro forma financial statement.
d. Financial forecast. (11/87, Aud., #11, 9911)

29A. An accountant may accept an engagement to apply agreed-upon procedures to prospective financial statements provided that
a. Distribution of the report is restricted to the specified users.
b. The prospective financial statements are also examined.
c. Responsibility for the adequacy of the procedures performed is taken by the accountant.
d. Negative assurance is expressed on the prospective financial statements taken as a whole. (11/94, Aud., #23, 5096)

30. Which of the following statements concerning prospective financial statements is correct?
a. Only a financial forecast would normally be appropriate for limited use.
b. Only a financial projection would normally be appropriate for general use.
c. Any type of prospective financial statement would normally be appropriate for limited use.
d. Any type of prospective financial statement would normally be appropriate for general use. (5/90, Aud., #23, 0424)

31. Accepting an engagement to compile a financial projection for a publicly held company most likely would be inappropriate if the projection were to be distributed to
a. A bank with which the entity is negotiating for a loan.
b. A labor union with which the entity is negotiating a contract.
c. The principal stockholder, to the exclusion of the other stockholders.
d. All stockholders of record as of the report date. (11/90, Aud., #9, 0420)

31A. Accepting an engagement to examine an entity's financial projection most likely would be appropriate if the projection were to be distributed to
a. All employees who work for the entity.
b. Potential stockholders who request a prospectus or a registration statement.
c. A bank with which the entity is negotiating for a loan.
d. All stockholders of record as of the report date. (5/94, Aud., #14, 4679)

32. An accountant's compilation report on a financial forecast should include a statement that the
a. Compilation does **not** include evaluation of the support of the assumptions underlying the forecast.
b. Hypothetical assumptions used in the forecast are reasonable.
c. Range of assumptions selected is one in which one end of the range is less likely to occur than the other.
d. Prospective statements are limited to presenting, in the form of a forecast, information that is the accountant's representation. (5/92, Aud., #9, 2762)

32A. An accountant's compilation report on a financial forecast should include a statement that
a. The forecast should be read only in conjunction with the audited historical financial statements.
b. The accountant expresses only limited assurance on the forecasted statements and their assumptions.
c. There will usually be differences between the forecasted and actual results.
d. The hypothetical assumptions used in the forecast are reasonable in the circumstances. (11/94, Aud., #83, 5156)

33. When an accountant examines a financial forecast that fails to disclose several significant assumptions used to prepare the forecast, the accountant should describe the assumptions in the accountant's report and issue a(an)
a. "Except for" qualified opinion.
b. "Subject to" qualified opinion.
c. Unqualified opinion with a separate explanatory paragraph.
d. Adverse opinion. (11/89, Aud., #21, 0432)

33A. An examination of a financial forecast is a professional service that involves
a. Compiling or assembling a financial forecast that is based on management's assumptions.
b. Limiting the distribution of the accountant's report to management and the board of directors.
c. Assuming responsibility to update management on key events for one year after the report's date.
d. Evaluating the preparation of a financial forecast and the support underlying management's assumptions. (5/95, Aud., #22, 5640)

34. Prospective financial information presented in the format of historical financial statements that omit either gross profit or net income is deemed to be a
a. Partial presentation.
b. Projected balance sheet.
c. Financial forecast.
d. Financial projection. (11/88, Aud., #27, 9911)

35. Which of the following is **not** an attestation standard?
a. Sufficient evidence shall be obtained to provide a reasonable basis for the conclusion that is expressed in the report.
b. The report shall identify the assertion being reported on and state the character of the engagement.
c. The work shall be adequately planned and assistants, if any, shall be properly supervised.
d. A sufficient understanding of the internal control structure shall be obtained to plan the engagement. (5/93, Aud., #4, 3900)

35A. Which of the following is a conceptual difference between the attestation standards and generally accepted auditing standards?
a. The attestation standards provide a framework for the attest function beyond historical financial statements.
b. The requirement that the practitioner be independent in mental attitude is omitted from the attestation standards.
c. The attestation standards do **not** permit an attest engagement to be part of a business acquisition study or a feasibility study.
d. **None** of the standards of field work in generally accepted auditing standards are included in the attestation standards. (5/94, Aud., #10, 4675)

36. An accountant may accept an engagement to apply agreed-upon procedures to prospective financial statements provided that
a. The prospective financial statements are also examined.
b. Responsibility for the adequacy of the procedures performed is taken by the accountant.
c. Negative assurance is expressed on the prospective financial statements taken as a whole.
d. Distribution of the report is restricted to the specified users. (11/92, Aud., #55, 2989)

37. Which of the following is the authoritative body designated to promulgate attestation standards?
a. Auditing Standards Board.
b. Governmental Accounting Standards Board.
c. Financial Accounting Standards Board.
d. General Accounting Office.
(5/90, Aud., #49, 0426)

38. An attestation engagement is one in which a CPA is engaged to
a. Issue a written communication expressing a conclusion about the reliability of a written assertion that is the responsibility of another party.
b. Provide tax advice or prepare a tax return based on financial information the CPA has **not** audited or reviewed.
c. Testify as an expert witness in accounting, auditing, or tax matters, given certain stipulated facts.
d. Assemble prospective financial statements based on the assumptions of the entity's management without expressing any assurance. (5/92, Aud., #60, 2813)

38A. In performing an attestation engagement, a CPA typically
a. Supplies litigation support services.
b. Assesses control risk at a low level.
c. Expresses a conclusion about an assertion.
d. Provides management consulting advice.
(11/93, Aud., #9, 4246)

39. Negative assurance may be expressed when an accountant is requested to report on the
a. Compilation of prospective financial statements.
b. Compliance with the provisions of the Foreign Corrupt Practices Act.
c. Results of applying agreed-upon procedures to an account within unaudited financial statements.
d. Audit of historical financial statements.
(11/89, Aud., #19, 0430)

40. An accountant's report on a review of pro forma financial information should include a
a. Statement that the entity's internal control structure was **not** relied on in the review.
b. Disclaimer of opinion on the financial statements from which the pro forma financial information is derived.
c. Caveat that it is uncertain whether the transaction or event reflected in the pro forma financial information will ever occur.
d. Reference to the financial statements from which the historical financial information is derived. (5/94, Aud., #68, 4733)

Solution 42-1 MULTIPLE CHOICE ANSWERS

Compilation and Review of Financial Statements (SSARS 1)

1. (b) AR 100.01 states, "The Statements on Standards for Accounting and Review Services define the compilation of financial statements and the review of financial statements of a nonpublic entity and provides guidance to accountants concerning the standards and procedures applicable to such engagements. The accountant should not issue any report on the unaudited financial statements of a nonpublic entity or submit such financial statements to his client or others unless he complies with the provisions of this Statement."

1A. (a) AR 100.01 states the accountant should not issue any report on the unaudited financial statements of a nonpublic entity or submit such financial statements to his or her client or others unless he or she complies with the provisions of SSARS. Answer (b) does not exist. Answers (c) and (d) apply to other specific types of engagements.

2. (c) Preparing a working trial balance (I) and preparing standard monthly journal entries (II) are **both** examples of other accounting services that are distinguished from a compilation and from a review and for which standards are not established under Statements on Standards for Accounting and Review Services (AR 100.02).

3. (c) SSARS are issued by the AICPA Accounting and Review Services Committee, the senior technical committee of the institute designated to issue pronouncements in connection with the unaudited financial statements or other unaudited financial information of a *nonpublic* entity.

4. (a) Neither a review nor a compilation engagement contemplates obtaining an understanding of the internal control structure or assessing control risk, testing of accounting records and of responses to inquiries by obtaining corroborating evidential matter, and certain other procedures ordinarily performed during an audit (AR 100.04).

4A. (d) AR 100.02 states that the SSARS do not establish standards or procedures for other accounting services such as consulting on accounting, tax, and similar matters, or processing financial data for clients of other accounting firms.

4B. (d) SSARS 1 indicates that the CPA must, at a minimum, comply with the provisions applicable to a compilation when submitting unaudited financial statements of a nonpublic entity. Submission of financial statement is defined as presenting to the client financial statements the accountant has generated, either manually or through the use of computer software. Answers (a), (b), and (c) are examples, per SSARS 1, of services that do not constitute the submission of financial statements.

5. (d) AR 100.29 states, "A review does *not* contemplate obtaining an understanding of the internal control structure or assessing control risk, tests of accounting records and of responses to inquiries by obtaining corroborating evidential matter, and certain other procedures ordinarily performed during an audit." Answers (a), (b), and (c) are usually performed by the accountant in a review engagement of a nonpublic entity.

6. (b) AR 100.05 states, " . . . whenever an accountant compiles or reviews financial statements of a nonpublic entity, he should issue a report prepared in accordance with the applicable standards . . . However, when the accountant performs more than one service (for example, a compilation and an audit), he should issue the report that is appropriate for the highest level of service rendered."

6A. (c) In a review of financial statements, where the CPA expresses limited assurance that the financial statements do not contain material deviations from GAAP, the accountant is required to obtain a knowledge of the accounting principles and practices of the industry in which the entity operates. This is required so that the CPA can determine and apply proper inquiry and analytical procedures. The review is not an audit and it is not intended that the CPA will apply the procedures listed in the other answers.

Compilation of Financial Statements

7. (a) The CPA need not be independent to perform compilation services; nor must he or she be independent to prepare a tax return for a client.

8. (b) AR 100.10 states, "The accountant should possess a level of knowledge of the accounting principles and practices of the industry in which the entity operates that will enable him to compile financial statements that are appropriate in form for an entity operating in that industry." Answers (a), (c), and (d) represent procedures beyond the scope of a compilation.

8A. (a) AR 100.13 states, "Before issuing his report, the accountant should read the compiled financial statements and consider whether such financial statements appear to be appropriate in form and free from obvious material errors. In this context, the term error refers to mistakes in the compilation of financial statements, including arithmetical or clerical mistakes, and mistakes in the application of accounting principles, including inadequate disclosure." A representation letter from members of management is not usually obtained in a compilation engagement. Inquiries of management concerning actions taken at meetings of the stockholders and the board of directors is an analytical procedure normally used in a review engagement [AR 100.27(d)] but not necessary in a compilation engagement. AR 100.12 states, "The accountant is not required to make inquiries or perform other procedures to verify, corroborate, or review information supplied by the entity."

9. (c) A compilation engagement, by definition, is one in which the accountant does not express *any* assurance, limited or otherwise, on the statements (AR 100.04). However, a compilation report would state the following: that the compilation was performed in accordance with Statements on Standards for Accounting and Review Services issued by the AICPA that the financial statements have not been audited or reviewed and that a compilation is limited to presenting in the form of financial statements information that is the representation of management.

9A. (b) According to AR 100.14, the compilation report should state, "A compilation has been performed in accordance with Statements on Standards for Accounting and Review Services issued by the AICPA." A compilation does not include the assessments and evaluations in answer (a) and thus would not be appropriate in a compilation report. Answers (c) and (d) are both items that should be in a report accompanying a review, but not in a compilation report.

10. (b) AR 100.14 states, "Financial statements compiled without audit or review by an accountant should be accompanied by a report stating that--(1) A compilation has been performed in accordance with Statements on Standards for Accounting and Review Services issued by the American Institute of Certified Public Accountants. (2) A compilation is limited to presenting in the form of financial statements information that is the representation of management (owners). (3) The financial statements have not been audited or reviewed and, accordingly, the accountant does not express an opinion or any other form of assurance on them."

10A. (a) An accountant would only explicitly discuss independence in the compilation report when he or she *lacks* independence. Thus, when the accountant is independent, it is not specifically stated in the report. AR 100.14 states that financial statements compiled by an accountant should be accompanied by a report stating that the financial statements have not been audited or reviewed and, accordingly, the accountant does not express an opinion or any other form of assurance on them; thus answers (b) and (d) are *explicitly* stated. Inquiry and analytical procedures are performed during a review engagement, not in a compilation.

11. (d) AR 9100.43 states, "When an accountant compiles financial statements that are presented in accordance with a comprehensive basis of accounting other than generally accepted accounting principles and that omit substantially all disclosures, paragraph 20 of <u>SSARS 1</u> [Section 100.20] requires disclosure of the basis of accounting. This disclosure may be in an attached footnote or in a note on the face of the financial statements. If disclosure is not made as part of the financial statements, modification of the accountant's compilation report would be required."

11A. (c) AR 100.14 prescribes the components of a compilation report; including the requirements noted in answer (c). Answer (a) is incorrect because it refers to GAAS. By using the term "limited assurance," answer (b) is referring to a review. The AICPA establishes the standards.

11B. (a) AR 100.20 notes that if financial statements which are compiled in conformity with a comprehensive basis of accounting other than GAAP do not include disclosure of the basis, the accountant must disclose the basis. Answers (b), (c), and (d) are not options mentioned in the Standards.

12. (d) AR 100.19 states, "The accountant may compile such financial statements provided the omission of substantially all disclosures is clearly indicated in his report and is not, to his knowledge, undertaken with the intention of misleading those who might reasonably be expected to use such financial statements." The reason for omission of the disclosures should be clearly indicated in the report. It need not be explained in the engagement letter and in the management representation letter. The financial statements do not need to be prepared on a comprehensive basis of accounting other than GAAP.

The financial statements do not need to be restricted to internal use only.

12A. (c) AT 200.16 states that the accountant's standard report on a compilation of prospective financial statements should include a statement that a compilation is limited in scope and does not enable the accountant to express an opinion or any other form of assurance on the prospective financial statements or the assumptions. The report should also include a statement that the accountant assumes no responsibility to update the report for events and circumstances occurring after the date of the report. AT 200.18 states that the accountant's report should include a separate paragraph that describes the limitations on the usefulness of the presentation.

12B. (c) AR 100.19 presents both requirements.

13. (c) If, during a review of the financial statements of a nonpublic entity, an accountant becomes aware of a lack of adequate disclosure, he or she should consider whether modification of the standard report is adequate to disclose the departure. If the accountant concludes that modification of the standard report is appropriate, the departure should be disclosed in a separate paragraph of his or her report (AR 100.39-.40).

14. (a) AR 200.05 states, "Compiled financial statements that omit substantially all of the disclosures required by GAAP are not comparable to financial statements that include such disclosures. Accordingly, the accountant should not issue a report on the comparative financial statements when statements for one or more, but not all, of the periods presented omit substantially all of the disclosures required by GAAP."

15. (a) "There is a presumption that the information required by a prescribed form is sufficient to meet the needs of the body that designed or adopted the form and that there is no need for that body to be advised of departures from generally accepted accounting principles required by the prescribed form or related instructions." (AR 300.03) The auditor does not have to disclose the details of the omissions (AR 300.03). The auditor should issue a standard form of compilation report for a prescribed form (AR 300.03). The auditor should not express any assurance on financial statements that have been compiled (AR 100.04).

15A. (a) AR 100.21 presents an example report of this situation. Further, AR 100.19 notes that when compiled financial statements omit substantially all disclosures, the accountant should indicate that substantially all disclosures are omitted. Answers (b), (c), and (d) are not options allowed by the Standards.

16. (a) AR 100.24 states, "The accountant should possess a level of knowledge of the accounting principles and practices of the industry in which the entity operates and an understanding of the entity's business that will provide him, through the performance of inquiry and analytical procedures, with a reasonable basis for expressing limited assurance that there are no material modifications that should be made to the financial statements in order for the statements to be in conformity with generally accepted accounting principles." The engagement referred to here is a review of financial statements. Answers (b), (c), and (d) are all examples of procedures performed in an audit engagement.

17. (d) AR 100.04 defines a review of financial statements as, "performing inquiry and analytical procedures that provide the accountant with a reasonable basis for expressing limited assurance that there are no material modifications that should be made to the statements in order for them to be in conformity with generally accepted accounting principles or, if applicable, with another comprehensive basis of accounting." Answer (a) describes an audit engagement. Answer (b) describes an attestation engagement. Answer (c) describes consulting services.

Review of Financial Statements

18. (b) An accountant's review procedures will include inquiry and analytical procedures. Analytical procedures are designed to identify relationships and individual items that appear to be unusual, and consist of (1) comparison of the financial statements with statements for comparable prior period(s), (2) comparison of the statements with anticipated results, if available, and (3) study of the relationships of the elements of the statements that would be expected to conform with a predictable pattern based on the entity's experience [AR 100.21(c)]. Answers (a), (c), and (d) are procedures that should be performed in an audit engagement.

19. (b) Inquiries and analytical procedures ordinarily performed during a review of a nonpublic entity's financial statements include inquiries concerning the entity's procedures for recording and summarizing transactions (AR 100.27b). They would not be concerned with corroborating evidential matter, management's assertions concerning continued existence, or the entity's attorney's opinion concerning contingent liabilities.

19A. (c) In reviewing the financial statements of a nonpublic entity, the auditor would most likely use ratio analysis as the analytical procedure for developing relationships among balance sheet accounts. Such ratios are useful in evaluating an entity's solvency. Ratio analysis that includes relationships between income statement accounts and balance sheet accounts are useful in evaluating operational efficiency and profitability. Ratio analysis provides an indication of the firm's financial strengths and weaknesses.

20. (c) AR 100.55 states, " A review of financial statements consists principally of inquiries of company personnel and analytical procedures applied to financial data. Because a review does not contemplate tests of accounting records and of responses to inquiries by obtaining corroborating evidential matter, among other things, the accountant is required to obtain a written representation from members of management to confirm the oral representations made to the accountant." A representation letter would not usually be obtained in a compilation engagement.

21. (a) AR 100.16 states, "Each page of the financial statements reviewed by the accountant should include a reference, such as 'See Accountant's Review Report.'"

21A. (c) AR 100.16 states, "Each page of the financial statements reviewed by the accountant should include a reference, such as 'See Accountant's Review Report.'"

22. (a) Financial statements reviewed by an accountant should be accompanied by a report stating that a review is substantially less in scope than an audit. A review report does not provide any assurance as to the entity's internal control structure; nor does it make a comparison of a review engagement with a compilation engagement. A review report does not state that it provides limited assurance as to fair presentation. It does, state that no material modifications should be made to the statements to make them conform with GAAP (AR 100.35).

23. (c) Among the statements set forth in AR 100.32 for inclusion in the standard report on a review of financial statements is, "the accountant is not aware of any material modifications that should be made to the financial statements in order for them to be in conformity with generally accepted accounting principles, other than those modifications, if any, indicated in his report." "A review consists principally of inquiries of company personnel and analytical procedures applied to financial data." Although a review report does not express an opinion, it does indicate *limited assurance.*

23A. (a) AU 504.14 states that when unaudited financial statements are presented in comparative form with audited financial statements in documents filed with the Securities and Exchange Commission, such statements should be clearly marked as "unaudited" but not referred to in the auditor's report.

23B. (a) The procedures in answers (b) and (d) are noted in AR 100.27c, and the procedures in answer (c) are noted in AR 100.27d as appropriate in a review.

23C. (b) Obtaining a client representation letter is required by AR 100.28. The procedures in (a), (c), and (d) are not mentioned.

23D. (c) AR 200.28 notes that if the accountant issues a report on the current period with a separate paragraph covering the prior period, the separate paragraph should include a statement that no auditing procedures were performed since the date of the previous report. Answers (a), (b), and (d) are not noted in AR 200.28.

24. (b) According to AR 100.37, the CPA may issue the review report on just the balance sheet "if the scope of his inquiry and analytical procedures has not been restricted." This is the only restriction provided for in the Code.

24A. (d) AR 100.10 states that for a compilation, and AR 100.25 states that for a review, the requirement that the accountant possess a level of knowledge of the accounting principles and practices of the industry in which the entity operates does not prevent an accountant from accepting a compilation or review engagement for an entity. It does, however, place upon the accountant a responsibility to obtain the required level of knowledge.

24B. (a) Per AR 100.41, if the accountant believes that modification of his or her standard report is not adequate to indicate the deficiencies in the financial statements taken as a whole, he or she should withdraw from the compilation or review engagement and not provide any further services regarding those financial statements. Answer (b) is incorrect because the accountant cannot be assured the financial statements would not be delivered to individuals outside of the firm. The accountant would follow the procedures in answer (c) if the modification of the report was considered adequate. Answer (d) is incorrect because there is no modified review report.

24C. (c) AR 100.41 states that when the accountant believes that modification of the standard report is not adequate to indicate the deficiencies in the financial statements as a whole, the accountant should withdraw from the compilation or review engagement.

25. (c) Independence shall be considered to be impaired if during the period of a professional engagement or at the time of expressing an opinion, a member or a member's firm had or was committed to acquire any direct or material indirect financial interest in the enterprise (ET 101.02). An accountant is precluded from issuing a review report on the financial statements of an entity with respect to which he or she is not independent (AR 100.38).

25A. (b) AR 100.38 states, "An accountant is precluded from issuing a review report on the financial statement of an entity with respect to which he [or she] is not independent." Judgments about independence should be guided by the AICPA Code of Professional Conduct. Rule 101 states that independence is considered impaired if there is *any* direct or material indirect financial interest.

26. (d) If the accountant concludes, based upon his or her professional judgment, that there is reasonable justification to change the engagement from an audit to a review, and if he or she complies with the standards applicable to the changed engagement, he or she should issue an appropriate review report. The report should not include reference to the original engagement, any auditing procedures that may have been performed, or scope limitations that resulted in the changed engagement.

26A. (c) AR 100.49 notes that when there is reasonable justification to change the engagement because of scope restriction, the report should not include reference to the original engagement, any auditing procedures that were performed, or the scope limitation.

Reporting on Personal Financial Statements Included in Written Personal Financial Plans (SSARS 6)

27. (d) A written personal financial plan containing unaudited personal financial statements may be submitted to a client without complying with the requirements of SSARS 1 if they will not be used to obtain credit. However, when the personal financial statement is to compiled and used to obtain a mortgage, the accountant must follow SSARS standards and procedures (AR 600.03).

28. (a) "An accountant may submit a written personal financial plan containing unaudited personal financial statements to a client without complying with the requirements of SSARS 1 when *all* of the following conditions exist: (1) the accountant establishes an understanding with the client, preferably in writing, that the financial statements will be used solely to assist the client and the client's advisers to develop the client's personal financial goals and objectives and *will not be used to obtain credit* or for any purpose other than developing these goals and objectives; and (2) nothing comes to the accountant's attention during the engagement that would cause the accountant to believe that the financial statements will be used to obtain credit or for any purposes other than developing the client's financial goals and objectives." (AR 600.03) Answers (b), (c), and (d) are not conditions required by AR 600.03.

28A. (d) AR 600.03 includes an agreement from the client that the financial statements will not be used to obtain credit as one condition of exemption from SSARS 1. The statements may be presented in comparative form and may be in conformity with GAAP or another comprehensive basis of accounting. The certification of the user financial planner is irrelevant to the issuance of the report.

Financial Forecasts and Projections

29. (d) AT 200.07 states, "Prospective financial statements are either *general use* or *limited use*. *General use* of prospective financial statements refers to use of the statements by persons with whom the responsible party is not negotiating directly, for example, in an offering statement of an entity's debt or equity interests. Because recipients of prospective financial statements distributed for general use are unable to ask the responsible party directly about the presentation, the presentation most useful to them is one that portrays, to the best of the responsible party's knowledge and belief, the expected results. Thus, only a *financial forecast* is appropriate for *general use*."

29A. (a) AT 200.49 states, "An accountant may accept an engagement to apply agreed-upon procedures to prospective financial statements provided that, ...(b.) distribution of the report is to be restricted to the specified users." The accountant does not have to examine, compile, or apply agreed-upon procedures to the prospective financial statements unless the accountant's compilation, review, or examination report on historical financial statements is included with the accountant-submitted document containing the prospective financial statements (AT 200.58). Responsibility for adequacy for the procedures performed is taken by the specified users, not the accountant (AT 200.49). AT 200.56 states, "When the accountant reports on the results of applying agreed-upon procedures, he or she should not express any form of negative assurance on the prospective financial statements taken as a whole."

30. (c) AT 200.08 states, "Any type of prospective financial statements that would be useful in the circumstances would normally be appropriate for limited use. Thus, the presentation may be a financial forecast or a financial projection." Only a financial forecast is appropriate for general use (AT 200.07).

31. (d) A projection, since it is not meant for general use, would be inappropriate for all stockholders of record, as it would be unreasonable to expect this group to be familiar with the basis of the projection or to be closely involved with those preparing it. The parties in answers (a), (b), and (c) parties would tend to have more direct knowledge of operations and of the basis used for the projection (AT 200.09).

31A. (c) AT 200.07 states that a projection, since it is not meant for general use, would be inappropriate for all stockholders of record and employees, as it would be unreasonable to expect this group to be familiar with the basis of the projection or to be closely involved with those preparing it.

32. (a) The accountant's standard report on the compilation of a forecast should include a statement that a compilation is limited to presenting in the form of a forecast information that is the representation of management and does not include evaluation of the support for the assumptions underlying the forecast (AT 200.17).

32A. (c) The standard report in AT 200.17 includes a statement that there will usually be differences between the forecasted and actual results. The items in answers (a), (b), and (d) are not in the standard report.

33. (d) When an accountant examines a financial forecast that fails to disclose several assumptions that, at the time, appear to be significant, the accountant should describe the assumptions in the report and issue an adverse opinion (AT 200.40).

33A. (d) AT 200.27 states, "An examination of a financial forecast involves evaluating the preparation of the prospective financial statements, evaluating the support underlying the assumptions, evaluating the presentation of the prospective financial statements for conformity with AICPA presentation guidelines, and issuing an examination report." This service does not include compiling the forecast, or assuming responsibility to update management on key events afterwards. The report may be for general use, in which case the distribution need not be limited.

34. (a) AT 200.67 states that a presentation which omits one or more of the applicable minimum items (which include gross profit and net income) is a partial presentation.

Statements on Standards for Attestation Engagements

35. (d) A sufficient understanding of the internal control structure for planning an engagement is not a requirement of the general, fieldwork, or reporting standards for an attestation engagement. AT 100.77 provides a comparison of the Attestation Standards with GAAS. Answer (a) represents the second standard of fieldwork, answer (b) represents the first standard of reporting, and answer (c) represents the first standard of fieldwork for an attestation engagement.

35A. (a) AT 100.05 states that an attest engagement may be part of a larger engagement such as a feasibility study, that includes an examination of prospective financial information. Answer (b) represents the fourth general standard for attestations. The two attestation field work standards are the same as the first and third standards of field work for audits, or GAAS.

36. (d) Among the items listed for inclusion in an accountant's report on applying agreed-upon procedures to prospective financial statements is a statement concerning the limitations on the use of the report because it is intended solely for the use of specified parties (AT 9100.42). The accountant is not precluded from applying agreed upon procedures only. There is no requirement that the prospective financial statements also be examined. The specified parties to whom the report is restricted take responsibility for the adequacy of the attest procedures. Answer (c) is incorrect because the negative assurance expressed is based on the application of the agreed upon procedures. Since these procedures are limited by the client to specific assertions within the financial statements, no assurance can be given as to the prospective financial statements taken as a whole.

37. (a) The Accounting and Review Services Committee, Auditing Standards Board, and Management Advisory Services Executive Committee are the senior technical committees of the Institute

designated to issue enforceable standards under the AICPA's Code of Professional Conduct concerning attestation services in their respective areas of responsibility.

38. (a) AT 100.01 states, "An attest engagement is one in which a practitioner is engaged to issue or does issue a written communication that expresses a conclusion about the reliability of a written assertion that is the responsibility of another party."

38A. (c) AT 100.01 states that an attest engagement is one in which a practitioner is engaged to issue or does issue a written communication that expresses a conclusion about the reliability of a written assertion that is the responsibility of another party. Answers (a) and (d) are specifically identified in AT 100.02 as examples of services not considered to be attest engagements. The CPA would not necessarily assess control risk during every attestation engagement.

39. (c) AT 100.59 states, "A practitioner's conclusion on the results of applying agreed-upon procedures to a presentation of assertions should be in the form of a summary of findings, negative assurance, or both."

Pro Forma Financial Information

40. (d) AT 300.12 states that the accountant's report on pro forma financial information should include reference to the financial statements from which the historical financial information is derived... The statement in answer (a) should not be made in any review engagement. Answer (b) is incorrect because the report on pro forma information is a different engagement from reporting on the financial statements from which the pro forma information was derived. A review report would not require a disclaimer because the accountant is not issuing an opinion. No reference to uncertainty should be made as that is assumed, based upon the nature of the engagement, and the accountant need only provide a conclusion as to whether any information came to his or her attention to cause him or her to believe management's assumptions do not provide a reasonable basis for the effects directly attributable to the transaction or event or that the pro forma column does not reflect the proper application of those adjustments to the historical financial statements.

PERFORMANCE BY SUBTOPICS

Each category below parallels a subtopic covered in Chapter 42. Record the number and percentage of questions you correctly answered in each subtopic area.

Compilation and Review of Financial Statements (SSARS 1)

Question #	Correct √
1	
1A	
2	
3	
4	
4A	
4B	
5	
6	
6A	
# Questions	10

Correct ________
% Correct ________

Compilation of Financial Statements

Question #	Correct √
7	
8	
8A	
9	
9A	
10	
10A	
11	
11A	
11B	
12	
12A	
12B	
13	
14	
15	
15A	
16	
17	
# Questions	19

Correct ________
% Correct ________

Review of Financial Statements

Question #	Correct √
18	
19	
19A	
20	
21	
21A	
22	
23	
23A	
23B	
23C	
23D	
24	
24A	
24B	
24C	
25	
25A	
26	
26A	
# Questions	20

Correct ________
% Correct ________

Reporting on Personal Financial Statements Included in Written Personal Financial Plans (SSARS 6)

Question #	Correct √
27	
28	
28A	
# Questions	3

Correct ________
% Correct ________

Financial Forecasts and Projections

Question #	Correct √
29	
29A	
30	
31	
31A	
32	
32A	
33	
33A	
34	
# Questions	10

Correct ________
% Correct ________

Statements on Standards for Attestation Engagements

Question #	Correct √
35	
35A	
36	
37	
38	
38A	
39	
# Questions	7

Correct ________
% Correct ________

Pro Forma Financial Information

Question #	Correct √
40	
# Questions	1

Correct ________
% Correct ________

OTHER OBJECTIVE FORMAT QUESTION

Problem 42-2 (15 to 25 minutes)

Problem 42-2 consists of 13 items pertaining to possible deficiencies in an accountant's review report. Select the **best** answer for each item. **Answer all items.**

Jordan & Stone, CPAs, audited the financial statements of Tech Co., a nonpublic entity, for the year ended December 31, 1991, and expressed an unqualified opinion. For the year ended December 31, 1992, Tech issued comparative financial statements. Jordan & Stone reviewed Tech's 1992 financial statements and Kent, an assistant on the engagement, drafted the accountants' review report below. Land, the engagement supervisor, decided not to reissue the prior year auditors' report, but instructed Kent to include a separate paragraph in the current year's review report describing the responsibility assumed for the prior year's audited financial statements. This is an appropriate reporting procedure.

Land reviewed Kent's draft and indicated in the *Supervisor's Review Notes* below that there were several deficiencies in Kent's draft.

Accountant's Review Report

We have reviewed and audited the accompanying balance sheets of Tech Co. as of December 31, 1992 and 1991, and the related statements of income, retained earnings, and cash flows for the years then ended, in accordance with Statements on Standards for Accounting and Review Services issued by the American Institute of Certified Public Accountants and generally accepted auditing standards. All information included in these financial statements is the representation of the management of Tech Co.

A review consists principally of inquiries of company personnel and analytical procedures applied to financial data. It is substantially less in scope than an audit in accordance with generally accepted auditing standards, the objective of which is the expression of an opinion regarding the financial statements taken as a whole.

Based on our review, we are not aware of any material modifications that should be made to the accompanying financial statements. Because of the inherent limitations of a review engagement, this report is intended for the information of management and should not be used for any other purpose.

The financial statements for the year ended December 31, 1991, were audited by us and our report was dated March 2, 1992. We have no responsibility for updating that report for events and circumstances occurring after that date.

Jordan and Stone, CPAs
March 1, 1993

Required:

Items a through m represent deficiencies noted by Land. For each deficiency, indicate whether Land is correct or incorrect in the criticism of Kent's draft.

Supervisor's Review Notes

a. There should be **no** reference to the prior year's audited financial statements in the first (introductory) paragraph.

b. All the current-year basic financial statements are **not** properly identified in the first (introductory) paragraph.

c. There should be **no** reference to the American Institute of Certified Public Accountants in the first (introductory) paragraph.

d. The accountant's review and audit responsibilities should follow management's responsibilities in the first (introductory) paragraph.

e. There should be **no** comparison of the scope of a review to an audit in the second (scope) paragraph.

f. Negative assurance should be expressed on the current year's financial statements in the second (scope) paragraph.

g. There should be a statement that **no** opinion is expressed on the current year's financial statements in the second (scope) paragraph.

h. There should be a reference to "conformity with generally accepted accounting principle" in the third paragraph.

i. There should be **no** restriction on the distribution of the accountant's review report in the third paragraph.

j. There should be **no** reference to "material modifications" in the third paragraph.

k. There should be an indication of the type of opinion expressed on the prior year's audited financial statements in the fourth (separate) paragraph.

l. There should be an indication that **no** auditing procedures were performed after the date of the report on the prior year's financial statements in the fourth (separate) paragraph.

m. There should be **no** reference to "updating the prior year's auditor's report for events and circumstances occurring after that date" in the fourth (separate) paragraph. (5/93, Aud., #2)

OTHER OBJECTIVE FORMAT SOLUTION

Solution 42-2 Report Deficiencies--Review Engagement

Land's criticism is

	Correct	Incorrect
a.	√	
b.		√
c.		√
d.		√
e.		√
f.		√

	Correct	Incorrect
g.	√	
h.	√	
i.	√	
j.		√
k.	√	
l.	√	
m.	√	

ESSAY QUESTIONS

Essay 42-3 (15 to 25 minutes)

The following report was drafted on October 25, 1990, by Major, CPA, at the completion of the engagement to compile the financial statements of Ajax Company for the year ended September 30, 1990. Ajax is a nonpublic entity in which Major's child has a material direct financial interest. Ajax decided to omit substantially all of the disclosures required by generally accepted accounting principles because the financial statements will be for management's use only. The statement of cash flows was also omitted because management does not believe it to be a useful financial statement.

To the Board of Directors of Ajax Company:

I have compiled the accompanying financial statements of Ajax Company as of September 30, 1990, and for the year then ended. I planned and performed the compilation to obtain limited assurance about whether the financial statements are free of material misstatements.

A compilation is limited to presenting information in the form of financial statements. It is substantially less in scope than an audit in accordance with generally accepted auditing standards, the objective of which is the expression of an opinion regarding the financial statements taken as a whole. I have not audited the accompanying financial statements and, accordingly, do not express any opinion on them.
Management has elected to omit substantially all of the disclosures required by generally accepted accounting principles. If the omitted disclosures were included in the financial statements, they might influence the user's conclusions about the Company's financial position, results of operations, and changes in financial position.

I am not independent with respect to Ajax Company. This lack of independence is due to my child's ownership of a material direct financial interest in Ajax Company.

This report is intended solely for the information and use of the Board of Directors and management of

Ajax Company and should not be used for any other purpose.

Major, CPA

Required:

Identify the deficiencies contained in Major's report on the compiled financial statements. Group the deficiencies by paragraph where applicable. Do **not** redraft the report. (11/90, Aud., #5)

Essay 42-4 (15 to 25 minutes)

An accountant is sometimes called on by clients to report on or assemble prospective financial statements for use by third parties.

Required:

a. 1. Identify the types of engagements that an accountant may perform under these circumstances.

2. Explain the difference between "general use" of and "limited use" of prospective financial statements.

3. Explain what types of prospective financial statements are appropriate for "general use" and what types are appropriate for "limited use."

b. Describe the contents of the accountant's standard report on a compilation of a financial projection. (5/88, Aud., #2)

Essay 42-5 (15 to 25 minutes)

For the year ended December 31, 1988, Novak & Co., CPAs, audited the financial statements of Tillis, Ltd., and expressed an unqualified opinion dated February 27, 1989.

For the year ended December 31, 1989, Novak & Co. were engaged by Tillis, Ltd., to review Tillis, Ltd.'s financial statements, i.e., "look into the company's financial statements and determine whether there are any obvious modifications that should be made to the financial statements in order for them to be in conformity with generally accepted accounting principles."

Novak made the necessary inquiries, performed the necessary analytical procedures, and performed certain additional procedures that were deemed necessary to achieve the requisite limited assurance.

Novak's work was completed on March 3, 1990, and the financial statements appeared to be in conformity with generally accepted accounting principles. The report was prepared on March 5, 1990. It was delivered to Jones, the controller of Tillis, Ltd., on March 9, 1990.

Required:

Prepare the properly addressed and dated report on the comparative financial statements of Tillis, Ltd., for the years ended December 31, 1988, and 1989. (11/82, Aud., #5)

ESSAY SOLUTIONS

Solution 42-3 Report Deficiencies--Compilation Engagement

Deficiencies in the report on the compiled financial statements are as follows:

Within the first paragraph:

- The financial statements are **not properly identified.**
- **Statements on Standards for Accounting and Review Services** issued by the AICPA should be **referred to.**
- The expression **"to obtain limited assurance"** should not be used.

Within the second paragraph:

- The information is not stated to be the **representation of management.**
- The phrase **"less in scope than an audit"** is **inappropriate.**
- Reference to the **financial statements not being reviewed** is omitted.
- Reference to **"any other form of assurance"** is omitted.

Within the third paragraph:

- Reference to the **omission of the statement of cash flows** is omitted.
- There should be a statement that the financial statements are **not designed for those uninformed about the omitted disclosures.**

- It is inappropriate to refer to **changes in financial position.**

Within the fourth paragraph:

- The **reason for the accountant's lack of independence** should **not be described.**

Inclusion of the fifth paragraph is inappropriate.

The accountant's compilation report is **not dated October 25, 1990.**

Solution 42-4 Reporting on Financial Projections

a. 1. An accountant who reports on or assembles **prospective financial statements for use by third parties** should perform any one of three engagements. The accountant may **compile, examine**, or **apply agreed-upon procedures** to the prospective financial statements.

2. **"General use"** of prospective financial statements refers to use of the statements by persons (creditors, stockholders, etc.) with whom the **responsible party** (management) is **not negotiating directly. "Limited use"** of prospective financial statements refers to the use of prospective financial statements by the **responsible party and third parties** with whom the responsible party is **negotiating directly.**

3. Only a **financial forecast is appropriate for general use,** but any type of prospective financial statements (either a financial forecast or a financial projection) would normally be appropriate for **limited use.**

b. The accountant's standard report on a compilation of a financial projection should include

- An **identification** of the **projection** presented by the responsible party.
- A statement that the accountant has **compiled** the **projection in accordance with standards established by the AICPA.**
- A separate paragraph that describes the **limitations** on the **use of the presentation.**
- A statement that a compilation is **limited in scope** and **does not enable** the accountant to **express an opinion** or any other **form of assurance** on the **projection** or the **assumptions.**
- A caveat that the **prospective results may not be achieved.**
- A statement that the **accountant assumes no responsibility to update** the report for events and circumstances occurring after the date of the report.

Solution 42-5 Review Report--Prior Year Audited

To the Board of Directors of Tillis Ltd.:

We have reviewed the accompanying **balance sheet** of Tillis, Ltd. as of December 31, 1989, and the **related statements of income, retained earnings,** and **cash flows** for the year then ended, **in accordance with Statements on Standards for Accounting and Review Services** issued by the American Institute of Certified Public Accountants. All information included in these financial statements is the **representation of the management** of Tillis, Ltd.

A review consists principally of inquiries of company personnel and **analytical procedures** applied to financial data. It is **substantially less in scope than an audit in accordance with generally accepted auditing standards**, the objective of which is the expression of an opinion regarding the financial statements taken as a whole. Accordingly, **we do not express such an opinion.**

Based on our review, we are **not aware of any material modifications** that should be made to the accompanying 1989 financial statements in order for them to be **in conformity with generally accepted accounting principles.**

The financial statements for the year ended December 31, 1988, **were audited by us**, and we **expressed an unqualified opinion** on them in our report dated February 27, 1989, but we **have not performed any auditing procedures** since that date.

Novak & Co.
March 3, 1990

NOTES

APPENDIX A
AUDITING FINAL EXAM

Problem 1 MULTIPLE CHOICE QUESTIONS (90 to 110 minutes)

1. On the basis of audit evidence gathered and evaluated, an auditor decides to increase the assessed level of control risk from that originally planned. To achieve an overall audit risk level that is substantially the same as the planned audit risk level, the auditor would

a. Increase inherent risk.
b. Increase materiality levels.
c. Decrease substantive testing.
d. Decrease detection risk.

2. The purpose of segregating the duties of hiring personnel and distributing payroll checks is to separate the

a. Human resources function from the controllership function.
b. Administrative controls from the internal accounting controls.
c. Authorization of transactions from the custody of related assets.
d. Operational responsibility from the record keeping responsibility.

3. For audits of financial statements made in accordance with generally accepted auditing standards, the use of analytical procedures is required to some extent

	As a substantive test	In the final review stage
a.	Yes	Yes
b.	Yes	No
c.	No	Yes
d.	No	No

4. A CPA establishes quality control policies and procedures for deciding whether to accept a new client or continue to perform services for a current client. The primary purpose for establishing such policies and procedures is

a. To enable the auditor to attest to the integrity or reliability of a client.
b. To comply with the quality control standards established by regulatory bodies.
c. To lessen the exposure to litigation resulting from failure to detect irregularities in client financial statements.
d. To minimize the likelihood of association with clients whose management lacks integrity.

5. An internal control questionnaire indicates that an approved receiving report is required to accompany every check request for payment of merchandise. Which of the following procedures provides the greatest assurance that this control is operating effectively?

a. Select and examine canceled checks and ascertain that the related receiving reports are dated **no** earlier than the checks.
b. Select and examine canceled checks and ascertain that the related receiving reports are dated **no** later than the checks.
c. Select and examine receiving reports and ascertain that the related canceled checks are dated **no** earlier than the receiving reports.
d. Select and examine receiving reports and ascertain that the related canceled checks are dated **no** later than the receiving reports.

6. The accounts payable department receives the purchase order form to accomplish all of the following **except**

a. Compare invoice price to purchase order price.
b. Ensure the purchase had been properly authorized.
c. Ensure the goods had been received by the party requesting the goods.
d. Compare quantity ordered to quantity purchased.

7. An auditor would consider internal control over a client's payroll procedures to be ineffective if the payroll department supervisor is responsible for

a. Hiring subordinate payroll department employees.
b. Having custody over unclaimed paychecks.
c. Updating employee earnings records.
d. Applying pay rates to time tickets.

8. To improve accountability for fixed asset retirements, management most likely would implement a system of internal control that includes

a. Continuous analysis of the repairs and maintenance account.
b. Periodic inquiry of plant executives by internal auditors as to whether any plant assets have been retired.
c. Continuous utilization of serially numbered retirement work orders.
d. Periodic inspection of insurance policies by the internal auditors.

9. Which one of the following would the auditor consider to be an incompatible operation if the cashier receives remittances from the mailroom?
a. The cashier posts the receipts to the accounts receivable subsidiary ledger cards.
b. The cashier makes the daily deposit at a local bank.
c. The cashier prepares the daily deposit.
d. The cashier endorses the checks.

10. A client erroneously recorded a large purchase twice. Which of the following internal control measures would be most likely to detect this error in a timely and efficient manner?
a. Footing the purchases journal.
b. Reconciling vendors' monthly statements with subsidiary payable ledger accounts.
c. Tracing totals from the purchases journal to the ledger accounts.
d. Sending written quarterly confirmations to all vendors.

11. Sound internal control policies and procedures dictate that defective merchandise returned by customers should be presented to the
a. Inventory control clerk.
b. Sales clerk.
c. Purchasing clerk.
d. Receiving clerk.

12. Which of the following statements is correct concerning the auditor's required communication of material weaknesses in internal control?
a. If the auditor does not become aware of any material weaknesses during the audit, that fact must be communicated.
b. Weaknesses reported at interim dates should be tested for correction before completion of the engagement.
c. Although written communication is preferable, the auditor may communicate the findings orally.
d. Weaknesses reported at interim dates must be repeated in the communication at the completion of the engagement.

13. After his consideration of an entity's internal control structure, the auditor decides to assess control risk at the maximum level for all financial statement assertions. Documentation may be limited to the auditor's
a. Understanding of the internal control structure.
b. Understanding of the internal control structure and his conclusion that control risk is at the maximum level.
c. Understanding of the internal control structure, his conclusion that control risk is at the maximum level, and his basis for that conclusion.
d. Completed internal control questionnaire.

14. The auditor would be **least** likely to be concerned about the internal control structure as it relates to
a. Land and buildings.
b. Common stock.
c. Shareholder meetings.
d. Minutes of board of directors meetings.

15. Which of the following is intended to detect deviations from prescribed Accounting Department procedures?
a. Substantive tests specified by a standardized audit program.
b. Tests of controls designed specifically for the client.
c. Analytical procedures as designed in the industry audit guide.
d. Computerized analytical procedures tailored for the configuration of EDP equipment in use.

16. While substantive tests may support the accuracy of underlying records, these tests frequently provide no affirmative evidence of segregation of duties because
a. Substantive tests rarely guarantee the accuracy of the records if only a sample of the transactions has been tested.
b. The records may be accurate even though they are maintained by persons having incompatible functions.
c. Substantive tests relate to the entire period under audit, but tests of control ordinarily are confined to the period during which the auditor is on the client's premises.
d. Many computerized procedures leave no audit trail of who performed them, so substantive tests may necessarily be limited to inquiries and observation of office personnel.

17. Which of the following symbolic representations indicates that a sales invoice has been filed?

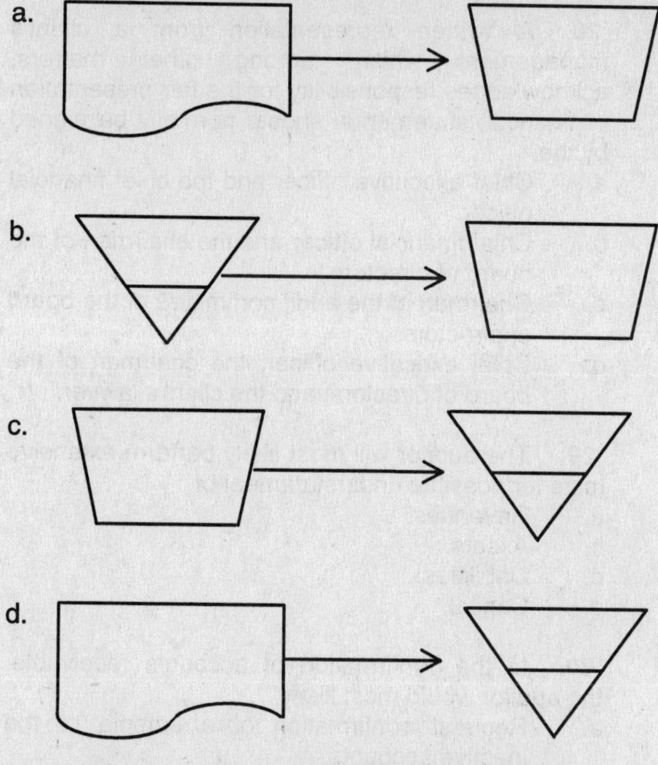

18. Which of the following statements best describes the auditor's responsibility regarding the detection of material errors and irregularities?
a. The auditor is responsible for the failure to detect material errors and irregularities only when such failure results from the nonapplication of generally accepted accounting principles.
b. Extended auditing procedures are required to detect material errors and irregularities if the audit indicates that they may exist.
c. The auditor is responsible for the failure to detect material errors and irregularities only when the auditor fails to confirm receivables or observe inventories.
d. Extended auditing procedures are required to detect unrecorded transactions even if there is no evidence that material errors and irregularities may exist.

19. When using the work of a specialist, the auditor may make reference to and identification of the specialist in the auditor's report if the
a. Auditor decides to express a qualified opinion.
b. Specialist's reputation or professional certification is being emphasized.
c. Auditor wishes to indicate a division of responsibility.
d. Specialist's work provides the auditor greater assurance of reliability.

20. When an auditor is unable to inspect and count a client's investment securities until after the balance-sheet date, the bank where the securities are held in a safe deposit box should be asked to
a. Verify any differences between the contents of the box and the balances in the client's subsidiary ledger.
b. Provide a list of securities added and removed from the box between the balance sheet date and the security-count date.
c. Confirm that there has been **no** access to the box between the balance sheet date and the security-count date.
d. Count the securities in the box so the auditor will have an independent direct verification.

21. The auditor's primary means of obtaining corroboration of management's information concerning litigation is a
a. Letter of audit inquiry to the client's lawyer.
b. Letter of corroboration from the auditor's lawyer upon review of the legal documentation.
c. Confirmation of claims and assessments from the other parties to the litigation.
d. Confirmation of claims and assessments from an officer of the court presiding over the litigation.

22. Which of the following might be detected by an auditor's review of the client's sales cut-off?
a. Excessive goods returned for credit.
b. Unrecorded sales discounts.
c. Lapping of year-end accounts receivable.
d. Inflated sales for the year.

23. An auditor would be most likely to consider expressing a qualified opinion if the client's financial statements include a footnote on related party transactions that
a. Lists the amounts due from related parties including the terms and manner of settlement.
b. Discloses compensating balance arrangements maintained for the benefit of related parties.
c. Represents that certain transactions with related parties were consummated on terms equally as favorable as would have been obtained in transactions with unrelated parties.
d. Presents the dollar volume of related party transactions and the effects of any change in the method of establishing terms from that of the prior period.

24. The permanent file section of the working papers that is kept for each audit client most likely contains
a. Review notes pertaining to questions and comments regarding the audit work performed.
b. A schedule of time spent on the engagement by each individual auditor.
c. Correspondence with the client's legal counsel concerning pending litigation.
d. Narrative descriptions of the client's accounting procedures and internal control structure.

25. Which of the following is **not** one of the independent auditor's objectives regarding the examination of inventories?
a. Verifying that inventory counted is owned by the client.
b. Verifying that the client has used proper inventory pricing.
c. Ascertaining the physical quantities of inventory on hand.
d. Verifying that all inventory owned by the client is on hand at the time of the count.

26. Prior to the acceptance of an audit engagement with a client who has terminated the services of the predecessor auditor, the CPA should
a. Contact the predecessor auditor without advising the prospective client and request a complete report of the circumstances leading to the termination, with the understanding that all information disclosed will be kept confidential.
b. Accept the engagement without contacting the predecessor auditor since the CPA can include audit procedures to verify the reason given by the client for the termination.
c. Not communicate with the predecessor auditor because this would violate the confidential relationship between auditor and client.
d. Advise the client of the intention to contact the predecessor auditor and request permission for the contact.

27. Two months before year-end, the bookkeeper erroneously recorded the receipt of a long-term bank loan by a debit to cash and a credit to sales. Which of the following is the most effective procedure for detecting this type of error?
a. Analyze the notes payable journal.
b. Analyze bank confirmation information.
c. Prepare a year-end bank reconciliation.
d. Prepare a year-end bank transfer schedule.

28. A written representation from a client's management which, among other matters, acknowledges responsibility for the fair presentation of financial statements, should normally be signed by the
a. Chief executive officer and the chief financial officer.
b. Chief financial officer and the chairman of the board of directors.
c. Chairman of the audit committee of the board of directors.
d. Chief executive officer, the chairman of the board of directors, and the client's lawyer.

29. The auditor will most likely perform extensive tests for possible understatement of
a. Revenues.
b. Assets.
c. Liabilities.
d. Capital.

30. In the confirmation of accounts receivable, the auditor would most likely
a. Request confirmation of a sample of the inactive accounts.
b. Seek to obtain positive confirmations for at least 50% of the total dollar amount of the receivables.
c. Require confirmation of all receivables from agencies of the federal government.
d. Require that confirmation requests be sent within one month of the fiscal year-end.

31. The auditor notices significant fluctuations in key elements of the company's financial statements. If management is unable to provide an acceptable explanation, the auditor should
a. Consider the matter a scope limitation.
b. Perform additional audit procedures to investigate the matter further.
c. Intensify the audit with the expectation of detecting management fraud.
d. Withdraw from the engagement.

32. The auditor is most likely to seek information from the plant manager with respect to the
a. Adequacy of the provision for uncollectible accounts.
b. Appropriateness of physical inventory observation procedures.
c. Existence of obsolete machinery.
d. Deferral of procurement of certain necessary insurance coverage.

33. Which of the following statements is correct concerning statistical sampling in testing of controls?
a. The population size has little or no effect on determining sample size except for very small populations.
b. The expected population deviation rate has little or **no** effect on determining sample size except for very small populations.
c. As the population size doubles, the sample size also should double.
d. For a given tolerable rate, a larger sample size should be selected as the expected population deviation rate decreases.

34. The diagram below depicts the auditor's estimated deviation rate compared with the tolerable rate, and also depicts the true population deviation rate compared with the tolerable rate.

Auditor's Estimate Based on Sample Results	True State of Population: Deviation Rate Exceeds Tolerable Rate	True State of Population: Deviation Rate Is Less Than Tolerable Rate
Deviation Rate Exceeds Tolerable Rate	I.	III.
Deviation Rate Is Less Than Tolerable Rate	II.	IV.

As a result of testing of controls, the auditor assesses control risk too high and thereby increases substantive testing. This is illustrated by situation
a. I.
b. II.
c. III.
d. IV.

35. The theoretical distribution of means from all possible samples of a given size is a normal distribution and this distribution is the basis for statistical sampling. Which of the following statements is **not** true with respect to the sampling distribution of sample means?
a. Approximately 68% of the sample means will be within one standard deviation of the mean for the normal distribution.
b. The distribution is defined in terms of its mean and its standard error of the mean.
c. An auditor can be approximately 95% confident that the mean for a sample is within two standard deviations of the population mean.
d. The items drawn in an auditor's sample will have a normal distribution.

36. The tolerable rate of deviations for a test of controls is generally
a. Lower than the expected rate of misstatements in the related accounting records.
b. Higher than the expected rate of misstatements in the related accounting records.
c. Identical to the expected rate of misstatements in the related accounting records.
d. Unrelated to the expected rate of misstatements in the related accounting records.

37. The most important function of generalized audit software is the capability to
a. Access information stored on computer files.
b. Select a sample of items for testing.
c. Evaluate sample test results.
d. Test the accuracy of the client's calculations.

38. Camela Department Stores has a fully integrated EDP accounting system and is planning to issue credit cards to creditworthy customers. To strengthen internal control by making it difficult for one to create a valid customer account number, the company's independent auditor has suggested the inclusion of a check digit which should be placed
a. At the beginning of a valid account number, only.
b. In the middle of a valid account number, only.
c. At the end of a valid account number, only.
d. Consistently in any position.

39. Totals of amounts in computer-record data fields which are not usually added for other purposes but are used only for data processing control purposes are called
a. Record totals.
b. Hash totals.
c. Processing data totals.
d. Field totals.

40. Auditing by testing the input and output of an EDP system instead of the computer program itself will
a. Not detect program errors which do **not** show up in the output sampled.
b. Detect all program errors, regardless of the nature of the output.
c. Provide the auditor with the same type of evidence.
d. Not provide the auditor with confidence in the results of the auditing procedures.

41. The principal auditor is satisfied with the independence and professional reputation of the other auditor who has audited a subsidiary but wants to indicate the division of responsibility. The principal auditor should

a. Modify only the scope paragraph of the report.
b. Modify both the scope and opinion paragraph of the report.
c. Modify the introductory, scope and opinion paragraphs of the report.
d. **Not** modify the report except for inclusion of a separate explanatory paragraph.

42. An auditor issued an audit report that was dual dated for a subsequent event occurring after the completion of field work but before issuance of the auditor's report. The auditor's responsibility for events occurring subsequent to the completion of field work was

a. Limited to the specific event referenced.
b. Limited to include only events occurring before the date of the last subsequent event referenced.
c. Extended to subsequent events occurring through the date of issuance of the report.
d. Extended to include all events occurring since the completion of field work.

43. After issuing a report an auditor concludes that an auditing procedure considered necessary at the time of the audit was omitted from the audit. The auditor should first

a. Undertake to apply the omitted procedure or alternative procedures that would provide a satisfactory basis for the auditor's opinion.
b. Assess the importance of the omitted procedure to the auditor's ability to support the opinion expressed on the financial statements taken as a whole.
c. Notify the audit committee or the board of director's that the auditor's opinion can **no** longer be relied upon.
d. Review the results of other procedures that were applied to compensate for the one omitted or to make its omission less important.

44. Management of Blue Company has decided not to account for a material transaction in accordance with the provisions of a FASB Standard. In setting forth its reasons in a note to the financial statements, management has clearly demonstrated that due to unusual circumstances the financial statements presented in accordance with the FASB Standard would be misleading. The auditor's report should include an explanatory separate paragraph and contain a(an)

a. Adverse opinion.
b. Unqualified opinion.
c. "Except for" qualified opinion.
d. "Subject to" qualified opinion.

45. The auditor concludes that there is a material inconsistency in the other information in an annual report to shareholders containing audited financial statements. If the client refuses to revise or eliminate the material inconsistency, the auditor should

a. Revise the auditor's report to include a separate explanatory paragraph describing the material inconsistency.
b. Consult with a party whose advice might influence the client, such as the client's legal counsel.
c. Issue a qualified opinion after discussing the matter with the client's board of directors.
d. Consider the matter closed since the other information is **not** in the audited financial statements.

46. An auditor includes a separate paragraph in an otherwise unqualified report to emphasize that the entity being reported upon had significant transactions with related parties. The inclusion of this separate paragraph

a. Violates generally accepted auditing standards if this information is already disclosed in footnotes to the financial statements.
b. Necessitates a revision of the opinion paragraph to include the phrase "with the foregoing explanation."
c. Is appropriate and would **not** negate the unqualified opinion.
d. Is considered an "except for" qualification of the report.

47. Which of the following subsequent events will be **least** likely to result in an adjustment to the financial statements?

a. Culmination of events affecting the realization of accounts receivable owned as of the balance sheet date.
b. Culmination of events affecting the realization of inventories owned as of the balance sheet date.
c. Material changes in the settlement of liabilities which were estimated as of the balance sheet date.
d. Material changes in the quoted market prices of listed investment securities since the balance sheet date.

48. The fourth reporting standard requires the auditor's report to contain either an expression of opinion regarding the financial statements taken as a whole, or an assertion to the effect that an opinion cannot be expressed. The objective of the fourth standard is to prevent

a. An auditor from reporting on one basic financial statement and **not** the others.
b. An auditor from expressing different opinions on each of the basic financial statements.
c. Management from reducing its final responsibility for the basic financial statements.
d. Misinterpretations regarding the degree of responsibility the auditor is assuming.

49. Jones, CPA, audited the 19X3 financial statements of Ray Corp. and issued an unqualified opinion on March 10, 19X4. On April 2, 19X4, Jones became aware of a 19X3 transaction that may materially affect the 19X3 financial statements. This transaction would have been investigated had it come to Jones' attention during the course of the audit. Jones should

a. Take **no** action because an auditor is **not** responsible for events subsequent to the issuance of the auditor's report.
b. Contact Ray's management and request their cooperation in investigating the matter.
c. Request that Ray's management disclose the possible effects of the newly discovered transaction by adding an unaudited footnote to the 19X3 financial statements.
d. Contact all parties who might rely upon the financial statements and advise them that the financial statements are misleading.

50. Which of the following will **not** result in modification of the auditor's report due to a scope limitation?

a. Restrictions imposed by the client.
b. Reliance placed on the report of another auditor.
c. Inability to obtain sufficient competent evidential matter.
d. Inadequacy in the accounting records.

51. The objective of the consistency standard is to provide assurance that

a. There are **no** variations in the format and presentation of financial statements.
b. Substantially different transactions and events are **not** accounted for on an identical basis.
c. The auditor is consulted before material changes are made in the application of accounting principles.
d. The comparability of financial statements between periods is **not** materially affected by changes in accounting principles without disclosure.

52. When comparative financial statements are presented but the predecessor auditor's report is **not** presented, the current auditor should do which of the following in the audit report?

a. Disclaim an opinion on the prior year's financial statements.
b. Identify the predecessor auditor who audited the financial statements of the prior year.
c. Make **no** comment with respect to the predecessor audit.
d. Indicate the type of opinion expressed by the predecessor auditor.

53. An auditor's report issued in connection with which of the following is generally not considered to be a special report?

a. Compliance with aspects of contractual agreements unrelated to audited financial statements.
b. Specified elements, accounts, or items of a financial statement presented in a document.
c. Financial statements prepared in accordance with an entity's income tax basis.
d. Financial information presented in a prescribed schedule that requires a prescribed form of auditor's report.

54. When an auditor reports on financial statements prepared on an entity's income tax basis, the auditor's report should

a. Disclose that the statements are presented in conformity with a comprehensive basis of accounting other than generally accepted accounting principles.
b. Disclaim an opinion on whether the statements were audited in accordance with generally accepted auditing standards.
c. **Not** express an opinion on whether the statements are presented in conformity with the comprehensive basis of accounting used.
d. Include an explanation of how the results of operations differ from the cash receipts and disbursements basis of accounting.

55. The objective of a review of interim financial information is to provide the accountant with a basis for reporting whether

a. A reasonable basis exists for expressing an updated opinion regarding the financial statements that were previously audited.
b. Material modifications should be made to conform with generally accepted accounting principles.
c. The financial statements are presented fairly in accordance with standards of interim reporting.
d. The financial statements are presented fairly in conformity with generally accepted accounting principles.

56. An auditor's report on the internal controls of a publicly held company would ordinarily be of least use to

a. Shareholders.
b. Officers.
c. Directors.
d. Regulatory agencies.

57. When an accountant is **not** independent of a client and is requested to perform a compilation of its financial statements, the accountant

a. Is precluded from accepting the engagement.
b. May accept the engagement and need **not** disclose the lack of independence.
c. May accept the engagement and should disclose the lack of independence, but **not** the reason for the lack of independence.
d. May accept the engagement and should disclose both the lack of independence and the reason for the lack of independence.

58. When an accountant compiles projected financial statements, the accountant's report should include a separate paragraph that

a. Describes the differences between a projection and a forecast.
b. Identifies the accounting principles used by management.
c. Expresses limited assurance that the actual results may be within the projection's range.
d. Describes the limitations on the projection's usefulness.

59. Which one of the following is generally more important in a review than in a compilation?

a. Determining the accounting basis on which the financial statements are to be presented.
b. Gaining familiarity with industry accounting principles and practices.
c. Obtaining a signed engagement letter.
d. Obtaining a signed representation letter.

60. When auditing an entity's financial statements in accordance with *Government Auditing Standards*, an auditor should prepare a written report on the auditor's

a. Identification of the causes of performance problems and recommendations for actions to improve operations.
b. Understanding of the internal control structure and assessment of control risk.
c. Field work and procedures that substantiated the auditor's specific findings and conclusions.
d. Opinion on the entity's attainment of the goals and objectives specified by applicable laws and regulations.

SOLUTIONS

Solution 1 MULTIPLE CHOICE ANSWERS

1. (d) AU 319.58 states that after considering the level to which the auditor seeks to restrict the risk of a material misstatement in the financial statements and the assessed levels of inherent risk and control risk, the auditor performs substantive tests to restrict detection risk to an acceptable level. As the assessed level of control risk decreases (or increases, for this question), the acceptable level of detection risk increases (or decreases, for this question). To increase control risk while maintaining the same audit risk level, the auditor could also reduce inherent risk; therefore, answer (a) is incorrect. If the auditor were to increase materiality levels, that would reduce the overall audit risk; therefore, answer (b) is incorrect. When the auditor increases control risk and thus decreases detection risk, substantive testing would need to be increased; therefore, answer (c) is incorrect.

2. (c) Incompatible functions are those that place any person in a position to both perpetrate and conceal errors or irregularities in the normal course of his or her duties. Therefore, a well-designed plan of organization separates the duties of authorization, record keeping, and custody of assets.

3. (c) AU 329.04 states that analytical procedures should be applied to some extent to assist the auditor in planning the nature, timing, and extent of the auditing procedures to be performed and as an overall review of the financial information in the final review stage of the audit.

4. (d) QC 90.23 states that policies and procedures should be established for deciding whether to accept or continue a client in order to minimize the likelihood of association with a client whose management lacks integrity. Answers (a) and (b) are incorrect because QC 90.23 states that the existence of such procedures does not imply that a firm vouches for the integrity or reliability of a client, nor does it imply that a firm has a duty to anyone but itself. Answer (c) is incorrect because the failure to detect irregularities in client financial statements will result in the same exposure to litigation regardless of whether the CPA has quality control policies and procedures. However, the existence of quality control procedures would reduce the likelihood of having such irregularities.

5. (b) The question requirement is to determine the best test of controls for an internal control procedure that calls for an approved receiving report to accompany every check. This control can be tested by selecting canceled checks and ascertaining that the related receiving reports are dated no later than the check. (In addition, the auditor would probably want to ascertain that the amount of the checks corresponds to the price of the goods received.) Answer (c) is incorrect because if the auditor selects receiving reports (rather than checks) to test this control, he or she will not become aware of instances where checks were written with no accompanying receiving report.

6. (c) The accounts payable department receives the vendor's invoice which contains the quantities, descriptions, and prices of the items subject to the bill. A copy of the purchase order will enable the accounts payable department to (1) compare the invoice price with the purchase order price [answer (a)], (2) ensure that the purchase was properly authorized [answer (b)], and (3) compare the quantity ordered to the quantity purchased [answer (d)]. The accounts payable copy of the purchase order will not ensure that the goods had been received by the party requesting the goods.

7. (b) Payroll checks should be distributed directly to employees, on proper identification, by treasurer's department personnel. The checks should not be returned to payroll for distribution since the payroll department would then have control over both preparing and paying the payroll. The payroll department supervisor should be responsible for hiring subordinate payroll department employees, updating employee earnings records, and applying pay rates to time tickets.

8. (c) Continuous utilization of serially numbered retirement work orders will provide assurance that the authorized retirements were in fact reflected in the accounting records. Continuous analysis of the repair and maintenance account [answer (a)] will provide assurance that capitalizable expenditures are not expensed. Periodic inquiry of plant <u>executives</u> [answer (b)] is not an effective procedure because such executives are not in a position to be aware of fixed asset retirements. Periodic inspection of insurance policies by internal auditors [answer (d)] will improve accountability of insurance expense, but some fixed assets may not be insured. The retirement of such assets would not be indicated in the insurance policies.

9. (a) Incompatible functions are those that place any person in a position to both perpetrate and conceal errors or irregularities in the normal course of his duties. An employee who has access to assets as well as the accounting records related to those assets performs incompatible functions. The cashier performs incompatible functions if he or she can both receive remittances and post the receipts to the accounts receivable subsidiary ledger. Answers (b), (c), and (d) are all functions normally performed by the cashier.

10. (b) By reconciling the vendors' monthly statements with the subsidiary payable ledger accounts, the error would be corrected in at most a month's time. Answer (a) is incorrect because footing the purchases journal would only verify the <u>mathematical</u> accuracy of the journal. Answer (c) is incorrect because the erroneous purchase amount in the purchases journal was originally carried through from the <u>client's</u> ledger accounts. Answer (d) is incorrect because the vendor may not confirm the fact that the client is <u>overstating</u> its liability for the purchases.

11. (d) Sound internal control procedures dictate that an employee should be responsible for performing a given function, and that the same employee should not perform an incompatible function. Thus, all incoming shipments, including returns by customers, should be processed by personnel in the receiving department. A receiving clerk should inspect the merchandise and prepare a receiving report. This employee should not have control over the inventory records because that

would enable him or her to divert merchandise without recording it.

12. (c) AU 325.02 states that the independent auditor should communicate to senior management and to the board of directors or its audit committee (or the equivalent level of authority, such as a board of trustees) any material weaknesses that come to his or her attention during the course of the audit of the financial statements if such weaknesses have not been corrected before they come to his or her attention. Preferably, the auditor's findings should be communicated in a written report to reduce the possibility of misunderstanding. If the auditor's findings are communicated orally, he or she should document the communication by appropriate notations in the working papers. Answer (a) is incorrect because if the auditor does not become aware of any material weaknesses in internal control during the audit of the financial statements, the auditor may, but is not required to, communicate that fact. However, he or she should not issue a written report stating that "no material weaknesses were noted" (AU 325.17). Answer (b) is incorrect because it does not pertain to the required communications of material weaknesses in internal control. Answer (d) is incorrect because AU 325.18 states, "because timely communication may be important, the auditor may choose to communicate significant matters during the course of the audit rather than after the audit is concluded."

13. (b) In addition to the documentation of the understanding of the internal control structure, the auditor should document the basis for the conclusions about the assessed level of control risk. However, for those financial statement assertions where control risk is assessed at the maximum level, the auditor should document his or her conclusion that control risk is at the maximum level but need not document the basis for that conclusion (AU 319.39).

14. (c) The independent auditor is primarily concerned with those internal control structure policies and procedures that are relevant to the audit. Generally, the policies and procedures relevant to the audit pertain to an entity's ability to record, process, summarize, and report financial data consistent with the assertions embodied in the financial statements (AU 319.06). Internal controls over land and buildings [answer (a)] and common stock [answer (b)] are of primary concern to the auditor because they relate directly to financial statement assertions. Internal control over meetings of shareholders [answer (c)] and the minutes of board of directors meetings [answer (d)] are in the nature of administrative controls. Although these controls are of secondary concern to the auditor, the controls over the minutes of board of directors meetings are more important than those over shareholder meetings because they relate directly to management's authorization of transactions. Shareholder meetings can only have an indirect impact on such authorization.

15. (b) Tests of controls directed toward the effectiveness of the design of an internal control structure policy or procedure are concerned with whether that policy or procedure is suitably designed to prevent or detect material misstatements in specific financial statement assertions (AU 319.34). Answers (a), (c), and (d) are all incorrect because they consist of substantive tests which are tests of details and analytical procedures performed to detect material misstatements in the account balance, transaction class, and disclosure components of financial statements.

16. (b) The primary purpose of substantive tests is to determine the validity or propriety of the accounting treatment of transactions, or, conversely, monetary errors or irregularities therein. Substantive tests may support the accuracy of underlying records, but these tests frequently provide no affirmative evidence of segregation of duties because the records may be accurate even though they are maintained by persons having incompatible functions. Tests of controls directed toward operation are used to provide evidence of segregation of duties since the primary purpose of these tests is to determine how the policies or procedures are applied, the consistency with which they were applied, and by whom they were applied (AU 319.35).

17. (d) Answer (a) represents that a document undergoes some kind of manual operation. Answer (b) represents that a file is accessed for some kind of manual operation. Answer (c) represents that an item is filed after being subject to some kind of manual operation.

18. (b) The auditor has the responsibility under GAAS to plan his or her audit to provide reasonable assurance of detecting errors or irregularities that would materially affect the financial statements. The auditor usually satisfies this responsibility by exercising due skill and care in the performance of the audit procedures considered appropriate under the circumstances. If these procedures indicate that material errors or irregularities may exist, the auditor should extend his or her audit procedures (AU 316.21).

19. (a) AU 336.12 provides that "If the auditor decides to depart from an unqualified opinion . . . as a result of the report or findings of a specialist, reference to an identification of the specialist may be made in the auditor's report if the auditor believes such reference will facilitate an understanding of the reason for the departure." Answers (b), (c), and (d) are incorrect because reference to a specialist should not be made if an unqualified opinion is expressed (AU 336.11).

20. (c) The bank should be asked to confirm that there has been no access to the box between the balance sheet date and the security-count date. If the client has had access to the box between those dates, the auditor should obtain from the client a list of securities added or removed, so as to reconcile the securities on hand on the count date to the securities listed in the subsidiary ledger on the balance-sheet date. Furthermore, the auditor should test the list of securities added or removed by tracing them to brokers' documents indicating sale or purchase of the securities. Answers (a) and (d) are incorrect because those procedures should be performed by the auditor, not by the bank's staff. In general, evidential matter is more persuasive when directly obtained by the auditor than when obtained from third parties. Answer (b) is incorrect because banks normally don't keep lists of contents of safe deposit boxes.

21. (a) A letter of audit inquiry to the client's lawyer is the auditor's primary means of obtaining corroboration of the information furnished by management concerning litigations, claims, and assessments (AU 337.08). Note that auditors are not presumed to be experts on legal matters and so are not required to review legal documentation [answer (b)].

22. (d) The main objective of the sales cut-off test is to determine that sales were recorded in the proper period. Answers (a) and (b) are incorrect because the auditor would test for excessive sales returns and discounts from a sample encompassing the entire period, not just the year-end work. Lapping of accounts receivable [answer (c)] would be detected by tracing payments received to postings in the appropriate receivable subsidiary ledger.

23. (c) It is difficult to substantiate representations that a transaction was consummated on terms equivalent to those that prevail in arm's-length transactions. Thus, if a footnote includes such a representation, the auditor should express a qualified or adverse opinion because of a departure from GAAP (AU 334.12). Answers (a), (b), and (d) are all proper disclosures with respect to related party transactions.

24. (d) The permanent file--as indicated by its name--contains information on the client which is <u>not</u> likely to change from year to year. This information should be periodically updated and it is often used as a basis for the preliminary design of the current year's engagement. Descriptions of the client's accounting procedures and internal control structure are the types of information found in this file. The types of information listed in answers (a), (b), and (c) mainly affect only the current year's engagement and so they are likely to be found in the current file, not the permanent file.

25. (d) It is common practice for inventory to be sold on consignment. When this is the case, it is not necessary for the consigned inventory to be on hand at the time of the count. However, the auditor should perform audit procedures to verify the existence and amount of consigned inventory. Answers (a), (b), and (c) are all audit objectives regarding the examination of inventory.

26. (d) AU 315.05 states, "The successor auditor should explain to his [or her] prospective client the need to make an inquiry of the predecessor and should request permission to do so." Answer (a) is incorrect because such an arrangement would cause the predecessor to violate the confidential relationship between the client and the predecessor. Answer (b) is incorrect because the predecessor should be contacted prior to acceptance of the engagement. Answer (c) is incorrect because the predecessor may communicate with the successor provided that the client grants permission for the contact. Such communication does not violate the auditor-client confidentiality.

27. (b) An analysis of bank confirmation information will reveal that the long-term liability accounts of the client are understated. Answer (a) is incorrect because the notes payable journal would not appear to be in error until the notes payable were confirmed. Answers (c) and (d) are incorrect because a year-end bank reconciliation and a year-end bank transfer schedule are used to verify the accuracy of the cash account which is not affected, in this case, by the bookkeeper's error.

28. (a) The written representation letter should be signed by members of management who the auditor believes are responsible for and knowledgeable, directly or through others in the organization, about the matters covered by the representations. Normally, the chief executive

officer and chief financial officer should sign the letter (AU 333.09). Answers (b), (c), and (d) are all incorrect because they suggest that the representation letter be signed by those who are not members of management, such as the chairman of the board of directors, the chairman of the board's audit committee, and the client's lawyer.

29. (c) The financial statements are the representations of management, who would like the financial position of the entity to appear as sound as possible. Thus, the auditor is concerned with possible overstatements of revenues [answer (a)], income, assets [answer (b)], and capital [answer (d)]. Conversely, the auditor is concerned with the possible understatement of any losses, expenses, and liabilities [answer (c)].

30. (a) By requesting confirmation of a sample of the inactive accounts, the auditor is seeking to determine the accuracy of the financial records with regard to the accounts. Due to their inactive nature, defalcations could occur in these accounts, e.g., through lapping or an improper writing-off of the account balance. Answer (b) is incorrect because the cost of obtaining positive confirmations for at least 50% of the total dollar amount of the receivables would far outweigh the benefits derived from such confirmations (AU 326.21). Answer (c) is incorrect because the auditor does not treat receivables from agencies of the federal government any differently than other receivables, i.e., they are subjected to selective testing, also. Answer (d) is incorrect because receivable confirmations can be sent as of any date.

31. (b) If management is unable to provide an acceptable explanation of significant fluctuations, the auditor should perform additional procedures to investigate those fluctuations further (AU 329.21). Answer (a) is incorrect because a scope limitation would only result if, after applying all the procedures considered necessary, the auditor is not able to explain the significant fluctuations. Answer (c) is incorrect because the existence of fluctuations is not necessarily indicative of management fraud. Answer (d) is incorrect because the auditor should consider withdrawal from the engagement if his or her audit indicates errors, irregularities, or illegal acts by clients. The discovery of significant fluctuations in the financial statements does not provide the auditor with enough evidence to indicate these types of problems.

32. (c) The plant manager has a thorough knowledge of the operation of the factory. This knowledge comprehends an awareness of the productive capability of all the machinery in the plant, as well as new machinery on the market. As a result, he or she would know whether a particular machine is obsolete. Answer (a) is incorrect because the plant manager has no contact with accounts receivable and, thus, is not in a position to know about the adequacy of the provision for uncollectible accounts. Answer (b) is incorrect because the auditor must determine the appropriateness of the inventory observation procedures. The plant manager, on the other hand, would be helpful in identifying the location of all the inventory. Answer (d) is incorrect because the plant manager is not responsible for procuring necessary insurance coverage and, therefore, would not be aware that such procurement was deferred.

33. (a) When a sample is small in relation to the population, the population size has little or no effect on the determination of an appropriate sample size. However, in the rare case when the sample size is greater than 10% of the population size, a finite population correction factor may be used, which tends to decrease the required sample size. Answer (b) is incorrect. The required sample size varies with the expected deviation rate. Answer (c) is incorrect. As the population increases in size, the sample size necessary to represent the population with specified precision and reliability will increase, but not in proportion to the increase in population size. Answer (d) is incorrect. The tolerable rate is the maximum population rate of deviations from a prescribed control procedure that the auditor will tolerate without modifying the nature, timing, or extent of substantive testing. For a given tolerable rate, a smaller sample size should be selected as the expected population deviation rate decreases.

34. (c) An auditor assesses control risk too high when the results of his or her testing of controls indicate that the deviation rate exceeds the tolerable rate, when in fact this is not the case for the population taken as a whole. Assessing control risk too high generally results in the auditor increasing his or her substantive tests of detail, thereby increasing the cost of the audit. In contrast, assessing control risk too low would tend to reduce the cost of the audit but would increase the risk of material misstatements in the financial statements.

35. (d) Upon repeated random samples of a given size from a population, the distribution of the means of those samples will be a normal distribution. The mean of the distribution is equal to the population mean and the standard error of the mean of the distribution equals the population standard deviation divided by the square root of the sample size [answer (b)]. Approximately 68% and

95% of the sample means will be within one and two standard deviations, respectively, of the mean of the distribution [answers (a) and (c)]. All of these characteristics relate to the distribution of sample means that results from repeated samples of a given size from a population. However, the distribution of the items drawn by the auditor in a particular sample may take on any form. Such a sample distribution is not necessarily a normal distribution, and therefore, the statement in answer (d) is not true.

36. (b) The tolerable rate of deviations is the maximum rate of deviations from a prescribed control procedure that the auditor is willing to accept without altering his or her assessed level of control risk. Deviations from pertinent control procedures do not necessarily result in misstatements because the transactions may still be recorded properly. Therefore, deviations from pertinent control procedures at a given rate ordinarily would be expected to result in misstatements at a lower rate (AU 350.33-.34).

37. (a) Accessing information stored on computer files is the <u>most</u> important function of generalized audit software (GAS) because it is the only function of GAS that the auditor cannot do for himself.

38. (d) A check digit is a redundant digit added to a code or identification number for validation purposes. It can be inserted into any position as long as it is inserted consistently. In this respect, the auditor is able to recompute the check digit to determine whether an invalid number has been created.

39. (b) A hash total is a sum that is formed for error-checking purposes by adding fields that are not normally related by unit of measure, e.g., a total of invoice serial numbers. Answers (a) and (d) are incorrect because they would provide useful information other than for control purposes. Answer (c) is not a valid term.

40. (a) If correct input data is processed by a program which contains one or more errors and the output does not reflect the errors in the program, the auditor will not detect any errors inherent in the program by testing the input and output of an EDP system. Answer (b) is incorrect because program errors which do not show up in the output will not be detected. Answer (c) is incorrect because the two different procedures may very well provide the auditor with different types of evidence. Answer (d) is incorrect because testing the input and output of an EDP system is an audit procedure in which the results may in fact provide the auditor with confidence.

41. (c) When the principal auditor decides that he or she will make reference to the audit of the other auditor, the report should clearly indicate, in the introductory, scope, and opinion paragraphs, the division of responsibility as between that portion of the financial statements covered by his or her own audit and that covered by the audit of the other auditor (AU 543.07).

42. (a) When an auditor dual-dates a report, his or her responsibility for events occurring subsequent to the completion of fieldwork is limited to the specific event referenced (AU 530.05).

43. (b) The omission of an auditing procedure that was considered necessary at the time of the audit does not necessarily imply that the opinion originally rendered is faulty, or that not enough auditing procedures were performed. Thus, the auditor should first assess the importance of the omitted procedure to his or her present ability to support the previously expressed opinion (AU 390.04). The results of other procedures originally applied or the results of subsequent audits may provide audit evidence of the audit opinion originally rendered. If at this point the auditor concludes that the omitted procedure is indeed necessary to support the opinion, then he or she should undertake to apply the omitted procedure (AU 390.05).

44. (b) An independent auditor <u>generally</u> cannot express an unqualified opinion stating that financial statements are presented in conformity with generally accepted accounting principles if such statements contain a departure from accounting principles promulgated by the designated body, and the departure has a material effect on the financial statements taken as a whole. However, an independent auditor can express an unqualified opinion on such statements if he or she can demonstrate that due to unusual circumstances the financial statements would otherwise be misleading (AU 508.14 and .15).

45. (a) AU 550.04 states, "If the other information is not revised to eliminate the material inconsistency, the auditor should consider other actions such as revising his [or her] report to include an explanatory paragraph describing the material inconsistency." Therefore, answer (d) is incorrect. Answer (b) is incorrect because the auditor should never consult with the client's legal counsel without first obtaining permission from the client. Answer (c) is incorrect because the issuance of a qualified opinion would be misleading since the financial

statements themselves are presented fairly in conformity with GAAP.

46. (c) In some circumstances, the auditor may wish to emphasize a matter regarding the financial statements, but nevertheless intends to express an unqualified opinion. For example, the auditor may wish to point out that the entity is a component of a larger business enterprise or that it has had significant transactions with related parties, or to call attention to an unusually important subsequent event or to an accounting matter affecting the comparability of the financial statements with those of the preceding period. Such explanatory information may be presented in a separate paragraph of the auditor's report. Phrases such as "with the foregoing explanation" should not be used in the opinion paragraph in situations of this type (AU 508.37).

47. (d) AU 560.07 states, "Subsequent events such as changes in the quoted market prices of securities ordinarily should not result in adjustment of the financial statements because such changes typically reflect a concurrent evaluation of new conditions." The financial statements are typically adjusted for subsequent events that (1) provide additional evidence with respect to conditions that existed at the balance sheet date and (2) affect the estimates inherent in the process of preparing financial statements. Answers (a), (b), and (c) are all examples of the type of subsequent events that typically result in adjustments to the financial statements, because they are examples of conditions which existed at the balance sheet date.

48. (d) AU 504.01 states, "The objective of the fourth reporting standard is to prevent misinterpretation of the degree of responsibility the accountant assumes when his [or her] name is associated with financial statements." Answers (a) and (b) are incorrect because the auditor is not precluded from reporting on one statement and not the others. Nor is he or she precluded from expressing differing opinions on the basic financial statements. Answer (c) is incorrect because management can never reduce its final responsibility for the basic financial statements.

49. (b) AU 561.04 provides that an auditor should, in this situation, discuss the matter with the client at whatever management levels he or she deems appropriate, including the board of directors, and request cooperation in whatever investigation may be necessary. Answer (a) is incorrect because the transaction arose before the balance sheet date, and the auditor is responsible for reporting on such an event. Answer (c) is incorrect because an <u>unaudited</u> footnote should not be added to the 19X3 financial statements. Answer (d) is incorrect because the client--not the auditor--is the party responsible for notifying those who might rely on the financial statements.

50. (b) When reliance is placed on the report of another auditor, the report should disclose the division of responsibility between the two auditors but would not necessarily modify the report (AU 543.07). Answers (a), (c), and (d) are all examples of restrictions on the scope of the audit which will result in modification of the report (AU 508.40).

51. (d) The objective of the consistency standard is (1) to give assurance that the comparability of financial statements between periods has not been materially affected by changes in accounting principles, or (2) if comparability has been materially affected by such changes, to require appropriate reporting by the independent auditor regarding such changes (AU 420.02). Answer (a) is incorrect because variations in the format and presentation of financial statements can be made without affecting the consistency standard. Answer (b) is incorrect because modification of an accounting principle necessitated by transactions or events that are clearly different in substance from those previously occurring does not involve the consistency standard (AU 420.16). Answer (c) is incorrect because although management will generally consult the auditor regarding changes in accounting principles, this is not the primary objective of the consistency standard.

52. (d) The current auditor should indicate in the introductory paragraph of his report (1) the date of the prior report, (2) the type of report issued by the predecessor auditor and (3) the reasons for any report other than a standard report (AU 508.83). Concerning answer (a), the current auditor expresses an opinion in the opinion paragraph only on the current period which he or she audited. The current auditor does not disclaim an opinion on the prior period statements, or mention them at all. Answer (b) is incorrect because the successor auditor should not name the predecessor auditor in his or her report unless the predecessor's practice was acquired by, or merged with, that of the successor auditor (AU 508.83). Answer (c) is incorrect because the current auditor comments on the predecessor auditor's report in the introductory paragraph, as mentioned above.

53. (a) AU 623.01 states that special reports include ". . . auditors' reports issued in connection with (1) financial statements that are prepared in conformity with a comprehensive basis of

accounting other than generally accepted accounting principles, (2) specified elements, accounts, or items of a financial statement, (3) compliance with aspects of contractual agreements or regulatory requirements related to audited financial statements, (4) financial presentations to comply with contractual agreements or regulatory provisions, and (5) financial information presented in prescribed forms or schedules that require a prescribed form of auditor's report." An auditor's report issued in connection with compliance with aspects of contractual agreements unrelated to audited financial statements is not considered to be a special report.

54. (a) When reporting on financial statements prepared on an entity's income tax basis, the auditor's report should include a paragraph which discloses that the statements are presented in conformity with a comprehensive basis of accounting other than GAAP. Answer (b) is incorrect. The auditor does not express an opinion on whether the statements were audited in accordance with GAAS. Answer (c) is incorrect. The auditor should report on whether the statements are presented in conformity with the basis used. Answer (d) is incorrect. The report should explain how the basis used differs from GAAP.

55. (b) The objective of a review of interim financial information is to provide the accountant, based on objectively applying his or her knowledge of financial reporting practices to significant accounting matters of which he or she becomes aware through inquiries and analytical review procedures, with a basis for reporting whether material modifications should be made for such information to conform with generally accepted accounting principles (AU 722.05).

56. (a) Reports on internal control are usually for the restricted use of management, specified regulatory agencies [answer (d)], and sometimes specified third parties. In this context, the term management includes directors [answer (c)], officers [answer (b)], and others who perform managerial functions (AU 642.02, footnote 2). Thus, reports on internal control are ordinarily of least use to shareholders [answer (a)].

57. (c) AR 100.22 states that "An accountant is not precluded from issuing a report with respect to his [or her] compilation of financial statements for an entity with respect to which he [or she] is not independent. If the accountant is not independent, he [or she] should specifically disclose the lack of independence. However, the reason for the lack of independence should not be described."

58. (d) When an accountant compiles projected financial statements, the accountant's report should include a separate paragraph that describes the limitations on the usefulness of the presentation.

59. (d) In a compilation, the accountant presents, in the form of financial statements, information that is the representation of management. No expression of assurance is contemplated in a compilation. In a review, however, the accountant makes inquiries and performs analytical procedures which should provide a reasonable basis for expressing limited assurance that there are no material modifications that should be made to the financial statements. Because of this increased level of responsibility in a review, the accountant is required to obtain a management representation letter. Answers (a), (b), and (c) are all incorrect because they each list one of the prerequisites for performing either a compilation or a review.

60. (b) In the *Government Auditing Standards* for financial audits, the third supplemental reporting standard states that the auditor should prepare a written report on his or her understanding of the entity's internal control structure and the assessment of control risk made as part of a financial statement audit or a financial related audit. Answer (a) is incorrect because this represents procedures to be reported in a performance audit, not a financial statement audit. Answer (c) is incorrect because specific procedures performed are not included in the auditor's report. Answer (d) is incorrect because the auditor does not provide an opinion on the entity's attainment of the goals and objectives as specified by laws and regulations; rather, the auditor provides an opinion on the fairness of the presentation of the financial statements taken as a whole.

ESSAY QUESTIONS

Essay 2 (15 to 25 minutes)

Loman, CPA, who has audited the financial statements of the Broadwall Corporation, a publicly held company, for the year ended December 31, 19X1, was asked to perform a review of the financial statements of Broadwall Corporation for the period ending March 31, 19X2. The engagement letter stated that a review does not provide a basis for the expression of an opinion.

Required:

a. Explain why Loman's review will not provide a basis for the expression of an opinion.

b. What are the review procedures which Loman should perform, and what is the purpose of each procedure? Structure your response as follows:

Procedure	Purpose of Procedure

Essay 3 (20 to 25 minutes)

Various types of "accounting changes" can affect the second reporting standard of the generally accepted auditing standards. This standard reads: "The report shall identify those circumstances in which such principles have not been consistently observed in the current period in relation to the preceding period."

Assume that the following list describes changes which have a material effect on a client's financial statements for the current year.

1. A change from the completed-contract method to the percentage-of-completion method of accounting for long-term construction-type contracts.

2. A change in the estimated useful life of previously recorded fixed assets based on newly acquired information.

3. Correction of a mathematical error in inventory pricing made in a prior period.

4. A change from prime costing to full absorption costing for inventory valuation.

5. A change from presentation of statements of individual companies to presentation of consolidated statements.

6. A change from deferring and amortizing preproduction costs to recording such costs as an expense when incurred because future benefits of the costs have become doubtful. The new accounting method was adopted in recognition of the change in estimated future benefits.

7. A change to including the employer share of FICA taxes as "Retirement benefits" on the income statement from including it as "Other taxes."

8. A change from the FIFO method of inventory pricing to the LIFO method of inventory pricing.

Required:

Identify the type of change which is described in each item above, state whether any modification is required in the auditor's report **as it relates to the second standard of reporting,** and state whether the prior year's financial statements should be restated when presented in comparative form with the current year's statements. Organize your answer sheet as shown below.

For example, a change from the LIFO method of inventory pricing to the FIFO method of inventory pricing would appear as shown.

Item No.	Type of Change	Should Auditor's Report Be Modified?	Should Prior Year's Statement Be Restated?
Example	An accounting change from one generally accepted accounting principle to another generally accepted accounting principle.	Yes	Yes

Essay 4 (15 to 25 minutes)

Rivers, CPA, is the auditor for a manufacturing company with a balance sheet that includes the caption "Property, Plant, and Equipment." Rivers has been asked by the company's management if audit adjustments or reclassifications are required for the following material items that have been included or excluded from "Property, Plant, and Equipment."

1. A tract of land was acquired during the year. The land is the future site of the client's new headquarters which will be constructed in the following year. Commissions were paid to the real estate agent used to acquire the land, and expenditures were made to relocate the previous owner's equipment. These commissions and expenditures were expensed and are excluded from "Property, Plant, and Equipment."

2. Clearing costs were incurred to make the land ready for construction. These costs were included in "Property, Plant, and Equipment."

3. A group of machines was purchased under a royalty agreement which provides royalty payments based on units of production from the machines. The cost of the machines, freight costs, unloading charges, and royalty payments were capitalized and are included in "Property, Plant, and Equipment."

Required:

a. Describe the general characteristics of assets, such as land, buildings, improvements, machinery, equipment, fixtures, etc., that should normally be classified as "Property, Plant and Equipment," and identify audit objectives (i.e., how an auditor can obtain audit satisfaction) in connection with the examination of "Property, Plant, and Equipment." **Do not discuss specific audit procedures.**

b. Indicate whether each of the above items numbered 1 to 3 requires one or more audit adjustments or reclassifications, and explain why such adjustments or reclassifications are required or not required. Organize your answer as follows:

Item Number	Is Audit Adjustment or Reclassification Required Yes or No	Reasons Why Audit Adjustment or Reclassification Is Required or Not Required

Essay 5 (15 to 25 minutes)

A CPA has been asked to audit the financial statements of a publicly-held company for the first time. All preliminary verbal discussions and inquiries have been completed between the CPA, the company, the predecessor auditor, and all other necessary parties. The CPA is now preparing an engagement letter.

Required:

List the **items** that should be included in the typical engagement letter in these circumstances and describe the **benefits** derived from preparing an engagement letter.

SOLUTIONS TO ESSAY QUESTIONS

Solution 2

a. A **review of interim financial statements** does **not provide a basis for the expression of an opinion** because a review is not an audit performed in accordance with generally accepted auditing standards. That is, a review **does not contemplate obtaining an understanding of the internal control structure or assessing control risk**, tests of accounting records and of responses to inquiries by obtaining corroborating evidential matter through inspection, observation, or confirmation, and certain other procedures ordinarily performed during an audit.

b. The procedures that Loman must perform consist primarily of **inquiries and analytical procedures** concerning significant accounting matters relating to the financial information to be reported. The **procedures** that Loman should apply ordinarily **may be limited** to the following:

Procedure	Purpose of Procedure
Inquiry concerning the accounting system with respect to the preparation of interim financial statements.	To obtain an understanding of the manner in which transactions are recorded, classified, and summarized in the preparation of interim financial statements.
Inquiry concerning any significant changes in the internal control structure.	To ascertain their potential effect on the preparation of interim financial statements.
Analytical procedures applied to interim financial statements.	To identify and inquire about relationships and individual items that appear to be unusual.
Reading the minutes of meetings of stockholders, board of directors and committees of the board of directors.	To identify actions that may affect the interim financial statements.
Reading the interim financial statements.	To consider, on the basis of information coming to the accountant's attention, whether the information to be reported conforms with generally accepted accounting principles.
Considering the types of matters that have previously required adjustments.	To give adequate consideration to matters that historically warrant consideration.
Obtaining reports from other accountants who may have been engaged to make a review of the interim financial information of significant segments of the reporting entity, its subsidiaries, or other investees.	As a basis, in part, for the report.
Inquiry of officers and other executives having responsibility for financial and accounting matters concerning-- (a) Whether the interim financial statements have been prepared in conformity with generally accepted accounting principles. (b) **Changes** in the entity's business activities or accounting practices.	In order to become aware of significant matters affecting the interim financial statements.

Procedure	Purpose of Procedure
(c) Matters about which questions have arisen in applying the foregoing procedures.	
(d) **Events subsequent** to the date of the interim financial statements that would have a material effect on the presentation of such statements.	
Obtain **written representation** from management concerning its responsibility for the financial information, completeness of minutes, subsequent events and other matters for which Loman believes written representations are appropriate.	In order to reduce the possibility of misunderstandings.

Solution 3

Item No.	Type of Change	Should Auditor's Report Be Modified?	Should Prior Year's Statement Be Restated?
1.	An accounting change involving a **change** from one generally accepted accounting **principle** to another generally accepted accounting principle.	Yes	Yes
2.	An accounting change involving a **change in an accounting estimate.**	No	No
3.	An **error correction** not involving an accounting principle.	No	Yes
4.	An accounting change involving a correction of an error in principle which is accounted for as a correction of an error.	Yes	Yes
5.	An accounting change involving a **change in the reporting entity** which is a special type of change in accounting principle.	Yes	Yes
6.	An accounting change involving both a change in accounting principle and a change in accounting estimate. Although the effect of the change in each may be inseparable and the accounting for such a change is the same as that accorded a change in estimate only, an accounting principle is involved.	Yes	No
7.	Not an accounting change but rather a **change in classification.**	No	Yes
8.	An accounting change **from one generally accepted accounting principle to another** generally accepted accounting principle.	Yes	No

Solution 4

a. "Property, Plant, and Equipment" normally includes only fixed tangible assets. Fixed tangible assets are capital assets with useful lives generally in excess of one year that are used in the operation of the business and that are not purchased for resale purposes. In connection with the examination of property, plant, and equipment (PP&E), the auditor must be satisfied that--

(1) **Internal controls** over PP&E and PP&E acquisitions are **adequate.**
(2) Assets included in PP&E **exist** and are being used in the normal operations of the business.
(3) Assets included in PP&E are **owned** by the company whose financial statements are being audited.
(4) Assets included in PP&E are **not encumbered by liens** or, if so, the facts are properly disclosed in the footnotes to the financial statements.
(5) **Depreciation** and/or amortization **methods** are **proper**.
(6) Amounts in the financial statements are in substantial **agreement** with the **supporting records.**
(7) Accounting for additions, disposals, and retirements is proper.
(8) **Maintenance accounts** do not include items that should be capitalized.
(9) The **valuation** and the **disclosure** of the method of valuation are acceptable.
(10) Important information relating to the assets is properly disclosed.

b.

Item Number	Is Audit Adjustment or Reclassification Required Yes or No	Reasons Why Audit Adjustment or Reclassification Is Required or Not Required
1.	Yes	**Commissions paid** to real estate agents are costs **directly related to the acquisition** of the property and **should be included** in the land cost. Costs of removing, relocating, or reconstructing property of others to acquire possession are costs that are directly **attributable to conditioning the property for use** and should be **included in land costs**. An adjustment is required for these items so that total land costs can properly be included in "Property, Plant, and Equipment."
2.	No	No adjustment is required because clearing costs are costs that are **directly attributable to conditioning the property for use** and **should be included** in land costs which are part of "Property, Plant, and Equipment."
3.	Yes	All costs relating to the purchase of machinery and equipment should be capitalized. For purchased items such costs would include invoice price, freight costs, and unloading charges. **Royalty** payments, however, **should not be included** in the cost of the machinery. Such payments should be charged to expenses as they accrue. The machinery costs, other than royalty payments, should be included in "Property, Plant, and Equipment."

Solution 5

The typical engagement letter generally includes the following:

(1) The **name** and address of the person or **persons who retained the auditor** to perform the auditing services.
(2) An opening paragraph that confirms the **understandings** of the auditor and the client.
(3) A summary of significant events that led to the retention of the services of the auditor.
(4) A general description of the CPA firm that will conduct the audit.
(5) A **statement that the audit will be performed in accordance with generally accepted auditing standards.**
(6) A **description of the scope** of the **services** to be rendered, which should establish the nature of the engagement.
(7) Any **scope restriction** or **special limitations** and their effect on the auditor's report.
(8) A statement regarding the **auditor's responsibility for the detection of fraud**.
(9) An indication of the possible **use of client personnel** in connection with the audit to be performed.
(10) A statement that the **auditor will provide a management letter** if required in the circumstances.
(11) The **method and timing of billings** as well as billing rates and fee arrangements.
(12) Space for the **client representative's signature**, which indicates "acceptance" of the letter and the understandings therein.

The benefits of preparing an engagement letter include the **avoidance of possible problems** between the CPA and the client concerning (1) the **scope** of the work, (2) the **service** to be rendered, and (3) the audit **fee**. In addition, the "in-charge" auditor conducting the audit can avoid misunderstanding the nature and scope of the engagement if the engagement letter is included in the permanent section of the audit working papers. The **letter should eliminate misunderstandings and confusion** about the type of financial statements to be audited, the estimated report date, and the type of opinion expected. In this respect, the letter lessens any problems associated with the first standard of field work, which requires the work to be adequately planned and assistants to be properly supervised. In addition to avoiding possible misunderstandings, any legal problems relating to the auditor's failure to perform certain procedures can be reviewed with reference to the contractual commitment assumed. (For example, if scope limitations prevent the auditor from performing normal audit procedures, the auditor cannot be legally responsible if an irregularity is not detected when clearly it would have been detected if such procedures were performed.)

The engagement letter is also useful as a **reference document** when preparing for future engagements.

NOTES

AUDITING INDEX

A

D

E

F

G

M

N

O

P

NOTES

NOTES

APPENDIX B

NOVEMBER 1995 UNIFORM CPA EXAMINATION

AUDITING

Number 1 (Estimated time--140 to 150 minutes)

1. In assessing the objectivity of internal auditors, an independent auditor should
a. Evaluate the quality control program in effect for the internal auditors.
b. Examine documentary evidence of the work performed by the internal auditors.
c. Test a sample of the transactions and balances that the internal auditors examined.
d. Determine the organizational level to which the internal auditors report.

2. In planning an audit, the auditor's knowledge about the design of relevant internal control policies and procedures should be used to
a. Identify the types of potential misstatements that could occur.
b. Assess the operational efficiency of the internal control structure.
c. Determine whether controls have been circumvented by collusion.
d. Document the assessed level of control risk.

3. Able Co. uses an online sales order processing system to process its sales transactions. Able's sales data are electronically sorted and subjected to edit checks. A direct output of the edit checks most likely would be a
a. Report of all missing sales invoices.
b. File of all rejected sales transactions.
c. Printout of all user code numbers and passwords.
d. List of all voided shipping documents.

4. Which of the following auditor concerns most likely could be so serious that the auditor concludes that a financial statement audit **cannot** be conducted?
a. The entity has **no** formal written code of conduct.
b. The integrity of the entity's management is suspect.
c. Procedures requiring segregation of duties are subject to management override.
d. Management fails to modify prescribed controls for changes in conditions.

5. Management philosophy and operating style most likely would have a significant influence on an entity's control environment when
a. The internal auditor reports directly to management.
b. Management is dominated by one individual.
c. Accurate management job descriptions delineate specific duties.
d. The audit committee actively oversees the financial reporting process.

6. Which of the following is a management control method that most likely could improve management's ability to supervise company activities effectively?
a. Monitoring compliance with internal control requirements imposed by regulatory bodes.
b. Limiting direct access to assets by physical segregation and protective devices.
c. Establishing budgets and forecasts to identify variances from expectations.
d. Supporting employees with the resources necessary to discharge their responsibilities.

Items 7 and 8 are based on the following flowchart of a client's revenue cycle:

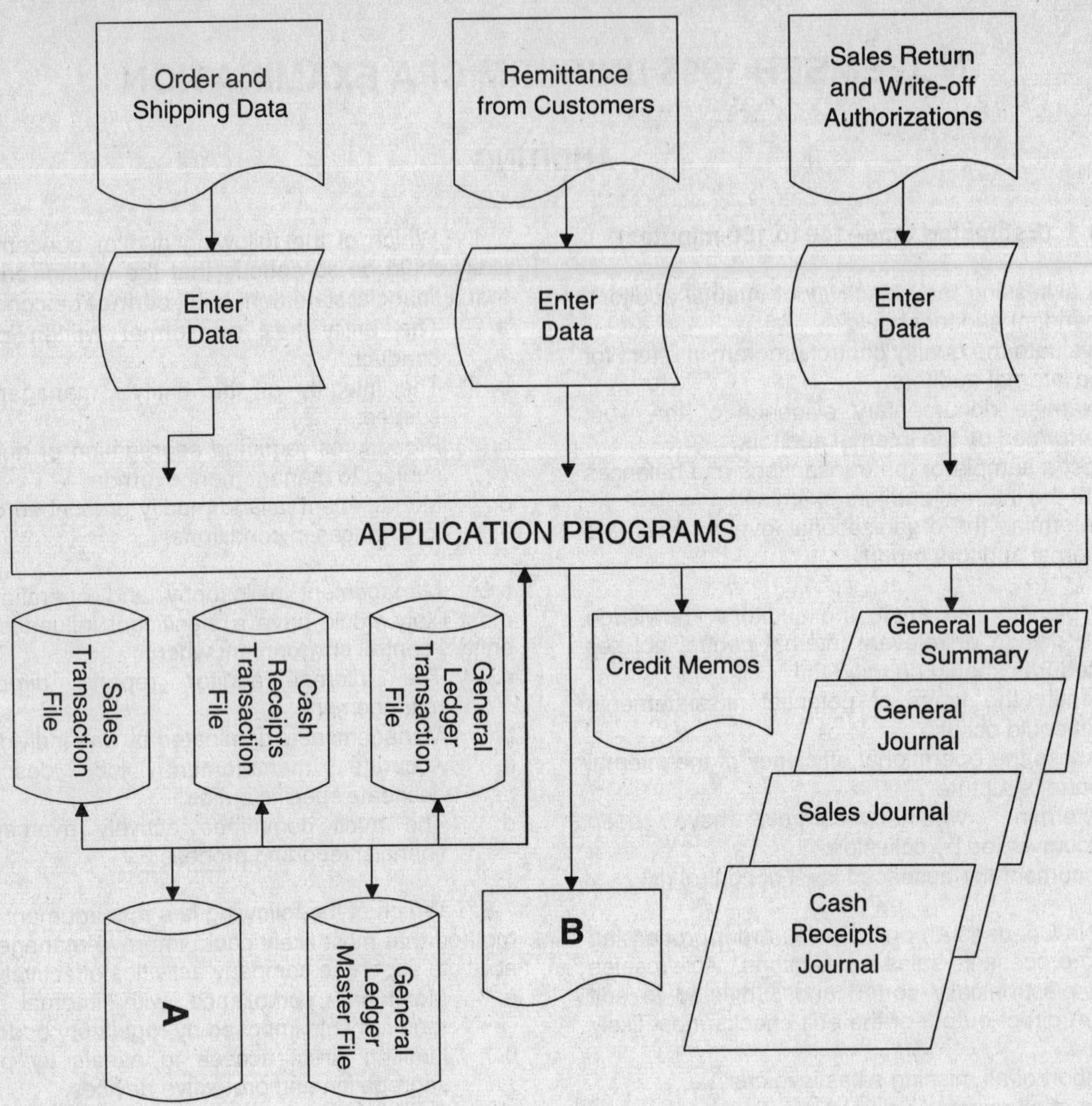

7. Symbol A most likely represents
   a. Remittance advice file.
   b. Receiving report file.
   c. Accounts receivable master file.
   d. Cash disbursements transaction file.

8. Symbol B most likely represents
   a. Customer orders.
   b. Receiving reports.
   c. Customer checks.
   d. Sales invoices.

9. In an audit of financial statements in accordance with generally accepted auditing standards, an auditor is required to

a. Document the auditor's understanding of the entity's internal control structure.
b. Search for significant deficiencies in the operation of the internal control structure.
c. Perform tests of controls to evaluate the effectiveness of the entity's accounting system.
d. Determine whether control procedures are suitably designed to prevent or detect material misstatements.

10. Which of the following is an example of a validity check?

a. The computer ensures that a numerical amount in a record does **not** exceed some predetermined amount.
b. As the computer corrects errors and data are successfully resubmitted to the system, the causes of the errors are printed out.
c. The computer flags any transmission for which the control field value did **not** match that of an existing file record.
d. After data for a transaction are entered, the computer sends certain data back to the terminal for comparison with data originally sent.

11. Which of the following types of evidence would an auditor most likely examine to determine whether internal control structure policies and procedures are operating as designed?

a. Gross margin information regarding the client's industry.
b. Confirmations of receivables verifying account balances.
c. Client records documenting the use of EDP programs.
d. Anticipated results documented in budgets or forecasts.

12. Which of the following internal controls most likely would reduce the risk of diversion of customer receipts by an entity's employees?

a. A bank lockbox system.
b. Prenumbered remittance advices.
c. Monthly bank reconciliations.
d. Daily deposit of cash receipts.

13. In obtaining an understanding of an entity's internal control structure policies and procedures that are relevant to audit planning, an auditor is required to obtain knowledge about the

a. Design of the policies and procedures pertaining to the internal control structure elements.
b. Effectiveness of the policies and procedures that have been placed in operation.
c. Consistency with which the policies and procedures are currently being applied.
d. Control procedures related to each principal transaction class and account balance.

14. Which of the following control procedures most likely could prevent EDP personnel from modifying programs to bypass programmed controls?

a. Periodic management review of computer utilization reports and systems documentation.
b. Segregation of duties within EDP for computer programming and computer operations.
c. Participation of user department personnel in designing and approving new systems.
d. Physical security of EDP facilities in limiting access to EDP equipment.

15. Which of the following is a control procedure that most likely could help prevent employee payroll fraud?

a. The personnel department promptly sends employee termination notices to the payroll supervisor.
b. Employees who distribute payroll checks forward unclaimed payroll checks to the absent employees' supervisors.
c. Salary rates resulting from new hires are approved by the payroll supervisor.
d. Total hours used for determination of gross pay are calculated by the payroll supervisor.

16. Which of the following controls would a company most likely use to safeguard marketable securities when an independent trust agent is **not** employed?

a. The investment committee of the board of directors periodically reviews the investment decisions delegated to the treasurer.
b. Two company officials have joint control of marketable securities, which are kept in a bank safe-deposit box.
c. The internal auditor and the controller independently trace all purchases and sales of marketable securities from the subsidiary ledgers to the general ledger.
d. The chairman of the board verifies the marketable securities, which are kept in a bank safe-deposit box, each year on the balance sheet date.

17. The diagram below depicts an auditor's estimated maximum deviation rate compared with the tolerable rate, and also depicts the true population deviation rate compared with the tolerable rate.

Auditor's estimate based on sample results	*True state of population*	
	Deviation rate is less than tolerable rate	Deviation rate exceeds tolerable rate
Maximum deviation rate is less than tolerable rate	I.	III.
Maximum deviation rate exceeds tolerable rate	II.	IV.

As a result of tests of controls, the auditor assesses control risk too low and thereby decreases substantive testing. This is illustrated by situation

a. I.
b. II.
c. III.
d. IV.

18. In assessing control risk, an auditor ordinarily selects from a variety of techniques, including

a. Inquiry and analytical procedures.
b. Reperformance and observation.
c. Comparison and confirmation.
d. Inspection and verification.

19. The risk of incorrect acceptance and the likelihood of assessing control risk too low relate to the

a. Allowable risk of tolerable misstatement.
b. Preliminary estimates of materiality levels.
c. Efficiency of the audit.
d. Effectiveness of the audit.

20. Which of the following statements is correct concerning an auditor's assessment of control risk?

a. Assessing control risk may be performed concurrently during an audit with obtaining an understanding of the entity's internal control structure.
b. Evidence about the operation of control procedures in prior audits may **not** be considered during the current year's assessment of control risk.
c. The basis for an auditor's conclusions about the assessed level of control risk need **not** be documented unless control risk is assessed at the maximum level.
d. The lower the assessed level of control risk, the less assurance the evidence must provide that the control procedures are operating effectively.

21. An auditor assesses control risk because it

a. Is relevant to the auditor's understanding of the control environment.
b. Provides assurance that the auditor's materiality levels are appropriate.
c. Indicates to the auditor where inherent risk may be the greatest.
d. Affects the level of detection risk that the auditor may accept.

22. Assessing control risk at below the maximum level most likely would involve

a. Performing more extensive substantive tests with larger sample sizes than originally planned.
b. Reducing inherent risk for most of the assertions relevant to significant account balances.
c. Changing the timing of substantive tests by omitting interim-date testing and performing the tests at year end.
d. Identifying specific internal control structure policies and procedures relevant to specific assertions.

23. After assessing control risk at below the maximum level, an auditor desires to seek a further reduction in the assessed level of control risk. AT this time, the auditor would consider whether

a. It would be efficient to obtain an understanding of the entity's accounting system.
b. The entity's internal control structure policies and procedures have been placed in operation.
c. The entity's internal control structure policies and procedures pertain to any financial statement assertions.
d. Additional evidential matter sufficient to support a further reduction is likely to be available.

24. When assessing control risk below the maximum level, an auditor is required to document the auditor's

	Understanding of the entity's control environment	*Basis for concluding that control risk is below the maximum level*
a.	Yes	No
b.	No	Yes
c.	Yes	Yes
d.	No	No

25. An auditor who uses statistical sampling for attributes in testing internal controls should reduce the planned reliance on a prescribed control when the
a. Sample rate of deviation plus the allowance for sampling risk equals the tolerable rate.
b. Sample rate of deviation is less than the expected rate of deviation used in planning the sample.
c. Tolerable rate less the allowance for sampling risk exceeds the sample rate of deviation.
d. Sample rate of deviation plus the allowance for sampling risk exceeds the tolerable rate.

26. In addition to evaluating the frequency of deviations in tests of controls, an auditor should also consider certain qualitative aspects of the deviations. The auditor most likely would give broader consideration to the implications of a deviation if it was
a. The only deviation discovered in the sample.
b. Identical to a deviation discovered during the prior year's audit.
c. Caused by an employee's misunderstanding of instructions.
d. Initially concealed by a forged document.

27. When there are numerous property and equipment transactions during the year, an auditor who plans to assess control risk at a low level usually performs
a. Tests of controls and extensive tests of property and equipment balances at the end of the year.
b. Analytical procedures for current year property and equipment transactions.
c. Tests of controls and limited tests of current year property and equipment transactions.
d. Analytical procedures for property and equipment balances at the end of the year.

28. An auditor suspects that a client's cashier is misappropriating cash receipts for personal use by lapping customer checks received in the mail. In attempting to uncover this embezzlement scheme, the auditor most likely would compare the
a. Dates checks are deposited per bank statements with the dates remittance credits are recorded.
b. Daily cash summaries with the sums of the cash receipts journal entries.
c. Individual bank deposit slips with the details of the monthly bank statements.
d. Dates uncollectible accounts are authorized to be written off with the dates the write-offs are actually recorded.

29. In testing controls over cash disbursements, an auditor most likely would determine that the person who signs checks also
a. Reviews the monthly bank reconciliation.
b. Returns the checks to accounts payable.
c. Is denied access to the supporting documents.
d. Is responsible for mailing the checks.

30. For effective internal control, the accounts payable department generally should
a. Stamp, perforate, or otherwise cancel supporting documentation after payment is mailed.
b. Ascertain that each requisition is approved as to price, quantity, and quality by an authorized employee.
c. Obliterate the quantity ordered on the receiving department copy of the purchase order.
d. Establish the agreement of the vendor's invoice with the receiving report and purchase order.

31. In determining the effectiveness of an entity's policies and procedures relating to the existence or occurrence assertion for payroll transactions, an auditor most likely would inquire about and
a. Observe the segregation of duties concerning personnel responsibilities.
b. Inspect evidence of accounting for prenumbered payroll checks.
c. Recompute the payroll deductions for employee fringe benefits.
d. Verify the preparation of the monthly payroll account bank reconciliation.

32. In obtaining an understanding of a manufacturing entity's internal control structure concerning inventory balances, an auditor most likely would
a. Analyze the liquidity and turnover ratios of the inventory.
b. Perform analytical procedures designed to identify cost variances.
c. Review the entity's descriptions of inventory policies and procedures.
d. Perform test counts of inventory during the entity's physical count.

33. Which of the following factors is(are) considered in determining the sample size for a test of controls?

	Expected deviation rate	*Tolerable deviation rate*
a.	Yes	Yes
b.	No	No
c.	No	Yes
d.	Yes	No

34. A weakness of internal control over recording retirements of equipment may cause an auditor to

a. Inspect certain items of equipment in the plant and trace those items to the accounting records.
b. Review the subsidiary ledger to ascertain whether depreciation was taken on each item of equipment during the year.
c. Trace additions to the "other assets" account to search for equipment that is still on hand but **no** longer being used.
d. Select certain items of equipment from the accounting records and locate them in the plant.

35. An auditor's letter issued on reportable conditions relating to an entity's internal control structure observed during a financial statement audit should

a. Include a brief description of the tests of controls performed in searching for reportable conditions and material weaknesses.
b. Indicate that the reportable conditions should be disclosed in the annual report to the entity's shareholders.
c. Include a paragraph describing management's assertion concerning the effectiveness of the internal control structure.
d. Indicate that the audit's purpose was to report on the financial statements and **not** to provide assurance on the internal control structure.

36. Brown, CPA, has accepted an engagement to examine and report on Crow Company's written assertion about the effectiveness of Crow's internal control structure. In what form may Crow present its written assertion?

I. In a separate report that will accompany Brown's report.
II. In a representation letter to Brown.

a. I only.
b. II only.
c. Either I or II.
d. Neither I nor II.

37. Computer Services Company (CSC) processes payroll transactions for schools. Drake, CPA, is engaged to report on CSC's policies and procedures placed in operation as of a specific date. These policies and procedures are relevant to the schools' internal control structure, so Drake's report will be useful in providing the schools' independent auditors with information necessary to plan their audits. Drake's report expressing an opinion on CSC's policies and procedures placed in operation as of a specific date should contain a(an)

a. Description of the scope and nature of Drake's procedures.
b. Statement that CSC's management has disclosed to Drake all design deficiencies of which it is aware.
c. Opinion on the operating effectiveness of CSC's policies and procedures.
d. Paragraph indicating the basis for Drake's assessment of control risk.

38. An auditor may achieve audit objectives related to particular assertions by

a. Performing analytical procedures.
b. Adhering to a system of quality control.
c. Preparing auditor working papers.
d. Increasing the level of detection risk.

39. The confirmation of customers' accounts receivable rarely provides reliable evidence about the completeness assertion because

a. Many customers merely sign and return the confirmation without verifying its details.
b. Recipients usually respond only if they disagree with the information on the request.
c. Customers may **not** be inclined to report understatement errors in their accounts.
d. Auditors typically select many accounts with low recorded balances to be confirmed.

40. Which of the following sets of information does an auditor usually confirm on one form?

a. Accounts payable and purchase commitments.
b. Cash in bank and collateral for loans.
c. Inventory on consignment and contingent liabilities.
d. Accounts receivable and accrued interest receivable.

41. An auditor's analytical procedures most likely would be facilitated if the entity

a. Segregated obsolete inventory before the physical inventory count.
b. Uses a standard cost system that produces variance reports.
c. Corrects material weaknesses in internal control before the beginning of the audit.
d. Develops its data from sources solely within the entity.

42. To measure how effectively an entity employs its resources, an auditor calculates inventory turnover by dividing average inventory into

a. Net sales.
b. Cost of goods sold.
c. Operating income.
d. Gross sales.

43. How would increases in tolerable misstatement and assessed level of control risk affect the sample size in a substantive test of details?

	Increase in tolerable misstatement	*Increase in assessed level of control risk*
a.	Increase sample size	Increase sample size
b.	Increase sample size	Decrease sample size
c.	Decrease sample size	Increase sample size
d.	Decrease sample size	Decrease sample size

44. An advantage of statistical sampling over nonstatistical sampling is that statistical sampling helps an auditor to

a. Eliminate the risk of nonsampling errors.
b. Reduce the level of audit risk and materiality to a relatively low amount.
c. Measure the sufficiency of the evidential matter obtained.
d. Minimize the failure to detect errors and irregularities.

45. The usefulness of the standard bank confirmation request may be limited because the bank employee who completes the form may

a. Not believe that the bank is obligated to verify confidential information to a third party.
b. Sign and return the form without inspecting the accuracy of the client's bank reconciliation.
c. Not have access to the client's cutoff bank statement.
d. Be unaware of all the financial relationships that the bank has with the client.

46. An auditor most likely would limit substantive audit tests of sales transactions when control risk is assessed as low for the existence or occurrence assertion concerning sales transactions and the auditor has already gathered evidence supporting

a. Opening and closing inventory balances.
b. Cash receipts and accounts receivable.
c. Shipping and receiving activities.
d. Cutoffs of sales and purchases.

47. Which of the following procedures would an auditor most likely perform in searching for unrecorded liabilities?

a. Trace a sample of accounts payable entries recorded just before year end to the unmatched receiving report file.
b. Compare a sample of purchase orders issued just after year end with the year-end accounts payable trial balance.
c. Vouch a sample of cash disbursements recorded just after year end to receiving reports and vendor invoices.
d. Scan the cash disbursements entries recorded just before year end for indications of unusual transactions.

48. An auditor traced a sample of purchase orders and the related receiving reports to the purchases journal and the cash disbursements journal. The purpose of this substantive audit procedure most likely was to

a. Identify unusually large purchases that should be investigated further.
b. Verify that cash disbursements were for goods actually received.
c. Determine that purchases were properly recorded.
d. Test whether payments were for goods actually ordered.

49. Which of the following explanations most likely would satisfy an auditor who questions management about significant debits to the accumulated depreciation accounts?

a. The estimated remaining useful lives of plant assets were revised upward.
b. Plant assets were retired during the year.
c. The prior year's depreciation expense was erroneously understated.
d. Overhead allocations were revised at year end.

50. Which of the following circumstances most likely would cause an auditor to suspect an employee payroll fraud scheme?

a. There are significant unexplained variances between standard and actual labor cost.
b. Payroll checks are disbursed by the same employee each payday.
c. Employee time cards are approved by individual departmental supervisors.
d. A separate payroll bank account is maintained on an imprest basis.

51. The objective of tests of details of transactions performed as substantive tests is to

a. Comply with generally accepted auditing standards.
b. Attain assurance about the reliability of the accounting system.
c. Detect material misstatements in the financial statements.
d. Evaluate whether management's policies and procedures operated effectively.

52. A primary advantage of using generalized audit software packages to audit the financial statements of a client that uses an EDP system is that the auditor may

a. Access information stored on computer files while having a limited understanding of the client's hardware and software features.
b. Consider increasing the use for substantive tests of transactions in place of analytical procedures.
c. Substantiate the accuracy of data through self-checking digits and hash totals.
d. Reduce the level of required tests of controls to a relatively small amount.

53. The work of internal auditors may affect the independent auditor's

I. Procedures performed in obtaining an understanding o the internal control structure.
II. Procedures performed in assessing the risk of material misstatement.
III. Substantive procedures performed in gathering direct evidence.

a. I and II only.
b. I and III only.
c. II and III only.
d. I, II, and III.

54. Which of the following statements is correct concerning an auditor's use of the work of a specialist?

a. The auditor need **not** obtain an understanding of the methods and assumptions used by the specialist.
b. The auditor may **not** use the work of a specialist in matters material to the fair presentation of the financial statements.
c. The reasonableness of the specialist's assumptions and their applications are strictly the auditor's responsibility.
d. The work of a specialist who has a contractual relationship with the client may be acceptable under certain circumstances.

55. Which of the following is an audit procedure that an auditor most likely would perform concerning litigation, claims, and assessments?

a. Request the client's lawyer to evaluate whether the client's pending litigation, claims, and assessments indicate a going concern problem
b. Examine the legal documents in the client's lawyer's possession concerning litigation, claims, and assessments to which the lawyer has devoted substantive attention.
c. Discuss with management its policies and procedures adopted for evaluating and accounting for litigation, claims, and assessments.
d. Confirm directly with the client's lawyer that all litigation, claims, and assessments have been recorded or disclosed in the financial statements.

56. Which of the following procedures would an auditor most likely perform to obtain evidence about the occurrence of subsequent events?

a. Confirming a sample of material accounts receivable established after year end.
b. Comparing the financial statements being reported on with those of the prior period.
c. Investigating personnel changes in the accounting department occurring after year end.
d. Inquiring as to whether any unusual adjustments were made after year end.

57. Which of the following matters would an auditor most likely include in a management representation letter?

a. Communications with the audit committee concerning weaknesses in the internal control structure.
b. The completeness and availability of minutes of stockholders' and directors' meetings.
c. Plans to acquire or merge with other entities in the subsequent year.
d. Management's acknowledgment of its responsibility for the detection of employee fraud.

58. Which of the following auditing procedures must likely would assist an auditor in identifying related party transactions?

a. Inspecting correspondence with lawyers for evidence of unreported contingent liabilities.
b. Vouching accounting records for recurring transactions recorded just after the balance sheet date.
c. Reviewing confirmations of loans receivable and payable for indications of guarantees.
d. Performing analytical procedures for indications of possible financial difficulties.

59. Cooper, CPA, believes there is substantial doubt about the ability of Zero Corp. to continue as a going concern for a reasonable period of time. In evaluating Zero's plans for dealing with the adverse effects of future conditions and events, Cooper most likely would consider, as a mitigating factor, Zero's plans to

a. Discuss with the lenders the terms of all debt and loan agreements.
b. Strengthen internal controls over cash disbursements.
c. Purchase production facilities currently being leased from a related party.
d. Postpone expenditures for research and development projects.

60. The permanent (continuing) file of an auditor's working papers most likely would include copies of the

a. Lead schedules.
b. Attorney's letters.
c. Bank statements.
d. Debt agreements.

61. Harris, CPA, has been asked to audit and report on the balance sheet of Fox Co. but not on the statements of income, retained earnings, or cash flows. Harris will have access to all information underlying the basic financial statements. Under these circumstances, Harris may

a. Not accept the engagement because it would constitute a violation of the profession's ethical standards.
b. Not accept the engagement because it would be tantamount to rendering a piecemeal opinion.
c. Accept the engagement because such engagements merely involve limited reporting objectives.
d. Accept the engagement but should disclaim an opinion because of an inability to apply the procedures considered necessary.

62. Which of the following statements is a basic element of the auditor's standard report?

a. The disclosures provide reasonable assurance that the financial statements are free of material misstatement.
b. The auditor evaluated the overall internal control structure.
c. An audit includes assessing significant estimates made by management.
d. The financial statements are consistent with those of the prior period.

63. An auditor may **not** issue a qualified opinion when

a. An accounting principle at variance with GAAP is used.
b. The auditor lacks independence with respect to the audited entity.
c. A scope limitation prevents the auditor from completing an important audit procedure.
d. The auditor's report refers to the work of a specialist.

64. An auditor most likely would express an unqualified opinion and would **not** add explanatory language to the report if the auditor

a. Wishes to emphasize that the entity had significant transactions with related parties.
b. Concurs with the entity's change in its method of computing depreciation.
c. Discovers that supplementary information required by FASB has been omitted.
d. Believes that there is a remote likelihood of a material loss resulting from an uncertainty.

65. An auditor would express an unqualified opinion with an explanatory paragraph added to the auditor's report for

	An unjustified accounting change	*A material weakness in the internal control structure*
a.	Yes	Yes
b.	Yes	No
c.	No	Yes
d.	No	No

66. Under which of the following circumstances would a disclaimer of opinion **not** be appropriate?

a. The auditor is unable to determine the amounts associated with an employee fraud scheme.
b. Management does **not** provide reasonable justification for a change in accounting principles.
c. The client refuses to permit the auditor to confirm certain accounts receivable or apply alternative procedures to verify their balances.
d. The chief executive officer is unwilling to sign the management representation letter.

67. Digit Co. uses the FIFO method of costing for its international subsidiary's inventory and LIFO for its domestic inventory. Under these circumstances, the auditor's report on Digit's financial statements should express an

a. Unqualified opinion.
b. Opinion qualified because of a lack of consistency.
c. Opinion qualified because of a departure from GAAP.
d. Adverse opinion.

68. The fourth standard of reporting requires the auditor's report to contain either an expression of opinion regarding the financial statements taken as a whole or an assertion to the effect that an opinion cannot be expressed. The objective of the fourth standard is to prevent

a. An auditor from expressing different opinion on each of the basic financial statements.
b. Restrictions on the scope of the audit, whether imposed by the client or by the inability to obtain evidence.
c. Misinterpretations regarding the degree of responsibility the auditor is assuming.
d. An auditor from reporting on one basic financial statement and **not** the others.

69. In which of the following circumstances would an auditor **not** express an unqualified opinion?

a. There has been a material change between periods in accounting principles.
b. Quarterly financial data required by the SEC has been omitted.
c. The auditor wishes to emphasize an unusually important subsequent event.
d. The auditor is unable to obtain audited financial statements of a consolidated investee.

70. An explanatory paragraph following the opinion paragraph of an auditor's report describes an uncertainty as follows:

> As discussed in Note X to the financial statements, the Company is a defendant in a lawsuit alleging infringement of certain patent rights and claiming damages. Discovery proceedings are in progress. The ultimate outcome of the litigation cannot presently be determined. Accordingly, no provision for any liability that may result upon adjudication has been made in the accompanying financial statements.

What type of opinion should the auditor express under these circumstances?

a. Adverse.
b. Qualified due to a scope limitation.
c. Qualified due to a GAAP violation.
d. Unqualified.

71. Which of the following phrases would an auditor most likely include in the auditor's report when expressing a qualified opinion because of inadequate disclosure?

a. Subject to the departure from generally accepted accounting principles, as described above.
b. With the foregoing explanation of these omitted disclosures.
c. Except for the omission of the information discussed in the preceding paragraph.
d. Does **not** present fairly in all material respects.

72. Kane, CPA, concludes that there is substantial doubt about Lima Co.'s ability to continue as a going concern for a reasonable period of time. If Lima's financial statements adequately disclose its financial difficulties, Kane's auditor's report is required to include an explanatory paragraph that specifically uses the phrase(s)

	"Possible discontinuance of operations"	*"Reasonable period of time, **not** to exceed one year"*
a.	Yes	Yes
b.	Yes	No
c.	No	Yes
d.	No	No

73. Mead, CPA, had substantial doubt about Tech Co.'s ability to continue as a going concern when reporting on Tech's audited financial statements for the year ended June 30, 1994. That doubt has been removed in 1995. What is Mead's reporting responsibility if Tech is representing its financial statements for the year ended June 30, 1995, on a comparative basis with those of 1994?

a. The explanatory paragraph included in the 1994 auditor's report should **not** be repeated.
b. The explanatory paragraph included in the 1994 auditor's report should be repeated in its entirety.
c. A different explanatory paragraph describing Mead's reasons for the removal of doubt should be included.
d. A different explanatory paragraph describing Tech's plans for financial recovery should be included.

74. In the first audit of a new client, an auditor was able to extend auditing procedures to gather sufficient evidence about consistency. Under these circumstances, the auditor should

a. Not report on the client's income statement.
b. Not refer to consistency in the auditor's report.
c. State that the consistency standard does **not** apply.
d. State that the accounting principles have been applied consistently.

75. When reporting on comparative financial statements, an auditor ordinarily should change the previously issued opinion on the prior-year's financial statements if the

a. Prior year's financial statements are restated to conform with generally accepted accounting principles.
b. Auditor is a predecessor auditor who has been requested by a former client to reissue the previously issued report.
c. Prior year's opinion was unqualified and the opinion on the current year's financial statements is modified due to a lack of consistency.
d. Prior year's financial statements are restated following a pooling of interests in the current year.

76. Jewel, CPA, audited Infinite Co.'s prior-year financial statements. These statements are presented with those of the current year for comparative purposes without Jewel's auditor's report, which expressed a qualified opinion. In drafting the current year's auditor's report, Crain, CPA, the successor auditor, should

I. Not name Jewel as the predecessor auditor.
II. Indicate the type of report issued by Jewel.
III. Indicate the substantive reasons for Jewel's qualification.

a. I only.
b. I and II only.
c. II and III only.
d. I, II, and III.

77. The introductory paragraph of an auditor's report contains the following sentences:

> We did not audit the financial statements of EZ Inc., a wholly-owned subsidiary, which statements reflect total assets and revenues constituting 27 percent and 29 percent, respectively, of the related consolidated totals. Those statements were audited by other auditors whose report has been furnished to us, and our opinion, insofar as it relates to the amounts included for EZ Inc., is based solely on the report of the other auditors.

78. March, CPA, is engaged by Monday Corp., a client, to audit the financial statements of Wall Corp., a company that is not March's client. Monday expects to present Wall's audited financial statements with march's auditor's report to 1st Federal Bank to obtain financing in Monday's attempt to purchase Wall. In these circumstances, March's auditor's report would usually be addressed to

a. Monday Corp., the client that engaged March.
b. Wall Corp., the entity audited by March.
c. 1st Federal Bank.
d. Both Monday Corp. and 1st Federal Bank.

79. Financial statements of a nonpublic entity that have been reviewed by an accountant should be accompanied by a report stating that a review

a. Provides only limited assurance that the financial statements are fairly presented.
b. Includes examining, on a test basis, information that is the representation of management.
c. Consists principally of inquiries of company personnel and analytical procedures applied to financial data.
d. Does **not** contemplate obtaining corroborating evidential matter or applying certain other procedures ordinarily performed during an audit.

80. Financial statements of a nonpublic entity compiled without audit or review by an accountant should be accompanied by a report stating that

a. The scope of the accountant's procedures has **not** been restricted in testing the financial information that is the representation of management.
b. The accountant assessed the accounting principles used and significant estimates made by management.
c. The accountant does **not** express an opinion or any other form of assurance on the financial statements.
d. A compilation consists principally of inquiries of entity personnel and analytical procedures applied to financial data.

81. A CPA's report on agreed-upon procedures related to management's assertion about an entity's compliance with specified requirements should contain

a. A statement of limitations on the use of the report.
b. An opinion about whether management's assertion is fairly stated.
c. Negative assurance that control risk has **not** been assessed.
d. An acknowledgment of responsibility for the sufficiency of the procedures.

82. When an accountant examines projected financial statements, the accountant's report should include a separate paragraph that

a. Describes the limitations on the usefulness of the presentation.
b. Provides an explanation of the differences between an examination and an audit.
c. States that the accountant is responsible for events and circumstances up to one year after the report's date.
d. Disclaims an opinion on whether the assumptions provide a reasonable basis for the projection.

83. Field is an employee of Gold Enterprises. Hardy, CPA, is asked to express an opinion on Field's profit participation in Gold's net income. Hardy may accept this engagement only if

a. Hardy also audits Gold's complete financial statements.
b. Gold's financial statements are prepared in conformity with GAAP.
c. Hardy's report is available for distribution to Gold's other employees.
d. Field owns controlling interest in Gold.

84. Which of the following statements is correct about an auditor's required communication with an entity's audit committee?

a. Any matters communicated to the entity's audit committee also are required to be communicated to the entity's management.
b. The auditor is required to inform the entity's audit committee about significant errors discovered by the auditor and subsequently corrected by management.
c. Disagreements with management about the application of accounting principles are required to be communicated in writing to the entity's audit committee.
d. Weaknesses in the internal control structure previously reported to the entity's audit committee are required to be communicated to the audit committee after each subsequent audit until the weaknesses are corrected.

85. Which of the following events occurring after the issuance of an auditor's report most likely would cause the auditor to make further inquiries about the previously issued financial statements?

a. An uninsured natural disaster occurs that may affect the entity's ability to continue as a going concern.
b. A contingency is resolved that had been disclosed in the audited financial statements.
c. New information is discovered concerning undisclosed lease transactions of the audited period.
d. A subsidiary is sold that accounts for 25% of the entity's consolidated net income.

86. A registration statement filed with the SEC contains the reports of two independent auditors on their audits of financial statements for different periods. The predecessor auditor who audited the prior-period financial statements generally should obtain a letter of representation from the

a. Successor independent auditor.
b. Client's audit committee.
c. Principal underwriter.
d. Securities and Exchange Commission.

87. An auditor is engaged to report on selected financial data that are included in a client-prepared document containing audited financial statements. Under these circumstances, the report on the selected data should

a. Be limited to data derived from the audited financial statements.
b. Be distributed only to senior management and the board of directors.
c. State that the presentation is a comprehensive basis of accounting other than GAAP.
d. Indicate that the data are **not** fairly stated in all material respects.

88. In auditing a not-for-profit entity that receives governmental financial assistance, the auditor has a responsibility to

a. Issue a separate report that describes the expected benefits and related costs of the auditor's suggested changes to the entity's internal control structure.
b. Assess whether management has identified laws and regulations that have a direct and material effect on the entity's financial statements.
c. Notify the governmental agency providing the financial assistance that the audit is **not** designed to provide any assurance of detecting errors and irregularities.
d. Render an opinion concerning the entity's continued eligibility for the governmental financial assistance.

89. In auditing compliance with requirements governing major federal financial assistance programs under the Single Audit Act, the auditor's consideration of materiality differs from materiality under generally accepted auditing standards. Under the Single Audit Act, materiality is

a. Calculated in relation to the financial statements taken as a whole.
b. Determined separately for each major federal financial assistance program.
c. Decided in conjunction with the auditor's risk assessment.
d. Ignored, because all account balances, regardless of size, are fully tested.

90. Which of the following statements represents a quality control requirement under government auditing standards?

a. A CPA who conducts government audits is required to undergo an annual external quality control review when an appropriate internal quality control system is **not** in place.
b. A CPA seeking to enter into a contract to perform an audit should provide the CPA's most recent external quality control review report to the party contracting for the audit.
c. An external quality control review of a CPA's practice should include a review of the working papers of each government duty performed since the prior external quality control review.
d. A CPA who conducts governments audits may **not** make the CPA's external quality control review report available to the public.

85/89 = 96

Number 2 (Estimated time—15 to 25 minutes)

Question Number 2 consists of 15 items. Select the **best** answer for each item.

Required:

Items 91 through 105 represent a series of unrelated statements, questions, excerpts, and comments taken from various parts of an auditor's working paper file. Below the items is a list of the likely sources of the statements, questions, excerpts, and comments. Select as the best answer for each item, the most likely source. Select only one source for each item. A source may be selected once, more than once, or not at all.

91. There are no material transactions that have not been properly recorded in the accounting records underlying the financial statements.

92. In connection with an audit of our financial statements, management has prepared, and furnished to our auditors, a description and evaluation of certain contingencies.

93. Provision has been made for any material loss to be sustained in the fulfillment of, or from the inability to fulfill, any sales commitments.

94. Fees for our services are based on our regular per diem rates, plus travel and other out-of-pocket expenses.

95. The objective of our audit is to express an unqualified opinion on the financial statements, although it is possible that facts or circumstances encountered may preclude us from expressing an unqualified opinion.

96. There have been no irregularities involving employees that could have a material effect on the financial statements.

97. Are you aware of any facts or circumstances that may indicate a lack of integrity by any member of senior management?

98. If a difference of opinion on a practice problem existed between engagement personnel and a specialist or other consultant, was the difference resolved in accordance with firm policy and appropriately documented?

99. Although we have not conducted a comprehensive, detailed search of our records, no other deposit or loan accounts have come to our attention except as noted below.

100. At the conclusion of our audit, we will request certain written representations from you about the financial statements and related matters.

101. We have no plans or intentions that may materially affect the carrying value or classification of assets and liabilities.

102. As discussed in Note 14 to the financial statements, the Company has had numerous dealings with businesses controlled by, and people who are related to, the officers of the company.

103. There were unreasonable delays by management in permitting the commencement of the audit and in providing needed information.

104. If this statement is not correct, please write promptly, using the enclosed envelope, and give details of any differences directly to our auditors.

105. The Company has suffered recurring losses from operations and has a net capital deficiency that raises substantial doubt about its ability to continue as a going concern.

List of Sources

(A) Partner's engagement review program.
(B) Communication with predecessor auditor.
(C) Auditor's engagement letter.
(D) Management representation letter.
(E) Standard financial institution confirmation request.
(F) Auditor's communication with the audit committee.
(G) Auditor's report.
(H) Letter for underwriters.
(I) Audit inquiry letter to legal counsel.
(J) Accounts receivable confirmation.

Question Number 3 consists of 15 items. Select the **best** answer for each item.

Required:

Items 106 through 120 represent a series of unrelated procedures that an accountant may consider performing in separate engagements to review the financial statements of a nonpublic entity (a review) and to compile the financial statements of a nonpublic entity (a compilation). Select, as the best answer for each item, whether the procedure is required (R), or not required (N) for both review and compilation engagements. Make two selections for each item.

106. The accountant should establish an understanding with the entity regarding the nature and limitations of the services to be performed.

107. The accountant should make inquiries concerning actions taken at the board of directors' meetings.

108. The accountant, as the entity's successor accountant, should communicate with the predecessor accountant to obtain access to the predecessor's working papers.

109. The accountant should obtain a level of knowledge of the accounting principles and practices of the entity's industry.

110. The accountant should obtain an understanding of the entity's internal control structure.

111. The accountant should perform analytical procedures designed to identify relationships that appear to be unusual.

112. The accountant should make an assessment of the control risk.

113. The accountant should send a letter of inquiry to the entity's attorney to corroborate the information furnished by management concerning litigation.

114. The accountant should obtain a management representation letter from the entity.

115. The accountant should study the relationships of the financial statement elements that would be expected to conform to a predictable pattern.

116. The accountant should communicate to the entity's senior management illegal employee acts discovered by the accountant that are clearly inconsequential.

117. The accountant should make inquiries about events subsequent to the date of the financial statements that would have a material effect on the financial statements.

118. The accountant should modify the accountant's report if there is a change in accounting principles that is adequately disclosed.

119. The accountant should submit a hard copy of the financial statements and accountant's report when the financial statements and accountant's report are submitted on a computer disk.

120. The accountant should perform specific procedures to evaluate whether there is substantial doubt about the entity's ability to continue as a going concern.

NOVEMBER 1995 UNIFORM CPA EXAMINATION
AUDITING UNOFFICIAL SOLUTIONS

1. (d) AU 322.10 states that, "When assessing the internal auditor's objectivity, the auditor should obtain information about the organizational status of the internal auditor including the organizational level to which the internal auditor reports". Answers (a), (b), and (c) would give an indication as to competency, not objectivity.

2. (a) AU 319.16 states that, "The auditor's knowledge obtained in planning the audit should be used to identify types of potential misstatements, consider factors that affect the risk of material misstatements, and design substantive tests." AU 319.17 refers to the auditor's consideration of operating effectiveness, not efficiency. Answer (c) refers to an inherent limitation, AU 319.15. AU 319.26, but this is not a reason for obtaining knowledge.

3. (b) The most likely output from an online sales order processing system is a file of all rejected sales transactions. Answer (a), sales invoices would be generated by the system. Answers (c) and (d) are not relevant outputs from the online sales order processing system, but would be outputs of other system applications.

4. (b) AU 319.18 states, "Concerns about the integrity of the entity's management may be so serious as to cause the auditor to conclude that the risk of management misrepresentations in the financial statements is such that an audit cannot be conducted." Answers (a), (c), and (d) should be considered by the auditor but are not necessarily serious enough to cause an auditability question.

5. (b) AU 319.66 states "Management philosophy and operating style encompass a broad range of characteristics. These characteristics have a significant influence on the control environment, particularly when management is dominated by one or a few individuals." Answers (a), (c), and (d) are aspects of other control environment factors.

6. (c) AU 319.66, paragraph 6, includes the use of budgets and forecasts as management control methods. Answer (a) is discussed under external influences. Answer (b) is a control procedure. Answer (d) is part of personnel policies and procedures.

7. (c) In the revenue cycle application process, the most likely output among the choices given is an accounts receivable master file, especially since there is a cash receipts transaction file. A remittance file (a) is not typically a separately constructed file. Answers (b) and (d) are not part of the revenue cycle.

8. (d) Sales invoices are the most likely output from the system at this point. The customer orders would most likely be at the beginning of the revenue cycle. Receiving reports are not part of the revenue cycle, and customer checks are not created by the system but are received from the customer.

9. (a) AU 319.26 states, "The auditor should document the understanding of the entity's internal control structure elements obtained to plan the audit." The auditor is required to evaluate the effectiveness of the entity's internal control structure, not search for significant deficiencies. The auditor performs tests of controls to evaluate the effectiveness of the entity's internal control procedures, not the accounting system. According to AU 319.29, an auditor is required to assess control risks which includes evaluating the effectiveness of control procedures designed to prevent or detect material misstatements, determining is beyond the requirements.

10. (c) A validity check ensures that only authorized data codes will be entered into and accepted by the system. Answer (a) is an example of a limit (reasonableness) check. Answer (b) is an example of an error report being generated. There is no comparison performed as in answer (d).

11. (c) When a client has documentation regarding the use of EDP programs, it is an effective internal control. Answer (b) is a substantive test. Answers (a) and (d) are analytical procedures.

12. (a) A bank lockbox system assures accountability control as cash enters the client's cash receipts system. Answers (b), (c), and (d) are cash receipt controls imposed after cash is captured in the system.

13. (a) According to AU 319.02, "In all audits, the auditor should obtain a sufficient understanding of each of the three elements of the internal control structure by performing procedures to understand the design of policies and procedures relevant to audit planning." Answers (b), (c), and (d) would be of concern later in the audit process.

14. (b) A control procedure for preventing employees from modifying programs to bypass programmed controls is to segregate the functions of programming and computer operations. Answers (a), (c), and (d) are all appropriate EDP controls but in themselves would not prevent employees from modifying programs.

15. (a) By promptly notifying the payroll supervisor of employee termination's, the personnel department would avoid a terminated employee from continuing to be paid. Unclaimed payroll checks should be forwarded to the Treasurer's office. Salary rates should be controlled in the personnel office. Total hours should be determined and approved prior to getting to the payroll department. Although answers (c) and (d) are good controls, they would not prevent employee payroll fraud.

16. (b) A bank safe-deposit box with two company officials in control of the asset provides strong physical control over the securities. Answers (a) and (c) would not safeguard the physical marketable security. Answer (d) does not provide for dual control throughout the year, as is preferred.

17. (c) Per AU 350.12-.14, when the auditor's estimate based on the sample results indicates that the maximum deviation rate is less than the tolerable rate, and the true state of the population shows that the deviation rate exceeds the tolerable rate, the auditor assesses control risk too low and does not plan sufficient substantive testing. Answer (b) is an example of the auditor accessing control risk higher than necessary and thereby increasing substantive testing. Answer (a) and (d) represent correct audit decisions regarding controls and planned substantive evidence.

18. (b) According to AU 319.47, in assessing control risk, an auditor selects from tests such as inquiry, observation, inspection, and reperformance of a policy or procedure that pertains to an assertion. Only one answer choice contains two of these tests. Answers (a), (c), and (d) contain substantive tests.

19. (d) AU 350.14 states, "The risk of incorrect acceptance and the risk of assessing control risk too low relate to the effectiveness of an audit in detecting an existing material misstatement." If the auditor incorrectly accepts an account as being materially accurate or incorrectly concludes that control risk is below the maximum, additional procedures that may detect this incorrect conclusion are either eliminated or reduced and the audit would prove ineffective in detecting misstatements. Answers (a) and (b) are incorrect because of an inappropriate combination of terms. In (a), risk should relate to exceeding tolerable misstatement levels. In (b), materiality is judged, not estimated and related to tolerable misstatement (AU 350.18) Audit efficiency is related to the risk of incorrect rejection or the risk of assessing control risk as too high. (AU 350.13)

20. (a) According to AU 319.40, obtaining an understanding of the internal control structure and assessing control risk may be performed concurrently in an audit. Answer (b) is incorrect because the opposite is true, according to AU 319.53. Answer (c), according to AU 319.39, is incorrect because when the auditor assesses control risk below the maximum level, the auditor is required to document the auditor's understanding of the entity's control environment and basis for concluding that control risk is below the maximum level. Answer (d) is incorrect because the opposite is true, the lower the assessed level of control risk, the more assurance the evidence must provide that the control procures are operating effectively. (AU 319.46)

21. (d) AU 319.45 states, "The assessed level of control risk is used in determining the appropriate detection risk to accept for those assertions and, accordingly, in determining the nature, timing and extent of substantive tests for such assertions. Understanding the importance of controls and inherent risk, come before control risk assessment. Auditor materiality judgments are inputs to the process.

22. (d) According to AU 319.30, assessing control risk at below the maximum level involves identifying specific internal control structure policies and procedures relevant to specific assertions that are likely to prevent or detect material misstatements in those assertions. Inherent risk is assessed separately and before control risk. According to AU 313.05, changing the timing of substantive tests by omitting interim-date testing and performing the tests at year end is a procedure that is either not affected or would go in the opposite direction.

23. (d) After the auditor obtains an understanding of the entity's internal control structure and assesses control risk, the auditor may want to seek a further reduction in the assessed level of control risk for certain assertions. In such a case, the auditor considers whether additional evidential matter is available to support a further reduction. Per AU 319.44, efficiency is a consideration regarding support for a reduced risk assessment. Answers (b) and (c) would have occurred prior to the initial control risk assessment.

24. (c) According to AU 319.39, the auditor is required to document the understanding of the entity's internal control structure and the basis for concluding that control risk is below the maximum level.

25. (d) When the sample rate of deviation plus the allowance for sampling risk, which is the upper deviation limit, exceeds the tolerable rate, the sample results do not support the assessed level of control risk and the auditor should reduce the planned reliance on a prescribed control. Answers (a), (b),

and (c) represent results that support planned reliance.

26. (d) According to AU 350.42, evidence that a deviation was covered up in a fraudulent manner would require the auditor to consider the implications of the deviation more closely. Answers (a), (b), and (c) give no causes for added concern.

27. (c) According to AU 319.63, regardless of the assessed level of control risk, the auditor should perform limited substantive tests for significant account balances and transaction classes. Answer (a) is the opposite, indicating extensive tests. Answers (b) and (d) do not include test of controls as would be required for a lower control risk assessment.

28. (a) Lapping involves the theft of one customer's payment and subsequently crediting the customer with payment made by another customer. Future remittances may be deposited but would be credited to the account from which funds were stolen, thus comparison of remittance dates would detect the scheme. Answers (b), (c), and (d) occur after the theft and would not show differences to pursue.

29. (d) A control for cash disbursements is for the person who signs the checks to compare them to supporting documents, cancel the documents, and to also mail them. The person who signs the checks should have access to the supporting documents in order to validate their legitimacy. Reconciliation of the monthly bank statement is a control that should be done by a person independent of cash transactions. The checks should not be returned or given to anyone who has responsibility in the cash disbursement process.

30. (d) The agreement of the documents will verify that the goods were ordered (purchase order), received (receiving report), and the company has been billed (vendor's invoice). The individual signing the checks, not accounts payable, should stamp, perforate, or otherwise cancel the supporting documentation. The purchasing department, not the accounting department, is involved with the approval of purchase requisitions, and blanking out the quantity ordered on the receiving department copy of the purchase order.

31. (a) Observing the segregation of duties concerning personnel responsibilities and payroll disbursement is a common audit procedure relating to the existence or occurrence assertion for payroll transactions. Inspecting evidence of accounting for prenumbered payroll checks would provide evidence related to the completeness assertion. Recomputing the payroll deductions for employee fringe benefits would provide evidence related to the valuation and the rights and obligations assertions. An auditor would likely review payroll checks and bank reconciliations to determine that all checks were cashed as part of obtaining evidence for the existence or occurrence assertion and not just verify the preparation of the monthly payroll account bank reconciliation.

32. (c) In obtaining an understanding of a manufacturing entity's internal control structure concerning inventory balances, an auditor would review the entity's descriptions of inventory policies and procedures. Analyzing inventory ratios, performing cost variance analytical procedures, and performing inventory test counts are substantive audit procedures.

33. (a) According to AU 350.38, both the expected deviation rate and the tolerable deviation rate are considerations in determining the sample size for a test of controls.

34. (d) A weakness in internal control over recording retirements of equipment most likely would result in assets that have been retired continuing to be carried in the accounting records. Tracing from the records to the actual assets would be an audit procedure designed to detect such errors. Tracing equipment in the plant to the accounting records would only provide evidence about equipment not yet retired. Depreciation is applied to assets carried on the books and thus depreciation would continue to be taken on retired equipment erroneously still on the books. A review of depreciation would not of itself indicate that certain equipment had been retired. Additions to the "other assets" account would be newly acquired other assets rather than retired equipment and would not likely give any evidence about retired equipment.

35. (d) According to AU 325.11, "Any report issued on reportable conditions [relating to an entity's internal control structure] should [1] indicate that the purpose of the audit was to report on the financial statements and not to provide assurance on the internal control structure, [2] include the definition of reportable conditions, and [3] include a restriction" that the report "is intended solely for the information and the use of the audit committee, management, and others within the organization," and, in some circumstances, specified regulatory authorities as appropriate (AU 325.10). A brief description of the tests of controls performed is not required. Reportable conditions are not required to be disclosed in the annual report to the shareholders. A paragraph describing management's assertion concerning the effectiveness of the internal control structure is not required.

36. (c) In accordance with AT 400.03, management may present its written assertion about the effectiveness of the entity's internal control structure in **either** of two forms; in a separate report that will accompany the practitioner's report, or in a representation letter to the practitioner.

37. (a) According to AU 324.29, one of the items that should be included in a service auditor's report expressing an opinion on a description of policies and procedures placed in operation at a service organization is a description of the scope and nature of the service auditor's procedures. A statement that management had disclosed all design deficiencies of which it is aware is not appropriate in the report. The report should also contain, per AU 324.29, a disclaimer of opinion on the operating effectiveness of the policies and procedures. A paragraph indicating the basis for assessment of control risk is not appropriate in the report.

38. (a) According to AU 329.04 and .10, one of the uses of analytical procedures is as a substantive test to obtain evidential matter about particular assertions. In the process of achieving audit objectives, the auditor should adhere to a system of quality control, prepare working papers, and may possibly increase the level of detection risk, however none of these actually cause the auditor to achieve audit objectives.

39. (c) The accounts receivable and sales audit objective related to the completeness assertion is to ascertain that **all** sales and receivables that should be recorded are properly recorded. Customers may not be inclined to report understatement errors in their accounts on a confirmation form, and thus not all the sales and receivables that should be recorded are necessarily recorded. It is not as likely that customers will merely sign and return the confirmation without verifying its details; the accounts they are verifying represent liabilities to them. It is more likely that the customers will not return them. It cannot be assumed that a nonresponse means that the recipient agrees with the information on the request; it could also mean that the intended recipient did not receive the request, has misplaced the request or has not processed the request, or has returned the request but it was delayed or lost in transit. Auditors typically select few accounts with low recorded balances to be confirmed and a higher percentage of accounts with large balances.

40. (b) A standard confirmation request sent to a financial institution at which the client has both a checking or savings account and a loan would include requests on one form regarding the cash balance and the loan balance and, in addition, a description of the collateral for the loan. While confirmation of accounts receivable is a generally accepted auditing procedure (AU 330.34), confirmation of accounts payable is not and is generally used only in cases of suspected fraud, sloppy or missing records, or suspected understatements. The entity holding inventory on consignment generally would not have information related to contingent liabilities. Accrued interest receivable would most likely be related to notes receivable rather than accounts receivable.

41. (b) AU 329.06 states, "the objective of the procedures is to identify such things as the existence of unusual transactions and events, and amounts, ratios, and trends that might indicate matters that have financial statement and audit planning ramifications." The use of a standard cost system that produces variance reports allows the auditor an opportunity to compare the output from the standard cost system with the financial information presented by management. Segregating obsolete inventory before the physical inventory count would likely facilitate inventory auditing procedures, but not necessarily the analytical procedures. According to AU 329.16, the auditor should assess the reliability of the data by considering the source of the data and the conditions under which the data was gathered. Stronger internal controls and independent sources of data enhance the reliability of data used in analytical procedures.

42. (b) The formula for Inventory Turnover is Cost of Goods Sold divided by Average Inventory. Cost of Goods Sold includes only inventory related expenses and thus is the best value to use to compare to average inventory to calculate inventory turnover. Net sales, operating income, and gross sales are all based on the prices charged the customers, not the actual costs to the company for the goods that were sold, and thus are not as closely related to the costs associated with inventory.

43. (c) According to AU 350.48, increasing the tolerable misstatement would lead to a decrease in the sample size. Increasing the assessed level of control risk would lead to an increase in the sample size.

44. (c) AU 350.04 indicates that both statistical and nonstatistical sampling plans can provide sufficient evidential matter if properly applied. Statistical sampling, as well as nonstatistical sampling, is subject to nonsampling errors (procedural mistakes or human error). Both methods of sampling may be used to reduce audit risk, but neither would affect the level of materiality. Both can be used to reduce the risk of failing to detect errors and irregularities, which is the risk of incorrect acceptance.

45. (d) AU 330.14 states, "The AICPA Standard Form to Confirm Account Balance Information With Financial Institutions is designed to substantiate information that is stated on the confirmation request; the form is not designed to provide assurance that information about accounts not listed on the form will be reported." The bank employee completing the form may be unaware of all the financial relationships that the client has with the bank and the request may not ask specifically about all the financial relationships, thus the usefulness of the confirmation in providing evidence for financial statement assertions may be limited. Responding to bank confirmation requests is a normal activity for a bank. It would be unlikely that a bank employee would not believe that the bank is obligated to verify confidential information to the third party, especially as the confirmation request is signed by the client authorizing the bank to release the information to the auditor. The bank would not have access to the client's bank reconciliation and thus would not inspect its accuracy. The bank does have access to the client's cutoff bank statements, but that information is not used by the bank to confirm year-end balances.

46. (b) When the auditor has already gathered evidence supporting cash receipts and accounts receivable, the same evidence would support sales. Thus, having already gathered this evidence and having assessed control risk as low for the existence or occurrence assertion regarding sales transactions, the auditor most likely would conclude that he or she has substantial evidence for sales and would limit substantive tests of sales transactions. Evidence supporting opening and closing inventory balances, shipping and receiving activities, and cutoffs of sales and purchases would give only limited information regarding sales.

47. (c) In searching for unrecorded liabilities, the auditor would most likely vouch a sample of cash disbursements recorded just after year end to receiving reports and vendor invoices to ascertain that payables had been recorded in the proper period. Tracing a sample of accounts payable entries recorded **just after** (not just before) year end to the year-end unmatched receiving report file, comparing a sample of purchase orders issued **just before** (not just after) year end with the year-end accounts payable, and scanning the cash disbursements entries recorded **just after** (not just before) year end for indications of unusual transactions may also aid in the detection of unrecorded liabilities.

48. (c) Tracing a sample of purchase orders and the related receiving reports to the purchases journal and the cash disbursements journal provides evidence to determine that purchases were properly recorded. Although during this audit procedure the auditor might identify unusually large purchases that should be investigated further, this would not be the prevailing purpose of this substantive audit procedure. To verify that cash disbursements were for goods actually received would require vouching from the cash disbursements journal to the receiving reports. To test whether payments were for goods actually ordered would require vouching from the cash disbursements journal to the purchase orders.

49. (b) When plant assets are retired, the accumulated depreciation account is debited for the amount of depreciation that has been recorded for those assets, which could be a satisfactory explanation for significant debits to this account. When the estimated remaining useful life of a plant asset is revised upward, the calculation for current and future depreciation is revised to reflect the new estimate of remaining useful life; accumulated depreciation is not affected. If the prior year's depreciation expense was erroneously understated, a correction would require a credit, not a debit, to accumulated depreciation. Revisions in overhead allocations would not affect the accumulated depreciation accounts.

50. (a) Significant unexplained variances between standard and actual labor cost could cause an auditor to suspect a payroll fraud scheme. Payroll checks disbursed by the same employee each payday, as long as that person has no other payroll responsibilities, employee time cards being approved by individual departmental supervisors, and a separate payroll bank account being maintained on an imprest basis are proper internal control procedures.

51. (c) According to AU 326.11, in selecting particular substantive tests to achieve the audit objectives developed, an auditor considers, among other things, the risk of material misstatement of the financial statements. Not performing test of details of transactions in some situations would not be a violation of auditing standards. Attaining assurance about the reliability of the accounting system and evaluating whether management's policies and procedures operated effectively are involved in assessing control risk.

52. (a) In the AICPA Audit Guide entitled "Computer Assisted Audit Techniques," one of the reasons for using generalized audit software (GAS) is that it enables the auditor to gain access and test information stored in the client's files without having to acquire a complete understanding of the client's EDP system. Although the use of GAS enables the auditor to deal more effectively with large quantities of data and produces economies in the audit while increasing the quality of the audit, it cannot replace analytical

procedures. Self-checking digits and hash totals are controls in the client system. Reducing the level of required tests of controls to a relatively small amount is the result of assessing control risk and applying preliminary tests of controls, not a result of using a GAS package.

53. (d) According to AU 322.12, "The internal auditors' work may affect the nature, timing, and extent of the audit, including (I) procedures the auditor performs when obtaining an understanding of the entity's internal control structure, (II) procedures the auditor performs when assessing risk, and (III) substantive procedures the auditor performs."

54. (d) According to AU 336.06, "Ordinarily, the auditor should attempt to obtain a specialist who is unrelated to the client. However, when the circumstances so warrant, work of a specialist having a relationship to the client may be acceptable." AU 336.08 states, "Although the appropriateness and reasonableness of methods or assumptions used and their application are the responsibility of the specialist, the auditor should obtain an understanding of the methods or assumptions used by the specialist to determine whether the findings are suitable for corroborating the representations in the financial statements." AU 336.02 states, "an auditor may encounter matters potentially material to the fair presentation of financial statements...that require special knowledge and that in [the auditor's] judgment require using the work of a specialist."

55. (c) AU 337.05 states, "Since the events ... that should be considered in the financial accounting for and reporting of litigation, claims, and assessments are matters within the direct knowledge and, often, control of management of an entity, management is the primary source of information about such matters. Accordingly, the independent auditor's procedures ... should include ... [inquiry and discussion] with management [concerning] the policies and procedures adopted for identifying, evaluating, and accounting for litigation, claims, and assessments." AU 337.08 states, "A letter of audit inquiry to the client's lawyer is the auditor's primary means of obtaining corroboration of the information furnished by management concerning litigation, claims, and assessments." However, the lawyer does not evaluate the client's ability to continue as a going concern or whether all litigation, claims, and assessments have been recorded or disclosed in the financial statements. Examination of the legal documents in the client's lawyer's possession would be an unusual procedure.

56. (d) Subsequent events occur between the period ending date and the issuance of the financial statements. AU 560.12 states that one of the auditor's procedures about the occurrence of subsequent events is inquiry of management concerning unusual adjustments after year-end. Confirming a sample of accounts receivable established after year end would be a secondary step in obtaining evidence about subsequent events, if it were done at all. Comparison between the current and the prior year financial statements is an analytical procedure unlikely to uncover evidence about the occurrence of subsequent events. Investigating personnel changes in the accounting department occurring after year end would be more likely when possible misconduct, rather than a subsequent event, is being considered.

57. (b) A management representation letter is from the audited entity's management to the auditor. AU 333.04 lists the third item to be included in a management representation letter as the completeness and availability of minutes of stockholders' and directors' meetings. Communications with the audit committee would be verbal or in a letter addressed to the audit committee from the auditor. Plans to acquire or merge with other entities in the subsequent year would most likely be included in the minutes of stockholders' and directors' meetings. Management's acknowledgment of responsibility for the detection of employee fraud is not explicitly stated in the representation letter.

58. (c) Loans receivable and payable would be more likely to be guaranteed by related parties than the other listed transactions are to involve related parties. The procedures in answer (a) might reveal related party transactions, but as a by-product. Answers (b) and (c) are more part of a search for unrecorded liabilities.

59. (d) According to AU 341.07, an entity's plans to reduce or delay expenditures would be one of an auditor's primary considerations in reviewing management's plans. Plans to discuss the terms of debt and loan agreements with lenders would not be given much weight. The availability of financing or existing or committed arrangements to restructure or subordinate debt would be more important. Strong internal control will not keep an entity from bankruptcy. Purchasing instead of leasing assets during an unstable period would generally work against plans to delay expenditures.

60. (d) AU 339 states that working papers serve mainly to provide the principal support for the auditor's report and to aid the auditor in the conduct and supervision of the audit. Permanent files contain items of continuing interest, such as debt agreements, flowcharts of internal controls, and articles of incor-

poration. The other items are of temporary interest only.

61. (c) According to AU 508.47, an auditor is not precluded from reporting on only one of the basic financial statements and not the others. A scope limitation would not exist if the auditor is able to apply all the procedures the auditor considers necessary. Such engagements involve limited reporting objectives. Acceptance of the engagement is not a violation of the profession's ethical standards, as the work can be expected to be accomplished. Per AU 508.73, a "piecemeal opinion" is an opinion on specific elements of the financial statements when the auditor has disclaimed an opinion on the statements as a whole and is unacceptable. A disclaimer of opinion would be unnecessary, because Harris will have access to all information underlying the basic financial statements, and thus could apply all the procedures he or she considers necessary.

62. (c) Per AU 508.08, the fourth sentence of the scope paragraph of an auditor's standard report states, "An audit also includes assessing the accounting principles used and significant estimates made by management, as well as evaluating the overall financial statement presentation." Answers (a) and (b) are not mentioned in the report. Per AU 508.34, consistency is only mentioned when it is absent, and requires explanatory language be added to the standard report.

63. (b) Since the CPA cannot be in accordance with GAAS if the CPA is not independent, the nonindependent CPA must disclaim an opinion. (AU 504.08 - .10) AU 508.38 provides for a qualified opinion when there is a material departure from GAAP. When there are scope limitations, AU 508.40 indicates that the auditor should qualify or disclaim an opinion. AU 336.10 allows reference be made to the work of a specialist when there is a departure from GAAP and such reference will help to clarify the reason for the qualification.

64. (d) According to AU 508.24, for a remote likelihood situation, an explanatory paragraph would not be added to the report. Per AU 508.11, answers (a), (b), and (c) would be appropriate for mention in explanatory language to an auditor's standard report.

65. (d) Per AU 508.59 - .62, a material unjustified accounting change would require that the auditor express a qualified or adverse opinion. Both require an explanatory paragraph. A material weakness in the internal control structure is generally not mentioned in the auditor's report.

66. (b) Per AU 508.59, an unjustified accounting change would require that the auditor express a qualified or adverse opinion. Answers (a), (b), and (c) represent various restrictions of the scope of the audit. A restriction of the scope of the audit, whether imposed by the client or circumstances, may require the auditor to express a qualified opinion (AU 508.40).

67. (a) The auditor's standard report implies that the auditor is satisfied that the statements are consistent with respect to GAAP, and such principles have been consistently applied *between periods*. Use of different cost principles for different inventories is not inherently inconsistent (AU 508.34).

68. (c) AU 508.05 states, "The objective of the fourth reporting standard is to prevent misinterpretation of the degree of responsibility the accountant assumes when his [or her] name is associated with financial statements." The auditor may express different opinions on the statements presented. Material scope restrictions result in a qualification or disclaimer of opinion. Per AU 508.47, an auditor is not precluded from reporting on only one of the basic financial statements and not the others.

69. (d) Per AU 508.42, the inability to obtain audited financial statements of a consolidated investee represents a scope limitation resulting in a qualified opinion or a disclaimer of opinion. Per AU 508.11, the circumstances in answers (a), (b), and (c) may require an explanatory paragraph, but they do not preclude an unqualified opinion.

70. (d) According to AU 308.11, existence of properly disclosed uncertainties may require explanatory language added to the auditor's (unqualified) standard report. AU 508.32 provides an example of an explanatory paragraph for an unqualified opinion similar to the illustrated paragraph.

71. (c) According to AU 508.56, the language generally used in this circumstance is "...except for the omission of the information discussed in the preceding paragraph..." "Subject to..." and "With the foregoing explanation..." is unacceptable language. The language in answer (d) is for an adverse opinion.

72. (d) AU 341.12 specifically requires the words "substantial doubt" and "going concern" be used, and a phrase similar to "substantial doubt about its ability to continue as a going concern" be used. "Possible discontinuance of operations" and "Reasonable period of time, not to exceed one year" are not mentioned.

73. (a) AU 341.16 states, "If substantial doubt about the entity's ability to continue as a going concern ... existed at the date of prior period financial

statements that are presented on a comparative basis, and that doubt has been removed in the current period, the explanatory paragraph included with the auditor's report ... should not be repeated."

74. (b) AU 420.23 states, "When the independent auditor has not audited the financial statements of a company for the preceding year, he [or she] should adopt procedures that are practicable ... to assure him [or her-] self that the accounting principles employed are consistent ... Where adequate records have been maintained by the client, it is usually practicable ... to gather sufficient competent evidential matter about consistency." Thus an auditor would issue an unqualified opinion in a standard report. According to AU 420.24, the auditor would not report on the income statement only if precluded from obtaining appropriate evidence as to consistency. The consistency standard does apply in first year audits. The standard report doesn't explicitly mention consistency.

75. (a) AU 508.77 states that if an auditor's previous opinion on financial statements was qualified or adverse due to a GAAP departure, and those statements are restated to comply with GAAP, the auditor should, in a reissued report, note that the statements are restated and express an unqualified opinion. Per AU 508.83, a successor auditor cannot change a predecessor auditor's opinion, but should inform the predecessor of the restatement and make note of it in the audit report. The prior year report is not affected. The current and updated report should refer to the prior year financial statements as restated.

76. (d) AU 508.83 states, "If the financial statements of a prior period have been audited by a predecessor auditor whose report is not presented, the successor auditor should indicate in the introductory paragraph of his [or her] report (a) that the financial statements of the prior period were audited by another auditor, (b) the date of his [or her] report, (c) the type of report issued by the predecessor auditor, and (d) if the report was other than a standard report, the substantive reasons therefore." AU 508.83 provides an example of such a report, in which the predecessor auditor is **not** referred to by name.

77. (a) AU 508.12 states, "When the auditor decides to make reference to the report of another auditor as a basis, in part, for his [or her] opinion, he [or she] should disclose this fact in the introductory paragraph of his [or her] report and should refer to the report of the other auditor in expressing his [or her] opinion. These references indicate division of responsibility for performance of the audit." AU 508.13 gives an example of such a report that is similar to the illustrated paragraph.

78. (a) AU 508.09 states that if the auditor is engaged to audit the financial statements of a company that is not the auditor's client, the report should be addressed to the client and **not** to the directors or stockholders of the company being audited.

79. (c) According to AR 100.32, "Financial statements reviewed by an accountant should be accompanied by a report stating that a review consists primarily of inquiries of company personnel and analytical procedures applied to the financial data." A review report *disclaims* an opinion concerning the fair presentation of the financial statements. An *audit* report mentions "examining, on a test basis, information that is the representation of management." A review report would not mention the items in answer (d).

80. (c) According to AT 100.14, "Financial statements compiled without audit or review ... should be accompanied by a report stating that ... the accountant does not express an opinion or any other form of assurance on the financial statements." One of the elements of a compilation report is that the "statements have not been audited or reviewed and, therefore, no opinion or other form of assurance is expressed on them." No reference to testing the financial information, or to assessing the principles and estimates used is made in the report. Testing the information supplied is not required in a compilation. A *review* consists primarily of inquiries of entity personnel and analytical procedures applied to financial data.

81. (a) According to AT 500.23, a report on an engagement consisting of applying agreed-upon procedures related to management's assertion about compliance with specific requirements should include a statement of limitations on the use of the report. A practitioner's report on the application of agreed-upon procedures ordinarily should also indicate that the work performed was less in scope than an examination and disclaim an opinion on the assertions. Negative assurance as to fair statement of the assertion is not allowed. Negative assurance concerning the assessment of control risk is not expressed. The CPA does not take responsibility for the sufficiency of the procedures.

82. (a) According to AT 200.33, the report contains a paragraph describing the limitations on the use of the presentation. The report does not provide an explanation of the differences between an examination and an audit. The accountant is not responsible for events occurring after the date of the

report. The standard report contains the phrase, "In our opinion, ...the underlying assumptions provide a reasonable basis for management's projection..."

83. (a) According to AU 623.16, "If the specified ... item is based upon an entity's net income ... the auditor should have audited the complete financial statements to express an opinion on the specified ... item." Hardy could express an opinion even if Gold's financial statements are not prepared in conformity with GAAP or if Field does not own controlling interest in Gold. A requirement that Hardy's report to be available for distribution to Gold's other employees is nonexistent; such disclosure might actually conflict with client confidentiality requirements.

84. (b) According to AU 380.09, "The auditor should inform the audit committee about adjustments arising from the audit that could ... have a significant effect on the entity's financial reporting process." It is common for the reports to the audit committee to be available to management, but not required, and occasionally, not appropriate (AU 380.02). The communication with the audit committee need not be in writing (AU 380.03). Internal control structure weaknesses need not be repetitively communicated if the audit committee has acknowledged its understanding and consideration of such deficiencies and the associated risks (AU 325.06).

85. (c) AU 561.04, "When the auditor becomes aware of information which relates to financial statements previously reported on ... not known at the date of his [or her] report, ... he [or she] should [follow up on the information]." Answers (a), (b), and (d) do not fit this requirement.

86. (a) AU 711.11 indicates that the predecessor auditor should, before reissuing a auditor report, obtain a letter of representations from the *successor auditor.*

87. (a) According to AU 552.09, an auditor's report on information accompanying the basic financial statements should include either an opinion on whether the accompanying information is fairly stated in all material respects in relation to the basic financial statements taken as a whole, or a disclaimer of opinion. The report should be limited to data that are derived from audited financial statements. There is no restriction on the distribution. The basis of accounting is not necessarily other than GAAP. The data are generally indicated as fairly stated in all material respects.

88. (b) According to AU 801.17 and .11, the auditor, when auditing a not-for-profit organization that receives governmental financial assistance should, "assess whether management has identified laws and regulations that have a direct and material effect on the entity's financial statements."

89. (b) According to AU 801.57, in auditing an entity's compliance with requirements governing each major federal financial assistance program in accordance with the Single Audit Act and OMB Circular A-128, the auditor considers materiality in relation to each program.

90. (b) Chapter 3 of the 1994 Yellow Book states, "Organizations conducting audits in accordance with these standards should have an external quality control review at least once every 3 years." and "Audit organizations seeking to enter into a contract to perform an audit in accordance with these standards should provide their most recent external quality control review report to the party contracting for the audit." There is no requirement that an external QC review include a review of the work papers of each government audit performed since the last review. QC 100.60 states, "The reviewed firm should not publicize the results of the review or distribute copies of the report ... until it has been advised that the report has been accepted by the state CPA society ... or the AICPA Quality Review Division." A CPA is not restricted from making an accepted external QC review report available to the public.

91. D

According to AU 333.04.d, the specific written representations obtained by the auditor in a representation from the client's management include "absence of errors in the financial statements and unrecorded transactions."

92. I

According to AU 337.04, the auditor should obtain evidential matter in an audit inquiry letter to legal counsel concerning the existence of a condition, situation, or set of circumstances indicating an uncertainty as to a possible loss arising from a contingency. AU 337a.01 illustrative inquiry letter contains this language.

93. D

According to AU 333.04.m, the specific written representations obtained by the auditor in a representation from the client's management include "losses from sales commitments."

94. C

Although engagement letters are not required by GAAS, they are recommended and should include a discussion of fees so that there are no misunderstandings.

95. C

Although engagement letters are not required by GAAS, they are recommended and should include a discussion of the objective of the audit.

96. D

According to AU 333.04.h, the specific written representations obtained by the auditor in a representation from the client's management include "irregularities involving management or employees."

97. B

According to AU 315.06, "The successor auditor should make specific and reasonable inquires of the predecessor" including "facts that might bear on the integrity of management."

98. A

The independent auditor is required to comply with Rule 202 of the Rules of Conduct of the Code of Professional Conduct which deals with quality control standards that relate to the conduct of a firm's audit practice as a whole. The quality control standards advise an auditor how to handle a difference of opinion. QC 90.16.2.d indicated the need for procedures to resolve differences.

99. E

According to AU 330.24, when designing confirmation requests, the auditor should consider the types of information respondents will be readily able to confirm.

100. C

Although engagement letters are not required by GAAS, they are recommended and should include that the auditor will request a management representation letter at the conclusion of the audit.

101. D

AU 333.04(j) states that the specific written representation from management ordinarily include, "Plans or intentions that may affect the carrying value or classification of assets or liabilities."

102. G

This statement is similar to one in the sample of an auditor's report with an explanatory paragraph in AU 508.32 and .35. AU 508.37 indicates a separate paragraph to emphasize a matter is acceptable.

103. F

AU 380.14 indicates that difficulties encountered in performing the audit (and gives this as an example) should be communicated to the audit committee. Such a statement would not appear in an auditor's report.

104. J

AU 330.20 describes a negative confirmation request. This statement is commonly found in negative accounts receivable confirmations.

105. G

AU 341.13 provides, for this situation, a sample auditor's report with an explanatory paragraph regarding substantial doubt about an entity's ability to continue as a going concern.

106. RR

AU 100.08 states, "The accountant should establish an understanding with the entity, preferably in writing, regarding the services to be performed." AU §100.08 applies to both the reviews and compilations.

107. RN

AR 100.27, applicable to reviews, lists several procedures that ordinarily are performed in a review, including "Inquiries concerning actions taken at meetings of stockholders, board of directors, committees of the board of directors, or comparable meetings that may affect the financial statements." AR 100.12, applicable to compilations, indicates that the accountant is not required to make inquiries about information supplied by the client.

108. NN

AR 400.08 states, " A successor accountant ... may wish to obtain access to the predecessor's working papers." This step is <u>not</u> required in either a review or a compilation.

109. RR

AR 100.10, applicable to compilations, states, "The accountant should possess a level of knowledge of the accounting principles and practices of the industry in which the entity operates that will enable him to compile financial statements that are appropriate in form for an entity operating in that industry." AR 100.24, applicable to reviews, states a similar requirement, but more comprehensive than for a compilation.

110. NN

AR 100.30 states, "A review does not contemplate obtaining an understanding of the internal control structure or assessing control risk, tests of accounting records and of responses to inquiries by obtaining corroborating evidential matter, and certain other procedures ordinarily performed during an audit." A compilation engagement is even more narrow in scope than a review.

111. RN

AR 100.27(c) describes such analytics for a review. AR 100.12 indicates that, for compilations, the accountant is not required to perform such procedures.

112. NN

According to AR 100.30, a review does not contemplate obtaining an understanding of the internal control structure or assessing control risk. A compilation is more narrow in scope than a review.

113. NN

AR 100.27 indicates various inquiries appropriate to a review, all of which are of client personnel. Inquiries of a client's lawyer would be considered corroborative evidence and is beyond the scope of a review. A compilation engagement is even more narrow in scope than a review.

114. RN

AR 100.28 states that the accountant is required to obtain a written representation from members of management in a review engagement. AR 100.12 indicates verifying evidence is not required in a compilation. A representation letter would not usually be obtained in a compilation engagement.

115. RN

AR 100.27 (c) identifies types of analytical procedures in a review. A study of the relationships of the elements of the statements that would be expected to conform with a predictable pattern based on the entity's experience is item (3). A compilation does not require analytical procedures.

116. NN

AR 100.08 states, "The understanding [with the client] should also provide (a) that the engagement cannot be relied upon to disclose errors, irregularities, or illegal acts and (b) that the accountant will inform the appropriate level of management of any material errors ... and any irregularities or illegal acts that come to his or her attention, unless they are clearly inconsequential." This guidance is applicable to both a review and a compilation.

117. RN

AR 100.27(g), applicable to a review, states, "Inquires of persons having responsibility for financial and accounting matters concerning ... events subsequent to the date of the financial statements that would have a material effect on the financial statements." A compilation does not require inquiries about subsequent events. (AR 100.12)

118. NN

According to AR 100.39 - .40 (footnote 18), as long as the change is appropriate and is appropriately disclosed in the financial statements, there is no requirement to alter the report. A compilation is even more narrow in scope than a review.

119. NN

There is no professional requirement that the accountant submit a hard copy of financial statements or the accountant's report for a review or a compilation.

120. NN

AR 100.27 states that, for a review, only inquires and analytical procedures are required. AR 100.12, for a compilation, indicates that no verifying procedures are required.

ERRATA

Due to last minute changes, the CPA Exam schedule times are listed incorrectly in Foreword F on page F-3. The correct times are listed below:

Section	Day	Time	Hours
Business Law & Professional Responsibilities	Wed.	9:00 - 12:00	3 hours
Auditing	Wed.	1:30 - 6:00	4 1/2 hours
Accounting & Reporting--Taxation, Managerial, and Governmental and Not-for-Profit Organizations	Thur.	8:30 - 12:00	3 1/2 hours
Financial Accounting & Reporting	Thur.	1:30 - 6:00	4 1/2 hours
			15 1/2 hours

Totaltape CPE & CPA Review

America's #1 Private Provider of Quality Multimedia CPE and CPA Review Helps You Succeed at Every Stage of Your Career

It went by in a "blink"—but Totaltape has been serving the accounting profession now for 25 years! Thank you for making us America's largest private provider of quality, multimedia CPE and CPA Review. We are the ONLY provider to offer you EVERY type of educational format...

- **CD-ROM & Software—interactive**
- **Video—broadcast quality**
- **Audio—digitally recorded**
- **Text On-line—instant libray at your fingertips**
- **Reference Book—valuable informational guides**

In addition, our CPE and CPA Review programs are the only materials that are officially licensed as Microsoft® Windows™ compatible.

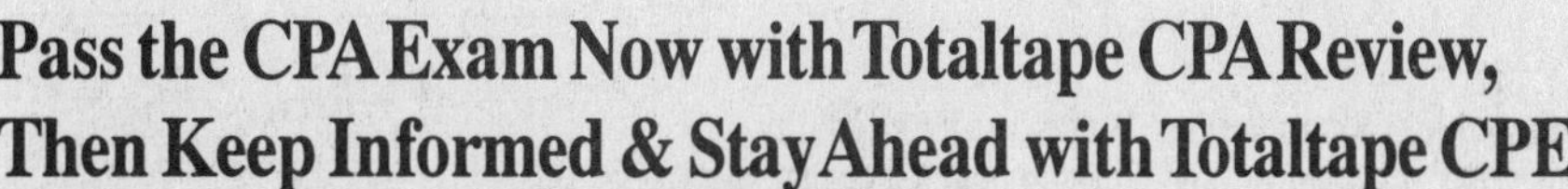

Pass the CPA Exam Now with Totaltape CPA Review, Then Keep Informed & Stay Ahead with Totaltape CPE

Totaltape's continuing professional education (CPE) programs are the most ideal and cost-effective way yet of fulfilling your mandatory CPE reporting requirements. You can earn the hours you need simply and conveniently in the comfort of your home or office, because with Totaltape's proven audio, video, software, CD-ROM and textbook self-study instruction, you determine how, when and where you study. All of our programs are written by the country's leading CPE experts in accordance with the AICPA and various State Boards of Accountancy Standards on Continuing Professional Education, and are completely up-to-date.

Choose from over 200 CPE programs in tax, accounting & auditing, business & industry, and computer video training. The following pages contain a small sampling of Totaltape's best-selling introductory programs, to provide beginning practitioners with the working knowledge they need to get off to a successful start!

For a FREE Totaltape CPEasy catalogue, or to place an order, call 1-800-874-7877.

Taxation

Guide to Limited Liability Companies

by William L. Raby, Ph.D., C.P.A.
Former National Director of Tax Services for Touche Ross & Past Chairman of the AICPA's Federal Tax Division

NEW

12 TAX CPE CREDIT HRS.

PREREQUISITE: None
KNOWLEDGE: Basic
*Video Coming Soon

Get the latest edition of our already popular Guide to Limited Liability Companies program! Packed with more topic coverage than ever, this comprehensive guide to LLCs provides you with a complete overview of what you need to know about working with limited liability companies, plus shows you how to save your clients money. The limited liability company offers an attractive alternative to traditional corporate or partnership entities. Income from an LLC is taxed at a single level like a partnership, but an LLC provides limited liability to the owners like a corporation. If you're not taking advantage of tax-saving opportunities now available through LLCs, try this program RISK-FREE. Learn how to set-up an LLC and the tax consequences of converting from various business forms to a limited liability company. Dr. William Raby, well-known as the "dean" of federal taxes, and former Chairman of the AICPA's federal tax division, focuses on problem areas and pitfalls to avoid in LLCs. Plus, tax-saving tips are stressed throughout. Understand your state requirements regarding limited liability companies. Included is a state-by-state summary (including New York and California) of enacted LLC legislation containing important filing information, aspects of formation, and classification issues. Sample state forms for forming, merging, and dissolving an LLC are also included. A detailed table of contents and comprehensive index enable you to access your information quickly and easily. New on video!

*Program Ordering Information:**

Audio. 6 Cassettes, Textbook & Quizzer	**Item No. CPE0590**	**$159.00** ($7.95 Shipping)
Video. 2 Hr. Video, Textbook & Quizzer	**Item No. CPE0597**	**$199.00** ($7.95 Shipping)
Extra Textbooks & Quizzers	**Item No. CPE0591**	**$70.00** ($3.95 Shipping)
Extra Quizzers Only	**Item No. CPE0596**	**$60.00** (Free Shipping)
Software. Windows-Disks, Textbook & Quizzer	**Item No. CPE0593**	**$159.00** ($7.95 Shipping)
Extra Disks & Quizzers	**Item No. CPE0594**	**$60.00** ($3.95 Shipping)

Basic S Corporation Taxation

by Nathan M. Bisk, J.D., C.P.A.,
and Stephen T. Galloway, J.D.

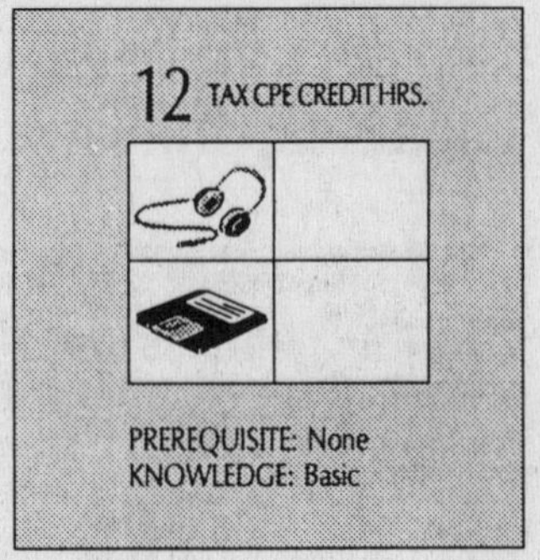

This practical guide provides a "nuts-and-bolts" working knowledge of S corporations. We discuss the eligibility requirements for S corp status and current tax considerations. Discover when you should and *should not* change from a "C" corporation to an "S" corporation. Plus, we identify opportunities and possible problem areas. We also cover how to utilize pass-throughs for shareholder benefit, retirement plans, acquisitions & liquidations, selected Code provisions, rulings and regulations, amendments made through all recent tax acts, special planning ideas, and practice problems.

Program Ordering Information:

Audio. 6 Cassettes, Textbook & Quizzer	**Item No. CPE0540**	**$159.00** ($7.95 Shipping)
Extra Textbooks & Quizzers	**Item No. CPE0541**	**$70.00** ($3.95 Shipping)
Extra Quizzers Only	**Item No. CPE0547**	**$60.00** (Free Shipping)
Software. Windows-Disks, Textbook & Quizzer	**Item No. CPE0545**	**$159.00** ($7.95 Shipping)
Extra Disks & Quizzers	**Item No. CPE0546**	**$60.00** ($3.95 Shipping)

Overview of Federal Income Taxation

by Nathan M. Bisk, J.D., C.P.A.

Totaltape CPEasy's Overview of Federal Income Taxation program is a perfect training tool for new "staffers"—as well as a good refresher for even the most seasoned pros! Its practical instruction will provide you with a thorough understanding of the fundamentals affecting individuals, corporations, shareholders, partnerships, and estates and trusts. Emphasis centers on the taxation of individuals, and all new tax acts are fully reflected.

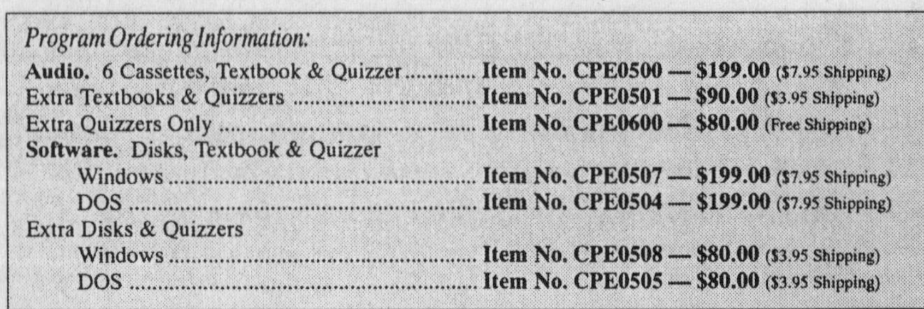

Program Ordering Information:

Audio. 6 Cassettes, Textbook & Quizzer	**Item No. CPE0500**	**$199.00** ($7.95 Shipping)
Extra Textbooks & Quizzers	**Item No. CPE0501**	**$90.00** ($3.95 Shipping)
Extra Quizzers Only	**Item No. CPE0600**	**$80.00** (Free Shipping)
Software. Disks, Textbook & Quizzer		
Windows	**Item No. CPE0507**	**$199.00** ($7.95 Shipping)
DOS	**Item No. CPE0504**	**$199.00** ($7.95 Shipping)
Extra Disks & Quizzers		
Windows	**Item No. CPE0508**	**$80.00** ($3.95 Shipping)
DOS	**Item No. CPE0505**	**$80.00** ($3.95 Shipping)

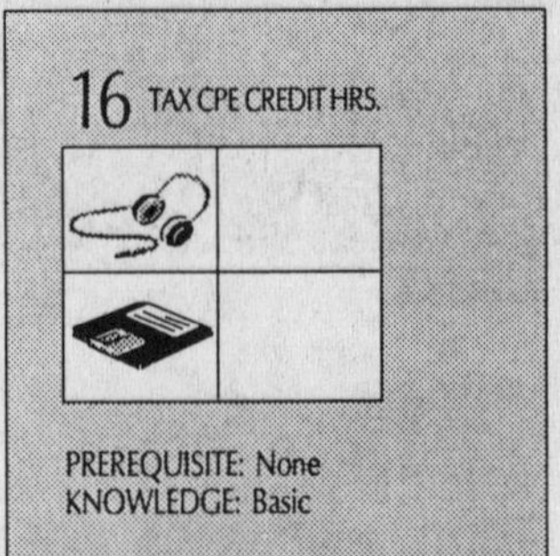

ORDER TOLL-FREE 1-800-874-7877

TAXATION

Form 1040: A Practical Guide

by Nathan M. Bisk, J.D., C.P.A.,Stephen T. Galloway, J.D., and George Schain, J.D.

Totaltape's Form 1040 practical reference guide features in-depth, line-by-line instructions on how to file all individual forms and schedules. We include key tax changes, helpful tax-savings tips *and* tax planning strategies, plus over 90 illustrations of important tax rules and calculations. Using real-world case studies, we show you how the forms work and how to properly apply them. We even provide you with over 100 examples to represent situations your clients could find themselves in. You get complete and comprehensive coverage on Form 1040 filing requirements; personal exemptions; gross income; compensation; depreciation; travel & entertainment; home business offices; at-risk limitations; NOLs; hobby losses; like-kind exchanges; the sale of a principal residence; related-party transactions; rental & pass-through income; passive activities; other income; adjustments to income; deductions from adjusted gross income; medical expenses; income tax computation; tax credits; AMT; tax payments; penalties; extended & amended returns; and claims for a refund. Sample charts, tables, and other reference materials are also included to greatly simplify the tax preparation process for you.

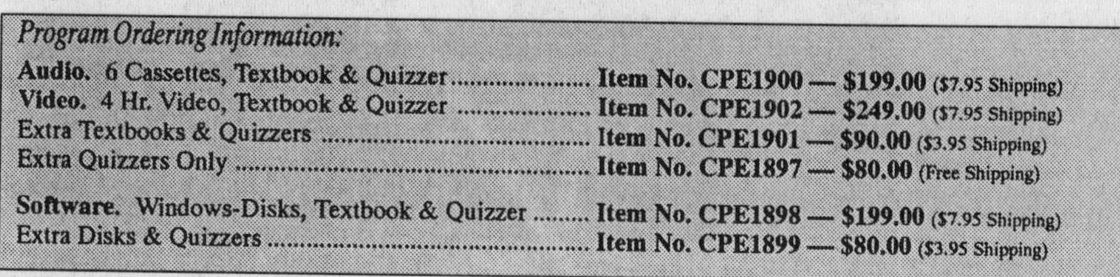

Program Ordering Information:

Audio. 6 Cassettes, Textbook & Quizzer .... **Item No. CPE1900 — $199.00** ($7.95 Shipping)
Video. 4 Hr. Video, Textbook & Quizzer .... **Item No. CPE1902 — $249.00** ($7.95 Shipping)
Extra Textbooks & Quizzers .... **Item No. CPE1901 — $90.00** ($3.95 Shipping)
Extra Quizzers Only .... **Item No. CPE1897 — $80.00** (Free Shipping)

Software. Windows-Disks, Textbook & Quizzer .... **Item No. CPE1898 — $199.00** ($7.95 Shipping)
Extra Disks & Quizzers .... **Item No. CPE1899 — $80.00** ($3.95 Shipping)

Form 1120: A Practical Guide

by Cris VanDenBranden, C.P.A.,Machen, Powers, Disque & Boyle, and Richard M. Feldheim,M.B.A., J.D., LL.M., C.P.A.

Save time, trouble, and money on your corporate tax returns with our step-by-step guide to filing Form 1120. Packed full of sample filled-in forms and comprehensive case studies you can apply directly to your clients' situations, this year-round tool is our best Form 1120 tax source yet. Not only do we make filing easier than ever, but we also supply you with specific tax-planning *and* tax-saving strategies. Plus, we take "complex" corporate tax issues and break them down into easily understood, straightforward explanations. Fully reflects all recent tax acts.

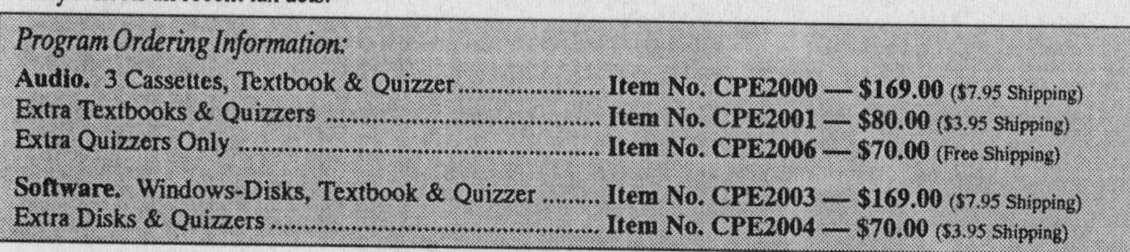

Program Ordering Information:

Audio. 3 Cassettes, Textbook & Quizzer .... **Item No. CPE2000 — $169.00** ($7.95 Shipping)
Extra Textbooks & Quizzers .... **Item No. CPE2001 — $80.00** ($3.95 Shipping)
Extra Quizzers Only .... **Item No. CPE2006 — $70.00** (Free Shipping)

Software. Windows-Disks, Textbook & Quizzer .... **Item No. CPE2003 — $169.00** ($7.95 Shipping)
Extra Disks & Quizzers .... **Item No. CPE2004 — $70.00** ($3.95 Shipping)

Form 1120S: A Practical Guide

by Nathan M. Bisk, J.D., C.P.A.,and Stephen T. Galloway, J.D.

Totaltape CPEasy's *Form 1120S* program provides you with the clear and concise guidance you need to prepare—and review—your S corporation returns...quickly and efficiently. Our coverage gives you step-by-step filing guidance, plus assists you in identifying opportunities and problem areas when preparing this often complex return. We also include all recent legislative, judicial, and regulatory changes, authoritative answers to tax return compliance questions, a realistic case study, and more.

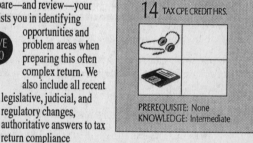

Program Ordering Information:

Audio. 6 Cassettes, Textbook & Quizzer
Item No. CPE4120 — $169.00 ($7.95 Shipping)
Extra Textbooks & Quizzers
Item No. CPE4121 — $80.00 ($3.95 Shipping)
Extra Quizzers Only
Item No. CPE4117 — $70.00 (Free Shipping)

Software. Windows-Disks, Textbook & Quizzer
Item No. CPE4118 — $169.00 ($7.95 Shipping)
Extra Disks & Quizzers
Item No. CPE4119 — $70.00 ($3.95 Shipping)

Forms 1040, 1120 & 1120S Xtra Value Package

XTRA VALUE! SAVE $50

Get all the practical, step-by-step guidance of Totaltape CPEasy's Forms programs on flexible audio tape, interactive software *for Windows* or our new, quick & efficient CD-ROM! We include complete coverage of our Form 1040 individual tax prep program, our Form 1120 corporate tax prep program, and our Form 1120S S corporation tax prep program (all featured on this page). SAVE $50 off our single program prices!

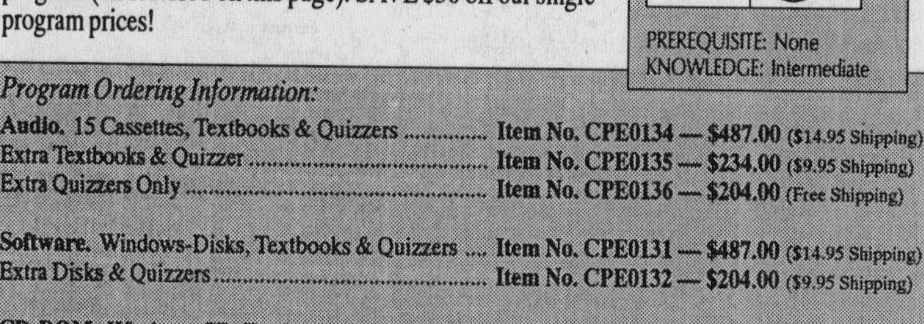

Program Ordering Information:

Audio. 15 Cassettes, Textbooks & Quizzers .... **Item No. CPE0134 — $487.00** ($14.95 Shipping)
Extra Textbooks & Quizzer .... **Item No. CPE0135 — $234.00** ($9.95 Shipping)
Extra Quizzers Only .... **Item No. CPE0136 — $204.00** (Free Shipping)

Software. Windows-Disks, Textbooks & Quizzers .... **Item No. CPE0131 — $487.00** ($14.95 Shipping)
Extra Disks & Quizzers .... **Item No. CPE0132 — $204.00** ($9.95 Shipping)

CD-ROM. Windows-CD, Textbooks & Quizzers .... **Item No. CPE0130 — $487.00** ($14.95 Shipping)
Extra CDs & Quizzers .... **Item No. CPE0133 — $204.00** ($9.95 Shipping)

ORDER TOLL-FREE 1-800-874-7877

If you're continually scrambling to read all the journals and written services that cross your desk to keep up with the latest and greatest tax changes—*STOP.*

Audio Tax Report...

does it for you. Call now!

At the touch of a button, Dr. Bill Raby, America's "dean" of federal taxes, provides you with his expert commentary every month on 8-10 of today's hottest tax topics, tax planning strategies, and much more...all on convenient audio tape!

Our full-time staff of tax experts continually monitors IRS rulings, wire services, and leading tax journals so you will always have the most up-to-the-minute information. You no longer have to read through time-consuming mounds of continually changing tax rules & legislation, because Audio Tax Report takes all the major developments that you'd normally have to find in dozens of publications and compiles them into **one, concise report**...and delivers it right to your door every month on convenient audio tape! Listen anytime, anyplace.

We give you "bite size" topics, presented in 10-15 minute segments that you can easily find time to listen to. And we bring in the "heaviest hitter" around, Dr. Bill Raby, former Chairman of the AICPA's Federal Tax Division and America's most respected tax analyst, to interpret all the major tax laws, court cases, and revenue rulings for you—plus provide you with effective tax planning strategies. A lively newsletter accompanies each issue, and acts as a word-for-word transcript of the audio tape...convenient for quick and easy reference! Best of all, you earn while you learn...up to 12 CPE credits per year. Order multiple CPE quizzers for additional staff members; you won't find a more cost-effective source of CPE credit anywhere else. Try your first issue RISK-FREE!

12 TAX CPE CREDIT HRS.

Monthly News & Information Service

PREREQUISITE: None
KNOWLEDGE: Update

Program Ordering Information:

Audio. 1 Year Subscription - 12 Cassettes, PLUS
Mthly. Transcripts, Yrly. Album, Index & Quizzers .... **Item No. CPE0001 — $225.00** ($15.00 Shipping)

2 Year Subscription - 24 Cassettes, PLUS
Mthly. Transcripts, Yrly. Albums, Indexes & Quizzers .... **Item No. CPE0002 — $395.00** ($30.00 Shipping)

Extra Quizzers - 1 Year .... **Item No. CPE0004-1 — $80.00** (Free Shipping)
Extra Quizzers - 2 Years .... **Item No. CPE0004-2 — $155.00** (Free Shipping)

Audio Financial Planning Report

by William L. Raby, Ph.D., C.P.A., C.F.P., Former National Director of Tax Services for Touche Ross, and Past Chairman of the AICPA's Federal Tax Division

Stay current on the latest financial planning trends & techniques with the help of Dr. Bill Raby, CFP, CPA, and former Chairman of the AICPA's federal tax division! Every month, Audio Financial Planning Report will bring his expertise on financial planning and tax law right into your home, office, or car—on convenient audio tape.

Dr. Raby will keep you up-to-date with the hottest financial planning issues, like:

Estate & Retirement Planning • Insurance Selection • Cash Management • Stocks & Bonds • Mutual Funds

...and more. He'll show you how to save your clients tax dollars and how to prepare for the future. Plus, you'll learn how to expand the scope of services offered by your firm, increase your client base, and keep your competitive edge! Each 60-75 minute audio report features 4-5 different financial planning topics. Plus, your audio report is accompanied by a lively newsletter, which acts as a word-for-word transcript of your audio tape. Audio Financial Planning Report also satisfies CFP ethics requirement of CFP Board of Standards. Try your first issue RISK-FREE! Call today!

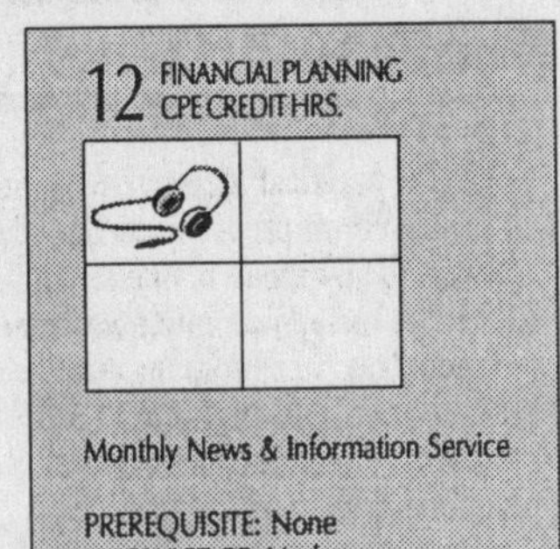

Program Ordering Information:

Audio. 1 Year Subscription - 12 Cassettes, PLUS
Mthly. Transcripts, Yrly. Album, Index & Quizzers .... **Item No. CPE2310 — $225.00** ($15.00 Shipping)

2 Year Subscription - 24 Cassettes, PLUS
Mthly. Transcripts, Yrly. Albums, Indexes & Quizzers .... **Item No. CPE2320 — $395.00** ($30.00 Shipping)

Extra Quizzers - 1 Year .... **Item No. CPE2311 — $80.00** (Free Shipping)
Extra Quizzers - 2 Years .... **Item No. CPE2321 — $155.00** (Free Shipping)

ORDER TOLL-FREE 1-800-874-7877

Accounting & Auditing

Corporate Financial Reporting Issues

by Paul Munter, Ph.D., C.P.A.

Dr. Paul Munter, the Florida Institute of CPAs' 1993 Outstanding Educator, shows you how to implement the latest changes in accounting principles, auditing standards, and more with Totaltape CPEasy's Corporate Financial Reporting program! He provides you with an analysis and professional advice on recently issued FASBs, SASs, and AcSec & EITF pronouncements—paying special attention to their impact on smaller companies and implementation issues. The program also features coverage on changes in reporting practices for not-for-profit organizations, accounting & reporting environmental clean-up costs, and legal liability for reform. Plus, Dr. Munter discusses how the auditor's responsibility for fraud detection has increased in the wake of these changes; consolidated financial reporting; a new approach to valuing impaired assets; accounting & reporting financial instruments; and the impact of an exposure draft to assign values to all stock compensation plans.

Program Ordering Information:

Audio. 4 Cassettes, Textbook & Quizzer .... **Item No. CPE1191 — $159.00** ($7.95 Shipping)
Video. 2 Hr. Video, Textbook & Quizzer .... **Item No. CPE1190 — $199.00** ($7.95 Shipping)
Extra Textbooks & Quizzers .... **Item No. CPE1192 — $70.00** ($3.95 Shipping)
Extra Quizzers Only .... **Item No. CPE1198 — $60.00** (Free Shipping)

Software. Windows-Disks, Textbook & Quizzer .... **Item No. CPE1194 — $159.00** ($7.95 Shipping)
Extra Disks & Quizzers .... **Item No. CPE1196 — $60.00** ($3.95 Shipping)

CD-ROM. Windows-CD, Textbook & Quizzer ...... **Item No. CPE1195 — $159.00** ($7.95 Shipping)
Extra CDs & Quizzers .... **Item No. CPE1197 — $60.00** ($3.95 Shipping)

Bisk GAAP Guide

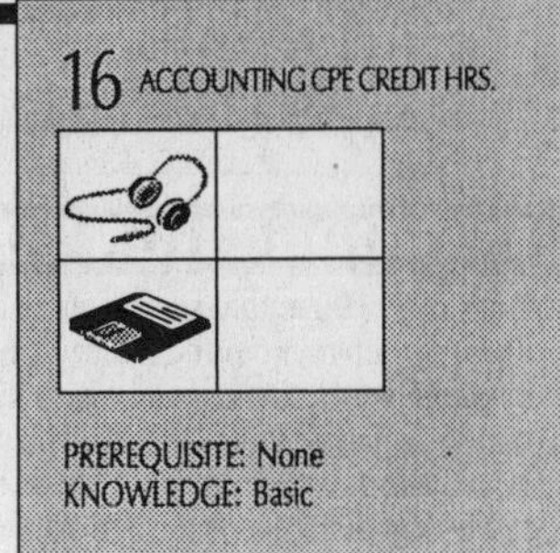

by Nathan M. Bisk, J.D., C.P.A., and Robert L. Monette, J.D., C.P.A.

Recent FASB Statements are having a major impact on financial statement presentation. But to learn only the newest pronouncements isn't enough...you must also understand how they have changed *existing* Standards. This program provides you with a current, comprehensive overview of all GAAP, and can help you avoid misapplications of accounting principles. Coverage includes current assets & liabilities; fixed assets & long-term liabilities; intangibles and R&D; stockholders' equity method; reporting the results of operations; statement of cash flows; deferred taxes; leases & pensions; business combinations; foreign operations, and more. Updated through FASB 119.

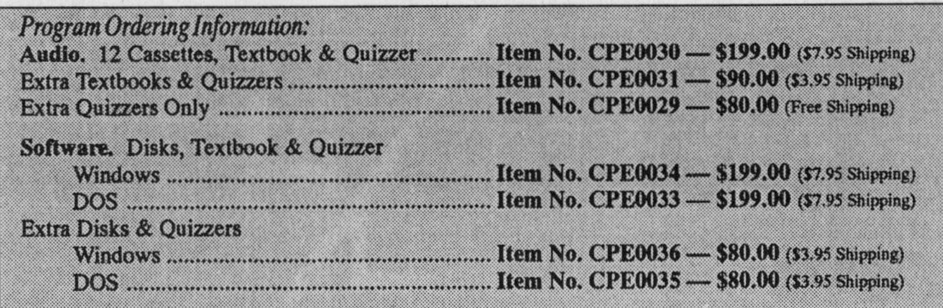

Program Ordering Information:

Audio. 12 Cassettes, Textbook & Quizzer .... **Item No. CPE0030 — $199.00** ($7.95 Shipping)
Extra Textbooks & Quizzers .... **Item No. CPE0031 — $90.00** ($3.95 Shipping)
Extra Quizzers Only .... **Item No. CPE0029 — $80.00** (Free Shipping)

Software. Disks, Textbook & Quizzer
Windows .... **Item No. CPE0034 — $199.00** ($7.95 Shipping)
DOS .... **Item No. CPE0033 — $199.00** ($7.95 Shipping)
Extra Disks & Quizzers
Windows .... **Item No. CPE0036 — $80.00** ($3.95 Shipping)
DOS .... **Item No. CPE0035 — $80.00** ($3.95 Shipping)

Bisk GAAS Guide

by Nathan M. Bisk, J.D., C.P.A.

This course thoroughly explains the SASs and how they change the way you should conduct an audit engagement. You'll get a clear overview of auditing standards, the code of professional conduct and standards applicable to other professional services such as compilations/reviews, tax and MAS work—plus, numerous illustrations of the wording and format required for most types of reports. We take an in-depth look at standards, ethics & related issues; internal control; audit sampling; audit evidence; programs & procedures; reports on audited financial statements; special reports; and other professional services. And we include a master status checklist and handy cross-reference index of all SASs and SSARs.

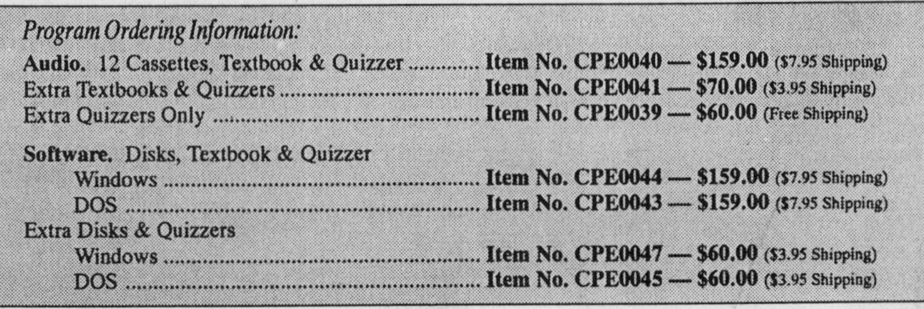

Program Ordering Information:

Audio. 12 Cassettes, Textbook & Quizzer .... **Item No. CPE0040 — $159.00** ($7.95 Shipping)
Extra Textbooks & Quizzers .... **Item No. CPE0041 — $70.00** ($3.95 Shipping)
Extra Quizzers Only .... **Item No. CPE0039 — $60.00** (Free Shipping)

Software. Disks, Textbook & Quizzer
Windows .... **Item No. CPE0044 — $159.00** ($7.95 Shipping)
DOS .... **Item No. CPE0043 — $159.00** ($7.95 Shipping)
Extra Disks & Quizzers
Windows .... **Item No. CPE0047 — $60.00** ($3.95 Shipping)
DOS .... **Item No. CPE0045 — $60.00** ($3.95 Shipping)

ORDER TOLL-FREE 1-800-874-7877

Test Drive Windows® 95 Today

Totaltape Puts You in the Driver's Seat with All the Information You Need to Upgrade to the Next Generation of Windows...Right Here, Right Now!

Get complete details on the new interface, new features, applications, hardware requirements, networking, and more. Totaltape's new, interactive training programs provide you with the efficient working knowledge you need to become a Windows® 95 expert.

NEW

12 ADVISORY SERVICES CPE CREDIT HRS. EACH*

PREREQUISITE: None for Intro. level programs. Prior to taking an Adv. level program, we recommend that you complete its introductory version, or have a working familiarity with the actual software program.
KNOWLEDGE: Basic & Advanced

Totaltape's computer training programs are perfect for in-house training. Maximize cost-effectiveness by training your entire staff.

INTRODUCTION TO WINDOWS® 95

With over 100 actual screen shots of Windows® 95's new user interface, this introductory program gives you an immediate grasp of the specific changes between your current Windows version and Windows® 95. Learn first-hand about the new printing, multimedia, and mobile computing enhancements, as well as how to use the new Task Bar, Wizards, Properties, Plug-and-Play features, and more. We show you how to gauge the best way to upgrade your current system to Windows® 95, plus address current questions about where familiar items may now be found; plus, how to use all of Windows® 95's new accessories, track incoming and outgoing messages, and how to network. With a thorough discussion of everything from the newly designed interface, to the power of the 32-bit architecture, to the multimedia technology—you'll feel as though you have your new Windows® 95 program right in front of you.

- Video, Textbook & Quizzer—**Item No. CPE1360**
- CD-ROM, Textbook & Quizzer—**Item No. CPE1363**
- Extra Textbooks & Quizzers—**Item No. CPE1361**
- Extra Quizzers Only—**Item No. CPE1362**

ADVANCED WINDOWS® 95

Utilizing step-by-step instructions and real-world examples, this hands-on training tutorial explores the more intricate workings of Windows® 95, like multitasking, integrating between applications that aren't possible in DOS, customizing Windows, and overcoming some of the problems you will face in upgrading to Windows® 95. Our Advanced Windows program shows you how to install, and uninstall, Windows® 95; how to use DOS programs with Windows® 95; how to avoid potential disasters; and how to effectively use the new enhancements, such as Explorer, the expanded help function, and Remote Access Services. We examine the types of hands-on topics related to using the system on a day-to-day basis, and show you how to quickly migrate to this much more powerful operating system while continuing to get the most from your PC...without a steep learning curve.

- Video, Textbook & Quizzer—**Item No. CPE1370**
- CD-ROM, Textbook & Quizzer—**Item No. CPE1373**
- Extra Textbooks & Quizzers—**Item No. CPE1371**
- Extra Quizzers Only—**Item No. CPE1372**

QUICK START WINDOWS® 95

Totaltape's new software/textbook program, Quick Start Windows® 95, was designed exclusively to ease the transition between "old and new" Windows, and to give PC users a fast leg-up on the significant changes they will face with the introduction of the new Windows® 95 operating system. An excellent, quick lesson on how to work with—and what to expect from—the new Windows program, Quick Start contains complete coverage on the features of the new operating system (like the Desktop, Taskbar, Shortcuts & Folders, Network Neighborhood, and Briefcase); the new Window layout; new accessories (such as Microsoft Exchange, Wordpad, Phone Dialer, Paint, and File Transfer); plus shows you how to customize your system using the Control Panel, how to add programs to the startup folder, and more.

- Software (3-1/2" disk) with Text On-line & Quizzer—**Item No. CPE1380**
- Extra Disk & Quizzer—**Item No. CPE1381**
- CD-ROM with Text On-line & Quizzer—**Item No. CPE1390**

**Not accepted for Continuing Education credit in Mississippi. Word processing, database, graphics & operating system programs are only accepted for "management" CPE credit in New York.*

ORDER TOLL-FREE 1-800-874-7877